CW01657291

A NEW COMPANION TO HOMER

A NEW COMPANION TO HOMER

EDITED BY

IAN MORRIS AND BARRY POWELL

BRILL
LEIDEN · NEW YORK · KÖLN
2011

This book is printed on acid-free paper.

Library of Congress Control Number: 96038925

This paperback was originally published in hardback under ISBN 978 90 04 09989 0 as volume 163 in the series *Mnemosyne, Supplements*.

ISBN 978 90 04 20608 3

In memory of Arthur Adkins

CONTENTS

List of Contributors xi
Editors' Introduction
IAN MORRIS and BARRY POWELL xiii

PART ONE

TRANSMISSION AND HISTORY OF INTERPRETATION

1. Homer and Writing
BARRY POWELL 3
2. Homer in Antiquity
ROBERT LAMBERTON 33
3. Homeric Papyri and Transmission of the Text
MICHAEL HASLAM 55
4. Homeric Scholia
GREGORY NAGY 101
5. The Homeric Question
FRANK TURNER 123
6. Oral Tradition and its Implications
JOHN FOLEY 146
7. Neoanalysis
MALCOLM WILLCOCK 174

PART TWO

HOMER'S LANGUAGE

8. Homer's Dialect
GEOFFREY HORROCKS 193
9. Homer's Meter
MARTIN WEST 218
10. The Formula
JOSEPH RUSSO 238
11. Homeric Style and 'Oral Poetics'
MARK EDWARDS 261
12. The Study of Homeric Discourse
EGBERT BAKKER 284

13. Homer and Narratology
IRENE DE JONG 305
14. Quantifying Epic
AHUVIA KAHANE 326

PART THREE

HOMER AS LITERATURE

15. The *Iliad*: Structure and Interpretation
SETH SCHEIN 345
16. The Structures of the *Odyssey*
STEPHEN TRACY 360
17. Modern Theoretical Approaches to Homer
JOHN PERADOTTO 380
18. Epic as Genre
ANDREW FORD 396
19. Myth in Homer
LOWELL EDMUNDS 415
20. Homer and the Folktale
WILLIAM HANSEN 442
21. Homer and Hesiod
RALPH ROSEN 463
22. The Homeric Hymns
JENNY STRAUSS CLAY 489

PART FOUR

HOMER'S WORLDS

23. Homer and the Bronze Age
JOHN BENNET 511
24. Homer and the Iron Age
IAN MORRIS 535
25. Homer and Greek Art
ANTHONY SNODGRASS 560
26. Homer and the Near East
SARAH MORRIS 599
27. Homeric Society
KURT RAAFLAUB 624
28. The Homeric Economy
WALTER DONLAN 649

29. Homeric Warfare
HANS VAN WEES 668
30. Homeric Ethics
ARTHUR ADKINS 694

Select Bibliography 715

Index 747

CONTRIBUTORS

Arthur Adkins was Edward Olson Professor of Greek and Professor of Philosophy and Early Christian Literature at the University of Chicago.

Egbert Bakker is Assistant Professor of Classics at the Université de Montreal.

John Bennet is Associate Professor of Classical Archaeology and Chair of the Department of Classics at the University of Wisconsin at Madison.

Irene De Jong is Professor of Classics at the University of Amsterdam.

Walter Donlan is Professor of Classics at the University of California at Irvine.

Lowell Edmunds is Professor of Classics at Rutgers University.

Mark Edwards is Professor Emeritus of Classics at Stanford University.

John Foley is Byler Professor of English and Classical Studies and Director of the Center for Studies in Oral Tradition at the University of Missouri at Columbia.

Andrew Ford is Associate Professor of Classics at Princeton University.

William Hansen is Professor of Classics at Indiana University.

Michael Haslam is Professor of Classics at the University of California at Los Angeles.

Geoffrey Horrocks is Lecturer in Classics at Cambridge University and Fellow of St. John's College.

Ahuvia Kahane is Assistant Professor of Classics at Northwestern University.

Robert Lamberton is Associate Professor of Classics at Washington University.

Ian Morris is Professor of Classics and History and Chair of the Department of Classics at Stanford University.

Sarah Morris is Professor of Classics at the University of California at Los Angeles.

Gregory Nagy is Francis Jones Professor of Classical Greek Literature, Professor of Comparative Literature, and Chair of the Department of the Classics at Harvard University.

JOHN PERADOTTO is Andrew V. V. Raymond Professor of Classics and SUNY Distinguished Teaching Professor at the State University of New York at Buffalo.

BARRY POWELL is Halls-Bascom Professor of Classics at the University of Wisconsin–Madison.

KURT RAAFLAUB is Professor of Classics at Brown University and Co-Director of the Center for Hellenic Studies in Washington, DC.

RALPH ROSEN is Associate Professor of Classics and Chair of the Classics Department at the University of Pennsylvania.

JOSEPH RUSSO is Professor of Classics at Haverford College.

SETH SCHEIN is Professor of Comparative Literature at the University of California at Davis.

ANTHONY SNODGRASS is Lawrence Professor of Classical Archaeology at Cambridge University, and Fellow of Clare College.

JENNY STRAUSS CLAY is Professor of Classics at the University of Virginia.

STEPHEN TRACY is Professor of Classics at the Ohio State University.

FRANK TURNER is John Hay Whitney Professor of History at Yale University.

HANS VAN WEES is Lecturer in Ancient History at University College, London.

MARTIN WEST is a Fellow of All Souls College, Oxford.

MALCOLM WILLCOCK is Professor Emeritus of Classics at University College, London.

Ian Morris and Barry B. Powell

EDITORS' INTRODUCTION

A generation has passed since the publication of Wace and Stubbings' original *Companion to Homer* in 1962. Yet this remains the only other English-language volume which claims to offer a broad survey of Homeric scholarship. A third of a century is a long time in the humanities; as in any field of classical scholarship, new interpretations and questions have emerged, and new archaeological finds have accumulated. But our *New Companion to Homer* is not simply an updated version of Wace and Stubbings. The years since the original *Companion* took shape have seen profound shifts in our notions of what Homeric studies should be.

When Heinrich Schliemann began digging at Troy and Mycenae in the 1870s, there was general agreement among classicists that Homeric society and the Trojan war were to all intents and purposes fictions of the eighth century B.C., helpful for understanding Greek values at the dawn of the Archaic age, but nothing more than that. Schliemann's discoveries shattered this orthodoxy, and by the time Wace began collecting contributions for the original *Companion* in the late 1930s, a new attitude dominated scholarship: the *Iliad* and *Odyssey* were basically Bronze Age poems, transmitted more or less intact across the Dark Age, accurately reflecting the realities of the Mycenaean world. The main aim of the original *Companion* was to give expression to this vision, explicating the poems' historical setting by means of the material record. Its first five chapters surveyed meter, style, composition, language, and Homer's relationship to other epic poetry; the next two introduced issues of textual transmission and the Homeric Question; but the final sixteen chapters—well over half the book—were devoted to archaeology and history.

The publication of the original *Companion* was long delayed by the Second World War and then by the deaths of the editor and his original assistant. By the time it finally appeared, in 1962, there had been a revolution in Homeric scholarship. Milman Parry had formulated his theories of oral composition—and had himself met an untimely death—in the days when Wace was still planning the *Companion*;

but his ideas only really began to gain ground in the 1950s. Further, in 1952 Michael Ventris announced his decipherment of Linear B, and in just the same years, archaeologists began imposing order on the previously confusing material from Iron Age Greece. Taken together, these developments undermined the older orthodoxy of a Mycenaean Homeric world, suggesting that the differences between heroic society and that of the Bronze Age palaces were much greater than had previously been realized. Some specialists argued that the society described in the poems accurately reflected the world of the tenth century B.C.; others, that it belonged in the eighth century; others still, that it was a poetic conflation of memories spanning a millennium of Greek prehistory. Some of the chapters in the *Companion* reflected the new attitudes of the 1950s, but most—and the overall archaeological-historical focus of the book—remained rooted in the debates of the 1930s. In fact, we might almost say that it has been *two* generations since anyone has tried to put together a comprehensive English-language survey of Homeric scholarship.

We can hardly claim to be the first people to have noticed this peculiar situation. Between 1985 and 1993, Cambridge University Press published a six-volume commentary on the *Iliad*, and between 1988 and 1990, Oxford University Press published a three-volume commentary on the *Odyssey* (originally published in Italian). And in 1995, three English-language collections of essays on Homer appeared—J.-P. Crielaard's *Homeric Questions* and Ø. Anderson and M. Dickie's *Homer's World* developing out of conferences, and J. Carter and S. P. Morris' *Ages of Homer* being a volume in honor of Emily Vermeule. But the *New Companion* is different from any of these books. We make no attempt to compete with the exhaustive coverage of the Cambridge and Oxford commentaries. There are no line-by-line analyses or encyclopedic displays of knowledge here. But on the other hand, the *New Companion* is far more systematic than the other recent volumes of articles (and indeed more systematic than the original *Companion*).[1]

Unfettered by the constraints imposed by the genres of conference-volume or Festschrift, we have reached for the chimera of comprehensive coverage of the major questions which dominate current Homeric scholarship. Yet despite the size of this volume, we are pain-

[1] J. Latacz's excellent *Zweihundert Jahre Homer-Forschung* (ed., 1991a) falls somewhere between the English-language conference volumes and this *New Companion* in terms of comprehensiveness, but most of the chapters are written in German.

fully conscious of how far we have fallen short of this goal, of those topics we have not been able to review, and those scholars whose voices we were not able to include. Inevitably, we were forced to make hard decisions, concentrating on certain areas at the expense of others. A truly comprehensive survey, leaving nothing unsaid, is as much a fantasy as a comprehensive commentary, but we believe that for all its flaws, a book like the *New Companion* has an important role to play in Homeric scholarship at the century's end.

The most obvious contrast between the *New Companion* and its predecessor is the reversal of the balance between archaeological and literary discussion. This reversal reflects what we perceive to have been a major shift in scholarly interests in the last generation (or two), away from traditional forms of historical analysis and toward more broadly cultural issues. As such, Homeric scholarship is merely following in trends which have affected all the humanities and social sciences. Historical and archaeological analysis remain important, but in the 1990s no longer provide an over-arching framework for Homeric studies.

A second major contrast between the *New Companion* and the original *Companion* is in the expected readership. Stubbings ([1962a] vi) explained that 'This *Companion* is intended primarily for those who are reading Homer in Greek, especially those who, in school or university, are reading him for the first time.' We expect the audience of the *New Companion* to include such readers, but we also look to those who read Homer in translation, who will be able to read most of our contributions with profit. Specialists, too, will be able to use the *New Companion* to find out what the latest questions and advances are in topics of Homeric scholarship which fall outside their own professional focus: the art-historian can learn where work on the formulae stands, and the expert on the papyri how the latest finds from the Bronze Age affect our reading of the poems. The first *Companion* appeared in an era when many scholars taught and wrote with equal authority on Homeric philology and archaeology, but such polymaths are now rare indeed. Literary, linguistic, archaeological, and historical methodologies have become increasingly sophisticated, and the sheer quantity of archaeological finds has increased rapidly. We hope that the *New Companion* will make it easier for specialists to transcend the forces of fragmentation which seriously threaten older ideals of the unity of classical scholarship. The *New Companion* provides a sense of the most important new work being done across the whole range of Homeric studies.

We have divided the thirty contributions into four groups. The first seven essays examine 'Transmission and History of Interpretation.' In the first chapter, Barry Powell treats the role of writing in the formation of the text, arguing in favor of the oral-dictation model. In Ch. 2, Robert Lamberton traces the reception of the texts across the next thousand years, through the Classical Athenian philosophers and poets to the schoolmasters and Neoplatonists of the Roman empire. Chs. 3 and 4 form a pair, dealing in different ways with the vast wealth of information contained in the scholia on Homer. In 'Homeric Papyri and the Transmission of the Text,' Michael Haslam provides a magisterial survey of the Egyptian evidence for the analysis and editing of texts of Homer from the third century B.C. through the tenth century A.D.; and in 'Homeric Scholia,' Gregory Nagy explores the implications of these documents for any attempt to reconstruct 'the original' text of Homer. In Ch. 5, Frank Turner follows 'The Homeric Question' from its inception in late eighteenth-century Germany through to the early twentieth century and the eve of Milman Parry's breakthrough. In Ch. 6, John M. Foley takes up the story where Turner leaves off, with Parry and Lord's work with Serbo-Croatian oral poets, and its revolutionary (if delayed) effect on the entire field of Homeric studies. Finally, in Ch. 7, Malcolm Willcock sets out the agendas and achievements of Neoanalysis, a school of thought which has still had relatively little impact in the English-speaking world.

The seven chapters of Part Two, 'Homer's Language,' cover both long-standing scholarly debates and fields which scarcely existed when the original *Companion* appeared. In Ch. 8, Geoffrey Horrocks explains recent advances in one of the longest-standing of all Homeric problems, the nature and historical formation of Homer's dialect; and in Ch. 9 Martin West does the same for Homer's meter. Chs. 10 and 11, by contrast, take up themes raised in Ch. 6, exploring the nature of Homeric formulae, which were so important for Milman Parry's theory of oral composition. In 'The Formula,' Joseph Russo surveys sixty years of modifications of Parry's initial definition of the formula, and what these have meant for theories of orality; and in 'Homeric Style and "Oral Poetics,"' Mark Edwards explores Parry's problematic claim that the formulas were nothing more than metrical space-fillers, devoid of meaningful content. The last three chapters in this section take up new areas of scholarship. In Ch. 12, Egbert Bakker discusses the implications of pragmatic theories in linguistics and the relationships between oral poetry and everyday speech; and in Ch. 13, Irene De Jong presents the contributions of narratology. In Ch. 14, Ahuvia Kahane describes some of the main ways in which quantitative techniques have changed our understanding of Homer's language in the last generation.

Part Three, 'Homer as Literature,' presented the toughest editorial problems. Homer's poetry survived because of its emotional power, and there are more people alive today who have read Homer for sheer literary pleasure than at any other time in history. Choosing just eight topics was very difficult, and doubtless every reader of the *New Companion* will feel that we have left out subjects which we should have brought in. Chs. 15 and 16 form another pair: Seth Schein examines the structure of the *Iliad*, and Stephen Tracy that of the *Odyssey*. Then in Ch. 17, John Peradotto goes on to review the contributions of 'Modern Theoretical Approaches to Homer,' ranging from Marxism and feminism through intertextuality and deconstruction. In Ch. 18, Andrew Ford examines the coherence of heroic epic as a genre and the poet's relationship to the Muses. In Ch. 19, Lowell Edmunds explores the relevance of modern concepts of 'myth' to Homer, and the relationships between myth and epic poetry. In Ch. 20 William Hansen looks at Homer's use (particularly in the *Odyssey*) of folktales which are found in the oral traditions of other cultures often far-removed in time and space from early Archaic Greece, and the ways in which Homer accommodated these traditions to the requirements of heroic epic. Chs. 21 and 22 set Homer into the context of related literature from Archaic Greece. In 'Homer and Hesiod,' Ralph Rosen reviews traditional questions about the chronological order and direction of influences between the two poets, and also newer concerns over subtle allusions in Hesiod to heroic poetry as a competing genre. In 'The Homeric Hymns,' Jenny Strauss Clay takes a similar approach to this relatively neglected corpus.

Part Four, 'Homer's Worlds,' brings us back to the archaeological and historical topics which so dominated the original *Companion*, but also shows the great changes which have overtaken Homeric scholarship in the intervening years. Whereas Stubbings ([1962a] vii) had nothing but scorn for Moses Finley's judgment, first published in 1957, that 'Homer is not only not a reliable guide to the Mycenaean tablets; he is no guide at all,' John Bennet is happy to close Ch. 24, on 'Homer and the Bronze Age,' by quoting these words. Bennet argues that Bronze Age archaeology is most valuable for providing the background to the early stages of the epic tradition, not as an external check on the reality of Homer's world. Ian Morris develops similar ideas in 'Homer and the Iron Age,' reviewing the variety of the material record and suggesting that we should see Homer and the monuments as two complimentary ways in which eighth-century Greeks talked about their world and its relationships to the past. In Ch. 25, 'Homer and Greek Art,' Anthony Snodgrass also argues against treating Homer and the material record as passive reflections of one another. Archaic vase painters, he suggests, had agendas every bit as complex as those of oral poets, and both groups drew on, and in the process transformed, a widely shared fascination with the heroic past. Sarah Morris, in 'Homer and the Near East,' tackles a theme entirely absent in the original *Companion*, but which fascinates many modern readers. She locates Homer's stories within a broader east Mediterranean mythological tradition. In Ch. 27, Kurt Raaflaub summarizes the emerging orthodoxy of the 1990s that the heroic society of the poems is based largely on Homer's own world of the eighth century B.C., rather than on the Mycenaean world, the earlier Dark Age, or an unhistorical conflation. Walter Donlan takes a similar approach in Ch. 28, showing the internal consistency of economic institutions in Homer and arguing that their most plausible context is in the real world of the eighth century. In Ch. 29, Hans van Wees takes up the *Iliad*'s central theme of heroic warfare, relating this to developments in the eighth and seventh centuries and the recent debates over whether Homer shows awareness of hoplite tactics. Finally, in Ch. 30, the last paper he wrote before his death in February 1996, Arthur Adkins takes up another theme missing from the original *Companion*: 'Homeric Ethics.' He argues that the individualistic values of the heroes were fundamentally at odds with larger goals of their society, creating ethical problems that were to remain central to Greek thought for the next three hundred years.

This volume is dedicated to Arthur's memory. We hope that it will stand as a monument to his love of Homer and his inspiring teaching, scholarship, and friendship; if not for all time, then at least until we are ready for another new companion to Homer.

Ian Morris
Boulder Creek, California

Barry Powell
Madison, Wisconsin

PART ONE

TRANSMISSION AND HISTORY OF INTERPRETATION

Barry B. Powell

HOMER AND WRITING

Central to the genesis of the Homeric poems is the question of writing. The poems exist in writing, but they emerge from an illiterate age and were generated through a technique of composition which does not require writing, which is even hostile to it. The *Iliad* and the *Odyssey* appear to date to the 8th century B.C., though precision is impossible, while most classicists place the invention of the alphabet around 800 B.C. Here, then, is the paradox: immensely long oral poems recorded in writing near the time when writing, for historical Greece, begins, virtually the same writing which supports the words on this page. The paradox is as real today as in 1795 when F. A. Wolf complained that 'if our forefathers had heard that serious doubts were raised as to whether Homer, the greatest of writers, used the art of writing, they would have cried out that the lovers of paradoxes no longer had any shame.'[1]

Since Wolf's day scholars have pursued two lines of argument to ease the paradox. One pushes the poet—the author of the poems as we have them, who we agree did exist—into the 'fully literate' period of the sixth century, when the massive effort and expense of recording such long works would seem *a priori* more likely. The other argument pushes back the introduction of writing to an earlier time.

But pushing Homer down into the 7th or 6th centuries B.C., to get some distance between him and the beginning of writing in Greece, generates recalcitrant problems of its own. No object or social practice in either poem, which contain rich descriptions of everyday life, can be securely placed later than 700 B.C. (see K. Raaflaub in this volume). It is idle to believe that circa 700 B.C., for unknown reasons, the *mise en scène* of the poems was frozen *without the aid of writing*. Furthermore, R. Janko's study of the evolution of certain linguistic features within early epic places the *Iliad* and the *Odyssey* somewhat before Hesiod and more before the Hymns, in a relative chronology

[1] Wolf (1985 [1795]) 71.

that agrees well with an 8th century date.[2] Only a written version can explain such linguistic fixity (cf. M. Haslam in this volume). Nor is it true that writing was better able to record long poems in the 7th or 6th centuries than in the 8th. It was a monumental task whenever performed, and Greeks of the 8th century as able to do it as any living later.

Arguments for an earlier date for the introduction of the alphabet are equally unfounded, but not so easily settled, because they are based on misapprehensions about the history of writing and about the nature of writing itself. We must now discuss these issues in some detail, if we wish to understand the paradoxical relation between writing and Homer.

The Nature and History of Writing[3]

We bring prejudgments to the study of writing and badly need a theory of the history of writing to sort out the complex data. Historical systems of writing come to us rife with the mistakes, confusions, and inventions of ancient peoples, for whom writing was never a scientific device, but a tool designed for practical ends by practical people, whose conditions of life were utterly different from our own. We are likely to think of writing as visible speech, according to de Saussure's dictum that 'the spoken language is primary and writing is essentially a means of representing speech in another medium.'[4] Only for a moment, however, in Archaic Greece, did writing come close to fulfilling de Saussure's misleading claim. In its obsession with phonetic accuracy, the Greek alphabet was a great anomaly in the history of writing, and many of its successors have gladly returned to earlier practices. In modern English, for example, not the sound attached to the signs, but the shape of the written word may determine which word is meant: hic*cough*, r*ough*, d*ough*, c*ough*, pl*ough*, or thr*ough*.

If we define writing as 'any system of human intercommunication by means of a set of visible marks with a conventional reference,'[5]

---

[2] Janko (1982).

[3] Best general theoretical study remains Gelb (1963); for a historical description of Aegean scripts, Heubeck (1979).

[4] Cf. F. de Saussure, *Course in General Linguistics*, tr. J. Culler (New York, 1959) 23–32.

[5] Bennett (1963) 99–100.

we realize how unsatisfactory is the notion that writing is frozen speech. Mathematical and musical notations and computer languages are also writing, as are wiring diagrams and the leaping deer on a roadside sign, but such forms of writing, called *semasiography* ('sign-writing'), do not require the intervention of speech to know what is meant. Semasiographic signs can be understood by speakers of any language, and modern international commerce encourages their proliferation in airports, in panels on photocopying machines, and in bewildering variety on computer screens.

The disadvantage of semasiography is that many forms of thought, and the best part of poetic expression, are closely wedded to speech. Historically, semasiography is older than *lexigraphy*, visible marks that *do* have a conventional reference to speech, though it is probably not possible to disentangle the historical transition from semasiography to lexigraphy in the Ancient Near East in response to the economic needs of early agricultural society. Early lexigraphic signs in the Near East seem to evolve from a neolithic system of keeping accounts by means of clay tokens, according to D. Schmandt-Besserat.[6] The varied shapes of clay tokens—circles, tetrahedrons, lozenges—at first represented commodities, one original token for one commodity. Later, impressed in clay envelopes, the mere shape of the token came to represent the category of commodity, e.g. ⊕ = sheep, beside which strokes were inscribed and other counting marks. From this usage the shape came to stand for an actual word, e.g. ⊕ = the word 'sheep.' Many think that 'writing' began with pictures, but the actual evidence suggests that in the Near East, whence our own writing descends, writing began with abstract designs.[7] This earliest stage of lexigraphic writing is *logography*, 'word-writing.'

'Semasiography' and 'lexigraphy' are the two categories of writing, and logography is one type of lexigraphy; Chinese writing is mostly logographic. Logography led to the discovery of *phonography*, the graphic representation of the sounds of speech, or rebus, in which a graphic shape ceases to have semantic value and stands for sound alone. Discovered evidently in order to record proper names, phonography made possible another category of lexigraphic writing,

---

[6] Schmandt-Besserat (1992). Summary of the argument in E. L. Bennett, Jr., 'Minos and Minyas,' in *Proceedings of the 10th International Colloquium of Mycenaean Studies*, Salzburg, 1996 (forthcoming).

[7] Writing in the Far East is another topic. Though many take Chinese writing as dependent on Near Eastern writing, the issue is unresolved.

syllabography, in which a sign represents a syllable. If ⊙ represents 'the sun' as a logogram, it may also stand for the sound 'sun' as in my 'son,' now a syllabogram, or, in conjunction with some other sign, 'sun'dae. The sign ⊙ as a syllabogram has the sound [sun], but as a logogram could stand for 'sun' in English, 'Sonne' in German, 'soleil' in French, and ἥλιος in Greek. Thus it is possible to detect the meaning of logographic writing when you know nothing about an underlying language, as in the signs '1, 2, 3,' universally recognized. The more phonographic writing becomes, the more closely tied it is to the special speech of a certain group of human beings. Apologists for Chinese writing, whose signs are not phonographic (though containing phonetic hints), always bring forth its independence from local mutually unintelligible dialects, and no doubt this very feature of Chinese writing has made possible the extraordinary stability of a polyglot Chinese civilization for millennia over vast territories.[8]

In history, syllabography combined with logography in two majestic *logosyllabic* systems, Mesopotamian cuneiform and Egyptian hieroglyphic. Logosyllabic writing also makes use of semasiographic elements, especially semantic complements ('determinatives'), which categorize a word but are neither phonographic nor logographic. Mesopotamian cuneiform and Egyptian hieroglyphic are highly abstract and far removed from subtle but transitory speech. A reader never knows from the signs how to pronounce a given word, but rather is reminded of a word in his native language through a web of suggestions, some semantic and some phonographic and some semasiographic. Scribes acquire a high facility for recognition of signs—that is, they read and write them easily—but the code they are using does not actually give them the approximate sound of the words in the language they are speaking. We cannot pronounce Sumerian or Akkadian, because Sumerian and Akkadian speakers are extinct. Such facts should not surprise us, when we consider the complexities of representing human speech by means of graphic signs within a traditional system with roots in the faraway past. But the effect of the distance between script and speech in historical logographic writings is that human thought communicated by such systems is simpler than thought common in speech, though with the obvious advantage of

[8] There is much debate how Chinese writing actually works, but a useful description in F. Coulmas, *The Writing Systems of the World* (Oxford, 1989) 91–136.

outlasting the speaker. Novelty of thought in logosyllabic writing, *tout court*, brings unintelligibility.

Nonetheless such writings functioned vigorously for more than three thousand years and were still used in the early centuries of the Christian era. Never did scribal classes show any interest to remove logographic elements in favor of phonographic ones, any more than we would want to throw away '1, 2, 3.' Egyptian and Mesopotamian writing was far more advanced than the writing used in China today, where one fourth of all humans live, if one equates the ability to communicate phonetic information with advancement in the history of writing, as many do.

The first wholly phonographic writings appeared at the fringes of the great Bronze Age centers of power in the first half of the second millennium. Parallel experiments in the Aegean and Levant rejected, by and large, the use of logograms and reduced writing to pure syllabaries, to phonetic representation alone. The emergence of mostly phonographic systems among formerly illiterate peoples exemplifies an important principle in the history of lexigraphic writing: structural change in the way the writing works occurs only when a writing is passed from one culture and its supporting language to another culture and language. Structural change within a system of 'graphic marks with a conventional reference' is avoided at all costs and unknown within the history of writing, for change of an arbitrary system introduces obscurity when clarity, not simplicity, is the supreme desideratum. When writing crosses cultural lines, underlying principles can be reassessed, if unconsciously, and new structures made.

Of the Aegean experiments, Linear B is the most familiar, with 87 separate signs to represent five vowels and a full range of consonant + vowel clusters, and many special signs, really logograms, for commodities. Initially designed for a Minoan language of unknown affinity, the system was applied to Greek by 1400 at the very latest. Hellenists sometimes decry how unsuited this writing was to recording Greek, noting that Linear B preserves only lists and accounts while alphabetic writing took down Homer. Such comparisons are unhistorical; in truth the Aegean syllabaries recorded with surprising accuracy the phonology of Greek speech. The later Cypriote syllabary, which belongs to the same tradition as Linear B, was even used side by side with the Greek alphabet on Cyprus from c. 800 down into the Hellenistic Period. The Aegean syllabic scripts were a major innovation over earlier logosyllabic systems, and one wonders why so advanced a writing should be found in the provincial Aegean: a good example of how outlying peoples are better positioned to make structural changes to a system of writing than those living in the great centers of power and influence.

By 1500 there appeared in the Levant another wholly phonographic family of writings, the West Semitic scripts, directly antecedent to Greek alphabetic writing. The idea of fashioning a wholly phonographic script may have come to the Levant from the Aegean, when one considers the archaeologically attested precedence in time of Cretan Linear A (18th century B.C.), presumably a syllabary like its descendant Linear B; persistent traditions report that the Philistines, visible in Gaza by the Late Bronze Age, were Minoans.[9] The actual model for the West Semitic scripts, however, must have been Egyptian logosyllabic hieroglyphic, because in both writings, uniquely, the only phonetic information provided is consonantal, while in Mesopotamian logosyllabic cuneiform, and in the Aegean syllabaries, vowels are always associated with consonants (so in Linear B 𐀴𐀪𐀡 *ti-ri-po* = τρίπους). Speakers of Canaanite West Semitic lived of course in cultural and geographical proximity with the Egyptians.

Phonograms in Egyptian are of three kinds, representing three consonants, two consonants, or one consonant. Being an outsider, the inventor of West Semitic writing[10] appears to have seen how an entirely different kind of writing, a purely phonographic script, could be fashioned from the 24 or so uniconsonantal phonograms in the Egyptian logosyllabic writing of around 700 signs. Because of the structural similarity between the Afro-Asiatic ('Hamitic') Egyptian language and Semitic languages, the inventor had at his disposal in the 24 Egyptian uniconsonantals, preformed, something close to the consonantal phonemic repertory of West Semitic speech.

The invention of the astonishingly simple and logical West Semitic linear writing by some unknown genius was an event of extraordinary importance in the history of culture. Modern Arabic script is essentially the same, and dozens of other scripts, including the Indic and the Greek alphabet, descend directly from it. Other revolutionary features of the West Semitic scripts, in addition to their small

---

[9] Recent overview in T. Dothan and M. Dothan, *People of the Sea: The Search for the Philistines* (New York, 1992).

[10] For writing systems as the inventions of single individuals, cf. Powell (1991) 10–12.

number of pure phonograms, are a fixed order of the signs and the naming of the signs in a rhythmical series as a mnemonic device to enable learning, as in our ABC song. The encoding of the sound of the sign in its name was a major innovation, and in this functional sense one can meaningfully speak of the 'acrophonic principle,' the rule that the first sound of the name of a sign is the sound of that sign.[11] Because of this mnemonic system it was easier to learn West Semitic writing than other writings.

What is an Alphabet?

We have been discussing the history of writing as a procession, within lexigraphy, from logography, to logosyllabic writing, to pure syllabaries. But West Semitic writing is universally called 'the alphabet' by Semiticists, and sometimes by others. The writing is so called according to the notion that an alphabetic sign stands for a phoneme, a class of sounds which are significantly different from other sounds (different enough to change the meaning of a word). Because each sign in the West Semitic repertory stands for a single consonant, obviously a phoneme, West Semitic writing must therefore be alphabetic, the first alphabet. Libraries carry any number of 'histories of the alphabet' that are really histories of West Semitic writing, with an appendix on the Greek alphabet. But if West Semitic writing was an alphabet, then ancient Egyptian must have been partly alphabetic too, as far as the functioning of the around 24, or so, uniconsonantal

[11] Unfortunately the phrase 'acrophonic principle' is also applied to a theory of the origin of West Semitic signs in early pictograms, whose names describe what is pictured. Hence the first sign *'alp* = 'bull' is supposedly so called because ∢ once represented the head of a bull, now rotated onto its side. Repeated in many handbooks, the theory presupposes that the inventor of West Semitic writing first fashioned a coherent phonemic repertory, then sought out Egyptian pictographic signs whose names in Semitic would encode that repertory! Furthermore, only some Semitic names are meaningful, and some signs have more than one name. See Gelb (1963) 111, 138. Cf. J. Teixidor, 'Lire et entendre en Ouest-Sémitique,' in Baurain et al. (1991) 96: 'Mais on ne peut pas faire valoir aux commencements de l'alphabet [= West Semitic] le principe dit acrophonique: son utilisation, justifiée pour des raisons pédagogiques, n'entra en jeu qu'après l'invention des signes alphabétiques [= West Semitic]. Isolés, ils étaient indéfinissables et imprononçables. Pourquoi la lettre beth, par exemple, aurait-elle eu une graphie qui ressemblait au dessin d'une maison? Quand on l'entendait prononcer, le son beth ne pouvait signifier autre chose que "maison". On ne commence pas par nommer ce qu'on ne connaît pas.'

hieroglyphic signs was concerned,[12] the very repertory isolated by the inventor of West Semitic writing. A common complaint tells how the Egyptians could always have discarded their repertory of 750 signs any time they wanted and written their 'language' solely by means of the 24 uniconsonantal signs. But if the 24 Egyptian uniconsonantals were 'alphabetic,' little sense remains to describing Egyptian writing as logosyllabic, which from the point of view of the history of writing it surely was. It is hardly likely that truly 'alphabetic' signs (one sign = one phoneme) would appear in combination with logograms and syllabograms, a point made long ago by I. J. Gelb.[13] An important reason the Egyptians never 'took advantage' of their 24 'alphabetic signs' is that these signs were not alphabetic; they were not perceived as different in kind from Egyptian syllabic biconsonantal and triconsonantal signs.

Viewed within the history of writing, West Semitic writing was really an odd sort of syllabary in which an individual sign stood not for a single phoneme, but for a consonantal phoneme *plus* an unknown vowel, or no vowel—a syllable in short. What does the sign *beth* represent phonetically? [bi], [ba], [bu], or, at the end of some words [b]. For example, a literate native speaker of Arabic, a West Semitic script, cannot know how to pronounce the word written KTB in isolation; only context reveals how the consonantal skeleton is to be vocalized, so that according to very different vocalizations the meaning could be 'writer,' 'he wrote,' 'book,' 'books,' 'bookseller,' or 'writing.' AEIΔE, by contrast, can be pronounced by someone who knows nothing at all about the Greek language and who does not understand what is being said. Similarities in form and letter-name between the Greek alphabet and West Semitic writing, and the shared system of learning through a mnemonic series of names, are evidence of historical relation, not of identity of system.

Another way to think about the essential difference between the West Semitic scripts and the Greek alphabet is that the individual *consonantal* signs in the Greek alphabet, taken alone, are not pronounceable, while in West Semitic writing they are. If asked how to pronounce T, an alphabet-user will say [ti] or something like that, but

---

[12] A. Gardiner's standard *Egyptian Grammar*³ (Oxford, 1957) does call them 'alphabetic signs.'

[13] Gelb (1963) 122–153; see also P. Swiggers, 'On the Nature of West-Semitic Writing Systems,' *Aula Orientalis* 2 (1984) 149–151.

really T is only pronounceable in combination with another sound, in this case represented graphically by a vowel sign. In West Semitic, on the other hand, the sign T is pronounceable as [ti], [ta], [tu], or it closes a syllable.

In fact the very concept of the phoneme descends from an analysis of the working of the Greek alphabet in its relation to speech, and some linguists deny the phoneme's objective reality; Chinese speakers not exposed to *Pinyin* ('spell sound,' Roman characters for recording Chinese) are unable to resolve syllables into phonemes, while those who have learned *pinyin* can do it easily.[14] An analysis of West Semitic writing could never lead to the concept of the phoneme, nor did it. West Semitic writing functions by providing the reader with phonetic hints of extreme ambiguity. When reading the Greek alphabet, by contrast, the reader sounds out the signs—as children do today—then recognizes from the aural, phonetic reconstruction what word is meant, a process that made silent reading rare until the end of the classical period. There is never clarity about mood, tense, or aspect in West Semitic writing, and the distance between the actual sound of speech and information encoded in the writing remains very great. The oblique narrative descriptions in familiar English versions of the Hebrew Bible, when compared with Homer's vivid descriptions, or the tragedians', reflect the inability of West Semitic writing to come close to natural language.[15] The profound phonetic ambiguity implicit in West Semitic writing is exemplified in the biblical story of Daniel (5.25–26), when West Semitic Aramaic writing appeared on the walls at Belshazzar's feast:[16]

Conventionally transliterated as MN ꜣ MN ꜣ TQL WPRSYN, the writing is evidently a money-changer's text, 'A mina, a mina, a shekel (in Aramaic = tekel), half-minas.' But Daniel, who understands West

[14] C. Read, Zhang Ynu-Fei, Nie Hong-Yin, and Ding Bao-Qing, 'The Ability to Manipulate Speech Sounds Depends on Knowing Alphabetic Writing,' *Cognition* 24 (1986) 31–44.

[15] E. Auerbach's famous distinction between Homeric and biblical style in the first chapter of *Mimesis* (1953) 1–19—the Homeric style being on the surface, explicit, encyclopedic; the biblical being allusive, implicit, elliptical—is false because it fails to take into account the relation between the technology of writing and style in written expression.

[16] For Aramaic characters from 5th to 3rd centuries, cf. H. Jensen, *Die Schrift in Vergangenheit und Gegenwart* 3rd ed. (Berlin, 1969) 293.

Semitic writing, unlike the soothsayers and scribes who write Akkadian in cuneiform script, draws prophecy from the ambiguity of the signs, reading MN Ʒ as 'numbered' (really MNH, and with different vowels: 'God has *numbered* your kingdom'); TQL as 'weighed' (really TQYLTH, with different vowels: 'You are *weighed* in the balance and found wanting'), and WPRSYN as 'and Persians' (really WPRS: 'Your kingdom is divided and given to the Medes *and the Persians*').[17]

The discovery of the phoneme in graphic representation was a Greek achievement, no doubt accidentally made and imperfect, but radical in its effects, and Greek alphabetic writing has established nearly irrevocable prejudgments for us about what writing is and what writing should do. It is hard for us to remember that it is only one kind of writing. While enabling highly refined forms of thought through its close alliance with speech, the Greek alphabet would badly disappoint the followers of Thoth, whose beautiful written signs were alive and able to harm or heal; or the Mandarin, whose signs could be read 2,000 miles away by someone who spoke a different language; or Daniel, who found the will of God in phonetic ambiguity.

Monogenesis and the Adapter

In being carried from one language and culture to another, the West Semitic syllabary was transformed into the world's first alphabet, but there was nothing inevitable or necessary about how alterations to its model were made. If you just have to have vowel-signs, why not use them only to clarify ambiguity, as the so-called *matres lectionis*, consonantal signs used as vowel markers, actually did function in some West Semitic scripts (but with inconsistent values and never in Phoenician writing). Even to an alphabet-user, the instinct to omit vowels is strong and natural, as in the experience of a five-year old child learning to write in America (Figure 1).[18]

The child has been taught to use vowels with consonants, and she is sensitive to vowel length, writing TOO for [tou] and WEE for [wē], but doesn't mind LITLL, LIZRS, LBSTRS, WR, and LBI5RD, and vrbdy knws y dnt nd vwls ll th tm. West Semitic writing has not been handed over unaltered in its essence to the Greeks. An inven-

[17] Cf. J. P. Brown, *Israel and Hellas* (Berlin, 1995) 50.
[18] My thanks to Laura Miller.

FIGURE 1. I WINT TOO JAMAICA WEE SAW LAWS UV LITLL LIZRS WEE SOW BIEBIE LBSTRS THEAY WR VAREE BIG WEE WIT SWIMU WEE SAW A BAIBEE LBI5RD THEAN WEE WINT BAC

tion has taken place for which we require an inventor, 'the adapter,'[19] who made abrupt and epoch-making changes to his Phoenician model. Somewhere, in real time, this man isolated the phoneme in graphic representation by requiring every vowel to be annotated explicitly (though not precisely, ignoring long and short). His law is never violated: nowhere in early Greek inscriptions do we find haphazard use or intentional omission of vowel signs.

The importance of understanding the historical role of the adapter makes it worthwhile to recreate his method, the problems he faced, and how he solved them. A Greek learning a phonetic system of writing from a Semite will, of course, struggle with the different phonologies of each language. The adapter receives from his informant the rule that the first sound in the name of the sign will be the phonetic value of the sign (the 'acrophonic principle'), but the rule breaks down on the very first Semitic character *'alf* 𐤀 (cf. Figure 2) because he cannot hear the initial phoneme, a glottal stop which is not phonemic in Greek. Hence, according to the informant's own rule about deriving the phonetic quality of the sign from the sign's name, *alp* 𐤀 should = [a]. Perhaps in this way the adapter discovered the principle that a sign can represent a quality of the vibration in the vocal chords, because he transforms Phoenician *hē* 𐤄 = [h^x][20] to Greek *ei* = [ε] (later called *epsilon*), and Phoenician *ḥēt* 𐤇 = an 'emphatic'[21] [ḥ^x] to Greek aspirate *hēta* = [h] (in some dialects later called *ēta* = [η] through psilosis), but the assignments might have gone the other way. The assignment of Phoenician *yōd* 𐤉 = [y^x] to Greek iota = [ι] is plausible enough, for consonantal [y] and vocalic [i] are related phonologically, and we might pause to complain of the chance lost to represent graphically the common Greek phonemic glide [y], accurately represented in the Cypriote syllabary. Nothing, however, about Phoenician *'ain* 𐤏 = a voiced pharyngeal fricative plus a vowel obviously suggested to the adapter Greek vocalic *ou* (later *omicron*) = [o], clear evidence of the adapter's craft, as is the treatment accorded to Phoenician *wau* 𐤅 = [w^x], retained in the Greek series as the consonant [w] and probably called *wau* (later *digamma*) = [w], but reshaped as Ϝ. The Phoenician shape 𐤅 was

[19] The term was first used by B. Einarson, 'Notes on the Development of the Greek Alphabet,' *Classical Philology* 62 (1967) 1–24.

[20] Superscript ^{x} stands for 'any vowel, or no vowel.'

[21] Conventionally so called to indicate pharyngealization or velarization, but we cannot reconstruct precisely the phonology of ancient Phoenician.

FIGURE 2. The Greek and Phoenician Signaries

	Hypothetical Phoen. name	Hypothetical Phoen. sound	9th–8th cent. Phoen. shape	Selected Greek shapes from epichoric varieties 8th–5th cent. (all forms-right-to-left)	Greek sound	Greek name	Greek shape in 4th-cent. Koinē left-to-right	Modern printed Greek shape
	a.	b.	c.	d.	e.	f.	g.	e.
1	ʾalf	ʾˣ	𐤀	𐤀 A	a	ἄλφα	A	A α
2	bēt	bˣ	𐤁	[illegible]	b	βῆτα	B	B β
3	gaml	gˣ	𐤂	7 ⟩ 7) ⟩ Λ	g	γάμμα γέμμα	Γ	Γ γ
4	delt	dˣ	𐤃	Δ ◁ ◁	d	δέλτα	Δ	Δ δ
5	hē	hˣ	𐤄	∃ ∃ ∃ ∃ ⊐	ĕ	εἶ, ἒ ψιλόν	E	E ε
6	wau	wˣ	𐤅	[illegible]	w	Ϝαῦ	-	-
7	zai	zˣ	𐤆	I I	dz, zd	ζῆτα (from ṣādē?)	I Z	Z ζ
8	ḥēt	ḥˣ	𐤇	8 ⊟ ⊟ H H H	h, ē	ἦτα	H	H η
9	ṭēt	ṭˣ	𐤈	⊗ ⊕ ⊙	th	θῆτα	Θ ⊙	Θ θ
10	yōd	yˣ	𐤉	[illegible]	i	ἰῶτα	I	I ι
11	kaf	kˣ	𐤊	[illegible]	k	κάππα	K	K κ
12	lamd	lˣ	𐤋	[illegible]	l	λάμβδα	Λ	Λ λ
13	mēm	mˣ	𐤌	[illegible]	m	μῦ, μῶ	M	M μ
14	nūn	nˣ	𐤍	[illegible]	n	νῦ	N	N ν
15	semk	sˣ	𐤎	⧧ Ξ ⊞ Ξ	ks	ξεῖ	Ξ Ξ	Ξ ξ
16	ʿain	ʿˣ	𐤏	o ⊘	o	οὐ, ὂ μικρόν	O	O o
17	pē	pˣ	𐤐	[illegible]	p	πεῖ	Π	Π π
18	ṣādē	tsˣ	𐤑	M M	s	σάν (from zai?)	-	-
19	qōf	qˣ	𐤒	Ϙ Ϙ	q	ϙόππα	[illegible]	-
20	rōš	rˣ	𐤓	[illegible]	r	ῥῶ	P	P ρ
21	šin	shˣ	𐤔	[illegible]	s	σίγμα (from semk?)	Σ	Σ σ s
22	tau	tˣ	𐤕	+ T	t	ταῦ	T	T τ
23	see wau above			Y Y V V	u	ῦ	Y	Y υ
24	(? φ [qof] >)			Φ Φ	ph	φεῖ	Φ	Φ φ
25	(? X, + [tau] >)			X +	ks, kh	χεῖ	X	X χ
26	(? Ψ [kaf] >)			[illegible]	ps, kh	ψεῖ	Ψ	Ψ ψ
27	o [ô μικρόν] >			[illegible]	ō	ὦ, ὦ μέγα	Ω	Ω ω

retained as the Greek character named *u* (later *upsilon*) = [ʊ] and placed at the end of the series after *tau*.

The arbitrary nature of the adapter's assignments are clear from the parallel adaptation of West Semitic writing to record Iberohispanic, where the Iberian inventor fashioned a syllabary consisting of signs for consonant + vowel, with five signs for pure vowels. As in the Greek signary, *'alf* becomes [a], but Semitic *'ain* o stands for [e] and Semitic *zai* ⌶ = [z^x] becomes the vowel [o]![22]

The adapter has decided consciously to fashion a full vocalic system. Though he has no words to describe what he is doing, he is thinking about phonemic range in his new technology. Realizing the advantage of a series of signs that can represent aspirated stops, so phonemically prominent in Greek,[23] as in πόρος/φόρος or κόρος/χόρος, the adapter adds to the end of the series after *upsilon* the so-called supplementals Φ, X, Ψ, naming them after the model of *pei* (Π) as *phei*, *khei*, and probably **ϙhei* with the values of [ph], [kh], and probably [*ϙh].[24]

The adapter has made no distinction between long and short vowels, and the choice of five vowel signs is itself arbitrary. By c. 600 B.C. the need for a long [ō] inspired a diacritical form of *omicron*, added to the end of the series and later called *omega*, the only addition ever made to the adapter's original signary, if we do not count such sportive epichoric forms, ignored by the κοινή, as Ionian *sampi* ϡ = [ss]. But the adapter's conservatism has set down conditions for later confusion, especially in his retention of ϙ = [k] at the back of the mouth before [o] and [u] and in some other circumstances, and in his apparent invention of a corresponding aspirate Ψ = **ϙhei* (?). These sounds were not phonemically distinct from K = [k] before [a], [i], [e] and X = [kh] in the same conditions, and before long ϙ = [k] and Ψ = **ϙhei* dropped from the signary or received altered values.

---

[22] The parallel is little known: see now J. De Hoz, 'The Phoenician Origin of the Early Hispanic Scripts,' in Baurain et al. (1991) 667–82.

[23] Except for Cretan: but the adapter is no Cretan.

[24] Long thought to be a later accretion, the supplementals must belong to the initial system: see Powell (1987). For a defense of the earlier view, see Wachter (1989). For a tempting explanation of ϙ and Φ as representing labio-velars, and for the phonology of the earliest alphabet in general, Cl. Brixhe, 'De la phonologie à l'écriture: quelques aspects de l'adaptation de l'alphabet cananéen au Grec,' in Baurain et al. (1991) 313–356.

The adapter's handling of the four Semitic signs for sibilants, when in Greek there was but a single [s] sound,[25] led to desperate perplexity. He might have kept one Phoenician sign for [s] and discarded the other three, but he did not wish to disturb, through omission, the integrity of the signary and its explicative row of names learned by heart; new signs he added at the end of the signary. We know from Roman authorities that the alphabet was learned, first, as a series of names and, second, as a series of graphic signs, over which the series of names was imposed. Quintilian (1.1.245) complained about this impractical system and recommended that the names be associated individually with the shapes. Because to the Greek ear all [s] sounds were pretty much the same, a careless exchange of names seems to have taken place in the memorized series very early in the history of the alphabet, perhaps at the adapter's own hands. The shape of Phoenician *zai* ⌶ = [z^x] became the shape of Greek *zēta* ⌶ = probably biliteral [ts]or [dz], but the name *zēta* appears to come from Semitic *ṣādē* ᛘ = [ṣ^x],[26] influenced by the names of succeeding *ēta, thēta* in the series. The shape of the Phoenician sign *šīn* w = [sh^x] became the shape of Greek *sigma* ϟ = [s] (its axis has changed), whose name seems to be taken from the Semitic letter *semk* ǂ = [unvoiced s^x] (perhaps *semk* > **sekm* > *sigma*). The Phoenician sign *ṣādē* ᛘ = [ṣ^x] appears to have given rise to the Greek sign M = [s] called *san*, which occupies the same place in the series as *ṣādē* (Figure 2), though the shapes are never quite the same; the name *san* is derived *faut de mieux* from Semitic *zai* ⌶. Semitic *semk* ǂ = [unvoiced s^x] gave rise to Greek ⊞, but now with the name *šin*(?) and the value [sh], which found no equivalent in Greek phonology: the name '*ksei*' must come after the value [ks] was given to it in the Eastern epichoric scripts,[27] apparently in the 6th century B.C. or earlier, at the same time that a reformer in the East gave a new value [ps] to Ψ (from its hypothetical original nonphonemic value of *ʕh, made obsolete by phonemic X = [kh] in Eastern scripts); still, literacy must have been restricted for such alterations to 'catch,' the only ones made deliberately to the adapter's model. In the Western scripts, ⊞ is not

[25] Though there were other affricates, as ͳ or Ͳ (apparently -ss-/-tt-) attest.

[26] Another so-called 'emphatic.'

[27] There is not room here to discuss A. Kirchhoff's division of the epichoric scripts into Red (Western), Blue (Eastern), and Green (Southern): A. Kirchhoff, *Studien zur Geschichte des griechischen Alphabets*[4] (Gütersloh, 1887); cf. Powell (1991) 53–54.

used at all, though fixed in the abecedarium, and Ψ settles on the phonemic value [kh] (Western X = [ks] is evidently a deaspirated simplification of the bigraph X$).[28] Early alterations to name and sound were canonized as the writing spread from a small group into the Greek world.

The partly arbitrary assignment of Semitic consonantal signs to Greek vowels and the extraordinary splitting of Semitic *vau* into two signs, one consonantal and one vocalic; the inviolable rule that a vocalic sign must accompany a consonantal sign; the creation of three additional signs to represent aspirates; and the confusion of the names and values of the sibilants are only explicable on a theory of monogenesis. It is contrary to the principles of historical criticism to suppose that a complexity of arbitrary changes will occur twice, let alone in the same place at the same time. A single man at a single time isolated the consonantal phoneme in graphic representation, basing his labors on a preexistent West Semitic syllabary. Depending on convention, as do all systems of writing, the Greek alphabet clung tenaciously to its initial principles, never slipping back into syllabography or logography and resistant for hundreds of years to a standard orthography. All over the Greek world a new technology recorded the actual sound of speech by breaking down the continuous stream of sound into a continuous stream of phonemic signs which at first wind back and forth (*boustrophedon*), then are stacked row after row, avoiding punctuation and preserving the bewildering array of local dialects with which Hellenists still struggle today.

When?

Without evidence, but proceeding from a theory that high cultures are literate, scholars of the 19th century believed that the alphabet was introduced to Greece early, in the late Bronze Age or early Iron Age at the latest. Rhys Carpenter argued against the traditional view in the 1930s,[29] when real epigraphic information about West Semitic writing was accumulating and the corpus of Greek inscriptions was already enormous. How could the Greeks, who wrote on pots and

---

[28] See Powell (1991) 58–63.
[29] Carpenter (1933); (1938).

stones from the moment when the earliest inscriptions appear around 750 B.C. or a little earlier, be supposed never to have behaved in this way before? The epigraphic record must be more or less coextensive with the existence of the writing itself, Carpenter argued, and most have followed. According to Carpenter's reasoning and on present evidence, the alphabet was, therefore, invented about 800 B.C., assuming (admittedly on no concrete basis) that a gap of a generation or so is necessary for the adapter's invention to spread, a 'decent' interval before our earliest extant inscriptions.[30]

Semiticists who do not accept the syllabic character of West Semitic writing, and who do not therefore consider the Greek alphabet to be structurally distinct from West Semitic, have recently questioned Carpenter's *argumentum ex silentio*. Their arguments have received a wide audience. Such scholars point out that in the Levant West Semitic inscriptions are extremely scarce until classical times (but they do exist), so perhaps all early Greek writing has simply been lost (but no Greek alphabetic writing before 775–750 B.C. has ever been found). They speak as if 'alphabetic' writing might have passed from East to West piecemeal, now this letter form and now that, and see no objection to the 'alphabet's' crossing more than once to the West. They ignore the hand of the adapter and dwell on minor features in script to support their arguments. J. Naveh, for example, suggests that Greek five-stroke *mu* and dotted *omicron* must depend on Semitic letter forms earlier than c. 1000 B.C.[31] (in truth neither five-stroke *mu* or dotted *omicron* appears in the earliest Greek inscriptions). When considering problems of external form and their relation to the fact of transmission, we must remember that neither Greek *san* M nor *iota* ʃ have shapes just like their Phoenician models: changes have taken place at the adapter's hands, or by early followers. On general principles it is informative to see, *mutatis mutandis*, how in Figure 1 the child has added an extra loop to *w* ɯ WINT [= went] and in WEE = [we], but not in the seven following examples. She makes

[30] Carpenter worked with later dates for the epigraphic finds. He also encouraged comparison between Greek and Phoenician letter forms, but this method has proven treacherous because of the small sample of West Semitic inscriptions and problems in dating them (debate continues, for example, over the earliest Phoenician inscription, on the coffin of King Ahiram, cut in the 13th *or* in the 10th century B.C.). For the comparative study of letter forms, McCarter (1975).

[31] J. Naveh, *Early History of the Alphabet* (Leiden, 1982) 181.

the J in *Jamaica* = ℯ the same as the E = ℯ in *biebie* [= baby] and the G = ℯ in *big*—she knows there is a loop, but is unsure where. She draws Z as ϟ in liz[a]r[d]s and as a 5 in *lb[?]iz[a]rd*, understanding that there is a bend, but confused about the details. The little girl has copy-books to hand, but prefers to act on learned principles of letter formation. In spite of her mistakes, her intent is intelligible because we understand these same principles. Odd shapes in the Greek epichoric scripts (e.g. ᒪΓ for *beta* in Corinth) must descend from just such stylistic or accidental variants to the adapter's original system, passed on as correct forms when the alphabet was known to few. The study of external form is useful paleographically, but of restricted value in assessing the historical change that took place when c. 800 B.C. someone altered the Phoenician syllabary to create the world's first alphabet.

Where?

'Where was writing transmitted from East to West?' we wonder, but we would better ask 'Where did the adapter live, and who was he?' At least we will need to place Greek and Phoenician together. Pressure from the Neo-Assyrian Empire on the Levant during the Iron Age encouraged the Phoenician settlement of Kition c. 900 B.C. on Cyprus, side by side with Greek-speaking communities; important West Semitic inscriptions have been found at Kition. Phoenician craftsmen may also have been living in Crete, where a bowl survives c. 900 B.C. with a Phoenician inscription.[32] Actual Assyrian occupation of the Levantine coast in the 8th century must stand behind the great Phoenician diaspora in the Western Mediterranean at this time,[33] and Greeks were caught up in the expanding nexus of international trade in metals, especially, which fed the Assyrian market.

In the Aegean, the most conspicuous role at this time was played by Euboians from, probably, the powerful Iron Age community at

---

[32] M. Sznycer, 'L'inscription phénicienne de Tekke, près de Cnossos,' *Kadmos* 18 (1979) 89–93. Other Phoenician objects on Crete are found in the Idaean Cave, at Knossos, and at Kommos, where a Phoenician-style stone temple has been found: J. W. Shaw, 'Phoenicians in Southern Crete,' *American Journal of Archaeology* 93 (1989) 165–83.

[33] M. E. Aubet, *The Phoenicians and the West. Politics, Colonies, and Trade* (Cambridge, 1993) 68–74.

Lefkandi (a modern name). Euboians seem to have had a permanent trading colony at Al Mina at the mouth of the Orontes, and an early Greek alphabetic inscription has been found there.[34] Phoenicians and Euboians rubbed shoulders in Pithekoussai, too, in the Bay of Naples, where both West Semitic writing and early alphabetic Greek inscriptions have been found. If Phoenicians did not actually live in Lefkandi on Euboia at the end of the Iron Age, their crafts are well represented in finds;[35] but they may have lived there, and our most important testimonium about the introduction of the alphabet into Greece, in Herodotus, supports the claim (5.57.1–58.2):[36]

> Now the Gephyraean clan, of which the slayers of Hipparchus were members, claim to have come at first from Eretria, but my own enquiry shows that they were among the Phoenicians who came with Kadmos to the country now called Boiotia. In that country the lands of Tanagra were allotted to them, and this is where they settled. The Kadmeans [i.e. Thebans] had first been expelled from there by the Argives [in the War of the Epigoni], and these Gephyraeans [companions of Kadmos but not living in Thebes] were forced to go to Athens after being expelled later by the Boiotians [the native Greeks]. The Athenians received them as citizens of their own on set terms, debarring them from many practices not deserving of mention here. These Phoenicians who came with Kadmos and of whom the Gephyraeans were a part brought with them to Hellas, among many other kinds of learning, the alphabet [γράμματα], which had been unknown before this, I think, to the Greeks.

Later (5.61.2) Herodotus adds that the Gephyraeans 'have certain set forms of worship at Athens in which the rest of the Athenians take no part, particularly the rites and mysteries of Achaean Demeter.' Otherwise unknown, the Achaean Demeter may be the Phoenician goddess Astarte/Ashtoreth, called Achaean because she is old and Demeter because she sponsors fertility. Γέφυραῖοι has been assimilated to γέφυρα = 'bridge,' but the word may be Semitic from KPR = 'village.'[37] It is not hard to see why the families of the aristocratic tyrant-slayers Harmodios and Aristogeiton would reject, as Herodotus

[34] For Euboians, D. Ridgway, *The First Western Greeks* (Cambridge, 1992); J. Boardman, 'An Inscribed Sherd from Al Mina,' *Oxford Journal of Archaeology* 1 (1982) 365–67.

[35] Popham et al. (1979–80) 355–69.

[36] Translation based on A. D. Godley in the Loeb Library.

[37] *KPRYM, 'villagers,' is not attested, but B'LY KPYRY, 'lord of the village,' is (my thanks to Michael V. Fox).

implies, a tradition that made them of non-Greek Phoenician descent, but their own account does not necessarily disagree. They came, they say, not from Tanagra, but from Eretria on Euboia, which we now know to have been settled c. 800–775 B.C., about the same time that Lefkandi was being abandoned. But Lefkandi may have been 'Old Eretria' before war over the Lelantine plain in the 8th century encouraged Lefkandiots to found classical Eretria, with which Athens always had strong ties.[38] The ancestors of Harmodios and Aristogeiton, then, whom Herodotus asserts were Phoenicians, may according to family tradition have lived in Lefkandi. Herodotus' assertion that the Gephyraeans brought γράμματα with them is justified by alphabetic scraps unearthed at Lefkandi, the earliest anywhere, while other finds from the cemetery prove unbroken commerce with the Near East through the Iron Age. On the basis of such evidence we may guess that the transmission took place near or on Euboia, perhaps in Lefkandi itself.

Herodotus' further remarks on the alphabet agree with this conclusion (5.58.2–58.3):

> As time went on the sound and the form [ῥυθμός] of the letters were changed. At this time the Greeks who were settled around them were for the most part Ionians, and after being taught the letters by the Phoenicians, they used them with a few changes of form. In so doing, they gave to these characters the name of Φοινικήια, as was quite fair seeing that the Phoenicians had brought them into Greece.

In fact the sound and the ῥυθμός of the letters *did* change, just as Herodotus describes, when the adapter assigned vocalic sounds to signs formerly consonantal; and he added new letters to the end of the series. Because Herodotus has placed Phoenician settlements in eastern Boeotia, his nearby Ionians ought to be West Ionians—Euboians.[39]

Early Inscriptions

We date the introduction of the alphabet by sliding back a little from the earliest inscriptions, so the earliest inscriptions ought to tell

[38] For the war, L. H. Jeffery, *Archaic Greece* (London, 1976) 64–67; Janko (1982) 94–98.

[39] For Euboia's role in the introduction of the alphabet, see now Ruijgh (1995) 36–39 in Crielaard (1995).

us a lot about how the alphabet was used in its early days. Stratigraphically dated by ceramic typology, the oldest Greek inscriptions are from Lefkandi, c. 750 or even 775, and one from Italy.[40] They are miserable scraps, a few letters which, in some cases may be parts of names, Αισχρι[ον?] or Σαμ[ος? From slightly later come other intriguing bits from Pithekoussai in the Bay of Naples. Because short West Semitic inscriptions are found here too, where Euboian and Phoenician lived cheek by jowl, some wonder if the alphabet did not arise here; but Euboia and Pithekoussai are Aegean and western nodes of a common nautical and international society. Most celebrated of the Pithekoussan finds is one of our oldest substantial inscriptions, the three line inscription on the so-called Cup of Nestor, c. 730, scratched retrograde on an imported Rhodian skyphos smashed in a cremation burial:

←
Νεστορος : ε̣[ιμ]ι̣ ευποτ[ον] : ποτ[[ο]]εριον
←
hος δ' α⟨ν⟩ τοδε πιεσι : ποτερι[ο] : αυτικα κενον
←
hιμερος hαιρεσει : καλλιστε̣[φα]ν̣ο : Αφροδιτες

I am the cup of Nestor, a joy to drink from.
Whoever drinks this cup, straightway
the desire of beautiful-crowned Aphrodite will seize.

The first line is probably prose, the second and third are hexameters, and the inscription appears to record a symposiastic skolion, where diners must 'cap' the line of a competing symposiast. The leader of the party begins with a joke that the Rhodian skyphos was the famous cup of Nestor (*Il.* 11.632–637). A second diner plays on the curse-formula attested on early Greek cups, 'Whoever steals this cup' (will suffer something horrible), but jokingly and appropriately changes 'steals' to 'drinks.' A third diner informs us *para prosdokian* that the punishment will be a pleasant sexual experience![41]

[40] See Powell (1991) 119–86 for early inscriptions in general. For the recently published inscription from Gabii in Latium, five letters (including ε, υ, ι, ν) on a pot fragment from an undisturbed tomb securely dated by archaeological context to c. 770 B.C., see E. Peruzzi, 'Cultura Greca a Gabii nel Secolo VIII,' *Parola del Passato* 47 (1992) 459–68.

[41] Probable fragments of another metrical three-line continuously retrograde inscription have now been found at Eretria: A. W. Johnston and A. Andriomenou, 'A Geometric Graffito from Eretria,' *Annual of the British School at Athens* 84 (1989) 217–20. It is unfortunately impossible to make sense from the 18 surviving letters.

We ought to be surprised at jocose and witty metrical exchange recorded at the very beginning of alphabetic literacy, but more surprising is an apparent deliberate reference to Homer's *Iliad*—unless one thinks that Homer's jape about a garrulous septuagenarian, able to lift huge cups, was common poetic fare. If the inscription refers to the text we know as the *Iliad*, or to a public performance based on that text, we have in the Cup of Nestor inscription a *terminus ante quem* for the text of our *Iliad*. Of course texts of the *Iliad* did come into being at some time, and were circulated and memorized. Those who refer the inscription to a *topos* in the oral tradition risk denying to the historical Homer the flare, humor, and poetic brilliance that have placed his poems above all else. The Cup of Nestor inscription is stunning in its improbability, and not so easily explained.

From the same date, or a little before, back on the Aegean nub of the Euboian/Phoenician circuit, comes another substantial inscription scratched through the glaze of an Attic oinochoe, the celebrated Dipylon Jug found in illicit digging in the Kerameikos cemetery. First published in 1871, it is perhaps the most discussed of all Greek inscriptions:

←
hος νυν ορχεστον παντον αταλοτατα παιζει το [= του] τοδε κ{μ}μ{ν}ν

As on the Cup of Nestor, the hexameter defines the condition under which something will happen, 'who now of all the dancers dances most gracefully, of him this . . .' i.e., he will get this pot *vel sim.* The remainder of the apodosis is lost in what seems a clumsy effort to write, in a second hand, the snippet from an abecedarium, κλμ.[42]

Both the Cup of Nestor and the Dipylon Jug inscriptions reflect secular, agonistic activity couched in traditional epic language that must reflect the same process of oral composition that produced the Homeric poems. As a symposium appears to stand behind the Cup of Nestor, a public dance contest, like those Homer places on Scheria in Book 8 of the *Odyssey*, must stand behind the Dipylon Jug inscription. We might expect early inscriptions to be clumsy or inchoate, but we discover the opposite; even the scraps from Pithekoussai and Lefkandi that we take to be simple names may be parts of longer writings. Many have held that the Greeks initially used their alpha-

[42] See Powell (1988) 65–86.

bet for commerce, but we look in vain in early alphabetic inscriptions for any business practice, not even any numbers until the second half of the 6th century B.C., fully 200 years after the alphabet was invented.

The Legend of Palamedes

We have seen how the West Semitic writing and the Greek alphabet are functionally disparate systems with separate origins, and how a Greek inventor made arbitrary changes to his model to create the first technology capable of preserving by mechanical means a facsimile of the human voice. We will be reluctant to think that without his invention he could never have used the Greek language to support written expression based on the West Semitic syllabary, when in history Greek supported two (related) syllabic scripts, Linear B and the Cypriote syllabary; the latter even functioned happily side-by-side with the alphabet. Before, there was the West Semitic syllabary; after, there was the Greek alphabet. What about the adapter, the man who first isolated the phoneme in graphic representation? Who was he? Greek rationalists thought Danaos a good candidate for the transmitter of writing from East to West, because he came from the high culture of Egypt; or Prometheus, who benefitted humankind in many ways; or Kadmos, in the speculation of Herodotus. Danaos and Kadmos are transmitters, and Prometheus a divine culture-bearer, but according to our earliest testimonium, 'Stesichorus [c. 630–555 B.C.] in the second book of his *Oresteia* says that Palamedes invented the alphabet [εὑρηκέναι τὰ στοιχεῖα]' (Page, *PMG* fr 213). We seek an inventor, and Stesichorus may have been right.

Never mentioned in Homer, the legendary Palamedes, son of Nauplios, seems first to have appeared in legend in the post-Iliadic *Kypria*, where he threatened the infant Telemachus to force Odysseus to join the Trojan campaign.[43] In the 5th century, Palamedes was the topic of plays by Aeschylus, Sophocles, and Euripides, who called Palamedes' invention 'the drug of forgetfulness, voiceless yet speaking' (Eur. fr 578N^2). Other stories told how, while the Achaeans were becalmed at Aulis, Palamedes showed how to use Phoenician letters to ration food; letters, στοιχεῖα, 'things in a row,' *are* numbers in the

[43] For a summary, see Gantz (1993) 576–78, 603–606.

so-called Milesian system, attested from the 6th century B.C. Palamedes also invented arithmetic and gaming with dice, an arithmetic game. He divided the army into units, discovered weights, measurement of space and time, military tactics, and how to read the stars. There were different versions of his betrayal and death, but in the best known account Odysseus planted on a captive a false letter implicating Palamedes. In a twist appealing to tragedy, the man who invented writing was undone by it, hoist by his own petard.

We need to explain Palamedes' place in Greek legend, which already had its trickster hero in Odysseus: small wonder stories told of their rivalry. If Palamedes were the actual name of the adapter, the man who fashioned the technology that preserved, then put an end to oral culture, we can understand why he has no place in Homer, whose contemporary he was. Legends are always in formation and no less so during the Archaic Period. Legends preserve facts, though they are not always easy to find. Palamedes' father was Nauplios, famed for seafaring, who lit beacons on Kaphereus at the southernmost tip of Euboia to lure the Greeks to their death after they treacherously murdered his son. Presumably Palamedes was a native of Euboia.

Writing in Homer

The forged letter that destroyed Palamedes is typical of the role that written documents will play in literature once alphabetic writing is wide-spread. We think at once of the note that Phaidra pinned to her breast, accusing Hippolytos (Eur. *Hip.* 856–865), or the tablet (δέλτος) that Iphigeneia wishes to send to her brother in Greece (Eur. *Iph.Taur.* 584), or the message that Harpagos sent to Cyrus, urging revolt (Her. 1.123). Homer's heroes, by contrast, are illiterate; writing is not part of their world. Homer mentions no scribes in the numerous passages where he speaks of occupations and the professions of his day. Nowhere in Homer's descriptions of shields, cups, or other artifacts does writing of any kind appear, not in descriptions of tombs actual or to come: while instructing his son Archilochos how to run the chariot race, Nestor cannot be sure whether a stone is the σῆμα of someone dead, or whether it is a turning post (νύσσα) for a race long ago (*Il.* 23.331–332). The word γράφω or ἐπιγράφω appears seven times in the Homeric poems, and in five cases means to scratch, chafe, or groove (*Il.* 4.139, 11.388, 13.553, 17.599; *Od.* 22.280). The remaining two cases require closer attention.

In *Iliad* 7.170–192, in order to determine who will meet Hector in single combat, Nestor advises the Achaean leaders each to mark a lot—οἱ δὲ κλῆρον ἐσημήναντο ἕκαστος (7.175). The lots are placed in a leather helmet, which is shaken, and out flies the lot of Aias. The herald carries the lot down the line of warriors. Each man denies it is his own, until the herald comes to Aias, who acknowledges that he has 'made the mark' ἐπιγράψας. This cannot be lexigraphic writing, because only Aias knew the sign; there is no conventional reference.

A single genuine allusion to writing appears in the Homeric poems,[44] in the story that Lykian Glaukos tells Diomedes about his ancestor Bellerophon and how he fell victim to the wiles of Anteia, lustful wife of Proitos, king of Ephyre. Being rebuffed, Anteia slandered Bellerophon. The angry Proitos sent Bellerophon to Anteia's father in Lykia, bearing 'baneful signs' σήματα λυγρά 'written on a folding tablet, many and deadly' γράψας ἐν πίνακι πτυκτῷ, θυμοφθόρα πολλά (*Il.* 6.168–170). When Bellerophon showed the tablet to his father-in-law αὐτὰρ ἐπεὶ δὴ σῆμα κακὸν παρεδέξατο γαμβροῦ (6.178–179), his father-in-law sent him against the Chimaira.

Did Homer, then, live in a literate age after all? Was writing part of his world, and did he know how to read and write because in the story of Bellerophon he describes baneful signs on a folded tablet? It is remarkable that only here does real knowledge of this controlling technology appear, omnipresent in Eastern civilizations since the beginning of the third millennium. We can nowhere find clearer evidence for the provincialism of Aegean society in Homer's day than this clumsy and passing reference. Homer calls the inscribed signs σήματα (not γράμματα *vel sim.*), just as in Book 7 the warriors 'made their mark' κλῆρον ἐσημήναντο ἕκαστος. It is misguided to wonder what was the 'original script' to which Homer refers—Linear B preferred by those who think Homer knows of the Mycenaean past, the alphabet by those who want a pen in Homer's hand. To Homer the σήματα are just marks, like those on the lots in the helmet, like those known to be made on 'folded tablets' ἐν πίνακι πτυκτῷ, a widespread writing medium in Mesopotamia and Anatolia; actual examples have been found in the Bronze Age shipwreck off Ulu Burun and in 8th century

[44] Though a scholiast thought a picture was intended: Sch. AE to Dionysius Thrax, in *Gramm. Graeci* I 3, 470, l.19–20, Hilgard.

B.C. wells in Nimrud.[45] Such tablets, covered in wax, are still shown in red-figured Athenian pots of the 5th century[46] and were used in the Roman period. For three thousand years they were the medium for learning to write cuneiform, West Semitic, and the Greek alphabet, as clay or papyrus was used for long records. The folding tablet/writing board must have come to Greece at the moment of transmission and the name δέλτος with it, from the Semitic DLT meaning 'door'; from the same word, no doubt at the same time, came the letter name *delta*.[47] Homer never uses δέλτος (first attested in Aeschylus), as he never mentions Palamedes, because writing and its traditions are not part of his world. Though he may have seen a folded tablet with marks on it, in the hands of rascal Phoenicians who sold gewgaws in Greek lands, σήματα λυγρά cannot refer to any specific script. The detail of 'the fatal letter' must come to Homer embedded in an Eastern dragon-combat myth, whose hero's name invokes the Semitic Storm-god Baal. 'A man, wishing to destroy his enemy, gave him a sealed letter to deliver on a far frontier. The letter read, "Kill the bearer."' The story appears in the biblical account of Solomon and Bathsheba (2 Sam. 11,1,2). Lykia, where Chimaira lived, whence the story must come, is contiguous with lands which used all kinds of scripts from a very early time.

Summary and Conclusions

We began with a paradox, the concinnity of the historical Homer and the date of the invention of the alphabet. The force of this paradox can be lost through clumsy descriptions of the history and nature of writing, or through clumsy models of how oral poems become written documents. As alphabet-users ourselves, it is natural to suppose that writing does for any literate people what writing does for us, and we live by the aphorism first *parole*, then *écrit*. But writing is a human invention which enables forms of thought impossible otherwise, not necessarily translatable into natural language. Natural

[45] G. F. Bass and C. Pulak, 'The Late Bronze Age Shipwreck at Ulu Burun: 1986,' *American Journal of Archaeology* 91 (1987) 321; D. J. Wiseman, 'Assyrian Writing Boards,' *Iraq* 17 (1955) 1–13; R. Payton, 'The Ulu Burun Writing-Board Set,' *Anatolian Studies* 61 (1991) 99–106.

[46] Best known is Berlin, Staatliche Museen F2285.

[47] Cf. Burkert (1992) 30.

language supported the logosyllabic writings of Mesopotamia and Egypt, yet remained surprisingly distant from written expression.[48] The West Semitic syllabaries achieved extraordinary simplicity by abandoning the semantic non-phonetic accoutrements that allowed clear communication in logosyllabic systems, but they paid dearly for the gain in simplicity by a corresponding heightened ambiguity. Certainly the sounds of natural language were not encoded in the Phoenician syllabary, which imparted phonetic information only about the consonantal skeleton of natural language.

The Greek alphabet, which isolated the phoneme in graphic representation, was an utterly different kind of writing. Even when the reader does not know the meaning, he can pronounce the words. Because writing *per se* does not require close intimacy with natural language, something about natural language in and of itself must have attracted the adapter's interest; that something, according to inscriptional evidence, was the complex meters and subtle artificial language of Greek hexametric poetry, a suggestion first made by H. T. Wade-Gery in 1952[49] and now received with approval by many students of Archaic Greece. The possessors of the early Greek alphabet were evidently aristocrats and in their social life audience to Homeric epic and Hesiodic wisdom, but they were not above sailing to Italy in small open boats in the pursuit of profits from the transport of metals for the international trade fostered by Assyrian militarism. In foreign outposts, on Pithekoussai, the earliest possessors of alphabetic literacy played capping games while drinking deeply, and they wrote their verse on cups (the Cup of Nestor). Like Odysseus on Scheria, they witnessed gymnastic contests and were proud of their victories (the Dipylon Jug).

The adapter received detailed information from a Phoenician about the West Semitic syllabary: the names of the letters, the rule that the sound of the sign was encoded as the first sound of the name, the order of the signs, and the shapes of the signs.[50] He changed the value of five signs, making them vowels, but maintained the consonantal value of Semitic *vau* and its place in the series (= Greek *digamma*)

[48] Cf. Bottéro (1992) 97–100.

[49] (1952) 11–14.

[50] In a similar fashion, and at the same time, stories were passing from East to West, no doubt by bilingual speakers, including the story of creation as dragon-slaying preserved in Hesiod's *Theogony*; but the details of such transmission remain obscure.

while adding a sign similar in shape to the end of the series after *tau* (= Greek *upsilon*). The adapter introduced the rule that every vocalic sound needed to be annotated explicitly, and he added three new signs at the end of the series. So did Palamedes add letters to the originals brought by Kadmos, according to several accounts.[51] Ambiguities in the phonology of the inherited system when applied to Greek, and obscure problems attending the original sounds of some letters, led to misunderstanding among early users and the formation of the epichoric scripts.

By every indication Euboia was the place of adaptation, where men maintained relations with the Near East through the Dark Ages.[52] Around 800 B.C., Euboians competed with Phoenicians in the exploration of the far West and left inscriptions there, as they did back home in Lefkandi. Athens, which enjoyed close relations with Euboia, offers examples of other early inscriptions, including that on the Dipylon Jug, long thought because of epigraphic oddities to have been inscribed by a non-Athenian (from Euboia?).[53] Herodotus received a tradition about the importation of writing to Greece by Phoenician immigrants, who lived in Euboia and nearby Boiotia; some of their descendants, including the families of Harmodios and Aristogeiton, went to Athens.

The Greek alphabet was as able to record the songs of Homer in 800 B.C. as in 600 B.C. or in 400 B.C. or at any other time.[54] As for media, papyrus is invisible in the archaeological record outside Egypt, but without doubt an Eastern import into the Aegean through

[51] Hyg. *fab.* 277; Plut. *Quaest. conviv.* 9.2; Pliny *NH* 7.56, 192.

[52] So did Crete, but the early epigraphic remains are on Euboia and in Euboian outposts; Euboia seems to have had permanent settlements in the East itself.

[53] Cf. Jeffery/Johnston (1990) 68.

[54] G. Nagy's 'evolutionary model' of the formation of the Homeric poems cannot stand: rejecting A. B. Lord's theory of the dictated text, Nagy writes that 'Any pattern of diffusion [of the Homeric poems in the fourth quarter of the seventh century] . . . can hardly be ascribed to any hypothetical proliferation of a plethora of manuscripts, in view of the existing physical limitations on materials available for writing down, let along circulating, a text of such monumental size as the *Iliad* or the *Odyssey*' (1995) 164. But papyrus, perishable outside Egypt, must have been widely traded in the Mediterranean long before the invention of the alphabet: for hard evidence cf. J. Smith, *Seals for Sealing in the Late Cypriot Period*, diss. Bryn Mawr College (1994) 63–65, 167 ff., esp. 169 fig. 30; J. Weingarten writes on Aegeanet 8/28/95: '. . . I will vouch for a sealing that truly sealed a papyrus document (indeed, the identification of it is mine) excavated by Jonathan Tubb at Tell el'Sa'idiyeh in Jordan, of Early Iron I date'; for indirect epigraphic evidence, 'The Byblos Syllabary: Bridging the gap between Egyptian hieroglyphs and Semitic alphabets,' *Journal of the Society for the Study of Egyptian Antiquities* 20 (1990) 115–124.

Phoenician Byblos by, say, 900 B.C.[55] For this reason Greek βύβλινον (*Od.* 22.390) means 'made of papyrus.' Whoever wrote down Homer's poems, whenever he did, was a man of means, able to afford a lot of papyrus. Such men certainly existed among far-traveled Euboians grown rich in the metals trade in the late Iron Age, coursing from Italy to Cyprus to the mouth of the Orontes. Seeking parallels in our own age of invention, it is not hard to find entrepreneurs who profit from technologies that roughly reproduce the live performance of others.

Because of his dialect, we think of Homer as Ionian, meaning he lived in Asia Minor, but the evidence is thin. The seafaring Euboians were Ionians too and a natural audience for song about a journey to very far lands and a man who through labor and intelligence made his way home; the *Odyssey* is a Euboian poem. Roots of the Trojan saga may penetrate to the Bronze Age, but modern finds in Euboia reveal a warrior aristocracy vigorous throughout the Iron Age, who at the beginning of historical times waged a bitter war over the Lelantine plain, which drew overseas allies on either side. Aulis, across the Euripos from Lefkandi, is an irrational point of embarkation for Argives going against Troy, but natural for inhabitants of Euboia or Boiotia. Achilles from southeastern Thessaly, just up the coast and over a bit, is best of the Achaeans, while Argive Agamemnon is a braggart, maybe a fool. To everyone's consternation, the first and longest and greatest entry in the Catalogue of Ships belongs to Boiotia, who shared Aulis with Euboian settlements, whither Gephyraeans brought Phoenician letters. The *Iliad* and the *Odyssey* contain traditional material, but Homer has tailored his songs for local consumption, flattering the experience and loyalties of men who lived in southern Thessaly, Boiotia, and island Euboia, site of the earliest alphabetic literacy. The *Iliad* and the *Odyssey* must have been written down there in the early 8th century B.C. Hesiod, who grew up in Boiotia in Ascra across the Euripos, belongs in the same cultural circuit; he sang, he says, in Chalcis on Euboia at the funeral games of Amphidamas (*Erg.* 665–669), who may have died during the Lelantine War. Most place Hesiod later than Homer, but no one has proved ungenuine Hesiod's 'In Delos, Homer and I, singers of oral song, sang

[55] Cf. K. A. Sheedy, 'A Prothesis Scene from the Analatos Painter,' *Mitteilungen des Deutschen Archaeologische Instituts*, Athenische Abteilung 105 (1990) 143.

of Phoebus Apollo, he of the golden sword, stitching together oral song in fresh hymns' (Fragment 357 Merk.-West). There is nothing against the same scribe recording both poets within a lifetime.

The scribe may well have been the adapter himself, who inspired the legend of Palamedes, son of Nauplios, inventor of the alphabet. From principles that govern the history of writing and from the early inscriptions, the adapter's desire was evidently to record metrical verse. What metrical verse? Only Homer and Hesiod can fulfill this role. The natural model is a refinement of the Parry-Lord description, placing the historical adapter in the role of Milman Parry. One man recorded Homer (and perhaps Hesiod), the other recorded Avdo Mejedovich.[56] Neither recorder was a poet, but each possessed his own purpose and an unfamiliar technology capable of making a permanent record of human speech; in the adapter's case, he himself invented this technology. We can never know the exact motives of such a man, but if the personality and songs of historical poets inspired his invention, we can resolve the paradox that has troubled Homeric studies so long. In the beginning, the adapter alone understood how to use his invention. But if you want to learn how to read and write, and with a little musical instruction sing like Homer, you need to work with an existing text. In this way, from the beginning, Homer and Hesiod became the educators of Greece.

[56] For the theory of the dictated text, A. B. Lord (1953) 124–134; cf. Janko (1990) 311–325; for later adjustments to the original text, see Lamberton (this vol.). *Acknowledgments*: My thanks to John Bennet, Emmett L. Bennett, Jr., and Ian Morris for commenting on drafts of this paper.

Robert Lamberton

HOMER IN ANTIQUITY

The question of the relationship of ancient audiences, first of listeners and then of readers, to our *Iliad* and *Odyssey* is bound up with the question of the origin of the poems themselves. What use was made of them, by whom, at what time? There are formidable obstacles to answering these questions for the centuries prior to the late Hellenistic period, when the text known as the vulgate, the basis for the strikingly uniform medieval manuscript tradition, came into being and when, for the first time, we can assume the existence of a uniform reading text closely resembling the poems as we know them. From that point on, we can apply a model of literary production, imitation, and interpretation of a sort relevant to subsequent periods of European literature. Before the vulgate became the norm—a process we probably owe to the Romans, who embraced Hellenic paideia in the second and first centuries B.C. and so stimulated a book trade of unprecedented scale to meet a demand for uniform texts of Homer—we find citations and a few papyri that provide testimony to the existence of considerably longer texts of the poems.

Before 400 B.C., we have only a handful of citations in Herodotus (11 verses), Thucydides (who cites as 'Homer's' one line from the *Iliad* and 13 from the *Hymn to Apollo*), and Aristophanes (whose quotations are problematic, subject as they are to comic distortion), along with a few Homeric phrases in Democritus and the Hippocratic corpus. One thing that emerges clearly is that the lost cyclic epics, completing the Troy tale and adding the saga of Thebes, were widely attributed to Homer in the fifth century, along with the *Hymns* and other material. Thus, even if we had a much larger volume of citations of 'Homer,' we might still be at a loss to specify whether fifth-century copies of the *Iliad* and *Odyssey* resembled our own, or how those poems were understood. Fourth-century citations are far richer and bear ample evidence of variation. Aristotle in particular has many lines not in the received text, and Plato's and Aeschines' citations of Homer include lines absent from the received text and omit canonical lines.

Beginning in the third century, the papyri tell a similar story. Textual deviation from the future vulgate was unevenly distributed in the manuscripts in circulation in the century after Alexander, but at one extreme, a single third-century papyrus containing about 90 lines of Book Eight of the *Iliad* introduces about 30 that were to disappear from our text. Three other papyri of the same century, ranging in length from 28 to 282 lines, have rates of 'added' lines of 10% or higher, as do two substantial papyri of the second century.[1] The papyri of the following two centuries show significantly greater resemblance to the vulgate. The sample is not large, but we can say with certainty that from the fourth to the second century, copies of the *Iliad* and *Odyssey* were being produced that were 10% longer than the poems we know, and sometimes a good deal longer yet.

Evidence for accretion is easier to find than evidence for deletion, and the tradition seems to have been reluctant to remove or suppress any received material.[2] Composed of the inventions of rhapsodes over a span of time we can only attempt to quantify, along with the literary interpolations of poets, of politicians, and ultimately of textual critics such as Crates of Mallos, the poems that lay before the unknown creators of the vulgate incorporated their own history. Those nameless editors carved them down and shaped them into the poems we know, finally a manageable and uniform oeuvre, with an author named Homer, who had a biography, an iconography, a style, a view of the world. Sophisticated and critical biographies of this poet came into existence and prefaces were written to introduce the first-time reader to his life, ideas, and importance. In the schools of the Hellenistic world, the Homer of the subsequent European literary tradition was invented. From that point, as Greek paideia spread through the Roman world, we can talk of interpretive communities, conflicting claims about the meaning of the poems and about the wisdom of Homer, its scope, its contemporary relevance.

The watershed of the Hellenistic vulgate will therefore divide our

---

[1] Though dated, the best account of this problem is in Allen (1923). For discussion of these examples, 250–70 (citations), 299–301 (papyri). See also M. Haslam in this volume.

[2] This impression is reinforced by a naive anecdotal scholion to Dionysius Thrax, where the claim is made that Peisistratus laid the basis for the first critical text of Homer by buying up all the scraps of Homer that could be found, indiscriminately, duplicates and all, and then appointing seventy-two scholars each to assemble his own version of the poems. Aristarchus (!) emerged as winner. See J. I. Porter (1992) 67–68 with n. 1.

inquiry here into two parts, within each of which we may examine the reception of the *Iliad* and *Odyssey* under the general rubrics of philosophy, literature, and education, categories that themselves changed significantly over time.

The Archaic and Classical Periods

Who first mentions Homer? The Homeric corpus we have is exceptionally stingy in the information it provides about its singer. Since the same does not hold true for other traditions of archaic Greek poetry stemming from oral traditions, either a fictional persona endowed with attributes, comparable to Hesiod, Orpheus, or Musaeus, never arose in the traditions of song about Troy, or did arise but was subsequently edited out as an accretion. The former hypothesis is the more attractive, and we might perhaps embrace it with confidence, if not for one anecdotally self-referential passage in the Homeric *Hymn to Apollo* (172–73). There, the self-advertising singer exhorts his audience to declare the best singer to be

> A blind man, and he lives in rocky Chios;
> His songs are all the best, from now on.[3]

The traditions of Homeric song, as we have them, left it to others to fill in the details.

Homer and the philosophers

The history of the Greek reception of Homer starts with the beginnings of Greek philosophy in sixth-century Ionia, and the first mention of Homer in preserved Greek literature is hostile. Within a decade or two of the year 550, Xenophanes of Colophon (frs. 11, cf. 14, 15, 16 DK), himself a poet, declared Homer's and Hesiod's representation of the gods to be implausible, inaccurate, and immoral. Xenophanes had his own notions about the gods that seemed to him superior to those of the earlier poetic 'theologians' (as the archaic hexameter poets were called, at least from the time of Aristotle ([e.g., *Metaph.* 938b28–29]). His denunciation of the anthropomorphism and immorality of Homer's account of the gods set an important precedent.

---

[3] The lines are singled out and quoted by Thucydides (3.104).

From these first stirrings of what came to be called philosophy, a traditional, received poetic world-view, evoked only to be criticized or revised, could be attributed to 'Homer and Hesiod.' To Heraclitus (fr. 56 DK), perhaps a half-century after Xenophanes, is attributed the observation that 'men make mistakes with reference to the knowledge of manifest things . . . [even] Homer, who was the wisest of the Greeks.' In a less charitable mood (fr. 42 DK) he said 'Homer should be thrown out of the contests and whipped—and Archilochus along with him.'

Thus Homer came to represent the old, poetic world-view, in head-on conflict with nascent philosophy. Heraclitus saw the poetic festivals (the 'contests' of fr. 42) as the arena in which that world view asserted and consolidated its hold over people's minds. Much the same view surfaced over a century later in the dialogues of Plato, projected back into the last decades of the fifth century and proclaimed through the persona of Socrates. The Socratic rejection of Homer, however, locates the struggle between poetry and philosophy not in the festivals but in the classroom. The *Iliad* and *Odyssey* must be banished from education both for practical reasons—stories that portray death as an evil and exemplary heroes overcome by emotion will not effectively mold future defenders of the city (*Rep.* 386a–389a)—and because their picture of reality, and particularly of theology, is faulty and pernicious (*Rep.* 376e–383a). The devaluation of all mimetic art as inherently divorced from reality, and hence misleading and useless in the pursuit of truth (*Rep.* 595a–601b), is an outgrowth of this displacement of Homer from his prominent position in education. Clearly, what was at stake, once again, was the conflicting claims of philosophy and its competitors.

From Plato's Socrates as well we get the first inkling of the habit, widespread from the Hellenistic period, of finding in actual lines of the *Iliad* and *Odyssey* the antecedents of later philosophical assertions. In the *Theaetetus* (152e), Socrates proposes to his interlocutor that Homer, 'when he said "Okeanos, the source of the gods, and mother Tethys" (*Il.* 14.201, 302) was saying that everything springs from flow and motion.' With whatever seriousness, the central doctrine of Heraclitus—*panta rei*—is here credited to the very poet Heraclitus said should be whipped. The competition of educational claims and practices is real. Homer, though, could be mustered to serve in that competition on the side of his adversaries. And for all the damning critique, the dialogues of Plato are so permeated with Homeric material that within two centuries of his death an Alexandrian scholar named Ammonius wrote on *Plato's Debt to Homer*, and later 'Longinus,' summarizing that scholarship in his flowery manner wrote that Plato had 'diverted to himself ten thousand streams from that Homeric spring' (De sub. 13.3).

The philosophical polemic against Homer faded from significance in Plato's own generation and there is little trace of it in Aristotle, though Homer as forerunner of philosophical doctrines is very much a part of Aristotle's intellectual world. When, for example, Aristotle observes (*De an.* 404a) that Empedocles, who identified soul and mind, found that same doctrine in Homer's description of the unconscious Hector as 'thinking other thoughts' (ἀλλοφρονέων [cf. *Il.* 23.698]),[4] Aristotle makes no commitment to the accuracy or inaccuracy of Empedocles' claim about Homer's knowledge or intent. But Aristotle goes on to observe a little later (*De an.* 427a) that people generally seem to believe that thought and judgment are forms of perception and himself takes the position that 'the Homeric phrase "for such is thought' (τοῖος γὰρ νόος ἐστίν, *Od.* 18.136) says the same" as Empedocles' more explicit claims on the matter.[5] The little work entitled *On the Universe*, which presents itself as a letter from Aristotle to Alexander, treats Homer as a theological authority (400a), and though the historical Arisotle is not implicated by this piece of pseudepigrapha, the work was widely known and translated, and served to give Aristotelian support to such thinking. Aristotle is also the earliest author known to have made a collection of *Homeric Questions*, or 'problems'[6] relating to specific Homeric words, phrases, or stories, followed by solutions (λύσεις). The testimony of the scholia and later commentators cannot be trusted when they claim that a given Homeric solution is Aristotle's own, but what is said and preserved of the collection does show that in the Peripatos there was interest in such problems and that the precedent was set there for the later collections of solutions, likewise mined by the scholiasts.

With the Stoa, the philosophical school founded by Zeno of Citium

[4] The word in fact occurs in the *Iliad* as we have it only to describe a competitor in the funeral games for Patroclus, Euryalos, who is 'knocked silly' by Epeios in a boxing match.

[5] The examples are discussed by H. Cherniss, *Aristotle's Criticism of Presocratic Philosophy* (Baltimore, 1935) 80, with n. 331.

[6] They are known variously as προβλήματα, ἀπορήματα, and ζητήματα. The fragments are collected in O. Gigon, ed. *Librorum Deperditorum Fragmenta = Aristotelis Opera*, v. 3 (Berlin, 1987), nos. 366–404.

in the Painted Stoa of the Athenian Agora at the end of the fourth century, opens the most problematic phase of the pre-vulgate history of the philosophical reception of Homer.[7] The testimony of such imposing but steadfastly anti-Stoic authorities as Cicero, Plutarch, and Galen paints the Stoics as habitually self-serving and intellectually dishonest readers of early poetry, who read their own ideas into Homer and Hesiod and 'tried to make out that they were Stoics before the fact' (Cicero *De nat. deorum* 1.41). The extent of Stoic commitment to allegorical interpretation and to the notion that the early hexameter poets were sages expressing truths consistent with Stoic models has been disputed.[8] Undisputed, however, is that from Zeno on, the Stoics took an interest in early poetry as a repository of useful information about reality. At the very least, a commitment to the notion that analysis of the divine names in the early poets could reveal hidden truths remained a characteristic element in the thought of many Stoics.[9]

In Plato and in Aristotle, as we have seen, the argument from poetic authority carries no weight. By the latter part of the fourth century, though, Homer was widely viewed as a proto-philosopher, helpful even for Aristotle in giving concrete expression to pre-philosophical notions about the world. With the claim that a hidden truth lay encoded in at least some of those archaic hexameters, the Stoa endowed Homer and Hesiod with an authority of a new kind.

Homer and the poets

The story of the interaction of Homeric poetry with the other Greek poetic traditions that emerged out of the preliterate past is no longer recoverable in detail. A mythic account of the relationship of Homeric and Hesiodic poetry in the form of a story about the competition of the two bards constitutes the earliest recorded attempt to clarify that interaction.[10] Many sources, including the biographies of Homer and the *Suda*, attribute works other than the *Iliad* and *Odyssey* to Homer—not only the cyclical epics and the *Hymns*, nearly universally granted

[7] For the traditional view of the matter, P. DeLacy, 'Stoic Views of Poetry,' *American Journal of Philology* 69 (1948) 241–71.

[8] See A. A. Long, 'Stoic Readings of Homer,' 44–66 in Lamberton and Keaney (1992).

[9] See Most (1989).

[10] *The Contest of Homer and Hesiod* (or *Certamen*) survives intact only in a form that is probably Hadrianic, but a Hellenistic papyrus guarantees that it was already centuries old in the second century A.D., and it may well belong to the archaic period. Text and translation in Evelyn-White (1914) 565–97. See also R. Rosen in this volume.

to the author of the *Iliad* and *Odyssey* in the fifth century, but such unlikely works as the partially iambic *Margites*, certified as Homeric by no less an authority than Aristotle (*Poetics* 1448b). There is every reason to believe that these disagreements concerning authorship stemmed from changing models of literary production and the retrospective accommodation of the body of Greek hexameter poetry stemming from oral traditions to criteria of authorship alien to the conditions of their production.

The skeptical Herodotus thought he could prove that the *Cypria* was not by Homer (2.117),[11] and doubted the Homeric authorship of the poem on the destruction of Thebes, the *Epigonoi* (4.132). Thus the first prose author we have who cites Homer is (like Xenophanes before him) a debunker. What sort of *Iliad* and *Odyssey* he had in front of him cannot be deduced from his limited citations, but certainly the fifth-century's *Iliad*s and *Odyssey*s must, in general, have resembled our own in story and perhaps in bulk. Like other pre-Hellenistic authors, Herodotus cites the *Iliad* by episode, not by book, and so lends support to the ancient observation that the division into books was first done 'by the grammarians of the school of Aristarchus' ([Plutarch] *De vit. hom.* 4).

Though Homer's name is generally evoked only by critics and competitors, echoes and adaptations of Homeric words, phrases, and lines are frequent in the surviving Greek lyric poetry of the seventh and sixth centuries.[12] At the proximal end of the archaic lyric tradition, Pindar represents an especially interesting and well-documented case. Pindar evokes Homer by name three times and the Homerids, the 'sons of Homer,' once. All these evocations serve the greater glory of both Homer and Pindar,[13] but one (*Nemean* 7, 20–30) explicitly corrects the Homeric account of Odysseus. Odysseus, Pindar asserts, has received more fame than he deserved 'thanks to Homer and his sweet words' and were it not for the capacity of 'cleverness' (σοφία) to mislead the 'blind heart' (τυφλόν . . . ἦτορ) of most of mankind, the disputed arms of Achilles would have gone not to Odysseus, but to Ajax. The story is that told in Sophocles' *Ajax* (perhaps half a century after Pindar wrote) and found in neither the *Iliad* nor the

[11] His argument is based on a supposed contradiction between the *Iliad* and the *Cypria*, but even if it in fact existed, such a contradiction would prove nothing about authorship in poetic traditions of this sort.

[12] See Allen (1923) 250, n. 1, for a list of 'allusions' in the lyric poets.

[13] Nagy (1990b) 202: '. . . [in] Pindaric song . . . the idealized poet of the past can be represented as "Homer" while the implicit poet of the present is Pindar.'

Odyssey. In Sophocles' play as in Pindar's ode, the confrontation of military and athletic prowess on the one hand (Ajax) and the manipulative skills of language and intellect on the other (Odysseus) is central. Pindar says clearly enough that the former *deserved* victory, and his epinician poetry was concerned primarily to celebrate those same military and athletic virtues. But the power of sweet words is also Pindar's own, and even here, where the Pindaric account seems most adversarial, it sets out not so much to correct the Homeric account as to absorb and supersede it.

If non-Homeric early Greek epic only gradually became distinct and distinguishable from the Homeric corpus, and the two centuries of archaic lyric poetry (650–450) constitute in their own way a development incorporating and appropriating Homeric poetry, tragedy notoriously began with Aeschylus' self-styled 'chops from Homer's banquets' (Athenaeus 8:347e). In fact, the surviving Athenian tragedies as well as the titles of those that have not survived suggest that the *Iliad* and *Odyssey* were infrequently the source of the stories from the epic tradition selected by the tragedians. The most Iliadic tragedies we know of were indeed by Aeschylus: an Achilles trilogy in which Achilles' alienation from the Greek army (*Il.* 1), and the delivery of his new arms (*Il.* 18.614–19.39) were put on the stage, and the final play, *The Phrygians*, or *The Ransoming of Hector*, must have somehow appropriated the famous passage of *Iliad* 24 where Priam faces Achilles in his tent. Nevertheless, among the nearly 80 titles of plays of Aeschylus known to us, this trilogy stands out as the conspicuous exception. Other stories—including the *Oresteia*—belonged to the cyclic epics (in that instance, the *Nostoi*), but there seems on the whole to have been a reluctance on the part of the tragedians to compete with the *Iliad* and *Odyssey*, which, after all, had their place in Athena's festival, not in that of Dionysus.

The larger picture of the relationship of Homer to Greek tragedy is again one of continuity rather than discontinuity. Aeschylus' Homeric 'banquets' designate the broad range of epic within which his generation did not yet single out the *Iliad* and *Odyssey* as a distinct oeuvre. Athenian tragedy itself constitutes the last flowering of that epic tradition and its stories into an artform addressed to an entire community. By the time the *Iliad* and *Odyssey* had become books like other books, the Greek cities in their evolving complexity had outgrown the capacity or the need for such shared reenactments of the old stories.

Homer and the educators

We have already seen that the philosophical polemic against Homer centered on the role of the *Iliad* and *Odyssey* in education. At issue in the archaic period was education of a deeply communal sort, located in the festivals that provided the context for competitions of poetic recitation and song. In the *Odyssey*, Homer claims that his own antecedents—Phemius, Demodocus, and the other bards within the poem—were entertainers who sang for princes at their feasting, but the earliest external evidence we have for the performance of the Homeric poems suggests a less aristocratic audience. The date at which musical (including rhapsodic) competition began in the Panathenaic festival in Athens is disputed, and the evidence of ancient authors is contradictory, but whether the Peisistratids in the third quarter of the sixth century or Pericles in the third quarter of the fifth should be credited with the innovation, it constituted a conspicuous appropriation of the *Iliad* and *Odyssey* to Athenian ends.[14] There is in any case no doubt that by the end of the sixth century rhapsodic performances of the poems did occur in Athens, presumably in an agonistic context, and such evidence as the fragment of Heraclitus cited above (fr. 42 DK) demonstrates that the phenomenon was widespread.

The nature of performance undoubtedly changed between the festivals of the sixth century and those observed by Plato, but his *Ion* presents our earliest portrait of a rhapsode, one specializing in the performance of Homeric poetry. It is hardly a complimentary portrait, concerned as it is with the familiar Platonic distinction between form and content, performance and true knowledge. The fatuous Ion is manipulated into presenting himself as an expert on the matters treated in the *Iliad* and *Odyssey*, only to be shown in fact to be a mere mouthpiece skilled only in esthetically engaging performance.

It is in the antecedents of the sixth-century contests, in turn the still remoter antecedents of Ion's displays, that we must imagine the 'Homeric encyclopedia'[15] functioning, and it is that body of wisdom

---

[14] Most recent scholars accept the testimony of Lycurgus (*In Leocr.* 102), [Plato] (*Hipparchus* 228b), or Diogenes Laertius (1.57) pointing to a sixth-century date for the innovation, but Wade-Gery (1952) 30, with n. 77, influentially embraced the Plutarchan evidence (*Pericles* 13) that Pericles made the change in 442, and could well be correct.

[15] E. Havelock's term for Homeric poetry as an all-encompassing bearer of archaic Greek traditional wisdom: (1963) 61–85.

that provoked the first philosophical reaction. Nevertheless, aside from the chance survival of remarks like that attributed to Heraclitus, we know very little about just how Homeric poetry shaped the perceptions of the Greeks of the archaic period. Elementary education in reading and perhaps writing seems to have been reasonably widespread in Athens, at least among the wealthy, by the end of the fifth century, but it is impossible to say just how many young Athenians may have had the opportunity to enjoy the services of a *grammatodidaskalos* at that time, and *a fortiori* in the sixth century.[16] Still, by the latter part of the sixth century higher education, both medical and philosophical, had arisen in Ionia and the Pythagoreans were developing the antecedents of the modern educational institution in Magna Graecia.

Homer's role in elementary education in the archaic and classical periods must be inferred from anecdotes, such as that of the obnoxious young Alcibiades punching a teacher who could not produce a book of Homer (Plutarch, *Alc.* 7). Plato's *Republic* assumes, as a foil for its own prescriptions, an elementary education system heavily committed to Homer, a picture clarified somewhat in the *Laws* (809e–810a), where a period of three years (no more, no less) of study of writing and literature (γράμματα)—including hexameter poetry—is prescribed, to begin at the age of ten, and to be succeeded by three years of lyre-playing between the ages of thirteen and sixteen.

With the expansion of literacy, then, the Homeric poems, already prominent in the shaping of Greek communities' perceptions about the world, became entrenched in the elementary level of education. Socrates' remark that they should be removed from that position 'whether they're allegorical or not' (*Rep.* 378d) lends strong support to the notion that by the end of the fifth century, elementary commentary and interpretation, some of it allegorical, was a part of that education. Socrates' efforts aside, Homer was not to be dislodged from the position of first author until long after the demise of polytheism, and the interpretive claims, at first sub-literary and confined to the classroom, were to mushroom into a vast literature of commentary.

In the generation of Socrates and the other sophists who brought higher education to Athens late in the fifth century, discussion of

---

[16] See Knox (1985), with the cautions expressed by R. Thomas (1992), passim and esp. p. 92 with n. 49.

poetry, and in particular Homeric poetry, was a salient feature of Greek intellectual life. In the *Protagoras*, Plato portrays Socrates as a reluctant participant in such discussion, a picture consistent with Plato's general dismissal of poetry as a tool in the pursuit of the truth. The fifth century saw some quite amazing claims about the true meaning of the Homeric poems—most memorably those of Metrodorus of Lampsacus who described the entire *Iliad* as a depiction, on the plane of the mortal characters, of the physical universe, and on the plane of the immortals, the component organs of the human body.[17] But most commentary on the *Iliad* and *Odyssey* down to the time of Aristotle is lost—both the elementary exegesis of the *grammatodidaskalos* and the interpretive claims put forward in more advanced educational contexts. A scholion, probably Porphyrian, provides the information that Theagenes of Rhegium—apparently a *grammaticus* of the late sixth century—was the inventor of both ethical and physical allegory. What Porphyry, writing c. A.D. 300, meant was that Theagenes was the first to find the true meaning of certain episodes in Homeric poetry in their ethical message, and that of others in their cryptic representation of the elements and forces of the universe (e.g. in the form of the gods of the theomachy of *Iliad* 20–21). On the surface of it, Porphyry's claim seems implausible, but taking it in conjunction with the evidence of Plato we can be certain that the claim that Homer allegorized—that he habitually 'said other things' from what his words superficially designated—were a familiar part of Greek education by the late fifth century and had been as long as anyone could remember.

Homer in the Hellenistic World and the Roman Empire

The conquests of Alexander liberated Greek literature and culture from their ethnic shell and fashioned an international Hellenism. Within two centuries, the Romans had appropriated that international Hellenic culture to their own needs and designs, and from there went on to make it into a world culture. We have already seen that this process probably had as one of its marginal effects the creation of the Hellenistic vulgate that forms the basis of all modern

[17] See Lamberton, 'The Neoplatonists and the Spiritualization of Homer,' 115–33 in Lamberton and Keaney (1992) 125 and N. J. Richardson (1975).

texts of the *Iliad* and *Odyssey*. Although the date of the formation of that vulgate is fairly clear from the disappearance of most of the 'wild' lines from papyri and citations after the second century B.C., the details of the process are elusive. One might have expected Aristarchus to prevail, but the vulgate text is not his. The scholia provide a great deal of information about the lines athetized, obolized, or bracketed (though almost never 'left unwritten') by the Alexandrian scholars, and the inescapable conclusion is that these scholars did not produce *Iliads* and *Odysseys* reduced and defined by their own ideas of what was authentic and what was not. Rather, they used marginal symbols to indicate their judgments, and either did not have the power or simply chose not to delete lines they doubted.[18]

The second century nevertheless did see a standardization of the text, accompanied by the elimination of many lines that appear in earlier papyri and citations. Subsequently, schools apparently had uniform texts, and if an aberrant author such as Plutarch transmits a relatively high percentage of variants from the vulgate, it may be because he cites at second-hand, from an intermediate author, not a contemporary text.[19]

The sixth, fifth, and fourth centuries forged a Homer out of disparate elements, with little agreement on the limits of the corpus or the details of the text. The vulgate represents the realization of that goal on the level of the text. Subsequent interactions with imitators and competitors are no longer the absorptions and supersedings we have seen to this point. In the Hellenistic world, Homer was admired from arm's length, with a sense both of the esthetic richness of the text—the key to its accessibility—, and of its distance in time, its strangeness. The vulgate opened the way for the complete individuation of the figure henceforth known, if somewhat preciously, as 'the Poet.'

Homer in the Roman schools

The education described in Plato's *Republic* and *Laws* was never realized in detail, but does provide us with a picture of an idealized and generalized aristocratic Athenian education. This was gradually transformed in the democratic Athenian society of the fifth and fourth

[18] Allen (1923) 304–305; Haslam, this volume.
[19] Allen (1923) 263–65.

centuries into something simultaneously more practical and more familiar. The emphasis shifted away from the aristocratic luxuries of music and athletics in the direction of language skills. Plato's uncomplimentary portraits of the sophists, or teachers, who competed with Socrates indicate the trend.

When the Romans took up that educational system, Homer was already installed at the base of the pyramid of instruction in the Greek language. He was the first Greek author studied in the schools of the empire, where to know Greek meant to have read Homer.[20] Like Shakespeare in the traditional twentieth-century pedagogy of the English language—an author remote in date and style, whose language could not in any immediate sense be taken as a model for composition—Homer served as an ideal of Greek eloquence and poetic power, an inspiration rather than a model for imitation.

The process did not stop with the elementary instruction of the *grammatodidaskalos*. Another of the anecdotes of education in Plutarch's *Alcibiades* (7) has the arrogant young man demand a copy of Homer of a *grammatodidaskalos* who in turn supplies one that he himself has corrected. Alcibiades' response is that this teacher should not be teaching children (presumably, ten to fourteen year olds) to read if he had the skills to correct a text of Homer, he should rather be teaching older teenagers (*neoi*). This probably meant (at least in Plutarch's time, if not in that of Alcibiades) that this *grammatodidaskalos* had the requisite skills to present himself as a *grammaticus*. If the student aspired to still more education, he would turn to a teacher of rhetoric, where Homeric *exempla* might again be studied.

Though in the Hellenistic and Roman periods we may assume access to complete texts resembling our own, we do not know just how much of the two poems was read in school at various levels. By the second century A.D., the poems were probably studied by means of anthologies. Numerous partial texts and copy texts, apparently from the schoolroom, survive, and although no complete copy of a school anthology has reached us, it is clear from the citations of Homer in Greek authors of the Imperial period that certain passages were better known than others, while some sections are rarely, if ever, cited. J. F. Kindstrand examined the abundant citations of Homer, many decorative and some substantial, in three major orators of the Second

[20] See e.g. Heraclitus, *Homeric Allegories*, ch. 1; [Plutarch] *Essay on the Life and Poetry of Homer*, ch. 1.

Sophistic: Dio Chrysostom, Maximus of Tyre, and Aelius Aristides, representing the literary elite of the late first and the second centuries A.D. Kindstrand concluded that, although the lines in the *Iliad* to which they referred were unevenly distributed, these three authors had first-hand knowledge of the entire poem. The *Odyssey* seems to have been less well known, even among the most educated. Kindstrand concluded that only Dio, of the three, knew the entire poem, as did Plutarch.[21]

One tremendously valuable text throws light on the teaching of Homer in the schools of the Roman empire. After serving as an introduction to the poems for many centuries, the work of unknown authorship lay neglected from the eighteenth century until our own time. Many passages echo Plutarch, under whose name it was known to the late Middle Ages and Renaissance. Apparently the work of a *grammaticus* of the late second or third century, and variously titled *De Homero* and 'On the Life and Poetry of Homer,' it presents itself as an introduction to the *Iliad* and *Odyssey* for the first-time reader.[22] The language of Homer (meter, dialect, tropes, and figures) occupies one third of the text (chs. 7–73), but the bulk concerns Homer's view of the world and his position as founder and source of subsequent literary and intellectual developments. We are introduced to Homer as the founder of historical discourse (chs. 75–90), the source of major ideas on physics and ethics (chs. 92–144), and of miscellaneous maxims of the sages and poets (chs. 145–60). Homer, the first-time reader is told, is likewise the founder of political discourse, and specifically, rhetoric (chs. 161–74). Homer also understands statecraft, social obligations, tactics, medicine, and seercraft and lies at the source of all the literary genres (chs. 175–217). The closing panegyric (ch. 218) observes, to the greater glory of Homer, that those who have come later have found in his poetry even what few things he himself did not include—an apparent reference to the allegorists—and goes on to point with approval to the *centones* or pastiches of Homer, current from at least the second century, in which Homeric phrases and lines were rearranged to express entirely alien notions.

---

[21] Kindstrand (1973) 104–105.

[22] An exemplary text has recently appeared: J. F. Kindstrand, ed., [Plutarchus] *De Homero* (Leipzig, 1990). For a bilingual with limited commentary see, J. J. Keaney and Robert Lamberton, ed. and tr., [Plutarch] *Essay on the Life and Poetry of Homer* (Atlanta, 1996).

The final chapter seems also to refer to divination by Homer—the Homeric version of the Romans' *sors vergiliana.*

This school-introduction of the imperial period presents a Homer at once familiar and strange. The treatment of Homer's language is, *mutatis mutandis*, not unlike what will be found in modern introductions, at least in its concerns (if not its conclusions). The claim that Homer is the source of all subsequent wisdom is easily traced back to the pretensions ridiculed in Plato's *Ion*, and the grand gesture of such a claim may well be inherited from classical pedagogy and before that, from the self-advertisement of the bards. Our *grammaticus*, however, adds something more. His Homer stands at the source of everything, but he also had and conveyed certain beliefs and rejected others—he had an identity and a definable view of the world, extraordinary in its scope and depth.

The appropriation of Homer into Christian education begins in the second century, but the issues do not come into clear view until the fourth.[23] By the reign of Julian (361–364), Christian teachers of the polytheist texts were a sufficient threat to the integrity of the tradition that the apostate emperor barred them by imperial decree from teaching them.[24] This heavy-handed move is revealing in a number of ways. First, it is clear that in the Greek-speaking world, the hostility to polytheist texts that continued to prevail in Latin Christianity (and notably Augustine) had been dissipated by the mid-fourth century. Texts like Basil's *Ad adulescentes*[25] make it clear just how Christians—whose scriptural canon, along with the history of its interpretation, was a powerful stimulus to hermeneutic sophistication—were able to neutralize the theological authority of polytheist texts and absorb this invaluable cultural property into Christian education. As in so much else, Julian here seems to have been right in assessing the threat, but naive in his belief that his own interpretive community could be saved, or the growing Christian one suppressed, by proclamation. The absorption of Homer into Christian Greek

[23] The early apologists—Justin Martyr and Tertullian—are generally hostile to all polytheist literature, but as early as Clement a more nuanced view begins to emerge.

[24] Julian, 'Rescript on Christian Teachers,' in W. C. Wright, ed., *The Works of the Emperor Julian*, vol. 3 (Loeb Library, New York, 1923) 117–23.

[25] See R. J. Deferrari, ed. and tr., *Saint Basil, The Letters*, vol. 4 (Loeb Library, Cambridge, Mass., 1931) 363–435.

education, completed by the fourth century, was extended and institutionalized in the Byzantine educational system, where expertise in the language and culture of the polytheist past remained the single skill most cultivated and most rewarded.[26] In fifth and sixth century Athens and Alexandria, polytheists continued, at least in the Platonic schools, to expound the glories of Homer in terms of which Julian might have approved, but the evidence points to an increasing emphasis on secrecy and exclusivity. By the time of Proclus (d. 485), the polytheist intellectuals still active viewed the *Iliad* and *Odyssey* as material fit only for the most advanced of students, those capable of reading the truth behind the screen of fiction.

Homer and the Hellenistic and Roman poets

When the vulgate took shape, Homer and Hesiod were no longer representative of shared poetic traditions that new practitioners had to absorb and incorporate in order to supersede them. Along with the other archaic poets, they were comfortably distanced: individual identities defined, circumscribed, and set in their place—and, of course, available for exploitation in the same manner as all of the other precious cultural baggage from the past. When Callimachus posed as Hesiod, receiving the poetic vocation from the Heliconian Muses (*Aitia* fr. 2, 112), that pose was something qualitatively different from that of all the performers who had performed *as* Hesiod over the preceding centuries. The voice of Callimachus remains his own and the mask of Hesiod is just a mask, symbolic of the poet's initiation. The extraordinary esthetic self-consciousness of Hellenistic poetry entails a constant distancing of the past that it persistently evokes, a marking of differences and a claim to a newness that can live with the old without competing with it.

Something similar happened to Homer at the same time, but because the Homeric persona was so featureless and the Homeric text so pervasive and powerful a cultural property, the procedures were somewhat different. It is important to realize as well that there were epic poets active continuously down to the time of Pericles and beyond: Herodotus' uncle, Panyassis of Halicarnassus, wrote an *Ionica* and a *Heracleia* (the latter about 3/4 as long as the *Odyssey*),[27] and

[26] See R. Browning, 'The Byzantines and Homer,' 134–48 in Lamberton and Keaney (1992).

[27] See Huxley (1969) 177–90.

Antimachus of Colophon, who wrote a *Thebaid*, was a contemporary of Plato and active well into the fourth century. Antimachus in fact wrote both hexameters and elegiacs and did textual work on Homer that is reflected in the scholia, and so stands as a transitional figure, anticipating the third-century scholar-poets of the Alexandrian library.

Apollonius with his *Argonautica* did not, then, appear out of nowhere, but this does not diminish the originality of his accomplishment. It is traditional to view Apollonius as a rebel against the Callimachean canons of taste, daring the long poem in defiance of the master's scorn for the *mega kakon*, though in fact it is far from clear just what sort of long poems Callimachus condemned, and various arguments have been made to show that the *Argonautica* is in its way a Callimachean poem.[28] Certainly it is not a Homeric poem, despite obvious formal similarities and its pervasive, complex dialogue with Homeric language. The speaker wears his Homeric persona much the way Callimachus wore that of Hesiod, while performing in a mode quite self-consciously divorced from Homeric esthetics. For example, the dragon guarding the golden fleece

> hissed monstrously, and all around
> the long banks of the river and the vast forest echoed.
> It was heard by those far beyond Titenian Aia
> who lived in the land of Kolchis at the mouth of the Lycus,
> which forks off from the rumbling river Araxes
> and joins its holy stream with the Phasis, and the two together
> flow forth into the Caucasian Sea driven on as one,
> and nursing mothers awoke in terror and threw their arms
> around their newborn children sleeping at their breasts,
> when they shuddered at the hiss. (4. 129–38)

There is an echo here of Andromache's description of the sleeping Astyanax in her lament for Hector (*Il.* 22.502) and a conspicuous juxtaposition of vocabulary that is elegantly Homeric (ἀγκαλίδεσσιν, 137) and elegantly unHomeric (ἀποκιδνάμενος, 133). The rapid shift of scale from the vast to the intimate is very Homeric, but too vertiginous for Homeric style to tolerate, and further exaggerated by the juxtaposition of the characteristically Hellenistic savoring of lists of place-names (here in the context of the Homeric taste for the fantasy of the earth viewed from heaven or Olympus), with the tactile, physical quality of the relationship of mother and newborn. And

[28] See Beye (1982) 6–10, and A. Cameron, 'Genre and Style in Callimachus,' *Transactions of the American Philological Association* 122 (1992) 305–12.

finally, the hiss is heard by the sleeping and the waking, crossing barriers of consciousness as it defies geographic probability in its scale.

It would be possible to examine the entire subsequent tradition of hexameter poetry in this way, from the bizarre obscurantism of Lycophron down to the *Posthomerica* of Quintus and ultimately the school of Nonnus in the fifth and sixth centuries. Each reappropriation of the medium is unique and asserts its uniqueness, its esthetic distance from Homer and from other hexameter poetry. Formally, the principal change is a gradual restriction of the range of the patterns of word-endings tolerated in the hexameter, so that Nonnus and Musaeus work in a medium far tighter and more demanding than the one the archaic bards had enjoyed. But the more important changes are on the level of the imaginative representation of experience. Each of the later hexameter poets had a clear sense of the nature and limits of the Homeric style and each formed his own style and his own esthetic in deliberate contrast to that style.

Beyond the sphere of narrative poetry, Homeric language increasingly permeated other media as well, as the universally accessible point of reference of the *Iliad* and *Odyssey* became the source for the great bulk of the poetic ornament used in prose. Citation and pastiche of Homer are increasingly common from the Hellenistic period on, and in the Greek prose of the Roman empire, Homeric echoes are heard line after line. In Lucian, in particular, scraps of Homer crop up everywhere, either held up in isolation or embedded in the syntax of his prose, and this exploitation of Homeric material constitutes one of the largest and richest categories in the range of his wit.

In the fourth century, Julian the Apostate so larded his orations with Homeric material that his manner has been compared with that of contemporary Christians with their scriptural citations and resonances. The comparison is misleading. The Homeric material that is so omnipresent in the Greek prose of the Roman empire is exploited, by and large, exclusively for esthetic effect. It is true that this period saw as well an extraordinary proliferation of exegesis, indicating profound changes in the understanding of the poems. But whether in the mouth of the mocking Lucian or the pious Julian, the Homeric material integrated into later Greek prose shows little trace of these developments. What is does show—and this is a matter to which Julian was acutely sensitive—is the degree to which a knowledge of Homer had become inseparable from a knowledge of Greek, and Homer himself and Homeric language had come to stand for the tradition of Greek literature itself. To understand those references and resonances was, along with sensitivity to the figures and tropes of rhetoric and the underlying rules of grammar and syntax, integral to participation in Greek culture.

Homer and the later philosophers

Stoic concern with certain aspects of archaic poetry was, as we have seen, an anomaly. The project of Greek philosophy throughout its long duration was the search for truth and only rarely did the notion surface in philosophical circles that the poems of Homer, Hesiod, or Orpheus might offer promising tools for gaining such access.

The various traditions of philosophical inquiry each had distinct views with regard to texts in general and early poetic texts in particular. Thinkers in the tradition of Plato began doing philosophy by commentary on the dialogues at least as early as the second century B.C. The myths of Plato—including the 'myth of Er' in the *Republic*, and the Atlantis story in the *Timaeus* and *Crito*—posed unique hermeneutic problems that were surmounted in various ways. We know from a casual remark of Plutarch's (*De gen. an.* 1013A–B) that one of the most characteristic interpretive strategies of later Platonism—the claim that mythic accounts routinely present in sequential narrative truths that are in fact simultaneous and eternal—is as old as the generation after Plato. Xenocrates used it to explain why, in the *Timaeus*, Plato seemed to say that the world-soul was created in time, when in fact he knew it to be eternal. Thus the strategies we see coming into play in philosophical commentary on the myths of the poets, when such commentary occurs, were in all probability developed for other purposes.

There is little surviving interpretive commentary on Homer that can confidently be attributed to Stoics, while there exists a rich and varied literature of commentary by thinkers explicitly in the tradition of Plato. Crates of Mallos, the Pergamene textual critic contemporary with the Alexandrians, who interpolated explanatory lines and wrote allegorical commentary, was probably not a Stoic, though he has frequently been represented as one.[29] The same can be said of the Heraclitus who, sometime in the first or second century, compiled

[29] See J. I. Porter (1992) 85–88.

the collection known as the *Homeric Allegories*.[30] True, many of his readings are either physical allegories—claims that the poems represent forces or elements of the natural world as gods—or ethical ones that stress edifying concealed messages, and such interpretations seem to have been endorsed by some Stoics. Heraclitus is nevertheless quite explicit about his project. He is concerned to defend this most basic of school texts against the charge of impiety. He has no particular philosophical ax to grind, nor does he use Homeric passages to support specific philosophical claims. His well-argued first principle is that poets have always used the trope of allegory—designating one thing through another (as Alcaeus' ship of state)—and that when Homer appears to say impious things, he can be seen to be doing the same. Heraclitus is hostile to Plato for his rejection of Homer (4), but he does not present himself as a philosopher, any more than the *grammaticus* who wrote the *Essay on the Life and Poetry of Homer*,[31] who may have been his contemporary.

On the whole, the issues addressed in pre-Hellenistic commentary on Homer are seldom relevant to our own experience of the poems. The Homeric problems and solutions reported as Aristotelian by the scholiasts are a good sample the range of concerns of early philosophical commentary, from problems about the meaning of odd, Homeric words to broadly allegorical readings. Aristotle's *Poetics* has a good deal to say about epic as a genre, but little about qualities of Homer that are prized today. In the odd essay 'On the Sublime' attributed to the third-century Athenian Platonist Longinus, certain qualities of ancient poetry and prose are first appreciated in a manner that anticipates the post-Renaissance experience of readers.[32] His appreciation of the Homeric sublime (ch. 9) stresses the vast scale of the theomachia and the contrast between human and divine experience as represented by Homer, noting at the same time, in much the same terms we find in Heraclitus, that 'if these passages are not taken allegorically' they are 'atheistic and exceed what is fitting' (9.7).

Despite this attention to Homer's apparent impiety, the truth-value of the poems is not an issue for 'Longinus.' The sublime, though it has an ethical dimension, remains fundamentally an esthetic phe-

[30] See Buffière (1956).

[31] See above, 46–47.

[32] See D. A. Russell's discussion of the date and attribution of the text, xxii–xxx in the 'Introduction' to his edition of the text (Oxford, 1964), along with the reasons for believing that the text in fact belongs to the first century.

nomenon—hence its modernity. By contrast, philosophical concern with early poetry, when it arose, was postulated on the idea that it contained, or gave access to, some truth. An obscure second-century Pythagorean named Numenius, who pointed to a primitive and widespread revelation of the truths of theology—later distilled into the works of Plato (Fr. 1, des Places)—clearly believed the *Iliad* and *Odyssey* formed part of that primitive revelation. He also wrote about *The Secrets in Plato* and used Homeric material (the description of the Cave of the Nymphs, *Od.* 13.96–112) in conjunction with the 'myth of Er' in the *Republic* to reconstruct a true picture of the fate of souls and the structure of the universe (Fr. 31, des Places).

This is the earliest passage we have in which the myths of Plato and the Homeric poems are juxtaposed in such a way, and where a commitment to the truth-value of both is clear. The Numenian material is preserved in the essay of the Neoplatonist Porphyry on *The Cave of the Nymphs in the Odyssey* (c. 300), where Porphyry elaborates claims of unprecedented scope about the meaning of the *Odyssey*. The whole poem is seen as the journey of a soul embodied—fallen into the sea of matter—but distinguished from other souls by its affinity to rational mind. After a journey aggravated by a premature attempt to escape the life of the senses by suicide (the blinding of the Cyclops), this privileged soul returns to its true home (that place in Tiresias' prophecy, so remote from the sea that an oar is no longer a familiar object).[33] Porphyry's essay is unique in surviving ancient literature for the imaginative range of its allegorizing. The *Odyssey* it addresses is a piece of public cultural property, a poem Porphyry was equipped, in other contexts, to discuss as a philologist,[34] but which he here reveals to be most richly meaningful on a level that is far from apparent, where its truths were those closest to Porphyry's own obsessions, the relationship of soul and matter and the return of the soul to its true home.

What we see in Porphyry's essay is presumably the highest level of the interpretation of Homer that a student frequenting Platonic teachers in Rome about the year 300 might have been offered. Porphyry's teacher Plotinus held classes open to all (Porph. *Vit. Plot.* 1), and

[33] For discussion, Buffière (1962) 421–49; Lamberton (1986) 108–33; (1983).

[34] His vast collection of *Homeric Problems*, was one of the sources most often mined by the scholiasts. See the edition by Schrader (1880–82); (1890).

Porphyry's presentation of hidden meanings in the Homeric text suggests that they as well were available for public scrutiny. He does not exploit Homer to add credibility to his own world view, as the Stoics were accused of doing; rather, he expands on the Numenian material to reach the core of the meaning of the Homeric passage before him. The results are presented as an appreciation, apparently for a general audience, of the rich texture of meanings to be found there.

Athens in the fifth century provides the last context in which we can gauge the fate of polytheist commentary on Homer. In the century and a half that separate the efforts of Porphyry from those of Proclus the function of Platonic commentary on such texts had changed radically. According to his biographer Marinus (*Vit. Proc.* 38), Proclus did not think his contemporaries should read Homer at all. In the fifth and sixth books of his *Commentary on the Republic* he offers a detailed reconciliation of the authoritative voices of Homer and Socrates. But now the audience is explicitly limited: his auditors are enjoined to close the door against the uninitiated and to keep these interpretations secret. At least for this little band of fifth-century polytheists, Homer was restricted material, reserved for an inner circle. Others, in ignorance of the complexities of his allegories, would be misled, perhaps with disastrous consequences (*In Rep.* 1.74–76). Only the secret commentary turns a text full of pitfalls into a rich revelation of truths. As we have already seen, however, a Christian interpretive and pedagogic tradition had long been at work on these texts, and it was this tradition, feared by Julian and implicitly by Proclus after him, that would ultimately reduce the gods of Homer to purely esthetic beings, divorced from any pretense to theological truth.

Michael Haslam

HOMERIC PAPYRI AND TRANSMISSION OF THE TEXT

When in 1779 Villoison unearthed Venetus A of the *Iliad* in the library of San Marco, it appeared that just about everything one could wish to know about the text as it existed in the heyday of Alexandrian scholarship was revealed. But it turns out that the scholia, immensely informative though they are, do not tell the whole story. Now we have actual Homer manuscripts of the period, and their texts are not at all what could have been predicted. The capacity of Homer papyri to surprise is no longer what it was when they first came on the scene, but they have lost none of their significance. They give us a direct if fragmented view of the transmission of the Homeric text over the course of a millenium, from the early 3rd century B.C. to the end of antiquity. For any attempt to trace the history of Homer in antiquity it is the ancient manuscripts themselves that constitute the only secure evidential base; they serve as a control on the nature and worth of the medieval tradition and on any reconstruction of the first four or five hundred years. The papyri show us the transmissional process in action. They will form the core of this chapter, which will explore the transmission not just of the 'authentic' or 'original' text, as problematic a concept as it is elusive an object, but of the text as it actually existed for its hearers and performers, its scribes and readers.[1]

The general picture is one of a very dynamic, open tradition, with diminution over time in the range of textual variation, offset to some extent by often short-lived incoming new variants. The papyri reveal

[1] Homeric papyri are referred to by their conventional numeration, as listed by Sutton (1991), extending earlier lists by (successively) T. W. Allen, P. Collart, and H. J. Mette; and normally also by their 'M(ertens)-P(ack)' number (Pack (1965); revision by P. Mertens forthcoming; in Mertens' revision the Pack² numeration will be unchanged; I am most grateful to Prof. Mertens for a preview). By familiar convention 'papyri' as a generic term is inclusive of ancient manuscripts written on parchment—inexact but justifiable, and practically unavoidable as long as the pernicious habit of confining the term 'manuscripts' to medieval manuscripts persists.

a transmissional watershed in the 2nd century B.C., a sort of textual standardization, delimiting the contours of the text inasmuch as it stabilized the number and sequence of verses and quite drastically cut down current variants. Just what kind of intervention this reflects is unclear. Thereafter the text continued to move in a constant state of flux, but a less volatile one; variants were multitudinous but minor, accretion was virtually confined to simple one-line additions, losses were strictly local and ephemeral. The text was subject to a certain amount of scholarly interference, but the effect of Alexandrian critical activity was slight, at least as far as the constitution of the individual verses was concerned. No discrete channels of transmission are in evidence. The text was much copied (the *Iliad* always more than the *Odyssey*), collation was fairly wide-spread (protecting against loss and disseminating accrual), and we have substantial pieces of manuscripts from every century down to the 7th: much activity, little change. Passage through the bottle-neck to the 9th and 10th centuries seems to have entailed overall relatively little loss of what had been current in the Roman period; the medieval tradition is a direct continuation of the ancient, inevitably attenuated but in its totality showing unusually good catchment of ancient readings (better for the *Iliad* than for the *Odyssey*), promiscuously distributed. The later minuscule manuscripts add little to what is found collectively in the earlier ones (the earliest extant being 10th cent.), except that extra readings from the Alexandrian scholarly tradition were imported into some.

That is a summary—very summary—outline of the traceable history of the rather Protean thing that is the written text of Homer.[2] Before we proceed further with its shifting constitution, a few words are in order on the changing nature of its physical form. Modern readers, and even post-modern ones, read texts which present them with a succession of words and of sentences. Readers in the 3rd century B.C. faced merely a succession of letters, uninterrupted except by verse-termini:

ανδραμοιεννεπεμουϲαπολυτροπονοϲμαλαπολλα
πλαγχθηεπειτροιηϲϊερονπτολιεθρονεπερϲεν

This goes deeper than graphic convention. In antiquity the written text is a given sequence of letters, whose articulation is effected by

[2] I do not confine the term 'text' to written text.

the reader in the act of reading.[3] The letters alone constitute the text: all else is interpretation.[4] Over time it became more common for scribes or readers to constrain interpretation by adding a modicum of lectional apparatus, but practice was always very variable: some 5th-cent. A.D. manuscripts have hardly any accents, others almost as many as our printed texts. Some punctuation becomes normal, though usually nothing more differentiated than a single stop; Nicanor in the 1st century worked out a philosophically based eight-grade system specially for Homer, but nobody used it. Elision was usually effected, less usually marked; scriptio plena is sometimes used to obviate syntactical ambiguity (e.g. *Il.* 1.567 ιοντιοτε in Ꝑ269, precluding ἰόντε and ἰόντα). Distinction between lower-case and upper-case letters is modern (and Homer was surely better off without it), as are quotation marks. In some manuscripts of the Roman period speech-termini are marked by the paragraphos (an interlinear dash at line-beginning), and the speaker's name—or 'poet,' on reversion to narrative—may be added in the left margin; this matches the practice used in dramatic and pseudo-dramatic texts (e.g. Plato), only in Homer the narrator is on a par with his characters, in accordance with Aristotelian analysis of epic discourse. Or a verse identifying the speaker could be added.

The medium too underwent change, from scroll form to codex. ('Roll' not 'scroll' is the usual form among classicists, after German 'Rolle,' but no-one speaks of the Dead Sea Rolls, and 'scroll' has the advantage of suggesting affinity with the process of 'scrolling' on a computer screen—though a papyrus roll was scrolled through not vertically but laterally, like 'print preview' on a computer—and then had to be scrolled back again.) There were Homer codices in Rome in Martial's time (Homer 'in pugillariis' is a Saturnalia gift, 14.83–4), but in Egypt the codex does not come in until the 2nd century. The

[3] This is practicable in Greek, as it would not be in English, a language with less consistent correspondence between phonemic constitution and graphic representation and with greater tendency to asyndeton. The reader processes the phonemes, thus simulating the oral-aural experience of live communication. Earlier texts will have used less fully differentiated spelling (ε not ει and ο not ου, perhaps ε not η and ο not ω (this contested by R. Janko, *The Iliad: A Commentary* IV. *Books 13–16* (Cambridge, 1992) 34–38), single not geminated consonants), requiring more disambiguation on the reader's part.

[4] Some articulations, e.g. that of καταϲνηϲτιν, were never settled. Systematic spacing between words, and with it the regrettable need to confer or withhold word status with regard to appositives, e.g. κατα, περ, κε, is modern.

codex was more capacious than the scroll, but still could not normally accommodate an entire *Iliad* or *Odyssey*. Each poem had to be split up. However, the 24-book division came about not because of the exigencies of the papyrus scroll but in spite of them: even the longest of the individual 'books'—'rhapsodies,' in the ancient terminology—are much shorter than the normal length of a scroll. We speak unthinkingly of 24 books, but that effaces what is surely the essence of the division. It is not a numerical system but an alphabetical one, and the α–ω partitioning must have been devised for its symbolism, advertising Homer's all-comprehensiveness (cf. 'I am the alpha and the omega,' and modern usage of 'A–Z'); if the contemporary alphabet had had only 20 letters, each epic would have been divided into 20 books (and who knows how many the *Aeneid* would have had?). This evidently had sufficiently strong appeal for the partitioning to be universally adopted in spite of its inconvenience and its artificiality (it cuts across traditional segments of the poems such as the Aristeia of Diomedes).[5] Some scholars link the system with the textual stabilization of the 2nd century, but it must be earlier.[6]

However that may be, scrolls of Homer might carry more than one book apiece; perhaps most of them did. Codices carried more. There seem to have been no standard groupings. Mild surprises abound. A scroll of the 1st cent. B.C. (*Il.*p449, M–P 980) consisted of bks. 19–22 of the *Iliad.* A 4th-cent. papyrus codex (*Il.*p60, M–P 870) consisted of bks. 11–16: we can only register the fact and wonder whether it was part of a complete set, and if so whether that set was in three volumes or four.[7] Correct sequence of scrolls was some-

[5] Once the book divisions were established, Diomedes' Aristeia was identified with bk. 5 (a recently published papyrus of bk. 5 (1st cent. B.C. or A.D.) has Διο]μήδουϲ [ἀριϲτ]εία in its end-title; similarly the medieval mss.), but Hdt. 2.116 quotes *Il.* 6.289–92 as from Diomedes' Aristeia.

[6] The symbolism seems distinctly unalexandrian. In some texts a book line-count is given in attic stichometry: that must be prealexandrian. The fact that it is the ionic alphabet that is used tells us little, except perhaps that the book-divisions will not be Pisistratean. The evidence for the date of introduction is well presented and discussed by S. West, *The Ptolemaic Papyri of Homer*, Papyrologica Coloniensia 3 (Köln-Opladen, 1967) 18–25 (prealexandrian), cf. Janko (1992) 39–40, G. Broccia, *La forma poetica dell'Iliade e la genesi dell'epos omerico* (Messina, 1967); recent discussions include N. J. Richardson, *The Iliad: a Commentary, vol. vi* (Cambridge, 1993) 20–21 (Alexandrian), O. Taplin, *Homeric Soundings* (Oxford 1992) 285–86 (Aristarchan), K. Stanley, *The Shield of Homer* (Princeton, 1993) 249, 397–98 n. 7 (pre-hellenistic). Nagy (1996a) 181, associates it with Athenian state organization of rhapsodic performance under Demetrius of Phalerum.

[7] B. Hemmerdinger, *Studi Italiani di Filologia Classica* n.s. 25 (1951) 85, associates

times ensured by writing the first one or two verses of the succeeding book at the end. But just as in rhapsodic performances some episodes were no doubt recited more than others (as Hipparchus' Panathenaic regulation seems to imply for the 6th cent. B.C.), so some Homeric books were read more than others, and were copied more—of the *Iliad* the earlier books, especially the first two, of the *Odyssey* bks. 4 (why?) and 11.[8] In classical Athens someone might own a complete Homer, but only an enthusiast or a potential rhapsode, or perhaps a schoolteacher.[9] A papyrus codex of the 3rd cent. A.D. (*Il.*p3, M–P 634) omits the Catalogue of Ships, as in turn do some of the medieval manuscripts. Presumably it was found boring.[10] But at all periods there is a strong sense of each poem as a whole, and this was not compromised by their physical fragmentation.

A switch from scroll to codex—the form of book we still use today—constitutes a radical change in the reading experience itself. You now face not an unbroken succession of adjacent columns, to be progressively unrolled to the right as you reroll what you have traversed to the left, but a set of pages. The difference is only palely reflected in the fact that the pages of a codex were usually numbered, the columns of a scroll rarely. Pages interfered with the line-by-line continuity of the poetic text even more rudely than columns did, but of course it was now easy to flip through and find whatever passage you wanted; in one early *Odyssey* codex (p28, M–P 1106) such reference is facilitated by the relevant book-number being repeated at the top of each right-hand page. Whether for aesthetic or for practical reasons, the abandonment of the scroll was fairly slow: codexes are common in the 3rd century A.D., but scrolls were still

this with Crates' diorthosis of *Iliad* and *Odyssey* in nine books (so the Suda), fantastically.

[8] J. A. Davison, *Akten des VIII internat. Kongresses für Papyrologie in Wien, 1955* (Vienna, 1956), 51–58; his figures are out of date but for the most part hold good proportionally. A 1st-cent. book-by-book list of library holdings apparently lacks *Od.* 7 and records duplicates of *Od.* 3–4 (P. J. Sijpesteijn and K. A. Worp, *Chronique d'Égypte* 98 (1974) 324–31).

[9] Xenophon *Memorabilia* 4.2.10, Plutarch *Alcibiades* 7.1.

[10] Rather this than that the Catalogue's status in the poem was in question, as has occasionally been suggested; the Catalogue's introduction (484–93) is always retained. Ludwich attributed the omission to an evil accident (*Homervulgata* 170)! According to Porphyry as reported by Eustathius (263.33), some cities required by law that school-children learn the Catalogue by heart. It is ignored in the Epimerismi (9th cent.), as also in Manuel Moschopoulos' paraphrase of *Il.* 1–2 (based on Ge?). Cf. Eust. 260.43, Dion. Hal. *de comp.* 16.17–19.

being produced in the 5th.[11] But however radical experientially, the change had little impact on the transmissional process itself, beyond increasing the amount of text that could be accommodated 'between two covers.'

The transition from papyrus to parchment was even slower, and did not enjoy the same success, at any rate in Egypt, where the native papyrus continued to be the dominant material. A parchment codex could carry more, or more comfortably (parchment typically being thinner than papyrus), and we have extensive remains of one written around the turn of the 3rd century which contained the entire *Odyssey*,[12] but even in late antiquity a Homer codex is still much more likely to be of papyrus. Writing styles changed too, though in most periods there was wide variety. From the 4th or 5th century onwards Homer texts tended to be written in the more or less standard kind of script sometimes known as uncial, but the distinction sometimes drawn between 'papyri' and 'uncials' has no validity.

* * *

Homer manuscripts now number well over a thousand. Most are ancient, but fragmentary—a few scrolls and codices largely intact, many scraps with only a few partial lines, most somewhere in between. More are published every year. Survival and provenance, as always, are determined by the water-table, archeologists' site-choice, and chance. From a wide variety of places mostly in Egypt come pieces of hundreds of Homer manuscripts ranging in date from the early 3rd century B.C. to the late 6th or 7th A.D.[13] Alexandria itself yields none, and Homer was so ubiquitously available that perhaps none of our manuscripts was written there.[14] Homer is far better represented than any other author, in every period, and the *Iliad* is constantly

[11] Scrolls were much easier to make. Psychological resistance will have played a role too (cf. Judaic prescription of scroll form for the Torah).

[12] p28 (M–P 1106), 3rd–4th cent.; the surviving leaves cover bks. 12–15 and 18–24, but a couple of quire-numbers reveal the original extent of the book.

[13] A few come from Nubia. The provenance of the Ambrosian *Iliad* (p1), an illustrated manuscript of the 5th or 6th cent. whose history can be traced through medieval and renaissance times, has been variously thought to be Italy, Constantinople, or Alexandria; R. Bianchi Bandinelli argued for Constantinople (*Hellenistic Byzantine Miniatures of the Iliad* (Olten, 1955)), but G. Cavallo has made a strong case for Alexandria (*Dialoghi di Archeologia* 7 (1973) 70–86). Homer is often quoted in texts from Herculaneum, but no actual Homer manuscripts have come to light there.

[14] But see preceding note.

favored over the *Odyssey* by 2:1 or better. No local peculiarities are in evidence. The nature of these texts ranges widely. There are ordinary commercial copies, there are careful copies and staggeringly careless copies, there are copies equipped with critical sigla, there are copies furnished with variant readings and annotations;[15] the variety and interplay of features is such as to defy systematic classification. The gap between the 7th-cent. arab conquest of Egypt and Syria and the 9th-cent. revival of hellenism in Constantinople is tenuously bridged by four leaves of an *Iliad* codex with poetic text and prose paraphrase on alternate lines discovered in St. Catherine's Monastery on Mt. Sinai in 1975 and written perhaps around the end of the 8th century.[16] Homer manuscripts in minuscule, which have the advantage of being often complete or nearly so, enter the scene in the 10th century, and thereafter become increasingly plentiful.

The Homeric text is evidenced in less direct forms too. Throughout antiquity schoolchildren used running vocabularies ('glossaries' or 'scholia minora'), medievally inherited in the so-called D[idymus]-scholia. The earliest manuscript of the *Iliad* D-scholia is assigned to the 9th century, earlier than any of the minuscule manuscripts of the poem itself, its *Odyssey* counterpart to the late 10th.[17] Their lemmas sometimes differ from the readings of the direct tradition. At the other end of the scale, scholars wrote treatises and commentaries. We have substantial papyrus remains of several, both Alexandrian and Pergamene, and they convey a wealth of information both about the contemporary text and about how it was treated. Their transmission in antiquity, like that of the scholia minora, was bibliographically independent, except insofar as their contents were sometimes

[15] Sigla: K. McNamee, *Sigla and select marginalia in Greek literary papyri* (Brussels, 1992); annotations: ead. in *Papiri letterari greci e latini*, ed. M. Capasso (Lecce, 1992), 13–51; cf. *Greek, Roman and Byzantine Studies* 22 (1981) 247–55.

[16] L. Politis, *Scriptorium* 34 (1980) 1–17 with pl. 8(b).

[17] *Il.*: Ve^1, split between Rome (Bibl. Naz. gr. 6) and Madrid (4626); written possibly as early as the first half of the century (N. G. Wilson, *Scholars of Byzantium* (London, 1983) 85, but it is doubly not 'an uncial copy of Homer'). *Od.*: Bodl.Lib. MS.Auct. V.1.51; cf. Wilson, op. cit. 148 (plate IV in L. D. Reynolds & N. G. Wilson, *Scribes & Scholars*^{3} (Oxford, 1991); dated to the 11th cent. by H. van Thiel, ed., *Homeri Odyssea* (Hildesheim-Zürich-New York, 1991) xix). On the *Iliad* D-scholia (where Ve^1 is known as C) see F. Montanari, ed., *Storia poesia e pensiero nel mondo antico: studi in onore di Marcello Gigante* (Naples, 1994) 475–481. The D-scholia differ from simple scholia minora in that they incorporate a collection of *historiae* too (the 'Mythographus Homericus'). In addition to their independent transmission, they are a component of the marginal annotations in Venetus A.

excerpted in margins of Homer texts. An impressive amount of this material was variously taken over into the margins of medieval manuscripts of the poems, to become our principal source of hellenistic scholarship. Commentaries also formed the basis of the Homer lexicon of Apollonius Sophista in the 1st century, which included Homeric quotations; this survives in papyrus fragments and in reduced form in a 10th-cent. manuscript, and surprisingly often attests a text different from that of the medieval tradition. In addition to all this paraliterary material, there is the indirect tradition in the conventional sense—Homeric quotations in posthomeric literature.

A very few of the ancient manuscripts may be listed.[18] The order is roughly chronological; papyrus scrolls unless stated otherwise.

Iliad

*Il.*p7 (M–P 819), III B.C.; remains of bk. 8, with plus-verses
*Il.*p12 (M–P 979), III B.C.; remains of bks. 21–23, with plus-verses
*Il.*p13 (M–P 998), I B.C.; remains of bks. 23–24
*Il.*p6c (M–P 952), II; bk. 18
*Il.*p2 (M–P 616, the Hawara Homer), II; remains of bks. 1–2, with critical signs and annotations
*Il.*p21 (M–P 778), II–III; remains of bk. 6, with critical signs and annotations
*Il.*p3 (M–P 634), III, papyrus codex; remains of bks. 2–4 (2.494–end omitted)
*Il.*p4 (M–P 697), III; remains of bks. 3–4, collated with a second exemplar
*Il.*p400–401 (M–P 736), III–IV, remains of bk. 5 and bk. 6 (two companion scrolls)
*Il.*p60 (M–P 870, the Morgan papyrus), IV, papyrus codex; remains of bks. 11–16
*Il.*p1 (Ambrosianus 1019, the Ambrosian *Iliad*), V–VI, illustrated parchment codex; remnants of most books
*Il.*p9 (Brit.Libr.add.MS. 17210, the Cureton *Iliad*), VI, palimpsested parchment codex, remains of bks. 12–24.

Odyssey

*Od.*p31 (M–P 1081), III B.C.; remains of bks. 9–10, with plus-verses
*Od.*p30 (M–P 1056), II B.C.; remains of bks. 4–5, with plus-verses

[18] See n. 1 for the conventions of reference.

*Od.*p3 + 43 (M–P 1039), I; remains of bk. 3, with annotations
*Od.*p28 (M–P 1106), III–IV, parchment codex; remains of bks. 12–15 and 18–24.

Commentaries include:

*Od.*h27 (M–P 1211.01), III B.C., on *Od.* 16–17
*Il.*h68 (M–P 1187.2, Erbse vol. VII 300–2), II B.C., on *Il.* 9
*Il.*h40 (M–P 1173, Pap. II Erbse), I B.C., on *Il.* 2
*Il.*h62 (M–P 1186, Pap. VI Erbse), I, on *Il.* 7
*Il.*h94 (M–P 1205, Pap. XII Erbse), II, on *Il.* 21
*Od.*h29 (M–P 1212.01), II, on *Od.* 20.

* * *

Our earliest Homeric manuscripts, those of the 3rd cent. B.C., are characterized by their startling degree of difference from the text that prevailed later, sometimes known as the 'vulgate.' We must beware of anachronism here, for we cannot simply assume that the vulgate was already in existence. Furthermore, the very term 'vulgate' is a misnomer. It designates no particular version of the text; there is no vulgate of Homer as there is a vulgate of the Bible. It is convenient to be able to refer to any given reading of all or most of the medieval manuscripts as the vulgate reading, but that is no more than a form of shorthand. By an extension of this shorthand the collectivity of such readings will be the vulgate text. But that is a construct which may never have had any existence in the real world, and it would be wrong to view any given manuscript as a more or less deformed version of it. What the manuscripts reflect is a host of concurrent variants jostling for preference, and there was no point in time at which this was not the case. Over time some variants dropped out, others came to the fore. The stabilization of the 2nd century B.C., however drastic, was still only relative. Manuscripts continue to show a great deal of textual variation (more than is sometimes made out), but its range is narrower than seems to have been the case earlier. In this context the 'vulgate' text may mean the collectivity not just of majority readings but of all readings in subsequent general circulation, as distinct from the different textual instantiations of the early Ptolemaic manuscripts. In this sense the vulgate text is a real thing, but far from being a uniform entity. A further complication is raised by references in Alexandrian scholarship to ἡ κοινή (sc. ἔκδοϲιϲ, unless λέξιϲ)—not to be equated with the subsequent vulgate; this will be taken up below.

We now have fragments of about forty Homer manuscripts written c. 150 B.C. or earlier.[19] In the course of the 2nd century, as Grenfell and Hunt were able to observe already in 1897, a distinct change occurred. As more evidence has accrued, the definiteness of the change has only been confirmed. The vulgate cannot have displaced divergent texts overnight, but the transition seems to have been remarkably rapid and complete. The earliest manuscript with a clearly vulgate text is assigned a date around 150 (*Il.*p271), whereas there are a couple of non-vulgate texts probably written in the latter half of the century (*Il.*p53, *Il.*p354) and even one assigned to the early 1st (*Il.*p51);[20] beyond that, the vulgate rules absolutely. It must be understood that dates are assigned ancient manuscripts mainly on the basis of palaeography, and can only be approximate. The most striking single characteristic of the texts falling on the upper side of the divide, as viewed from the standpoint of the text that subsequently established itself, is the large number of additional verses that they contain. These 'plus-verses,' however, are just the most conspicuous feature of a larger pattern of difference: there are also minus-verses, and much difference in the form of verses in common. The text has a different physiognomy. These early Ptolemaic texts of Homer are conventionally dubbed 'wild' or 'eccentric,' as are their counterparts for Euripides, Plato, and other authors. Such labels have the advantage of convenience, but not only are they anachronistic—for we have learned that there was nothing abnormal about these texts in their day—they also beg a few questions. It cannot actually be proved, for instance, that the variation which obtained among the early Ptolemaic manuscripts was any greater than that which obtained later. Only rarely do we have the same part of the Homeric text extant in more than one of these manuscripts, and when we do, there can be a surprising amount of agreement. In the brief stretches

[19] Those published before 1966 are conveniently and reliably accessible in S. West (1967), where earlier treatments are cited. More have appeared since, none very extensive. Cf. also A. di Luzio, 'I papiri omerici d'epoca tolemaica e la costituzione del testo dell'epica arcaica,' *Rivista di cultura classica e medioevale* 11 (1969) 3–152.

[20] On the date see G. Cavallo in D. Harlfinger, G. Prato, eds., *Paleografia e codicologia greca* (1991) 17. The text has critical signs (diplai and apparent obelos), and some lines coinciding with lines in the pseudo-Hesiodic *Shield* (*Il.* 18.608a–d ~ *Sc.* 207/8, 209/11–13) are marked with diplai. Di Luzio (1969) 116–7 argues that it is not really to be grouped with the early Ptolemaic papyri.

of text represented both by *Il.*p432 (3rd cent. B.C.) and by *Il.*p217 (2nd cent. B.C.), we find in both manuscripts two separate verses unknown to the later tradition (12.189b and 190a) as well as a version of 192 quite different from the vulgate's.[21] But the provenance of neither papyrus is known, and it is clear that the tradition was not uniform: there is one clear discrepancy between these two manuscripts (12.130a, present only in p432), and others elsewhere.[22]

Several of these early manuscripts give evidence of having been collated with another exemplar (so 'wild' is hardly the word for them), and sometimes reveal that 'vulgate' readings coexisted alongside 'eccentric' ones. The existence of individual vulgate *readings* does not of course mean that vulgate *texts* were current, and the papyri provide no evidence that they were. Of the variants entered from the second exemplar in the most extensive of the early *Iliad* papyri (p12), four coincide with the vulgate (21.413 οὕνεκα for εἵ κεν, 23.119 ἐπειγόμενοι for ἀμειβ-, 123 ἀνώγει for -εν, 128 Ἀχιλλεύϲ for Ἀχαιοῖϲ, cf. also 21.307), four others give non-vulgate readings where the primary text coincides with the vulgate (21.377 βοῶπιϲ πότνια for θεὰ λευκώλενοϲ, 397 ὑπονόϲφιον with Antimachus for πανόψιον, 406 ἀϲπίδα for αὐχένα, 23.123 ὥϲ περ for ὡϲ γὰρ), while in four other places both the primary text and the entered variant seem to have differed from the vulgate (21.378, 412, 23.156, 182), and in many other places the text is non-vulgate and no variant is entered. A similar picture is presented by the most extensive of the early *Odyssey* texts, p31. Only two of the papyri written probably before the middle of the 2nd century display no significant difference from the vulgate, and these are too short and damaged to count for much (*Il.*p460, remains of *Il.* 2.127–40, and *Il.*p496, remains of *Il.* 12.228–38, 246–65), although one of them (*Il.*p496) does lack a plus-verse which is found in *Il.*p217 (*Il.* 12.250a); a succession of ten or even twenty lines without a plus-verse is of small evidential value, especially since the more extensive early texts make it clear that the distribution of plus-verses is very uneven, as is only to be expected. *Il.*p41 has also been adduced as

---

[21] The verses represented in common are only 128–31 and 189b–92; actual textual overlap is virtually nil, but the restorations seem secure.

[22] p217 shows several discrepancies vis-à-vis p496 (III B.C.; the area of overlap is *Il.* 12.249–263); in these cases the earlier manuscript agrees with the vulgate. *Il.* 2.674, though present in p40 (early II B.C.), was apparently absent elsewhere (om. Zenodotus, Galen, ?Euripides). p12 has *Il.* 23.223ab, a quotation in ps.-Plutarch has 223bc.

indicating (or 'confirming') the pre-Alexandrian existence of the vulgate,[23] but it does nothing of the kind. It has a plus-verse, *Il.* 4.69a, is without 4.89 and 5.527, and has several non-vulgate readings (3.388, 4.57, 88/89, 5.530, 797); it was certainly no vulgate text. A couple of interesting features are (i) that its version of 4.88–9 coincides with that reported in the scholia for Zenodotus, showing either Zenodotus' effect on contemporary texts or vice versa, and (ii) that it also 'omits' 3.389, absent from several later papyri too but from none of the medieval manuscripts—a token of the readiness with which interpolations are capable of spreading.

The Homer of readers in the 3rd and early 2nd century, at any rate in Egypt (not that there is any reason to think the situation was different in places more distant from Alexandria), was appreciably more flaccid than the Homer of subsequent readers. The texts are longer, and what makes them longer is verses which slow the pace of the narrative without materially altering the action. Many of the verses recur elsewhere in Homer, or are composed of two such half-verses; the vulgate too contains many such recurrences, but not in such quantity. A few examples will suffice to give a sense of the sort of thing that is typically involved; I take them from the first part of *Od.* 5, all from one manuscript of the 2nd cent. B.C.[24] Such are the paradoxes of the Homeric transmission that the readings of this our oldest manuscript are not even recorded in either von der Mühll's or van Thiel's critical editions of the poem. The oldest manuscripts are not necessarily the best manuscripts, but in no other author would they be treated as negligible.

• 23–4, Zeus to Athena:

> οὐ γὰρ δὴ τοῦτον μὲν ἐβούλευϲαϲ νόον αὐτή,
> ὡϲ ἤτοι κείνουϲ 'Οδυϲεὺϲ ἀποτίϲεται ἐλθών
> οἶϲιν ἐνὶ μεγάροιϲ, ἢ ἀμφαδὸν ἠὲ κρυφηδόν;

The last line does not occur in 'our' *Odyssey*, but both halves of it do, and both in the context of Odysseus' return (1.269, 14.330 = 19.299).

---

[23] van Thiel, *Odyssea* vi n. 9.

[24] *Od.*p30, with remains of some 170 lines of bks. 4–5. I print the lines in conventional modern form, and I dispense with square brackets and sublinear dots where the restoration is in no doubt, but I do not say that a papyrus 'has' or 'gives' a certain reading unless it is extant. I omit several plus-verses whose text is beyond recovery. The verses are defended by di Luzio (1969) and accepted into the text by G. D'Ippolito, *Lettura di Omero: il canto V dell''Odissea'* (Palermo, 1977).

• 41–2, Zeus to Hermes. The vulgate text is

ὣϲ γάρ οἱ μοῖρ' ἐϲτὶ φίλουϲ τ' ἰδέειν καὶ ἱκέϲθαι
οἶκον ἐϲ ὑψόροφον καὶ ἑὴν ἐϲ πατρίδα γαῖαν.

In the papyrus this occupied not two lines but three:

οὐ [γάρ οἱ τῆιδ' αἶϲα δόμ]ων (unless φίλ]ων) ἄπο τῆλ' ἀλαλῆϲθαι[25]
ἀλ[λ' ἔτι οἱ μοῖρ' ἐϲτὶ κτλ.

These three lines occur in Hermes' subsequent report of Zeus' message, 113–5, except that 113 ends φίλων ἀπονόϲφιν ὀλέϲθαι (likewise the papyrus there); we have δόμων ἄπο τῆλ' ἀλάληϲο at 3.313, cf. 15.10. In the papyrus the corresponding passages evidently corresponded more closely than in the vulgate.

• 103–4, Hermes to Calypso:

ἀλλὰ μάλ' οὔ πωϲ ἔϲτι Διὸϲ νόον αἰγιόχοιο
οὔτε παρεξελθεῖν ἄλλον θεὸν οὔθ' ἁλιῶϲαι
ὃϲ νῦν με προέηκε τεὶν τάδε μυθήϲαϲθαι.

The last line occurs in our *Odyssey* not here but (with ἣ for ὃϲ) at 4.829 (image of Iphthime to Penelope, with reference to Athena), cf. *Il.* 11.201.

• 110–11, still Hermes to Calypso:

ἔνθ' ἄλλοι μὲν πάντεϲ ἐπέφθιθον ἐϲθλοὶ ἑταῖροι
τὸν δ' ἄρα δεῦρ' ἄνεμόϲ τε φέρων[26] καὶ κῦμα πέλαϲϲε.

The papyrus continued with an unknown verse:

[c. 9]ωϲ μετὰ [κ]ύμαϲι νυκτὸϲ [ἀμολγῷ].

This has no close congeners elsewhere in Homer, though each of the phrases appears earlier in the poem (μετὰ κύμ. 3.91, νυκ. ἀμ. 4.841). That Odysseus had landed at night is attested at 12.447.

• 230–2, the dressing of Calypso. The papyrus had two extra lines at the end:

κρηδέμνωι δ' ἐφύπερθε καλύψατο δῖα θεάων
καλῶι νηγατέωι, τό ῥα οἱ τεθυωμένον ἦεν.

---

[25] The scribe miswrote τηλελαϲθαι, imperfectly corrected by supralinear λη.

[26] The papyrus has not φερων but κακοϲ, evidently a scribal error induced by ανεμον τε κακον in the same position two lines before.

This pair of lines occurs in the vulgate as *Il.* 14.184–5, the dressing of Athena, except that the latter half of 185 is not τό - ἦεν but λευκὸν (v.l. λαμπρὸν) δ' ἦν ἠέλιος ὥς; τὸ - ἦεν occurs a few lines earlier at 172, with reference not to the veil but to the robe, ἀμβροσίῳ ἑδανῷ/ἑανῷ. In all texts the sequence robe-belt-veil is common to both scenes, with the Iliadic being fuller; Athena's dressing occupies 16 lines, while Calypso's, in the vulgate, is covered in three (230–32 = *Od.* 10.543–5, the dressing of Eos), finishing with (232) κεφαλῇ δ' ἐπέθηκε (ἐφύπερθε Aristarchus) καλύπτρην. The papyrus apparently juxtaposes two descriptions of the donning of the veil, an incoherence.[27]

Had these verses, or some of them, always been part of the Homeric text? Or did they enter in the course of transmission, only to disappear again? I pose the questions as alternatives, but it is possible to deconstruct the disjunction: does the Homeric text have a definable starting-point? In any event, we must account for their elimination. As with the variants and the 'omissions,' it is rarely easy or even possible to determine the age and authority of the non-vulgate elements of the early Ptolemaic texts on internal grounds, or not without recourse to subjectivity or to circular argument. This flabbier Homer is not the one we are familiar with, and may not be one we like, but how are we to ground our taste? From a transmissional point of view, however, it is easier to view plus-verses as accretions which did not gain a sufficiently firm hold to be perpetuated than as pristine material which was dropped. The verses' disappearance cannot be imputed to Alexandrian athetesis: that would not have effected their loss. Evidently the verses' presence in contemporary texts was not universal. Still, manuscripts with such verses must have been known at Alexandria, and the silence of the ancient scholarly tradition is remarkable; either they were considered negligible, or mention of them was erased in the course of the scholarly tradition's abridgement. Whatever kind of a history they have behind them, the verses existed, and while editors whose quest is the original Homer may not see fit to admit them or even to report them, the fact remains that they were effectively just as much a part of the Homeric text as verses whose subsequent life was longer.

---

[27] With the papyrus' text, the κρήδεμνον must be imagined as being put on over the καλύπτρη (cf. di Luzio (1969) 98–100). Of the latter part of 232 in the papyrus, what survives is actually κεφαληι̣ δ̣' εμ̣[, with some supralineation (not suitable for επεθηκε, apparently) above μ̣[, but it looks impossible to construct a text which would remove the awkwardness.

The parameters of variability are not adequately defined by simple line-count; the entire text was unstable, showing a degree of volatility more characteristic of texts whose transmission is oral.[28] Some variants are clearly secondary, e.g. subjunctive for optative at *Il.* 6.453 (p317); Wecklein had conjectured the subjunctive, following the same urge for syntactical normalization. In other cases (e.g. *Il.* 11.827, 12.192, *Od.* 21.390) editors' preference is determined solely by the presumed authority of the vulgate. Most of the variants, whether plus-verses or other, are best viewed not as the product of deliberate alteration but as a reflex of the same sort of textual dynamism that is witnessed in, for instance, English ballads.[29] They merit study as testifying to the kinds of improvisation in which rhapsodes engaged. To have such texts being written as late as the 2nd century B.C. is extraordinary.

* * *

Another body of information about the text in the 3rd century B.C. is the Alexandrian scholarly tradition, as preserved in remnants of ancient commentaries and marginalia and in the scholia. It is to this tradition that we owe what little knowledge we have of the 'city editions' and of individual scholars' 'editions' (αἱ κατ' ἄνδρα); some of the latter are pre-alexandrian (most notably Antimachus) and one of them Pergamene (Crates).[30] Just what these were is far from clear. The city-texts are cited simply as ἡ Χία (ἔκδοϲιϲ) etc., or collectively as αἱ ἀπὸ τῶν πόλεων or the like, the κατ' ἄνδρα texts similarly as ἡ 'Ριανοῦ or ἡ κατὰ 'Ριανόν or the like; the city-texts were presumably just manuscripts obtained from the places in question, while the κατ' ἄνδρα texts are likelier to have been critical notes than actual

[28] P. Zumthor's term 'mouvance' (first in *Essai de poétique médiévale*, Paris, 1972) has been aptly enough applied to Homeric epic in its oral phases, and for Zumthor himself it is applicable only to orally transmitted texts (cf. *Introduction à la poésie orale* (Paris, 1983), 245–262; *Yale French Studies* 67 (1984) 25–42). But the critical factor appears to be not the actual mode of transmission so much as the performer's (or writer's) interiorization of the text; the orality need only be potential.

[29] R. Finnegan, *Oral Poetry, Its Nature, Significance and Social Context* (Cambridge, 1977).

[30] The city-texts are surveyed by V. Citti, *Vichiana* 3 (1966) 227–67, cf. H. Marx, *Rheinisches Museum* 83 (1934) 373–76; some new attestations in *Od.*h29 = P.Oxy. LIII 3710 (the first attestation of the Cyprian *Odyssey*) and forthcoming Oxyrhynchus papyri. It is clear both from the uneven distribution of testimony among the various bodies of scholia and from the fuller reports in papyrus commentaries that only a small fraction is preserved in the scholia.

continuous texts. In the 'city' class we have the poet's reputed birthplace Chios, and far-flung places such as Marseilles (this one cited in the extant scholia much more frequently than any other) and Sinope, which may possibly indicate a calculated desire to get texts from peripheral areas; the full list is (West to East) Marseilles, the Argolid, Crete, Chios, the Aeolid (*Odyssey* only), Cyprus, and Sinope. To have even such highly selective reports of texts from outside Egypt is potentially very valuable indeed.[31] What may be thought most remarkable about them is their paucity of distinctiveness. Surprisingly often several of them agree with one another, against the vulgate; such agreements range from matters of form (e.g. μαχήcομαι not μαχέccομαι *Il.* 1.298, ἠΰτ' ὄρευc not εὖτ' ὄρεοc *Il.* 3.10) to substantively different versions (at *Il.* 19.76 f., where the medieval manuscripts all give τοῖcι δὲ καὶ μετέειπεν ἄναξ ἀνδρῶν Ἀγαμέμνων / αὐτόθεν ἐξ ἕδρηc οὐδ' ἐν μέccοιcιν ἀναcτάc, the Marseilles and Chios texts reportedly each offered τοῖcι δ' ἀνιcτάμενοc μετέφη κρείων Ἀγαμέμνων/ μῆνιν ἀναcτενάχων καὶ ὑφ' ἕλκεοc ἄλγεα πάcχων).[32] Particularly striking are two cases of agreement between city-texts and quotations in 4th-cent. Attic authors.[33] Such concordances leave the vulgate isolated. The city-texts are unlikely to be very old, and some of their reported readings are clearly secondary[34]—which makes their distribution all the more notable. However the readings are judged, the reports

[31] For van der Valk, *Textual Criticism of the Odyssey* (Leiden, 1949) 14–21 and *Researches on the Text and Scholia of the Iliad* (Leiden, 1963–64) II 1–9, they are valueless (they are 'of no value in textual matters,' their readings being 'arbitrary conjectures to which no value can be attributed'), but he does not concern himself with the transmission. In categorizing readings he operates with an opposition between 'original, old readings' and 'only subjective conjectures' (1949 15, assigning all the city-text readings to the latter category), a schematization that is surely too simple to cope successfully with the complex vicissitudes of the Homeric text.

[32] The city-text version of 76 was also Zenodotus' (the same variation between τοῖcι δὲ καὶ μετέειπε and τοῖcι δ' ἀνιcτάμενοc is presented by A at 9.52), 77 being absent. That may be the primary text (Bolling, 1925, 40, 185–6), or Zenodotus may be dependent (as again on the Chios text at *Il.* 17.133, see M. J. Apthorp, *The Manuscript Evidence for Interpolation in Homer* (Heidelberg, 1980) 76), and have rejected 77.

[33] *Il.* 23.77 οὐ μὲν γὰρ codd., οὐ γὰρ ἔτι Aeschines (*in Tim.* 149), reported by sch. A for 'some' of the city-texts; *Il.* 24.82 κῆρα codd., πῆμα Plato (*Ion* 538D), reported by sch. A again for 'some' of the city-texts. The Alexandrian scholarly tradition was apparently unaware of these agreements. Few will believe them due to 'fortuitous coincidence' (van der Valk (1949) 19).

[34] At *Il.* 21.576, where the vulgate is εἴ περ γὰρ φθάμενόc μιν ἢ οὐτάcῃ ἠὲ βάλῃcιν, the city-texts (no doubt the original report was more specific) had not μιν but τιc—surely pointing to a primary text with neither? Cf. e.g. *Od.* 15.436, ὅρκῳ πιcτωθῆναι ἀπήμονά (μ') οἴκαδ' ἀπάξειν, where FW have not μ' but δ'—and CD and Eustathius are without either.

afford us a welcome glimpse of what texts were like in other parts of the world.

Another text cited in the Alexandrian scholarly tradition is ἡ κοινή—'the vulgate,' no less. The medievally transmitted scholia vacillate between ἡ κοινή and αἱ κοιναί, but the singular is consistently given when such annotations occur in papyri.[35] Whatever this was, it was not the same as our vulgate. At *Il.* 2.397, for instance, ἡ κοινή had γένηται, while our manuscripts have γένωνται; at *Il.* 22.478 αἱ κοινότεραι had ἐνὶ οἴκῳ (so does Strabo), while our manuscripts have κατὰ δῶμα; at *Il.* 24.214 αἱ κοιναί had οὔ τι (so does p14, 2nd cent.), while the medieval tradition is οὔ ἑ. The list of discrepancies is quite long, and becomes still longer if we take αἱ εἰκαιότεραι and αἱ δημώδεις as terms equivalent to the koine, as it appears we should.[36] Little more than half the recorded readings coincide with our vulgate. It has been proposed that the koine is in fact another city-text, none other than the Athenian, not identified as such because it was indeed the 'standard' text.[37] This is a neat idea: it simultaneously explains the curious absence of any reference to Athenian texts in the Alexandrian tradition and the Attic overlay of the poems' texts in their transmitted form. But it is hard to think that the koine would make such a poor showing in the scholarly tradition if it were in fact the Athenian city-text, even if we take the clearly pejorative connotation that the word has in the scholia (where the 'common' texts are evidently equated with the 'inferior' or 'vulgar' or 'bad' copies) as an ignorant post-Aristarchan development, as the theory would require that we do. It is rather the early Ptolemaic papyri that we may see as specimens of the 'common' text(s).[38] The new orthodoxy that Aristarchus should have stuck to the koine instead of preferring αἱ χαριέστεραι rests on a very fragile basis. The difference between the koine and the subsequent vulgate is not to be elided.

Then there are the readings of the Alexandrian scholars themselves. 'Aristarchus' readings, it is now admitted, were all or nearly

[35] *Il.*p235 (M–P 950, Pap. *XI* Erbse), 2nd cent.; *Il.*p2 (M–P 616, Pap.I Erbse), 2nd cent.; *Il.*p21 (M–P 778, Pap.IV Erbse), 2nd–3rd cent. Among them they have six citations, none of which is preserved in the medievally transmitted scholia (in one case, *Il.* 2.397, ἡ κοινή is replaced by τινες)—an indication of the severely reduced nature of the scholia.

[36] T. W. Allen, ed., *Homeri Ilias I: Prolegomena* (Oxford, 1931) 277.

[37] M. S. Jensen, *The Homeric Question and the Oral-formulaic Theory* (Copenhagen, 1980) 109. The idea is taken up by Nagy (1996a) 187 ff.

[38] Cf. S. West (1967) 26. A small item of support: *Il.* 12.33 ἵεν or ἴεν codd., ιει the koine: 21.382a (= 12.33) ιει p12 (3rd cent. B.C.).

all taken from MSS extant in his time.' So it could be said in 1910.[39] Nowadays, in the wake of van der Valk, the pendulum has swung back: the prevailing opinion is that Aristarchus invented them, that is, conjectured them. The problem is still more acute with Zenodotus, the earliest in the line of Alexandrian 'correctors' of Homer, whom like Aristophanes of Byzantium we reach only through the filter of Aristarchus a century later.[40] If it is true (and it is) that 'Aristarchus and his pupils did not understand the principles on which Zenodotus had worked,'[41] it is not likely that we shall do better. The best-known case of a Zenodotean reading, οἰωνοῖcί τε δαῖτα not οἰωνοῖcί τε πᾶcι at *Il.* 1.5, may not in fact be typical (and without Athenaeus we would not even know of it), but what gives it its abiding importance is that the reading was apparently current in 5th-century Athens yet finds no representation at all in our manuscript tradition.[42] Nauck's suggestion that πᾶcι was a conjecture by Aristarchus was unduly provocative, but it must remain uncertain whether Zenodotus even knew the reading that was to prevail.[43] How wide and how good his manuscript base was, there is no telling, nor what use he made of it.

The only real clue to his procedures is his use of a mark, probably a marginal dash (the 'obelos'), wherewith he 'athetized' verses. Modern scholars sometimes speak of verses' being 'deleted' or the like, but this is misleading on more than one count. Ancient scholars were not so much editors as critics, and deletion was not the function of athetesis. The classic example is Pindar *Ol.* 2.27 φιλέοντι δὲ Μοῖcαι interpolated at stanza end: athetized by Aristophanes, it stayed in all manuscripts, in defiance of metrical response. Exceptions are rare: the absence of *Il.* 1.296 from a 2nd-cent. papyrus (p377) is so anoma-

---

[39] T. W. Allen, 'The text of the *Odyssey*,' *Papers of the British School at Rome* 5.1 (1910) 82.

[40] On Zenodotus see K. Nickau *Untersuchungen zur textkritischen Methode des Zenodotos von Ephesos* (Berlin-New York, 1977), id. in *Paulys Real-Encyclopädie der classischen Altertumswissenschaft* 10A (Stuttgart, 1972) cols. 20–55. On Aristophanes see W. J. Slater, *Aristophanis Byzantini fragmenta* (Berlin-New York, 1986), 205–10. A Zenodotean reading which can hardly be a conjecture is ἐc Κρήτην at *Od.* 1.93 and 285.

[41] S. West, ed., with A. Heubeck and J. B. Hainsworth, *A Commentary on Homer's Odyssey* vol. 1 (Oxford, 1988) 42, after Nickau.

[42] Cf. G. Pasquali, *Storia della tradizione e critica del testo*, 2nd ed. (Florence, 1954) 236–7, R. Pfeiffer, *History of Classical Scholarship* (Oxford, 1968) 111–14; the most important passage is the earliest, Aesch. *Suppl.* 800–1, κυcὶν δ' ἔπειθ' ἕλωρα κἀπιχωρίοιc ὄρνιcι δεῖπνον. Nickau (1977, 42 n. 32) endorses van der Valk's scepticism (*Researches* II 66–68). Zenodotus athetized verses 4–5.

[43] On the illegitimacy of assuming that our vulgate was already known to Zenodotus see Nickau (1977) 32; cf. A. Rengakos, *Der Homertext und die hellenistischen Dichter*

lous that we should either deem it accidental or imagine that the papyrus independently continues a line of transmission from which the verse was absent. That Zenodotus athetized on the basis of manuscript evidence, as Bolling and Pfeiffer supposed, may be doubted.[44]

He also 'omitted' (that is, reportedly 'did not write') a number of lines which Aristarchus subsequently recognized or athetized.[45] Since the obelos afforded an escape from the either/or dilemma to write or not to write, it seems reasonable to suppose that verses not included by Zenodotus were absent from at least some of his manuscripts; but even this is beyond proof, and there is always the possibility that he had more cavalier predecessors. Nor is it clear just what form his critical work took. An 'edition' in the form of a continuous written text would be unexpected, but if his diorthosis consisted of annotations, whether marginal or bibliographically independent, his 'omissions' become problematic. It has recently been suggested that οὐκ ἔγραφεν—the imperfect is the usual form—means 'he did not want to write' or 'he suggested that one not write,' which would imply not that the verses in question were unknown to him but precisely the reverse.[46] But that puts more weight on the tense than it will comfortably bear (the usage is parallel to οὐκ ἐφέροντο, οὐκ ἦcαν, of verses not carried by particular manuscripts),[47] and it may be preferable to suppose that the notation derives from the absence of the verses from whatever copy Zenodotus' readings were recorded in. However that may be, as far as the transmission is concerned three things are reasonably clear: (i) Zenodotus' text, whatever we understand by that, was slightly shorter than Aristarchus' and the vulgate; (ii) some of its readings had been earlier current (and were popular with contemporary

(Stuttgart, 1993) 38–48, exposing the prejudice-driven character of van der Valk's work.

[44] Pfeiffer (1968) 113–4, pointing to two egregious atheteses in response to Plato's criticism of the poet (*Il.* 1.225–33, cf. Pl. *Rep.* 389e, and *Il.* 16.432–58, cf. Pl. *Rep.* 388cd), supposed the verses were omitted from copies available to Zenodotus. But there is no reason to think that Plato ever induced actual excision in manuscripts of the poet. (Cf. Nickau, 1977, 219.)

[45] Zenodotus is also reported to have 'bracketed' (περιγράφειν) certain passages, i.e. marked them for deletion, I would presume on the basis of collation. (Literary papyri offer several instances of such bracketing, and P.Oxy. 2387 fr. 1 has a note on a passage of Alcman 'bracketed in Aristonicus' copy but unbracketed in Ptolemy's.') On these and other terms applied to Zenodotus' textual operations cf. Nickau (1977) 6–30.

[46] van Thiel (1991) ix–x ~ xxviii.

[47] Even with ἀθετεῖν the imperfect is common. If the present and perfect are commoner, it is because the Aristarchan athetesis is still there, in the form of the obelos.

poets)[48] but were now to disappear; and (iii) its discernible effect on the subsequent transmission is slight.

To Aristarchus we shall have to return. But perhaps we should now try to move in the other direction, back towards Homer himself.

* * *

The documentary evidence for the text prior to the 3rd century is not easy to control. The numerous quotations, the earliest Simonides' of *Il.* 6.146 but mostly by 4th-cent. Athenian prose-writers, were marshalled by Ludwich in an attempt to show that the vulgate had pre-Alexandrian existence, something that the early Ptolemaic papyri had rather forcibly called into question.[49] The attempt fails, for few of the quotations are at all extensive. Many of them, moreover, show discrepancies from the vulgate, discrepancies not all to be accounted for by postulating inadvertent or deliberate misquotation.[50] A notable instance is the indirect quotation of a series of 'Homeric' verses in the pseudo-Platonic *Second Alcibiades* (149d), reconstructible as:

ἔρδον δ' ἀθανάτοιϲι τεληέϲϲαϲ ἑκατόμβαϲ·
κνίϲην δ' ἐκ πεδίου ἄνεμοι φέρον οὐρανὸν εἴϲω
ἡδεῖαν· τῆϲ δ' οὔ τι θεοὶ μάκαρεϲ δατέοντο
οὐδ' ἔθελον· μάλα γάρ ϲφιν ἀπήχθετο Ἴλιοϲ ἱρή
καὶ Πρίαμοϲ καὶ λαὸϲ ἐυμμελίω Πριάμοιο,

where the vulgate has only the second of these (*Il.* 8.549).[51] But much the lengthiest, as well as the most illuminating, is Aeschines' quota-

---

[48] Rengakos (1993). This does not mean they are not conjectures: if anything, the reverse.

[49] *Homervulgata*. The quotations are usefully surveyed by T. W. Allen, *Homer: The Origins and the Transmission* (Oxford, 1924) 249–70. For Plato's citations see J. Labarbe, *L'Homère de Platon* (Liège, 1949), not without G. Lohse, 'Untersuchungen über Homerzitate bei Platon,' *Helikon* 4 (1964) 3–28, 5 (1965) 248–325, 7 (1967) 223–31.

[50] The weakness of Ludwich's case was shown by B. P. Grenfell & A. S. Hunt, *The Hibeh Papyri, Part I* (London, 1906) 68–75, who point out that the quotations are 'easily reconcilable with an inference exactly opposite to that drawn from them by Ludwich' (73).

[51] The last of them recurs at *Il.* 4.47, but it appears to be the bk. 8 passage that [Plato] has in mind; Wilamowitz assigned the verses to the *Little Iliad*, however (but also believed that the composer of bk. 8 took them over). It is by a quirk of the modern transmission that the five verses are accorded continuous numbers as if they were part of the medievally transmitted text (*Il.* 8.548–52), to be duly rendered in e.g. Lattimore's translation. Likewise with *Il.* 11.543, Ζεὺϲ γάρ οἱ νεμέϲαϲχ' ὅτ' ἀμείνονι φωτὶ μάχοιτο, quoted after 11.542 by Aristotle (*Rhet.* 1387a34) but absent from all Homer manuscripts. Hippocrates quotes as from Homer ὡϲ δ' ὁπότ' ἀϲπάϲιον ἔαρ ἤλυθε

tion (*in Tim.* 149) of *Il.* 23.77–91 (Patroclus to Achilles). This is worth giving in extenso.

	Aeschines	Hom. codd.
77	οὐ γὰρ ἔτι ζωοί γε φίλων ἀπάνευ θεν ἑταίρων	οὐ μὲν γὰρ ζωοί γε φίλων ἀπάνευ θεν ἑταίρων
78	βουλὰϲ ἑζόμενοι βουλεύϲομεν, ἀλλ' ἐμὲ μὲν κὴρ	βουλὰϲ ἑζόμενοι βουλεύϲομεν, ἀλλ' ἐμὲ μὲν κὴρ
79	ἀμφέχανε ϲτυγερή, ἥ περ λάχε γινόμενόν περ·	ἀμφέχανε ϲτυγερή, ἥ περ λάχε γιγνόμενόν περ·
80	καὶ δὲ ϲοι αὐτῷ μοῖρα, θεοῖϲ ἐπιείκελ' Ἀχιλλεῦ,	καὶ δὲ ϲοι αὐτῷ μοῖρα, θεοῖϲ ἐπιείκελ' Ἀχιλλεῦ,
81	τείχει ὕπο Τρώων εὐηγενέων ἀπολέϲθαι	τείχει ὕπο Τρώων εὐηγενέων ἀπολέϲθαι
81a	μαρνάμενον δηίοιϲ Ἑλένηϲ ἕνεκ' ἠυκόμοιο.	*om.*
82	ἄλλο δέ τοι ἐρέω, ϲὺ δ' ἐνὶ φρεϲὶ βάλλεο ϲῇϲιν·	ἄλλο δέ τοι ἐρέω καὶ ἐφήϲομαι, αἴ κε πίθηαι·
83	μὴ ἐμὰ ϲῶν ἀπάνευθε τιθήμεναι ὀϲτέ', Ἀχιλλεῦ,	μὴ ἐμὰ ϲῶν ἀπάνευθε τιθήμεναι ὀϲτέ', Ἀχιλλεῦ,
83a	ἀλλ' ἵνα πέρ ϲε καὶ αὐτὸν ὁμοίη γαῖα κεκεύθῃ	*om.*
83b	χρυϲέῳ ἐν ἀμφιφορεῖ τόν τοι πόρε πότνια μήτηρ,	*om.*
84	ὡϲ ὁμοῦ ἐτράφεμέν (ἐτράφομεν Scaliger) περ ἐν ὑμετέροιϲι δόμοιϲιν	ἀλλ' ὁμοῦ ὡϲ ἐτράφην περ (ἐτράφημεν v.l.) ἐν ὑμετέροιϲι δόμοιϲιν
	. . .	. . .
91	ὣϲ δὲ καὶ ὀϲτέα νῶϊν ὁμὴ ϲορὸϲ ἀμφικαλύπτοι,	ὣϲ δὲ καὶ ὀϲτέα νῶϊν ὁμὴ ϲορὸϲ ἀμφικαλύπτοι,
92	(*om.*, add. alii)	χρύϲεοϲ ἀμφιφορεὺϲ τόν τοι πόρε πότνια μήτηρ.'

The Aeschines version stands in just the same sort of relation to the vulgate as do the early Ptolemaic papyri. The most notable individual features are the plus-verse 81a and especially the two verses following 83, which correspond to the vulgate 92 (presumably absent from Aeschines' text). Like most of their counterparts in the Ptolemaic texts, these have left no trace either in the later manuscript tradition or in the scholarly tradition (which shows no awareness of the quotations to be found in Aeschines). 92, on the other hand, was known to Aristarchus: he athetized it, thereby securing its subsequent

βουϲὶν ἕλιξιν, but whether from a divergent text or from a poem of the Cycle there is nothing to show.

transmission. He was quite right to athetize, as the Aeschines version shows by its offering 83ab: the addition of 92 and the addition of 83ab were evidently alternative means of effecting the equation of the ϲορόϲ of 91 with the golden amphora which Thetis provides for Achilles' bones at *Odyssey* 24.73–77.[52] It is perhaps a little surprising that he knew the verse at all, for it is absent from a mid-3rd-cent. B.C. *Iliad* manuscript (p12) which covers part of this same passage; but since 83ab had come into being, the competing 92 cannot have been far behind if it was to triumph. This is one of the very few passages where we are able to make a direct comparison between a pre-Aristarchan Homer manuscript and a certifiably pre-Aristarchan quotation; but the papyrus text is lost between verses 1 and 85, so that there is no knowing whether or not 81a and 83ab were present, and we cannot gauge the extent of the affinity between Aeschines and the papyrus beyond the absence of 92.[53] But that is enough to make it clear that the Aeschines quotation and the papyrus text cannot be dismissed as merely aberrant. It is also clear that Aristarchus did at least on occasion have manuscript authority for his atheteses.[54] This gives some reassurance that he would not actually omit verses which were present in all his manuscripts.

The other variations in Aeschines' version seem less important, but the Homer scholia attest 77 οὐ γὰρ ἔτι for 'some' of the city-texts (originally the notice will have been more precise), so that too is unlikely to be a casual aberration on the part of Aeschines or his manuscript tradition. 82 banalizes, in line with many such variants both in the early Ptolemaic texts and among the medieval manuscripts themselves. Aeschines' version of 84 is conditioned by the accession of 83ab.[55]

This quotation of Aeschines', and others in the same speech, may

[52] See further *Transactions of the American Philological Association* 121 (1991) 35–45. A contrary assessment is given by van der Valk (1963–64) II 326–31.

[53] Except inasmuch as the papyrus has ἀμφικαλύπτῃ in 91, and the oldest Aeschines manuscript (f, 10th cent.) is reported as having -ῃ or -ει. Some of the Homer mss have -ει, a common variant form of -ῃ but here more probably derived from -οι, the vulgate reading.

[54] He would not have athetized without internal evidence against the line, however. Cf. Apthorp (1980) 49–53, and more generally D. Lührs, *Untersuchungen zu den Athetesen Aristarchs in der Ilias und zu ihrer Behandlung im Corpus der exegetischen Scholien* (Hildesheim-Zürich-New-York, 1992) 10–13.

[55] So it is hard to share Pasquali's enthusiasm for ὡϲ ὁμοῦ ἐτράφομέν περ (1954, 244). As to the split in the medieval tradition, the plural is supported by two later papyri (p258, 3rd cent., p9, 5th–6th cent.).

be supposed to have been taken from an ordinary written text of the day.[56] Likewise with Lycurgus' quotation of *Il.* 15.494–499 in his speech against Leocrates (103), showing similar verbal variation.[57] With Aristotle it is different, or can be. Discussing the association of courage with passion (*Eth.Nic.* 1116b 24), Aristotle produces a slew of Homeric phrases: cθένοc ἔμβαλε θυμῷ; μένοc καὶ θυμὸν ἔγειρε; δριμὺ δ' ἀνὰ ῥῖναc μένοc; ἔζεcεν αἷμα—which do indeed sound Homeric (except perhaps the last), but turn out none of them actually to occur in our texts of the poet. It need not be supposed that Aristotle had ever read or heard these precise phrases in Homer. Even so, to call them misquotations (and to identify them with specific verses) is misleading. With Homeric phraseology thoroughly interiorized, he came up with them out of his head, much as a rhapsode might, recomposing in performance; the phrases are, as it were, potentially Homeric.

Before leaving the non-vulgate texts exemplified by the early Ptolemaic papyri and by earlier quotations, we should note that while such texts find no representation in the post-Aristarchan direct tradition, they do quite often crop up in much later writers, Plutarch and Strabo especially. These writers are probably not to be thought of as having access either to pre-Aristarchan Homer manuscripts[58] or to contemporary manuscripts whose texts had somehow escaped the 2nd-cent. standardization; their access to non-vulgate versions comes by underground descent from their now lost sources.[59] The quotations

[56] I assume Aeschines provided the clerk of the court a copy of the text with the relevant places marked (with paragraphos, cf. Isoc. *Antidosis* 59). The published speech represents the orator as reading out the first passage himself (§ 144, six verses), then calling on the clerk for the rest (§§ 148, 149, 150).

[57] 494 διαμπερέc not ἀολλέεc, 497 νήπια τέκνα not παῖδεc ὀπίccω, 498 κλῆροc καὶ οἶκοc not οἶκοc καὶ κλῆροc, 498 ἵκωνται (ἥκωνται fere codd.) not οἴχωνται.

[58] Preservation of papyrus scrolls over so long a period is not unthinkable in itself—Galen handled scrolls he thought were 300 years old (xviii.2 p. 638 Kühn)—but hard to imagine with an author as common as Homer. The anecdote in Diogenes Laertius (9.113) about Timon's recommendation to Aratus to seek out old copies (τὰ ἀρχαῖα ἀντίγραφα) instead of corrected ones (τὰ ἤδη διωρθωμένα) is much rehearsed in modern scholarship, but what counts is that it is about *Timon*, sceptic composer of *Silloi*; the pose is not to be taken as in any way representative of contemporary popular attitudes.

[59] The basic studies are H. Amoneit, *De Plutarchi studiis homericis* (Königsberg, 1887), H. Bidder, *De Strabonis studiis homericis* (Königsberg, 1889). For post-Aristarchan quotations in general see A. Ludwich, *Über Homercitate aus der Zeit von Aristarch bis Didymos* (Königsberg, 1897). As an alternative it has been proposed that well-to-do literary families would have had their worn-out Homer manuscripts privately recopied rather than buying new ones (Jensen, 1980, 107); but whether or not that is so, I find no

in these late authors constitute a substantial augmentation of our knowledge of the pre-stabilized text. To take one instance, again from *Il.* 23: in Plutarch(?) *Consolatio ad Apollonium* (117d), the simile that introduces Achilles' mourning as he burns the bones of Patroclus is expanded vis-à-vis the vulgate:

222 ὡϲ δὲ πατὴρ οὗ παιδὸϲ ὀδύρεται ὀϲτέα καίων,
223 νυμφίου, ὅϲ τε θανὼν δειλοὺϲ ἀκάχηϲε τοκῆαϲ,
223b ἄρρητον δὲ τοκεῦϲι γόον καὶ πένθοϲ ἔθηκε, (~ 17.37)
223c μοῦνοϲ τηλύγετοϲ πολλοῖϲιν ἐπὶ κτεάτεϲϲι, (~ 9.482)
224 ὣϲ Ἀχιλεὺϲ κτλ.

223bc are not in our Homer manuscripts—at least, 223c is not: 223b is in one, namely the 3rd-cent. B.C. papyrus adduced above in connection with Aeschines. This has a version comparable but not identical with ps.-Plutarch's: again two plus-verses after 223, but the first is

223a χήρωϲεν δ[ὲ γυναῖκα μυχῷ θαλάμοιο νέοιο (~ 17.36)

and the second is 223b. Whether or not the papyrus version and the Plutarch version are mutually independent, as Stephanie West believes, it is most interesting to observe how they differently deploy other Homeric scenes to heighten the pathos, and also to observe the vulgate's successful insulation, confirming the pre-Aristarchan nature of the version in ps.-Plutarch. It is also worth noting that the quotations from Euripides and Plato in the *Consolatio* have readings which are regarded by editors as superior to those of the direct tradition. Only in Homer is the direct tradition treated as having exclusive authority.[60]

It is in this context that we confront the notorious case of the passage alleged by Plutarch (*de aud. poet.* 26 f.) to have been expelled by Aristarchus from Phoenix' tale in *Il.* 9: Ἀρίϲταρχοϲ ἐξεῖλε ταῦτα τὰ ἔπη φοβηθείϲ, 'Aristarchus removed these verses, out of fear' (an unusual motive). The verses in question, 458–61, are not in any of our Homer codices (including one of the 3rd century), and probably Plutarch's charge, or his source's, is nothing but an inference, based on the observed discrepancy with the vulgate: if the verses were not

case of an 'eccentric' quotation which is unlikely to be at second-hand, directly copied as it stood in the source.

[60] van Thiel (1991, iii–iv ~ xxi–ii) expressly treats readings not only of the indirect tradition but even of the papyri as conjectures!

there, it must be because Aristarchus had expelled them. Since there is no comment on the verses in the scholia, Aristarchus probably never knew them. If all his manuscripts had had them, he would have retained them, athetized or not.[61] But they can hardly have originated in post-Aristarchan times. It seems we have here another sample of an 'eccentric' text. That puts the lines on a par with the plus-verses of the early papyri and quotations, unusual only in their uniqueness. Such verses are much more readily accounted for as additions which did not permeate than as excisions which did.[62]

* * *

To try to get further back involves us in The Homeric Question. The poems' transmission is very different, according as they attained their monumental form in the 8th century or only in the 6th. How critical a role Athens played in the poems' evolution and transmission is much disputed: how real is the Pisistratean recension? No less disputed are questions of the poems' being written down: when, and why, and what difference did it make? Such questions are as fundamental as they are complex, and a comprehensive and impartial survey is impossible. Some things there is no disputing, e.g. that the medium was predominantly oral down to the 5th century or beyond, and for many centuries was both oral and written, with various kinds of mostly unfathomable interplay between the two.[63] We are tracing the history of poems whose primary instantiations for centuries took not the form of written text, something still there after the event, but the momentary form of what was sung and heard. The poem may continue, but in what sense is it the same? A scribe's job is to copy the letters that another has written, and his degree of success is measurable. But is it a singer's job to sing the words that another has sung? To pose such questions is to remind ourselves that oral

[61] So Bolling (1925) 121; cf. S. West, *Liverpool Classical Monthly* 7 (1982) 84–86, Apthorp (1980) 91–99.

[62] Contra Janko (1992) 28, according to whom Aristarchus' preferred sources (i.e. 'unreliably emended texts') 'surely deleted some recalcitrant verses, and formed the model for Zenodotus' practice.' That seems unlikely to me.

[63] Cf. M. L. West, 'Archaische Heldendichtung: Singen und Schreiben,' in W. Kullmann and M. Reichel, eds., *Der Übergang von der Mündlichkeit zur Literatur bei den Griechen* (Tübingen, 1990), 33–50, and more generally J. Goody, *The Interface between the Written and the Oral* (Cambridge, 1987).

transmission differs essentially from written, not only in its nature but in its object.

The matter of writing makes perhaps the best entry-point into the maze. One theory holds that there were no written texts of the Homeric poems until the middle of the 6th century.[64] Another has the first writing down of the poems coincide with their composition and/or performance by the poet.[65] Both theories associate written form with definitive form. Both involve a host of other, interlocking propositions; clearly each understands something different by 'Homer,' and will define the relationship between Homer and his tradition in different terms. Both encounter powerful objections, along with empty ones. Against the latter theory may be urged difficulties both practical and motivational, as well as its arguable implication in a literacy-bound view of the conditions under which great poems may be produced. Even the most naively optimistic scholar may feel uneasy when invited to believe that what we have happens to be just what Homer sang, and it is a troubling presupposition that 'Homer' is a theoretically identifiable individual to whom the composition of the *Iliad* and/or the *Odyssey* is axiomatically to be attributed, as if unitarian views can be validated by ex cathedra pronouncements.[66] But where the former theory founders, it seems to me, is in its inability adequately to account for the early textual fixation implied by certain details of the linguistic constitution of the poems. Janko's comparative statistical study of the incidence of a variety of older linguistic features in early epic poems, enabling firm relative dating (*Iliad, Odyssey*, Hesiod, in that order), shows that the Homeric poems' linguistic evolution was arrested at a very early point.[67] It seems impossible to explain this arrest except in terms of the fixity provided by writing. We are free to postulate rhapsodic performance of a memorized text,

[64] E.g. E. Heitsch, *Hermes* 96 (1968) 641–60 ('Diese in Athen vollzogene Niederschrift des Epos war für unsere Ilias die erste, einzige und endgültige' 659), G. Nagy (1996a) and elsewhere, cf. R. Seaford, *Reciprocity and Ritual* (Oxford, 1994) 152–154.

[65] E.g. Janko (1992) 38 and elsewhere, favoring dictation (and a single poet for both poems); S. West (1988) 33 (different authorship for each poem); B. Powell, *Homer and the Origin of the Greek Alphabet* (Cambridge, 1991).

[66] Thus for Janko there are three *a priori* possibilities for how the text of Homer was written down (*Classical Antiquity* 9 (1990) 327–28): all three take a single composer for granted.

[67] R. Janko, *Homer, Hesiod and the Hymns: Diachronic Development in Epic Diction* (Cambridge, 1982). For a sceptical view see A. Ballabriga, *Revue des études grecques* 103 (1990) 16–29, and cf. West (1995) 204 f.

but unless this was controlled by an invariant, i.e. a written text, some linguistic development would have been inevitable. If there is one thing that research into oral traditions has shown, it is that they are inherently labile: change, however imperceptible to performers and audiences, does not stop. Yet it did stop, prior to Hesiod: this can only be due to writing.[68]

To record in writing in the 8th century poems of the length of the *Iliad* and the *Odyssey* would have been an enterprise so remarkable that it is hard to credit; the difficulties which the hypothesis encounters are not to be minimized. But it seems that it was done.[69] The poet himself would derive no advantage from having a script, nor would he have the facilities to produce one; the initiative must have come from a wealthy admirer. With others, I see no alternative to dictation: which may have resulted in the poems' being longer than hitherto. The material will have been papyrus, obtained from Egypt perhaps via Phoenicia (whence also the alphabet); for such long texts that is surely more probable than animal-skin, i.e. leather or parchment. What effect the written text had on subsequent performance is not easy to gauge, and the nature of early diffusion is obscure. The *Odyssey* poet appears to be familiar with the *Iliad* (readily explained if it was his poem), and, more important, the Boeotian Hesiod with at least some of the *Odyssey*.[70] Acquaintance with both epics in some form, along with other of the 'Homeric' sagas, seems to be evidenced in the Peloponnese before the end of the seventh century, and with the *Iliad* on Lesbos.[71] The Homerids of Chios will have performed hereditary functions, and perhaps the poems, but little is really known of their activities or their authority; likewise with the Creophyleans of Samos.[72] A change in mode of performance is signalled by the

[68] G. Nagy (1992) 38 and elsewhere, correlates width of diffusion with strictness of adherence to a normative and unified version, but even if the correlation holds good, I do not see that it will sufficiently account for the early fixation of the text. He posits a 'relatively static' phase of oral transmission lasting some two centuries (ib. 52); the objections which A. Parry brought against Kirk ('Have we Homer's *Iliad?*' *Yale Classical Studies* 20 (1966) 175–216) apply no less strongly here.

[69] On the material factors see A. Heubeck, *Archaeologia Homerica* x, 'Schrift' (Göttingen, 1979), esp. 152–6. Cf. B. Powell's article in this volume.

[70] If Hes. *Theog.* 84–92 is dependent on *Od.* 8.170–3, as I believe it is. Cf. H. Neitzel, *Homer-Rezeption bei Hesiod* (Bonn, 1975).

[71] *Il.*: K. Friis Johansen, *The Iliad and Early Greek Art* (Copenhagen, 1967); *Od.*: Alcman fr. 80, after *Od.* 12.47; Lesbos: Alcaeus fr. 44.

[72] The main evidence for the Homerids is Pind. *Nem.* 2.1–4 and the scholium thereon (Hippostratus *FGrHist* 568 F5). Cf. Allen (1923) 42–50, W. Burkert, *Museum*

switch from the Homeric lyre to the Hesiodic staff: Homer sang (at least, his bards do), rhapsodes recited. A welcome nugget of information is that there were rhapsodic contest-performances of Homer at Sicyon early in the sixth century.[73] No doubt there were at other places too, Ionian as well as Dorian. But the first detailed testimony concerns later 6th-century Athens. An Athenian tradition had it that Pisistratus' son Hipparchus was the first to bring the Homeric poems into Attica. That is surely too late, and has been interpreted as referring to a book-text, but the weight falls on the second limb of the story, that Hipparchus compelled the rhapsodes at the Panathenaea to 'go through them in order,' each taking up where the last left off—implying, what there is every reason to believe, that hitherto parts of the poems had been sung independently or out of sequence.[74] A tradition first attested in Cicero, ascribing the arrangement of the Homeric books to Pisistratus himself, seems to be a garbled variant of this, and the story becomes one of a *compositio membrorum* on the model of an Actaeon or a Pentheus.[75] In this context belongs the unattributed tradition found in a T-scholium on *Il.* 10.1 that the Doloneia (*Il.* 10) was originally separate, and was incorporated in the *Iliad* by Pisistratus. The Panathenaic institutionalisation under Hipparchus receives confirmation from the efflorescence of Iliadic scenes in contemporary vase-painting,[76] and it seems to have crystallized the delimitation of 'Homer' to the *Iliad* and *Odyssey*. But the 'Pisistratean recension' itself is controversial, some assigning to it the definitive formation of the Homeric poems, others denying it transmissional

Helveticum 29 (1972) 74–85 ('schon für die Antike kaum mehr als ein Name' 78–79), D. Fehling, *Rheinisches Museum* 122 (1979) 193–210 (extreme).

[73] Hdt. 5.67.1 ('Clisthenes put a stop to rhapsodes competing in Sicyon because of the Homeric epics, because they are full of celebration of Argives and Argos'). There is no telling how long the institution had been in place. R. Sealey's inference that the songs belonged to Theban not Trojan saga (*Revue des études grecques* 70 (1957) 348) is unwarranted, as is J. Svenbro's inference of use of a fixed text (*La parole et le marbre* (Lund, 1976) 44–45): singers of Homer in any form would have found it hard to avoid mentioning Argives.

[74] ἐξ ὑπολήψεως ἐφεξῆς αὐτὰ διιέναι [Plat.] *Hipparchus* 228b. The regulation was assigned to Solon by the Megarian Dieuchidas (*FGrH* 485 F6). In Spartan tradition the first to bring Homer into the Peloponnese was Lycurgus (Aristotle *Lac.Pol.*, fr. 611.10). Homer was first sung at Syracuse by the Chian Cynaethus in 504 B.C., according to Hippostratus (ap. schol. Pind. *Nem.* 2.1, *FGrH* 568 F5): again later than is credible, but cf. W. Burkert in *Arktouros: Hellenic Studies presented to Bernard M. W. Knox* (Berlin-New York, 1979) 53–62.

[75] On its mythical features cf. Nagy (1992) 43–51.

[76] Friis Johansen (1967) cf. H. A. Shapiro, *Art and Cult under the Tyrants in Athens* (Göttingen, 1990) 43–46.

importance beyond the diction's acquisition of an attic veneer.[77] What seems clear, although even this depends on accepting atticisms as such, is that the poems passed through Athens, and in written form, on their way to Alexandria and us. If one accepts their early textual fixation, they were not drastically affected in the process.

Signs of Athenian interference with the text are nugatory. There is nothing Athenocentric about the Athenians' most prominent Homeric appearance, their entry in the Catalogue of Ships (*Il.* 2.546–56), featuring not a Theseid but the obscure Menestheus. Even the suspicion attaching to verses 553–5, boosting Menestheus, has to contend with the Athenian appeal to those verses before Gelon of Syracuse (Hdt.7.161), which could hardly have been made if the verses had not been by then canonical. There was a story that the plus-verse 2.558, placing Ajax' ships with the Athenians', was added by Solon to support the Athenian claim to Salamis. This could even be true (in which case an established text prior to Pisistratus is implied), though it seems more probable that the verse was invented as an embellishment to the story, according to which the Megarians countered with their own version of the Ajax entry; 558 made its way into some of the medieval manuscripts of the poem, but only in modern times gained an established place in the text.[78] The singular brevity of the Ajax entry, with or without 558, is one of several instances of this hero's underrepresentation in the *Iliad*, with which Athens probably has nothing to do.[79] The Megarian Hereas alleged that *Od.* 11.631, mentioning Theseus, had been added by Pisistratus, who complementarily deleted an offending line from Hesiod (fr. 298 M–W)—an interesting form of political mudslinging, but nothing more. Another verse mentioning Theseus was interpolated at *Il.* 1.265 from the pseudo-Hesiodic *Shield*; but the interpolation is post-Aristarchan, and in line with other Hesiodic additions (*Il.* 24.45, 16.608a–d, *Od.* 11.604). The most amusing testimony closes bk. 18 of Julius Africanus'

[77] The former: Jensen (1980) providing (128–31) summaries of important discussions prior to her own (Allen's, Merkelbach's, Davison's, Mazon's); cf. most recently R. Seaford, *Reciprocity and Ritual* (Oxford, 1994) 144–54. The latter: Allen (1923) 225–48, cf. Janko (1992) 29–32.

[78] Cf. Apthorp (1980) 165–77. The manuscript evidence would suggest a post-Aristarchan origin for the verse (it is absent from the vulgate), but it is already parodied by Matro, normally dated to the 4th century; evidently the verse made its way into Homer texts via the story.

[79] Cf. D. L. Page, *History and the Homeric Iliad* (Berkeley, 1959) 232–35. But see also M. Finkelberg, *Classical Quarterly* 38 (1988) 31–41.

24-book *Kestoi*, dedicated to Severus Alexander. The author is unsure whether a magical incantation set in the context of a farrago of verses from the Nekuia was suppressed by the poet himself or by the Pisistratids when they were stitching together the rest (τὰ ἄλλα ϲυνράπτοντεϲ ἔπη); but he assures his reader that the whole work is preserved in the archives (ἐν τοῖϲ ἀρχαίοιϲ) of Jerusalem, and at Nysa in Caria, and up to line 13 'in the fine library in the Pantheon which I personally designed for the emperor.'[80] This has no bearing on the historicity of the Pisistratean recension, but it warns us not to believe everything we read.

* * *

Just how the vulgate came to *be* the vulgate is an unsettled question. As to the part played by Alexandrian scholarship, diametrically opposed views have been arrived at. For Bolling, the vulgate represented the edition of Aristarchus: 'all our MSS are reproductions of that edition.'[81] For Allen, Aristarchus had no effect on the text at all.[82] Both positions rest on hard evidence. The number and sequence of verses in our manuscripts (unevenly attested verses excluded) conform with near perfect exactitude to the verses recognized by Aristarchus (verses which he athetized included): hence Bolling. At the same time, the proportion of Alexandrian scholars' readings in the vulgate is very low: hence Allen. The relation between Aristarchus and the post-Aristarchan vulgate is thus a highly curious one: there appears to be simultaneously match and mismatch. A sort of compromise explanation of the paradox has won wide acceptance, framed in terms of the book trade. Booksellers made their texts conform to the Aristarchan line-count, but did not bother to revise the actual wording, about which most readers would neither know nor care.[83] But the solution seems more facile than plausible, and the hypothesis does not really resolve the contradiction. If we imagine an Aristarchan text available to proprietors of scriptoria, it has to be explained why

[80] P.Oxy. III 412.

[81] *American Journal of Philology* 35 (1914) 128.

[82] 'Homeric critics had no effect upon the published text,' Allen (1924) 326–7.

[83] P. Collart, *Revue de Philologie* ser. 3 7 (1933) 52–54, cf. G. M. Bolling, *The athetized lines of the Iliad* (Baltimore, 1944) 22–23; the most persuasive presentation in English is by S. West (1988) 47–48 (similarly 1967, 16–17); endorsed in turn by Apthorp (1980) 9–10, Janko (1992) 22.

they should not simply have reproduced it. We are invited to envisage a public so insistent on having Aristarchan texts that all non-Aristarchan lines were cancelled, yet so ignorant and uncaring that Aristarchan readings could be routinely passed over. And the hypothesis only highlights the problem of Aristarchus' 'edition' itself. If we ask what form an ancient scholar's critical edition took, we shall normally do better to think in terms of commentary or marginal annotation than of a newly produced text incorporating the scholar's preferred readings.[84]

It would at least resolve the paradox of the vulgate's constitution if we view it rather as the result of Aristarchus' work of recension. Alexandrian scholars' proposals for amelioration of the text consisted of (a) atheteses and (b) individual 'readings' (as we call them): Zenodotus, Aristophanes and Aristarchus athetized verses which they thought the text might be better off without, and wherever the text seemed to admit of improvement they proposed it. (The proffered reading—what a given scholar 'writes'—would not necessarily be original to the scholar in question, though many of them are clearly conjectural in character; likewise with the atheteses.) Neither their atheteses nor their readings were meant to supplant the given text, nor did they: they were scholarly apparatus in attendance on the received text. But the received text was a very varied thing, as the early Ptolemaic papyri are enough to show. It seems that the Alexandrians, and Aristarchus in particular, more or less established it. This is what we know as the vulgate. If it had any discrete pre-Alexandrian existence, it is clear that it did not become the vulgate, the standard text, until the time of Aristarchus. Quite how it came about that texts in circulation were brought within the contours set by Aristarchus is still far from clear (strong links between the Museum and the book trade are implied, a virtual Alexandria University Press), but at least we are free to see the standardized text as an internally consistent entity—the received text as determined by Aristarchus. The presence of lines which he athetized and the absence of readings which he would have preferred are now on a par.

This means that Aristarchus' edition, if by that we understand the text which he annotated, was effectively the archetype of the

[84] Cf. H. Erbse, *Hermes* 87 (1959) 275–303; M. W. Haslam, *Illinois Classical Studies* 3 (1978) 67; H. van Thiel, *Zeitschrift für Papyrologie und Epigraphik* 90 (1992) 1–32; Lührs (1992) 6–10.

subsequent tradition. Some flexibility is provided for by the somewhat indefinite nature of that text, and also by a certain amount of filtering back of excluded material. In search of common errors in the tradition that would demonstrate the existence of an archetype, Bolling found a lacuna in *Il.* 18:

380 ὄφρ' ὅ γε ταῦτ' ἐπονεῖτο ἰδυίῃϲι πραπίδεϲϲι,
381 ⟨τόφρα οἱ ἐγγύθεν ἦλθε θεὰ Θέτιϲ ἀργυρόπεζα.⟩
382 τὴν δὲ ἴδε προμολοῦϲα Χάριϲ λιπαροκρήδεμνοϲ . . .

Missing in now three papyri (p11, 1st–2nd cent., p239, 2nd–3rd cent. p647, 3rd cent.), verse 381 is present in only a few of the medieval manuscripts; clearly it was absent from Aristarchus' edition, and if genuine, as Bolling then believed, must have been reintroduced by some back-channel. Pasquali accepted that the verse was genuine, but nonetheless, such was his aversion to archetypes, dismissed the probative value of its absence by suggesting that its omission arose independently in the various manuscripts which lack it.[85] That is not credible. If the verse is pristine, we do indeed have here firm evidence for a defective archetype. But it is better regarded as an interpolation, added for obvious reasons;[86] hence it does not signify. More significant is the insecure hold of *Il.* 23.804, unknown to Nicanor and absent from the oldest vulgate witnesses (p13, 1st cent. B.C., the earliest):

802 ἄνδρε δύω περὶ τῶνδε κελεύομεν, ὥ περ ἀρίϲτω,
803 τεύχεα ἑϲϲαμένω ταμεϲίχροα χαλκὸν ἑλόντε
804 ⟨ἀλλήλων προπάροιθεν ὁμίλου πειρηθῆναι.⟩

The text is intelligible without the verse (at least, Nicanor found it so), but it is hard to believe it interpolated. The case is unique, and puzzling.[87] But it does look as if there was towards the middle of the second century B.C. an actual copy of Aristarchus' recension of the transmitted Homeric text (possibly equipped with critical signs but not incorporating emendations), from which the subsequent tradition mainly derives.

What real authority the vulgate has, there is no telling. Ludwich's

---

85 (1954) 219–20.

86 Bolling later recognized this (1925, 18–19). Exhaustive discussion at Apthorp (1980) 137–40, cf. 154–55.

87 Cf. Apthorp (1980) 128–34; he postulates that Aristarchus did include the verse, but it was erroneously omitted in the copy that served as the archetype. He adds *Od.* 4.432 as a possible case in the *Odyssey*.

belief in its pre-Alexandrian existence was ardent, and some scholars today are of the same persuasion. Van Thiel's ringing declaration that 'the Alexandrians knew no other than our text' has fallen on sympathetic ears.[88] But the evidence is lacking. What the Alexandrians knew was a multiplicity of texts, all different. No doubt all or most of the components of the subsequent vulgate were in existence, but the vulgate itself is apparently an Alexandrian product. What authority we choose to invest it with should depend on what view we form of the manuscripts available and the use made of them. 'Chaos' is the word applied by Wilamowitz and many since to the situation confronting Zenodotus.[89] That seems overstated. But there is no warrant for positing an authoritative base text. We can weave pleasant fantasies around attested or hypothesized candidates. Was there an official Athenian text, as there reputedly was for the tragedians? How about Alexander's *Iliad*, corrected by Aristotle himself, the so-called ἐκ τοῦ νάρθηκος ('from the casket')? What role was played by Demetrius of Phalerum, the link-figure between Athens (and Aristotle) and Alexandria?[90] Within the limits of the evidence, we may tell what stories we wish. A newly fashionable attitude, owed to van der Valk, is to revere the vulgate and condemn the Alexandrians for tampering with it. The quality of the vulgate is indeed phenomenal, and it gives us poems which we could well believe are the genuine article, practically word for word; but it is the Alexandrians' sifting and restraint that are responsible for it.

* * *

Thereafter, the text travelled within the contours set by Aristarchus, in much less freewheeling fashion. A number of one-line interpolations gradually crept in, many of them still contaminating the texts we use today,[91] and there is much surface variation, partly in the form of interchange of Homeric phrases, particles, etc., induced by the nature of Homeric verse and the scribes' drearily intimate

---

[88] *Odyssea* vi ('Auch die Alexandriner kannten keinen anderen als unseren Text'); endorsed by R. Janko, *Gnomon* 66 (1994) 291.

[89] *Die Ilias und Homer*, 2nd ed. (Berlin, 1920) 7.

[90] Cf. the ingenious constructions of Nagy (1996a).

[91] Most of them are conveniently listed by Bolling (1925) 16–30. They are nearly all Homeric verses, and while they make no difference to the action, they affect the texture of the poem. So they do matter.

familiarity with it, and partly the consequence of modernization of forms and syntax, prosodic easements, etc., in perhaps less conscious response to the same impulses that generated the interpolations. Schoolchildren were hauled word by word through *Iliad* A (just as were their successors in 14th-cent. Byzantium), and holiday entertainments included Homerists' dramatizations of popular scenes.[92] Scholars collated copies and excerpted or recycled commentaries. Most manuscripts appear to be regular commercial copies, corrected desultorily if at all. But collation is sometimes discernible even where not evidenced directly (e.g. *Il.*p9's unmetrical γεραιὸϲ ξεϲτοῦ at 24.322, conflating the competing variants γεραιὸϲ ἑοῦ and γέρων ξεϲτοῦ), and medievally attested variants can appear in one and the same ancient manuscript (e.g. *Od.*p171 has 4.623 ἔνεικαν as the primary reading, with ἔπεμπον registered by m.2, cf. 4.767 αὐδῆϲ m.1, ἀρῆϲ m.2). The amount and nature of variation seem to remain fairly constant, but in such dynamic conditions trivial and more or less imperceptible degeneration was inevitable, and some readings disappeared, to survive only in back-channels such as Apollonius Sophista. By the same token, large-scale change was precluded.

That the number of Homer manuscripts diminishes from the 5th cent. A.D. no doubt reflects the general decline of traditional Greek culture. But Panopolis could produce a Nonnus, literature of all sorts continued to be copied, and an elaborately annotated 6th-cent. Callimachus from Oxyrhynchus, a forerunner of the medieval text-plus-scholia format, is an impressive sample of the sort of work that could be found even outside the major centers.[93] At one such center, Gaza, Procopius composed his prose Paraphrases of the *Iliad*; we know that Photius read them in the 9th century (as we do not know that he read the poem itself). The Ambrosian *Iliad* (p1) is a beautiful illustrated parchment codex produced perhaps in Alexandria around the end of the 5th century: coffee-table book par excellence, we may doubt that it was ever read. There is nothing special about its text.[94] Pieces of more than a dozen more normal-looking codices are assigned to the 6th century, and recent years have seen the publication of several which may well belong to the 7th, from various towns in

[92] Byzantium: R. Browning, *Viator* 6 (1975) 16. Homerists: G. Husson, *Journal of Juristic Papyrology* 23 (1993) 93–99.

[93] P.Oxy. 2258.

[94] It is sometimes said to be related to that of Venetus A, but it is not, or not specially.

Egypt.[95] For the next manuscripts of either poem, apart from the few pages of the *Iliad* codex Sinaiticus already mentioned, we must await the 10th century, but Homeric studies were not dead in the interim. The Epimerismi perhaps to be associated with George Choeroboscus grammatically dissected the *Iliad* line by laborious line,[96] and it is clear that Homer enjoyed his share of the philological resurgence of the 9th century. An epigram of Cometas (flor. 855–66, Constantinople) speaks of punctuating and renovating the Homeric texts,[97] and we have a set of scholia minora to the *Iliad* copied in minuscule around the same period.[98]

The history of the medieval tradition is uncharted territory. No one has attempted to ascertain how many ancient manuscripts feed directly into it, and it is doubtful that any such attempt could succeed. The interrelationships of the manuscripts have not been sorted out, and may never be. What makes it difficult is not that there are so many of them, but the very nature of the transmission—in particular, its openness, both ancient and medieval. Distribution of inherited readings among the medieval manuscripts is extremely tangled. This is partly the result of the multiplicity of earlier manuscripts that evidently inform the medieval tradition (ancient manuscripts themselves showing a similarly tangled distribution of readings), and partly the result of textual interplay ('contamination') among the medieval manuscripts themselves. And since only a fraction of the manuscripts are extant, the task is all the more difficult. Research in this area has been virtually at a standstill since T. W. Allen's labors at the turn of the century.[99] In the wake of Ludwich and Leaf, Allen made considerable headway with sorting the manuscripts, grouping them into

---

[95] 6th–7th cent. MSS of *Iliad*, all published since Pack²: p456d, p483a (Antinoopolis), p606 (Hermupolis), p625, p633, p636 (Hermupolis); of *Odyssey*: p219, p12 (?Fayum), p123 (Antinoopolis), p96 (Oxyrhynchus).

[96] C. Theodoridis, *Byzantinische Zeitschrift* 72 (1979) 1–5, id. ib. 73 (1980) 341–45, A. R. Dyck, *Epimerismi Homerici I* (Berlin-New York, 1983) 5–7.

[97] AP 15.38, cf. 36–37; see B. Baldwin, *Hermes* 113 (1985) 127–8. 'Renovating' (γράψας ἐκαινούργησε) seems to imply making new transcripts, presumably from uncial into minuscule; the old books are described as ἐφθαρμένας τε κοὐδαμῶς ἐστιγμένας; 'punctuating' (στίξας) could refer not just to stops but to accents etc.

[98] See n. 17 above.

[99] The only contribution of note has been N. Tachinoslis' *Handschriften und Ausgaben der Odyssee* (Frankfurt, 1984), whose collations enable some refinements to be made to Allen's groupings of *Odyssey* manuscripts (e.g., for the *a* family, L⁷ has affinity with C and R⁴ only in the first eight books—though that might already have been guessed from the selection of readings listed by Allen). Tachinoslis presents his work as exposing the worthlessness of Allen's ('Allens Versuch der Familienbildung ist ein

'families' on the basis of the incidence of various classes of demonstrably premedieval readings.[100] His methods were rudimentary but not, as is often charged, fundamentally flawed. Where he went wrong, from a tactical point of view, was in calling his groupings 'families.' He used the term in the normal genealogical sense, whereby membership of one family does not exclude membership of another, and family relationships vary in degree of closeness. As a heuristic model this actually answers very well to the realities of the transmission. Ancestors multiply as you go back through the generations, and the genetic relationship (if we may think of readings as genes) becomes less close; synchronically, an individual's genetic make-up will define one's relationship to the rest of the population, and family members will be more or less recognizably distinct from non-family members. This is a model that is hard to beat, though certainly Allen's use of it is open to criticism. In the critical apparatus of the Oxford Classical Text editions of the *Iliad* and the *Odyssey*, family sigla are attached to readings which may not be carried by all of the designated family members, a sacrifice of precision to compendiousness guaranteed to deceive all but the most well informed users.[101] But it is Allen's classification itself which has incurred the severest criticism. Allen of course knew that his families were without clear-cut definition, and constantly warned of their lack of integrity; but this did not save him from being criticized by Pasquali for their 'mechanical' and 'inconclusive' nature.[102] These criticisms seems to me misguided, but they have been routinely echoed in subsequent scholarship, often in heightened form.[103]

Fehlschlag gewesen,' 45), but in fact it leaves Allen's groupings mostly intact, and makes no advance in method.

[100] 'The text of the *Iliad*,' *Classical Review* 13 (1899) 110–116, revised in (1931); 'The text of the *Odyssey*,' *Papers of the British School at Rome* 5.1 (1910) 3–85.

[101] So I dare not call the procedure justifiable; but if the alternative is strings of dozens of alphabetically arranged sigla of individual mss, as in his ed. maior of the *Iliad* (1931), the need for *some* more informative and accessible system of presentation is clear. The solution, obviously, is selective use and reporting: but without Allen's labors, selection would be blind.

[102] (1954) 208–10.

[103] Pasquali's honest failure to come to terms with Allen's sorting principles becomes vicious in Tachinoslis (n. 99 above). Recent condemnations of Allen's family groupings via endorsement of Pasquali and Tachinoslis include S. West, *Classical Review* 99 (1985) 377–8 (Allen's *Odyssey* families falsely labelled 'illusory'), Janko (1992) 20 n. 3 (all Allen's *Iliad* familes except *h* 'do not survive Pasquali's criticism'), N. G. Wilson, *Proceedings of the British Academy* 76 (1990) 316 (a startlingly ungenerous assessment which ignores the fact that Allen did not claim to have made word-for-word

For more advanced methods of classification we turn to the natural sciences, where we find that numerical taxonomy, which depends on statistical clustering, has been largely replaced by cladistics, which seeks to reflect evolutionary history.[104] Instead of putting all variants for purposes of analysis on an equal footing, cladistics distinguishes shared derived characteristics from shared primitive characteristics, and classifies on the basis of the former (the problem, predictably, is deciding which are which). Read 'common errors' for 'shared derived characteristics' and this begins to sound familiar, and for our situation unpromising. Furthermore, classification is not only hierarchical but monophyletic, that is, a taxon (e.g. a family) includes all and only the descendants of a single ancestor. This is indeed just about what classicists normally understand by a manuscript family (hence much of the criticism of Allen, no doubt), but the exclusivity would seem to render it inapplicable to a tradition as open as Homer's. It is clear that the Homeric manuscripts do not admit of classification at all, in any taxonomically acceptable sense. Nonetheless, striking success with an admittedly less complex manuscript tradition has been reported for a cladistics computer program, and as programs become more powerful and sophisticated, much light could doubtless be thrown on the interrelations of the Homer manuscripts by such means.[105] First, however, full and accurate collations would have to be made and put into suitable form; the prospect of that seems remote, and the utility of the results would in any event be limited. Advance may more realistically be expected from (a) routinely conducted *recensio*, utilizing shared absence of interpolated verses as stemmatically significant;[106] and (b) investigations into the history of

collations of more than four *Iliad* manuscripts). The allegation that in his editio maior (1931), 'in the face of Pasquali's criticism' (published 1934), 'he abandons his attempt to classify the Homeric MSS' (Janko (1990) 332 n. 19, cf. West l.c.) rests on a serious misunderstanding of what Allen was doing. It is ironic that Allen's understanding of the workings of contamination in the tradition was superior to Pasquali's. Pasquali was content to see only 'contaminazione totale o quasi totale' (exempting Allen's families *h* and *i*), while Allen recognized that meaningful (though not watertight) groupings are discernible, with contamination becoming increasingly generalised over time.

104 Cf. John Maynard Smith, 'Dinosaur Dilemmas,' *New York Review of Books*, April 25, 1991, 5–6.

105 *Bryn Mawr Classical Review* 3 (1992) 331–37; it is noted however that the program's 'greatest difficulties lay in the areas of contamination and coincident variation' (335).

106 Interpolations spread, whereas omissions are made good (cf. *Illinois Classical Studies* 3 (1978) 66); the absence of an interpolation behaves like an omission, i.e. is

the various manuscripts, considered not merely as textual vehicles but more holistically as historical documents.

In the meantime, Allen's collations, imperfect though they are, enable a certain amount to be done without much trouble. The earliest extant *Iliads* written in minuscule are two very different 10th-cent. manuscripts. One is known as D (Laur. 32.15), the other is the celebrated A or Venetus A (Marc.gr.454).[107] D is a very careless piece of work and full of superficial error; it clearly has an ordinary text of later antiquity as its exemplar.[108] A stands at the opposite pole. It is an exquisite scholarly production, a painstakingly controlled copy systematically furnished with inherited scholarly apparatus (critical signs and two sets of largely text-critical scholia, elaborately formatted), evidently a premium-grade product of a distinguished center of learning; it draws, mostly at a remove, on several different sources. These two manuscripts are mutually independent. To the 11th century are assigned B (Marc.gr.453); T (Brit.Lib. Burney 86, the 'Townley' manuscript), dated A.D. 1059; E^3 (Escor. 291; loss at beginning and end); E^4 (Escor. 509); and perhaps C (Laur. 32.3). B T E^3 C all have scholia (mostly exegetical), copied by the original scribes. Stemmatically significant relation among the Homer texts of B, E^3, and C is clear;[109] evidently they have a common hyparchetype (C updates B's accentuation); the many divergencies among them will be due mostly to individual use of other sources. T stands apart.[110] In the *Iliad* text of E^4, on the other hand, I see nothing that looks independently inherited with the exception of Φηρίῃ at 2.766.[111] So far, by my reckoning, we have evidence for the copying into minuscule of at least four

indicative of vertical descent. Unevenly attested verses (inadvertent omissions excluded) are normally interpolations.

[107] D was heavily used and suffered accordingly: bks. 1–4 were supplied in the 12th cent., and various other losses have been repaired at various times. A was always treasured; it is assigned to the last quarter of the century by E. Mioni, *Annali della Facoltà di lettere e filosofia dell'Università di Padova* 1 (1976) 185–93, cf. A. Diller, *Serta Turyniana* (Urbana, 1974) 523–24, rejecting Hemmerdinger's attribution to the scribe Ephraim.

[108] There is one outcropping of critical sigla, obeli in attendance on 18.444–56. If these are by the original scribe, the exemplar may have had more.

[109] E.g. om. 11.825 γὰρ, 23.674 αὖθι, 779 ἕλε.

[110] E.g. exempt from 2.320, 9.44 (ath. Ar.), 17.74, 316; om. Catalogue of Ships (cf. p3); 12.374 ἐελδομένοιcι (ἐπειγομένοιcι cett.), 16.137 ἀμφίθαλον κυνέην θέτο τετραφάληρον (ἰφθίμῳ κ. εὔτυκτον ἔθηκεν cett.), 788 γάρ οἱ (γάρ τοι cett.). For the interrelationships of the scholia of these manuscripts, similar but apparently not identical, see Erbse, *Scholia Graeca* I xlviii–lviii.

[111] Perhaps it is a copying error induced by Φηρητιάδαο three lines earlier; it

ancient manuscripts, perhaps c. 6th–7th cent.; others were evidently collated. If the medieval tradition of the Demosthenic corpus rests on minuscule transcription of four ancient manuscripts,[112] it should not surprise that at least as many Iliadic ones were transcribed. Thereafter the picture gets murkier. Of 12th-cent. manuscripts, O^{5} (Bodl.Lib. Auct.T. 2.7) may have some inherited readings not in earlier manuscripts, though it is difficult to be quite sure;[113] likewise with V^{10} (Vat.gr. 903);[114] with V^{12} (Vat.gr.1315) the case is perhaps clearer, though the haul is small;[115] likewise with V^{16} (Vat.gr.1319).[116] Various fragments of 12th-cent. manuscripts are more or less negligible.[117] Infiltration from the inherited scholarly tradition, occasionally in evidence in the above 12th-century manuscripts, becomes more systematic in the manuscripts of Allen's *h* family (principally U^{4}, M^{1}, U^{2}, all variously defective), for which it seems we must postulate a lost medieval hyparchetype. Some of their readings are imported from the exemplar of the main A-scholia, which was used also by Eustathius (obit c. 1195); presumably they were first entered in the margins or above the line (as sometimes in A itself), and transferred into the main text

could be a guess, but that would be out of character for this manuscript. The reading is reportedly shared with Macrobius; the medieval paradosis is Πιερίῃ (condemned by the ancient commentary h40, P.Oxy. 1086), and Πηρ(ε)ίῃ, attested by papyri, Eustathius, and Stephanus of Byzantium, apparently does not put in an appearance among the medieval manuscripts until later. The only other reading to give momentary pause is παναριϲτῆεϲ 'Αχαιῶν for ἀριϲτῆεϲ Παναχαιῶν at 7.328, evidently due to misplaced restitution of omitted παν-.

[112] See *Liverpool Classical Monthly* 1 (1976) 4.

[113] 14.491 ὄπαζε not ὄπαϲϲε, 15.180 ἄνωγε not ἀνώγει, 407 ἀμύνεϲθαι not ἀπώϲαϲθαι, 20.143 ἀναλκίῃϲι for ἀνάγκῃ ἶφι, 23.622 ἀποδύϲεαι not ἐϲ-. These as well as some of its errors (e.g. 10.88 γνῶθι for γνώϲεαι) variously recur in various later manuscripts, whether drawn from it or from a common source. Its unique omission of 21.195 (om. Zenodotus) seems more likely to be inadvertent (perhaps due to homoeomeson, -ρεί-) than induced by scholium or siglum.

[114] 21.403 Παλλὰϲ 'Αθήνη for χειρὶ παχείῃ could come from the margin of A or could be spontaneous; 22.64 προτὶ ἄϲτυ (with Stobaeus) for π. γαίῃ is probably just a slip; the omissions of 9.700 and 21.433 are mechanical.

[115] The most significant seem to be 16.151 'Ηριδανοῖο for ὠκεανοῖο, 11.788 ἐπακοῦϲαι for ὑποθέϲθαι (these two otherwise first appear in Eustathius), 11.300 ὤρεξεν (l. ὄρεξεν) for ἔδωκεν, 22.330 ἐξ ὀχέων for ἐν κονίῃϲ, 23.300 τήν τόθ' (v.l. in A). But I cannot rule out the scholarly tradition as the source.

[116] Most notably 13.6 δικαιοτάτων τ' (τ' om. cett.), 13.9 ἑῆοϲ (also ap. Eust.) not ἑοῖο, 437 ἀπόμοργνυ (also V^{12}) not ἀπέμεϲϲεν or ἀπέμαϲϲεν. Three omissions of athetized lines (5.808, 9.694, 16.261) represent contemporary (not ancient) response to the athetesis.

[117] Bm^{1} (Marc.gr. 453) is a single leaf of a lost codex. Et (Etonensis 139) survives up to 5.84 but apparently has nothing to contribute. P^{20} (Bibl.Nat. suppl.gr. 679) has little more than 100 lines surviving.

at a subsequent copying; but others may come from yet another ancient manuscript of the poem. In the Palaeologan revival of the late 13th and early 14th centuries further ancient manuscripts were probably acquired; the most suggestive indication is the copying of a uniquely rich strain of exegetical scholia on *Il.* 21 in Ge (Genavensis 44, belonging to Manuel Moschopoulos), scholia miraculously matched by a 2nd-cent. papyrus commentary on the same book (h94, P.Oxy. 221, the 'Ammonius' commentary). Less cursory investigations would readily improve all these results.

Early minuscule manuscripts of the *Odyssey* are surprisingly few, even after allowance is made for the normal imbalance between the two poems, and there is nothing to compare with Ven. A of the *Iliad*. Only two antedate the 13th cent.: G (Laur. 32.24, Allen's L^4), 10th cent., and F (Laur.conv.soppr. 52, Allen's L^8), 11th, both now missing their ends.[118] Both are plain texts without scholia, and once again, their history is unknown. Next comes P (Heidelberg, Palatinus 45, Allen's Pal), dated 1201, with some scholia (relinquished after bk. 7). It is clear that these three manuscripts have each a different ancient exemplar. Thereafter, as with the *Iliad*, things get more mixed up, but several of the dozen or so 13th or early 14th cent. manuscripts have manifestly inherited readings not in the earlier manuscripts. The possibility must be borne in mind that the ancient manuscripts utilized may have carried variants themselves, so variants in a medieval manuscript do not necessarily imply more than one immediate source; but the result is the same. Some carry scholia, some carry vv.ll. (M, Marc. 613, is exceptionally well supplied) and explicitly attest collation with a second exemplar; a few have firm provenance and milieu, a couple being associated with Planudes. Many of the renaissance manuscripts have close connections with one or other of the early ones. Several attractive and some irresistible readings which first appear in the 15th century are assumed by Allen to be inherited, but perhaps are conjectured.[119] Alexandrian readings, especially Aristarchan, appear in greater proportions and less unevenly distributed among the *Odyssey* manuscripts than the *Iliad* ones; here too,

[118] G is later than A of the *Iliad*, according to Diller (1974) 524.

[119] The phenomenon is especially noticeable in Allen's *d* family, e.g. 3.278 Ἀθηνέων for -ῶν (GFM) or -αίων; other reported readings coincide with modern emendations (unless these were actually made on manuscript authority), e.g. 4.293 om., 11.580 ἕλκυϲϲε, 20.86 ἀμφεκάλυψεν.

since such readings are mostly absent from the papyri, they will be infiltrators from the scholia. The manuscripts were sorted by Allen, and his data and results remain fundamental, but the history of the tradition has yet to be written. The most recent editor uses the oldest representative of each of Allen's thirteen 'families,' plus one (T) which Allen labelled 'independent.' (It takes some effort to discover this, since the manuscript sigla are different and the editor expresses nothing but contempt for Allen, whose work is condemned as 'methodisch verfehlt.')[120] This may be too many: it is not clear to me that they all have independent value. It may also be too few.[121]

The medieval tradition, it is clear, has good access to ancient tradition, though less good in the *Odyssey* than the *Iliad*, and papyri confirm the antiquity of much of its large pool of variants. Since variants were freely distributed in antiquity, it is unlikely that any of the primary medieval manuscripts (I necessarily use 'primary' in a loose sense, meaning those which are relatively close to being apographs of ancient ones) has much greater authority than any other, though of course some may be better than others. In the *Iliad* A is special, but it is doubtful that its main text merits any greater respect than BCE^3 or T or the underlying text of D. Attempts are sometimes made to press the papyri into stemmatic service by establishing affinity between a given papyrus and some particular component of the medieval tradition (usually the beloved A), but all such attempts fall foul of the transmissional realities. Papyrus texts consistently show inconsistent agreement: collation spreads readings unsystematically: there are no separate lines of transmission. On the other hand, papyri may enhance the authority of under-appreciated manuscripts. Papyrus evidence secures a significant place for the 14th-cent. cod. U of the *Odyssey* (Monacensis 519B), for instance (perhaps still undervalued), and shows that e.g. the 13th-cent. cod. V^1 of the *Iliad* (Vat.gr.26) is entitled to more attention than it might otherwise receive.[122] There are more than a dozen *Iliad* minuscules written prior

[120] van Thiel (1991) iii, repeating Tachinoslis (n. 99 above). Eleven manuscripts are cited systematically, others only occasionally; also used are a still imperfectly known 13th-cent. Moscow manuscript recorded by Allen but unavailable to him, the 14th-cent U, the editio princeps (1488), and the oldest manuscript of the D-scholia.

[121] For instance, 24.496 ἔδυνον, apparently the reading of p28 (3rd–4th cent.), is reported by earlier editors as a v.l. in Y (Vindob. 56, 15th cent.); this reading was preferred by Bekker. All van Thiel's manuscripts have δύοντο.

[122] V^1 readings not found in any of the earlier minuscules include *Il.* 11.352 ἐρύκετο

to the end of the 12th century, but an edition which used no later ones would be cutting out much ancient tradition not found in any of them.

But if papyri certify the antiquity of medieval variants, and show that most of the readings in circulation in late antiquity were successfully carried through into one or another of the minuscule manuscripts, they also show that not all of them were. This was in fact already clear from the medievally transmitted D-scholia, which sometimes have lemmas not represented in the direct transmission of the poems. And the authority of the D-scholia is sometimes bolstered by papyri. At *Il.* 13.84 a 4th-cent. papyrus (p60) and the D-scholia agree in ἀνέψυχθεν φίλον ἦτορ, where the medieval manuscripts of the poem all have ἀνέψυχον.[123] Editors' preference for the latter is based on a blanket-like faith in the exclusive authority of the medieval paradosis which is no longer tenable.[124] At *Il.* 1.344 the medieval paradosis is μαχέοιντο, homerized by Bentley to μαχεοίατο: no fewer than three papyri, along with the D-scholia, have μαχέονται. There are similar agreements between papyri and the indirect tradition. It is clear that the medieval manuscripts of the poems do not enjoy a monopoly of access to ancient readings. At *Il.* 14.403, the medieval tradition is ἔγχει, ἐπεὶ τέτραπτο πρὸϲ ἰθύ οἱ, οὐδ' ἀφάμαρτε, but for πρὸϲ ἰθύ οἱ Monro conjectured πρὸϲ ἰθύν, and that is the reading of all three ancient manuscripts that preserve the passage.[125] The proposition that 'the tradition was rich enough to ensure the survival, somewhere in the early [medieval] codices, of all the readings and interpolations preva-

with p60 (ἐρύκακε vulg.), 13.207 ἐνὶ κρατερῇ ὑϲμίνῃ with p9 (ἐν αἰνῇ δηϊότητι vulg.), 15.183 ἐμοὶ with p9 and p60 (οἱ vulg.), 18.222 αὐδήϲαντοϲ with p239 (and v.l. in P[3]: Αἰακίδαο vulg.), 20.317 om. with p9 (cf. 22.363 om. with p9, p255 and D); 22.228 προϲέφη γλαυκῶπιϲ Ἀθήνη with p254 (ἔπεα πτερόεντα προϲηύδα vulg.), 23.626 om. with p13. Also notable is the 13th-cent P[10]: 11.339 οὐδέ οἱ with p60 (and Vi[5] U[13]: οὐ γάρ οἱ vulg.), 618 ἀλλ' with p481 (and Vi[5]: οἱ δ' vulg.), 739 Αὐγείδαο with p75 and p60 (and Vi[5]: Αὐγείαο vulg.), cf. 1.344 μαχέωνται. These manuscripts are not among the fifteen early minuscules (10th–12th cent.) listed by Janko (1992) 21 which he labels the 'good MSS.'

[123] The phrase recurs at *Il.* 10.575; there most of the medieval manuscripts preserve ἀνέψυχθεν, but some have ἀνέψυχεν. These -θεν forms gave constant trouble.

[124] E.g. *Od.* 24.180 D-schol. βέλεμνα implies the verse-ending ϲτονόεντα βέλεμνα, where all the medieval MSS of the poem have βέλεα ϲτονόεντα. The authority of the D-scholia is confirmed by papyrus agreement (in this case p28, 3rd–4th cent.).

[125] p438 (3rd cent.), p60 (4th cent.), and p9 (6th cent., ἰθυμ induced by the resultant θυμου?), probably all of different provenance. The last of these was published before Monro (*Grammar of the Homeric Dialect* (Oxford, 1891²), 338), but he does not adduce it.

lent in later antiquity,'[126] even with the qualifications of 'prevalent' and 'later,' is hard to sustain.

Ancient manuscripts vary among themselves in much the same ways as the medieval, only more so. That is, the same kinds of variants were floating around, but in greater numbers. Any reasonably extensive papyrus text will have a sprinkling of readings which might well have found a place in the medieval tradition but happened not to. A 3rd–4th cent. codex of *Il.* 5 (p400, M–P 736) offers a generous sample. Some involve interchangeable phrases (e.g. 294 ἤριπε δὲ πρηνής, 529 καὶ αἰδῶ θέcθ' ἐνὶ θυμῷ, 616 διὰ ζωcτῆροc ἔλαccεν, 753 εὗρον δ' εὐρύοπα Κρονίδην, 757 ὁρῶν, 785 ἡμὲν δέμαc ἠδὲ καὶ αὐδήν, 856 ἐπέρειcε δὲ ἶν' ἀπέλεθρον); this kind of variability is ubiquitous within the tradition. Also notable are 486 not ὤρεccι but ὀάρεccι, matching the open forms elsewhere in the poem (9.327 etc.); 603 not πάρα εἷc but πάρ' ἔειc (παρεειc corr. from παραειc), giving the peculiar form found at Hes. *Theog.* 145 and conjectured here by Nauck to avoid the untoward hiatus; 636 not εἶναι but ἔμμεναι, as independently printed by van Leeuwen (ἔμμεν'); and 822 not αὐτόc τ' ἀναχάζομαι but αὐτὸc ἀποχάζομαι, giving mid-line hiatus and the compound attested at *Od.* 11.95. There are also verses absent—most through scribal inadvertence, usually assisted by homoeoteleuton or the like (172, 233, 584, 604, 669–70), but others should be viewed as verses which have infiltrated the tradition: 457 (~ 362) and 808 (~ 4.390), the latter missing from another papyrus too and reportedly absent from Aristarchus' editions.[127] These minus-verses are offset by plus-verses; 522a (= 11.28), out of place here, is a token of the text's susceptibility to such 'concordance interpolations' which we find everywhere in the tradition.

More or less indifferent variants are multiplied, and in consequence, some of the differentiation of the medieval tradition is nullified. At *Il.* 14.283 most of the medieval manuscripts have Ἴδην δ' ἱκέcθην πολυπίδακα, at 15.151 they all have ἵκανον; the lines are otherwise identical. Perhaps the verse was sung in both forms by Homer. The

[126] Janko (1992) 21.

[127] The case is rather unusual, in that the verse is apparently pre-Aristarchan (A-schol. on 807). Its presence in a third papyrus (p295, 2nd–3rd cent.) is less surprising than its absence from the two minuscules V^{16} (12th cent.) and L^{9} (mid-15th)—perhaps due either to Aristarchus-induced excision or to homoeomeson (808 7 litt. τοιηοιεγων, 809 5 litt. τοιμενεγωπ). See Apthorp (1980) 4–6 and nn.

Morgan papyrus (p60, 4th cent.), however, presents ἱκέcθην in the bk. 15 instance. At 6.472 the medieval tradition is αὐτίκ' ἀπὸ κρατὸc κόρυθ' εἵλετο, at 15.125 τοῦ δ' ἀπὸ μὲν κεφαλῆc κόρυθ' εἵλετο. The papyrus gives κρατὸc in the latter verse. ἀνέψυχθεν vs. ἀνέψυχον at *Il.* 10.575 and 13.84 we have already viewed. There are many similar cases. The practical upshot of such equalization of variants, as it might be termed, is that it may be a mistake to place reliance on whatever particular form the medieval manuscripts happen to transmit in any given place. *Il.* 5.791 and 13.107 are identical except insofar that in bk. 5 most of the medieval manuscripts have δὲ ἑκὰc while in bk. 13 they all have δ' ἕκαθεν (with Aristarchus, against Zenodotus and Aristophanes who read δὲ ἑκὰc); but the papyrus gives δὲ ἑκὰc in bk. 13. δ' ἕκαθεν was evidently generated by discomfort with the hiatus consequent on the loss of digamma. An argument has nonetheless been made for δ' ἕκαθεν in bk. 13, precisely because it is different.[128] But such extreme faith in the vagaries of the medieval tradition receives no comfort from the papyrus evidence.

Various kinds of degeneration are observable within the medieval tradition itself: in antiquity the degeneration is less advanced. Interpolation is one category, of which I shall say only that the papyrus evidence has still not been fully exploited. Replacement of adjective by adverb is another.[129] Elimination of hiatus is another. At *Od.* 2.211, for instance, where H (13th cent.) preserves τὰ ἴcαcι, its descendants have succumbed to τά γ' or τάδ'. At *Il.* 21.399 ὅccα (μ') ἔοργαc, only p1 and D are without μ'. At *Od.* 4.555–6, where according to the medieval tradition the Old Man of the Sea identifies the third man in these words:

υἱὸc Λαέρτεω, Ἰθάκῃ ἔνι οἰκία ναίων·
τὸν δ' ἴδον ἐν νήcῳ θαλερὸν κατὰ δάκρυ χέοντα,

Bentley, discoverer of the digamma, deleted δ'. A 1st or 2nd cent. papyrus published in 1979 is without it.[130] Better known cases are *Il.* 23.198 ὦκα δὲ Ἶριc (p12, 3rd cent. B.C., already conjectured by Bentley) vs. ὠκέα δ' Ἶριc and *Il.* 3.103 οἴcετε ἄρν' (p3, 3rd cent.) vs.

[128] Janko (1990) 332–33.

[129] ἀντίον vs. -οc, πληcίον vs. -οι, etc., cf. at P.Oxy. 3710 i 23; similarly in e.g. Thucydides, cf. at P.Oxy. 3878.7.

[130] p171 (M. Manfredi, *Papiri dell'Odissea* (Florence, 1979), no. 5); hardly an accident, because the papyrus has been collated, and variants entered. Cf. e.g. *Od.* 10.285 μενέειc δὲ cύ γ' ἔνθα περ ἄλλοι: om. γ' p115 (6th cent.).

οἴcετε δ' ἄρν'. The 2nd–3rd cent. p21 at *Il.* 6.493 gives not πᾶcιν, ἐμοὶ δὲ μάλιcτα (so the med.mss.) but πᾶcι, μάλιcτα δ' ἐμοί, which is how we have it in the *Odyssey* ([1.359] = 11.353 = 21.353); this preserves the digamma of Ἰλίῳ in the second half of the line, τοὶ Ἰλίῳ ἐγγεγάαcιν, and leads in turn to *Il.* 17.145 οἶοc cὺν λαοῖc{ι} τοὶ Ἰλίῳ ἐγγεγάαcιν and *Od.* 8.495 οἳ {ῥ'} Ἴλιον ἐξαλάπαξαν (confirmed by Eustathius). It is notoriously difficult to know how far to carry extrapolations such as this. The tendency today, an extreme reaction to earlier excesses, is to refuse them altogether and to lay down a strictly hands-off policy, allowing Homer to sing nothing unattested. But it should be possible to recognize the difficulty of pinpointing places at which change has occurred without denying that change *has* occurred. If we decide we have no choice but to follow the manuscripts, we ought not delude ourselves into thinking that they give us Homer pristine.

* * *

It may be helpful to add as coda a brief note on where some modern editions in current use stand in relation to the tradition. For the *Iliad*, the Monro-Allen Oxford Classical Text edition is still the standard text (ed. 3 1920, often reprinted). It is an eclectic text, restrained in its acceptance of ancient scholarly readings but still choicer than commands assent today. Few interpolations are signalled (Allen knew full well that the text is riddled with identifiable interpolations but printed them out of piety to the dead weight of tradition: not all readers have shared the editor's knowledge of their nature). Its apparatus is not wholly reliable but is more accurate than is sometimes made out. In his ed. maior (1931) Allen reproduced the Aristarchan marginal signs and gave precise (if only laboriously accessible) reports of manuscript readings; and he could avail himself of more papyri. Bolling's *Ilias Atheniensium* (1950), an attempted reconstruction of the Pisistratean text from which Bolling believed the tradition to derive, treats all verses omitted or athetized by Alexandrian scholars as interpolations, and attempts to restore 6th-cent. Attic forms. Van Thiel's new edition (1996), by contrast, privileges the medieval vulgate (see below). For the *Odyssey*, Allen's Oxford Classical Text edition (ed. 2 1916, often reprinted), constructed on the same principles as its *Iliad* counterpart, has acquired a variety of competitors. Von der Mühll's stimulating edition (1946) is relatively radical, though more so in its apparatus than in its actual text. The edition in the Scrittori greci e latini series, edited by A. Heubeck and others (1981–86), is on the same lines. Very different is van Thiel's edition (1991). This is founded on the premise of the exclusive authority of the vulgate.[131] As reviewers have not failed to point out,[132] it prints even more interpolations than the OCT, but its apparatus is unusually reliable: an exemplary 'conservative' edition,[133] destined to be highly influential.

[131] His standpoint, like Janko's, was articulated by Monro nearly a century ago: 'Unde colligas libros nostros non ex Alexandrina aliqua fabrica, sed e vetustissimis exemplaribus fluxisse. Dicat fortasse quispiam, si res eiusmodi se habeant, profecto dandam esse operam ut solis codicum testimoniis utamur, neglecta importuna grammaticorum eruditione' (*praefatio* to the *Iliad* OCT, xiii). But if van Thiel has read those words, he has rejected the follow-up: 'Hoc vero ita esset Scyllam vitare ut in Charybdin incideres.'

[132] *Gnomon* 66 (1994) 289–95 (Janko), *Classical Review* n.s. 43 (1993) 228–30 (Apthorp).

[133] Not that there is actually anything conservative about preferring medieval manuscripts to ancient ones.

Gregory Nagy

HOMERIC SCHOLIA

As of this writing, Homeric scholarship has not yet succeeded in achieving a definitive edition of either the *Iliad* or the *Odyssey*. Ideally, such an edition would encompass the full historical reality of the Homeric textual tradition as it evolved through time, from the pre-Classical era well into the medieval. The problem is, Homeric scholarship has not yet reached a consensus on the criteria for establishing an edition as 'definitive.' The ongoing disagreements reflect a wide variety of answers to the many serious questions that remain about Homer and Homeric poetry. Crucial to most of these questions is the information provided by the Homeric scholia.

The relevance of the scholia (plural of *scholion*), that is, of the marginal and/or interlinear notes (also glossaries and lexica) that accompany the text of Homer in a wide variety of manuscripts, was first made manifest to the world of modern Homeric scholarship in 1788, when Jean Baptiste Gaspard d'Ansse de Villoison published the tenth-century Venetus A codex manuscript of the *Iliad* of Homer (codex Marcianus 454). In his *Prolegomena*, Villoison assesses the impact of the A-scholia on Homeric scholarship:

> By way of these scholia, never before published, the greatest light is shed on Homer's poetry. Obscure passages are illuminated; *the rites, customs, mythology, and geography of the ancients are explained; the original and genuine reading is established; the variant readings of various codices and editions as well as the emendations of the Critics are weighed*. For it is evident that *the Homeric* contextus, *which was recited by the rhapsodes from memory and which used to be sung orally by everyone, was already for a long time corrupt*, since it would have been impossible for the different rhapsodes of the different regions of Greece not to be forced by necessity to subtract, add, and change many things. *That Homer committed his poems to writing is denied by Josephus* at the beginning of Book I of his *Against Apion*, and this opinion seems to be shared by an unpublished Scholiast to Dionysius Thrax, who narrates that the poems of Homer, which were preserved only in men's minds and memory and were not written, had become extinct by the time of Pisistratus, and that he accordingly offered a reward to those who would bring him Homeric verses, and that, as a result, many people, greedy for money, sold Pisistratus their verses as if they

> were Homeric. The *Critics* left these spurious verses in the *Edition*, but marked them with the obelus. (Villoison [1788] xxxiv. Translation and emphases mine)[1]

This assessment in Villoison's 1788 Prolegomena anticipated in some significant details the ultimately far more influential views of Friedrich August Wolf in his *Prolegomena ad Homerum*, published in 1795 (English-language edition 1985; see Turner, this vol.).[2] In other details, however, Wolf's assessment diverged radically from that of Villoison. This divergence is crucial for weighing the importance of the Homeric scholia and, by extension, even for determining the criteria for editing Homer. The point of disagreement centers on what the scholia tell us about the ancient *kritikoi* or Critics, as Villoison refers to them in the passage just quoted.

These critics are the scholars responsible for the textual transmission of Homer in the Library of Alexandria, founded in the early third century B.C., the era of Zenodotus of Ephesus, who is credited with the first Alexandrian 'edition' of Homer. There were subsequent 'editions' by Aristophanes of Byzantium, who became head of the Library around the beginning of the second century B.C., and by a later director, Aristarchus of Samothrace, the culmination of whose work is dated around the middle of the second century B.C. It is the 'edition' of Homer by Aristarchus, as frequently cited by the Homeric scholia, that constitutes the primary authority of the Homeric scholia.

Here we come to the central point of divergence between Villoison and Wolf: whereas Villoison viewed the A-scholia as an authoritative witness to an authoritative edition of Homer by Aristarchus, Wolf swerved from this position by questioning the authoritativeness of the scholia and, more fundamentally, the authority of Aristarchus as an editor of Homeric poetry. This swerve away from Villoison's position is reflected in the fullest single collection of data currently

---

[1] I leave untranslated Villoison's use of *contextus*, which conveys the metaphorical sense of 'fabric, structure' (cf. the verb *con-texô*). On the *rhapsôidoi* or 'rhapsodes,' professional performers of Homeric and other Archaic poetry, see nn. 22 and 28 below. The obelus is a horizontal mark, placed next to a verse in the left-hand margin of a text, to indicate the editor's doubts about the authenticity of the verse: see n. 48 below.

[2] Besides translating Wolf's original Latin text into English, Grafton, Most, and Zetzel have written an introduction and notes focusing on Wolf's influence on Homeric scholarship. Pp. 7–8 give their translation of the passage from Villoison (1788) xxxiv quoted above. They do not stress Wolf's fundamental debt to this specific formulation by Villoison. On that subject, see Pierron (1869) I, xxiii; II, 509 n. 1.

available on the Homeric scholia, Hartmut Erbse's edition of the *Iliad* scholia.[3]

Erbse's edition aims to encompass two main components of the scholiastic tradition on Homer: (1) 'Ap.H.,' the archetype of the A-scholia and a main source for the twelfth-century Homer commentator Eustathius (as also for the *Etymologicum Genuinum*),[4] and (2) c, the archetype of the b- and the T-scholia.[5] Erbse's edition excludes, however, the so-called D-scholia.[6] Erbse also excludes the material from the *Homeric Questions* of Porphyry (third century A.D.).[7]

Erbse divides what he calls the 'major scholia' of Homer, as represented by A, b, and T, into two categories: (1) the data culminating in A, stemming from the so-called *Viermännerkommentar*, that is, the 'four-man commentary,' or VMK for short, and (2) the data culminating in c, archetype of b and T, the so-called 'exegetic' scholia.[8] As for the D-scholia, they are assigned by default to a more amorphous category, the 'minor scholia,' about which more below. Also, there are Homeric 'scholia' in papyri from the Hellenistic and Roman

[3] Erbse (1969–88). More below on the other scholia. On the problems of dating the origins of compilations of scholia in general, see N. G. Wilson, 'A chapter in the history of scholia,' *Classical Quarterly* 59 (1967) 244–56; also the reactions in the addenda of Erbse (1969–88) II, 547, with specific reference to the Homeric scholia.

[4] Erbse (1969–88) I, xlvii. See pp. xlv–xlvi on the wording in Eustathius 47.13: ἐν τοῖς Ἀπίωνος καὶ Ἡροδώρου εἰς τὸν Ὅμηρον ὑπομνήμασι 'in the Homer commentaries of Apion and Herodorus [probably corrupted from Heliodorus],' whence the abbreviation 'Ap.H.' On Heliodorus, see A. R. Dyck, 'The fragments of Heliodorus Homericus,' *Harvard Studies in Classical Philology* 95 (1993) 1–64. Editions of Eustathius: M. van der Valk, ed., *Eustathii archiepiscopi Thessalonicensis Commentarii ad Homeri Iliadem* (4 vols., Leiden 1971–88) and J. G. Stallbaum, ed., *Eustathii Commentarii ad Homeri Odysseam* (2 vols., Leipzig 1825).

[5] Erbse (1969–88) I, li traces the b-scholia (the family of the B manuscript, as also of C, E^3, and others) and the T-scholia back to a larger family c, which may also have been a source for Eustathius.

[6] For more on the D-scholia (formerly known, wrongly, as the Didymus-scholia), see below; also Haslam (this vol.). These scholia can be found in the editions of the A, B, and T traditions by Dindorf (1875–88). Vols. V–VI contain the T scholia, edited by E. Maass.

[7] See Schrader (1880–82); (1890). See also A. R. Sodano, ed., *Porphyrii Quaestionum Homericarum liber* I (Naples 1970).

[8] Erbse (1969–88) I, xi–xii. The c scholia may also contain fragments of the VMK (p. lii). Although these scholia often reflect views that contradict those advocated by the school of Aristarchus at the Library in Alexandria, they are not necessarily to be traced back to the rival school of Crates at the Library in Pergamum: see Erbse (1969–88) I, xii. See also Haslam (1994) 44, arguing that the c-scholia derive from commentaries and that the term 'exegetical' is a misnomer.

periods, some of which are cognate with but qualitatively different from the D-scholia.[9] More below on the papyrus scholia as well.

Erbse's categories of Homeric scholia apply also to the textual tradition of the *Odyssey*, not just the *Iliad*, but here we find much less textual evidence. The two earliest minuscule manuscripts of the *Odyssey*, G (tenth century) and F (eleventh century), are without scholia.[10] There is nothing remotely comparable to the A-scholia of the *Iliad* in the textual history of the *Odyssey*. Nor is there an edition of the *Odyssey* scholia that matches the scale of Erbse's work on the *Iliad* scholia.[11]

Focusing on the A-scholia of the *Iliad*, Erbse ([1969–88] I, xii, xlvii) traces their data back to the VMK. The *subscriptio* that we find at the end of each of the 24 books (except for a lacuna at the end of book 17 and an omission at the end of book 24) of the Venetus A *Iliad* gives the basic information about the VMK: παράκειται τὰ Ἀριστονίκου σημεῖα καὶ τὰ Διδύμου Περὶ τῆς Ἀρισταρχείου διορθώσεως, τινὰ δὲ καὶ ἐκ τῆς Ἰλιακῆς προσῳδίας Ἡρωδιανοῦ καὶ ἐκ τοῦ Νικάνορος Περὶ στιγμῆς: 'placed in the margins are the signs of Aristonicus and work of Didymus entitled "On the Aristarchean edition" [*diorthôsis*], and some material also from the "Iliadic prosody" of Herodian and from the work of Nicanor entitled "On punctuation".'[12] Thus the VMK combines the Homeric scholarship of Didymus (on variant textual readings),[13] Aristonicus (on critical signs),[14] Nicanor (on punctuation),[15] and Herodian (on accent).[16] The VMK authors are to be dated as

---

[9] Erbse (1969–88) I, xiii. See also Erbse (1960) 170–71.

[10] Haslam (this vol.).

[11] An early edition: Dindorf (1855). See also A. Ludwich, ed., *Scholia in Homeri Odysseam α 1–309 auctiora et emendatiora* (Königsberg, 1888–90).

[12] Erbse (1969–88) I, xv; see also p. xlvii, where he argues that the source of the VMK data in A is an archetypal codex that had merged the four distinct commentaries (Erbse adduces scholia A to 10.398, ἐν μέντοι τῇ τετραλογίᾳ Νεμεσίωνος οὕτως εὗρον περὶ τῶν στίχων τούτων. Erbse conjectures that Nemesion lived in the fifth or sixth century A.D.). There is reason to dispute this argument, on the basis of comparative evidence discussed by M. Haslam, 'Apollonius of Rhodes and the papyri,' *Illinois Classical Studies* 3 (1978) 71.

[13] M. Schmidt, ed. *Didymi Fragmenta* (Leipzig, 1854); A. Ludwich, ed., *Didymi commentarii* in Ludwich's *Aristarchs Homerische Textkritik nach den Fragmenten des Didymos* I (Leipzig, 1884) 175–631.

[14] L. Friedländer, ed., *Aristonici Περὶ σημείων Ἰλιάδος reliquiae emendatiores* (Göttingen, 1853); O. Carnuth, ed., *Περὶ σημείων Ὀδυσσείας* (Königsberg, 1869).

[15] L. Friedländer, ed., *Nicanoris Περὶ Ἰλιακῆς στιγμῆς reliquiae emendatiores* (Königsberg, 1850). Cf. D. L. Blank, 'Remarks on Nicanor, the Stoics, and the ancient theory of punctuation,' *Glotta* 61 (1983) 48–67.

[16] A. Lentz, ed., *Herodiani technici reliquiae* (= Grammatici Graeci III 1–2; Leipzig,

follows: Didymus in the second half of the first century B.C. and beginning of the first A.D.; Aristonicus, a younger contemporary of Didymus; Nicanor, under Hadrian; Herodian, about 200 years after Didymus, under Marcus Aurelius. The data provided by the VMK are based ultimately on the Homer edition and commentary of Aristarchus, as we learn from the testimony of the first of the 'four men,' Didymus, as mediated by the scholia.

On the basis of data derived primarily from the Homeric scholia, Rudolf Pfeiffer reconstructs the history of Aristarchus' edition of Homer as follows: first, Aristarchus wrote a *hupomnêma* or 'commentary' on the *ekdosis* or 'edition' of Homer produced by his immediate predecessor as head of the Library of Alexandria, Aristophanes of Byzantium; then, Aristarchus produced his own 'edition' and wrote a revised 'commentary' to accompany it; later, the members of his school produced a revised 'edition.'[17]

Here we return to the divergence, going all the way back to Villoison and Wolf, about the value and even the nature of the work accomplished by the 'editors' of Homer, especially Aristarchus, in transmitting the Homeric textual tradition. Depending on how we interpret the information attributed by the Homeric scholia to Aristarchus and other such scholars, there is room for a wide variety of different ideas about what exactly the definitive text of Homer may have been, and even whether there had existed such a thing as a 'definitive' text.

In order to grasp the essence of this divergence, we may focus on the wording of Villoison's original formulation, as highlighted by emphases in the passage quoted at the beginning. According to Villoison, the Homeric scholia provide essential background on the following three aspects of the Homeric tradition: (1) the historical context, (2) the text itself, and (3) the oral traditions underlying but also 'undermining' that text.

Starting with the first aspect, we see that Villoison valued the Homeric scholia for their providing a background on 'the rites, customs, mythology, and geography of the ancients.' For Villoison, the

1867–1870). Cf. A. R. Dyck, 'Aelius Herodian: recent studies and prospects for future research,' in W. Haase and H. Temporini, eds., *Aufstieg und Niedergang der römischen Welt* 2.34.1 (Berlin, 1993) 772–94.

[17] Pfeiffer (1968) 217. On the second 'edition' of Aristarchus, supposedly produced by his students, see Apthorp (1980) 132. On his *hupomnêma* or 'commentary,' see Lührs (1992) 10, who describes it as a combination of an *apparatus criticus* and a *commentarius criticus*.

Homeric scholia put the Homeric text back into its historical context(s). As Grafton et al. explain:

> Villoison's hopes for the usefulness of the scholia—and the wide interest his huge, highly technical edition of them provoked—owed much to views of Homer that sprang up largely outside the professional tradition in philology, and in particular to a new sense of the poet's *historicity* that grew out of the criticisms of him voiced during the Quarrel of the Ancients and Moderns. (In Wolf [1985] 8. Emphases added)[18]

Turning to the second aspect, the Homeric text, we have already noted that the 'Critics' to whom Villoison's formulation primarily refers are the three Homer scholars of the Library or Museum at Alexandria who were credited with producing 'editions' of Homer: Zenodotus of Ephesus, Aristophanes of Byzantium, and, especially, Aristarchus of Samothrace. The publication of Venetus A and its scholia, with over 1,000 references to Aristarchus, produced a quantum leap of information about the premier Alexandrian editor of Homer. There was a sense of euphoria about prospects of recovering the Homer edition of Aristarchus, along with the commentary produced by his school. Villoison could hope to establish 'the original and genuine reading,' on the basis of examining 'the variant readings of various codices and editions as well as the emendations of the critics.' The A-scholia of Homer seemed to bring Aristarchus back to life.

As we can see from his quoted formulation, however, Villoison's optimism about restoring, through the scholia, the 'original and genuine' text of Homer was tempered by his intuition about an oral tradition that transmitted but also 'corrupted' this 'text.' Here we come to the third of the three aspects of Homeric tradition highlighted by Villoison. His point about an oral Homeric transmission by way of rhapsodes was seized on by Wolf, whose own elaborations on this third aspect of the Homeric tradition led ultimately to a destabilization of scholarly perspectives on the second and even the first aspects, concerning the Homeric text and its contexts as elucidated by the scholia. To this day, the destabilization continues, though most experts

[18] The contributions of the A-scholia to an understanding of the historical context are more than matched by the bT-scholia: for an illuminating survey, see M. Schmidt, *Die Erklärungung zum Weltbild Homers und zur Kultur der Heroenzeit in den bT-Scholien zur Ilias* (Munich, 1976). On the mythological world of the D-scholia, see P. Lünstedt, 'Untersuchungen zu den mythologischen Abschnitten der D-Scholien' (Ph.D. dissertation, Hamburg University, 1961).

fail to agree on a unified explanation for the inherent instability of the ancient Homeric textual tradition.

Wolf's reformulation of Villoison's assessment centers on the testimony of Josephus, *Against Apion* 1.12–13, as invoked by Villoison in the passage quoted above. Since Josephus (first century A.D.) in his polemics with the Homer scholar Apion (also first century) seems to be arguing from the premise that no *original text* of Homer survived, Wolf infers that the Homer scholars of Alexandria must have accepted this premise. Otherwise, Wolf reasons, Josephus could not get away with arguing, against an authoritative Homer scholar like Apion (he was a student of Didymus), that Homer did not write. Here is Wolf's interpretation of the Josephus passage:

> ... the ancients themselves ascribed the *origin* of variant readings to the rhapsodes, and located in their frequent performances the principal source of Homeric *corruption and interpolation.* And this judgment, which began with the Alexandrian critics [footnote 76], is clearly supported by consideration of the nature of the case. (ch. 25; Wolf [1985] 111. Emphases added)

At note 76, Wolf cross-refers to an earlier part of his treatise (ch. 18), where he argues not only that Homer did not use writing in composing his poetry but also that the Homer scholars of Alexandria must have known this:

> This is the only clear, authoritative testimony about the question. But it is weightier because it was written against the most learned Homeric commentator, and no ancient defender of a different or contrary opinion survives. Therefore, however the overall credibility of Josephus may be assessed, that passage will have all the force that clear words have. Recently he was reinforced by a certain scholiast [note 39], a coadjutor unworthy of any mention had he not gathered his tale, one soon corrupted by the stories of later grammarians, from the same Alexandrian remains. For it is clear that they did not draw it from Josephus (ch. 18; Wolf [1985] 94–95).

At note 39, Wolf specifies that this additional testimony comes from the scholia to Dionysius Thrax published by Villoison himself in his *Anecdota Graeca* 2.182 [*Grammatici Graeci* 3.179]: the Greek text of the scholiast is translated thus: 'For the works of Homer were lost, as they say. For in those days they were not transmitted by writing, but only by training so that they might be preserved by memory, etc.' (Wolf [1985] 95 n. 39).

The implications of Wolf's inference are far-reaching: if he is right, then the Homer text inherited by the scholars of Alexandria has been 'corrupted' by oral transmission, and whatever 'corrections' they make are likely to be conjectures. By extension, the evidence of the scholia, which reflect the work of the Alexandrian scholars, is devalued.

The Greek text of Josephus' *Against Apion* 1.12–13, as we have seen it invoked by both Villoison and Wolf, is as follows:

> ὅλως δὲ παρὰ τοῖς Ἕλλησιν οὐδὲν ὁμολογούμενον εὑρίσκεται γράμμα τῆς Ὁμήρου ποιήσεως πρεσβύτερον, οὗτος δὲ καὶ τῶν Τρωϊκῶν ὕστερος φαίνεται γενόμενος, καί φασιν οὐδὲ τοῦτον ἐν γράμμασι τὴν αὑτοῦ ποίησιν καταλιπεῖν, ἀλλὰ διαμνημονευομένην ἐκ τῶν ᾀσμάτων ὕστερον συντεθῆναι καὶ διὰ τοῦτο πολλὰς ἐν αὐτῇ σχεῖν τὰς διαφωνίας·
>
> In general, no commonly recognized writing is found among the Greeks older than the poetry of Homer. But he too seems to have been later than the Trojan War, and they say that not even he left his poetry in writing, but it was *preserved by memory* [*diamnêmoneuomenên*] and *assembled* [*suntethênai*] later from the songs. And it is because of this that there are so many *inconsistencies* [*diaphôniai*] in it. (Wolf [1985] 94)

As we see from the wording of Josephus, he claims that the poems of Homer were preserved by memory *and assembled later from the songs*. The idea of an 'assembling' of a text 'from the songs' suggests that the premise of Josephus' argumentation is the historical reality of a narrative tradition that told of a recension of the Homeric poems commissioned by the Athenian tyrant Pisistratus.[19] Still, the historical reality is not necessarily what the stories say about a Pisistratean Recension, as Wolf argues, but merely the stories themselves—or, better, the narrative tradition. It can be argued, *pace* Wolf, that the stories of the Pisistratean Recension result from a political myth, fostered by the dynasty of Pisistratus himself, that pictured the tyrant as a culture hero who rescued and restored the poems of Homer, which had formerly become neglected, fragmented, and even lost.[20] It can also be argued that such a story is characteristic of a type of charter myth, attested not only in other Archaic Greek traditions but also in those of a wide variety of different cultures, that serves to explain the genesis of a centralized oral tradition in the metaphorical

[19] On the stories about a 'recension' commissioned by Pisistratus or at least by a member of the dynasty of the Peisistratidai, see G. Nagy (1996) 65–106. See also pp. 103–105 for arguments in support of dating the story of the Pisistratean Recension at least as far back as the fourth-century B.C., the era of Dieuchidas of Megara (FGH 485 F 6, by way of Diogenes Laertius 1.57).

[20] Nagy (1996) 70–75.

terms of written traditions, so that the gradual evolution of an oral tradition into a centralized institution is imagined by the myth as an instantaneous re-creation of a lost or at least obsolete archetype of an ultimate Book.[21]

There is reason, then, for resisting what both Villoison and Wolf infer from the stories of the Pisistratean Recension. These stories center on the notion of a lost text, and they make no explicit reference to the reality of oral transmission by Homeric performers called rhapsodes. Although there is indeed evidence to support both Villoison and Wolf in their arguing for the concept of a rhapsodic phase in the history of Homeric transmission,[22] the point is that the Alexandrian scholars argued for an altogether different concept: for them, especially for Aristarchus, the idea of an original written text of Homer was not so much a metaphor but a historical reality.[23] For Aristarchus, it appears that Homer was an Athenian who lived around 1000 B.C., in the time of Athenian migrations (cf. scholia A to *Iliad* 13.197);[24] moreover, the scholiastic tradition stemming ultimately from Aristarchus implies that Homer *wrote* his poems (scholia A to *Iliad* 17.719) and that Hesiod actually had a chance to *read* them (scholia A to *Iliad* 12.22a).[25] Although earlier traditions did indeed accept the idea of a rhapsodic transmission of Homer and Hesiod,[26] even picturing the poets themselves as rhapsodes,[27] the later exegetical traditions of scholars like Aristarchus seem to have rejected this model, positing instead a literate Homer and Hesiod.[28]

Thus Wolf seems unjustified in thinking that the Homer scholars of Alexandria posited a phase of oral transmission to account for the variations that they found in the history of the Homeric text. The problem is, Wolf does not make a distinction between earlier and

---

21 Ibid. Cf. Tzetzes, *Anecdota Graeca* 1.6 ed. Cramer.

22 Cf. the scholia to Pindar, *Nemean* 2.1e [ed. Drachmann]; note the usage of *apangellô* in the sense of 'perform,' with reference to the performance of rhapsodes in the circle of Cynaethus (οἱ περὶ Κύναιθον . . . τὴν Ὁμήρου ποίησιν . . . ἐμνημόνευον καὶ ἀπήγγελλον), to be compared with the usage of the same word in Herodotus 7.142.1. On the relationship of master and disciple in the traditions of the rhapsodes (cf. οἱ περὶ Κύναιθον), see pp. 23–24 of Zs. Ritoók, 'Die Homeriden,' *Acta Antiqua* 18 (1970) 1–29.

23 Nagy (1995a) 150–51.

24 Cf. Janko (1992) 32 (n. 53), 71.

25 See J. I. Porter (1992) 83.

26 E.g., [Plato], *Hipparchus* 228b–c; Plato, *Ion* 531a, 532a.

27 E.g., Plato, *Republic* 600d.

28 Wolf (1985) ch. 25, in arguing that the textual instability of Homeric poetry is

later views of Homer in ancient criticism: the premise of Josephus reflects an earlier Homeric model, while that of Apion promotes a later one, of Aristarchean provenance (to repeat: Apion was a student of Didymus).[29] Wolf's thinking on this point turns out to be a cornerstone for his overall theory that patterns of relative instability in the earlier phases of the Homeric textual tradition can be explained by positing even earlier phases of Homeric oral tradition. Grafton, Most, and Zetzel suggest that 'Like Villoison, he [Wolf] saw the early oral transmission of the Homeric poems as the chief source of early variants and the chief stimulus for the development of textual criticism.... Unlike Villoison, however, Wolf insisted that the ancient critics had not had old enough materials to give their critical work a firm foundation' (in Wolf [1985] 17). In other words, Wolf questions, in varying degrees, the reliability of the scholia and of their primary authorities—Zenodotus, Aristophanes, and even Aristarchus—as sources that can lead to the recovery of the 'original' Homer text.

Villoison, by contrast, claims that these scholia establish the 'original and genuine reading,' thereby affirming his conviction that the Alexandrian Homer scholars, especially Aristarchus, did indeed come close to recovering an 'original' Homer text. Thus Villoison's Homer text is Aristarchean, in contrast to Wolf's, which is meta-Aristarchean. Essentially, Villoison's claim about the A-text and the A-scholia of the *Iliad* seems to match the goal of Aristarchus himself, who sought to recover an 'original' text.[30] To be sure, we may disagree fundamentally with the premise of Aristarchus, who searched for variants

due to the rhapsodes, and that the Alexandrian critics made the same inference, cites an account claiming the authority of Aristarchus, in the scholia on Pindar, *Nemean* 2.1c, e [ed. Drachmann] and Eustathius 6.39–40. According to this account, Cynaethus the Rhapsode (on whom see n. 22 above) 'interpolated' his own verses into the poetry of Homer (on the dating of Cynaethus' performance of Homer at Syracuse at 504 B.C., see Haslam [this vol.]). Granted, the idea that Cynaethus is a rhapsode implies an oral tradition; and yet, he is represented as 'interpolating,' which implies a written tradition. If indeed Aristarchus is the source for this account, for him it is still a matter of *textual* instability.

[29] See M. S. Jensen (1980) 155, who argues that Josephus accepted an earlier model, which she outlines on p. 150. For Apion, see S. Neitzel, ed., *Apions Γλῶσσαι Ὁμέρικαι*, in vol. 3 of *Sammlung griechischer und lateinischer Grammatiker* (Berlin, 1977).

[30] Nagy (1995a) 107–152. On Aristarchus' apparent lack of interest in the performative traditions of Homeric rhapsodes, see Nagy (1995a) 130, 151. For what seems to be a vestigial reference in the Homeric scholia to such performative traditions, see scholia T to *Iliad* 16.131 (where it is prescribed that verses narrating the arming of Patroclus be performed at an allegro pace) and the comments of N. J. Richardson, 'Literary criticism in the exegetical scholia to the *Iliad*,' *Classical Quarterly* 30 (1980) 287.

in Homeric textual transmission in order to find in each case *the* authentic variant. Instead, we may wish to argue for an evolutionary model, accounting for a plethora of different authentic variants at different stages (or even at any one stage) in the evolution of Homeric poetry *as an oral tradition*; variations in the textual tradition would reflect different stages in the transcribing of this oral tradition. Such a model is fundamentally at odds with the theories of Villoison, who puts his trust in Aristarchus, validating that Alexandrian scholar's case-by-case search for *the* authentic reading in the text of Homer.

Such an evolutionary model is also at odds with the theories of Wolf, who distrusts Aristarchus' ability to recover authentic readings in general. Whereas Aristarchus—and Villoison—may have gone too far in positing *the* authentic reading in any given case throughout the Homeric text, there is no reason to doubt that any Homeric variant attributed to Aristarchus can be considered *an* authentic reading. For Wolf to cast general doubt on variant readings attributed to Aristarchus may well be going too far in the opposite direction.

In this regard, there is room for disagreement with Grafton et al., the editors of the 'English Wolf,' who set up the following dichotomy between Villoison and Wolf: 'where Villoison heaped up without structure or order texts and data from all periods of Greek literature,' they claim, 'Wolf moved systematically through the scholia, assembling what he took to be characteristic corrections attributed to the ancient readers and critics' (in Wolf [1985] 18). This is to put the best light on Wolf's general practice of discrediting not only Zenodotus but also Aristophanes and even Aristarchus (Wolf [1985] 8). According to this assessment, Wolf's pessimistic formulation supposedly helps put Homer into a historical context. Pursuing this train of thought, the editors of the 'English Wolf' quote the verdict of Pfeiffer on Wolf as the man 'who opened the eyes of his contemporaries and of posterity to the unique *historical* position of the Homeric poetry' (emphasis in original).[31]

Ironically, Villoison's optimistic formulation, articulating the goal of recovering the genuine Homer through Aristarchus, can lead to a clearer perspective about the earlier history of Homeric transmission, while Wolf's pessimism about verifying the testimony of the three major Alexandrian Homer scholars, including Aristarchus, leads to a

[31] Pfeiffer (1968) 214, quoted in Wolf (1985) 29.

default mentality that finds certainty only in the later history of this transmission. To follow this mentality is to rely mostly on what Wolf considers the only verifiable historical reality, that is, the Homer text that evolved *after* the era of Aristarchus. As one of Villoison's defenders puts it, the *Iliad* of Wolf is the *Iliad* of Longinus and Porphyry.[32]

There are other possible approaches to the Homer scholia, and one of them is even more optimistic than that of Villoison: we may consider any variant—whether it is found in the textual traditions or is attributed by the scholia to Zenodotus, Aristophanes, Aristarchus, and other Homer scholars—to be a *potentially* authentic written reflex of the oral poetic system of Homeric diction.[33] Let us focus for the moment on the three major Alexandrian Homer scholars. For Wolf, whenever Aristarchus is 'right' about a reading and Zenodotus is 'wrong,' or vice versa, the inference is that *neither* can be trusted. From the standpoint of oral poetics, however, it can be argued that we cannot establish which given reading is 'right' and which is 'wrong' as we study the variants that survive in the Homeric textual tradition: all we can determine is what seems to be authentic or not, and we may even leave room for more than one authentic reading in any given situation—if we take into account the historical evolution of Homeric poetry in performance.[34]

In investigating the historical layers separating the Homeric scholarship of Zenodotus, Aristophanes, and Aristarchus, Wolf manages to discredit all three to the extent that none of them can lay claim to be the consistent transmittor of 'the' authentic reading. Here is where a return to Villoison helps broaden the perspective. His A-text of the *Iliad*, along with the A-scholia, helps reconstruct the earlier history of Homeric transmission, even if he overprivileges the testimony of Aristarchus against that of Zenodotus and Aristophanes, let alone the earlier Athenian transmission.[35]

---

[32] Pierron (1869) cxl.

[33] Nagy (1995a) 132–149, defending the validity of editorial testimony attributed to Zenodotus and Aristophanes as well as to Aristarchus. For the editorial methods of Zenodotus, see the indispensable work of Nickau (1977). For Aristophanes of Byzantium, see W. Slater, ed., *Aristophanes Byzantii Fragmenta* (Berlin, 1986).

[34] Nagy (1992); (1995a); (1996). This 'evolutionary model' differs from various dictation theories, e.g., that of Janko (1982) 228–31, who proposes 750–725 B.C. and 743–713 B.C. as definitive dates for the text-fixation of the *Iliad* and *Odyssey* respectively. It also differs from the dictation theory of M. L. West (1995), who argues for a *terminus post quem* of either 688 or perhaps 678 B.C. See also Powell in this volume.

[35] That Zenodotus, in the process of editing Homer, did indeed produce his own

In this light it is instructive to study, as a historical model, the reissuing of the Iliadic A-text and A-scholia by A. Pierron.[36] Pierron built on the work of K. Lehrs, the moving force of the 'Königsberg School,' who consistently defended the value of Aristarchus' Homeric scholarship as transmitted primarily through the A-scholia.[37] Pierron's reissue represents at least an approximation, however fragmented, of Aristarchus' own editorial work on the *Iliad* text.[38] Such an Aristarchean edition of Homer, achieved primarily by way of the A-scholia, is valuable not so much for its avowed goal of pinpointing the singular text that Aristarchus had hoped to recover but for its illustrating the variety of multiple readings that were apparently still available to this ancient scholar in his ongoing quest to find in each case the one true reading. What the Homeric scholia reveal, however imperfectly, is that Aristarchus' attempt to reconstruct the single truth of an original Homeric text had led him to scan a multiplicity of existing Homeric texts. Attracted to the idea of that singularity, Villoison placed his trust in Aristarchus. Facing the reality of multiple Homeric textual transmission, Wolf despaired of ever recovering the original Homer text.

The differences between Villoison and Wolf in weighing the importance of the Homeric scholia have left to this day a legacy of uncertainty about the criteria needed for editing Homer. As of this writing, the Homer edition used by most English-speaking Classicists as the definitive or near-definitive text, the Oxford Classical Text of T. W. Allen (with D. B. Monro), has been seriously called into question.[39] As we contemplate the most recent and purportedly most definitive edition of Homer, encompassing both the *Iliad* and the *Odyssey*, we find that its editor, H. van Thiel,[40] condemns Allen's earlier

text is argued by Rengakos (1993) 12–14. He also argues that Aristarchus had direct access to the Homer edition of Zenodotus, even if Didymus and Aristonicus may not have ([1993] 14). So too Apollonius of Rhodes and Callimachus, both contemporaries of Zenodotus, had access to such a text (ibid.).

[36] Pierron (1869).

[37] K. Lehrs, *De Aristarchi Studiis Homericis* (3rd ed. Leipzig, 1882).

[38] See especially Pierron (1869) 564 n. 2, referring to the criticism of Wolf by Lehrs in the second edition of his work on Aristarchus (Königsberg, 1833).

[39] Cf. Janko (1990) 332, 334, on Monro and Allen, eds. (1920). See also Janko (1990) 332 n. 19 on the editorial strategy of the *editio maior* of Allen (1931). Even the intellectual integrity of Allen as editor has been called into question: see N. Wilson, 'Thomas William Allen, 1862–1950,' *Proceedings of the British Academy* 76 (1990) 311–19. For a more balanced assessment of Allen's methods, see Haslam (this vol.).

[40] van Thiel (1991); (1996).

edition as fundamentally defective in its methodology,[41] and he reinforces his condemnation by deliberately making his manuscript sigla different from those of Allen.

It is open to question, however, whether van Thiel's own Homeric editions are any more definitive than Allen's: as M. Haslam points out (this vol.), with specific reference to van Thiel's *Odyssey* (1991), such an edition 'is founded on the premise of the exclusive authority of the vulgate.' By his shorthand reference to the 'vulgate' text of Homer, Haslam means the medieval transmission, as distinct from readings attested in the scholia, in papyri, or in the indirect tradition (Homer quotations and the like). The editorial method espoused by van Thiel is to treat as mere conjectures the variants attributed by the scholia to the Alexandrian editors. In response to current descriptions of such a method as 'conservative,' Haslam points out: 'not that there is actually anything conservative about preferring medieval manuscripts to ancient ones.' It is also essential to keep in mind, as Haslam succinctly puts it, that many medieval variant manuscript readings are 'infiltrators from the scholia.' Also, there were many Homeric readings that the medieval tradition simply did not preserve.

Even the inconsistencies of modern usage in applying the word 'vulgate' to various different phases of a reconstructed Homeric text illustrate the ongoing uncertainties in establishing a definitive text of Homer. For A. Ludwich, the 'vulgate' Homeric text is pre-Alexandrian, derived from an Athenian prototype, which is the ultimate source for the medieval manuscript tradition.[42] Similarly for M. van der Valk ([1963–64] I, 609), a pre-Aristarchean 'vulgate' had 'preserved the authentic text,' and this text 'was also transmitted by the vulgate of the medieval manuscripts.' For both Ludwich and van der Valk, this 'vulgate' is distinct from the Homer 'editions' of the Alexandrians, especially that of Aristarchus. For van der Valk, however, the readings of the 'vulgate' are generally more authentic than the variant readings attributed by the Homer scholia to scholars like Aristarchus, which he generally takes to be 'conjectures'; for Ludwich, by contrast, such variants are not 'conjectures' but authentic readings preserved by the scholia from the Alexandrian editions of Aristarchus and others.[43] For Ludwich, the Alexandrian 'edition' of Aristarchus

---

[41] See especially van Thiel (1991) iii; cf. Haslam (this vol.).
[42] Ludwich (1898); cf. Allen (1924) 327.
[43] Cf. Nagy (1995a) 185.

represents a quantum leap beyond the pre-Alexandrian 'vulgate'; for van der Valk, by contrast, the pre- and post-Alexandrian 'vulgate' text is relatively superior to the Alexandrian 'edition' of Aristarchus, which may not even be deserving of the term 'edition.'

The term 'Wolfian vulgate' has been applied to post-Wolf editions of Homer that tend to discount the judgments of Alexandrian critics, especially with reference to criteria of excluding lines in the Homeric corpus.[44] Such an edition is the Monro-Allen 1920 Oxford Classical Text of the *Iliad*. In other respects, though, this edition follows the criteria of Aristarchus, occasionally adopting the variant readings attributed by the Homer scholia to Aristarchus or to his Alexandrian predecessors.[45] By contrast, the most recent Homer editions of van Thiel go beyond Monro-Allen and most other previous editions in moving toward the 'Wolfian vulgate' as the definitive text. Ironically, this impetus toward privileging the 'Wolfian vulgate' and challenging most of the Alexandrian editorial criteria transmitted by the scholia has been championed by the editor of the major *Iliad* scholia, H. Erbse.[46] R. Pfeiffer, in his summary of the efforts of Lehrs and others to rehabilitate the authoritativeness of Aristarchus as editor of Homer ([1968] 214–15), singles out Erbse's minimizing of the authority of the Alexandrian editors. Pfeiffer begins by saying ([1968] 215): 'it looks to me as if by a sort of unconscious counter-revolution Wolf has now been put back on the throne from which Lehrs had driven him.'

It may well be an overstatement to say that Wolf has been reinstated as the driving force behind Homeric studies. Still, the 'Wolfian vulgate' version of the Homeric text is once again ascendant, culminating in the monumental editions of van Thiel. A key to this ascendancy is the work of Erbse, culminating in his commensurately monumental edition of the *Iliad* scholia. As we have seen, the centerpiece of Erbse's edition, as also of Villoison's, is the testimony of the A-scholia. Much as Villoison had supplemented the testimony of the A-scholia with those of the B-scholia, so also Erbse with that of the c-branch comprised of the b- and T-scholia.

And yet, Erbse's edition cannot provide a complete picture of the Homer scholia. The corpus encompassed by this edition, massive as

---

44 Apthorp (1980) xiii, enhancing the arguments of Bolling (1925).
45 Janko (1990) 332–34.
46 Cf. Erbse (1959).

it is, preserves but a fraction of the information that had once been available and is still sporadically visible in the Homer commentaries of papyri from the Hellenistic and Roman eras. Moreover, Erbse's edition omits the D-scholia, as we have already noted. This is a major loss, since these scholia supplement considerably the picture of ancient Homeric scholarship.

To be sure, there are counter-trends to the trend of accepting the default of a 'Wolfian vulgate.' There are those who systematically argue for validating the editorial standards of the Alexandrians (Zenodotus and Aristophanes as well as Aristarchus), especially with reference to their choices of variant readings.[47] As I write, they are in a minority. Still, some aspects of their views are gaining ground: a case in point is the growing acceptance of arguments for the validity of Aristarchus' criteria in establishing the 'authentic' *numerus versuum*, a fixed number of verses deemed genuine in the text of the Homeric poems.[48]

A systematic edition, not yet realized, of the D-scholia would considerably enhance our knowledge of ancient Homeric scholarship, though of course it too would fall far short of the whole picture. Moreover, the textual history of these scholia is even more complicated than that of the A-scholia. In order to grasp the essence of the D-scholia, we must start with the broader concept of 'minor scholia,' a category that includes the D-group. The minor scholia can be divided into four categories:[49]

---

[47] See especially Rengakos (1993).

[48] See especially Apthorp (1980). For an extreme formulation of the *numerus versuum* principle, see Bolling (1950) 1–16. For Bolling (p. 7), the canonical length of 'archetype' Π of the *Iliad*, going back to the sixth century B.C., is c. 14,650 lines. It is of course primarily the testimony of Aristarchus, as mediated by the scholia, that makes it possible to reduce to this low number the accretive 'Alpha Text' of c. 15,600 lines, which supposedly goes back to the fifth century. Though his concept of 'archetype' Π is questionable, let us follow through on the implications of Bolling's formulation: Aristarchus reduced c. 15,600 lines to c. 14,650 by systematically adding in the left margin, next to suspect lines in the 'Alpha Text' that he used as his point of departure, the editorial sign of the obelus. The obelus marks the judgment of athetesis; when a line is athetized by Aristarchus, it is not deleted from his 'Alpha Text': rather, it is simply marked as textually suspect, the result of 'corrupting' accretion. The fundamental problem with the methodology of Bolling is that he allows only for expansion, never for compression, in the evolution of Homeric poetry. If we apply the perspective of diachronic studies in oral poetics, Bolling's assumptions about a tradition that can only add, never subtract, are unjustified.

[49] This classification follows the valuable analysis of Henrichs (1971); (1974). See especially (1971) 100–101.

1) marginal or interlinear scholia written in papyrus texts of Homer (some of these scholia derive from school-texts, others from learned disquisitions) and interlinear scholia written in medieval manuscripts; the interlinear scholia found in the Homer texts of A and T, which stem from the D-scholia, were published by W. Dindorf and E. Maass in vol. II;[50]

2) Homer glossaries, found in papyri and in medieval manuscripts; the basic format: start with a *lemma*, that is, with an individual word or phrase taken from the Homer text, and then explain that *lemma*

3) Homer lexica found in papyri and in medieval manuscripts

4) running paraphrases in prose, found in papyri and in medieval manuscripts

The *lemmata* of the papyrus scholia can sometimes be traced back to the writings of Alexandrian scholars, though much of the information found in these texts comes from less scholarly authority.[51] We may note in general that the papyrus 'scholia,' like the medieval ones, often omit the name of the scholar whose authority had been invoked, and that the actual sources vary from sophisticated scholarly epitomes and disquisitions (some of which must have had direct access to the work of Alexandrian scholars) all the way to unsophisticated schoolmasterly or schoolboyish paraphrases.[52]

What is remarkable about the corresponding medieval D-scholia is their tendency to preserve the relatively more learned versions of the ancient sources.[53] Also, the D-scholia sometimes 'have lemmas not represented in the direct transmission of the poems.'[54] The bulk of the 'minor scholia' transmitted by the 'archetype' of the medieval manuscript versions of the D-scholia as well as the codex of the lexicon of Apollonius Sophista and of the codex of the lexicon of Hesychius, must have been very similar to what is already a fairly consolidated corpus of information as reflected in the Homer papyrus

[50] Henrichs (1971) 101 n. 11.
[51] Henrichs (1971) 102.
[52] See especially Haslam (this vol.) on the medieval manuscript Genavensis 44, containing exegetical scholia on *Iliad* 21 that are 'miraculously matched' by a second-century papyrus commentary on the same book.
[53] Henrichs (1971) 105.
[54] Haslam (this vol.).

scholia of the Roman period (most of the Homer papyri stem from this period).[55] This much said, it is important to keep in mind that the D-scholia preserve only a part of the traditions reflected in the Homer papyrus scholia.[56] Finally, the D-scholia tradition preserves another important component of scholarly heritage stemming from the period of Alexandrian Homer scholarship, drawing on the scholarly genre of the mythological *historia*; the chief source is a 'complex' known as the Mythographus Homericus.[57]

We may perhaps detect a general sense of hesitation on the part of most contemporary Homerists about the prospect of tracing the information found in medieval manuscript scholia back to corresponding information in papyrus scholia. Such reluctance can be explained in part as a lingering reaction to the excesses of earlier scholars who thought that they had recovered Aristarchean realities from the scholia. As Haslam argues (this vol.), constructions of stemmata linking the scholia of papyri and medieval manuscripts prove impossible even for the 'beloved' A-manuscript, since 'collation spreads readings unsystematically: there are no separate lines of transmission.' The point is well taken, though there may be a danger in going too far in the other direction by not crediting the scholia of the A-manuscript with an authority comparable to that of other scholia: in the case of the D-scholia, for example, it is fair to say that their 'authority' is often 'bolstered by papyri.'

There is perhaps a further danger: an undervaluing of the A-scholia leads to an undervaluing of the Homer editions of Aristarchus, Aristophanes, and Zenodotus, which in turn leads to an overvaluing of the 'Wolfian vulgate.' In order to find a balance, we may consider the testimony of the Homer scholia themselves on the concept of 'vulgate.'

Applications of the term 'vulgate' to various aspects of the Homeric

---

[55] Henrichs (1971) 106–107. Cf. Haslam (1994; this vol.).

[56] Henrichs (1971) 109. There are two branches of sources for the Iliadic D-scholia: a-1, edited by V. de Marco from select manuscripts (Rome, 1932, 1941), and a-2, edited by J. Lascaris (Rome, 1517). There is an edition of the Odyssean D-scholia by F. Asulanus (Venice, 1528).

[57] Montanari (1979) 14; also p. 24 n. 35 on the contributions of van der Valk in defining the Mythographus Homericus. Cf. Haslam (this vol.); 'A new papyrus of the Mythographus Homericus,' *Bulletin of the American Society of Papyrologists* 27 (1990) 31–36; 'On P.Oxy LXI 4096, Mythographus Homericus,' *Zeitschrift für Papyrologie und Epigraphik* 110 (1996) 115–17. For an example of a *historia* preserved by way of the D-scholia, see Haslam (1991) 37.

textual tradition can be traced back ultimately to the usage of Aristarchus—or at least of Didymus, the epitomator of Aristarchus—as reflected especially in the Homer scholia. According to the scholia, the *khariesterai* or 'more elegant' texts of Homer were (1) those 'edited' by previous scholars and (2) the so-called *politikai* or 'city editions' stemming from Chios, Argos, Cyprus, Sinope, Massalia, and so on, while the texts of Homer that were *dêmôdeis* ('popular') or *koinai* ('common') did not belong to the previous two privileged categories.[58] In the context of such negative comparisons, the usage of plural *koinai* and singular *koinê* can be equated with Latin *vulgata*, or 'vulgate.'[59] But the biblical Latin analogy can mislead: in Jerome's *Epistle to Sunnia and Fretella*, the word *koinê*, which he glosses in Latin as the *vulgata* or 'vulgate,' is applied to two 'common' Greek versions of the Hebrew Bible, one of which is the *editio* or 'edition' of Lucian and the other, the *editio* of Origen—that is, the Septuagint as edited in the *Hexapla* of Origen.[60] As in the usage of the Homer scholia, there is an element of negative comparison here as well: conceding that the Greek term *koinê* is applicable to both of the Greek-language biblical 'editions' in question, Jerome goes on to contrast the 'old corrupt edition' of Lucian with the 'uncorrupted and immaculate' version that serves as the source for Jerome's Latin vulgate translation (κοινή *autem ista, hoc est* communis, editio *ipsa est quae et septuaginta, sed hoc interest inter utramque quod* κοινή *pro locis et temporibus et pro voluntate scriptorum* vetus corrupta editio *est, ea autem quae habetur in* ἑξαπλοῖς *et quam nos vertimus ipsa est quae in eruditorum libris* incorrupta et immaculata *septuaginta interpretum translatio reservatur*).[61] In other words, the 'edition' of the Septuagint that Jerome uses as his own textual source is *koinê* to the extent that it is 'common' in the sense of 'general' or even 'universal,' but it transcends the designation of *koinê* to the extent that it is a 'corrected' text, freed from 'corruptions' associated with a text that is

---

[58] Haslam (this vol.). For a defense of the authenticity of variant readings found in the 'city editions,' see Nagy (1995a) 147–48, following Citti (1966).

[59] Allen (1923) 317.

[60] Jerome, *Epistles* 106.2, as discussed by Allen (1924) 317, 319. See in general B. Neuschäfer, *Origenes als Philologe* (Basel, 1987: Schweizerische Beiträge zur Altertumswissenschaft 18.1/2). Cf. also Lührs (1992) 8 on Origen's editorial policy of avoiding personal emendations or conjectures in editing the text of the Septuagint.

[61] Ibid. Jerome also makes it clear here that Origen and Eusebius referred to the edition of Lucian as *koinê*. By implication, Origen would hardly have called his own edition a *koinê* version.

'common' in the sense of 'vulgar.' The word *koinê* has the aura of an authoritative but relatively 'uncorrected' text.

Similarly in the case of Aristarchus, it can be argued that his category of *koinai* or 'common' texts of Homer, mentioned throughout the Homeric scholia, may be traced back to an authoritative but relatively 'uncorrected' textual source, and the most likely reconstruction is an Athenian 'City Edition,' perhaps stemming from the fourth century.[62] A piece of evidence that may be cited in favor of this reconstruction is the fourth-century Athenian usage of the adjective *koinos* as 'common' in the ideological sense of 'general, standardized, universalized';[63] such a description would fit the *Iliad* and *Odyssey* as 'owned' by the state of Athens on the occasion of seasonally-recurring performances at the festival of the Panathenaea.[64] Another piece comes from the papyri: whereas we see a pervasive fluctuation between plural *koinai* and singular *koinê* in the medieval Homer scholia, the few instances where we find the matching testimony of marginalia written on papyri consistently reveal the distinctive singular.[65] Here too, as in Jerome's assessment of the word *koinê*, we may detect the aura of an authoritative but relatively 'uncorrected' text.

Thus the argument that the *koinê* Homer text stems from an Athenian City Edition cannot be countered by suggesting that Aristarchus would surely have preferred an Athenian City Edition, if indeed he had access to such a thing, over other editions.[66] The Homer scholia make it clear that Aristarchus' criterion for distinguishing a superior from an inferior *ekdosis* or 'edition' is the variable scholarly quality of the editing process, that is, of *diorthôsis* or 'correction'—in the sense of *restoring 'genuine' or 'original' readings to a 'corrupted' text.* To the extent that the *koinê* Homer is 'common' in the privileged sense of a 'general, standardized, universalized' text stemming from an earlier past, we can expect Aristarchus to value it; to the extent that this same

[62] Nagy (1995a) 187–200, following (in part) M. S. Jensen (1980) 109. This possibility is entertained but ultimately resisted by Haslam (this vol.).

[63] Cf. Lycurgus 1.102 and Demosthenes 18.170; also Isaeus 7.16, on the care taken in the recording of legitimate records: only after full verification 'are they to be written down into the *koinon grammateîon*' (εἰς τὸ κοινὸν γραμματεῖον ἐγγράφειν). This expression confirms that ἐν κοινῷ goes with *both* γραψαμένους *and* φυλάττειν in [Plutarch], *Lives of the Ten Orators* 841 f., as discussed by Nagy (1995a) 175 n. 77.

[64] Nagy (1995a) 189.

[65] Haslam (this vol.). As he points out, the fuller and more accurate reporting found in the papyri indicates 'the severely reduced nature of the scholia.'

[66] So Haslam (this vol.).

koinê is 'common' in the default sense of 'vulgar,' we can expect him to prefer the more 'corrected' editions from the more recent past, including those of Aristophanes and Zenodotus. This pattern of preference could only be expected to intensify in the post-Aristarchean era, by which time the privileged sense of *koinê* would have eroded further.

According to an explanation that differs from the one offered here, the mentions of *koinai* in the Homer scholia refer simply to 'the early Ptolemaic papyri that we may see as specimens of the 'common' text(s).'[67] This is to assume, however, that *koinai* and the more distinctive *koinê* mean 'common' only in the default sense of 'vulgar.' It is also to assume that *koinê* is merely a foil, an inferior copy. Rather, it may be an authoritative point of departure for the process of scholarly *diorthôsis* that ostensibly leads to the editing of a superior text.

The authenticity of *koinê* readings, where the designation *koinê* is actually made explicit by the scholia, can be confirmed on the basis of two independent criteria: (1) comparative linguistics and (2) oral poetics.[68] But this is not to discredit the authenticity of non-*koinê* readings that the scholia attribute to the *diorthôsis* or 'corrective editing' of scholars like Aristarchus. In many instances, the variant readings attributed to Aristarchus or Aristophanes or Zenodotus can likewise be confirmed on the basis of those same two independent criteria of comparative linguistics and oral poetics.[69] Thus it is unjustified to assume, as have many Homeric scholars, that the variant readings resulting from the *diorthôsis* of Alexandrian critics are as a rule scholarly conjectures. Many of these variants stemming from the learned editions prove to be just as authentic, from the standpoint of oral poetics, as the variants stemming from the City Editions or from the *koinê* texts in general.

Ironically, an assumption that Wolf had made about oral traditions led him to take as a given one of the two working assumptions of Alexandrian critics like Aristarchus. These critics assumed both that the Homeric text was 'corrupted' and that they could 'correct' these corruptions by combining the internal evidence of Homeric diction with the external evidence of variant manuscript traditions. Though Wolf did not accept the assumption of the Alexandrian critics

---

[67] Haslam (this vol.), following S. West (1967) 26.
[68] Janko (1992) 26.
[69] Nagy (1995a) 148–49; cf. Muellner (1976) 58–62.

that they had the means to 'correct' the 'corruptions,' he took as a given their assumption that there were indeed 'corruptions' in the first place. For a scholar like Aristarchus, such 'corruptions' were a matter of textual traditions that had gone awry. For Wolf, they became something else, a matter of oral traditions that had made the textual traditions go awry.

The study of living oral traditions refutes this assumption: the process of composition-in-performance, typical of oral traditions, does not 'corrupt' an 'original' song. Even the concept of 'original' misleads in such a context, in that any performance in an oral tradition can re-create a given composition into a new 'original'—though of course the degree of re-creation may vary considerably, depending not only on the nature of the given tradition but also on a wide variety of historically-determined contingencies. Still, it can be said about the process of recomposition-in-performance that different authentic variants can be generated by the same oral tradition at different historical points of its evolution. The principle of variation in living oral traditions extends to the actual length of a given composition-in-performance, which can vary over time in degrees of relative expansion or compression.

In sum, the Homer scholia help reconstruct the full diachronic dimensions inherent in the evolution of Homeric textual traditions. Different Homeric textual traditions may have been definitive at different historical moments, but no single Homeric textual tradition can be deemed definitive beyond its own historical context.[70]

[70] Haslam (this vol.) argues that the text of A merits no greater respect than the text-family of B C E[3] or the text of T or the underlying text of D.

Frank M. Turner

THE HOMERIC QUESTION

Homer and Homeric composition have been discussed, probed, and criticized since ancient times.[1] The *Homeric Question*, however, is a distinctly nineteenth-century invention, created by the philological enterprise, the romantic concepts of composition, and the historicism of the age. Research and argumentation over the Question were pursued within distinctly nineteenth-century intellectual institutions. The Question was, however, in fact a series of questions about the composition of the *Iliad* and the *Odyssey*. Those included: Did the two epics have a single author? Under what conditions were the epics composed? Was there an original core to the *Iliad* or to the *Odyssey* upon which a later longer poem had been composed? What was the relationship of the *Iliad* to the *Odyssey*?

These became issues of genuinely European scope, because unlike works of later literature, the *Aeneid* being the only exception, the Homeric epics were read and admired across the continent, providing humanistic scholars with a body of material that could be debated transnationally. But it was the emergence of philology as a core discipline in German universities that made the questions surrounding Homer problematic for a significant group of scholars. The Homeric Question became a vehicle whereby philologists worked to assert their cultural authority in European and more particularly German intellectual life. Homeric criticism constituted an arena in which academic philological virtuosos could display their skills in transforming two of the monumental works of Western literature into objects of academic analysis. Philologists wrested Homer from the world of poets and literature and placed him at the mercy of modern scientific criticism, just as they wrested the Christian scriptures from the realm of sacred reverence.

---

[1] J. E. Sandys, *A History of Classical Scholarship* (New York, 1967; first published 1903–1908), Vol. 3; U. von Wilamovitz-Moellendorf, *History of Classical Scholarship*, trs. A. Harris (London, 1982; first German edition, 1921); Davison (1962b); Turner (1981) 135–186.

The eighteenth century had seen much debate over the character of Homeric poetic genius, and the first modern exploration of the physical landscape described in the poems.[2] This debate went on within the arena now denoted by cultural historians as the Republic of Letters. Eighteenth-century commentators as different as Richard Bentley, Giambattista Vico, and Jean Jacques Rousseau raised questions about the nature of Homeric authorship and composition that directly foreshadowed and laid much of the groundwork for the Homeric Question that dominated so much nineteenth-century classical scholarship.[3] Alexander Pope's translation of Homer for a time ensconced the poetry into the confines of neoclassicism, but the epics would not long be so contained. The eighteenth-century debate over the character of poetic genius, as seen in Thomas Blackwell's *An Enquiry into the Life and Writings of Homer* (1735; German translation, 1766), along with the new emphasis that emerged in the second half of the century on poetic originality, brought Homer to the fore of taste over the long-standing respect accorded to Virgil.[4] Homeric poetry stood not in the glacial confines of neoclassical marble but as one of many manifestations of an ancient and less polished or civilized Mediterranean life and culture. To grasp Homer in all his fullness required that the imagination escape to a different time and place. Blackwell, for example, had argued that readers must set themselves into the audience of ancient warriors who understood all of the customs that Homer's verse described and recounted. Not unimportantly, while Blackwell's book worked its way through English and European intellectual circles, biblical critics like Archdeacon Robert Lowth were bringing the narratives of the Hebrew Bible into a similar world of historical analysis and empathy. There was a strong intellectual and spiritual sense that the critical fate of Homer and the fate of the scriptures stood closely linked.

In addition to the growing awareness of history, the late eighteenth century witnessed a new appreciation for the topographical accuracy

---

[2] Simonsuuri (1979).

[3] Bentley had written, 'Homer wrote a sequel of songs and rhapsodies, to be sung by himself for small earnings and good cheer, at festivals and other days of merriment; the Iliad he made for the men, the Odysseis for the other sex. These loose songs were not collected together into the form of an epic poem until 500 years after.' Richard Bentley, 'Discourse of Freethinking, by Phileleutherus Lipsiensis,' (1713) quoted by Grote (1869) I:151 fn.

[4] F. M. Turner, *Contesting Cultural Authority: Essays in Victorian Intellectual Life* (Cambridge, 1993) 284–321.

of the Homeric descriptions of landscape. Robert Wood, in *An Essay on the Original Genius of Homer* (1769), had emphasized the poet's accuracy of historical and geographical detail. Wood had also speculated on the conditions under which the epics had been composed, and had suggested that Homer could not write. Anticipating late nineteenth-century anthropological criticism, Wood also believed that much could be learned about Homeric society by comparing it with modern Bedouin life in the Middle East. Only by making such leaps in the imagination, he thought, could readers begin to see how different Homer's world was from that presupposed by neoclassical writers. Wood's analysis, like Blackwell's, became well known in Germany.[5]

These and other eighteenth-century compositions that to one degree or another addressed Homer did not provoke ongoing controversy or discussion. They left Homer largely in the realm of belle lettres, not connecting the criticism of Homer to any larger cultural issue. It was the publication of *Prolegomena ad Homerum* in 1795 by the young F. A. Wolf (1759–1724) that established the foundation of the Homeric Question for the next century, and transferred Homeric criticism into the expanding realm of professional scholarship. Wolf's essay is one of the most remarkable modern works of philology. It helped establish the discipline as a force for generating additional scholarship, and also probably constituted the last major work of European intellectual history to be composed and published in learned Latin. It was also a relatively brief work on a major subject which the author never followed up.

As Wolf's contemporaries and more recent scholars have observed, much of the essay's content was not especially original. Wolf's own footnotes make this clear. He did not answer or fully explore many of the issues that he had raised. By leaving his own contribution in a somewhat truncated form, he allowed others to define further and to redefine the issues that he had first set out. In that regard, the Homeric Question very much grew on itself and again and again was transformed as it passed into the hands of later scholars. The comment of a major nineteenth-century commentator is important: 'Vielleicht niemals hat ein philologishes Werk, selbst Bentleys Schrift über die Brief des Phalaris nicht, den Fortschritt der gesammten

[5] F. Meinecke, *Historicism: The Rise of a New Historical Outlook* (New York, 1972; first published, 1959) 203–209.

Wissenschaft so mächtig gefödert als Wolfs Prolegomena.'[6] It is fundamental to understanding the Homeric Question as a nineteenth-century phenomenon to realize that it was philology and philological careerism rather than concern for Homer that fueled the Question. It was the case of a modern methodology making its way in the world by addressing a subject of long-standing interest. Consequently the nineteenth-century Homeric Question was in large measure as much a quarrel about arguments as it was a dispute over Homer.

Wolf wrote the *Prolegomena* while a Professor at Halle. The subtitle of the work was 'Concerning the Original and Genuine Form of the Homeric Works and Their Various Alterations and the Proper Method of Emendation.' From a consideration of these issues, other questions soon presented themselves. Wolf primarily concerned himself with the character of the most recent Homeric texts and the manner in which they did or did not, could or could not, relate to the original composition of the epics. He entertained no illusions about achieving the Homeric ur-text, and commented: 'If we demand the bard in simon-pure condition, and are not content with what contented Plutarch, Longinus, or Proclus, we will have to take refuge either in empty prayers or in unrestrained license in divination.'[7] The fundamental problem was not that an ur-text of Homer was not available, but why it was not. Wolf asked how anyone could separate what Homer had written from what later ages had changed, removed, or added. The text could not be regarded as impure or incorrect simply because it did not mesh with modern taste. Nor could the text of Alexandrian times be regarded as authoritative because it had itself been made to read in accordance with that ancient taste.

The genuinely problematic issues emerged as Wolf discussed why it was impossible to achieve the ur-text and ultimately also impossible to discover an original Homer. First, there was quite simply the problem of the transmission of the ancient manuscripts once the poems had been committed to writing. These difficulties had been made all the more evident in Wolf's day by the publication by Villoisin of the Venetian Scholia which presented a vast array of changes and emendations made by ancient critics. A. Grafton has made the important point that Wolf sought to understand the history of the ancient criticism itself. This process was what Wolf termed 'the internal critical

---

6 L. Friedländer (1853) 1. See also Grafton (1991) 214–243.
7 Wolf (1985) 46.

history of these poems.'[8] He sought to understand what the Alexandrian critics had done to the earlier text of Homer. He demanded that those ancient critics for whom he had much respect be interpreted as functioning as creatures of their own intellectual climate and not as modern professional scholars.[9] They had added or changed the received text according to their own taste rather than according to critical philological principles. They were revisers of Homer not restorers of his original purity. Wolf explained:

> But if above I properly related the text of ancient writers to the consideration of *historical facts*, then in establishing the text no appearance of plausibility drawn from one's sense of elegance, but pure and sufficiently old exemplars must take the first place. It is one thing to combine the laws of history with usage, learning, and taste when examining the credibility of the best witnesses; a very different thing to be propelled by this volatile sense [of taste] as by a gust of wind, so that we believe that any pretty and appropriate reading which crops up is also the true one.[10]

The ascertaining of an original text had nothing to do with a modern aesthetic judgment about changes which had been imposed by ancient critics on the grounds of their own sense of taste. Indeed, for Wolf critical taste must give way to critical judgment.

In considering how the poems has been composed and emended in ancient times, Wolf engaged in a project of historicist thinking that was remarkable even for his day in its rigor and determination. Blackwell and Wood had introduced historicity in the sense of arguing that Homer must be read, understood, and interpreted in light of the society and geography of his own day and not in terms of universalizing neoclassical categories. Wolf further demanded that the act of composition as well as the content of the epics be understood in regard to the historical situation. The problem lay at the fountainhead of the poems themselves. Drawing upon hints and suggestions from earlier eighteenth-century Homeric commentators, Wolf asked:

> But what if the suspicion of some scholars is probable—that these and the other poems of those times were not consigned to writing, but were first made by poets in their memories and made public in song, then made more widely available by the singing of the rhapsodes, whose

[8] Wolf (1985) 57.
[9] Grafton (1991) 227–233.
[10] Wolf (1985) 59.

> peculiar art it was to learn them? And if, because of this, many changes were necessarily made in them, by accident or design, before they were fixed, so to speak, in written form? And if for this very reason, as soon as they began to be written out, they had many differences, and soon acquired new ones from the rash conjectures of those who rivaled one another in their efforts to polish them up, and to correct them by the best laws of the art of poetry and their own usage? And if, finally, it can be shown by probable arguments and reasons that this entire connected series of the two continuous poems is owed less to the genius of him to whom we have normally attributed it, than to the zeal of a more polite age and the collective efforts of many, and that therefore the very songs from which the *Iliad* and *Odyssey* were assembled do not all have one common author?[11]

At the end of the day the epic existed, but at the beginning of the day there may have been no Homer. Authorship of the Homeric epics had passed from the one to the many. This assertion first posed in the form of a question and then driven home by Wolf with one argument after another set the stage for the next half-century of Homeric scholarship.

The issue of Homer to a very considerable extent became the question of the existence of the skill of writing in ancient times, and in the minds and work of many scholars it would remain so until the late twentieth century. As important as was (and is) the question of writing and of poetry in a predominantly oral culture, no less important for the history of the Homeric epics in the West was the transfer of critical and scholarly attention from the poems themselves to the mode of the composition and transmission. Suddenly, scholars could think about the poems in a very different way that gave them a different character and might appeal to a different standard of literary taste, but in fact at the same time the evaluation of the poems rapidly centered on their mode of composition rather than upon their content.

Nowhere was this redirection of attention clearer in Wolf's work than in his consideration of writing in the age of Homer. Wolf's skepticism regarding the possibility of an ancient poet using writing at the time of the composition of the Homeric poems was deeply rooted in romantic historicist thinking rather than in enlightenment rationalism with which Wolf has frequently been associated. Wolf declared:

[11] Wolf (1985) 69–70.

> Now we have begun to examine the natures of ancient monuments more profoundly and to judge each event by the mental and moral habits of its time and place, while keeping the strictest law of history—that we do not call into doubt things which are true and supported by honest witnesses, and that we do not take as established things which are passed down in any way whatever or adorned with the name of some author or other.[12]

Historicizing the factor of writing in Homer constituted part of the process of removing him from the confines of neoclassicism. It also implicitly raised the issue of the character of authorship, which Wolf never really explored in detail.

This section of his essay was important for two reasons. First, just as it was necessary to recognize that the Alexandrian critics had not behaved like modern critics, it was also necessary to understand that Homer's works could not be considered as books in a modern library. Wolf thought it quite likely that even if writing of some kind had existed in Homer's day, Homer himself would not have had any dexterity in writing. Wolf attempted to analyze early writing from a cultural standpoint. He suggested that in Homer's day, when poetry was associated with memorized song or recitation, it would have demeaned the work as poetry to have committed it to writing. Second, Wolf's discussion of ancient writing or the absence thereof became quite technical. He pointed out that Homer did not discuss or portray writing, and he emphasized the importance of memory in that age. This long discussion of writing presaged later nineteenth-century discussions of Homeric poems in allowing the actual poems themselves to disappear behind detailed analysis. Repeatedly in discussions of the Homeric Question, virtually everything but the poems came to be discussed, analyzed, and criticized.

Had Homer himself composed the poems alone, as had long been uncritically assumed, he would have needed not only his imagination, tongue, and lungs, but pens and a writing table. In one of his most memorable passages, Wolf concluded:

> If as the only man of his time to have such equipment, he had completed the *Iliad* and the *Odyssey* in their uninterrupted sequence, they would in their want of all other suitable contrivances have resembled an enormous ship, constructed somewhere inland in the first beginnings of navigation: its maker would have had no access to winches

[12] Wolf (1985) 71.

> and wooden rollers to push it forward, and therefore no access to the sea itself in which he could make some trial of his skill.[13]

Rendered skeptical by such historicist analysis, Wolf could not envision a solitary Homer writing his poems at an ancient writing desk that never possibly existed:

> But as for me, whether I contemplate the progress of the Greeks themselves or that of other races, I find it impossible to accept the belief to which we have become accustomed: that these two works of a single genius burst forth suddenly from the darkness in all their brilliance, just as they are, with both the splendor of their parts and the many great virtues of the connected whole.[14]

Wolf could not deny that the two Homeric epics stood at the head of the Western literary tradition, but he could not believe they had been the work of a single author. Rather the poems revered in the modern age had been recited and revised by ancient rhapsodists, and then variously altered, interpolated, corrected, and emended from the age of Solon down to that of the Alexandrians.[15] There had first been the Homeric songs, then their repetition and revision by the rhapsodists, and finally their commitment to writing in the age of Pisistratus. Only in that last act had any real stability come to the text, and even thereafter numerous changes were introduced by later critics. Wolf argued that the Homeric poems had in this fashion emerged gradually over time, just as his contemporary J. Hutton, the Edinburgh geologist, argued about the formation of the earth.

Wolf understood that he was presenting the Homeric poems as the product of a long passage of time and that some would see his views as analogous to those who presented the world as having developed over time. He seemed to have removed a guiding mind from Homeric composition just as the geologists and other scientific theorists would be accused of removing the mind of God from the development of nature. In this regard, Wolf himself presciently anticipated certain of his later disparagers, when he wrote:

> There once were philosophers who decreed that this universal framework of all things and bodies were not made by a divine mind and will but instead was born and developed by accident and chance. I do not fear that anyone will accuse me of like temerity if I am led by the

[13] Wolf (1985) 116.
[14] Wolf (1985) 148.
[15] Wolf (1985) 209.

> traces of an artistic framework and by other serious considerations to think that Homer was not the creator of all his—so to speak—bodies, but rather that this artistic structure was introduced by later ages. For we find that this was not done suddenly by chance, but that instead the energies of several ages and men were joined together in this activity.[16]

Just as in much contemporary theology, a transcendent deity was giving way to an immanent one that worked its way in the world in a tentative fashion, a collective Homer immanently and tentatively constructing his poems was replacing a transcendent author.

Wolf's *Prolegomena* stood in its day and remains a tour de force of historicism and philology. The power of both new intellectual forces to recast the entire manner that an ancient piece of literature could be understood and interpreted had been established. Despite accusations from Heyne and others that he had said little or nothing original, Wolf's achievement stood. He also demonstrated the kind of work and authority that could grow out of the new German university culture. Indeed, the reformers of the German universities laboring under the guidance of Humboldt used Wolf's work to demonstrate the relevance and power of philological science and thus connected the traditional study of the classics to the powerful new method. Contemporary poets might debate Wolf's views and come to differing opinions at differing times, but the opinion of the poets and men of letters was no longer decisive. The day of the professional Homeric scholar had dawned. The power and influence of such scholarly method would become mutually reinforcing across classical scholarship, and early in the next century the Roman historian B. G. Niebuhr would dissect the early books of Livy's history into folk lays analogous to the rhapsodist lays Wolf had discerned in Homer.

The next major step in the development of the Homeric question came in the late 1830s with the work of K. Lachmann (1793–1851). Lachmann was also a philologist, who had established a scholarly reputation through analysis of the *Nibelungenlied.* He had asserted that the German epic was a collection of separate songs or lays each of which told parts of the story, but had little or no relationship to each other until gathered together in the thirteenth century. Lachmann had carried out an extensive correspondence with the Grimm brothers over the character of the *Nibelungenlied* and the nature of its authorship.

---

[16] Wolf (1985) 131.

This discussion took place in the larger context of thinking about the relationship of the German nation and the German *Volk* to the *Nibelungenlied* and its composition.[17]

Lachmann published relatively brief articles on the *Iliad* in 1837 and 1843, and republished them, with some additional material, in 1847.[18] They constituted little more than a pamphlet. Indeed many nineteenth-century journal articles were much longer than Lachmann's influential comments on Homer. Lachmann contended that the *Iliad*, like the *Nibelungenlied*, represented a collection of eighteen separately composed ancient lays which had been gathered together over the years, most importantly by Pisistratus. This mode of analysis differed distinctly from Wolf's and some of his later commentators. For Wolf and others, there did exist an *Iliad* which had developed organically over time as generations of rhapsodists had embellished earlier songs, and this *Iliad* constituted a more or less unified work of art. Lachmann's approach also differed from Wolf's in that his analysis was not particularly historicist. Rather, for each of the lays Lachmann imposed his own sense of what should constitute a particular kind of narrative. He raised virtually no questions about how ancient Greeks might have thought about these narratives, or the narratives' relationships to each other. In that regard, Lachmann's theory, though set forth by a German scholar, represented the kind of a priori criticism and the imposition of modern literary standards that Wolf had so deplored and associated with the French.

According to Lachmann, the *Iliad* had not existed until the various separate and unrelated songs composed by different authors had been collected into the epic. His analysis opened the way for two not necessarily disparate views of the Homeric epic. First, the authorship of the *Iliad*, like that of the *Nibelungenlied*, could be seen as in some way originating in the collective genius of the Greek people. In this regard, the destruction of the unity of Homeric authorship opened the way for the erection of a collective ancient genius. Some commentators, such as Niebuhr, thought this mode of composition embodying the spirit of an entire people gave the Homeric epics a standing higher than works of a single poet such as Virgil.[19] Second,

[17] A. Leitzmann, ed., *Briefwecksel der Brüder Jacob and Wilhelm Grimm mit Karl Lachmann* (Jena, 1927). See also M. Thorp, *The Study of the Nibelungenlied* (Oxford, 1940).

[18] Lachmann (1847).

[19] B. G. Niebuhr, *The History of Rome*, trs. J. C. Hare and C. Thirlwall (3d ed., Philadelphia, 1844) I:111.

Lachmann's analysis set the stage for an ongoing effort that would continue for many decades to take the *Iliad* to pieces in an effort to discover its ancient building blocks.

Lachmann and later scholars writing in his spirit discerned the Homeric building blocks through discovering inconsistencies of narrative, language, and metaphors. On the basis of these, they argued that the *Iliad* had been composed by joining together these earlier materials. The main counter-argument was that such inconsistencies had not been noted by ancient listeners or readers, or if noted, had not bothered them. As W. D. Geddes observed with a quiet irony late in the century, 'Possibly the Homeric Greeks were not so much disturbed as some moderns at such inconsistencies.'[20] Nonetheless, Lachmann laid the foundation for approaching the epics in search of any kind of inconsistency that might suggest they were the product of combining previous much shorter poems. This outlook would, in the second half of the century, be carried to the analysis of the *Odyssey*. The problem that arose, however, was the incapacity of any two scholars to discern quite the same building blocks.

Lachmann's very influential theory appeared at the end of a decade that had seen an exploration of the composition of pre-Homeric Greek poetry that partially recovered an original Homer. In a number of books and articles, G. W. Nitzsch (1790–1861) of the University of Kiel attempted to combine a view of the *Iliad* and the *Odyssey* that acknowledged the presence of earlier songs and poems but portrayed Homer as having through his own poetic genius drawn these together and improved upon them.[21] In this respect, Homer the poet appears much later than his subject matter, uses the work of lesser predecessors, but sets his own stamp of unquestioned genius on the poems. In this analysis Homer marks a fundamental second stage in the development of epic poetry in which epic works of enduring power and quality were achieved by a single author. In effect there is for Nitzsch a single Homer who like other poets of genius profited from predecessors but whose genius qualitatively surpassed theirs. Nitzsch also made a case for the existence of writing in Greece at a date earlier than thought by Wolf. He finally argued vigorously that the Cyclic poems, previously researched by F. G. Welcker (1784–1868),

---

[20] In H. T. Peck, ed., *Harper's Dictionary of Classical Literature and Antiquities* (New York, 1897) 839.

[21] Nitzsch (1830–37; 1841; 1852). See also Browne (1908) 148–150.

presupposed the existence of the Homeric poems more or less in the form that they had appeared in classical Greece and beyond. In the middle and second half of the nineteenth century Nitzsch was regarded by unitarians as having set forth the most powerful refutation of the Wolfian school.

There were other efforts to rescue some kind of Homeric composition by a single author. In what proved to be a theory of very considerable long-term influence, G. Hermann (1772–1848) in essays of 1831 and 1832 argued that there had been an original Homer, and that he had composed original poems much shorter than the present *Iliad* and *Odyssey*. Later poets had then expanded these, interpolating their own work. This approach became known as the 'kernel theory.' In a very real sense, it tied a unitary Homer to a Wolfian theory of finalized composition of the two epics. Hermann believed there had been some earlier songs or lays, but the original Homer had not only drawn upon these but had also established the basic structure of the *Iliad* and the *Odyssey*. Later poets expanded and reworked the two poems, but their audiences' expectations of hearing the main elements of the earlier poems inhibited fundamental modifications.

Just before the middle of the century the first major English voice joined the debate and drew upon Hermann's insight. In 1846 George Grote published the first two volumes of *A History of Greece*, a work that had enormous influence not only in the English-speaking world but also on the continent. For the first time, a discussion of Homer appeared in a work of expansive historical and literary scholarship that commanded a wide audience. The first volume contained Grote's important discussion of early Greek history which questioned the historical content of any of the Greek myths. Grote described the stories of the myths including the myth of the Homeric wars as 'a past which never was present,—a region essentially mythical, neither approachable by the critic nor measurable by the chronologer.'[22] The second volume contained a no less influential analysis of the Homeric poems. Grote denied the historicity of the Trojan War narrative but embraced the details of Greek life in the epics.

In terms of Homeric composition, Grote followed the direction of Wolf, but not the same path; he accepted part of Lachmann's outlook, but not the details; and he found a kernel, but not Hermann's.

---

[22] Grote (1869) I:43.

Grote also pointed out with his usual clarity that the 'disallowance of the historical personality of Homer is quite distinct from the question, with which it has been often confounded, whether the *Iliad* and *Odyssey* are originally entire poems, and whether by one author or otherwise.'[23] Grote agreed that writing probably had not existed in the era of Homeric composition and that the poems had been communicated and passed through the generations orally. Blackwell and Wood had historicized the Homeric setting and Wolf the nature of composition. Grote historicized the audience for the ancient poems as much as their composition. He thus made the audience as important as the author. He reminded his readers:

> In appreciating the effect of the poems, we must always take account of this great difference between early Greece and our own times—between the congregation mustered at a solemn festival, stimulated by community of sympathy, listening to a measured and musical recital from the lips of trained bards or rhapsodes, whose matter was supposed to have been inspired by the Muse—and the solitary reader with a manuscript before him; such manuscript being, down to a very late period in Greek literature, indifferently written, without division into parts and without marks of punctuation. As in the case of dramatic performances in all ages, so in that of the early Grecian epic—a very large proportion of its impressive effect was derived from the talent of the recitor and the force of the general accompaniments, and would have disappeared altogether in solitary reading.[24]

Grote emphasized this oral recitation in part because he believed the development of writing had come quite late. Indeed, Grote found 'the existence of trained bards, gifted with extraordinary memory' to be 'far less astonishing than that of long manuscripts in an age essentially non-reading and non-writing, and when even suitable instruments and materials for the process are not obvious.'[25] There would have been no reason for the poems to have been committed to writing until there existed a 'reading class' of persons in Greece.[26] Grote thought such a class could not possibly have emerged any earlier than the seventh century.

Grote sharply rejected the view of German scholars from Wolf through Lachmann that the *Iliad* and *Odyssey* were produced as unified

[23] Grote (1869) I:134.
[24] Grote (1869) I:136.
[25] Grote (1869) I:144.
[26] Grote (1869) I:149.

written works under Pisistratus. In the first place the poems displayed too few elements of the tyrant's age. Pisistratus had attempted to bring new solemnity to the great religious festivals. He would not therefore have undertaken so vast an innovation as having previously separate lays gathered together into a new work. His very purpose suggested the bringing forward of works already known and revered. Grote thought it impossible for persons at the time of Pisistratus to have forgotten the separate identities of the lays allegedly gathered and forged into a unity at that late date. So late a unified epic would have commanded none of the reverence and respect accorded to Homeric poetry.

Grote believed that the Wolfians and, more importantly, the adherents of Lachmann's views, needed to admit that the *Iliad* had a certain, even if imperfect, unity, and that they must account for that unity as well as for the departures from it. The German emphasis on the disparate character of the ancient lays allegedly collected into the poem at some later time created as many difficulties as it solved. Grote was able to conceive a rough and ready unity to the *Iliad* that centered about Achilles because unlike Wolf half-a-century earlier, he did not see himself as resisting the rules of neoclassical criticism.[27] Grote thoroughly historicized the composition of the *Iliad*, but did not exclude the possibility of an original work from which the later epic had grown and developed. Grote, in the spirit of Dr. Johnson's comment on the dancing bear, thought the imperfect unity of the *Iliad* far more impressive than its lack of perfect unity.

In the middle of the century there existed an effective draw between Wolfians and non-Wolfians. As L. Friedländer, the most important mid-century commentator on the Homeric question wrote, 'Die Lösung der Homerischen Frage kann immer nur eine hypothetische sein.'[28] But the world of scholarship and commentary was not willing to leave the matter as an hypothesis. Nor were the scholars of the second half of the century willing to concentrate only on the *Iliad*. Grote

---

[27] Grote contended that the *Iliad* had emerged over time from a single earlier poem which had outgrown it original purpose and organization. He argued that Books 1, 8, and 11 through 22 constituted the original poem which had sung of the exploits and wrath of Achilles. Books 2 through 7, 10, 22, and 24 had been added later to expand the poem to encompass additional themes. The embassy from Agamemnon to Achilles in Book 9 Grote considered spurious. Grote found a central core poem which could very well have the product of a single mind.

[28] L. Friedländer (1853) 71.

had declared, 'If it had happened that the *Odyssey* had been preserved to us alone, without the *Iliad*, I think the dispute respecting Homeric unity would never have been raised.'[29] In 1887 R. J. Jebb declared, 'It is in the *Iliad* . . . that the main interest of the Homeric question must always be centered.'[30] But despite such assertions, philologists in the second half of the century set the *Odyssey* front and center in their considerations.

The assault began in 1859 when A. Kirchhoff (1826–1908), a Berlin professor, contended that the *Odyssey* had itself grown from an original core with various parts being added to it later. The original poem had concerned itself with the Return of Odysseus to which a sequel, which had never stood alone as a poem, had been added. Still later was added material on the adventures of Telemachus. Kirchhoff elaborated his views in essays and in a commentary on Homer. Two decades later in *The Problem of the Homeric Poems* (1878), W. D. Geddes (1828–1900) of the University of Aberdeen suggested there had been two Homeric poets. The first had created the original core of the *Iliad* (the *Achilleid*), and then one or more additional poets added major sections to it. This later poet or poets had also in turn written the *Odyssey*.

The most influential scholar to follow upon Kirchhoff was von Wilamowitz-Moellendorff (1848–1931), who published his *Homerische Untersuchungen* in 1884. In his effort to point out inconsistencies in the *Odyssey* that indicated more than one author, Wilamowitz made harsh comments about the quality and character of Homeric poetry such as had not appeared among the Wolfians of the first part of the century. For example, Wilamowitz described the *Iliad* as 'a miserable piece of patchwork.'[31] Other critics of the *Odyssey* did likewise. Fick declared, 'The present *Odyssey* is a crime against human intelligence.'[32] Muelder observed that 'It is really too bad that the poet of the *Odyssey* tried his powers in a species of poetry for which he had neither the creative ability nor the powers of expression.'[33] Consequently, by the end of the century, one German scholar after another had pronounced the unsatisfactory poetic character of the two epics as evidence for

[29] Grote (1869) II:165.
[30] Jebb (1887) 131.
[31] Wilamowitz, as quoted in Scott (1921) 75–76.
[32] Quoted in Scott (1921) 76.
[33] Quoted in Scott (1921) 76.

either the absence of a poet of genius working alone or forging previous lays or a multiplicity of authors. Wilamowitz noted the irony of that situation as early as 1884:

> Homer is zur zeit kein viel gelesener dichter mehr. . . . Homer is eine macht, aber eine überwundene. Selbst die philologen kennen ihn meist so schlect wie die frommen die bibel.
>
> Aber die homerische frage is populär. Das interesse dafür hat sich verschoben, aber interesse dafür is vorhanden. Der 'gebildete' fühlt sich verbunden in der einen oder andern weise dazu stellung zu nehmen.'[34]

The Homeric debate had taken on a life of its own that overwhelmed the poetry. For the sake of scoring points against opponents, it had become scholarly practice to disparage the ancient epics themselves. The ghost of Wolf must have wept at the sight.

In England strong sentiment in favor of some kind of unitary Homer continued, but the attitude was generally regarded as one of sentiment. W. Leaf (1852–1927), the most influential late-century English commentator, could on the one hand speak of 'the magical power which the poem [the *Iliad*] has held over the mind of man from the very earliest days,' but at the same time insist that upon close examination of the epic 'we find ourselves face to face with various matters which make us pause and think that they are not such as we should expect to find in the work of a poet composing a long poem with his mind fixed throughout on the subject as a single whole.'[35] Leaf even contended that the late additions to the poems, the work of the interpolators, was the place where 'we find as a rule most of the passages of noble pathos which sink deepest into our hearts.'[36] There were also parts of the *Iliad* that Leaf asserted 'might be absent without any great loss.'[37] Leaf went so far as to confess, 'To try to keep one level of interest in the *Iliad* from beginning to end is to most readers a disheartening task, which ends only in their fancying that they have not the power of poetic appreciation.'[38] For Leaf the problem was not the lack of poetic power on the part of the composers of the epic but the conditions under which they had worked.

---

[34] Wilamowitz (1881) 381.
[35] Leaf (1892) 18, 23.
[36] Leaf (1892) 27.
[37] Leaf (1892) 28.
[38] Leaf (1892) 28.

Yet it was not philology alone that recast both the criticism of the poems and the dimensions of the Homeric Question in the second half of the century. No less important was the work of archaeologists, and most famously, Heinrich Schliemann (1822–1890). From his own day to the present controversy has swirled over this merchant turned self-advertising archaeologist.[39] The exploits of Schliemann touched the Homeric question in at least three ways. First, he was himself a thoroughgoing unitarian who trusted Homer to guide him to the location of Troy. His unitarian faith had appeared to be rewarded and thus gave courage to other unitarians who were themselves often readers outside the various university systems and the philological profession.

Second, Schliemann's excavations at Troy and Mycenae set the recitation of the poems into a new context. Gone were the happy ancient volkpoets who had composed the ancient lays of Lachmann and his followers. Their replacements were courtly bards who sang their songs to royalty in a rich setting. By the end of the century, in the words of Leaf, it had become widely believed that the epics were 'essentially and above all court poems.'[40] As Leaf explained, 'They were composed to be sung in the splendid palaces of a ruling aristocracy, and the commonalty have no part or lot as actors in them.... This is the first point which must be clearly grasped by those who would enter into the spirit of Homer: that the poems are aristocratic and courtly, not popular.'[41] Without ever admitting the fact, the late-century commentators had made the composition of the Homeric epics whether by a single poet or by several rather resemble Virgil's composition of the *Aeneid* for a court and a strong emperor. This new setting for the origin of the poems also made them the product of a civilized rather than a primitive age, a civilized age that had been brought to an end by the Dorian invasions.

Third, Schliemann's excavations moved some of the discussion of the Homeric Question from the world of philology to the examination of artifacts. Arguments focused on shields and swords. Reverting to the praise of Homeric topographical and social realism voiced by Robert Wood over a century earlier, Leaf asserted:

> It must not be forgotten that the world of Homer is a real world, not a world of fancy. This is evident in every line. The surroundings among

[39] For the most critical recent biography, see Traill (1995).
[40] Leaf (1892) 2.
[41] Leaf (1892) 2–3.

> which the heroes move are as vivid and real as the heroes themselves; and they are as different as possible from the surroundings of poets composing in Ionia. It is not as if we were transported into a mere realm of fairyland, where the poet could imagine and impose upon us such scenery as he thought fit. Wherever we can test the actualities of the poem we find that they are at all events possible, and in many points they coincide in a surprising way with the results which recent discoveries have shown us.[42]

Still again the ancient poetry lay submerged in the wake of nineteenth-century science. Among scholars who were bedazzled by the archaeological, there was a tendency to become so concerned with the implements of everyday life and warfare as to verge on triviality. This is particularly clear in the work of A. Lang (1844–1912), who filled his volumes with pictures of discoveries intended to prove his argument for a unitary Homer or for at least no more than two ancient authors of the epics.[43] The emphasis on the everyday in ancient life also worked to separate the world of Homer from anything that might seem relevant to the life of a modern reader.

The involvement of archaeology and later of anthropology in the Homeric Question toward the close of the century was simply the last of the modern intellectual movements and enthusiasms that had originated and shaped the Homeric Question and given it a vibrancy and relevance unavailable through literary concerns alone. Wolf's original critics had been correct that his ideas where not wholly original, but the cultural climate of the century after he published imparted new importance and ramifications to them. And those ramifications had much to do with the significance and passions which Victorians across the Western world linked to both the Homeric Question and the Homeric poems. As the redoubtable J. S. Blackie of the University of Edinburgh declared in 1866:

> If the Wolfian theory with regard to the origin and composition of the Homeric poems be looked at beyond the surface, it will be found to underlie a great number of the most important literary, historical, and theological questions that stir the mind of England at the present hour.[44]

Those comments applied to Europe at large as well as the intellectual life of the British isles.

---

[42] Leaf (1892) 11–12.
[43] Lang (1893; 1919).
[44] Blackie (1866) I:184.

The Homeric Question was the child of philology. By the middle of the century philology had become one of the most powerful and all-embracing humanistic sciences.[45] Philologists were actively involved in the establishment of national literatures which might or might not have had a genuinely long existence, and by implication with the process of modern nation-building. They were using their scientific analysis to raise the most serious questions about the composition and veracity of the Bible. Philological theory seemed capable of addressing itself to human beings in all locations and conditions. Philology was literally reshaping the way learned Europeans and Americans were thinking about themselves in the past and the present. Indeed philology was to the cultural life of the mid-nineteenth century what structuralism and post-structuralism were in the late twentieth century. It was an intellectual tool that undertook the criticism (and often the destructive criticism) of the political, religious, and cultural status quo. Classical scholars from Wolf onward were by profession associated with philology, but they also realized that the more they tied their writings to that powerful intellectual impulse, the more influence they could exert within their universities and cultures.

The Homeric Question from the time of Wolf onward also manifested the growing controversy and tension within the literary world between the artist and the critic. The critics—whether philologists, historians, or literary commentators—had by the middle of the century established their dominance over the ancient poems themselves. Throughout the learned academic circles of Europe it was the criticism of Homer, rather than the power and content of the poems, that commanded attention and made academic careers. Furthermore, the critics, using the term in its broadest sense, had managed to dissolve what the eighteenth century commentators had regarded as the genius of Homer. One can only wonder how this destruction of the ancient epic artist affected in Germany the agenda of a Richard Wagner who during the 1850s was as a single author writing his epic *Ring of the Niebelung* and proclaiming it a 'total work of art.' In that regard Wagner represented a modern besting the ancients. It was to be a modern embodying the romantic concept of genius who would produce a masterpiece to be sung on a series of evenings. It was also to be a masterpiece that bespoke the Middle Ages and

[45] It is difficult to grasp the intellectual authority and power assigned to nineteenth-century philology. See 'Philology,' *Encyclopaedia Britannica*, Eleventh Edition.

Germany. In this respect the destruction of the unitary Homer undermined the cultural authority not only of the ancient epics but also of the universal values that had traditionally been associated with ancient Greece whether in the Archaic or Classical period of its history.

The final large cultural element that rendered the Homeric Question such a lively area of controversy was its relationship to the Bible. Wolf's *Prolegomena* had emerged from his earlier training at Göttingen University, where Heyne had already been applying philological methods to the analysis of the Bible. In the *Prolegomena* Wolf had seen parallels between a disparate authorship for the *Iliad* and the disparate authorship of the Hebrew Bible. He also saw similarities between the stories of Homeric composition and transmission and those relating to the Hebrew Bible. Except for the early Germans, most attention to Homer and the Bible tended during the first three quarters of the century to inhibit the critical discussion of the latter. Whatever affected the credibility of Homer might be seen as affecting the credibility of the Bible.

In this respect, the mid-century English discussion of Homer always took place in a somewhat different cultural arena than did the German. The English had seen almost from the beginning of the debate in Germany that the question of Homeric composition could influence the understanding of the composition of the Bible. Grote's analysis made English Christians all the more sure of that. Grote was a philosophic radical, associated with the political circles of Jeremy Bentham, James Mill, and John Stuart Mill. He and his companions were known to be skeptical about Christianity, though they were always very circumspect in what they wrote and said. Grote's discussion of Homer firmly established in the English mind an association between the higher criticism of Homer and the higher criticism of the Bible. First, if the narrative historical content of the Greek epics stood in doubt as Grote argued it did, so might the historical character of the Biblical narratives. There was a clear parallel between Grote's view of ancient myths as representing the mind of a particular age and the analysis of biblical myth by D. F. Strauss.

In England at least, the key cultural association of the Homeric Question was the fear that any critical analysis of Homer would spill over to the critical approach to the Bible. As E. B. Pusey, the great Tractarian leader and Oxford Professor of Hebrew, declared in 1854: 'The skepticism as to Homer ushered in the skepticism on the Old

Testament.'[46] In that he was later joined by T. H. Huxley who observed that Homeric criticism manifested the scientific spirit examining the previously unexamined idols of the day.[47] Repeatedly in England writers returned to the apprehension that Wolf himself had voiced that his analysis of Homer would be seen to resemble those who thought the universe had been created by chance and with no clear purpose. As Elizabeth Barrett Browning wrote in *Aura Leigh*:

> Wolf's an atheist
> And if the *Iliad* fell out, as he says,
> By mere fortuitous concourse of the old songs,
> We'd guess as much, too, for the universe.[48]

Such comments fulfilled Wolf's apprehension that his literary criticism would be detrimentally associated with a nontheistic or at least nonteleological vision of physical nature.

Wilamowitz was the scholar who as a relatively young man clearly and openly linked Homeric and biblical criticism in his *Homerische Untersuchungen*. He dedicated this work to his teacher J. Wellhausen, who was one of the most distinguished and advanced of German biblical scholars. In his preface he declared:

> Die analyse der homerischen gedichte is zunächst wie die des pentateuchs lediglich eine aufgabe philologisher kritik. Bibel und Homer müssen zudem zunächst allein aus sich heraus verstanden und analysirt werden, und selbst die art ihrer überlieferung, die textgeschichte, fordert die parallelisirung heraus.[49]

Wilamowitz believed such analysis would not only illuminate the textual debates but would also expand the knowledge of the history of both the Greeks and the Hebrews. He regarded the Bible and Homer as 'die beiden wurzeln aller unserer geistigen bildung.'[50] Such an evaluation was a two edged sword. Wilamowitz, as already noted, used philology to discredit the poetic value of the Homeric epics. The same philology could be seen undermining the spiritual authority of scripture. Indeed there would continue to be a parallel between the attack on the quality of Homer's poetry and on the veracity and

---

[46] E. B. Pusey, *Collegiate and Professorial Teaching and Discipline in Answer to Professor Vaughn's Strictures* (Oxford and London, 1854) 62.
[47] T. H. Huxley, *Collected Essays*, 9 vols. (New York, 1895) V:32–33.
[48] E. B. Browning, *Aurora Leigh* (London, 1847), Book V.
[49] Wilamowitz (1881) iii.
[50] Wilamowitz (1881) iv.

spiritual quality of the Bible. Poets would continue to value Homer, and believing Christians, the Bible. But in the world of scholarship both Homer and the Bible became objects of naturalistic analysis. The touch of cold philology disenchanted both worlds.

Among some commentators the influence of biblical scholarship also influenced the reading and interpretation of Homer. Perhaps the best known example of biblical scholarship working in this manner was G. Murray's *The Rise of the Greek Epic* (1907). Murray (1866–1957) contended that the Homeric epics like the Bible and other works such as the *Song and Roland* and the *Niebelungenlied* were traditional books. Such works had developed over time and were not the product of a single mind or author. In associating Homer with traditional books, Murray was drawing upon the work of William Robertson Smith and S. R. Driver on the Pentateuch. Smith and Driver contended that the Pentateuch was a book that had developed over time and reflected the effort to make it conform over time to monotheism. The books displayed signs of polytheism and of efforts to remove that polytheism. Murray argued that the Homeric poems displayed a similar expurgatory development. Murray posited the presence of a body of ancient verse, now lost, but originally containing much morally repugnant material that over the course of time and through a series of editings had come to constitute the Homeric epics. The unknown editors embodied what Murray termed the 'Homeric Spirit.'[51] In particular, these editors had removed evidence of homosexual practices. The editors had also purged elements of earlier chthonic religion and presented the Olympian religion in all of its glory. The work of the Homeric Spirit allowed Murray to give the poems a new value. He had surrendered the idea of a unitary Homer and the historical reality of the Trojan War, but the *Iliad* and the *Odyssey* could still stand as monuments to the achievement of civilized humanity in the West. In this respect the poems came to represent models of humanistic achievement that might substitute to some extent for the biblical faith that stood so fully under siege.

The Homeric Question represents one of the first great topics of modern humanistic scholarship to generate long-standing, career-making quarrels in the European academy. The nineteenth-century Homeric Question stands as one of the major examples of the professionalization of scholarship encroaching upon a subject that had

[51] G. Murray (1907) 116.

once been addressed by amateurs from a variety of fields. To be sure, many nineteenth-century commentators remained amateur Classicists: Grote and Leaf made careers at banking, and Schliemann at commerce. But the fundamental thrust of classical scholarship was toward the professionalism growing out of the German universities. With the exception of Grote and Leaf, virtually all the major voices addressing the Homeric Question did so from university posts. By the time that Milman Parry transformed the grounds of debate over Homer, both classics and classical scholarship had become limited almost entirely to the university world. The twentieth century would witness remarkable new work on Homer and the issues debated by nineteenth-century scholars. What would, however, be missing would be the links between the classics and public life that existed in the Victorian age. At the same time, paradoxically, the expansion of the university population in the twentieth century and the appearance of new translations have meant that more people have read Homer than at any other time in human history. Perhaps to the chagrin of the scholarly world, no doubt most of the twentieth-century readers of Homer rarely or never contemplated the issues of composition that so shook the philological minds of the previous century.

John Miles Foley

ORAL TRADITION AND ITS IMPLICATIONS

This chapter focuses on the modern rediscovery of ancient Greek oral tradition and its implications for the study of Homeric epic. It will thus be concerned not only with the demonstration of the poems' oral traditional nature—an interesting and important phenomenon in itself—but more fundamentally with the question 'So what?' If Homeric verse emerges from an unwritten art of poetry and is committed to text only quite late in its development, how does this cultural, historical, and technological circumstance affect the way we read the *Iliad* and *Odyssey*? The discussion will consist of four sections: (I) a brief history of the early research conducted by Milman Parry and Albert Lord; (II) a sketch of the most prominent features of the so-called Oral Theory; (III) significant replies to and revisions in the Theory; and (IV) the implications of oral tradition for Homer's art.[1]

The Modern Rediscovery of an Ancient Technique

When the American classicist Milman Parry came on the scene in the mid-1920s, the Homeric Question had two basic answers, neither of them definitive. One faction, much the stronger and better organized, argued for what amounted to many Homers: these Analysts treated the *Iliad* and *Odyssey* as a kind of archaeological dig, searching for textual strata of different authorship and assuming a

[1] I limit my remarks primarily to the Oral Theory (also called the Oral-Formulaic Theory), which was developed in Homeric studies and which, with the spread of this approach to more than 100 language areas, has become much more than theoretical. In doing so let me also note the important contributions of E. Havelock (esp. 1963 and 1986), W. Ong (esp. 1982), and others who have treated the 'oral culture' of ancient Greece. Since an exhaustive bibliography and history of Oral Theory already exists elsewhere (see respectively J. M. Foley (1985), with updates in the journal *Oral Tradition*, and Foley (1988), rpt. 1992; J. Foley, ed., *Teaching Oral Traditions* (New York, Modern Language Association, forthcoming), the first section will be relatively brief. See especially M. W. Edwards's three-part essay on 'Homer and Oral Tradition' (1986b; 1988; 1992).

master editor who joined the originally separate pieces together into coherent wholes. On the other side stood the Unitarians, who maintained a firm faith in a single gifted individual solely responsible for creating both poems. While one school utilized apparent discrepancies in language and narrative logic to map the edges of supposed 'tectonic plates' in the extant poems, the other submerged such minor infelicities in a theory of unitary authorship and composition.

Parry's great achievement was to offer a third alternative that rationalized the disparate evidence presented by both factions and moved the discussion to a new level. That alternative was the hypothesis of a Homeric oral tradition, a generations-old technique of verse-making that was the collective inheritance of many singer-poets, or *aoidoi*, in ancient Greece. The poems as we have them, he reasoned, were neither the pastiches of the Analysts nor the modern, free-standing products envisioned by the Unitarians; rather they represented the culmination of a process that brought the stories from probable roots in the Mycenaean period through the textless Dark Age to their eventual recording. Their most important vehicle was neither tablet nor papyrus, he contended, but the spoken word.

Parry began his research by ascribing the Homeric poems to a *tradition*, an important emphasis to which we will return below. That is, his first approximation, as presented in the 1925 M.A. thesis and the two doctoral theses of 1928,[2] contained no mention of the 'oral' term in the equation, but concentrated exclusively on establishing the inherited compositional technique behind the *Iliad* and *Odyssey*. Basing his conception of the poems' pre-textual origin and dynamics on a meticulous study of the texts, Parry demonstrated the systematic nature of much of the diction, pointing out the degree to which Homer (and now his tradition) depended on familiar, repetitive phrases such as 'much-suffering divine Odysseus,' 'swift-footed Achilles,' or 'gray-eyed Athena.' Such phrases he called *formulas*, defining this unit of phraseology as 'an expression regularly used, under the same metrical conditions, to express an essential idea.'[3] Formulas—understood as 'chunks' of language—recurred because they were useful to the composing poet, because they were part of his poetic tradition.

---

[2] 'A Comparative Study of Diction as One of the Elements of Style in Early Greek Epic Poetry,' M.A. thesis (University of California, Berkeley), 1925, first published in Parry (1971) 421–36; 'The Traditional Epithet in Homer' and 'Homeric Formulae and Homeric Metre,' tr. by A. Parry, op. cit. 1–190 and 191–239.

[3] In 'The Traditional Epithet in Homer' (1971) 13.

Eventually Parry would posit a companion structure, the 'formulaic system,' to accommodate those families of phrases with both a constant and a variable element, a flexible pattern that could fit varying situations.[4]

The concept of a formulaic language as the medium for a continuous poetic tradition did not spring full-grown from Parry's head. His ideas emerged in the dual context of linguistics, especially German philology,[5] and contemporary anthropology. From the linguists he drew his conclusions on the interdependence of meter and phraseology, a mainstay of what was to become the Oral Theory, as well as an initial impression of what that interdependence meant for the history and development of the specialized dialect of language used by Homer and his predecessors. What Parry accomplished in the 1925 and 1928 theses, in turn, was a revolutionary expansion of a few philological insights into a sustained and coherent explanation of poetic composition, thereby dissolving the impasse of Analyst versus Unitarian and bringing to the forefront the contribution of a long-standing method of composition. While not yet glimpsing the 'necessity' that this poetic tradition also be *oral*, he had already begun to unlock the secret of Homer's repetitive, recursive style.

The next step in the process of rediscovery was to move from the study to the field, from the library of texts to the living laboratory of oral traditional performances. Pivotal in this regard was Parry's mentor for the 1928 doctoral theses, Antoine Meillet, whom Parry credits with leading him 'to see, dimly at first, that a true understanding of the Homeric poems could only come with a full understanding of the nature of oral poetry.'[6] Meillet also arranged for Matija Murko, a Slovenian philologist who spent his summers doing field research on oral epic in the former Yugoslavia, to be present at the thesis defense. This experience was to prove formative for the young classicist, who would soon acknowledge that 'it was the writings of Professor Murko more than those of any other which in the following years led me to the study of oral poetry in itself and to the heroic poems of the South Slavs.'[7]

---

[4] See 'Studies in the Epic Technique of Oral Verse-Making. I. Homer and Homeric Style,' *Harvard Studies in Classical Philology* 41 (1930): 73–147; rpt. in Parry (1971), 266–324, esp. 272–79.

[5] On the substantial contributions of J.-E. Ellendt, Heinrich Düntzer, and Kurt Witte, see Foley (1988), 6–10.

[6] 'Ćor Huso: A Study of Southslavic Song,' in Parry (1971) 439.

[7] Parry (1971) 439. See M. Murko, 'The Singers and Their Epic Songs,' trans.

Before the great adventure of fieldwork could begin, however, Parry had first to follow out the implications of his doctoral work for Homer, and this he did in a pair of seminal essays published in 1930 and 1932 under the joint title 'Studies in the Epic Technique of Oral Verse-Making.'[8] The former forged a crucial link between tradition and orality in Homer, explaining the ready-made diction, the formulaic language, as a response to the continuous pressure of composition in performance. The poets used traditional phraseology, so went the argument, because it served a pressing need; beyond any other concern, it was first and foremost a useful instrument. The companion essay, less influential at the time but of major importance later for both ancient Greek and many other traditions, described the multidialectal language of Homer as symptomatic of traditional oral style. The variety of forms that marked the language of the *Iliad* and *Odyssey* as an artificial dialect or *Kunstsprache*—spoken by no single individual in any one place at any one time for any conventional, everyday purpose—could be accounted for, Parry maintained, by remembering the special dynamics of traditional composition. Thus Homeric vocabulary and morphology were dependent not on what was current in the spoken language of any given time or place, but on what had entered this special poetic dialect over many centuries under the aegis of the hexameter.[9] In these two essays the traditional process of verse-making is reconceived as driven by the challenge of oral composition in performance.

It was to test this set of hypotheses, all developed exclusively through close study of texts, that Parry and his assistant Albert Lord embarked on their collecting expeditions to the former Yugoslavia in 1933–35. Their reasoning was straightforward; if the conclusions drawn about the phenomenon of Homer's formulaic language were correct, then a living oral poetry should reveal the same principles at work:

---

by J. M. Foley, *Oral Tradition* 5 (1990) 107–30. Cf. also the influence of other ethnographers, as detailed in J. M. Foley (1988) 10–18. Especially important was W. Radloff, who conducted extensive fieldwork on central Asian epic; see his 'Preface to *The Dialect of the Kara-Kirgiz*,' tr. by G. B. Sherman with A. B. Davis, *Oral Tradition* 5 (1990) 73–90.

[8] Parry, 'Studies II' (1971) 325–64.

[9] Cf. the nature of Homeric armament as an achronological mixture of artifacts from different periods that could appear as a single ensemble only within the traditional compass of the epic poems, as pointed out quite early by Lorimer (1950) esp. 452–54. Cf. also the similarly specialized language of South Slavic traditional oral epic, which, even in the present political situation, contains Serbian and Croatian as well as archaic and modern elements alongside one another.

preliterate singers who composed their epic songs using a similar kind of traditional phraseology. The engaging story of their novel foray into South Slavic epic tradition—complete with a specially constructed recording apparatus, their native assistant Nikola Vujnović (who was himself a singer or *guslar*), and the enormous cache of recorded epic performances that began the Parry Collection of Oral Literature at Harvard University—is told in detail elsewhere.[10] For the present purpose it is enough to say that their efforts produced an archive unmatched anywhere in the world, with more than sufficient evidence to establish what they had set out to do: to show that the South Slavic oral poets employed a formulaic language in many ways parallel to the language of the *Iliad* and *Odyssey*. At this level, at least, Parry's textual hypothesis seemed to have been confirmed by a brilliant and unprecedented experiment in the laboratory of South Slavic oral epic.

Parry was not to live to carry out his plans for an extended comparison of the two poetries; that task fell to Lord, who would wholly redefine the nature and goals of the inquiry. Not only did his *The Singer of Tales*[11] expand the comparative investigation to medieval English, medieval French, and Byzantine Greek, pointing the way toward an interdisciplinary approach that would eventually touch on scores of areas, but it also offered a close-range view of a living oral tradition. Alongside examples of formulaic language drawn from the heroic songs (*junačke pjesme*) of the South Slavs, he located and described other traditional units: the recurrent typical scene or 'theme' and the yet larger 'story-pattern' that underlay entire epics.[12] In addition, he provided a detailed description of the apprenticeship of the singer, from the time the young boy first becomes interested in performance through his mature appropriation of the craft. This degree of concentration on the South Slavic analogue *per se* went far beyond what Parry had planned, and it played a significant role in the overall development of the Oral Theory. Together with the gradual publication of the recorded performances in the series *Serbo-Croatian Heroic Songs* (from 1953 onward; hereafter, *SCHS*) and his many other writings,[13] Lord brought both a widening of the comparative dimen-

---

[10] See 'General Introduction' by Lord, in *SCHS* I, 3–20; also Foley (1988) 31–34.
[11] Cambridge, Mass., 1960; rpt. New York, 1968 et seq.
[12] On the theme, see Lord (1960) 68–98; on story-pattern, 99–123 and 'The Theme of the Withdrawn Hero in Serbo-Croatian Oral Epic,' *Prilozi za književnost, jezik, istoriju i folklor* 35 (1969) 18–30. Examples of both units are cited below in section II.
[13] See esp. (1991).

sion and a more precise focus on the South Slavic singers and their songs as parallels to Homer and 'his' songs.

One manifestation of this shift in emphasis was Lord's long-term attention to Avdo Medjedović, most Homeric of South Slavic singers, and his dictated masterpiece, *The Wedding of Smailagić Meho*, together perhaps the most direct argument for the analogy between ancient Greek *aoidos* and contemporary *guslar*.[14] At 12,311 lines, or about the length of the *Odyssey*, this elaborate tale rehearses a narrative sequence well known to the epic tradition—a young man's coming of age, a summons to marriage, an epochal battle, and denouement in a wedding that unites ruling families. And yet it far outstrips, not just in length but also in fullness and artistry, typical performances by Avdo's peers. Here was living proof, Lord reasoned, that traditional oral epic could reach Homeric proportions in the hands of a talented singer, proof that the inherited and shared compositional style could yield a poem of imposing size and rewarding depth.[15] In cognate fashion, this research cleared the way for serious consideration of the ever-increasing array of witnesses from the world's oral traditions, both living and text-based. Before two decades had elapsed, the Oral Theory would affect more than one hundred language areas as disparate as Chinese, African, Australian, and Native American.[16] As we shall see below, this welcome enrichment of the sample from which analogies are drawn has both led to new insights into Homeric epic and called into question the easy generalizations that characterized earlier comparative work. That is to say, Lord's work has fostered a second growth in our understanding of Homer as an oral traditional poet.

The Singer's 'Words' and the Scholar's Theory

Let us begin this brief sketch of Oral Theory by soliciting the opinion not of a classical philologist or an anthropologist but of an actual practitioner of the craft: a South Slavic *guslar*. In response to questions

[14] Lord, in *SCHS* vols. 3 and 4.
[15] As we shall see below in section III, the issue of artistic quality has often been ignored or deflected by adherents of Oral Theory. See further section IV on the contribution of 'traditional referentiality' to Homeric art.
[16] For examples, see Foley (1985).

posed by Parry and Lord's assistant Nikola, singers often offered comments such as those of Mujo Kukuruzović on an issue as fundamental as the identity of a 'word' (or *reč*):[17]

Nikola: Let's consider this: 'Vino pije lički Mustajbeže' ['Mustajbeg of the Lika was drinking wine']. Is this a single *reč*?
Mujo: Yes.
Nikola: But how? It can't be *one*: 'Vino-pije-lički-Mustajbeže.'
Mujo: In writing it can't be one.
Nikola: There are four *reči* here.
Mujo: It can't be one in writing. But here, let's say we're at my house and I pick up the *gusle* [accompanying instrument]—'Pije vino lički Mustajbeže'—that's a single *reč* on the *gusle* for me.
Nikola: And the second *reč*?
Mujo: And the second *reč*—'Na Ribniku u pjanoj mehani' ['At Ribnik in a drinking tavern']—there.

For Mujo Kukuruzović and his colleagues a 'word' was obviously a unit of utterance rather than typography. Instead of construing the 'atom' of linguistic expression as something visually defined by white space or lexically isolated in a dictionary, as is the case with these words you are presently reading, they prescribed a whole decasyllabic line of verse as the smallest *reč*, the smallest meaningful unit of utterance. Anything less was a partial word, an unmeaningful subdivision that might pass muster in writing but is irrelevant in the idiom of oral tradition. Consider an analogy: a speaker of contemporary English who is asked to subdivide the common noun 'boat' will inevitably discover that the phonemes [b], [o], and [t] prove to be atoms of sound but not of sense. Just as with Kukuruzović's word, it is possible to fragment this unit beyond its ability to mean. Further probing by Nikola established other possible interpretations of *reč* as a group of lines, a speech, a scene, or even a whole poem. The important point is that this notion of 'word'—whatever the actual size of the increment—insists upon its compositional reality and function. Like the Homeric *epos* and Anglo-Saxon *word*,[18] South Slavic *reč* names the various kinds of expressive units that actually constitute the epics.

With this insight from the singers in mind, we can then define a formula in their terms as a 'phraseological word,' a unit of utterance

[17] Quoted from Parry Collection conversation *6619*, my trans. For related comments, see, e.g., the report on a similar conversation with the *guslar* Ibro Bašić in Foley (1990) 44–45.
[18] See Foley (1990) 137–55 (*epos*) and 219, 223 (*word*).

at the level of diction. Parry's noun-epithet formulas, such as πολύτλας δῖος Ὀδυσσεύς ('much-suffering divine Odysseus') are customarily invariable, with their intelligibility dependent on that absolute regularity. Such unitary words combine with other phrases to constitute a whole hexameter line, as in the following example cited by Parry:[19]

αὐτὰρ ὁ μερμήριξε (1)	
αὐτὰρ ὁ βῆ διὰ δῶμα (1)	
αὐτὰρ ἐπεὶ τό γ' ἄκουσε (1)	πολύτλας δῖος Ὀδυσσεύς
τὸν δ' αὖτε προσέειπε (8)	
ἔνθα καθέζετ' ἔπειτα (1)	

But [he] pondered	
But [he] went through the house	
But when [he] heard it	much-suffering divine Odysseus
And in turn [he] addressed him	
Then [he] sat down there	

A variety of actions can thus be matched to a single character, who is consistently named whether he is pondering, going through the house, hearing something, addressing someone, or sitting down. The matching process works because the noun-epithet formula is metrically suitable for combination with the various verb phrases; together they make a whole line. When one multiplies this expressive variety by the hundreds of noun-epithet 'words' for people and divinities in the *Iliad* and *Odyssey*, it is easy to see how the formulaic method provided Homer and his tradition a ready and generative means of composing in performance.

Of course, not all of the phraseology could be as invariant as the noun-epithet formulas, a fact that Parry realized as he moved from his 1928 theses to the 1930 essay on Homeric style. To cover the greater flexibility of much of the diction, he postulated the existence of 'formulaic systems,' which amount to singers' 'words' with rule-governed variability or substitution. Instead of occurring in precisely the same form each time, they could modulate to fit the situation, as in the family of phraseology cited below:[20]

[19] Parry (1971) 11.
[20] Parry (1971) 276 (selections).

αὐτὰρ ἐπεὶ
- < δείπνησε (2)
- < κατέπαυσα (1)
- < τάρπησαν (3)
- < ῥ'
  - < ἕσσαντο (3)
  - εὔξαντο (4)
  - < ἵκοντο (3)
  - < ἐνέηκε (1)

But when
- < he or she took a meal
- < I ended
- < they enjoyed
- < [and so]
  - < they clothed themselves
  - they prayed
  - < they reached
  - < he or she sent into

This group of related formulas could be labeled the 'But when X' family, where X stands for the action of the verb. Some of them also include the 'and so' particle in ancient Greek (full enclitic form ῥά), introduced as a phonological bridge between 'when' (*epei*) and those verbs beginning with a vowel or diphthong.[21] This formulaic system—and many others constructed similarly—can then participate in line-building with the comprehensive array of noun-epithet formulas, giving the poet myriad possibilities for matching characters and actions. Nor does this kind of subject-predicate template exhaust the compositional potential of formulaic language: numerous other sorts of combinations, some verbatim and some variable within limits, can and do occur as the singer makes his *epea* or 'words.'[22]

At another level Homer and his tradition use 'themes' or 'narrative words' to build the singular poem from traditional materials. In this case the words amount to whole scenes, familiar in their general outline and content but also plastic enough to be molded to accord with the immediate context. Thus the Feast scene[23] so prevalent in the *Odyssey* will always follow a preliminary anointment and seating of the guest(s), and will always consist of a maidservant bringing water

---

[21] This kind of phonological bridge is very common in South Slavic epic; see Foley (1990) 90–91.

[22] I limit examples of formulaic language to these two groups of phrases; see Russo's essay in this volume for a more detailed treatment. For a history of scholarship on the formula in Homer, see Edwards (1986, 1988).

[23] For a full discussion of this typical scene, see Foley (1990) 265–76.

for washing, a table being placed before guest(s) and hosts, a housekeeper providing bread and other foodstuffs, and a carver passing out meat and golden cups. Likewise, after the elaborate preparatory description is finished, the Feast's consummation will dependably be marked by two formulaic lines:

> They put their hands to the good things that lay ready before them.
> But when they had put away their desire for eating and drinking....

These signals mark the passage as a known quantity, furnishing evidence that the Feast 'word' is an established entry in Homer's traditional lexicon. At the same time, however, the suitors' noisy arrogance in Book 1 makes the breaking of bread an uncomfortable compromise for Telemachos and his guest Mentes (Athena in disguise). No such anxiety pervades the occurrence of this typical scene in Book 4, where Telemachos can only wonder at the sumptuousness of Menelaos' reception; the 'word' spoken here is fundamentally the same, and yet different. Still another combination of traditional and situation-specific characterizes Circe's proffered meal in Book 10, a meal that Odysseus stubbornly refuses until she changes his men back from swine. As these and other instances make clear, the Feast *epos* allows the poet both a standard, recognizable set of descriptive details and a latitude in suiting the 'word' to any one particular context.

Such typical scenes abound in Homeric epic, as in the South Slavic analogue that Lord first used to establish their tectonic importance.[24] M. Edwards's major categories for narrative *epea* in the *Iliad* and *Odyssey* include Battle, Social Intercourse, Travel, Ritual, and Speeches and Deliberation, with the second of these broken down into Hospitality in General (with six sub-types); Messengers; Dreams; Divine Visit; Conference, Conversation, and Greeting; Assembly and Dis-

[24] Lord defines 'themes' as 'groups of ideas regularly used in telling a tale in the formulaic style of traditional song' (1960, 68). The concept may be traced to Arend (1933) and Parry's review of Arend, 'On Typical Scenes in Homer,' *Classical Philology* 31 (1936) 357–60; rpt. in Parry (1971) 404–407. Examples from South Slavic include the ubiquitous 'Shouting in Prison' theme, in which the incarcerated hero laments so loudly that a bargain is struck for his release, and the 'Letter-writing' theme, in which a tsar or beg transmits a series of invitations to battle, his child's wedding, or both. Especially prominent in Old English are the 'Beasts of Battle,' who devour the carrion after a fight, and the 'Exile' theme, which uses the conventional imagery of winter to reflect a state of mind or a shifting social context. On these and other examples, see Foley (1990) 278–328 (South Slavic) and 329–58 (Old English).

missal; Supplication; Dressing and Adornment; and Allurement and Seduction.[25] Furthermore, like smaller 'words,' themes can exhibit considerable variety and plasticity. Not only are some larger and more complex than others, but all of them can be fleshed out to varying degrees, affording the poet a substantial degree of freedom in suiting the ready-made increment to the particular narrative purpose. And just as multiple combinations of formulas and formulaic systems make for virtually innumerable possibilities in the diction, so multiple arrangements of variable themes make for enormous narrative resources. Although the lexicon may have finite limits, as does any linguistic instrument, the poet's available 'words' are rich in expressive potential.

The largest-scale *reč* or *epos* in Oral Theory—the story-pattern—is perhaps best illustrated by paraphrasing an extremely common tale from the South Slavic epic tradition.[26] The story opens with an imprisoned hero, a miserable fellow whom we later learn was summoned to a faraway war on or near the eve of his engagement or marriage (or its consummation), or soon after the conception of a son. He cries out so loudly and unceasingly from captivity that, through the agency of a powerful female, he gains release and begins the often arduous trek home. After certain adventures he reaches his own community, only to find his fiancée or wife pursued by unwanted suitors, his property under siege, and his son (if he has one) despairing. As yet unrecognized because of his 'disguise' as a long-incarcerated prisoner, the hero goes about testing the fidelity of his son, his relatives, his servants, and finally his wife, meanwhile defeating the usurping suitors in what is usually the ritual combat of athletic competition but can evolve into something more deadly. If the wife proves faithful, all is well and the story comes to an end, with the marriage fulfilled or resumed, the son reassured of his patrimony, and order restored.[27] One might add that it is not unknown for the

[25] M. W. Edwards (1992). Also recommended are the discussions of 'Type-Scenes and Expansion' and 'Battle Scenes,' 71–77 and 78–81 in M. W. Edwards (1987) and, for an example of type-scene analysis at close range, Reece (1993).

[26] It should be noted that the story-pattern is the least studied of the three levels of 'words' in Oral Theory. For definitions and morphology, see note 12 above and Foley (1990) 359–87. For story-patterns in the *Odyssey*, cf. Powell (1977).

[27] If the wife proves unfaithful (a possibility that, while less common, is always in the cards), the song continues in a sequel that features the hero's initial defection to the enemy before all is finally set right. See further Foley (1990) 369–86.

hero to be marked by a scar (*beleg*) on his leg or for his wife to be glimpsed weaving.

Of course we recognize the story of the *Odyssey* from Homeric tradition, but what may come as a surprise is the fact that there exist literally hundreds of recorded versions of this Return Song narrative in South Slavic, many of them collected by Parry and Lord, and many more in areas as widely dispersed in space and time as medieval England, nineteenth-century Russia, Albania, Bulgaria, Turkey, and central Asia.[28] According to Lord's schema, the Return Song or *nostos* conventionally begins with the hero's Absence, which prescribes Devastation for himself in captivity and for his loved ones left behind. After some negotiation he accomplishes a Return, followed by Retribution exacted against his challengers and a Wedding (or re-wedding) with the Penelope figure. In symbolic terms the 'map' for such stories is

$$A > D > R > Rt > W$$

This pattern is quite flexible enough to accommodate such features as paired or substitute heroes, the presence or lack of a son, complications on the journey homeward, various kinds of interactions with the suitors, and differing outcomes to the hero's tests for fidelity. This largest of 'words' exhibits, in short, the same kind of variation within limits and the same opportunities for individual manipulation of traditional patterns as do formulas and themes. Proceeding by analogy, we can see that it is along this variable superstructure that Homer's tale of Odysseus is told.

A few additional points deserve mention before leaving this sketch of Oral Theory. A corollary measurement, the quantitative density of formulaic language, was at one time considered a litmus test for distinguishing 'oral' from 'literary' poems, and was applied widely to Homer and numerous other areas. Now largely discarded, this kind of measurement assumed the paramount feature of formulaic phraseology to be its utility to the orally composing poet, an overemphasis that long obscured artistic concerns. Utility also lay behind what Parry identified as 'thrift' in Homeric epic, that is, 'the degree in which [a formula type or system] is free of phrases which, having the same metrical value and expressing the same idea, could replace one

---

[28] See, e.g., M. P. Coote, 'Lying in Passages,' *Canadian-American Slavic Studies* 15 (1981) 5–23.

another.'[29] This precept—only one solution for each compositional problem—has proven more a characteristic of ancient Greek epic than of traditional oral poetry in general,[30] and it should be stressed that it is Homeric 'words' (and not their referents) that exhibit such thoroughgoing thriftiness. Another property of Homeric verse studied by Parry was its characteristic mode of enjambement, in simplest terms its tendency toward completing the basic sentence unit by the end of a hexameter line. Lord later framed discussion of this feature as the 'adding style' of South Slavic epic, pointing toward its value as a comparative index of traditional composition.[31]

When a poet composes by 'adding' together units that have semi-independent lives of their own apart from any one combination, there will be occasions when the fit between units is less than perfect. This was the guiding principle in Parry's explanation of metrical flaws that occur at the juncture-points between formulas in Homer, and it also informed Parry and Lord's view of the narrative inconsistencies long cited by the Analysts as evidence for viewing the epics as conglomerates of originally separate compositions.[32] Parallels from South Slavic epic—wherein a hero changes name or a horse changes color from one scene to another, for example—seemed to confirm this hypothesis, and thus to rob the Analysts of a precious kind of proof at the same time that it diminished the importance of such supposed rough edges by placing them against the ever-shifting background of an oral tradition. Finally, the question of how this oral tradition was eventually recorded found a fresh answer in Lord's argument for the *Iliad* and *Odyssey* as 'oral-dictated texts' of the sort they had recorded in the former Yugoslavia. Some *guslari*, it seemed, could perform songs at greater length with greater elaboration if they learned to forgo the normal speed and rhythm of oral performance in favor of the slower pace of dictating to an amanuensis. The quality of Homer's songs, Lord argued, marked them as the productions of a bard accustomed to the oral-dictated mode of composition.[33]

---

[29] Parry (1971) 276.

[30] On the lack of thrift in South Slavic epic and Old English verse, see Foley (1990) 163–64 and 354–55, respectively.

[31] See esp. Parry (1971) 251–65; and Lord (1960) 54.

[32] See 'Homeric Formulae and Homeric Metre' in Parry (1971) and A. B. Lord, 'Homer and Huso II: Narrative Inconsistencies in Homer and Oral Poetry,' *Transactions of the American Philological Association* 69 (1938) 439–45.

[33] (1953); rpt. in Lord (1991) 38–48. On the various kinds of performances and texts recorded by Parry and Lord and their characteristics, see Foley (1990) 40–42.

In summary, the first stage of Oral Theory strove to establish Homer's vocabulary of tectonic 'words,' his and his tradition's basic repertoire of expressive units. These units are not coincident with more modern, textual words; rather they constitute a kind of language dedicated to a different mode of representation, one in which the important elements are defined not by typography or morphemic structure but by their usefulness as compositional 'bytes.' Such 'words' live and serve their function not by fossilization within the feedback loop created by print, but by variation within limits. Given this situation, we must agree with the many *guslari* who steadfastly maintained, even as they sang versions that scholars showed to be variants, that their performances were always 'word for word' (*rečima po rečima*) the same each time. According to their much more pertinent conception of 'word,' they were absolutely right.

Replies and Revisions

Like any approach, the Oral Theory has followed a predictable and natural life-cycle. The pioneering statements of Parry, Lord, and others, which had to be strong and radical enough to shake the sinecure of established opinion, were found to be in need of further articulation and revision. In this section I examine the most important and far-reaching replies to their opening statements, concentrating for the most part on issues and perspectives rather than specific contributions.[34] The discussion will cover four major topics: the limits of analogy, the 'literary quality' of South Slavic epic, the relationship between Homeric texts and Homeric oral tradition, and the charge of mechanism leveled at Oral Theory.

As the comparative program initiated by Lord began to mature, the concept of 'oral tradition' or 'oral literature' began to expand and diversify accordingly. Reports from the field and from the study started to indicate what has since become starkly evident: that oral traditions are yet more various than the formidable selection of written genres with which we are usually much more familiar, and that such variety needs to be weighed against the facile generalizations and unitary model that seemed so fundamental only a few decades

[34] For individual contributions, the best source remains M. W. Edwards's three-part article on 'Homer and Oral Tradition' (1986b, 1988, 1992).

ago. Alongside the genres privileged by the existence of well established counterparts in written literature—epic, lyric, ballad, and so on—stands a large group of genres virtually unknown to the book or the manuscript and therefore almost invisible to (literary) history and criticism: praise poetry, charms, genealogies, laments, and many more. Even the presumably unified category of epic has proven remarkably diverse: Homer's poems are simply not entirely of a piece with, for example, the widely distributed Sirat Bani Hilal tales of the Arabic Middle East, the Son-Jara performances from Mali, or the Geser cycle along the Silk Roads in China, Mongolia, and central Asia.[35] The wholesale expansion of studies in oral tradition since about 1975 has led to the necessary conclusion that responsible comparison must also involve careful discrimination of differences, a philologically sound attempt to understand each different form on its own terms.

This more realistic perspective on the world's oral traditions, living and textualized, has at least one important implication for Homer and all other areas. Because of the inherent variety of witnesses, a useful poetics for traditional oral forms must balance comparison through similarities against the principles of tradition-dependence, genre-dependence, and medium-dependence. That is, we must be willing to stipulate differences among individual traditions (according to language and history), individual genres (e.g. epic versus charm), and individual media (performances and texts of various sorts). This is in fact what Parry and Lord did when they chose to consult South Slavic *Moslem* epic, which matches Homeric epic rather closely in many of its formal linguistic characteristics and particularly in its subgeneric features. With Moslem epic they could study firsthand a tradition of long and elaborate tales whose *reči* happened to correspond rather well to Homer's *epea*.[36] This congruity made for an effective analogy, but at the same time it obscured those aspects that were not parallel and, more significantly for the field at large, pointed toward a monolithic model of oral tradition that could not bear the weight of attested international diversity.

---

[35] See, e.g., B. Connelly, *Arab Folk Epic and Identity* (Berkeley, 1986); J. W. Johnson, ed. and tr., *The Epic of Son-Jara: A West African Tradition*, text by Fa-Digi Sisòkò (Bloomington, 1986); and the collection of essays on the Silk Roads epics in *Oral Tradition* 11, i (1996).

[36] Cf. the shorter, less elaborate, and in effect more textual subgenre of Christian epic, which Parry and Lord chose largely to ignore because of its lack of congruency with Homeric epic; see further Foley (1991) chs. 3–4.

As well suited an analogue as South Slavic Moslem epic provided for the *Iliad* and *Odyssey* in many ways, it was not, and could not be, merely a matter of superimposition.[37] In addition to variance in formal features, some classicists have been eager to remark what they see as another important discrepancy: the disparity in 'artistic quality' between Homer's and the *guslars*' songs. As early as 1962, G. S. Kirk deprecated the 'simpler Yugoslav poet,' and 'an effect of monotony and lack of imagination' in his poems. This shortcoming Kirk attributed to the South Slavic oral poets' position in his four-part ontogeny of oral traditions (originative, creative, reproductive, and degenerate): Homer was at stage two, the *guslar* past his prime at stage three.[38] More recently, H. Lloyd-Jones echoed Kirk and a number of other scholars in claiming that 'the epics in question are hardly as distinguished as, say, Sir Walter Scott's long poems *Marmion, The Lady of the Lake, The Lay of the Last Minstrel.* It seems clear enough that they cannot be compared with Homer.'[39]

In response to these two critics, it should be emphasized that, as argued above, the comparison of oral traditions must not only admit but actually stipulate differences as well as similarities. Points of incongruity must be as welcome as points of correspondence in a responsible poetics. On the specific issue of quality, however, one may reasonably doubt the opinion of commentators who do not read the South Slavic material in the original language; Kirk's observations and evolutionary hypothesis, along with Lloyd-Jones's error-riddled presentation of the analogy, are unfortunately based entirely on a small selection of translations.[40] Yet more fundamentally from a historical perspective, the argument over 'quality' is tautological. Not only does the diversity uncovered by comparative research render such value judgments parochial, but the unique position of Homer at the source of Western literary aesthetics automatically disqualifies

[37] The hexameter and the decasyllable do not entirely match in structure, and so the two phraseologies show differences as well. Typical scenes and story-patterns exhibit similarities, but diverge not only in substance but also to some extent in dynamics. On the divergent 'traditional rules' that inform the morphology of these units, see further Foley (1990) chs. 4–5, 7–8.

[38] Kirk (1962) 86, 95–98.

[39] 'Becoming Homer,' *New York Review of Books* 39, v (5 March 1992) 55.

[40] Kirk consulted only the English translations of songs from the Novi Pazar singers [*SCHS* vol. 1], while Lloyd-Jones seems to have read only the example passages from Lord's *The Singer of Tales*, which he quotes with numerous misspellings, and a German translation of 84 lines total in F. Dirlmeier's *Das serbokroatische Heldenlied und Homer* (Heidelberg, 1971) 34–39.

all competitors for his throne—especially competitors outside the Western mainstream. We would do better to leave aside untenable judgments and to concentrate on what any given analogue can (and cannot) tell us about Homer.

The third topic for response and revision concerns the complex problem of the textual medium in which Homeric epic reaches us, and how this text relates to ancient Greek oral tradition.[41] At the root of one objection against Oral Theory has been the uncertainty about the role of writing in the recording and transmission of the oral performances postulated as the basis for our *Iliad* and *Odyssey*. As in so many other respects, this controversy arose from oversimplification and absolutism on both sides. On the one hand, the Parry-Lord approach at first mandated an immediate death for oral tradition from the moment writing entered a culture; only if Homer were himself an unlettered bard, so went the original explanation, could he have composed the epics. Since there could be no 'transitional text,' the only recourse for recording would be dictation to an amanuensis, along the lines of Avdo Medjedović's dictation of *The Wedding of Smailagić Meho* to Nikola Vujnović.[42] On the other hand, proponents of a literate and literary Homer argued that such magnificent and complex works as the *Iliad* and *Odyssey* could be managed only if composed with the help of writing, and that the advent of this technology in archaic Greece, in whatever form, was enough to prove the fundamental role of literacy in the making of the poems.

Now that a more nuanced evaluation of literacy in the ancient world is starting to emerge, the interrelationship of Homeric oral tradition and Homeric texts, while still susceptible to different explanations,[43] appears less mysterious. W. V. Harris' research has revealed that while ancient Greece certainly had a degree of scribal literacy, the kind of mass literacy we moderns imagine was unthinkable.[44]

---

[41] The answers to such questions lie in part beyond the scope of the present essay, and I will concentrate here only on the issues that pertain most closely to our subject. See esp. the chapters in this volume on 'The Homeric Question' (F. Turner), 'Writing and Homer' (B. Powell), and 'The Transmission of the Text' (M. Haslam).

[42] But note Lord's eventual acceptance of the 'transitional text' (1986) and 'The Transitional Text,' in Lord (1995) 212–37.

[43] Compare, for example, the recent arguments by R. Janko for an oral-dictated text (1990, 326–34); by G. Nagy for a 'Panhellenic fixation' without writing (1990b, 77–81); and by B. Powell for an alphabet invented for the purpose of writing down Homer's poems (1991).

[44] He concludes that there is 'no epigraphical or literary evidence to suggest that

Likewise, his discussion lays bare the diversity of activities we too crudely subsume under the heading of literacy: where possible, distinctions must be made between writing and reading and also among their various applications (history, record-keeping, legal matters, religious purposes, letter-writing, the transmission of 'literature,' and so on). His well supported view that 'the diffusion of literature . . . always remained more oral than is generally realized' (29) agrees in principle with R. Thomas' examination of the mixture of oral tradition and written records in classical Athens.[45] In these sources, and elsewhere in scholarship focused on different areas and periods,[46] the picture coming into focus is one of a very gradual (and never complete) shift from one technology to the other, with a continuing persistence of oral traditions and their expressive strategies long after the appearance and adoption of literacy for certain activities. While we will probably never know the exact relationship between the Homeric oral tradition and the surviving Homeric texts, we can at least cease positing a Great Divide between the two. Homer's 'words,' however they were committed to text, are also oral traditional 'words.'

In this spirit, it seems wise to discard absolute categories of oral versus written and to conceive of the *Iliad* and *Odyssey* as *oral-derived traditional texts.* By allowing the possibility that writing played a role in the transmission or even the creation of the poems as we know them, we avoid advocating a theory of exclusivity that analogues in other areas would discourage. At the same time, by insisting on the oral-derived and traditional nature of these same texts, we maintain the perspectives initiated by Parry and Lord and modified to take account of further investigations. In short, the designation of oral-derived traditional text amounts to the maximum defensible assumption about the poems that have reached us. Furthermore, as we shall

---

more than a very small percentage of Greeks were literate before 600 (1989, 49)'. More account needs to be taken by future investigators of the actual media technology available to the ancient world, and of its effect on the institutions of authorship and readership.

[45] In (1989) 285–86, she comments: 'The presence of literacy and writing complemented the oral traditions but did not destroy them;' further, 'we should consider not the mere presence of literacy nor its "extent," but how and where it was used.'

[46] See esp. J. Boyarin, ed., *The Ethnography of Reading* (Berkeley, 1993); Finnegan (1977); and B. Stock, *The Implications of Literacy* (Princeton, 1983). On the importance of oral traditional strategies in Anglo-Saxon manuscripts, see K. O'Brien O'Keeffe, *Visible Song: Transitional Literacy in Old English Verse* (Cambridge, 1990), and A. N. Doane, 'Performance as a Constitutive Category in the Editing of Anglo-Saxon Poetic Texts,' *Oral Tradition* 9 (1994) 420–39.

see below, this designation not only agrees with the preponderance of comparative research, but also puts the emphasis where it belongs—on the 'words' and their inherent artistic potential.

More than any other single aspect, those who disagreed with the initial Parry-Lord conception of Homeric poetry have cited the issue of mechanism. From G. Calhoun's early refusal to accept Parry's contention that the formula 'winged words' was primarily a metrical stop-gap through P. Vivante's and J. Griffin's emphasis on what they see as Homer's decidedly literary style,[47] many critics have voiced essentially the same objection: the attractive hypothesis of an oral poet's ready-made diction and narrative patterns simply leaves no room for verbal art. How can we understand the *Iliad* and *Odyssey* as masterpieces, they ask, if all the poet is doing is obeying the constrictive rules of the tale-telling game? Is the contribution of individual genius to be submerged entirely in a collective poetic tradition? Is each occurrence of a particular formula or typical scene to be taken merely as a mechanical solution to the challenge of composing in performance? Is Homer then to be understood as wholly insensitive to the narrative situations in which he deploys the traditional structures, so that suitability to immediate context is never a concern? These were and are perfectly reasonable questions, and to the extent that the Oral Theory engendered them, it must also address the impasses they expose.

In fact, we can trace those impasses—mechanism versus art, tradition versus the individual, and generic versus context-sensitive meaning—to a single shortcoming of Oral Theory in its initial form: a virtually exclusive attention to composition at expense of reception. Because Parry and Lord were seeking to explain the phenomenon of Homeric epic, first as a traditional and then even more radically as an oral poetry, they naturally concentrated on the apparent miracle of how a preliterate poet could have produced such an imposing pair of monuments—nearly 30,000 lines of hexameter verse—without the cognitive prosthesis of writing. In an attempt to discover and define the system of 'words' that made this feat possible, they and most of their successors accepted Parry's mechanical notion of an 'essential idea,' namely, that 'swift-footed Achilles' meant simply Achilles, 'ox-eyed Hera' merely Hera. If the most important quality

[47] Calhoun (1935); Griffin (1980); Vivante (1982).

of a phrase was its utility in constructing hexameter lines, and the most important quality of a typical scene was to furnish a dependable, ready-made way to continue the performance—if in short the one prime function of the 'words' was composition, then it is not difficult to understand how art could give way to mechanism, individual creativity to a collective tradition, and context-sensitivity to the 'essential ideas' of generic meaning. Nor is it difficult to understand that such a one-sided view of the poems needed to be rebalanced, to address not only the singer's feat of verse-making but also and equally the audience's and reader's feat of interpretation. In the next section I will consider how rebalancing the equation of composition and reception can lead to a fuller appreciation of Homer's art.

The Implications of Oral Tradition

The most important question raised by studies in oral tradition is 'So what?' If there is an ancient Greek oral tradition in the background of the *Iliad* and *Odyssey*, as now seems certain, what difference does that make to our understanding of the poems? In facing this challenge, I will first be reexamining the assumptions behind the term 'oral tradition,' and then turning to a consideration of *traditional referentiality* as a key to dissolving the false dichotomy of mechanism versus art. The object of the inquiry will be to provide a perspective on oral tradition in the Homeric poems that satisfies three criteria: (1) it must avoid oversimplification and allow for the complexity attested among international witnesses, both living and textualized; (2) it must incorporate what is useful from the successes of Oral Theory at the same time that it responds thoughtfully to cogent criticisms of that approach; and (3) it must explain the way in which Homeric art emerges not in spite of but through the unique agency of oral tradition.

Let us begin at the most basic level of terminology. Over the years since Parry's initial research, *oral* has become the more prominent member of the phrase that names the pre-textual medium. Because it denotes the opposite of 'written,' 'textual,' and 'literate'—three labels for our own (often unexamined) way of doing things—'oral' has seemed to designate a singular alternative, the 'other' way of proceeding. But as many anthropologists have pointed out, both orality and literacy—and their stepchildren 'oral and literate cultures'—are abstractions so broad as to have little meaning once applied to real situations.[48] Since it can mean simply 'spoken,' whether from spontaneous composition, from memory, or even from a text, the term oral is not diagnostic of an important single property or characteristic; real people in actual cultures display a whole repertoire of communicative channels, some of them dependent on the exchange of writing and texts and some of them not. Although a global concept such as orality may initially impress a highly literate and now electronic generation as identifying a unified technology of communication, the fact is that it can obscure more than it illuminates.

No less in need of deconstruction is the other term in the equation, *tradition*.[49] Originally employed by Parry as the fundamental concept in his reconception of the Homeric poems, tradition soon took on an inert, fossilized nature in the minds of many, a nature in one sense suggested by the Oral Theory's concentration on words as prefabricated parts, as items ready for useful deployment. Ironically, the same philological analysis that uncovered the system of phraseology and narrative patterns also tended to fragment the poetic tradition into a series of underlined parts and titled scenes, purportedly oral units that were located and described as tacitly visual, typographic entities. Tradition became the handy tool-kit that made composition possible, and little if anything more.

But what if tradition were understood not as a collection of inert products on the page but as the vital process imaged in language? We might conceive of such a resource as 'a dynamic, multivalent body of meaning that preserves much that a group has invented and transmitted but which also includes as necessary, defining features both an inherent indeterminacy and a predisposition to various kinds of change or modification.'[50] Like language itself, such a conception of tradition would undoubtedly provide, even ensure, a degree of continuity. But note also some other, equally functional characteristics. Tradition would be not only capable of but predisposed to rule-governed change (like language); it would comprise a signifying system

[48] For the strong thesis of orality versus literacy, necessary to break theoretical ground but now in need of further articulation, see Ong (1982) and Havelock (1963). Cf. the anthropologically based findings of Finnegan (1977); (1988), and B. Street, *Literacy in Theory and Practice* (Cambridge, 1984).

[49] On some ways in which this term has been applied, see D. Ben-Amos, 'The Seven Strands of *Tradition*: Varieties in Its Meaning in American Folklore Studies,' *Journal of Folklore Research* 21 (1984) 97–131.

[50] Foley (1995) xii.

with its own brand of referentiality (like language); and it would entrust the process of communication to the performer's and audience's negotiation of what remains unsaid (like language). Such a notion of tradition frees us from a monolithic model and its focus on static products, and redirects attention toward the ongoing process that informs Homeric composition and reception.

Under this aegis the 'words' so painstakingly and successfully mapped out by the Oral Theory are understood as indexes of traditional meaning. Instead of serving simply as counters in an elaborate board game, they are apprehended as nodes in a network of signification, as keys that unlock what the Anglo-Saxon poets called the 'wordhoard' of myth and story, as signs that point the way down the Homeric *oimê*[51] or song-path. In short, the recurrent phrases and scenes that characterize Homeric epic and numerous other such narratives are credited with more than mere compositional convenience; because their *traditional referentiality* is fully taken into account, we no longer have to contemplate sacrificing artistic depth to an adequate theory of structure, or vice versa. The 'words'—the *epea* of Homer, the *reči* of the South Slavic *guslar*—do more than make possible a traditional oral performance; they actively enable traditional oral art.

Thus the first step in rebalancing composition and reception must consist of establishing the traditional field of reference for the various kinds of 'words' that constitute the specialized Homeric vocabulary. Under the 'swift-footed Achilles' headword (πόδας ὠκὺς Ἀχιλλεύς), for example, the lexicographer must include more than merely the Parryan essential idea of 'Achilles' and more than an etymological definition that somehow suits the various situations in which the phrase occurs; otherwise, in any given case we will have to choose between a flat, repetitive accommodation to metrics and a questionable fit between instance and context. Either the great Achaean hero will once again be burdened with his only too tiresome appellation or we may be left to ponder how his celebrated speed could possibly pertain to this or that action. But if the Homeric epic lexicon offers as its primary definition something like the following—'the entire heroic portrayal, complete with its mythic history and contradictions,

[51] See line 1 of the Anglo-Saxon poem 'Widsith': '[The singer] Widsith spoke, unlocked the wordhoard' (K. Malone, ed., Copenhagen, 1962), my translation. On *oimê*, see esp. *Od.* 22.347; also 8.74, 481.

as known to the tradition and as signaled by this phrase,'[52] then we will see this and other noun-epithet formulas for what they are: a species of characterization. Such telegraphic characterization depends upon the nominal meaning of the components of the 'word' and the traditional meaning of the composite 'word' as an expressive unit. What is more, it operates under a general and extremely widespread rule for representation in traditional oral works, with the concrete part ('swift-footed Achilles') standing for the untextualized and literally untextualizable whole (the entire character).

The *pars pro toto* relationship between the unit and its traditional meaning extends beyond the characterization of the noun-epithet formulas to the phraseology as a whole. Two examples of this enhanced referentiality must suffice.[53] When a particular figure is introduced as 'looking darkly' (*hupodra idôn*), as J. Holoka has shown, much more is traditionally implied than a portentous glare; this phrase specifically 'conveys anger on the part of a speaker who takes umbrage at what he judges to be rude or inconsiderate words spoken by the addressee.'[54] This headword in the Homeric lexicon prescribes two speakers exchanging words under a particular verbal contract, and it thus contributes to setting the scene and developing their relationship by framing the singularity of the immediate situation in a resonant traditional context. Likewise, the modest-sized phrase *pukinon epos* ('intimate word') does more than denote a secret or carefully guarded speech. Via traditional referentiality it consistently signals 'a message or communication of great importance, one that if properly delivered and received would change the present course of events.'[55] Thus, for example, Priam dispatches his herald Idaios in *Iliad* 7 in a futile attempt to end the Trojan war; Nestor tells Patroklos of his father's wish that he provide Achilles a *pukinon epos*, and then sug-

[52] Of course, there are other ways to name Achilles (e.g., 'Peleus' son,' Πηληιάδεω 'Αχιλῆος, gen. sing.), not all of them absolutely in line with Parry's concept of thrift (see Shive, 1987). But the point is that each traditional 'word,' whether metrically unique or not, serves as a traditionally approved pathway to Achilles' characterization. Comparisons with traditions that (like South Slavic) do not feature thrift illustrate how metrical uniqueness is not the operative principle in this mode of characterization.

[53] For illustrative purposes, I choose two examples with substantial, focused referentiality. In practice, Homeric (and other) traditional oral epic reveals a spectrum of signification, from the most workaday, literal formula (such as those that introduce speeches) to 'words' such as the two phrases below.

[54] (1983) 4.

[55] Foley (1991) 155.

gests borrowing the great hero's armor (Book 11); Andromache laments the fact that she will never again share a *pukinon epos* with the dead Hektor (Book 24); and Zeus works through Iris to instruct Thetis to intervene with Achilles and mandate the release of Hektor's corpse (Book 24). Each of these actions marks a major turning point in the narrative, and each unique moment is enriched by the traditional frame associated with the 'intimate word.'

The same principle of traditional referentiality informs the dynamics of typical scenes in Homer, as in the case of the ubiquitous Feast. As pointed out above, this theme consists of a number of regularly recurring details alongside the specific coloring it takes on in any given situation. To the highly individual instance—whether the qualified feast on Ithaca (Book 1), the interrupted sequence on Circe's island (Book 10), or any of the others—the recurrent pattern counterposes a sameness, a sense of order that may be reinforced or contradicted by what is happening at that particular juncture. Moreover, the Feast as a typical scene participates in a larger design, which is also both tectonic and traditionally resonant. The larger sequence moves from Assembly (for group debate or mourning) through Anointment to Feast and on to Mediation,[56] forecasting a goal or result by providing a traditional map with which to negotiate even the most singular of proceedings. Whether it is Achilles refusing preliminary washing and nourishment through most of the *Iliad* until he finally breaks bread with Priam, or whether it is Odysseus observing the rites of anointment and seating of the guest that lead inevitably to the long-deferred feast with Penelope,[57] this extended and coherent sequence of actions lends a trademark momentum to the unique events it helps to portray. The necessary link between Anointment and Feasting as well as the expectation of Mediation to follow are implicit, immanent connections prescribed not by the power of the singular instance—however estimable—but by the context of traditional referentiality.

Such referentiality is the property not of isolated units but of language, more exactly an idiom or *register* of language that exists solely

[56] See Foley (1991) 174–89.

[57] Notice that of all seven instances of Anointment (or Bath), this occurrence in Book 23 is the only one that does not give way to a literal feast. The artistic potential of traditional convention is, however, apparent in the fact that after the requisite washing and seating comes Odysseus and Penelope's 'feast' of recognition and reunion. See Foley (1990) 256–57.

to serve one expressive function, the transmission of ancient Greek epic. Registers, defined by D. Hymes as 'major speech styles associated with recurrent types of situations,'[58] are familiar enough categories for speakers of all languages, ancient or modern. Consider the variance among the idioms you use for the classroom, an intimate tête-à-tête with a friend or family member, and a legal proceeding; most of us will carry on all of these conversations in English, but each setting will demand a specific register of English, with its own somewhat divergent vocabulary, sentence structure, and perhaps gestures, all engaged in order to constitute the speech-act. The Homeric epic register is no different: a language marked by its archaisms and dialect mixture, as well as by its own distinctive array of 'words,' becomes the dedicated medium for the composition and reception of the poems. In its very idiosyncrasy, long misunderstood as a curious blend of forms fossilized into convenient building blocks, lies the secret to its success as a signifying instrument. This 'way of speaking' designates a channel for communication, a precise wavelength for both the making and the receiving of Homeric epic. Far from being a limitation or an awkward hindrance that leads to a nodding Homer, it is a uniquely empowering medium, full of traditional implication at every level. From the mere fact of its use as the medium of communication, the language of the *Iliad* and *Odyssey* represents the best of both worlds: the individual, inimitable event emerging against the rich background of the poetic tradition.

Recognizing that Homer's phraseology and narrative patterns amount to such a register has another liberating consequence: it effectively bridges the Great Divide between 'orality' and 'literacy.' The fact that any given culture or individual commands a variety of registers proves blanket generalizations about orality and literacy much too crude to be useful. Examples abound worldwide of individuals who compose fluently within oral traditions and yet can also manipulate texts—a kind of code-switching quite expectable within a repertoire of situational idioms.[59] Nor need we any longer struggle to

[58] 'Ways of Speaking,' in *Explorations in the Ethnography of Speaking*, 2nd ed. (Cambridge, 1989), 440.

[59] Cf. P. Lutgendorf, *The Life of a Text: Performing the* Rāmcaritmānas *of Tulsidas* (Berkeley, 1991) on North Indian verbal art, which emerges from 'a society possessing a literary heritage dating back three millennia, but much of which has always been orally transmitted and performed; a mixed literate and illiterate culture that supports an extraordinarily broad range of performance genres and an intricate text/

explain how traditional oral forms persist into texts. The 'words' continue to appear because the poets are employing the single linguistic instrument best suited to their purpose. What reason could they have, whatever the medium, to abandon the 'mother tongue' of traditional tale-telling for a foreign idiom? And how could they expect others to follow and appreciate a story if the new idiom is just as foreign to audience as to poet? Leaving behind the Homeric register entails forsaking all that is encoded in that special medium by losing the vital connection to the poetic tradition. Indeed, to the extent that critics have failed to grasp the traditional referentiality of Homer's 'words,' it is not he but they who have nodded.

If register names the special language of exchange used for the composition and reception of the *Iliad* and *Odyssey*, then the place where that exchange takes place can be called the *performance arena.* In its most basic sense, this term designates the actual physical site where an oral poet and audience collectively experience a live performance. Parry, Lord, and Nikola Vujnović, for example, recorded South Slavic epic in hundreds of performance arenas, each of them geographically distinct from the others. But in a larger sense, to the extent that each *guslar* tapped into the epic register as the framing medium for his singular poetic achievement,[60] all of them performed at precisely the same 'site.' This seems to be the chief message of the standardized proems (or *pripjevi*) with which so many of the South Slavic songs begin, as in these common lines: 'Eh, long ago it was in time,/Long ago, now we are remembering/In this place and in every other.'[61] Indeed, the *guslar* specifies and respecifies the locus for composition and reception with every line he sings, speaking the dedicated dialect for epic exchange and deploying the 'words' that make up his language of implication.

Once a traditional oral poem has become textualized, as with the Homeric epics, the performance arena obviously has no physical reality. Nonetheless, one thing is certain: the rhetorical persistence of

performance relationship that should rarely be excluded from any comprehensive study of either text or performance.'

[60] It should be added that traditional poetic registers—again like languages in general—exist in idiolectal and dialectal variants; for illustration in South Slavic, see Foley (1990) chs. 5, 8.

[61] Quoted from Salih Ugljanin's *Pjesma od Bagdata* (*SCHS* 2:8, ll. 8–10, my translation), but very common elsewhere. On the structure and function of *pripjevi*, see further Foley (1991) 68–75.

cues for entering the arena, understood as above in the larger sense. For example, proems invoking performance also begin both the *Iliad* and *Odyssey*, the latter poem's tenth line effectively imploring the Muse to let this poet and audience join the ranks of their traditional forebears: τῶν ἁμόθεν γε, θεά, θύγατερ Διός, εἰπὲ καὶ ἡμῖν ('From some point *speak also to us* of these things, O goddess, daughter of Zeus'). On a much broader canvas, and just as with the South Slavic tradition, the composite, artificial dialect and the various levels of *epea* reinforce that invocation with every hexameter verse. Although the signals for reception now occur outside the spoken medium, for the suitably fluent audience they still bear a wealth of associations, made possible through the traditional referentiality of the Homeric register.

Because Homer and his audience utilize the dedicated register within the performance arena, the exchange between them takes place with great *communicative economy*.[62] Because so much can be said and heard with so few 'words,' the transaction is uniquely intense and efficient. Of course, as parallels in other traditions confirm, such economy of expression results from the narrow focus of this way of speaking: the more specialized a variety of language becomes, the more useful it is for that particular activity and the less useful it is for general, run-of-the-mill verbal activities.[63] On the other hand, an unmarked, standard variety of a language may prove extremely adaptable to a wide spectrum of applications, but quite unwieldy when devoted to a purpose as specialized as epic composition and reception. Homer uses the inherited hexameter language—complete with its special 'words' and their unmatched economy—because its very limitations make for a built-in allusiveness, because whatever characters and actions he describes will frame the individual situation in the resonant context of the traditional, because its inherent economy of signification makes possible a distinctive kind of verbal art.

In summary, then, what are the implications of oral tradition for the contemporary reader of Homer, millennia removed from the original context of the *Iliad* and *Odyssey*? To an extent, the poems

---

[62] This kind of economy, which designates the relationship between the dedicated register and its array of traditional meanings, should be clearly distinguished from Parry's concept of 'thrift,' which is a morphological feature of the poetic language.

[63] In some cases, as with the magical charms still prevalent in South Slavic oral tradition, the register can become almost impenetrable to outsiders, whether because of vocabulary, syntax, background mythology, or performance features such as volume and speed of articulation. See further Foley (1995) ch. 4.

will always be understood against a contemporary backdrop; they must in some way fit the world of the reader, however distant it may be from the world in and for which they were made and remade. But we must also take account of their background in oral tradition, not only because their composition involved a special set of circumstances and 'words,' but especially because those 'words' carry a special brand of meaning—traditional referentiality—that lies at the heart of Homeric art. Does this attention to the implications of oral tradition demand a wholly new poetics? Here I believe the answer must be firmly in the negative, since 'literary' and 'traditional oral' strategies will sometimes overlap or even coincide, and since experience has taught us the perils of a policy of segregation in such matters. Our responsibility should rather be integrative: to hear the resonance in Homer's 'words,' to contextualize the individual and immediate in the traditional and recurrent. Just as studies in oral tradition began with the modern rediscovery of an ancient technique of composition, so now another rediscovery awaits us: the linked technique of reception. Only then can Homer and his tradition truly εἰπε[ῖν] καὶ ἡμῖν, 'speak also to us.'

Malcolm Willcock

NEOANALYSIS

Neoanalysis is a term invented by the late J. T. Kakridis, the leading Greek Homeric scholar of this century, to denote a new approach to the interpretation of the *Iliad*. Its reception by western scholarship has been bedevilled by a number of accidental circumstances: the war (for Kakridis' book, expanded from articles dating back into the 1930s, was first published in modern Greek as Ὁμηρικὲς Ἔρευνες, in 1944); the fact that the English version, *Homeric Researches* (1949), which ought to have had a massive impact on readers, for it is among the most attractive books ever written about the *Iliad*, was relatively inaccessibly published in Sweden, vol. XLV in a series called *Skrifter utgivna av Kungl. Humanistiska Vetenskapssamfundet i Lund*; take-over by powerful voices in the German tradition; misunderstanding by reviewers and critics, even by proponents; apparent conflict with the emergent and expansive American oral poetry industry. It is best therefore first of all to define neoanalysis, then to sketch the history of its development and reception in the last fifty years, then to consider its position in present-day Homeric studies and what it has to offer to general consensus and understanding.

Definition

Neoanalysis is consciously and explicitly unitarian, starting from the belief that the *Iliad*, virtually as we have it, is the work of one great poet. It was a reaction against the century-long German tradition of analytical scholarship, separatist in its view of the authorship of the epic. However, neoanalysis is not simply unitarianism under another name, for it too analyses the text and draws conclusions from consideration of the details. Its essential approach is to see behind some of the incidents of the *Iliad* into the content of pre-Homeric poetry in the belief that it can be shown that 'Homer' consciously or subconsciously reflects scenes from that broader background. The most obvious and central example of this is to be found in the mourning for the dead Patroclus, especially at the beginning of *Iliad* 18, where there are apparent echoes of that far more important moment in the Greek war against Troy when the body lying on the ground and mourned by Thetis and the Nereids was not that of Achilles' friend Patroclus, but that of Achilles himself.[1]

Neoanalysis is an attitude of mind. What makes it exciting is that it brings us close to the thought processes of the poet Homer himself; we feel that we are looking over his shoulder, *nel laboratorio di Omero*, to use a fine phrase created by V. Di Benedetto for his improvements to the Parry theory of formulaic composition. When the learned scholar A. Heubeck wrote his survey of twentieth century Homeric research in 1974 (*Die homerische Frage*), he divided the approaches to the *Iliad* into four categories: Analysis, Neoanalysis, 'Unitarismus,' and (set against these three) Oral Poetry Research. (For the *Odyssey*, he used the other three categories, but not Neoanalysis.) There is nothing inherently inconsistent between neoanalysis and oral poetry theory; indeed the two attitudes could quite easily be assimilated. Yet this important approach has had little impact on the English-speaking world; we must see why.

The First Stages (Kakridis and Pestalozzi)

In 1945, one year after the Greek version of Kakridis' book, but completely independent of it, there appeared in Switzerland H. Pestalozzi's *Die Achilleis als Quelle der Ilias*. Short (only 52 pages), and attractively written, it provided the direct impulse of much of the neoanalytical writing that followed. Pestalozzi, who of course was unaware of the term 'neoanalysis,' differs from Kakridis in concentrating specifically on a single model for the *Iliad*, an 'Achilleis,' which had some connection with the cyclic *Aithiopis*. This introduces the Epic Cycle into the equation, the succession of poems which in due course provided a continuous treatment of the Trojan War story from the judgement of Paris to the death of Odysseus—*Cypria, Iliad, Aithiopis, Little Iliad, Iliupersis, Nostoi, Odyssey, Telegony*, for the lost poems of which we possess a prose summary by Proclus' accessible to the present day reader in numerous publications.[2] From the time of Pestalozzi

---

[1] Kakridis (1949) 65–95. He had written on this subject years before, in Ἀθηνᾶ 42 (1930) 66–78.

[2] For example, Vol. V of the Oxford Classical Text of Homer; the Loeb *Hesiod, the Homeric Hymns and Homerica*; Kullmann (1960) 52–7; Davies (1988).

on, neoanalysis has tended to be equated with 'the *Aithiopis* theory,' and the wording of Proclus' summary of that poem taken to be a précis of the contents of the presumed model of the *Iliad*.

Pestalozzi brought into play two considerations which have affected discussion ever since. First, not being concerned with thoughts about oral poetry, and sharing that European disregard for Milman Parry and his followers which pertained until the 1960s and the work of A. Lesky, he assumed that the model used by Homer for the *Iliad* was a pre-existing poem available to him; secondly, in allowing it to appear that that poem could have been the *Aithiopis*, he raised the intricate problem of the date of composition of the *Iliad* and its relationship to the poems of the Epic Cycle. It had for a long time been assumed that the cyclic epics, including the *Aithiopis*, were composed later than the *Iliad* and the *Odyssey*, and indeed that their function was to complete the story of the Trojan war, starting off from the existence of those two great epics. The *Aithiopis* was ascribed to a historical author, Arctinus of Miletus, often nowadays assigned to the sixth century B.C., the *Iliad* having been composed according to most scholars betwen 750 and 700. Suddenly scholars were questioning whether the *Iliad* needed to be so early or the *Aithiopis* so late, and suggesting that because the *Iliad* appears to echo features known to have appeared in the *Aithiopis*, that poem may have antedated the *Iliad*.

Before we proceed further, we should identify the two most important scenes of the *Aithiopis* which appear to be echoed in the *Iliad*. First, the events surrounding the death of Patroclus in the *Iliad* mirror those in the *Aithiopis* relating to the death of Achilles. The relevant sentences in Proclus' summary are as follows:

> τρεψάμενος δ' Ἀχιλλεὺς τοὺς Τρῶας καὶ είς τὴν πόλιν συνεισπεσὼν ὑπὸ Πάριδος ἀναιρεῖται καὶ Ἀπόλλωνος· καὶ περὶ τοῦ πτώματος γενομένης ἰσχυρᾶς μάχης Αἴας ἀνελόμενος ἐπὶ τὰς ναῦς κομίζει, Ὀδυσσέως ἀπομαχομένου τοῖς Τρωσίν. ἔπειτα Ἀντίλοχόν τε θάπτουσι καὶ τὸν νέκρον τοῦ Ἀχιλλέως προτίθενται. καὶ Θέτις ἀφικομένη σὺν Μούσαις καὶ ταῖς ἀδελφαῖς θρηνεῖ τὸν παῖδα.
>
> Achilles having put the Trojans to flight and rushed into the city with them, is killed by Paris and Apollo. And after a fierce battle over the corpse, Ajax lifts it up and brings it back to the ships, Odysseus fighting off the Trojans. Then they bury Antilochus and lay out the body of Achilles. And Thetis comes with the Muses and her sisters and laments for her son.

In the *Iliad*, disregarding events in Book 16 which bear some similarity to the first sentence here, we concentrate on the end of 17 and the beginning of 18. In the former book, after a prolonged and stubborn battle over the corpse of Patroclus, Ajax arranges that it shall be carried back to the ships by Menelaus and Meriones, while he and the other Ajax fight off the Trojans. At the beginning of 18, Antilochus, the young son of Nestor, sent for this purpose by Ajax, arrives at Achilles' hut and gives him the news of the death of his friend. Three things then happen: first, Achilles lies on the floor of his hut, αὐτὸς δ' ἐν κονίῃσι μέγας μεγαλωστὶ τανυσθεὶς | κεῖτο 'but he lay stretched out in the dust, mightily in his might' (18.26–7); then his mother Thetis and her sisters the Nereids come out of the sea to share his sorrow (35–69); thirdly, when she reaches her son, Thetis takes his head in her arms (71).

All three of these images, in different but complementary ways, would be much more appropriate in a poem about the death of Achilles himself:

1). The phrase about the mighty body lying in the dust has a fascinating resonance. It is part of a formula filling a line and a half, and used as an epitaph for Hektor's brother and charioteer Kebriones at 16.775–6:

ὁ δ' ἐν στροφάλιγγι κονίης
κεῖτο μέγας μεγαλωστί, λελασμένος ἱπποσυνάων

> he lay in a swirl of dust, mightily in his might, forgetful of his horsemanship.

It also, and surely significantly, appears about Achilles himself in the exact context we are envisaging, i.e. his own death. In the scene in the underworld in Book 24 of the *Odyssey*, when the descending suitors come upon Agamemnon and Achilles conversing, Agamemnon is telling Achilles of the events that occurred at his (Achilles') death, and says among other things

σὺ δ' ἐν στροφάλιγγι κονίης
κεῖσο μέγας μεγαλωστί, λελασμένος ἱπποσυνάων
(*Od.* 24.39–40).

It has an extraordinarily powerful effect to find part of this epitaph used of Achilles when he has collapsed on the ground at the news of the death of his friend.

2). Thetis and the Nereids had more reason to join the lamentation when Achilles was dead than when he was mourning the death of Patroclus. And we have seen in the summary of the *Aithiopis* that they did exactly that in that poem; and, again in the underworld scene in the last book of the *Odyssey*, Achilles is told by Agamemnon of the fear inspired in the Greek army at the eery cry that rose from the sea when Thetis and her sisters came to mourn (*Od.* 24.47–9)

> μήτηρ δ' ἐξ ἁλὸς ἦλθε σὺν ἀθανάτῃς ἁλίῃσιν
> ἀγγελίης ἀίουσα· βοὴ δ' ἐπὶ πόντον ὀρώρει
> θεσπεσίη, ὑπὸ δὲ τρόμος ἔλλαβε πάντας Ἀχαιούς

> Your mother came out of the sea with the sea goddesses when she heard the news; and a strange cry arose over the sea, and trembling came over all the Greeks.

Essentially, Patroclus does not rate Nereids: Achilles does.

3). The gesture of the mother holding the head of her son is one appropriate to mourning for the dead. This can be found in *Il.* 24.724, when Andromache holds Hektor's head as his body is being brought back to Troy—

> Ἕκτορος ἀνδροφόνοιο κάρη μετὰ χερσὶν ἔχουσα

(cf. also Achilles at the funeral of Patroclus at 23.136).

The indication of these three scenes seems to those of a neoanalytical persuasion quite incontrovertible. The *Iliad* poet is making use of images from the death of Achilles as he describes the death of Patroclus. In some other examples of parallels between *Iliad* and *Aithiopis* the influence might equally be the other way, the later poet imitating an effective scene from the *Iliad*. But these three only make sense in the way we have described, and they influence our judgement about the earlier scene of the carrying of the body of the dead Greek leader back to camp—by Menelaus and Meriones in the *Iliad*, by Ajax in the *Aithiopis*. We cannot so absolutely demonstrate priority here, but in the light of the first eighty lines of Book 18, it is difficult not to adopt the same explanation of the final scene in 17. And once one has accepted that argument, one finds the case supported by some minor indications: the greater importance in the history of the war of the corpse being rescued in the *Aithiopis*, and the greater economy of that scene, with just the two pre-eminent heroes Ajax and Odysseus in action, compared with the mixed group of four in the *Iliad*.[3]

---

[3] The fight for Achilles' body is referred to by Odysseus at *Od.* 5.309–10

In addition to the images relating to the corpse of Patroclus at the end of 17 and the beginning of 18, another scene in the *Iliad* is central to the beliefs of neoanalysts—what German scholars call *Nestors Rettung*, 'the rescue of Nestor.' The scene is that at 8.78–99, a key moment in the *Iliad* plot, when Zeus has just taken positive action to fulfill his promise to Thetis in Book 1 by throwing a thunderbolt at the Greeks. All the leaders retire, but not Nestor, because his horse has been shot (a) by Paris (b); Hektor (c) is rapidly approaching to take advantage of Nestor's difficulty; Diomedes (d) observes the danger and calls out to Odysseus to come and help. Odysseus, however, is ambiguously inattentive, being on his way to the Greek ships. So Diomedes goes back on his own and rescues the old man. The scene, rich in characterisation, has no significant consequences.

The *Aithiopis* appears to have had a closely similar scene. Proclus' summary merely says, καὶ συμβολῆς γενομένης 'Αντίλοχος ὑπὸ Μέμνονος ἀναιρεῖται, ἔπειτα 'Αχιλλεὺς Μέμνονα κτείνει, 'the battle begins and Antilochus is killed by Memnon, then Achilles kills Memnon.' Not much detail there, but the picture is filled out in the myth of Pindar's *Sixth Pythian*:

ἔγεντο καὶ πρότερον 'Αντίλοχος βιατὰς
   νόημα τοῦτο φέρων,
ὃς ὑπερέφθιτο πατρός, ἐναρίμβροτον
ἀναμείναις στράταρχον Αἰθιόπων
Μέμνονα. Νεστόρειον γὰρ ἵππος ἅρμ' ἐπέδα
Πάριος ἐκ βελέων δαιχθείς· ὁ δ' ἔφεπεν
κραταιὸν ἔγχος· Μεσσανίου δὲ γέροντος
δονηθεῖσα φρὴν βόασε παῖδα ὅν,
χαμαιπετὲς δ' ἄρ' ἔπος οὐκ ἀπέριψεν· αὐτοῦ
   μένων δ' ὁ θεῖος ἀνὴρ
πρίατο μὲν θανάτοιο κομιδὰν πατρός. (*P.* 6.28–39)

Mighty Antilochus was born in earlier days with this attitude of mind, he who died for his father, facing the murderous commander of the Ethiopians, Memnon. For the horse was impeding Nestor's chariot, smitten by Paris' arrow; and he (Memnon) was bringing his powerful spear; the old Messenian leader's mind was distraught, and he shouted for his son; and his words did not fall useless to the ground; but that

---

ἤματι τῷ ὅτε μοι πλεῖστοι χαλκήρεα δοῦρα
Τρῶες ἐπέρριψαν περὶ Πηλείωνι θανόντι

'on that day when a vast number of Trojans hurled bronze-tipped spears at me over dead Achilles.' This shows at least that a post-Iliadic Arctinus did not invent Odysseus' involvement in this scene on the model of *Iliad* 17, unless we place the *Odyssey* later than the *Aithiopis*.

divine man stayed there, and bought his father's safety at the price of his own death.

Here we see close similarities to the *Iliad* story: Nestor's horse has been shot (a) by Paris (b); Memnon (c) is rapidly approaching to take advantage of Nestor's difficulty; Antilochos (d), Nestor's own son, rescues him, but at the cost of his own life.

We might wonder whether Pindar's myth is an exact version of what appeared in the *Aithiopis*, in the light of arbitrary changes he can be shown to have made to myths in other poems (e.g. *O.* 1); but, although neither *Odyssey* 4.188 nor Quintus Smyrnaeus 2.243–59 mentions that Antilochus died to save his father, though both tell that he was killed by Memnon, other ancient authorities support the facts as given by Pindar,[4] and it seems very probable that Virgil imitated Antilochus' filial devotion in the death of Lausus to save his father Mezentius, the source for Virgil being much more probably the epic cycle than a hypothetically divergent Pindaric myth.[5]

Assuming therefore that the details of Antilochus' death as given by Pindar represent the picture in the *Aithiopis*, we have another example of coincidence between *Aithiopis* and *Iliad*, to add to the images of *Iliad* 17 and 18; and we naturally once again consider the question of priority. Neoanalysts believe that in this case also the apparently earlier imitates the ostensibly later. They take the view that the more organic tale, in the sense of more important structurally to the plot, is likely to have been prior to the episodic; and the more emotional (death of a son for his father) likely to have been prior to the merely narrative. Critics of neoanalysis react differently; they argue that it is equally possible that a passing incident in the *Iliad* inspired imitation by a later poet telling the tale of Memnon.

The incident as it appears near the beginning of *Iliad* 8 certainly shows the invention of the poet Homer: it fits his method of character-drawing by repetition of behaviour, every one of the figures involved acting in the way that is characteristic of him, with a broad touch of Homeric humour in the treatment of Odysseus. It highlights a key moment in Homer's plot. It could of course be total invention; but, in the light of what we saw with Patroclus, it is dis-

---

[4] Welcker (1882) 174 n. 5, gives a list, to which could be added Xenophon *Cynegetica* 1.14.

[5] S. J. Harrison *Vergil, Aeneid 10* (Oxford, 1991) on *Aen.* 10.789–832; E. Fraenkel, *Philologus* 87 (1932) 243–8.

tinctly more likely that Homer has made use of a story pattern known to him from elsewhere as the origin of his creativity.[6]

We are discussing the inspiration either of the *Iliad* or of the *Aithiopis*. We must not forget that the *Aithiopis* is generally assumed to have been later than the *Iliad*; on the other hand it may well have been a written version of myths circulating in oral form before Homer. Apart from the figure of Antilochus, to whom we shall return, it is clear that the plot of this part of the *Aithiopis* was in essentials identical with the plot of the *Iliad*: the enemy leader (Memnon, Hector) kills Achilles' close friend (Antilochus, Patroclus) and Achilles, the greatest warrior, takes vengeance for his friend by killing the killer. It is natural to assume that one of these versions is a variation on the other; where the priority lies is the question of debate.

Hector is much more central to the Trojan story than Memnon, the finest son of King Priam of Troy compared with the far-away king who came as an ally to help, no less a probable addition to the legends of Troy (even if son of Tithonus, Priam's brother) than Penthesilea, queen of the Amazons, whose arrival to defend the doomed city also appeared in the *Aithiopis*. That suggests priority to the *Iliad* (Hector/Patroclus) version. On the other hand, some have felt that Hector (a 'speaking name,' the 'Upholder' [ἔχω] of Troy) might even have been the invention of the *Iliad* poet; he has little mythological significance outside the *Iliad*. So did the *Aithiopis* poet imitate the plot of the *Iliad* in this part of his work? Or did the *Iliad* poet reflect, as the basic action in his plot, a myth of Memnon and Antilochus that appeared in pre-Iliadic poetry and was later recorded in the *Aithiopis*? Or is there some other explanation? This is of central importance, for it faces the question of the actual composition of the *Iliad*, and may also involve the change from oral poetry to the use of writing.

One thing is certain: the *Iliad* poet knew the *Aithiopis* story. From the moment in 17 when Ajax decides that Antilochus is the proper person to give Achilles the bad news about the death of Patroclus, to his presence with Achilles in 18, holding Achilles' hands for fear he will kill himself, to his verbal exchanges with Achilles in 23 after the chariot race and the foot-race, where he even makes Achilles smile (23.555), it is obvious that Homer is preparing for future events by establishing a relationship between these two which will be the

[6] Pestalozzi (1945) 10–11.

background to the later story of Antilochus, and the fights with Memnon. Thus one of the possible solutions to the double sequence is shown to be false. Arctinus of Miletus did not invent the Memnon/Antilochus tale on the model of the Hector/Patroclus tale in the *Iliad*. The fate of Antilochus was already known to Homer.

Significantly, also, both tales were known to the *Odyssey* poet. For on two occasions in his underworld scenes he introduces Achilles down there accompanied by a small group of three close friends:

ἦλθε δ' ἐπὶ ψυχὴ Πηληιάδεω Ἀχιλῆος
καὶ Πατροκλῆος καὶ ἀμύμονος Ἀντιλόχοιο
Αἴαντός θ', ὃς ἄριστος ἔην εἶδός τε δέμας τε
τῶν ἄλλων Δαναῶν μετ' ἀμύμονα Πηλείωνα.

> The ghost of Achilles, son of Peleus, came up, and that of Patroclus and of the faultless Antilochus, and of Aias, who was best in appearance and stature of the other Greeks, after the faultless son of Peleus. (*Od.* 11.467–70 = 24.15–18, though in the latter with εὗρον δὲ ψυχήν ['they came upon the ghost'] at the beginning).[7]

In the light of all this, either Homer modelled his Patroclus plot on a previously existing Antilochus story, inventing or expanding the figure of Patroclus, and the *Odyssey* poet gave a passing nod to his predecessor by introducing Patroclus and Antilochus together in Achilles' entourage, or the two versions had already been conflated by the time of the composition of the *Iliad* and *Odyssey*. If that is so, we are back in the tradition of oral poetry before the *Iliad*. Antilochus, son of Nestor, is a key figure in neoanalytical argumentation.[8]

That these two features of the *Iliad*, the mourning for Patroclus' recovered corpse and the rescue of Nestor, echo pre-existing story patterns is the bedrock of neoanalysis, and they will naturally find their place in any discussion by its adherents. Both appear in both Kakridis and Pestalozzi. Neither in fact was a wholly new perception, as Heubeck carefully points out.[9] The echoing of the death of Achilles himself in that of Patroclus was argued by the unitarian D. Mülder in 1910 in a book whose other tenets are no longer of interest to us;[10] while the thesis that 8.78–99 is based on the tale of the killing of Antilochus by Memnon was held by several analysts,

---

[7] Patroclus and Antilochus are associated also at *Od.* 3.110–12 and 24.77–9.
[8] Willcock (1983).
[9] Heubeck (1974) 40, 42.
[10] Mülder (1910) 193.

notably Bethe and Wilamowitz.[11] However, these analysts had used the argument to demonstrate a late stage in the growth of their composite *Iliad*; the mental attitude that saw in this perception a view into the mind of the individual poet Homer was new.

Nor did Kakridis and Pestalozzi see eye to eye in other matters. For Kakridis the 'Patroclea,' as he called it, was only one of several instances of an influence upon the *Iliad* of pre-existing myths; he spends in fact more time on an argument that poetry about Meleager influenced the picture of Hector in *Iliad* 6, a view that would find few adherents today; and his general approach is influenced by nationalism, in the (undoubtedly interesting) view that modern Greek folk poetry may help to explain superficially inconsistent features in Homer. Pestalozzi on the other hand developed the evidence in these two cases into a coherent 'Aithiopis' theory, i.e. he identified the precise model for the composition of the *Iliad* in a single pre-existing poem which he called the *Achilleis* and viewed as virtually identical with the relevant part of the cyclic *Aithiopis*. This was the way neoanalysis went for the next twenty years, and the dogmatic assumption of a single model was the cause of the harsh criticism by anglophone critics, convinced of the Parry/Lord oral theory. Kakridis did not go so far.

Further Development (Schadewaldt and Kullmann)

Just as Homer wisely held back his big guns at the beginning of the fighting in the *Iliad*, letting the at that time minor character Antilochus begin the action on the Greek side before Ajax and Odysseus joined in,[12] so Pestalozzi was the precursor of two powerful German scholars, W. Schadewaldt and W. Kullmann.

Schadewaldt accepted Pestalozzi's theory in its entirety, even to the extent of apologizing (p. 157) for a statement in *Iliasstudien* which had been queried by both Kakridis 94 n. 50 and Pestalozzi 11.[13] His treatment, 'Einblick in die Erfindung der Ilias. Ilias und Memnonis,' was published in a Festschrift for Reinhardt in 1951, and reprinted in the second and later editions of his *Von Homers Welt und Werk*. He

[11] Bethe (1914) 110–11; Wilamowitz (1915) 45–46.

[12] *Il.* 4.457–94.

[13] Schadewaldt (1966) 97 n. 2; he had doubted the dependence of the scene in 8 on the parallel scene in the *Aithiopis*.

set out the evidence for the *Iliad*'s dependence on a pre-existing poem about Memnon as he saw it, listing seven mutually supportive features: two are supplied by what Kakridis called the 'Patroclea' (Thetis' lament, and the description of Achilles lying on the ground), and there is naturally also the rescue of Nestor; the others are less compelling (the operation of the 'scales of Zeus,' the removal of Memnon's/Sarpedon's body by Sleep and Death, Thetis' warning to her son, and Achilles' unmotivated and immediately withdrawn decision to attack Troy at *Iliad* 22.381); the idea that they too were taken over into the *Iliad* from a Memnon poem only becomes arguable if one has already accepted the pre-existence of that poem from the other evidence. Schadewaldt is now seen by many as the greatest Homeric scholar of the twentieth century, surpassing even Wilamowitz; so his adherence to neoanalysis carried weight in European circles, and brought Pestalozzi's little book to a wider readership than it would otherwise have had. Indeed Schadewaldt's whole work might be included in a broader definition of neoanalysis, for in *Iliasstudien* he had used the technique of the analysts, the precise logical discussion of the detailed text, to support a firmly unitarian stance; and in that book he had encouraged the search for Homer's sources (*Quellen-Analyse*) as the future role of analysis.[14]

In 1960 appeared the biggest contribution to Homeric studies of W. Kullmann, *Die Quellen der Ilias*. His research was directed to the external evidence that we have for features in the *Iliad*. It is surprising that this work had not been done before. The book is not restrictedly 'neoanalytical,' encyclopaedic rather. But it relates closely to the contents of the Epic Cycle, as it searches for evidence of the presence of Iliadic figures in Trojan war legends both before and after the time span of the *Iliad*. The central chapter (pp. 227–357) runs through every sentence of Proclus' prose summary of the contents of the cyclic epics, and considers any possible connections with features in the *Iliad*.

Kullmann then, as later, was a defender of neoanalysis. On pp. 29–50 he replied to recent German criticism, particularly of the seven features concentrated on by Schadewaldt, defending all of them and adding others, all as showing a pre-Iliadic source for what we see in the *Iliad*.

The question was now urgent, whether that pre-Iliadic source was

---

[14] Schadewaldt (1966) 164, quoted by J. A. Davison in his review of Pestalozzi in *Classical Review* 61 (1947) 29.

in fact the cyclic *Aethiopis*. On this, both Kakridis and Pestalozzi had been uncommitted. Kakridis would evidently have liked the *Aithiopis* itself to have preceded the *Iliad*, because of the exceedingly close parallels which he finds between them, but he is unwilling to be drawn into the complicated arguments about the time of composition of the Epic Cycle and the scope of its constituent poems. However, he shows his preference when he argues (p. 89) that if Homer's model was not the cyclic *Aithiopis*, it must have been a poem with the same content. Pestalozzi calls his model an 'Achilleis,' but uses Proclus' summary of the *Aithiopis* as evidence for what it contained. It was the powerful and assured Schadewaldt who came down firmly for the pre-existence of the cyclic *Aithiopis*, or at least of the four of its five books which, according to him, told the tale of Memnon, the single book covering Penthesilea, queen of the Amazons, being probably a later addition: '*Wir nennen "Memnonis" die eigentliche Aithiopis, nämlich die Geschichte von Achilleus' Kampf mit dem Aithiopen Memnon, seinem Sieg über ihn und seinem eigenen Tod—ohne die bereits in der Antike gesondert angeführte Amazonia.*'[15] This view is not totally impossible, but it runs contrary to our previous assumption that the *Aithiopis* was composed much later than the *Iliad*, probably in the sixth century, an assumption based on (a) the lower quality of the cyclic epics,[16] (b) Aristarchus' description of their authors as νεώτεροι,[17] (c) a named and located author (Arctinus of Miletus) in contrast to the shadowy 'Homer,' and (d) the apparent construction of the Cycle around an already existing *Iliad* (and *Odyssey*). Kullmann is well aware of this difficulty, and in his defence of neoanalysis on pp. 29–50 of his book he repeatedly insists (pp. 31, 35, 36, 40, 41, 45, 48) that it makes no difference to the validity of the neoanalytical thesis whether the material imitated by the *Iliad* was the cyclic *Aithiopis* or an earlier version of its contents. In his summary conclusions at the end of the book, however, where he draws together the consequences of his research (pp. 360–79), he keeps such an open mind as to suggest that all solutions to the question are equally possible (he offer six scenarios, three to unitarians and three to analysts), while nevertheless indicating that his personal preference is for the two which place the *Aithiopis* earlier than the *Iliad*. His discussion is not limpidly clear, perhaps, and

[15] Schadewaldt (1965) 158; cf. 174.
[16] Aristotle in *Poetics* 1459a30–b16; J. Griffin in *Journal of Hellenic Studies* 97 (1977) 39–53.
[17] See Severyns (1928) 83–101.

consequently other Homerists have got a stronger impression than he probably intended, so that he has more recently claimed that he has been misunderstood.[18]

Thus a certain lack of clarity allowed critics to assert as fact that Kullmann had placed some of the cyclic epics earlier than the *Iliad*. And even without that the attitude which saw the *Iliad* as indebted to a particular recognizable pre-existing poem was anathema to those devoted to oral poetry theories, who were taught by Milman Parry and A. B. Lord that there were no definitive versions in oral poetry. In consequence, influential reviewers (Combellack and Page) were unsympathetic, attacking Pestalozzi, Schadewaldt, Kullmann, and the later, more doctrinaire, Schoeck,[19] mostly disregarding Kakridis, and not seeing the essential rightness of the approach.[20] These reviews probably added to the general neglect of neoanalysis in the English-speaking world.[21]

From the Sixties to the Nineties and Beyond

Not a great deal of importance has been written on neoanalysis since 1961 (it is not necessary to mention here every allusion or imaginative theory), apart from several presentations by Kullmann himself. He evidently feels, and rightly so, that the mantle of Kakridis has fallen to him, and he has endeavoured to justify this approach to a wider scholarly audience: see Kullmann 1968, 1981 (dedicated to J. T. Kakridis on his eightieth birthday), 1984 (written in English, attempting a rapprochement between neoanalysis and oral theory), and 1991 (to J. T. Kakridis on his ninetieth birthday), all four reprinted in the 1992 collection *Homerische Motive*. In the course of time Kullmann has moved away from the term 'neoanalysis' and come to prefer '*Motivübertragung*,' 'the taking over of motifs,' and (for the activity) '*motivgeschichtlich*,' 'relating to the history of motifs.'[22] This makes

[18] Kullmann (1968) 19 n. 18; (1981) 33 n. 76; (1991) 429 n. 24.

[19] In his *Ilias und Aithiopis* (1961).

[20] For the rightness, see Heubeck (1991) 451 n. 1; (1978) 9.

[21] An important exception is Fenik (1964), the thesis of which is clearly neoanalytical (that the Doloneia reflects a pre-existing version of the Rhesus story, the details of which we can deduce from the tragedy attributed to Euripides). Fenik shows his awareness of neoanalytical parallels on pp. 8–9.

[22] Kullmann (1981) 6; (1984) 309; the titles of 1991 and 1992.

quite a difference from Kakridis's original conception of echoes in the *Iliad* from non-Iliadic situations; for now all evidence of Homer's awareness of events in the Trojan war outside his immediate scope, and indeed of events in other cycles of Greek mythology, falls within the definition. Such an approach does still look behind the *Iliad* as we have it, but no longer gives one the feeling of closeness to the mind of a particular poet. The attempt at scientific completeness reaches the point in the latest treatment (Kullmann, 1991) where parallels that have been found between details of the *Iliad* story and non-Greek middle-eastern literature and religion are also treated as grist to the neoanalytical mill. Many may feel that this dilutes the concept of neoanalysis too much, making it indeed nothing more than 'Motivübertragung.'

Kullmann has strong views also about the use of writing. Like other German scholars, he refuses to believe that the *Iliad* can have been orally composed, thinking that such an accurate and considered composition necessarily implies the use of writing[23] (though he has no difficulty with a background of oral poetry before Homer); and he at one time tended to take the same view of the hypothetical poem about Memnon which was Homer's source, not easily seeing how the necessarily floating material of oral poetry could have occasioned such precise cross-references.[24] Later he felt the need to change this stance also and deny that it was neoanalytical dogma that the sources of the *Iliad* were in written form.[25] Belief in a written Homer, however, has been another barrier in the way of the acceptance of the results of neoanalysis by Parryists in America, as was pointed out by J. P. Holoka in the same volume in which Kullmann 1991 appears.[26]

Perhaps it would be best if neoanalysis abandoned the all-inclusiveness of allusion and reference which it has reached in Kullmann's latest writing, and returned to Kakridis's original perception, accepted also by Heubeck,[27] which restricted the scope of neoanalysis to certain

[23] Kullmann (1981) 29–30; he gives a list of scholars who share his belief in an *Iliad* composed with the help of writing on p. 30 n. 68.

[24] (1960) 372–3 n. 3, 374.

[25] *Gnomon* 49 (1977) 531; Kullmann (1991) 429.

[26] 'The majority of Neoanalyst practitioners, however, insist on a literate Homer,' in Latacz (1991) 467.

[27] Heubeck (1978) 9, refers to the objects of neoanalysis as 'narrative elements in Homeric poetry that were previously used in other contexts and only later were adapted by Homer for his own narrative.'

Iliad situations which actually reflect more significant occasions in the story of the Trojan war; for it is by this more limited definition that we find ourselves truly observing Homer at work. Other instances, to add to the 'Patroclea' of 17–18 and the rescue of Nestor in 8, are: Paris and Helen going to bed in 3, the expedition of Diomedes and Odysseus behind the Trojan lines in 10, Paris shooting Diomedes in the foot in 11, the aggressive and unpleasant character of Oilean Ajax in 23, Telamonian Ajax and Odysseus wrestling in the same book. That each of these is a specific, probably intuitive rather than conscious, allusion to a more famous occasion will be seen by any Homerist. They differ from much of what Kullmann wishes to include in his 'history of motifs.' Their relationship to the poetry known to Homer is best seen, not as some kind of imitation of a particular pre-existing poem, whether written or oral, but as the result of conditioning of the mind of the poet by the material with which he was familiar. Indeed, the most important and convincing example of all, the one we began with, the reflection of dead Achilles behind dead Patroclus, surely derives from the fact that Homer himself, the composer of the *Iliad*, had on other occasions sung of the death of Achilles in the Skaean gate, the recovery of his body, and the arrival of Thetis and the Nereids to mourn. There is no need to hypothesize an external source.[28]

Students of oral poetry distinguish, among the repeated elements in the system, between 'formulas' and 'typical scenes' (or, in A. B. Lord's term, 'themes'). Improvements in the discussion of formulaic composition[29] have made distinctions among the formulas themselves between those which were part of the common stock, available for use by the poet at will, and those that carried with them a particular aura from previous use or origin. Similarly with typical scenes or themes, some will have been part of the poet's regular repertoire (armings, arrivals, sacrifices), others more indicative of the conscious or intuitive artistry of the poet, as echoes or reflections or foreshad-

[28] When Homer sang, on other occasions, of the death of Achilles, he doubtless included the lavish funeral of the hero and magnificent funeral games; these are mentioned in *Od.* 24.63–84 and 85–92 in the speech of Agamemnon quoted above. *Iliad* 23 no doubt carries the resonance from that other song, for, as with the Nereids, Patroclus does not, in heroic terms, rate the honors paid to him: Heubeck (1991) 465–6.

[29] See Austin (1975), di Benedetto (1986), Shive (1987).

owings (the four soliloquies, the four warnings of Polydamas).[30] Into this latter category may be seen to fall the scenes identified in the original definition of neoanalysis; they show parallels with different situations in the oral poetry known to the poet, and so may be included in the description of 'composition by theme.' Along these lines there can be a close similarity of approach between neoanalysis and oral poetry theory; the two schools can fruitfully cross-pollinate. In alliance with oral theory, neoanalytical perceptions, by drawing attention to some sources of Homer's creativity, may be described as restoring the poet to the poetry.

[30] Willcock (1990).

PART TWO

HOMER'S LANGUAGE

Geoffrey Horrocks

HOMER'S DIALECT

Introduction

In the Archaic and early Classical periods dialectal heterogeneity, spoken and written, was a natural concomitant of the political fragmentation of the Greek world, which lacked any politico-cultural basis for the establishment of a single 'standard' language before the emergence of Athens as the focus of intellectual life and the later rise of Macedonia as a military power.

The language of the earliest Greek poetry therefore displays a clear dialectal character, but interestingly one which never corresponds exactly to the 'official' dialect of any given city or region (in so far as these are known to us). Instead each genre employs a form of language which exhibits certain distinctive 'markers' of the dialect group to which the spoken and official varieties of its supposed region of origin belonged, but which conventionally eliminates narrow linguistic parochialism in favour of a more stylised diction which conveys its dialectal affiliations in a rather neutral way and which, in varying degrees, reflects authorial ambitions to reach a panhellenic audience.

Wherever poetry of a particular kind came to be composed outside its 'traditional' region (not necessarily the region of origin but at least the region where it had undergone its most significant developmental phase), the associated 'literary' dialect was then routinely adopted as a genre-specific standard by all practitioners, regardless of their native speech. A good example is the 'literary Doric' of choral lyric, a genre which enjoyed an important developmental phase in Laconia (cf. Alcman), but whose dialect in its mature form (e.g. the works of Pindar and Bacchylides, neither of whom was of Dorian birth) employs little that is distinctively Laconian, or indeed that is specifically localizable within the Doric-speaking regions.

This state of affairs reflects a conception of 'poetic diction' that owes much to the precedent established by the earliest surviving poetry of all, namely the Homeric corpus, dating originally perhaps from the mid/late 8th century. This revered panhellenic possession formed a central part of Greek education and crucially employed a dialect which, while displaying an obviously Ionic character overall, was distanced from all contemporary varieties by its generally archaic 'feel' and the integration of 'foreign' elements of non-Ionic origin. It is the purpose of this chapter to investigate the origins and development of this linguistic amalgam which was to prove so influential for all later poetic activity.

The Problem of the Text of Homer

In any investigation of the language of 'Homer' we are obviously at the mercy of the material which has been transmitted to us, and it is immediately clear that we are dealing not with a transcription of what the monumental poet(s) might have composed but rather with a manuscript tradition that goes back to the great Alexandrian editors of the 2nd century B.C. Prior to this it is clear that 'personal' and 'official' editions proliferated, and that earlier still (taking it as given that the poems show evidence of oral composition)[1] we must allow at least for the possibility of a period of oral transmission before the poems were first written down, an interlude during which considerable modifications might have taken place.[2]

The problem is further exacerbated by the likelihood that the earliest texts were written in archaic local alphabets, which did not mark word division or double consonants, or distinguish between ε, η and (secondary)[3] ει, or between ο, ω, and (secondary) ου, so that later transcription into the standard orthography of the reformed/Ionic alphabet, introduced in Athens at the end of the 5th century B.C., must have presented problems with the spelling of relatively unfamiliar archaic or dialect forms.[4] To illustrate the nature of the difficulty we may cite a few examples of the textual uncertainty that arises

---

[1] This standard assumption goes back to the pioneering work of M. Parry collected in *The Making of Homeric Verse* (1971) and has been extensively developed by many scholars since, e.g., Hainsworth (1962) and (1968); Hoekstra (1965), (1969), (1981); Kirk (1962), (1966a, b), (1976); Lord (1960); Notopoulos (1960), (1962), (1964); Pavese (1972), to mention only a few.

[2] See Powell (1991) for a recent discussion of the complex issues involved.

[3] I.e., the product of a sound change such as contraction or compensatory lengthening.

[4] *Pace* Goold (1960).

when one of the possible modernized variants cannot be automatically selected for metrical reasons:[5]

1) (a) ΚΡΕΣΟΝ/ΜΕΖΟΝ: regularly written in their Attic form κρείσσων/μείζων rather than in their 'true' Ionic forms κρέσσων/μέζων.
   (b) ΚΑΙΡΟΣΕΩΝ (¯ ˘ ˘ ¯, η107): displays a suspicious absence of synizesis in the gen. pl. suffix (by which -εω- normally scans as one heavy syllable); the original form was probably καιρουσσέων (¯ ¯ ¯) < καιροεσσέων, the feminine of καιρόεις, with contraction of -οε- and synizesis in the final syllable.
   (c) ΤΕΘΝΕΟΣ (¯ ¯ ¯): sometimes written τεθνηώς, as preferred by Aristarchus, sometimes τεθνειώς (alongside the more modern τεθνεώς (¯ ¯) with antevocalic shortening of -η- and the usual synizesis).

In such circumstances it is clearly futile to try to establish 'Homer's text'. What we can do, however, is to employ our knowledge of the early history of Greek, supplemented where appropriate by standard methods of reconstruction and our understanding of the history and principles of epic meter (cf. M. L. West's chapter in this volume), to try to establish at least the general properties of the language of the tradition to which, in its final stages of development, the monumental poet(s) belonged.

Innovation and Archaism: Some Issues in Dialectology

Dialectological methodology requires that varieties be characterized on the basis of distinctive linguistic innovations not shared with other varieties. This is because archaisms preserved at any given time in one or more dialects of a language can often be shown previously to have characterized the language as a whole (with later local loss and replacement). Retention of an archaism in a particular dialect at a particular time is not therefore a criterion for determining the dialectal status of that form in earlier periods. This obviously has implications for the assignment of features in the language of the Homeric poems to particular dialect 'sources'.

---

[5] This is perhaps the best place to acknowledge once and for all the pervasive debt in what follows to P. Chantraine's (1965/1973) monumental *Grammaire Homérique*, an indispensible source of information and sound judgement on virtually all the central issues of Homeric usage. Other important surveys include Palmer (1962) and Hainsworth (1988) 24–32.

For example, the initial syllable of a word such as τόσ(σ)ος may scan as either light or heavy in 'Homer' and so, by convention, be spelled with either one or two sigmas. This metrically useful choice extends to many words in which the historic Ionic dialects (and Attic) had medial /s/ and the Aeolic (and Doric) dialects had medial /ss/. Since the primary dialectal layers of Homeric diction are Ionic and Aeolic (see below), we might be tempted to take τόσος as Ionic and τόσσος as Aeolic. But the forms with /s/ are simplifications of earlier forms with /ss/, and it may therefore be the case that those with /ss/ are simply 'prehistoric Ionic', retained alongside the newer forms because of their metrical utility in the preservation of established formula systems.[6] Thus while the metrically guaranteed presence of τόσος (alongside other Ionic innovations) justifies the assumption that Ionic provides an important layer of Homer's language, the fact that the historic Aeolic dialects preserve τόσσος etc. does not of itself entitle us to regard these as Aeolicisms. This would follow only if there were also evidence that either 2)(a) or 2)(b) was correct:

2) (a) the ancestor of Ionic already had /s/ in the relevant words even in the Bronze Age.
   (b) the Ionic epic tradition began relatively 'late,' i.e. after the simplification of /ss/.

We shall return to these questions below. In the meantime we must accept that, given the 'traditional' character of the epic language, much of it may prove to reflect 'common Greek' archaisms that were subsequently replaced in some or all later dialects, and that such features cannot tell us much about dialectal origins but themselves need to be 'interpreted' in the context of a reconstructed chronology of dialectal innovations and the development of epic diction.

Homeric Archaism

Homeric-Mycenaean correspondences

The decipherment of Linear B in the 1950s opened up important new lines of enquiry vis-à-vis the language of the Homeric poems.[7]

---

[6] Cf. D. G. Miller (1982), who seeks to demonstrate the continuity of the Ionic component of the epic by amassing arguments of this general kind.

[7] The basic text here is still Ventris and Chadwick (1973), though there is of

In particular, many apparently non-Ionic phenomena previously categorized as 'Aeolic' could now be shown to have parallels in 'Mycenaean' (i.e. the Greek dialect of the Linear B tablets).[8] Morphological examples include:

3) (a) masculine genitive singulars in -ᾱο (1st declension) and -οιο (2nd declension).
(b) genitive plurals in -ᾱων (1st declension).
(b) the 'oblique' case ending -φι (previously independently attested only in the isolated Boeotian ἐπιπατρόφιον).

In addition a large stock of shared vocabulary items was also discovered. For example:

4) a-pi-po-re-we /amphiphorêwes/ (KN Uc 160)	ἀμφιφορεύς
wa-na-ka /wanaks/ (KN Vc 73)	ἄναξ
di-pa /dipas/ (KN K 875)	δέπας
e-ke-si /enkhesi/ (PY Jn 829.3)	ἔγχος
ta-ra-nu /thrânus/ (PY Ta 707)	θρῆνυς
ko-ru /korus/ (KN G 5670)	κόρυς
o-ro-me-no /oromenos/ (PY Ae 134)	ὄρομαι
te-me-no /temenos/ (PY Er 312)	τέμενος
te-tu-ko-wo-a /tetukhwo(h)a/ (KN Ld 871)	τεύχω
pa-ka-na /phasgana/ (KN Ra 1540)	φάσγανον

Two things remained to be shown, however, if these parallels were to be of real significance: first that the Mycenaean world enjoyed a tradition of dactylic poetry from which this material had been inherited (the relevant forms and words might after all have been preserved for a time in ordinary spoken dialects, with epic poetry as we know it actually beginning in the Dark Age), and secondly that the elements in question came into the epic specifically from the poetry of the speech communities that produced the Mycenaean documents rather than from some other Bronze Age dialect(s) that might also have shared them (see below for further discussion on both items).

The 'new' dialectology of Greece in the Bronze Age

These questions could only begin to be answered in the context of a convincing theory of Bronze Age dialectology, which was duly provided

course now a vast specialist bibliography on specific points of detail. See in particular Ruijgh (1985).

[8] See for example, Chadwick (1958) 116–122 and Shipp's critique (1961).

by the pioneering work of W. Porzig and E. Risch.[9] The resultant renewal of interest in the prehistory of Greek soon led to a number of radical revisions of the previously standard view, going back to P. Kretschmer,[10] that Greek was brought to the Balkans ready-made by three successive 'waves' of invaders speaking Ionic, Achaean (the putative ancestor of Arcado-Cypriot and Aeolic) and Doric varieties respectively. It will therefore be useful at this point to attempt a consensus view of the 'new' dialectology.[11]

Greek is now widely believed to be the product of contact between Indo-European immigrants and the speakers of the indigenous languages of the Balkan peninsula beginning c. 2,000 B.C. As Mycenaean, known from documents of the second half of the 2nd millennium B.C., has been shown to have undergone key innovations characteristic also of the 'East Greek' dialect group of later times, i.e. Arcado-Cypriot and Attic-Ionic, it is clear that 'West Greek' varieties, a group later represented by Peloponnesian Doric and North-West Greek, must have coexisted in the Bronze Age. Since Linear B tablets have been found at various sites across the Peloponnese and as far north as Thebes, it is generally assumed that East Greek was at that time widely diffused over southern Greece, and that West Greek was spoken primarily in the north-west, with a later influx of speakers into the south (the 'Dorian invasion') either occasioning or exploiting the Mycenaean collapse c. 1200 B.C.[12]

According to this theory Mycenaean itself represents a standardized 'official' language of East Greek type, and both Arcado-Cypriot and Attic-Ionic are assumed to have evolved from a complex of only weakly differentiated East Greek spoken dialects during the course of the Dark Age; the first pair are supposed to be fairly direct descendants of this dialect continuum (Arcadian being the residue of East Greek in the central Peloponnese after the putative Dorian invasion, Cypriot the language of early colonists), while the second pair seem to have undergone more radical development, perhaps partly under

---

[9] Porzig (1954); Risch (1955).

[10] Kretschmer (1896).

[11] Cf. for example Chadwick (1956), (1963), (1976b); Cowgill (1966); García-Ramón (1975: reviewed by J. Chadwick, 'The Origin of the Aeolic Dialects,' *Classical Review* 28.2 (1978) 292–293) and C. J. Ruijgh in *Bibliotheca Orientalis* 30, 5/6 (1978) 418–423); see also Wyatt (1970).

[12] This standard view has been challenged in a radical way by Chadwick (1976b), who argues for West Greek as the dialect of the lower classes in the Mycenaean world (cf. Risch (1979) for a reaction).

the impact of a West Greek variety or varieties.[13] Crucially, the emergence of distinctively Ionic dialects (in eastern Attica and across the Aegean) is seen to be a largely post-Mycenaean development beginning in the 12th century B.C., following migration and population mixture in the wake of the destruction of the Mycenaean civilization.

It has similarly been argued that Aeolic too is an essentially post-Mycenaean development. Initially we seem to be dealing here with elements of East Greek admixture (e.g. ἱερός and 1st plural verb forms in -μεν for West Greek ἱαρός and -μες) into a subgroup of the West Greek dialects once spoken in Thessaly (i.e. in territory adjacent to the Mycenaean South); but all the truly distinctive Aeolic innovations seem again to have occurred in the two to three centuries after c. 1200 B.C.[14] East Thessalian is seen as the closest descendant of this proto-Aeolic in later times, with west Thessalian and Boeotian evolving under the continued influence of neighbouring North-West Greek, and Asiatic Aeolic, carried across the Aegean by Dark Age colonists from Thessaly some time before c. 1,000 B.C., and surviving as Lesbian, becoming partially assimilated to the neighbouring Ionic.

Implications for our interpretation of Homeric Greek

Assuming the essential correctness of this approach, the terms 'Ionic' and 'Aeolic' become anachronistic in the context of Bronze Age Greece, and it follows that if the epic tradition did indeed go back to Mycenaean times (and perhaps beyond: see below), its linguistic vehicle at that time must have been of a broadly East Greek or West Greek type. And since there is no good evidence for any exclusively West Greek innovations in the epic dialect as we know it,[15] it follows that, if Bronze Age dactylic poetry did indeed exist, it must have employed an East Greek (i.e. Mycenaean-like) dialect. Assuming this to be so, the simplest account of the archaisms in 3) and 4) would be that they entered the tradition from a dialect very like that of the Linear B tablets and were preserved subsequently because of their centrality to the formula systems which exploited them.

[13] Cf. Risch (1955); idem (1979), or see Chadwick's (1956) summary of the earlier work.

[14] García-Ramón (1975).

[15] Cf. Morpurgo-Davies (1964).

Although the notion of Aeolic dactylic poetry prior to the Mycenaean collapse can be rejected in the context of the dialectological framework above, we must nevertheless allow for the emergence after c. 1200 B.C. of a 'proto-Aeolic' branch of the tradition in Thessaly. Note, for example, that the Homeric poems contain such East Thessalian forms as ποτί alongside Ionic/Lesbian πρός (and indeed that the central character of the *Iliad* is a Thessalian). It is possible, then, that (elements of) an established East Greek tradition passed into just those adjacent parts of West Greek territory which display other signs of linguistic and cultural contact with the South, and that this material was developed and progressively Aeolicised as the local dialect evolved its own distinctive character in the early Dark Age.

Two possible interpretations of the Homeric dialect now become available. On the one hand the old East Greek (soon to be Ionic) tradition and the new Aeolic tradition may have evolved in parallel, with reciprocal diffusion of features and material that continued throughout the Dark Age after they had both been carried across the Aegean by colonists; the Ionian tradition as we know it would then represent a particularly brilliant phase of development that eventually eclipsed its Aeolic partner. Alternatively the tradition may have thrived initially only in Thessaly, with the old East Greek branch effectively dying out, and only the former being exported to the East. Since we know that Ionic, once established in the eastern Aegean and Asia Minor, expanded steadily at the expense of both Doric to the South and Aeolic to the North, it might then be the case that the Aeolic tradition was first assimilated and Ionicised during this process of expansion, and then extensively developed in its new guise. This highly controversial issue will be taken up below.

Whatever the true story, the Dark Age development of dactylic poetry not only in Ionia ('Homer') but also in Lesbos and adjacent territory in Asia Minor seems certain in the light of Sappho 44 ('the wedding of Hector and Andromache'), a narrative poem in 'Aeolic' dactyls on a traditional theme, which has been plausibly interpreted as providing evidence for a long poetic tradition similar to, but partly independent of, its Ionian counterpart.[16]

[16] See for example, M. L. West (1973a), (1988); Nagy (1974), Hooker (1977).

Bronze Age dactylic poetry?

The likelihood of Bronze Age dactylic poetry in an East Greek dialect has been reinforced by the observation that Homeric Greek has preserved a syntactic construction, so-called 'tmesis' (i.e. the separation of a preverb from its verb), which is clearly of Indo-European origin (see below) but which, in the absence of examples in the Linear B corpus, had probably already been eliminated not only from Mycenaean itself but also from contemporary spoken varieties of East Greek too, in so far as written languages are inherently more conservative than their spoken counterparts.[17]

Tmesis, however, is extremely common in Homer and indeed is central to a number of Homeric formula systems, as we can see from the example in 5):

5)	3		4	5		6	
	– ⏑ ⏓		– ⏑ ⏓	– ⏑ ⏓		– ⏓	
				δάκρυα		λείβων	(N658)
			(κατὰ)	δάκρυ χέ	-	οντα	(ξ280)
	τέ	-	ρεν κατὰ	δάκρυ χέ	-	ουσα	(Γ142)
	θαλε	-	ρὸν κατὰ	δάκρυ χέ	-	οντα	(δ556)

Since West Greek is assumed to be irrelevant to the epic tradition, it follows that even if tmesis was preserved in some Doric dialects for a time, the survival of such a grammatical archaism in the epic can most naturally be explained on the assumption that it was already, even before the period of our earliest Linear B tablets, ineradicably embedded in a number of key formula systems within the context of an East Greek tradition of dactylic poetry.

It is, however, possible that tmesis, having perhaps survived for longer in spoken West Greek, continued into proto-Aeolic as this began to emerge as a distinct group in the period after c. 1200 B.C. It might therefore have been incorporated into the developing Aeolic traditions of both lyric (cf. κὰδ δέ μ' ἴδρως ψῦχρος ἔχει . . ., Sappho 31.13, if Page's conjecture is correct) and dactylic poetry in post-Mycenaean times, and then been 'borrowed' by the Ionian tradition in a later period (cf. above).

We should note, however, that apocopation of prepositions or preverbs is common in West Greek and Aeolic, and is particularly

[17] Cf. Horrocks (1980).

prevalent in Thessalian. Presumably, then, this must already have been at least a characteristic tendency of the proto-Aeolic exported to the East, a view confirmed by the usage of the archaic poetry (cf. the line from Sappho above) and later official documents that survive from Lesbos. It is, however, very rare indeed in Ionic, and it is clear that the formula systems that rely on tmesis in Homer routinely employ the full forms of the prepositions concerned. Unless, then, we are prepared to believe that all the Ionic formulas exploiting tmesis were built at a 'late' date in the tradition on the basis of metrically distinct (apocopated) Aeolic models, surely a very difficult assumption given the very high frequency of such constructions in Homer and the heavily developed character of the formula systems concerned, it follows that the Ionian tradition must indeed have preserved the construction independently and that it therefore represents a continuous line of development from dactylic poetry of the Bronze Age.

Note that tmesis is in any case quite rare in surviving Lesbian poetry, and that the examples attested all involve the 'sandwiching' of a subject by preverb and verb, with the preverb typically standing in initial position in the clause (e.g. Alcaeus 326.6, 338.5). Though this pattern is shared with Homer and well attested in other early Indo-European languages, the other regular Homeric pattern, in which a separated preverb and its verb sandwich a direct object, as in the example in 5), is not apparently employed by the Lesbian poets at all, even though this too is paralleled in Vedic and so presumably also of Indo-European origin.[18] The at least partial independence of the Ionian tradition in this respect seems undeniable, and its continuity from the Bronze Age follows directly.

In support of this conclusion, we may also note the presence in the Ionian tradition of archaisms that clearly did not survive into any of the spoken dialects of the post-Mycenaean period and which had almost certainly already disappeared from East Greek by the time of the Mycenaean documents. Formulaic antiques such as that in 6), for example:

6) (a) λιπουσ' ἀνδροτῆτα καὶ ἥβην (Π857)
˘ |– – ˘ ˘ | – ˘ ˘ | – – ||

(b) .... */a+ nro+ tâ+ta/ ....
˘ | – ˘ ˘ | – – ˘ ˘ | – – ||

[18] Cf. Horrocks (1980).

where ἀνδροτῆτα does not scan in its 'modern' form, suggest that this must have originated in a prehistoric period before the intrusive /-d-/ had been inserted (already present in Mycenaean, cf. a-di-ri-ja-te /andriantei/, PY Ta 707, '(inlaid) with the figure of a man'), thus permitting the second syllable to scan light, assuming the syllabification given in 6)(b).[19] This again points clearly to the existence of a Bronze Age tradition which continued through and beyond the later Mycenaean era. Assuming once again the irrelevance of West Greek, such an early tradition can only have been of East Greek type; and once the existence of such a tradition is accepted, it is inconceivable that it would have abandoned a flexible constructional variant as central to the formulaic *Dichtersprache* as tmesis.

Innovation and the 'Abuse' of Inherited Characteristics

It should not, however, be imagined that the generations of bards who inherited such archaisms simply preserved them in the form in which they had first entered the language. On the contrary, new forms from the contemporary vernacular were continuously admitted throughout the history of the tradition, not only as useful metrically distinct alternatives to the older forms, but also more generally as replacements, whenever they could be introduced without undue metrical damage. While we should certainly not underestimate the deliberate retention of 'colourful' antique formulas and vocabulary, we should never forget that comprehensibility was a primary consideration for bards who made a living by entertaining audiences whose tolerance of 'archaism for its own sake' was surely limited.

By and large, then, the retention of archaisms seems to have been motivated by the degree to which they were embedded in an unmodifiable form within elaborated formula systems. Nevertheless, many such features of traditional diction were routinely ignored when they threatened to restrict creativity just as readily as they were artificially

[19] Cf. Watkins (1964). It is possible that Mycenaean retained a 'syllabic' /r/ (cf. A. Heubeck), 'Syllabic r̥ in Mycenaean Greek?' *Acta Mycenaea* 2 (1972) 55 and that this is indirectly attested here. This view has not prevailed, however, and it is perhaps simpler to assume development to /ro/, with the group /nr/ treated as tautosyllabic (cf. note 19), thus permitting the initial ἀ- to scan as a light syllable. The /d/ is a natural intrusion introduced after the creation of the formula, presumably.

extended when they proved themselves useful. Examples of such developments, internal to the language of the epic, are given below.

Digamma (ϝ)

/w/ was still a 'common Greek' feature at the very beginning of the 1st millennium B.C. But while the majority of dialects retained it (written ϝ) at least into the archaic and early classical periods, Ionic had already lost it in the period before alphabetic inscriptions begin. Homer's predecessors, however, certainly spoke a dialect (or dialects) which contained /w/, and many phrases and formulas first entered the tradition at a time when this was a phonetic reality. But by the time of monumental composition it had evolved into a 'silent,' though highly convenient, metrical convention, to be followed or ignored at will. Thus certain words beginning with a vowel behave metrically, within the context of inherited phrases and formula systems, as if they begin with a consonant, with the inaudible element in question serving both to block hiatus, 7)(a), and 'make position', 7)(b):

7) (a) ἐξαύδα, μὴ κεύθε νό- |ῳ, ἵνα | (ϝ)εἴδομεν | ἄμφω (A363)
(b) ἐσθλὸν δ' οὔτε τί πω εἶ- |πες (ϝ)ἔπος | οὔτε τέλεσσας (A108)
– ⏑ ⏑

The contemporary artificiality of these conventions is demonstrated by examples where the phantom consonant is ignored. Thus in 8)(a) we find elision of the vowel of δέ, and in 8)(b), where a light syllable is required in the 'weak' part of the foot, the potential to 'make position' is conveniently forgotten:

8) (a) ἐκπέρσαι Πριάμοιο πόλ- |ιν εὖ δ' | (ϝ)οἰκαδ' ἱ- |κέσθαι (A19)
(b) μάντι κακῶν, οὐ πώ ποτέ μοι τὸ | κρήγυον | (ϝ)εἶπες (A106)
– ⏑ ⏑

Since /w/ was not a phonetic reality for the bards working at the latter end of the Ionic tradition, its physical disappearance was frequently compensated for by adaptations of traditional formulas, involving devices such as the introduction of the characteristically Ionic 'movable -ν':

9) ἢ | ἄνδρασιν | (ϝ)ἶφι μάχεσθαι (A151)

This option is not, however, systematically employed everywhere it might be. Consider, for example, the 'normal' early Ionic dative plurals of 1st and 2nd declension nouns in -οισι(ν)/-ῃ/σι(ν). These normally undergo elision of the final -ι before an initial vowel in a following word (written -οις-ης), and sometimes therefore after the loss of an original initial /w/. This may then engender a characteristically 'epic' metrical restoration involving the addition of an extra syllable to the following word when this belongs to the neuter s-stem declension (with e/o alternation in the suffix, e.g. ἔπος/ ἔπε(σ)-ος):

10) ἀταρτηρ- | οἷς ἐπέ- | εσσιν || (A223)
< * ἀταρτηρ- | οἷσι ϝέπ- | εσσι ||

This oddity requires some explanation, given the availability in principle of movable -ν. To avoid paradigmatic 'irregularities' such as πο-σί (< * ποδ-σί) beside πόδ-ες etc., the Aeolic dialects introduced a 'new' dative plural in -εσσι (e.g. πόδ-εσσι), perhaps via the following analogy:

11)	1st declension:	nom. pl.	-αι	:	dat. pl.	-αι + σι
	2nd declension:	nom. pl.	-οι	:	dat. pl.	-οι + σι
	3rd declension:	nom. pl.	-ες	->	dat. pl.	-εσ + σι

This new dative plural suffix was then added to the s-stem type in the epic language in a way unparallelled in surviving 'real' Aeolic, perhaps on the basis of the analogical parallel in 12):

12)	πράγματ - α	:	ἔπε - α
	πραγμάτ - ων	:	ἐπέ - ων
	πραγμάτ - εσσι	->	ἐπέ - εσσι

Since movable -ν might well have been exploited here, this adaptation must originally have been carried out by Aeolic bards, with later adoption of the resultant forms by Ionic poets. And since Lesbian was the only Aeolic dialect both to prefer 1st/2nd declension dative plurals in -αισι/-οισι (forced by the fact that the corresponding accusative plurals end in -αις/-οις), and to experience relatively early loss of initial /w/ (thus forcing elision of the final -ι of the adjectives above before (ϝ)ἔπεσσι etc.) it seems, as expected, that we must look specifically to 'late' Asiatic Aeolic for an explanation of at least some of the non-Ionic features of Homer's dialect (cf. further below).[20]

Such hyper-Aeolicisms soon became part of the poets' stock-in-trade, however, and many examples, such as that in 13):

13) ἐρητύ- | ειν ἐπέ- | εσσιν || (B75)

---

[20] Cf. e.g., Janko (1982) 91–92.

are clearly not conditioned adaptations but involve 'original' creations guaranteed by the metre.

Correption

This conventional shortening of any long vowel or diphthong in hiatus must have originated with the natural prevocalic pronunciation of -αι and -οι as as short vowel + consonantal 'y':

14) Ἀτρεΐδ- |αι τε καὶ| ἄλλοι (A17)
– ᴗ ᴗ

This option, however, was soon extended, regardless of phonetic plausibility. Thus long diphthongs too can be shortened in this way, where, even after allowing for a consonantal pronunciation of the final -ι, the remaining long vowel still ought to form a heavy syllable. An extreme example is provided by 15), where even -εῳ (with synizesis) counts as a single light syllable:

15) χρυσέῳ ἀ- | νὰ σκήπτρῳ (A15)
– ᴗ ᴗ

The extension of the license to 'simple' long vowels was then only a matter of time.

Note, however, that this applies only in the weak part of the foot where light syllables are needed; wherever a long vowel or diphthong in hiatus is required to make position, correption does not take place:

16) ἡμετέρ- |ῳ ἐνὶ | (ϝ)οἴκῳ (A30)
– ᴗ ᴗ

Variable syllabification

Ordinarily a short vowel before a consonantal group consisting of a plosive + a liquid/nasal forms a heavy syllable (i.e. is syllabified VC + C); but in the weak part of the foot such a combination is regularly treated as a light syllable for metrical convenience (i.e. is divided V + CC):[21]

[21] I.e. a syllable containing a short vowel counts as light is it is not 'closed' by a consonant.

17) ἔπεα πτερό- | εντα προσ- | ηύδα (A201)

– ⏑ ⏑

This latter syllabification is particularly useful for words which would otherwise be unmetrical:

18) 'Αφροδίτη (V + CCV + CV̄ + CV̄ : ˘ ˘ | ¯ ¯)

Indeed, taking the use of digamma, correption, and variable syllabification together, it should by now be clear that they constitute a series of inter-related conventions that allow for the convenient creation of heavy syllables in the strong part of the foot and light syllables in the weak part of the foot, as required.

Contraction

There are many contractions in our text of Homer that would certainly have been lacking in earlier stages of the tradition (which was therefore very much more 'dactylic'). Consider the genitive singular of 2nd declension nouns in -ου, which derives from -οιο (/oj-jo/, as attested in Mycenaean and preserved as a metrically useful alternative in Homer) through simplification and eventual loss of /-jj-/ followed by later contraction of -oo.

The contracted form is often metrically guaranteed:

19) πολέ- |μου δ' ἀπο- | παύεο | πάμπαν || (A422)

– ⏑ ⏑

But wherever this suffix occurs in the weak part of a foot it is at least possible that it represents a modernization of earlier -oo (itself a liberating early innovation, since inherited -οιο could only fill the weak part of a foot, as a single heavy syllable, when its final -o was elided before a following vowel). This is particularly likely in cases where contraction produced a highly disfavoured spondee in the fourth or fifth foot:

20) | δήμου | φῆμις || (ξ239)

– –

Thus while some contractions are clearly 'original,' because metrically guaranteed, as in the famous formula:

21) ἔπε¯ |α πτερο- | έντα προσ- | ηύδα || (< *-α¯ε)

others almost certainly represent modernizations of more archaic phraseology with originally uncontracted vowels. Note once again, however, that bards did not hesitate to modernize their material in line with developments in the spoken language (whenever this could be done without collateral damage), or to exploit the new forms freely in building up new phraseology.

Limited damage (entailing further adjustment) was, however, clearly tolerable, and apparently sometimes preferable to the simple retention of archaic forms. Consider, for example:

22) || βῆν εἰς | Αἰό- | λου κλυτὰ | δώματα (κ60)
– ⏑

where the 2nd foot is unmetrical unless we assume artificial lengthening of the -ο- or doubling of the following -λ- (on which see *Metrical lengthenings*). If, however, we assume an original *Αἰόλοο the problem is resolved, since the final -ο before the group κλ- naturally constitutes a heavy syllable in the strong part of the foot:

23) || βῆν εἰς | Αἰόλο- | ο κλυτὰ | δώματα
– ⏑ ⏑ –

Similarly in 24)(a), the lengthening of the penultimate vowel in ἀδελφειοῦ (the word is normally ἀδελφεός) can also be explained as consequential upon the contraction of -οο in an 'original' 24)(b):

24) (a) οὐ δ' ἔτλη περιβῆναι ἀ- | δελφει- | οῦ κταμέν-| οιο || (E21)
– – – ⏑ ⏑

(b) οὐ δ' ἔτλη περιβῆναι ἀ- | δελφεό- | ο κταμέν-| οιο ||
– ⏑⏑ – ⏑ ⏑

It is, of course, impossible to know whether 'Homer' was responsible for all such changes (many contracted forms are guaranteed, after all), or whether some at least reflect later efforts to restore a metrical text following mistaken 'transcription' from archaic texts into the Ionic alphabet (if O could represent not only -ο, -ω, and -ου, but also -οο).

Distension

While regular contracted forms of verbs in in -άω are often metrically guaranteed and seem well-established in the tradition in their own right (cf. 21), the modernization of uncontracted traditional phraseology again sometimes led to unmetrical structures. In these circumstances the long contracted vowel was 'distended,' i.e. repeated, to restore the meter. Such forms demonstrate particularly clearly the 'internal' evolution of epic diction independently of normal spoken varieties.

Consider the examples in 25), where the original forms appear on the left, the contracted forms in the middle, and the distended Homeric forms on the right:

25) (a)	ὁρά-οντες (ᾰ)	>	ὁρῶντες	>	ὁρό-ωντες	(˘ ˘ – ˘̲)
(b)	μενοινά-ει (ᾱ)	>	μενοινᾷ	>	μενοινά-ᾳ	(˘ – – –)

In the third column the length of the initial element of the distended vowel corresponds to that of the stem-final -α- in the original form of the first column, where normal antevocalic shortening of the originally long -ᾱ- was naturally inhibited whenever the product would lead to an unmetrical sequence – ˘ –. Where a graphic distinction exists between long and short vowels, and the length of the second element of the distended vowel is not metrically determined (e.g. ὁρόοντες would be equivalent to the attested ὁρόωντες), we generally find the spelling which most closely reflects the standard orthography at the time of the transposition into the Ionic alphabet.

Metrical lengthenings

Many artificial lengthenings can be seen to fit a rather general pattern deriving from the treatment of certain prehistoric consonant clusters involving liquids (/l, r/) and nasals (/m, n/). In 'core' Aeolic (i.e., Thessalian and Lesbian, excluding Boeotian) the usual product was assimilation to the liquid/nasal producing gemination (doubling), but elsewhere we typically find simplification of the cluster to the liquid/nasal alone accompanied by 'compensatory lengthening' (i.e. lengthening of a short vowel before the surviving liquid/nasal in order to preserve the heavy syllable previously guaranteed by the cluster: VC + C > V + C > V̄ + C):

26)		*original*	*Thessalian/Lesbian*	*Ionic*
	(a)	*κριν-jω	κρίννω	κρῑνω
	(b)	*φθέρ-jω	φθέρρω	φθείρω

27)		*original*	*Thessalian/Lesbian*	*Ionic*
	(a)	*στάλ-νᾱ	στάλλα	στήλη
	(b)	*ἐσ-μι´	ἔμμι	εἰμί
	(c)	*ἔ-μεν-σα	ἔμεννα	ἔμεινα

Consider now past tense verb forms such as those in 28):

28) *ἔ-σλαβ-ε > ἔλλαβε
*ἔ-σνε-ον > ἔννεον
*ἐ-σρύ-ην > ἐρρύην

in which the heavy syllable before the liquid/nasal is metrically guaranteed. If we assume gemination to be a stage through which non-Aeolic dialects passed, the conventional spelling with a doubled consonant perhaps reflects here a phonetic reality of old Ionic, though the surviving Aeolic usage must have strengthened the position of such forms in the system. These etymologically 'motivated' forms remained in use alongside more modern Ionic forms with a single liquid/nasal (the absence of the usual lengthening being conditioned by the inhibiting effect of the 'standard' form of the augment in ἐ-), and bards soon felt able to exploit the coexistence of ἔλλαβε/ἔλαβε etc. to allow single intervocalic liquids/nasals occasionally to be doubled for metrical convenience even when there was no comparable etymological justification. We have already seen examples such as 22), where there is no graphic indication of the process and 'compensatory lengthening' might equally well be assumed (cf. 31) below). There are, however, a few examples of artificial gemination directly represented in the conventional spelling of the text:

29) ἔμμαθε (ρ226)
ἐλλίσονθ' (I585)

and these clearly represent the product of the 'internal' generalization of a once etymologically motivated metrical alternation (though again the development was supported by (Asiatic) Aeolic, where liquids and nasals are sometimes similarly doubled.)[22]

Parallel to gemination, however, we more usually find artificial vowel lengthenings before liquids and nasals, based on the corresponding 'modern Ionic' pattern of compensatory lengthening. In texts written in archaic alphabets the two options would, of course, have been indistinguishable, but lengthening was perhaps favoured graphically at the time of the transposition into the Ionic alphabet because this was particularly characteristic of the East Ionic dialects, spoken in the region where the epic tradition underwent its last major developmental phase (cf. below). These had, for example, gone further than

[22] Cf. Lesbian κάλημμι etc.

most other varieties in displaying compensatory lengthening even after the simplification of groups involving liquids/nasals + /w/:

30)	*original*	*E. Ionic*	*Other Ionic/Lesbian*
	*ξένϝος	ξεῖνος	ξένος
	*κόρϝᾱ	κούρη	κόρη/-ᾱ
	*καλϝός	κᾱλός	κάλος

Examples of metrical lengthenings involving the 'internal' extension of this development include:

31)	ᾱ̓νήρ (B553)	beside	ἀνήρ (B673)
	Οὔλυμπον (A221)	beside	Ὄλυμπον (A402)
	μείλανι (Ω79)	beside	μέλανα (H265)

The license was again especially useful in dealing with words that would otherwise have been unmetrical:

32) Πειρίθοος (- ⏑ ⏑ ⏒, for Περίθοος ⏑ ⏑ ⏑ ⏒)
εἵνεκα (- ⏑ ⏑ , for ἕνεκα ⏑ ⏑ ⏑ , cf. Myc. e-ne-ka with no /w/)

Over and above such examples of word-internal consonant doubling/metrical lengthening, we can also point to phenomena such as that in 33), where an etymological initial group involving a liquid/nasal still makes position:

33) ὄρε- | ϊ (ν)νιφό- | εντι || (N754: < *σνιφόεντι)
– ⏑ ⏑

Since such groups were simplified to a single liquid/nasal in all dialects prehistorically, making position in this way (whether by vowel lengthening or consonant doubling in actual performance) must have been a simple matter of convention from very early on in the tradition—another indication, if any were needed, of its great antiquity. Once again, however, we soon find examples such as those in 34), where no initial consonant cluster had ever existed:

34) (a) ἅμα | δὲ νέφος | (Δ274)
– ⏑ ⏑

(b) ὄφ- | ρα λεί- | ψαντε (Ω285)
– –

We cannot know, of course, whether 'Homer' himself doubled his liquids/nasals or lengthened the preceding short vowels in such cases, and the later orthography simply adopts the spellings standard at the time of the transposition into the Ionic alphabet.

Ionic and Aeolic

Although many features of the Homeric dialect are archaisms, or artificial adaptations or extensions of inherited archaic characteristics, there is an unmistakably Ionic quality overall to the text as we have it, and in some cases a specifically East Ionic quality (cf. 30). This points to a major period of development in Asia Minor and/or the adjacent islands, which is, of course, the region where 'Homer' is most persistently located by tradition. Characteristic Ionic innovations, or choices from inherited options, include the following (some of which, irrelevantly, are also Attic):

35) (a) original *ᾱ > η even after ε/ι/ρ (cf. βίη, χώρη etc.).
(b) quantitative metathesis, e.g. (*-ᾱο>) -ηο- > -εω- (cf. Πηληιάδεω etc.).
(c) movable -ν.
(d) athematic infinitives (i.e. of -μι verbs, which lack the 'thematic' linking vowel, cf. τίθε-μεν and λύ-ο-μεν, etc.) in -ναι.
(e) extension of 3 plural aorist indicative suffix -σαν in place of inherited -ν (cf. ἔθε-σαν, ἦ-σαν etc.).
(f) the modal particle ἄν.
(g) ἤν for ἐάν.
(h) ἡμεῖς/ὑμεῖς for forms based directly on *n̥s-sme/*us-sme (e.g. Lesbian ἄμμε-ς/ὔμμε-ς etc.).
(i) agent nouns in -της for earlier forms in -τηρ/-τωρ.
(j) characteristically East Ionic compensatory lengthening in forms such as ξεῖνος, μοῦνος etc. (cf. 30 above).

Nevertheless, a residue of distinctively Aeolic innovations remains stubbornly in place, despite the fact that many features which were once thought of as Aeolic can often, as we have seen, be reinterpreted as simple archaisms:[23]

36) (a) labial reflexes of inherited labio-velars (i.e. /kw, gw, khw/, still preserved in Mycenaean) even before front vowels, where Ionic has a dental (cf. πίσυρες, πελώριον, etc.).
(b) thematic infinitives in -έμεν (Thessalian and Boeotian, and possibly once also Lesbian, e.g. ἀκουέμεν etc.).
(c) athematic infinitives in -μεν (Thessalian and Boeotian, but probably originally Lesbian too).
(d) perfect participles in -ων / -οντος (e.g. κεκλήγοντες (μ256); but many 'strange' perfects with the long vowel of the nominative

[23] See Strunk (1957) for an extreme attempt to eliminate Aeolicisms, and Ruijgh (1957) for a general survey of the issues.

singular extended to the rest of the paradigm, e.g. μεμαῶτες (B473), perhaps conceal earlier Aeolic forms in -οντες.

(e) analogical doubling of -σ-, based on the inherited s-stem type ἐτέλεσ-σα, in aorists with short-vowel stems (e.g. (ἐ)κάλεσσα).

(f) generalization of the singular stem to the plural of the aorists of athematic verbs in Thessalian and Lesbian (e.g. (ἔ)θηκ-αν, beside the usual Ionic (ἔ)θε-σαν, both for original (ἔ)θε-ν, the latter with -σαν taken from regular aorists, cf. 35)(e)); such forms are also attested sporadically in early post-Homeric Ionic poetry, and may be partly an independent levelling, partly the product of contact with Aeolic varieties.

(g) dative plurals of consonant-stem nouns in -εσσι (including the artificial s-stem forms in -έεσσι, cf. 12) above).

(h) athematic infinitives in -μεναι (Lesbian), perhaps from the influence of Ionic -ναι on proto-Aeolic -μεν.

This Aeolic element of Homeric diction does not correspond exactly to the usage of any single Aeolic dialect as known to us from inscriptions or literature, but this is hardly surprising given that our knowledge of these varieties is quite limited and based largely on 'late' documents and papyri or manuscript copies containing a very restricted corpus of archaic poetry. The Homeric forms belong to an earlier tradition which almost certainly comprised inputs from different periods and different places (cf. above). According to García-Ramón (1975), of the features given above, 36)(a)–(e) represent either inherited archaisms (the athematic infinitive in -μεν) or innovations that took place before c. 1125 B.C. Of the remainder, 36)(f) and (g) are placed between 1125 and 1000 B.C., leaving only 36)(h) as a specifically Lesbian innovation from the period after 1000 B.C. (i.e., after the Aeolic migrations when the dialect came under Ionic influence). It should be noted, however, that Ionic provides the predominant dialect base and that the Aeolic forms appear routinely only where they offer an alternative metrical shape to their Ionic equivalents. Consider the examples in 37):

37) (a) ἄμμες/ὔμμες before consonants are metrically equivalent to ἡμεῖς/ὑμεῖς and so do not appear there; prevocalically, however, they provide a light final syllable where the Ionic forms offer a heavy one.

(b) ἔμμεν/ἔμμεναι (including artificially 'degeminated' ἔμεν/ἔμεναι, beside εἶναι.

(c) (ἐ)κάλεσσα etc. beside Ionic (ἐ)κάλεσα.

(d) θεᾱ́ (nom./voc.) for Ionic θεός/θεέ, 'goddess'.

Diffusion or 'Aeolic Phase'?

As noted, Homer's Aeolicisms might represent the product of continuous borrowing and subsequent Ionicisation of formulas, themes, and episodes from a parallel Aeolic tradition, beginning in the early post-Mycenaean period and continuing through the Dark Age, especially in the eastern Aegean. Surviving Aeolicisms would then represent a residue of forms that could not be replaced by contemporary Ionic equivalants for metrical reasons, but which were subsequently exploited freely for their metrical utility.

Alternatively, the East Greek tradition of the Bronze Age might have died out with the demise of the Mycenaean civilisation. If so, elements of that tradition, having taken refuge in Thessaly, could have formed there the basis for an exclusively Aeolic phase of the tradition which was later exported to Lesbos and adjacent territory on the mainland of Asia Minor. The Ionic phase would then represent the later 'rediscovery,' Ionicisation, and development of this material by the Ionians as they expanded northwards into formerly Aeolic territory.

The idea of an Aeolic phase in the development of the epic goes back at least to Fick (1885), and has been vigorously defended by various supporters ever since.[24] While often disagreeing about the scale of the Ionian contribution and the timing of the 'takeover,' all proponents of such a theory agree that a line of Aeolian bards stands between the origins of the genre and the later Ionian epic. We should note, however, that the assumption of diffusion in a later period is not *per se* incompatible with a theory which supposes that the initial post-Mycenaean development of the epic took place exclusively in areas where Aeolic speech was developing.

First challenged by Sittl (1884), this theory of successive phases has become rather unfashionable in recent years, perhaps in line with our growing understanding of the complexities of dialect contact and the almost unlimited possibilities, given favourable conditions, for linguistic diffusion.[25] The fundamental question, of course, is whether characteristically Ionic features peter out as we work back in time,

---

[24] Fick (1885) 195–246. See, for example, M. Parry 'Studies in the Epic Technique of Oral Verse Making. II. The Homeric Language as the Language of an Oral Poetry,' in Parry (1971), Palmer (1962), Hoekstra (1965), Wathelet (1971), Janko (1982).

[25] Sittl (1884) 1–31. See the work of, amongst others, Webster (1958), Wyatt (1969), (1975), Hooker (1977), D. G. Miller (1982).

leaving a 'gap' between the earliest recoverable Ionic forms and their East Greek antecedents in the Bronze Age; any such gap would constitute *prima facie* evidence for the putative Aeolic phase. Most recently, Janko (1982) has argued strongly for the existence of such a gap, while Miller (1982) has argued equally forcefully that the most characteristic Ionic innovations have a complete phonological history in the Homeric poems. Clearly both cannot be right, and an attempt to evaluate the arguments has been made by Horrocks.[26]

Consider first of all the chains of development given in 38):

38) (a) *στᾱ́-ο-μεν > στεί-ο-μεν (O297) > στέ-ω-μεν (Λ348)
(b) *νᾱ(ϝ)-ός > νη-ός (A476) > νε-ός (O423)

Here we have the interaction of two sequential Ionic innovations *vis-à-vis* common Greek, the shift of *ᾱ > η and quantitative metathesis (the latter restricted to antevocalic shortening in 38)(b) because of paradigmatic pressure to avoid an irregular genitive singular ending in -ως). The sequence in each example represents first the 'common Greek' form, then the earliest Ionic form (-ει- in 38)(a) is an erroneous transposition of the archaic spelling E), and finally the 'modern' Ionic form of the later stages of the tradition. On the face of it such evidence would appear to vindicate Miller, and advocates of an Aeolic phase are clearly faced with a problem.

But before jumping to conclusions, we should also note the counter-examples in (39), first noted by Meister (1921),[27] and central to anti-diffusionist argumentation ever since:

39) (a) -ᾱο > *-ηο > -ε͜ω (gen. sg. masculine a-stems)
(b) -ᾱων > *-ηων > -ε͜ων (gen. pl. a-stems)

The Homeric poems have large numbers of examples of both the initial (common Greek) and the final (modern Ionic) endings in each sequence, the latter normally scanned as a single heavy syllable with synizesis; but of the reconstructed endings in the middle (putative old Ionic, with e-spellings and heavy-light scansion) there is no trace. This apparent gap in the phonological history of Ionic clearly supports the theory of an Aeolic phase, and diffusionists too are apparently confronted with some inconvenient facts.

As noted, the 'Aeolic phase' account requires us to postulate a reason for the delayed operation of quantitative metathesis/antevocalic

[26] Horrocks (1987).
[27] Meister (1921).

shortening in forms such as those in the central column of 38), so that this particular subset of 'intermediate' forms could survive in vernacular Ionic for longer than those in 39), and crucially for long enough to be incorporated from that source directly into the Ionic poetic tradition once it eventually got under way. But even if a suitably plausible account could be constructed (cf. Horrocks (1987) for an attempt), it would fail to explain the evidence presented above in favour of the continuity of the East Greek tradition. In any case, the theory of an Aeolic phase presupposes the disappearance of the Bronze Age poetic tradition throughout the old Mycenaean (and new Ionic-speaking) territories, in a period when, if Kirk (1962, 1976) is right, conditions were such as to promote heroic poetry.

'Diffusionists,' then, have overall plausibility on their side, but the apparent early loss of the 'old Ionic' forms in 39), alongside their retention in 38), still has to be accounted for. On this approach, since there would have been no reason to retain any original/archaic forms such as -ᾱο / -ᾱων alongside the metrically equivalent old Ionic forms with -η-, it must instead be supposed that the latter were actually replaced relatively late in the Ionian tradition by metrically equivalent Aeolic forms (which also happened to be conservative) whenever the Ionic vernacular evolved more modern variants of a different metrical value. This would require us to believe that contemporary 'foreign' inflectional morphology was in principle favoured over Ionic archaism, according to the following hierarchy:

40) (a) if possible, replace archaic and/or Aeolic morphology in borrowed material with contemporary Ionic.
(b) failing this, retain the Aeolic forms, and exploit them to replace archaisms, whether original or specifically Ionic, in both native and borrowed material.
(c) failing this, retain the archaisms.

In favour of this (initially perhaps not very appealing) hypothesis, consider again the endings -ᾱο and -ᾱων, not now as graphic but as phonetic forms within the context of the phonological system of early Ionic. These would in fact have been felt to fit quite naturally into a paradigm in which the element -ᾱ- /a:/ was already well established in the accusative plural (earlier -ανς > -ᾱς). But it is vital to note here that Ionic in fact lacked the phoneme /a:/ altogether until the simplification of the consonant cluster and compensatory lengthening in forms of this kind. The change probably took place in the early 8th century, since, as Chadwick (1956) has pointed out, the

Persian word *Māda* is borrowed as Μῆδος in Ionic (though as Μᾶδος in Cypriot), and Medes could hardly have become known to the Greeks before the 9th century at the very earliest; if /a:/ had existed at that time in Ionic, the word would have been borrowed as Μᾶδος. The genitive endings -ᾱο and -ᾱων must therefore have been incorporated into the East Greek/Ionian tradition as replacements for -ηο and -ηων sometime after both the onset of quantitative metathesis, around the end of the 9th century B.C. (cf. Janko 1982: 93), and the emergence of new long -ᾱ- (/a:/), perhaps early in the 8th century B.C. Prior to that time it is clear that Ionian bards, in the absence of /a:/ in their own dialect, would simply have pronounced these endings with a phonetic reflex of the phonologically corresponding /ε:/, i.e. as -ηο and -ηων, and that the subsequent treatment of them could not then have been distinguished from that of the native forms, a patently false account of the phenomena.

Here, of course, lies the fatal flaw in the theory of an Aeolic phase; if the Ionian tradition could not have incorporated phonetic elements assignable to a phoneme /a:/ until the early 8th century, we are forced to accept a date for the assumed Ionian 'takeover' which is far too late to allow for the emergence of the *Iliad* (more or less as we have it) by c. 750 B.C. The only alternative is to accept that the Ionian tradition had been around for a very long time prior to the introduction of -ᾱο and -ᾱων, exactly as the diffusionists argue. The disappearance of -ηο and -ηων cannot therefore be taken to support the existence of an exclusively Aeolic phase in the tradition, despite initial appearances to the contrary, and the hypothesis summarised in 40) would appear, after all, to be essentially correct.

The retention of the old Ionic forms in (38) must, of course, still be explained (again cf. Horrocks (1987) for an attempted account), but assuming a reasonably convincing treatment of the problem to be available, it seems clear that standard assumptions about the chronology of sound changes in early Greek force an interpretation of key Aeolicisms that ties in well with other evidence about the continuity of an East Greek/Ionic tradition of dactylic poetry and which generally supports the theory that diffusion lies at the heart of the 'mixed' dialect of the Homeric poems as they come down to us. At the very least proponents of an Aeolic phase have some very difficult questions to answer before such an approach can be revived as a fully plausible rival.

Martin West

HOMER'S METER

The Homeric poems are composed in a single meter throughout. The same metrical pattern governs every line, and the pattern recurs, line after line, for many thousands of verses. This does not mean that every line is metrically identical, because the pattern has several tolerances built into it: it admits certain variant forms as equivalent. But the essential structure of the verse remains uniform.

This principle of line-by-line repetition is characteristic of epic poetry in many cultures. It is normal to find the same meter used throughout a poem, however long. The only common modification of this simple 'stichic' principle is that in some traditions it has become the practice to group verses together into stanzas, whether of fixed or changing length. There is no sign of such grouping in Homer.

What did stichic structure mean in oral performance? The Iliad and Odyssey are written texts, but their poets describe men 'singing' heroic poetry to the accompaniment of a lyre, and they were no doubt accustomed to do so themselves. If every verse has the same metrical pattern, does that imply that it was sung to the same melody, repeated over and over again? That might be thought impossibly monotonous; yet it is supported by the analogy of many other epic traditions.[1] There is one scrap of Greek evidence: a fragment of a hymn in the epic meter, inscribed on stone at Epidaurus, with musical notation provided for the first line only, as if to serve for all. The inscription was cut in the third century A.D., but the hymn and its music may be many centuries older, and the practice of using the same melody for every line is more likely to have been inherited

[1] I have cited several, with references, in M. L. West (1986) 42–43. For others see S. M. Pandey, *The Hindi Oral Epic Canain* (Allahabad, 1982) 58; E. Gerson-Kiwi in *The New Grove Dictionary of Music and Musicians* (London, 1980) ix. 638 (Yemen); various authors in *Traditions of Heroic and Epic Poetry*, ed. A. T. Hatto (London, 1980–9), i. 107 (D. J. A. Ross: Old French), 202 (R. Auty: Serbo-Croat), 225 (G. F. Cushing: Ob-Ugrian), 294–5 (C. R. Bawden: Mongol), 304–5 (A. T. Hatto: Kirghiz); ii. 98 (K. Reichl: Uzbek). In some cases the singers have more than one melody at their disposal, and alternate them in different types of context.

from the archaic period than introduced later. On the other hand, there is reason to believe that the Homeric singer was able to preserve the natural pitch accents of the words, the musical rises and falls that were an inherent feature of the classical Greek language. These formed a different pattern in every line. But it may have been possible to reconcile them with a repeating melodic scheme, provided that it had a certain elasticity.[2]

Prosody

Before the scheme of the Homeric verse is considered, it is necessary to explain the principles of prosody. The meter of Homer, like that of all classical Greek verse, is 'quantitative,' based on the opposition of long and short syllables, not (like English verse) on the opposition between accented and unaccented elements. In Greek the distinction between long and short was for the most part clear-cut. In any given word each vowel was in itself either long or short; only in occasional special cases could it fluctuate.[3] The length of *syllables*, which is what counts for meter, depended partly on the length of the vowels that they contained, and partly on whether the syllable was 'open' (ending with the vowel) or 'closed' (with a consonant following the vowel before the syllabic boundary).

For this purpose the whole verse is treated as a continuum and analysed into syllables without regard to word division. The syllable begins with the consonant (if any) preceding each vowel, or if there is none, with the vowel itself. When two consonants occur together (other than at the beginning of the verse), the second initiates the following syllable, while the first is (normally) allocated to the preceding one, making it closed.[4] The *spiritus asper* is ignored. For example, in the line

πέπλον μὲν κατέχευεν ἑᾱνὸν πατρὸς ἐπ' οὔδει

[2] On this question (and other aspects of performance) see M. L. West (1986) and (1992) 208–209 and 328.

[3] The vowels ε and ο are short; η, ω, and diphthongs are long; α, ι, and υ are short in some words, long in others. In this chapter they will be printed ᾱ, ῑ, ῡ where they are long (unless they carry a circumflex accent, which is a sufficient indication); otherwise they should be assumed to be short.

[4] The double consonants ζ [zd], ξ [ks], ψ [ps] are likewise divided between syllables.

(*Il.* 5.734) the syllabification is

πεπ-λον-μεν-κα-τε-χευ-ε-νε-ᾱ-νον-πατ-ρο-σε-που-δει.

Any closed syllable counts as long, even if its vowel is short (as in the first three syllables in the example). An open syllable with a long vowel or diphthong is long, at any rate if the next syllable begins with a consonant (see below). An open syllable with a short vowel is short. The line quoted therefore scans

– – – ⏑ ⏑ – ⏑ ⏑ – – – ⏑ ⏑ – –

These basic rules are subject to certain qualifications and exceptions.

1. A long vowel or diphthong at word-end is usually shortened when the following word begins with a vowel. This is called epic correption. Thus in

Ἀτρεΐδαι τε καὶ ἄλλοι ἐϋκνήμῑδες Ἀχαιοί

the diphthongs in καὶ and ἄλλοι are both shortened. In cases where the shortening does not take place, we speak of 'hiatus' (a term also applicable when a short final vowel is not elided before another vowel).

Internal correption, that is, shortening before a vowel in the same word, occurs exceptionally, as in *Il.* 1.489 υἱός scanned ⏑ –, 13.275 οἷός ἐσσι ⏑ ⏑ – ⏑, 16.235 χαμαιεῦναι ⏑ ⏑ – –, *Od.* 20.379 ἔμπαιον οὐδὲ – ⏑ ⏑ – ⏑.

2. Sometimes two adjacent vowels, or a vowel and a diphthong, are run together to make one long syllable. This is called synecphonesis or synizesis. It is regular with the case-endings -εω (from -ᾱο) and -έων (from -άων). Synecphonesis of vowels in different words is rare but can be striking, as in *Il.* 17.89 ἀσβέστωι· οὐδὲ, 18.458 ἐμῶι ὠκυμόρωι, *Od.* 1.226 εἰλαπίνη ἠὲ, 24.247 ὄγχνη, οὐ. The text is not certain in all these instances.

3. To be distinguished from the above class is the occasional reduction of a short ι before a long vowel to a non-syllabic [y] in order to accommodate in the verse a proper name of awkward metrical shape: *Il.* 2.537 Ἱστίαιαν, 749 Αἰνιῆνες, 9.382 Αἰγυπτίᾱς, each scanned as only three syllables and pronounced *Histyaian, Ainyēnes, Aiguptyās*. These names could not otherwise have been used, because the verse scheme does not admit the sequence – ⏑ –.

4. A plosive consonant (π β φ, τ δ θ, κ γ χ) followed by a liquid (λ or ρ) is occasionally treated as syllable-releasing, so that a preceding short open syllable remains unlengthened. This is called Attic correp-

tion, because it is typical of Attic verse. Thus the name Ἀφροδῑτη is syllabified Ἀ-φρο-δῑ-τη, leaving the first syllable short; otherwise it could not have been used. This type of correption occurs more often when the plosive + liquid begin a word, as in the formula ἔπεα πτερόεντα προσηύδᾱ.

5. It happens also with a few names and other words beginning with σκ or ζ (Σκάμανδρος, Σκαμάνδριος, σκέπαρνον, Ζάκυνθος, Ζέλεια) that a preceding short open syllable remains unlengthened, because the sequence – ⏑ – would otherwise be created.

6. Initial continuants (λ, μ, ν, ῥ, σ) are sometimes treated as doubled consonants, so that a preceding short open syllable becomes closed and long.

Some further freedoms and anomalies will be considered later.

The Metrical Scheme

The meter of the Homeric epics is known as the hexameter, that is, the 'six-measure';[5] or, to give it its full title, the dactylic hexameter catalectic. The terminology reflects a traditional analysis of the verse as consisting of six metra or feet of dactylic nature (– ⏑ ⏑), the sixth one being 'catalectic,' truncated by one position. In any of the first five feet the two shorts may be contracted into one long; this is often described as substituting a spondee for the dactyl. The sixth foot may be represented either by – ⏑ or by – –, since the final syllable of any verse may be either long or short. The scheme, then, is:

1 – ⏕ 2 – ⏕ 3 – ⏕ 4 – ⏕ 5 – ⏕ 6 – ⏒ ||

The double vertical bar at the end indicates that there is no prosodic continuity between one line and the next; a word cannot overrun, and a vowel at line-end cannot be elided.[6]

For some purposes it is convenient to analyse each of the first five feet into two parts, the 'princeps' and the 'biceps.' A princeps is a

[5] The term first appears in Herodotus, who uses the phrases ἐν ἑξαμέτρωι τόνωι (1.47.2, 62.4, 5.60; then without τόνωι in 5.61.1) and ἐν ἔπεσι ἑξαμέτροισι (7.220.3). Some writers (Pl. *R.* 400b following Damon, Arist. *Po.* 1460a3, etc.) speak of the 'heroic' rhythm or metre, ἡρῶιος/-ον, ἡρωϊκόν.

[6] The archaic form Ζῆν, which occurs in three places (and once in Hesiod) at line-end, was misunderstood as elided Ζῆνα by Aristarchus, and perhaps already by early poets, since in each case they start the next line with a vowel. See M. L. West (1966) 399–400.

metrical position that calls for a long syllable; a biceps is a pair of short positions that may be replaced by one long. Despite the interchangeability of two shorts with one long in this context, ancient rhythmical theorists taught that the princeps in the hexameter was shorter in duration than the biceps by an amount which they could not quantify. Various features of Homeric versification (to be mentioned below) support this, and suggest that the ratio was something of the order of 5:6. This presumably reflects the fact that the average long syllable was about five-sixths of the length of two average shorts in ordinary speech, or five-thirds of the length of one short.[7]

One effect of this is that when the biceps is occupied by one long syllable instead of two shorts, a slight strain is put on the rhythm: either the long syllable in question has to be prolonged slightly beyond its natural duration, or the progress of the verse is momentarily accelerated. It is observable that words containing three consecutive long syllables are generally placed so that only one of them occupies a biceps: – ⏕ –, or at verse-end ⏕ – –, rather than ⏕ – ⏕. By the same token, words with four long syllables are normally placed at verse-end so that only one biceps needs to be contracted.

Contraction is more frequent in the first half of the line than in the second. In each of the first two feet it occurs in about 40% of verses; in the third foot in about 15%; in the fourth, in about 30%; in the fifth, in only 5%. There are half a dozen lines in which every biceps is contracted, as at *Il.* 23.221,

ψῡχὴν κικλήσκων Πατροκλῆος δειλοῖο.[8]

Caesuras and Pauses

Every verse without exception has a caesura (word-end) at one of three places: (1) after the first syllable in the third foot ('masculine' or penthemimeral caesura); (2) between the two shorts in the third foot ('feminine' or κατὰ τρίτον τροχαῖον caesura); or (3) after the first syllable in the fourth foot (hephthemimeral caesura). Over 98%

[7] See West (1982a) 18–20. The term 'princeps' is my invention (loc. cit.); 'biceps' was coined by Paul Maas, but I use it in a more restricted sense than he did (see 1982a, 192).

[8] For detailed statistics see J. La Roche, 'Zahlenverhältnisse im homerischen Vers,' *Wiener Studien* 20 (1898) 1–69.

of lines have one of the third-foot caesuras, and of these the 'feminine' – ⏑ | ⏑ predominates over the 'masculine' – | ⏕ in the proportion 4:3.

This regular incidence of caesura in the third foot effectively divides the verse into two not quite equal cola, differentiated by the feature that the first begins in 'falling' rhythm, the second in 'rising.' Cola of similar forms occur independently in lyric verse, and it is these, rather than the notional 'feet' of paper analysis, that constitute the essential components of the hexameter. Many of the traditional formulae of epic diction are shaped to fill one or other colon and thus especially easy to combine, as in a verse such as αὐτὰρ ἐπεὶ τό γ' ἄκουσε + Ποσειδάων ἐνοσίχθων.

In the small remainder of verses that have only a hephthemimeral caesura, a long word extends across the whole of the third foot and into the fourth, as in *Il.* 1.218,

ὅς κε θεοῖς ἐπιπείθηται, | μάλα τ' ἔκλυον αὐτοῦ.

In such lines the caesura may be regarded as displaced from its normal third-foot location to the next position that yields a similar effect, namely division of the line into unequal cola and contrast of falling with rising start.[9]

The caesura may depend on an elision, as in the second line of the Iliad:

οὐλομένην, ἣ μυρί' | Ἀχαιοῖς ἄλγε' ἔθηκεν.

The enclitics δέ, μέν, γάρ, κεν, ἄν, the proclitics καὶ, ἀλλὰ, and the monosyllabic prepositions are felt to cohere so closely with the preceding or following word that no valid caesura can exist between them. Certain other clitics, however, are occasionally found divided by the caesura from the word on which they lean, such as οὐ (*Il.* 1.132), ποτε (*Il.* 3.205), the definite article (*Od.* 21.245), and disyllabic prepositions such as ἀνά (*Il.* 1.53).

The converse of a caesura is a 'bridge,' a place in the verse where word-end is avoided. There is one significant bridge in the Homeric hexameter, discovered by Gottfried Hermann in 1805 and consequently known as Hermann's Bridge.[10] It links the two shorts of the

[9] The examples of this caesura are listed by K. Lehrs, *Jahrbücher für classische Philologie* 6 (1860) 513–31.

[10] G. Hermannus, *Orphica* (Leipzig, 1805) 692–4. Exceptions are listed by J. van

fourth foot, between which word-end seldom occurs. Again, clitics are regarded as cohering with the preceding or following word, so that the rule is not infringed by lines such as

ἄμφω ὁμῶς θῡμῶι φιλέουσά-τε κηδομένη-τε

or τὴν μὲν ἐγὼ σὺν νηΐ τ' ἐμῆι καὶ-ἐμοῖς ἑτάροισιν.

But it is breached by a line such as

πολλὰ δ' ἄρ' ἔνθα καὶ ἔνθ' ἴθῡσε | μάχη πεδίοιο.

Sentence- and phrase-structure is not closely tied to the verse-structure, but not altogether independent of it. The strongest sense-pauses, such as those preceding the introduction of a new topic or a new development in the narrative, occur at the end of a verse. Some 63% of all lines have a syntactic break at the end sufficient to call for some punctuation in a modern edition. After that, the commonest places for a sense-pause are at the caesura or at the end of the fourth foot. For the rest, sense-pauses are practically confined to the beginning of the line, in the first foot or at latest after the first syllable of the second. These occur either when the verse begins with a very short sentence, such as ὣς φάτο, or when a sentence overruns from the preceding verse. The poets are much more inclined to let a sentence overrun by a word or so than to bring it to a conclusion shortly before the end of a verse.[11]

Word-shape and Placement

It is an important feature of Homeric versification that for words of any given metrical shape there are certain preferred positions in the line.[12] For words of three syllables there will be at most three favored places; for longer words, seldom more than two. These limitations are explained partly by the constraints of the caesura, partly by the tendency to avoid more than one contracted biceps per word. The effect of the caesura was not just the negative one of ruling out certain

---

Leeuwen, *Mnemosyne* 18 (1890) 265–76. Their average frequency is about once in 550 lines.

[11] Much effort has been devoted to the study of enjambement. See M. Parry (1971) 251–65; Kirk (1966a) 105–50; Sicking (1993) 75 n. 27 with references.

[12] Shown in detail by O'Neill (1942).

placements that would conflict with it. It meant that the poets were composing within a frame

– ⏑ ⏑ . . . ⏑ – – ⏑ | ⏑ – – ⏑ ⏑ . . . ⏑ – – ‖ or – ⏑ ⏑ . . . ⏑ – | ⏑ ⏑ – ⏑ ⏑ . . . ⏑ – – ‖

which called for particular sorts of word-shape at four points. Words—particularly polysyllables—which were of the right shape for the beginning or (especially) for the end of one or other colon tended to be assigned to that position rather than to other possible, colon-internal positions. Thus words shaped ⏑ – –, or ending with that sequence, tended to be put at the end of the verse; those ending ⏑ – ⏑ or – – ⏑ either there or before the caesura; those beginning – – ⏑ ⏑ or ⏑ ⏑ – ⏑ ⏑ or ⏑ – ⏑ ⏑ after the caesura; those scanning – – – or – ⏑ ⏑ – at the beginning or end of the first colon.

Hermann's Bridge may be explained as a consequence of this principle. It is another way of saying that words shaped ⏑ ⏑ – ⏑ or ⏑ – ⏑ or – – ⏑ are not normally placed at the beginning of the second colon.[13]

Words with a long penultimate syllable and a short vowel in the final syllable tend not to be so placed that a collocation of consonants lengthens that syllable. Thus a word such as ἄλλον or Ὀδυσῆος, if not at verse-end, would normally be followed by a word beginning with a vowel. Again this is something which was differently formulated in the early nineteenth century when one manifestation of it was observed, namely that where there is word-end after a spondee in the fourth foot, the last syllable of the word in question usually has a long vowel.[14] The second foot shows a similar tendency, though less markedly. In general, word-end after contracted biceps is frequent only in the first foot.

Wilhelm Meyer's three Laws may be mentioned here, though they were formulated for Alexandrian hexameter verse, not for Homer, who is so impudent as to break all three of them in the very first line of the Iliad. Meyer's First Law states that words which begin in the first foot do not end between the shorts of the second foot, or at the end of that foot. This follows from the preferences noted above for the placing of words of the relevant shapes. But they are only preferences, and exceptions that transgress Meyer's rule occur every

[13] M. L. West (1982b) 281–97, at 294–5, and (1982a) 37–38.

[14] This is commonly known as Wernicke's Law, after F. A. Wernicke, *Tryphiodori Ilii excidium* (Leipzig, 1819) 173, but it was actually first stated by E. Gerhard, *Lectiones Apollonianae* (Leipzig, 1816) 147–57.

twenty or thirty lines in Homer. His Second Law states that disyllables scanning ˘ ¯ are avoided immediately before the caesura. In Homer they are indeed much more often placed after the caesura, or so as to end in the second princeps, but again there are many exceptions. The Third Law concerns the avoidance of word-end following the third and simultaneously the fifth princeps.[15] In Homer's unruly incipit,

μῆνιν ἄειδε θεᾰ̀ Πηληϊάδεω Ἀχιλῆος,

ἄειδε breaks the first law, θεᾰ́ the second, and Πηληϊάδεω the third.

Prosodic Freedoms and Apparent Anomalies

Homeric verse shows, in comparison with later Greek poetry, some remarkable freedoms in the accommodation of words to the meter.[16] Certain words which might seem impossible to fit into a hexameter are adjusted by means of the 'metrical lengthening' of one vowel. Two particular patterns may be noticed. The commoner is that in a word containing three or four consecutive short syllables one of the vowels is lengthened, usually the first. Thus ἀποδίωμαι becomes ᾱ̓ποδίωμαι, κυάνεος becomes κῡάνεος, ἀνέρι and ὕδατι become ᾱ̓νέρι and ῡ̔δατι,[17] ἀνεμόεις becomes ᾱ̓ν- and then ἠνεμόεις, Πολυδάμας becomes Πουλυδάμας, συβόσια becomes συβόσῑα, ὄνομα becomes οὔνομα, γενόμενος becomes γεινόμενος. (Note that lengthened ε and ο are written ει and ου in our text by a post-Homeric convention.) The less common pattern is that a word scanning ˘ ¯ ¯ ˘ has its first vowel lengthened: Ἀ̄πόλλωνα, Οὐλύμποιο.

Many apparent anomalies have historical explanations. The poets of the *Iliad* and *Odyssey* were the heirs to a long and continuous tradition of epic composition reaching back to the Mycenaean age. In the course of that time various changes took place in Greek, and the epic language for all its conservatism could not avoid being affected by them. The consequence was that some formulae which had

---

[15] W. Meyer, *Sitzungsberichte der philosophisch-philologischen und historischen Classe der Königlichen Bayerischen Akademie der Wissenschaften zu München*, Jahrgang 1884, 980–6.

[16] See W. Schulze, *Quaestiones epicae* (Gütersloh, 1892), usefully summarized by Leaf (1900–1902), i. 590–8; Meister (1921) 34–40; Chantraine (1953) 97–112; (1973).

[17] Hence by analogy the poets often scan the first vowel of these words long in the nominative or vocative: ᾱ̓νήρ, ᾱ̓νερ, ῡ̔δωρ.

originally been metrical became, strictly speaking, unmetrical, or at any rate metrically imperfect, yet they continued to be used. Hence we often find in our text verses which become metrically more satisfactory when we translate them back into an older form of the language. Sometimes it is simply a matter of resolving a vowel contraction, as in the line

ἔνθα δ' ἀποβρίξαντες ἐμείναμεν ἠῶ δῖαν (*Od.* 9.151 = 12.7)

and a series of others where ἠῶ occupies the fifth foot. This is a wholly abnormal placement for a word consisting of two long syllables, but quite normal for a word scanning ¯ ˘ ˘ as the earlier form ἠόα had done.

The most famous case is that of the digamma. Greek once possessed a sound like English w, which occurred in very many words. Some dialects still possessed it in historical times, and wrote it with the letter ϝ, called *wau*, which stood after ε in the alphabet.[18] Later grammarians called it *digamma* (because its shape resembled a double gamma) or the *Aeolica littera*. In other dialects, including the Homeric, it ceased to be pronounced sometime before the introduction of the alphabet and was accordingly not written. But for the most part, especially where the diction is formulaic, Homer's verses are scanned as if the lost consonant were still present:

Ἀτρεΐδης τε (ϝ)άναξ ἀνδρῶν καὶ δῖος Ἀχιλλεύς.
ἐσθλὸν δ' οὔτέ τί πω (ϝ)εῖπας (ϝ)έπος οὔτ' ἐτέλεσσας.
ὣς ἔφατ', ἔδ(ϝ)εισεν δ' ὁ γέρων καὶ ἐπείθετο μύθῳ.

This was the epoch-making discovery announced in 1732 by Richard Bentley, who knew of the *Aeolica littera* from the grammarians. In the nineteenth century certain enthusiasts such as Richard Payne Knight, Immanuel Bekker, and August Fick published editions in which the digamma was 'restored' to the text of the poems, or of a presumed Aeolic antecedent text. But although the digamma is 'observed' in over three thousand places, there are still some six hundred in which it is 'neglected.' There is little doubt that it had disappeared some considerable time before the composition of the extant epics, and that there was never a text of Homer in which it was written.[19]

[18] The Latins took it over into their alphabet in the same position, but used it for the sound [f] which they had in their language and which the Greeks did not at that time have.

[19] But cf. Powell (1991) 64.

Its ghostly effectiveness is due to the continued use of formulaic language that was coined at an earlier period.[20]

The digamma may not have disappeared from the epic dialect until the ninth or eighth century. There were other sounds that lost their consonantal value at a much earlier date. Initial or intervocalic [s] developed into [h]. The Linear B tablets show that this had already happened by the thirteenth century. For example, the word for 'lengths of cloth,' originally **phárwesa*, is written *pa-we-*a_2, i.e. *phárweha*. But perhaps this [h] still had consonantal value; we cannot tell. Anyway, some Homeric forms go back to a stage when there was still an effective consonant there. ἀγχίαλος, ἀμφίαλος, ἀμφίεπον, ἐπιάλμενος still have prefixes unelided before roots that once began with [s]: ἅλς ≈ Latin *sal*, ἕπ- ≈ *sequ-*, ἅλλομαι ≈ *salio*. ὑπείρ instead of ὑπέρ in ὑπεὶρ ἅλα and ὑπείροχος represents the restitution of original long syllables in **uper sálm̥*, **upér-sokhos*, or (at a later stage) **uper ḥála*, **upérḥokhos*, where 'ḥ' represents an [h] that still has consonantal value. In the formula Διῑ̀ μῆτιν ἀτάλαντος, the syllable τιν gets its length from an original [s] or [ḥ] at the beginning of ἀτάλαντος (from **sm̥ò-talantos*, 'of one weight with').

Words that originally began with [sw], where both consonants disappeared, leaving only an aspiration, are occasionally still treated as if they began with two consonants:

> αἰδοῖός τέ μοί ἐσσι, φίλε (σϝ)ἑκυρέ, δ(ϝ)εινός τε (*Il.* 3.172).
> ἢ δὲ μέγα (ϝ)ι(ϝ)άχουσα ἀπὸ (σϝ)έο κάββαλεν υἱόν (*Il.* 5.343).

In words that originally began with [wr], [sr], [sl], [sm], or [sn], only the second consonant remained; but again, such words are sometimes treated as if they began with two consonants, so that the final syllable of the preceding word, though ending in a short open vowel, is lengthened:

> τὴν δ' ἐφόρει μέγα κῦμα κατὰ ῥόον (**sróworn*) ἔνθα καὶ ἔνθα (*Od.* 5.327).
> Πηλιά<u>δα</u> μελίην (**smel-*) τὴν πατρὶ φίλωι πόρε Χείρων (*Il.* 16.143).
> τῶν δ' ὥς <u>τε</u> νιφάδες (**snig*^{w}*h-*) χιόνος πίπτωσι θαμειαί (*Il.* 12.278).

It was by analogy with such cases (presumably) that poets came to admit lengthening by any initial ϝ, λ, μ, ν, ρ, or occasionally σ, even

[20] There is a partial analogy in the Eddic poems, where the disappearance of initial [w] before [r] in Old Icelandic left some eleven verses with w-alliteration defective. But here the [w] must still have been sounded when the poems were composed.

where there had never been a second consonant. In oral delivery they no doubt doubled the initial consonant, and in the Ptolemaic papyri it is regularly written double in such cases.[21] A point to notice is that the lengthened syllable normally occupies the princeps part of the foot, that is, the shorter part. Lengthening in the biceps is practically confined to the first foot, as in *Il.* 21.368,

πολλὰ (λ)λισσόμενος (ϝ)έπεα πτερόεντα προσηύδᾱ.

Original initial [y], like [s], developed into [h]. In this case there are still traces of the original sound in Linear B, where the relative pronoun (**yós* > classical ὅς) is sometimes written with *yo-*, sometimes with *o-*; but it was clearly well on the way out. Yet in Homer the comparative particle ὥς (< **yō̃s*) is often treated in formulae as if it had an initial consonant: θεὸς ὥς and ὄρνῑθες ὥς with ος and θες as long syllables, λύκοι ὥς with no correption of κοι. The formula πότνια Ἥρη, with the short α surprisingly unelided, presumably goes back to a time when Hera's name began with a consonant ([y] or [s], certainly not [w]).

Another early sound-change was the development of [r̥] (sonant r, that is, r functioning as a short vowel between consonants) into [or], [ro], [ar], or [ra], according to dialect. In the Mycenaean dialect, at least, this change had taken place by the time of the Linear B tablets. But there are a few Homeric formulae which only scan properly if we go back to the time before the change. Νὺξ ἀμβρότη (*Il.* 14.78) stands in the verse where the meter requires – ⏑ ⏑ –, but to restore this scansion we have to go back to an original **Núx amr̥ta*, syllabified *a-mr̥-tā: mr̥* became *mro* and with a glide consonant *mbro*, altering the prosody of the word irrevocably. The verb form ἀμβροτάξομεν (*Il.* 10.65) likewise offers the unmetrical sequence – ⏑ –, but the difficulty is resolved by going back to an ancient **hamr̥táxomen*. The soul that departs to Hades λιποῦσ' ἀνδροτῆτα καὶ ἥβην (*Il.* 16.857 = 22.363) leaves us with a similar problem, and it has a similar solution (**anr̥tâta*). The formula Ἐνῡαλίωι ἀνδρειφόντηι (*Il.* 2.651 et al.) can be scanned as it stands only by assuming synecphonesis of ῡα or (more horribly) of ωι-α. But originally, no doubt, the epithet was **anr̥gʷhóntāi*, scanning ⏑ ⏑ – –. The **anr̥-* evolved into **anro-*, ἀνδρο-, and this was replaced by ἀνδρει- in an attempt to restore a metrical phrase.

---

[21] S. West (1967) 113.

In a number of places the third-declension dative ending -ι is scanned long although it is by nature short.[22] We find this, for example, with Zeus' name in the compound διΐφιλος (which can equally well be written as two words, Διῒ φίλος) and in the formula Διῒ μῆτιν ἀτάλαντος (which we have seen to contain another indication of high antiquity). It must go back to the time when there was a separate dative ending in -ει and a locative in -ι. Originally these formulae had the form Διϝεί, but later, after the -ει ending disappeared and the locative ending took over the dative function, Διϝί was substituted. Similarly with the ancient hero Ajax: of the six passages in the Iliad where his name occurs in the dative, no less than three give it the metrical value ¯ ¯ ¯, reflecting the old form Αἰϝάντει. In the Linear B tablets the dative of this declension still appears for the most part as *-e* (i.e. -ει), but *-i* has already begun to make inroads.

Another formula that has become unmetrical through linguistic change is

ἕως ὃ ταῦθ' ὥρμαινε κατὰ φρένα καὶ κατὰ θυμόν.

There are several other places where we find ἕως or τέως in the text but the meter calls for ¯ ˘. The words had earlier been *ἧος, *τῆος, but they suffered the 'quantitative metathesis' typical of Attic-Ionic, just as βασιλῆος became in Attic βασιλέως. It may be debated whether the poets actually came to recite these lines with ἕως[23] or the introduction of the later form was an error of the written tradition.

In another case the written tradition does seem to be to blame. At *Il.* 22.6,

Ἰλίου προπάροιθε πυλάων τε Σκαιάων,

to mend the meter we have to restore Ἰλίοο, a genitive form which is not attested but which must have existed as an intermediate step between the older -οιο and the later -ου (= -ō), both of which are common in Homer. Ἰλίου προπάροιθε may have been a formula established many generations before Homer; but there are altogether some eighteen places where the poets seem to have intended the -οο form, and they are not all fixed formulae. The manuscripts in each instance give the contracted -ου.[24]

---

[22] Hartel (1873) 56–60.

[23] As I argued in 'Epica,' *Glotta* 44 (1967) 135–9.

[24] La Roche (1975) 164–5; Wathelet (1970) 239–42; M. L. West (1992) 174.

Not all prosodic anomalies can be put down to the replacement of older forms. Some result from the adaptation or juxtaposition of formulae by the poets.[25] For example, in *Il.* 2.5–8,

> ἥδε δέ οἱ κατὰ θῡμὸν ἀρίστη φαίνετο βουλή,
> πέμψαι ἐπ' Ἀτρεΐδηι Ἀγαμέμνονι οὖλον Ὄνειρον·
> καί μιν φωνήσᾱς ἔπεα πτερόεντα προσηύδᾱ·
> 'βάσκ' ἴθι, οὖλε Ὄνειρε, θοᾱ̀ς ἐπὶ νῆας Ἀχαιῶν,'

the poet first uses an accusative formula οὖλον Ὄνειρον, and then adapts it into the vocative, resulting in a hiatus after the short -ε of the epithet. At 18.288 the common genitive formula μερόπων ἀνθρώπων is exceptionally turned into the nominative:

> πρὶν μὲν γὰρ Πριάμοιο πόλιν μέροπες ἄνθρωποι,

where a long syllable for the fifth princeps is obtained only by the irregular syllabification -πες-αν- instead of -πε-σαν-.

It is in fact not rare for final syllables closed by a consonant (ν, ρ, or ς) to stand in the princeps—but not the longer biceps—before an initial vowel, as in *Il.* 3.24,

> εὑρὼν ἢ' ἔλαφον κεραὸν ἢ' ἄγριον αἶγα.

Occasionally even short open syllables are allowed to occupy the princeps:[26]

> διὰ μὲν ἀσπίδος ἦλθε φαεινῆς ὄβριμον ἔγχος (*Il.* 3.357).
> φίλε κασίγνητε, κόμισαί τέ με δὸς δέ μοι ἵππους (*Il.* 5.359).
> μήτε σύ γ' Ἄρηα τό γε δείδιθι μήτέ τιν' ἄλλον (*Il.* 5.827).
> ἐπεὶ δὴ νῆάς τε καὶ Ἑλλήσποντον ἵκοντο (*Il.* 23.2).
> ἀλλὰ τά γ' ἄσπαρτα καὶ ἀνήροτα πάντα φύονται (*Od.* 9.109).
> ναύλοχον ἐς λιμένα, καί τις θεὸς ἡγεμόνευεν (*Od.* 10.141).

Aristotle (*Po.* 1458b5) records that one Euclides, a comic poet or iambographer, made fun of such arbitrary lengthenings in epic verse. Later critics classified them as στίχοι ἀκέφαλοι (those with a short syllable in the initial position) or λαγαροί (those with a short in place of a long within the verse). Another term, μύουρος ('mouse-tailed') or μείουρος, was applied to *Il.* 12.208,

> Τρῶες δ' ἐρρῑ́γησαν ὅπως ἴδον αἰόλον ὄφιν,

---

[25] For a full discussion see 'Homeric Formulae and Homeric Metre' in Parry (1971).
[26] Hartel (1873) 60–4; La Roche (1869) i. 65–7.

where the sixth foot appeared to have a short syllable occupying its princeps, but there is some reason to assume an Ionian pronunciation ὄπφιν.[27]

The other common irregularity is hiatus, where a short final vowel is left unelided, or a long one unshortened, before an initial vowel. Many instances, as we have noted, derive from an earlier period when the second word had begun with ϝ or another consonant that was later lost. But there remain many cases of hiatus that have no such justification. After short vowels it occurs especially at the feminine caesura or at the so-called 'bucolic caesura,' that is, at the end of the fourth foot after uncontracted biceps, where word-end is frequent. Formulae commonly begin or end at these points, and the hiatus is often the result of their improvident combination. Long vowels in hiatus (again, when original ϝ is not involved) stand mostly in the princeps; the first foot is the most tolerant of exceptions, as at *Il.* 17.734,

πρόσσω | ἀΐξᾱς περὶ νεκροῦ δηριάασθαι.

Mimetic Use of Meter

The freedoms and irregularities described above do not appear to have been adopted for the sake of any special artistic effect. They are rather an indication that epic poets were more concerned with fluent and coherent utterance than with polished versification. We should not expect, therefore, that they would seek seek to make conscious artistic use of versification to mirror or enhance the sense. In the whole of the *Iliad* and *Odyssey* there are only one or two passages where this can plausibly be claimed. They are, however, noteworthy. At *Il.* 7.238 Hector assures Ajax of his ability to manipulate his shield and to parry blows from right or left, saying

οἶδ' ἐπὶ δεξιά, οἶδ' ἐπ' ἀριστερὰ νωμῆσαι βῶν.

The rhythm is unusual. The line has a legitimate caesura after the second οἶδ', but the phrasing cuts across the verse cola and divides the hexameter into three equal segments. οἶδ' ἐπὶ δεξιά in feet 1–2 exactly matches οἶδ' ἐπ' ἀριστερά in feet 3–4, and seems to express

[27] Ath. 632ef; sch. *Il.* 12.208c, 22.379ab, with testimonia cited by Erbse; M. L. West (1982a) 173.

Hector's equal dexterity on both sides. The uncontracted dactyls of these phrases contrast with the heavy ending νωμῆσαι βῶν; contracted fifth biceps is relatively uncommon, and its combination with a final monosyllable even more so. If the dactyls suggest dextrous movement, the spondees suggest solid defence, climactically encapsulated in the implacable βῶν. There is no telling whether such subjective reactions correspond at all to the poet's sense of what he was doing, but if the features in question were not the product of design, the accident was a most felicitous one.

A longer passage that calls for quotation in this connection is the account of Sisyphus' underworld labor at *Od.* 11.593–600:

> καὶ μὴν Σῐ́συφον εἰσεῖδον, κρατέρ' ἄλγε' ἔχοντα,
> λᾶαν βαστάζοντα πελώριον ἀμφοτέρῃσιν·
> ἤτοι ὃ μὲν | σκηριπτόμενος | χερσίν τε ποσίν τε
> λᾶαν ἄνω | ὤθεσκε ποτὶ λόφον· ἀλλ' ὅτε μέλλοι
> ἄκρον ὑπερβαλέειν, τότ' ἀποστρέψασκε κραταιΐς·
> αὖτις ἔπειτα πέδονδε κυλίνδετο λᾶας ἀναιδής.
> αὐτὰρ ὅ γ' ἂψ | ὤσασκε τιταινόμενος, | κατὰ δ' ἱδρώς
> ἔρρεεν ἐκ μελέων, κονίη δ' ἐκ κρᾱτὸς ὀρώρει.

In lines 595–6 and 599 the long participles (σκηριπτόμενος with deferred caesura; τιταινόμενος), the word-ends after princeps at the places marked (giving a rising rhythm), and the hiatus in ἄνω ὤθεσκε all seem to contribute to the portrayal of the great physical effort involved in pushing the boulder up the hill. By contrast, the word-ends after the short positions in 598 (falling rhythm) and the uncontracted dactyls irresistibly suggest the momentum of the boulder as it rolls down again to the bottom, after which the straining begins all over again.

Origins of the Hexameter

We have seen that certain Homeric formulae appear to go back to the Mycenaean period. There are those that presuppose the third-declension dative in -ει, which was already starting to be replaced in the time of the Linear B tablets. There are those coined when initial [y] or [s/ḥ] still had the force of a consonant; [y] is well on the way out in the tablets, and [s] has already changed into some sort of [h]. An even earlier date has to be assumed for those formulae that ceased to be metrical after sonant r developed into [ro/or] or [ra/ar], which it had done by the time of the tablets. Such formulae would seem to be at least as old as the fourteenth century. The conclusion is strengthened if it is correct to suppose that the formula ἀσπίδος ἀμφιβρότης, with its tolerable but abnormal short syllable before βρ, goes back to **aspídos amphimr̥tās* and so belongs with the sonant r group; for archaeology confirms that the 'shield that encircles a man,' the so-called body shield, had its heyday before 1400.

These formulae are inseparable from the hexameter. They imply that this was already the meter of heroic epic in the fifteenth or fourteenth century. It may be that one or two whole lines from that early period have been preserved in the *Iliad* with only superficial modernization. The recurrent formulaic line about the Cretan hero Meriones may be such a case:

Μηριόνης ἀτάλαντος Ἐνυαλίωι ἀνδρειφόντηι, or
Māriónās hatálantos Enuwalíōi anr̥qʷhóntāi.

Ἐνυαλίωι ἀνδρειφόντηι is linguistically very old, as we have seen; we have found ἀτάλαντος in another early formula, Διὶ μῆτιν ἀτάλαντος; and Meriones' name may be identical with *maryannu*, the Hurrian word that spread all over the Near East in the sixteenth and fifteenth centuries as the designation of the elite chariot warrior.[28]

Evidently the hexameter that we find in Homer was no recent creation. It had been established for seven centuries or more. But can we say any more about its origins?

It has sometimes been argued that a dactylic meter is not naturally suited to the Greek language, and that therefore the hexameter is likely to have been taken over from some other people.[29] There are three things to be said against this.

Firstly the premise is unsound. It would be difficult to find a language *better* suited to dactylic rhythm than the Greek of the late Bronze Age or early Iron Age. The rule that the comparative and superlative endings -ότερος and -ότατος become -ώτερος and -ώτατος following a short stem syllable, as in μαλακώτερος, and the preference for θανατηφόρος over θανατοφόρος, illustrate the language's tendency to impose a dactylic pattern on a longer run of shorts. Of course there were many words that did not fit into dactylic meter, but that

[28] F. Schachermeyr, *Atti e Memorie del I Congresso Internazionale di Micenologia* (Roma, 1968) 306. Cf. M. L. West (1988) 156–59.

[29] Meister (1921) 58, 231; Meillet (1923) 58–63.

was bound to be the case with any meter based on patterns of syllabic quantity.

Secondly we know of no other people with whom the Greeks might have come into contact and who had anything remotely like a dactylic meter. All Semitic verse of the relevant periods (Akkadian, Ugaritic, Hebrew) is based on the rhetorical arrangement of accentual cola, not on the counting of syllables. The same seems to be true of Egyptian poetry, and, so far as we can see, of Hurrian and Hittite. There may have been other Anatolian traditions that are not recorded, and we know nothing of the verse-forms of Minoan Crete or of the pre-Hellenic people(s) of mainland Greece. But to derive the hexameter from their hypothetical influence would be to explain *ignotum per ignotius.*

Thirdly the obvious point must be made that the hexameter exists in, and must have originated in, that tradition of quantitative meter to which all classical Greek verse belongs, and which is inherited, if not from proto-Indo-European times, at any rate from the time when the ancestors of the Hellenes were together with those of the Phrygians, Armenians, and Indo-Iranians. This may be inferred from the similarities between the principles of Greek and Vedic verse. Vedic verse too is strictly quantitative, and its rules of prosody are essentially the same as those that obtain in Greek: the verse is treated as a continuum; the first of two adjacent consonants is allotted to the preceding syllable and makes it long even if its vowel is short; final long vowels and short diphthongs generally suffer correption before an initial vowel. The long diphthongs *-āi* and *-āu*, however, became *-āy* and *-āw* before a vowel and preserved their length; and it corresponds to this that in Homer the long diphthongs (-ηι, -ωι) are less liable to suffer correption than the short ones.[30] There are also significant similarities between Vedic meters and some of those used in Greek lyric, especially those of Sappho and Alcaeus, tending to confirm the continuity of the tradition.[31]

Now, there is nothing like dactylic rhythm among the Vedic meters, let alone anything like the hexameter. Nor do we find in India, until a later period, the principle of the interchangeability of a long and two shorts, which seems already to have operated at the time when the oldest identifiable hexameter formulae were coined. The conclusion

[30] E. B. Clapp, *Classical Philology* 1 (1906) 241–9, gives statistics. Note the non-correption of *-ōi* in the reconstructed old formula *Enūwalíōi anr̥q*^{w}*hóntāi.*
[31] See Meillet (1923); M. L. West (1973) 162–70.

must be that the hexameter does not go back to the period of Greco-Aryan unity but is a later development, probably a purely Greek development, within the inherited tradition of quantitative verse.

This still leaves the question of its nearer antecedents. It has often been conjectured that a verse of such length (twelve to seventeen syllables) must represent the conjunction of two shorter verses.[32] An analogy would be the meter of Indian epic, the sixteen-syllable *śloka*, which is formed from the union of two eight-syllable verses of a kind common in the Vedas. We have seen that the hexameter does divide naturally into two cola, with caesura at the join. That these might once have functioned as independent verses is suggested by the fact that cola of similar form, (×) – ⏑ ⏑ – ⏑ ⏑ – (×), are often found in lyric poetry in other combinations. In a fragment from a dithyramb of Bacchylides (Carm. 20 Snell-Maehler) we find a narrative composed in a series of verses of the form × – ⏑ ⏑ – ⏑ ⏑ – or × – ⏑ ⏑ – ⏑ ⏑ – × ||: hardly a direct survival of Bronze Age practice, but it illustrates the possibility.

The assumption would be that in the early Mycenaean epic tradition these cola came to be paired, and regulated in such a way that the first of each pair began in falling rhythm and the second in rising. Again the *śloka* provides an analogy: its two halves are regularly differentiated by ending in contrasted ways, the first normally ending – – ×, the second – ⏑ ×. A further regulation necessary in the hexameter was that the beginning of the second colon be adjusted to the end of the first so that the dactylic rhythm was not disturbed. There is in fact a very small number of verses in Homer where the two cola are not properly adjusted and the rhythm does suffer disturbance:

> λᾱῶν οἵ (ϝ)οἱ ἕποντο | Τρί(κ)κης ἐξ ἱπποβότοιο (*Il.* 4.202).[33]
> εἵλετο κρῑνάμενος | τρῐηκόσι' ἠδὲ νομῆας (*Il.* 11.697).
> ἀργύρεοι δὲ σταθμοὶ | ἐν χαλκέωι ἕστασαν οὐδῶι (*Od.* 7.89).

They are so rare that we should perhaps regard them as accidents rather than exploitations of an ancient licence; but at least they illustrate the poets' tendency to think in cola.

---

[32] T. Bergk, *Ueber das älteste Versmaß der Griechen* (Progr. Freiburg im Breisgau, 1854) = *Kleine philologische Schriften*, ii (Halle, 1886) 392–408, and many others; Sicking (1993) 70–71, with references.

[33] Most manuscripts give Τρίκκης, and this is the form of the name at 2.729; some copyists write Τρίκης in an attempt to mend the meter. One might suppose that the poet himself mutilated the name in order to fit it in; but there was no pressing need to do so.

Whatever the process by which the hexameter was fashioned, it proved an ideal vehicle for epic narrative. For at least seven centuries down to the time of the *Iliad* and *Odyssey* it seems to have remained essentially unchanged, despite the considerable renovations which that lapse of time effected upon the Greek language and perhaps upon the nature of the epic tradition itself. But that was far from being the end of the story. Throughout antiquity, down to the time of Nonnus in the fifth century A.D., the hexameter remained the standard meter for epic, besides being a common one for other purposes such as hymns, oracles, and didactic poetry. From the early second century B.C. it was taken up at Rome and acquired comparable status in Latin poetry. It was a Roman's use of it that inspired Tennyson to acclaim it as

> the stateliest measure
> ever moulded by the lips of man.

Joseph Russo

THE FORMULA

> In fact the 350 species [of sharks] found in the world vary immensely, so much so as to stretch the definition of the very word *shark*.
>
> E. O. Wilson, *The Diversity of Life*, p. 113

Prologue: The Current Situation

Writing on the Homeric formula in 1996 allows us to review the major 'paradigm shift' that Milman Parry brought to the interpretation of the earliest Greek poetry, and to evaluate it with the advantages of hindsight. There are many features of style and content that suggest that the Homeric epics are products of a long oral tradition, but the cornerstone of Parry's edifice has always been the formula. I shall not attempt to survey all that has been said on this subject,[1] but to focus on some key issues and problems that have been with us from Parry to the present. Scholars' attempts to define the formula have been frequently beset with ambiguities that often derive from Parry's own words. And yet, paradoxically, it is the very open-endedness of the concept that has given it much of its force.

Investigations of the formulaic element that characterizes Homeric style have always embodied, at least implicitly, a search for the mysterious chemistry whereby gifted poets transmute mere words into verbal art. In Homer's case the mystery is especially compelling, because his words are largely conventional. The controlling force of tradition, with its constant pressure toward use of familiar-sounding

[1] That was well done by M. W. Edwards (1986b; 1988) in two surveys that are close to annotated bibliographies. Among other reviews of the development of formula studies since Parry, the most important among European scholars are Latacz, ed., (1979) 1–44, an attempt to reconcile the German and the Parryist traditions; Fantuzzi (1980), with good bibliography and critical assessment of problems; Cantilena (1982), 19–103, who comments insightfully on some serious questions of theory, definition and methodology that have characterized formula studies since Parry; and Holoka's admirable survey (1991). Hainsworth (1993) 1–31 offers a fine and detailed discussion of the important problems in the relation between Homeric diction and composition.

diction and typical thematic structure, to modern taste seems an obstacle to attainment of the highest poetic excellence, especially of originality of any kind. Therefore Parry's theory of an oral Homer who composed only through formulaic diction—a mixture of verbatim formulas and related expressions derived by analogy or modification—initially met with strong resistance in America from would-be defenders of the 'literary' excellence of the *Iliad* and *Odyssey*, and was virtually ignored by most European Homerists.

The reverse of this situation eventually came about: the oral view of Homer became the prevailing orthodoxy, and is now the position against which dissenters must argue. This orthodoxy, however, has considerably diminished its claims. There has been constant revision of Parry's more extreme judgements, e.g. that Homer's diction is essentially all formulaic and traditional.[2] Also, adherents of the oral theory speak less often of 'proof' of Homer's orality (whether by formula-count or other indices), and more cautiously refer to a probable oral genesis or to the epics as oral-derived texts.[3] The paramount role supposedly played by Parry's relatively fixed formulaic phrases and systems has been significantly reduced from his estimation of their omnipresence, and replaced by a hierarchy of linguistic levels at which 'something formulaic' may exist. In addition, the poet's ability to incorporate rare single words that occur only once (termed *hapax legomena*) is now freely admitted by scholars who consider themselves within the oralist tradition.[4]

After a comparative lull in formula studies, recent years have shown renewed interest in the significance of Parry's work and the reconceptualization of the formula. This is an opportune juncture, then, at which to review critically the main issues in formula studies, with the intention of re-framing some of the difficulties and controversies they have inspired in the hope of a better understanding of Homer's verbal art. But first, as preparation for some considerations of formal structure, we need a brief look at the internal structure of the Homeric hexameter.

---

[2] As Parry (1971) 324, 335, put it: 'At no time is [the poet] seeking words for an idea which has never before found expression . . . his poetry remains throughout the sum of longer and shorter passages which he has heard.'

[3] J. M. Foley (1990); (1991) has coined the useful term 'oral-derived text.'

[4] See Hainsworth (1993) 6–7; M. W. Edwards (1991) 53–55.

Formula, Meter, and Colon

A new era in the colometry of the hexameter began with H. Fränkel's famous 1926 study.[5] His four-colon conception of hexametric structure, while subjected to challenges and revisions, is still persuasive to most metricians.[6] But the analyses of Fränkel and his successors revealed some disagreement over crucial questions: the degree to which cola were sense-units, the exact length allowable for each colon, and whether a significant minority of verses were better analyzed as having two or three cola. Nevertheless, after several thorough re-evaluations, there is general agreement that the four-colon verse is the 'norm' and that cola often provide the metrical structures into which formulas conveniently fit. A flexible model of hexameter colon-structure, incorporating the preferences of Rossi and Porter with those of Fränkel, would be as follows:

A A A A AA B B C C C
– ¦ ⏑ ¦ ⏑ | – | ⏑ ¦ ⏑ ¦ – | ⏑ ⏑ – | ⏑⏑ | – ¦ ⏑⏑ – ⏑

Broken verticals indicate the less frequent caesural positions. The significant detail is the great variability of the A caesura compared to the restriction of B and C.[7]

Given the highly formulaic nature of Homeric verse, it is undeniable that formular shape and colon shape have been mutually interdependent for a long period in the history of the hexameter. Assigning

---

[5] Fränkel (1926), most accessible in a concise version in Fränkel (1975) 30–34.

[6] H. N. Porter (1951) made modifications in Fränkel's A and C caesural positions and tried to shift emphasis from cola as sense units to cola as defined by statistically prominent word-ends. Rossi (1965) accepted Fränkel's view generally but argued for greater prominence of longer (3 ½ to 4-morae) first cola and short single-word third cola. Kirk (1966b); (1985) 17–37, believed two- and three-colon verses to be far more common than Fränkel allowed. Ingalls (1972), Barnes (1986), and Beck (1972) essentially re-affirm Fränkel's four cola. Beekes (1972) seems an anachronistic attempt to go back to the earlier conception of negative rules of word-end inhibition instead of Fränkel's more positive and organically cohesive approach. See the pragmatic approach of Kahane (1994) 17–42, who reconciles the metrical and semantic concepts of cola at a functional level by allowing for a wide range of possible caesural positions, identified neither as 'correct' nor 'irregular' but rather ranked in sequence by higher or lower audience expectation of word-end.

[7] If one favors the sheer statistics of word-end over the sense-unit, more A caesuras at 2 and 3 can be counted and fewer (or none, according to Porter) at the alternative positions. Conversely, more acceptance of purely semantic boundaries leads to more A caesuras at 1, 1 ½, 3 ½, and 4. See Kahane (1994) for a judicious evaluation of the differences.

priority to either formula or meter seems pointless, since metricians' speculations about the antiquity and evolution of the hexameter vary and can never be conclusive. Whether theme generates formula which then generates meter as G. Nagy believes, or metrical structures have diachronic priority according to the diverse theories of hexameter evolution offered by B. Gentili and G. Giannini, A. Hoekstra, M. L. West, and others, it is clear that the articulation of the epic verse into cola is a manifestation, on what O'Neill (below, n. 23) called the inner-metrical level, of an accumulation of specific realities on the verbal level.[8]

Parry was well aware of this interdependence of formula and verse-segment (although the four-colon theory as such was unknown to him). He explicitly described (1971:9) formulas as characteristically filling the spaces between what we nowadays call Fränkel's B and C caesuras and the end of the verse, or the first half of the verse up to the B caesura. Regarding the A caesura, by far the most problematic of the three because of its extreme fluidity of placement and its frequent bridging, we may see some acknowledgment of this structural feature in Parry's study of the runover word in the enjambment characteristic of orally-derived hexameter verse (1971: 251–65); and also in his specific illustration of the schematization of Homeric diction with the series οὐλομένην ἥ, νήπιοι οἵ, δύσμορος ὅς, σχέτλιος ὅς, νηλεὲς ὅς, etc., all of which are verse-initial.[9]

The formula studies of most of Parry's successors have retained this connection between formula and colometry, and proceeded to amplify it both theoretically and empirically. As we shall see, both Lord and Notopoulos conceived of their analogical formulas as filling characteristic slots in the verse, and the concept of the structural formula consisted of joining this approach more specifically to the

[8] G. Nagy (1976); Gentili and Giannini (1977); Hoekstra (1981) 33–53; M. L. West (1973a); (1973b) 161–87. Gentili and Giannini's argument is especially attractive, offering an important place to both formula and meter and placing special emphasis on their interaction to yield, over time, the finished product that is the hexameter as we know it. Gentili views the hexameter as a relatively late creation, whose constituent units are essentially those filled by many of Parry's formulas: adonic, alcmanian, enoplian, reizianum, and hemiepes. These formula shapes made available 'preferred' structural units which were joined to make the eventually polished hexameter.

[9] In principle Parry never considers single words as complete formulas, but in practice he occasionally does. See his comments on ὀλοόφρονος (1971) 71, Homer's regular use of ἡρώων and Ἀργείων to begin the verse, (1971) 313, and the middle participle plus enclitic περ, (1971) 314.

O'Neill-Porter-Fränkel tradition of emphasizing favored localization for words and colon-length phrases. Even in the most recent reconsiderations of the identity of the formula and its possible relation to more variable, less formulaic diction, we see a continuation of the view that formula and meter are inextricably bound up with one another.

Finding the Formula: 1928 *to* 1980

It has become an inaccurate commonplace to assert that the series of formula studies inspired in the sixties and seventies by Milman Parry's research led to a deadlock or a blind alley. A better formulation would be that the impossibility of finding consensus on a definition of the formula, and any agreement on whether formula density was a true index of orally composed texts, brought into clarity for the first time the full complexity of the verbal phenomena that scholars were attempting to pursue with inadequate conceptual and methodological tools. Such clarification could only be a good thing. As I argue below, there need be no unitary, accepted definition of the formula for the concept of formularity to be a productive one, with a stimulating effect on our reading of Homer and our appreciation of why his style succeeds so well both functionally and aesthetically. But first a review of the definitions and expanding concepts of the formula, from Parry to the present.

In 1928 and 1930 Milman Parry offered a virtually identical definition of the formula: 'a group of words which is regularly employed under the same metrical conditions to express a given essential idea.' He added the further stipulation that a formula be 'made up of at least four words or five syllables, with the exception of noun-epithet phrases, which may be shorter, such as φίλον ἦτορ.[10] Such formulas were the most distinctive mark of orally composed epic poetry, which he saw as essentially formula-dependent and entirely traditional in thought.[11] He went on, however, to say there was more to the formula than his strict definitions allowed: analogical construction played

[10] Parry (1971) 272 (cf. 13), 275 n. 1.

[11] He does allow for an individual poet to add a new epithet, phrase, or verse to the traditional diction, but asserts there could be only 'a few' such creations for any one singer, and they would have to blend in perfectly with the traditional style in order to enter the diction and keep a place there: (1971) 324, 330.

a significant role in Homer's creation of formulas.[12] When these modifications kept some identical wording they were accorded formulaic status and included in Parry's formal textual analyses as phrases marked with broken underlining. Others, constructed on identity of grammar, rhythm and location within the verse, were more informally suggested as possibilities still to be explored. 'But there are more general types of formulas, and one could make no greater mistake than to limit formulaic material to what is underlined,' he says ([1971] 313), and goes on to note such similarities as Ἀχαιοῖς ἄλγε' ἔθηκε and ἐπ' αὐτῷ κῦδος ἔθηκε, πολλὰς δ' ἰφθίμους ψυχὰς and πολλὰς δὲ δρῦς ἀζαλέας, τεῦχε κύνεσσιν and δῶκεν ἑταίρῳ, and even the tendency to use the single words ἡρώων and Ἀργείων at the beginning of a verse, followed by a new clause.

Parry's followers saw the usefulness of this more broadly defined formula, which moved beyond mechanical-seeming repetition and allowed the freedom of substitution that characterizes the flexibility of living language itself. Hence a series of definitions that moved quickly to the level of analogical constructions via syntactic patterns with substitutable elements, which required less strict dependence on specific words and word order than did Parry's original definition.

The prime articulation of analogical formula construction is that of A. B. Lord in *The Singer of Tales*. Because he was studying a traditional, oral, and formulaic diction that was still alive and creatively functioning, Lord was aware, perhaps even more than Parry, of the realities of what he calls 'basic formula patterns' that the skilled singer manipulates by *substitution* of words and the *adjustment* of phrases so created to fit the metrical and musical requirements to produce successful verse.[13] The flexibility inherent in Lord's conception contains the kernel of all important theorizing about the formula that has since appeared. In essence, he says that more basic than the formulas themselves are the syntactic patterns that underlie them and give the singer the capacity to generate new formulaic phrasing according to a poetic 'grammar' analogous to the grammar used by the speaker of ordinary language. Here we may see an embryonic version of M. N. Nagler's *Gestalt* theory of formulaic production (discussed below). Lord even anticipates the later attempts of scholars to identify formula

---

[12] Parry (1971) 68: 'Analogy is perhaps the single most important factor for us to grasp if we are to arrive at a real understanding of Homeric diction.'

[13] A. B. Lord (1960) Ch. 2, and especially pp. 35–45.

shape and length with colometric units of the hexameter, although Lord is of course making the observation specifically about Serbo-croatian decasyllabic verse: 'Closely allied to the word-boundary patterns, and to no small extent helping to form them, are the syntactic patterns of the formulas.'[14]

Lord's emphasis on the importance of analogical phrase formation was followed by J. Notopoulos (1962), who applied the tracing of syntactic patterns to Greek hexameter diction, specifically that of the four major Homeric Hymns. Notopoulos called attention to the frequent use of analogical syntax, in such phrases as Κύνθιον ὄχθον, καμπύλα κύκλα, θούριδος ἀλκῆς, οἴνοπα πόντον, ὄβριμον ἔγχος, etc., all metrically identical and localized at the end of the line. But his analysis also contains many unsupported claims of formular analogy according to 'similar' patterns whose resemblance is clearly inadequate. For example, he underlines τρομέουσιν ἰόντα, indicating that ἰόντα in its verbatim repetition is a formula and τρομέουσιν is substitutable by analogical formation. Yet the parallels he cites for τρομέουσιν[15] exhibit neither the same metrical form nor the same grammar, and do not even have the kind of similarity of sound upon which some plausible formulaic relationship may be built. Whether ἰόντα by itself in end-line position is formulaic is a point that would need some argument, not simple assertion.[16] Notopoulos' other supporting evidence for analogical patterns is similarly uneven, as will be evident to anyone who follows up all his references. The resulting set of statistics he gives for formular density are therefore unreliable, and not adequate proof of the oral genesis of these texts. It is important to note, however, that his intuition of wide-ranging formularity in the Hymns seems accurate. In an impressively thorough formula-analysis of the entire corpus of Hymns, applying the more stringent

[14] A. B. Lord (1960) 41. This is precisely the point demonstrated in detail for the hexameter in Russo (1966) (especially pp. 236–40); Ingalls (1972); and Gentili and Giannini (1977).

[15] θᾶσσον *Il.* 17.654, ἐπ' ἀλλήλοισιν 3x, κολοσυρτὸν *Il.* 12.147, κλισίηθεν *Il.* 12.336, and Οἰχαλίηθεν in verse-initial instead of verse end combination, *Il.* 2.596.

[16] I myself have argued for single words and word-types as formulaic when they are heavily localized (1963); (1966), but recognize that such a claim can cover too broad a range of phenomena to be illuminating. I would now say that single-word formularity becomes significant in certain words and forms whose metrical shape ideally fills one of the verse-cola. C. J. Ruijgh (1957) 29–55, 87 has suggested single word formularity for the heavily localized αὐτὰρ and μερμηρίζω, and Kirk (1962) 67–68 for ἦτορ and δῶμα, and in (1966b) 104 for γενέσθαι, γένηται, γένοντο, and γένοιτο.

criteria developed by W. M. Minton (1975), M. Cantilena also came up with a high formula content that would seem to strengthen Notopoulos' and Lord's arguments that orality may be inferred from formular density (although he disagrees with their high percentages).[17]

Homerists continued to develop conceptions of the formula that might offer some escape from the constraints of Parry's 'official' definition and thus answer his critics' charges that 'mechanistic' verse production had replaced poetic creativity for Parry's Homer. To this end three significant new definitions of formula were conceived during the 1960s: the 'structural' formula, the 'flexible' formula, and the formula as variable manifestation of a pre-verbal *Gestalt.*

My conception of the structural formula was an attempt to carry the analogical constructions seen by Lord and Notopoulos one step further, by grounding them in syntactic-metrical patterns inherent in the hexameter itself. I attempted to locate formular generativity in the localization of word-types with clear grammatical identities, whose combination into phrases often created familiar metrical cola of the type documented by Fränkel and Porter. The impressively patterned word-type localizations had been demonstrated by E. G. O'Neill, Jr. (1942), but with no data as to what *kinds* of words filled in the abstract metrical shapes. Porter's revision of Fränkel's four-colon theory was unsuccessful in some details, but had the great advantage, through building on O'Neill's work, of showing exactly what word-type combinations most characteristically constituted each of the four cola. It seemed opportune to me, as Porter's student, to investigate the grammatical nature and syntactic relationship of the word-types that entered into the most frequent or characteristic colon-filling combinations, i.e., a synthesis of the O'Neill-Porter patterns of localized word-types and the Parry-Lord suggestion that epic diction was pervaded by syntactic patterns generating new formulaic phrases by analogy.

In this view of Homeric diction, the long series or 'system' documentable by juxtaposing the phrases ἄλγε' ἔθηκε, κῦδος ἔθηκε, κῦδος ἔδωκε, εὖχος ἔδωκε, εὖχος ἀπηῦρα, etc., could be understood as the structural formula $\overset{\text{N}}{-}\smile | \smile \overset{\text{V}}{-}$x localized at 12, the verse-end. The middle-passive verse-initial participial form seen in οὐλομένην, εὐχόμενος, ἀχνύμενος, λισσόμενοι, ἐρχόμενος, etc., and the verse-ending form seen

[17] Cantilena (1982) 82–89 finds a formular density of around 50% for the Hymns, close to the approximately 54% he calculates for the Homeric epics. See p. 83 n. 70 for a generous appreciation of Notopoulos' contributions to oral studies.

in ἐρχομένοιο, ἐρχομενάων, κηδομένη περ (τε), ἀχνύμενός περ, περθομένη τε, etc. would be the single-word structure $-\overset{\text{pcp}}{\smile\smile}-$ localized at 3 or in the combination $-\overset{\text{pcp}}{\smile\smile}-$ x at 12.

These localized combinations (and occasional significantly used single word-types) may be seen as abstract linguistic structures or matrices from which new epic formulas are generated.[18] As a piece of theory synthesizing current ideas in Homeric studies and seeing how far they might be taken, this was attractive, and remains so in my judgment. Applied to the analysis of Homeric texts, the 'structural' approach had the virtue of exposing more regularities of diction than were previously apparent, and of suggesting how new phrases could be created on the model of existing ones. But it is clear in retrospect that my structural formulas were too loosely defined, and their suggested all-pervasiveness deprived them of value as decisive indicators of the orality of hexametric texts.[19]

At this point the inability of even the most inclusive conceptions of analogy and syntactic-metrical structure to define clearly the parameters of the formulaic led to two new and opposite-seeming approaches. The first was that of J. B. Hainsworth (1964); (1968) and A. Hoekstra (1965), who saw the poet's formula-generating capacity in his ability to improvise new formulaic phrases out of existing ones by significantly altering their *structure* but preserving their *content*. This was a radical departure from Parry's conception of a phrase regularly employed under the same metrical conditions: these scholars offered evidence to support a conception of the formula as

---

[18] Russo (1963); (1966). Some unease about giving the name 'formula' to what were conceived as formula-generating *potentialities* is seen in the suggestion that the structural patterns should perhaps be thought of as 'shadows of formulas' ([1963] 239), a phrase that even to a severe critic of the structural approach is, 'however misleading, still the most illuminating and suggestive' (Minton [1975] 253.)

[19] See the appropriate warnings of Hainsworth (1964) and Minton (1965) about the dangers of using high percentages of loosely defined analogical/structural formulas to argue for oral composition. It should noted that, unlike Lord and Notopoulos, I never calculated percentages of formulas to prove oral composition, well aware that their boundaries were too fluid to allow strict quantification. I simply assumed oral composition as the likeliest hypothesis (as I still do), and claimed that structural patterns were one sign of such a style. One part of Minton's argument (repeated by Packard [1976]) that the presence of structural formulas in Apollonios' *Argonautica* invalidates any claim that their presence in Homer points to oral composition, fails to allow for the historical precedence of Homer as the poet who established norms of hexameter dictional patterns that later poets were bound to follow. As I have argued (Russo [1976]), frequency of structural formulas may fairly be considered a necessary but not sufficient condition for an oral hexameter style.

eminently 'flexible,' while denying significance to structural or analogical substitution-systems as formula generating matrices.[20] The second new approach was that of M. N. Nagler (1967); (1974), who saw the basic formula-generating mechanism as an abstract, preverbal *Gestalt* or template in the poet's mind. This was a radical departure from the attempt to see formulas phenomenologically as concrete and measurable phenomena related by *either* structure *or* content: it denied the possibility of precisely identifying and counting formulas, while offering as consolation an intellectually appealing basis for this impasse. Let us consider each of these approaches in detail.

Hainsworth's 1968 monograph was the most influential of this group of post-Parry reconceptualizations of the formula. It opened a range of new possibilities by departing radically from Parry's requirement of 'the same metrical conditions' and replacing it with the simpler one that there be bonds of mutual expectancy between two or more words for them to be treated by the poet as formulas. These bonds would keep the words connected even when their metrical shape and position changed. The processes of change include (1) mobility (2) expansion, (3) separation, including (3a) splitting a word group over two lines of verse, and modification through such 'adjustments' as (4) inverted word order, (5) use of an alternate case-form or suffix. Any of these may be combined, and the results further altered through elision. Each category may be illustrated by the following examples: (1) ξίφος ὀξύ, φίλος (-ον, -οι) υἱός (-όν, -α, -ες), et al. are mobile between three different positions in the verse; (2) ⟨φόνον καὶ⟩ κῆρα μελαινον (simple addition); or the even simpler addition of adverbs like μέγα, πολύ or μάλα to existing formulas; or ἄλλοι ⟨μάκαρες⟩ θεοὶ as a conflation of θεοὶ ἄλλοι and μάκαρες θεοί; (3) αἴγεον ἄσκον and ἄσκῳ ἐν αἰγείῳ, κακὰ πολλὰ and πολλ' ⟨ἐπὶ τοῖς πάθομεν⟩ κακά, (3a) δεξιὸν ὦμον and ὦμον/δεξιόν, (4) χεῖρας ἀάπτους and ἀάπτους χεῖρας, (5) πᾶσι δόλοισι and πάντεσσι δόλοισι.

Some modifications of this type had been described by A. Severyns, and were certainly present in Parry's view of formular behavior.[21] They were developed within a diachronic linguistic perspective in Hoekstra's 1965 study, where conjugation and declension of formulas,

[20] Hoekstra (1965) 11–20 and Hainsworth (1968) 14–19 explicitly reject the use of analogical substitution systems as indices of oral style.

[21] Severyns (1946) 49–61. Parry's *Homeric Formulas and Metre* ([1971] 191–239) is entirely concerned with modification, juxtaposition, conflation, etc. of formulas, approached from the perspective of the metrical anomalies caused by these adaptations.

splitting by the introduction of another word, replacement of archaic forms by newer ones, and the removal of formulas from traditional positions are studied in detail. Hoekstra shows the loosening effect exerted upon the diction by historical innovations like quantitative metathesis, loss of diagamma, introduction of movable nu, and the emergence of newer versions of archaic forms generally.

Hoekstra's was in fact the first book-length treatment of the Homeric formula since Parry and the first serious critique of the oral hypothesis. Neither a 'true believer' nor a debunker, the Dutch scholar keeps an open-minded view of the possibility that Homeric poems were composed orally, but with deliberate rehearsal and memorization as opposed to the 'improvisation' theory he (mistakenly but understandably) attributes to Lord.[22] His review on pp. 8–20 of the development of Parry's theory and methodology from the French theses to the subsequent American articles, and of its further extension by Lord and Notopoulos, is full of cautions about over-extension of definitions of the 'formulaic' element and the automatic assumption that formularity equals orality. Hoekstra equates formularity with traditional style but not necessarily with oral style. This monograph, together with Hainsworth's, significantly broadened our vision of how Homer and his predecessors could innovate within the confines of their traditional style.

Hainsworth, however, is a convinced oralist, and presents the abundant evidence for formular flexibility as exemplifying the suppleness and adaptability of the technique of improvisational composition. Focusing his argument specifically to challenge a key element of Parry's definition of formula, that it is always used under the same metrical conditions, he concentrates on the behavior of two word groups, shaped – ⏑ ⏑ – x and ⏑ ⏑ – x. The first is a staple of Parryist formulaic studies, providing the frame for numerous end-line formulas, particularly epithet-noun combinations. When its final syllable is short, however, Hainsworth shows that it exhibits great mobility, with a 'scatter' over four positions within the verse. The second is a relatively neglected phase shape, allowed by Parry as an exception (when it was epithet-plus-noun) to his requirement that a formula have at least

[22] Hoekstra (1965) 18–20. Lord repeatedly rejected the term improvisation because of its suggestion of ad hoc creation, and preferred instead to call the oral creative process '(re-)composition in performance.' See most recently A. B. Lord (1991) 76.

four words or five syllables, which was meant to exclude brief and trivial word combinations. The brevity of ⏑ ⏑ – x limits it to rather humble formulaic phrases like the familiar φίλος υἱός μέγα ἄστυ, βροτὸς ἀνήρ, βροτὸν ἄνδρα, μέγα δῶμα, δύο δοῦρε, θεοὶ ἄλλοι, κακὰ πολλά, πρόπαν ἦμαρ, κλέος εὐρύ, etc. Some of these do not ideally meet Parry's criterion of epithet-noun combination, and can seem rather trivial compared to formulas that afford the composing poet more significant cola as building blocks for his hexameter line. This shorter phrase-type also gains considerable mobility when its final syllable is short, as Hainsworth points out, because of the ease with which it can avoid limitations of placement imposed by the internal bridges of hexameter structure (p. 47).

One limitation of Hainsworth's illuminating study is that in his emphasis on the role of flexibility in generating new formular variants, he believes it necessary to minimize the importance of other sources of formula creation and extension. His original purpose, acknowledged in his Preface, is 'to correct an emphasis on certain structuralist standpoints which seemed mistaken.' A previous study of his revealed the conviction that 'pattern and structure of the phrases, interpreted strictly, do not play a predominant part in the creation of new diction.'[23] And as a consequence of his avoidance of structural/analogical considerations, he ends up with a high number of 'unique expressions,' many of which could easily be seen as structural or analogical variants of familiar existing formulas. These phrases are 'unique' in the literal sense, but remain such close kin to other phrases similarly constructed that it seems obdurate not to classify them all within one formular substitution system.[24]

Hainsworth's approach leaves some questions of detail perhaps

---

[23] Hainsworth (1964) 164. His 1962 article contains the more moderate judgment that 'formula-types . . . are not the sole technique used in composition by formulae' (p. 59). This study shows the origins of Hainsworth's conviction that schematization represents tradition whereas flexibility means invention (pp. 64–65), which makes understandable his emphasis on the latter for an appreciation of the oral poet's creativity.

[24] At (1968) 132–33 νηλέι θυμῷ and νηλέι χαλκῷ are listed as 'regular formulae' while the obviously kindred νηλέι δεσμῷ and νηλέι ὑπνῷ, because they occur only once, are classified as 'unique expressions.' The same is true of the 'unique' δείελον ἦμαρ despite the well-established system νηλεὲς (ἱερὸν, δούλιον, αἴσιμον, μόρσιμον, νόστιμον) ἦμαρ (pp. 136–8); and the 'unique' σήματα λυγρά and ἔχθεα λυγρά despite κήδεα (ἄλγεα) λυγρά (3x, 2x) and the ἕλκεα λυγρά classed with 'possible formulas and derivative expressions' (pp. 136–7). Many other 'unique expressions' may be similarly reconsidered.

disputable. Among minor modifications, for example, 'expansion' in some cases demonstrates no more than that Homer could place another word next to his formula. Viewing this new combination as an 'extended formula' begs the question of formular identity: it is simply a formula plus another word, often a weak word like μάλα or the definite/demonstrative article. Among major modifications, one could criticize those examples of separation which create such a different pattern that the new configuration seems not so much a formula as a new word group composed of the elements of a sometime formula. Thus one recent scholar worries that the concept of the flexible formula may carry 'the seeds of its own destruction.'[25] The problem again is nomenclature: it seems imprecise to describe *both* the many Homeric regularities *and* their several degrees of variation and deviation as all 'formulas' of one kind or another.

By the late 1960s, then, the concept of formula seemed in a confused state, with no agreed upon definition but a shared uncritical assumption that the term must refer to a single phenomenon of diction. The conceptual expansion of the formula had taken essentially two opposite directions: either holding on to meter, order, and syntax and loosening requirements of close word repetition, or keeping close word repetition but loosening the other requirements. Each of these criteria permitted an analysis that could find new formulaic expressions related to existing ones; but each also allowed ambiguous boundaries between clearly accepted formulas and possibly related expressions.

A thoroughly new approach was offered by M. N. Nagler's conception of the 'generative' nature of the formula. Nagler (1974) begins from the impasse to which various conflicting theories of the formula had led. In an opening chapter called 'The Traditional Phrase,' he demonstrates that for any set of phrases that seem to be variants of the same formula, it is always possible to add still other phrases that share some resemblance, so as to form a continuous chain of diminishing connectedness. He illustrates this principle by juxtaposing the following phrases, of which the first two were cited by Parry ([1971] 72) as having what he called a punning relationship:

---

[25] Higbie (1990) 166–68 shows how formulas like εἶπον + μῦθον and βάλλω + δουρί can be 'altered almost beyond recognition,' citing instances where 'a flexible formula carries the seeds of its own destruction' and is more plausibly 'construed as individual words and not as a formula.'

ἀμφήλυθεν θῆλυς ἀυτμή	[*Od.* 12.369]
ἀμφήλυθε θῆλυς ἀυτή	[*Od.* 6.122]
θείη δέ μιν ἀμφέχυτ' ὀμφή	[*Il.* 2.41]
δεινὴ δὲ θεείου γίγνεται ὀδμή	[*Il.* 14.415]
. . . θῆλυς ἐέρση	[*Od.* 5.467]
βοῶν δ' ὣς γίγνετο φωνή	[*Od.* 12.396]
περὶ φρένας ἤλυθ' ἰωή	[*Il.* 10.139]
ἀκούετο λαὸς ἀυτῆς	[*Il.* 4.331]
ἕκαθεν δέ τε γίγνετ' ἀκουή	[*Il.* 16.634]

Of the seven phrases he has added to Parry's original two, Nagler claims that 'two have the same commonly found noun-epithet combination after the bucolic diaeresis [although this is not really true or λαὸς αυτῆς], while the remaining five share another, but not unrelated, syntactic pattern' ([1974] 3). He further suggests that there are still more phrases that might be incorporated into this sequence, and proceeds to construct other sequences even more elaborately diffuse. The resemblances, he claims, are 'more than coincidental'; they may not be groups of formulas according to definitions hitherto accepted, but 'one is justified in feeling that . . . they are groups of *something*' (p. 11). Here the fact that Nagler has titled his chapter 'The Traditional Phrase' may take on added significance: we may infer that 'traditional phrase' would be a more useful term than 'formula' to name these fluctuating phenomena.

With such subtle and varied grounds for group coherence, it would seem arbitrary to declare a firm cut-off point where membership in the group might be denied. These observations lead the author to introduce into formula studies the concept of the 'open-ended family' (pp. 11–13). Such open-endedness is not merely descriptive but has a theoretical center, an abstract, pre-verbal mental template for which no English term exists and which may be called a Gestalt. It is closely similar to the concept called *sphota* by Sanskrit grammarians and has looser resemblances to the Platonic idea, the Jungian archetype, and the Lévi-Straussian structural model of myth. It is at this level of phenomena that the true formula exists, as a mental potentiality; all the actual verbalizations made by the reciter are called 'allomorphs' of this one entity.

Nagler has offered an ingenious solution to the problem of relating similar-seeming expressions under one unifying identity. His emphasis on resemblances that are more subtle than those commonly documented by formula-hunters must appeal to the intuitions of every reader of Homer. On the other hand, several of his assertions of similarity must strike most readers as subjective and unconvincing (e.g., he adduces *Il.* 16.634 for its supposed similarity to 14.415). A more serious theoretical problem raised by this approach is that it removes the formula from the manifest realm where we can observe and measure its forms, and transposes it to a realm where it is potential rather than actual and thus no longer analyzable. So while the formulation makes elegant theory, it renders our concordance-compiled repetitions of limited use in finding the allomorphs of any *Gestalt*, leaving us with no investigative tool as a replacement except for each individual researcher's 'nose' for formulas.

We have reviewed a constant shifting of definitions that allowed formulas to look less and less like those of Parry. Although sometimes deplored, I believe that the development of multiple competing definitions has helped broaden our understanding of the aesthetics of Homeric style. Anyone who reads Homer in Greek becomes eventually aware that repetition is constantly at play, some of its forms being more immediately evident than others. The uniquely satisfying effect that Homeric style has upon us derives from our perception, at different levels ranging from fully conscious to subliminal in varying degrees, that patterns of sentence, phrase, word, rhythm, and sound are repeatedly returning, and recalling one another with a subtlety that defies precise definition and classification. It is this refusal of the formulaic to be defined and classified, and its increasing identification with the organized functioning of language on multiple levels simultaneously, that the studies of the sixties and seventies successfully, even if sometimes unintentionally, brought to light. Milman Parry's definition was a good beginning, but only a first attempt to capture the infinite variety of verbal patterning within Homeric diction. Parry saw and defined with clarity the 'tip of the iceberg,' and clearly intuited the existence of much of the supporting sub-structure. The subsequent expansions should not be seen as the abandonment of rigor or the 'debasement' of some primeval gold, but as extensions outward to capture some of the less manifest (but no less poetically, rhetorically, and psychologically effective) patterns through which Homer imposes poetic form on hexametric language.

Recent Directions (Since 1980)

The epithet reconsidered

In 1982, Paolo Vivante published a book-length study of Homeric epithets that took a position directly opposite to Parry's: epithets are never simply functional or ornamental, but always evoke the 'fullest materialization' and 'visual focus' ([1982] 14) of the person or thing named, giving them a 'fresh sense of reality' (p. 173). Vivante is probably correct to some degree, but it remains difficult to estimate just how much fullness and focus πόδας ὠκὺς adds to Ἀχιλλεύς or πολυμῆτις to Ὀδυσσεύς, and whether it is the same in all contexts.[26] And for all his desire to challenge Parry's vision, it may be that Vivante's position was to some extent anticipated by Parry, whose judgments, as already noted, sometimes carry the seeds of their own revision and correction. We tend to think of Parry's view of epithets in terms of his more absolute pronouncements, such as 'the use of the ornamental epithet in Homer is entirely dependent on its power to facilitate versification' ([1971] 23). But he also says that the ornamental fixed epithet 'adds to the combination of substantive and epithet an element of nobility and grandeur' ([1971] 127), a conception that is surprisingly close to Vivante's.

Vivante also reminds us ([1982] 22–26, 94–100) that there are many instances where the epithet may have been used but was omitted, and invites us to look beyond the more mechanical needs of verse-construction to possible semantic factors, such as the poet's wish *not* to dwell on the full presence of the person but to focus attention elsewhere. This is an attractive idea, and seems supported by the examples the author has collected. But then again, it is inherently problematical to collect passages where it may be safely claimed that the poet *chose* not to use a traditional epithet *because* he wished to shift his focus elsewhere. The most important contribution of Vivante's study remains his insistence on the possibility that function and poetic value need not be seen as constantly opposed to one another, which was the rigid view that could be extracted, perhaps

[26] In an earlier challenge to the Parry orthodoxy, Whallon ([1961], expanded in Whallon [1969]) argued that epithets are so true to character that they in fact influence characterization, and in specific contexts assume vivid semantic presence. This approach, like Vivante's, must contain a kernel of truth, and similarly runs the risk of subjective interpretation.

unavoidably, from Parry's writings, but need not be the only position for an oralist aesthetic.

The formula reconsidered

After an apparent moratorium in the struggle to find acceptable definitions of the formula, a new impulse has come from two recent attempts to reconsider its essential nature. Both share the interesting idea that not all members of a formulaic phrase need be equally stable or essential: there is semantic nucleus surrounded by more peripheral or variable elements. E. Visser proposed this approach in his 1987 German dissertation, summarized in 1988 as an English article. He acknowledges the seed of this important difference in Parry's original distinction between the fixity of the noun and the variability (lexical and prosodic) of the modifier in the intensely studied noun-epithet combinations. Visser develops this idea into a major principle for discriminating between semantically 'nuclear' words, necessary for the poet to use to express his 'essential idea,' and the more optional and variable words and phrases which adapt that idea to the exigencies of hexameter versification.

A good example is found in the frequently used whole lines within 'killing scenes' in which Homer says the equivalent of 'A killed B.' From a collection of many such single verses—which allow a control on the data through similarity of idea and form—Visser draws several conclusions. The names of killer and victims can take a wide range of metrical shapes, so they must be positioned first; then the verb of killing must be fitted into whatever metrical slot(s) is (are) most typical for localization of that type (following O'Neill). Thus the nuclear material is placed according to semantic needs, and the remaining 'fillers,' which do not convey crucial sense but functionally complete the verse, are fitted in wherever possible. The example afforded by *Il.* 5.43 is analyzed in the 1988 article, with the assumption that we can dissect its components to reconstruct Homer's versification technique.

Ἰδομενεὺς δ'ἄρα Φαῖστον ἐνήρατο, Μῄονος υἱόν.

The subject Idomeneus is localized in the place commonest for choriambs, – ⏑ ⏑ –, perhaps a plausible claim, though it scants O'Neill's evidence ([1942] 144) for approximately equal use in position 5 and some use in 9 and 11. Then when 'Phaiston,' in Visser's explanation, 'a trochee or spondee, is set in relation to the choriambic and when we consider the structure of the caesurae in the hexameter [here a ref. to Fränkel's colometry, discussed above], we get the following most natural disposition: Ἰδομενεὺς ⏑ ⏑ Φαῖστον ⏑ – – ⏑ ⏑/– ⏑ ⏑ – x//.' Here the argument grows less compelling, because it is not explained by what principles 'Phaiston' is *bound* to be placed where it is by Frankel's scheme of caesurae, since as a trochee or spondee it can have, according to O'Neill, five or six favored positions. (Five if we count 20% or more of occurrences as constituting a 'favored' position, six if we accept 14% as our threshold, according to O'Neill's data on pp. 141–42.)

For the other nuclear element, the verb ἐνήρατο, it is perfectly true that this shape ⏑ – ⏑ ⏑ localizes strongly before the bucolic caesura; but Visser omits the possibility that the poet could use many of the 27 verb forms Visser himself lists to express the idea 'killed.' Not all would fit equally well into a verse that had to contain the words Idomeneus and Phaiston, but the poet's choices seem far less mechanically restricted than Visser claims. Also doubtful is the claim that the two shorts after Idomeneus are 'usually filled by the . . . connective element,' therefore 'the only possible completion can be δ'ἄρα (Visser [1988] 35–36). The concordances show seven Iliadic uses of the metrically equivalent ἕλε in this position, of which four are descriptions of killing. This verse therefore could have been constructed

Ἰδομενεὺς δ' ἕλε Φαῖστον ἀμύμονα, Μῄονος υἱόν

or

Ἰδομενεὺς Φαῖστον μὲν ἐνήρατο . . .

leaving it to the poet to complete the verse in a manner compatible with the needs of meter and sense. And still other possibilities exist. Even keeping δ'ἄρα in the second metron we could have

Ἰδομενεὺς δ' ἄρα Φαῖστον ἀμύμονα θυμὸν ἀπηῦρεν.

Visser's theory is an interesting expansion of Parry's conception of the formula, and certainly redirects needed attention to the fact, oddly under-appreciated, that *some members of formulaic combinations are more 'formulaic' than others.* Thus it suggests a useful corrective—at least in some cases—to Hainsworth's conception of the 'mutual bond of expectancy' between members of a formulaic word-group, which had implied an *equal status* for each member.

But it is not a major challenge to oral theory. Moreover, Visser's argument is weakened by the all-or-nothing form in which he casts his conclusions: 'Homer obviously thought in categories of single words and not in formulaic word-blocks' ([1988] 36). This is a monolithic vision as overstated as Parry's oft-regretted claim that the poet composes entirely in pre-existing formulas. One wonders what prevents Visser from seeing the evident truth that Homer thinks and composes *sometimes* in formulaic phrases (the evidence of the Concordances and Schmidt's *Parallel-Homer* is mighty) and *sometimes* in single words.

Visser's 'nuclear semantics' approach has been recently adapted by E. J. Bakker and F. Fabbricotti (1991) and developed further on the theoretical plane. They view Homer's diction as oral and spontaneous, consisting regularly of nuclear words with associated 'peripheral' elements, and differing importantly from written versification 'in the degree to which it makes *systematic* use of flexible, metrically adaptable material.' As an application of the theory, they offer a close analysis of Homer's use of dative expressions centering on the words for 'spear' δόρυ and ἔγχος. Like Visser, they analyze battle scenes where these phrases normally constitute material that the poet treats as peripheral, i.e., 'reactive,' to his more important main ideas, the names of slayer and slain and the verb of killing, which are called 'determinative.' The variability of this material is clear evidence of the poet's technique for adapting what he wants to say to the metrical constraints that bind him; whereas the selection and placement of nuclear words shows him operating in a sphere of relatively free choice.

Like Visser, the authors are concerned to show that Homer composes far less through pre-made formulaic blocks than 'hard Parryists' have tended to believe. But they differ from Visser in that they use the nuclear-peripheral distinction to support the likelihood of oral composition. With an essentially Parryistic vision, they see the poet as an oral bard who used peripheral material to improvise completions to verses centered on the placement of the more determinative nuclear material. Visser, on the other hand, follows Latacz (whose student he is) in imagining a poet who had recently left behind the old style but can still utilize it, while also having recourse to writing to achieve the 'excellence' of his poetry.

An important question left unanswered by these recent investigations is whether Homeric diction consists entirely of nuclear words deliberately and relatively freely selected and placed within the verse in combination with relevant peripheral phraseology, or whether this phenomenon is concentrated in the more stereotypical subject matter. All the verses analyzed represent the relatively simple structures and ideas found in battle passages. To echo Chantraine's one reservation about Parry's work ([1929] 299), they have chosen the most favorable material for their thesis. Since Bakker and Fabbricotti view peripherality as recursive—that is, every peripheral element may itself have a nuclear and a peripheral part—one imagines that attempts to view less stereotypical passages in nuclear-peripheral terms may yield analyses of increasing complexity and diminished clarity. Nonetheless, Bakker here and in other publications has brought a new dimension of linguistic sophistication to the study of Homeric diction, relating it to oral discourse through a variety of shared rhetorical features exclusive of formular phraseology as traditionally conceived (see below).

Two other recent studies have had some success in a project analogous and complementary to those just discussed: distinguishing the formulaic from the non-formulaic component in order to show that Homer could be both an oral poet and a composer of some originality. Both M. Finkelberg (1989) and W. M. Sale (1989) have shown admirable methodological rigor and freedom from bias toward an oral or a literate Homer. Letting themselves be led by the evidence, both authors arrive at a similar evaluation of different areas of Homeric diction, Finkelberg studying the verbal expressions for joy and Sale the epithets for Trojans. Each author sees approximately 70% formulaic diction, with the remaining 30% an indeterminable mixture of free expression and under-represented formulas. This seems consistent with the general judgement passed a generation ago by C. M. Bowra ([1952] 230–31, 252–53), who said that while the oral poet must rely greatly on formular expressions there is also a part of his diction in which he chooses words freely, and in the better poets this part increases.

Discourse theory

Most recently, applying a linguistic approach based on contemporary discourse theory, E. J. Bakker raises an interesting challenge to the fundamental assumption that formulas are a unique characteristic of oral poetic style. He argues that formulas, along with other distinctive features of Homeric discourse, are not so much the differentia between oral and written literary style as phenomena of spoken language itself. 'Homeric discourse,' he says, 'is stylistically and metrically a stylization of the cognitive production of ordinary speech.' Any oral speech-production is characterized by composition through intonation units rather than the clauses and sentences defined by traditional grammar, which was developed to analyze *written* style. The other key feature of oral style is the use 'discourse markers,' which in Homer are primarily ἄρα and δέ, and to a lesser extent μέν and δή.[27] Bakker's approach offers an original re-conceptualization of our approach to Homeric style, inviting us to re-locate what we have understood as a formulaic and paratactic style within a larger conceptual scheme which sees speech production as close to the act of cognition and therefore obeying some of its constraints and habits of organization.

A Homerist might worry that Bakker's emphasis undervalues the fundamental importance of metrical form, if such form were to be viewed as a kind of second-level phenomenon whose role is essentially to support 'regularization' or 'stylization' of the discourse flow rather than to create it. But Bakker says,

> Far from minimizing the difference between Homeric metrical discourse and ordinary speech, I contend that the specific nature of Homeric diction is not so much a matter of simply being removed from the realm of ordinary speech with its dysfluencies and hesitations, as, paradoxically, an age-old strategy precisely to *prevent* those hesitations and dysfluencies. By putting metrical constraints on the flow of discourse, Homeric diction is able to obviate the cognitive constraints that are inherent in speech production. (Bakker [1993] 8)

This is a promising beginning to acknowledging the complexities involved in such an approach. Given the intrinsically deep connection of many formulas and formulaic substitution systems to firm metrical structures (usually colometric units), the discourse-centered approach to Homeric style should proceed next to more detailled consideration of the role of meter, which is in fact Bakker's intention in a work in progress.

---

[27] Bakker (1993a); quotations from pp. 3, 8. See also Bakker (1990); (this vol.), for analyses of Homeric text according to 'intonation units' rather than the traditional ones of formula, colon, and verse.

Conclusion

We arrive, then, at a vision of Homeric diction as an amalgam of elements covering a spectrum from highly formulaic to nonformulaic, a view that may be considered both unsurprising and uncontroversial. What readers of Homer will still debate are the proportions allocated to different components of the amalgam, the location of the boundaries that separate them, and the literary or aesthetic effects achieved by the poet's strategies of choice and combination. A useful scheme for envisioning this picture is that of M. Cantilena ([1982] 70), to which I have added a few details in brackets.[28]

	Metrical Identity	Non-metrical Identity
tradition	traditional formula	
↓		traditional phrase
	formulaic expression	
	[flexible formula]	
	structural formula	
	[localized single word]	free phrase [or word]
	non-traditional formula	
individuality	[hapax?]	[hapax?]

It should now be more than clear that much of the disagreement over how best to define formulas was created by a limitation in terminology. The word formula proved to be a poor thing, hopelessly inadequate to cover the different *kinds* of formulaic realities in Homeric

[28] If 'traditional phrase' is to refer to all members of Nagler's formular 'family,' it might be moved to the margin of metrical identity, closer to the Hainsworthian flexible formula. My suggestion of the flexible formula's 'liminal' status comes from its frequent appearance in identical metrical shape but transposed to a less usual place in the verse (there is some ambiguity in whether 'the same metrical conditions' covers only metrical shape or location as well). The uncertainty of where to locate the hapax reflects the possibility of a pull towards localization according to its metrical word-type, following O'Neill's evidence.

diction. And it is reasonable to assume that the talented traditional poet would always have been capable of some non-formulaic, original language, including the strategic handling of individual words. Creation on all these levels is essential to the total epic diction.

Parry's theory remains impressive for its durability in the face of so many challenges and revisions on particular points. Like other theoretical revolutions in this century that required us to re-think the nature of well-studied but partially misunderstood phenomena, Parry's vision continues to shape our thinking even as we continually alter its details. It is inevitable that today no reader of Homer can fail to be in some sense a Parryist.

Mark W. Edwards

HOMERIC STYLE AND ORAL POETICS

Introduction

In this chapter I shall survey what seem to me to be the most significant current ideas about Homer's use of conventional verbal expressions, indicating the developments which have taken place in the more than three decades since the Wace-Stubbings *Companion to Homer* of 1962. I shall not include a historical account of work since Milman Parry, since several diachronic surveys already exist;[1] instead, I shall discuss the progress made in certain specific areas, beginning with the realization of the problems Parry's discoveries caused for appreciating Homer's creative genius, and continuing with the modifications made to his theory; subsequent studies of the relationship of formulae to the hexameter verse; our better understanding of the antiquity of the formulae and the way in which older expressions give way to new; the extent to which Homeric diction is formulaic; the depth of meaning that should be attributed to a formulaic expression; the attention paid to formulae in recent commentaries on Homer; and the contribution made by recent studies of oral poetry and the grammar of speech.

Occasionally I may be guilty of trying to fit a certain significant study into an area where it does not quite belong, for the sake of simplicity of exposition; and I am afraid that my discussion may seem to be dominated by the work of American and British scholars. To some extent at least this apparent favoritism can be justified by the comparative slowness (with important exceptions) with which Parry's work was appreciated in Europe, which has meant that new theoretical studies on the nature of formulae have been slow to appear there.

[1] See J. Russo's chapter in this volume (prepared independently). My present chapter fills the gap left by the never-completed § 9, 'Homer and the criticism of oral poetry,' of my survey article (M. W. Edwards [1988]). There is a brief survey in J. M. Foley (1985), and a fuller one in Foley (1988); see also Latacz (1979); Boedeker (1988); Holoka (1991). An admirably full systematic analysis and discussion of the phenomena of Homeric formulae may be found in Hainsworth (1993) 1–31.

After Parry: the Call for an 'Oral Poetics' (i)

The Wace-Stubbings *Companion* contained three chapters by Maurice Bowra, 'Metre,' 'Style,' and 'Composition,' and a fourth by Albert Lord, 'Homer and Other Epic Poetry', which was up-to-date enough to refer in a footnote to his *The Singer of Tales* (1960). At that time Parry's work was well known to Homerists in the US and Britain, and had not yet been modified or amended; instead of constructive criticism there was a certain amount of unhappy and emotional rejection by those who felt that Homer's individuality and genius were being infringed upon. Bowra, however, had worked on heroic poetry himself and was sympathetic towards Parry's results, and much of what he says in his second and third chapters would (I think) be considered unexceptionable nowadays (though his chapter on meter shows no knowledge of the contribution of H. Fränkel and is badly outdated). He declares that 'a given set of words is normally used for a like occasion whenever it occurs' ([1962] 28), complains mildly that 'At times it looks a little mechanical, as when certain epithets are not so much otiose as out of place,' and mentions the familiar problems of the beggar Irus' 'lady' mother and cases where 'the familiar epithet is retained in its usual place in the verse, even though it conflicts slightly with the sense' ([1962] 29). He also allows for times when Homer 'abandons the stock form for something more elaborate.... No doubt he does this because he wishes to make something special of the occasion and to give it its own appropriate poetry' ([1962] 30). Nowadays, however, some would feel reservations when Bowra suggests that the appeal of noun-epithet formulae 'is dulled by repetition, and the original audiences, who were more accustomed to them than we are, must have been no less unresponsive' ([1962] 34). His conclusion is that Homer 'was still free to make the most of his technique and to apply it as he thought most suitable to the different elements in his tale' ([1962] 73). Lord's chapter includes a short section on formulaic and thematic structure ([1962] 186–88), but is mostly devoted to broader topics in oral poetry. In his monumental *The Singer of Tales* (1960) he stressed that 'the percentage of demonstrably formulaic lines or part lines is truly amazing' ([1960] 142; according to his analysis, 90%), but he discussed mainly the 'themes' in the *Iliad* and *Odyssey*.

Influential about this time was an article by F. M. Combellack. Pointing out that 'An important conclusion Parry drew from his materials was that the oral poet tends to use his formulas primarily because they are convenient and not because their meaning is especially appropriate in a given passage,' Combellack concluded that 'one result of Milman Parry's work on the Homeric style has been to remove from the literary study of the Homeric poems an entire area of normal literary criticism' ([1959] 193). But he still insisted that Parry had not 'remove[d] the creative poet from the *Iliad* and *Odyssey*' (the formulation of the horrified Wade-Gery, which he quotes), but that 'If Parry's conclusions are sound, it is now hard, or impossible, to find artistry in many places in the Homeric poems where critics of the pre-Parry age found beauty and where contemporary critics often still find it' ([1959] 196). Using as an example Ruskin's comment about 'the high poetical truth' of φυσίζοος αἶα (*Iliad* 3.243), 'the earth . . . our mother still, fruitful, life-giving' even when it covers Helen's dead brothers, Combellack declared that 'we can no longer with any confidence urge that the adjective φυσίζοος was deliberately chosen by the poet because of any kind of peculiar appropriateness of meaning' ([1959] 197–98).[2] He concluded by reasserting that 'The difficulty is not that Parry's work has proved that there is no artistry in these features of Homer's style, but that he has removed all possibility of any certitude or even reasonable confidence in the criticism of such features of Homeric style. . . . The hard fact is that in this post-Parry era critics are no longer in a position to distinguish the passages in which Homer is merely using a convenient formula from those in which he has consciously and cunningly chosen *le mot juste*' ([1959] 208).

Even before Combellack, J. Notopoulos ([1949] 1) had begun an article: 'This paper poses the question, do the same principles of literary criticism apply to both written and oral literature? The answer is no.' The article was subtitled 'A New Approach to Homeric Literary Criticism,' and later Notopoulos published another which included a section headed 'Toward a Poetics of Early Greek Oral Poetry' (1964). But though he pointed out some of the pitfalls of approaching Homer as if he were a familiar literate poet, and declared 'The new question which challenges our times is centered on the effect Parry's work will have on literary criticism' ([1964] 47), Notopoulos did not provide any very coherent alternative principles. A

[2] There is a particularly good appreciation of these lines in A. Parry (1966) 197–98, and a recent full discussion in J. M. Foley (1991) 247–52.

little later, Lord similarly concluded a long article highly critical of some of the preceding work on Homer by saying 'Surely one of the vital questions now facing Homeric scholarship is how to understand oral poetics, how to read oral traditional poetry. Its poetics is different from that of written literature because its technique of composition is different' ([1967] 46).

Taking up the same topic, a few years later J. B. Hainsworth published 'The Criticism of an Oral Homer' (1970), in which he pointed out that 'the oral poem properly speaking is knowable only through its performances. There is no "real" or "original" form ... all that can ever be heard is the "version" of a poem' ([1970] 90). Besides anticipating the present interest in performance, Hainsworth made a significant contribution by emphasizing that in appreciating Homer one must evaluate both the basic structure and the importance of elaboration or ornamentation, and of good proportion in its use ([1970] 97).[3] But the topic of 'oral poetics' was far from settled.

The First Modifications of Parry's Work

In the mid-1960s two important supplements to Parry's ideas appeared, both of them emphasizing the flexibility inherent in Homeric usage of formulae. Parry had discussed the metrical irregularities which sometimes arise from the juxtaposition of two formular expressions ([1971] 202–221) and the occasional neglect of initial or medial digamma ([1971] 222–34, 391–403); now A. Hoekstra published a monograph (1965) studying the ways in which traditional formulae could be made more flexible in shape by taking advantage of three linguistic changes in the Greek language (the exchange of quantity from -ηο to -εω and synizesis of the vowels, the dropping of initial digamma, and the optional addition of a final -ν to certain verb and noun forms), which allowed a freer declension of nouns, a freer conjugation of verbs, changes of positioning in the verse, and the insertion of particles. The work is of fundamental importance because it demonstrates clearly for the first time that the presence in a verse of later linguistic elements is no proof of interpolation, but merely shows the poet making use of innovations in the language to facilitate

[3] I tried to demonstrate the importance of observing the poet's elaboration or abbreviation of type-scenes in my analysis of *Iliad* 1 (M. W. Edwards [1980]).

composition. No longer could simple observance or neglect of the digamma be used as an indication of genuine or 'interpolated' verses.

The second significant work was that of J. B. Hainsworth (1968), who studied noun-epithet (*not* name-epithet) formulae which commonly occur in a certain metrical shape (e.g., καρτερὰ δεσμά) but also have the flexibility to appear in other metrical forms (e.g., κρατερῷ ἐνὶ δεσμῷ, δεσμοῖο ˘ - κρατερου, δεσμοῖς ˘ ˘ - κρατεροῖσι). Such phrases do not fall under Parry's famous definition of a formula ('an expression regularly used, under the same metrical conditions, to express an essential idea': [1971] 13, etc.; see Russo, this vol.) because of the metrical differences, but nevertheless the forms are clearly associated in some way; and Hainsworth ([1968] 35–36) proposed a new (rather loosely-worded) definition of the formula: 'a repeated word-group' where 'the use of one word created a strong presumption that the other would follow. This degree of mutual expectancy I choose as the best differential of the formulaic word-group.' This 'mutual expectancy' of the elements of a formula, despite various re-arrangements of sequence and changes in shape of each part, is the most valid approach to a definition, at least for Homeric Greek.[4]

Both Hoekstra and Hainsworth give appreciative summaries of Parry's results, but include some criticisms of his definition and his application of it, and of his tendency to generalize too broadly from the special case of nominative name-epithet expressions.[5]

The Formula and the Hexameter

In 1926 H. Fränkel published a highly original and significant article (revised version in Fränkel 1968) on the structure of the Greek hexameter, dividing it not into metrical feet (dactyls and spondees) but into 'cola,' sections of the verse separated by word-boundaries and often by pauses in the sense (see also Russo, this vol.). The commonest divisions fall at the well-known break in the middle of the verse and at the often strongly-marked 'bucolic diaeresis' before the final

[4] The poet's adeptness in modifying formulae in this way has been used in Postlethwaite (1979) to identify the stylistic habits of individual poets in the Homeric Hymns, and (Postlethwaite [1981]) in an attempt to determine if the conclusion of the *Odyssey* (23.297 to the end) is by the same poet as the rest of the work.

[5] Bakker (1995) 97–100 gives an excellent summary and appraisal of Parry from today's viewpoint.

five syllables; and usually there is another division at some point within the first half of the verse (an accessible and sound description can be found in Kirk [1985] 18–24)[6]. Parry was unaware of Fränkel's work; but it is immediately obvious that the verse-divisions indicated by Fränkel (together with the end of the verse) also mark the commonest points for the beginning and end of formulae (again, for examples see Kirk [1985] 24–30). In the 1950s and later several scholars studied the relationship of cola and formulae (see M. W. Edwards [1986b] 178–88), and in an article of my own (M. W. Edwards 1966) I examined the sense-units (single words and formulae) which tend to occur in each of the four sections into which the caesurae articulate a verse, and the ways in which verses which are otherwise identical are modified by the exchange of metrically equivalent but semantically different phrases in certain of their sections. By coincidence, in the same year G. S. Kirk published an article which dealt with many of the same issues from a slightly different viewpoint (Kirk 1966b).[7]

After a number of years, a significant advance has recently been made by Visser (1987; the substance of this is given in English in Visser [1988]). Basing his argument on a study of all verses in the *Iliad* in which one warrior kills another, Visser distinguishes the semantically most important elements, the names of killer and killed, from the less-stressed items—the verb, whose semantic content is already expected in the situation, and the conjunction(s); and then goes on to show that the highly functional and metrically inflexible names appear in the verse at the places most suitable for their shape, and the remaining and less stressed material, the verb and conjunction(s), is adapted for the needs of the verse by means of a range of metrically different synonyms available in the poet's traditional technique (one only for each metrical shape—Parry's principle of economy is re-affirmed). Visser lists ([1988] 31) twenty-seven metrically different verb-forms found in 'killing'-scenes, ranging in length from ἕλ' to ὑπὸ γούνατ' ἔλυσεν, and nine different lengths for the conjunctions, running from δ' to δ' ἄρ' ἔπειτα.[8] But to make all this possible there must be extra space available, a little elbow-room; and this is

[6] But note that normally the alternative mid-verse caesurae (labelled by Kirk M or F) are termed B^1 or B^2, and the third caesura (labelled by Kirk B) is termed C.
[7] I discuss G. Nagy's ideas on formulae and cola in the next section.
[8] The lists are reprinted in Riggsby (1992) 100. This article is an extension of Visser's type of analysis to speech introductions, with interesting remarks on theory of formulae.

filled by loosely connected material such as epithets and adverbial expressions.

Visser's insights into how these ultra-regular 'killing'-verses are formed have been extended by E. J. Bakker in two articles (Bakker and Fabbricotti [1991]; Bakker and van den Houten [1992]). The elements Visser identifies as essential or non-essential (his terms are actually 'semantic and metrical components') Bakker and Fabbricotti speak of as 'material that is *peripheral* to a *nucleus*' ([1991] 64), as (for instance) δῖος is peripheral to Ἀχιλλεύς. Bakker examined the dative expressions for 'with a (his) spear' to see if they can be described as peripheral to verbs of killing, and found this is usually the case; he lists 9 expressions of different lengths (Bakker and Fabbricotti [1991] 70) to demonstrate the metrical variability and interchangeability of this semantic unit. Bakker holds, however, that though the expressions are neutral to the context, they are not meaningless (as Parry said), but their meaning is subservient to the ultimate goal, metrical utility.

The related issue of enjambement, the running-over of a sentence from one verse to the next, which Parry himself ([1971] 251–65) and a number of others have worked on, has recently been exhaustively studied by Higbie (1990), and cannot be summarized here.[9] The positioning of formulae and sense units in the hexameter of early elegiac verse, which is different from that in the stichic hexameter, has been studied briefly in Greenberg (1985) and more fully in unpublished work by H. R. Barnes.

How Old are Homeric Formulae?

The question falls into two parts: how old are the oldest formulae? and are new formulae still being introduced in Homer's time?

On the answer to the first question, probably the most authoritative voice from the linguistic side[10] is that of C. J. Ruijgh, who has argued ([1985]; [1995]) that the hiatus appearing in (βοῶπις) πότνια Ἥρη shows that the formula goes back to Mycenaean times, when

[9] See also Cantilena (1980); Bakker (1990); the review article by Barnes (1991); and Clark (1994).

[10] I will not attempt here to discuss the archaeological evidence, on which see Bennet, I. Morris, and Snodgrass (this vol.); I give some of the older bibliography in M. W. Edwards (1986b) 207–210.

the initial *h-* functioned like a normal consonant and prevented the metrical irregularity (the memory was powerful enough to prevent Homer, but not Hesiod, from using the form in the accusative); the same strong Mycenaean initial *h-* also preserved the heavy syllable before the last word of Διῒ μῆτιν ἀτάλαντος (the final iota of the first word would have been -εί at that time). He lists other Homeric expressions which also show traces of this consonantal *h-* (Ruijgh [1995] 78–85), and holds that the oddities of scansion in the full-verse formula Μηριόνης ἀτάλαντος Ἐνυαλίῳ ἀνδρειφόντῃ go back to proto-Mycenaean, even earlier than the language of the tablets (sixteenth-/fifteenth-century; Ruijgh [1995] 85–91).

G. Nagy argues that the hexameter arose from a pherecratean verse expanded by three dactyls, and supports this view by a listing of formulae which have alternative forms with a dactylic expansion ([1974]; [1976] 250–52). He holds that Greek meter is cognate with Indic, where the patterns of rhythm emerging from favorite traditional phrases suggest that Greek formulae similarly shaped the hexameter verse, and supports the Indic parallel by claiming a phraseological correspondence between the Homeric κλέος ἄφθιτον and a postulated Vedic *śrávа(s) ákṣitam* (reconstructed from two other verbal combinations), both deriving from an Indo-European prototype. The idea has not won general acceptance, and the argument continues.[11]

M. L. West (1988) draws a number of other parallels between expressions in other early Indo-European languages and in Mycenean and Homeric Greek. Like Ruijgh, he feels that features of Homeric Greek belong to an earlier stage of the language than that of the Linear B tablets, and adds to the list of Homeric words and formulae which fit the meter better when lost consonants are restored; for him, 'Mycenaean heroic poetry was cast in hexameters from at least as early as the fourteenth century' ([1988] 158).[12]

The second question, that of the obsolescence and replacement of formulae, has been a particular interest of J. B. Hainsworth ([1964]; [1978]; [1993] 28–30). He has shown that formulae including mundane epithets spread at the expense of the old dramatic ones (e.g.

[11] The κλέος ἄφθιτον correspondence has been challenged, especially in Finkelberg (1986); Nagy has replied in (1990a) 122 n. 3. The latest entry into the conflict is that of Olson (1995) 224–27. M. L. West (1988) 152 appears to agree with Nagy.

[12] Among other work on the history of the hexameter, I should mentioned Hoekstra (1981). Janko (1992) 8–19 has recently summarized the arguments, with further evidence and examples.

θεὰ λευκώλενος Ἥρη for βοῶπις πότνια Ἥρη; the commonplace χάλκειος of a helmet, for the mysterious τετραφάληρος). 'The formula becomes outmoded. Its colour turns first into the rust of archaism, and finally into the magnificence of the unknown and incomprehensible: at which stage the old formula is ripe for replacement by the neutral product of generative processes, and the cycle begins anew' ([1978] 50). Changes in the language (see Hoekstra [1965]) allowed the development of new forms (e.g., μελιηδέος οἴνου, with neglect of initial digamma and the later -ου form of the genitive) in place of the old (μέλανος ϝοίνοιο), and even for the august Zeus the stately πατὴρ ἀνδρῶν τε θεῶν τε faces competition from the more flexible Κρόνου πάϊς (ἀγκυλομήτεω), which includes metathesis and synizesis of vowels and can be shortened if desired (Hainsworth [1993] 30).

Finally, one must mention Janko 1982, an impressive study which examines linguistic changes in the Homeric poems and the use of innovative and archaizing diction in Hesiod and the *Homeric Hymns*.

How Formulaic is *Homer?*

There are several different ways to attempt to answer this question. First of all, both Parry ([1971] 301 ff.) and Lord ([1960] 143 ff.) printed short extracts from the Homeric text in which they had underlined the formulae, and others have followed them.[13] The results depend, of course, on the definition of formula which is used, and are on the whole useful mainly for the particular purpose for which each analysis has been performed.

Important here, however, is an original and very promising new approach to the understanding of Homeric formulae has been worked out during the last ten years by W. M. Sale. His first relevant article (1984) argued that the set of formulae in which the home of the gods is Olympus is earlier than the set locating them in Ouranos, because the latter (much smaller) set seems to exist in order to fill a metrical gap in the former. A little later (1987), Sale studied how often formulae occurred in expressions giving the sense 'in (to, from) the Greek camp' and 'in (to, from) Troy,' showing that formulae for 'in Troy' and 'from Troy' are significantly fewer than the others. He

[13] See the listing in M. W. Edwards (1988) 42–53; and add now R. P. Martin (1989) 167 ff.; J. M. Foley (1990) 141 ff.

concluded that 'This means that .when Homer was composing the *Iliad* there were few or no formulae available to him meaning "in Troy-city"' ([1987] 35). The rigorous procedure for categorizing formulae and the methods of statistical analysis which Sale has developed are applied even more intensively in Sale (1989), which focuses on the fact that the formulae for the Trojans are repeated many times fewer than the average; regular formulae in the nominative occur a minimum of six times, but the Trojans have no nominative formula occurring more than four times. The reason seems to be that the Trojans, like the suitors in the *Odyssey*, have formulae which include hostile epithets, and these are not used in the poet's own voice (cf. Griffin 1986). Sale suggests 'the traditional poets shared the Achaean attitude towards the Trojans and handed on to Homer a set of formulae that he could not employ as R[egular] F[ormulae] because he looked upon the Trojans with much greater favor than they did' ([1989] 378–79). In Sale (1993a) and (1993b), he makes a statistical comparison of the use of formulae in the *Iliad*, the *Odyssey*, and the *Chanson de Roland*, finding the poems very similar. He also discusses ([1993a] 135–42) the birth of infrequent formulae for metrical or semantic reasons, including a discussion of forty 'semantic-aesthetic' alternatives to regular formulae, where (for instance) Thetis is 'weeping' instead of 'silver-footed,' or Telemachus refers to Odysseus as 'my father, noble Odysseus' instead of using the normal 'much-enduring. . . .' Sale's results are a valuable indication of which ideas in Homer may be new and not covered by the traditional diction.

M. Finkelberg, recognizing the problem posed by a unique expression which we might or might not call a formula, depending upon whether or not a second, or a third, instance happened to survive to our day, set out to avoid this uncertainty by examining a verbal rather than a nominal idea; she looked at the phrases by which Homer expresses joy, which always involve forms of the verbs γηθέω, γάνυμαι, and χαίρω (Finkelberg [1989]). She found that 'of the one hundred expressions examined, sixty percent proved to be formulae or modifications of attested formulaic patterns, while the rest (40%) could be categorized as isolated or remained unqualified' ([1989] 191). She further acutely notes that 'the distribution of the formulaic and nonformulaic expressions is anything but fortuitous. Instead of evenly covering all possible situations requiring an expression of joy, the formulaic system for this idea only provides expressions that occur in the third person of the aorist indicative or imperfect and express joy as an immediate emotional response or as a feeling accompanying the main action.... Just as the traditional poet found it 'thrifty' to have formulae for all recurring ideas and standard narrative situations, so he found it equally thrifty not to overload his formulaic apparatus with expressions for just any idea and situation' ([1989] 196–97). Though unsurprising in itself, her conclusion is unusually well-documented.

Hapaxes, words which occur only once in Homer (sometimes defined as once in the *Iliad* or once in the *Odyssey*) and hence are in most cases unformulaic by definition, have been discussed in four recent studies: Pope (1985), Kumpf (1984), N. J. Richardson (1987b), and M. W. Edwards (1991) 53–55. In brief summary: a word which appears only once in Homer occurs on the average every 9.4 verses of the *Iliad* and every 11.8 verses of the *Odyssey*;[14] some of these are common words which just happen to occur only once, some are everyday but highly specific words (often found in the similes), and some words are rare or unique, perhaps even newly-coined compounds. It is hard to draw any generalizations about the circumstances where *hapaxes* occur. But the authors reach similar conclusions: 'Homer was as much concerned with the individual word as other poets and prepared to coin a new one if he felt it necessary' (Pope [1985] 8); 'The very high frequency of [Homer's] *hapaxes* does not accord well with the theory of a composer tied to the apron-strings of his tradition' (N. J. Richardson [1987b] 183); '[Homer] was completely at ease in employing in his verse words which are not only non-formular but which must be considered (on our limited evidence) foreign to the usual epic vocabulary' (M. W. Edwards [1991] 55).

N. Austin (1975), checking the formulae for 'Odysseus' in the *Odyssey*, pointed out that in the nominative the name alone (without epithet) is as common as a name-epithet formula, and that in the oblique cases the unaccompanied name forms considerably the larger part of the instances. Thus it is only the nominative which supports Parry's ideas of a system marked by extension and economy. He also notes that these formulae are used almost entirely by the narrator; the characters most often use more personal expressions like 'father,' 'child,' or a pronoun in addressing or referring to him. The attempt of D. Shive (1987) to show that many more expressions for 'Achilles' were used by the poet than Parry allowed for seems to me unsuccessful,

[14] These figures are from Kumpf, and include those *hapaxes* which are proper names.

as many of the 'equivalent' formulae he lists are not in fact semantically identical (e.g., 'Αχιλλεύς, αὐτός, and υἱός; Shive [1987] 21).[15]

Do Formulaic Epithets have any Meaning?

Before Parry's work began to be criticized for his over-generalizing from his study of name-epithet formulae to the whole Homeric diction, he attracted overwhelming attention because of his repeated and uncompromising statements denying that formulaic epithets could have any meaning. 'The technique of epithets, as we have studied it, is solely designed to help the poet to fit a noun into a line of six feet; once the noun has been fitted in and the line is complete, the epithet has no further function' (Parry [1971] 165); 'In the matter of the generic meaning of the epithet as in that of its ornamental meaning, we can conclude that the poet was guided in his choice by considerations of versification and in no way by the sense' ([1971] 149); 'What was this constraint that thus set Homer apart from the poets of a later time, and of our own time, whom we see in every phrase choosing those words which alone will match the color of their very own thought? The answer is not only the desire for an easy way of making verses, but the complete need of it. Whatever manner of composition we could suppose for Homer, it could be only one which barred him in every verse and in every phrase from the search for words that would be of his own finding' ([1971] 317).[16] Combellack remarked on the implications of this view for literary criticism (Combellack [1959]; see above); others grabbed their pens to argue (or angrily assert) that the ornamental element is often, or always, responsive to its immediate context. The fullest and most effective arguments were those of W. Whallon, who in a series of studies attempted to show that the metrically identical ἀνδρόφονος, ἀντίθεος, and ἱππόδαμος are used appropriately for certain heroes (Whallon [1961]; [1979]), that the epithets of some heroes may have had enough weight to influence their characterization (Whallon

[15] Among many studies of the adaptation of formulae I would note those of V. Di Benedetto in *RFIC* 114 (1986) 257–85, 385–410; 115 (1987) 257–87.

[16] In his full account of Parry's work and its reception, J. M. Foley quotes several of Parry's scholarly predecessors in the study of epic formulae who said much the same as Parry, and just as categorically (J. M. Foley [1988] 6–10). See also Bakker (1995) 97–100.

[1969]), and that other considerations than metrical convenience affect the Homeric phrases for 'shield' (Whallon [1966]). In a number of books and articles, P. Vivante has emphasized the meaning it is possible to see in the usage of epithets, though his ideas are often rather subjective and some of the phrases he suggests it was open to Homer to use, instead of what actually appears in our text, are improbable or even impossible (Vivante [1970]; [1982]).[17]

Often how much semantic weight and poetic effect is attributed to a formulaic epithet must be left to the taste of the individual reader. But a few points can be established with some certainty. First of all, to some extent the interpretation must depend upon the particular formulaic word in question: δῖος, which is used of twelve different men (mostly with names scanning ⏑ - -)[18] in the nominative, ranging from Achilles to the swineherd slave (royally-born and devoted though he is), seems to be little more than a polite honorific like 'Mr.'; whereas ποδάρκης 'swift-footed' and πολύτλας 'much-enduring' have a clear meaning—even though in the *Iliad* Achilles is unable to overtake Hector by his speed and Odysseus has not yet undergone his toil-some adventures.

Second, it has long been noticed that occasionally Homer is sensitive enough to the meaning of a formulaic epithet to provide a substitute when it is particularly inappropriate to its context: Sale ([1993a] 139–40) lists twelve such cases (cf. Combellack [1976] 53–54), including the change of 'cloud-gathering' Zeus to 'lightning-gathering' when he is *dispersing* the clouds (*Iliad* 16.297–98; Janko [1992] 356 refers to this 'unique makeshift' as 'gauche'), and others might be added (for instance, Thebes has 'wide dancing-floors' instead of the usual 'seven gates' when the city is still 'unfortified', *Odyssey* 11.264–65; Penelope is 'noble' instead of the usual 'having good sense' when she is specifically *said* to have good sense, *Odyssey* 24.194). It has recently been pointed out that Diomedes, usually βοὴν ἀγαθός 'loud-voiced', never receives that epithet during his night-time raid on the Trojan camp in *Iliad* 10, where silence is much more desirable.[19]

[17] See also Austin (1975) 65–80; M. W. Edwards (1966) 153–54, 164–67, 169–70; (1968).

[18] So Parry (1971) 149; the epithet occurs 183 times with such names, compared with 5 times with names scanning differently.

[19] So Machacek (1994) 331–33. I have difficulty accepting the other arguments in this article.

And third, it must be remembered that Homer always has (and often avails himself of) the option of not taking advantage of the opportunities offered by the formulaic diction but of substituting something fitting the context and quite untraditional, so far as we can see. This is especially the case in the last five syllables of the verse, following the bucolic diaeresis (cf. M. W. Edwards [1966] 167–75; Bakker and Fabbricotti [1991]), where the place of a common verse-ending is often taken instead by a new enjambing phrase. A very simple case is ὣς οἱ μὲν μάρναντο δέμας πυρὸς αἰθομένοιο 'So they fought | like fire | blazing' (3 times in the *Iliad*); once the place of the concluding participle is taken by the enjambing phrase οὐδέ κε φαίης | . . . (*Il.* 17.366), and once the places of both the short simile and the participle are taken by a new (and unique) enjambing phrase, σιδήρειος δ' ὀρυμαγδὸς | . . . (*Il.* 17.424). Among many other examples, 'Αχαιῶν after the mid-verse caesura is often followed by χαλκοχιτώνων |, often not. Homer's technique supplies δουρὶ φαεινῷ and similar convenient phrases if they are required, but does not *obligate* a poet of Homer's genius to use them.

Besides these prosaic practical considerations of fitting within the verse words which may or may not be really meaningful, scholars have proposed theoretical principles which are relevant here. One of the first applications of modern linguistic theory (generative grammar) to Homeric verse was made by M. N. Nagler in a very important book (1974). Beginning with comments on the 'puns' or phonological repetitions Parry ([1971] 72) had noted in Homer, Nagler speaks of 'the operation of psychological cola or rhythmical groups of some sort' ([1974] 8), and soon drops the word 'formula' in favor of 'allomorph,' which is 'a derivative not of any other phrase but of some preverbal, mental, but not quite real entity underlying all such phrases at a more abstract level' ([1974] 12), a 'preverbal template' or 'Gestalt' realised in the appropriate spoken form at the moment of utterance. Besides other values, this approach is a very salutary reminder that whether in the case of formulae, type-scenes, or story patterns, one must beware of the tendency to identify one form (perhaps the commonest) as a model or prototype upon which others are based. In another chapter ([1974] 27–63) Nagler opens up another virtually new field in discussing the poetic significance and symbolism obvious in some formulae, using as an example the particularly rich associations of κρήδεμνον 'head-binder; veil; battlement; seal' with chastity and its loss.

A similar expansion and deepening of the meanings and associations of formulae has been suggested by other scholars. At almost the same time that Nagler's book appeared, G. Nagy suggested in a conference on 'Oral Literature and the Formula' that 'A particularized epithet is like a small theme song that conjures up a thought-association with the traditional essence of an epic figure, thing, or concept' ([1976] 244 = [1990a] 23, with 'distinctive' for 'particularized'). Recently this idea has been broadened still further in the work of the well-known scholar of oral poetry, J. M. Foley. For a number of years Foley has written on the work of Parry and Lord and its application to ancient Greek, Anglo-Saxon, and Serbo-Croatian epic, contributing to our understanding of these three disciplines by his unrivaled knowledge of the languages and texts in question and of the whole field of scholarship on these and other oral poetries. In Foley (1991)[20] he propounded the concept of 'traditional referentiality,' what he calls '. . . a modified form of Receptionalism' ([1991] xv), based on the *Rezeptionsästhetik* of W. Iser and H. R. Jauss and akin to the theory of P. Zumthor ('The formulaic style can be described as a discursive and intertextual strategy: it inserts and integrates into the unfolding discourse rhythmic and linguistic fragments borrowed from other preexisting messages that in principle belong to the same genre, sending the listener back to a familiar semantic universe by making the fragments functional within their exposition' [Zumthor (1990) 89–90]). In Foley's words, 'Traditional elements reach out of the immediate instance in which they appear to the fecund totality of the entire tradition, defined synchronically and diachronically, and they bear meanings as wide and deep as the tradition they encode. . . . Traditional referentiality, then, entails the invoking of a context that is enormously larger and more echoic than the text or work itself, that brings the lifeblood of generations of poems and performances to the individual performance or text. Each element in the phraseology or narrative thematics stands not for that singular instance but for the plurality and multiformity that are beyond the reach of textualization' (Foley [1991] 7). This is *metonymy*, the part standing for the whole; and Foley applies the principle not only to name-epithet formulas but also to type-scenes and story-patterns.

Foley gives numerous examples of the results of applying this theory; as an example, one may quote his comment on the line introducing

[20] Cf. also J. M. Foley (1995).

Achilles' sharp response to Priam's refusal of his offer of a seat, τὸν δ' ἄρ' ὑπόδρα ἰδὼν προσέφη πόδας ὠκὺς Ἀχιλλεύς (*Iliad* 24.559): 'A sensitive audience would thus invest the language of line 559 with two different but complementary associations. By virtue of the noun-epithet phrase, indivisible as a unit of meaning, Achilleus is brought before us in full immanence, with his pride, choler, and arrogant intransigence boiling just beneath an apparently calm surface. Likewise, the *hypodra idôn* phrase characterizes the situation as one of those traditional Homeric confrontations in which a perceived insult is about to elicit an indignant response' (Foley [1991] 143). The conclusion is not far from those of Vivante, but much better based on theoretical argument; and it is congenial to the ideas of Nagy (quoted above) and R. P. Martin ('only a deracinated, print culture would view Homeric formulas as devices to aid the composition of poetry. Rather, they belong to the 'composition,' if you like, of personal identity in a traditional world' [1989] 92). Bakker has well pointed out ([1995] 102–103) that 'Metonymic relationships are at the heart of wider ranging strategies of epic poets to locate their discourse with respect to the larger realms of human experience', quoting as further examples Homeric similes, catalogues, *androktasiai*, *aristeiai*, and the use of 'epic τε' to mark generic statements. Use of the characteristic epithet of a god or hero distinguishes him and gives him *kleos*; an epithet is 'a small-scale, routinized and recurrent re-enactment within the encompassing framework of the epic re-enactment as a whole' ([1995] 102), a 'miniature-scale myth' ([1995] 109). We are not far from one of Aristarchus' principles for explaining apparently incongruous epithets, οὐ τότε ἀλλὰ φύσει, 'not at that moment, but in general,'[21] extending it to cases where the epithet is *not* inappropriate. The theory adds depth to our appreciation of the epic, and reminds us that the listeners to a traditional oral poem were more attuned to the song than we can be.[22]

Other work on the meaning of Homeric formulae and words must be dealt with summarily. In *The Language of Heroes*, R. P. Martin includes an exceptionally sensitive and careful analysis and discus-

---

[21] See Parry (1971) 120–124; Combellack (1987) 206–209.

[22] Of course writers too create and make use of the expectations of their readers; Foley comments on this, briefly and not very clearly (Foley [1995] 211–12). This does not, however, diminish the cogency of the theory for oral poetry. There is a thoughtful, well-measured summary and review of Foley's work by W. M. Sale in *Bryn Mawr Classical Review* 7 (1996) 13–21.

sion of the formulas in Achilles' superb speech in *Iliad* 9.308–429 ([1989] 160–205). T. Jahn, in a highly significant piece of research (1987), investigating the semantic field of the various words meaning 'spirit, heart (etc.)', has demonstrated that both in the nominative and in the oblique cases κῆρ, φρήν, ἦτορ, θυμός, στῆθος, φρένες, κραδίη, and πραπίδες (and combinations of these) are all metrically different (fulfilling Parry's principle of economy), and so the poet's choice on any particular occasion is likely to be determined by the structure of the rest of the verse rather than by any semantic difference we may try to identify. This finding immediately renders suspect the results of many past investigations of Homeric psychology. A very heavy weight of association is attributed to single words ('theme-words') such as ἄνδρα, μῆνιν and νόστον, especially when initial in the verse, in Kahane (1992); (1994). P. Pucci probably goes further than most Homerists would follow in his identification of cross-references in the phraseology of the *Iliad* and the *Odyssey*, when (for instance) he declares that the use of a couplet describing Dawn at *Odyssey* 5.1–2, which recurs only at *Iliad* 11.1–2, 'cannot be purposeless' and 'forces the audience to remember the Odysseus of the *Iliad*' ([1987] 21 n. 10), and that when a verse appears in Calypso's words to Odysseus about his wish to return home (*Odyssey* 5.204), and also in Athena's words to him when the Greek army is dashing for the ships (*Iliad* 2.174), 'the reader is made aware that, in the *Odyssey*, "wily" Odysseus does not realize the foolishness of his rash departure and fails to persuade himself of his error' ([1987] 35). As usual, however, the decision is subjective: I would not follow Pucci in seeing allusions here, but I have no doubt that there is an intended significant allusion produced by the reservation of *Iliad* 16.855–57 and 22.361–63 to describe the deaths *only* of Patroclus and Hector. Finally—this is not always relevant to formulas, but very clearly illustrates Homer's individuality and freedom of choice in his diction—Jasper Griffin in a very important article (1986) has identified differences between the vocabularies of the narrative and the speeches in Homeric epic, finding that moral judgements, negative epithets (those beginning with alpha-privative), and the superlative forms of adjectives occur only or mainly in speeches; and that the speeches of different characters also show strong differences, those of Achilles (for instance) showing more asseveration, more exaggeration, more use of similes, and a more imaginative vocabulary than those of Agamemnon.

The New Commentaries

Within the last decade, each of the old English university presses has produced a full-scale *Commentary* on one of the Homeric poems. G. S. Kirk edited a six-volume set on the *Iliad* for the Cambridge University Press (books 1–4, Kirk [1985]; books 5–8, Kirk [1990]; books 9–12, Hainsworth [1993]; books 13–16, Janko [1992]; books 17–20, M. W. Edwards [1991]; books 21–24. N. J. Richardson [1993]). The three volumes of the Oxford *Odyssey* commentary, a revised version of the six-volume Italian-language edition, with text and translation, published by Mondadori in successive years from 1981 to 1986, were edited by Heubeck, West, and Hainsworth ([1988], books 1–8), Heubeck and Hainsworth ([1989], books 9–16), and Russo, Fernández-Galiano, and Heubeck ([1992], books 17–24). Of the *Iliad* editors, four had studied their Homer in England, one in the USA.[23] The *Odyssey* editors (a slightly larger group) included scholars from Britain (J. B. Hainsworth again, S. West), the USA (J. Russo), Germany (A. Heubeck, the general editor), the Netherlands (A. Hoekstra), and Italy (M. Fernández-Galiano). It would be unwise to expect, or to try to construct, a consensus among these ten Homerists about oral poetics—Homerists are often surprised at what is confidently declared to be 'the consensus' or 'orthodox opinion'—but the two Commentaries may well help to *form* a consensus among readers who do not themselves specialize in Homeric language and style; so it is worth while to check what aspects of the subject the various editors feel is important.

Kirk's first volume includes an introductory section (pp. 24–30) on 'The formular style and its operation,' which deals with the mechanical aspects of fitting phrases within the verse cola but says nothing about meaning. In the unique case of the place-name epithets in the Catalogue of Ships, after a detailed discussion he concludes that they are 'for the most part very general in meaning' and 'also usually arbitrary in distribution, depending as they do to some considerable extent on the rigid and conventionalized arrangement of these particular verses' ([1985] 177), which is true enough. His index is not very informative, and does not give a breakdown of topics under 'formulas' or under proper names. But Kirk is not unsympathetic towards

[23] Myself; my interest in Homeric formulae began after I came to the USA, in conversations with J. Notopoulos.

the poet's individuality; after a careful analysis of the formulae for the coming of dawn he concludes 'These [other expressions], too, display less formular economy than might be expected, but it is with the highly artistic variations of dawn appearing (or spreading, rising, or bringing light) over hills or sea that a departure from normal oral economy of means can be detected. Several such verses occur at the beginning of an important new episode. . . . In these circumstances the singer can be seen seeking both colour and drama in his expression, and a special kind of poetical deliberation and effort is apparent' ([1985] 119–20).

Kirk's second volume contains an introductory section on direct speech which continues the work of Griffin on vocabularies (Kirk [1990] 28–35; Griffin [1986]), remarking that 'The formular style imposes a degree of uniformity, but it is notoriously overriden by the prolix impetuosity of Akhilleus' utterances to the Embassy in bk. 9, and can also be tempered in more subtle ways' ([1990] 34). The index under 'formulas' is not analyzed, but a quick check shows mainly comments on highly formulaic or unformulaic passages. His sympathetic approach to the meaning of epithets appears, however, when he notes that Homer keeps the 'formidable μέγας κορυθαίολος' for Hector when he addresses Helen, Hecuba, and Andromache, when use of the 'less martial φαίδιμος' would have been possible, and terms the phrase 'significant' as it begins the speech preceding the fright of Hector's infant son (*Iliad* 6.440; Kirk [1990] 207, 219).

Hainsworth's volume includes an introductory section in which he sets out and discusses phenomena about formulae under 17 headings, including the question of what exactly a formulaic epithet adds to its noun ([1993] 21–22), deciding sensibly that 'an epithet that is neutral in most contexts acquires force when sense and context chime together.' His general conclusion is quotable: 'ἀοιδοί, guided by an infrastructure of habits in localization and sentence structure, could invent, improve, improvise, and expand their diction according to their competence as well as reproduce a traditional language, but their imagination could only feed on what was familiar to them, their own world' ([1993] 30–31). His commentary sometimes draws attention to formulaic usage, and five times he identifies 'underrepresented formulae.'

R. Janko's is the longest volume in the *Iliad* set, and his index is by far the fullest. His introductory section on 'The origins and evolution of the epic diction' (Janko [1992] 8–19) includes a good deal of information about the early history, linguistic form, and modifications (as the language changed) of formulae, and the splendid index directs the reader to numerous entries under such rubrics as 'equivalent formulae' (i.e., violations of economy), 'formulae . . . conjugated . . ., declined . . ., displaced . . ., misapplied . . ., under-represented' and many other sub-divisions; and each significant proper name has a listing under 'epithets of.' I cannot attempt to summarize the immense value of this volume to anyone who wishes to understand how Homeric formulae actually *work*.

My own volume contains a section on metaphors, many of which occur in formulaic expressions, and another on *hapax legomena* ([1991] 48–55). Subdivisions under the listing for 'formulae' include 'formular epithet with significant sense' (twenty entries) and 'innovative use or adaptation of . . .' (forty-four entries). Anyone who checks these will probably find lots of room for disagreement. Finally, N. J. Richardson's volume again has many entries under 'epithets: significant', and he comments sympathetically on such usages as Achilles πτολίπορθον (*Iliad* 21.550) that 'it may suggest Akhilleus' rôle as the *potential* destroyer of Troy itself' [1993] 100); on Deiphobus λευκάσπιδα (22.294) that 'It is as if Hektor were looking all around the battlefield for this conspicuous sign of his brother's presence . . . only to find emptiness and silence' ([1993] 136); on Antilochus διοτρεφές (23.581) that 'it is as if Menelaos is appealing to Antilokhos' own sense of honour, and suggesting that it is not in his true character to act as he did' ([1993] 232), and on several epithets which occur in the meeting of Priam and Achilles ([1993] 322–25). Uniformly, these scholarly editors are very ready to give a traditional epithet the benefit of the doubt, and attribute a meaningful sense to it when it seems at all appropriate.

In the Oxford *Odyssey* comments on formulae are less frequent, but not very different in approach. In his General Introduction to the first volume Heubeck, after describing the oral poetry theory as 'gaining ground steadily since the thirties, particularly (though not exclusively) in Anglo-American circles,' says that 'In many important respects Parry's views were undoubtedly correct', but gives very little account of formulaic diction (Heubeck et al. [1988] 8–9), and neither does Hainsworth's section on the epic dialect ([1988] 24–32). The index lists a number of references to formulae, especially those which are 'metrically equivalent,' but they are almost entirely to comments on books 5–8 (edited by Hainsworth). The second volume includes a section by Hoekstra on Homeric diction, which (not surprisingly) refers occasionally to formulae (Heubeck and Hoekstra [1989] 149–60). The index to this volume lists a number of references to the declension, evolution, modification etc. of formulae, and under 'epithets: not "ornamental"' refers to several comments by Heubeck where he attributes a significant sense to a traditional epithet (ὀλοόφρων for Aeetes 'hints at the danger to come' (*Odyssey* 10.137; [1989] 52); δῖον (rather surprisingly) 'is significant: Memnon is son of Tithonus and Eos' (11.522; [1989] 108) and to one by Hoekstra in νύκτα διὰ δνοφερήν (15.50) 'the epithet is not "ornamental" . . .: without good visibility a journey through the Peloponnese must have been a risky affair' ([1989] 234). In the third volume Russo discusses Parry's ideas and those of his critics at the beginning of his work (Russo et al. [1992] 18) and comments several times on 'epithets: distinctive'; all three editors point out the practical workings of the formulaic system, but not very much attention is paid to the possible significance of traditional epithets.

Oral Poetry and the Grammar of Speech

At the 1976 conference on 'Oral Literature and the Formula' (Stolz and Shannon, eds. [1976]) one of the most important presentations was by a participant trained in linguistics, who presented a fundamental comparison of Homeric formulae to the 'bound expressions' or clichés of everyday language ('foregone conclusion,' 'perfect stranger,' etc.), and introduced Homerists to a conception of oral poetry as embodying the grammar of speech which has recently become highly significant (Kiparsky [1976]). Kiparsky approved Hainsworth's abandonment of the metrical criterion as part of the definition of a formula, and was careful not to single out one particular form as the prototype from which others could be generated by analogy. Once presented, the application of the grammar of speech to oral poetry is obviously appropriate, and applicable both to the shaping of his performance by the poet and to the perception of it by his listeners; but it was not carried forward until E. J. Bakker began to apply to Homeric epic the ideas of the linguist W. L. Chafe (Bakker [1990]; [1993a]). Under the name 'pragmatics,' S. R. Slings (1992) has similarly studied certain phenomena of Homeric language as reflecting the ways and means of oral communication.

This and related aspects of Homeric diction are discussed by Bakker (this vol.), and I need not describe them further here.[24] His work is building an up-to-date foundation in linguistics for the ideas of today's Homerists, much as Devine and Stephens (1984) did for our understanding of the hexameter.

The Call for an 'Oral Poetics' (ii)

What has been accomplished in our understanding of Homer's poetic use of formulae since Notopoulos ([1949] 1) called for new principles of literary criticism nearly fifty years ago? It is, on the whole, the last ten years which have been the most productive, and which make the future exciting. To summarize our progress (with the names of some of those particularly responsible);[25] we better understand: the structure and composition of Homeric verse, and the oral nature of its grammar (Visser, Bakker); the age of formulae, the speed of their obsolescence and replacement, and their relative pervasiveness in the diction (Ruijgh, Hainsworth, Sale, Finkelberg); the characteristics of an oral culture and its relationship to the power of writing (Nagy, Foley, and others); differences in vocabulary between speech and narrative, and between characters (Griffin, Martin); the significance and power of association a traditional word or phrase may convey to the listeners in an oral culture (Foley); the possible ways in which Homer's song eventually became a fixed written text (Nagy [1995a]); and we have new commentaries on the poems, paying more attention to formulaic structures than any have done previously (Kirk, Heubeck and their collaborators).[26]

These accomplishments encourage continuation and extension. And to help, we have new tools. Besides our well-worn Concordances, now over a century old, we have the *TLG* and the capacity to search it; more convenient access to the papyrus fragments of Homer (thanks to Sutton [1991]); better editions of the *Iliad* scholia and of Eustathius'

---

[24] I am grateful to Professor Bakker for sending me a typescript of his chapter prior to publication.

[25] I am very conscious that I am omitting much valuable work and many scholars who have made large contributions, and what I mention has inevitably been chosen in accordance with my own idiosyncratic preferences. I can claim only a long familiarity with the topic.

[26] Though they are not closely dependent upon formulae, I would like to mention here the aesthetic effects of expansion of verbal expressions and of type-scenes, discussed respectively by Russo (1994); M. W. Edwards (1980); (1992).

commentary (Erbse, van der Valk); the indices and lists of Dee, Kumpf, Paraskevaïdes, and Strasser; and we may be moving towards better texts of the poems, constructed with understanding of the nature of an oral-derived, at some stage oral-dictated text.[27] We eagerly anticipate the new books on Homeric discourse and performance announced in E. J. Bakker's chapter in this volume (Bakker [1996]; Bakker and Kahane, eds. [1997]).

New approaches continue to appear (for instance, the questions recently raised about Homer's relation to earlier poets by Johnson [1994]); and despite new discoveries the old questions often will not go away. Let me close with an example. J. M. Foley's application of 'traditional referentiality' to *Iliad* 24 ([1991] 135–89) is immensely sympathetic toward the evocative effects of the traditional diction and the skill of the poet in manipulating it; but in the penultimate line of the poem, δώμασιν ἐν Πριάμοιο διοτρεφέος βασιλῆος, and in its last line, ὣς οἵ γ' ἀμφίεπον τάφον Ἕκτορος ἱπποδάμοιο, he refuses to allow any special significance to the final occurrence of the heavy formula for Priam ('. . . the vision of Homer's direct (and literary) manipulation of the phraseology would thus appear illusory.' [1991] 144) and for Hector's familiar epithet, on the grounds that the phrases occur elsewhere without special significance ('The simple form *Hektoros hippodamoio* thus betrays neither the poet's singular manipulation of the diction to sound a coda to the *Iliad* nor his mindless accession to a compositional imperative, but rather his harnessing of the inherent meaning of the epithetic phrase to convey a richness of signification otherwise unachievable:' ([1991] 146). My own feeling is that Homer is intentionally repeating, for the last time, the effect he so memorably produced at the death of Patroclus, when he gave him the name of his beloved friend for his last words: '. . . χερσὶ δαμέντ' Ἀχιλῆος ἀμύμονος Αἰακίδαο' (*Iliad* 16.854). It remains a matter of individual choice; which is, of course, just as it should be.

[27] See Janko (1990), and his review of H. van Thiel's new text of the *Odyssey* (Hildesheim 1991) in *Gnomon* 66 (1994) 289–95.

Egbert Bakker

THE STUDY OF HOMERIC DISCOURSE

In this chapter, Homeric poetry is discussed within the wider contexts of spoken language and communication. Taking the Homeric text as a *transcript* of an earlier speech, rather than as a modern text in our sense, we shall be concerned with Homeric discourse as *speech*, and discuss a number of salient properties of Homeric style and syntax that are amenable to the analysis applied to spoken language data as practiced in modern *discourse analysis*. The discussion will furthermore focus on some basic problems in the study of 'oral style,' arguing for an awareness of how much of our usual notional apparatus for the study of Homer and other traditions of epic poetry is explicitly or implicitly textual.[1]

Orality and the Formula

Most scholarly work carried out in the wake of Parry's and Lord's groundbreaking studies[2] has focused on the question what makes oral poetry oral. The central concern was to define oral poetry in terms of its chief constitutive building-block, the formula, which led to a strong preoccupation with the *definition* of this concept, as well as with the question how much of the *Iliad* and *Odyssey* could be called formulaic and how much not.[3] For Parry ([1971] 328), the notion of formula defined oral poetry as such in a conception in which the oral, the formulaic and the traditional were intimately connected:

---

[1] The argument of this chapter is presented at greater length in Bakker (1996). See also Bakker (1990); (1993a).

[2] Parry (1971); A. B. Lord (1960).

[3] Both practices go back to the last phase in Parry's work: cf. his own definition of the formula ('a group of words which is regularly used under the same metrical conditions to express a given essential idea,' [1971] 272; cf. [1971] 13) as well as his well-known formulaic analysis of the first 25 lines of the *Iliad* and *Odyssey* (Parry [1971] 301–314; cf. Lord [1960] 143). Just how large a portion of the debate on the formula in the 1970s was devoted to problems of definition can be gleaned from most of the papers in Stolz and Shannon, eds. (1976). See also Russo, this vol.

'The nature of Homeric poetry can be grasped only when one has seen that it is composed in a diction which is oral, and so formulaic and so traditional.'

Parry also held ([1971] 377) that on account of its formulaic nature, oral poetry could be opposed to *written* poetry, which was conceived of, by implication, as non-formulaic: 'Literature falls into two great parts not so much because there are two kinds of culture, but because there are two kinds of *form: the one part of literature is oral, the other is written.*'

The binary opposition between oral and written poetry has met with considerable criticism in recent years, particularly from students of medieval formulaic poetry, who point out that formulas in the Parryan sense can be easily imitated in written composition. This led to a conception in which the *compositional* aspects of the formula recede in favor of their *receptional* aspects, their recognizability to a (listening) audience, an aspect neglected by Parry and Lord.[4]

What concerns us here, however, is the *perspective* implied by an opposition between oral and literate poetry. The opposition is meant to create an objective binary contrast, with the formula as the specific difference between the two members of the pair. In reality, however, it hides a conception that is intimately bound up with the perspective of the researcher. If oral poetry is defined as a kind of literature that is formulaic and traditional, then the general background against which Homeric discourse is viewed is that of literature, or poetry, of which *oral* literature or poetry is the special case. This perspective, however, does not match that of the epic singer himself, whose activities take place in a situation in which literature in our sense does not exist and in which writing has at best marginal relevance. It is with this perspective that the present chapter is concerned.

Oral vs. Literate Style

The literary perspective is also apparent in the study of Homeric syntax, which is commonly characterized with such terms as 'paratactic

[4] For formulas and writing, see Bäuml (1987); Schaefer (1988); (1992) 59–87; Bakker (1996) ch. 2. For the meaningfulness of 'old' information in the epic performance, cf. also Bakker (1993b).

style' or 'adding style.' Such labels are meant to designate a way of linking clauses that is considered 'primitive' with respect to the more sophisticated hypotactic style of written literature. In the paratactic style clauses are simply added to what precedes, without there being syntactic hierarchies, stylistic subtleties, or means to differentiate important ideas from less important ones.[5] The very first lines of the *Iliad* will serve as a characteristic and straightforward example of this phenomenon:

> Μῆνιν ἄειδε, θεά, | Πηληϊάδεω Ἀχιλῆος |
> οὐλομένην, | ἣ μυρί' Ἀχαιοῖς ἄλγε' ἔθηκε, |
> πολλὰς δ' ἰφθίμους ψυχὰς Ἄϊδι προΐαψεν |
> ἡρώων, | αὐτοὺς δὲ ἑλώρια τεῦχε κύνεσσιν |
> οἰωνοῖσί τε πᾶσι, | Διὸς δ' ἐτελείετο βουλή,
> ἐξ οὗ δὴ τὰ πρῶτα διαστήτην ἐρίσαντε |
> Ἀτρεΐδης τε ἄναξ ἀνδρῶν καὶ δῖος Ἀχιλλεύς.

Clauses containing a verb are linked to the preceding discourse either with the particle δέ or in the form of a paratactic or 'digressive' relative clause (ll. 2, 6); a phrase without a verb, on the other hand, such as Πηληϊάδεω Ἀχιλῆος (l. 1) or ἡρώων (l. 4) is simply 'heaped upon its predecessor.'[6]

In the earlier literature on the style of Archaic Greek poetry, historical, or even genetic, perspectives are offered, in which paratactic style was seen as an 'early' stage in the development of literature, or of the human mind, to be overcome in due course.[7] Parry's work and the 'discovery' of orality did much to weaken support for these ill-founded 'evolutionary' ideas, yet the perspective did not change: instead of a sign of 'primitive' language, paratactic and adding style came now to be seen as due to circumstances of composition that are quite different from those of written literature, but the frame of reference remained written literature:

> Oral versemaking by its speed must be chiefly carried on in an adding style. The Singer has no time for the nice balances and contrasts of unhurried thought: he must order his words in such a way that they leave him much freedom to end the sentence or draw it out as the story and the needs of the verse demand. (Parry [1971] 262)

---

[5] On paratactic style, see e.g., Fränkel (1968) 40–96; Notopoulos (1949); Thalmann (1984) 4–6.

[6] Kirk (1976) 152. Kirk speaks of 'cumulation' in this respect.

[7] E.g., Kühner and Gerth (1904) 226, 347; Norden (1958 [1909]) 37 n.

Even though Parry and his approach firmly established oral poetry as a 'legitimate' form of literature, passages such as these still betray a perspective in which writing and written language is a norm, somehow, to which oral language does not (yet) conform, and with respect to which it is defined. The view, often in veiled and implicit form, of written language as the dominant form of language, is still widespread, even among linguists who subscribe in theory to the primacy of spoken language, or students of oral poetry, who try to devise a poetics other than our own.

Part of this situation seems to be due to a failure to recognize two different senses of 'oral,' the distinction of which is important for the solution of the problem. Scholars who speak of 'oral style' conceive of 'orality' as a psychological or intellectual phenomenon: the degree to which an individual's mental habits are *not* governed by the conventions of (formal) written discourse. By this criterion, a discourse may be oral to a higher or lesser degree, according to the absence or presence of a number of formal or communicative features. In this first sense, 'oral' denotes the *conception* of a discourse, its being unplanned or informal as opposed to planned and formal.[8] In addition, however, there is a quite different sense in which a discourse can be oral. The term can simply mean that a discourse is spoken, 'phonic,' a matter of sound and voice as opposed to the graphic nature of a written discourse. In this sense, 'oral' denotes a *medium*, the way in which a discourse is realized. And as a *medium*, orality is not the absence of writing or its imperfect and clumsy ('early') use, but simply a way of using language that is different from, and opposed to, written communication.[9] A 'medially' oral discourse may be formal or informal, just as a conceptionally oral discourse may be spoken or written: the two senses operate in different dimensions.

The distinction between the two senses of 'oral' is important in a number of ways. Not only does it restrict common usage in Homeric studies and classical philology in general to just one use of the term; more importantly, it enables us to put Homeric discourse, as well as epic discourse in general, in the right perspective. If oral discourse,

---

[8] Critique of a simple 'oral-literate'-opposition can be found in Beaman (1984); Koch and Oesterreicher (1985); Oesterreicher (1997). See also Bakker 1996, ch. 1.

[9] On the medial opposition between written language and spoken language, see the articles in Tannen, ed. (1982) and Olson et al., eds. (1985). On Ancient Greek, see Slings (1992). The distinction between 'conception' and 'medium' is borrowed from the work of Oesterreicher, see the previous note.

in the strong sense of Parry and Lord, is simply a use of language that is different from writing, not governed by any of its conventions, then the need to define it with respect to writing is obviated. Indeed, this definition becomes distinctly misleading, inasmuch as it amounts to a comparison between incomparable magnitudes: Homeric orality as a *medial* phenomenon and writing as a *conceptual* phenomenon. Furthermore, instead of being the properties of 'early' discourse, or the product of a (still) unsophisticated or primitive mind, parataxis and the other 'oral features' of Homeric style become characteristic properties of language used in the spoken medium. Such properties will appear in some form in any spoken discourse, including that of the highly literate scholar when he or she speaks and does not write.

Consciousness and Spoken Language

The consequences of this maneuver are obvious: if Homeric Greek can be viewed as a language that differs from written literature as to its medium, it becomes pertinent to study it against the background of spoken discourse in general. The possibilities for such a study were until relatively recently quite limited in the field of linguistics. Due to the almost automatic conception of language as written language as described above, spoken discourse has not often been studied for its own sake, its dysfluencies, parataxis and other salient features having been dismissed as irrelevant in a way not dissimilar to the philologists' treatment of archaic style as 'early' or 'primitive.'[10]

Since the 1970s, however, some linguists have been studying speech without prejudice as to its status with regard to writing and with an open mind for its specific features, contributing to an area of interest that has become known as *discourse analysis*, an interdisciplinary crossroads of linguistics, sociology, and anthropology.[11] Of particular importance for the study of Homeric discourse is the work of W. Chafe.[12] This linguist has elaborated the central thesis that language is intimately connected with *consciousness*, and that a number of salient

[10] Cf. the low esteem in which the notion of 'performance' (the actual use of language in concrete situations, characterized by such grammatically 'irrelevant' features as false starts, memory-lapses etc.) is held; cf. Chomsky (1965) 3–4.

[11] Cf. Chafe (1994); Tannen (1989); Hymes (1974). For surveys of the various possibilities, see Brown and Yule (1983); Schiffrin (1994).

[12] Most recently and most fully Chafe (1994).

properties of speech can be explained by this connection. Consciousness is the mental representation of anything 'thought about,' but, as Chafe notes, the capacity of the human mind in this regard is quite limited:

> Although every human mind is devoted to modeling a larger reality within which it (or the organism it inhabits) occupies a central place, only one small piece of that model can be *active* at one time. At any given moment the mind can focus on no more than a small segment of everything it 'knows.' I will be using the word *consciousness* here to refer to this limited activation process. Consciousness is an active focusing on a small part of the conscious being's self-centered model of the surrounding world. (Chafe [1994] 28)

Consciousness is, just as vision, not only limited in terms of *quantity*, but also in terms of *time*: conscious experience—introspective or perceptual—is 'restless, moving constantly from one item of information to the next' (Chafe [1994] 29). Consciousness, in other words, is what Chafe calls a *flow*, a process through time. This flow is not a smooth one, but rather a sequence of different *foci of consciousness*, units of experience that are replaced in an ever shifting present moment.

Language and speech are obviously the result of conscious activity, but in the perspective proposed by Chafe, consciousness is not only a *source* of speech, but also a *constraint*. Indeed, speech (or language as spoken *medium* in the terms discussed above) is intimately bound up with what appear to be the crucial properties of the flow of consciousness. The linguistic reflex of the focus of consciousness is the spurt-like, segmented nature that each spoken discourse displays, if studied carefully and without literate prejudice. Chafe calls these speech-segments *intonation units*. Intonation units are the verbalization of foci of consciousness; they are typically four or five words long, may be separated by a brief pause (which may or may not be due to respiration), but are most typically characterized prosodically.[13] The following fragment is a typical example of a sequence of intonation units in speech:

a. Like óne day I was just
b. . . I was . . uh càrrying my garbage,
c. to the garbage dùmp.
d. . . . And this gùy came by on a mótorcycle.

[13] Chafe (1994) 56–61; cf. also Brown and Yule (1983) 155–69.

e. And thèn he went bàck in the óther dirèction,
f. and wènt back in the óther dirèction,
g. .. I was still carrying my gárbage.
h. And thén,
i. .. I'm walking =,
j. .. like bàck to my hóuse and,
k. .. this... mòtorcycle gets sló=wer and slówer and slówer,
l. ... and like it's like .. ró=lling,
m. and fínally this gùy is sàying,
n. ... I lòve you.
o. .. I love you.
p. .. I love you.[14]

This discourse may look unsophisticated on paper, but this is simply due to its *transferral* from one medium (speech) to another, to which it does not properly belong (writing).[15] This is not a specimen of poor writing, but simply spoken language that is presented under communicative conditions that are quite different from those of a written discourse. Its syntactic structure is not a concession to the fact that the more sophisticated structures we associate with written discourse were unattainable; this syntax serves its own purposes. The structure of the passage does not reflect the referential object of the discourse, as written syntax is supposed to do; rather, it reflects the speaker's *mental processes* in re-activating, remembering the event. The units in which it divides represent the successive ideas in the speaker's mind while recalling the event, each representing a 'focus of consciousness.' And the way in which they are linked reflects the *transition* from one idea to the other.

The ubiquitous particle *and* in particular plays a central role here: rather than effecting what would be in literate terms an indefinitely prolonged *coordination* (the linkage of sentences of one and the same syntactic level), the particle serves the purpose of *continuation*: it signals that 'more is to come,' that the unit in question is part of a chain of ideas verbalized.[16] In short, the passage is a *process* rather

[14] Chafe (1994) 208. = signals lengthening of a preceding vowel.

[15] During academic conferences one can frequently witness the opposite transferral: discourses that are 'medially' spoken but written as to their *conception*, and that accordingly often do not meet the reception conditions of speech.

[16] Various linguists stress that this use of *and* has no counterpart in written language; cf. Beaman (1984), 47, 60–61, who speaks of a 'filler word'; Halliday and Hassan (1976) 238, who distinguish an 'additive' use of *and* from its coordinative use. Cf. also Schiffrin (1987) 128–52 and Chafe (1988) 10–12.

than a *product*, a written text, and its speaker is not so much a maker (the idea of 'author' or 'owner' we commonly associate with a written discourse) as a 'doer' who engages in communicative *behavior*. To apply to it the conceptual apparatus that has been developed for the study of written products would be to misrepresent its dynamics and its very communicative purpose.

Homeric Discourse as Speech

In terms of the stylistics of Archaic Greek poetry, the passage just discussed is clearly 'paratactic' and 'adding': clausal intonation units are mostly linked to what precedes by the conjunction *and* (d–f, h, l–m) and there are units that are loosely added to the previous one, to provide explanatory detail (c, j). Yet the discourse is not 'archaic'; nor is there any reason to suppose that its speaker is particularly childlike or primitive (the properties usually attributed to 'oral style'). Instead, we might consider the alternative possibility. Could it be that Archaic Greek poetry, and Homeric discourse in particular, displays the characteristics of speech as it can be observed all around us? This would mean that we may have been dealing in textual terms with a phenomenon that in reality belongs to the opposite medium. And it could imply that a partial overhaul of the notional apparatus of Archaic Greek stylistics is necessary, which would do justice to the ways in which Homeric discourse resembles ordinary speech *and* to the obvious ways in which it is different.

Let us first present the beginning of the *Iliad* again, this time in the format of Chafe's example, with the units into which the passage easily divides presented as separate 'lines':

a. μῆνιν ἄειδε, θεὰ,	Sing of the wrath, goddess,
b. Πηληϊάδεω Ἀχιλῆος	of Achilles, son of Peleus,
c. οὐλομένην	the accursed <wrath>,
d. ἣ μυρί' Ἀχαιοῖς ἄλγε' ἔθηκε,	that caused numerous woes for the Achaeans,
e. πολλὰς δ' ἰφθίμους ψυχὰς	and many valiant souls,
f. Ἄϊδι προΐαψεν	<it> sent <them> forth to Hades,
g. ἡρώων,	<souls> of heroes,
h. αὐτοὺς δὲ ἑλώρια τεῦχε κύνεσσιν	and themselves as prey it put to the dogs,
i. οἰωνοῖσί τε πᾶσι,	and to all the birds,
j. Διὸς δ' ἐτελείετο βουλή,	and the will of Zeus was fulfilled,

k.	ἐξ οὗ δὴ τὰ πρῶτα	<starting> from the moment at which for the first time
l.	διαστήτην ἐρίσαντε	<they> stood apart in quarrel,
m.	Ατρεΐδης τε ἄναξ ἀνδρῶν	Atreus' son lord of men,
n.	καὶ δῖος 'Αχιλλεύς.	and godlike Achilles.

The translation added to the passage is more 'rugged' than most renderings; yet it brings out more accurately what happens in the Greek. One might prefer not to read the entire *Iliad* in this way, but that is precisely my point: the *Iliad* was never meant to be read in our sense of the word, and the written form in which it has come down to us is closer to a transcript such as Chafe's rendering of his taped discourses than it is to a written text as we conceive of it.

We are concerned, then, with 'detextualizing' the salient properties of Homeric style and with re-describing them in terms of the spoken discourse of which our text is the transcription. And this applies most of all to the syntactic articulation of the passage, which brings us to the units as presented above and their interrelationships. The typical segmentation of this and similar passages was already recognized, as we saw, in the older stylistic analysis of Archaic Greek poetry, but we are now in a position to move beyond stylistics and put the passage in a different perspective. The units into which *Il.* 1.1–7 divides may be seen as different steps not only in the verbalization of the passage, but also in the flow of consciousness underlying this verbalization. The passage, in fact, not only derives from a verbalizing consciousness; it is also meant to accommodate the hearer's consciousness, as well as a *future* verbalizing consciousness in the re-performance of the *Iliad*.

But how do the units relate to each other? The passage constitutes the first 'sentence' of the *Iliad*: we usually print μῆνιν with a capital and put a full stop after δῖος 'Αχιλλεύς (l. 7, unit n). Yet is it really a sentence in our sense, with a beginning and an end? There is certainly a great deal of coherence in these crucial first moments of the Iliadic performance, but it is worth asking where the coherence comes from. We *know* what these lines 'are about,' so that we are able to construe the succession of phrases as meaningful. But this coherence does not result from the transcription as it stands. What the text actually gives us is a series of short speech units that are more or less loosely connected syntactically. By themselves, if approached without prejudice or foreknowledge as to their content, these units do not do much more than guiding our attention through a series of island-like ideas.

The 'logic' of this process may be quite different from our idea of organic sentential composition, yet it is perfectly logical in its own specific way. The first unit we might compare to a 'preview' or a 'checklist': the two closely related ideas which it contains, 'wrath' and 'sing,' are taken up and focused on successively, 'wrath' in units b–j, and 'sing' in units k–n, each series being the verbalization of a number of details pertaining to each basic idea. The transition from the one to the other in unit k we may find awkward syntactically—one has to connect ἐξ οὗ with the too distant ἄειδε of the first unit—but such a construal presupposes, again, a sentence, with which this speaker is not concerned. The 'previewing technique' has more to do with *orientation*, the creation of context for a listening audience, than with syntactic correctness.[17] And it equally applies to 'supra-syntactic' levels, dealing which discourse units larger than any 'sentence.' Indeed, the proem as a whole functions as preview with respect to discourse to follow in due course.[18] The very essence of Homeric composition and discourse progression, then, is reflected in the way Homeric speech moves through what are for us sentences on the printed page.

In what follows I organize the discussion of this Homeric syntax into two parts, dealing with the two major ways in which speech units in Homeric discourse can be related to each other: addition and continuation.

Addition

We return to the beginning of the *Iliad*, the first three units of which constitute a characteristic example of Homeric discourse progression:

a. μῆνιν ἄειδε, θεὰ,	Sing of the wrath, goddess,
b. Πηληϊάδεω Ἀχιλῆος	of Achilles, son of Peleus,
c. οὐλομένην,	the accursed <wrath>,

As we saw, the discourse starts from what may be called a 'core clause' and proceeds by way of additions specifying various aspects of the central idea of that clause, the Wrath. The b-unit is a noun-epithet formula for Achilles in the genitive case and the c-unit is

[17] On consciousness and 'orientation,' see Chafe (1994) 30, 128–29.

[18] Cf. Krischer (1971) 132, who speaks of 'katalogische Stil,' in which a poet moves from the general to the particular in the treatment of a given topic, as a camera zooming in on details. For more details, see Bakker (1996) ch. 5.

what is usually called a 'runover word,' a term deriving from the study of Homeric enjambement. What is important to emphasize, however, is that the three units do not form one integrated sentence, the equivalent of 'Muse, sing of the accursed wrath of Achilles the son of Peleus.' In cognitive terms, such a structure would be too large and complex an aggregate of information to be verbalized as one single phrase; it has to be broken down into its component parts for the verbalizing consciousness to grasp it, piece by piece.[19]

This analysis of the first moments of the *Iliad* as a sequence of more or less 'fragmented' speech units is corroborated by the findings of a quite different line of research, the study of Homeric Greek in a historical perspective and against the background of Indo-European linguistics. A. Meillet has repeatedly stressed the autonomous nature of the word in the Indo-European phrase: the grammatical agreement in case, number, and gender between two nominal elements or in number between a noun and a verb (see below) is less a matter of 'government' ('*rection*') than of *apposition*:[20] words mark by themselves the role they play in the discourse, and are thus more like elliptic clauses ('<it was the wrath> of Achilles son of Peleus | <the wrath was> accursed'). The relevance of this for the present chapter is that rather than due to 'poetic style' the word order in question is a matter of the movement of one idea to the other, yielding semantically as well as intonationally discrete speech segments.

The fragmented, appositional nature of Homeric discourse is also apparent in the typically Homeric use of names in the nominative case. The end of our passage yields a good example (Ἀτρεΐδης τε ἄναξ ἀνδρῶν | καὶ δῖος Ἀχιλλεύς). In a sentential analysis, these names would be the subject of the preceding verb διαστήτην, and this is how *noun-epithet formulas* are treated by Parry in his famous discussion of these phrases (e.g., [1971] 10–13). The autonomy-principle of Meillet, however, applies here, too: the relation between a substantival subject (such as a proper name) and a verb is very often just as much a matter of apposition. Greek verbal forms, in contrast to the English verb, do not need a subject to be syntactically 'complete'; accordingly, when the name or noun does occur, it is often not

---

[19] Chafe (1994) 108 ff. speaks of the 'one new idea constraint' here; cf. Givón (1984) 258–63, who speaks of the 'one chunk per clause principle.'

[20] Meillet and Vendryes (1979) 572, 598. Cf. Meillet (1937) 358; Chantraine (1953) 12.

governed in the way in which a subject in English is governed by its verb. The same applies to unit e, where the accusative can be seen as independent from the verb in the following unit:

e. πολλὰς δ' ἰφθίμους ψυχὰς	and many valiant souls,
f. Ἄϊδι προΐαψεν	<it> sent <them> forth to Hades.

A clear example of this phenomenon is also:

a. αὐτὰρ ὁ βοῦν ἱέρευσεν	but he, he sacrificed a bull,
b. ἄναξ ἀνδρῶν Ἀγαμέμνων	ruler of men Agamemnon,
c. πίονα πενταέτηρον	fat, five years old,
d. ὑπερμενέϊ Κρονίωνι.	to the sovereign son of Kronos. (*Iliad* 2.402–403)

Just as in the case of the first moments of the *Iliad* we see a unit that serves as a 'checklist,' verbalizing an event in the most general way by means of the combination of an object and a verb (βοῦν ἱέρευσεν, 'sacrificed a bull,' cf. Μῆνιν ἄειδε, 'sing the wrath'). To this core idea detail is then added, in three installments, each being a separate intonation unit and representing a separate focus of consciousness, and one of them (unit b) being the loose addition of the name of the agent in the event. This phrase is not the subject of the clause, nor is the dative noun-epithet phrase in d its indirect object. Both are additions, appositions to the clause in a, details filling in the picture. The nominative phrase in b agrees with the pronoun ὁ in a, just as the accusative phrase in c agrees with the object βοῦν ('bull') in a.

There is a difference, however, between the idea of Agamemnon and the other ideas in the example just cited. The idea verbalized in unit a is the idea of an *event* and c–d verbalize details of this event; they are of a transient nature in the flow of ideas and of speech. The idea of a *participant* in an event, on the other hand, and that of the *agent* in an event in particular (as Agamemnon in the sacrifice-event just presented), is different. The idea of a participant, especially if he is the *protagonist* in a story, is likely to remain longer in the speaker's consciousness.[21] Such longer-lasting concepts need a certain amount of management to serve their purpose in the epic story: there are always other characters on the scene with whose actions the activities of a given protagonist interact; or the concept of a protagonist may have to be re-activated in the minds of the audience once it has dropped out of focus.

[21] Cf. Chafe (1994) 71–81.

When the last mention of the character was only moments ago, a mere 'topic switch' (verbalized as ὁ δέ or αὐτὰρ ὁ, 'and he,' 'but he') suffices to restore the idea of the participant in question. When the last mention was somewhat longer ago, a new mention may be necessary, in the form of an added noun phrase. This is what happens in the example just cited: the noun-epithet phrase ἄναξ ἀνδρῶν 'Αγαμέμνων helps restore the idea of the leader after some intervening, and potentially distracting discourse (lines 394–401 in our text). In the prologue, the mentions of Agamemnon and Achilles are no restorations, of course, because the two heroes were not mentioned before. Yet the two names are nonetheless syntactically optional additions: the preceding unit διαστήτην ἐρίσαντε ('they stood apart in quarrel') is complete as it stands, and probably intelligible as such by most audiences. The function of the two names is not so much to identify the subject of διαστήτην and to provide new information as to 'stage' the two principal characters for the first episode of the tale.

The name may also *precede* the clause, which becomes then, conversely, an addition to the name. This may happen when the last mention of the character in question is so long ago that a direct 'naming,' rather than a topic switch is in order:

a. αὐτὰρ 'Οδυσσεὺς	but Odysseus,
b. ἐς Χρύσην ἵκανεν	he arrived at Khruse,
c. ἄγων ἱερὴν ἑκατόμβην.	leading the sacred hekatomb. (*Iliad* 1.430–1)

In this example the narrator resumes the thread (the return of Chryseis to her father by an embassy led by Odysseus) that was left more than hundred lines ago (l. 312), before the attention was directed to Thetis' visit to Achilles. In other examples, the name precedes the clause not as a sign of reactivation but as a strategy to effect *contrast*:[22]

a. Ὣς ὁ μὲν ἔνθα καθεῦδε	so he slept there,
b. πολύτλας δῖος 'Οδυσσεὺς	much-suffering godlike Odysseus,
c. ὕπνῳ καὶ καμάτῳ ἀρημένος·	worn out with sleep and fatigue,
d. αὐτὰρ 'Αθήνη	but <as for> Athene,
e. βῆ ῥ' ἐς Φαιήκων ἀνδρῶν	she went to the Phaeaceans'
f. δῆμόν τε πόλιν τε	their people and city (*Odyssey* 6.1–3)

Examples like this provide evidence that such verbal figures as hysteron proteron or chiasm, the arrangement of two pairs of elements in an

[22] On 'contrast' as a factor determining word order, see Givón (1984), 187 ff.; Mithun (1992); Ward (1988).

order *abba*, are not by themselves a matter of 'style' without further ado; they are quite normal in living speech, where they result from a natural sequence in the flow of ideas and their verbalization. The idea of Odysseus triggers the idea of the other participant in the scenes depicted before, which is verbalized, in unit d, in direct contrast with what precedes.

Units d and e are interesting, furthermore, in that the separate status of αὐτὰρ Ἀθήνη can be demonstrated on the basis of the presence of ῥ' (an attenuated phonetic realization of the particle ἄρα) in unit e. This particle, according to the so-called Wackernagel's Law, ought to occupy, as an enclitic, the second position in the clause, which it does: the clause starts with βῆ, and the preceding αὐτὰρ Ἀθήνη is prosodically a distinct unit.[23]

We conclude, then, that names in Homeric narrative tend to be used, not as subjects to any clause, but as syntactically autonomous 'tracking devices,' reminders of who is active at a given point, or steps in the manipulation of ideas of characters through time. In uttering them, the speaker is not so much concerned with new 'information' or with complementing verbs syntactically as with channeling the flow of speech and making sure that a given event is seen in the right perspective.

Continuation

For the second characteristic feature of Homeric syntax we turn again to the first lines, or moments, of the *Iliad*:

a. μῆνιν ἄειδε, θεά,	Sing of the wrath, goddess,
b. Πηληϊάδεω Ἀχιλῆος	of Achilles, son of Peleus,
c. οὐλομένην,	the accursed <wrath>,
d. ἣ μυρί' Ἀχαιοῖς ἄλγε' ἔθηκε,	that caused numerous woes for the Akhaeans,
e. πολλὰς δ' ἰφθίμους ψυχὰς	and many valiant souls,
f. Ἄϊδι προΐαψεν	<it> sent <them> forth to Hades,

After the loosely added non-restrictive ('appositive') relative clause of unit d, the discourse continues in unit e with what appears to be, in syntactic terms, a new main clause, marked by the first occurrence of the particle δέ in the *Iliad* (πολλὰς δ' ἰφθίμους . . .). From our

[23] On this issue see Ruijgh (1990); see also Devine and Stephens (1994) 422–23 (on the position of the modal particle ἄν). More examples in Bakker (1996) 101.

sentential perspective we would rather expect an extension of the relative clause ('which . . . . . and which . . . . .'), bringing out the syntactic hierarchical relationships involved. However, what 'ought' to be a subclause is not marked as such at all: the clause with δέ differs in no way from an ordinary independent clause. The reverse phenomenon also frequently occurs: a clause that 'ought' to be a main clause with respect to a subclause is not marked as one. See for example the following case, not much later in the *Iliad*:

a. οἳ δ' <u>ἐπεὶ</u> οὖν ἤγερθεν	and they when they had gathered,
b. ὁμηγερέες τ' ἐγένοντο,	and had assembled together,
c. <u>τοῖσι δ'</u> ἀνιστάμενος μετέφη	and to them standing up he spoke,
d. πόδας ὠκὺς Ἀχιλλεύς·	Achilles swift of foot. (*Iliad* 1.57–9)

Unit c is to our sense of style and syntax a main clause (apodosis) that is preceded by a subclause (protasis) and as such quite different from a main clause preceded by another main clause. Yet the 'coordinative' particle δέ is used as if the latter is the case; in Greek linguistics the amazement at this fact is expressed in the term 'apodotic δέ', specifying the *locus* where the particle 'should not' occur.[24]

Instead of assuming that a syntactic rule has been violated, we do better to realize that such a rule, based on a 'categorial' difference between subclauses and main clauses in their hypotactic interrelationships, simply did not exist at the time this discourse was produced and presented in its original setting, the epic performance. And if this kind of syntactic articulation was not a goal aimed at by the Homeric performer, we should not impose on this kind of discourse what belongs to an entirely different conception of language and its use. What concerns the epic poet, rather, is the kind of structure that is connected with *movement*, the flow of ideas through consciousness. And the particle δέ in Homeric discourse marks just that: movement, the step to a new idea focused on and verbalized in the flow of narrative.

The use of δέ in Homer is comparable to that of *and* in spoken English discourse as shown above, and its 'processual' character is even more rigorous. Its central function is not coordination, the creation of longer, more complex 'sentences' out of smaller ones. Nor does it serve as an adversative particle to mark antithesis, an opposition between two referents or a contrast in style.[25] Rather, its func-

---

[24] E.g. Denniston (1954) 177–78.

[25] For a discussion of the differences between δέ in Homer and after see Bakker

tion is dynamic, to mark the act of *continuation*, the step to a new idea. It is used by default whenever a new 'fact' is touched upon, regardless of the degree of cohesion between the new idea and the previous one. Thus in our passage the first instance of δέ marks a closely related idea:

d. ἣ μυρί' Ἀχαιοῖς ἄλγε' ἔθηκε,	that caused numerous woes for the Akhaeans,
e. πολλὰς δ' ἰφθίμους ψυχὰς	and many valiant souls,
f. Ἄϊδι προΐαψεν	<it> sent <them> forth to Hades.

But somewhat later, the particle marks a step to a new idea that is only thematically related, in a less obvious way (j. Διὸς δ' ἐτελείετο βουλή, 'and the will of Zeus was fulfilled'); and in numerous other cases the particle marks an entirely new scene or episode. What all these cases have in common is that the discourse does not stop, the speaker assuming that his audience is prepared to take the next step with him, regardless of where it will lead.

δέ is used whenever another, more specific connective particle is inappropriate. The most characteristic of these is μέν, with which δέ in post-Homeric discourse forms a correlative pair (ὁ μὲν. . . . ὁ δέ, 'the one. . . . the other'). In Homeric discourse, however, μέν is just as 'processual' as δέ: it does not mark 'the one' *referent* vis-à-vis 'the other' but one *unit* with respect to another. A speaker using μέν makes a statement that has no purpose in and by itself; rather, it serves as a basis for statements to come, setting up the appropriate context. This may in practice have the effect of a *concession*, a speaker giving way at some point only to prepare the way for a point he really wants to make. This is what happens in the following example, the first 'characters' speech' in the *Iliad*:

a. Ἀτρεΐδαι τε	sons of Atreus,
b. καὶ ἄλλοι ἐϋκνήμιδες Ἀχαιοί,	and other well-greaved Achaeans,
c. ὑμῖν μὲν θεοὶ δοῖεν	may the gods give to you,
d. Ὀλύμπια δώματ' ἔχοντες	holding their Olympian dwellings,
e. ἐκπέρσαι Πριάμοιο πόλιν,	to destroy the city of Priam,
f. εὖ δ' οἴκαδ' ἱκέσθαι·	and to return home safely,
g. παῖδα δ' ἐμοὶ λύσαιτε φίλην,	and/but may you give back my dear daughter,
h. τὰ δ' ἄποινα δέχεσθαι,	and accept the ransom,
i. ἁζόμενοι Διὸς υἱὸν	honoring Zeus' son,
j. ἑκηβόλον Ἀπόλλωνα.	far-hitting Apollo (*Iliad* 1.17–21)

(1993c). Cf. also (1990) 5–6; (1993a) 11–12; and (1996) ch. 4.

In unit c the old priest lays the basis for the point he wishes to make in his address to the Greek army. The μέν he uses is 'answered' by δ' in unit g. But there is no opposition between ὑμῖν and παῖδα, as there would be in Attic Greek; nor is the 'answering' unit g marked as such and differentiated from the two continuative units (marked by δέ) between which it is wedged. All the Greek text gives us is an instance of μέν, followed by a series of moments marked for continuation.

Homeric Discourse as Special Speech

The discussion presented above has been silent on such quintessential topics of Homeric stylistics as *meter* and the *formula*. Yet these topics do play a role, of course, to the extent that Homeric discourse, in spite of the strong similarities, is not identical to ordinary spoken language. Everyday speech does not display the degree of formulaic repetition and metrical regularity offered by Homeric discourse. But the perspective offered here provides a way to account for this difference while at the same time doing justice to the similarity. In other words, the most characteristic features of Homeric discourse in the quality of 'oral poetry' in which it has been studied are amenable to an analysis in terms of speech. Or more precisely, they can be analyzed as *enhancements, stylizations* of the basic properties of speech.

The cognitively determined intonation unit thus becomes the background against which the Homeric formula may be assessed. It may be right to say, with Parry, that prefabricated phrases may be necessary to fill the metrical space of the verse in a satisfactory way; but it is equally right to say that such a process of formulaic composition cannot be carried out without accommodating human consciousness, its requirements and its limitations. Formulas, then, as the primary 'bits' of Homeric discourse, correspond to intonational phrases, the primary bits of ordinary discourse. Rather than setting Homeric discourse apart, as 'oral poetry,' from literate poetry, the formula sets it apart, as *special speech*,[26] from ordinary speech. But in doing so it highlights what is most natural to speech, turning what results from the

[26] See G. Nagy (1990b) 33–39, who speaks of 'unmarked' and 'marked' speech in an anthropological perspective.

most essential properties of the human mind into (what is for us) poetry, while retaining the basic properties of the spoken word, its conception and reception.

The stylization of everyday speech should probably be seen as a diachronic process, the gradual regularization of the intonational contour of the speech units into rhythm. This process is not the imposition on language of something external; rather, the emergence of rhythm amounts to the regularization of what is already there, in naturally occurring speech.[27] In the case of Homer, the earliest stage of the process, that is, the origin of the hexameter, is still obscure and continues to delude us, but the outcome, as it can be observed in our text, is of an unprecedented complexity and sophistication. In contrast to many other poetic traditions around the world, the metrical vehicle for Homeric discourse, the dactylic hexameter, does *not* coincide with the cognitively necessitated length of the speech units: it is simply too long. This leads to considerable variety in the way in which the speech units—or metrical *cola* in this respect—may occupy the metrical space of the verse. In one of the examples cited above, for example, we see that the break between the first and second units coincides with the trochaic caesura:

a. ‖ Ὣς ὁ μὲν ἔνθα καθεῦδε	so he slept there,
b. πολύτλας δῖος Ὀδυσσεὺς ‖	much-suffering godlike Odysseus.

This may be considered the most common relation between the linguistic and metrical levels: two units per line, divided at the main caesura. But the next two units of the example divide at what is commonly called the bucolic diaeresis:

c. ‖ ὕπνῳ καὶ καμάτῳ ἀρημένος·	worn out with sleep and fatigue,
d. αὐτὰρ Ἀθήνη ‖	but <as for> Athene,

And the last two units have a dividing-point at yet another place, the 'hephthemimeres':

e. ‖ βῆ ῥ' ἐς Φαιήκων ἀνδρῶν	she went to the Phaeaceans'
f. δῆμόν τε πόλιν τε ‖	their people and city (*Odyssey* 6.1–3).

And in other frequent cases the 'trithemimeres' functions as unit-boundary; examples are οὐλομένην and ἡρώων at *Iliad* 1.2 and 1.4. The different and regularly recurring *cola*-lengths are of course reflected

[27] Cf. Devine and Stephens (1993) 399–400.

in the formulaic systems for the naming of the major gods and heroes described by Parry.

Yet Homeric discourse quite frequently moves even beyond this level of colometric complexity. This takes us to the range of phenomena that are commonly described under the general heading of 'enjambement,' the mismatch between verse-end and sentence-end.[28] In the perspective presented here, however, where the notion of 'sentence' recedes in favor of the intonation unit, this concept is not likely to remain unchanged.[29] In the example just cited, for example, there would be a case of what Parry ([1971] 253) called 'unperiodic' enjambement between unit b and c, the least severe form of enjambement, where line-end coincides with a natural break within the sentence. The transition from unit c to d, on the other hand, would be a case of 'necessary' enjambement, defined by Parry as the separation by the end of the line of two constituents that syntactically belong together (a subject and its verb).[30]

We have seen, however, that 'subject' is a particularly inappropriate characterization of unit d, and in fact in both cases of enjambement the end of the line coincides with a unit-boundary. This does not mean, of course, that there is no difference between the two cases: by the end of unit b a sense of closure prevails (unit c is a syntactically optional addition), whereas unit e is more 'necessary:' even though unit d is intonationally and syntactically independent, it creates a strong anticipation as to what will come next. Yet such an anticipatory, announcing function for a unit occurs in ordinary speech, too, and what the placement of the unit at the end of the line does is nothing other than enhancing the effect: the line-final position reinforces the 'hanging' nature of the preposed name. Instead of a mismatch between the linguistic and metrical levels, then, we might say that there is an *interaction* between the two levels: a cognitively inevitable boundary is put to greater poetic and rhetorical effect.

Mismatch between the metrical and the linguistic levels does occur in Homer, however. In the perspective presented here this means not so much enjambing sentences *as enjambing intonation units*: a unit, usually beginning at the bucolic diaeresis, may continue across the

---

[28] Cf. M. W. Edwards (1966); Kirk (1966a); Higbie (1990); Clark (1994); Parry (1971) 251–65.

[29] Cf. Bakker (1990).

[30] Note that Kirk (1966a) and Higbie (1990) have more refined classifications than Parry's tripartite scheme (no enjambement; unperiodic; necessary).

verse-boundary into the next verse.[31] This is in itself already a remarkable feat of versification, but it is made even more significant by the fact that it tends to occur in *clusters*, yielding areas of metrical turbulence whose full impact can be realized only if we conceive of Homeric discourse as speech, that is, as sound and rhythm. Consider, for example, the words of Andromache in which she expresses her agonizing uncertainty as to the fate of her husband Hector:

a. αἰδοίης ἑκυρῆς ὀπὸς ἔκλυον,	I heard the voice of my honored mother-in-law,
b. ἐν δ' ἐμοὶ αὐτῇ ‖ στήθεσι πάλλεται ἦτορ	and within me my heart is pounding in my breast,
c. ἀνὰ στόμα,	up to my mouth,
d. νέρθε δὲ γοῦνα ‖ πήγνυται·	and my legs below cannot move,
e. ἐγγὺς δή τι κακὸν Πριάμοιο τέκεσσιν.	Yeah, something terrible is close to Priam's children,
f. αἳ γὰρ απ' οὔατος εἴη ἐμεῦ ἔπος·	may the word be far from my ear:
g. ἀλλὰ μάλ' αἰνῶς ‖ δείδω....	but terribly I fear... (*Iliad* 22.451–5)

Here the usual flow of epic speech, in which the one unit builds on the other within the confines of the metrical structure, is temporarily upset. Units b, d, and g 'break through' the metrical structure, producing a halting, unhexametric rhythm.[32] One might want to consider cases like this[33] as a deviation from the safe regularity of meter that is uncharacteristic of oral composition and not likely to occur in the practice of improvisation.[34] Yet from the point of view of performance and audience attention, that is, poetry and rhetoric, one cannot help finding them very effective, indispensable even, to avoid a metrically too correct and therefore potentially dull sequence of cognitive units.

---

[31] See Higbie (1990) 115–16.

[32] One might argue that unit b consists, after all, of two cognitive units separated by the end of the verse, but in that case the cohesion between them would be so strong that the effect produced would be in practice the same as described here.

[33] Cf. also *Iliad* 8.125–29; 18.245–48 among many others. Fuller discussion in Bakker (1996) ch. 6.

[34] Cf. Kirk (1976) 168–69 on *Iliad* 16.306–350.

Conclusion

The above presentation was meant to show that a perspective in terms of speech enables us to account for many features of Homeric poetry that does more justice to their original function than does the usual notion of 'oral style.' Such a notion compares Homer with a form of language use ('written style') that has relevance only for the researcher and therefore inevitably betrays a perspective that is not only inappropriate but even harmful for a correct understanding of Homeric linguistic expression: psychological or even 'evolutionary' explanations have to be adduced to account for phenomena that are observable all around us, and in which we participate ourselves whenever we speak.

The speech perspective allows us also to view the 'poetic' elements in Homeric style in a different way. From the point of view of the Greek epic tradition and its performers, 'formulas' are not what separates epic style from other poetic styles and what makes epic style 'oral.' Formulas derive from the very nature of spoken language, as a regularization of its basic segment, the cognitively determined intonation unit. Once this regularization has resulted in a fixed metrical form, one of the functions of the formula is obviously the one highlighted by Parry and Lord: facilitating composition in performance. But this function is not the only one and maybe not even the most important. Formulas are speech units and the essence of speech is being heard. It is the recognizeability of the formula as a moment in the flow of speech that constitutes not only one of the main poetic effects of Homeric discourse but at the same time its close connection with the social dynamics of the speech of everyday.

Irene de Jong

HOMER AND NARRATOLOGY[1]

Introduction

The term 'narratology' was coined in 1969 by T. Todorov.[2] Like drama theory, it is a branch of literary criticism which deals specifically with one group of texts, narrative texts. The term 'narrative text' is used here in a broad sense and includes historiography, the bible, and even film and painting. The aim of narratology is to provide a set of descriptional and analytical tools with which to tackle the narrativity of the texts under discussion. As such it is a typical product of two important currents in twentieth-century literary theory: formalism (which focuses on *literaturnost*, the specific literariness of literature) and structuralism (which is concerned with the universals of cultural products).[3]

Of course, an interest in narrative technique is not exclusive to the present century. Ancient literary criticism already knew a rich terminology for analysing narrative or, what they referred to as rhetorical effects. To take only one example, the technique of anticipation (prolepsis or flashforward) was well known to the Homeric scholiasts as *proanaphonesis*. If I focus in this chapter, in accordance with the aims of this book, on recent contributions to our understanding of Homer's narrative technique, I do so in the full awareness that much of what follows has firm roots in antiquity. Further, not all contributions mentioned here are narratological in the strict sense of the word, i.e., making use of the terminology and concepts developed by modern narratologists. I use the word 'narratology' in the title of this chapter in a broad sense, to include all studies which deal specifically with narrative aspects or techniques of the Homeric epics.[4]

[1] I wish to thank S. R. van der Mije and S. Richardson for reading through an earlier version of this text, Mrs. B. Fasting for correcting my English.

[2] Todorov (1969) 10.

[3] For a historical overview of the development of narratology in this century, see W. Martin (1986).

[4] For other recent overviews of Homeric narratology, see Schwinge (1991); M. W. Edwards (1991) 1–7.

Narrators and Narratees

Primary narrator

One of the defining elements of a narrative text is the presence of a subject of narration, the narrator, and beneficiaries of that narration, the narratees. Both may be seen as the text-internal representatives of the author, on the one hand, and the hearers/readers of flesh and blood, on the other. To speak of a narrator rather than the author or the poet, as narratologists are wont to do, is typical of twentieth-century literary criticism, turning as it does away from the biographical fashion of the nineteenth century. The narrator is referred to as the primary narrator, whenever we want to distinguish him from characters functioning as (secondary) narrators.

In the case of the Homeric epics, the interest in the narrator has long centered around three issues: the Muses, the apostrophe, and the figure of the singer within the text. Only recently have more comprehensive descriptions of the Homeric narrator been undertaken.

The Homeric narrator is a somewhat hazy figure, who seldom steps forward to reveal his persona. One of these rare occasions is the Muse invocation, which is more common in the *Iliad* than in the *Odyssey*. A central issue here is the division of labor between goddess and narrator; while some scholars tend to see the narrator as a mere mouthpiece of the Muse, others stress his initiative. A solution might be to view the activities of Muse and narrator in terms of 'double motivation,' i.e., both are involved at the same time, just as an athletic victory is viewed through Archaic eyes as the accomplishment of both god and athlete.[5]

The discussion of the role of the Muses is part of a larger issue, namely the question of truth and fiction in the Homeric epics. On the one hand, the patronage of the Muses seems to guarantee a completely truthful representation of the past (cf. in particular 'for you, who are goddesses, are there [sc. at the place of action] and you know all things [from first-hand experience]:' *Il.* 2.495). On the other hand, the figure of Odysseus, an arch-liar and yet often compared to a singer, should alert us to the possibility that the main narrative, too, may be a mixture of true and fictional elements.[6]

---

[5] Recent discussions include De Jong (1987a) 45–53; Finkelberg (1990); Ford (1992).

[6] Advocates of the first position include Rösler (1980) and Ford (1992); of the second, Bowie (1993) and Pratt (1993).

Andersen (1990) takes an interesting different approach to the question, pointing out that when Homeric characters recall events of the past, their versions may differ from that of the narrator or of another character. Thus in *Il.* 17.24–28, Menelaus says that Hyperenor had taunted him before he was killed. If we look at the incident in 14.516–19, we see that no speech by Hyperenor is reported. The crucial point here is that *such differences are not commented upon* by either narrator or characters: as Andersen says ([1990] 29–30), 'Homer accepts, as his characters must do and his audience would do and we should do, that the past is not fixed but fleeting.' In other words, the Homeric narrator claims to tell the truth, yet his conception of the truth—and here he seems to anticipate Herodotus and Thucydides[7]—is different from the Rankean 'wie es eigentlich gewesen.' It would be worthwhile to pursue this line of thought, applying the insights of modern philosophers of historiography like H. White (1973) to ancient historiographical texts, including Homer.

Another device by which the narrator reveals himself is the apostrophe, when he addresses one of the characters. A good deal of debate has already been devoted to the question of whether these apostrophes are merely a metrical convenience which makes it possible to fit in certain names (Patroclus, Eumaeus) or whether they also have a narrative significance. The former view was defended most recently by Yamagata (1989). Together with the scholia,[8] I myself would opt for the second view: the apostrophe signals the narrator's compassion for Patroclus and his sympathy for Eumaeus, whom only he, Odysseus, Telemachus, and Penelope address by name (as opposed to the bare 'swineherd' used by the suitors).

The figure of the singer within the text, notably Phemius and Demodocus in the *Odyssey*, is generally taken as a self-representation of the narrator, who is himself a singer, as is clear from his invocations of the Muse, patroness of the professional singer, and from *Il.* 2.489–90 ('not if I had ten tongues and ten mouths, not if I had a voice never to be broken and a heart of bronze within me'). An

[7] See Woodman (1988).

[8] See especially the scholion ad *Il.* 16.787: 'the apostrophe shows that he [the poet] condoles with you, O Patroclus, who were loved so much by Achilles, who had exerted yourself to save your fellow Greeks, who had patiently endured Nestor's garrulity, who had lovingly tended Eurypylus, who had shed tears because of the [disaster of the] Greeks, who had persuaded unyielding Achilles, who had secured a way out [for the Greeks] at the cost of your own life. By relating all this to the apostrophe one can detect its highly pathetic meaning.'

analysis of the passages in which these singers appear offers us important information about the functions of epic song (to provide 'entertainment,' but also to keep alive the memory of the past, i.e., to serve as a kind of proto-historiography) as well as its effects.[9]

A more comprehensive description of the Homeric narrator has been undertaken by S. Richardson (1990) and myself (De Jong [1987a]), both making use of (mainly French and Anglo-Saxon) narratological concepts. They show that the activities of the largely invisible narrator can, in fact, be traced at many points: *if not*-situations, e.g., 'there the sons of the Achaeans might have taken gate-towering Ilion under the hands of Patroclus, if Apollo had not taken his stand on the tower . . .' (*Il.* 16.698–701, also studied by Lang, Nesselrath, and Morrison);[10] prolepses and analepses; summaries, e.g., 'seventeen days he sailed, making his way over the water' (*Od.* 5.277); pauses, e.g., the description of Agamemnon's scepter (*Il.* 2.101–108); bird's-eye views, e.g., 'when they had strengthened their ranks on both sides, Trojans and Lycians, Myrmidons and Achaeans, they threw themselves together in battle over the dead body' (*Il.* 16.563–65); and narratorial comments, e.g., 'but then Zeus, the son of Cronus, took the wits away from Glaucus, who exchanged with Tydeus' son, Diomedes, armor of gold for bronze, the worth of a hundred oxen for that of nine' (*Il.* 6.234–36; the *nepios* comments have most recently been studied by S. Edmunds [1990]).

Together, these passages show the hand of the narrator, making it clear that the Romantic idea of the Homeric epics as an objective genre, in which the events 'tell themselves,' is not in fact appropriate. Rather 'we move through the *Iliad* with Homer constantly at our elbow, controlling rigorously our beliefs, our interests, and our sympathies.'[11] An important contribution to the unravelling of the implicit rhetoric of the Homeric epics has been made by Griffin ([1980] 103–143), who discusses the way in which pathos is conveyed by certain similes, digressions ('obituaries') and motifs ('death far from home,' 'death near friends,' 'bereaved parents,' 'beauty brought low').

The relation between narrator and characters also forms the object

---

[9] Maehler (1963) 9–34; Svenbro (1976); Macleod (1983) 1–15; Walsh (1984) 3–21; Ford (1992) 90–130.

[10] M. Lang (1989); Nesselrath (1992) 5–38; Morrison (1992) 23–33.

[11] Booth (1961) 4–5. I discuss the alleged objectivity of the Homeric epics in De Jong (1987a) 14–26; cf. S. Richardson (1990) 165.

of a study by Di Benedetto (1994), who, alongside such well-known topics as the apostrophe and narratorial comments, draws attention to verbal echoes between narrator-text and speeches, e.g., the narrator's ἀρνευτῆρι ἐοικώς (*Il.* 16.472) preparing for Patroclus' κυβιστᾷ (16.745, 748).

Secondary narrators

Homeric characters, particularly those of the *Odyssey*, are wont to act as (secondary) narrators, as was noted long ago by Longinus: τῆς δὲ Ὀδυσσείας τὸ πλέον διηγηματικόν (*On the Sublime* 9.13). The narratives of these characters concern either a past which is also recounted in the main story (internal analepses or 'mirror-stories') or a more remote past, which lies outside the time covered by the main story (external analepses). Homeric mirror-stories are found, e.g., in *Il.* 1.365–92 (Achilles recounting to Thetis the initial events of the *Iliad*, the mission of Chryses, the plague, and the quarrel between himself and Agamemnon) and *Od.* 7.261–97 (Odysseus telling the Phaeacian king and queen about Calypso, the storm, and his encounter with Nausicaa); they have been studied by Létoublon (1983) and myself (De Jong [1985]; [1987a] 210–18). On the level of the characters their function is informative: one character tells another character what has happened to him. For the primary narratees, the interest lies in the comparison between the version of the character and that of the narrator. Thus Achilles calls Apollo's arrow (which brought the plague to the Greek camp) a κακὸν βέλος (1.382), whereas the narrator had earlier stressed its effectiveness, calling it a βέλος ἐχεπευκές (1.51).

The more numerous external analepses often function as paradigms: thus Nestor recalls a heroic exploit from his youth to exhort the Greek leaders (e.g., *Il.* 1.259–74) or Athena recalls Orestes' revenge on Aegisthus in order to spur Telemachus on (*Od.* 1.298–302).[12] A useful extension of the notion of paradigm has been introduced by Andersen (1987), who suggests that a distinction should be made between argument function, i.e., the function which an embedded narrative has for the characters in the story, and key function, i.e., the function it has for the primary narratees. Thus the argument

[12] See Austin (1966); Pedrick (1983); Held (1987); Hölscher (1990) 297–310; Olson (1995) 24–42.

function of the Meleager story, told by Phoenix to Achilles in *Iliad* 9, is to exhort Achilles to accept Agamemnon's gifts and take up fighting again, while its key function is to prefigure the outcome of the main story: Achilles will not accept the gifts and will re-enter the battle only when he is forced to do so by the death of Patroclus.[13]

The most important secondary narrator of all is, of course, Odysseus. In the first place, he presents the *Apologos*, an enormous external analepsis, which describes his adventures on the way home from Troy up until Calypso, i.e., the beginning of the *Odyssey*. Here the Odyssean narrator has boldly expanded a technique which is familar from the *Iliad*, viz. having characters fill in the 'prehistory' of the poem. Instead of *a number of* characters sketching in the nine years before Troy, he here has *one* character narrate the nine years of his wanderings in *one* continuous story. Many scholars have analysed the structure of Odysseus' long tale, the most recent being G. W. Most (1989a), who, on the basis of his analysis, suggests the following argument function of the *Apologos*: to convey, indirectly and subtly, Odysseus' refusal of Alcinous' offer of Nausicaa's hand. In the second place, there are Odysseus' numerous lying-tales, which show a highly effective blend of fictional and true elements (cf. 19.203–209), whereby the former are often only thinly disguised allomorphs of his real adventures. Thus no one will fail to recognize Nausicaa in the Thesprotian prince, who led 'the Cretan,' overcome by weariness, to the palace of his father and gave him clothes (14.317–20).[14] As early as the scholiasts the idea was voiced that the *Apologos*, too, is in fact a lying-tale; this idea has recently been convincingly refuted by H. Parry (1994).

A very special type of secondary narrator is formed by the singers Phemius and Demodocus. Their songs are never quoted to us in the form of speeches, as are the stories of Odysseus and other heroic narrators. The (primary) narrator begins by quoting them indirectly ('he sang how . . .'), but after a few lines he relinquishes this form in favour of the independent style. As a result, the voices of the (primary) narrator and the singers in the text blend naturally, as S. Richardson ([1990] 86) says, 'an implied statement of [the narrator's] identification with' those singers.

---

[13] For analyses of embedded narratives which pay special attention to its key functions, see, e.g., Rosner (1976); Andersen (1977); and Olson (1989).

[14] E.g., Trahman (1952); Haft (1984); Emlyn-Jones (1986).

Primary and secondary narratees

Like the primary narrator, the primary narratees are largely invisible in the text. The few traces which can be found—mainly second-person passages like 'then *you would* not have seen divine Agamemnon slumbering nor cowering, nor being unwilling to fight, but showing eagerness for the fighting which brings men glory' (*Il.* 4.223–25)—are discussed in De Jong ([1987a] 54–60) and S. Richardson ([1990] 174–78). The *implicit* presence of the narratees, however, is felt in almost every line. Thus, in many passages containing a negation, the narrator contradicts the expectations of the narratees, e.g., 'only the spear of splendid Achilles he [Patroclus] did *not* take, the heavy, large, and strong one' (*Il.* 16.139–40); the taking of a spear was one of the stock elements of an arming scene. Or, in numerous γάρ-clauses the narrator provides his narratees with explanations of things he has just told them which they might find puzzling, e.g., 'the leader of the Aetolians was Thoas [possible reaction of the narratees: why Thoas and not Meleager?], for (γάρ) there were no sons of Oeneus left, he himself had died and Meleager' (*Il.* 2.638–42).

The secondary narratees, characters listening to stories told by other characters, have traditionally figured in discussions of the effects of heroic song, notably those of Macleod ([1983] 1–15) and Walsh (1984), but recently have become the object of a special monograph by Doherty (1995). We may distinguish between unaffected and affected audiences: the Phaeacians, who enjoy listening to Demodocus' songs, versus Odysseus and Penelope, who start weeping when they listen to Phemius and Demodocus. The difference in reaction is related to the degree of involvement in the events recounted. The Phaeacians, who live a life of isolated peace, can enjoy listening to songs about the Trojan war. For Odysseus these same songs are a source of sorrow, because, although victorious in that war, he still has not managed to reach home. Similarly, Penelope cannot bear to listen to Phemius when he sings about the return of the Greeks, because Odysseus has not—yet—returned. Only afterwards, when everything is over, can a person enjoy the tale of his woes, says Eumaeus (*Od.* 15.400–401). Thus after they are reunited, we see Penelope and Odysseus in bed telling each other of their adventures (23.301–343). It has been suggested by Walsh that we, the hearers/readers of *Iliad* and *Odyssey*, should take the detached Phaeacians as a model for our own responses. In my opinion, Eumaeus, who reacts with a mixture of enjoyment (17.515–21) and emotional involvement (14.361–62), is a better candidate.

Focalization (Point of View)

The point of view or focalization (this term will be explained below) in a narrative text is one of the most hotly debated issues in narratology. The discussion was triggered by novelists (Flaubert and Henry James), taken over by literary critics (Percy Lubbock) and systematized by narratologists (Stanzel and Genette, to mention only two of the most influential ones). Where the Homeric epics are concerned, the question of point of view has until recently seldom been raised. Only Delasanta (1967) and Suerbaum (1968) have drawn attention to the difference between the omniscience of the primary narrator and the restrictions of Odysseus as a first-person narrator in the *Apologos*. The primary narrator commutes effortlessly between the Trojan and the Greek camp, between earth and Olympus, between a fairytale destination like Scheria and Ithaca; he is able to read the minds of his characters, and knows how the story will end.[15] Odysseus, however, has to rely on informants to know what is going on elsewhere (e.g., 10.251–60), is only able to present the thoughts of his companions when they are later recounted to him (as in 10.415–20), and is uncertain about the exact divine motivation behind certain events (e.g., 9.142: θεός).

This neglect of the epic point of view appears to be due to several factors: where the narrator's point of view is concerned, the alleged objectivity of the epic style suggests that he was not expressing a point of view at all, since 'the events tell themselves.' The presentation of the story through the eyes of one of the characters (in Stanzel's terminology: figural narration), a technique cherished by nineteenth- and twentieth-century novelists, was unthinkable for ancient texts like the Homeric epics. Thus, in the highly influential chapter on Homeric narrative technique in his *Mimesis* (1953), Auerbach declared figural narration (which he called 'the subjectivistic-perspectivistic procedure') 'entirely foreign to the Homeric style.' A similar conclusion was reached by Effe (1975), who submits that figural narration 'could not develop' in Homer, but was invented by Heliodorus in his *Aethiopica*.

[15] See also S. Richardson (1990) 109–140, 'special abilities.'

Effe's verdict on Homer is the result of the narratological model he uses: Stanzel's tripartite typology (authorial, figural, first-person). Thinking in terms of a typology means that one is looking for the *dominant* narrative situation in a text, which in the case of Homer indeed is the authorial one. Since that time, however, other narratological models have been developed, which offer not typologies, but flexible analytical instruments. By drawing on the narratological models of Genette (1980) and Bal (1985) I have been able to arrive at a more refined analysis of point of view in Homer, as the next section will show.[16]

Forms of focalization

The hearers/readers of a narrative text do not perceive the events in that text directly, in the way they perceive events in the real world; rather events are perceived *for* them by an agent in the text, the focalizer, just as these perceived events are told *to* them by a narrator. Focalization involves not only seeing or hearing, but also feeling, thinking, remembering, in short, any kind of mental activity. The focalization in a text normally resides with the primary narrator (I), or, in the case of a speech, with a character (III). But the primary narrator can also embed the focalization of one of his characters in the narrator-text (II). Embedded focalization (= Stanzel's figural narration) means that we see events through the eyes of a character, without that character himself or herself verbalizing his or her perception. The following passage will illustrate these three forms of focalization (*Il.* 5.134–76):

I simple narrator-text
Τυδεΐδης δ' ἐξαῦτις ἰὼν προμάχοισιν ἐμίχθη . . .
Ἔνθ' υἷας Πριάμοιο δύω λάβε Δαρδανίδαο
εἰν ἑνὶ δίφρῳ ἐόντας, Ἐχέμμονά τε Χρομίον τε.
ὡς δὲ λέων ἐν βουσὶ θορὼν ἐξ αὐχένα ἄξῃ
πόρτιος ἠὲ βοός, ξύλοχον κάτα βοσκομενάων,
ὣς τοὺς ἀμφοτέρους ἐξ ἵππων Τυδέος υἱὸς
βῆσε κακῶς ἀέκοντας . . .
II complex narrator-text (embedded focalization)
Τὸν [Diomedes] δ' ἴδεν Αἰνείας ἀλαπάζοντα στίχας ἀνδρῶν . . .
III character-text (speech)
'. . . ἀλλ' ἄγε τῷδ' ἔφες ἀνδρὶ βέλος, Διὶ χεῖρας ἀνασχών,
ὅς τις ὅδε κρατέει καὶ δὴ κακὰ πολλὰ ἔοργε
Τρῶας, ἐπεὶ πολλῶν τε καὶ ἐσθλῶν γούνατ' ἔλυσεν·'

[16] See De Jong (1987a); (1987b); (1991); (1994).

In I, the primary narrator-focalizer recounts how Diomedes kills a succession of Trojans. Although the narration is factual, the focalization of the narrator reveals itself in the lion simile, which glorifies Diomedes and sympathizes with his Trojan victims (note, in particular, the *hapax* πόρτις, 'calf'), and in a qualification like κακῶς, which need not have a moral undertone, but certainly has an emotional one (this is confirmed by the observation that this adverb is found mainly in speeches, 17 times out of a total of 21 instances). In II, the same event (Diomedes' slaying of many Trojans) is focalized (ἴδεν) by Aeneas. The emotions of the Trojan, who sees his compatriots being killed one after the other, are reflected in the strong expression ἀλαπάζοντα, 'thinning the ranks of' (again a word which is found mainly—seven times in speeches). And finally, in III, Aeneas himself—as secondary narrator-focalizer—describes his perception (note τῷδ' ὅδε). His focalization is clear from the fact that he does not know who 'this man' is and from his reference to the killing as κακὰ πολλά. In the *Iliad* 50% of the text is presented by the primary narrator-focalizer, 5% by secondary focalizers, and 45% by secondary narrator-focalizers. The figures for the *Odyssey* are: 28%, 5%, and 67%.

Within the category of embedded focalization, we may distinguish between *explicit* embedded focalization, i.e., signalled by a verb of seeing, thinking, feeling, etc. (as in passage II above), and *implicit* embedded focalization, where such a signal is lacking. An example of implicit embedded focalization is *Il.* 24.478–79: κύσε [Priam] χεῖρας [of Achilles] |δεινὰς ἀνδροφόνους, αἵ οἱ πολέας κτάνον υἷας. Achilles' hands are focalized by Priam; at the moment he kisses them he realizes that these are the very hands which killed so many of his sons. To back up this interpretation, I draw attention to (i) the presence of the 'sympathetic' dative οἱ, which according to the grammarians indicates an affectionate relationship between the sons and their 'possessor' Priam, and (ii) the fact that not long afterwards Priam refers to Achilles in a speech as ἀνδρὸς παιδοφόνοιο (506; the adjective is a *hapax*).[17] The category of implicit embedded focalization is, of course, a somewhat subjective one, depending primarily on the intuition of the commentator. But, it is an interesting one and, provided it is argued for as fully as possible (along the lines suggested above: the

[17] For examples of implicit embedded focalization from Virgil, see D. Fowler (1990).

presence of emotional or evaluative words and the comparison with speeches), deserves a place in our interpretations.[18]

The following subsections will demonstrate how focalization has been—and could be—used in the interpretation of the Homeric texts.

Focalization and plot

Focalization by characters, whether expressed in embedded form or in a speech, is an important expedient by which the narrative is given shape. Characters may look back in anger, look forward hopefully or anxiously, make plans, and so forth. In her recent study of Penelope, Felson-Rubin (1994) uses the concept of focalization to distinguish different plot types. Focalized by the returning warrior, a *nostos* may consist of death at Troy, death at sea, death upon arrival, or crime and punishment. Focalized by the wife at home, a *nostos* may involve marriage to a suitor, dalliance and courtship, seduction by a stranger, disdain and cunning tricks, or death. It is against the backdrop of these options that the characters in the story—and we, too—must judge Penelope.

The focalization of the gods often has a structuring function. Their plans, presented in speeches, and intentions, presented in embedded focalization (final clauses), help the narratees to grasp the structure of the story. Examples are Zeus' speeches of *Il.* 8.470–6 and 15.64–71, in which he reveals the chain of events culminating in Achilles' return to battle and the death of Hector; Athena's speech in *Od.* 1.84–95, which lists the contents of books 1–4, the Telemachy; and Athena's embedded focalization in *Od.* 6.112–4, which prefigures the content of book 6, the confrontation between Odysseus and Nausicaa. Passages like these are the invaluable signposts of an oral narrative, which has to do without a table of contents or chapter headings.

There is also a very different way in which passages of embedded focalization may have a plot function. Embedded focalization means

[18] In my opinion, too sweeping a use of focalization is made by R. Martin (1993). On p. 239 he argues that the opening scenes of the *Odyssey* are focalized by Telemachus, because the suitors are spoken of without any introduction and only Telemachus is sufficiently keyed in to the situation on Ithaca to allow such a casual reference. However, the opening scenes are focalized by the primary narrator, who, relying on the foreknowledge of his primary narratees, can permit himself casual allusions to the suitors. Only lines 1.115–17 are an instance of (embedded) focalization by Telemachus, as is clear from the optative and the reference to Odysseus as πατέρ' ἐσθλόν.

that the thoughts and emotions of a character are revealed to the primary narratees only; since the focalizing character does not speak, other characters do not get to know what is going on inside his or her head. As long as there are no other characters present or the thoughts and emotions are no secret, this characteristic of embedded focalization is not particularly significant. But it can also be exploited to create a (pathetic, ironic, or suspenseful) discrepancy between the knowledge of the narratees and that of the characters in the story. This is what frequently happens in the *Odyssey*, e.g., in 18.90–94: (spurred on by the suitors, the 'beggar'/Odysseus and the beggar Irus engage in a wrestling contest)

> δὴ τότε μερμήριξε πόλυτλας δῖος Ὀδυσσεὺς
> ἢ ἐλάσει' ὥς μιν ψυχὴ λίποι αὖθι πεσόντα,
> ἦέ μιν ἦκ' ἐλάσειε τανύσσειέν τ' ἐπὶ γαίῃ.
> ὧδε δέ οἱ φρονέοντι δοάσσατο κέρδιον εἶναι,
> ἦκ' ἐλάσαι, ἵνα μή μιν ἐπιφρασσαίατ' Ἀχαιοί.

The narratees learn about what is going on in Odysseus' head, his impulse to kill Irus which is tempered by reason. The suitors have no idea of the inner thoughts of 'the beggar,' the fact that he is consciously restraining himself, the fact . . . that he is Odysseus. Time and again, passages of embedded focalization in the *Odyssey* give the narratees insight into the minds of cool-headed Odysseus, prudent Penelope, youthfully impatient Telemachus, and hypocritical suitors (De Jong [1994]).

Although this exploitation of embedded focalization for purposes of creating secrecy is found mainly in the *Odyssey*, there are also some examples in the *Iliad*, e.g., 24.582–86:

> δμῳὰς δ' ἐκκαλέσας λοῦσαι κέλετ' [Achilles] ἀμφί τ' ἀλεῖψαι,
> νόσφιν ἀειράσας, ὡς μὴ Πρίαμος ἴδοι υἱόν,
> μὴ ὁ μὲν ἀχνυμένῃ κραδίῃ χόλον οὐκ ἐρύσαιτο
> παῖδα ἰδών, Ἀχιλῆϊ δ' ὀρινθείη φίλον ἦτορ,
> καί ἑ κατακτείνειε, Διὸς δ' ἀλίτηται ἐφετμάς.

These are Achilles' motives for washing and anointing the body of Hector outside his tent. It is interesting to note that in his unexpressed thoughts Achilles goes much further than in his earlier speech to Priam: there he said he was afraid to *chase* the old man away, if he continued to irritate him (568–70); here he is even afraid of *killing* him (586).

This 'secretive' use of embedded focalization, which would later be brought to such perfection by twentieth-century novelists, points up the unexpected modernity of the Homeric epics.

Focalization and vocabulary

Until recently, scholars working on Homeric vocabulary paid virtually no attention to whether a word or formula occurred in a speech or in narrator-text. However, research of the last ten years has revealed that there is, in fact, a marked difference between the language of characters and the language of the narrator. Thus Griffin (1986) shows that emotional and evaluative words are used primarily by characters in speeches. He lists some 170 words, e.g., σχέτλιος (29 times in speech versus once in narrator-text) δαιμόνιος (30:0), ὕβρις (26:3), αἰδώς (24:1), or ὑπερφίαλος (23:5). Austin ([1975] 11–80) demonstrates that characters far less often than the narrator refer to Odysseus by a name-epithet formula: 90 times out of 280 occurrences. Instead, they prefer to use only his name or circumlocutions like 'your father' or 'my master.' Similarly, Shive (1987) shows that Achilles is referred to in many other ways than by name-epithet formulas alone. Even though he does not address the question of how these two types of naming—name-epithet formula or by other means—are distributed over characters and narrator, a casual glance at his discussion shows that it is again the characters who most often use the alternative ways of 'naming Achilles.'

The studies by Griffin, Austin, and Shive take the opposition 'narrator-text versus speech' as the point of departure for their distinction between narrator-language and character-language. I have argued that this boundary should be refined.[19] Many of the rare occurrences of emotional language outside speeches are found in embedded focalization, e.g., ὁρμαίνουσ' ἤ οἱ θάνατον φύγοι υἱὸς ἀμύμων, ἦ ὅ γ' ὑπὸ μνηστῆρσιν ὑπερφιάλοισι δαμείη (*Od.* 4.789–90). This is Penelope's focalization (ὁρμαίνουσ') and from her point of view, it is not surprising that the suitors are called ὑπερφιάλοισι, 'overbearing.' Likewise, passages of embedded focalization often contain the kind of indirect references to characters ('son,' 'father,' etc.) which Shive and Austin have pointed out in the speeches. Thus, in the passage just quoted, Telemachus is referred to as υἱὸς ἀμύμων, 'her illustrious son.' The line of demarcation between the language of characters and that

[19] De Jong (1987a) 136–47; (1987c); (1992); (forthcoming).

of the narrator is therefore determined by focalization rather than narration: character-language comprises words or formulas which are found exclusively or predominantly in direct speech or embedded focalization.

The subject of character-language has only just begun to be explored. It is to be expected that many more categories of words might be fruitfully investigated, for example, particles and pronouns. The question also arises whether Homer is unique in this respect. In the case of at least one author, Apollonius Rhodius, Hunter ([1993] 109–116) has already given the answer: '[i]t is clear that the Homeric division between the lexicon of speech and that of narrative is blurred and weakened, but not entirely abandoned.'

Closely related to the question of character-language versus narrator-language is that of 'denomination,' the manner in which a character is referred to (De Jong [1993]). This may be by means of his name or a circumlocution, in which case we are dealing with periphrastic denomination. An example of the latter is: Ἕκτωρ δ' ὡς ἐνόησεν ἀνεψιὸν ὀφθαλμοῖσιν | ἐν κονίῃσι πεσόντα (*Il.* 15.422–3), where we find 'his nephew' instead of the name Kaletor, because Hector is focalizing (ἐνόησε). The substitution of a 'relative term' for a proper name here has an obvious pathetic effect. Another example is the periphrastic denomination πόσις for Odysseus: out of a total of 45 occurrences in the *Odyssey*, 26 refer to Odysseus. Most of these 26 instances occur in speeches (by or to Penelope). But there are also 6 instances outside speeches. One of the most intriguing of these is 23.86, the moment when Penelope descends from her room and enters the megaron, where she has been told she will find Odysseus: πολλὰ δέ οἱ κῆρ | ὅρμαιν', ἢ ἀπάνευθε φίλον πόσιν ἐξερεείνοι, | ἦ παρστᾶσα κύσειε κάρη καὶ χεῖρε λαβοῦσα. At this stage Penelope is still not fully convinced that the man she is approaching is Odysseus (cf. 84) and if we ascribe πόσις to her—since she is, after all, focalizing (ὅρμαιν')—then it must mean 'the man they say is my husband.' However, it is also possible to ascribe it to the narrator, who wishes to underscore the pathos or irony of the situation: Penelope deliberating whether or not to kiss the husband for whom she has been longing for twenty years!

Periphrastic denomination may also be used by the narrator to convey irony (as when Eumaeus speaks to 'his master' about his absent master: 14.36) or pathos (when Odysseus laments 'his fatherland,' not knowing that he finds himself on Ithaca: 13.219), or to underscore themes (we find a sudden increase in the narrator's use of πόσις = Odysseus and ἄλοχος = Penelope in book 23, dealing with the reunion of husband and wife, and of πατήρ = Odysseus and υἱός = Telemachus in book 16, dealing with the reunion of father and son).

Another aspect of the relation between focalization and vocabulary concerns characterization by means of speech, i.e., the question of whether Homeric characters, at least the most important ones, employ an individual vocabulary. Studies by Friedrich and Redfield (1978) and Griffin (1986) suggest that the answer may be 'yes'. Thus there are some 58 words which are used in the *Iliad* by Agamemnon only. R. P. Martin ([1989] 146–230) has undertaken a similar investigation of Achilles' individual use of formulas.

Time

Time is one of the best researched aspects in narratology. The Russian formalists were the first to distinguish between 'fabula' and 'suzjet,' i.e., the events in their chronological sequence vs. the events as they appear in the text. The relationship between these two levels can be investigated from a number of angles: rhythm (the amount of time spent on the narration of an event), frequency (the number of times an event is narrated), and order. Order, in particular, has attracted the attention of narratologists and Homerists alike. As I mentioned in my introduction, the ancient scholia already provided excellent analyses of one of the best known forms of change of order, the anticipation or prolepsis.

Prolepses

The Homeric prolepses have been in detail, and taken together, these studies have yielded a fairly detailed picture of the uses of the prolepsis in the *Iliad* and *Odyssey*.[20]

In the first place, we can distinguish between clear anticipations, like Zeus' announcement of Hector's death in *Il.* 15.68, and more vague foreshadowings, like the simile in *Il.* 12.41–50, where a hint of the hero's impending death can be heard (cf. in particular ἀγηνορίη

[20] Duckworth (1933); Schadewaldt (1965); De Jong (1987a) 81–91; S. Richardson (1990) 132–39.

δέ μιν ἔκτα, which recalls φθίσει σε τὸ σὸν μένος, Andromache's words to Hector in 6.407).

In the second place, it is important to realize who is making the prolepsis: (1) the narrator, (2) a focalizing character, or (3) a speaking character. (An example of a prolepsis in embedded focalization is *Il.* 16.646–55, where Zeus meditates upon Patroclus' death.) In the case of (1) and (2), the information reaches only the narratees, not the characters in the story. Thus in *Il.* 10.336 the narratees are fore-warned about Dolon's death, just as he is enthusiastically embarking on his mission. Even in the case of (3), the information may not reach all characters, viz. when the prolepsis is voiced on Olympus. Thus the death of Patroclus is announced no fewer than eight times in the *Iliad*, but never to the hero himself or to other mortal characters.

In the third place, a distinction can be made between internal and external prolepses: those falling *within* the time boundaries of the story and those falling *outside* those boundaries. An example of an internal prolepsis is the anticipation of Hector's death, while the anticipations of the deaths of Achilles or Odysseus (on the latter of which see Peradotto [1990] 59–93) are external prolepses.

In the last place, it may be instructive to compare the prolepses in the *Iliad* with those in the *Odyssey*. In the *Iliad* the prolepses, concerning mainly the deaths of Patroclus, Hector, and Achilles, and the fall of Troy, reinforce the tragic nature of this story. We see heroes striding towards their death, unaware of the fate in store for them (Hector, Patroclus) or, perhaps even more moving, fighting in the certain knowledge that they will be killed (Achilles) or defeated (Hector). In the *Odyssey*, the prolepses are concerned mainly with the impending death of the Suitors. Since they are repeatedly warned about the criminal nature of their behaviour, the tone of these prolepses is very different. Here, irony and even grim satisfaction are discernible, e.g., in 20.392–94:

> δόρπου δ' οὐκ ἄν πως ἀχαρίστερον ἄλλο γένοιτο,
> οἷον δὴ ταχ' ἔμελλε θεὰ καὶ καρτερὸς ἀνὴρ
> θησέμεναι· πρότεροισι γὰρ ἀεικέα μηχανόωντο.

Within hours, Odysseus will have his revenge on the suitors. The metaphor of the 'unpleasant meal' is particularly ironic, since the suitors are just having a meal, have been seen carousing all through the story, and will be killed during a banquet.

Misdirection

For a long time scholars were convinced that there were no surprises to be found in the Homeric epics. It is precisely because of the profusion of prolepses that the narratees are fully informed about the way in which the story will develop. On the other hand, the scholia were already familiar with the phenomenon of the ἀπροσδόκητος, 'the unexpected.' Indeed, we need only think of Odysseus' encounter with Arete in Book 7 of the *Odyssey* to see that the element of surprise is not entirely absent: the queen does not immediately react to Odysseus' supplication, despite two anticipations of her important role, and then, when everything seems settled for Odysseus, she suddenly asks the stranger an anxious question. The classic analysis of this passage is still Fenik ([1974] 5–130).

A recent monograph by Morrison (1992) offers an extensive study of one form of surprise: misdirection, the creation of false expectations among the narratees. These expectations may be based on foreknowledge, familiarity with the epic tradition, or predictions made in the text either by characters (prophecies, prayers, threats, etc.) or by the narrator. One form of misdirection is what Morrison calls 'false anticipation,' when the fulfilment of a prediction is delayed. This is, in fact, the well-known epic technique of retardation (Reichel [1990]). An example is the long retardation between Achilles' announcement in Book 18 that he will go after the murderer of Patroclus, Hector, and the final confrontation between the two heroes in Book 22.[21] Another form of misdirection is 'epic suspense,' when an untraditional episode is inserted, without the narrator making clear whether the traditional course of events is going to be resumed and how this will be accomplished. An example is the duel between Paris and Menelaus in *Iliad* 3, which for some time suggests that the war may come to an end without the capture of Troy. The narrator gives no clues about the outcome of the fight, leaving out, for example, the customary divine reaction to a prayer (when Menelaus asks Zeus to grant him victory).

In the past the mismatch between announcement and fulfilment was often seen by scholars as a mistake, and 'corrected' by atethesis, attributed to multiple authorship, or glossed over as the characteristic error of an oral poet. Today, the concept of misdirection

[21] See Bremer (1987).

offers the possibility to see it as a conscious and effective narrative technique.

Simultaneity

One of the characteristics of the Homeric epics is their constant forward movement: the narrator never retraces his steps, and when time moves on in one place, it moves on everywhere else as well, and by roughly the same amount of time. For example, at *Od.* 15.300, we leave Telemachus at night, as he sails towards Ithaca; we then turn to Odysseus and Eumaeus, who are having their supper (301–302) and, after their conversation, retire to bed (494); then breaks dawn (495) and we return to Telemachus, who has now reached the coast of Ithaca (495–98).

It is due to two scholars, Zielinski and Delebecque, that this 'law of succession' in Homer has been revealed.[22] The former, however, has gone even further. According to Zielinski, certain events which are described successively *should be thought of as simultaneous.*[23] For example, the missions of Iris and Apollo in *Il.* 15.168–218 and 220–62 or those of Athena and Hermes in *Odyssey* 1 and 5, should in fact be understood as taking place simultaneously. Thus when the narrator indicates that the first mission has been completed when the second takes place (e.g., when Zeus tells Apollo in 15.222–24 that Poseidon 'already has left the battlefield,' sc. as a result of Iris' mission), this should be considered a 'false synchronization.' Zielinski even goes so far as to call Homer's presentation the 'apparent' one and the one reconstructed by himself the 'real' one ('scheinbare' vs. 'wirkliche Handlung'). In his eyes, the 'law of succession' is an aesthetic weakness, leading to all kind of 'distortions' ('Störingen'). Since Zielinski's extended version of the 'law of succession' was better known than Delebecque's more moderate version, the—in my opinion, incorrect—idea that 'successive = simultaneous' became canonical.[24] Even Krischer, who has considerably refined certain aspects of Zielinski's views, leaves this aspect of the theory intact:

---

[22] Zielinski (1899–1901); Delebeque (1958).

[23] The same idea seems to be implied in the scholion ad *Il.* 12.2: ὅταν τὰ ἅμα γινόμενα οὐ δύναται ἅμα ἐξαγγέλλειν. But contrast Aristotle: ἐν δὲ τῇ ἐποποιίᾳ διὰ τὸ διήγησιν εἶναι ἔστι πολλὰ μέρη ἅμα ποιεῖν περαινόμενα (*Poetics* 1459b).

[24] See, e.g., C. H. Whitman and R. Scodel, 'Sequence and Simultaneity in *Iliad*,' *Harvard Studies in Classical Philology* 85 (1981) 1–15; S. Richardson (1990) 90–95 (93: 'falsifying the "true" temporality'). One of the few adherents of Delebecque is M. J.

> es ist Zielinskis großes Verdienst, gesehen zu haben, daß wir es hier *mit einem trügerischen Schein* zu tun haben. Immer wieder wirden uns Handlungszusammenhänge, die *bei genauerem Zusehen nur als Parallelhandlungen verständlich sind*, als rein suksessive Ereignisse berichtet. (Krischer [1971] 91; emphasis mine)

Only recently has the 'successive = simultaneous' theory been challenged by Patzer (1990). He claims that when the Homeric narrator presents events successively, he *meant them to be understood as successive*, and that the so-called 'false synchronizations' are not false but real, in short, that it is Homer's text which is 'real' and not Zielinski's reconstruction. The successive presentation at times may look a little strange to us, it may originally be the result of some technical handicap (just as the difficulties involved in—orally—maintaining indirect speech over a long stretch of text led to a restricted use of this form in Homer), but in the end the Homeric narrator has made it clear that this is what he wanted. By way of conclusion, let us take a closer look at one example. In Book 1 of the *Odyssey* two missions, those of Athena to Telemachus and Hermes to Calypso, are announced. Books 1–4 then describe Athena's mission and the outcome: the assembly, Telemachus' voyage to Pylos and Sparta and the suitors' conspiracy against him. Then, in book 5, in a new divine council—the first having taken place four books before—Hermes is sent to Calypso. In comparison with Book 1, his mission has become all the more urgent, both objectively (a new threat to the house of Odysseus has been added: the danger threatening Telemachus) and subjectively (the narratees now have 'seen for themselves' the deplorable situation in which Odysseus' palace and Ithacan society at large find themselves). Thus the successive order of presentation yields a highly effective structure.

Conclusion

In this overview of narratological (in the broad sense) research on Homer, it has not been possible to cover all aspects of this extensive

---

Apthorp, 'The Obstacles to Telemachus' Return,' *Classical Quarterly* 30 (1980) 1–22. He mentions Zielinski in a footnote (14), apparently without realizing that there is a for his argument crucial difference between Delebecque's and Zielinski's version of the 'law of succession'. B. Hellwig, *Raum und Zeit* (Hildesheim, 1964), mentions Zielinski in her discussion of parallel storylines (115–25), but does not repeat his idea that successive actions should be understood as simultaneous.

field, such as 'space,' for example. Various suggestions for further research were made, and in this conclusion I would like to mention one major aspect which, in my opinion, merits closer investigation: characterization. In a broad sense, one could say that in this century the study of Homeric characterization has been discouraged by the theories of Snell (if Homeric characters are not perceived by either themselves or the narrator as a unity, can we speak of characters at all?) and Parry (does the oral-formulaic nature of the epics enable the creation of individual characters?). A number of scholars took up the challenge and produced successful character studies all the same. Recently, there has even be a 'boom' in Penelope studies. What seems to be lacking, however, is a discussion of the concept of Homeric characterization itself, such as we do have for dramatic characterization.[25]

A major issue in any such discussion would be the question of whether Homeric characters are capable of development. The *communis opinio* is that they are static or 'flat.' Thus a recent paper by Race shows how the first appearance of a character in the *Odyssey* already reveals *in nuce* his or her essential characteristics. For example, Eumaeus' first appearance in *Odyssey* 14 shows him to be hardworking (Odysseus finds him while he is cutting new leather sandals), kind (in his haste to quiet the watchdogs attacking Odysseus, he drops the piece of leather he was working on), loyal to the memory of his master (in his opening speech to 'the stranger,' he almost immediately refers to Odysseus), and scrupulously observant of the rules of hospitality (he slaughters some of his own pigs to set before his guest and improvises a comfortable seat for him). The picture should perhaps be modified, however, for certain characters, who do seem able to develop over the course of time: Achilles, Odysseus, and Telemachus. The changes are not radical but rather gradual developments of latent and potential characteristics. Thus Odysseus' self-restraint is apparent even before his travels and incognito return to the palace: as he sat inside the Wooden Horse, he stopped his fellow Greeks from responding to Helen who calls out their names (4.271–89). The Homeric style of characterization would seem to reflect the way Greeks thought about real-life character development: the main characteristics are already present at the moment of birth. Thus in Greek mythology there are many examples of a person's youth prefiguring

[25] See most recently Easterling (1990).

his later behaviour: e.g., baby Heracles strangling the snakes or young Hermes stealing Apollo's cattle and then fooling him.

In this discussion narratology might offer its services again, such as the interesting theoretical study on characterization by Phelan (1990). One complication here is that many Homeric characters are not created *e nihilo*—like most characters in novels—but are, to a certain extent, part of the tradition. Thus the mechanisms of character construction will in certain respects differ.[26] It would be of interest to both Homeric scholarship and narratology, if someone came up with a framework for the analysis of this particular type of (traditional) character.

[26] This has been overlooked by Sternberg (1978) 56–128 in his otherwise highly interesting analysis of Odysseus.

Ahuvia Kahane

QUANTIFYING EPIC

Einmal ist niemals, zweimal ist immer.
U. von Wilamowitz-Möllendorff.

Once is happenstance, twice is coincidence, three times is enemy action.
I. Flemming.

'All right,' said the computer, and settled into silence again. The two men fidgeted. The tension was unbearable.
'You're really not going to like it,' observed Deep Thought.
'Tell us!'
'All right,' said Deep Thought. 'The Answer to the Great Question . . .'
'Yes . . .!'
'Of Life, the Universe and Everything . . .' said Deep Thought.
'Yes . . .!'
'Is . . .'
'Yes . . .!!! . . .?'
'Forty-two,' said Deep Thought, with infinite majesty and calm.
D. Adams

Homer's poetry contains many repetitions and is therefore an ideal subject for quantitative study. Indeed, quantified analysis has been used as a tool in the study of many aspects of Homer: metre, formula, grammar, dialect, style, theme, poetics, and so on. The range and variety of uses made of statistical methods make it almost impossible to provide a detailed survey, especially if we wish to avoid repeating matters discussed in other, dedicated chapter of this book. What follows is thus not quite a historical survey, but rather an analytic description of the field.

We must give numbers neither more nor less than their due. Statistical studies are sometimes regarded as free from subjectivity. This is inaccurate. Abstract numerical relations may be objective, but 'objectivity' within concrete social contexts is something altogether different.[1] Certainly statistical approaches to literature are not about

[1] The classic critique of scientific (and largely quantitative) methodology is T. Kuhn, *The Structure of Scientific Revolutions*, 2nd ed. (Chicago, 1970). Most recently see T. M. Porter, *Trust in Numbers: The Pursuit of Objectivity in Science and Public Life* (Princeton, 1995) who argues that 'objectivity' is sometimes an attempt to present an 'impersonal strategy' in social contexts where trust and authority are lacking. In

numbers in the abstract. Mathematics apart, quantified data can only be made significant through an interpretive process.[2] Before counting we must, for example, decide what to count (and what not to count). After counting we must decide what the figures mean. Such decisions affect our results profoundly, but they are not 'numerical.'

Assume that we wished to count abstract nouns in Homer. This task is not as simple as it seems. What, for example, would we make of the following (Il. 14.200–201, cf. the highly similar 14.301–302, and also 14.244)?

εἶμι γὰρ ὀψομένη πολυφόρβου πείρατα γαίης,
'Ωκεανόν τε, θεῶν <u>γένεσιν</u>, καὶ μητέρα Τηθύν

'for I am going to see the limits of fertile earth,
Okeanos *begetter* of gods and mother Tethys ...' (tr. Kirk and Raven)[3]

In formal terms *genesis* is a verbal abstract noun (*-sis*) meaning 'source,' or 'origin.'[4] But clearly here Okeanos is the male counterpart of *mother* Tethys. *Genesis* may even be a metrically convenient substitute for *patera*, 'father' (in Homer the last syllable of the accusative *patera* is always lengthened by position to form a dactyl—not possible in this context). Not surprisingly Kirk and Raven translate *genesis* as 'begetter.' Are we then to follow formal lexical principles, lexical pragmatics, the semantic implications of metrical substitution, or indeed higher poetic considerations?[5] Here we would probably determine what it is we wanted to count at least in part on the basis of what we wanted to find. In other words, part of our expected conclusions may precede our premises. Strictly speaking this is 'interpretation' not 'mathematics'.

Consider another, perhaps broader case. One of the most important applications of quantified method in Homer is the study of the formula. Thus, for example, many scholars have tried to compare

fact he considers the possibility that 'the sciences have been compelled to redefine their proper domain [i.e., in terms of objective, quantified method, AK] in order to monopolize it' and that 'much of what passes for scientific method is a contrivance of weak communities, partly in response to the vulnerability of science to pressures from outside' (12). We should keep this argument in mind, although it may, or may not apply to our case.

2 See the introduction to A. J. P. Kenny, *The Computation of Style: An Introduction to Statistics for Students of Literature and Humanities* (Oxford, 1982).

3 Kirk, Raven, and Schofield (1983).

4 Chantraine (1933) 274 ff. (esp. 277, sect. 219).

5 The implication is that we must first consider whether we can treat items *en masse*, or whether each case must be evaluated individually before counting.

what is known as 'formular density', i.e. the relative proportion of formulae, in hexameter texts. The potential of such studies is considerable: Some opinions hold that different levels of formular density allow us to distinguish between oral and literate works.[6] Essentially, the assumption is that formulae are the hallmark of oral style, and that the formular density of oral poetry will generally be higher than that of literate compositions.

Some aspects of the relation between formularity and orality are discussed elsewhere in this volume;[7] here I merely note that alongside substantial possible gains, there are also some risks. Clean cut figures, e.g. 72%/60% 'formularity' for Hesiod, or 90% for Panyassis, compared, for example, to lower levels in Apollonius of Rhodes, suggest conclusions that are often too elegant.[8] To begin with, the comparison of precise figures requires a precise definition of the unit counted, in this case the formula. And of course, the definition of the formula is a matter of some dispute. Even assuming that we have agreed on a common definition, it is still necessary to be sure that in each case this definition was applied equally, that data were obtained under controlled conditions, and above all, that the basic *interpretation* of any possible differences conforms to certain methodological standards. Sometimes easier said than done. Milman Parry himself was not, it seems, incapable of error (see further below, the example of whole line formulaic verses). Where careful attention to methodology is paid, as in R. Janko's well known *Homer, Hesiod and the Hymns*, the results can be important and indicative, but as a whole they present a generally cautious, perhaps even tentative perspective on formularity and epic development.[9]

Homer's meter and rhythm is another important area for quantified analysis.[10] Scholars have thus collected metrical pauses, sense pauses, metrical word-shapes, localization (the place of certain words or word types in the line), and the like.[11] Martin West, for example,

---

[6] For a general survey see M. W. Edwards (1988) 42–53 (part II.8).

[7] See Russo in this volume.

[8] See A. Kahane, review of M. Fantuzzi, *Ricerche su Apollonio Rodio* (Rome 1988) in *Classical Review* 43 (1993) 19–20. Fantuzzi cites statistics by Matthews (1974); McLeod (1966) 95–110; Minton (1975) 25–54. See also Janko (1982) 19 for similar comments on Notopoulos (1962) 337–68 and Pavese (1972).

[9] Janko (1982) 188–99.

[10] Job (1981).

[11] See O'Neill (1942) 105–78; H. N. Porter (1951) 3–63; J. T. McDonough, *Struc-*

suggests that 'sense-pauses are practically confined to the following positions' in the hexameter verse (% of lines):[12]

```
0.6  2  6  7        12  9    3   11        63
 – | ⏑ | ⏑ | – | ⏑ ⏑ – | ⏑ | ⏑ – | ⏑ ⏑ | – ⏑ ⏑ – – |
```

These quantified data are useful because they present an overall relationship effectively and concisely. However, West offers no information as to how the figures were obtained (what exactly is a 'sense pause'? What is the size of the sample? Where was the sample taken from?), and any attempt to take their numerical precision literally (or at least without relying on other, more clearly defined counts) could be misleading.[13] For example, a clean figure of 63% sense-pauses at the end of the verse may gloss over the extended debate over Homeric *enjambment*, or run-over lines, where the sentence, or sense-unit extends beyond the end of the verse. *Enjambment*, of course, is not merely a 'stylistic' phenomenon. It has often been viewed as an important factor in the debate over orality—and much of the discussion of *enjambment* has been carried out by quantitative methods.[14]

Paradoxically, the simpler our countable units, the more significant our interpretive, i.e. 'non-objective' decisions; and surely among the 'simplest' of all countables in literature is the 'word.' Consider that words have metrical shapes, and metrical shapes generally tend to be localized, i.e. to be often used only in specific positions in the verse.[15] The statistics about localization can tell us much about 'metrical predisposition' for the ordering of words, regardless of their 'meaning,' and are therefore an important tool for the understanding of epic verse structure. But what is a 'word'? Is it simply the black thing between white spaces in our written text? If so, are *appositives* (οὐκ γάρ, not to mention elided monosyllables such as γ' and μ') independent words?[16] Is it right to rely on a distinctly *textual* and

---

tural Metrics of the Iliad (diss. Columbia Univ., 1966); Kirk (1966a,b); Hagel (1994–95) 77–108.

[12] M. L. West (1982a) 36.

[13] See further in Kahane (1994) ch. 2.

[14] Notably by Parry himself. See Higbie (1990) for survey and discussion. See also further below on Parry's discussion of whole-line formulaic verses.

[15] See O'Neill (1942), H. N. Porter (1951), Higbie (1990), Hagel (1994–95).

[16] Devine and Stephens (1984); idem (1994). For problems of application see, e.g., Clayman (1981) 110–13. According to Hagel (1994–95) 81 the total number of 'words' (*Wörter*, words separated by spaces) in the *Iliad* is 106,668; the total number of 'word-groups' (*Wortbilder*, with appositives not counted separately) is 79,631, a reduction to 74.64%!

hence *literate* definition of words ('the black things . . .') in a study of poetry that is assumed to be *oral* in nature? But then, do phonetic or vocal units fully correspond to cognitive, or to conceptual units?[17] And, in an oral setting, should we consider repeated noun + generic-epithet formulae as two different words? After all, Parry suggested that the semantic function of many epithets is minimal (rather, in Parryan terms, the formula expresses an 'essential idea'). But Parry's views on this point have often met with opposition.[18] Furthermore, if, as many scholars assume, the extant texts of the *Iliad* and *Odyssey* are representations of an otherwise fluid *oral tradition*, then what part of that tradition are we counting exactly? What relation would our figures then bear to the otherwise unknown traditional whole? In such cases, the conception of our basic building blocks relies heavily on our image of the edifice as a whole. Quantified analyses are thus tools that can tell us a great deal about many aspects of Homer, but we should bear in mind that they are indeed *special types of interpretation*, not generally separable from our broader perceptions of Homer.

There is another important aspect to the question of interpretation. Quantitative studies of literature are widely thought to deal with 'technicalities.' Quantitative studies may indeed deal with technical aspects of language, meter, composition, etc., and they do generally incorporate a technical apparatus in the form of tables, lists, or mathematical calculations. But the ultimate applications and value of quantitative studies are neither more nor less technical than those of non-quantitative investigations. Admittedly, most human attitudes, emotions, and beliefs are not formally tabulated, but for this very reason the interpretation of 'innocent' countable data can provide important insights.

Consider briefly two examples. First J. Griffin's 'Homeric Words and Speakers.'[19] Griffin's work is not openly quantitative, nor indeed technical. The argument itself is concerned with what are otherwise 'literary' issues, namely, the distinctions between the narrator's dis-

---

[17] On cognition and phonetic units see e.g. W. Chafe, *Discourse, Consciousness, and Time: The Flow and Displacement of Conscious Experience in Speaking and Writing* (Chicago, 1993).

[18] E.g., Nagler (1974); Austin (1975). Bibliography in M. W. Edwards (1988) ('formula and meaning'). See recently J. M. Foley (1991) and his notion of 'traditional referentiality.'

[19] (1986). Cf. S. Kelly, 'Homeric Correption and the Metrical Distinctions Between Speeches and Narrative' (Harvard diss. 1990).

course and character speeches. And yet Griffin does make use of quantified data.[20] Apologizing for his use of numbers, he observes that in Homer there is 'a ratio of 4 or 5 to one' between abstract nouns in speeches and in narrative. It is suggested that abstractions and an analytic approach may have been regarded by the poet as appropriate to his characters, but less so to the recounting of events by the singer, who is 'the mouthpiece of the goddess [i.e., the Muse].'[21] The sum of these 'figures' is hardly technical.

The second example is W. M. Sale's 'The Trojans, Statistics, and Milman Parry.'[22] Sale asks why the Trojans, mentioned more often than many familiar Homeric characters, 'have no formula at all in the nominative case repeated more than 4 times.' This study uses mathematical statistics and applies such mathematical formulae as chi-square (a statistical test for the significance of proportions) and Pearson correlation coefficients (a formula for expressing the degree of similarity between sets of data).[23] But ultimately the argument is about how to say 'Trojans' in Homer, and about how the Trojans are integrated into the poet's traditional diction. The scarcity of nominative expressions such as *Troes hyperphialoi* ('the haughty Trojans') in the extant text of the *Iliad* is a 'fact.' However, this fact cannot be left in a vacuum. It must be contextualized and 'given meaning.' In a narrow sense Sale illuminates the use of specific formulae and the mechanics of Homeric verse-making. Sale deliberately (and perhaps rightly) restricts the application of his argument, but he is well aware of its potential in terms of literary values. Noting that the nominative formula for the Trojans resembles the formula *mnêstêres hyperphialoi*, 'the haughty suitors' in the *Odyssey*, he asks, 'can it be that, traditionally, the Trojans were as villainous as the Suitors but that the *Iliad* disagrees?'[24] This, of course, is not a technical question.

Two somewhat different 'statistical' approaches are presented above.

---

[20] Here it may be useful to remember our cautionary comments about the classification of abstract nouns.

[21] Griffin (1986) 37.

[22] Sale (1989) 341–410.

[23] For these and other mathematical procedures see e.g., Kenny (1982); Rowntree (1981).

[24] This may be an indication of competing voices in Homer ('polyphony' in M. Bakhtin's terms). Compare the ideas by the 'Harvard school' about 'public and private' voices in Virgil's *Aeneid* (e.g., A. Parry, 'The Two Voices of Virgil's *Aeneid*,' *Arion* (1963) 66–80).

In Griffin's study the use of quantitative data was based on common-sense, and no special mathematical formulae were used. In Sale's study mathematically structured data and mathematical statistics were used. Both a common-sense approach and a mathematical approach can be very insightful, but each also requires caution. Milman Parry in his famous 'The Distinctive Character of Enjambment in Homeric Verse' collected data for the frequency of one line sentences in Greek epic from Homer and Apollonius. He found that the such sentences were twice as frequent in Homer (about once every five or six lines) as in Apollonius.[25] These are 'common-sense' statistics which he eventually used, along with evidence for the coincidence of sentence structure and verse structure (otherwise expressed as the tendency towards enjambment, for which see above) as a criterion for orality.[26] Here, however, Parry made a simple, but significant error. He failed to sample widely enough, and as a consequence he told only half the truth. As D. Clayman points out, in other, clearly literate hexameter Greek poetry, for example in Nicander of Colophon's *Alexipharmaka*, the number of sentences ending at the verse-end is even higher than in Homer.[27] Clayman suggests that Parry might still be essentially right in his view of enjambment as a factor of orality, but she stresses that we must also take account of more complex mechanisms of imitation in otherwise literate compositions, that might explain the high coincidence of sense and metrical structures.

As for mathematical statistics, R. Schmiel, for example, in a study of the relationship between *ictus* and *accentus* develops a complex computational formula for distinguishing between lines where the two accentual systems correspond or clash respectively. Schmiel's statistical model is carefully detailed, but he ends up dividing *all* Homeric hexameters into two rhythmical types—'homodyne' and 'heterodyne' (having selected what he openly admits is a somewhat arbitrary cut-off point).[28] This binary taxonomy may be useful as a tool, but it is, I believe, fundamentally at odds with the subtle richness of Homeric rhythmic structure.

The above discussion exemplifies some of the scope and potential, as well as some of the limitations of quantitative method. Statistics

---

[25] Parry (1971) 255.
[26] Parry (1971) 388–89.
[27] Clayman (1981) 114–15.
[28] Schmiel (1981) 10–11.

are a varied, flexible tool, which may be used either in dedicated researches, or as an ancillary element in other types of arguments, and which may thus be found in studies of almost every aspect of Homeric poetry.

And yet there is one feature common to all quantitative studies of Homer, which has perhaps the greatest importance. By counting individual occurrences and by sorting them into groups we can extract general conclusions that rely on detail, but transcend any single context in our extant *text* of Homer. A quantitative approach therefore enables us to learn about a *non-textual* or rather a *hyper-textual*[29] version of Homer. This version is perhaps better known simply as *the epic tradition* (which, of course, is assumed to be larger and more fluid than our extant *Iliad* and *Odyssey*).

As suggested at the beginning of this chapter, the volume of quantitative work on Homer is already too large and varied to be surveyed in full. And yet, we are arguably only now beginning to make use of quantified studies. The simple reason for this is that advances in technology are making it increasingly less tedious to count more and more phenomena.[30] Two brief illustrations follow. The first deals with specific detail, the second concerns a very wide perspective. The objective here is not so much to argue for any particular theory or interpretation, as to illustrate how statistical arguments are presented, developed and concluded.[31]

I. *A statistical glance at Dawn: Odyssey* 5 describes Odysseus' parting from Calypso, as he begins his final journey home. The narrative opens with the rise of Dawn, who is also mentioned elsewhere in the book:

> Ἠὼς δ' ἐκ λεχέων παρ' ἀγαυοῦ Τιθωνοῖο
> ὤρνυθ', ἵν' ἀθανάτοισι φόως φέροι ἠδὲ βροτοῖσιν (5.1–2)

---

[29] The term may be a-la-móde, but is also accurate: 'Hypertext' and 'Hyper Text Markup Language' (HTML, the basis of World Wide Web pages on the Internet) describe flexible access formats that make any one sequence of 'pages' in an electronic document dependent on any one instance of 'reading' it on-screen.

[30] See, e.g., C. Schäfer, *Computer und antike Text*, vol. I (St. Katharinen, 1993) and J. Solomon, ed., *Accessing Antiquity: The Computerization of Classical Studies* (Tucson, 1993). But the field is advancing faster than the surveys. Many studies that incorporate computerized searches of one sort or another often do not even mention this any more.

[31] Data analysis, including sorting, tabulation and statistical calculations below was done using custom-processed, tagged *TLG* texts, a variety of commercial and custom processing and concordancing software, and statistical software.

'Now Eos rose from her bed, where she lay by haughty Tithonos, carrying light to the immortal gods and to mortals.'

ὥς μὲν ὅτ' Ὠρίων' ἕλετο ῥοδοδάκτυλος Ἠώς (5.121)
'So it was when rosy-fingered Dawn chose Orion'

ἦμος δ' ἠριγένεια φάνη ῥοδοδάκτυλος Ἠώς (5.228)
'When rosy-fingered Eos, the early one, appeared'

ἀλλ' ὅτε δὴ τρίτον ἦμαρ ἐυπλόκαμος τέλεσ' Ἠώς (5.390)
'But when Eos of fair-locks brought the third day'

The Greek *êôs* is both a common noun denoting 'dawn', and a proper name (proper names are not capitalized in ancient texts nor, of course, in oral discourse). Dawn's relationship with the mortal Tithonos is, on the one hand, a counterfoil to Calypso's relationship with Odysseus, as is openly stated in the example of 5.121, a mythological exemplum adduced by Calypso as she complains of the gods' adversity to mortal and divine relationships (the example is not used to describe time). On the other hand the formula ἦμος δ' ἠριγένεια φάνη ῥοδοδάκτυλος Ἠώς ('When rosy-fingered Eos, the early one, appeared') is regularly used (21x in *Odyssey*) to describe the time of day. Should we then regard the occurrence of *eos* in Homer as an elaborate, conventional way of saying 'at dawn,' which, on a few occasions, has been developed into personified description? Or should we regard mention of *êôs* essentially as 'the epiphany of a goddess,'[32] which has also been conveniently applied to more practical end of telling time?

Many literary, mythological, formulaic, and anthropological matters must be considered in order to answer this question. But a quantitative approach can offer some interesting evidence. Consider these data:

Table 1: Usage of *êôs* in *Odyssey* 5 and in the whole of the *Odyssey*

Text/Case	Nominative	Accusative	Dative	Genitive	Vocative	(*-thi*)[33]
Od. 5	4	–	–	–	–	1
Od. (all)	40	17	9	3	–	2

Distinctions between *êôs* and *Êôs* are here ignored. The *-thi* form is included for reference only.

[32] Austin (1975) 67. Note that Book 5 is framed by personified representations: Dawn in 5.1, Sleep in 5.493.

[33] ἠῶθι (with πρό): Likely adverbial, but may be 'locative.'

Usage of the word *eos* in the *Odyssey* spans all grammatical cases except the vocative. The data for *Odyssey* 5 reflect and enhance the polarities of overall usage, since the nominative, the most common case for this word in the *Odyssey*, is attested repeatedly in Book 5, while all other cases, less often attested in the whole, are absent in Book 5. Consider this in the context of the general distribution of grammatical-case frequency for proper names and common nouns.

Table 2: Rank-order and absolute frequency of grammatical case (common nouns and proper names in *Odyssey* 5)

Rank-order/ Part of speech.	1	2	3	4	5	total
common nouns	acc. 287	nom. 177	gen. 136	dat. 131	voc. 11	742
proper name	nom. 59	gen. 24	acc. 16	dat. 12	voc. 5	116

The four attestations of *eos* in *Odyssey* 5 are excluded from the count.

Note that the most frequent case is the accusative for common nouns, but the nominative for proper names. Note also that proportionally there are far less vocatives (1.48% of total) for common nouns than for proper names (5.8% of total) in Book 5.

I submit that these data reflect basic semantic properties. The majority of names (and indeed in the nominative) in Homer are those of persons.[34] Now, broadly speaking a person is more of a *doer*, an *agent*, than an inanimate object. And agents are most commonly grammaticalized by the nominative (the 'subject case'). By contrast, common nouns, a tree, a raft, a ship, a spear, spoken words, more often *have things done to them* (words are spoken, rafts are built, spears are cast, etc.). They therefore tend to appear less often in the nominative (although there are, of course, examples to the contrary), and more often in other cases, indeed, primarily in the accusative (the 'object case'). The vocative may be similarly explained: speeches are usually addressed to persons, not to inanimate things or to animals, hence common noun vocatives are proportionally less frequent. In fact, the 11 common noun vocatives in Book 5 all describe persons (πάτερ, θεοί 4x, τέκνον, θεά 3x, ἄναξ 2x).[35] It seems, then that relative case frequencies, and especially acc./nom. proportions, reflect

[34] Data in Kahane (1994). A glance at the concordance, e.g., under *Odysseus* (name of a person) and *Ithaca* (place name) will illustrate this amply.
[35] Typical of the whole of Homer. See Wendel (1929).

inherent general differences between common noun and proper name usage in Homer.[36]

This may serve us as the basis for interpreting our third, and final set of data:

Table 3: Rank-order and absolute frequency of grammatical case: *Odysseus* (*-s-* and *-ss-* forms) and *eos* (regardless of common noun/proper name distinctions in printed text) for the whole of the *Odyssey*

Name/ Rank-order	1	2	3	4	5	total
Odys(s)eus	nom. 252	gen. 131	acc. 66	voc. 35	dat. 32	516
êôs/Êôs	nom. 40	acc. 17	gen. 9	dat. 3	voc. –	69

Non surprisingly, the rank order for Odysseus is generally very similar to the overall rank order for proper names in Table 2.[37] There are, of course, significant differences at the level of detail, for example, the vocative for Odysseus is proportionally far more common than the vocative for proper names in general.[38] But then, Odysseus is the most prominent user of words in the epic tradition. He speaks often and is hence also often addressed.

What is important for us is that the rank order for *Êôs/êôs* for the whole of the *Odyssey* shows important similarities to both the pattern for proper names and for common nouns but does not fully replicate either (consider e.g. relative frequency of the nominative, the accusative, and the vocative). If our suggestions and method are accepted, the implication is that *Êôs/êôs*, in general, is part 'person' part 'thing.' Indeed, mathematical tests and the absence of vocative examples for *Êôs/êôs* may even indicate slightly greater proximity to common nouns than to proper names.[39]

And yet, the most memorable and common way of saying *dawn* involves the *nominative* formula ἦμος δ' ἠριγένεια φάνη 'ροδοδάκτυλος

[36] In mathematical terms the *rank correlation factor* (hence RCF) between the two sets of data is 0.700 (a factor of 1.00 = two rank orders are absolutely identical; a factor of −1.00 = two order display no shared features). The *Chi-square value* df = 4, 1 cell with expected counts less than 5.0) is 52.013, indicating statistically very significant differences. See Kenny (1982), Rowntree (1981).

[37] RCF 9.00.

[38] The Chi-square value for the two sets of data is (df = 4) 68.1, indicating considerable significance.

[39] Usage of *eos* may even be closer to that of common nouns: RCF when compared with common nouns 8.00, with proper names 7.00.

Ἠώς ('When rosy-fingered Eos, the early one, appeared'). Likewise in *Odyssey* 5 the *nominative* was the only attested case. And nominatives are, as we have argued, a prominent characteristic of proper name usage. Here, then, usage of *Êôs/êôs* moves closer to what is typical of proper names.[40] One possible inference from this is that in contexts where *Êôs/êôs* is given more attention, as in the frequent 'rosy-fingered dawn' formula or in *Odyssey* 5, she does take on more of the usage characteristics typical of proper names, and becomes just a little more of a 'person.'

Let us state again, however, that the main objective in presenting this example is not to argue for any particular interpretation of *Êôs/êôs*. Rather it is to show how a quantitative approach can be used as a tool for the study of a detail.

II. *The statistics of verse-making*: Our second example is more complex, and concerns not so much any individual verse, as the very nature of Homer's discourse. This discourse, we know, is highly 'formulaic'. Now, the definition of 'formulaic style' is a complicated and controversial matter; it is discussed by J. Russo elsewhere in this volume. We shall not here enter the fray. Rather, keeping in mind that the names of heroes are often the basis of formulae, let us see what happens, quantitatively speaking, when, for example, the *Odyssey* mentions its eponymous hero by name and makes him to be the subject of action. Put a little more dryly, we shall ask, what numeric tendencies can be observed concurrent to nominative usage *Oduseus* and *Odusseus* (i.e. both single and double sigma forms) in the *Odyssey*?

There are, as it happens, 323 examples of these two nominative forms in the *Odyssey*.[41] Now, in general, the analysis of systems of formulae (rather than of individual formulaic expressions) tends to

---

[40] The RCF for Book 5, when compared with common nouns is 0.354, and with proper names 0.707. There is evidence that using the name in verse-terminal position is most typical of the proper names of important heroes (e.g., Odysseus, Achilleus, Agamemnon, etc. See Kahane (1994) ch. 5.

[41] The list of examples is readily available electronically, via a *TLG* search engine. But the essence of analysis and interpretation lies in the sorting process. Available lists use only one sorting criterion: sequential line order. Such order is not un-important, but it commonly fails to expose, indeed, it may even obscure many grammatical, metrical, syntactic, thematic, and poetic tendencies (or any combinations thereof). For example, the kind of tendencies (or 'systematic relationships') implied by Parryan formula systems are *not* self-evident in concordances, indeed for several millennia they drew little attention. What is required is a flexible searching and sorting utility. For the purposes of this discussion an analytic concordance was

lay greater emphasis on substantival elements—as in noun-epithet combinations.[42] But most 'complete' utterances (a grammatical sentence is, for example a 'complete' utterance) normally contain not only substantival, but also verbal elements. What, then, of the verb when the *Odyssey* says *Odusseus/Oduseus*?

Our statistics show that almost two thirds of the examples (198 examples = 61.3%; perhaps more, depending on our selection criteria) contain a verb (or verb + appositives) placed immediately next to the nominative *Oduseus/Odusseus* (with or without corresponding epithets). On the whole, and where practically possible the verb appears immediately left of the nominative expression. A small selection of examples will suffice to illustrate our point. It also illustrates that the essential subject/predicate relationship spans a range of metrical configurations, sentence constructions, lexical items, and semantic categories. Furthermore, almost all of the examples below represent larger groups of examples displaying various structural similarities that extend beyond the nominative expression (the nominative expression and the verb are underlined. In the translations they are sometimes separated, for the sake of English grammar):

ἦλθ' Ὀδυσεὺς καὶ οἶκον ἱκάνεται, ὀψέ περ ἐλθών· (23.7)
'*Odysseus is here*, he has reached the house, though late in his coming'

ὠτρύνοντ' Ὀδυσεύς τ' ἰέναι καὶ δῖος ὑφορβός. (17.183)
'*Odysseus* and the noble swineherd *were stirring themselves* to go . . .'

τοῖος ἐὼν μνηστῆρσιν ὁμιλήσειεν Ὀδυσσεύς· (1.265)
'I wish that such an *Odysseus would come now* among the suitors'

οἷά ποτε Τροίηνδε κιὼν κατέλειπεν Ὀδυσσεύς, (16.289)
'like what *Odysseus left behind* when he went to Troy'

Ὣς ὁ μὲν ἔνθα καθεῦδε πολύτλας δῖος Ὀδυσσεὺς (6.1)
'So long suffering great *Odysseus slept* in that place'

τὸν δ' αὖτε προσέειπε πολύτλας δῖος Ὀδυσσεύς· (14.148 etc.)
'Then long suffering great *Odysseus said* to him in answer'

τὴν δ' ἀπαμειβόμενος προσέφη πολύμητις Ὀδυσσεύς· (5.214 etc.)
'Then resourceful *Odysseus spoke* in turn and answered her'

ἔνθ' αὖτ' Εὐρυδάμαντα βάλε πτολίπορθος Ὀδυσσεύς, (22.283)
'This time *Odysseus, stormer of cities, struck down* Eurydamas'

---

generated, in which composite sorting criteria involving metrical shape, grammatical category, syntactic relationships, etc. were used.

[42] See Russo in this volume.

εἰ δ' Ὀδυσεὺς ἔλθοι καὶ ἵκοιτ' ἐς πατρίδα γαῖαν, (17.539)
'But *if Odysseus could come*, and return to the land of his fathers'

ἀλλ' Ὀδυσεὺς κατέρυκε καὶ ἔσχεθεν ἱεμένω περ. (4.284)
'But *Odysseus pulled us back* and held us, for all our eagerness:

ἐξ οὗ Ὀδυσσεὺς δῖος ἔβη κοίλῃσ' ἐνὶ νηυσί. (2.27)
'Since *great Odysseus went away* in the hollow vessels'

The fact that these examples and so many others reveal such proximities with regard to the verb and the nominative subject may suggest a structural principle, e.g.: **verb [+ postpositives] + nominative proper-name based expression**, commonly anchored either to the beginning of the verse or to the end of the verse. A generative rule may also be involved, e.g.: **if the order verb + nominative is metrically impossible or is overruled by stronger patterns, invert to nominative + verb order.**

The significance of this pattern may be more- or less technical. It may have to do with the making of Homeric hexameters, or it may have to do with oral poetics, or with some other aspect of epic discourse. Let us note, however, that this pattern cannot be described in Parryan formulaic terms (for which see Joseph Russo's contribution to this volume) since the verb + nominative structure cannot be reduced to an 'essential idea', nor can it be said to operate 'under the same metrical conditions' in the commonly accepted sense of this Parryan expression. At the same time, the lines containing the pattern also involve many noun-epithet combinations that are the very essence of Parryan formulaic systems (e.g., *polymêtis Odusseus*). To the extent that an epic bard used formulae to make his verses, he would have also had to acknowledge—as he made the lines—the syntactic pattern implied by the above. But this syntactic pattern does not operate within the framework of Parryan 'economy' and 'extension' of systems. This state of affairs may indicate an inherent insufficiency on the part of Parryan systems as explanatory models for verse-making.

Likewise, the verb + nominative pattern cannot simply be described as a 'structural' formula since it contains important lexical and probably even poetic elements—it seems to rely heavily on the nominative of Odysseus, the protagonist of the poem.[43] Is it also not possible

[43] The nominatives of proper names tend to be localized in part according to their narrative roles. Indicative in this sense is that, for example, the names of the two protagonists of the *Iliad* and the *Odyssey* respectively, which are metrically identical, both having single- and double consonant forms; for both protagonists the

to describe the pattern in terms of 'peripheral' and 'nuclear' elements, as some formulaic expressions have recently been described,[44] since it is obvious that both basic elements of the pattern (the verb and the nominative expression) are semantically and grammatically essential within their contexts. Furthermore, our pattern relies on a highly systematic verbal element, while existing discussions of the formula stress, on the whole, the nominal components of epic discourse.[45] We are left with an important question-mark concerning the use of verbal elements, generated, essentially, by quantitative observations.

The list of different uses to which these data can be applied is considerable. For example, it is the case that all of the lines containing combinations of a longer epithet + *Odusseus* are anchored to the end of the verse, and of these almost all are directly preceded by *a verb of saying or thinking* (90 out of a total of 105 = 85.7%). This strongly suggests that the so-called 'technical' system of formulaic extension (on which see the chapter by J. Russo) is not technical at all, but is rather firmly linked to semantics and to theme. At the same time the above seems to imply that speech introductory expressions of the common type

> τὸν δ' ἀπαμειβόμενος προσέφη πολύμητις Ὀδυσσεύς·
> 'Then resourceful Odusseus spoke in turn and answered him'

are, at a deeper level, merely a specialized segment of a much broader pattern of diction.

But, yet again, it is not our objective here to pursue any particular Homeric question *per se*, nor to argue for any particular interpretation. For our purposes what is important is firstly, that the above data suggest the existence of potentially significant features of Homer that are not adequately covered by existing theory, and secondly, that such data would not 'exist' but for quantitative methods of analysis. A quantitative approach may thus be regarded as type of

---

double consonant form is localized at the end of the verse. By contrast, none of the names of the suitors (who are *not* heroes) is suitable for terminal localization. See further in Kahane (1994) ch. 5.

[44] See e.g., Visser (1987); idem (1988) 21–37; Bakker and Fabricotti (1991) 63–84.

[45] 'The name-plus-epithet system is much the clearest instance in Homeric poetry of what could be though to be a thoroughgoing formulaic system. Verbs do not, on the whole, lend themselves so neatly to tabulation in columns of exact repetition.' in Griffin (1995) 34. For a bibliography of works on verbal formulae see M. W. Edwards (1988) 18–24.

verbal 'lens', a microscope or a telescope device, allowing us to observe 'objects' that are otherwise 'invisible'. Some of this 'optical' potential is already in plain view. Milman Parry's work, although not mathematical, inherently relied on grouping examples and quantifying data. And arguably Parry's studies have revealed to us a Homer previously unknown. Quantifying epic thus has some power to make 'new' epic verse.[46]

Finally, even our brief glance at the data reveals that although it is easy to detect patterns in Homeric verse, many of our detected features display a 'family resemblance' to other features. Everything is, as it were, connected to something else, in what may well be an 'open-ended system.'[47] And indeed, it is likely that if we were to generate analytic lists for one or more of the elements of the *Oduseus/Odusseus* verses, e.g. one of the common nouns, one of the verbs, an appositive such as αὐτάρ, or indeed one of the grammatical or metrical categories, we would find yet more patterns emerging, partially overlapping those we have noted. We may find the thought of such sprawling 'networks' and 'family resemblances' bewildering. Certainly in upholding complex networks we risk losing the elegant simplicity of Parryan and similar systems. Complex networks do not provide neat 'algorithmic' answers (i.e., a simple set of basic instructions that allows us to generate, e.g., epic verse) to questions about Homer and Homeric poetry. However, it may be argued that the unruly complexity of our suggested networks is more true to life, that it ultimately provides a better representation of the complexity inherent to Homer, his language, and his poetry. And, finally, our discomfort at the thought of losing a simple explanatory algorithm may stem from our own highly literate way of reading texts (especially in scholarly contexts!). We seek the finality of a visual object, a written text, where the poetry of Homer is something broader, more evasive, and at least partly affected by the inherent fluidity of oral discourse.[48] And this is just where quantitative approaches may help. A pattern of proper names and verbs such as we have seen, shared by, e.g. 61.3% of all examples in the *Odyssey* is likely to have some significant implications, but it also leaves ample scope for variation

[46] M. W. Edwards (1988) 49–50 commenting on future trends still holds true.

[47] The phrase was introduced in Nagler (1974).

[48] See J. Foley, 'Writing Bellerophon's Tablet,' in E. J. Bakker and A. Kahane, *Written Voices, Spoken Signs: Tradition, Performance, and the Epic Text* (forthcoming, Harvard University Press, Cambridge, Mass.).

in the remaining 38.7% of the examples. Paradoxically, then, a quantitative approach gives us *both* precision *and* flexibility. It allows us to read the text very closely, while making statements that extend far beyond any single context. This type of elliptic relationship in which the part can somehow stand for the whole may be a reflection of a deeper ellipsis. As some scholars have recently argued, epic is fundamentally 'elliptic', inasmuch as it embodies the plurality of epic tradition as a whole.[49] If we accept this, then there is something singularly appropriate about quantifying epic.

[49] See G. Nagy, 'Ellipsis in Homer,' in Bakker and Kahane (see note above, forthcoming). Needless to say, Nagy's argument is far more complex than its brief mention here.

PART THREE

HOMER AS LITERATURE

Seth L. Schein

THE *ILIAD*: STRUCTURE AND INTERPRETATION[1]

The *Iliad* is organized according to two complementary, structural principles, one related to its narrative action and traditional mythological content, the other to its traditional style and the artistic norms of the eighth century B.C. The latter principle may be called static and symmetrical: its main characteristics are 'balance, responsion, contrast, and repetition, in an orderly syntax,'[2] and it is, in a sense, independent of the plot of the poem. The former principle is dynamic and linear or progressive: it involves the movement of the poem from beginning to end toward the death of Achilles in the context of the ultimate destruction of Troy, and it consists, broadly speaking, of three stages, each of which uses and reuses traditional motifs in ways that gradually accumulate meaning.[3] Of course, neither principle excludes the other, and the two reciprocally reinforce one another: the symmetrical balance and repetition in the poem is, in part, a balance and repetition of elements of the plot, and the linear progress through three stages involves the repetition of specific narrative motifs as well as of specific diction.

The principle of symmetry can be seen in the frequently observed balance between the first three books of the poem and the last three. In Book 1, Agamemnon rejects the supplication of Chryses and refuses to release his daughter for a ransom; in Book 24, Achilles accepts the supplication of Priam and releases the body of his son for a ransom. In each instance, Apollo is instrumental in setting the action in motion: at 1.43–52, he responds to Chryses' prayer by descending from Olympus and sending a plague against the Greek army; at 24.33–54, he chides the other gods for being willing to assist Achilles in his defilement of Hector's body, and begins the discussion that ends in Zeus' decision to have Achilles accept a ransom for the corpse.

[1] In this essay, I have drawn freely, and sometimes verbatim, on parts of Chapter 1 of Schein (1984).

[2] Whitman (1958) 101.

[3] Cf. Whitfield (1967) 15–27, who also distinguishes two structural principles, the one 'static' and 'analogical,' the other 'dynamic' and 'logical.'

Furthermore, this scene on Olympus near the beginning of Book 24 corresponds to the scene at the end of Book 1; each book also includes a meeting between Zeus and Thetis in which they discuss Achilles. Even the pattern of days in the two books is almost exactly balanced: in Book 1, the day of Chryses' supplication is followed by nine days of plague, one day on which the Greeks appease Apollo after Achilles and Agamemnon quarrel, and a twelve-day break until the gods return from the land of the Aithiopes; in Book 24, after Achilles mistreats Hector's corpse for twelve days while the gods argue about what to do, there is the day of Iris' errand to Priam from Zeus and the old man's ransom of Hector's corpse, followed by nine days during which the Trojans gather wood to burn the body, its cremation on the tenth day, and its burial on the eleventh.[4] This eleventh day, like the confusion over how long the gods were arguing (above, n. 3), disrupts the exact correspondence-in-reverse between the two books, but the two long stretches of time in the opening and closing books, unparalleled elsewhere in the *Iliad*, effectively frame the action of the poem and, as it were, throw into relief the wrath of Achilles and its deadly consequences.

The correspondences between Books 2 and 23 and 3 and 22 are less detailed than those between Books 1 and 24 but equally significant. Books 2 and 23 present descriptions of the Greek army assembled as a large group: the catalogue of ships and men introduces the main leaders of the army, the funeral games are a kind of farewell to them. The catalogue and the recollections by Odysseus (2.299–322) and Nestor (2.350–56) of the omens and prophecies of ten years past allude to the beginning of the war, while the success and failure of particular heroes in the games foreshadows their known mythological destinies beyond the time frame of the *Iliad*. Books 3 and 22 are clearly parallel to one another because of the duels between Paris and Menelaus and Hector and Achilles. That between the two husbands of Helen, the first combat in the poem, is appropriate to and recapitulates the beginning of the war; that between Hector and Achilles, the final combat in the poem, resolves the war, because the death of Hector is in effect the fall of Troy.

---

[4] Whitman (1958) 351 n. 18, points out that the gods in Book 24 are roused to action on the twelfth day (24.31) but Zeus later says they have been arguing for nine days (24.107); he suggests that 'the confusion over twelve and nine is likely enough in oral composition,' and that the main point is that the two long time-gaps in Book 24 correspond to those in Book 1.

The polar or reverse symmetry evident in Books 1–3 and 22–24 reflects on a large scale a basic technique of poetic composition and organization within the poem, and in early Greek literature generally, known as ring composition. Ring composition means that a topic mentioned near the beginning of a speech or narrative unit is repeated, sometimes verbatim and sometimes in more or less similar language, at the end of the passage, which thus is framed and set off as a discrete poetic entity.[5] Ring composition is found in the *Iliad* in almost every direct speech that begins and ends with an explicit statement or other indication in the text that somebody spoke. It also is illustrated by certain digressive passages, such as, for example, Nestor's recollections of his youth at 1.259–74 and 7.129–60. In addition, ring composition can be a more subtle structural device than such simple frames. Often, a series of topics or ideas mentioned in the first half of a speech or description recurs in reverse order in the second half. For example, Achilles, urging Priam to eat at 24.599–620, tells him: a) your son is ransomed and tomorrow at dawn you will see him and take him away (24.599–601), b) 'now let us be mindful of supper' (24.601), c) even Niobe was mindful of food (24.602), d) the story of Niobe (24.603–12), c), she was mindful of food (24.613), b) so let the two of us think of food (24.618–19), a) you can weep for your son tomorrow, when you take him back to Troy (24.619–20).[6] There also can be ring composition between two speeches: that of Achilles at 24.599–620 is a 'mirror image' of Priam's earlier speech (24.518–51) 'in its content, overall structure, in many details.'[7] Just as individual speeches and scenes are framed or structured according to the principle of ring composition, so the entire poem, with its corresponding scenes at the beginning and end, is organized according to a principle of balance and polar correspondence. This correspondence may be 'logical,' as when supplication accepted in Book 24 stands in contrast to supplication rejected in

[5] Whitman (1958) 252–56. Cf. Lohmann (1970) 5–8, who refers to W. A. A. van Otterlo, *De ringkompositie als opbouwprincipe in de epische Gedichten van Homerus*, Verhandelingen der Koninklijke Nederlandse Akademie van Wetenschappen, Afd. Letterkunde, no. 51.1 (Amsterdam, 1948).

[6] Lohmann (1970) 13. The overall ring form of the speech is unmistakable, whether or not, as many scholars since antiquity have thought, lines 24.614–17 were interpolated into the poem at a later date. Cf. Kakridis (1949) 96–105.

[7] Nagler (1974) 191. For a thoroughgoing demonstration of the extent and importance of ring composition within and among speeches in the *Iliad*, see Lohmann (1970).

Book 1; or it may be merely 'analogical,' as when a group scene in Book 23 is parallel to one in Book 2, with no specific point of contrast.[8] In either case, the 'use of polarities as a structural principle' is clear.[9]

Such artistic organization calls to mind the Geometric designs on Greek painted pottery of the eighth century B.C.[10] The structural analogies between the *Iliad* and Geometric art suggest that the balance and symmetry of the poem are not unique but rather indicative of a contemporary feeling for form characteristic of the age.[11] This feeling for form would have enabled the opening of the poem, or of a speech or narrative subunit, to create an expectation in the minds of a contemporary audience that the closing of the ring would later have satisfied. Thus, the effect of its formal, geometrical symmetry is to impart to the *Iliad* a sense of completion and fulfillment.[12]

On the one hand, the *Iliad* is characterized by this formal symmetry, but its narrative action and mythological content move in a certain direction and are neither completed nor rounded off by a balance of corresponding parts. The direction of this movement is toward death—the death of Hector, the death of Achilles, the fall of Troy—and in the mortal world of the poem, the movement toward death is a one-way movement, an overriding reality that lends the poem much of its power as a representation of the tragically urgent and limited human condition. The story of the wrath of Achilles and its consequences unfolds in apparently straightforward fashion, with events being told in the order that they occur by the poem's implied narrator. Past events are paradigmatically evoked, recalled, or related, usually when one character wishes to persuade another to a particular course of action, but there is nothing like the extraordinarily complex narrative form of the *Odyssey*, with its multiple plots, its movement back and forth in time, its numerous internal narrators

[8] Whitfield (1967) 13, uses the term 'analogical' in a slightly different sense, when he speaks of the 'analogical coherence between [Books 1 and 24], based on themes and salient features . . . which are common to them both.'

[9] Whitman (1958) 256. Cf. Schadewaldt (1965) 51, 95, 214, on the compositional importance of 'polarity' and 'opposition' in the *Iliad.*

[10] On the geometric structure of the *Iliad*, cf. Myres (1932); Whitman (1958) 87–101, 249–84. Both Myres and Whitman were influenced by J. T. Sheppard, *The Pattern of the Iliad* (1922; reprint, London, 1969).

[11] For interesting attempts to situate Homer in the late eighth century B.C., see Schadewaldt (1965) 87–129; G. Nagy (1979) 7. Cf. Schein (1984) 49, 169.

[12] Cf. Whitfield (1967) 26.

(including, of course, Odysseus himself) and narrative perspectives, and its constant changes of locale.[13]

Generally speaking, the narrative of the *Iliad* consists of three parts or stages: Books 1–7, Books 8–17 (perhaps excluding Book 10, the *Doloneia*, as intrusive and not originally part of the poem), and Books 18–24. These parts may correspond to or reflect units of oral performance/composition; structurally, they are more important than the conventional division of the text into twenty-four books.[14] In general, the first stage presents the traditional or normative picture of the Greeks and Trojans as aggressors against and defenders of Troy, respectively. Diomedes, whose *aristeia* in Books 5 and 6 is the major heroic exploit of this part of the poem, embodies traditional heroic values of courage while fighting for the sake of honor and glory and respect toward his commander Agamemnon (4.401–402) and toward the gods (6.128–31). Although he wounds both Ares and Aphrodite on the instructions of Athena and with her direct assistance, he prudently retreats before Ares (5.600–606) and gives way to Apollo (5.439–44), thus remaining within his mortal limits. The *aristeia* of Diomedes shows a conventional type of hero successfully and in a morally uncomplicated way living up to traditional norms and values. In Whitman's words, '[H]is is the heroic pattern without thought, victory without implicit defeat.'[15]

The second stage of the poem, with its depiction of the alienation of Achilles and its consequences—the success of Hector and the

[13] Cf. Slatkin (1992) 223–24.

[14] Taplin (1992) 13, 285–93, argues strongly against there being any structural or poetic significance in the traditional division of the text into 24 books. His views on the structure of the *Iliad* are grounded primarily in his understanding of how the poem shapes narrative time. For Taplin, 'the three-part structure matches and arises from Homer's own performance; the forward-markers to "tomorrow" in *narrative-time* also serve as forward-markers in *performance-time*'. (26). Taplin argues that the first part of the poem ends at 9.712, the second at 18.353. He considers that Book 10 'does not fit in the structure as a whole, and that it contains elements intrusively alien to the character of the rest of the *Iliad*' (11). Cf. Danek (1988), who argues that Book 10 was composed by a poet who was familiar with the *Iliad* as a fixed text. For a contrasting judgment on the division into twenty-four books, see Stanley (1993), who sees in each book 'a remarkable structural integrity' as well as 'an equally striking coherence in the groups comprising them' (249). For Stanley, as for myself, these groups consist of Books 1–7, Books 8–17, and Books 18–24. Though one may differ on details of overall narrative construction, Stanley's detailed interpretations of the individual books and of these three groups are consistently instructive and stimulating, as are his discussions of such topics as ring composition, digressions, and the relation between oral theory and the poem's narrative structure.

[15] Whitman (1958) 167.

Trojans, followed by the death of Patroclus—raises moral and intellectual issues that go beyond anything in Books 1–7, and perhaps beyond anything in the poetic tradition; this stage is distinctively *Iliadic.* The major heroic exploit of this section of the poem, apart from the Zeus-given, temporary success of Hector, is the *aristeia* of Patroclus in Book 16. In contrast to that of Diomedes, which is, so to speak, traditional and in character, that of Patroclus is uniquely motivated and reflects an odd dislocation of values. For Patroclus is not fighting for his own honor and glory but 'so that we might honor the son of Peleus, who is the best/of the Argives beside the ships' (16.271–72). It is appropriate, then, that he fights in Achilles' armor and deliberately assumes his identity to deceive the Trojans. When he puts on the armor of his comrade and with it his comrade's triumphant power, Patroclus loses his own identity and his characteristic gentleness. Homer refers to him, and makes other characters refer to him, as 'amiable' (*enêês,* 17.204; 21.96; 23.252, 648), a word used of no one else in the poem; but when he assumes Achilles' role and power, his 'amiability' (*enêeiê,* 17.670) disappears and Patroclus cannot retain his sense of himself and his mortal limits. When Apollo warns him to retreat, in the same language in which he warns Diomedes (16.706–709 = 5.440–42), Patroclus gives way temporarily but then presses on against the Trojans 'equal in weight to swift Ares' (16.784), until Apollo himself opposes him, strips him of his armor, and stuns him, leaving him an easy target for Euphorbus and Hector (16.788–821).

Achilles' *aristeia* in the final stage of the poem, culminating in the killing of Hector and mutilation of his corpse, is even more dislocated and untraditional than that of Patroclus, and in comparison with Diomedes, Achilles stands out as a deadly and daemonic force of destruction barely acknowledging his human limits. For example, at the beginning of Diomedes' *aristeia,* fire blazes from the hero's helmet and spear 'like the star in the late summer, which most/brightly shines, when it has been washed in the Ocean' (5.5–6); the reflection from Achilles' armor is compared to the same star, Sirius, which is, however, described as 'the brightest, and it is made as a sign of evil/and it brings high fever to wretched mortals' (22.30–31).[16] Whereas Diomedes observes his mortal limits in refusing to fight with a god, Achilles, with the aid of Athena, Poseidon, and

[16] Ibid.

Hephaestus, successfully opposes the river Scamander and even says that he would 'pay back' Apollo, 'if only I had the power' (22.15). With the results of Achilles' *aristeia*—the death of Hector, Achilles' own impending death, and the inevitable fall of Troy—the *Iliad* returns, as it were, to the traditional mythology of the Trojan War. The three stages of the poem, marked by the *aristeiai* of Diomedes, of Patroclus, and of Achilles, are progressive stages leading toward this death and destruction.

Each of the three parts of the poem includes near its beginning a crucial action of Achilles: his quarrel with Agamemnon and withdrawal from combat in Book 1, his refusal to accept Agamemnon's gifts in Book 9, and his decision to die at once if he can avenge Patroclus in Book 18. Other actions and motifs similarly recur in the poem, marking its movement toward death. For example, in Book 1 Zeus promises Thetis he will honor Achilles by granting Hector and the Trojans victory and destroying many Greeks (1.517–26). At 8.473–83, he prophesies to Hera that Hector will be triumphant until he kills Patroclus and reaches the ships, thus inciting Achilles to rejoin the fighting. At 15.61–77 he speaks in more detail and goes even further, telling Hera that Hector will rout the Greeks until Achilles rouses Patroclus to fight; Hector will kill Patroclus, after Patroclus has killed Sarpedon; Achilles then will kill Hector in revenge, after which the Trojans will be pushed back toward the city until it is taken; all this will happen in accordance with his promise to Thetis in Book 1. Zeus' promise and prophecies unfold his plans as the poem unfolds. They set Achilles' actions, and all human actions, in a divine perspective that imparts to them an ironic and tragic dignity. Each of Zeus' statements of his developing plans follows an intervention into the action or expression of resentment by Hera in support of the Greeks: at 1.555–59 she voices her fear that Zeus has promised to destroy many of the Greeks; at 8.201–207 she tries to persuade Poseidon to intervene on behalf of the Greeks contrary to Zeus' command, then at 8.352–56, after she raises the subject with Athena, the two are on their way to the battlefield when Zeus deters them by his threats (8.402–405, 416–19); in Book 14 Hera deceitfully seduces Zeus so that Poseidon can help the Greeks while he is distracted. In each instance Zeus' plans develop in response to Hera's attempt to aid the Greeks. The repeated motif of their divine quarreling gradually clarifies the movement of the *Iliad* toward its tragic conclusion on the mortal plane.

Together the divine and human forces impart to the poem a linear momentum that complements the balanced, ring compositional symmetry of its Geometric form. The result is a dual structure that is simultaneously harsh and harmonious, incomplete and fulfilled. This structure, arising from the combination of two opposed, conventional, structural principles, gives the *Iliad* its distinctive artistic organization.

One striking feature of this organization is the use of allusion and indirect suggestion to refer to numerous incidents in the Trojan War that, in the poetic tradition, took place before or after the events narrated in the poem. In effect, Homer works the story of the entire war into the *Iliad*. Much of this story, though known from later sources such as fragments and summaries of the Epic Cycle and Archaic and Classical vase paintings, is in fact pre-Iliadic, at least in its general features. Audiences schooled in the oral poetic tradition would have recognized the poem's use and transformations of the traditional mythology in accordance with its distinctive themes and values. This recognition in turn would have enhanced their appreciation of the form and thought of the new epic, of how the plot of the *Iliad* is, as it were, a digression in the story of the entire war, which in a sense it interrupts, and of how the poem manages to include within this digression the greater narrative whole.[17]

Following Achilles' quarrel with Agamemnon and the outbreak of his wrath in Book 1, Books 2–4 recall in numerous details the beginning of the war. In these books the linear plot of the poem progresses from episode to episode, but at the same time these episodes evoke events which took place nine years earlier. Thus, as many scholars have pointed out, the Catalogue of Ships (2.494–760) really belongs to, and probably derives from, a traditional description of the Greek army and fleet assembling at the port of Aulis before sailing to Troy. This description is adapted to the circumstances of the poem: for instance, in mentioning Protesilaus (2.698–709) and Philoctetes (2.718–25), the former killed 'as he leapt from his ships, far the first of the Achaeans' (2.701), the latter 'languishing on the island, suffering

[17] Cf. Heubeck (1950) 17–36. For a thoroughgoing study of the poem's adaptation of traditional mythology, see Kullmann (1960). Kullmann emphasizes the 'Anpassung der überkommenen Sage an die Thematik der Ilias,' the 'allgemeinen Tendenz dieses Epos, vorliegende Sagen mehr oder weniger gewaltsam ihrem eigenen Thema anzugleichen' (29), as well as the 'symbolic repetition' of the whole conflict in the course of the poem (366). Cf. the same author's 'Vergangenheit und Zukunft in der *Ilias*,' *Poetica* 2 (1968) 15–37.

overwhelming pains,/on sacred Lemnos, where the sons of the Achaeans left him' (721–22), the implied narrator says that although their men longed for these leaders, they were not leaderless, because Podarkes and Medon commanded their respective contingents. Both Protesilaus and Philoctetes would have been included in a catalogue of the army gathering at Aulis, and the poem does what is necessary to account for their absence in the *Iliad*.[18] In a more general way, it adapts the traditional description to the circumstances of the poem by specifying the number of ships in each contingent only as a kind of addendum, emphasizing instead the number of men, the names of the leaders, and their ancestry, homelands, and special qualities. That the poem is transforming a traditional catalogue of the army assembling at Aulis is made more likely by Odysseus' recollection of the omens they saw there and of how Calchas interpreted them (2.299–330), as well as by Nestor's recalling the favorable lightning from Zeus when the Greeks set sail for Troy (2.350–53).

The *Iliad* also suggests the beginning of the war in the contrast between the silent Greeks and the noisy Trojans marching to battle, and in the simile about the dense cloud of dust they raised as they were crossing the plain (3.1–14). It is significant that the Trojans are compared to cranes who aggressively initiate battle—'bringing slaughter and death to the Pugmaian men/and at daybreak they bring on the evil conflict' (3.6–7)—while the Greeks are described in terms of their defensive intent—'eager in their hearts to protect one another' (3.9). Because the Greeks are attacking Troy and the Trojans are defending their city, one would expect the Trojans to be described in terms of defense and the Greeks as aggressors. But this opening contrast between the armies begins a consistent pattern in which the Trojans initiate not only the battle but the war, as aggressors and transgressors who are morally responsible for their own ruin. This moral responsibility is emphasized in Book 4 when Athena, at Hera's urging and Zeus' command, incites Pandarus to break the truce, 'so that the Trojans might begin first/to do harm to the highly renowned Achaeans in violation of their oaths' (4.66–67 = 71–72). In this way the Trojans are made to reenact their original guilt in abducting

[18] See Mülder (1910) 176–77, cited by Heubeck (1950) 32, for the suggestion that the detail that Protesilaus' ship is the first to be set on fire by Hector and the Trojans (16.122–23; cf. 15.704–706) is a reflection of the story that he had been the first Greek killed in the war.

Helen and violating the religiously sanctioned guest-host relationship (3.46–51; cf. 13.621–27). Their inevitable destruction for breaking their oaths is emphasized by Agamemnon (4.270–71) and later by Antenor in the Trojan assembly (7.351–53). This symbolic reenactment of the original Trojan guilt, like their description as aggressors, effectively calls to mind the beginning of the war.

In the same way, the characterization and actions of Paris and Helen in Book 3 contribute to the sense that the poem is retelling the origin of the war without actually narrating it. The single combat between the two husbands of Helen to settle the conflict, and the view from the wall where Helen points out the prominent Greek heroes to Priam as if for the first time (3. 161–242), 'belong naturally to the first year of the war and are out of place in the ninth.'[19] The same is true of the recollection by Antenor of Menelaus' and Odysseus' embassy to Troy to demand Helen's return (3.204–224). Furthermore, Helen and Paris are portrayed as the attractive lovers whose elopement brought on the war. When Paris, saved from death by Aphrodite, urges Helen to come to bed with him, he himself mentions that he desires her even more than when they made love for the first time after leaving Sparta (3.441–46).

Just as Books 2–4 recall the beginning of the war, so the final books repeatedly suggest events that an audience familiar with the poetic tradition would have known took place later (in mythological time) than the action of the *Iliad*. Chief among these events is the fall of Troy. In addition to the prophetic words of Agamemnon (4.164–65), Hector (6.448–49), and Zeus (15.70–71), other references to and predictions of the city's doom are so numerous that it becomes clear that the life of the city is inextricably bound up with that of Hector.[20] Priam makes this explicit at 22.56–57, where he foresees the fall of the city immediately after anticipating his son's death. When Hector is slain, the implied narrator describes the lamentation and groaning as 'most like what it would have been, if all/beetling Ilion were being consumed utterly by fire' (22.410–11). Finally, Andromache, in her lamentation for her dead husband, says, (24.727–30),

> the son whom you and I bore in our ill fortune—I do not
> think he will reach his youthful prime, since sooner this city will be utterly

---

[19] Whitman (1958) 265.
[20] Cf. Schadewaldt (1965) 156–57, n. 4.

sacked. For you, its guardian, have perished, who used to save
it, and you protected its careful wives and infant children. . . .

By the end of the *Iliad*, the situation for the Trojans is superficially not unlike what it was before Achilles' wrath: they are penned in their city, afraid to come out of the gates to fight. But as a result of the action of the poem, with Hector dead, the city itself has virtually been destroyed, and its ultimate doom is fully present to the minds of an audience or reader. Although this action is only a brief episode in the tenth year of the war, within the time frame of this episode the poem has actually told the story of the entire war from the judgment of Paris, referred to at 24.28–30, to the fall of the city, and even beyond.[21]

This 'beyond' is reflected in certain details of the funeral games for Patroclus in Book 23 that foreshadow mythical 'events' known to have taken place after the action of the *Iliad*. The wrestling match between Odysseus and Ajax the son of Telamon mirrors in a harmless way their fatal conflict over the arms of Achilles, which was narrated in the *Aithiopis* and *Little Iliad*. When Athena causes Ajax the son of Oileus to slip on some dung during the foot race, the scene anticipates his doom in retribution for his rape of Cassandra at Athena's altar during the sack of Troy. The most important later event referred to but not narrated in the *Iliad* is the death of Achilles. The poem repeatedly makes it clear that Achilles' doom will follow closely after that of Hector and portrays Achilles as virtually dead from the beginning of Book 18 on,[22] but it does not and cannot show the death of Achilles, because, in a mythological innovation fundamental for its structure and meaning, it uses the details (and perhaps some of the specific diction) traditionally associated with the death of Achilles to tell of the death of Patroclus. This makes it possible simultaneously to represent Achilles' terrible isolation and self-reproach at his comrade's fall and to evoke in an audience or reader the sense that, with the death of Patroclus, Achilles himself dies.

The death of Achilles was narrated in the post-Homeric *Aithiopis* on the basis of older mythical traditions. In that epic, according to Proclus' summary, Achilles kills the Aethiopian prince Memnon, a Trojan ally and son of the goddess Eos, after Memnon slays Achilles' dearest friend, Antilochus. Eos and Thetis beseech Zeus each for

[21] Cf. Heubeck (1950) 25.
[22] See Schein (1984) 128–32, 143–44.

the victory of her own son, and Zeus decides, after weighing the heroes' lives on his scales, that Achilles will conquer. Subsequently Achilles routs the Trojans and, as he presses on to sack the city, is slain by Paris and Apollo. His corpse is rescued by Odysseus and Ajax son of Telamon; then Thetis and the Nereids come with the Muses to mourn the dead hero, whose funeral, with athletic contests in his honor, is followed by a dispute between Ajax and Odysseus over his arms. In the meantime, the body of Memnon has been taken away by Eos, who with Zeus' approval confers on him a posthumous immortality.

It seems clear that the *Iliad* has selectively and creatively borrowed for Patroclus this tradition about the death of Achilles. Patroclus slays the son of Zeus and Trojan ally Sarpedon (16.462–505), after Zeus and Hera discuss whether he should intervene to save his son (16.433–57). Zeus sends Death and Sleep to convey the corpse of Sarpedon to his native Lycia for burial and worship in a hero cult (16.456–57), which implies an immortality analogous to that of Memnon in the *Aithiopis*.[23] Patroclus presses on, drives the Trojans toward their city, and is killed there by Euphorbus, Hector, and Apollo. At one point, when he is about to take the city (16.698–99), Apollo beats him back and tells him: 'It is not allotted/to sack the city of the mighty Trojans beneath your spear,/nor beneath that of Achilles, who is far better than you' (16.707–709). Thus, just before his death, Patroclus, who is fighting in Achilles' armor, is linked to the son of Peleus by Apollo's words as well as by the general narrative of his exploits and his death. After he dies, his body is rescued by Ajax son of Telamon (Odysseus has been wounded and is not fighting) and mourned by Thetis and the Nereids. In Book 23, Homer describes Patroclus' funeral and the games in his honor with constant reference to the later death and burial of Achilles.[24]

In thus adapting and transforming the death of Achilles into that of Patroclus, the *Iliad* is not merely playing with traditional mythological motifs. Rather, for an audience familiar with the poetic tradition, Patroclus, with whom Achilles has a uniquely close and tender friendship, becomes a substitute or surrogate for his comrade.[25] On

[23] On Sarpedon's hero cult, see Schein (1984) 48; G. Nagy (1983). On the parallel between his mortality and Memnon's, see Heubeck (1950) 27–28.
[24] Cf. Schein (1984) 155–56, with references.
[25] Cf. Heubeck (1950) 30 with n. 1; Whitman (1958) 200–202.

the one hand, this makes it possible for the poem to include within itself the story of Achilles' death, along with other mythological events in the war that were known to have occurred earlier or later than its time frame. On the other hand, and more importantly, by having Achilles 'die' while he is still alive, the poem is able to suggest how far beyond normal human limits his dislocation, isolation, and suffering extend.

Just as the poem gives Patroclus traditional mythological features of Achilles and Antilochus, so it gives aspects of Memnon to Sarpedon and to Hector.[26] Sarpedon resembles Memnon in that he is a Trojan ally of divine parentage who attains immortality after his death in battle on the Trojan plain. Hector resembles Memnon in being the slayer of Achilles' dearest comrade and the occasion of Achilles' death; in both poems, Achilles knows that his own death must follow soon after his revenge. Both Hector and Memnon (as we know from the *Aithiopis*) are represented as the last hope of Troy; in each case, then, Achilles' triumph constitutes virtually a sack of the city.

The *Aithiopis* cannot have been a direct source or model for the *Iliad*: like the other Cyclic Epics, it was composed later. Nor, given the nature of oral composition/performance and the absence of a fixed text in an oral poetic tradition, can Homer simply have transferred incidents and speeches from a preexistent *Achilleis* or *Memnonis* to new characters and contexts in the *Iliad*.[27] Rather, the *Iliad* and *Aithiopis* both descend from the same oral poetic tradition and are not dependent the one upon the other. Undoubtedly, certain traditional motifs and diction associated with Achilles' death and funeral in the *Aithiopis* are associated with the death and burial of Patroclus in the *Iliad*, but the scenes and characters in each poem were created for their place in that poem, not transferred *en bloc* from a preexistent source or model.

The *Iliad* achieves its results not only by transforming specific mythological episodes into events in its own dramatic action but, as K. Reinhardt pointed out, by reshaping traditional stories and story patterns into dramatic structures and 'situations.'[28] For example, the 'judgment of Paris' is mentioned in the poem only once, in passing, at 24.28–30, and is in no way significant for the story. On the other

[26] Heubeck (1958) 34–35.
[27] As suggested by Pestalozzi (1945), and Schadewaldt (1965) 155–202.
[28] Reinhardt (1960), 16–36; cf. pp. 5–15.

hand, it explains, as it were, a significant 'situation' that pervades the *Iliad*: the favor Aphrodite shows to the Trojans, especially Paris, in contrast to Athena's and Hera's intense hatred toward them. The unconditional and unvarying partisanship of these three goddesses is otherwise unmotivated: no reason for it, other than Paris' rejection of Athena and Hera and choice of Aphrodite as the most beautiful, is anywhere mentioned. Yet the *Iliad* does not tell this story, which was developed in the cyclical epic known as the *Cypria*; it would make sense, as Reinhardt observed, only as an introduction to the story of the fall of Troy, and since that fall is not actually the story the poem is telling, the poem has no direct use for it. On the other hand, just as the deserved fall of Troy occurs symbolically, or proleptically, within the *Iliad*, so the story of the judgment of Paris is, as it were, assumed throughout in the conflict between the Olympians. The transformation of story into structural 'situation' is exemplified also in the contrasts between Hector and Paris in Books 3 and 6 and Hector and Polydamas in Book 18. These contrasts reflect dramatically a story not developed in the poem, but elsewhere associated with the destiny of Troy—a story about the good and bad brothers who were respectively the blessing and bane of their city. Such transformations of traditional stories and story patterns are frequent in the *Iliad* and are one of Homer's characteristic ways of exploiting the mythological tradition behind the poem.[29]

The *Iliad* looks back to a heroic age that had long since vanished and that its original audience knew had vanished. Whether or not earlier poets in the oral tradition had endowed the heroes whose imperishable glory and timeless actions they celebrated with the quality of transitoriness that informs the *Iliad*, there is throughout the poem a structural tension between the vivid, present immediacy of the narrative and the distance which separates the race of heroes from Homer's (and our) own era. This distance is evident in similes that move from the world of the poem to that of its audiences' or readers' daily lives; in occasional references to Ajax or Hector easily hurling a rock so heavy that two men 'today' could barely lift it; in the description of the shield of Achilles at 18.478–608, which refers outside the poetic world of which the shield itself is part, setting that

[29] For a far-reaching study of how the *Iliad* attains not only narrative resonance but metaphysical depth by its exploitation of traditional mythology—in this case, the traditional mythology associated with Thetis—see Slatkin (1991).

world in a 'continuity of life' that actually seems to have passed it by;[30] and most powerfully at 12.10–35, where, in the midst of the fighting, the implied narrator comments how, after the sack of Troy and the Greeks' departure, Poseidon and Apollo restored the shore to its pristine appearance by utterly leveling the wall the Greeks had toiled to build and beneath which both armies had fought and died. Only in this passage does the word *hêmitheoi*, 'demigods,' occur to describe characters in the poem—the same word Hesiod uses in *Works and Days* 160 to distinguish the race of heroes from the men of his own day. In this passage, the implied narrator looks back at a past heroic age in much the same way in which his description of the shield of Achilles sets the hero's brilliant deeds and the Trojan War as a whole in an ironic perspective that makes them intensely affecting.[31] Such a perspective is a structural feature of the *Iliad* that infuses its creative transformation of traditional mythology with added meaning. The result is that meditation on death and on the tragic limitations of the human condition—for even the greatest heroes—which is distinctive and characteristic of the poem.

[30] Reinhardt (1961) 405–406.

[31] See Bowra (1964) for other examples of epic poetry describing 'events so staggering [that they] can only have been carried out by a superior breed of men' (26), and for discussion of the relation between the society of the poet and his audience and that of his heroes.

Stephen V. Tracy

THE STRUCTURES OF THE *ODYSSEY*

Works of art do not occur randomly. They are created.[1] Their creators dispose their material in such a way that it usually exhibits some organization or pattern, such as balance or symmetry, to take but one example. This, to put it in the simplest terms, is largely what I mean by structure.[2] In the case of poetry, the use of structuring devices doubtless both aids the poet in shaping or, in some cases surely, in controlling his material and certainly guides the audience in apprehending it. Form and meaning tend to cohere; the structure, in short, will often reinforce the meaning by throwing emphasis on what is important. At the same time, poets tend to exploit a variety of structures and sometimes seem to take delight in employing more than one at the same time. To cite an excellent example from Latin poetry—it is well-known that Vergil has organized the books of the *Aeneid* so that relatively calm books, the odd numbered ones, alternate with more emotionally charged books, the even numbered ones. The work also falls into two halves that show a fair amount of parallelism and into a tripartite structure of three groups of four books. Homer too uses, as one might expect, a variety of structures, sometimes in combination. The following essay seeks to delineate some of the more important ones; it obviously makes no claim to offer a complete structural analysis of the poem. That is an unattainable goal.

[1] There can be little question that the Homeric epics are the products of a living oral tradition (A. B. Lord, 1960 and 1991). The progressive creation/fixation of the texts is the subject of much discussion which it is not my place to rehearse here (see Nagy, 1992, 17–60). However the text that we have came into being, my assumption is that it exhibits a careful organization and essential unity. This is in marked contrast to the analytic approach to Homer that has dominated much of European, especially German, scholarship. On its affect on approaches to structural studies of the *Odyssey*, see Hölscher (1991) 415–422.

[2] Critics interested in structure focus on 'the internal dynamics of a literary work.' See the article on structure in Preminger and Brogan (1993) 1222–1224, esp. 1222 and the bibliography there. On the importance of the disposition of the material in the *Odyssey*, Kitto (1966) 116–152. Also to be consulted are the sensible remarks of Rutherford (1985) 133–134 on structure in the Homeric epics.

Some Common Structural Patterns in the Odyssey

Ring composition

Ring composition that has the shape a b c, c b a occurs frequently and appears to be a device which derives from the habits of ordinary speech.[3] One tends to respond to a series of questions by picking up with that asked last and replying in reverse order. An excellent example occurs in book 11 lines 171 to 203. There in conversation with his mother in the underworld Odysseus asks her about her death, about his father, about his son, and finally about his wife.

τίς νύ σε κὴρ ἐδάμασσε τανηλεγέος θανάτοιο;
ἦ δολιχὴ νοῦσος ἦ Ἄρτεμις ἰοχέαιρα
οἷς ἀγανοῖς βελέεσσιν ἐποιχομένη κατέπεφνεν;
εἰπὲ δέ μοι πατρός τε καὶ υἱέος, ὃν κατέλειπον,
ἢ ἔτι πὰρ κείνοισιν ἐμὸν γέρας, ἦέ τις ἤδη
ἀνδρῶν ἄλλος ἔχει, ἐμὲ δ' οὐκέτι φασὶ νέεσθαι.
εἰπὲ δέ μοι μνηστῆς ἀλόχου βουλήν τε νόον τε,
ἠὲ μένει παρὰ παιδὶ καὶ ἔμπεδα πάντα φυλάσσει
ἦ ἤδη μιν ἔγημεν Ἀχαιῶν ὅς τις ἄριστος;

What bane of terrible death overcame you?
A long illness or did Artemis rejoicing in her arrows
coming strike you down with her gentle darts?
Tell me of my father and son whom I left behind.
Is my honor still with them or does some other
man have it since all claim that I will no longer return?
Tell me of my wedded wife, her will and intention.
Does she remain by her child and guard everything steadfastly
or has some other, best of the Achaeans, already married her?[4]

In responding she takes his questions in exactly the reverse order: wife, son, father, and lastly her own death which receives thereby strong emphasis:

καὶ λίην κείνη γε μένει τετληότι θυμῷ
σοῖσιν ἐνὶ μεγάροισιν· ὀϊζυραὶ δέ οἱ αἰεὶ
φθίνουσιν νύκτες τε καὶ ἤματα δάκρυ χεούσῃ.
σὸν δ' οὔ πώ τις ἔχει καλὸν γέρας, ἀλλὰ ἕκηλος
Τηλέμαχος τεμένεα νέμεται καὶ δαῖτας ἐΐσας

[3] The presence of repetition of ideas and themes (or their opposites) in this pattern constitutes ring composition. See the discussions of ring composition and bibliography in Gaisser (1969) 3–5 and in Stanley (1993) 6–9.
[4] The translations throughout are my own.

δαίνυται, ἃς ἐπέοικε δικασπόλον ἄνδρ᾽ ἀλεγύνειν·
πάντες γὰρ καλέουσι. πατὴρ δὲ σὸς αὐτόθι μίμνει
ἀγρῷ, οὐδὲ πόλινδε κατέρχεται· οὐδέ οἱ εὐναὶ
δέμνια καὶ χλαῖναι καὶ ῥήγεα σιγαλόεντα,
ἀλλ᾽ ὅ γε χεῖμα μὲν εὕδει ὅθι δμῶες ἐνὶ οἴκῳ
ἐν κόνι ἄγχι πυρός, κακὰ δὲ χροῒ εἵματα εἷται·
αὐτὰρ ἐπὴν ἔλθῃσι θέρος τεθαλυῖά τ᾽ ὀπώρη,
πάντῃ οἱ κατὰ γουνὸν ἀλωῆς οἰνοπέδοιο
φύλλων κεκλιμένων χθαμαλαὶ βεβλήαται εὐναί·
ἔνθ᾽ ὅ γε κεῖτ᾽ ἀχέων, μέγα δὲ φρεσὶ πένθος ἀέξει
σὸν νόστον ποθέων· χαλεπὸν δ᾽ ἐπὶ γῆρας ἱκάνει.
οὕτω γὰρ καὶ ἐγὼν ὀλόμην καὶ πότμον ἐπέσπον·
οὔτ᾽ ἐμέ γ᾽ ἐν μεγάροισιν ἐΰσκοπος ἰοχέαιρα
οἷς ἀγανοῖς βελέεσσιν ἐποιχομένη κατέπεφνεν,
οὔτε τις οὖν μοι νοῦσος ἐπήλυθεν, ἥ τε μάλιστα
τηκεδόνι στυγερῇ μελέων ἐξείλετο θυμόν·
ἀλλά με σός τε πόθος σά τε μήδεα, φαίδιμ᾽ Ὀδυσσεῦ,
σή τ᾽ ἀγανοφροσύνη μελιηδέα θυμὸν ἀπηύρα.

Truly she abides with enduring heart
in your home and bitter nights always
wear her down and days too, weeping.
No one yet has your fine honor; rather, secure
Telemachus disposes your holdings and feasts fine
feasts, such as befits a ruling lord to care about.
All call on him. Your father abides out there
in the field and does not come to town nor does he have
beds with frames, spreads, and shiny sheets;
in the winter that man sleeps in the house where
the slaves do, in ash near the fire, and wears dirty clothes.
But when summer and verdant spring come,
indiscriminately along the flat land of the vineyard
beds of piled leaves are thrown on the ground for him.
There he lies in pain and great suffering grows in his heart
longing for your return. Harsh old age is on him.
So too did I perish and meet my end.
Neither did the archeress rejoicing in her arrows coming
strike me down in the house with her gentle darts
nor did some disease come on me, which especially
with hateful withering took the breath from my limbs.
No, desire for you, your counsels, and your dearness,
brilliant Odysseus, took the sweet life from me.

Odysseus has been solicitous to ask her first about herself. We may well suspect that she in reply speaks of his wife first out of kindness because she knows his eagerness to learn of Penelope. In any case, it is not any sense of modesty which forbids her to speak of herself first. Rather her response carefully builds up to and, thus, emphasizes the suffering that his absence has caused, particularly to his parents. His father grieving for Odysseus' return has retreated to the solitude of the country (195–196), while longing for him has actually killed her (202–203). The structure emphasizes the point and, as harsh as it may be, seems designed to impress on Odysseus the importance of his own return home.

Larger stretches of the narrative also reveal careful ring composition at the thematic level. A disclaimer, however, is necessary before proceeding. Although there is controversy about the book divisions as we have them, both about when and by whom they were made, there is no doubt that the poem falls into sections that the book divisions often reflect.[5] I will therefore for convenience, and because I know no other way (practically speaking) to do it, refer to the books of the *Odyssey*. The 434 lines on the bow of Odysseus contained in our book 21 are arranged in a concentric ring. The focus of this section of the poem is on the bow and the stringing of it. The passage forms a unit that begins with Penelope going to fetch the bow and ends with Odysseus still in disguise stringing it. The structure may be laid out as follows:

a. Penelope and the bow (1–79)
b. Eumaios brings the bow to the suitors and is rebuked. (80–100)
c. Telemachus (101–139)
d. Leodes and Antinoos (140–187)
  The Recognition (188–244)
d. Eurymachos and Antinoos (245–272)
c. Odysseus (273–358)
b. Eumaios brings the bow to the beggar amidst rebukes. (359–379)
  [Eurykleia and Philoitios lock the hall.] (380–392)
a. Odysseus with the bow (393–434)

The ring composition of this section is unmistakable. It is also marked on the verbal level at the opening and close by identical phrases used of the actions of Penelope as she sent the key home (ἧκε . . . ἄντα τιτυσκομένη 47–48) and of Odysseus as he shot the arrow (ἧκε . . . ἄντα τιτυσκόμενος 420–421).[6] Since, as a practical matter, Eumaios is needed to carry the bow to the beggar, the book centers (188–244)

[5] See Heubeck et al. (1988) 33–48, for the view that the divisions pre-date Aristarchus and Stanley (1993) 249–293 for the argument that they are early, perhaps of the sixth century.
[6] See further Tracy (1990) 123–124.

on Odysseus' use of the scar to reveal himself to his two loyal servants, Eumaios and Philoitios, whose help he will shortly require. The importance of this short scene is thus emphasized. Moreover, the recognitions have a crucial function to play in the second half of the poem; through them Odysseus re-establishes himself in his various roles to the people on Ithaca. The major ones are recounted at some length, as for example the recognition with Telemachus (16.172–320), with Eurykleia (19.357–502), Penelope (23.1–240), and Laertes (24.219–360). This one necessarily must be told quite briefly, so the poet has made it central to the structure as a means of underlining its importance.

Tripartite structures

Narrative sections often reveal a tripartite structure, which is frequently another (simpler) type of ring composition since the second of the three parts is inevitably framed by the other two.[7] The account of Odysseus' arrival at his palace (17.166–491), for example, is surrounded by passages arranged in a ring that depict Penelope. She hears predictions that Odysseus will return and wishes that it would be so (17.157–165, 525–540). Moreover, she requests news of Odysseus in each section and is rebuffed initially, in the first by Telemachus (44–51) and in the second by Odysseus himself (544–573). Penelope's fixed position in the palace has been established from the opening book. Indeed, she and the palace have become one for the audience and for Odysseus, at once a goal and a symbol of the steadfast quality of the house and their union. Her presence in the narrative at this point framing his return, just as the poet frames him visually in the door of his palace as he enters it (339–341), is very satisfying. Artistically, we have here a variation on the type of a picture contained within a picture.

The next book, by almost a mirror technique, features Penelope at the center of a tripartite structure as she appears before the suitors and beguiles gifts from them (18.158–303). Just as she tricks the suitors, so on each side of her we now see Odysseus besting the suitors and their minions (1–157, 304–428). These side panels have parallel development—in the first section of each Odysseus receives

[7] See J. L. Myres' attempt to analyze the entire poem as a series of triptychs: (1952) 1–19.

abuse from a 'follower of the suitors (Iros, Melantho), deals with one of the ringleaders (Antinoos, Eurymachos), and gets the better of them. In the second part the suitor Amphinomos behaves in a civilized manner (120–157, 412–428).'[8] The narratives of books 17 and 18 thus play off against one another to emphasize effectively husband and wife, the two protagonists who will be brought face-to-face next in the narrative, during their tête-à-tête before the fireside in book 19. There exists no better illustration of the poet's ability to manipulate the disposition of his narrative elements and to exploit simple structural devices to excellent effect.

Structures that Inform the Poem as a Whole

Six-part division

Homer, like Vergil who probably copied him, was the master of combining structures. There is no doubt that the poem falls both into two halves as well as into tetrads, six groups of four books. Indeed, it is perhaps easiest to keep the poem in mind by noting that the latter arrangement is thematic. The first four books deal with Telemachus, portray him beginning to come of age and, with Athena's help, making a journey to Pylos and Sparta in search of news of his father. Real news is not to be had, but he learns from Nestor at Pylos and from Helen and Menelaos at Sparta what sort of man his father was. By learning about his father, Telemachus in reality learns about himself. That one's father is an important determiner of one's identity is true in most societies, but especially true of the ancient Greek world, for, in their naming system, a young man was named using his father's name; he was always x, son of x. His identity, then, was explicitly bound up with that of his father. Telemachus' journey in short becomes one of maturing and of learning about himself.[9] These books serve the added function of introducing us to the situation on Ithaca. We see the unruly behavior of the suitors, the desperation of Penelope, and naturally become aware of the great need for Odysseus at home.

---

[8] Tracy (1990) 105.

[9] For the formulaic ways in which Telemachus is characterized, see R.P. Martin (1993).

In book 5 we meet Odysseus for the first time marooned on Calypso's island, but longing for home. Books 5 to 8 take Odysseus out of the land of his adventures to the island of the Phaeacians, his last stopping point before coming home. Having escaped the attractive, as well as dangerous demi-goddess Calypso, he now encounters the innocent, but, by this very token, even more dangerous, princess Nausicaa who has marriage much on her mind. It is an extremely delicate situation which the poet develops fully by exploiting the folk-motif of the contest for the hand of the princess. In essence, Odysseus defeats the Phaeacians in an athletic contest and wins her hand, but he can not complete the final part of the story because he has a wife and child at home.

In books 9 to 12 Odysseus tells his adventures since leaving Troy to the Phaeacians, thus identifying himself to them. He takes over the role of the singer. Since singers have the power to confer what heroes want above all else, namely *kleos*, fame on the lips of men,[10]—the only kind of immortality that counts for men in Homeric poetry—the fact that Odysseus becomes the singer and sings his own song takes on powerful significance. He confers *kleos* on himself, that is to say, by singing he guarantees his own survival. In a real sense his narrative also establishes his identity for the other audiences of the poem, namely the present hearers and, in a most important way, himself. It is not inaccurate to claim that Homer here portrays via a concrete example what, thanks to relatively recent psychological theory, we can characterize as the notion that if a person can talk about his past, he has come to understand it.

After a leisurely beginning in which the poet sets the stage in the initial books, the pace quickens and tautens right through the recital of the adventures in books 9 to 12. Such a pace cannot be maintained. To begin the second half of the poem, the poet then deliberately varies things by slowing the action. Books 13 to 16 bring Odysseus and Telemachus back to the Ithacan countryside. Athena returns to the fore to aid Odysseus; this she does largely by altering his appearance to that of an old beggar. Odysseus encounters the swineherd Eumaios whom he finds to be completely loyal and in book 16 is reunited with his son. Together they begin to plot the overthrow of the suitors.

Books 17 to 20 at first continue the leisurely pace, but the tension

[10] G. Nagy (1979) 16–17, 317–319.

of the situation, the inevitable doom of the suitors, soon grips the hearer. Odysseus and Telemachus go to the palace separately. In these books the theme of the abuse of a guest is emphasized, indeed in three of the four books the disguised Odysseus is actually struck by one of the suitors. The first book focuses on Odysseus as he enters his palace for the first time in twenty years, the next portrays Penelope besting the suitors by beguiling gifts from them; these carefully prepare for the emotionally charged night meeting between the two of them in the nineteenth book. The next book returns to the suitors to give us one last portrait of their blindness to the situation. The supreme irony that results from the audience's knowledge that the suitors unknowingly abuse Odysseus accounts for much of the appeal that these books undeniably exert.

The final section of the poem has four discrete subjects—the stringing of the bow (book 21), the slaughter of the suitors (book 22), the reunion with Penelope (book 23), and the necessary wrap-up, viz. the reunion with Laertes and the resolution with the families of the suitors (book 24). The final book brings the poem efficiently to an end. Some have found the ending abrupt or somewhat unsatisfying.[11] Indeed, the last book may have the feel of a hasty tidying up—this is a matter of taste—but there is no question that the reunion with Laertes and the resolution of the quarrel with the families of the suitors is an integral part of this poem's design.[12] For one thing, Odysseus' identity can not be complete without the reunion with his father. Furthermore, he can not simply kill, no matter how justified his action may be, the sons of all the leading families in Ithaca and the surrounding territory without expecting some retaliation from their families. Ancient custom demanded that they react. This problem must be dealt with, especially since the issue is specifically raised at book 23 lines 118 to 122, or else the poem will be intolerably incomplete.[13]

Who is to say, however, that Homer has not shown good judgment in bringing his story rapidly to an end? The climax of the work came at the close of book 21, the stunning moment when Odysseus strings the bow and plucks it. And, as Homer remarks, 'it sang forth beautifully like a swallow' (21.411). There is a lesser

[11] Eustathios on 23.296 reports that the Alexandrian scholars Aristophanes and Aristarchus regarded this verse as the end (πέρας) of the poem. Page (1955) 101–136, in a characteristically vigorous attack, styles the end of the poem '*The Continuation*.'

[12] See, for example, Stanford (1965) 5–20 and Wender (1978).

[13] Tracy (1990) 140–143.

crescendo in book 23, when Penelope turns the tables on Odysseus with her deceit about their marriage bed (23.177–180). It is somehow especially fitting that she outwits him; she alone, we are made to understand clearly, is a true match for him. After these great moments a serious anticlimax could be avoided only by winding up the remaining threads rapidly.

Division into halves

The first half brings Odysseus in the narrative from Troy through his adventures to Phaeacia. The second half brings him home to Ithaca and to his rightful place in the palace. Almost exactly in the middle dividing the poem is book 11, the crucial journey to the underworld. The poet has gone to some trouble to place book 11 as close to the mid-point as possible. Indeed, I would contend that one of the primary purposes for Odysseus' narration of his past adventures to the Phaeacians in books 9 to 12 is precisely to gain this position for the account of the underworld. Why?

Conquering death constitutes logically the most difficult labor a hero can perform; thus Homer has made it central in the structure as well as in thematic importance. It is perhaps accurate to say of Odysseus that he does not conquer death by going to the underworld so much as that he symbolically dies and is reborn. In any case, he learns there what it means to be a mortal, i.e. that death is inevitable, and he also experiences the shadowy, insubstantial nature of what awaits in the underworld. It is not insensitive, then, to see the first half of the poem as a journey of self-knowledge for Odysseus in preparation for the second half in which, having gained that knowledge, he can re-establish his identity to the people on Ithaca who, one and all, have given him up for dead. And on the narratological level, of course, he does return to Ithaca almost directly from the land of the dead.

Not only is the journey to the underworld central, Homer has carefully marked Odysseus' final voyage home, with which the thirteenth book opens, as a second beginning. He has done this on a verbal level by recalling in lines 5 to 6 and again (as that journey comes to an end when the Phaeacian ship actually reaches Ithaca) in lines 90 to 92 of book 13 phrases from lines 1 to 4 of book 1.[14] Note

[14] On this point, see Kahane (1992) 120–121.

especially how παλιμπλαγχθέντα (5), μάλα πολλὰ πέπονθας (6), μάλα πολλὰ πάθ' ἄλγεα ὃν κατὰ Θυμὸν (90), and ἐπεπόνθει (92) specifically echo the themes of wandering and suffering sounded in the initial lines of the poem.

> Ἄνδρα μοι ἔννεπε, Μοῦσα, πολύτροπον, ὃς μάλα πολλὰ
> πλάγχθη ἐπεὶ Τροίης ἱερὸν πτολίεθρον ἔπερσε·
> πολλῶν δ' ἀνθρώπων ἴδεν ἄστεα καὶ νόον ἔγνω,
> πολλὰ δ' ὅ γ' ἐν πόντῳ πάθεν ἄλγεα ὃν κατὰ θυμόν . . .
>
> Tell me Muse of the man of many turns, who wandered
> very much after he sacked the holy citadel of Troy.
> Many men's cities he saw and minds he knew,
> many the pains on the sea he suffered in his own heart . . .

There can be no doubt that whoever made the division of the poem at this point did so in response to these clear textual indications. There is here a new beginning that points clearly to a conception on the part of the artist of two halves. Another way, then, to look at the poem is to realize that Odysseus journeys from Troy, from the killing fields, as it were, to home where he must re-establish himself as king. The journey covers roughly the first half of the poem; the re-establishing himself as lord of his realm the second half. The *nostos*, the return home, for a warrior, perhaps for everyman, is hard, almost impossible. In some sense you can't go home again; things are never the same, but this is especially true for a soldier who has been gone for many years. By placing the underworld at the center of the journey, Homer seems to say that the only way you can accomplish it is to die and be reborn, to go through hell. One has the overwhelming sense that he knew war and its aftermath first-hand.

Other overarching designs

In the work as a whole, there are certainly other overarching structures and designs. For example, there is a grand tripartite arrangement on the level of basic subject matter. The first four books deal with Telemachus and the twenty-fourth deals importantly, if not solely, with Laertes; these books surround the others, the major part of the poem, which focus on Odysseus. The hero, then, is situated structurally between his son and his father, the two parameters of his existence. This arrangement underlines the theme of fathers and sons which plays a fundamental role, as we have noted above, in the poem. The son of a hero, in the epic mind-set, should grow up to be worthy of his father. Thus Orestes, who avenged the murder of his father, is several times held up as an example to Telemachus in the first four books (1.298–302, 3.304–316, 4.546–547).

Baths cleanse; the act of bathing, then, can easily take on symbolic meaning, e.g. renewal and purification. For example, Aphrodite, as Demodokos tells the story in book 8, caught *in flagrante* with her lover Ares, returns home to Paphos on Cyprus where the Graces bathe and anoint her with oil (8.362–364). The poet also associates baths with feeding guests, often newly arrived (4.48–49, 10.364, 450, 17.87–88). And Calypso washes Odysseus before he sails away on his raft (5.264). While not heavily emphasized, the baths mark these events. In addition, each of the family members of Odysseus undergoes a bath from which or after which he is transformed. The poet explicitly avails himself of the symbolic power naturally associated with baths by adding in every instance but one a simile or a description of Athena actually transforming the individual in question.

These major baths are carefully placed, both tying the narrative together and marking important junctures in it. Telemachus' bath comes at a point when he has completed the first stage of his journey (3.464–468), Laertes' immediately after his recognition of Odysseus (24.365–367). Odysseus is bathed and transformed just after he has met Nausicaa (6.224–227) and is bathed again just before she bids him farewell (8.449–456). She has posed a real challenge to him, just as Penelope does. Not surprisingly, then, he is also bathed and transformed in preparation for the final recognition scene with his wife (23.153–155). Finally, the motif is used to suggest a parallel between husband and wife; each rejects a bath, Penelope just prior to her appearance before the suitors (18.178–179), Odysseus during his interview with Penelope (19.314, 336–348). Each apparently desires to avoid the transformation inherent in the act. But neither can quite escape it, for Athena puts Penelope to sleep and beautifies her (18.187–196), while Eurykleia recognizes her master as she washes his feet (19.392, 467–475). The bath—even the non-bath—rejuvenates or, in the case of Telemachus, marks his maturation; it also underlines crucial moments facing Odysseus and his family. Hardly anyone else, it appears significant, takes a bath in the poem.

One can see, if one isolates these major baths and what is associated closely with them in the narrative, an extended ring composition of some complexity as follows:

a. Bath of Telemachus (book 3)
  1. Athena (371)
  2. Nestor and his sons (386–387)
  3. Bath and simile (464–469)
  4. Journey (477–497)

b. Bath of Odysseus (book 6)
  1. Encounter with Nausicaa (127–197)
  2. Bath and clothes (224–228)
  3. Transformation by Athena and extended simile (229–235)

  [Second bath (book 8)
    2. Clothes and bath (449–456)
    1. Farewell to Nausicaa (457–468)]

c. Penelope (book 18)
  1. Refuses bath (178–179)
  2. Athena puts her to sleep and transforms her (187–196).
  3. Story about Odysseus at the time of his departure for Troy (257–271)

c. Odysseus (book 19)
  1. Refuses bath (336–348)
  2. Eurykleia washes his feet (386–392, 467–471).
  3. Story about Odysseus, his birth and his scar (393–466)

b. Bath of Odysseus (book 23)
  2/3. Bath/transformation by Athena and extended simile (153–163)[15]
  1. Recognition and reunion with Penelope (166–296)

a. Bath of Laertes (book 24)
  4. Metaphorical journey (345–355)
  3. Bath (365–367)
  1. Transformation by Athena (368–371)
  2. Dolios and his sons (387)

The baths of Odysseus in books 6 and 8 form within the larger ring an inner ring composition with each other; while the two non-baths at the center have their elements arranged parallel to each other.[16]

As the poem ends, the poet naturally returns to the beginning. We return to the palace and Penelope, the place where we started. The twenty-fourth book additionally has some specific responsions

[15] Note that the extended simile here is the same as the one in book 6 (23.157–162 = 6.230–235).

[16] For another overarching ring composition based on the theme of wooing and winning the princess/queen, see Tracy (1990) 139.

with the opening of the poem.[17] It begins with an apparent digression, the trip to the underworld (1–204), just as the poem as a whole began with another apparent digression, the Telemacheia. Moreover, in this final book an assembly in which the relatives of the suitors are in vain advised to give up their wrath against Odysseus motivates Athena to intercede with Zeus (421–471). In the opening two books Athena's intervention with Zeus leads to the thwarting of Poseidon's wrath at Odysseus and eventually to the assembly in book 2. There Telemachus pled in vain with the suitors to give up the siege of his household. Finally, the appearance of Athena disguised as Mentor at the end establishing the truce (24.546–548) recalls her appearance as Mentes at the start (1.105 ff.) to spur Telemachus to action. While there is no fully developed ring composition shaping the entire epic, these thematic responsions/echoes at the extremities of the poem do suggest a ring pattern that brings it in a satisfying way full circle.[18]

A dominant structural pattern: parallelism

If there is any one dominant structural mode in the *Odyssey*, it is parallel or balanced structures of the shape a b c, a b c. Indeed, one can observe between the three tetrads of the first half of the poem and the three of the second certain specific thematic parallels:

a. Books 1–4
- Ithaca
- Athena and Telemachus
- Suitors' failure to observe proper modes of hospitality
- Telemachus' journey to Pylos and Sparta
- The suitors plot the death of Telemachus.

b. Books 5–8
- Journey to the palace of Alkinoos
- Conflict/contest with the youngmen
- Latent marriage contest for the princess
- Identity of Odysseus unknown

c. Books 9–12
- Odysseus identifies himself and becomes the singer.
- Tells his adventures to the Phaeacians

---

[17] See Bertman (1968) 115–123, esp. 121–122.

[18] There is a thoroughgoing responsion between the first and last books of the *Iliad* that has often been noted. S. E. Bassett indeed has argued for a general structural similarity between the *Iliad* and *Odyssey* (1919) 557–563.

Wins the support of Queen Arete
Underworld/mother/heroes of Troy

a. Books 13 to 16
Ithaca
Athena and Odysseus
Eumaios' exemplary hospitality
Telemachus' return from Sparta and Pylos
Odysseus and Telemachus plan the death of the suitors.

b. Books 17–20
Journey to the palace of Odysseus
Fight with beggar and conflict with the suitors
Latent contest for the hand of the queen
Identity of Odysseus unknown

c. Books 21–24
Odysseus identifies himself to the suitors and becomes the bowman.[19]
Wins the confidence of his queen
Recounts his adventures to Penelope
Underworld/heroes of Troy/father

These correspondences do occur in the text. It should not be surprising nor a matter sparking incredulity that a storyteller, especially one working in a tradition that employs frequent type-scenes as a device of composition, could create these thematic resemblances between the larger parts of his narrative.[20] They, afterall, naturally emerge from and complement the technique of recurring narrative patterns. These patterns themselves, moreover, reinforce one's sense of a story told with multiple parallels. For example, children regularly appear in the tale before their parents. This is not just the case with Telemachus and Odysseus, it is almost invariably so. Peisistratos, the son of Nestor, is introduced before his father, Nausicaa before her parents, Antinoos (and all the suitors) before his father Eupeithes (and the other parents), Melanthios and Melantho before their father Dolios, and, capping the series, Odysseus before Laertes.

Female figures who first pose a threat and then help the hero are another staple of this story. The major ones, of course, are Calypso, Nausicaa/Arete, and Circe; but, Athena in book 13, Eurykleia in book 19, and Penelope in books 19 to 21 also fit this mold. The

---

[19] See Rutherford (1985) 141–144, for a sensitive discussion of the parallels between Odysseus' self-identification in books 9 and 21.

[20] For an attempt to discern a single thematic pattern, repeated in rich variety, as lying behind much of the poem, see Powell (1977).

poet also exploits this pattern in Helen's description of her encounter with Odysseus who had stolen into Troy in disguise to spy (4.244–258). Though she recognized him, she did not give him away, but helped him. Likewise, a narrative strategy that includes numerous doublets contributes strongly to this feeling of recurrent parallels. This is most easily perceived in the case of character doubles such as Calypso and Circe, Mentor and Mentes, the two mother figures Antikleia and Eurykleia, the bards Phemios and Demodokos, the loyal servants Eumaios and Philoitios, the traitorous Melanthios and Melantho, and the leading suitors Antinoos and Eurymachos, to specify some of the most obvious.[21]

Moreover, in the extensive narrative dealing with Telemachus and then with Odysseus, Homer has created many thematic parallels between father and son. They often have the same or similar experiences. One telling example—Eurykleia is said to have been nurse to each of them (Telemachus: 1.435, Odysseus: 19.482–483). Clearly the poet has done this to reinforce the audience's perception that Telemachus is truly his father's son. How much he has become his father's equal is shown to us during the contest of the bow towards the end of the poem (21.128–129) where Odysseus must nod Telemachus off, else on the fourth attempt he would have strung Odysseus' great hunting bow. Odysseus, of course, strings the bow with consummate ease, but none of the others save Telemachus can even come close.

I confine myself here to noting some parallels between Telemachus in books 1 to 4 and Odysseus in books 5 to 8. Of course, the general situation of the two at the start of the respective sections is the same. A god (Athena, Hermes) arrives to set events moving. Telemachus sits among the suitors despondent; Odysseus weeps at the shore alone. After a somewhat emotional interchange with the mistress of the house (Penelope, Calypso), the hero departs on a journey. In each case the woman does not want him to go.[22] Once on their way, these parallels cannot, I think, be pursued very fruitfully. The journeys and their purposes differ strikingly. Still, certain parallels of a specific nature are notable. Athena enhances the appearance of each so that the people admire him as he goes to the assembly (2.12–

[21] For a thorough discussion of doublets, including thematic and narrative doublets, see Fenik (1974) 133–232.

[22] See also Bertman (1966) 18–19, 24 fig. 7.

13, 8.17–20). Telemachus weeps and covers his face when he hears his father's name (4.114–115); Odysseus does likewise as he listens to Demodokos' song about himself and Achilles (8.83–86). Both hear accounts of the wooden horse on Troy's final night (4.265–290, 8.492–520). Alkinoos' palace makes a gleaming impression on Odysseus just as Menelaos' did on Telemachus (7.84–85 = 4.45–46). While in the overall story of the poem the parallels between father and son suggest their essential similarity, these parallels in the opening books surely are meant to underline the audience's perception that Odysseus in books 5 to 8 has experiences much like his son's in books 1 to 4. Indeed, he undergoes a series of encounters that bear a striking resemblance to the growing pains of a young man. Symbolically reborn at the close of book 5 (see p. 378 below), Odysseus meets a marriageable young maiden in book 6, her parents in 7, and bests the young men in the contest for her hand in book 8.

Let us now consider the parallel structure of a single episode, namely Odysseus' underworld experience (11.51–627). Odysseus recounts his meetings with six figures in the underworld and lists others briefly. The poet separates them with the intermezzo; otherwise they are arranged in two parallel sets of three (the first group in ascending order of length, the second in descending).[23]

a. Elpenor (lines 51–83) 33 lines
   Odysseus speaks first.
   Elpenor speaks of his own humble death and asks for burial, making his appeal more poignant by reminding Odysseus of Penelope and Telemachus.

b. Tiresias (90–151) 62 lines
   Tiresias speaks first and asks how it is that Odysseus has come.
   Speaks of the situation at Odysseus' home
   Speaks of Odysseus' future

c. Antikleia (152–224) 73 lines
   Antikleia speaks first.
   Odysseus attempts in vain to embrace her.
   Died because of Odysseus

d. Catalog of Women (225–327)
   Intermezzo (328–384)

a. Agamemnon (387–446) 80 lines
   Odysseus speaks first.

---

[23] Adapted from Tracy (1990) 72–73.

Agamemnon relates his own unseemly death and mentions Odysseus' wife and son.

b. Achilles (467–540) 74 lines
   Achilles speaks first and asks how it is that Odysseus has come.
   Wants to know the situation at his own home
   Odysseus relates the past at Troy.

c. Ajax (543–565) 23 lines
   Ajax stands off silent and so Odysseus must speak.
   Odysseus attempts in vain to converse.
   Died because of Odysseus

d. Catalog of Men (568–627)

The first three spirits tell him about his personal future and his family; the second three are figures from his past, who teach him by their actions—they care only about what is going on in the upper world—that death, a wraithlike shadowy state, holds nothing for a hero.[24] Odysseus gains from this experience in the underworld the determination to go on in spite of the obstacles. By contrast, before it he had been increasingly discouraged and, upon being blown back from Ithaca to Aiolos' island, had even contemplated suicide (10.51). After it, even though at the end completely alone, he clings for dear life to the fig tree above Charybdis (12.431–441).

Similarly, the adventures recounted by Odysseus in books 9 to 12, although they reveal more than one structure, have fundamentally a parallel design.[25] After the sack of the Kikonian city (a doublet of Troy), these adventures fall into two sets of four arranged around a core of ring composition (Circe/underworld/Circe) as follows:[26]

a. Lotos eaters
   Eastern or orientalizing motif
   Temptation to forget home
   Odysseus takes his companions away by force.

b. Polyphemos
   Monster in a cave
   Six companions are devoured.
   Odysseus thinks of using his sword, but realizes he must outwit the monster.

---

[24] See Griffin (1980) 100–101.

[25] Following a suggestion made by C. H. Whitman (1958) 288–289, most have seen a ring structure in this account—see Niles (1978) 46–60; Most (1989a); and Garrison (1989) 117–123.

[26] Adapted from Tracy (1990) 55–56.

c. Aiolos
   Island of the wind god
   Odysseus sleeps.
   Companions disobey Odysseus.

d. Laestrygonians
   Cannibalistic giants
   Doublet of the Cyclops
   Odysseus and his crew alone survive.

Circe/underworld/Circe

a. Sirens
   Eastern motif
   Temptation to forget home
   Odysseus' companions forcibly remove him.

b. Scylla (and Charybdis)
   Monster in a cave
   Six companions are devoured.
   Odysseus arms to kill Scylla, but can't even see her.

c. Helios
   Isle of the sun god
   Odysseus sleeps.
   Companions disobey Odysseus.

d. Charybdis (and Scylla)
   Odysseus alone escapes the storm.
   Odysseus retraces the route to Charybdis.
   Doublet of a sort with Scylla

Calypso

In each set Odysseus is progressively stripped of the outward accoutrements of a hero, namely his men and ships, with the result that at the close of book 12 he faces Charybdis alone desperately riding a spar from his wrecked ship. Each set leads him to a demi-goddess to whom he makes love and from whom ultimately he has difficulty escaping. Both goddesses have strong associations with death.[27]

As to be expected, there are other organizational principles at work here as well. Violent adventures in which lives are lost alternate with non-violent ones. Excepting the underworld, the adventures also occur in groups of three, two that are shorter and one longer; thus, we

[27] On Calypso, whose name signifies concealer or buryer, see just below; that Odysseus encounters Hermes on his way to Circe (10.277 ff.) assures her underworldly associations. Hermes is also (be it noted) associated with Calypso; he is sent by Zeus at the opening of book 5 to intercede with her on behalf of Odysseus. For more on Circe's and Calypso's connections with the underworld, Crane (1988) 15–60.

find the groupings Kikones, Lotos-eaters, Polyphemos; Aiolos, Laestrygonians, Circe; Sirens, Scylla (and Charybdis), and Helios. Since the last three adventures are told twice in the twelfth book, there are six adventures before the underworld and six afterwards. These latter schemes, however, all but ignore the encounter with Charybdis that closes the adventures. They are not then to my mind very persuasive ways to look at the structure of these adventures, for, in coming last, the episode at Charybdis attains a structural as well as thematic importance that needs to be addressed.

Form in the *Odyssey* effectively reinforces the subject matter, for these parallel structures underscore the primary theme of the poem, namely, the parallel journeys of the hero, of his son, and of his father. These journeys lead home to the palace on Ithaca and become in the telling more than geographical in nature. Telemachus' journey is one of growth and self-discovery, Odysseus' one of finding out what it means to be a mortal, and Laertes' one of reinvolvement in life. Telemachus breaks the apron strings exerted by his mother and his nurse Eurykleia by physically leaving the palace. Odysseus and Laertes both symbolically die and are reborn on their journeys.

Indeed, each one of Odysseus' journeys involves elements of death and rebirth. Most obviously the journey home from Troy via the underworld in the eleventh book carries this connotation. When, moreover, he arrives at the land of the Phaeacians at the close of the fifth book, he has escaped Calypso (the buryer) with the aid of Leukothea (the white goddess). He emerges from the sea naked. The symbolism could not be clearer. Furthermore, when Odysseus finally comes home aboard the Phaeacian ship at the opening of book 13, a deep sleep holds him, and, lest we miss the symbolism, the poet specifically describes the sleep as 'most like death' (θανάτῳ ἄγχιστα ἐοικώς, 80). He arrives on Ithaca at daybreak (93–95) and is deposited near an olive tree and cave (102–103)—all symbols of life and rebirth. Finally, even the short journey that he makes from Eumaios' hut in the countryside to his own palace at lines 200 ff. of book 17 has unmistakable elements of a journey to the underworld. Evening approaches as Eumaios and Odysseus depart (191). They meet a darkling figure, Melanthios, on the road (212–253)[28] and arrive at a palace in front of whose gates they encounter a dog (291).

This motif has been so consistently present in Odysseus' journeys

[28] Melanthios' name derives from the word *melas* meaning 'black.'

that when we encounter Laertes' momentary faint at the realization that Odysseus is home and his immediate recovery (24.345–349) we readily perceive it as a mini-death and rebirth. Laertes is then rejuvenated by Athena (367–369)[29] and takes the lead in facing the relatives of the suitors, in fact slaying their ringleader Eupeithes, father of Antinoos (523–525). His 'journey' has been less a physical one than an emotional one, from total discouragement and lack of involvement in the affairs of his family to total involvement, indeed leadership, as head of the household. In fact, as he kills the leader of the suitors' relatives, he momentarily displaces his son as leader.

The three heroes together, son, father, and grandfather, armed for battle (24.505–515) mark the fulfillment of these journeys and the poem. It is a striking moment, easy to visualize, tableau-like in affect. Writers have often in discussing the arrangement of the poem sought comparisons from architecture; in particular they liken such scenes to pedimental sculptures of temples.[30] This is highly appropriate. After all, we have a sense at the end of having experienced not chaos, but rather a beautifully-crafted, monumental work of art.[31]

---

[29] The phrase used is 'larger and stouter to look upon.' In short, Athena makes him his most impressive just as she had done for his son in the encounter with Nausicaa and the Phaeacians (6.229–230, 8.19–20) and again in preparation for his reunion with Penelope (23.156–157). Penelope too is transformed in this way by Athena as she prepares to go before the suitors (18.195).

[30] See, for example, Bassett (1919) 563; Myres (1952) 1; and, very recently, R. P. Martin (1993) 239. This comparison to architecture also occurs frequently in German scholarship (Hölscher [1991] 417).

[31] I owe special thanks to Richard Martin and June Allison for their helpful comments on a preliminary draft of this and to Will Batstone for bibliographic advice on modern works discussing structure.

John Peradotto

MODERN THEORETICAL APPROACHES TO HOMER

'Modern' and 'theory' are notoriously imprecise terms. Before attempting to define their use in the present essay, it would be naive not to draw attention to the inevitable impermanence of any study with the word 'modern' in its title. When the present *New Companion* has aged as much as Wace and Stubbings' original *Companion to Homer* now has, what critical shifts will have taken place to render this essay passé, and will the *Iliad* and the *Odyssey* continue to float somehow intact above these sea-changes? Let me insist that any despondency engendered by this eventuality is misplaced, as I hope to show in my discussion of the postmodern condition and its unabashed distrust of the search for permanent verities.[1]

Wace and Stubbings contained no chapter remotely corresponding to the present one. That volume itself had been first conceived, and some of its chapters actually written, more than twenty years before its publication in 1962. During that entire period between conception and publication what would have passed for 'contemporary theory,' at least among the community of classicists, would have been what we call New Criticism and archetypal criticism inspired

[1] There have been many rich and thought-provoking literary studies of Homer with little involvement, at least little *explicit* involvement, in contemporary theory. Regretfully, the present study is constrained by limits of space to take little notice of them. (For twentieth-century critical trends, chiefly Parryism and reactions to it, prior to structuralism, poststructuralism, deconstructionism and postmodernism, see J. P. Holoka's masterful (1991) essay, 'Homer, Oral Poetry, And Comparative Literature: Major Trends and Controversies in Twentieth-Century Criticism.') Neither shall I have much to say of studies that claim a contemporary theoretical approach but do not live up to the claim, 'theory' being in such cases no more than a fashionable overlay for more traditional critical (often New Critical) practice. Neither will I consider studies whose primary focus is narratology, the theory of oral poetry, or myth analysis, all of which involve explicit theory, but which are dealt with elsewhere in this volume. As for those scholars and works actually considered, the present essay makes no attempt to be exhaustive, but rather selective and exemplary of method, providing samples rather than full reviews of arguments which are far too complex for treatment within the limited scope of an essay such as this.

Portions of the present essay are drawn from Peradotto (1990).

by Jungian psychology. But these influences would be all but overshadowed by the most important development in Homeric studies in the twentieth century. For Wace and Stubbings as for most homerists of the period, Milman Parry's investigations of Homer's work as oral poetry, slow to merit much attention or to catch hold in the United States, was now the thing to be looked at, for it seemed to offer a defensive profession the chance of taking a giant step in its aspiration to become a 'hard science' and to forswear the soft belletrism and impressionistic aestheticism that had characterized so much of its literary appreciations. Few literary analysts would be able (or perhaps even willing) to match the way in which C. Whitman, in *Homer and the Heroic Tradition* (1958), blended an appreciation of Parry's findings with the sensitivity to verbal texture, symbol, image, structure, ambiguity, and irony central to the New Criticism. Despite the brilliance with which he managed this, many, if not most, homerists believed the devices designed for the interpretation of written literature simply incompatible with Parry's theory of Homer as oral poetry. Perhaps the most extreme read on the implications of Parry's thesis was expressed by F. Combellack in a 1959 article:

> The hard fact is that in this post-Parry era critics are no longer in a position to distinguish the passages in which Homer is merely using a convenient formula from those in which he has consciously and cunningly chosen *le mot juste*. For all that any critic of Homer can now show, the occasional highly appropriate word may, like the occasional highly inappropriate one, be purely coincidental—part of the law of averages, if you like, in the use of the formulary style.[2]

With varying degrees of emphasis the same attitude taken toward formulaic phraseology was taken also toward the artistic manipulation of traditional *narrative themes*. Since then there have been a number of studies which, without contesting the powerful influence of a traditional style, structure, and set of narratives, still portray a poet in control of that tradition, capable of originality and innovation, to counter the questionable image of a compliant replicator and a frozen tradition.[3] Nevertheless polemics are still prevalent in a clash

---

[2] (1959) 208.

[3] One of the best of the oral theorists, J. M. Foley, while insisting on a performance-based orientation to oral texts, recognizes the potential contribution of contemporary theory (especially Bakhtinian dialogism) to the elucidation of oral texts. He also distinguishes himself from the older Parryites by his awareness of the thorny problematics involved in reconstructing any 'tradition.' See especially Foley (1995) xi–xii.

between those more inclined to espouse the cause of the innovative artist and those more inclined to insist on the sway of tradition.

In the classical community, contemporary debate about what constitutes an appropriate scholarly reading tends to represent it as taking two forms.[4] One faces toward the past and concerns itself with sources, origins, historical considerations. The other faces forward and emphasizes the context and situation of the modern reader. More traditional (or, in the parlance of the opposition, 'reactionary') theories identify with the backward-facing form and look to recover original truth or original authorial intent or original audience response as governing protocols that will yield readings more or less impervious to change. They argue that anything departing from or adding to original authorial intent and original audience reception is an inauthentic, contaminated reading. More contemporary (what the opposition calls 'radical') theories favor the forward facing form that affirms the large part played by the reader in the production of meaning and harbors an abiding skepticism about immutable meanings. They argue that what Gadamer calls the modern reader's 'horizon' is inescapable,[5] that original authorial intent and original audience reception are themselves 'contaminated' reconstructions that simply shift the problem of interpretation to a different (often more inaccessible) level and to different texts, and that the literary artifact leads an unintended ontological afterlife in an unpredictably altered state of its own language and other signs.[6]

This linear, oppositional metaphor of reading is challenged by Robert Scholes, properly, I think. In its place he offers a slightly better one based on the paired notions of centrifugality and centripetality, alerting us nonetheless to the danger it shares with the metaphor of backward- and forward-looking:

> Centripetal reading conceives of a text in terms of an original intention located at the center of that text. Reading done under this rubric will try to reduce the text to this pure core of unmixed intentionality. Centrifugal reading, on the other hand, sees the life of the text as

---

[4] See F. Danker, *A Century of Greco-Roman Philology: Featuring the American Philological Association and the Society of Biblical Literature* (Atlanta, 1988) 218. A. J. Boyle ('Intellectual Pluralism and the Common Pursuit: Ramus Twenty Years,' *Ramus* 20, 1991, 116–18) cautions against the too simplistic view that some have taken of an opposition between 'old philology' and 'new theory.'

[5] H.-G. Gadamer, *Truth and Method*, tr. G. Barden and J. Cumming (New York, 1975; orig. *Wahrheit und Methode*, Tübingen, 1960), 269–74.

[6] See Peradotto (1990) 12–14, and Holoka (1991) 479.

> occurring along its circumference, which is constantly expanding, encompassing new possibilities of meaning. . . . But this is still a two-term or binary system, all too easily shifted into an invidious polarity of centrist conservatives and marginal radicals, reducers and expanders, truth-seekers and sophists, or what you will.[7]

We are conditioned to think of classical philology as defined more by backward-looking or centripetal reading than by the other kind. That is of course far less true of the eighties and nineties than of the period in which Wace and Stubbings was written and published. A profound change has taken place to erode the institutional resistance to centrifugal reading. To be sure, this change was taking place when and even before Wace and Stubbings was published. The difference is that now it is impossible to ignore. We call it the postmodern condition. That is what 'modern' in my title refers to, for I have chosen deliberately to ignore the misleading chronological and historical association of the term 'postmodern.' I have also chosen deliberately to use 'postmodernism' not in a narrow sense to designate one among a variety of contemporary theoretical approaches, but rather as a generic term that focuses on presuppositions, questions, strategies, methods of analysis common to these otherwise different theoretical approaches.[8]

As a condition of reading and thinking, the postmodern condition is not likely soon to disappear, even if, and however often, some new name is conjured up to designate the set of theoretical and epistemological stances that characterize it. Indeed, it may be said always to have been there, but ignored or suppressed. 'Paradoxically,' as J. McGowan has observed,

> most of the materials for a radical questioning can be found in the tradition itself if we look in different places (noncanonical works) or with new eyes at familiar places . . . a Western tradition that now appears more heterogeneous than previously thought even while it appears insufficiently tolerant of (open to) multiplicity. At the very least, postmodernism highlights the multiplication of voices, questions, and conflicts that has shattered what once seemed to be (although it never really was) the placid unanimity of the great tradition and of the West that gloried in it.[9]

---

[7] *Protocols of Reading* (New Haven, 1989) 8.

[8] See Goldhill (1994) for a fine discussion of the losses that result from insisting too resolutely on the discreetness of different theoretical enterprises.

[9] 'Postmodernism' in *The Johns Hopkins Guide to Literary Theory and Criticism*, eds. M. Groden and M. Kreiswirth (Baltimore, 1994) 587.

It is for this reason (and for others I shall mention later), that Homeric studies finds itself not uncomfortably at home in so-called postmodern territory.

It is crucial not to misunderstand what we are talking about. The postmodern condition was brought about by what R. Rorty called the twentieth-century's 'linguistic turn.' Fundamentally, it involves a dismantling of the encoded forms of folk epistemology dominant in what has been called 'Standard Average European' and perhaps in all Indo-European language and thought.[10] In this view, the one postmodernism assails with questions, 'reality,' the 'world,' is composed of more or less stable substances, 'things,' which are given more or less directly to awareness, predominantly visual. Language, when it is 'true to' this direct perception, represents, literally represents, things pretty much as they are in themselves. 'Postmodern' and similar (e.g., Heraclitean) readings of the world are accordingly dismissed as aberrant, questioning, as they do, not only the priority of 'substances' over 'accidents,' 'qualities,' 'attributes,' 'relations,' 'actions,' 'events,' but the very ontological status of 'substances.' Such questioning seems easy to discredit for it flies in the face of unreflective, everyday experience. It also seems often to fail in consistency and clarity, to fall into oxymoron and paradox, doomed as it is to express itself in a language which collaborates with the realist position, because it is the chief means whereby that position is maintained and disseminated. Your realist man-in-the-street knows in his heart that you *can* step into the same river twice. He knows this because that is what he *sees*. He also knows in his heart that, grammatically speaking, nouns (substantives) are more real than verbs, because nouns stand by themselves, while verbs are predicated of nouns, mirroring the fact that substances are what 'stand under' (Aristotelian *hypokeimena*) changes, actions, appearances, while actions must be actions *of* something. He knows this because that's what he *sees*. S. Tyler offers a tidy summary of this way of looking at the world and of what it implies:

1) *Things*, both as fact and concept, are hegemonic in Standard Average European language and thought.
2) The hegemony of things entails the hegemony of the visual as a means of knowing/thinking. *Seeing* is a privileged sensorial mode and a key metaphor in S[tandard]A[verage]E[uropean].

[10] The term 'standard average European' is Whorf's. See Tyler (1987) 149–50.

3) The hegemony of the visual, among other things: (a) necessitates a reductive ontological correlation between the visual and the verbal; (b) creates a predisposition to think of thinking/knowing as seeing; (c) promotes the notions that structure and process are fundamentally different and that the latter, which is only sequentiality, can always be reduced to the former, which is simultaneity, and thus being dominates becoming, actuality dominates possibility.

4) The hegemony of the visual, of this way of seeing things, is not universal, for it, (a) has a history as a common sense concept in Indo-European influenced particularly by literacy; (b) is not 'substantiated' in the conceptual 'structures' of other languages; and (c) is based on a profound misunderstanding of the evolution and functioning of the human sensorium.[11]

This last observation, being the summary of a complex argument, not the argument itself, certainly does not disprove the realist's view, but it should at very least raise a suspicion in his mind that what he holds, what he *sees*, is not something that 'goes without saying,' and that the relationship between words and things, between texts and facts, may be more problematical than he thinks. His epistemology will prevent him from making any sense of the main focus in what has been called 'postmodern anthropology,' which is characterized by Tyler, in sharp opposition to naive realism, as follows:

> Postmodern anthropology is the study of man—'talking.' Discourse is its object and its means. Discourse is both a theoretical object and a practice, and it is this reflexivity between object and means that enables discourse and that discourse creates. Discourse is the maker of the world, not its mirror, for it represents the world only inasmuch as it is the world.... Postmodern anthropology replaces the visual metaphor of the world as what we *see* with a verbal metaphor in which world and word are mutually implicated, neither having priority of origin nor ontic dominance. Berkeley's *esse est percipi* becomes 'to be is being spoken of.' Postmodern anthropology rejects the priority of perception, and with it the idea that concepts are derived from 'represented' sensory institutions that make the intelligible, the sensible 'resigned.'[12]

So much for narrowing (or has it been expanding?) the sense of 'modern' in my title. What of 'theory'? There is a problem here if by 'theory' we understand an unassailable, foundational 'master narrative'

---

[11] Tyler (1987) 149–50.
[12] Tyler (1987) 171.

or, in Stanley Fish's representation, 'an attempt to *guide* practice from a position above or outside it' or 'an attempt to *reform* practice by neutralizing interest, by substituting for the parochial perspective of some local or partisan point of view the perspective of a general rationality to which the individual subordinates his contextually conditioned opinions and beliefs.'[13] Theory, so understood, would be incompatible with the postmodern perspective, which disputes decontextualized, nonlinguistic, nonsituational sources of justification.

In speaking of theory, one may distinguish at least two fundamental operations in current literary discussion: description and theory-development. To describe is, in T. Todorov's neat formulation,

> to try to obtain, on the basis of certain theoretical premises, a rationalized representation of the object of study, while to present a scientific work [i.e. a theory] is to discuss and transform the theoretical premises themselves, after having experienced the object described.[14]

(Reading is distinct from both of these operations, though obviously it may be affected by them.) Classicists themselves have had little to do with literary theory-formation, tending to apply to classical texts theoretical premises developed elsewhere. Opposition to theory arises mostly from the belief that it inserts something alien (a contaminant) between the reader and the text. 'The simple response to this,' in T. Eagleton's often quoted remark,

> is that without some kind of theory, however unreflective or implicit, we would not know what a 'literary work' was in the first place, or how we were to read it. Hostility to theory usually means an opposition to other people's theories and an ignorance of one's own.[15]

In the long run, 'theory' as applied to the reading and analysis of Homer, as of any text, offers one among many explicitly considered frameworks for reading the text, for giving a rational account of it, as opposed to a reading that proceeds within a framework either inexplicit or unknown to the reader.[16]

Unfortunately, there is an unnecessary but not infrequent discrepancy between most theoretical writing and a style that is clear, coherent

[13] *Doing What Comes Naturally* (Durham, 1989) 319.
[14] *Littérature et signification* (Paris, 1967) 7.
[15] *Literary Theory* (Minneapolis, 1983) viii.
[16] See especially C. Martindale, *Redeeming the Text: Latin Poetry and the Hermeneutics of Reception* (Cambridge, 1993) 11–18.

and aesthetically appealing, something cherished if not always practiced by classicists. This has played no small part in creating the climate of impatience with and distrust of theory among literary scholars who come out of a tradition that ranks stylistic clarity and elegance high in its list of cherished humanistic values. Even more sinister in their eyes is the damaging effect theory may be perceived to have on the aesthetic appeal or pleasure one derives from 'reading' a text. There are many who, even if they concede the legitimacy and importance of theory, still consider it isolable from the act of reading literature and insist on its suspension if the work is to be enjoyed. They would argue that to expose the rules of the game, the process and devices of construction that ground and authenticate the representational surface of the work, is to spoil the pleasure we derive from that representational surface. But much of what I am calling contemporary theory forces us to question how far this suspension of disbelief can really go, or should really go. Such 'innocent' reading of any texts can be morally alienating and socially damaging. In other words, much of contemporary theory goes beyond giving an 'account' of texts within an explicit theoretical framework to become *social criticism*. 'It reveals,' says Umberto Eco (speaking particularly about semiotics), 'ways in which the labor of sign product can respect or betray the complexity of . . . a cultural network, thereby adapting it to (or separating it from) *the human labor of transforming stages of the world*.'[17] Sign production—with Homeric poetry we are concerned mainly with *narrative* sign production—may constrain or enhance the human enterprise of transforming the world to its own desire and design, or it may sustain and authorize the interests of one social group to the detriment of another in that enterprise. Contemporary theory questions the powerful unquestioned assumption that language, particularly narrative language, functions according to principles which are the same as, or even remotely like those of the phenomenal world or that literature is a reliable source of information about anything other that its own language.[18]

The 'ways in which the labor of sign product can respect or betray the complexity of . . . a cultural network' is, of course, more explicitly, if not exclusively, the concern of Marxists and feminists than it is of those whose transaction with the text reveals little moral, social

[17] Eco (1976) 297, emphasis added.
[18] See De Man (1982) 11.

or political motivation, not to speak of those who openly insist that such motivation is either inappropriate or futile.

P. Rose, in the first two chapters of *Sons of God, Children of Earth: Ideology and Literary Form in Ancient Greece*,[19] develops a Marxist analysis of the Homeric texts that shows a subtle sensitivity to postmodern epistemology and a sure grasp of its tools, even as he maintains a stout historicist stance. No naive seeker after authorial intent or 'original' audience response, he yet tries to reconstruct the historical crises that engendered these texts. He finds the *Iliad* torn between two representations, one that validates an ideology linking kingship with divine genealogy and another that criticizes 'the irreversible trend toward plutocracy represented by Agamemnon' and insists on 'claims of inherited excellence as valid only when demonstrated through risk taking and actual success on the field and in the trials of community deliberations' (90). As for the *Odyssey* Rose disputes the way in which the ambiguities in the text, its self-conscious preoccupation with punning and naming and with the potential duplicity of poetry are hypostatized by purely literary analysts as results of the inherently polysemous nature of all discourse and sign systems. He prefers rather to see these qualities primarily as 'creative responses to the political, social, economic, and psychological ambivalences of specific historical actors at a specific historical juncture,' and as products of 'a concrete crisis in text production itself associated with the transition from an oral to a literate culture' (139). He draws from the text a credible picture of a poet whose 'ambiguous allegiance results, on the one hand, from his role as the bearer of the elite culture and partial dependent of the aristocratic ruling element, and on the other, from his status as a wandering craftsman and his proximity to the discontented peasants and marginal elements in society' (139).

As with Marxism, so also with feminist approaches, the social, reformative aim is primary, explicit and insistent. The most recent and perhaps most insistent of these in Homeric studies is L. E. Doherty's *Siren Songs: Gender, Audiences, and Narrators in the Odyssey*.[20] The

---

[19] Rose (1992). For those little conversant with Marxism, Rose's introduction, 'Marxism and the Classics,' should be required reading. In it he traces the development of Marxist theory culminating with a summary of F. Jameson's concept of the double hermeneutic.

[20] Doherty (1995). As the present essay was being written, Doherty's book was still in press, but the author kindly supplied me with page proofs of her two introductory segments where her purposes and methodology are most explicitly enunciated.

larger framework within which her reading of the *Odyssey* takes place is an active critique of the androcentric (and to a lesser extent the class-based) assumptions she sees informing not only Homeric epic, but also contemporary social conditions, including what becomes especially problematical for feminist classicists, the limited canon of works the focus of which is almost wholly androcentric. Using mainly tools associated with narratology and audience-response criticism, she focuses on two questions: (1) Is the *Odyssey* a *closed* (redundant) text, i.e., 'one that by its self-consistency and adherence to convention seeks to limit the possibilities of interpretation,' or an *open* (plural) text, i.e., one that 'disrupts its own structural patterns or the conventions of its genre, thereby making room for—even requiring—more interpretative activity'; and (2) What strategies are available to feminist readers of the *Odyssey*? Her conclusion, a not uncontroversial one, is

> that the *Odyssey* presents itself primarily as a closed text, and that this has serious consequences for female readers, whose responses it models in elaborate and seductive ways. At the same time, the existence of conspicuous narrative breaks or silences interferes with the text's redundancy. These 'openings' represent opportunities for the reader who would resist textual determinacy.

As one would expect, the feminist movement has brought keener attention to Homer's female characters, Penelope in particular, even in studies in which a feminist agenda is muted or barely perceptible.[21] N. Felson-Rubin's *Regarding Penelope: From Character to Poetics*[22] adroitly supports a moderate feminism with perspectives drawn from narratology, possible-world semantics, audience-oriented criticism, Peircean semiotics and Bakhtinian dialogism in exploring the character of Odysseus' embattled spouse.[23] Speaking of an audience's capacity to occupy the subject position of the poem's characters, Felson-Rubin maintains that 'the division between the genders is not necessarily so

[21] The publication of *The Distaff Side: Representing the Female in Homer's Odyssey*, edited by B. Cohen (Oxford, 1995), occurred when the present essay was nearly complete. Among the highly commendable essays in this collection, a quick perusal turned up the following essays with a more or less explicit contemporary theoretical perspective: S. L. Schein, 'Female Representation and Interpreting the *Odyssey*,' S. Murnaghan, 'The Plan of Athena,' L. Doherty, 'Sirens, Muses and Female Narrators in the *Odyssey*,' and F. Zeitlin, 'Figuring Fidelity in Homer's *Odyssey*.'

[22] Felson-Rubin (1994).

[23] For the remarkable but late-to-be-appreciated work on semiotics and the theory of the sign of C. S. Peirce, turn-of-the-century American philosopher and logician, cf. N. Felson-Rubin, 'Semiotics and Classical Studies,' *Arethusa* 16 (1983).

restrictive as scholars commonly imagine.' Accordingly, she finds in the text a more deliberate and effectual critique of its own androcentric tradition than Doherty would probably want to concede. In this reading, Penelope is seen as the most enigmatic and puzzling character in the *Odyssey*, a judgment powerfully confirmed by the observation that, while the actions of Odysseus, the suitors, even the gods themselves are routinely forecast, leaving fairly little doubt about the poem's major eventualities, no authoritative voice ever makes clear what Penelope will do, before she does it. Instead, a number of hypothetical narrative outcomes (chiefly the Argive plot of Clytemnestra's treachery) are kept constantly within the range of possibility before finally yielding to the actual conclusion of successful second courtship and reunion.

Felson-Rubin eschews that strain of postmodernism that distances the reader/critic from what she calls the 'emotional content' of the text. This stance, combined with her desire to bring as much coherence as possible to the fictional world of the *Odyssey*, makes her deliberately less skeptical about the problematics of artistic unity and of psychologizing character than many late twentieth-century theorists are inclined to be. They tend to stress the gaps, the disjunctions, inconsistencies, contradictions and indeterminacies in literary characters and plots. M. A. Katz takes this tack in *Penelope's Renown: Meaning and Indeterminacy in the Odyssey*,[24] diverging in a fundamental way from Felson-Rubin,[25] even though their books otherwise exhibit frequent points of convergence. Katz turns into a virtue the textual inconsistencies that scandalized the analysts, and refuses to settle for a sense of unity derived either from simplistic notions of authorial intent or from audience-oriented criticism. The referentiality of the poem is, as she says, 'forever open to question.' And 'it is the figure of Penelope through whom this indeterminacy is encoded into the text.' As for character, she is relentless in her assault upon the uni-

---

[24] Katz (1991).

[25] In *Disguise and Recognition in the Odyssey* (1987), Murnaghan, who seems to occupy a tense middle ground between these two positions, sums up admirably the dilemma of dealing with literary character (128): 'The figure of Penelope in the *Odyssey* exemplifies with particular clarity the double life led by most characters in literary plots, as both figures in an orderly artistic design and as representations of human beings making their way through experiences whose patterns they cannot perceive or predict. In Penelope's case these two aspects of her role in the poem yield perspectives on her character and behavior that are so different that they cannot easily be reconciled.'

tary notion of the subject—'the idea, that is to say, that character is constituted around a core of true being represented by certain "characteristics," rather than, as Katz insists, around narrative exigencies.' However, the indeterminacy in Penelope's case is not unproductive. The 'absence of integrity' in the development of her character, Katz concludes,

> can be understood instead as performing a specific function in the text, that of calling into question the relation between semblance and being, between disguise and truth. This disruption of the fixity of Penelope's character, then, functions, like Odysseus's disguise, as a strategy of estrangement—we do not know, in a certain sense, 'who' Penelope is. Her 'character' is thus rendered so as to represent an analogue to her state of sociological indeterminacy, which is defined by her lack of a *kyrios* or authorizing agent.

Katz's suspicion regarding the stable subject and consistency and continuity of character and her insistence that character is subservient to narrative exigencies are shared in my own *Man in the Middle Voice: Name and Narration in the Odyssey*, where I argue that from this austere and, for the conventionalist, discomfiting point of view, 'Outis' turns out to be the only *proper* name for the emptiness that in reality all narrative persons share, but that is nonetheless the improper ground on which their spurious claims to absolute distinctness rest. Odysseus's deliberate abrogation of distinctness in Polyphemus' cave displays him as the narrative agent par excellence, as therefore capable of becoming *any* character, of assuming *any* predicate, of doing or enduring *anything*, of being, in a word, *polytropos*—the negativity capable of the fullest and most polymorphic narrative development. This theme develops out my own larger analytic frame, which views the *Odyssey* as a tense, never resolved opposition between tragic 'myth' and optimistic 'folktale,' recognized as vehicles for contrasting ideological opinions on the world. With terms drawn from M. Bakhtin's concept of 'dialogism,' the poem's two voices are characterized as 'centripetal' and 'centrifugal'—the one associated with dominant political power, with the conventional, the official, and the heroic; the other with the personal, the disempowered and the popular, with the antics of the Autolycan trickster and outlaw. I find an analogous polarity between two views of poetic activity revealed in the *Odyssey*, distinguished from one another by the extent of their subservience to the external pressures of tradition and verisimilitude. One is a discourse of *representation*, embodied in the blind Phaeacian bard Demodocus, who gracefully repeats a fixed tradition given to him in inspiration by the Muses to keep the past intact; the other is a discourse of *production*, embodied in Odysseus himself, who freely designs fictions out of his own ingenuity to control present circumstance and to serve his purpose for the future.

Most of the studies referred to so far are in varying degrees *intertextual*. Intertextuality, understood in the weakest, least provocative sense of the term as a set of relations among texts, is certainly no new phenomenon in the literary critical lexicon of classicists. A familiar practice of traditional philology has been the search for one text's allusions to others, especially its sources (*Quellenforschung*), but also including such non-literary 'texts' as social, political, biographical codes, influences and institutions that constitute the 'context' of the text under study.[26] But allusiveness in traditional studies, with the privilege it attached to recovering 'original' meaning or the 'original' performance, was understood to be strictly bound by time's arrow: the texts alluded *to* had to be earlier or contemporaneous with the text under study. When it came to Homer, this restriction generally sanctioned the study of allusions to the *Iliad* in the *Odyssey*, but looked with grave suspicion on any that might be considered to move in the other direction, (even though, with ironic inconsistency, the prior composition of the *Iliad* has had no solid proof).

But intertextuality in the strong or postmodern sense disavows, or at least refuses to privilege the premises on which this more traditional study of allusiveness is based, foremost among them, the view that texts are self-sufficient, with more or less absolute closure and resolution. By contrast, postmodern intertextual practice views texts as fragmentary, referring endlessly to other texts, the way a dictionary definition refers explicitly or implicitly to other definitions, no single one of them occupying a privileged, stable, univocal center. Accordingly, authors lose their authority, failing, as all language users necessarily fail, in their attempt to make language their own. Their intentions, even where they can be somehow demonstrated (as in Homer they obviously cannot), carry less weight than the incessant allusiveness of the language they use. Furthermore, the very notion of a privileged, autonomous 'literal' meaning, to which a connotational

[26] See Rosenmeyer (1988) 40–42, where the author prefers the term 'contextual' to 'intertextual'.

allusive meaning must be considered additional and superfluous, is itself an arbitrary construct.[27]

In Homeric studies, P. Pucci's *Odysseus Polutropos: Intertextual Readings in the Odyssey and the Iliad*[28] makes most extensive and daring use of this and other deconstructive premises.[29] One should not be misled by the title. Although the work could be described as a dialectic or, perhaps better, a duel between the two Homeric texts, the site on which it is played out is mainly the *Odyssey*. But this is definitely not to say that Pucci privileges it over the *Iliad*. On the contrary, he sees the two poems and their heroes as representing 'two opposite economies of life, two exemplary extremes in conceiving our relationship with life and death and accordingly two different ways of writing and circumventing our anxiety about death' (173). But these two poetic representations imply or, perhaps better, implicate one another, irrespective of their temporal relationship: 'the textual force of the *Odyssey* and of the *Iliad* lies in their linguistic relationships, differences, and similarities. This textual relationship is to some extent indifferent to the priority of one text over the other' (48). There is a yet bolder implication in this, the invitation to understand the two texts as giving one another what Pucci calls a 'specular reading': 'One text would rewrite the other, but it would simultaneously be written by the other' (42). There is, however, a moment when Pucci forgets this complicated balancing act and does seem to authorize the Odyssean perspective. It is a *felix culpa*, if *culpa* at all: a brilliant reading of Odysseus as reader of the *Iliad* (226):

> Through the song of Demodocus, the *Odyssey* has induced us to read its own reading (of Odysseus' reading) of his own tradition and to become conscious of the thematic continuity and difference that the text constantly maintains with respect to the heroic tradition. Odysseus has become a fellow reader of the heroic tradition: he is no longer a hero of that genre but is now the character whose pathos points at the business of survival and pleasure. This business is epitomized by his transformation from an actor in the Trojan War into a passionate and pitiful reader of that war's story.

---

27 For the special pertinence of this observation to Homeric studies see especially Pucci (1987) 236–45.

28 For a detailed and sympathetic reading of this demanding book, see Pedrick (1994) 75–96.

29 The exception to this generalization may well be the consistently provocative work of A. Bergren: (1980), (1981), (1983a), (1983b).

That what I have been calling postmodern concerns in fact correspond to the conceptual environment of the Homeric poems is a premiss on which these and other contemporary studies proceed. And that this is especially the case with the *Odyssey*[30] shows itself in the steady stream of books on that poem in recent years, ranging from those whose perspective combines the best in traditional philological analysis with an equally traditional humanist aesthetic, to Derridian, deconstructionist, intertextual readings of the poem. And there are others, and not a few, yet in the works.[31] One may, of course, find other explanations for this concentration on the *Odyssey*. It is certainly no new discovery that this text is extremely self-reflexive about the processes of its own poetic production[32] and of its relation to the narrative tradition that lies behind it. But those attuned to current theoretical discussions have turned these into major concerns. They would argue further that the *Odyssey* is a truly perplexed and disruptive text, and was no less so to nineteenth- and twentieth-century philologists who, to blunt its scandal, scanned and dissected it, stratified it into earlier and later parts, better and worse parts, sifted it for inconsistencies, all in the search for an uncontaminated original to match their own implicit model of the work of art as an organic and harmonious whole, and of the human subject as a consistent and harmonious whole. However, in the wake of theoretical movements culminating in the set of perspectives comprised by the term postmodernism, this same perplexed and disruptive text becomes a para-

[30] My sampling of theoretical approaches has concentrated on works addressed to the *Odyssey* for the obvious reason that its own preoccupation with textuality, with signs, with the problematics of language, the poetic transaction, subjectivity and other concerns of postmodernism are more patent. One should by no means overlook the brilliant, if often obscure, study of the *Iliad*, by M. Lynn-George (1988), in which the tools of deconstruction and Bakhtinian dialogism are wielded with uncommon skill. M. Naas's *Turning from Persuasion to Philosophy: A Reading of Homer's Iliad* (1995), which promises a sensitive postmodern reading, appeared as the present essay was being completed.

[31] Among authors of recent *Odyssey* studies C. Segal deserves special mention for a consistently remarkable stream of work on Homer bridging the period between the publication of Wace and Stubbings and the present. This work ranges from elegant, discriminating *explication de texte* (as in his 1962 *Arion* essay 'The Phaeacians and the Symbolism of Odysseus' Return') to the latter half of *Singers, Heroes, and Gods in the Odyssey* (Ithaca, 1994), where his focus is on many of the issues dear to contemporary theory, e.g., the poem's self-reflexive character, the strategies of its internal narrators, the reactions of their audiences, and the clues these provide to the *Odyssey*'s moral dimension.

[32] For an extensive bibliography on the self-reflexive poetics of the *Odyssey*, see Goldhill (1991) 57, note 98.

digm for a less authoritative, less confident, more dialectical view of text production—writing, and of text reception—reading, and indeed for a more discordant view of the human subject. No one should expect any of this to make reading Homer any easier, but, in Pucci's words (225),

> Readers of the *Odyssey* are expected to possess the same intellectual gifts as the poet and the character of the poems: otherwise they will read this amazingly subtle and complex text as a mere fable for grown-up children.

Andrew Ford

EPIC AS GENRE

To call the *Iliad* and *Odyssey* 'epics' today can evoke two quite different sets of comparable works. The first grouping would put Homer at the head of a Western tradition of literary epic that runs from Apollonius of Rhodes through Vergil, on to the Renaissance and beyond.[1] The second, with equal justice, would view Homeric poetry as one instance of a type of traditional oral narrative to be found the world over, including cultures far outside the influence of the West.[2] For all their divergence, these two classes of 'epic' are not unrelated: the traditional oral art embodied in Homer was, after all, what Aristotle took as his exemplar when he laid the groundwork for the theory of Western epic in the *Poetics*. Between these two aspects of epic is yet a third way of defining the genre, in relation to the other forms of song that were named and recognized in Archaic Greece. This chapter will attempt a definition of Greek epic in such terms, asking how Homer's poems were presented to and accepted by contemporary audiences as instances of a particular kind of singing. Defining the genre in historical and culturally specific terms may offer an enriching perspective on the works, and may make clearer the connections between Homer the oral poet and Homer the father of classical epic.[3]

We do not know when the Greeks began to sing what we now call epics, for the *Iliad* and *Odyssey* derive from oral traditions reaching back to the Bronze Age (see Horrocks, this vol.; Bennet, this vol.). Because the Myceneans did not write their songs down, we can only conjecture that they may have had songs about notable ancient kings which they distinguished from cult songs or praises of living

[1] Valuable overviews of the classical epic tradition are Newman (1986); Hainsworth (1991).

[2] For an introduction to the vast and ongoing research on oral poetics, see A. B. Lord, 'Oral Poetry' in *The New Princeton Encyclopedia of Poetry and Poetics*, ed. A. Preminger and T. V. F. Brogan (Princeton, 1993), 863–66.

[3] A. Fowler (1982) argues powerfully for the continuing usefulness of genre criticism in these terms.

men.[4] It is in any case generally agreed that the Greek 'Dark Age' was crucially important for developing the themes and the special style we see in the Homeric poems.[5] By the end of the eighth century, the Ionian version of this ancient art had triumphed over all others as *the* way to sing the exploits of heroes and gods. This style, entailing formal features such as a characteristic meter and dialect as well as larger narrative patterns, amounted to a distinct genre in the sense that it could be expected of a certain class of singers when they performed certain themes, no matter where they came from or where they sang.

This genre appears to have had at first no particular name, though Greek critics eventually named it 'epic.' When the Western critical tradition was founded in Plato and Aristotle, Homeric poetry was popularly called ἐποποιία, meaning something like 'verse composition' or 'hexameter composition.' Although Aristotle objected to naming kinds of literature according to the meter used,[6] he recognized that trial and error had established the dactylic hexameter as the only proper vehicle for heroic narratives, and he took account of meter in defining epic.[7] His conception of ἐποποιία as a distinct genre, however, also includes historical, 'natural,' and thematic considerations: epic was the ancestor of tragedy, each genre satisfying a human impulse to imitate the actions of serious or elevated men; the shared themes and aim of epic and tragedy distinguished them from such genres as mock-epic and comedy, while they were distinct from each other in formal terms: epic was longer and greater in scope; it used a single meter throughout which was intoned without the full musical range employed in tragic odes or other songs such as the dithyramb; epic could not dispense with an element of narrative. For Aristotle, these features and the genres they marked were far from arbitrary conventions; on his view, literary genres were rooted in natural aptitudes and appetites but evolved historically as poets discovered the kinds of representations that most fully and efficiently achieved their particular aims. (Aristotle notoriously specified the aim of tragedy as a catharsis of pity and fear; some ancestral

[4] Cf. Webster (1953) 91–135.

[5] Kirk (1976) 19–39; M. L. West (1988).

[6] Because the poet's essential task is not versification but imitation: *Poetics* 1447a28–47b23; cf. 1451a37–b5, 1451b27–29.

[7] *Poetics* 1459b31–60a1. Cf. Aristotle's brief formulas for epic: 'the mimetic art in hexameters' (1449b21) or 'the art of narrative imitation in recited meter' (1459a17).

form of this is often assumed to have been the aim of epic).[8]

Aristotle's teleological outlook disposed him to view epic in relation to tragedy, and indeed to rank the later-arising form higher for its intense and economically achieved effects (ch. 25). Yet he influentially singled out the *Iliad* and *Odyssey* as paradigms of the epic art, and his acute observations on these poems[9] came to have prescriptive force as canons future poets would be wise to observe: the most effective epics had been predominantly naturalistic representations of the deeds of notable figures from legend; the stories were framed within a third-person, past-tense narrative, though the speeches of characters could be given in the first person; the plot, which could begin *in medias res*, normally progressed in a linear sequence, subsuming many episodes under a single main topic; large size, scope, and a relative degree of unity were valued.

Literary conceptions of genre clung to the poems when they entered Rome, where Homer remained a staple of liberal education and the proper approach to a classic work (the *praelectio*) demanded an understanding of its genre. By the time the poems had come to dominate Roman literary practice, Greek critics were speaking of 'epic poetry,' ἡ ἐπικὴ ποίησις, and Roman schoolmasters and littérateurs of *epicum poiema* and *epicus poeta*.[10] When Vergil subsumed the Greek models and critical ideas of epic in his *Aeneid*, Homer's name and the idea of epic were ensured a lasting place in the literary traditions of the Latin west. The rich and multifarious tradition of classical epic achieved its greatest prestige and most rigidly defined form in the seventeenth century, but it is worth remembering that a now canonical exemplar like *Paradise Lost* challenged that form as much as it continued it. The decline in the prestige and practice of formal epic after the eighteenth century did not entirely extinguish the genre, since Romantic long poems or modernist epic novels implicitly invoke the classical mold if only so that their departures from it may have more force. Hence Aristotle's analysis of epic may be said to have shaped much of Western theory and literary practice from the fourth century B.C. through the present.

---

[8] On Aristotle's notion of genre, see Rosenmeyer (1985).

[9] Surveyed in Hogan (1973).

[10] Cicero, *de Opt. Gen.* 1, 2; Quintilian, *Inst.* 10.1.51, 62 (where the broad range of 'epic' poets is noteworthy). The Greek phrase is first attested in Dionysius of Halicarnassus, *On Composition* 22 (where it is a very probable emendation); on ἔπος as a name for the genre (e.g., Horace, *Satires* 1.10.43), see Koster (1970) 86–91.

In the twentieth century the epic corpus expanded exponentially to accommodate traditional narratives from other cultures ranging from Bosnia, northern Russia, and Asia to the Americas and Africa. Interest in non-canonical epics can be traced to the eighteenth century, but the researches of Milman Parry and Albert Lord into how oral poems are composed and handed down gave a deeper understanding to the formal dynamics of such works. For example, Aristotle explains Greek epic's predilection for archaic and exotic words (γλῶτται) as a matter of choosing diction 'appropriate' to its dignified meter and themes (*Rhetoric* 1406b3; *Poetics* 1459b35); oral formulaic theory adds that many such forms were retained in the poetic language through centuries because they were ready to hand, metrically convenient, and inseparable from the tale as heard and performed. The study of epics as products of oral composition in performance has also made it possible to specify a further array of formal patternings which were, even if executed unthinkingly, so frequent as to have been hallmarks of the form: the paratactic style, composition by type-scenes, the use of formulaic expressions, extended similes, and ring composition.[11]

The comparative study of epic conceives of genre not as a series of texts linked in a conscious literary tradition but as a cross-cultural type or kind: in part because Aristotle had defined the form so influentially, the definition of oral epic is not substantially altered from his (a lengthy recitation, usually sung or chanted, which treats the quasi-historical exploits of notable heroes from the culture's past); but the sample from which such a definition is drawn makes it clear that each of its terms (length, recitation, history, heroes) is relative and is only fully significant in relation to specific cultural norms. Hence defining Homeric epic may include asking how the archaic Greek version of this kind of singing was conceived by its poets and understood by its earliest audiences.

An inquiry into the early conception of epic cannot confine itself to descriptive analysis. Terms that might be adequate to sort written texts into classes are not necessarily sufficient or even relevant for an oral culture in distinguishing kinds of songs (cf. Bynum [1976]; Rosenberg [1978]). Aspects of performance, for example, are less evident in a text than its formal properties, yet in Archaic Greece the social context in which songs were performed played a major

[11] For a full description, see M. W. Edwards (1987) 29–123.

role in determining their formal requirements. Outlining the sorts of considerations that went into classifying kinds of singing in Homer's time suggests that epic and all archaic Greek poems were defined in relation to four major categories: (1) the context of the song, (2) its 'form' or the ways it marked its language, (3) its 'contents' or themes, and (4) the relations between the poet and the audience. Let us consider these categories in order, devoting most attention to the latter two which will prove the most significant.

Like any complex society, Archaic Greece organized its singing along with the rest of social life, recognizing only certain kinds of speech, rhythm, melody, and movement as appropriate on certain occasions. Thereby particular contexts generated corresponding types of song, with social and religious notions playing as large a role in their definition as formal and aesthetic criteria.[12] Most of the named kinds of songs in Homer are tied to particular ritual or communal occasions, such as the *hymenaios* (ὑμέναιος, *Il.* 18.493) for weddings, the *threnos* (θρῆνος, 24.721) for funerals, or the *linos* song (λίνος, 18.570) for harvesting (see Diehl [1940]). But epic performance was confined to no particular settings, times or places. The poems suggest that such songs were particularly at home at banquets (*Od.* 8.99; cf. 9.2–11, 13.7–10), but other evidence makes it likely that epic poetry was also performed in the marketplace or at contests held in connection with funerals and national religious festivals (Kirk [1962] 274–81). The only contextual requirement for epic performance, then, appears to have been leisure, a break from normal business sufficient to hear a long account of ancient deeds.

The context of Archaic song also determined its formal requirements, for the kinds of music and rhythms favored in particular contexts depended both on the actions to be accompanied by the song (e.g., dancing, processions, pantomimes) and also on how performing roles were to be distributed among participants. *Threnoi*, for example, not only required suitably lugubrious themes and music, but also restricted solo singing to select participants based on their age, gender, and status relative to the deceased: in *threnoi* described by Homer, women kin offered a short song to which the larger group responded antiphonally (Alexiou [1974]). This pattern in which a single performer 'leads' the rest of the group was used in other types

[12] R. P. Martin (1989) 43–44 argues that 'social genres' are primary and that literary genres vary according to a society's ideas of performance.

of song as well and was marked with a particular word for 'leading' (ἐξάρχειν).[13] A different formal pattern folded all participants into one homogeneous choral group singing in unison: in Homer this is exemplified in the soldiers' paean, a collective prayer to Apollo: provided it expresses group solidarity, the paean is equally suitable in situations of distress (*Il.* 1.472–73) or of triumph (22.391–94). Epic performance would appear to represent the other extreme from these practices, to judge from the singers Homer represents: they perform solo, accompanying themselves on a stringed instrument;[14] there is normally no dancing, and the audience is specifically designated as still, seated in rapt silence (*Od.* 1.325–26). Although the music of epic performance can only be guessed at, the vocabulary for 'singing' indicates that it was a sort of recitative, felt to lie above plain speech but below fully melodic singing.[15] This mode of performance would have distinguished epic from the melodic songs the Greeks called μέλος (including most of what we call 'lyric' poetry), but not from solo recitatives in other stichic meters such as iambics and trochaics.

Neither performative contexts nor their formal requirements, then, gives us more than the most general definition of archaic Greek epic: we can only say that already for Homer it was a traditional kind of non-melic poetry, adaptable to many situations but identified with none and so without a particular name. What most obviously set epic apart from other non-melic forms in iambo-trochaic meters was the themes it treated. To turn to the contents of epics, the invocations offer important evidence.

Evidence from Homer and other early epics shows that the narrative proper was regularly announced with an invocation, a prayer that the Muse 'sing' or 'tell' a certain story; the invocation could be repeated later in the song to make a transition to new themes or

---

[13] E.g., *Il.* 24.723 (Hector's mother 'leads off' the laments for her son); *Od.* 4.15–19 (a musician and tumblers lead a wedding song); Archilochus leads the Dithyramb and the 'Lesbian Paean' (120, 121, M. L. West, ed., *Iambi et Elegi Graeci*, Second edition [Oxford 1992]). Further varieties in *Lexicon des Frügriechischen Epos*, ed. B. Snell et al. (Göttingen, 1979–) s.v. ἄρχω, B I 2e and B II 2 (Hereafter, *LfgrE*).

[14] On musical instruments in Homer, see Barker (1984) 4–17, 25. By the Classical period, epic performers had dispensed with the lyre altogether; how early this occurred is unclear: see M. L. West (1966) on Hesiod *Theog.* 30. G. Nagy (1990b) 21–24 cautions that the portrayal of poets in Homer may not directly reflect contemporary practice in every respect.

[15] For a musical reconstruction of epic recitative, see M. L. West (1981), who also discusses the terms for singing.

inset pieces.[16] Invocations had a relatively set form: an imperative, vocative ('sing, Goddess,' 'tell me, Muse'), and a brief naming of the theme which would have served as a kind of title for the song: 'the Wrath of Achilles,' is Homer's title for what was called the *Iliad* in the classical period, and 'the Man of Many Turns . . .' his title for the *Odyssey*.[17] Other songs mentioned within the poems are identified in the same format (Ford [1992] 18–23): 'The Baleful Return of the Achaeans' (*Od.* 1.326–27), 'The Quarrel of Odysseus and Peleus' son Achilles' (8.75), 'The Destruction of the Achaeans/As much as they wrought and suffered and as much as the Achaeans toiled' (8.489–90), 'The Fashioning of the Wooden Horse' (8.500–501), 'The Destruction of the Argive Danaans and of Ilion' (8.578). Invocations next regularly emphasize the great scope of the action, its pathetic quality, the nations involved, and the presence of the gods throughout. At the end of the invocation the poet specifies from what point the tale is to begin: the *Iliad* is to be sung 'from the time when the son of Atreus and Achilles first stood apart in contention' (1.7–8); the poet of the *Odyssey* asks the Muse 'of these things, starting from some point, tell us now' (1.10).

The first seven lines of the *Iliad* and the first ten of the *Odyssey* promise a kind of poem that Bowra (1925) has well described as 'heroic epic.'[18] The poet's 'sing' or 'tell' means the song is fundamentally a narrative, as Aristotle noted (1462a16–17), although Homeric poetry is half dramatic speeches. The narrative will concern the actions of great men and women from the nation's past who suffered and strove beside the gods; it will be a large and complex story, but only a part of a much larger story that might be told. With the recognition that the Muse is taking up the story from a certain point, the poet reminds us, as Aristotle noted too (*Poetics* ch. 8), that any particular epic is carved out of a notionally larger whole. In Lord's words ([1960] 123), 'a song in tradition is separate, yet inseparable from other songs.' This larger story, even if only an abstraction, is significant

---

[16] In addition to *Il.* 1.1–7 and *Od.* 1.1–10, cf. Hesiod *Theog.* 104–115; *Thebais* fr. 1, ed. M. Davies (1988); Antimachus; *Thebais* fr. 1 Wyss. Transitional invocations: *Il.* 2.484 ff., 2.761–62, 11.218–20, 14.508–510, 16.112–13; Hesiod *Theog.* 965–68, 1021–2. See especially Fränkel (1975) 6–25.

[17] Cf. Lord (1960) 99: 'When one asks a singer what songs he knows, he will begin by saying that he knows the song, for example, about Marko Kraljevic when he fought with Musa, or he will identify it by its first lines.'

[18] Cf. Hainsworth (1993) 32–53.

because it would appear to constitute the theoretical limits of the epic repertoire, and limiting content is a major component in defining this genre.

To delimit the themes of epic for Homer means in the first instance describing the kinds of songs that the Muses inspire professional singers to sing. For among the many divinities (*Il.* 1.604; *Od.* 10.254) and mortals (*Il.* 1.473; *Od.* 14.464) who 'sing' (ἀείδειν) in Homer, some are singled out as professional singers with the title ἀοιδοί. The word is only used of professional singers in Homer and Hesiod, those who may be listed among the society's itinerant craftsmen along with carpenters, seers, healers, and heralds (*Od.* 17.382–85).[19] The professional singers in Homer are masters of 'singing and dancing' (*Od.* 1.152) for any occasion: Priam summons *aoidoi* to the palace to 'lead' the threnos for Hector (*Il.* 24.720–22), and Odysseus can require a song to accompany a wedding dance from Phemius, the *aoidos* on Ithaca (*Od.* 23.133 ff.); Phemius seems to play and sing a *molpê* while the suitors sport (1.150–55), and the Phaeacian Demodocus can accompany acrobatic dancing by troops of young men (8.261–64) or perform a burlesque hymn in the agora (8.266 ff.). Nevertheless, to infer from this picture that the epic performer in Homer's time was a jack-of-all-songs may be erroneous. For it seems reasonable to suppose that poets would have had to specialize to produce epics of such length and complexity, and no melic poems were ascribed to Homer in Greek tradition.

Homer seems aware of a distinction between the singers' heroic narratives and the other kinds of song they provide when he describes Phemius' 'Return of the Achaeans' (*Od.* 1.328) and Demodocus' 'Destruction of the Achaeans' (8.498) with the formula, θέσπις ἀοιδή, 'singing filled with the words of god.'[20] The epithet is also applied to professional singers, who are the only mortals said to be 'filled with the words of a god' (θέσπιν ἀοιδόν),[21] referring evidently to the central role the Muses have in defining this kind of poetry. For the modern observer, what made a professional epic poet was a long apprenticeship in learning its themes and style; in Homer's terms, it is the Muses who make some singers *aoidoi*, and presumably make their singing superior to that of amateurs.

[19] *LfrgE* s.v. ἀοιδός and ἀοιδή.

[20] Cf. *Il.* 2.600, *Od.* 12.158; *Hom. Hymn Hermes* 442.

[21] *Od.* 17.385; cf. Hesiod fr. 310.2 R. Merkelbach and M. L. West, *Fragmenta Hesiodea* (Oxford, 1967), hereafter M–W.

The search for a Homeric term that would describe in general what poets sing has focused on the phrase κλέα ἀνδρῶν, as when Achilles sings 'the fames of men' to a lyre (*Il.* 9.189). The dedication of a kind of poetry to conferring 'fame' on its subjects derives from epic's very ancient connection with Indo-European praise poetry (Schmitt [1967] 61–102). Preserving and disseminating 'fame' was especially the concern of poets: *aoidoi* are said to 'confer fame' upon their subjects by celebrating them in song (κλείουσιν, *Od.* 1.338; cf. Hesiod *Theogony* 32; *Works and Days* 1); Hesiod speaks of an *aoidos* 'the servant of the Muses,' who 'celebrates the fames of earlier men' (κλεῖα προτέρων ἀνθρώπων, *Theog.* 100; cf. *Hom. Hymn* 32.18–20). Although κλέα ἀνδρῶν is clearly a traditional term for oral heroic traditions, other uses of κλέος in Homer show that professional epic poets claimed to present these traditions with an authority unavailable even to Achilles.

The *Odyssey* offers valuable evidence for the way poets regarded their repertoire when Homer describes a poet beginning a heroic theme:

Μοῦσ' ἄρ' ἀοιδὸν ἀνῆκεν ἀειδέμεναι κλέα ἀνδρῶν,
οἴμης, τῆς τότ' ἄρα κλέος οὐρανὸν εὐρὺν ἵκανε,
νεῖκος Ὀδυσσῆος καὶ Πηλεΐδεω Ἀχιλῆος,
ὥς ποτε δηρίσαντο θεῶν ἐν δαιτὶ θαλείῃ

the Muse then stirred up the singer to sing the fames of men
from that *oimê* whose fame at that time reached broad heaven,
the Quarrel of Odysseus and Achilles, son of Peleus,
how they once contended with each other at the rich feast of the gods
Od. 8.73–76

An individual story a bard might perform, such as 'the Quarrel of Odysseus and Achilles,' is here given the quasi-technical name οἴμη, possibly understood metaphorically as a 'path' of song.[22] A professional poet like Phemius knows many such stories: 'the Muse has made οἶμαι of every kind grow in my heart' (*Od.* 22.347–48; cf. 8.479–81). The aggregate of οἶμαι are the κλέα ἀνδρῶν (8.73). The κλέα ἀνδρῶν, however, include any account of earlier men of note, not just those purveyed by poets. Κλέος basically means 'what is heard,' and κλέα include whatever is handed down from mouth to ear. Indeed, simply as 'what is heard,' κλέος may be casual talk, second-hand

[22] On the meaning and etymology of *oimê*, see Ford (1992) 42 n. 78 and the literature there cited; a different view in Nagy (1990b) 28.

report, or mere rumor (e.g., *Od.* 3.83; 4.317; 16.461; 23.137).[23] Phoenix tells, without 'singing' and without invoking the Muses, an old story about Meleager which he ascribes to the 'fames of men': 'so we hear tell of the fames of men of long ago, the heroes' (τῶν πρόσθεν ἐπεύθομεθα κλεα ἀνδρῶν / ἡρώων, *Il.* 9.524–5). Genealogies may circulate in the same way, and are identified with κλέα when Aeneas compares his lineage with Achilles':

> ἴδμεν δ' ἀλλήλων γενεήν, ἴδμεν δε τοκῆας,
> πρόκλυτ' ἀκούοντες ἔπεα θνητῶν ἀνθρώπων·
> ὄψει δ' οὔτ' ἄρ πω σὺ ἐμους ἴδες οὔτ' ἄρ' ἐγὼ σούς.
>
> We know each other's lineage, we know each other's parents
> from hearing the sayings that have been heard before among mortal men;
> but as for actually seeing them, you have never seen my parents, nor I yours.
>
> *Il.* 20. 202–204

Oral genealogical traditions arise as each generation 'hears' from the one before, and not particularly from singers, the names of ancestors. But Aeneas significantly contrasts such knowledge (ἴδμεν, 202) as mortals may have of their past with the first-hand knowledge an eye-witness might have (ὄψει, 204). This opposition is significant because Homer uses it at a key point to distinguish his own inspired poetry from humanly transmitted κλέα ἀνδρῶν as a source of knowledge about the past.

In his extended invocation to the catalogue of ships Homer distinguishes the account his Muses inspire from the general run of oral tradition: 'For you [Muses] are goddesses, and are present, and know all/but we hear only and do not know anything' (*Iliad* 2.485–6: ὑμεῖς γὰρ θεαί ἐστε, πάρεστέ τε, ἴστε τε πάντα, / ἡμεῖς δὲ κλέος οἶον ἀκούομεν οὐδέ τι ἴδμεν). The Muses 'know' these things in the root sense of that word, they 'have seen' them (ἴστε) and so bring the authority of eye-witnesses to the events of which the poet wishes to speak. The poet and his generation do not 'know' the past in this way (οὐδέ τι ἴδμεν); for them, as for Aeneas, knowledge of the past without the Muses is mere report (κλέος οἶον). These same distinctions are deployed in the *Odyssey* when the hero praises a heroic singer: 'very rightly you sing the destruction of the Achaeans ... as if you had

[23] Cf. Redfield (1975) 32–34.

been there in person or had heard about them from someone who was' (ὥς τέ που ἢ αὐτὸς παρεὼν ἢ ἄλλου ἀκούσας, *Od.* 8.489–91). The implication is that the blind bard has an eyewitness' knowledge from the Muses.

Among the functions of the Muses, then, is to underwrite the claim by professional poets that their songs about the past are superior to the many other accounts available in the society. The Muses' favor and assistance make the difference between 'mere' κλέος and θέσπις ἀοιδή. Although the poet and the gentleman hero may share an interest in the fames of men, the poet's status depends on confining 'true' epic to what the Muses give. Accordingly, the range of epic is the range of songs that Muses inspire *aoidoi* to sing. Bowra's notion of 'heroic epic' well expresses the ethos of these poems, but a comparison with the Hesiodic corpus suggests that the range of 'heroic' song should be interpreted broadly.

Although the preeminence of the *Iliad* and *Odyssey* may incline us to identify θέσπις ἀοιδή with heroic poetry, the range of themes the Muses inspire is in fact wider. After all, Hesiod also invokes the Muses, and much of the poetry that went under his name shares the diction, meter, dialect, and legends to be found in Homer. A consideration of Hesiodic poetry shows that the repertoire of the Muses' singer extended beyond the doings of 'heroes,' and that it is better defined, in Homer's terms, as 'the deeds of gods and men that singers celebrate' (ἔργ' ἀνδρῶν τε θεῶν τε, τά τε κλείουσιν ἀοιδοί, *Od.* 1.338) or, in Hesiod's terms, as 'the fames of men of former times/and the blessed gods who hold Olympus' (κλεῖα προτέρων ἀνθρώπων / ὑμνήσει μάκαράς τε θεοὺς οἳ Ὄλυμπον ἔχουσιν, *Theog.* 100–101).

It used to be common to distinguish between an Ionian (Homeric) 'school' of heroic epic and a Boeotian (Hesiodic) school of didactic or catalogue poetry. But the opposition of epic to didactic is wholly inapplicable to the Archaic period,[24] and such a gross dichotomy obscures important conceptual affinities that Homer's poetry had with at least some of Hesiod's (Thalmann [1984] xi–xiii, 75–77). The epic singer, after all, must be knowledgeable (*Od.* 1.337–39), and later Greece put Homer on an equal footing with Hesiod as a teacher.[25]

---

[24] The most influential formulation was the fourth-century grammarian Diomedes: E. R. Curtius, *European Literature and the Latin Middle Ages*, tr. W. R. Trask (Princeton, 1973) 440. Cf. W. Kroll, 'Lehrgedichte,' *Pauly-Wissowa Realencyclopädie der classischen Altertumswissenschaft* 12.2 (1925) 1843.

[25] For Homer as teacher: Xenophanes B 10 DK (H. Diels and W. Kranz, *Die*

Moreover, the *Theogony* at least (I postpone discussion of *Works and Days*) is closer to Homer's poems than a strict epic/didactic dichotomy allows. In its proem Hesiod appears very much like a Homeric singer: he learned the art of singing, ἀοιδή, from the Muses (*Theog.* 22; cf. *Od.* 8.481; 488) who breathed into him a 'voice filled with the words of a god' (αὐδὴν θέσπιν, *Theog.* 31–32). He initiates his theme in much the same fashion as Homer, invoking the Muses to 'celebrate the holy race of the gods' and bidding them to 'tell me these things... from the beginning' (*Theog.* 104–115). Hesiod's theme is undoubtedly sacred history, but it is also a narrative of noteworthy deeds, and deeds that are far from unconnected to heroic history.

A bridge between the Hesiodic *Theogony* and Homeric epic is provided by his *Ehoiai* or *Catalogue of Women* which is blended into the end of our *Theogony*. After the ascendancy of the Olympians is secured, the *Theogony* changes its theme with a transitional invocation at 963–68: 'sing the tribe of goddesses . . . who lay with mortal men and produced godlike children.' Another invocation at 1019–22 switches to the converse of this theme, asking for the 'race of [mortal] women' who consorted with gods and the heroic descendants of these unions. With this latter invocation a transition is effected to the *Catalogue of Women.*[26] What we may call Homer's 'heroic' tales follow logically and chronologically on this *Theogony-Catalogue* continuum: one divine-mortal union that was recounted in the *Catalogue* (at some length and with a dramatic speech) was that of Thetis and Peleus (Fr. 210–211 M–W), but the union of Achilles' parents is equally an epic theme, as in the cyclic *Cypria.* From this perspective, epics appear not as secular stories about heroic mortals as opposed to gods, but as later stories in a single continuous history. The same comprehensive vision informed the epic cycle, which not only filled in the prologue and aftermath of the Trojan war but reached back to describe the Titanomachy and perhaps too the birth of the gods.[27]

Firm distinctions begin to become perilous here, for one may usefully describe the catalogue poem as a separate genre, a type of poetry that may be paralleled in Greece and elsewhere.[28] Even on such a

---

Fragmente der Vorsokratiker, 6th ed. [Berlin, 1952]), Heraclitus B 56. Xenophanes paired Homer with Hesiod in denouncing their portrayal of gods: B 11, A 1.18 DK; Herodotus joined them as the source of Greek ideas about the gods (2.53).

[26] Hesiod fr. 1 M–W. On these transitions, see M. L. West (1985) 49, 126–27.

[27] Bernabé (1988) 8; against any recoverable cyclic *Theogony*, see Davies (1989) 13.

[28] M. L. West (1985) 3–11.

view, however, catalogue poetry will often function as sub-genre or narrative mode within epic: the catalogue style, for example, is also at home in telling tales of Troy (e.g. *Il.* 2.484 ff., 12.89–104), and Homer no less than Hesiod may need to list a number of rivers (*Il.* 12.17–23; cf. *Theog.* 337–45) or Nereids (*Il.* 18.37–49; cf. *Theog.* 240–64). Even the characters within heroic narratives may have reason to list their ancestors at some length (e.g. *Il.* 6.150–211, 20.200–258). In a notable passage from Odysseus' account of his visit to the underworld (*Od.* 11.225–332), the hero catalogues for his audience the noble women he saw there, thus taking up the themes and much of the manner of a poem like the *Catalogue of Women.*

Whether one wishes to view catalogue poetry as a distinct genre or as a mode of heroic narrative, Hesiod's *Theogony* and *Catalogue of Women* suggests that theogonies were not set apart as distinctively didactic poems but were, like Homeric epic, narrative and sometimes dramatic accounts of earliest history. In the repertoire of the Muses, the κλέα ἀνδρῶν were connected to theogonies, and the whole embraced a discrete mythic epoch beginning with the birth of the gods and ending when the Trojan war resulted in a breach of the close intercourse between gods and mortals (Hesiod Fr. 1.6 ff. and Fr. dub. 264; cf. *Od.* 7.201–203). Although some nobles at epic performances may have claimed descent from the great dynasties mentioned, their world was irretrievably cut off from that age, most obviously because the gods no longer mixed as freely with mortals on earth.[29]

Archaic epic, then, was significantly defined by the themes it could treat. The Homeric and Hesiodic conception of Muse-inspired poetry was based on this mythic age and not on a division between poetry about mortals versus poetry about gods (which is essentially, and perhaps originally, a Platonic way of dividing poetry).[30] The restriction of epic to themes from this imaginary time held force for a very long time in Greece; as far as we can see, it was not breached until the fifth century when Choerilus of Samos, with much fanfare in his proem about innovation, gave epic treatment to Greece's wars with Persia.

[29] M. L. West (1985) 9–11, 29–30, remarks that early Greek catalogue poems are relatively unusual among other genealogical traditions in concentrating on the heroic age and not continuing lineages up to the 'present' time.

[30] The differentiation of 'hymns' (ὕμνοι) for gods from 'encomia' for mortals is found first in Plato (*Republic* 607a, etc.); see Càssola (1975) x–xii.

Other poems attributed to Hesiod appear to have been Muse-inspired narratives of ancient times, such as the *Marriage of Ceyx*, *Descent of Pirithous*, and *Aegimus*. Yet to call all of Hesiod 'epic' may be reductive: if we consider the fourth respect in which archaic poetry defined itself, the poet's relation to the audience, we will realize that Greek epic also involved a quite distinctive rhetorical stance of the poet toward his audience.

Hesiod's *Works and Days* begins with an invocation and so might be immediately taken as a form of Muse-inspired epic. But this invocation is in fact the reverse of those in Homer and the *Theogony*, and it establishes a relationship between poet and addressee that differs vastly from that of epic's to its audience. Hesiod bids the Muses to perform, but not to perform the *Works and Days*. They are asked to tell of Zeus and celebrate his justice (1 ff.): at the end of the proem, the poet turns to a certain Perses and proclaims that '*I* would tell [you] true things' (10). The actual poem will thus be Hesiod's speech to his brother, not the speech of the Muses.[31] This is not to say that the poet wished to sever his own song form from the true and authoritative song of the goddesses, but it does mean that *Works and Days* will not be a narrative, a fact reinforced by its many subsequent addresses to Perses. Hesiod will relate parts of divine and heroic history (such as the stories of Pandora and Prometheus), but always as a particular speaker advising a particular auditor, in order to draw lessons about what Perses should do in this morally ordered cosmos.[32] By contrast, Homer's epics and Hesiod's extended narratives present stories of the past in the first instance as coming from the lips of the Muses, and never explicitly indicate how to apply these tales to their auditors' lives.[33] Whereas the *Works and Days* establishes a highly individualized persona for both poet and addressee (as, presumably, the *Precepts of Cheiron* did also), the epic narrator's

[31] The gnomological *Theognidea* also opens by addressing the Muses and other deities before the poet resumes the first person to direct advice to a certain Cyrnos (esp. 27 ff.).

[32] Because the story of the *Theogony* involves the founding of the moral order of the world, it too sometimes briefly comments on the present effects of past actions, as when Oath is characterized as 'the one who most vexes perjurers on earth' (231–32). But even in lengthier excursuses on why the world works as it does now (e.g. the moralizing that follows the Prometheus-Pandora story, 590–616), the *Theogony* avoids appealing to a 'you' and quickly resumes its narrative thrust (cf. 612).

[33] De Jong (1987a) shows the many ways in which the epic narrator may to move away from the impersonal voice of the Muse and closer to his audience, but always to a degree of involvement that falls far short of direct exhortation.

relation to his audience is far less specific: its projected audience is a nameless collectivity, a weaker and more ignorant generation of mortals living long after the heroes (e.g., *Il.* 5.302–304; 12.380–83).

These differences in the way the poet orients himself to his audience suggest that the *Works and Days* is less close to the *Theogony* than to other hortatory, non-narrative Hesiodic poems such as the *Precepts of Cheiron*, *Bird Divination*, and *Astronomy*. Slicing up genres is particularly perilous here, but much as these poems may share with epic in diction, meter, dialect, legends, and morals, the personas of poet and addressee are quite different, and their themes could hardly be summed up as ἔργ' ἀνδρῶν τε θεῶν τε, τά τε κλείουσιν ἀοιδοί. When Greeks wished to draw a clear distinction between Homer and Hesiod, the latter's poetry is exemplified with *Works and Days* as forming a clear contrast to Homer: Aristophanes' list of useful ancient poets includes Hesiod who taught 'working the land, seasons and harvests and farming' and Homer, the teacher of 'battle formations, courage, and armor.'[34] Whatever name or status one may wish to give these Hesiodic works, they clearly derive from a different tradition than epic, one that may be called 'wisdom poetry' (M. L. West [1978] 3–25). To be sure, the hortatory mode of wisdom poetry may appear in epic too: Phoenix is giving instruction through heroic legend when he recounts the Meleager story to Achilles (9.524–605). Once incorporated into the *Iliad*'s hexameters, the Meleager tale may look like an 'epic within an epic'; but the whole is preceded and followed by direct, second-person instructions to Achilles on how to apply the story to his situation (9.513–23, 600–605). In a somewhat subtle variant, Nestor tells Patroclus one of his own youthful exploits (*Il.* 11.670–761): this Pylian cattle raid is recounted with typically heroic form and structure (see Hainsworth [1991] 22); but it is presented as the personal reminiscence of an elder warrior to a youth, and it is framed with pointed remarks contrasting Achilles' present behavior (11.663–668, 761–63).[35]

Archaic Greek epic must thus be defined in formal, thematic, and rhetorical terms. It was a long, solo song performed in a rhythmical

[34] *Frogs* 1033–36; Hesiod wins the *Contest of Homer and Hesiod* (233.207–210 Allen) on the grounds that he calls the people to 'farming and peace' whereas Homer urges them on to 'war and slaughter' (see Rosen, this vol.).

[35] The dramatic situation of this moral instruction suggests, again, the *Precepts of Cheiron*, and even more strongly Hippias of Elis' 'Trojan Oration,' which he performed (at schools) as a prose sermon from Nestor to the young Neoptolemos (Plato, *Hipp. Maj.* 286B).

recitative; it narrated on the authority of the Muses the deeds of gods and early heroes. The themes epic treated, the 'paths' it could take, were extensive but firmly circumscribed by a mythic conception of a long-lost golden age. The stories were presented dramatically and without explicit cues for how to apply them to their auditors' lives. This discreet attitude toward its audience and its lack of a fictional addressee distinguished epic from exhortative recitatives such as the *Works and Days*; it also would have distinguished epic from such melic poetry as offered extended mythic narrative but explicitly applied the stories to the present ceremony and community.[36] The combination of this limited range of themes, the poet's discreet way of rendering them, and the solo recitative was sufficient to distinguish epic formally and thematically from all contemporary lyric songs and from all non-narrative recitations.

Having achieved this much of a definition of epic in Archaic terms, it remains to add that manipulating these shared conventions offered the poet possibilities for subtly expressive effects. A simple but resonant example is Odysseus' deliberate misapplication of the rules governing wedding songs. After the slaughter of the suitors, Odysseus commands Phemius to produce a wedding song so that passersby might infer that Penelope has at last decided to marry (*Od.* 23.133 ff.). By applying a specific kind of song to the wrong context the hero strategically miscommunicates what has gone on in the palace. A wedding song is hardly what one expects to follow a blood bath, and yet such a song is ironically appropriate when the hero is about to be reunited with his wife.

In a more subtle example Homer discreetly evokes the Archaic genre of maiden's songs (later called *partheneia*) to provide a background to the scene of Odysseus' first meeting with Nausicaa. When the hero first spies the princess, she is amusing herself by playing a ball game with her maids and leading them in an antiphonal song and dance (ἄρχετο μολπῆς, *Od.* 6.101). The narrator does not tell us the song's theme but gives the performance a specific coloration when he compares it to the virgin goddess Artemis sporting with her nymphs in the wild (6.102–109). Such a conceit was typical in maiden's songs, which could be performed antiphonally and for which Artemis and her chorus provided a divine archetype.[37] The tableau moves Odysseus

---

[36] On the generic relations between epic and lyric narratives in the Archaic period, see Burkert (1987).

[37] See Calame (1977) II, 90–91; Ford (1992) 118–19.

to make the same comparison and to venture how well Nausicaa must dance in choruses; he adds that his only comparable experience was on Delos, which was famed for its women's choirs (6.151–63). Once again these subtle intimations of non-epic song are particularly appropriate to the scene, for the partheneion ceremony functioned as a kind of 'coming out' ball in which well-born women might attract the amorous glance of a spectator (cf. *Il.* 16.179–83), and the possibility of taking this princess to wife will soon present itself in the story.

The *Iliad* exhibits a particular versatility in exploiting another non-epic genre, the *threnos*. In drawing to a close, the poem modulates from epic narrative to first-person women's lament with a protracted presentation of the threnodies for Hector (24.723–776). It exploits this genre both for its themes of pathos (a tone also borrowed for the speeches of Andromache and Hecuba in *Iliad* 6) and for its antiphonal structure which allows Helen herself, as the final threnodist, to reflect on the war being fought for her sake. But the conventions of the *threnos* are significantly evoked throughout in the *Iliad*, especially in connection with the death of Patroclus. At Patroclus' lavish funeral in book 23, his comrade-in-arms Achilles 'leads' laments while the Myrmidons in full panoply respond (23.1–17). The verb suggests that Patroclus is being given a formal *threnos*, at least insofar as the battlefield allows. Earlier uses of the word place this male *threnos* for Patroclus in a series of more or less spontaneous laments which anticipate, albeit imperfectly, the final ceremony of 23. When Patroclus' body was being prepared, Achilles embraced the corpse and 'led' lamentations for the Achaeans who groaned in response (18.314–17, 354–55). This spontaneous lament resembles a *threnos*, though it is not formally constituted as one; and Achilles promises Patroclus another lament, that women will mourn him (18.338–42). This comes true in an unforeseen way: Briseis catches a glimpse of the body and 'leads' a lament to which her companions respond with groans (19.282–302). The multiplication of these scenes (also 19.314–39) dramatically emphasizes the loss Achilles feels rather than reflecting any precise set of funeral practices (M. W. Edwards [1986]). Two further quasi-antiphonies which begin the series suggest that the poet keeps returning to the form as a way of exploring how raw suffering may be transmuted into artistic structure. When news of Patroclus' death is first announced, Achilles falls to the ground in an orgy of grief, groaning, and self-defilement. These sounds arouse the captive women in his tent who come running and collapse around him beating their breasts (18.22–31). The actions are perfectly comprehensible in themselves even as the tableau suggests an antiphonal lament; it is as if the poet is deliberately superposing on the elemental and impassioned expression of grief its most proper and ceremonious form (its genre). That form is soon repeated when Thetis hears the cries and comes with her Nereids to comfort the hero. Taking Achilles' head in her arms, in another conventional gesture of mourning (18.72; cf. 24.712, 724), she 'leads the groaning' for the nymphs who beat their breasts in response (18.50–51). Her ensuing complaint (18.52–64) thus becomes at once highly pathetic and a generic anomaly: a god's lament in prospect for the son she knows will die. The *threnos*, then, serves the poet of the *Iliad* as a source of pathetic themes, as an evocative pattern for structuring action, and as a way to intimate the great pathos of an event that lies beyond the limits of the story he has to tell.

Generic conventions offer no less suggestive material when the genre being represented is epic itself. The *Iliad* does not show us epic singers performing; Priam has professional singers summoned to Hector's funeral, though their singing is not subsequently described (24.721–22). Their presence, however, suggests that epic's noble pedigree reaches back even to praises offered heroes at funerals, an idea that may contain a grain of truth.[38] The *Odyssey* offers more extensive representations of epic singing which dramatize Homer's definition of epic, affirming the distinction drawn above between epic and non-inspired accounts of the past.

The *Odyssey* twice suggestively juxtaposes epic song to nonpoetic accounts of heroic deeds: in book 1, Phemius sings about the return of the heroes while Telemachus privately discusses the same topic with a well-traveled guest (in reality, a disguised Athena); on Phaeacia, Odysseus praises Demodocus as a nonpareil epic performer, then goes on to recount his own adventures in a kind of 'prose' sequel to the poet's Trojan tales. In both cases the unique access that the Muses give to the past for Homer's generation is ironically reaffirmed: if epic poetry was once an entertainment worthy of heroes, it will be all the more valuable in a post-heroic age when gods do not so readily appear on earth bearing news, and heroes no longer give their own accounts of their actions. The contrast between song in a heroic context and song in Homer's own day is further underlined by the response of the audience. Penelope's tears at Phemius' song are set

[38] Reiner (1938) 62–67, 116–20; Bowra (1952) 8–10.

against the pleasure taken in the same song by the suitors, and Odysseus' repeated sobbing at songs of Troy provokes the curiosity of the pacific and music-loving Phaeacians (1.325 ff., 8.83 ff.). For non-heroic mortals, pleasure is the normal response to epic: when a man hears songs about earlier men, 'straight away he forgets his sad thoughts and does not think about his cares' (Hesiod, *Theog.* 102–103); even an embittered Achilles finds pleasure (φρένα τερπόμενον, *Il.* 9.189) in the κλέα ἀνδρῶν because the men in question are of former times. Because Penelope and Odysseus are not of the generation of later mortals, but are personally involved in the actions described in song their response differs heroically from the norm.[39]

A final outstanding example of Homer manipulating the conventions of his own genre is Odysseus' *apologos* in *Odyssey* 9–12. In a tour de force the poet assumes a persona which liberates him from three fundamental conventions of epic narrative: he narrates the story in the first person; as a vagabond sailor, he incorporates fantastic and supernatural tales otherwise out of place in Homeric poetry; finally, he boldly flashes back to tell at length events that preceded the beginning of the poem. But we are not quite allowed to forget the epic narrator who has modulated his own voice into that of his character. Odysseus too casts a singer's spell over his audience (*Od.* 11.333–34 = 13.1–2; cf. 1.337–40), and King Alcinous explicitly compares him to a singer (11.363–69). If the *apologos* reveals to the Pheacians that the apparent vagabond is really a hero, it also reminds Homer's audience that behind this hero stands a poet no less skilled in disguising himself.

Our ability to appreciate the ways in which Homer relies on and exploits his contemporaries' notions of genre rests on a very limited sample of Archaic songs. Although there is much we cannot know, nonetheless we may claim that a notion of epic genre helped the poet to guide the expectations of his audience and helped the audience place new songs in relation to ones it had heard. If at times the conventions of epic were pressed to their limits, the result would still be an epic, a tale of the vast but not infinite past delivered by the Muses to the skillfully recreative singer.

---

[39] A related ironic reversal of a fundamental epic norm is Telemachus' defending Phemius' heroic theme on the grounds that men love best the 'newest' song (*Od.* 1.350–52). Only in a heroic age can epic be 'new.'

Lowell Edmunds

MYTH IN HOMER[1]

In recent years, the concept of Greek myth has been challenged. In *The Creation of Mythology*, Marcel Detienne pointed to the non-existence of any ancient Greek terminology for 'myth,' 'legend,' etc. and, in particular, to the absence of any collective expression for what we call 'Greek myth,' i.e., a related set of stories about gods and heroes.[2] In anthropological terms, it was not, he and others have inferred, a 'native category.' According to Detienne, Greek myth was invented in the modern period, beginning in the eighteenth century, and retrojected onto Greek antiquity. It might, then, be naive to undertake a chapter on myth in Homer, on Homer's relation to the supposed category of Greek myth, unless one first gives this category some credibility.

In establishing the category of myth, one has to begin by conceding that the vocabulary of ancient Greek is impoverished in this area. *Mythos*, the word that ought to be the most useful, is disappointing. Whatever it means, it never in the archaic and classical periods refers to a category of stories corresponding to 'myth' as in our expression 'Greek myth.' And yet already in Homer, there is a use of *mythos* that points to a foundation for 'myth' and for 'Greek myth.' In his study of the speeches in Homer, *The Language of Heroes* (1989), Richard Martin showed that those called *muthoi* consist of three types: commands, boast-and-insult contests ('flyting'), and recitation of remembered events. On the basis of speech-act theory and comparative ethnological evidence, he described these *muthoi* as 'performances of self'; further, he argued that they must be imitations of styles of speaking actually practiced by those who listened to the poems. Because the stories of remembered events are what we would call

[1] I am grateful to Susan Edmunds, Richard P. Martin, Nancy Worman, and Barry Powell for comments on this chapter.

[2] Trans. M. Cook (Chicago, 1986). First published as *L'Invention de la mythologie* (Paris, 1981). Detienne's line of inquiry has been extended by C. Calame in 'Mythe' et 'rite' en Grèce: Des catégories indigènes? *Kernos* 4 (1991) 179–204 and in other earlier articles cited therein.

'myths,' we can say that for Homer and his audience, our 'myth' is the oral performance of a story with intent to sway an audience.

From this point of view, it seems that the question of Greek myth has been wrongly posed by Detienne and others. Instead of assuming that, if there was Greek myth in antiquity, it would have been Greek myth as defined in the modern period, one should ask if the modern concepts were the right ones in the first place. Could some other concept be formulated that would in fact correspond to an ancient 'native category'? The category, as Martin's findings suggest, is oral storytelling. In other words, myth can be understood in terms of a practice, not a subject-matter, and it is unnecessary to look for some ancient concept and/or term meaning 'story about gods or heroes.' There is in fact a fairly consistent set of terms that refers to this practice.[3] So, on this hypothesis, the question that should be addressed to the ancient Greek evidence is not 'Did the Greeks have a category of, or a terminology for, myth?' but 'Did the Greeks have a practice of oral storytelling and was this practice accorded any particular status?'[4] Homeric epic already provides clear answers to these new questions.

Both the *Iliad* and the *Odyssey* contain numerous representations of oral storytelling. In the *Iliad*, Nestor tells how he fought against the Centaurs (1.260–73; cf. 2.740–43), against Augeas, the Eleans, and the Moliones; and how he competed in the funeral games for Amaryngceus (11.670–762; 23.629–43).[5] Phoenix tells the story of the anger of Meleager (9.524–605); Achilles tells the story of Niobe (24.599–620); Agamemnon tells about Atē's influence on Zeus at the time of the birth of Heracles (19.91–133). *These are not stories that Homer tells in his*

[3] Cf. L. Edmunds, 'Oral Story-telling and Hexameter Poetry in Archaic Greece,' forthcoming in the Actas of the V Coloquio Internacional de Filología Griega.

[4] Cf. Hansen (1983), making more or less the same observation that Calame (n. 1 above) has recently made ('The Greeks did not abstract from all these kinds of traditional narratives a general concept of traditional oral story'), concludes that it is time for 'Hellenists . . . to operate with one inclusive category of the oral story, whether we wish to call it mythology or something else, and however we may wish to divide it up into genres' (108). My contribution to this volume, pursuing myth in Homer from this oral perspective, begs the notoriously difficult question of the transition from the oral to the written. On this question see Buxton (1994) 45–52 ('Performance into text').

[5] Cf. the *muthoi* that Nestor and Machaon are said to tell one another (not reported by Homer!). N.b. *enepontes* 'narrating' (*Il.* 11.643), which describes how they told *muthoi*, and, for the semantics of this verb, see Risch (1985).

own voice; these are stories that Homer represents as told by the heroes. And there are many other, less extensive examples of such storytelling on the part of the heroes.[6] In the *Odyssey*, besides Odysseus' recounting of his adventures and the five 'lies' that he tells upon his return to Ithaca, there are Penelope's two stories concerning the daughters of Pandareus (19.518–24; 20.66–78) and Antinous' recounting of the drunkenness of the Centaur, Eurytion (21.295–304). Unlike the heroes, Homer is not a storyteller; he limits himself for the most part to the narration of the forty-odd days covered in each of the epics.[7] His reference to both Trojan War and non-Trojan myth outside the time-frame of the epics is infrequent and concise.

The distinction between poetry and storytelling assumed by Homeric epic is especially clear in the passages set in the palace of Alcinous where Odysseus recounts his adventures. Alcinous, Odysseus' host, has in his retinue a professional bard, Demodocus, who on three occasions sings songs for the entertainment of those gathered for a meal. He accompanies himself on a lyre. When Odysseus proceeds to give his account of his adventures, he does not accompany himself on a lyre. He is *like* a bard, as Alcinous and later Eumaeus say (11.368; 17.518–21), but he is not a bard. He is a storyteller.[8] This distinction between poetry and oral storytelling, already articulated in Homer, remains a fundamental one down through the Classical period.[9]

---

[6] For example, when a hero gives his genealogy, he sometimes is led to tell a story about one or another ancestor: Glaucus (*Il.* 6.152–211); Diomedes (*Il.* 14.113–27). Other examples: Tlepolemus tells how Herakles came to Troy with six ships in order to get the horses of Laomedon and sacked the city (*Il.* 5.638–42; cf. *Il.* 14.250–61). Ajax tells how he and Teucer had received Lycophron, son of Mastor, after he had killed a man in his native Cythera (*Il.* 15.430–41). Diomedes tells of the crime of Lycourgus against Dionysus (*Il.* 6.130–40).

[7] See L. Edmunds (1993) chs. 7–8.

[8] Athena tells Odysseus that he is best of mortals at deliberation and *muthoi* (*Od.* 13.298), without mentioning poetry, and the Sirens give him the epithet *poluainos*, meaning that he is a man 'of many fables,' i.e., tells many *ainoi* or has many *ainoi* told about him (*Od.* 12.184).

[9] Pind. *P.* 1.92–94; *N.* 6.29–30; Thuc. 6.2.1; Plato *Rep.* 366e, 392d. Cf. Pind. *N.* 6.45–46; *N.* 3.52–53. The distinction is implicit at Thuc. 4.24.5, where Thucydides refers to the strait between Rhegium and Messene as the Charybdis through which Odysseus is said (*legetai*) to have sailed. Thucydides refers not to Homer, who provides no such identification of Charybdis, but to popular reconstruction of the voyage of Odysseus.

On the basis of myth as oral storytelling and the distinction between myth and poetry, several questions can be posed. First, what is the function in Homer of myth as oral storytelling by characters in the epics? What is Homer's attitude toward it? Second, what is the relation of Homer's own narratives in the *Iliad* and the *Odyssey*, including the larger story of the Trojan War presupposed by these narratives, to other versions of the same myths? What choices has Homer made? Third, how innovative is Homer? Does he invent myths? All of these questions bear on the function of myth in the poetry of Homer, an area that tends to be neglected in favor of research on the origins of Homeric myth and its relations to history and religion. These approaches will be briefly surveyed at the end of this chapter.

The Function of Myth as Oral Storytelling by Characters in Homer

The status of oral stories in Homer is, perhaps unexpectedly to us, who hold Greek myth in high esteem, dubious. Although oral storytelling is performative and self-assertive, most stories in Homer fail. Odysseus' stories are the big exception (and for Odysseus' audience these stories, aside from the Catalogue of Heroines, are not about the distant past but the storyteller's recent adventures). The only other real success is Achilles' retelling of the story of Niobe (24.601–20).[10] A good example of failure is Antinous' story of the drunken Centaur, Eurytion.[11] The archery contest is underway. Penelope has agreed to marry whichever of the suitors can shoot an arrow through a row of axes. After some of the suitors have failed to bend the bow, Odysseus, still disguised as a beggar and still unknown to Penelope, asks to be allowed to try. Antinous then rebukes him for his presumptuousness.

> Wretched guest, isn't it enough for you that you dine with us haughty men at your ease, and do not lack for a dinner, but listen to our words and speeches? No other guest and beggar listens to our words. Honey-sweet wine is wounding you, as it hurts others, too—whoever

[10] M. Lang, 'Reverberation and Mythology in the *Iliad*,' in *Approaches to Homer*, ed. C. A. Rubino and C. W. Shelmerdine (Austin, 1983), 142–43 observes; 'Thus the epic comes full circle . . .: a *paradeigma* that fails to persuade [Nestor's at 1.259 ff., the first in the *Iliad*] opens up the wrath-story, which is finally brought to a close with a *paradeigma* that succeeds in persuading [Achilles'].'

[11] The following discussion is adapted from L. Edmunds (1993) ch. 6.

> gulps it down and does not drink moderately. Wine infatuated the Centaur, too, glorious Eurytion, in the hall of great-hearted Peirithous, when he came to visit the Lapiths. When wine had infatuated his mind, he went mad and did criminal deeds in the house of Peirithous. And grief took the heroes, and they sprang up and dragged him outside, through the courtyard. They cut off his ears and his nostrils with the pitiless bronze. He, because his mind had been infatuated, went away bearing his guilt in his reckless spirit. From this time, there has been conflict between Centaurs and men, but he was the first to pay the penalty for his drunkenness. (*Od.* 21.287–304)

Antinous goes on to say that, like Eurytion, Odysseus will be punished if he tries to string the bow (305–310), i.e., Odysseus' offense is the equivalent of Eurytion's. Antinous did not have to specify the offense, because everyone knew it. The incident to which Antinous refers took place at the wedding of Peirithous to Hippodameia in Thessaly (Pindar frag. 166 S–M). Peirithous, king of the Lapiths, invited the Centaurs to the wedding. Unaccustomed to wine, they soon became drunk. Eurytion tried to carry off the bride; other Centaurs tried to carry off her attendants. A brawl erupted, and a continuous war between Centaurs and Lapiths ensued (*Il.* 1.260–73).

In Antinous' use of the story, wine is the point of contact between the story and the situation in which Antinous is speaking. The moral or application of the story is: do not drink in excess. Antinous adds an aetiological conclusion: this was the beginning of enmity between Centaurs and men, i.e., not only was Eurytion's drunkenness bad for him but it led to a new, worse phase in the relations between Centaurs and human beings. But the story has implications of which Antinous is unaware and that suggest a meaning the opposite of the one he intends. In fact, Antinous and his friends are the ones who are violating the laws of hospitality, and they are the ones who are going to be punished. The implicit connections between the story and the situation are the real ones.

The following aspects of Antinous' use of the Eurytion story are typical of how Homeric characters use stories. (1) Antinous finds a particular point of contact between the story and the situation to which he wishes to apply it (the drinking of wine). (2) He uses the story as an argument.[12] He finds a moral in the story: do not drink

[12] In the two Homeric Hymns that contain a narrative within the poet's narrative, the practical use of story-telling observed in the *Iliad* and the *Odyssey* is clear. Hermes' theogonic song has the purpose of softening the anger of Apollo at the

in excess. (3) Because of (1) and (2), he tells the story in an elliptical form. He leaves out a great deal. He assumes that his addressee already knows (Homer assumes that his audience already knows) the story. He slants the story toward the moral with which he will conclude. (4) The story has a meaning beyond the one intended by Antinous.[13]

Variation and Homer's Own Narratives in the Iliad and the Odyssey

While the stories told by characters in Homer are traditional (to repeat, the internal addressee's and the audience's prior knowledge of the story is assumed),[14] each telling of a story, because it has a particular motivation, is different from another. Against the traditionality of myth and its meaningfulness as a collective expression of society— these are the core of Walter Burkert's definition—,[15] must be set the consideration that a traditional story can survive only if it can be retold, and it can be retold only if it can be applied to new circumstances. (In the case of Antinous, one saw a misapplication that reflected ominously on the teller.) A story, or myth, is therefore, in retrospect, a set of variants on a fundamental pattern, while, on the occasion of any retelling, the present, individualist version is the authoritative one. Myth occurs, one could say, at the juncture of performance with tradition.[16] Here also alien, borrowed 'mythical ideas,' or narrative 'conceptual foci,' to use Robert Mondi's expres-

theft of his cattle, and the song is successful: Apollo says that it is worth fifty cows (*h. Merc.* 436–37). Aphrodite establishes the precedents for her union with Anchises by telling the stories of Tros (*h. Ven.* 200–217) and of Tithonus (*h. Ven.* 218–38). The latter story also explains why the mortal Anchises cannot become her husband.

[13] Other examples are discussed in Edmunds (1993) 35–39, 61–64.

[14] They appeal to 'memory.' Cf. Moran (1975).

[15] Burkert (1979b) 29; translated and paraphrased in G. Nagy (1990a) 8; again, perhaps Burkert's fullest definition, in (1993).

[16] Cf. L. Edmunds, ed. (1989) 15–16; followed by J. Bremmer, *Greek Religion* (Oxford, 1994) 57. This principle applies equally to the vase painter's use of myth, as S. Lowenstam has shown (1992).

sions, are articulated in stories and thus domesticated.[17] Outside of stories, it is doubtful that they could survive in a new land.

This principle of the juncture of performance with tradition and of borrowing, with variation as a result, applies to Homer's own narratives. It operates both within these narratives and as between these narratives and other versions of the same stories. The *Iliad* contains a notable example of internal variation in the two throwings of Hephaestus from Olympus. At the end of Book 1, in support of Achilles' desire to disgrace Agamemnon, Thetis goes up to Olympus and secures Zeus' promise to make the Trojans victorious. Hera, who favors the Achaeans, quarrels with Zeus, her husband. He threatens her with physical harm (565–67). At this point, Hephaestus intervenes and urges Zeus and Hera not to quarrel (573–76). He turns to his mother and reminds her of the great power of Zeus (577–83, 586–89). As an example, he reminds her of how, once before, when he had tried to defend her, Zeus had seized him by the foot and thrown him from Olympus. He fell all day and landed on Lemnos, where the Sinties rescued him (590–94). It is likely, but not certain, that in this version Zeus is the father of Hephaestus (the word 'father' in 578 is ambiguous: it might refer to Zeus as 'the father of gods and men'; but at *Od.* 8.312 Zeus is the father of Hephaestus). It is likely, but not explicit, that the lameness of Hephaestus is the result of his fall. (For the occasion on which Hephaestus had tried to defend his mother against Zeus, see under *Innovation?* below.)

In Book 16, Thetis goes to the house of Hephaestus, where she is warmly welcomed by Charis, his wife. (Compare *Odyssey* Book 8, where Aphrodite is the wife of Hephaestus.) Charis calls her husband. He comes from his workshop. Even before Thetis can make her request, Hephaestus says why he owes her a favor. Once upon a time, Thetis and Eurynome, the daughter of Ocean, had saved Hephaestus, after Hera, his mother, threw him off Olympus because she was ashamed of his lameness. He lived with Thetis and Eurynome for nine years in a cave beneath the ocean, and fashioned various ornaments for them.

These two contradictory versions of the throwing of Hephaestus appear within the same poem. They are an oddity. No other inconsistency of this magnitude is found within either the *Iliad* or the *Odyssey*.

[17] Mondi (1989).

The expression 'Even Homer nods' means that sometimes even a genius like Homer makes mistakes; but the inconsistency between the two versions of the throwing of Hephaestus seems to reflect a far greater inattentiveness than mere nodding. In order to explain the version in Book 18, it has been suggested that Homer invented it in order to motivate Hephaestus' willingness to make the armor. But did Homer have to motivate this willingness? If he did, could he not have found some other way? Why did he invent a motivation that created a contradiction of a kind unparalleled elsewhere in his poems? What might seem a gain for the immediate situation in Book 18 is a loss for the coherence of the poem as a whole.

The *Iliad* then contains two clearly distinct variants of the same story. From the formal and esthetic point of view, this contradiction is a defect (though the two versions are so distant from one another in the poem that there is nothing especially jarring about the contradiction). We expect, and Homer's audience clearly expected, self-consistency and coherence in an epic poem. Given these formal and esthetic requirements of epic poetry, it is to be expected that a poet will choose a particular version of a myth and narrate that version. The contradiction between the two throwings of Hephaestus in the *Iliad* is, then, an intrusion of the extra-poetic condition of myth, i.e., its variability, into a poem. This contradiction is a lesson in the difference between myth and poetry.[18]

Turning to variation among Homer's own narratives (as distinguished from storytelling by characters in the poems) and other versions of the same stories, the *Iliad* and the *Odyssey* presuppose a particular version of the Trojan War myth. The main identifying characteristic of this version is that Helen is at Troy. Another version, for which the earliest source is Stesichorus, held that she was detained in Egypt and that a phantom of Helen went to Troy.[19] Because Stesichorus is

[18] Cf. the formulation of the difference by Burkert (1985) 120–21: 'Scholars ... speak ... of early epic art. This art grows up on the foundation of myth, but is not identical with it. If myth is defined as a complex of traditional tales in which significant human situations are united in fantastic combinations ... to illuminate reality, then Greek epic is both less than this and more than this. It is less because it concentrates on heroic motifs, the struggles of heroes of an earlier age in a world which is conceived to some extent realistically, and it is more because it shapes these tales to the highest formal perfection with a technique which is equally sophisticated stylistically, metrically, and compositionally.'

[19] Herodotus has a rationalized version that omits the phantom: Helen was detained in Egypt as a runaway adulteress; Paris returned to Troy; when the Achaeans

the earliest source, he is often held to have invented this version, but comparative evidence shows that it is a common variant of an international folktale type that could be called The Abduction of the Beautiful Wife.[20] In this type, the beautiful wife is sometimes supernatural, possessing a double nature. Stesichorus did not have to invent the phantom Helen.[21] The *Odyssey* places Helen and Menelaus in Egypt but on their return from, not on their way to, Troy (Book 4), and thus perhaps recognizes the variant.

As for the return of Odysseus in the *Odyssey*, again Homer has chosen a particular version. Aristotle summarized the story of this poem thus: 'The account that one can give of the *Odyssey* is not lengthy. A man is away from home for many years; he is watched closely by Poseidon; further, things at home are such that his property is being wasted by suitors and his son is being plotted against. He arrives, storm-tossed; he causes certain recognitions. Attacking, he survives, and destroys his enemies. This is proper [to the *Odyssey*]; the rest is episodes' (*Poetics* 1455b17–23). To Aristotle's summary one would want to add Penelope, the wife of Odysseus, with whom he wants to be reunited and with whom he is reunited at the end of the story just when she is about to choose a new husband from amongst the suitors.

One of the poems of the Epic Cycle, the *Telegony*, which is known from fragments and summaries in later authors, provides a variant of the return of Odysseus, starting at the point at which he has finally reached his home.[22] Odysseus goes off to visit the famous stable of Augeas that Heracles had had to clean out. Odysseus is entertained

arrived at Troy, they refused to believe that Helen was not there; thus, according to this version, the Trojan War was fought for nothing (2.112–120). In both versions, Menelaus eventually finds Helen in Egypt and returns to Lacedaemon with her.

[20] Motifs of this myth are all found in the complex of folktales grouped by Aarne and Thompson (1961) under 400 ('The Man on a Quest for his Lost Wife'; cf. 465 'The Man Persecuted Because of His Beautiful Wife'). For an Indo-European Helen, cf. C. Grotanelli, 'Yoked Horses, Twins, and the Powerful Lady: India, Greece, Ireland, and Elsewhere,' *Journal of Indo-European Studies* 14 (1986) 125–52.

[21] Cf. M. Griffith, 'Contest and Contradiction in Early Greek Poetry,' in *Cabinet of the Muses: Essays on Classical and Comparative Literature in Honor of Thomas G. Rosenmeyer*, ed. M. Griffith and D. Mastronarde (Atlanta, 1990) 196–97.

[22] The *Telegony*, attributed to Eugammon of Cyrene (6th c. B.C.), is later than the *Odyssey*, but the story, as distinguished from the poem, could be as old as, or older than, the story of the *Odyssey*. In fact, there is considerable evidence that the *Iliad* and the *Odyssey* are aware of the narrative traditions of the Epic Cycle. Cf. the references to Neoanalysis in n. 57 below.

by Polyxenus, the grandson of Augeas. Then he goes to the land of the Thesprotians, where he performs the sacrifice that Teiresias had stipulated. There he marries the queen, Callidice, and defends her country in battles against its neighbors. They have a son, Polypoetes. In the meantime, Telegonus, Odysseus's son by Circe, is growing up on Circe's island. (There is no such son in the *Odyssey*.) Odysseus is succeeded by Polypoetes and returns to Ithaca. Telegonus, who has now grown up, goes off to look for his father and arrives at the island of Ithaca, not knowing that it is the land of Odysseus. He raids the cattle of Odysseus. A fight breaks out. The son unwittingly kills his father. Then Telegonus takes Telemachus and Penelope back to the island of Circe. Telegonus marries Penelope, and Telemachus marries Circe.

A major difference between the *Odyssey* and the variant is that in one, Odysseus is homeward bound or centripetal, whereas in the other, he is outward bound or centrifugal.[23] In the prophecy of Teiresias, the *Odyssey* acknowledges, and repudiates, the variant represented by the *Telegony*. This prophecy rather clearly acknowledges that the wanderings of Odysseus were not over when he returned to Ithaca after the Trojan War, but strictly coordinates these further wanderings with the homeward bound or centripetal Odysseus of the *Odyssey*. The variant of the return is also alluded to in the fourth of the 'lies' told by Odysseus, pretending to be a certain Aithon who in some ways resembles the centrifugal Odysseus (19.165–202).

The *Iliad* is more difficult to explain as the variant of a traditional story. The particular difficulty of the *Iliad* is its narrow focus on the anger of Achilles, provoked by Agamemnon, the commander of the Achaeans, when he took Briseïs from Achilles. Briseïs was a woman who belonged to Achilles, having been given to him as part of the spoils of war. To retaliate against Agamemnon, Achilles, the best Achaean warrior, withdrew from the fighting. The Trojans then began to prevail. Agamemnon sent an embassy to the hut of Achilles, in order to persuade him to rejoin the ranks. Achilles refused. Finally, in the absence of Achilles, a Trojan counter-offensive carried the battle up to the Achaeans' ships. At this point, Achilles' closest friend, Patroclus, joined the fighting and rallied the Achaeans. He was killed

[23] These terms are taken from Stanford (1963) ch. 6 ('Developments in the Epic Cycle').

by Hector, the greatest of the Trojans. Achilles then reentered the battle to get vengeance for his friend by killing Hector. Achilles' death does not take place in the *Iliad* but has been prophecied to follow soon after Hector's.

There are only very slight indications that the anger of a hero and his temporary withdrawal from battle was a traditional story (cf. Paris, *Il.* 6.326; Aeneas, 13.460).[24] The story of Meleager's withdrawal, narrated by Phoenix at the time of the embassy in Book 9, is ostensibly a precedent for Achilles,'[25] but, as will be shown, it has a quite different implication. The anger of Achilles in the *Iliad* is in fact best seen as an episode in the larger life-story, or hero myth, of Achilles. Hero myth is a definable type within Greek myth.[26] Typically, this myth begins with the marriage or union of the hero's parents and ends with his death. The *Iliad* includes a brief account of the marriage of Achilles' parents, Peleus and Thetis (24.59–63). The death of Achilles is foreshadowed in the *Iliad* several times. Most notably, when Achilles renounces his anger against Agamemnon in order to get vengeance on Hector, Thetis tells him that his own death will come soon after Hector's (18.91–99). In this way, the end of the anger story is linked to the end of the life-story.

Meleager

The story of Meleager told by Phoenix to Achilles illustrates all four of the points made above apropos of Antinous. But the meaning that goes beyond the one intended by Phoenix comes partly from comparison with a version of the story that Phoenix' version suppresses.

Phoenix begins by saying: we know that in the old days the heroes would accept gifts and were open to persuasion. Thus the speech starts out as an example of what Achilles should do. (The speech ends, rather maladroitly, on a different note.) Meleager lived in Calydon, a city in Aetolia in Northwestern Greece. His father was Oineus (who was also the father of Tydeus, the father of Diomedes). Oineus neglected a sacrifice to Artemis, and in anger she sent a wild boar to

[24] Cf. Gresseth (1975).

[25] Note Phoenix' opening; cf. Moran (1975).

[26] See the typology of E. Pellizer, *La peripezia dell'eletto: Racconti eroici della Grecia antica* (Palermo, 1991) 15–28.

ravage the territory of the Calydonians. Meleager gathered allies from a nearby city to fight the boar. These were the Curetes. After they killed the boar, they began to fight amongst themselves over the trophies, the boar's tusk and the hide. In the fighting, Meleager happened to kill his uncle on his mother's side, one of the Curetes. Meleager's mother then cursed him. In anger against his mother, because of the curse, Meleager withdrew from the fighting and spent all his time with his wife, Cleopatra. The Curetes then began to get the upper hand, and the elders of the Calydonians sent him a series of embassies, offering him gifts. The series represents an ascending 'scale of affection.'[27] First are priests; second, Oineus, Meleager's father; third, his mother; fourth, his friends. None of these succeeds. Only when the Curetes are on the walls of the city does a fifth party succeed in persuading Meleager, and this is his wife, Cleopatra, who thus proves to rank highest in the scale of affection. Meleager then drives back the Curetes, without, Phoenix points out, having received any gifts. (Phoenix does not tell the death of Meleager but, from other sources, it is clear that this version culminated with the death of Meleager at the hands of Apollo in the continued fighting against the Curetes.[28] Apollo sided with the Curetes.) Phoenix thus ends his story by saying: don't be like Meleager and reenter the fighting without the gifts that have been offered you, though he began by implying that Meleager would be an example of what Achilles should do.

Phoenix conveys messages of which he is apparently unaware. One has to do with the person who ranks highest in the scale of affection. For Meleager, this person is his wife, Cleopatra. For Achilles, this person will prove to be Patroclus, whom he values more than anyone else (18.80–81) and whose death will cause him to reenter the fighting. This is not a message that Achilles himself can grasp at the time of the embassy in Book 9 but it is there for Homer's audience, who know the outcome. The connection between the highest positions in the two scales of affections, Meleager's and Achilles', is even reflected in the names of the persons who occupy these positions. Each name is a compound (Kleo [A]-patra [B] and Patroklos, who is also called Patro [B]-kleēs [A]), and the compound consists of the same two semantic elements (*kleos* 'glory' and *pater* 'father,' thus 'glory

[27] Kakridis (1949) 141–54.

[28] Hesiod, frags. 25.12; 280.2 Merkelbach-West; Pausanias 10.31.3, referring to a now lost poem called *Minyas*.

of the fathers') in different sequences (A–B, B–A).[29] Phoenix thus unwittingly calls attention to the unfortunate circumstances under which Achilles will decide to reenter the fighting.

Phoenix' use of the Meleager myth has still further implications for Achilles, which become clearer if his version of the myth is compared with another ancient version, one which Homer's audience can probably be assumed to have known. This version is attested for the first time in a fragment of the tragedian Phrynichus (6th–5th c. B.C.),[30] and is found in Aeschylus' *Libation Bearers* (602–11). It is told by Apollodorus (1.8.2–3) and in an elaborate romanticized version by Ovid (*Metamorphoses* 8; written sometime after 2 A.D.).[31] When Meleager was seven days old, the Fates decreed that Meleager would die when a piece of wood in the fire burned up. His mother put the piece of wood in a chest. Meleager grew up to be a noble and invulnerable man. His father, Oineus, neglected a sacrifice to Artemis, as in Phoenix' version, and the Calydonian boar hunt ensued. Oineus promised the trophies to whoever killed the boar. A dispute broke out over the rightful winner of the spoils. Meleager killed two of his maternal uncles. In her grief, Meleager's mother burned up the piece of wood and Meleager died.

Whether Homer's audience thought of the death of Meleager at the hands of Apollo, presupposed in Phoenix' version, or of the death caused by his mother in the other version, this early death of the hero was an essential ingredient of the myth. Phoenix thus conveys not only the cause of Achilles' eventual return to the fighting, i.e., the death of Patroclus, but also the further effect of that return, the death of Achilles, which will soon follow Achilles' killing of Hector in vengeance for Patroclus. By returning to the fighting, Achilles chooses the short glorious life (cf. the element *kleos* 'glory' in the name of Patroclus), one of the two alternatives of which his mother had told him (9.410–417). The myth of Meleager therefore has greater relevance to the life of Achilles, in the contexts of the *Iliad* and of the Trojan War myth as a whole, than does the parallel insisted upon by Achilles—according to him, Agamemnon has committed

---

[29] First pointed out by E. Howald, 'Meleager und Achill,' *Rheinisches Museum* 73 (1924) 411. Cf. G. Nagy (1979) 102–108. In order to bring out the semantics of the names, I have here transliterated the Greek *kappa* by the Roman *k*.

[30] Paus. 10.31.4.

[31] *Ode* 5.94–154 of Bacchylides combines the two versions.

exactly the same wrong against him as the one Paris committed against Menelaus (9.336–43). And the myth of Meleager certainly has relevance far beyond Phoenix' point about accepting gifts, which miscarries completely. Achilles is far from persuaded to reenter the fighting. The myth is more useful, one could say, to Homer than to Phoenix.

Innovation?

The distinction between Homer's and a Homeric character's intentions for a myth is directly relevant to the question of mythical innovation in Homer. In the first place, most of the myths narrated in the *Iliad* and the *Odyssey* are narrated by characters in speeches. Homer narrates The Anger of Achilles and The Return of Odysseus but spends little time on non-Trojan War myths and on Trojan War myths that fall outside the time-frame of the epics. He provides only abbreviated genealogies, allusions, or brief comments (e.g. the aside on Castor and Polydeuces already dead and buried in Lacedaemon, *Il.* 3.243–44). The introduction of Theoclymenus (*Od.* 15.223–55) and the flash-back on the scar of Odysseus (19.391–466) are Homer's longest mythical excursions in his own voice. Homer's characters are the ones who narrate myths.

This simple fact tends to be overlooked by scholars interested in myth in Homer. They have often referred to 'mythological innovation' in Homer or to Homer's 'invention' of mythical details or even of whole myths (e.g. Thetis' assistance to Zeus at the time of a palace revolution on Olympus, *Il.* 1.393–407, discussed below).[32] It would be fitting to refer not to Homer but to the speaker and to the speech in its context in the poem. For it is the speaker who creates the 'innovation' in a myth, in reponse to the demands of the situation in which he or she is speaking. Thus it would be more accurate to say that *Homer represents his characters as innovating* than it is to say that Homer innovates.

---

[32] See J. March, *The Creative Poet: Studies of the Treatment of Myth in Greek Poetry*, Bulletin of the Institute of Classical Studies, Suppl. 49 (London, 1987) and her bibliography. For a critique of the notion of mythological invention in Homer, see G. Nagy, 'Mythological Exemplum in Homer,' in *Innovations of Antiquity*, ed. R. Hexter and D. Selden (London, 1991) 311–31.

Against the background of Homer's practice of presenting myths through his characters' speeches, one can return to the myth of Meleager recounted by Phoenix in *Iliad* Book 9. This myth is the one most often chosen by scholars as evidence of Homeric innovation. Phoenix' version of the Meleager myth, which omits the life-token (the piece of wood that, when consumed by fire, will cause the death of Meleager), can hardly have been invented by Phoenix (i.e., by Homer for Phoenix). To grasp this point, it is only necessary to think of the situation and of the intended effect of the speech on Achilles, i.e., a change of mind on his part. Phoenix speaks not only for himself but for the other members of the embassy, who as a group speak for the imperiled Achaean army. If Phoenix should here for the first time introduce such a radical revision into the Meleager myth as the deletion of the life-token and thus confront Achilles with something that Achilles knew (and Homer's audience knew) was untrue of the story, Phoenix would lose the chance of persuading him. (His speech fails in its purpose, but that failure is not to be explained by mythical 'innovation.') In fact, it is known from other sources, cited above, that there was a version of the myth in which Apollo, not the life-token, was the cause of Meleager's death. Although Phoenix says nothing of the death of Meleager, he must be assuming that it is caused by Apollo.

In Phoenix' version, the curse of Meleager by his mother replaces the burning of the life-token as her reaction to the killing of her brother (9.566–72).[33] One can compare the absence of the huntress Atalanta and the love motif in Phoenix' version, in which Meleager already has a wife. Another example of such variation within a motif is the curse on Phoenix: as he says earlier in the same speech in which he narrates the Meleager myth, he was cursed by his father for having slept with his father's concubine (9.454–57). In another version, Phoenix was not cursed but blinded by his father (Aristophanes, *Acharnians* 421; Apollodorus 3.13.8).

In the version of the Meleager myth told by Phoenix, anger is Meleager's reaction to his mother's curse, and anger is the explicit

[33] I.e., something folkloric is replaced by something more acceptable in the heroic setting. Cf. the self-mutilation of the protagonist of the folktale ('The Ogre Blinded') that lies behind the Cyclops episode in the *Od.* Self-mutilation cannot be taken over into the epic and is replaced by the No Man motif. See Edmunds (1993) ch. 3.

point of connection with the situation at hand: Achilles had the right to be angry up until now, when his friends have come to him and have offered him gifts in the name of Agamemnon. In olden times, Phoenix says, when heroes were angry, as Achilles is, they would accept gifts and were open to persuasion (9.515–26). As anger is the point of connection, so the giving up of anger is the announced moral. We have seen in the case of Antinous' use of the wedding of Peirithous, that the speaker typically focuses on a small detail as the point of connection, a detail that may be only an inference, as in the case of Niobe's taking food (24.599–620).[34] The anger of Meleager, causing his withdrawal from the fighting, is thus another example of how characters in Homer apply myths to the situation at hand. The anger would have been a lesser motif in the received version of the myth, which largely concerned the Calydonian Boar Hunt, one of the principal myths of Western Greece. Given Phoenix' purpose, it is not surprising that the Boar Hunt itself is narrated sketchily, as being well known, in twenty lines (9.529–49). Peleus, the father of Achilles, is not mentioned, though he was a famous participant and appears regularly in the many vase paintings of the Boar Hunt from the period 590–540 B.C. The curse, the anger, and so on are narrated at more than twice the length of the Boar Hunt, in forty-eight lines (9.550–98). In other words, Phoenix' emphasis on the anger of Meleager as an episode in the Calydonian Boar Hunt corresponds to Homer's emphasis on the anger of Achilles in the Trojan War, although, to repeat, the intention of Phoenix, as represented by Homer, is quite different from Homer's intention, which emerges from the context of Achilles' life-story as a whole. Homer's audience knows this story as a whole; Phoenix does not know the future.

In Phoenix' elaboration of the anger of Meleager, when he first gives the name of the hero's wife, he digresses on an incident in her life before she was married to Meleager: Cleopatra is

> the daughter of the fair-ankled Marpessa, daughter of Euenus, and of Idas, who was the mightiest of mortal men in those days, and he drew his bow against the lord Phoebus Apollo on account of the fair-ankled maiden [i.e., Marpessa], and her parents in their hall called her [Cleopatra] Alcyone by name because her mother, suffering the fate of the much-grieving kingfisher [in Greek, 'alcyon'], wept because

[34] Hainsworth (1993) 132.

> Phoebus Apollo the far worker had snatched her [Marpessa] away. (9.557–64).

Phoenix' account of the recovery of Marpessa (as interpreted in the preceding quotation) is borne out in Pausanias: Idas drew his bow against Apollo in order to recover Marpessa after Apollo had carried her off (Pausanias 5.18.2). In other words, Apollo had abducted the beautiful wife of Idas. Phoenix' digression is prompted by the name 'Cleopatra,' and its purpose is to explain why she was also called 'Alcyone.' In this way, Phoenix acknowledges that in the tradition the wife of Meleager has two names.

Scholars who maintain that there is 'mythological innovation' in Homer sometimes take the name 'Cleopatra' as an example, in the belief that it was invented for the sake of the parallelism with 'Patroclus.' There are two reasons why this name is not likely to be an invention. First, there is the matter of the expectations of Phoenix' primary addressee, Achilles, who is clearly assumed to know the myth (cf. the comment above on the sketchiness of the narrative in the first part of Phoenix' speech). A new name would be jarring and detract from the persuasiveness of the story. Second, the parallelism between 'Kleopatra' and 'Patroklos' points to the death of Patroclus, which, as Homer's audience knows, will set off the chain of events leading to Achilles' own death—the death of Patroclus at the hands of Hector will cause Achilles to reenter the fighting; Achilles will kill Hector; Achilles' own death will follow not long after Hector's (it is not narrated in the *Iliad* but is foreshadowed, especially in Thetis' words to Achilles at 18.95–96). It would be completely tactless of Phoenix to suggest Achilles' death to him, just when Achilles has stated his decision to return to Phthia (9.356–63), choosing the long life without glory over the short life with immortal glory (9.410–16).

The tragic implications of the parallelism of the names, as well as of the Meleager analogue as a whole, are intended, but they are intended by Homer for his audience, not by Phoenix for his. As in the case of other myths already discussed, Phoenix' use of the Meleager myth carries implications that go beyond the speaker's own intention. The same is true even of the digression discussed in the two preceding paragraphs. In the first part of the digression, Phoenix refers to a hero's confrontation of Apollo in combat. In the context of the Meleager story, the analogy with Meleager himself is difficult not to notice: Meleager died at the hands of Apollo. The digression thus, despite its overt function as an explanation of the name 'Cleopatra,' seems to point to an event, the final event, in the story of Meleager, which Phoenix does not mention, because, as has just been argued, it is not something appropriate to his purpose. But the death of Meleager at the hands of Apollo inevitably suggests to Homer's audience two other deaths. Apollo participates in the death of Patroclus, stunning him so that he can be killed by Hector (16.787–800); and Achilles knows that Apollo will assist Paris when the time comes for Paris to shoot him with an arrow. Xanthus, Achilles' horse, prophecies that Achilles will die at the hands of a mortal and god, without naming them (19.408–17); Hector says that Achilles will die at the hands of Paris and Apollo (22.359). Achilles himself says that he will die by a shaft of Apollo (21.277–78).

The excursus on the abduction of Alcyone is thus a miniature replica of larger narratives. The confrontation of Apollo by Idas is a replica of the conflict between Apollo and mortal hero seen in the death of Meleager and also in the parallel deaths of Patroclus and of Achilles—except that in all these other cases, the mortal loses. The excursus could also be understood as a miniature replica of The Abduction of the Beautiful Wife, in which the hero succeeds in recovering his wife from her divine abductor.[35] The understanding of the implications of the excursus, as of Phoenix' Meleager myth as a whole, depends upon the audience, especially because these are not implications that Phoenix intends.

Another myth that is often spoken of as an innovation on Homer's part is the divine strife to which Achilles refers in Book 1 of the *Iliad.* His mother Thetis, he says, went to the aid of Zeus when Hera, Poseidon, and Athena intended to bind him. Mabel Lang has shown that this story is part of a larger story of divine conflict that has to be pieced together from scattered references in the *Iliad.* In the following list, the letters indicated the sequence of the parts of the story as presented in the *Iliad*: The speaker appears in parentheses.

A 1.396–400 Thetis' aid to Zeus vs. Hera, Athena, Poseidon (Achilles)
B 1.586–94 Hephaestus tried to help Hera; thrown to earth by Zeus (Hephaestus)
C 5.638–42 Heracles sacked Troy when defrauded by Laomedon (Tlepolemos)

[35] For the concept of replica, see L. Dällenbach, *The Mirror in the Text,* trans. J. Whitely (Chicago, 1989).

D 14.247–62 In support of Hera, Hypnos lulled Zeus to sleep (Hypnos)
E 15.18–24 Hera punished by Zeus (Zeus)
F 15.24–30 Hera drove Heracles off course (Zeus)
G 20.145–48 Wall built for Heracles to protect him from sea monster (Homer in his own voice)
H 21.441–57 Poseidon and Apollo punished by Zeus; serve Laomedon (Poseidon)

Lang puts the story together as follows: 'the conflict on Olympus [1.396] led to the enforced servitude of Poseidon and Apollo, Poseidon's dispatch of a sea-monster to punish Laomedon's failure to pay for their service, Laomedon's hiring of Heracles to dispose of the sea-monster, Heracles' sack of Troy to punish Laomedon's failure to pay up, Hera's bribing of Hypnos to distract Zeus so she could drive Heracles off course, Zeus' punishment of Hera and threat to hurl to earth anyone who tried to help her, and Hephaestus being thus hurled for trying.' If one *numbers* the separate elements (indicated by *letters* above) to show the chronology of the story, the relation of the two orderings is:

1 A
2 H
3 G
4 C
5 D
6 F
7 E
8 B[36]

The poem defies the chronology of the story, as different characters (G is exceptional) tell different parts of it for their own purposes (cf. what was said above apropos of Antinous). Part A looks like a Homeric innovation only if it is seen in isolation. In fact, the story of pre-Trojan War divine strife is complex and consistent. Homer presupposes his audience's knowledge of the whole story, to which it can

36 Note that the throwing of Hephaestus in Book 16, i.e., by Hera, does not fit into this myth of divine strife, and remains one element of 'a doublet in the tradition,' to use Lang's phrase (op. cit., n. 10 above, p. 153).

relate the speakers' typically allusive and self-interested applications of various episodes.

Other Approaches

Up to this point, the approach to myth in Homer in this chapter has been more or less contextual. An enormous amount of research, however, has gone into the origins and background of Homeric myth. This research can be divided roughly into two kinds. One looks for a historical basis of Homeric myth in either political history or Greek religion. The other looks for an origin of Homeric myth in Indo-European or Near Eastern myth or folklore.

Myth and history

The historian Thucydides believed that the Trojan War had taken place (1.9–12). Plato represents Socrates at his trial in 399 B.C. as hoping to be able to question 'the leader of that great host against Troy' in the underworld (*Apology* 41B). Several Greek cities claimed to have been founded by heroes returning from Troy. The canonical date of 1184 B.C. for the sack of Troy goes back to the so-called Marmor Parium or Parian Marble (3rd c. B.C.), on which a list of dates is inscribed.

The ancient belief in the historicity of the Trojan War returned in a new form at the end of the nineteenth century with Heinrich Schliemann's identification of the Troy of Homeric epic with level VIIa of his excavation at Hissarlik in modern Turkey. It became possible to combine the traditional date for the Trojan War with Hissarlik as its site. The discovery by Milman Parry of the oral, formulaic nature of Homeric poetry meant that a historical record of this late Bronze Age event had been passed down orally to the time of the formation of the epics as we have them. The Catalogue of Ships at the end of Book 2 of the *Iliad* could be seen as the survival of a list of Bronze Age sites.[37] The epics themselves encouraged this picture. Scholars observed that Homer tends to 'historicize' his subject-matter: he suppresses certain aspects of his own time, which was, on

[37] Hope Simpson and Lazenby (1970).

the usual understanding of the matter, the end of the Dark Age and the beginning of the Archaic Period, in favor of an idealized period that could be identified with the Bronze Age.[38] For example, Homeric heroes fight with bronze weapons but in Homer's time iron was in use. If Homeric myth had a historical backbone, it made sense also to retrace the wanderings of Odysseus and to identify each of his landfalls with a historical place.[39]

The historicity of the Trojan War is now challenged, however. First, the archaeological and historical record is far from unambiguous. Both the site and the event have been put in doubt.[40] Recently, the character and veracity of Schliemann have come under scrutiny.[41] Second, comparative study of oral epic poetry has raised questions about its reliability as a historical source.[42] Third, the discernment in the Homeric epics of traditional story-patterns at all levels (see below in this chapter) tends to weaken their basis in historical fact.

The historical truth of Homeric myth may be general, not particular. Many sieges of cities like the one in the *Iliad* would have taken place in the Bronze Age, and many warriors would have had a difficult time returning home. Fifteenth-century B.C. frescoes discovered in 1972 on the island of Thera depict a seaborne expedition and the siege of a city. The Trojan War theme is thus already established as an artistic subject (the possible relation between these frescoes and epic *poetry* is another question). The siege in the *Iliad* could, then, be regarded as generic, a siege that reflects not one but many historical sieges that took place over several centuries during the Bronze Age.

Myth and religion

According to the old 'myth-ritual' view of the matter, myths arose to explain religious or cultic rituals. If myth was the narrative basis of

[38] Cf. I. Morris (1986). See J. Bennet, this volume and I. Morris, this volume.
[39] For another example of what might be called romantic archaeology, consider an article in the *The New York Times*, Feb. 23, 1993, p. C1 on a geomagnetic survey of Schliemann's site. The headline was 'A New Clue to the Splendor That Was Troy,' and the sub-head, 'Find may be wall around which Achilles ran'!
[40] Survey in C. G. Thomas (1993).
[41] Calder and Trail (1986).
[42] Kirk (1990) 36–50 ('History and fiction in the Iliad').

Homeric epic, then epic, too, had to have a fundamental basis in ritual. Not surprisingly, considering the Cambridge ritualists' long-influential preoccupation with the dying and rising god, the ritual basis of the *Iliad* was discovered in Achilles' 'ritual experience of death.'[43] The story of Achilles was the story of the hero's withdrawal (symbolizing death), devastation in his absence, and his life-bringing return.[44]

Although myth-ritual interpretations, of more limited scope and with defineable Indo-European bases, still appear from time to time,[45] few scholars, if any, would now take an absolutizing myth-ritualist view of the relation of myth and religion in Homer. The Trojan War myth as narrated (and presupposed) by Homer in the *Iliad* and the *Odyssey* seems to have its own rights vis-à-vis religion. Scholars have often observed the striking divergence of religious practices as represented in these epics from those of Homer's audience.

The most obvious case is hero cult. Its emergence belongs to the same era in which the *Iliad* and the *Odyssey* were taking their present shape, but is unknown to the characters in these poems.[46] This divergence is explained by the Panhellenic tendency of Homeric epic. 'The hero of cult must be local because it is a fundamental principle in Greek religion that his power is local. On the other hand, the *Iliad* and the *Odyssey* are Panhellenic.'[47] This tendency goes far to explain other divergences of the religious practices of Homer's characters from those of Homer's audience.[48] Homeric epic 'greatly played down . . . not only fertility-based cults but also public religious festivals, temple-based worship and most of domestic religion.'[49]

---

43 A. B. Lord (1962) 204, in the section 'Ritual and Magical Origins of Epic.'

44 A. B. Lord (1960) 186–97; cf. M. L. Lord, (1967); repr. in Helene Foley (1994) 181–89; M. Nagler (1974) ch. 5 (on 'withdrawal, devastation, and return' theme); M. W. Edwards (1987) 61–63.

45 For a survey, see Graf (1991) 358–59.

46 Cf. C. Antonaccio (1995).

47 G. Nagy (1979) 116.

48 As R. Martin has pointed out to me, it may also explain the different versions of the throwing of Hephaestus, discussed above in this chapter. The version in Book 1 would be Lemnian; that in Book 18 Panhellenic.

49 Kirk (1990) 13.

This independence of Homeric epic from contemporary religion suggests that the old myth-ritual approach in fact reversed the direction of the influence. It was not from religion to myth but vice versa. Scholars now speak of the 'Homerization' of Greek religion,[50] and, already in the fifth century B.C., Herodotus said that Homer and Hesiod created a theogony for the Greeks.[51] The two are notably in agreement on the kingship of Zeus. Zeus' father, Kronos, and the Titan Iapetos sit at the outermost limits of the world, with Tartaros about them (8.478–81; 14.203–4; cf. Hes. *Th.* 850–52). Typhoeus is battered by Zeus' thunder in the land of the Arimi (*Il.* 2.781–83); in Hesiod, Zeus throws him into Tartarus (*Th.* 868).[52]

Homeric myth is thus one of the first steps in creating what we call 'Greek myth' or 'Greek mythology,' a related set of stories about gods and heroes.[53] It pushes local myths (which may or may not have had their own local epic traditions) to the side (e.g., the myths of Northwestern Greece in the case of the centrifugal Odysseus).[54] It reinforces supra-local systematization that had already taken place in other kinds of epic, notably the kind reflected in the Catalogue of Women in *Odyssey* Book 11.[55]

Comparative approaches

There are four comparative approaches to myth in Homer. One, the folkloristic, has its own chapter in this volume. Another, called

---

[50] See Burkert (1985) 182–85 on the 'Homerization' of Greek religion; Bremer (1994) 11–14. Cf. Kirk (1990) 13–14.

[51] 'Whence each of the gods came and whether they all existed always and of what sort they were in appearance, they [the Greeks] did not know until yesterday or the day before, so to speak. For I think that Homer and Hesiod lived four hundred years before my time. These are the ones who created a theogony for the Greeks and gave the gods their names and distinguished their honors and arts and indicated their appearances' (2.53). See R. Rosen, this volume.

[52] The most pronounced difference between Homer and Hesiod is in the first stage of theogony: in the *Iliad*, Hera speaks of Tethys and Okeanos as the parents of the gods (14.201); in Hesiod, they are descended from Gaea (*Th.* 126 ff.) See Janko (1992) 180–82.

[53] As Graf (1991) 355 observes.

[54] Another example: myths connecting Aeneas with Lesbos after the time of the Trojan War. See Aloni (1986).

[55] Heubeck and Hoekstra (1989) 90–91.

Neoanalysis, deals with what it calls narrative 'motifs,' which are compositional units less fixed than A. B. Lord's 'themes.'[56] These units are established mainly by comparison of the *Iliad* and the *Odyssey* with Theban epic and with the Epic Cycle.[57] This approach thus belongs to the poetics of Homeric epic and not to the study of Homeric myth. Two approaches, however, focussing on Indo-European and on Near Eastern myth, belong to the subject of the present chapter. For both of these approaches, the big questions are: what (myths or elements of myths), how (oral transmission or writing), and when (date). For Indo-European reflexes in Homeric myth, the answer to the second question is relatively straight-forward. Greek is an Indo-European language, and there is some evidence in Greek epic for inherited Indo-European poetic diction, as well as for an inherited tradition of prose narrative.[58] Indo-European myth is thus, at least hypothetically, in the genes, so to speak, of Greek myth. It is surprising, then, that Greek myth in general and Homeric myth in particular seem bastardized—far less Indo-European than the mythologies of other languages in its linguistic family. The Greek pantheon itself consists of composite figures and 'affords rather slim pickings for comparative Indo-European mythology.'[59] As for the question of what myths in Homer can be shown to have Indo-European origins, again the pickings are slim. Scholars have for the most part been able to point not to whole stories but to mythical ideas (in R. Mondi's sense) or to motifs (in the folkloristic sense)—for example, the idea that the sun travels in a chariot (not in the *Iliad* and the *Odyssey* but in *Homeric Hymns: h. Cer.* 88–89; *h. Merc.* 68–69).[60] For this reason, the links that are discovered are often between Homeric myth and Indo-European institutions or ideology.[61] Sometimes, a motif, like

[56] Lord (1960) 68–98; G. Nagy (1992) 27 on theme. Cf. M. Willcock, this volume.

[57] Kullmann (1991) 425–55; cf. M. W. Edwards (1991) 16–18.

[58] For inherited poetic diction, see *Indogermanische Dichtersprache*, ed. R. Schmitt (Darmstadt, 1968); M. L. West (1988). For prose narrative, see Risch (1985).

[59] Puhvel (1987) 138.

[60] West (1988) 153.

[61] Cf. Graf (1991) 358–59. J. Baldick, *Homer and the Indo-Europeans: Comparing Mythologies* (New York, 1994) pursues parallels between the *Iliad* and the *Ramayana* and between the *Odyssey* and the *Mahabarata* with reference to Dumézilian tripartite ideology, not to myths or story-patterns.

Zeus's desire to alleviate the overpopulation of the earth, will be claimed as Indo-European by one scholar and Near Eastern by another.[62] But the dubiety conveyed in this series of generalizations may be diminished by the time that this volume is replaced by a new companion to Homer. The comparative Indo-European approach to Greek myth and thus to Homeric myth in particular is still in its beginning stages.[63]

The rather pervasive influence of Near Eastern myth on Greek myth is attributed to different periods (the Bronze Age; the 'orientalizing' period of 750–650 B.C.) and to different modes (oral transmission by merchants and by itinerant craftsmen and seers).[64] All of these modes are likely to have played a part; both of the two time-periods might have seen transmission, though direct literary influence would probably have had to take place in the later one. As for the question of what came from the Near East, in the case of Homer, the list of myths is extensive. First, the Panhellenic kingship myth (cf. above under *Myth and religion*) has a Babylonian antecedent and Phoenician parallel.[65] Second, Burkert has argued for what would now be called an 'intertextual' relation between certain passages in the *Iliad* and Near Eastern texts: the division of the cosmos (15.187–93; cf. *Atrahasis* I.7–10); Oceanus and Tethys as parents of the gods (14.201 = 302; 246; *Enuma Elish* I.1–5); Aphrodite's complaint to Dione (5.330–431; *Gilgamesh* VI.1–91). In this connection, Burkert suggests that the divine strife to which Achilles refers (1.396–400), which others have considered a Homeric innovation (cf. above under *Innovation?*), goes back to the *Atrahasis*.[66] Third, various other Homeric myths are linked to Near Eastern antecedents: for example, Bellerophon;[67]

[62] See Nagy (1990a) 15–16 on this motif and the *Cypria*; Burkert (1992) 100 ff. on this motif and *Atrahasis*.

[63] See J. F. Nagy (1989) 199–238 for an overview of the whole matter.

[64] See S. Morris, this volume.

[65] M. L. West (1966) 20–31; (1988) 156 observes that the hostility between the weather god (Greek Zeus) and his father/predecesor (Greek Kronos) is best attested in three texts in Indo-European languages: Greek, Vedic and Hittite.

[66] (1992) 106.

[67] Burkert (1983) 51–53. For an Indo-European connection, see Baldick (1994): Siyawush in the Persian *Book of Kings*.

the Achaean Wall (*Il.* 7.433–66; 12.3–35);[68] the prayer of Penelope (*Od.* 4.759–67).[69]

Conclusion

This chapter began with the notion of myth as a particular practice, i.e., oral storytelling, and thus belongs to the larger tendency of the research surveyed and carried forward by R. Thomas in *Literacy and Orality in Ancient Greece*.[70] This research has done much to strengthen our sense of the complexity of archaic oral culture, and, in particular, of the implications of orality for the understanding of the written literature that survives. By focussing on myth in the speeches of characters in Homer, it is possible to get a sense of the dynamics of myth as oral storytelling, as a social practice. In this perspective, myth and epic poetry are quite different things, and the latter implicitly comments on the former. Typically, a character's intentions for a myth that he or she narrates miscarry, while some further meaning, of which the character is unaware, becomes apparent in the context of the epic as a whole.

No story is told without a pragmatic purpose that leads to some degree or other of narrative reshaping, of variation of a received story. Although Homer shows considerable detachment from and even irony toward this fundamental condition of Greek myth, he himself is not immune. The two versions of the throwing of Hephaestus in the *Iliad* show the intrusion of this condition into epic. Further, Homer's epics as wholes can be shown to consitute particular variants of myths. Because of their monumentality and millenial predominance, their versions now seem authoritative, which is the same as saying that they seem no longer to be versions.

The striving of characters to make a point through the stories that they tell sometimes leads to a degree of variation that looks like innovation or 'creativity' on Homer's part. It is true that Homer composed what the characters are saying, but it is also true that this

---

[68] Scodel (1982) 33–50 argues for a background in the myth of destruction by flood in the Babylonian epic *Atrahasis*.

[69] *Gilgamesh*: Burkert (1992) 99.

[70] R. Thomas (1992) 104.

innovation is confined to the speeches of the characters and that, in every case, it can be explained pragmatically with reference to the context and thus as characterization.

A sense of the oral side of Greek culture has been strangely lacking in the debate over Greek myth that began in the early 1980s. It is as if the problem of orality can be confined to discussion of epic. But both epic and oral storytelling are modes of social memory, one more highly formalized, the other less.[71]

[71] For the concept of social memory, see Fentress and Wickham (1992) ch. 1; for a comparison of oral epic and folklore, ch. 2.

William Hansen

HOMER AND THE FOLKTALE

In 1857 Wilhelm Grimm published an essay on the story of Polyphemos and its analogues in international oral tradition, in which he concluded that both the Homeric and the later texts were essentially independent realizations of an international oral story. Following this work scholars have identified and compared numerous other stories that are found both in Homer and in international oral storytelling.[1] These investigations can cast light on the narrative sources of the Greek epic tradition, on the techniques of Homeric composition and storytelling, and on difficult passages in the poems.

Basic Concepts

Before turning to some of these narratives let me consider a number of concepts that have proven useful in the study of oral narrative. These are *type*, *genre*, and what can be called, for want of an established term, *genre variance*.

The following two texts, collected from oral tradition, are given here in summary.

> There was a young fellow who wanted to get married, but only to a girl who did not know anything about salt water and boats. So he

[1] Grimm (1857). Surveys include G. Gerland, *Altgriechische Märchen in der Odyssee: Ein Beitrag zur vergleichenden Mythologie* (Magdeburg, 1869), F. Bender, *Die märchenhaften Bestandtheile der homerischen Gedichte* (Darmstadt, 1878), Radermacher (1915), Calhoun (1939), Page (1973), Petersmann (1981), Hölscher (1990), and Bertolini (1989). Of the early treatments, those of Gerland and Bender are too outdated to be of much interest now.

> made a little oar, put it in his pocket, and traveled until he came to a farmhouse. When a young woman came to the door, he showed her the oar to see if she knew what it was. She said it looked like an oar, so he did not want anything to do with her. The next morning he went on to another farmhouse, where he showed the oar to another young girl, asking her what it was. She said it looked like her mother's pudding stick, so he decided that she was the girl for him. He stayed there, and they got married. When he went to bed on his wedding night he found his bride undressed on the bed, lying flat on her back with her legs sticking up in the air. When he asked her what she was doing, she said that there had been a squall, and she had gotten everything clewed up, and now she was scudding on the bare poles. So he found out that she knew something about salt water.

> A certain Curro Pérez, who had courted many women in his two years as a sailor, now decided to give up his sailor's ways, get married, and live according to God's will. Tired of his life at sea, he wanted a wife who knew nothing of the sea or of sailors. So he set out inland with an oar on his shoulder. When he came upon a good-looking girl in a village, he showed her the oar and asked her if she knew what it was. She said it was an oar. He moved on, asking the same question in village after village and receiving the same answer. Finally, in one village he met a girl who said the oar was a beam or stick. Pleased that he had found a girl who knew nothing of the sea, he told her of his love and married her a month later. On their wedding night he went to bed, but she hesitated to join him. When he asked her why, she said she would like to know if she was getting in on the port or starboard side.

The first text is an American comic tale collected in 1956 from Frank Alley, a retired lobster fisherman in Maine, and the second is a Spanish tale from Andalusia that was published at the end of the nineteenth century.[2] In both narratives, (1) a sailor decides that he wants a wife who knows nothing of the sea. (2) He sets out inland carrying an oar, and (3) at every farmhouse (or village) shows the oar to a young girl, asking her what it is. (4) When the girl identifies it as an oar, he moves on. (5) When finally he encounters a girl who misidentifies the oar as something else, (6) he remains there and marries her; however, (7) on their wedding night she unexpectedly speaks of her body (or of the bed) as a ship, revealing that she is well-acquainted

[2] R. Dorson, 'Collecting Folklore in Jonesport, Maine,' *Proceedings of the American Philosophical Society* 101, No. 3 (June 1957) 287; Dorson told me that he had also heard this tale in a bar in Chicago but neglected to write it down. K. Ranke, ed., *European Anecdotes and Jests*, trans. T. Buck (Copenhagen, 1972) 28, No. 12, citing *Chascarrillos andaluces* (Madrid, 1898) 115.

with seafaring. The ribald implication seems to be that, just as she is not innocent of the sea, she probably is not innocent of seamen either.

These texts illustrate what folklorists mean by *type*, that is, a traditional, migratory story whose texts, though varying in details, share a fairly constant core of coherent action. What is crucial to grasp here is that oral stories transmitted from generation to generation and/or spread laterally from region to region can show remarkable stability over very long periods of time and great geographical distances. Folklorists have catalogued and described such tale-types in a number of indices, of which the most useful for our purpose is Antti Aarne's and Stith Thompson's *The Types of the Folktale*, a listing of folktales that have been attested in oral tradition in the lands stretching from Europe in the West to India in the East.[3]

Like literary works, oral stories can be grouped according to *genres*. Native genres are those which a people employs for its own traditional stories; inevitably, such categories differ from nation to nation. Analytic genres are those which scholars impose upon data cross-culturally for their own convenience, and in comparative, cross-cultural studies it is generally more convenient to employ analytic categories. I follow folkloristic practice here in alloting traditional oral stories to three broad classes: myth, legend, and folktale; and I offer the following as working definitions, which simplify the issue of genre but will suffice for our discussion.[4]

Folktales are traditional fictions, that is, entertaining, instructive, or consolatory tales in which the issue of historicity is unimportant. Generally such tales are set in the indefinite past, transpire in vaguely defined or generic locales, and feature human or animal characters who are unnamed or bear generic names. Thus in the folktale texts given above the sailor and the girls are unnamed, the temporal and spatial setting is indicated only vaguely, and the events are not earnestly represented as having actually happened.

Legends differ notably from folktales in that, although they need not have any historical basis, they are recounted as reports of historical events or at least as reports that invite an evaluation of their

---

[3] Aarne and Thompson (1961).

[4] For a basic discussion see W. Bascom, 'The Forms of Folklore: Prose Narratives,' *Journal of American Folklore* 78 (1965) 3–20. On the nature of belief see L. Dégh and A. Vázsonyi, 'Legend and Belief,' *Genre* 4 (1971) 281–304. For the application of these and other narrative categories to ancient storytelling, see W. Hansen (1988) 2:1121–1130.

own historicity. Accordingly, they usually are situated in a definite time in human history or transpire in a definite locale or both, and feature purportedly real human beings. With the preceding folktale texts compare the following legend text, given here in full.

> St. Elias was once a seaman. On account of his endless rowing, the man got tired (rowing while eating, that's the way they had it in those days). He put an oar on his shoulder and left to go to find a place where they didn't even know the name of it. He walks to the village, he asks, 'What is this called?' 'An oar,' they say. He walks to another village, he asks, 'What is this called?' What the devil! He became desperate. Keeping on with his inquiry he finally asks at one village situated at the very top of the mountain, 'What is this called?' 'A piece of wood.' Thank God! He sets the oar straight up, builds a hut, and resolves to remain there for the rest of his life. For this reason they always put St. Elias on mountaintops.[5]

In this text from Greece the protagonist is a historical character, St. Elias, that is, the Old Testamental prophet Elijah. The character gives the story its dramatic date. The historicity of the events is implied by the fact that the protagonist is a historical personage and also by the narrator's final remark, which makes an aetiological connection between the saint's quest and a familiar feature of the present-day landscape, the many chapels dedicated to St. Elias that crown mountains all over Greece.

Finally, *myths* are traditional narratives about gods and monsters. They are set in definite locales, sometimes in the distant past when the world was receiving its basic character, sometimes in the more recent past, and are accounts of allegedly true events.

Although many narrative types are found in oral tradition only as myths or as legends or as folktales, other types are found expressed in one genre at one place or time and in another genre at another place or time. I call this phenomenon *genre variance.* It is illustrated here by the story of the Sailor and the Oar, which in Greece is told as a legend and elsewhere is told as a folktale; accordingly, these texts reflect different branches of the same story, the quest of a sailor for a girl who knows nothing of the sea, which is presented as a comic and purely fictional event, and the quest of St. Elias for a community of people who know nothing of the sea, which is recounted

---

[5] N. Πολίτης, Μελέται περὶ τοῦ Βίου καὶ τῆς Γλώσσης τοῦ Ἑλληνικοῦ Λαοῦ· Παραδόσεις (Athens, 1904) 2:801–2, No. 207. The story was told to Polites by Andreas Karkabitsas in 1903.

as a non-comic, historical event with implications for present cultic practice. In most discussions of folktales in the Homeric poems the question of genre and the phenomenon of genre variance are treated vaguely.

Homeric Stories with International Analogues

Herewith follows a survey of Homeric stories that have analogues in nineteenth- and twentieth-century oral tradition. I include stories regardless of their genre, for the genre in which the story is cast is less important than the information about form, content, and sometimes context that the analogues may provide. Limited space requires that this survey be brief and selective, and the reader is referred to the scholarly literature for more extensive discussion. I exclude stories to which Homer merely alludes (e.g., the ruse of the Trojan Horse); isolated motifs, except in the case of simple stories that are sometimes called motifs (e.g., *Potiphar's Wife*); and folk beliefs that are not expressed in the form of a story (e.g., the notion that there are floating islands). The discussion is a commentary upon the *Table of Stories* that appears below.

Of these stories the most complex are the Return of Odysseus, which provides the basic story of the *Odyssey*, and the encounter of Odysseus and Polyphemos.

Return of Odysseus. The story of *The Homecoming Husband*, the man who returns home after a long absence just in time to prevent the remarriage of his wife, is a folktale and legend that is primarily romantic and realistic in atmosphere. In addition to prose narration, this international story frequently takes the form of song, both ballad and epic.[6]

In the oral story, a man leaves his wife shortly after their marriage to make a journey to a distant land (e.g., to go to war). He may instruct his wife to wait a certain number of years for his return, after which she is free to remarry (or he says that he will return at

[6] For the story in Muslim Serbo-Croatian epic see A. B. Lord (1960) 121, 242–259, and J. M. Foley (1990) 359–387; for the Central Asian epic of Alpamysh see H. B. Paksoy, *Alpamysh: Central Asian Identity Under Russian Rule* (New Britain, 1989) 126–41. For the international story in general see Tolstoi (1934), and O. Holzapfel, 'Heimkehr des Gatten,' *Enzyklopädie des Märchens* (Berlin, 1990) 6:702–7.

a certain time, or he simply goes). After he is absent at war (in prison) for a long time, his wife finally decides to choose a new husband because the stated period of time has passed (or for other reasons). The hero is mindful that the period of time that he asked his wife to wait is nearly up (or unexpectedly learns of his wife's imminent wedding). He returns, sometimes with wondrous speed (e.g., a supernatural helper magically transports him home in one night as he sleeps). Back home the hero is unrecognizable because of changes due to time and climate (or because of years in prison or because he is disguised). Although humans remain unaware of his true identity, one of his animals (dog, horse, camel) may recognize him. With his humble appearance he gains admittance to the house where eventually he himself is recognized, usually by means of a token (e.g., half a ring that matches his wife's half) or by other means (e.g., a song that he sings, a birthmark, a feat that he accomplishes). If his wife is loyal, the couple is reunited, but if not, he punishes her. Similarly, if the suitor is innocent of misconduct, he is reconciled with the hero, but otherwise he flees or is slain.

So in a French folktale published in the nineteenth century, a devout nobleman and his beautiful, upright wife were childless, so that the nobleman vowed to the Virgin to go to the Holy Land for seven years to fight the enemies of the Lord if his wife should have a child. When his wife gave birth to a boy, the man told his wife of his vow. He warned her that men would tell her he had perished there and would ask for her hand in marriage, but she should not believe them. Since she might not recognize him upon his return, he cut their marriage contract in two, giving half to her; when he should produce the other half upon his return, she would know that it was he. He departed, fought for a year, and was captured and imprisoned, after which no one heard any news of him. So three wicked brothers went to the nobleman's wife, declared that he was dead, and said she must wed one of them. She refused, since there was no proof of his death, but the brothers moved into her chateau anyway and treated it as their own, feasting there and gambling with the money from the harvest. When the husband had been gone for five years, the brothers again pressed the woman to marry, and she said she would wear black and be in mourning for a year, after which she would choose one of them as husband. At the end of the sixth year, the brothers again pressed the woman, who said she needed a year to sew her wedding dress. When only three months remained until the wedding, the devil went to the imprisoned husband, informed him of the events, and offered to convey him home in return for a portion of the first meal taken by the man and his wife, a proposition to which the man agreed. The devil flew for three days carrying the man and deposited him near his chateau. At nightfall, the unkempt man knocked at the door and was informed that the mistress of the house was to be married on the morrow. He dashed upstairs, killed the three brothers, and informed the mistress that as payment she must marry him, but she refused to do so. Then he produced the marriage contract, proving that he was her husband. After they had dined, he gave the devil his due. The nobleman and his family lived happily ever after, and when they died they went to paradise.[7]

The only supernatural element that is regularly, though not invariably, a part of *The Homecoming Husband* is the hero's magical conveyance home from a distant land in time to prevent his wife's remarriage.[8] This feature also occurs in Homer, who relates how Phaiakians convey Odysseus home to Ithaka overnight in a supernaturally swift ship while he sleeps, twenty years after his departure for Troy. Phaiakian ships are as swift as a bird or as thought, they travel without pilots or rudders, they know men's thoughts, they are acquainted with all cities and lands, and they are wrapped in mist, that is, are invisible (7.36, 8.557–562). In particular, the ship carrying Odysseus moves more swiftly than a falcon, swiftest of birds (13.86–87). Since the hero's marvelous return is an element of the folktale, it is unnecessary to explain the motif by appeal to ideas that are foreign to the folk narrative and to Homer, such as shamanism.

Part of the Return of Odysseus is the recognition scene of Odysseus and Penelope.

Penelope's Test. Although the long-absent husband may have to prove his identity to his wife and although the way in which he does so varies, the curious identity-test that Odysseus undergoes is not one such way; rather, it is reminiscent of a kind of identity test found in certain popular ballads. These songs are similar to the *The Homecoming Husband* in that they also tell of the return of a husband after a long absence, but they differ in that their entire focus is upon the

---

[7] L. Edmunds (1993) 81–84, citing J.-F. Bladé, *Contes Populaires de la Gascogne* (Paris, 1885) 1:43–53.

[8] On this motif see G. Huet, 'Le retour merveilleux du mari,' *Revue des Traditions Populaires* 32 (1917) 97–109, 145–163.

recognition scene of the husband and wife. The ballad is international, and hundreds of texts have been collected in Greece.

In the ballad the returning husband comes to the door of his house and asks his wife to let him in, but she is unsure of his identity and makes him prove it by his knowledge of domestic matters. Thus, in a Russian song the husband first says that in her yard there is a nut tree. To this the wife replies that a neighbor could have told him that. Then the husband says that in her room there is a bed of brown ebony. The wife replies that the nurse could have told him that. Finally he says that she has a mark between her breasts. She opens the door.

So the husband provides progressively more intimate knowledge, from yard to bedroom to body, each instance of which his suspicious wife dismisses as inconclusive until the final, very intimate piece of knowledge, which she accepts as conclusive.

The identity test administered by Penelope is of the same sort, has some of the same motifs (notably a knowledge of the couple's bedroom) in the same sort of situation, and so no doubt reflects the same tradition as that which the ballad does. The differences are also instructive. Whereas the wife in the ballad tests openly, Penelope tries to entrap the claimant. Moreover, her test avoids the progressive, climactic structure of the ballad and instead goes directly to the decisive test, which in the Homeric story concerns knowledge of the couple's bedroom. This token, corresponding to the second level of intimacy in the ballad rather than to the third, is in harmony with the decorum of Greek epic, in which an intimate description of Penelope's body would be inappropriate.

The other two tokens appear in Odysseus' recognition scene with his father Laertes on the following day (24.327–344), and it has been conjectured that Homer has redistributed the traditional three tokens of the husband-wife recognition scene over these two scenes.[9] In the latter scene Odysseus proves his identity by displaying his scar (cf. level three) and by giving an exact description of the fruit trees and vines (level one) that he owns.

Polyphemos. The tale of the clever hero who blinds the cannabalistic ogre in whose power he finds himself, and escapes from the ogre's lair by pretending to be a sheep, is a very popular and widely-known international folktale, and it has also proven popular with scholars,

[9] Kakridis (1971) 151–163.

who have devoted more attention to it than to any other international story in Homer.[10] Aarne-Thompson label it *The Ogre Blinded*.

In the tale a man (sometimes with companions) comes to the dwelling of an ogre, usually a giant. The cannabalistic ogre keeps him in his lair. In self-defense the hero destroys the ogre's eyes (or his only eye) by means of a spit (or boiling liquid). Subsequently he covers himself with a sheepskin, joins the ogre's sheep, and crawls out of the lair. Having escaped from the ogre's dwelling, the hero sometimes mocks the ogre, and often the monster throws him a magic ring, but when the hero puts it on, the ring repeatedly yells 'Here I am,' thereby guiding the blinded ogre to him. Since the ring cannot be removed, the man is obliged to cut off his finger, after which he escapes, taking with him the ogre's valuables.

A memorable feature that appears commonly in the folktale texts but not in Homer is the episode of the magic ring by means of which the blinded ogre makes a last attempt to get hold of the hero. A trace of the ruse can probably be discerned in Polyphemos' offer of guest-gifts to the departing Odysseus,[11] an offer that the hero wisely ignores in view of the fact that Polyphemos' previous guest-gift was his granting to Odysseus the privilege of being eaten last. It appears that the Ring Episode in its usual form has been suppressed, probably because a talking ring that obliges the hero to cut off his finger would be incongruous in Greek heroic epic, and the trick might seem too cunning for a rogue so stupid as to fall for the Nobody ruse, not to mention the fact that the presence of so splendid a ring in Kyklopean society with its rudimentary technology might seem to call for an explanation. Very likely the Ring Episode persists in transformation as the ogre's curse, which like the magic ring does the hero some harm but fails to prevent his escape. The curse also links the Kyklops adventure with the remainder of Odysseus' return by motivating Poseidon's anger at Odysseus and so requiring the eventual reconciliation of Odysseus and the sea god.

In Homer, the story of Odysseus and Polyphemos also includes the trick of the deceptive name.

Noman. The Noman ruse is ordinarily the central feature of a simple traditional narrative told as a folktale or legend, in which a human

---

[10] Grimm (1857), Nyrop (1880–82) 216–55, Hackman (1904), Germain (1954) 55–129, Page (1955) 1–15, Röhrich (1962) 48–71, Glenn (1971) 133–181, Mondi (1983).

[11] Page (1955) 19, note 15; Glenn (1971).

being encounters a supernatural creature and, when asked, gives out his or her name falsely, usually as 'Myself.' When presently the human does harm to the supernatural being and the latter cries out, his fellows ask what is the matter, but hearing him reply that 'Myself has harmed me' they ignore him, concluding of course that he is the cause of his own distress.[12]

Thus, in a British oral narrative Jock decided to pass the night in a haunted mill. Eventually there entered a roguish man who was three feet high, looked eighty years old, and acted like eighteen. He asked Jock what his name was, and Jock said he was 'Mysel' and mysel'.' When the intruder became aggressive, Jock scalded his face with a duck he was roasting. The creature cried out in terror, attracting other similar beings to the place who asked him who did it. 'Mysel' and mysel',' he explained. 'An' if it was yoursel' and yoursel',' they answered, 'who can help that?'[13]

The Homeric narrative combines *Noman* and *The Ogre Blinded* into a single adventure, adding thereby another instance of Odysseus' cleverness and the Kyklops' stupidity.

In addition to *The Homecoming Husband*, two other narratives treat romantic or erotic themes, one seriously and the other comically.

Bellerophon and Anteia. Anteia lusted after the handsome youth, Bellerophon. When she was unable to seduce him, she urged her husband, King Proitos of Corinth, to kill Bellerophon, saying that she had been fighting off the youth's advances. So Proitos dispatched Bellerophon to Anteia's father in Lycia with a message instructing the Lycian king to put Bellerophon to death.

The legend is a version of an international story conventionally referred to as the *Potiphar's Wife* story (or motif), from the well-known Hebrew legend in which Joseph rejects the advances of the lustful wife of Potiphar (*Gen*. 39:1–20).[14] The plot of the oral story, told sometimes as a tale and sometimes as a legend, is as follows. An older, married woman makes a pass at an attractive youth, who virtuously rejects her advances. Angry at the rejection or fearing that the youth may inform her husband, the woman tells her husband that the youth made a pass at her. The husband believes her and angrily punishes the youth.

---

[12] Nyrop (1880–82) 246–251; Hackman (1904).

[13] K. Briggs, *A Dictionary of British Folk-Tales in the English Language* (Bloomington, 1971) Part B, 1:222–224.

[14] S. Trenkner, *The Greek Novella in the Classical Period* (Cambridge, 1958) 64–6.

Although the story is logically self-sufficient in its own right, in oral tradition it is regularly told not as an independent tale but as an episode within another tale. So also in Greek legend the dealings of Bellerophon and Anteia constitute one of many episodes in the traditional biography of Bellerophon.

Ares and Aphrodite. The story of the love affair of Ares and Aphrodite appears to be a mythologized novella, a ribald story of cuckoldry and intrigue that has been transferred from the world of ordinary humans to the celestial village of Olympos. Homer presents it as a comic myth.

Close counterparts to the Homeric story have been collected sporadically in oral tradition.[15] A man learns that his wife has a lover, and acquires a magical device that will make the two unable to disengage from their erotic embrace. When his wife's lover comes to his house, the cuckold employs the magic against them so that they stick together. Then he makes a public mockery of them.

Two narratives portray the interaction of a human and the supernatural.

Meleager. In the modern folktale, conventionally called *Meleager* after the Greek legend, a supernatural being or beings (goddesses of fate, angel, etc.) declare that a newborn child will live until a certain piece of wood, which is then burning in the stove, is burnt up. Overhearing this, the child's mother immediately removes the wood from the fire, extinguishes it, and puts it away in a chest for safekeeping. Sometime after the child grows up, the mother or another person (wife, father) to whom she has confided the secret becomes angry with him for one reason or another, retrieves the wood, and relights it. As soon as the wood is consumed, the man dies.

The plot of the Meleager legend in the form in which it seems to have been best known in Greek antiquity agrees in essence with the modern folktale.[16] Meleager's mother overheard the Moirai speaking her son's fate, declaring that he would live until a certain burning brand should have been consumed, whereupon she rescued the brand from the hearth. After Meleager grew up he killed his mother's brother

---

[15] Petersmann (1981) 52; W. Hansen (1995) 2–3. These texts resemble both Aarne-Thompson (1961), AT 1733B*, *Blacksmith Ties Wife and Lover Together*, as well as the urban legend known as *The Stuck Couple*, neither of which has been extensively studied.

[16] Kakridis (1949) 11–42, 127–48. For more recent literature on the issues in Homer's account of Meleager see Hainsworth (1993) 130–2.

(or brothers) during a quarrel at a boar hunt, incurring the anger of his mother, who returned the brand to the fire and thereby brought her son's life to an end. The principal difference between the international tale and this form of the ancient legend is that the Greek legend develops the role of the men so that they too are important actors, whereas women dominate the folktale.

The Meleager legend is recounted in part in the *Iliad* in the course of the embassy to Achilleus, in which Phoinix cites Meleager as a negative paradigm for Achilleus, an example of how he should not behave. The narrative that Phoinix recounts differs in some ways from the form of the legend given above, which appears to have been its usual form. Among the differences is the absence of the motif of the brand with which Meleager's life is bound, and so also the Moirai who declare his fate; in their place are his mother's curse and the Fury who responds to it. The version featuring the curse appears to be an epic modification of the version with the brand.

According to Homer the quarrel during the boar hunt led to Meleager's killing his maternal uncle, which in turn provoked his mother Althaia to anger. She pounded upon the earth, calling upon Persephone to kill her son, and a Fury hearkened to her cries. Enraged at his mother's curse, Meleager refused to join his fellow Calydonians in defending the city from attack. When finally the enemy pressed at the gates and his wife begged him to fight, he joined battle but gained nothing for his pains, presumably because (although Phoinix himself does not say so explicitly) he perished in the fighting.

Menelaos and Proteus. Stranded on the island of Pharos, Menelaos lay in ambush and captured Proteus, the Old Man of the Sea, whom he forced to reveal to him what god was preventing his sailing and how he might return home. Proteus revealed that he must perform a certain sacrifice that he had neglected. Then Menelaos probed Proteus for information about his comrades Aias, Agamemnon, and Odysseus, and Proteus answered him, after which the sea-deity foretold Menelaos' own fate and disappeared into the sea.

The notion that marine deities are prophetic is found in other traditions as well, and there is at least a general similarity between the legend of Menelaos' dealings with the Old Man of the Sea and a legend tradition attested in Scandinavia in which a man catches a mermaid. When the captured mermaid offers to answer a question (or three questions), the man asks one or more ordinary questions (for example, 'What is the strongest material for a flail?'), and she answers it, sometimes adding that he could have asked a more valuable question.[17]

In both the Homeric and Northern legends, (1) a man captures a marine spirit, (2) as a result of which he is entitled to ask him/her questions. (3) He does so, and (4) receives truthful answers. Unlike his Northern counterpart, however, the noble Menelaos chooses his questions well and is not chided for a lack of imagination.

Two narratives appear to be constructed around popular beliefs.

Bag of Winds. When Odysseus asked Aiolos for help in furthering his return home, Aiolos placed the harsh winds in a leather bag, which he entrusted to Odysseus. For Zeus had made Aiolos steward of the winds. The mariners had almost reached home when the exhausted Odysseus fell asleep, and his companions, thinking that the bag probably contained gold and silver, opened it, releasing the winds. The ship was driven back to Aiolos' isle.

Different forms of magic for the control of the winds are attested among different peoples. Among the ancient Greeks the idea of catching the winds in sacks is attested here and in a legend about the philosopher Empedokles. When once the etesian winds were blowing so hard that they were harming crops, Empedokles ordered the people to flay donkeys, make leather bags from their skins, and position them along the hilltops to capture the winds. After the winds ceased blowing, he was given the nickname Windstopper.[18]

In more recent tradition a common kind of wind-magic involves the use of 'wind knots,' which is found both in folk belief and as a motif in legend.[19] Sailors acquire from an old woman a handkerchief or cord in which she has tied three knots, instructing them to undo one knot for a mild wind and a second knot for a stronger wind but under no circumstances to undo the third knot. They untie the first two and then, somewhat like Odysseus' companions, whose poor

[17] R. Christiansen, *The Migratory Legends*, FF Communications 175 (Helsinki, 1958), Type 4060, *The Mermaid's Message*. For a text in English translation see R. Kvideland and H. K. Sehmsdorf, eds., *Scandinavian Folk Belief and Legend* (Minneapolis, 1988) 261–2, No. 52.4.

[18] Diog. Laert. 8.60. Thompson (1955), Motif C322.1, *Bag of winds*.

[19] Radermacher (1915) 18–21; R. Strömberg, 'The Aeolus Episode and Greek Wind Magic,' *Acta Universitatis Gotoburgensis* 56 (1950) 73–84; Page (1973) 73–78. On ancient and modern Greek wind magic see also R. Hampe, *Kult der Winde in Athen und Kreta*, Sitzungsberichte der Heidelberger Akademie der Wissenschaften, phil.-hist. Klasse, 1 (1967) 14–17.

judgment impels them to open the bag of winds, cannot resist untying the third, which produces a great storm.

So in a Danish legend collected from a man in Strandby, a few men who were fishing over in the west wanted to return home and were unhappy that the wind was still, for they would have to row. They were chatting with an old woman, and one of them jokingly asked whether she could get them a little wind. Yes, she could do that. Taking an old handkerchief she tied three knots in it, gave it to them, and said that when they were ready to sail they should undo one knot in order to get wind, and if they thought it was too little, they could undo the second; but they should beware of undoing the third. When they were ready to sail, they untied one knot and got a nice wind. The second man then proposed that they untie the second knot to see how it went. This time they got all the wind they could handle. When they were in sight of home the third man asked if they shouldn't try the third knot. The others agreed that nothing could go wrong now, but such a storm arose that they barely made it to land alive.[20]

The Petrified Ship. As the Phaiakians who had brought Odysseus to Ithaca were sailing back home to Scheria, Poseidon angrily struck their ship with his hand, turning it to stone and rooting it to the bottom of the sea.

There are modern legends according to which a certain offshore island is a ship that was supernaturally turned to stone.[21] According to a Faeroese legend, two viking ships once came and were ravaging the communities. When the ships were approaching the settlement at Oyndarfjord an old witch came out of her house and put a spell on them so that they were transformed into two large rocks, which she condemned to remain there and sway in the water for all eternity.[22]

A modern Greek legend collected in Kerkyra (Corfu) similarly recounts how there is a petrified ship with masts and all in the sea opposite the monastery of Paliokastritsa. Originally the ship was coming to plunder the monastery, and the monks saw it in the distance.

---

[20] E. T. Kristensen, *Danske Sagn* (Aarhus, 1900) 6:415–16, No. 1223. For texts in English translation see Kvideland and Sehmsdorf (1988) 150–51, No. 32.1, and 262–63, No. 52.6. The story in this form has been attested since at least the fifteenth century.

[21] Radermacher (1915) 35–6.

[22] O. Jiriczek, 'Færöische Märchen und Sagen,' *Zeitschrift des Vereins für Volkskunde* 2 (1892) 23–4, No. 24.

One man prayed: 'If this ship is well-intentioned, let it arrive safely, but if ill-intentioned, let it remain there as marble.' Hearing him God turned the ship into marble, and it has stood there ever since.[23] Indeed, more than one islet off of Kerkyra is, according to local lore, the actual petrified ship of the Phaiakians, a tradition that probably goes back to antiquity when, at least by classical times, the island was commonly identified with the land of Homer's Phaiakians. So Pliny (*NH* 4.12.53) says that off a promontory of Kerkyra there is a rock that because of its shape is said to be the transformed ship of Odysseus.

Since the modern texts are quite similar they may reflect a migratory legend; however, this story is really not the same as that which Homer tells. Although they do have in common the idea of a ship and crew that is punished by being transformed into an offshore rock, and could be genetically related, the texts are rather simple and could have arisen independently of one another.

Finally, there is the legend of Odysseus' last quest, a type that I have already discussed at some length above.

Odysseus and the Oar. Odysseus walked inland with an oar on his shoulder in search of a community that was ignorant of the sea. He knew he had found them when a man mistook his oar (the mariner's characteristic implement) for a winnowing shovel (a common agricultural tool that resembles an oar). There Odysseus sacrificed to Poseidon, appeasing his wrath (presumably by introducing the cult of the marine deity at a place where it previously was unknown), and returned home again.

Because Odysseus' quest takes place after the point in the story at which Homer brings the *Odyssey* to a close, the poet foretells this adventure rather than narrating it as a past event: Teiresias announces it to Odysseus as something that he must do upon settling matters in Ithaka, and Odysseus later announces it to Penelope. Consequently the reader of Homer is unaccustomed to encountering this story in the past tense, but outside of the epic poem it was simply one of the adventures traditionally attributed to Odysseus, and Pausanias (8.44.4) describes seeing on a mountain-top in Arkadia the ruins of a temple built by Odysseus for Poseidon and Athena, like the mountain-top chapels of St. Elias in the Greece of today.

---

[23] Πολίτης (1904) 1:156–7, No. 286 (text), 2:867–69 (comments). Polites also gives texts from Samos and Poros about petrified ships (Nos. 287–88).

As we have seen above, the story of *The Sailor and the Oar* is attested today in Greek tradition, in which it is told as a legend attached to St. Elias and also to St. Nikolaos, and in British and American tradition, in which it is related as a folktale. The story circulates mostly among persons whose livelihood has to do with the sea.[24]

Folktales in Homer

Very few texts in Homer are themselves actually folktales by any reasonable definition of the genre. Marginal exceptions are two relatively uncommon forms of fable. One is the *short fable*, or *fable-proverb*, a very brief metaphorical narrative that is intermediate in form between the fable and the proverb.[25] 'A mountain was in labor and gave birth to a mouse' (Diogeneianos 8.75) is a well-known ancient Greek instance, while 'Curiosity killed the cat' is familiar from contemporary America. In the *Iliad* we find the short fable, 'The fool learned after the event.'[26]

The *Odyssey* contains one instance of the *personal-experience fable*.[27] Odysseus came in the guise of a beggar to the hut of the swineherd Eumaios, who hospitably took him in and shared his meal with him. In the evening the weather turned cold. Hoping to induce Eumaios to allow him the use of a cloak, Odysseus declared that he was going to express a wish in the form of a story. He proceeded to recount how once he and his comrades at Troy had encamped for the night, the weather turned bitterly cold, and he alone had neglected to bring along a cloak; but he mentioned his plight to his commander, who arranged in a clever way for him to have the use of another man's cloak. Eumaios, expressing his delight with the tale, provided his guest with warm clothing for the evening (*Od.* 14.457–522).

The riddling tale that Odysseus recounts to Eumaios is a brief fiction devised extemporaneously in order to convey a message indirectly, in this case allowing the guest to hint to his host in a tactful

[24] W. Hansen (1976), (1977), and (1990). See also Moser (1976).

[25] For a discussion see B. E. Perry, 'Fable,' *Studium Generale* 12 (1959) 19, 25. He calls them 'metaphorical proverbs.'

[26] *Il.* 17.32: ῥεχθὲν δέ τε νήπιος ἔγνω.

[27] On the device see B. E. Perry, 'Fable,' *Studium Generale* 12 (1959) 23–25, and W. J. Verdenius, 'AINOΣ,' *Mnemosyne* 15 (1962) 389. 'Personal-experience fable' is suggested as an English term by W. Hansen (1988) 1122–23. On the Homeric passage see further G. Nagy (1979) 235–41.

and also entertaining way about an unmet need that he feels. A man who employs this rhetorical strategy invents a realistic tale of his own and reports it as something he has experienced; that is, the device is traditional but the material is not. Because the speaker's meaning is expressed indirectly, his listener has the option of acknowledging him on either the literal or the metaphorical level. The personal-experience fable is not easily classified in relation to the familiar oral-narrative genres, since it does not fit comfortably into the analytic classes defined above.

If the presence of actual folktales in Homer is therefore a somewhat uncertain matter, the Homeric use of narrative structures that are familiar from folktales is clear. A narrative sequence found in many folktales is the encounter of hero and donor.[28] When the protagonist of a folktale sets out to accomplish a task (in other words, when the protagonist has a major problem to solve), a stranger may suddenly appear, out of nowhere as it were (e.g., an old woman in the woods), who provides the protagonist with precisely the information or magical object that will prove to be essential to the successful accomplishment of the task that lies ahead. Often the donor's gift is given in return for an act of kindness shown by the hero to the donor (e.g., he generously shares his meager meal with the humble stranger).

The Homeric passage that is most like such a donor sequence is the appearance of Hermes to Odysseus on Aiaia (*Od.* 10.274–309). As the hero was making his way to the house of the witch Kirke, who had already transformed some of his companions into swine, he was suddenly accosted in the woods by Hermes in the form of a young man. The god gave him the plant moly to protect him against Kirke's enchantments and also explained exactly how he should deal with her. Then Hermes departed for Olympos, and Odysseus proceeded to Kirke's house, where with the help of the plant and Hermes' instructions he dealt successfully with the witch.

The similarity of this incident to the donor sequence of a folktale is obvious enough, but equally telling are the differences. First, there is no testing of the hero. Odysseus is not required to prove himself worthy of the donor's help by virtue of his kindness or generosity; he is simply granted it. Second, in the Odyssean adventure there are

[28] Petersmann (1981) 64–8. For the role of the donor in folktales see V. Propp, *Morphology of the Folktale*, 2nd ed. (Austin, 1968) 39–50.

two expeditions to Kirke and so two opportunities for the donor to appear. A group of men led by Eurylochos went to her house, where she transformed most of them into swine, after which Odysseus himself went, escaped her snares, and arranged for the disenchantment of the earlier group. If this story were a folktale, the donor would likely have appeared first to Eurylochos, who would have rebuffed him (or her) unkindly and so received no aid, and subsequently the donor would have appeared to Odysseus, who in contrast would have treated the stranger kindly and so received the crucial boon. But in the Homeric story Hermes appears only to Odysseus, for the Homeric world is not a place of equal opportunity. Supernatural helpers do not appear to Eurylochos precisely because he is merely Eurylochos, whereas supernatural helpers abound for Odysseus, who is favored by the gods and need not even prove himself.

Table of Stories

The following table lists all the stories recounted by Homer for which I find clear or suggestive analogues in international oral tradition, including the legend of Kirke, whose relationship to traditional tales is too complicated to discuss in small compass; that is, this is a catalogue of types in the folkloric sense.[29] For each story I give the Homeric citation and a reference to the international tradition (to a type or motif, to a conventional title, or as a last resort to a title that I have devised). 'AT' refers to Aarne-Thompson's *The Types of the Folktale*, 'Motif' to Thompson's *Motif-Index of Folk Literature*, and 'ML' to Christiansen's *The Migratory Legends*. I follow the sequence in which the stories appear in the poems.

A. *Iliad*

Bellerophon and Anteia (*Il.* 6.152–70)
ref: Motif K2111, *Potiphar's wife.*

Meleager (*Il.* 9.524–99)
ref: AT 1187, *Meleager.*

[29] For Kirke see A. Scobie, *Apuleius and Folklore: Toward a History of ML 3045, AaTh 567, 449A* (London, 1983) 229–57.

B. *Odyssey*

Menelaos and Proteus (*Od.* 4.351–586)
ref: resembles ML 4060, *The Mermaid's Message.*

Ares and Aphrodite (*Od.* 8.266–369)
ref: AT 1733B*, *Blacksmith Ties Wife and Lover Together*, and *The Stuck Couple* (urban legend).

Polyphemos (*Od.* 9.105–542)
ref: AT 1137, *The Ogre Blinded.*

Noman (*Od.* 9.355–414)
ref: Motif K602, *'Noman'.*

Bag of Winds (*Od.* 10.17–79)
ref: Motifs C322.1, *Bag of winds*, and D2142.1.2, *Wind raised by loosing certain knots.*

Odysseus and Kirke (*Od.* 10.133–468)
ref: *Ass-Tale Tradition IIA.*

Phaiakan Ship Turned to Stone (*Od.* 13.70–184)
ref: resembles *The Petrified Ship.*

Return of Odysseus (*Odyssey* as a whole)
ref: AT 974, *The Homecoming Husband.*

Penelope's Test (*Od.* 23.1–230)
ref: *Identity Test: Returning Husband's Intimate Knowledge.*

Odysseus and the Oar (*Od.* 11.121–37 & 23.265–87)
ref: *The Sailor and the Oar.*

Summary and Conclusions

The Homeric poems contain around a dozen stories that have more or less close parallels in international oral tradition. The source stories show considerable variety, ranging from such complex and widely-distributed folktales as *The Ogre Blinded* to such simple and sparsely-distributed legends as *The Petrified Ship.* Most of them occur in the *Odyssey*, for which reason the poem has been called a *Märchenepos*, a folktale epic, but this appellation is misleading. It would be truer to say that about a dozen stories in Homer have parallels in international oral tradition, most of them occurring in the *Odyssey*, where they are told as legends.

Homer is not likely to have been the inventor of the stories in question, nor do the international analogues derive from the Homeric poems; rather, the Greek bards drew independently upon the international tradition. The only story in which the question of priority has been much debated is that of *The Ogre Blinded*, and even here nearly all scholars have concluded that Homer's version is not the source of the international tale but an independent realization of it. In a couple cases the ancient and modern parallels may not be genetically related at all.

There is a tendency in studies of folk narratives in Homer to link the notions *folktale* and *fabulous*. This coupling can have undesirable consequences because realistic stories may be excluded from the consideration of traditional stories in Homer and because Homer's use of folktales may be regarded as being the same as his employment of the fantastic, which it properly is not, since not all folktales contain fabulous motifs and not all fabulous motifs belong to, or derive from, folktales. For example, there is nothing fantastic in the story of *The Sailor and the Oar*, however unlikely the means that the protagonist employs to accomplish his quest may be (a man seeking a community unfamiliar with the sea would probably make verbal inquiries rather than walk inland with an oar), and the erotic dueling of Bellerophon and Anteia is neither fantastic nor unrealistic.

In order to draw upon fabulous stories, Homer (by whom I mean the poet and/or his tradition) transforms some fabulous motifs into something non-fabulous, as when the magic brand of the Meleager story and the magic ring of the Polyphemos story are changed, as it seems, into curses. More often Homer retains the fabulous while distancing it in some way from the main story. Thus the fabulous adventures recounted in Books 9–12 take place in very distant lands that are set off from the familiar Achaean world, and their narration is assigned to a character within the poem, thereby transferring some responsibility for them to the internal narrator. Although Homer's epics teem with fabulous elements, they are not distributed randomly throughout the poems. The regulated presence of the fabulous adds charm and wonder, while the dignity and seriousness of the central story is maintained by the poet's emphasis on realism and natural causation.

There are apparent exceptions to these practices, such as the magical ship of the Phaiakians. In the folktale magical conveyance is employed in order to bring the hero home in an impossibly short period of time so that he may arrive before the remarriage of his wife, which he has learned is imminent. But Odysseus faces no such crisis, for Penelope has scheduled no wedding date, and in any case Odysseus has no precise knowledge of events in Ithaka. In this instance the poet retains the element of the fantastic from the folktale and narrates it in his own voice, but he decouples the role it plays in the folktale from the workings of the epic plot, retaining the wonder of the phenomenon but making nothing crucial depend causally upon the supernatural speed of the Phaiakian vessel.

Some non-fabulous motifs have also been modified because in their original form they did not suit the dignity of Greek heroic poetry. It would not be seemly to make Odysseus cut off his finger to rid himself of a magic ring, as the hero of *The Ogre Blinded* does, nor to have Odysseus prove his identity to his wife by describing her body intimately. The poet's solution is to transform the magic ring into a curse and to content himself with a less intimate level in the *Identity Test*.

Ralph M. Rosen

HOMER AND HESIOD

One of the most frustrating aspects of Homeric studies is that so little literary material outside the Homeric corpus itself survives to enhance our understanding of the cultural landscape of the period. Recent scholarship suggests that a large and diverse poetic tradition lay behind the figure we refer to as 'Homer,' but little of it survives. Indeed we have little continuous written Greek for another century. The one exception is Hesiod, who composed two extant poems, the *Theogony* and *Works and Days*, and possibly several others, including the *Shield of Heracles* and the *Catalogue of Women*. As we shall see, while Hesiodic poetry was not occupied specifically with *heroic* themes, it was part of the same formal tradition of epic, sharing with Homer key metrical, dialectal, and dictional features.

There are many reasons, beyond chronological proximity, to draw connections between Homer and Hesiod. Both poets composed in the dactylic hexameter, the traditional meter of Greek epic, and in an oral formulaic tradition. Like Homer, Hesiod was primarily concerned with transmitting traditional material in oral performance. Comparative analysis of Homeric and Hesiodic diction indicates that both poets drew on a common store of traditional formulas.[1] The particular ways in which this heritage manifests itself in both poets suggests that epic was driven by a 'panhellenic' impulse, a desire to appeal to as many city-states as possible. In language and theme alike, therefore, Homeric and Hesiodic poetry represent a movement away from epichoric composition, toward performances that could be intelligible and meaningful virtually anywhere in Greece.[2]

These linguistic and formal similarities led ancient critics to see

---

[1] See G. P. Edwards (1971) 190–207 for a summary of his conclusions.

[2] As G. Nagy (1982) 44, puts it, in discussing the particularly Panhellenic representation of the Olympian gods in Homer and Hesiod: 'Homeric and Hesiodic poetry systematized the city-states' diverse ideologies about the gods into a set of attributes and functions that all Hellenes could accept.' See also Nagy (1990b) 70–71. Equally revealing of Panhellenic tendencies are the glaring cases where localization occasionally seems to surface; see Nagy (1995b).

both poets as part of a unified tradition known as *epos* ('epic' poetry), although the contrasts between their works in length, subject matter, and authorial self-presentation challenge modern conceptions of the 'epic' genre. We tend to think of epics as poems like Homer's—very long narrative poems, dealing with heroes, often at war. Hesiod's poems, however, are short (*Theogony*: 1022 lines; *Works and Days*: 828 lines), have little to do with heroes, and are not much concerned with war, at least not among humans (the *Theogony* narrates divine battles, and humans play little part). Indeed, the *Theogony* and *Work and Days* themselves are quite unlike *each other* in many ways. Each seems to owe its character to distinct poetic sub-genres ('theogonic' or 'didactic-wisdom' traditions, respectively)[3] appropriate to different occasions.[4] As we shall see, the conspicuous differences between the poems of Hesiod and between Hesiod and Homer existed in tension with the unified poetic tradition of *epos*, to which these works belonged at the broadest level. By considering how Homer and Hesiod situated themselves within this larger tradition of hexameter *epos* and in relation to each other, we will understand better their sophisticated poetic culture, their generic self-consciousness, and the dynamics of intertextual composition in Archaic poetry.[5]

The Question of Priority

Since antiquity, scholars have debated the absolute and relative dating of Homer and Hesiod and the chronology of their works. They

[3] For the 'theogonic' traditions that inform Hesiod's *Theogony*, see M. L. West (1966) 1–16; for the didactic traditions of 'wisdom literature' behind the *Works and Days* see West (1978) 3–30.

[4] For some recent discussions of the generic identity of Hesiod's poetry, see Thalmann (1984); Ford (1992) 13–56, esp. 29–30; West (1978) 3–25; Hunt (1981).

[5] 'Intertextuality' might not, perhaps, seem an ideal critical term for discussing oral traditions, where the very notion of a 'text' is somewhat anachronistic. Still, Homer and Hesiod survive for us as texts, and as texts they allow us to analyse their constituent parts, even if these parts originally evolved from an essentially non-literary process of composition. In fact, 'intertextuality' as a term to describe how a group of texts (and authors) influence the composition and character of each other, is more appropriate for oral poetry than, for example, a concept such as 'allusion,' since the very force of a poetic *tradition* makes it difficult to ascribe influence to one particular poet who happens to survive, instead of to another one who does not. As we shall see below, the uncertainty about the chronology of Homer and Hesiod in particular makes it all the more dangerous to posit a chronology or direction of textual influence in cases where textual similarities (linguistic, thematic, metrical or otherwise) seem to exist.

have approached this problem with many motives—political, moral, or aesthetic[6]—and our own age is no different. While we may no longer be interested in establishing whether Homer or Hesiod was the better poet by fixing their dates, our reasons for pursuing this problem amount to more than idle curiosity. For if we could fix their chronology, we might gain a better sense of their relationship. In cases where one poet seems to allude to the other, for example, we could grapple more effectively with intertextuality within a dynamic oral tradition. And if we could plausibly isolate in one poet consciousness of the other's work, we could perhaps address less diffidently the tension between the oral poet as 'author' and as purveyor of tradition. Such concerns reflect a persistent obsession with authorship and an author's identity in our own era,[7] and chronology and historical context form the obvious starting point for addressing these issues.

We cannot fix the dates of Homer and Hesiod with much certainty, but a general consensus has developed in recent decades that the two poets' activity falls in the century 750–650 B.C. The issue is complicated by the fact that these poems must originally have been composed without writing; questions of dating have to address the problem of when our texts became fixed.[8] Still, it is probably no coincidence that our first texts, no matter when they were finally fixed in their current form, reflect poetic activity from the period when the introduction of the alphabet seems to have fostered the development of literature (Powell, this vol.). Scholars have applied external evidence from linguistics, archaeology, and history to Homer and Hesiod to date each poet individually. But because they both can be placed in the same general period, and because we cannot

[6] Lefkowitz (1981) 8 notes some of the agendas lying behind theories of priority in the past.

[7] Even some critical methodologies of recent decades that question the legitimacy of framing interpretative questions around the figure of a historically situated 'author' (new criticism, structuralism, deconstruction, and some phenomenological approaches, for example) have had to confront in their own ways the fact that all texts imply a relationship between an author and an audience, both of which are ultimately elusive to an individual critic. It is especially difficult to find stable meaning in texts composed within an oral tradition, because their oral provenance implies a certain measure of authorial anonymity—an individual poet may be responsible for the text as we have it, but his necessary reliance on traditional material (that is, the work of countless other oral poets) blurs the lines between innovation and poetic inheritance. For a sensitive appreciation of the critical dilemmas that a poet such as Hesiod poses for the modern reader, see Lamberton (1988) 34–37.

[8] Cf. G. Nagy (1995b) 174.

narrow down their dates to periods of time less than several decades, the question of which 'came first' requires further strategies. As we shall see, the situation is further complicated by a persistent ancient tradition that Homer and Hesiod were not only contemporaries, but even met in a poetic contest intended to contrast their individual styles.

Modern scholars generally assume that Homer composed earlier than Hesiod, although this rests on little more than subjective evaluations. Homeric epic somehow 'feels' older than Hesiod, as if the former's heroic, military themes must precede the more 'refined' sensibility which the latter's theogonic or didactic poems allegedly reflect.[9] The arguments have grown more sophisticated in recent decades, and the consensus in favor of an earlier date for Homeric survives, but the issue is not settled, and it may be worthwhile to mention here several representative discussions.

The fundamental debate is over the relative merits of internal and external criteria. Should we concentrate on establishing absolute dates for each poet by comparing his work with the historical and archaeological records, and from there making a circumstantial case for a relative chronology? Or will analysis of details of language, diction, and poetics offer better evidence for the relationship between the two, even if we cannot determine absolute dates?

M. L. West, in his commentary on the *Theogony*, exemplifies the external method, and is one of the few recent scholars to argue for Hesiod's priority ([1966] 40–48).[10] West sets himself in a tradition going back at least to fifth-century Greece, when the earliest poets were listed, presumably in chronological order, as Orpheus, Musaeus, Hesiod, and Homer. West suggests ([1966] 46) that 'the *Theogony* may well be the oldest Greek poem we have.' His *terminus post quem* of c. 750 B.C. for Hesiod, based on archaeological and historical evidence, seems secure; but dating the actual composition of the *Theogony* to the eighth century is another matter. To do this, West relies on

[9] See Walcot (1966) 124: '. . . the difference between the two poets in technique of composition and in language is thought to imply a lapse of time.' Walcot is impatient with this assumption and urges us first to establish dates for each poet independently before attempting to discuss their relationship.

[10] Others who have maintained priority for Hesiod include: Bethe (1914–27) II.299–339. Sellschopp (1934) argued that much of the *Odyssey* must have been composed later than Hesiod; for an attempt to repudiate this position, see G. P. Edwards (1971) 167–189.

a series of controversial premises about the dating of historical events, notably the so-called Lelantine War, an apparently intermittent conflict between Eretria and Chalcis.[11] Even if we accept this argument, Hesiod's priority also rests on the controversial view that Homer's poems as we have them cannot be older than c. 700.[12]

Until quite recently, however, nearly all scholars have relied on internal criteria. They found common ground between the two—shared themes, identical phraseology, unusual diction—and then tried to decide whether one was borrowing from or alluding to the other. These attempts to date the poets now seem problematic, especially as scholars explore the nature of oral poetry with increasing sophistication. The success of the method must be judged on a case-by-case basis.[13] Even champions of internal criteria lament that they encourage subjective evaluations: what strikes one commentator as 'naive' strikes another as 'sophisticated'; one person's idea of 'derivative' or 'ornamental' will seem 'original' and 'effective' to another.[14] The most explicit verbal and thematic parallels have been collected and sifted by several generations of scholars,[15] and just one example can illustrate the method.

Toward the end of the *Theogony*'s proem, honoring the Muses for their inspiration, Hesiod rounds off a list of the nine Muses with a

---

[11] M. L. West (1966) 43. For problems in dating the Lelantine war, see Janko (1982) 94–98.

[12] See West (1966) 46 n. 2, where he notes the archaeological evidence for an early sixth-century date for Homer (cf. E. Cook [1995]). Of course, the issue of assigning a date to Homer is all the more complicated by the necessity to separate Homeric *texts* as a product of a dynamic and fluid oral tradition, unsusceptible by nature to firm dating, and Homer the historical figure who lived some time in the eighth or seventh century B.C. See G. Nagy (1992) 51–53; (1995a) on the evolution of an oral poem from performance to fixed text.

[13] Some scholars have registered categorical disapproval of the method: 'A more insidious type of argument can result from the a comparison of passages in Homer and Hesiod whose contents or phrasing are similar' (Walcot [1966] 124). Walcot's objection is based on the nature of oral poetry: 'If poets trained in an oral tradition share formulas and themes, it is inevitable that we meet coincidence of phrasing when their subject-matter is similar' (p. 125).

[14] H. Neitzel (1975), for example, is concerned specifically with the passages in Hesiod that seem redolent of Homer (note, of course, how his title presupposes a chronology and direction of literary influence), though he sees his own work as more 'scientific' than that of his predecessors: see his introductory survey of the history of the problem, pp. 1–15.

[15] In addition to Neitzel's monograph (see previous note), one may consult the principal works that address the relationship between Homer and Hesiod: Schwenn (1934); Sellschopp (1934); Krafft (1963).

digression about their special relationship with kings (*basilêes*). The Muses, he says, pour sweet dew on the king's lips, which accounts for their honey-sweet speech (83–84). Hesiod then continues the description of the king:

> οἱ δέ νυ λαοὶ
> πάντες ἐς αὐτὸν ὁρῶσι διακρίνοντα θέμιστας
> ἰθείῃσι δίκῃσιν· ὁ δ' ἀσφαλέως ἀγορεύων
> αἶψά τι καὶ μέγα νεῖκος ἐπισταμένως κατέπαυσε·
> τούνεκα γὰρ βασιλῆες ἐχέφρονες, οὕνεκα λαοῖς
> βλαπτομένοις ἀγορῆφι μετάτροπα ἔργα τελεῦσι
> ῥηιδίως, μαλακοῖσι παραιφάμενοι ἐπέεσιν·
> ἐρχόμενον δ' ἀν' ἀγῶνα θεὸν ὣς ἱλασκόνται
> αἰδοῖ μειλιχίῃ, μετὰ δὲ πρέπει ἀγρομένοισι.
>
> *Theogony* 84–92

[... and the peoples all look to him as he decides what is to prevail with his straight judgments. His word is sure, and expertly he makes a quick end of even a great dispute. This is why there are prudent kings: when the peoples are wronged in their dealings, they make amends for them with ease, persuading them with gentle words. When he goes among a gathering, they seek his favor with conciliatory reverence, as if he were a god, and he stands out among the crowd.]
(trans. West)

This passage has long reminded scholars of Homer, *Odyssey* 8.165–77, where Odysseus angrily responds to Euryalus, who had just ridiculed Odysseus's unathletic appearance (159–64). Odysseus states that the gods bestow different gifts on different men, but that the eloquent man is especially envied:

> ἄλλος μὲν γὰρ εἶδος ἀκιδνότερος πέλει ἀνήρ,
> ἀλλὰ θεὸς μορφὴν ἔπεσιν στέφει, οἱ δέ τ' ἐς αὐτὸ
> τερπόμενοι λεύσσουσιν· ὁ δ' ἀσφαλέως ἀγορεύει
> αἰδοῖ μειλιχίῃ μετὰ δὲ πρέπει ἀγρομένοισιν,
> ἐρχόμενον δ' ἀνὰ ἄστυ θεὸν ὣς εἰσορόωσιν.
> ἄλλος δ' αὖ εἶδος μὲν ἀλίγκιος ἀθανάτοισιν,
> ἀλλ' οὔ οἱ χάρις ἀμφιπεριστέφεται ἐπέεσσιν,
> ὡς καὶ σοὶ εἶδος μὲν ἀριπρεπές, οὐδέ κεν ἄλλως
> οὐδὲ θεὸς τεύξειε, νόον δ' ἀποφώλιός ἐσσι.
>
> *Odyssey* 8.169–77

[... One man has a weak appearance, but god adorns him with eloquence, and people look upon him with pleasure. That man speaks flawlessly in public with conciliatory reverence, and distinguishes himself from the crowd, and they regard him as a god as he goes through the city. Another man, however, may have a physical appearance like the immortal gods, but his words are not suffused with charm. So in your case, you have a distinguished appearance, god has seen to that, to be sure, but you're really a fool.]

The similarities between these passages are close enough to suggest some sort of relationship (even if only one that has them drawing independently on the same traditional material), yet they are different enough to make it difficult to argue that either directly depends on the other. The difference in context—the one a hymnic invocation, the other a scene in a secular narrative—does not suggest interdependence based on the notion of a 'theme' and 'variation;' yet the main rhetorical point of each passage is strikingly similar. The *Theogony* passage praises the just king and describes the respect he receives; in the *Odyssey* passage, Odysseus notes the pleasure that the people take in the gifted speaker. Both the Hesiodic king and the Odyssean orator rely on the quality of their discourse and owe their talents to the gods.

Scholars have puzzled over these passages since Wilamowitz,[16] who felt that the Hesiodic one was probably the earlier. In his commentary on the *Theogony*, West also suspected that the Hesiod passage came first, although he does not assume that the author of the *Odyssey* therefore depended on Hesiod. West sees the difficulty in establishing a relative chronology, but his remarks on the passages' diction typifies a common argument. West ([1966] 183) suggests that 'Homer seems the further removed from the original or traditional application of the language involved. αἰδοῖ μειλιχίῃ ['with conciliatory reverence'] is much less appropriate to the tone of an eloquent man (*Od.* 8.172) than to the respect with which the people regard an αἰδοῖος βασιλεύς ['revered king'] (*Th.* 92), and mere eloquence . . . does not make a man who is εἶδος ἀκιδνότερος ['weak in appearance'] conspicious in a crowd . . . Kingship does.'

Every point West makes here is controversial: we have no access to an 'original or traditional application of the language involved,' and his assessment of what is 'appropriate to the tone of an eloquent man' oversimplifies a complex issue.[17] Other scholars have criticized West's subjectivity on this point, but are themselves little more 'objective.'

[16] von Wilamowitz-Moellendorff (1915) 477–79. See also Neitzel (1977) notes 3, 4, and p. 44.

[17] For criticism of West's subjectivity, see Butterworth (1986) 35; Solmsen (1954). Solmsen, Butterworth, and Neitzel (1977) argue that Homer's thought and language in this passage is coherent and precise (contra West).

H. Neitzel, for example, felt that the key point was that in Homer the god who bestows gifts on men and determines their natures in life is not named, whereas in Hesiod the divine benefactors appear as the Muses. Why, he asks, would Homer have neglected to mention the Muses if he were imitating Hesiod?[18] In fact, we can imagine any number of reasons why Homer might choose to do so or not to do so. The argument does nothing to establish priority, even if it does offer useful observations about how the two poets chose to handle traditional material.

Most recently, J. Butterworth has argued that although the phrase αἰδοῖ μειλιχίῃ ['with conciliatory reverence'] is found in both passages, its appearance in Homer was more traditional, and therefore that Homer was the earlier of the two. In the end, however, he too relies on an argument like West's (albeit in reverse form), that the phrase αἰδοῖ μειλιχίῃ *seems* to the sensibility of one critic to fit its context naturally in the one case (Homer), and awkwardly in the other (Hesiod).[19]

The ways in which scholars have confronted the similarities between these passages highlight the questions most commonly asked when parallel passages are detected, and the methods used to answer them. An obsession with chronology runs as a leitmotif through most attempts to explicate parallel passages, and this obsession has intensified as we become more confident about at least the approximate dating of the two poets, and about the mechanics of the oral poetic tradition in which they composed. But it is too often forgotten that discussing the relationship between any two poets by assessing similar passages involves an act of interpretation by the critic, and that such acts of interpretation presuppose, whether we choose to admit it or not, beliefs about the author's intentions which will never be verifiable. We seek, in other words, a simple answer to a simple

---

[18] Neitzel basically is following Solmsen (1954) 9 on this point.

[19] His argument may be schematized as follows:

(a) μειλίχιος is always applied in Homer to words, with the exception of this passage, where it is used of αἰδώς.

(b) μειλίχιος can be considered a traditional adjective applied to words.

(c) αἰδοῖ μειλιχίῃ is a unique phrase in Homer and Hesiod.

(d) In the *Odyssey* passage, the phrase is used more traditionally in that it at least refers to the verbal qualities of the eloquent man.

(e) The use of the phrase in Hesiod is awkward in its context (see also Neitzel [1977] 43) and untraditional in its usage (not referring to words), and therefore must come later than the Homeric passage.

question—who was first, Homer or Hesiod?—but the interpretation of the poetry itself cannot provide an answer.

This is not to say that the discussions of parallel passages are without insight or value, even if their ultimate goal of determining priority is unattainable.[20] Few would disagree with West, Neitzel, or Butterworth that the similarities between the *Theogony* and the *Odyssey* passages are more than coincidental, or that each poet was using in some way traditional material. Indeed it is precisely the similarities between the two passages which suggest the presence of traditional material. But even more remarkable, perhaps, is the fact that diction so similar is found in such different contexts. This ought to encourage us to focus more on how each poet manipulates traditional material within the individual work, rather than on trying to determine whether one must have borrowed from the other, and must therefore be judged the clumsier for it.

Both these passages, for example, although the narrative contexts are so different, depict as their central moral exemplum a figure who acquires public renown through intelligence and eloquent speech. By comparing its appearance in our two passages we begin to see how an oral poet could put his own stamp on traditional material. Although we will probably never have an accurate chronology for the passages, we can see a relationship between them that goes beyond verbal allusion. Despite the different stories that each poet is telling, the notion of a distinguished public speaker and arbiter resonates in both contexts.[21] Hesiod's kings are revered explicitly for their ability to mollify quarreling parties (86–87). In the *Odyssey* passage, the distinguished public speaker's moral qualities are less obvious, but Odysseus's exemplum highlights Euryalus' moral deficiency in contrast to his own more refined sensibility, based on eloquence and wit. Moreover, the dispute between Odysseus and Euryalus is precisely the sort of affair that Hesiod's judicious kings resolve, though Odysseus himself makes no overt connection between the gifted speaker

[20] In this regard, P. Pucci's remarks ([1987] 234 n. 14) about the question of the priority of Homer and Hesiod seem unnecessarily extreme: 'Even if it were proved that Hesiod's text follows the *Odyssey*'s . . . no serious critical consequence should stem from this assumption . . .'

[21] See R. P. Martin (1984), who argues that both passages are examples of the genre known as 'Instruction of Princes.' Martin emphasizes the traditional link between *aidos* and kingship (pp. 41–43), and notes how this link allows us to see Odysseus in the Homeric passage as commenting on the appropriate behavior of kings, and, in effect, enacting such behavior himself (see p. 44).

and a reconciliation with Euryalus. The passages are related in their use of the same traditional motif, but each poet deploys it in an idiosyncratic way. Whereas Hesiod offers a straightforward description of the idealized king, Homer weaves the motif into the passage with remarkable narratological economy. Homer has Odysseus counter Euryalus's taunts, contrast his own public eloquence to Euryalus's feeble-mindedness, and emphasize his own kingly stature. As R. P. Martin puts it: 'What is explicit in *Theogony* 86 ff.—that it is the king who speaks faultlessly, winning *aidos* and solving a *neikos* in the *agora* thereby—is acted out in the *Odyssey*.'[22]

Neither external nor internal criteria in the end settle the dating question conclusively, even if the questions they elicit about the poets' literary relationship may lead us down more productive critical paths. But one other recent attempt to address chronology deserves mention as a judicious amalgamation of external and internal arguments, avoiding many of the methodological pitfalls of each. R. Janko (1982) uses linguistic phenomena to establish a chronology of Archaic hexameter poetry. Janko works in a well established tradition of linguistic analysis[23] that sees signposts of poetic development in the evolution of dialect and the formulas of oral composition. But his careful collation of a broad spectrum of texts, his application of statistical methods, and his sensitivity to oral theory and poetic genre distinguish his study from most treatises that analyze the technical and formal aspects of epic. Janko sums up his method as follows ([1982] 189): '. . . one expects old formulae and archaisms to diminish in frequency through the generations, as innovative phraseology and language creeps in; and if this could be quantified, it might prove a yardstick useful for assigning approximate relative dates to the poems.' Janko orders the poems as follows: *Iliad, Odyssey, Theogony, Works and Days*.[24] This conclusion is hardly revolutionary, as he himself points out, and he acknowledges the inadequacies of our evidence, such as the impossibility of fixing absolute dates, the amount

[22] See Martin (1984) 44. Martin cautions on p. 45 that the typological connections between the two passages need not imply any direct influence of either one on the other.

[23] In the case of Hesiod, Janko is particularly indebted to G. P. Edwards (1971), who established with reasonable certainty that Homer and Hesiod were products of the same linguistic and dialectal tradition.

[24] See Janko (1982) 189–200; cf. G. Nagy (1995b) 174, who thinks of text-fixation as a more fluid process than Janko does.

of material now lost,[25] and the problem of literary 'allusion' in an oral tradition.[26] But he has taken the debate a step forward, offering cogent support for the widespread consensus that Homer composed before Hesiod.[27]

The Certamen: the Contest of Homer and Hesiod

No matter what relative chronology of Homer and Hesiod we ultimately choose to believe, no one would dispute that the two poets lived close enough in time to each other, between the middle of the eighth and the middle of the seventh centuries B.C., to make it plausible for their lifetimes to have overlapped. Indeed, for much of antiquity, it was assumed not only that the two poets were contemporaries, but even that they competed against one another in a contest of poetic styles. The story of a contest between Homer and Hesiod, even though clearly a fiction contrived by early biographers of the poets,[28] represents an early attempt to confront several fundamental questions perhaps even more significant than that of chronology, namely how a common epic tradition could produce such different poets as Homer and Hesiod, and how the distinctive character of each poet's work might reflect a difference in moral value and utility within an evolving canon.

The Contest of Homer and Hesiod exists for us in its fullest form in a text dating from the second century A.D., traditionally referred

---

[25] Janko (1982) 9: 'At least as much epic poetry has been lost as has survived, leaving aside oral poetry there may have been which was never recorded.'

[26] On the utility and legitimacy of investigating *exemplum* and *imitatio* in oral epic, cf. Janko (1982) 225–28; Butterworth (1986).

[27] Just how meaningful even this general formulation can be is uncertain, of course, given the fact that we know so little about the actual mechanism by which they were fixed in writing. To say that Homer composed before Hesiod implies that the texts we have of them reflect in some way the chronology of their composition. Given what we know generally about the transmission of Homeric and Hesiodic texts in the historical period of Greece, we have to be cautious about how much we make of the issue of priority. But until we have more information, for example, about influence of the rhapsodic tradition on textual fixation, it is reasonable for us to assume that our texts of Homer and Hesiod, taken as a whole, provide us with a serviceable record of a moment of fixation close to the period of original composition. For reservations about this assumption, however, see Nagy (1995b) 174.

[28] See Lefkowitz (1981) 4–5; Lamberton (1988) 5–7; also M. L. West (1967); Heldmann (1982). The story was repudiated by Plutarch (according to the fifth-century A.D. commentator Proclus), and in *Quaest. Conv.* 674 f. he regards the contest as a tedious topic; see West (1978) 319.

to by its Latin title, the *Certamen*.[29] Although this treatise is relatively late, there is persuasive evidence that it was based on a work by the sophist and rhetorical theorist Alcidamas of the fourth century B.C.,[30] which leads one to suspect that the tradition originated even earlier. The author of the *Certamen* takes a disarmingly catholic view of the background to his subject, opening the work in almost Herodotean fashion by recounting various traditions about the genealogical and geographical provenance of Homer and Hesiod, while committing himself to none in particular.[31] On the matter of the chronology of Homer and Hesiod, the author simply relates the divergent theories: 'Some say that [Homer] came before Hesiod, while others say that he was younger and related to him' (ἔνιοι μὲν οὖν αὐτὸν προγενέστερον Ἡσιόδου φασὶν εἶναι, τινὲς δὲ νεώτερτον καὶ συγγενῆ, 44–5). Although the author proceeds to offer a genealogy that makes Homer and Hesiod cousins through a lineage stretching back to Apollo himself, the anecdote that will occupy the rest of the treatise seems to assume that the two were unrelated: 'Some people say that [Homer and Hesiod] were active at the same time, and so were able to compete with one another at Chalcis in Euboea' (τινὲς δὲ συνακμάσαι φασὶν αὐτοὺς ὥστε καὶ ἀγωνίσασθαι ὁμόσε ἐν Αὐλίδι τῆς Εὐβοίας . . ., 54–55).[32] This version of the story has Homer and Hesiod meet by chance (καὶ οὗτοι οὖν ἐκ τύχης, ὥς φασι, συμβαλόντες ἀλλήλοις ἦλθον εἰς τὴν Χαλκίδα, 66–68) when they came to compete in the funeral contests held in honor of Amphidamas, the king of Euboea. It has long been recognized that the contest between the two poets at Euboea almost certainly arose from the famous passage in the *Works and Days* in which Hesiod claims that the only sailing he ever engaged in was the short voyage from the mainland to Euboea precisely in order to compete in the funeral games for Amphidamas. No mention is made of Homer in that passage, although as we shall see below, the whole passage is suffused with diction paralleled in Homer, which may help explain why later audiences found the funeral games to be an ideal

---

[29] The Greek text can be found in Allen (1912) V. 225–38 (Oxford Classical Texts series), and an English translation in Evelyn-White (1914) 567–97 (Loeb Classical Library).

[30] On the modern history of the question of Alcidamas's influence on the *Certamen*, which began with a two-part article by F. Nietzsche (1870–73) see O'Sullivan (1992) 63–66.

[31] The author does, however, give particular credence to information gleaned from the Pythia (line 41). On the narrative style of the *Certamen*, see Lefkowitz (1981) 19.

[32] The reading Εὐβοίας follows F. Nietzsche's emendation of Βοιωτίας.

venue for a meeting between the two poets.[33] For the author of the *Certamen*, in any event, the historicity of the events he relates or the reliability of the biographical facts about Homer and Hesiod seem far less important than the ethical and aesthetic ramifications of the contest itself.

The format of the contest of Homer and Hesiod in the *Certamen* certainly reveals a complex and puzzling agenda. Hesiod himself essentially controls the proceedings, at first asking Homer a series of questions, and then engaging him in an exchange of verses in which Homer has to complete a series of lines begun by Hesiod. The very first question posed by Hesiod establishes that the poets were to be judged especially for their philosophical contributions:

> υἱὲ Μέλητος Ὅμηρε θεῶν ἄπο μήδεα εἰδὼς
> εἴπ' ἄγε μοι πάμπρωτα τί φέρτατόν ἐστι βροτοῖσιν; (75–76)
>
> [Homer, son of Meles, whose thoughts come from the gods,
> tell me first of all what is best for mankind?]

That Hesiod orchestrates the contest seems to imply that his poetry was felt to be inherently didactic and philosophical, whereas Homer's was less explicitly so, and so had to prove itself on this score. But while the *Certamen* leads us to assume at the outset that Hesiod will expose his adversary's inability to hold up under Hesiod's rigorous challenges, in fact, Homer acquits himself successfully, at least in the eyes of the audience. When Homer, for example, answers Hesiod's second question (81–82) about what is the 'finest thing' for mortals (καλλίστον, 82, with aesthetic and moral overtones) by quoting the famous passage from the *Odyssey* about the splendors of the banquet (*Od.* 9.6–11), the audience is enormously impressed: ῥηθέντων δὲ τούτων τῶν ἐπῶν, οὕτω σφοδρῶς φασι θαυμασθῆναι τοὺς στίχους ὑπὸ τῶν Ἑλλήνων ὥστε χρυσοῦς αὐτοὺς προσαγορευθῆναι . . ., 90–92 ['when these verses were uttered, they were so greatly admired by the Greeks that the lines were called "golden". . .']. This reaction annoys Hesiod (ὁ δὲ Ἡσίοδος ἀχθεσθείς, 94) and forces him to pose more 'difficult'

[33] West (1978) 32, 44–45, has suggested that the *Theogony* itself was actually composed for performance at the funeral games for Amphidamas; see Janko (1982) 94–95. The *Certamen* mentions at lines 213–14 that when Hesiod won the tripod at Chalcis he dedicated it to the Muses with an inscription boasting of his victory over Homer. Pausanias, writing in the second century A.D. records that he saw the tripod at Mt. Helicon (9.31.3). On the tradition of Hesiod's victory tripod see O'Sullivan (1992) 97.

questions (τὴν τὸν ἀπορῶν . . . ἐπερώτησιν, 95). Homer continued to perform well in the exchange that ensued, and the crowd finally called for the victory crown to go to Homer (176–77). But the contest then takes an unexpected turn, when King Paneides intervenes and orders both poets to recite what they consider their finest passage. After Hesiod quotes from the *Works and Days* (383–92) and Homer from *Iliad* (13.126–39), the audience once again judges Homer the victor. But the King sees things otherwise, and awards the victory to Hesiod, '. . . saying that it was just that he win the prize who urged people to practice farming and live in peace, and not the one who recounted wars and slaughter' [. . . εἰπὼν δίκαιον εἶναι τὸν ἐπὶ γεωργίαν καὶ εἰρήνην προκαλούμενον νικᾶν, οὐ τὸν πολέμους καὶ σφαγὰς διεξιόντα, 208–210].

This conclusion to the contest is rather unexpected in view of the fact that throughout the *Certamen* Homer is portrayed much more favorably than Hesiod, and the crowd's consistent preference for Homer certainly bears this out. It is difficult to decide how significant it is, therefore, that in spite of the story's apparent anti-Hesiodic bias, that poet still ends up with the prize. Any attempt to address this problem fully must confront the complicated issues surrounding the provenance of the *Certamen*, as well as the relationship between this treatise and other traditions of the contest for which we have some evidence.[34] N. O'Sullivan reminds us ([1992] 96–97) in his recent study of this topic that although differing versions of the contest circulated at various points in antiquity—some in fact more disposed towards Hesiod throughout—they all agree that Hesiod won the contest in one way or another. This fact alone makes him suspect that a tradition of Hesiod's victory arose simply from an early tendency to assume that the passage in *Works and Days* where Hesiod claims to have won a victory tripod (651–57) in Chalcis must have referred to a contest with Homer. As such, the story of a contest that can be traced ultimately to a competition at Chalcis had to have Hesiod win in the end, even if the individual treatments of the event invested the narrative with idiosyncratic significance.[35]

---

[34] See O'Sullivan (1992) Ch. 3, esp. 96–98.

[35] O'Sullivan, for example, stresses the likelihood that the *Certamen* derives from Alcidamas' (a sophist of the fourth century B.C.) treatise *Peri Sophiston*, and that Alcidamas saw the contest between Homer and Hesiod as emblematic of a contemporary debate between two opposing rhetorical styles (where Homer represented the 'grand,' Hesiod the 'slender' styles, Alcidamas himself championing the former). O'Sullivan (1992) 98 notes other interpretations of Hesiod's victory.

Clearly the traditions of a contest between Homer and Hesiod tell us more about the ways in which subsequent cultures conceived of these poets than about how they may have actually interacted in their own lifetimes. Yet the cultures that generated these stories were grappling with the same sorts of questions about the very nature of Homeric and Hesiodic poetry which continue to intrigue us today: Can we, for example, characterize Homer and Hesiod meaningfully according to the contents of their poems? Can we, in the end, ever hope to define 'epic' poetry in the face of the differences between the two poets? Imagining a contest between Homer and Hesiod during which their poetic skills were articulated, compared and judged is just one way of arriving at answers to critical questions such as these. In the next section we will consider more recent strategies for understanding the specifically literary relationship between Homer and Hesiod in their own time.

Homer, Hesiod and the Character of Archaic Epic

We noted earlier that the *certamen*-tradition arose in the first place most likely because in the *Works and Days* Hesiod recounts his participation in the poetic contest at the funeral games for Amphidamas at Chalcis. Homer, of course, is not actually mentioned in that passage (even if ancient commentators assumed that he was in fact Hesiod's rival on that occasion), but in recent years scholars have detected there strong indications that Hesiod was attempting to contrast his own poetry to that of Homer's. The passage occurs in a section of the poem commonly referred to as the *Nautilia*, or 'Sailing' (619–94), where the poet offers advice about seafaring.[36] At lines 648–50 Hesiod introduces a digression about his own experience on the sea:

> δείξω δή τοι μέτρα πολυφλοίσβοιο θαλάσσης,
> οὔτέ τι ναυτιλίης σεσοφισμένος οὔτέ τι νηῶν·
> οὐ γάρ πώ ποτε νηί γ' ἐπέπλων εὐρέα πόντον,
> εἰ μὴ ἐς Εὔβοιαν ἐξ Αὐλίδος, ᾗ ποτ' Ἀχαιοί
> μείναντες χειμῶνα πολὺν σὺν λαὸν ἄγειραν
> Ἑλλάδος ἐξ ἱερῆς Τροίην ἐς καλλιγύναικα.
> ἔνθα δ' ἐγὼν ἐπ' ἄεθλα δαίφρονος Ἀμφιδάμαντος

[36] Scholars have often felt uneasy about this passage, since it seems out of place in the poem, and some have even proposed to delete it. See West (1978) 55–56, and Lamberton (1988) 131.

Χαλκίδα τ' εἲς ἐπέρησα· τὰ δὲ προπεφραδμένα πολλὰ
ἆθλ' ἔθεσαν παῖδες μεγαλήτορος· ἔνθά μέ φημι
ὕμνῳ νικήσαντα φέρειν τρίποδ' ὠτώεντα.
τὸν μὲν ἐγὼ Μούσῃς Ἑλικωνιάδεσσ' ἀνέθηκα,
ἔνθά με τὸ πρῶτον λιγυρῆς ἐπέβησαν ἀοιδῆς.
τόσσόν τοι νηῶν γε πεπείρημαι πολυγόμφων·
ἀλλὰ καὶ ὣς ἐρέω Ζηνὸς νόον αἰγιόχοιο·
Μοῦσαι γάρ μ' ἐδίδαξαν ἀθέσφατον ὕμνον ἀείδειν.

(*Works and Days* 648–62)

[I will show you the measure of the resounding sea—quite without instruction as I am either in seafaring or in ships; for as to ships, I have never yet sailed the broad sea, except to Euboea from Aulis, the way the Achaeans once came when they waited through the winter and gathered a great army from holy Greece against Troy of the fair women. There to the funeral games for warlike Amphidamas and to Chalcis I crossed, and many were the prizes announced and displayed by the sons of that valiant; where I may say that I was victorious in poetry and won a tripod with ring handles. That I dedicated to the Muses of Helicon, in the original place where they set me on the path of fine singing. That is all my experience of dowelled ships, but even so I will tell the design of Zeus the aegis-bearer, since the Muses have taught me to make song without limit.]

(trans. West)

Readers have frequently been struck by the fact that Hesiod would glorify a trip from Aulis to Euboea—a distance over water of some several hundred feet—by referring to it as an example of sailing, but other details in the passage suggest that sailing in the literal sense may be only part of what the poet has on his mind here. The mention of Aulis at line 651, for example, is followed immediately by a reference to the mustering of the Achaean ships as they prepared for their expedition to Troy,[37] and the much more substantial sea-voyage that the Achaeans had to make, contrasting starkly with Hesiod's short voyage, is expressed in distinctly Homeric diction.[38] The obvious connections with Homer and Homeric poetry, which in their immediate context appear gratuitous at best, and the immediate transition to an account of Hesiod's poetic victory at Chalcis (654–57), has led G. Nagy ([1982] 66) to wonder whether the passage 'reveals an intended differentiation of Hesiodic from Homeric poetry.' Hesiod, in fact, spends the last five lines of the passage recounting how he

[37] West (1978) 320: 'It shows how strong was the interest in heroic poetry, that Hesiod cannot mention Aulis without thinking of the Atreidai and their expedition.'
[38] West (1978) 320–21; G. P. Edwards (1971) 80.

dedicated his victory tripod to the Muses, and the fact that his focus has suddenly shifted from an apologia about his explicitly 'non-Homeric' expertise in sailing to a proud proclamation of his success as a poet,[39] makes it very likely that at some level he was equating sailing metaphorically with his poetic production.[40]

However much force we might choose to give to a metaphorical reading of Hesiod's account of his sailing, it is worth emphasizing, as we noted earlier, that the autobiographical digression within the *Nautilia* inspired ancient readers to suppose that Hesiod's antagonist at Chalcis was none other than Homer, and that the contest between them became emblematic of their divergent styles. This need not necessarily mean, of course, that in antiquity the digression was itself read allegorically as Hesiod's declaration of a poetic program, but the fictions of a *certamen* that arose from the passage had to presume for the age of Homer and Hesiod that it was plausible for the two poets to have been able to think critically and self-consciously about their own work. Clearly even ancient readers reacting to Hesiod's autobiography in the Nautilia sensed that Hesiod himself was attempting to claim a certain authority for his poetry, an authority that can only be secure when the poet has successfully articulated the very nature of his poetic activity. The authors of the various *certamen*-stories, therefore, seem to have been motivated by a central paradox: they felt that Homeric and Hesiodic poetry were somehow related (sharing poetic form, diction, and some aspects of theology, for example), but at the same time acknowledged that the two poets composed fundamentally different sorts of poetry.

What does the poetry itself of Homer and Hesiod, then, reveal to us about how they may themselves have actually understood the differentiation of their respective genres from the other? Hesiod's *Theogony* and *Works and Days*, in fact, conspicuously call attention to their formal affiliation with an epic tradition that we associate with Homer, particularly in their opening lines. Both Hesiodic poems open with an invocation to the Muses as the source of the singer's inspiration (*Th.* 1: Μουσάων 'Ελικωνιάδων ἀρχώμεθ' ἀείδειν . . .; *WD* 1:

[39] Note the peculiar summary line at 660: (τόσσόν τοι νηῶν γε πεπείρημαι πολυγόμφων, ['that is all my experience of dowelled ships']) where τόσσον ['that' or 'that much'] implies that the whole passage somehow relates to his expertise in sailing, even though the immediately preceding lines have been concerned with his competition at Chalcis.

[40] I have pursued this argument in detail in Rosen (1990).

Μοῦσαι Πιερίηθεν, ἀοιδῆσι κλείουσαι . . .), as do the Homeric poems (*Il.* Μῆνιν ἄειδε, θεά . . .; *Od.* 1.1: ἄνδρα μοι ἔννεπε, Μοῦσα . . .). Certainly, the function of the Muses in Archaic Greek poetry is not monolithic. Sometimes they are invoked as a source of knowledge (e.g., the implication that Hesiod can sing of sailing because the Muses have taught him, or Homer's invocation to the Muses at the beginning of the 'Catalogue of Ships,' *Iliad* 2.484–87),[41] at other times, they account for the poet's technical skill and aesthetic prowess (e.g., *Th.* 94–97).[42] But the epic Muse embodies in particular a force of commemoration, whose primary function seems to be to aid the poet in recollecting and recounting traditional narratives,[43] and both Homer and Hesiod call attention to this notion at various points in their poetry. Indeed the commemorative aspect of the Muses inheres in their mythological pedigree, which names Mnemosyne ('Recollection' or 'Memory' personified) as their mother.[44] In Archaic epic, then, one of the main functions of the Muses is to call to the poet's mind the 'things that have been heard,' or κλέα, about the gods, men and the world.

The human beings who have garnered for themselves a reputation that is deemed worthy 'to be heard' are naturally 'heroes' of the sort we find in Homeric epic.[45] But Hesiod, even as he invokes the Muses as bestowers of *kleos*, is interested in a rather different sort of commemoration than Homer, one that is not primarily concerned strictly speaking with the 'deeds of famous men.' In a famous passage from the *Theogony*'s proem, for example, Hesiod describes the character of his inspiration by the Muses:

> ἐνέπνευσαν δέ μοι αὐδὴν
> θέσπιν, ἵνα κλείοιμι τά τ' ἐσσόμενα πρό τ' ἐόντα,
> καί μ' ἐκέλονθ' ὑμνεῖν μακάρων γένος αἰὲν ἐόντων,
> σφᾶς δ' αὐτὰς πρῶτόν τε καὶ ὕστατον αἰὲν ἀείδειν.
>
> *Theogony* 31–4

41 See Pratt (1993) 12–17 (on the Iliadic passage), 48–49 (on the *WD* passage). In spite of such passages that call upon the Muses for 'information,' Pratt argues more broadly that the primary function of Archaic poetry was aesthetic, rather than to offer access to some notion of 'truth.'

42 Cf. Pratt (1993) 31–32.

43 Cf. Pratt (1993) 33–43 on the commemorative aspects of Archaic poetry.

44 Cf. G. Nagy (1979) 17 § 3 n. 2.

45 The song of Demodocus among the Phaeacians in *Odyssey* 8, a song about Odysseus and witnessed by Odysseus, has often been seen as a self-conscious reflection of the entire commemorative enterprise of heroic epic. Cf. Nagy (1979) 17–20. Pratt (1993) 43–47, discusses the passage with an eye to the question of poetic 'truth.'

> [... and they breathed into me wondrous voice, so that I should celebrate (= 'give *kleos*' to) things of the future and things that were aforetime. And they told me to sing of the family of blessed ones who are for ever, and first and last always to sing of themselves.]
>
> (trans. West)

The Muses invoked at the beginning of the *Works and Days* are likewise singled out for their ability to offer *kleos* (Μοῦσαι Πιερίηθεν, ἀοιδῇσι κλείουσαι..., [Muses from Pieria, who offer *kleos* with songs...], *WD* 1), though Hesiod promptly makes clear that he intends to compose a *mythos* directed against his brother Perses, containing 'true things' (ἐγὼ δέ κε Πέρσῃ ἐτήτυμα μυθησαίμην. [... but I would tell (= 'make *mythoi* about')[46] true things to Perses 10), rather than a narrative of the past heroes and their exploits.[47]

Clearly then, while Homer and Hesiod are at some fundamental level united by a desire to endow their subject matter with *kleos* in a commemorative project orchestrated by the Muses, they differentiate themselves from each other explicitly in what they choose to sing about. Homeric epic can be characterized generally as hexameter poetry that celebrated the deeds of the heroes of the past[48] with the pretense of objectivity and impersonality. By contrast, Hesiod's concerns in the two major poems that have come down to us lie elsewhere, and an insistent subjective voice runs through both of them. The *Theogony*, for example, has as its main theme the ascendancy of the Olympian gods, their genealogies, struggles and ultimate moral victory, and the poet highlights his personal relationship with the Muses as the source for the theogony proper that he proceeds to recount. But even though Hesiod's subject matter in the *Theogony* seems alien to that of heroic epic,[49] recent scholarship has aligned that poem intimately with the dynamics of performance associated with Homer. The *Theogony*, after all, can be regarded formally as a

---

[46] On the semantics of *mythos*, see Detienne (1986) 47–51; R. P. Martin (1989) 1–42. Martin's working definition of *mythos* is an 'authoritative speech-act performed in detail' (p. 39; and see pp. 12–13). On the verbal form, *mytheomai*, which occurs in the Hesiodic quotation above, see Martin, p. 40.

[47] On the meaning of *etetyma* ['true things'] in Hesiod, with bibliography tracing the long history of the problem, see Pratt (1993) 95–113.

[48] Ford (1992) 17 formulates a definition of Homeric poetry as 'that subclass of epos that offers a Muse-sponsored presentation of the past.'

[49] Indeed, we may legitimately speak of a 'tradition' of theogonic literature with an existence independent of hexametric epos. See M. L. West (1966) 1–16 for a survey of world theogonic literature.

prelude or prooimion to a work that would immediately follow in performance. Hesiod's poem, to be sure, is an elaborate and expansive version of such a form, but the formal parallels with the *Homeric Hymns*, many of which were clearly intended as proems to heroic epic, strongly suggest that the *Theogony* was composed along the same lines.[50] The likelihood, moreover, that the Hesiodic *Catalogue of Women*, a poem that catalogued famous women of a heroic and mythical past, picked up literally where the *Theogony* left off reinforces the idea that the *Theogony* could have functioned as a prooimion.[51]

Although the *Iliad* and *Odyssey* have not come down to us with formal prooimia in place, it is likely that in performance they were preceded by one, and the longer *Homeric Hymns* provide possible analogues for this.[52] If this is true, however, the traditional view that Homer and Hesiod differ fundamentally in their respective authorial stances must be considerably modified. While it is true that the poet Homer rarely intrudes into the narrative, whereas Hesiod dwells self-consciously on his own role as composer and teacher, some scholars have found it more appropriate to regard this contrast merely as reflecting the different stages of an epic performance rather than a fundamental difference in authorial orientation. Through a proem, then, Homer too would have had his opportunity to situate himself and his reputation in the broader context of the poetic tradition, as Hesiod could do in his expansive way in the *Theogony*.[53] With a model for performance such as this, we might more easily imagine how an

[50] Cf. Nagy (1982) 53: 'The proposition that the *Theogony* is, from a purely formal point of view, a complex prelude that invokes all the gods can be tested by adducing the larger *Homeric Hymns* as simplex preludes, each of which invokes one god.' On the Homeric Hymns as preludes, see Koller (1956). Nagy regards lines 1–963 of the *Theogony* as '. . . not a single, but rather a composite, hymn in comparison with most *Homeric Hymns*' (p. 54). Nagy, in fact, finds three discrete theogonies in this section of the poem; for details see pp. 54–55.

[51] At *Theogony* 963 Hesiod makes a transition from the Olympian gods to goddesses who slept with mortal men, and the heroes who were born from such unions. Although in antiquity the *Catalogue* was generally regarded as Hesiodic, modern scholars have expressed serious doubts. See M. L. West (1985) 124–38. For our purposes, however, it matters little whether the Hesiod of the *Theogony* also composed the *Catalogue*. The point remains that the *Theogony* could serve a prooimic function in antiquity.

[52] For bibliography on the *Homeric Hymns* as preludes to epic performances see Ford (1992) 24 n. 23; Nagy (1982) 53.

[53] See Ford (1992) 28–29: 'Short or long, [the proem] could allow these poets . . . to assert themselves and then sublimate themselves into the transcendental voice of the Muses. The proem carries the poet and audience from the personal to the traditional, from the local to the Penhellenic, from the present to the eternal.'

actual competition between two poets such as Homer and Hesiod might have played itself out.[54]

So far we have seen that Hesiod's *Theogony*, in spite of its many apparent differences from Homeric poetry in terms of subject matter, narratology, and authorial perspective, is in fact very much a part of the same performance context. We will probably never be able to determine exactly how the *Theogony* came to be the elaborate pastiche of autobiography, theology, and mythography that it is for us, and whether its current form reflects the idiosyncratic force of one individual poet or the vagaries of transmission. But its affiliation with the Homeric tradition both in form and occasion allows us at least to assume a very productive intertextual relationship between them. The *Works and Days*, on the other hand, has often proven less easy for scholars to align with Homer, largely because of its 'domestic,' non-heroic, subject matter and explicitly didactic program. M. L. West, for example ([1978] 3), has situated the poem in the context of 'wisdom literature,' by which he means 'works of exhortation and instruction,' and few would deny that, at least in its overall structure and professed intention, the *Works and Days* exhibits the characteristics of this type of poetry.[55] Certainly as well, the insistent autobiographical stance of the poem, the drama of a quarrel with his brother Perses, still active in the fictive present of the poem, offer a striking contrast to Homer's poetic voice, with its pretense of objectivity and only oblique connections with its audience (Ford [1992] 30–31). But even though the *Works and Days* clearly derives much of its ethos from literary genres distinct from heroic epic, we must remember that formally it too, like the *Theogony*, belonged to the same oral hexameter tradition as Homer, and as such, we may suppose that Hesiod created the *Works and Days* under similar conditions of performance and composition.

[54] A central question remains, however, as Lamberton (1988) 47–48 rightly stresses: why were the *Theogony* and *Works and Days* transmitted to us with prooimia in place, while Homer was not. Lamberton speculates that part of the reason for this has to do with the fact that by the Hellenistic period, the persona and text of Hesiod were institutionally connected with a festival for the Muses at Mt. Helicon, near Hesiod's birthplace, Ascra.

[55] See Ford (1992) 30. Ford classifies the *Works and Days* as 'parainetic' or 'advice' poetry, and distinguishes its 'ethos' from that of Homer, or even the *Theogony*: '. . . its fundamental "ethical" difference from epos is in its constant oscillation from sacred time back to its present auditor in order to draw lessons about the human place in the moral order of the world.'

Recently, in fact, a number of scholars have been arguing that, well beyond matters of diction, meter, and formula, the *Works and Days* was perhaps even more profoundly engaged in the Homeric tradition than the *Theogony*. The *Works and Days*, after all, is a poem explicitly about cosmic justice (*dikê*) as it manifests itself in the daily lives of human beings. *Dikê* is certainly a multivalent term in Archaic Greek thinking, but as it emerges in the *Works and Days*, it can be summarized as that sense of balance and order in human activity most conducive to personal and social well-being in a precarious world. At first glance, this may seem like a theme rather alien to the predominantly heroic and militaristic world of Homer, where individual *kleos* often holds the spotlight and little systematic moralizing can be found on mundane social or domestic issues. But Homeric epic also concerns *dikê*, even if it is there articulated in different ways than it is in the *Works and Days*. In the broadest sense, the *Iliad* and *Odyssey* tell one grand story about how *dikê* operates throughout all stages of human relations, from the interpersonal to the international. The story is told with the kind of authorial distance we come to expect of the epic poet, and there is no pretense, as there is in the *Works and Days*, of offering practical 'advice' to an audience construed in the second person. But while a didactic thread may be less easily traced through Homer than it can in the *Works and Days*, the fundamental ethical issues that inspired the tale of Troy and the *nostoi* ('homecomings') are not far removed from Hesiod's. In fact, the mythical cause of the Trojan War itself—the abduction of Helen by the foreigner Paris—was a violation of *dikê* at an interpersonal level of the sort that interested Hesiod most. Indeed, throughout the *Iliad* and the *Odyssey* the delicate issues of social and material equity, a concern for the proper balance of giving and receiving, for *timê* ('honor') and *philia* ('friendship'), are continually dramatized in some of the most pivotal scenes of both poems: we may recall the quarrel between Agamemnon and Achilles over Briseis (the event that occasions the very plot of the *Iliad*), the failed embassy to Achilles' tent, the behavior of the suitors toward Telemachus at Ithaca, or the complex social dynamics at work in Odysseus' behavior with the Cyclopes, to name just a few.

The dispute between Hesiod and his brother Perses over an inheritance of land, which ultimately motivates the composition of the *Works and Days* (or so Hesiod claims), can be situated in the same general realm of moral discourse as the Homeric examples, even if the players are now supposed to be 'contemporary' rather than heroic.[56] Perses' violation of *dikê* prompts Hesiod to offer him a prolonged sermon on the dangers of unjust behavior and the need for self-sufficiency through hard work in an agricultural economy. Hesiod's moralizing, simply put, seeks to promote a world in which humans coexist peacefully, resolve their disputes though law, and regard violence as itself a violation of *dikê*. Homer's narrative, by contrast, offers a considerably more complex response to wrongful behavior than Hesiod's in its focus on heroic figures, who have acquired their exalted status primarily through military expertise and the desire for *kleos*.[57] This is a simplistic evaluation, of course, which hardly does justice to the subtle treatment of the many individual Homeric heroes, but taken together these heroes do represent a contrast to the system of values envisioned by Hesiod. Happy landowners living at peace with each other, constructing their lives in accordance with the rhythms of nature certainly did not form the focus of heroic epic. Homer and Hesiod, in short, confront the same moral, social and even psychological dilemmas shared by all human beings, but their solutions seem widely divergent, and often in direct conflict.

Hesiod himself seems to call attention to such a conflict in the famous 'Myth of the Ages' at *Works and Days* 106–274, and I would like to conclude with a discussion of this passage because it exemplifies so well the intertextual possibilities within Archaic epic. In this parable, directed explicitly at Perses, Hesiod traces the history of humankind as a sad decline from a state of paradise through periods of moral degeneration and misery. Hesiod uses the metaphor of metals to characterize the successive ages, from an age of gold, to silver, bronze and iron, each metal representing a successive stage of decline. Between the bronze and iron ages, however, Hesiod locates a fourth, and calls it a 'divine race of heroes' (159). This age is actually

[56] On the figure of Perses as he is portrayed in *Works and Days*, and the question of whether or not he is a fictitious character, see West (1978) 33–40, who himself opts for a middle ground, namely that Perses was a real figure, but that Hesiod invented various details about him to suit his own purposes. Nagy (1979) 312–13 has pointed out that the *neikos* ('quarrel') between Hesiod and Perses which occasions the poem functions analogously to the *neikos* between Achilles and Agamemnon at the opening of the *Iliad*. Both poems, that is, begin with a dispute, and both portray explicitly the working out of *eris*.

[57] On *heros* see West (1978) 370–73; Nagy (1979) 115–17; Ford (1992) 139–40. The term came to refer to great figures of the past who had acquired cult status after death, though its precise connotation in Homer is not entirely clear, especially since, as West notes, Homer applies the word to living men.

a brief improvement over the preceding one (δικαιότερον καὶ ἄρειον, ['more just and superior'], 158), and Hesiod notes its close relationship with his own (iron) age (προτέρη γενεὴ κατ' ἀπείρονα γαῖαν, ['the race before us on the limitless earth'], 160).[58] Scholars have long been puzzled by this obvious interruption of an otherwise coherent progression, but one clue to its significance certainly seems to be the fact that Hesiod has in mind specifically literary heroes, the heroes who populate traditional epic poetry:[59]

> καὶ τοὺς μὲν πόλεμός τε κακὸς καὶ φύλοπις αἰνή
> τοὺς μὲν ὑφ' ἑπταπύλῳ Θήβῃ, Καδμηίδι γαίῃ,
> ὤλεσε μαρναμένους μήλων ἕνεκ' Οἰδιπόδαο,
> τοὺς δὲ καὶ ἐν νήεσσιν ὑπὲρ μέγα λαῖτμα θαλάσσης
> ἐς Τροίην ἀγαγὼν Ἑλένης ἕνεκ' ἠυκόμοιο.
>
> *Works and Days* 161–65

[And as for them, ugly war and fearful fighting destroyed them, some below seven-gated Thebes, the Cadmean country, as they battled for Oedipus' flocks, and others it led in ships over the great abyss of the sea to Troy on account of lovely-haired Helen.]

(trans. West)

This passage contains the one sentence describing the activity of the heroes on earth, and it is striking that its grammatical (and thematic) subject is 'evil war' (πόλεμος κακός) and the 'horrible cry of battle' (φύλοπις αἰνή). The heroes of Thebes and Troy are defined solely in terms of their military exploits, and their fate as humans hardly sounds enviable: they fight over issues which, in their brief mention, appear to be trivial ('the flocks of Oedipus,' 'fair-haired Helen')[60] in comparison to the genocide that they effect, and in the end the heroes can claim no *kleos* other than their death in battle.[61] Most of these

---

[58] Translating with West ad loc., 'the race before ours.'

[59] See West (1978) 174. Scholars have long noted that the diction of the passage is especially Homeric. See von Wilamowitz-Moellendorff (1928) on 161; Krafft (1963) 119.

[60] See Verdenius (1985) 101. The diction of these phrases is of course synechdochal, as R. Renehan, 'Progress in Hesiod' [Review of West, *Works and Days*], *Classical Philology* 75 (1980) 347, has noted, but the specific causes of these two great wars noted here are especially resonant in the context of the *Works and Days*. The 'flocks of Oedipus' refers to a dispute over land and inheritance, the very cause of the quarrel between Hesiod and Perses. As for Helen as the cause of the Trojan War, not only is she too treated here as an object of disputed property, but her appearance here occurs in a passage that immediately follows the story of another seductive and lethal woman, Pandora.

[61] West's dry description of the passage ([1978] 191) is revealing: 'Hesiod has

heroes receive a merely generic sort of death (. . . τοὺς μὲν θανάτου τέλος ἀμφεκάλυψεν, [the finality of death covered over some of them] 166), although a few of the élite are granted a semi-divine existence on the 'Islands of the Blessed' (171).[62] Hesiod calls these select heroes 'happy' (ὄλβιοι ἥρωες, 172), although this is a happiness that comes only at the expense of any sort of humanity: Zeus provides them with a livelihood and habitat 'apart from mankind,' and settles them at the 'ends of the earth' (τοῖς δὲ δίχ' ἀνθρώπων βίοτον καὶ ἤθε' ὀπάσσας Ζεὺς Κρονίδης κατένασσε πατὴρ ἐν πείρασι γαίης . . ., 167–8). Indeed, the entire passage is suffused with ambivalence about the race of heroes, and one wonders whether this ambivalence also reflects Hesiod's attitude towards the kind of poetry that celebrated such heroism. Hesiod may indeed believe that the familiar heroes of traditional epic were 'more just and superior' (158),[63] that their exploits were worthy of admiration in some sense, but his bleak description of their lot also seems to imply that in the end they can tell us little about living productively and morally in the world.

This reading of the Myth of the Ages suggests an ongoing engagement with the Homeric tradition, and as such may even be one of our earliest examples of literary criticism. The didactic stance of the *Works and Days* certainly comes into sharpest focus when viewed in relation to the values that pervade heroic epic, and when we understand that Hesiod was exploring the dynamics of the great epic themes—*eris, dikê*, the desire for *kleos*, among others—in a non-heroic setting which would include his own audience as well as future generations of people living in the real world. This tension in the *Works and Days* between a heroic past and the realities of life ultimately reflects a quite different conception of humankind than that of Homeric epic. While Homer is full of stories that celebrate the attempts of heroic figures to transcend their limitations as humans, Hesiod emphasizes that *dike* can really only be achieved when humans behave in accordance with a natural order configured for them by Zeus.[64]

---

nothing special to tell us of these people's way of life, and passes straight on to the manner of their death. It is exactly the same as that of the Bronze race: they killed each other off. But he puts it in a more favorable light.'

[62] See Verdenius (1985) 101 on the 'Islands of the Blessed.'

[63] See Lamberton's discussion of this issue, (1988) 119.

[64] As Hesiod himself reminds us in one of the most symbolic myths of the *Works and Days*, Prometheus and Pandora (47–105), this 'natural order' which governs human

Although, as we have seen, the connections between Homer and Hesiod in terms of dialect, meter, diction and compositional technique, have by now been well established, much work remains to be done on how Homer and Hesiod situated themselves within the larger tradition of Greek epos, and how their individual poetic voices were shaped by it. Our consideration of such questions here offers only a few of the possibilities that a comparative literary analysis of the two poets can yield, yet it reveals clearly that the interaction between them operated at a much deeper level than that of form and technique. All audiences of Homer and Hesiod have been struck by the differences between them in terms of subject matter and even moral vision, but careful attention to their respective poetics has begun to suggest that each was profoundly self-conscious about his place within a highly diverse poetic tradition, and that each could most fully articulate his individual poetic identity, to himself as well as his audiences, by constructing it in relation to the many alternatives available within this tradition.

existence came about when Prometheus angered Zeus at Mekone by trying to deceive him with an inferior apportionment of meat. In response to Prometheus's behavior, Zeus hid fire and so began the separate lives of humans and gods, and the need for humans to work.

Jenny Strauss Clay

THE HOMERIC HYMNS

ἀνοῖξαι πίθον ὕμνων

The Homeric Hymns consist of a heterogeneous collection of 33 hexameter poems, composed in the epic *Kunstsprache*, and dedicated to divinities. They range from 3 to 580 lines in length and come from the 8th to the 2nd century B.C. and later.[1] The context of their manuscript transmission is indicative of their uncertain status: a few MSS include them with the Homeric poems, while the majority transcribe them with a variety of poetry from the Hellenistic and even later periods.[2] The *Hymn to Demeter* is preserved in only one manuscript, where it follows the final lines of what must have been a fairly extensive *Hymn to Dionysus*.[3] The relatively small number of extant manuscripts and ancient quotations, the lack of scholia, and sparse papyrus fragments point to the general neglect of these poems in antiquity. While some ancient authors attribute the Hymns to Homer, the scholars of Alexandria must have disassociated the corpus from the poet, a fact which led to their subsequent obscurity.

Very little is known for certain about their dates, provenance, or circumstances of composition and performance, which were doubtless as diverse as the poems themselves. One thing, however, is fairly clear: while sharing many features with prayers and cult hymns, our Hymns show little connection with ritual practice.[4]

---

[1] The major modern editions are Allen (1912) vol. 5; Allen, Halliday, and Sikes (1936); Humbert (1936); and Càssola (1975). The *Hymn to Ares* (8) is generally recognized to be later than the rest. See M. L. West (1970); Gelzer (1987) 150–167, attributes *Ares* as well as *H. 31* and *32* (to the Sun and Moon) to Plotinus' circle.

[2] For a description of the manuscripts, see Allen, Halliday, and Sikes (1936) xi–lviii.

[3] Nine other lines from near the beginning of the Dionysus Hymn are preserved in Diodorus 3.66.3.

[4] See Norden (1923); Keyssner (1932); Meyer (1933); and Fröhder (1994) 17–60. Outside the opening and closing formulas, the 'Du-Stil' is relatively rare in our Hymns: *Dionysus* 1–7; *Apollo* 19–29, 127–129, 149–150, 179–181, 207–230, 242–246; cf. *H. 8, H. 21, H. 24, H. 29, H. 30.*

Linguistic Criteria for Dating

Because the Hymns offer little in the way of solid internal evidence for their dates or provenance, in the hope of discovering objective dating criteria, scholars have turned to linguistic evidence to determine the relation especially of the four major Hymns to Homer and the Hesiodic corpus. O. Zumbach focused on what he considered innovative, i.e. post-Homeric, features.[5] On the basis of the neglect or observance of digamma, Allen, Halliday, and Sikes concluded that *Apollo* is the oldest, followed by *Aphrodite, Demeter*, and quite a bit later, *Hermes*.[6] In the wake of Parry's discoveries, and refuting Notopoulos' claim that linguistic phenomena could not be used for dating oral poetry, Hoekstra's study also included modifications of formulaic diction, but his results did not diverge much from earlier conclusions.[7] Finally, by systematically gathering a large number of linguistic features and attempting to correlate them statistically, R. Janko has undertaken the most extensive investigation to date to determine the relative chronology of not only the Hymns, but also of Homer and Hesiod.[8] Janko also deals with the issues of oral composition, false archaisms, epic imitation, and regional variations in the diction of the Hymns. On this basis, he sets out to refute the position of C. O. Pavese who argues that the Hymns and Hesiod belong to a school of Continental poetry distinct from the Ionian epic of Homer. According to Pavese, these traditions are parallel and synchronic rather than earlier and later; hence linguistic criteria cannot be used to trace their diachronic development.[9] Janko's arguments are too complicated to summarize here, but his conclusions situate *Aphrodite* in a somewhat divergent northern Aeolic tradition as the earliest of the major Hymns (675 B.C.), followed by Delian *Apollo* (660 B.C.) in a line closer to the Ionian tradition, with *Demeter* (640 B.C.) more closely related to the Hesiodic tradition, and finally, Pythian *Apollo* (585 B.C.), descended from the line of the Delian Hymn, but showing special affinities to the *Odyssey*.[10]

---

[5] Zumbach (1955).

[6] Allen, Halliday, and Sikes (1936) xcvi–cix.

[7] Notopoulos (1962) 337–68; Hoekstra (1969). Hoekstra did not include *Hermes* in his study.

[8] Janko (1982). Like many others, Janko divides *Apollo* into two poems. Cf. the review by A. Hoekstra, *Mnemosyne* 39 (1986) 158–64, who questions some aspects of Janko's methodology.

[9] Pavese (1974); and (1972) 111–165.

[10] See Janko's stemma on p. 200.

Oral Composition

Issues of language and diction are inevitably linked to the question of traditional poetry, oral composition, and the use of writing. If no universal consensus on these questions exists for the Homeric epics, its absence in discussions of the Hymns will not surprise. As with Homer, the main approaches have been quantitative: having ascertained a statistical measurement of formulaic density in the *Iliad* and the *Odyssey*, one then compares it to figures reached by the same criteria from, for the most part, the longer Hymns.[11] Immediate problems arise first from the relative brevity of the Hymns and, more generally, from the lack of unanimity as to what constitutes a formula.[12] Even setting such issues aside, the question remains how to interpret the statistical evidence and how to account for divergent results.

For the first generation of Parryists, with their rather straightforward lines of demarcation between orally-composed works and written poems, a lesser degree of formulaic density clearly indicated texts no longer improvised in performance, but composed with the aid of writing. But with the recent blurring of these lines, in part through comparative studies of a wide range of oral traditions, and with the discovery that orality and literacy can coalesce, as can premeditation and improvisation, the issues have become more clouded and complex.[13] While a general consensus still considers the Hymns post-Homeric and representative of a 'sub-epic' stage of composition, new interpretations of divergences from Homeric practice, now agreed not to be monolithic, have raised questions concerning the prevailing diachronic view. Pavese and his followers, for example, insist that, while both the Hymns and the Hesiodic poems are fully oral compositions, their linguistic and dictional divergences from Homer point not to post-Homeric origin, but to a parallel mainland tradition of epic song, which includes Hesiod.

In addition to the supposedly objective quantitative criteria for determining degrees of orality, qualitative judgments involving fluency and facility in using traditional formulaic techniques are often invoked to separate the 'genuine' oral style of Homer from a derivative

[11] Cantilena (1982) offers a formulaic analysis of all the Hymns and attempts to calculate their formulaic density. Cf. R. Janko's review, *Phoenix* 37 (1983) 271–73. See also Postlethwaite (1979) 1–8.

[12] Cf. J. Russo in this volume.

[13] See, for example, A. B. Lord's recent discussion of the 'transitional text' (1995) 212–237.

and self-conscious use of that style. Such judgments are notoriously subjective, and it is instructive to compare G. S. Kirk's analysis of the *Hymn to Apollo* with C. Segal's similar analysis of the Demeter Hymn.[14] Kirk finds the Delian section, although containing 'post-Homeric exaggeration' and 'odd and non-oral kind of repetition,' 'purer' than the Pythian, which frequently demonstrates a 'typical sub-epic lack of accuracy and taste.'[15] Without disputing Kirk's judgments of individual passages, one can nevertheless clearly discern his presuppositions. In his discussion of *Demeter*, Segal views some of the same features noted by Kirk—lack of formulaic economy, elaboration of epithets, and self-conscious use of repetition—in a far more positive light. He also emphasizes that shorter narrative poems like the Hymns may exploit repetition of phrases and themes for subtle and sophisticated ends and hence achieve a denser texture, but not necessarily a more literate style.[16] In the same volume, B. Hainsworth sensibly cautions against the equation, Homer = oral, non-Homeric = imitative and/or literate.[17] A good first step might be to ban the term 'sub-epic,' with its inevitable overtones of inferiority and decadence, from discussion of the Hymns. Secondly, even without accepting Pavese's arguments for a continental school of poetry, one may postulate that the Hymns form a separate genre within hexameter *epos*, a genre with its own prehistory and evolution, utilizing traditional diction and techniques which may parallel and sometimes overlap with, but also diverge from, those of heroic epic.[18] If the tales of Troy were already traditional for Homer and his audience, how many times and in how many ways must the story of Persephone's abduction or Apollo's slaughter of the Pythian dragon have been told? Moreover, the familiarity of the material and its smaller scale may have invited experimentation and innovation in both diction and narrative technique.

[14] Kirk (1981) 163–82; and Segal (1981) 107–162 in the same volume.

[15] Kirk (1981) 166–67, 177.

[16] For repetition as a stylistic device, see also Porter (1949) 249–72; and Pellizer (1978) 115–44.

[17] Hainsworth (1981) 3–27.

[18] For some common stylistic features, see van Groningen (1958); and Thalmann (1984).

Opening and Closing Formulas[19]

The opening and closing formulas are among the most characteristic features of the Hymns. In addition to invocations to the Muse or Muses (known also from epic proems) to sing of a divinity (9x), and an invocation of the god to be celebrated (3x), the most common opening formula (20x) announces in the first person present or future 'I sing' or 'I begin to sing' a divinity. The *Hymn to Apollo* and the shorter *Hymn to Dionysus* (7) offer variant formulas μνήσομαι οὐδὲ λάθομαι and ἀμφὶ Διώνυσον . . . μνήσομαι.[20] The announcement 'I will remember' or 'call to mind' is thus the equivalent of 'I will sing.' Both imply that the act of singing will reveal and make present the divinity. The suggestion is that, at least in the longer Hymns, the subsequent narrative, though it recounts events from the distant mythic past, will make the gods present to the audience, will bring about their epiphany through an account of their deeds.

The closings of Hymns are likewise highly formulaic. All (except *H. 12*) have a farewell (χαῖρε) to the divinity, often followed by a brief prayer for favor (2x), general prosperity (9x), or pleasing song (3x), and, in one case, a request for victory 'in this contest' (*H. 6*); in another, the request 'to return here joyfully next year and for many years to come' (*H. 26*) suggests an annual festival; both appear to allude to the setting of the Hymns' performance. Frequently, a promise concludes: 'having begun from you, I shall go on to another *hymnos*,' μεταβήσομαι ἄλλον ἐς ὕμνον (3x). Finally, in the two late Hymns to the Sun (31) and Moon (32), the following song is explicitly described as heroic epic.

The most common closing—'I will remember you and another song' (12x)—is usually interpreted as equivalent to the μεταβήσομαι formula, that is, as a transition to another song. But it seems just as possible to take the phrase to indicate the promise of a future hymn to the self-same divinity; the present hymn may be completed, but the task of praise is merely interrupted and will be taken up either immediately or on some future occasion.[21]

---

[19] For a typology of the Hymns, see Janko (1981) 9–24; and Pavese (1993) 155–178.

[20] The ἀμφί formula seems to derive from the kitharodic *prooimion* and occurs in *H. 7, 19, 22,* and *33*. On μιμνήσκομαι, see Moran (1975) 195–211.

[21] Cf. N. J. Richardson (1974) on line 495, for various explanations of this obscure formula; also Rudhardt (1991) 20, n. 72; and De Martino (1980) 232–40.

Middle Sections

The middle sections of the Hymns are far less formulaic than their beginnings and endings. Introduced by a relative pronoun and sometimes one or more epithets, they may either describe the divinity in the present tense through an account of his typical haunts, pursuits, gifts to mankind, and characteristic activities, or recount a myth about him, often a birth story and an account of his first arrival on Olympus, which may be quite short or go on for hundreds of lines. The mythic and the descriptive modes both serve to reveal the deity's essential and eternal nature, whether in his characteristic habitual actions or through his unique history. The 45-line *Hymn to Pan* combines the two modes by first depicting his typical activities, scampering among the mountain nymphs, who then sing a hymn recounting his birth, his introduction to Olympus, and the amused amazement of the gods at his peculiar appearance.[22] *Hymn 33 to the Dioscuri* inverts the pattern by briefly recounting their birth, then their characteristic activity of rescuing sailors at sea, and ending with a brief narration in the aorist of such a rescue.

The verb forms used here and scattered throughout the Hymns resemble the Indo-European injunctive, which characterizes the timeless activities of the gods.[23] To recount a unique event in a god's history means simultaneously to represent him as he always is. The *Hymn to Dionysus* (7), whose 59 lines place it between the long and short Hymns, clearly exemplifies this feature of hymnic narrative: the story of the unrecognized god, whom Tyrrhenian sailors abduct and try to bind, and who reveals his divinity, punishing the impious and rewarding those who acknowledge him, constitutes both a singular event in the god's story and, at the same time, an eternal manifestation of his divinity.

Prooimion

The manuscripts entitle our collection 'Hymns of Homer,' but no modern scholar would ascribe it to the author of the Homeric epics.

---

[22] Cf. *H. 27 to Artemis*. For the middle-length Hymns, see Fröhder (1994).

[23] The injunctive looks like the unaugmented Greek aorist, but is a relic of the Indo-European verb system and could be employed for present, past, or future,

Other collections of hymns to the gods circulated under the names of Olen, Pamphos, and Orpheus, and there were doubtless many such poems that have not survived. But the term ὕμνος was not originally restricted to compositions dedicated to divinities, but simply meant 'song.'[24] Pindar and Thucydides call our Hymns προοίμια; Pindar (*Nemean* 2.3) describes the usual practice of the Homeridae to begin from a *prooimion* to Zeus, while Thucydides (Thucydides 3.104) calls *Apollo* a *prooimion* to Apollo.[25] Relying on these testimonia and the closing formulas that indicate a transition to another ὕμνος, epic recitation, or a request for victory, Wolf argued in 1975 that the Hymns were preludes to the recitation of Homer at formal contests and festivals,[26] and his view still forms the scholarly consensus. But Wolf may have been wrong to posit a single origin for all the Hymns. It is, for instance, striking that Pindar speaks of a Διὸς ἐκ προοιμίου, but our collection contains only the briefest of compositions in honor of Zeus (*H. 23*). Moreover, most of the Hymns which unambiguously refer to another song (ὕμνος) or epic recitation to follow are late.[27] Finally, *prooimion* is not so much a generic-descriptive as a functional term, later applied not only to all kinds of poetry, but even to prose, and signifies both a prelude or exordium or a separate introductory composition.[28] Even the etymology and the formation of the word is opaque: is it what comes before (πρό) the song (οἴμη) proper or is it the first οἴμη in what may be a series of songs?[29] The question is

---

depending on context. See M. L. West (1989) and Pelliccia (1985). Cf. the remarks of Gonda (1956) 39, on the *Rigveda*: 'In myth past and present coincide, or the events take place in timeless space. Moreover, the mythical occurrence is repeated and re-actualized by the ritual acts which belong to the present or are described as such.' In the case of the Hymns, re-actualization may be thought to occur through the act of 'remembering.'

[24] The sole occurrence in Homer is *Od.* 8.429. For a discussion of the term, see Harvey (1955) 165–168; and Calame (1974) 119–22. The restriction in meaning to songs dedicated to divinities is attested in Plato, but how much earlier it may have occurred is unclear, a question of some importance for assessing the μεταβήσομαι ἄλλον ἐς ὕμνον formula.

[25] Pindar, *Nemean* 2.3; Thucydides 3.104.

[26] Wolf (1985) 112–13.

[27] The exception is the long *Hymn to Aphrodite*, which concludes with the μεταβήσομαι ἄλλον ἐς ὕμνον closing and is followed by a short Hymn to the same divinity (*H. 6*). The formula was evidently taken literally: two manuscripts run the poems together.

[28] Cf. Cassolà (1975) xix; and Costantini and Lallot (1987) 13–27, for an attempt to describe the history of the term. Also Böhme (1937) 10–24, for the testimonia.

[29] For the etymology of οἴμη, see Chantraine (1968–80) *s.v.* Meyer (1933) 24–32, interprets πρό as 'hervor, heraus, an die Öffentlichkeit' and the noun as originally

important because the answer will define the Hymns either as an independent genre of poetry with its own pre-history or as a subgenre dependent on the diffusion of rhapsodic recitations within the context of formal poetic competitions.[30] To this question must be added the issue of the relation of the long to the short Hymns. Are the long Hymns expansions of what were originally brief preludes preceding the recitations of epics; or, on the contrary, are the short Hymns abbreviated versions, containing only the hymnic openings and closings, vessels, as it were, intended to be filled with extended narratives drawn from the lives of the gods?[31] Clearly a few of the short Hymns appear to be abbreviations of longer ones,[32] but their preservation in our collection would seem to indicate they had some practical utility.[33] Some have argued that the major Hymns are simply too long to serve as preludes to epic performances—a few brief lines of introduction would do;[34] others have suggested that the scale of the long Hymns would not be disproportionate as an introduction to the recitation of epics on the scale of our *Iliad* and *Odyssey*.[35] Even without taking account of the middle-length Hymns (those from 20–60 lines), the questions cannot be resolved, but undeniably scale is a generic marker.

Poems of varying length may have been used on different occasions at different periods, and the evidence from Homer points in both directions. In the *Odyssey*, the Phaeacian bard Demodocus sings of the Trojan horse, and his song is introduced by the words: 'roused, he began from the god, and showed forth his song' (8.499). This 'beginning from the god' closely resembles Pindar's statement describing the Homeridae who introduce their songs with an invocation to Zeus. One line of a proem, said to introduce an old edition

---

meaning 'das Herausgesagte.' One might also wonder whether the iota infix is adjectival or diminutive. And what should one make of Fr. 241 (L.P.) of Stesichorus: μέτειμι δὲ ἐπὶ ἕτερον προοίμιον?

[30] By rhapsodic, I mean only the mode of performance, that is, unaccompanied recitation of, mainly hexameter, verse in contrast to performance accompanied by the lyre. I take no position on the rhapsodes' possible use of memorization or writing. Cf. Ford (1988).

[31] See Lenz (1975) 278–86. Fröhder (1994) argues for the integrity of the middle-length Hymns.

[32] E.g., *H. 13*, cf. *Hymn to Demeter* 1–2; *H. 17*, cf. *H. 33; H. 18*, cf. *Hymn to Hermes* 1–9; *H. 25*, cf. *Theog.* 94–97.

[33] Cf. Lenz (1975) 284; Fröhder (1994) 14.

[34] E.g. Allen, Halliday, and Sikes (1936) xciv–xcv.

[35] E.g., N. J. Richardson (1974) 4.

of the *Iliad*, invokes Apollo and the Muses;[36] it has no particular thematic links to the epic which follows and could be reused for any occasion. The lengthier invocation to the Muses that introduces the *Theogony* (lines 1–104) contains many hymnic elements such as opening and closing formulas, but it is clearly specifically composed for the poem to which it is attached,[37] as is the hymnic proem to Achilles, which opens the newly discovered *Battle of Plataea* by Simonides.[38] The relatively brief but expandable *prooimion*, reusable as a generic prelude to any composition, may well have given rise to the proem in our sense, which, while preserving the opening and closing formulas as well as other features of the *prooimion*, was closely integrated with the rest of the poem to which it forms a hymnic introduction.

There is evidence for a second type: in Book 8 of the *Odyssey*, the bard has sung another song, the 'Lay of Ares and Aphrodite,' which, with its dialogue and somewhat ribald humor, closely resembles the elaborate narrative and tone of the longer Hymns. It may be significant that Demodocus' two performances take place in different contexts; whereas the heroic episodes from the Trojan War are sung as after-dinner entertainments in Alcinoos' palace, the other is performed at what is apparently a public festival in the *agora*, accompanied by athletic contests and dancing. To be sure, the Homeric performances depict a bardic tradition where the *aoidos* accompanies himself with the lyre, but they may well reflect the pre-history of our collection of Hymns and their double origin: the full length autonomous divine narrative and the brief invocational prelude. The shift from an aoidic to a rhapsodic mode of performance, that is from short after-dinner presentations of heroic episodes accompanied by the lyre, to public rhapsodic recitations of the monumental epics, may have occurred as early as the 8th century. Within that development, there may have been a parallel evolution of the two strands of hymnic poetry into the rhapsodic period, with the short prelude introducing heroic narratives coalescing alongside the independent large-scale narrative hymn. A fragment of Hesiod, in fact, suggests a competition involving hymns to Apollo.[39] When, however, both heroic epic and hymnic

[36] See Erbse (1969) 3.

[37] Cf. Friedländer (1966) 277–294 (= *Hermes* 49 (1914) 1–16); and Minton (1970) 357–77.

[38] Simonides, Frag. 10 and 11.20 (West[2]); but cf. Theognis 1–4, which could preface almost any elegaic poem.

[39] Frag. 357 (Merkelbach-West).

poetry were performed, the hymn, or even a series of hymns, would naturally precede, but not necessarily be subordinate to, the heroic narrative. Phemius in the *Odyssey* can sing the 'deeds of gods and men;' In *Apollo* the Muses first intone 'the immortal gifts of the gods' and then 'the sufferings of men,' and the Delian Maidens, the Muses' mortal counterparts, 'first hymn Apollo, and then in turn, having recalled (μνησάμεναι) Leto and Artemis, they sing a song of men and women of old' (158–160).[40]

The history and prehistory of the compositions that have come down to us as the Homeric Hymns may, then, not be monolithic, but complex and multiple with varied functions at different periods, adapted to changing situations and occasions of performance.[41] The short Hymns need not all be considered abbreviations of long ones, but may, as they appear in our collection, be preludes to other songs and never have formed a completely independent genre. The long narrative Hymns, on the other hand, may not constitute expansions of the short ones, or be dependent on epic, but may represent an autonomous genre of hexameter epos, developing alongside, and complementary to, heroic epic.

The Major Hymns

Viewed as derivative, the four major Hymns long languished in the shadow of Homer, and scholarship on the Hymns inevitably followed the trends of Homeric criticism. Thus, during the 19th and early 20th centuries, analysts and unitarians debated the integrity of the compositions, followed later by Parryists and their opponents who attempted to ascertain the oral or written character of these poems.

---

[40] The *Hymn to Apollo* and the proem to the *Theog.* can be understood as a hymn-complex (cf. Minton (1970) 376–77). Such stringing together of hymns might account for the joining of *Aphrodite 5* and *6* and Stesichorus' odd phrase (above n. 27).

[41] Koller's theory (1956, 159–206) of the origins of the hexameter *prooimion* from the kitharodic *prooimion*; followed now by G. Nagy (1990, 353–61) offers a different scheme of development. For him, a short solo song dedicated to a divinity and accompanied by the lyre introduced the kitharodic *nomos*, a choral song and dance. That kitharodic *proimion*, once detached from the following *nomos*, became the ancestor of our shorter Hymns. According to Koller, the long Hymns and indeed the epic itself developed through expansion of the narrative sections. Böhme (1937) argues that the long Hymns *are* kitharodic *nomoi*. But Quintilian 4.1 indicates that the *prooimion* was short (*pauca illa*).

Others focused on the Hymns as sources for the history of religion or on questions of date and provenance. Recently, however, there has been a revived interest in the Hymns as works of literary art and religious thought. New approaches include studies in the encomiastic rhetoric of the Hymns, structuralist analyses of the myths embedded in the poems, narratological studies, as well as applications of psychoanalytic and feminist theory. With their charm, humor, and pathos, the Hymns have finally begun to be restored to their proper τιμή in the history of Greek literature and thought.[42]

The four major Homeric Hymns all possess an extensive narrative middle section; with the epic they share not only formulaic diction but also narrative techniques such as dialogue and type scenes as well as plot types also found in many kinds of traditional storytelling.[43] But certain recurrent features seem to characterize the long Hymns as a genre. The celebration of the chosen divinity takes the form of a dramatic mythological narrative in which the god is the protagonist and which defines the divinity's essential function and character through his words and deeds. Despite their differences in style and subject matter, the long Hymns are also linked by a common mythological framework that gives these compositions a generic unity. Each Hymn recounts a critical moment in the mythological history of the Olympians; the actions and events that occurred then among the gods have permanent consequences for gods and men and inaugurate a new era in both the divine and human cosmos. Temporally, the framework can be more narrowly defined: the heroic epic reveals the fully perfected and stable Olympian pantheon in its interaction with the heroes; cosmogonic poetry, like Hesiod's *Theogony* recounts the origins of the primal gods, the emergence of the Olympians, and culminates in the accession of Zeus to the kingship of the gods. Generically, then, the narratives of Hymns fill the gap between theogonic poetry and heroic epic. Like the panhellenic epic and the great panhellenic shrines of Delphi, Delos, Eleusis and Olympia, the Olympian pantheon whose development the Hymns describes is a panhellenic construct, in which various divinities with their varied origins and local cults are organized into an ordered

[42] Cf. Parker (1991) 1: 'In any history of Greek mythological writing, the longer *Homeric Hymns* deserve a place of honor. They are the almost unique vehicle of a distinctive and important form of narrative about the divine world.'

[43] Cf. Sowa (1984).

panhellenic hierarchy, with each god possessing his characteristic prerogatives, functions, and modes of action under the aegis of Zeus. Consequently, the narratives demonstrate an avoidance of local cults and legends and reworkings of local myths in the interests of a panhellenic Olympian orientation.[44]

Typical components of hymnic narrative include conflict, aetiology, epiphany, and an Olympian scene.[45] The birth narratives of *Apollo, Hermes*, and, doubtless, the fragmentary *Hymn to Dionysus* constitute ideal subjects since the birth of a new god inevitably precipitates a crisis within the existing order, which is only resolved when he establishes his sphere of influence and is integrated into the Olympian hierarchy. *Demeter* and *Aphrodite* likewise proceed from a challenge to Zeus' order on the part of female deities, whose outcome leads to a new ordering of relations, not only among the gods, but also between gods and mortals.

As the supreme dispenser of τιμαί among the Olympians, Zeus plays a critical, if sometimes unobtrusive, role in the major Hymns. It is he who sanctions his childrens' privileges and legitimates them in *Apollo* and *Hermes*; he also can modify them by increasing or diminishing the prerogatives of the gods as he does in *Demeter* and *Aphrodite*. But Zeus reigns as father not only of gods, but also of men. While the Hymns offer a divine perspective with the gods as the major players, nevertheless, human beings are inevitably involved in these divine dramas. Their roles, in fact, often provide much of the humor and charm in these poems, whether it be Anchises cowering under the bed-clothes as Aphrodite reveals herself, or the naively ignorant daughters of Celeus who welcome the disguised Demeter, or the terrified Cretans who find their ship guided by a giant dolphin. But, on a more serious level, the divine conflicts and their resolutions serve to define the human condition: both *Apollo* and *Hermes* entail improvements in the primitive state of mankind by instituting closer communication between gods and men through Apollo's oracle and Hermes' mediating and civilizing functions. *Aphrodite* insists on

[44] Incidentally, this feature forms an argument against the proem theory, since the Hymns do not, as Aloni (1992) esp. 107–10, has most recently argued, demonstrate an interest in the specific local occasion of performance, but insist, on the contrary, on a panhellenic scenario. The apparent exception, the description of the festival on Delos in the *Hymn to Apollo*, cannot simply be self-referential, since the performance there described is choral/mimetic rather than rhapsodic.

[45] Cf. Lenz (1975) 9–21.

the gulf separating gods and men and our distance from an earlier era of greater intimacy, while *Demeter* likewise demonstrates the impossibility of immortality for mankind, but holds out some hope against the absoluteness of death.

Apollo

Since Ruhnken (1782), the central issue in discussions of *Apollo* has been its unity and the relation of the Delian section to the Pythian.[46] It was long held that the two were separate poems, stitched together by a transitional section, or that the Pythian part was added to an older Delian poem.[47] The separatists drew support from an erroneous interpretation of Thucydides 3.104.3, who ascribes the poem to Homer, the blind man of Chios. A scholium to Pindar's *Nemean 2* apparently attributes the Hymn to Cynaethus, who is said to have tried to pass it off as a composition of Homer's and to have introduced the poems of Homer into Syracuse in the 69th Olympiad (504/501), a date many regard as corrupt and too late, although some scholars defend both it and the authorship of Cynaethus.[48] While the Delian section is simply regarded as very old (7th or 8th century), an argument supported by the reference to its being inscribed on a *leukoma* in the temple of Artemis at Delos,[49] presumed historical references in the Pythian portion to the First Sacred War and the destruction of Crisa, its silence concerning the chariot races at Delphi (instituted in 586 B.C.) and the Alcmeonid temple, suggested a *terminus ante quem* of 585 B.C. However, every one of these claims has been controverted.[50] Recently, Burkert has revived the authorship of Cynaethus and argued that the occasion for uniting the two parts of the poem was the great festival of Apollo on Delos put on by Polycrates of Samos in 522 for his political aggrandizement.[51]

While the authorship and circumstances of the Hymn's composition and performance remain obscure, its overall unity has now

[46] For a survey of the scholarly literature, see Förstel (1979), esp. 20–62.

[47] But M. L. West (1975) 130–45, maintains the priority of the Pythian half.

[48] Cf. Förstel (1979) 92–101; Wade-Gery (1936) 56–78.

[49] Cf. Förstel (1979) 71–81.

[50] See Clay (1989) 87–89.

[51] Burkert (1979) 53–62. Cf. Janko (1982) 112–15. Aloni (1989) argues for a second Athenian version produced by the Peisistratids.

become more widely accepted on structural, rhetorical, and thematic grounds. The stylistic and narrative parallels between the first and second half, such as the geographical catalogues, the Olympian scenes, and the alternations of fear and joy provoked by the god's epiphanies, can now be viewed not as imitations, but as unifying devices. The transition between the two narratives of Apollo's birth and his founding of the Delphic oracle, once regarded as a clumsy attempt to join disparate poems, is now regarded as a skillful and self-conscious manipulation of hymnic conventions, bridging the two narratives.[52] *Apollo* may in fact offer an example of the linking of a series of hymns, implied by the conventional closing formulas, which finds a parallel in the *Theogony* where Hesiod first invokes the Heliconian Muses and moves on to the Olympian ones.[53] There is little justification for separating these two as for separating Delian and Pythian Apollo.[54] They are one and the same, and by celebrating both simultaneously, the poet emphasizes Apollo's panhellenic character.

In the course of the narrative, Apollo founds his two most important panhellenic sanctuaries, both of which depend on the god for their wealth and prosperity. The geographic catalogues throughout the Hymn likewise emphasize the god's universal character. Moreover, Apollo acquires many of his various epithets (*Pythios, Telphusios*, and *Delphinios*) and the three τιμαί he claimed at the moment of his birth: archery, the lyre, and prophecy. The account of the foundation of the Delphic oracle insists on the absence of a previous oracle on the site and thus emphasizes Apollo's innovation. The so-called digressions from the main narrative (the opening scene on Olympus and the 50 line account of the birth of Typhaon) take on their significance within the larger theogonic context. The mighty new god, whose birth was first universally feared as a threat to the Olympian order and in fact opposed by the insubordinate Hera in alliance with the chthonic pre-Olympian powers, becomes Zeus' greatest supporter by disseminating his father's unfailing will to mankind through his oracle, whose first pronouncement brings the Hymn to a close.

---

[52] See A. M. Miller (1985) 57–67; and (1979) 173–86.
[53] See above, n. 38.
[54] Cf. Pindar *Paean* 2.96 ff. (Snell-Maehler); and Clay (1989) 93–94.

Demeter

Demeter's combination of charm and solemnity, its familiar and moving narrative of mother and daughter, which links the cosmic phenomena of the seasons with the divine drama of loss and renewal, has long made it a favorite among the Hymns.[55] Culminating in the foundation of the Mysteries at Eleusis, the poem, with its overt aetiological passages, has had special interest for historians of Greek religion, who have discovered in the narrative a counterpart to the initiatory rituals carried out in the sanctuary. Yet the Hymn clearly does not violate the prohibition, enunciated at its end, against revelation of the secret rites. Its date and occasion remain obscure, although the Hymn's silence concerning Athens has suggested a date before the Athenian takeover of the Mysteries, and many scholars have assigned its performance to a local Eleusinian festival.[56] Recently, however, doubts have been raised concerning the author's knowledge of Eleusinian geography and ritual, as well as Eleusis' early independence from Athens.[57] At any rate, the Hymn cannot be read as the script for the sacred *dromena* at Eleusis, nor does it present purely local traditions, or those current in 6th century Athens but possibly far older in origin, but rather a unique synthesis designed to reinforce its panhellenic message.

Of late, *Demeter* has also attracted attention as a psychological drama embodying archetypal patterns of female experience, first by Jung and Kerenyi, and more recently, by feminist scholars.[58] The sympathetic focus on women's lives, not altogether common in Greek myth, the moving portrayal of the emotional bonds between mother and daughter, the anger and grief of the mighty goddess with its cosmic consequences, the vulnerability of her daughter, violently tricked into marriage, and the joy of the (conditional) reunion of mother and daughter have offered fertile ground for feminist interpretations. Yet despite the humanity of the story, one must not forget that the main actors are gods and that the abduction, which sets off the cosmic crisis of the Hymn, is no ordinary marriage.[59] On the other hand,

[55] See the excellent commentary of N. J. Richardson (1974), and the volume of H. P. Foley (1994), which includes a selection of the secondary literature.

[56] Cf. Richardson (1974) 5–12.

[57] For the issues involved, see Foley (1994) 169–75.

[58] See the good selection of essays in Foley (1994).

[59] Cf. Rudhardt (1978) 1–17.

Demeter's almost human suffering of loss, her encounter with human frailty and mortality, and the recognition of the interdependence of gods and men motivates the foundation of the Mysteries that promise a better fate to mortals after death.

A comparison with the many versions of the story of the rape and return of Persephone throws into relief some of the peculiarities of the Hymn's narrative,[60] which earlier critics explained through interpolation or the conflation of different accounts. Although the unity of the Hymn is no longer questioned, narrative problems persist. The Hymn culminates in the foundation of the Mysteries, not the gift of agriculture as some variants have it, where it is usually the reward to the local inhabitants for helping the goddess in her search for her daughter. Since Demeter learns of Persephone's abduction early on from Helios, the goddess' journey to Eleusis and her attempt to immortalize Demophoon appear unmotivated. Moreover, her stay in Eleusis brings her no closer to her goal. The famine, which in other versions, accompanies her search, is here delayed until after the events at the Eleusinian palace, and the final compromise arrived at for the division of Persephone's time above and below the earth is unique to the Hymn.

The divine conflict in the Hymn involves all parts of the cosmos—Olympus, the earth, and the underworld—and reveals their interdependence; the divine conflict and its resolution frames the events at Eleusis. The singular narrative structure of the Hymn transforms an old agrarian myth into an Olympian drama, in which Zeus' plan to give his daughter to the Lord of the Dead first meets with Demeter's resistance, but finally allows Mother and Daughter to forge a link between the world below and that above, and, through their Mysteries, to mitigate human mortality.

Aphrodite

Often called the most Homeric of the Hymns, *Aphrodite* most closely resembles the epics in its style, diction, and subject matter. This resemblance provoked numerous discussions concerning the Hymn's relation to the *Iliad*.[61] Enhanced understanding of the workings of

---

[60] See N. J. Richardson (1974) 74–86; H. P. Foley (1994) 97–103.
[61] See Lenz (1975) 84–277.

traditional poetry has muted the debate about priority. Anomalously, the Hymn presents neither a birth story nor a cult foundation. The now discarded theory that the poem was composed in the Troad in honor of the noble clan of the Aeneiadai of Skepsis, who traced their lineage to the legendary hero, by a poet who also inserted the *aristeia* of Aeneias in Book 20 of the *Iliad*, seemed at least to provide a plausible occasion for the poem's composition, its Anatolian setting and perhaps its 'secular' tone.[62] Loosed from its presumed mooring, the Hymn has benefited from renewed attention to its narrative.

The story of the Love Goddess' seduction of a mortal has many parallels, especially in the Near East.[63] But the particular character of this much admired composition within the generic boundaries of the Hymns has often been overlooked. Both the Hymn's diction and the digressions on Ganymede, Tithonus, and the tree Nymphs insistently emphasize human mortality and the distinction between gods and men. Situated between theogonic poetry and heroic epic, both of which recount in their different contexts and for different purposes the outlines of the story,[64] the Hymn locates itself in the period preceding the Trojan War and on Mt. Ida, where soon the fatal Judgment of Paris will precipitate another seduction that unleashes the war that marks the end of the heroic age.[65] The account elaborated in the Hymn shapes its meaning from an element usually absent from other versions: the action of Zeus. No ordinary amour of god and mortal, nor even a tale of the biter bit, the incorporation of Zeus' plan to stop the Love Goddess from bringing about such unions transforms this delightful tale of seduction into a world-historical event that signals the end of the era when gods and mortals united to produce the demi-gods called heroes.[66] Aphrodite's abrupt departure for Olympus signals the end of an epoch when gods and mortals shared a now vanished intimacy. No longer an insubordinate daughter of Zeus, Aphrodite warns against overstepping the boundaries separating gods and men and rejoins the gods. The Hymn thus combines a celebration of Aphrodite and her universal powers of

---

62 See Smith (1981b) and van der Ben (1980) 40–77.

63 Cf. Sowa (1984) 39–94; Friedrich and Redfield (1978); and Boedeker (1974), who insists on Aphrodite's Indo-European origins.

64 *Il.* 2.819–21 and 20. 208–241; and *Theog.* 1008–10. Cf. Pellizer (1978) 137–43.

65 Cf. *Il.* 12.13–33; *Works and Days* 157–65; and Frag. 204 (Merkelbach/West).

66 Cf. Rudhardt (1991) 8–20; Clay (1989) 165–201; van der Ben (1981) 69–107.

seduction with a singular narrative whose outcome radically alters the configuration of the cosmos and all future relations between gods and mortals.

Hermes

A birth hymn like *Apollo, Hermes* has delighted readers with its humorous tale of the outrageous and inventive newborn, the eternal trickster, but also civiliser, who, from his humble beginnings, wrests his honors from his big brother Apollo by theft, lies and bargaining, and finally finagles his way to a place among the Olympians. Generally regarded as substantially later than the other major Hymns, *Hermes'* dictional peculiarities, narrative leaps, and textual problems, have made interpretation difficult. Moreover, the text gives no indication of its provenance, although it has been assigned an Athenian or Boeotian origin.[67] Once again, the Hymn shows a panhellenic orientation and an attempt to define the god through a narrative of his words and deeds, which is itself as complex and shifting as the polytropic divinity it celebrates.[68] While Apollo is born early in Zeus' reign, Hermes appears at a later stage when the various prerogatives of the gods have already been distributed. Moreover, because of the clandestine circumstances of his birth far from Olympus, he is not at first even certain of his divine status, as his attempt to eat the meat he has prepared reveals. Only after his return to the cave can he declare to his mother his intention of acquiring divine honors equivalent to those of Apollo, but his ambiguous status abides as he becomes the god closest to human beings.

As last born of the Olympians, the new god must acquire his privileges through his inventiveness and trickery and through theft and 'deeds of exchange,' which include all manner of speech and rhetoric, that the Hymn declare to be his sphere of influence. The lyre he invents, the cattle he steals, and his rhetoric, both deceptive and seductive, become the means and bargaining chips for his acquisition of his place within the Olympian family. In a comic version of

[67] See Janko (1982) 140–50, for discussion of date and provenance. For questions of style and 'orality,' see T. Van Nortwick, 'The Homeric *Hymn to Hermes*: A Study in Early Greek Hexameter Style,' Ph.D. Dissertation Stanford, 1975; and Herter (1981) 183–201.

[68] Note the unusual introductory string of seven epithets in lines 13–15.

the standard hymnic motif of a new god's first arrival on Olympus, Hermes contrives to smuggle himself into Zeus' presence, dragged into court as a thief and a liar by his illustrious brother. That Hermes acquires his τιμαί through a series of confrontations with Apollo derives from their respective modes of action: Apollo is the guardian of boundaries, limits and hierarchies, whereas Hermes traverses them.[69] The final reconciliation of the two brothers reveals their mutual interdependence. As transgressor of limits, Hermes simultaneously reaffirms them, becoming a friend to men, and mediator between gods, men, and the underworld.

[69] See Kahn (1978) and Vernant (1965) 124–84.

PART FOUR

HOMER'S WORLDS

John Bennet

HOMER AND THE BRONZE AGE

Framing the Question

What do we mean by 'Homer and the Bronze Age'? In what sense, if any, is an eighth-century oral poet related to a period of Greek history—as defined by modern scholars—that ended some four-hundred years before his own day? Superficially the very idea that there may be any relation seems highly implausible and, indeed, seemed so until the archaeological discoveries of Heinrich Schliemann late in the last century.[1] Once Schliemann had declared that he had found Priam's Troy and Agamemnon's Mycenae, however, the idea that Homer in some sense preserved knowledge of events that could be situated in a Bronze Age world came to exercise a powerful hold on the scholarly and popular imagination. Indeed, Schliemann's approach—although not his archaeological methodology—laid the foundations for the systematic study of the archaeology of prehistoric Greece.

In the wake of his discoveries, works such as Lorimer's *Homer and the Monuments* and chapters in Wace and Stubbings' *Companion to Homer* examined in great detail the relationship of the Homeric corpus to a 'real,' material world. Indeed a series of works under the general title *Archaeologia Homerica* has been underway since 1967 in order to present just this type of data. A particularly strong case was mounted for the historicity of the Iliadic 'Catalogue of Ships,' notably by Page and by Hope Simpson and Lazenby.[2] Lorimer's conclusions, however,

---

[1] Schliemann (1875); (1880); (1881); (1884); (1885). There is now a large bibliography on Schliemann's methods (e.g., Calder and Traill [1986]; Traill [1995]), and on the 'treasure' lost since the war but now rediscovered in the Pushkin Museum (D. F. Easton, 'Priam's Gold: The Full Story,' *Anatolian Studies* 44 [1994] 221–44; 'The Troy Treasures in Russia,' *Antiquity* 69 [1995] 11–14). On the 'Homeric question' in general, see Turner (this vol.).

[2] Lorimer (1950); Wace and Stubbings (1962); F. Matz and H.-G. Buchholz (general eds.), *Archaeologia Homerica: Die Denkmäler und das Frühgriechisches Epos* (Göttingen, 1967–). The Catalogue: Page (1959); Hope Simpson and Lazenby (1970); Giovannini (1969). A good idea of the hold exercised on the popular imagination is the BBC-

were not in favor of a substantially Bronze Age date for most of the picture presented by Homer:

> Our review of the material civilization depicted in the Homeric poems has led us to the conclusion that while features of Bronze Age culture are undoubtedly preserved in them, these are much less considerable than was at one time supposed. It was an inevitable result of Schliemann's excavations and their astounding success that the extent of the Bronze Age tradition was exaggerated... (Lorimer [1950] 452)

Although Lorimer had raised serious qualifications to the idea of an entirely Bronze Age Homeric world, Moses Finley in his *World of Odysseus*—first published in 1954, in the wake of the decipherment of Linear B—initiated a modern skeptical trend that sees the world of the epics as consistently post-Bronze Age. This trend has continued—with conclusions differing in detail—in publications by Snodgrass, Dickinson, I. Morris, Raaflaub, and others, all of whom see Homer's picture as entirely post-Bronze Age, although for Snodgrass it is not an internally consistent view.[3] As a result of this reassessment of the society reflected in the epics, Homer's poetry is now used as evidence for reconstructions of Greek social behavior in the eighth century, and—significantly—as comparative evidence for social transformations from the Bronze Age to the later, historical periods.[4]

It is not difficult to see why such a radical reassessment should have taken place. In the first place, our knowledge of the archaeology of the period between 1200 and 700 B.C.—loosely the 'Dark Age'—has improved immensely through the work of scholars such as Desborough, Coldstream, and Snodgrass. These developments have allowed the recreation not only of a social and material culture background to the Homeric epics, but also a rationale for the use of Homeric poetry as one of a number of strategies for creating a heroic past in the context of the emergent Greek poleis ('city-states'). Second, over a century of archaeological exploration in Greece and adjacent areas has improved our understanding of the material culture of the Bronze Age. One of the basic results of this research is

---

TV series 'In Search of the Trojan War,' subsequently published as a book: Wood (1985).

[3] Finley (1978); cf. Finley (1982) 199–212, originally published in 1957–58; Snodgrass (1974); Dickinson (1986); I. Morris and Raaflaub (this vol., with references to earlier work).

[4] E.g., Carlier (1984); J. R. Lenz (1993). Also important work by, e.g., Qviller (1981); Donlan (1989a; 1989c).

the realization that the societies of Late Bronze Age Greece were much more complex than the Homeric picture would have suggested. Third, our understanding of the nature of oral poetry has radically altered our perspective on the ways in which Homer's poetry was composed and its likely relationship to the society in which he lived. Apart from elucidating the techniques of composition and the feasibility of long, orally composed epic poems, studies of oral traditions have demonstrated that such traditions are in a process of constant reformulation in the context of contemporary societies. Finally, the decipherment of Linear B has transformed our understanding of the economic workings and—to a lesser extent—the social organization of the Late Bronze Age palatial societies. The decipherment has helped reinforce the picture developed through archaeological research of a more complex society, a society that knew literacy and employed it as a relatively sophisticated means of monitoring economic activity. The decipherment has also transformed the study of the history of the Greek language and its dialects, demonstrating that the Homeric language is not a direct descendant of the language used by the administrators of Mycenaean palaces.[5]

As a result of these developments, the substantial differences between the world of Homer's epics and that of the Late Bronze Age have become clear, while the similarities with the Iron Age have become more obvious. Indeed, the very implausibility of the idea that Homer could ever have embodied a 'real' picture of the Bronze Age has been thrown into sharper focus. Perhaps 450–500 years separate Homer's time (c. 800–700 B.C.) from that of the latest palatial phase of the Bronze Age palaces of Mycenae, Tiryns, Pylos, Athens and Thebes (c. 1200 B.C.), a minimum of twelve generations, perhaps as many as eighteen. Accurate memories of life in the Bronze Age would have to have been handed down intact throughout this period, without the aid of writing, and in a period—as most agree—of great social upheaval and movement.[6]

[5] See I. Morris (this vol.) on Iron Age archaeology and J. M. Foley (this vol.) on oral poetics. For archaeological advances, McDonald and Thomas (1990) is a useful introduction. For the decipherment and some of its implications, see Chadwick (1967; 1976a). On the position of Homeric *Kunstsprache*, see Janko (1982).

[6] Burkert (1995) considers the implausibility of later Greek attempts to date events around the Trojan War through genealogies, concluding (p. 145) that none went back as far as that time. For the period in general and the upheavals throughout the Mediterranean world, see Ward and Joukowsky, eds. (1992).

Leaving aside the chronological separation, there is the issue of geography: where would such a tradition have been preserved? Later accounts associate Homer with Ionia (specifically Smyrna or Chios), yet the major Bronze Age polities were primarily a feature of mainland Greece and Crete, although Mycenaean Greeks were almost certainly resident in coastal western Anatolia. Close parallels between the historical dialects of Arcadia and Cyprus and that preserved in the Linear B tablets of the Late Bronze Age suggest that Mycenaean speakers migrated to the interior uplands of the Peloponnese and to Cyprus, yet Homeric epic is not associated with these regions of the Greek world, either by content or by authorship.

The Homeric *Kunstsprache*—although not a dialect ever actually in common usage—seems to be primarily Ionic, yet most scholars agree that it embodies some features of Aeolic Greek. These data suggest two possible scenarios: that there was an 'Aeolic phase' in the development of the dialect (and the poetry it carried), or that there were parallel poetic traditions in Ionic- and Aeolic-speaking areas, the Aeolic tradition affecting the Ionic by a process of 'diffusion.' The first presupposes a tradition that surfaced in Ionia (perhaps western Ionia), but goes back to (or even originated from) a tradition in the northern mainland, unless one assumes that the tradition originated entirely in northwest Anatolia—the region of Troy?—in an Aeolic milieu, before being taken over by Ionic speakers to the south. The second scenario assumes parallel Aeolic and Ionic poetic traditions, and that Aeolic features were incorporated from the adjacent Aeolic region into the Ionic epic as part of the constant modification of the poetic language.[7] In either case, there is no direct linguistic connection with the actual dialect of Bronze Age Greek preserved in the Linear B tablets, although I shall have more to say on this question below.

Given these conclusions, why even devote space in a work summarizing late-twentieth-century Homeric scholarship to what might seem to be a non-question? One answer is that, like all aspects of Homer, there are new views on the topic resulting from the scholarly developments outlined above.

---

[7] For a summary of the two possibilities and arguments for the latter, see Horrocks (1987). In support of the the 'Aeolic phase,' based both on poetic language and content, see, e.g., M. L. West (1988).

Late Bronze Age Greece[8]

Perhaps the best way to initiate our discussion of this topic is to examine the picture that many scholars would now accept of the Late Bronze Age of mainland Greece, the Mycenaean period (Late Helladic I–IIIB: c. 1750–1200 B.C.).[9] In the first instance, most scholars would agree that the inhabitants of mainland Greece at this time spoke a language that was recognizably Greek. Although the phenomenon of the so-called 'coming of the Greeks' has become less of an obsession with archaeologists since the days of Caskey, the evidence of the Linear B tablets demonstrates the use of the Greek language on Crete as early as ca. 1400 B.C., presumably introduced from the mainland.[10] Whenever speakers of the language that was to develop into Greek actually entered the area, it seems that they were certainly present by the time of the emergence of distinctive Mycenaean cultural and social features at the transition from the archaeological phase called Middle Helladic to that of Late Helladic. The Mycenaean Greeks of the 'high' Mycenaean period (Late Helladic IIIB, roughly the thirteenth century B.C.)—some 300–400 years later—would presumably regard their Late Helladic I predecessors as their ancestors and the founders of the major polities of Late Helladic IIIB.

---

[8] For a recent review of current archaeological work in mainland Greece in the pre-palatial Bronze Age, see J. Rutter, *American Journal of Archaeology* 97 (1993) 745–97; for the palatial Late Bronze Age, see C. W. Shelmerdine, *American Journal of Archaeology* 101 (1997). The most recent book-length general treatment of the Bronze Age is Dickinson (1994).

[9] The mainland Bronze Age is referred to as Helladic, to distinguish it from those of Crete (Minoan) and the islands (Cycladic); the Late Helladic period is often referred to as the 'Mycenaean' period. Absolute dates for the period have recently come under intense scrutiny as a result of the proposed redating of the eruption of Thera c. 1628 B.C., summarized by Manning (1995) 200–216. Contrast: Warren and Hankey (1989) 137–44, and P. M. Warren, 'Summary of Evidence for the Absolute Chronology of the Early Part of the Aegean Late Bronze Age Derived from Historical Egyptian Sources,' in D. A. Hardy and C. Renfrew (eds.) *Thera and the Aegean World* III.3 (London, 1990) 24–26.

[10] J. L. Caskey, *CAH* I[3] 771–807, now thoroughly reexamined—with an emphasis on continuity rather than disjunction—by J. Forsén, *The Twilight of the Early Helladics. A Study of the Disturbances in East-Central and Southern Greece Towards the End of the Early Bronze Age* (Jonsered, 1992). For the implication that the earliest preserved archive at Knossos (that of the Room of the Chariot Tablets) belongs to ca. 1400 B.C., see Driessen (1990). The recent discovery near Olympia of a pebble incised with Linear B script, dating to the end of the Middle Helladic period (before ca. 1700 B.C.?), has called into question the antiquity of the Linear B script and the location of its adaptation from Minoan Linear A: Godart (1995).

That such a notion is plausible is strongly suggested by the way Grave Circle 'A' at Mycenae—the area of the Shaft Graves first uncovered by Schliemann, belonging to the beginnings of Mycenaean culture—was 'landscaped' in the Late Helladic IIIB period when the massive Cyclopean walls were built around the citadel. Not only were the Shaft Graves included within the circuit, but a circular peribolos wall was built around the area. We see a similar phenomenon in Messenia, where the tholos tomb (tholos IV) built by the Late Helladic I inhabitants of Bronze Age Pylos continues in use (presumably as a burial place for the ruling elite) into Late Helladic IIIB, although many tholos tombs associated with surrounding settlements have gone out of use. The fact that other early Mycenaean burials—those in Grave Circle 'B'—at Mycenae were not incorporated in the fortifications or 'landscaped' implies that such memories were not perfect—or were 'selective'—over a three- or four-century span.

The richness of early Mycenaean burials—particularly the Mycenae Shaft Graves, but also the early tholos tombs in Messenia and Laconia—struck archaeologists immediately from Schliemann's day on, prompting his famous remark—fictitious or not—that he had gazed on the face of Agamemnon. Recently, however, archaeologists have begun to see the richness of the burials, the strongly Minoan features in the grave goods, and the elaboration of the sepulchers themselves as characteristic features of emergent social complexity, as elites vied with each other for social control. A powerful weapon in such competition was the conspicuous display and disposal of wealth in tombs, together with the presentation of martial prowess in images of warfare and hunting. Exotic knowledge—reflected in the Minoan and Minoanizing objects that imply direct connections with the contemporary palatial civilization of Crete—also played a significant part. Knowledge of Minoan cult practice and the ideology of rulership formed an important element in this exotic knowledge. It seems that the Mycenaean ideal of kingship, represented in the person (and title?) of the *wanax*, was formed in this early Mycenaean environment. The development may have been perceived as explicitly foreign, if the term *g^w^asileus* (Linear B *qa-si-re-u*, later βασιλεύς) preserved in the Linear B tablets in fact does represent the title of a local-level authority figure inherited from pre-Mycenaean society.[11]

[11] For discussion of the early Mycenaean origins of the *wanax*, see Kilian (1988), and Carlier (1984) on the relationship between the terms βασιλεύς and ἄναξ. Two

Burials form a major part of the archaeological evidence for early Mycenaean society because the large palaces and citadels of the mature and late Mycenaean phases often obliterated the remains of the early Mycenaean settlements. We are not in a very good position to discuss how such structures might have looked,[12] but we can be certain that by the Late Helladic IIIA period, there were substantial structures similar in function, if not in form, to the palaces of Minoan Crete. That is, complex structures providing residences for the elite, storage space for staples, workshops for palace-sponsored crafts, and cult areas for rituals associated with the ruling elite. The latest phases of these centers in some cases demonstrate considerable architectural sophistication, most notably the massive defensive circuits of Mycenae and Tiryns in the Argolid. Mycenaean engineering abilities extended to the construction of roads, and major hydraulic works such as the draining of the Kopaïs basin to create additional farmland and the construction of a dam near Tiryns to divert a dangerous river.[13]

By this period, major Mycenaean centers existed throughout southern and east-central Greece, from Pylos in the southwest to Volos/Iolkos in the northeast—the core area of Mycenaean culture (Fig. 1, see p. 534). Each of these centers had come to dominate large territories, as large or even larger than those of even the largest poleis of the historical period. For example, by Late Helladic IIIA the palace-center at Bronze Age Pylos probably dominated much of the western coast of Messenia, west of the Aigaleon range and was probably already using Linear B in its administration. By Late Helladic IIIB, it had incorporated the Messenian valley to the east, making a total

---

more recent studies emphasize the use of Minoan features in the context of socio-political development in early Mycenaean Greece: Palaima (1995); Wright (1995). Palaima discusses the issue of the *g^w^asileus* at pp. 123–25. Wright's discussion owes much to the anthropological work of Helms (1988), much of which is coincidentally applicable to the emergence of centers like Lefkandi in the Iron Age. For the use of burial as a social and political strategy in the Argolid from Late Helladic I to Late Helladic IIIB see most recently Voutsaki (1995).

12 Discussion of possibilities in Kilian (1987); Barber (1992).

13 W. A. McDonald, 'Overland Communications in Greece During LH III, With Special Reference to Southwest Peloponnese,' in E. L. Bennett, Jr., ed., *Mycenaean Studies* (Madison, Wisconsin, 1964) 217–40 (roads in general). Kopaïs: J. Knauss, B. Heinrich, and H. Kalcyk, *Die Wasserbauten der Minyer in der Kopais: Die älteste Flussregulierung Europas* (Munich, 1984); J. Knauss, *Die Melioration des Kopaisbeckens durch die Minyer im 2 Jh. v. Chr.: Kopais 2—Wasserbau und Siedlungsbedingungen im Altertum* (Munich, 1987). Tiryns: E. Zangger, 'Landscape Changes around Tiryns during the Bronze Age,' *American Journal of Archaeology* 98 (1994) 189–212.

area controlled of ca. 2,000 km^2.[14] It is likely that the emergent economic and political structures of the early Mycenaean period had become institutionalized by Late Helladic IIIA–B and that we can legitimately refer to these polities as states.

However, by Late Helladic IIIA, Mycenaean power and influence were no longer confined to the mainland of Greece. The use of Linear B at Knossos on Crete certainly by 1400 B.C. to record the Greek language implies that Mycenaeans were in control there, probably as a result of conquest. A similar pattern is visible throughout the Aegean: predominantly Minoan sites among the islands and on the west Anatolian mainland (in particular Miletus) come to have a predominantly Mycenaean material culture, although Linear B documents have not yet been found there.[15] These features certainly reflect the supremacy—cultural and political?—of the mainland Greeks in the Aegean, and probably also indicate the existence of Mycenaean inhabitants. Further afield, there is good evidence that Mycenaean trade connections extended beyond the Aegean to the east (the Troad, Cyprus, Syro-Palestine), the south (Egypt), and the west (south Italy, Sicily, Sardinia), although surprisingly they do not seem to have penetrated inland Anatolia, the area controlled by the Hittites, leading at least one scholar to suggest a possible Hittite embargo on trade with the Mycenaeans.[16] Studies such as those of Cline and Gale have provided a convincing context in which materials and ideas could travel between the east and the Mycenaean world. It is even plausible to see the trade links—to both west and east—of the Iron Age not as newly established links, but as more intense use of links that had never been totally lost since the Bronze Age.

An important feature of overseas connections in the context of possible relationships between Homer's poetry and the Bronze Age cultures of Greece is the likelihood of Mycenaean involvement in coastal western Anatolia, particularly the area of Troy. We have some

---

[14] See Bennet (1995).

[15] For a recent review of the archaeology of the Aegean islands in the Bronze Age, see J. L. Davis, *American Journal of Archaeology* 96 (1992) 699–756.

[16] Trade connections: Cline (1994); Gale, ed. (1991). The discovery of a thirteenth-century B.C. wreck off the south coast of Turkey at Uluburun has provided a great deal of direct information about the content and nature of such trade: G. F. Bass et al., 'The Bronze Age Shipwreck at Ulu Burun: 1986 Campaign,' *American Journal of Archaeology* 93 (1989) 1–29, and recent reports in *The Institute of Nautical Archaeology Quarterly*. An interesting find was a wooden diptych writing tablet: Payton (1991).

evidence for this in the material culture, Mycenaean pottery being fairly well attested at sites along the coast, including Troy itself, particularly from Troy VId onward. Further support is offered by the presence on the Linear B tablets from Pylos of female dependent workers whose ethnics seem to imply an origin in Asia Minor, particularly Knidos (*ki-ni-di-ja*), Halikarnassos (*ze-pu₂-ra₃*, apparently from Ζεφύρα, an old name for the site: Strabo 14.2.16), Miletus (*mi-ra-ti-ja*), Lemnos (*ra-mi-ni-ja*), possibly Chios (*ki-si-wi-ja*). Perhaps the most controversial evidence relates to the identity of a place referred to in the Hittite records as Aḫḫiyawa. Although there are some phonological problems with identifying Hittite Aḫḫiyawa with a probable Greek form 'Αχαιϝία, they are not insurmountable, given the fact that the term is crossing a language boundary. One possible construction of the Aḫḫiyawa references is that they refer to Mycenaean Greeks—either from the mainland, or from the eastern Aegean—who were involved in Hittite activities in western Anatolia from the fifteenth to the thirteenth centuries B.C. Whether we can go so far as to link such references to a specific series of historical events associated with the site of Troy itself is less clear, although some scholars have made the attempt.[17]

Finally, we should note that the recent campaign of excavations at Troy under the direction of M. Korfmann has demonstrated that the settlement around the citadel itself in Troy VI was quite large, and was bounded by a ditch and wall, probably of mudbrick on a stone foundation. Korfmann estimates the size of the total settlement as twenty hectares, roughly comparable, for example, with that of the overall settlement at Mycenae, and ten times larger than Schliemann's citadel alone. Korfmann sees parallels between the new fortification and the layout of citadel plus lower town with those of other Bronze Age Anatolian towns, suggesting that Troy—by virtue of its

[17] The name does appear to occur in the Linear B tablets from Knossos (as *a-ka-wi-ja-de* = */Akhaiwiande/*? [KN C (2) 914.B]), although this may refer to a Cretan place-name, known, for example, to the scholia on Apollonius of Rhodes, *Argonautica* 4.175: K. F. Kitchell, 'Topographica Cretica': 'Topoi' of Classical Crete with Testimonia' (Ph.D. diss., Loyola University of Chicago, 1977) 43–50. Cline (1994) 68–74, 121–25 collects and discusses the Aḫḫiyawa references. For a Hittitologist's view, see H. Güterbock (1983); (1986). C. Watkins, in the same volume, considers 'The Language of the Trojans' (pp. 45–62). The discovery in 1995 of a Luwian seal in a level dated to Troy VII (C. B. Rose, Aegeanet e-discussion list, 10–31–95) could be seen as offering confirmation that Luwian was the Trojan language, although the seal may have been deposited (rather than manufactured) at Troy.

strategic position on the Dardanelles—was an important center in the Late Bronze Age. Regarding the Anatolian nature of the site, we could also note the newly-discovered Luwian seal and the fact that, although Mycenaean pottery is present in Troy VI and VII, local Anatolian types make up 98% of the total assemblage.[18]

Another significant feature of Mycenaean material culture is the variety of burial types. Most striking, in contrast to the picture in Homer's epics, is that inhumation was the exclusive rite throughout Mycenaean Greece in the Bronze Age until its very end, when cremation creeps in. Moreover, tombs designed for multiple use are typical from the late Middle Helladic period onwards: the Shaft Grave type, the tholos tomb, and the chamber tomb. Burials are made in these structures and the tomb is sealed. When a new burial is made, the tomb is reopened, room is cleared for the new interment, the interment made and the tomb resealed. One aspect of Bronze Age funerary architecture that bears a resemblance to Homeric practices is the tumulus, particularly common in Middle Helladic Messenia. Tumuli again are multiple burial sites, in which the dead are normally interred within large pots. G. Korres has plausibly linked the tumulus to the tholos tomb, seeing the latter as a built version of the tumulus' burial container with a large mound heaped over it.[19] As I. Morris remarks (this vol.), multiple burial becomes much rarer on mainland Greece after the Bronze Age, while cremation becomes widespread, although far from ubiquitous.

Finally, one of the most interesting results of the decipherment of Linear B is that we are able to understand Mycenaean social organization in a more specific manner than we could were we dependent on material data alone, although it is worth noting that our most consistent evidence comes from a single site, Pylos. The pinnacle of the Mycenaean social structure was the *wanax* (*wa-na-ka*; later ἄναξ), whose actual duties are somewhat dim, as a result of the predominantly economic nature of the tablets as preserved. Nevertheless, there is evidence for ritual associated with the coronation of the *wanax*, ritual that demanded supplies acquired through the palace system. The *wanax* also seems to have owned land called a τέμενος, of some

[18] Korfmann (1995) and ongoing reports in the journal *Studia Troica*. For Mycenaean pottery in Troy VI and VII, see Mee (1984).

[19] On tumuli, see O. Pelon, *Tholoi, tumuli et cercles funéraires* (Paris, 1976); S. Müller, 'Les tumuli: où? Quand? Comment?' *Bulletin de correspondance hellénique* 113 (1989) 1–42. Dickinson (1994) 208–33 summarizes Aegean burial practices.

size, three times larger than that belonging to an official called the *lawagetas* (*ra-wa-ke-ta*), assumed, by etymology of the title ('leader of the host'), to have been the second most powerful member of the ruling elite. The opposition between the terms *wanakteros* and *lawagesios* seems to reflect a distinction between the two offices and their establishments. It seems likely that the epithet *wanakteros* could also mean something like 'palatial' when applied to products or workers.

We have therefore an individual in charge called a *wanax*, a term very difficult to etymologize as Indo-European, and therefore probably borrowed, perhaps from Minoan Crete (see above). This individual is apparently not named on the tablets, although it was once thought that he was to be identified with the name *e-ke-ra*$_2$*-wo* (perhaps *Enkheliawon*). In any event, we might expect him to have had his own private establishment and also to have had control over a large part of the production within his territory as *wanax*. The figure next in importance and power was the *lawagetas*, also perhaps with his own establishment, and perhaps responsible for military matters, if the etymology of his title is significant. There is some evidence also for important subordinate individuals. One group, the *ek*^{w}*etai* (*e-qe-ta*), may have functioned—presumably among other things—as officers in charge of contingents apparently responsible for coastal guard duty. Another group, sometimes referred to by scholars as 'collectors,' seem to have been given responsibility for (and benefit from?) certain aspects of the economy. They do not have a title, but appear by name.[20]

The term *qa-si-re-u* does seem to be the same word as later Greek βασιλεύς, but its function in Linear B is rather obscure. The local level of palatial administration seems to have been in the hands of titled officials (the *ko-re-te*, and the *po-ro-ko-re-te*, perhaps 'X' and 'vice-X'). The function of the *qa-si-re-u* may have been as a truly local official, not appointed by the palace, but recognized by the community. It has even been suggested that as a status term *qa-si-re-u* is an inheritance from pre-Mycenaean times, and reflects a situation prior to the introduction of Minoan-style palatial kingship with its territorially-powerful *wanax*. Retained at the local level, the term

---

[20] For much of the information we can deduce about individuals and their status, see Lindgren (1973). *E-qe-ta*: Deger-Jalkotzy (1978). 'Collectors': papers by Bennet, Carlier, Driessen, and Godart in Olivier, ed. (1992), pp. 65–101, 159–66, 197–214 and 257–83.

resurfaced as the title of a leader of a community when the *wanax*-dominated palatial system collapsed.[21]

The Linear B tablets also offer a detailed picture of palatial control over some sectors of the economy. One of the most striking areas is that of the wool industry centrally monitored from Knossos, but carried on over much of central and west-central Crete, involving detailed censuses of flocks (totaling up to 100,000 sheep, it seems), shearing, transfer of wool to weaving workgroups, finishing of cloth, and—finally—storage of finished cloth in the palace at Knossos (Knossos Ak, Da–g, Dk, Dl, Dn, L- series). In some cases the cloth is described as *ke-se-nu-wi-ja* (*xenwia*), perhaps 'for export,' or *e-qe-si-ja*, 'for members of the *ek*^{w}*eta*-class.' A similar, but more centralized industry for the production of linen cloth existed in the Pylos polity (Pylos Aa, Ad, L- series, Na), while Pylos alone boasts an extensive series of records detailing male work groups to produce bronze (Pylos Jn). Other documents list regular offerings to divinities (Knossos Fp, Gg; Pylos Fr; Un), details of land-holdings (Pylos E- series), including measures of area, and yearly tax assessments and receipts on the sub-units of the polity (Pylos Ma; perhaps Knossos Mc). An apparently unusual feature of the Linear B documents is that, apart from examples like the reference to *xenwia* cloth mentioned above, there are very few unambiguous references to trade, particularly overseas trade. The absence can perhaps be explained by assuming that such trade took place only intermittently, and we do not happen to have documents belonging to a period when it was going on, or that it was carried out at a different level of administration, either without written records or with records on a perishable medium, such as papyrus or skin.[22]

The picture we can reconstruct of the Aegean Late Bronze Age is therefore one in many ways at odds with the picture Homer constructs as an eighth-century oral poet of his own heroic past.[23] There

---

[21] On the *wanax* and *g*^{w}*asileus*, and their relationship, see Carlier (1984) and J. R. Lenz (1993). For the idea that the *g*^{w}*asileus* belongs to a pre-Mycenaean stage: T. G. Palaima (forthcoming); Morpurgo Davies (1979). For a dissenting view on the post-Bronze Age revival: J. R. Lenz (1993).

[22] For an excellent general discussion of the Mycenaean economy, with extensive reference to studies of individual areas, see Killen (1985). Recently Killen (and others) have suggested that a Pylos text (Un 443) implies payment by the palace to an individual for an imported commodity, alum: Killen (1995).

[23] See W. Donlan (this vol.), and compare the vivid picture of storage in *Od.* 2.337–47.

is a significant difference of scale: large, palatial complexes, with large dependent workforces, dominating extensive territories, with subordinate centers within them. Burial—or at least its visible residues—seems to be on a larger, more monumental scale. There are also qualitative differences: writing is intimately bound up with the administration of these centers and the social hierarchy appears more complex, with a single ruler (the *wanax*) and a relatively complex group of subordinate, titled elites. It is clearly very difficult to connect the specifics of either world, but is there any point of intersection between the two?

Connecting Homer to the Bronze Age?

Clearly, any investigation of the topic 'Homer and the Bronze Age' must take into account the issue of the chronological and spatial separation of one from the other. In the light of the above discussion, can we demonstrate a continuous tradition of epic song extending back in time from Homer to the Greek Late Bronze Age? If we can provide an affirmative answer to this question, then it makes more plausible the transmission of some 'real' Bronze Age features preserved in the 'amber' of a continuous epic tradition, although we must not assume that the content of such poetry will remain constant.[24] I deal first with the question of continuity of epic song, since, in my opinion, it embodies elements that are—to some extent—independently verifiable. If we can demonstrate its continuity, then we can speculate on the means by which Bronze Age poetry might have become transformed over the Dark Age into epic poems like the *Iliad* and the *Odyssey*.

The most convincing evidence of the existence of epic in the Bronze Age is linguistic, because such elements are subconsciously incorporated in the very fabric of the poems. Some years ago, Janko (1982) demonstrated that Homer's epic *Kunstsprache* (and that of Hesiod and the Homeric Hymns) was entirely consistent with the eighth-century linguistic situation in the Ionic-speaking Greek world and that the language was in dynamic transition even within the relatively short span encompassed by Homer, Hesiod, and the composers of the

[24] For a discussion of possible phases in the development of epic from the early Mycenaean period through the Dark Age, see Sherratt (1990).

hymns. Against this background, certain linguistic features stand out as being of considerable antiquity and, with the hindsight afforded by the decipherment of Linear B, it is possible to demonstrate that some of these features must have their origins in the Bronze Age.

Most significant among these are elements independent of Greek phonology, a complex area to explore using the syllabic Linear B evidence and the Homeric text as we have it in its essentially post-Alexandrian form. The most convincing feature in the area of syntax is the use of tmesis (the separation of verbs from verb particles or preverbs) in Homer. Horrocks (1980; 1984) has shown that the separation of verbs from verb particles or preverbs belonged to an early phase of Greek and was also paralleled in Sanskrit. The probability is that this feature of early Greek syntax was retained in the epic, poetic language because of the flexibility it offered in developing formulae within the constraints of the meter. Using Mycenaean evidence as a comparison, however, Horrocks demonstrated that the prose language preserved in the Linear B tablets (dating from c. 1400–1200 B.C.) appears to use verbal prefixes much as later Greek did, suggesting that this element of the Homeric language went back to a time before that of Linear B:

> Since these rules are inherited, since in all probability they have already disappeared from the Mycenaean prose language, since there are no plausible alternative lines of descent, and since their preservation in Epic is clearly and strongly motivated by the need to maintain the array of compositional techniques intact, we must conclude that dactylic poetry did indeed have a role to play in the Bronze Age narrative tradition and that certain aspects at least of that tradition passed in a direct line down to the Dark Age. (Horrocks [1980] 9)

If Horrocks is correct, then tmesis must have been retained in a poetic language before the time of the Linear B tablets as we have them, certainly before 1200 B.C., the end of the Late Helladic IIIB phase from which the archives at Pylos, Mycenae, Thebes and Tiryns date, possibly even by 1400 B.C., the date of the earliest preserved Knossos texts. It is not difficult to imagine why the feature would have been retained in poetic language, but the fact that it is not reflected in the (perhaps equally specialized?) language used by the Linear B scribes may have implications for the separation of these different spheres, literate and non-literate (on which, see below).

Less convincing are arguments based on phonology and/or on issues of scansion, since we do not know exactly what rules of scansion

Homer—subconsciously—held himself to, and in fact might expect there to have been more freedom in scansion than is reflected in our normalized text. Nevertheless, linguists have shown that certain features of Homer's language retain archaic forms where meter demands them. A simple example of this phenomenon is the frequently attested o-stem genitive in -οιο, the only o-stem genitive preserved in Linear B, but not preserved in any later Greek dialect, and in the process of being ousted in Homeric epic by the more recent form -ου, where the meter would accommodate it.[25] This particular example cannot be used to prove the existence of Mycenaean epic, since -οιο may have survived the Bronze Age and been incorporated into epic language within its intervening Dark Age stages.

However, other larger line segments in Homer do not scan in the form in which they are preserved, but would if certain historical forms are restored, some of which also reflect forms already archaic by the time of the Linear B tablets.[26] Here are two examples of formulaic phrases which 'scan' when transformed into plausible Mycenaean versions:

e.g., βίη̄ Ἡ|ρᾱκλη̄|είη̄ (*Il.* 11.690 etc.) Ἀχ̆ῑλλῆ̄|ος θεῖ|οῖο̆ (*Il.* 19.279 etc.)
γʷῑ|ᾱ Hη̄|ρᾱκλε̆ϝε̆|hεῑᾱ Ἀχ̆ῑλλῆ̄|ϝος θε̆hῐ|οιο̆

In these examples, the spondaic fifth feet disappear if Mycenaean forms are restored. In the second example, however, even the Mycenaean form θέhιος will not scan in the nominative, so the alternative formula δῖος Ἀχιλλεύς (*Il.* 1.7 etc.) is used, containing the adjective δίϝyος attested in Mycenaean. We might hypothesize a Mycenaean alternation between an adjective δίϝyος in the nominative and θέhιος in non-nominative cases.

Such examples merely take us back as far as the Mycenaean period, and even then, presume a rigidity of scansion rules that may not necessarily have applied. In order to prove the existence of Mycenaean epic, we need to isolate features that appear already to have been archaic in Mycenaean as attested in Linear B. An example of such a feature is the following line:

---

[25] E.g., Janko (1982) 50–54.

[26] E.g. Ruijgh (1985) 158–63 (in the context of a wider summary of the relationship between Homeric and Mycenaean Greek, now more fully developed in Ruijgh [1995]). See also M. L. West (1988) 156–59, with qualifications by Chadwick (1990) 175–76.

Μη̄ρῐό|νη̄ς ἀτᾰ|λᾱντŏς Ἐ̆|νυᾱλίῳ ϝᾱνδρεῑφ|ϝόντῃ̄ (*Il.* 7.166, etc.), -

which can be recreated as:

Μη̄ρῐό|νᾱς hᾰτᾰ|λᾱντŏς Ἐ̆|νῡᾰλῐ|ϝῳ ἀν|χʷό̄ντᾱͅ

Here the metrical irregularities can be resolved by reconstructing a form with a vocalic-r for the final word. However, forms in Mycenaean such as *a-re-ka-sa-da-ra* ('Αλεξάνδρα) demonstrate that the stem ἀνδρ- had already spread, a fact that implies that a line such as that above must predate the period of the Linear B documents.

The identification of such archaic features of the epic language can take us fairly certainly back to the period of the Linear B documents (at least to c. 1200 B.C.) and, in the case of the example of tmesis, probably some time before that. Whether one can speculate on the basis of linguistically older passages about the likely content of early Mycenaean epic is less clear, although M. L. West ([1988] 158–59) and others have made the attempt. One can see how older linguistic features could have been retained in traditional poetry while subject matter changed.

It is worth pausing briefly to speculate on when such poetry might have originated. Ruijgh, following Meillet, has suggested that the Greek hexameter was inappropriate to the Greek language and suggests that a possible source might be the Minoan culture known to have been so influential on early Mycenaean Greece. While such an hypothesis is very difficult to prove, and has been rejected by others, archaeologists and Mycenologists are increasingly attracted by the idea that the emergent Mycenaean chiefdoms of the Shaft-Grave period appropriated elements of Minoan elite culture and, probably, status terminology (as we saw above). In such a context, the adaptation of Minoan poetry (in praise of a ruler and his family?) to a Mycenaean elite context—perhaps reflected in the Pylos lyre-player fresco (see below)—seems more plausible.[27]

An important point here is that not only do such reconstructions demonstrate a Mycenaean antiquity for some features of the Homeric language, but also a rationale for the preservation of those features linked to the composition of hexametric verse. Whatever the origins

[27] Ruijgh (1985) 150–53, following Meillet (1923) 57–63. For a divergent account, see M. L. West (this vol.) and Chadwick (1990) 176. For two recent studies of the appropriation of Minoan features in the wider cultural context of early Mycenaean Greece, see Wright (1995) and Palaima (1995).

of the hexameter—native or Minoan—we can hypothesize the existence of hexametric verse as early as the fourteenth or fifteenth centuries B.C.

If Mycenaean poetry existed, is there any contemporary Mycenaean evidence—other than linguistic—to support its existence? Recently two scholars—S. P. Morris and S. Hiller—have proposed that the miniature fresco found in the West House of the settlement of Akrotiri on Thera supports such a conclusion, suggesting that it represents an elaborate visual narrative.[28] Taking the Shield of Achilles as his starting point, Hiller—alluding to Ruijgh's belief that the hexameter was Minoan in origin—has argued that the Minoan scenes on Thera form a plausible model for the structure of the Shield narrative, implying the transmission of such structures to Homer's day through the medium of Mycenaean culture. S. P. Morris sees in the visual images of the fresco parallels with poetic themes, formulae, and episodes.

Iconographic representations such as the Thera miniature fresco demonstrate the probability of narrative; it is difficult to see how the representation could not have been verbalized as a narrative. Or, perhaps it was itself a visual version of a pre-existing verbal narrative. The specifics are lost to us, however, since it was never the custom of Bronze Age artists to label scenes in a way later Greek artists frequently did, and we do not have sufficient clues as to where to begin and to determine, for example, whether the representation embodies a single time-frame or a sequence of events. Whether we can go as far as S. P. Morris and suggest that the individual scenes resemble thematically scenes in epic is uncertain, but there is no reason to doubt the existence of a parallel verbal narrative that embodied the events depicted in the fresco. It is likely that other scenes among the Thera frescoes—our best preserved source of Aegean imagery—embody narrative: for example, a scene from Xeste 3 showing a woman apparently injured in the foot.[29]

These representations belong to an essentially Minoan cultural

---

[28] S. P. Morris (1989); Hiller (1990). The idea is not entirely new; see, e.g., Warren (1979) 129. For a comprehensive treatment of the fresco, see L. Morgan (1988), who rejects the idea of a specific narrative, preferring to see the scenes as reflecting an annual ceremony celebrating the opening of the sailing season. Illustrations in Doumas (1992) 58–85.

[29] P. Rehak, 'Women's Myth and Ritual in Prehistoric Thera: The Wall-Paintings from Xeste 3 at Akrotiri,' paper delivered in Madison, Wisconsin, 1993; Doumas (1992) 136–37.

context now dated to the later seventeenth century B.C., nearly a millennium before Homer. However, there are many (more fragmentary) examples of narrative art in Mycenaean contexts. One of the earliest is the silver rhyton with a depiction of a siege found in shaft grave IV at Mycenae, roughly contemporary with the Thera miniature fresco. From the same archaeological context, a similar narrative content might also be argued for the inlaid dagger showing a lion hunt from shaft grave IV and for the scenes on stelae that originally marked the shaft graves in Grave Circles A and B. Indeed, L. Morgan has argued that the scenes on one dagger—a human lion hunt on one side; lions attacking deer on the other—act as a visual simile: just as lions overcome the deer, so do men overcome lions (and by implication, the user of this dagger will overcome his enemies)?[30] By the mature Mycenaean period (Late Helladic III), there are a number of fresco representations from the Mycenaean palaces of Mycenae, Tiryns, Orchomenos, and Pylos that depict battle or hunting scenes.[31]

All of the above examples suggest the presence of narrative in the Late Bronze Age, as embodied in visual representations. However, they do not prove the existence of poetic narrative. The 'missing link' between linguistic evidence for the Mycenaean antiquity of verse techniques and iconographic evidence for narrative is perhaps the small amount of evidence of musical (presumably vocal) performance in the context of Minoan and Mycenaean elite culture, much of it apparently connected with ritual.[32] Although any representations of

---

[30] L. Morgan (1988) 47–48.

[31] Shaft Graves period: McDonald and Thomas (1990) 101–102, fig. 43 (siege rhyton); Xenaki-Sakellariou and Chatziliou (1989) 25 (inlaid dagger); R. Hampe and E. Simon, *The Birth of Greek Art from the Mycenaean to the Archaic Period* (New York, 1981) pls. 52–53, S. Hood, *The Arts in Prehistoric Greece* (New York, 1978) 100, fig. 81 (examples of stelae). On narrative in Mycenaean painting in general, Immerwahr (1990) 122–34. For specific scenes on wall-paintings, ibid., pls. 64–65 (Mycenae); pls. 66–67, 73–74 (Pylos); pls. 68–70 (Tiryns); fig. 35b (Orchomenos). For other painted representations, Immerwahr (1990) pl. 84 (limestone stele painted in Late Helladic IIIC, Mycenae) pls. 85–87 (the Warrior Vase, Mycenae) pl. 90 (chariot krater, Tiryns) pl. 91 (pinax or larnax with warrior head, Tiryns). For a comprehensive presentation of pictorial representations on pottery, including scenes with chariots, see Karageorghis and Vermeule (1982).

[32] Perhaps the most famous representations are those of the lyre-players from the megaron at Pylos (e.g., Immerwahr [1990] pl. XVIII) and on the Minoan Agia Triada sarcophagus (Immerwahr [1990] pl. 50). These and other Bronze Age representations—mostly on pottery—are discussed and illustrated in Maas and Snyder (1989) 1–23. J. Younger, *Music in the Aegean Bronze Age: The Physical Evidence* (forthcoming)

lyre-players on their own might suggest sung poetic performance, the most convincing example of performance in a special public context is the famous representation on the wall of the main megaron (room 6) at the so-called Palace of Nestor in Messenia, Bronze Age Pylos.

Although there are some problems in interpreting the scene—not least the fact that the figure is apparently not playing, but merely holds his lyre—the fact that the scene can be placed in a festival context adds to its importance. According to the most recent reconstruction of the fresco program in the main megaron, the lyre-player is part of a larger scene of feasting, involving the sacrifice of a bull depicted on an altar to the right of the lyre-player and groups of people seated at tables 'toasting' with kylikes just like those found in their thousands in the palace storerooms off the opposite side of the megaron. This scene of feasting is placed to the right of an elaborate seat (that of the ruler?), to the left of which are depicted a large griffin and lion, presumably as supernatural protectors of the occupant of the seat. When we add this visual representation to the evidence from the Linear B documents for the procurement of supplies for feasts held to mark major events in the Pylian state, it is plausible to assume that the lyre-player may well have delivered song in praise of the ruler, the *wanax*.[33]

It seems, therefore, that we can link the poetry of Homer (and presumably others like him) with a tradition of poetic performance that had its origins in the Mycenaean Bronze Age. It is even possible that the status of bards such as Phemius or Demodocus in the Homeric poems—apparently permanently attached to the courts of Odysseus or Alcinous, unlike Homer or Hesiod?—may reflect the status of singers employed by the Mycenaean *wanaktes* to perform in the context of festivals centered on their palaces.

An issue here, of course, is the extent of Bronze Age literacy. Would these Mycenaean singers have used Linear B as an aid to their poetic

---

provides a comprehensive collection of the Bronze Age Greek evidence for musical instruments and performance. For similar problems in identifying rhapsodic performers on Greek painted pottery: Burkert (1987); H. A. Shapiro, 'Hipparchos and the Rhapsodes,' in C. Dougherty and L. Kurke (eds.), *Cultural Poetics in Archaic Greece. Cult, Performance, Politics* (New York, 1993) 92–107.

[33] Megaron frescoes: L. R. McCallum, 'Decorative Program in the Mycenaean Palace of Pylos: The Megaron Frescoes,' unpublished Ph.D. dissertation, University of Pennsylvania, 1987, 68–141. Linear B evidence for feasting: Killen (1994).

performance? If they had, would they then have been true ἀοιδά, composing like Homer on the spot without the aid of writing? If they did use writing, then in what sense, if any, are they predecessors of the oral poets of Homer's time? The overwhelming evidence from silence in the Mycenaean world tells against the use of writing for any purpose other than bureaucratic. There are no plausible examples of the use of Linear B for recording anything other than economic information. Furthermore, the total absence of text in Aegean iconography is striking, in contrast to contemporary examples in Egypt and the Near East. We may also contrast this situation with that in the Minoan world, where Linear A is found not only on clay administrative documents, but also as continuous text (i.e., without accounting symbols and numbers) on items of personal adornment (pins, rings) and on objects dedicated in sanctuaries (stone 'offering tables' and ladles), not to mention the existence of parchment documents to which sealings were affixed.

The absence of wider examples of literacy in the Mycenaean world may be sufficient evidence to support the idea that Bronze Age bards would have had no use for writing to aid their performance, despite the fact that performances might have been linked to state events, for which supplies were mobilized through the literate administration.[34] But perhaps the most telling argument is to ask for whom the writing would have functioned. The Linear B tablets were used as part of an administration, the information presumably being consulted by literate administrators at least on a yearly basis. The literacy they reflect was a very specialized literacy, a fact that is further reinforced by its total disappearance in the aftermath of the collapse of the palaces. What would the literate audience have been for written versions of songs about the ruler of Pylos? Surely the performance of such songs—and other associated festivities—was the crucial element. Scribes may have recorded the ingredients required by ideology from members of the state, but they could not record the spectacle of the festivals themselves. There may be an analogy with the Linear B offerings texts which tell us very little other than the name (and address) of the dedicatee (e.g., 'To Amnisos, to all the

[34] Mycenaean literacy: Palaima (1987). Examples of Linear A texts on media other than administrative documents: L. Godart and J.-P. Olivier, *Recueil des inscriptions en linéaire A. Vol. IV. Autres documents* (Paris 1982). Powell (1991) 109–115 discusses the suitability of syllabic script (specifically the Classical Cypriot syllabary) for recording hexametric poetry.

gods'), and the amount of whatever commodity is being offered (e.g., '20 liters of olive oil'), but nothing of the associated ritual.

Closing the Frame: the Bronze Age and Homer

It seems that there are a number of senses in which we can relate Homer's epic poems to the Greek Bronze Age. In the first case, we can plausibly link the techniques of epic oral composition to the world of the Bronze Age palaces, demonstrating a more-or-less continuous tradition of epic song at least from the early Mycenaean period (c. 1700 B.C.) to Homer's day. The initial development (or elaboration) of such a tradition seems plausible in the context of the reorganization of Mycenaean society that took place in the Shaft Grave period at Mycenae itself and elsewhere, as Sherratt observed (1990). Given that continuity, we can go some way to explaining how some features of the material world of the Bronze Age were preserved in Homeric poetry, while, in our present knowledge of oral poetics, we can well understand why social features—and many linguistic features—were systematically and subconsciously modernized through time.[35]

Is there any way in which Homer the poet self-consciously composed about the Bronze Age? He was creating an epic world explicitly situated in the past. From Hesiod's excursus on the different ages (*Works and Days* 156–65), we can see that contemporary Greek poets understood their past in terms of a transitional generation—the race of heroes—between the age of bronze and their own time, that of iron.[36] Although Homer—because of the nature of his poetry—does not make the reference explicit like Hesiod, we can assume that this was the age to which he would have attributed the events of his tales. But by the very construction of the system of ages and by the explicit comparison between then and now, Homer and Hesiod both link their eighth-century present to the time of the traditional Trojan War. The real disjunction was the collapse of the Mycenaean palace

[35] For the notion of the creation of epic poetry in the context of early Mycenaean society and its reformulation—in keeping with contemporary society—at key periods of major social change at the end of the Bronze Age and in the eighth century, see Sherratt (1990).

[36] For the view that not all Iron Age poets shared the same view of a heroic age: M. L. West (1978) 370–73.

societies and the period of instability in most parts of Greece that was ushered in after this collapse. For eighth-century Greeks it was an unbridgeable gap: it was impossible to demonstrate genealogical continuity across it (i.e., eighth-century inhabitants could not give themselves genealogies extending back into the Bronze Age) and it was equally impossible to demonstrate continuity of authority across the same time period (i.e., eighth-century rulers did not trace their own lineage back to Bronze Age heroes). It seems most likely to me that this disjunction is responsible for much of the explicit aggrandizing of the past in Homer, and that Bronze Age epic would have lacked such self-conscious inferiority about contemporary life.[37]

Because of this disjunction, Homer deliberately creates an 'epic distance' between his audience and the events of the poems. For example, although iron appears (particularly in similes, elements that need to be most accessible to contemporary audiences, or as a prize in the games of Patroclus [*Il.* 23.826–35]), bronze is the major metal for weapons in the poems.[38]

A converse—and more complex—example is the use of writing. Writing is almost entirely absent from the poems and in this respect, we assume Homer's picture reflects his own society and indeed his own status as an oral poet. Yet we know that at least a certain element of Mycenaean society was literate—an apparent contrast. It is possible, however, that Homer preserves a memory of Bronze Age literacy in the famous Bellerophon episode and introduces it as yet another example of 'epic distance.' Although this is possible, perhaps a more convincing explanation is that the medium—a diptych tablet—is the most significant element in the story, reflecting eastern writing practices contemporary with Homer himself, or belonging to the Bronze Age (as the Uluburun diptych now attests).

We might think of metals (along with armor, etc.) and writing as elements that Homer deliberately employed to give historical color to his poetry. Other elements, where we have some Bronze Age evidence seem to follow a regular pattern. In particular, certain material culture features and status-terms common in the Mycenaean palatial world are attributed to gods in Homer. Athena's lamp is a

---

[37] On genealogical continuity, see Burkert (1995). On the problems of royal succession, see Finkelberg (1991). The idea that heroic poetry is only possible *after* a preceding 'dark age' goes back to Chadwick and Chadwick (1932).

[38] Cf. Lorimer (1950) 453.

good example, while the status term ἄναξ is in transition, commonly applied to gods, but also to human rulers along with βασιλεύς. Recently, Cynthia Shelmerdine has shown how Bronze Age practices of textile treatment have been transformed into examples of shining or fragrant cloth in Homer's poetry.[39]

Continuities and discontinuities, then. We have traced a plausible origin for the poetic techniques used by Homer (and others like him) in the Mycenaean world. We can isolate—and many have played this game—features in Homeric epic that are Bronze Age in origin and are either preserved or misunderstood in his eighth-century B.C. context. We can also point to many features—linguistic, social, and material—that belong to Homer's time. One of the most striking features of the question, however, is perhaps why Homeric epic sprung up where it did. If we return to the map (Fig. 1), we note that the traditional location for Homer is Ionia (Smyrna) or Chios. Hesiod, a Boeotian bard, whose poetic persona claims to have sung in a contest at Chalcis on Euboea (see Rosen, this vol.), puts epic on the mainland and Euboea close to Homer's own time. A location on Euboea for an epic about the heroic past would not surprise us, since Euboea is the location of some of the most advanced Iron Age societies in Greece.[40] Clearly there is little geographical overlap between the world of the Bronze Age bard and that of the Iron Age bard (Fig. 1). Any attempt, then, to link Homer's poetry to (that of bards singing in) Bronze Age Greece not only has to bridge up to sixteen generations, but has to trace the development of the tradition from the dying embers of the Mycenaean centers of mainland Greece to the emergent poleis of Ionia, Euboea, or Boeotia. Such a quest might well be of great cultural interest, but, if we wish to 'use' Homer as a guide to the societies of Bronze Age Greece, we are likely to find ourselves in agreement with M. I. Finley, who concludes: 'Homer is not only not a reliable guide to the Mycenaean tablets; he is no guide at all.'[41]

---

[39] On lamps, see, for example, Powell (1991) 201–202. On kingship terms, see Carlier (1984). On 'shining cloth,' see C. W. Shelmerdine (1995).

[40] A view put forward by M. L. West (1988).

[41] Finley (1982) 232.

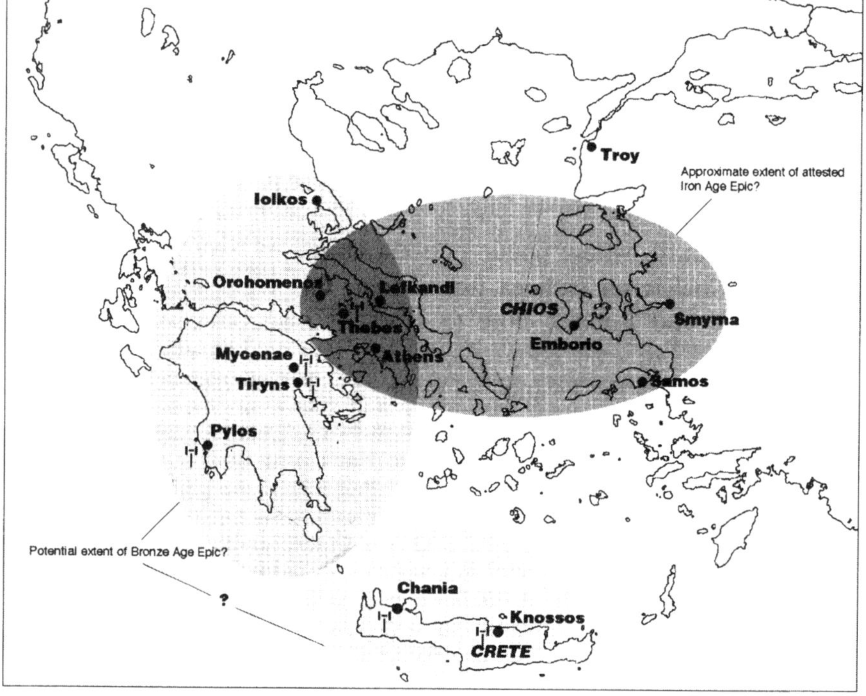

Figure 1: The Aegean, Showing Significant Sites, and the Distribution of Epic in the Bronze and Iron Ages.
(The presence of a Linear B sign next to a site indicates the find-spot of Linear B administrative documents.)

Ian Morris

HOMER AND THE IRON AGE[1]

In this chapter, I discuss the place of Iron Age archaeology in Homeric scholarship. I begin by briefly reviewing the relationships of these fields across the last 125 years, and then turn to the picture of Iron Age Greece which archaeology now provides, and its relevance to Homeric studies.

---

[1] I would like to thank John Bennet, Jan Paul Crielaard, and Barry Powell for reading an earlier version of this chapter and improving it substantially. They are of course not responsible for what I have done with their advice, or for the errors that remain.

There has been an explosion of archaeological evidence in the last twenty-five years. I limit myself to citing in the notes general studies, which have further bibliography, and reports on sites which I specifically mention in the text. This means that I must omit many important studies, but even so, I have to refer to a great many reports, mainly preliminary accounts in the Greek journals. This calls for a departure from the bibliographic procedures in the rest of the volume. I refer to monographs and interpretive articles in the regular format, by author's name and date of publication, but for preliminary reports, give only references by conventional abbreviated journal titles. These brief reports are not included in the consolidated bibliography at the end of the volume.

I use the following abbreviations:

AA	*Archäologischer Anzeiger*
AAA	*Athens Annals of Archaeology*
AD	*Arkhaiologikon Deltion*
AE	*Arkhaiologiki Ephemeris*
AEMTh	*To Arkhaiologiko Ergo sti Makedonia kai Thraki*
AJA	*American Journal of Archaeology*
AM	*Mitteilungen des Deutschen Archäologischen Instituts, Athenische Abteilung*
AR	*Archaeological Reports* (supplement to *Journal of Hellenic Studies*)
ASAA	*Annuario della Scuola Archeologica di Atene*
BSA	*Annual of the British School at Athens*
Ergon	*Ergon tis en Athinais Arkhaiologikis Etaireias*
IM	*Mitteilungen des Deutschen Archäologischen Instituts, Istanbuler Abteilung*
OJA	*Oxford Journal of Archaeology*
ÖJh	*Jahrshefte des Österreichischen Archäologischen Instituts*
Op Ath	*Opuscula Atheniensa*
Praktika	*Praktika tis en Athinais Arkhaiologikis Etaireias*
PZ	*Prähistorische Zeitschrift*

Homeric Criticism and Iron Age Archaeology[2]

There has long been interest in the material culture of the poems, but modern Homeric archaeology began with Heinrich Schliemann. Going against the scholarly orthodoxy of the 1870s, Schliemann believed passionately that Homer told the story of a real Trojan war. From this preliminary assumption, he drew the conclusion that the objects and places described by Homer reflected a real, external world; and he then took the logical next step, of further assuming that excavation could *prove* the reality of Homer's heroic age. To everyone's surprise, at Troy and Mycenae Schliemann found things which suggested that he might be right, and that Homer really did describe a lost civilization of bronze-armed heroes. There were heated debates over his finds for some years, but these were gradually settled in Schliemann's favor. By 1913, readers of the revised edition of J. B. Bury's *History of Greece* could learn that 'Our earliest written record, the *Iliad* of Homer, refers to the people and civilisation of Greece in the thirteenth century . . . the picture which Homer presents is a consistent picture, closely corresponding, in its main features and in remarkable details, to the evidence which has recently been recovered from the earth.'[3] There was general agreement that Bronze Age archaeology elucidated the epics, while that of the Iron Age did not. Since there was also general agreement that elucidating texts was the major goal of classical archaeology, the newly defined Iron Age—often described as a 'Dark Age'—received little attention.

This only began to change after 1945. As Milman Parry's and Albert Lord's researches into oral poetry slowly reached a wide audience (see Foley, Edwards, and Russo, this vol.), many classicists started to suspect that it was *a priori* unlikely that Homer was faithfully describing a society half a millennium before his own day. This feeling grew in strength after 1952, when Michael Ventris deciphered Linear B, revealing forms of Mycenaean bureaucratic control unlike anything described in Homer. Schliemann's Bronze Age was starting to look less like the world of the poems; and at just the same time, new excavation reports, like K. Kübler's *Kerameikos* volumes, and new

---

[2] This section condenses the arguments of my article 'Periodization and the Heroes' (I. Morris 1997).

[3] J. B. Bury, *A History of Greece* (2nd ed., London, 1913) 5, 50.

syntheses, like V. R. Desborough's *Protogeometric Pottery*, made Iron Age materials more accessible.

In 1950, H. L. Lorimer surveyed all the known finds from 1600 to 700 B.C. in her *Homer and Monuments*, and discussed their similarities to the objects described by Homer. She modified older views, arguing that while Bronze Age objects were prominent in Homer, they were much less so than had been thought. She suggested that the material culture of the poems conflated objects spanning almost a millennium. Much of her book focused on what this view of Iron Age archaeology meant for theories of Homeric composition. In Lorimer's view, Homeric material culture was as much an amalgam as the Homeric *Kunstsprache*, bearing no more relationship to any real situation than Homer's language did to any spoken tongue.[4]

Lorimer used archaeology to challenge some of Schliemann's conclusions, while retaining his assumption that the goals of archaeology were to elucidate the text and, if possible, to date the real heroic world described there. But the post-war re-evaluation of the Iron Age also had more radical results. In 1953, C. G. Starr began work on his *Origins of Greek Civilization*, aiming to use Iron Age archaeology not as a footnote to literary scholarship, but as a major source for social history. For Starr, Homer was most important as a central figure of what he called 'the age of revolution' (c. 750–650 B.C.), in which Classical Greek civilization took shape.[5]

In the 1970s, A. M. Snodgrass (1971), V. R. Desborough (1972), and J. N. Coldstream (1977) each published a detailed synthesis of Iron Age archaeology. All three books had a massive impact on scholarship, but Snodgrass' *Dark Age of Greece* seems to have been the most influential, taking up Starr's historical approach. Snodgrass saw the Iron Age artifacts as revealing a period of poverty, isolation, and simplicity, a true 'Dark Age.' He took Lorimer's conflation model of Homeric society further, bolstering it with a comparative argument that Homeric marriages also conflated incompatible practices from different historical periods (Snodgrass [1974]). Like Starr, Snodgrass saw the epics primarily as evidence for the cultural vigor of eighth-century Greece.

---

[4] M. Parry (1971); Chadwick (1967 [1958]); Kraiker and Kübler (1939); Kübler (1943); (1954); Desborough (1952); Lorimer (1950).

[5] Starr (1961); I would like to thank Professor Starr for discussing the background to his book with me.

These syntheses dominated Iron Age archaeology throughout the 1980s. The footnotes to the papers from the four major international conferences on the Iron Age held between 1979 and 1988 treat Snodgrass' conclusions as virtually proven.[6] By the mid 1980s, Homerists generally agreed that Iron Age archaeology, rather than Bronze Age, was vital for understanding the context of the poems, and felt that they had to fit their interpretations to the archaeologists' syntheses. By the end of the decade, however, a backlash against the new consensus began. P. James and his co-authors (1991) rejected the new orthodoxy by arguing that the five-century 'Dark Age' really lasted for only 250 years, and that Mediterranean chronologies all rested on a flawed reading of the Egyptian king lists. Few archaeologists have been impressed by this thesis. A second argument, still a minority position at the time of writing but steadily gaining supporters, holds that the 1970s 'Dark Age' models exaggerated the scale of disruptions after 1200. Those who hold this view sometimes assert that Homerists should return their focus to the Bronze Age.[7]

In the remainder of this paper, I present a summary of the archaeological evidence now available from Iron Age Greece (by which I mean the period roughly 1100–700 B.C.). I have two goals in taking this approach to the issue of 'Homer and the Iron Age.' The first is that for most Homerists, the 1970s syntheses are still the obvious place to go for an understanding of the material record. New finds have accumulated at an astonishing rate in the last twenty-five years, and although I can only provide a brief sketch in this short chapter, it may nevertheless provide a useful introduction to the newer materials.

My second aim is to show through a collection of the evidence that the kind of assumptions which have guided 'Homeric archaeology' for most of its brief history—that the archaeologist's job is to compare the finds with the texts, either to date the real society which Homer describes, or to chart the evolution of our the poems through time—are inappropriate. The evidence we now have produces an extremely complex picture, with significant differences between regions,

---

[6] For the conferences, Di Vita et al., eds. (1983–84); Hägg, ed. (1983); Deger-Jalkotzy, ed. (1983); Musti et al., eds. (1991).

[7] S. P. Morris (1989; 1992) is the most influential exponent of this view. See Bennet (this vol.).

and also major changes through time. As archaeologists since Lorimer have repeatedly insisted, the material world described by Homer cannot be paralleled by the excavated record from any single region of Greece at any single point in time within the Iron Age. Archaeologists have generally assumed that this means that a series of Dark Age poets described the lost race of heroes in terms of the material culture of their own times, that oral composition somehow 'froze' different bits and pieces of the material world into the poems, and that in Homer we have a mixture of all these chronological layers, which we can excavate (much like an archaeological site).[8] Instead, I make an argument much like Snodgrass' (this vol.): material culture and poetic culture were two ways in which people in eighth-century Greece constructed the social world within which they moved. Both were important arenas in which people fashioned images of what they wanted their world to be, and challenged competing constructions which they did not like. Reducing either to a passive reflection of the other is simplistic. I conclude that there is no way to use Iron Age archaeology to fix Homer in time or space; rather, Iron Age verbal and non-verbal representations must be read together, as sources for a fuller cultural history.

Strong regional variation is typical of Iron Age Europe, and Greece is no exception. Consequently, I divide the Greek world into four areas. Central Greece, where Homer's supposed homes of Smyrna and Chios lie, has attracted most archaeological activity, and I describe it in rather greater detail that the other regions.[9]

Central Greece

Chronology

I divide the evidence into five chronological phases, and call each by the pottery style associated with it. This has drawbacks, but is the clearest way to present the material. Although I give absolute dates for each phase, only the beginning and end of the period are securely

[8] The argument is made most explicitly by Sherratt (1990).

[9] The relevant sections of Snodgrass (1971), Desborough (1972), and Coldstream (1977) summarize the older finds, and I. Morris (forthcoming) Chs. 5–7, the newer ones. I only give references in the notes for sites which I mention in the text.

fixed. Any date between c. 1150 and 800 is a conventional estimate, and should be treated accordingly.[10]

Late Helladic IIIC (c. 1200–1075 B.C.)[11]

The Mycenaean palaces were destroyed and abandoned around 1200. Linear B, monumental stone architecture, and other 'high' skills disappeared. Population fell by perhaps 75% between 1250 and 1100. Emigration from the core areas of Mycenaean civilization, famine, and disease must all have been involved. The palaces had controlled much of the agricultural economy, and their destruction perhaps spelled economic disaster.

At some sites, dislocations were fairly small: at Tiryns, the area where the palace had stood (the 'Oberburg') was virtually abandoned, and a new town began to flourish below it on the 'Unterburg.' But many sites were evacuated. It seems that people from the Argolid made new homes in the Cyclades, Chalcidice, western Greece, and as far afield as Cyprus and the Levant. However, there may also have been migrations into Greece from the north at this time. Later traditions speak of Dorian invaders, and Egyptian records describe movements of 'Sea Peoples' in the early twelfth century. These large population movements must be connected with the events in Greece around 1200, either as a cause or a consequence (or both). It is difficult to document migrations archaeologically, but the handmade burnished ware ('Barbarian Ware') found on some twelfth-century sites may belong to northerners.

These were traumatic events, but we should not exaggerate their effects. There was something of a Mycenaean renaissance by 1150, perhaps a golden age for local aristocracies, now freed from palatial control. At Koukounaries on Paros, a Mycenaean-style mansion flourished in these years, and tombs at Perati include Near Eastern imports. But this revival collapsed around 1100.

---

[10] See the papers collected in *Acta Archaeologica* 67 (1996).

[11] Generally, Ward and Joukowsky, eds. (1992); Rutter (1990; 1992); Bennet, this vol. Tiryns: *AA* 1978, 449–70; 1979, 379–411; 1981, 149–94; 1982, 393–430; 1983, 277–328. Koukounaries: Schilardi (1984). Perati: Iakovidis (1970). Foxhall (1995) presents a different view of agriculture in this period.

Submycenaean (c. 1075–1025 B.C.)[12]

Central Greek material culture changed abruptly in the early and mid-eleventh century. Pottery remained basically Mycenaean, but its variety and quality declined. Individual inhumation in cist graves replaced the Mycenaean practice of multiple burial in chamber tombs, and single-roomed oval or apsidal houses replaced multi-room, rectilinear buildings. Cist graves and apsidal houses had been common in the Middle Bronze Age, and Submycenaean culture partly revived much older Greek traditions. At many sites where occupation continued, cist graves were cut into the old Mycenaean habitation areas; at other sites, occupation broke off altogether. Material evidence for cult ends at most Mycenaean shrines, although worship may have continued in forms which have low archaeologically visibility.

This was also a time of virtual symbolic anarchy. Submycenaean grave goods were very varied. Most graves were poor, but a handful had (by Iron Age standards) considerable riches, including a bronze helmet in one burial at Tiryns. The overall impression is that Mycenaean styles of life were being abandoned as irrelevant or impossible in the middle of the eleventh century, but no alternative vision of social order had yet taken hold. If any period can truly be called a 'Dark Age,' it is this.

Protogeometric (c. 1025–900 B.C.)[13]

There are further changes at the end of the late eleventh century. The amount of evidence (now almost entirely from graves) declines still further, and within each region of central Greece the burials are very homogeneous, particularly in Middle Protogeometric. People in most areas continued to inhume the dead in cists, but at Athens urn cremation was now preferred for adults, and in Euboea and some of the other islands, primary cremation in cist graves took over. Almost all graves were poor, with just a few pots and one or two metal

[12] Generally, Styrenius (1967). Tiryns: *AM* 78 (1963) 10–24.

[13] Bronze shortage model, Snodgrass (1971) 228–68; see also Karageorghis, ed. (1994). Exclusion hypothesis, I. Morris (1987); (forthcoming) Ch. 5. Chiefly cult, Mazarakis-Ainian (forthcoming). Isthmia, *Hesperia* 61 (1992) 6–22. Lefkandi, *BSA* 77 (1982) 213–48; *Antiquity* 56 (1982) 169–73; *AR* 1988/89, 117–29; 1993/94, 18; 1994/95, 31; *OJA* 14 (1995) 103–107, 151–57. Popham et al. (1980); (1993); Catling and Lemos (1990).

objects. In Middle Protogeometric and most of Late Protogeometric, almost all these metal goods, whether weapons or ornaments, were iron. Bronze, gold, and silver all but disappear.

Snodgrass argues that the shift to iron grave goods around 1025 was the start of a true iron-using economy. He suggests that central Greeks learned iron-working from Cyprus before 1050, but by 1025 long-distance trade had collapsed. Cut off from tin and copper, central Greeks began to make all their metal objects out of iron, even delicate ornaments. He saw this as but one facet of a broader transformation: as population continued to fall, large areas of Greece were left empty altogether, and new egalitarian, tribal, and perhaps pastoral/nomadic social forms emerged.

This is a powerful thesis, but there are other facets of the evidence which also need to be brought out. The fall in numbers of graves is partly caused by a change in their age structure: few child burials dating to the period after 1025 have be found, and fewer still after 900. The only demographically plausible interpretation of these age structures is that most children were disposed of in Protogeometric through Middle Geometric times in ways which have low archaeological visibility. I have argued that the visibility issue goes further, and that a new ritual system emerged around 1025/1000, imposing order on the chaos of Submycenaean times. The new funerary regime drew boundaries within the community: not only between adults and children, but also among the adults, between an elite and a larger, lower group. The elite represented itself as internally egalitarian, while the lower classes—like the children—received relatively informal disposal. Gender distinctions within the elite were only lightly marked.

There is good evidence for Snodgrass' model of a collapse of trade at the end of the eleventh century, since Greek objects disappear from Near Eastern contexts in this period, and Philistine pressure on the Phoenician cities provides a plausible context. But we must also understand the exclusive use of iron grave goods in ritual context: regardless of economic realities—or perhaps because of them—iron was a potent symbol. It drew lines between the present and the bronze-using past, and between the local soil, the source of iron ore in most parts of Greece, and the broader eastern world from which exotic items and the raw materials for making bronze came. As Hesiod was later to say, this was truly a race of iron.

Protogeometric burials are homogeneous and restrained, as is the rest of the material record, from styles of vase painting to house design. The houses of these years were flimsy structures. As a result, few are known, but there is little variation between most of them, and domestic finds are simple. Evidence for the worship of the gods is still rarer. At Isthmia a handful of pots go back to c. 1000, and a few bronzes at other sites may be as old. A. Mazarakis-Ainian argues that religious rites went on in chiefs' houses, effectively drawing another symbolic line within the community, between an elite group which had access to rituals and a larger group which did not.

As recently as 1980, this would have been an adequate summary of the Early and Middle Protogeometric evidence; but in 1981 new finds from Lefkandi Toumba changed the picture. Some time between 1000 and 950 B.C., a man's cremated bones were placed in a twelfth-century Cypriot bronze amphora, along with his weapons. Next to him was a female inhumation, decked out in gold jewelry. One piece was already a thousand years old when buried, and came from Babylon. An adjacent shaft held four horses. Over the graves was a giant krater and a fifty-meter long apsidal building. The building was deliberately filled in and converted into a tumulus.

Some archaeologists claim that these finds destroy the image of this period as a 'Dark Age,' but saying this means ignoring the other 99% of the archaeological record. However, those who defend the traditional Dark Age model have had trouble explaining the Lefkandi evidence. The most important thing about these finds is not that they are just richer than contemporary burials: rather, their symbolism turns on its head everything that we see in the rest of central Greece. Where other burials are inward-turned and homogeneous, cutting the present off from the past, and the Aegean off from the Near East, these graves do just the opposite. The offerings archaize and orientalize, linking the dead to a lost past and a grander, wider world. The rituals represented these two people as breaching conventional constructions of time and space.

Who could do such a thing? The excavators hinted at the answer in their initial report, calling the dead man 'the hero of Lefkandi.' This package of rites—cremation in a metal urn, weapons, horse sacrifice, the grave mound—was associated with the concept of the hero for the next millennium. Its parallels with Homeric heroic funerals (especially *Il.* 23.108–261) are well known. It was perhaps in the turbulent years around 1000 B.C., when every aspect of ritual was changing, that the Greek concept of the hero crystallized, as the mirror image of the present as a sadly declined race of iron. The concept of a vanished time when heroes walked the earth would have given central Greeks a usable past, making sense of the giant ruins which surrounded them. As in later times, a handful of men could show in death that they too merited semi-divine status, being heroized in their funerals. Such a system of myth and ritual was perhaps central to the new 'Dark Age' order.

Early and Middle Geometric (c. 900–750 B.C.)[14]

This Protogeometric order fragmented by 900 B.C. According to the Old Testament (1 Kings 9:10), Tyrian trade revived under Hiram I (969–936 B.C.). Phoenicians began sailing to the west Mediterranean, coming into the Aegean along the way.

Central Greek grave goods escalated at the end of Protogeometric, with bronzes becoming common again. At Lefkandi a sequence of rich graves in the Toumba cemetery began after the hero burials, probably around 950, and continued until c. 825. Near Eastern objects were deposited in these graves well before 900; at Athens, Argos, Tiryns, and other sites imports appear in quantity slightly later.

There were important changes in death-rituals around 900. The age structure contracted further, hardening adult/child distinctions. J. Whitley suggests that Athenians now selected even the decoration on the pots which they put in graves with a view to symbolic statements about the status of the dead. The old system of grave goods emphasizing the locality and the present weakened, and offerings reconnected the dead with the wider world and the past. By 900, a series of burials from Naxos to Vranezi included heirlooms, and echoed elements of the Lefkandi heroic rites.

Settlement expanded across the Aegean around 900. Few sites in the islands or Ionia have earlier evidence. Euboean pottery characterizes the new sites in the north Aegean, and Attic those in the south. At the Atticizing sites houses are more prominent than graves, and there were tentative experiments with domestic space, including rectilinear houses and substantial town walls. This anticipated what was to happen all over central Greece 150 years later.

The worship of the gods also began to change. Finds appear for the first time at a series of open-air shrines. The new Cycladic sites

[14] Pottery: Whitley (1991b). Naxos: Lambrinoudakis (1988). Koukounaries: Schilardi (1988). Vranezi: *Praktika* 1904, 39–40; 1907, 109; *AE* 1985, 57–84. Al Mina: Boardman (1990). Kearsley (1995) suggests that the Greek finds at Al Mina only begin c. 750.

at Koukounaries and Minoa had shrines from their first days. However, the deposits were very modest, with no metal. Even the few potsherds found may be residues from sacred meals rather than votives.

Grave goods peaked around 850, and then stability returned. This is sometimes interpreted as a break in contacts with the east, but other evidence shows that trade intensified after 825. At Al Mina on the Syrian coast, Euboean pottery was common by 800. If this was not a Greek trading post, then Syrian merchants were in close contact with the Aegean. Corinthian and Euboean pottery also appears in Italy by 800. Central Greeks were in contact with the outside world, but chose not to put imports in their graves and sanctuaries. In the early eighth century, something of the stability of the tenth-century order had been restored.

Late Geometric (c. 750–700 B.C.)[15]

This stability was short-lived. The whole Mediterranean world changed dramatically around 750. There is a huge increase in evidence; at Athens, Late Geometric burials are seven times as common as those of the earlier Iron Age. Snodgrass argued that this shows that population grew at about 4% per annum, roughly as fast as populations have ever been known to grow. He linked this increase to a shift from pastoralism to arable farming, and suggested that it triggered political centralization, more intense warfare, and the emergence of the cultural forms we associate with the city-state.

The population increase may have been exaggerated: child burials reappear after 750, cutting the growth rate in half. I have argued

[15] Athenian burial and demography: Snodgrass (1977); (1980) 20–24; (1987) 170–210; I. Morris (1987); (forthcoming) Ch. 5; '*Burial and Ancient Society* After Ten Years,' in R. Étienne, J.-F. Salles, and M.-T. Le Dinahet, eds., *Nécropoles et sociétés antiques* (Lyon, forthcoming); Whitley (1991b); S. Houby-Nielsen, 'Interaction Between Chieftains and Citizens? 7th Cent. B.C. Burial Customs in Athens,' *Acta Hyperborea* 4 (1992) 343–74; '"Burial Language" in Archaic and Classical Kerameikos,' *Proceedings of the Danish Institute at Athens* 1 (1995) 129–91. Sanctuaries: de Polignac (1995); Hägg et al., eds. (1988). Ephesus: *ÖJh* 58 (1988) 1–38; 63 (1994) 30–39. Iria: *AE* 1992, 201–216. Ayia Irini: M. E. Caskey, 'Ayia Irini, Kea: The Terracotta Statues and the Cult in the Temple,' in Hägg and Marinatos, eds. (1981) 127–35. Megara Hyblaea: Vallet and Villard (1976). Zagora: Cambitoglou et al. (1971); (1988); Cambitoglou (1981). Pithekoussai: *Expedition* 14 (1972) 34–39. Miletus: *IM* 23/24 (1973/74) 68–89; 29 (1979) 115–37; 37 (1987) 7–13; 49 (1990) 40–48; 42 (1992) 100–104; G. Kleiner, *Die Ruinen von Milet* (Berlin 1967). Domestic space and gender: see particularly D. Cohen, *Law, Sexuality, and Society: The Enforcement of Morals in Classical Athens* (Cambridge, 1991); L. Nevett, 'Gender relations in the classical Greek household,' *BSA* 90 (1995) 363–81. Tomb cult: I. Morris (1988); Antonaccio (1995).

that the reduction of the ritual distinctions between old and young was only part of a broader collapse of funerary distinctions, with the elite/commoner boundary also vanishing. The Late Geometric graves would thus represent a broader cross-section of the status structure than in the earlier Iron Age, as well as a broader cross-section of the age structure. At first grave goods and monuments escalated, perhaps as a way to preserve distinctions within the changing ritual order, but by 700 spending declined. Intramural burial virtually disappeared, and by the end of the eighth century, most sites had large, homogeneous, and poor 'citizen cemeteries' spreading along the roads leading out of town.

These cemeteries were part of a new spatial order, defining the Archaic city-state. The worship of the gods changed even more drastically. Suddenly, every village had its own sanctuary, usually with a stone altar and walls marking it off as a special space, and often with a temple too. Practices changed: even at small shrines, tens of thousands of pots were dedicated, and by 700 often expensive metal objects too. Most poleis set up two big sanctuaries, one at the town center, and one on a frontier, defining the community's spatial limits. These could be very impressive. *Hekatompeda*, hundred-foot-long temples, appeared by 700, and monumental all-stone temples by 650. A vast amount of wealth was drained into religious architecture. Some sites had spectacular votives, including thousands of bronzes and impressive Near Eastern and Egyptian objects. Weapons, rich jewelry, and Near Eastern imports disappeared from central Greek graves at just the time that they became common in sanctuaries, and Snodgrass ([1980] 54) has argued that 'There is a big social change with the redirection of attention towards the communal sanctuary and away from the individual grave.'

Some eighth-century sanctuaries may have been sacred across the whole Iron Age. At Ephesus and Iria on Naxos there are hints of continuous activity, but in most cases where temples stood above Bronze Age shrines material evidence breaks off by 1100, and there is a stratigraphic gap until 900 or later. Ayia Irini on Kea is an intriguing case. Here, the head of a Mycenaean figurine was used as a cult image in the sixth century, while the body lay sealed in a twelfth-century layer. There are many possible explanations for these finds, but the most economical is that cult continued across the eleventh and tenth centuries, but in forms which left few material traces, only to change drastically around 750.

The space of the living was transformed just as much as the spaces of the dead and the gods. At Megara Hyblaea, a colony founded in Sicily in 728, the settlers left an open space in the center of the town for an agora. For the first time, circuit walls become common around 700, protecting settlements against attack but also marking them off from the countryside. The most profound changes came within settlements. Multi-room, rectilinear houses focused on internal courtyards replaced the old Dark Age curvilinear single-room houses. At Zagora, the process was almost complete before 700, and in the Euboean colony of Pithekoussai an oval hut was rebuilt as a rectilinear house around 725. At Miletus, oval huts continued alongside more complex structures in the seventh century, but here too one hut was rebuilt as a rectangular house before 650, and by 600 the shift to courtyard houses was complete.

The courtyard house was an important innovation. To live among such closed-in houses, which could only be entered through a narrow door onto the street, was a different experience from the open space of a Dark Age village. This may have been most important in gender ideologies: in later literature the enclosed, dark, inner rooms of a house were associated with the female and opposed to the open, light, public spaces of male citizens.

Yet another spatial transformation was the collapse of distance. Thucydides (1.13) claimed that the trireme was invented around 700,[16] and we see a huge increase in finds of Greek pottery in other parts of the Mediterranean. Thucydides (6.3–5) also dates the first colony in Sicily to 733, and cross-dating with Egypt roughly confirms this. Thousands of Greeks emigrated between 750 and 700, which supports the picture of rapid population growth. Colonization probably played a key part in the feverish social experiments of these years.

A reordering of time paralleled this reordering of space. Another Near Eastern import, writing, provided new ways to fix information across time, and was crucial to the formation of the epics themselves (Powell, this vol.). Some Semiticists argue that 'the alphabet' was invented as early as the eleventh century; there is no direct evidence for this, but even if such claims prove to be correct, there was nevertheless a drastic change in the use of writing in Greece after 750. After more than four centuries in which no example of writing

[16] H. T. Wallinga, *Ships and Sea Power Before the Great Persian War* (Brussels, 1993) disputes Thucydides' statement.

entered the archaeological record, suddenly writing is everywhere, on potsherds and stone. At the very least, there was a massive widening of the uses of writing around 750. New art styles, again with Near Eastern prototypes, were used to portray what seem to be heroizing scenes (see Snodgrass, this vol.), and some people began to leave offerings at Bronze Age tombs. There are heated debates over what exactly eighth-century Greeks thought they were doing, but there can be no doubt that the evidence points to a tremendous new interest in the past, with the epics as the most important expression.

This social revolution—no other expression does justice to the breadth and depth of the changes—may have had economic causes, although so far there is little concrete archaeological evidence to support Snodgrass' suggestion of a shift toward more intensive arable farming. But however we interpret the details, we cannot doubt that in the second half of the eighth century the old Dark Age order collapsed. No two regions of central Greece experienced this in precisely the same way: Boeotia and Ionia, for example, only followed in some of the features described above; and Athens may even have rejected the new developments altogether after 700. But nonetheless, Iron Age society was permanently transformed. The world of the city-states had been created, a world of farmer-citizens unlike anything we find in the rest of the Iron Age Mediterranean.

Western Greece

Chronology

There is little agreement on the absolute dates in the west, or on its cross-links with the Aegean. I divide the evidence into three broad phases.

Early Dark Age (c. 1200–1000)[17]

Messenia had been one of the core areas of the Mycenaean world, and suffered a huge population decline after 1200. Pylos remained

[17] Pylos: M. R. Popham, 'Pylos: Reflections on the Date of its Destruction and on its Iron Age Reoccupation,' *OJA* 10 (1991) 315–24. Kephallenia/Achaea: Snodgrass (1971) 211. Laganidia: *Ergon* 1987, 88–91; 1988, 24–26. Amphikleia: *AD* 26:2 (1971)

occupied, but otherwise settlement apparently contracted to just three clusters of villages. There was emigration to Achaea and the Ionian islands, which became important centers in the twelfth century. Collective burial continued, though usually in small tholoi rather than in chamber tombs, and the pattern varied from place to place. Chamber tombs remained the norm into the tenth century on Kephallenia, in Achaea, at Laganidia in Elis, and at Phthiotian sites like Amphikleia and Elateia, but individual cist graves appeared perhaps as early as 1000 at Elis and Marmara, grouped under large mounds at the latter site. Dakoronia (1987) interprets these mounds as evidence for an invasion from the northwest Greece or the Balkans. Generally, there was a shift toward pithos burial for adults, which remained typically west Greek until Hellenistic times.

There is little true Submycenaean or Protogeometric pottery in the west. Plainer wares, normally simply called 'Dark Age,' were favored. Little iron is known till 900, and even the bronzes seem typologically backward. Snodgrass argued that the west, like central Greece, was cut off from the outside world around 1025, but did not go over to an iron-based economy (or symbolic order), instead recycling older bronzes for more than a century.

Overall, with the partial exception of Messenia, west Greek culture diverged rapidly from the Aegean after 1100. At Kynos Livanaton in Locris, Late Helladic IIIC buildings continued in use through Submycenaean times, but even here the settlement was abandoned by 1000. Poor imitations of Mycenaean lifestyles may have survived in the Ionian islands into the tenth century, but the general picture is of a virtually empty landscape.

Middle Dark Age (c. 1000–750)[18]

Burials are rare in tenth-century western Greece, but religious sites become quite common. There may have been continuous worship

231–32. Elateia: *AD* 40:2 (1985) 171; 43:2 (1988) 229–32; 44:2 (1989) 175; 45:2 (1990) 183–84. Elis: *AD* 17:2 (1961/62) 124–26; 19:2 (1964) 180–82; 23:2 (1968) 163. Marmara: Dakoronia (1987). Villages: W. D. E. Coulson, *The Dark Age Pottery of Messenia* (Göteborg, 1986). Kynos: *AD* 41:2 (1986) 68–69; 42:2 (1987) 234; 43:2 (1988) 223–24; 44:2 (1989) 171; 45:2 (1990) 177–78.

[18] Generally, C. A. Morgan (1990). Kalapodi: *AA* 1980, 38–123; 1987, 1–99. Ithaca: *BSA* 35 (1934/35) 43–73; *Praktika* 1992, 200–210; *Ergon* 1995, 63–67. Olympia: Morgan (1990) 57–105. Thermon: *AE* 1990, 191–200; *Praktika* 1992, 88–128; *Ergon* 1993, 44–56; 1994, 43–49; 1995, 36–42. Kombothekra: *AM* 96 (1981) 25–71. Aegira: *AAA*

from the Bronze Age through Archaic times and beyond at Kalapodi, Ithaca, and Olympia, but overall, few of the sites have a Mycenaean predecessor. C. A. Morgan sees these shrines as meeting places for local chiefs leading small, shifting groups. The only site which may have religious architecture is Thermon.

Olympia probably stood out from the beginning. Its early votives consist largely of bronzes; pottery is rare until 700. Bronze figurines and some jewelry were being dedicated by 950, and tripods probably by 850. The preference for bronze is paralleled at Kombothekra, Polis cave on Ithaca, and Aegira. But while other sites attracted only local offerings, Olympia always received Argive bronzes, and perhaps Argive participants in its festivals.

Messenia remains unusual. No early sanctuaries are known, except for Akovitika, near the border with Laconia. However, at Nichoria apsidal houses like those from central Greece have been found. The large Unit IV–1 was used as a house through the tenth and ninth centuries, and perhaps also for a chiefly cult of the kind Mazarakis postulates for central Greece.

Burial changed little, although iron grave goods appear after 900. The most interesting cemeteries are at the eastern edge of the region, in Locris. Pithos and cist graves with gold and rich bronzes have been found at Tragana and Atalandi. In this region central and western Greek customs mixed. Graves at Medeon contain much Corinthian pottery. It seems likely that Corinthians were regularly sailing down the Gulf from 900 on.

Late Geometric (c. 750–700)[19]

After 750, western Greece moved into the Aegean orbit. Olympia and Delphi became panhellenic sanctuaries. The Olympic victor lists mention only local athletes at this time, but Aegean, Near Eastern, Balkan, and Italian objects were being dedicated. The oracle at Delphi

11 (1978) 152. Akovitika: *AAA* 2 (1969) 352–57. Nichoria: McDonald et al. (1983), with *Op Ath* 17 (1990) 33–50; 19 (1992) 75–84. Tragana: *AD* 36:1 (1981) 1–57; 41:2 (1986) 74; 42:2 (1987) 235–38. Atalandi: *AD* 40:2 (1985) 165–67; 42:2 (1987) 226–28. Medeon: C. Vatin, *Médéon de Phocide* (Paris, 1969).

[19] Tegea: *AR* 1991/92, 19–20; 1992/93, 22–23; 1993/94, 18; *Op Ath* 20 (1994) 89–141, and general discussion of Arcadian sanctuaries in M. Voyatzis, 'Geometric Arcadia,' in C. Morris, ed., *Klados* (London, 1995) 271–83. Pharai: *AD* 20:3 (1965) 207. Anavra: *AD* 32:2 (1977) 104–105. Tragana: see n. 18 above. Sparta: R. Dawkins, ed., *Artemis Orthia* (London, 1929); *AR* 1976/77, 24–42.

now played a major role in central Greek decision-making. Visitors from central Greek states were probably common. As in central Greece, sanctuaries proliferated after 750, and votives got richer. Religious architecture remains rare, but recent work at Tegea suggests that early diggers may have missed traces of flimsy buildings. Apart from Messenia, where the first known sanctuary is at Pharai around 700, the spread of evidence for cult seems to extend an older pattern rather than breaking with it radically, as in the Aegean.

Burials become more common only in the seventh century. Customs vary, but adult inhumation in pithoi is popular at many sites. This rite and the increase in numbers of warrior graves after 700 contrast with central Greece. Locrian tombs are again rich; at Anavra, 22 LG graves yielded 116 bronzes, and pithos gr. Π-9 at Tragana (c. 750 B.C.) contained another fifty bronzes, one of them a bowl inscribed *Muzawi* in Neo-Hittite.

Messenian peculiarities continued. Like central Greece, but unlike the rest of the west, offerings began at Mycenaean tombs around 750. There was a general shift in settlement patterns after 750, perhaps as a result of the Spartan conquest (traditionally c. 730–710). Nichoria was abandoned. There is little evidence from Sparta itself in the Dark Age. Finds begin c. 900 in the sanctuaries at Amyklai and Artemis Orthia, and both have late eighth-century monumental buildings, perhaps paid for by the Messenian War. Worship of Helen began at the Menelaion by 700; but otherwise there are few finds until the late seventh century.

Except for the transformation of Olympia and Delphi, which may have had more to do with central- than with west-Greek dynamics, the eighth-century changes in the west are less striking than those in Aegean Greece.

Northern Greece

Chronology

Again, problems are acute. Absolute dates suggested by different archaeologists for some of the tombs at Vergina vary by several centuries. As a result, I treat the whole period down to the introduction of Late Geometric as a single phase.

Early Iron Age (c. 1200–750 B.C.)[20]

The northern frontier of Mycenaean culture seems to have been around Mt. Olympus. Imitation Mycenaean pottery is found at Assiros and Kastanas until well after 1200. K. A. Wardle suggests that the fall of the Greek palaces affected the local economies; but overall, Macedonian material is strongly Balkan.

As in Italy, the Mediterranean/central European cultural frontier retreated to the south after 1200. Thessaly became a buffer zone, with its own Protogeometric style, but with typically Balkan forms like the cutaway-necked jug occurring as far south as Iolkos. Thessalian burials were varied, and contained both cremations and inhumations. Tholos tombs had been common here in Mycenaean times, and miniature versions continued across the Iron Age. At Stavros chamber tombs continued during Protogeometric times. But cists (single or multiple) were also common, used across the whole Dark Age at Nea Ionia and Stylis. A group of tenth-century cairns was excavated at Halos, but on the whole large mounds are rare. However, a salvage excavation in 1990 provides a salutary reminder of just how quickly the picture can change in such a little-known region. A huge mound (27 meters in diameter, and preserved 5 meters high) at Ayioi Theodoroi near Karditsa turned out to be covering a large tholos tomb (diameter 5.5 m., height 4.1 m.) containing iron weapons and pottery spanning at least 200 years of the Protogeometric and Geometric periods.

Further north, mounds were common. In Epirus, cist graves were

[20] Mt. Olympus: *AD* 40:2 (1985) 240–43; *AEMTh* 1 (1987) 201–208; 2 (1988) 173–80. Assiros: *BSA* 75 (1980); 82 (1987) 313–29; 83 (1988) 375–87; 84 (1989) 447–63. Kastanas: B. Hänsel, *Kastanas. Die Grabung und die Baubefunde* (2 vols., Berlin, 1989). Iolkos: E. Sipsie-Eschbach, *Die protogeometrische Keramik aus Iolkos in Thessalien* (Berlin, 1991). Stavros: *AD* 33:2 (1978) 136–37. Nea Ionia: *AD* 18:2 (1963) 140–41; 36:3 (1981) 252; 39:2 (1984) 140–42; 42:2 (1987) 254. Stylis: *AAA* 15 (1982) 261–65; *AD* 36:2 (1981) 212–14; 38:2 (1983) 167–68. Halos: *BSA* 18 (1918) 1–30. Ayioi Theodoroi: *AD* 45:2 (1990) 204–205. Kalbaki: *AE* 1956, 114–15. Kato Meropi: *AD* 35:2 (1980) 303–304; 36:3 (1981) 272–73; 37:3 (1982) 259; 38:3 (1983) 229–30; 43:2 (1988) 302–304. Vergina: *AD* 17.1 (1961/62) 218–88; 18:2 (1963) 217–32; 25:3 (1970) 395–96; 26:3 (1971) 411–12; *PZ* 64 (1989) 86–151; M. Andronikos, *Vergina* I (Athens, 1969). Pateli: N. G. L. Hammond, *A History of Macedonia* I (Oxford, 1972) 340–43. Phiki: *AAA* 17 (1984) 74–87. Chalcidice generally, Snodgrass (1994); contra, Papadopoulos (1996). Torone: *Praktika* 1981, 38; 1982, 73–77; 1984, 44–50. Mende: *AEMTh* 1 (1987) 281; 2 (1988) 331–35; 3 (1989) 414–16; 4 (1990) 411–23. Koukos: *AEMTh* 1 (1987) 284–85; 2 (1988) 357–70; 3 (1989) 425–38. Arta: *ASAA* 60 (1982) 78–89. Vitsa: I. Vokotopoulou, *Vitsa* (3 vols., Athens, 1986).

grouped under large tumuli at Kalbaki and Kato Meropi. The earliest may pre-date 1200 (although the chronology is poor), and some archaeologists use the cists to trace an invasion from northwest Greece into the Aegean in the eleventh century. In Macedonia, more than 350 Early Iron Age graves have been found at Vergina, mostly under large mounds. Cists and pithoi were normal here. Further east, in Thrace, megalithic tombs may have continued through the Iron Age, but the problems of dating are even more acute.

Some graves at Vergina and Pateli are very rich in bronzes. Iron was used for weapons from c. 1000, but (unlike central Greece) bronze remained in use for ornaments. Snodgrass suggests that Macedonia kept up contact with Balkan metal sources. This also seems to be true of Thessaly, where two particularly rich graves of c. 1000–950 have been found at Phiki.

North of Thessaly there is generally little evidence for contacts with central Greece. The great exception is Chalcidice, where recent digs have transformed the picture, finding Athenian-style Submycenaean and Protogeometric pots at Torone, and Euboean-style pottery spanning the Dark Age at Mende. These were probably twelfth-century refuge sites, perhaps with new Euboean settlers arriving in Late Protogeometric, when Euboean pottery replaces Athenian at Torone, and appears at Koukos. A few Athenian and Euboean pots of c. 900 have turned up near the Macedonian coast, but the Chalcidian sites had very little impact on the hinterland. The villages at Assiros and Kastanas were more complex than anything known in the Aegean. In Epirus, a few Corinthian pots reached Arta by 800, and were buried in graves at Vitsa.

Late Geometric (c. 750–700 B.C.)[21]

Thessaly remained a transitional zone. It had its own Late Geometric style, and the number and wealth of graves increased c. 750,

[21] Nea Ionia: see n. 20 above. Krannon (Ayios Yeoryios Larisis): *AAA* 11 (1978) 156–82; *AD* 34:2 (1979) 220; 38:2 (1983) 203–204, 208–11; 39:2 (1984) 150–51; 42:2 (1987) 274–76. Iolkos: *Praktika* 1915, 157–59. Thessalian bronzes from sanctuaries: K. Kilian, *Fibeln in Thessalien von der mykenischen bis um archaischen Zeit* (Munich, 1975 [Prähistorische Bronzefunde 14.2]). Pherai temple: *Praktika* 1992/24, 107. Other possible early temples: *Praktika* 1910, 189, 252–58; 1925/26, 39–41. Corcyra graves: *AD* 17:2 (1961/62) 204–205; 20:3 (1965) 398; 23:3 (1968) 314; 24:3 (1969) 260–62; 25:3 (1970) 323–25; 27:3 (1972) 480–81; 35:3 (1980) 350–51, 355; 38:3 (1983) 258–61; 41:2 (1986) 125; 42:2 (1987) 341. Mon Repos: *AD* 18:3 (1963) 161–80; 19:4

especially at Nea Ionia. However, there was no decline in grave wealth after 700, and the richest warrior burials come from Archaic chamber tombs near Krannon and at Iolkos, filled with cremations in urns. Some sanctuaries have a few bronzes going back to 900, but huge numbers were dedicated beginning around 700. Only Pherai has definite traces of a temple, but once again clumsy digging in the early years of this century may account for this.

Epirote contacts with the Aegean strengthened. The best evidence is from Vitsa, perched 1000 meters above sea level, and perhaps a base for transhumant pastoralists. Here Corinthian pots were concentrated in a few rich graves, while at Arta, near the coast, they were widely distributed in the settlement. Imports were probably more valued in the mountains. At Dodona, Corinthian bronzes and a single Late Geometric sherd appear after 750. Corinthian influence on the coast may have been strong, especially after the colonization of Corcyra in 733 (possibly after expelling an earlier Euboean colony). The settlers brought central Greek practices with them. Only four out of roughly 100 published eighth- and seventh-century graves on Corcyra have bronzes, while the sanctuary at Mon Repos has rich votives and a monumental temple.

But Macedonia remained strongly Balkan. Some Late Geometric pottery is found along the coasts, but only a handful of Corinthian bronzes comes from inland. The cemeteries at Vergina and Pateli give the impression of powerful, rich, and warlike aristocracies. These burials increase in numbers and wealth in the eighth century and decline in the seventh century, paralleling trends in central Greece; but the many unprovenanced seventh-century bronzes strongly suggest that rich burials continued. Macedonian society was very different from the Aegean city-states. There is no clear evidence for hierarchy at Kastanas and Assiros, but these were small villages. Even in the eighth century, there is little evidence for Macedonian religion.

Except for narrow coastal strips in Chalcidice, Epirus, and (after the foundations of Thasos and Abdera) Thrace, the north remained distinct from the Aegean, although that was to change in Archaic times.

(1964) 317–28; 20:3 (1965) 381–91; 21:3 (1966) 317–21; 22:3 (1967) 360–66; 23:3 (1968) 303–313; 32:2 (1977) 182. Bronzes: *PZ* 50 (1975) 84–103; J. Bouzek, *Graeco-Macedonian Bronzes* (Prague, 1973).

Crete

Chronology

Here the evidence is better, although the overlaps between Late Protogeometric, Protogeometric B, and the Geometric styles cause confusion, and the east and central Cretan styles may have developed at different rates.

Late Minoan IIIC (c. 1200–1050 B.C.)[22]

The destructions of 1200 B.C. violently disturbed Cretan settlement. Most thirteenth-century sites were abandoned. In east Crete, there was a major shift toward remote mountain-top sites. These varied greatly: Karphi had a population of several hundreds, while Khalasmeno and Katalimata had only a few families. Until recently, it was taken for granted that population fell drastically; but in the light of the large number of refuge sites now known, the dominant demographic trend may in fact have been relocation rather than decline. In central Crete, the finds still suggest a demographic collapse, but some lowland sites survived. Knossos perhaps never fell below 1,000 residents, and Phaistos too remained a small town. In west Crete, the palace at Chania may have survived until 1150, but before 1100 the area lost its population. Only two refuge sites are known. The Dark Age was probably darker here than anywhere else on the island.

Subminoan/Protogeometric (c. 1050–800 B.C.)[23]

Despite the profundity of the twelfth-century upheavals, continuities were much stronger on Crete than in the Aegean. House forms changed little. Even at the remote site of Karphi, structures are

---

[22] Karphi: *BSA* 38 (1937/38) 57–145. Other refuge sites: *Hesperia* 92 (1993) 229–30, 303–337; *BSA* 89 (1994) 235–68. Knossos: S. Hood and D. Smyth, *An Archaeological Survey of the Knossos Area* (London, 1981, British School at Athens Supp. Vol. 14).

[23] Kastro: *Hesperia* 64 (1995) 101–107. Siteia: *AD* 29:4 (1973/74) 931–32; 31:3 (1976) 381–82; 32:3 (1977) 336–38; 33:3 (1978) 390–92. Vronda: *Hesperia* 52 (1983) 389–409. Teke: *Kadmos* 18 (1979) 89–93. Idaean Cave: E. Kunze, *Kretisches Bronzereliefs* (Stuttgart, 1931); J. Boardman, *The Cretan Collection at Oxford* (Oxford, 1961); *Praktika* 1983, 415–500. Kato Symi: A. Kanta, 'Cult, Continuity and the Evidence

recognizably Minoan, and Building G at Kavousi Kastro may have been occupied without a break from the twelfth century until the mid-eighth. Before 1000, the populations of many of the east Cretan refuge sites were drifting back toward lower ground.

Cretans continued to bury their dead collectively in chamber or small tholos tombs until about 600. During the tenth century urn cremation (with the urns collected in chamber tombs) replaced inhumation in central Crete, although in east Crete inhumation remained normal at Siteia and Vronda into the ninth century. Tombs were more varied and often richer than those on the mainland in this period, although between c. 1050 and 925 Near Eastern imports declined, as did finds of Cretan objects in Cyprus and the Levant. Grave goods revived around 900, and a tomb at Teke near Knossos even included a bronze bowl with a Phoenician inscription on it.

Religion also shows significant continuities. Activity went on without a break in the Idaean cave and at Kato Symi Viannou from Neolithic into Archaic times, and changes in practice were much less drastic than on the mainland. Religious iconography likewise shows some remarkable continuities. At Kommos, however, the small Temple B of the early ninth century contained a tripillar shrine so like Levantine examples that it is hard to avoid the conclusion that it was built by or for Phoenician sailors who used Kommos as a stopping point on their way to the west Mediterranean.

Cretan pottery was more conservative than mainland styles. Protogeometric only made headway in the late tenth century, and clearly Subminoan styles survived in some areas into the late ninth. The late-ninth century Protogeometric B style was in part a Minoan revival and in part an adaptation of Near Eastern influences.

Ninth-century Cretan culture was less inward-turned than that of central Greece. Cretan material culture proclaimed connections with the past and openness to outside influence. Athenians, Argives, and Euboeans used eastern imports and materials as grave goods between about 925 and 825; but Cretans used them much more, in sanctuaries as well as cemeteries, and their interest continued to grow after 825. Boardman argues that Levantine craftsmen settled at Knossos by 800. Cretan society seems more varied than that of the mainland, and the limited evidence for housing suggests a more complex hierarchy.

---

of Pottery at the Sanctuary of Syme Viannou, Crete,' in Musti et al., eds. (1991) 479–505. Kommos: *AJA* 93 (1989) 165–83.

The eighth century[24]

Settlements and burials multiply after 750, and new sites appear in west Crete. As in central Greece, grave goods are richer, but Near Eastern objects are much more common in Crete, and warrior burials continue down to 600. Urn cremation in chamber tombs remained normal, although new work at Vronda reveals a more complex burial regime. One funeral at Eleutherna may even have involved human sacrifice.

New sanctuaries appeared, and at older sites like the Idaean cave and Kato Symi the number of votives (particularly bronzes) increased. By 700, stone temples had been built at Prinias, Dreros, and Gortyn. This parallels central Greek changes, but as in western Greece, Cretan developments were more an expansion of an older system than a radical break with the past. The gods had been given bronzes throughout the Iron Age, albeit in smaller numbers; and stone temples were built in the tenth century not just at Kommos but also at Smari, and perhaps even earlier at some of refuge sites. Evidence for Near Eastern settlers on Crete in the late eighth century is strong.

Crete shared in some Aegean trends, but overall its Iron Age was very different. Continuities from the Bronze Age were strong, and there was great openness to the east. There were few significant Mycenaean survivals in central Greece after 1000, and even in outlying areas like Ithaca, these elements disappear in the tenth century. But Crete enjoyed something of a Minoan revival in the ninth century; and even the eighth-century changes had a Minoan coloring.

Conclusion

Iron Age society changed rapidly, with particularly intense transformations in the years 1025–1000, 925–850, and 750–700; and the differences between the four regions which I identify are just as striking as their similarities. Although Homer was clearly aware of eighth-

[24] Vronda: *Hesperia* 55 (1986) 376–84; 57 (1988) 283–98; 60 (1991) 152–67; 64 (1995) 74–88. Eleutherna: N. Stambolidis, *Elefthema* I (Athens, 1993); II (Athens, 1994); 'Homer and the Cremation Burials of Eleutherna,' in Crielaard, ed. (1995) 289–308. Prinias/Dreros: I. Beyer, *Die Tempel von Dreros und Prinias A* (Freiburg, 1976). Gortyn: G. Rizza and V. Scrinari, *Il santuario sull' acropoli di Gortina* I (Rome, 1978). Smari: *AAA* 13 (1980) 44–53.

century developments in material culture,[25] it has not proved possible to identify a single region and period with a material culture exactly like that in the epics. Most archaeologists have reacted like J. N. Coldstream in his magisterial survey of the ninth and eighth centuries ([1977] 18): 'Homer we cannot use; his epics, set in the heroic past, are coloured by an amalgam of anachronistic details, accumulated over centuries of oral transmission; thus Homeric society cannot be assigned to any single period.' J. Whitley ([1991a] 344) has also emphasized how the regionalism of the record should reinforce this skepticism, suggesting that 'Homeric society indeed is an amalgam, a poetic conflation of a number of diverse, *contemporary* societies' (emphasis added). For him, as well as dealing with chronological layering, 'the problem [is] of sifting out those aspects which may refer to one type of society, and those which refer to another.'

These are important observations, but both approaches seem to me to lose sight of the fact that the epics and the material record were both produced by real people, acting in pursuit of their own goals in a period of dramatic change. They represent the relationships between verbal and non-verbal culture as being mechanical: for Coldstream and Whitley, and for many other archaeologists (and historians), Homer is a mirror to an external materiality, but a defective one. Our job is then to smooth out his distorting surface to produce a clear reflection of the realities of Homer's world. Against these views, I would insist that the epic was not some kind of bad history. It was a poetic creation, what *some* eighth-century Greeks thought the heroic world *ought* to have been like. I suggested above that in the rituals which produced the archaeological record, Iron Age Greeks manipulated material culture as a non-verbal language through which they debated who they were and where they stood relative to each other, the larger east Mediterranean world, and the lost heroic past. The ritualized performance of epic poetry, although its only material trace is a body of texts refracted through centuries of reworking and copying,[26] was also a key part in this process. The poets described the heroes as using specific kinds of objects in order to create desired states of mind among their hearers. In doing so, they doubtless drew on everyday experience, but they shaped this to suit their own artistic ends.

---

[25] See the detailed survey in Crielaard (1995).

[26] A fact captured nicely by J. M. Foley's phrase (this vol.) 'oral-derived text.'

G. Nagy ([1990a] 10) suggests that Homer 'synthesizes the diverse traditions of each major city-state into a unified pan-Hellenic model that suits the ideology of the polis in general, but without being restricted to the ideology of any one polis in particular.' Similarly, Homer uses objects—some contemporary, some ancient, some invented—to evoke the past in the present, creating an 'epic distance.' Objects were as manipulable as language, religion, and the laws of physics, and there is no point in trying to pull Homer's picture apart, reassembling it in 'layers' which can then be correlated with the artifacts found in discrete archaeological strata. We should rather think of the epics themselves as artifacts—arguably the most important, for modern classicists as for ancient Greeks—generated in the great upheavals of the eighth century. The poems and the archaeological record can only be properly understood when read alongside each other and woven together, as remnants of competing eighth-century efforts at self-fashioning, out of which classical Greek civilization was created.

Anthony Snodgrass

HOMER AND GREEK ART

Ever since an approximate historical setting was established for the final form of the Homeric poems, it has been natural to look for comparisons with other phenomena of the same era, and especially with the visual arts. Today there is a long-standing consensus that, in art-historical terms, that setting is to be placed within the epoch of the Geometric style, and more specifically toward its latter end.

Geometric art has therefore been the favored field for this kind of comparative study; but that is not the whole story. For such study may have many different goals: to measure the impact of the poems on Greek society, either initially or in the longer term; to add precision to the dating of the poems; to interpret the works of art in the light of the poems; to discern common structures in the literary and artistic creations. Some of these approaches involve extending the investigation to later periods of art as well. Nearly all of them share another assumption, that first place must be given to the better understanding of the poems. Such a priority will come naturally to anyone who knows Homer but, again, it should not be the whole story. It may not be coincidental that one of the most fruitful fields of investigation has been one which to some extent adopts the opposite priority: the study of those passages in Homer that describe or refer to works of art, in the light of the surviving art of the period. It is, for example, a neat and objective confirmation of the relative dating of the *Iliad* and the *Aspis* that the artistic description of the Shield of Achilles in the former suggests an object stylistically earlier than the Shield of Herakles in the latter.[1]

In this chapter, however, I must be selective. I will concentrate on the art of the period which has the best claim to have fallen within the actual lifetime of Homer, the Late Geometric: a conservative choice, but one modified by the adoption of a less traditional aim, that of keeping the literary and the visual elements in more or less equal balance. For the truth is that the well-tried approaches have

---

[1] For this general topic, see Fittschen (1973); Canciani (1984).

been less fruitful than their early exponents must have hoped. They have suffered by sharing a form of positivism that is very familiar in archaeology: the belief that what survives today, because it is all that we have as a basis for inference, must be assumed to have held a place of equal prominence in its own world. In this case there is, on the literary side, every encouragement for that belief: the Homeric poems are part of what survives, and the testimony to their exceptionally influential and prominent position in Greek life, extending far beyond the purely literary sphere, is almost limitless. Yet even here, prominence is not the same thing as near-isolation, which is their position today. Other equally early epic poetry with legendary content (even the surviving work of Hesiod; see Rosen, this vol.) and, above all, other orally-transmitted mythology in non-literary forms, are often forgotten in the urge to match the two surviving epics with the visual material—with the former almost always filling the role of the model, the latter that of the naive imitator. The artistic material too, with much less justification, is regularly assumed to be at least a representative sample and sometimes more, the very cream, of what the Greeks of the age could produce. Thus the stage has been set for the long and, in my view, unsuccessful history of the attempts to identify legendary episodes—if possible, specifically Homeric episodes—in the figure-scenes shown in Geometric art.

But the underlying assumptions could hardly have survived a prolonged and cool reflection on the facts of the case. We know of too many legends that are not contained in the *Iliad* and the *Odyssey*, and we can prove that contemporary artists knew of them too. We can infer, not least from a reading of Homer himself, the existence of other media for artistic representation for which the physical evidence no longer survives. With such material as does survive, we have few reasons for thinking that it occupied a central place in the cultural life of Greece as a whole. Finally, there are chronological questions still open to discussion today: we cannot be so precise in the relative dating of the literary and the artistic evidence that we can always deduce the direction in which a perceived influence was travelling.

Once we acknowledge the fragmentary and, in the case of the artistic material, fortuitous nature of our evidence, it becomes clear that fresh approaches are needed. Instead of 'matching' one class of material with another, we shall do better to concentrate on integrating all of it into a very incomplete picture of the intellectual life of the period. At the most, we may discover what could arouse the enthusiasm of a few scattered and probably socially exclusive groups in different parts of the Greek world, a world that had already grown to the point where two of its communities could be living a thousand miles apart.

We may turn to the comparison of 'Homer' and contemporary 'Greek art,' in the realization that it is going to be difficult to keep the comparison a balanced one. Where Homer was treasured by later Greeks, Geometric art was not; where Homer grew to be a panhellenic figure, the art of Geometric Greece was divided into a number of regional styles which had a limited appeal beyond their own orbit. A further problem arises, in that there is at first sight so great a discrepancy in sophistication between the poetry of Homer and the work of his contemporaries the graphic artists, working mainly but not entirely in the medium of painting in silhouette on vases of the Late Geometric style, that it seems a presumption to compare or link them. To take first just the issue of characterisation: on the one hand, we have a mastery of presentation that uses words and actions to give individuality to even quite minor characters, and at times gives them even their own pattern of speech. On the other, we have the apparently jejune convention of two-dimensional, dark-on-light depiction which seems to allow only of grouping humankind into basic categories: there are men, women and children; within the category of men, warriors and non-warriors; within the category of warriors, winning and losing warriors; but that appears to be as far as characterisation can go. It is hard for these two art-forms reach out and touch each other. The conventional response has been to try to extract specific correspondences of episodes between the poems and the paintings but, as already indicated, that path will not be followed here.

The contrast that I have just drawn is not entirely imaginary; but it is, from one point of view, an unfair one. No one now doubts that Homer was the heir to a very long tradition of poetic composition in the same medium that he used himself. Homer's genius was his own, but what really set him apart from the visual artists was the wealth of pre-existing material which he could re-shape and elaborate in his own style. There were his predecessors, treating of the same or allied topics, and there were the formulae of poetic phrasing which he either took over from them or else invented himself and then used repeatedly. By contrast, the visual artists were only in his lifetime re-inventing a means of representing the human figure in scenes of action. Their art was at a stage of development that epic poetry had passed through generations earlier. But on top of all the inherited skills that Homer could use, there was a new element: the written word (see Powell, this vol.).

The interaction between alphabetic writing and the Homeric epic is admittedly controversial, but we at least know that the recording of hexameter lines was one of the earliest uses to which the new script was put in the Greek world; and that sooner rather than later it was used to record Homer's masterpieces for posterity. By contrast, once again, the uses of the written word in the visual arts were apparently not yet conceived of. Long before the notion arose of giving a title to the complete work of art, the simpler expedient of labelling one or more figures in a composition with their names was adopted, thus adding a second means, together with the action portrayed, to help the spectator read the narrative. But Homer's contemporaries made do without even this modest aid. For about a hundred years, at a time when the use of painted or incised 'caption' inscriptions was both technically and intellectually a possibility, it was avoided: when painted inscriptions do first appear on vases, they are not of this kind. We tend to explain this avoidance, as we do most things in the art of this period, as the result of pure lack of development; to imagine the possibility that it might have been deliberate is to take a first, speculative step toward re-assessing the purposes behind these early compositions.

The introduction of this word, 'composition,' is likewise an opening for one kind of comparison between literature and art. In the visual arts, the word has a rather specialized and specific use. It is a very rough synonym for 'arrangement;' it covers the way in which a painter or sculptor arranges the components of his work. It may include the way in which individual figures are posed, especially if they are on a large scale in relation to the work as a whole; but not, for example, their physiognomy or their coloring. As such, it covers decidedly only a part of the artist's whole range of activity. In literature or in music, by contrast, 'composition' is so absolutely central to the artist's activity that it is often used as a term for his whole art. Nevertheless, in the case of Homer we have special circumstances, as we have already seen. For Homer was presenting characters many of whom would be already familiar to his audience, through either the medium of earlier poetry or that of vernacular legend; the outline of his plots, too, would be a given element shared with his listeners. What 'composition' meant for him, what raised him above all his predecessors and his successors alike, was a matchless skill in filling out these characters and plots through his gift for language, and in adding whole new elements to both. Some characters, mostly minor but conceivably including such a memorable figure as Patroclus in the *Iliad*, we suspect him of having invented himself.

There were limits to what the visual artists could do to match this: we have seen some of the inhibitions under which they labored. The vase-painters chose to follow an austere set of conventions, which we believe were first devised by a single personality, known to specialists as the 'Dipylon Master' and working in Athens in the years around 750 B.C. Neither, at first, did artists in other media make any radical departure from these conventions, for at this time the art of vase-painting in Greece appears to have enjoyed more influence than ever again. Not only was the general principle of silhouette representation taken over from the painted figures on the Geometric vases and, as far as was appropriate, applied to other arts—in three-dimensional compositions, for instance, arrangement into a single plane was adopted, so that a clear profile view predominated; but the actual style of the vase-painter's silhouettes was also widely imitated, with such features as the human torso in the form of an inverted isosceles triangle, or the flaring muzzle of the horse, appearing across a range of different media.[2]

These conventions were, as has been said, austere ones: they prescribed a fairly narrow range of attitudes for the human figure, in which the delineation of the body itself was modified as little as possible. This meant that there was no easy way for one figure to be made distinguishable from others. Yet it would be wrong to conclude that all potential for narrative was thereby excluded. It was still possible to depict distinctive situations, especially those involving a number of figures, in which the relation between the figures gave the whole work a fairly clear narrative content. It was even possible, in principle at least, to make that content unique, not just in a trivial sense of combining details in a way not exactly matched before, but in that of conveying a unique meaning to the onlooker. Even in such a case, 'composition' would still not be achieving quite the aim that it did in Homer's hands, but there are parallels. The term

[2] This important argument was first advanced by Robertson (1951).

'formula' has often been used of Geometric painting as well (cf. Schein, this vol.), to denote the recurrent elements or 'building blocks' with which the artists, like Homer, worked. Just as Homer could compose memorable passages using almost entirely formulaic phrases, so as we shall see the painters could combine their convention-bound figures into memorable scenes.

There is also a different point that could be made about the subjects of the paintings. It has been universally assumed that these are works with a conscious message that the viewer was expected to pick up: that is, works with a 'subject' or implicit 'title.' But suppose that we return to our point about composition, and make a quite different assumption, that 'subject' or 'title' were secondary adjuncts for the artists, and that their prime concern was with composition for its own sake. We could then invoke the parallel of many painters of later millennia, who allocated titles and subjects, almost casually, to compositions which they had already executed. One such painter who is notorious, justifiably or otherwise, for having given subjects to his paintings without apparently modifying them in more than marginal ways, is Claude Gellée, or 'le Lorrain' (1600–1682). An exhibition of his works was mounted in the National Gallery in London in 1994, with the aim of counteracting the view that I have just referred to, by emphasizing 'how important the subjects of his pictures were to the artist and his patrons, and how far they determined the form of his compositions.' But I would still venture the opinion that on many occasions Claude did not let the entitlement of his pictures, with or without the addition of appropriate human figures, distract him from his main aim, of composing one hauntingly beautiful landscape after another.

If the Geometric vase-painters, like Claude and others, were less interested in the subjects of their pictures than in the way that their scenes were composed; if their dominant aim was the effect of the composition as a composition, then not only would this then ally them more closely with Homer and the literary act of composition, but it would profoundly affect the way in we would look at their products. Instead of feeling frustration at our failure to pick up the intended message—and, *a fortiori*, to match it with a story in Homeric or other mythology—we could view and at times admire their figure-scenes as pure exercises in composition. The virtual absence of landscape and background detail, the restricted use of the dimension of depth, and the complete reliance on a simple dark-on-light contrast, are of course severe constraints on the effect that they could achieve with their medium; in this sense, the proper comparison is with line-drawing rather than with landscape painting. Our prime concern is with the figure-scenes, but it must always be remembered that these comprise only a fraction of the painters' output: the greater part of their time was spent in applying the apparently abstract geometric decoration which has given its name to the style of the time, and which covers many complete vases, as well as the subsidiary zones of those which carry figure-scenes. If, as has sometimes been argued, elements of this 'abstract decoration' in fact carried objective connotations, then it is all the more essential to associate the human figures, equally 'geometric' in their own way, with the overall design of the vessel, when we attempt to assess the aims of the artists.

It is time to turn to some examples of their work, which I will present in what is believed to be their approximate chronological order. The Dipylon Master himself painted a funerary scene on a huge mixing-bowl or krater, which stood as a marker over an Athenian grave of about 750 B.C. (Plate 1). There is some independent evidence that bowls of this type were reserved for male graves, and so it is appropriate that here we are shown the lying in state of a deceased male, and that the scenes are of an inherently male content. The dead man lies on the bier, surrounded by adult and juvenile male mourners. The otherwise common rule of a single base-line for the human figures is violated here. Above, on a higher plane, seated female mourners share the same gesture of the hands raised to the head, perhaps tearing at their hair. Other mourners are grouped in 'boxes' at the upper left and upper right. Two prominent chariots drive by, each with a driver and a warrior with a distinctive type of shield that we shall see again repeatedly; a further wheeled vehicle was also probably present in the upper left box, and there are more in the next zone below. A warship is visible under the handle to the right. Much of the representational repertoire of the Geometric painter is already deployed here: man, woman, child, the living and the dead, bier, horse, chariot, ship and an unmistakeable form of shield. What we are seeing is perhaps less how a prominent Athenian was buried, than how he would wish to have been buried: it is an impressive scene, with well over forty participants, and details such as the chariots and the warship are often supposed to be allusions to the man's experience in life. But then we look round the main zone, out of the picture to the left, and we find that there is a rival focus of activity to the standard funerary ritual; for a duel or confrontation is apparently taking place in which a striding figure on the left (we have only the legs) faces a pair of warriors standing very close together in identical pose. To understand this part of the composition, we shall have to look at some better-preserved examples of the theme: for the moment, we must content ourselves with the fact that it is a recurrent theme; that it does offer the artist an unexpected opening for something which I have said was otherwise difficult for him, the creation of a figure or figures that were distinguishable from others; and that the inclusion of this theme may prove hard to reconcile with the orthodox interpretation of this scene as an episode of real life, or rather real death, in contemporary Athens.

Next, an artist from the same circle painted an action scene on a krater of the same purpose (Plate 2), perhaps a little later than the first. Here the picture is preserved in even more fragmentary form, but the action nonetheless appears less intractable to interpretation. In the upper zone, a grim land-battle is taking place: three warriors with rectangular shields are at grips with their enemies, with varying fortunes: one delivers a coup de grace, a second has been shot through the head by an archer, a third is again delivering a death-blow to an opponent with the distinctive shield that we saw in the previous scene, as he falls from a raised platform that is probably a wheeled vehicle, on which are visible the limbs of dead or wounded companions, lying like their stricken counterparts to the left. Below, three more bearers of this type of shield hurry along, with raised left feet, no doubt to join the fray before it is too late. But then, to the left of them, we are brought up short by another apparition: a shieldless warrior again confronts a pair standing close together: this time, a little more of the combatants is visible and the pair look as if their bodies are actually joined together. The theme has made its second appearance, and I would cut short further speculation by showing a third instance (there are fourteen in all in early Greek art), this time painted on a vessel from Argos, not from Athens (Plate 3). Here I think it is hard to doubt any longer that what we are looking at is a pair of Siamese Twins, a conclusion that will seem less outlandish when we take other evidence into account later. But we must also acknowledge the orthodox, or at any rate the skeptical, interpretation, which is that this motif has changed its meaning with the passage of time: the Argive piece is somewhat later, perhaps around 720–710 B.C., and this view would have it that the image had previously been intended to convey nothing more remarkable than two warriors standing side by side, just as we saw horses side by side and overlapping in the first picture, until someone thought to give it a new twist by converting or distorting it into a portrayal of Siamese Twins. I comment no further at this stage.

Our next vase is of a different type, a wine- or water-jug now in the Louvre, whose state of preservation is such that it must have been buried actually within an Athenian grave of perhaps 730 B.C (Plate 4). It has been known for a long time, but it had to wait until 1961 before the scene on it was given a really convincing interpretation.[3] Fifteen human figures and one still unexplained apparition are shown. Four of them—numbers 3, 6, 11 and 13 in the projected drawing—adopt gestures that we have not previously seen in quite this form: 6 and 11 grab at the helmet-crests of their opponents with, once again, the distinctive form of shield (5 and 10); while 3 and 13 are lunging for the side-arms carried by their similarly-equipped opponents, 2 and 12. This is surely a scene of the disarming of defeated prisoners. But something more sinister is going on as well: no. 9 has drawn his sword, evidently to use it on no. 8, whom he is gripping by the arm (this detail is obscured by the division of the projected drawing at this point), while further round no. 1 is also on the point of drawing his sword—note the violently flexed elbow. With the enemy already in a state of submission, this is unexpected. But an explanation is given by the collapsing no. 4, and the apparently already dead nos. 7 and 14. The enemy are being disarmed and then butchered: the three figures already stricken are presumably meant to have been laid low by the outstretched weapons which their left-hand neighbours, 3, 6 and 13, still hold above their bodies. The conventions of the human figures are fundamentally unchanged: most of them stand on a common base-line, and they all share the Geometric convention of profile heads and legs, combined with frontal torsos. Four—all on the losing side—carry a type of shield that we have seen repeatedly, together with the regular sword and dagger at the waist. But within the Geometric conventions, one artist at least shows us what composition can do: consider the effect that he achieves by gesture, from the vain pleading of no. 8 to the grim determination of no. 9, and the way that no. 13 rocks back on his heels, reveling in the violence.

[3] See Himmelmann-Wildschütz (1961).

Next we turn to another jug, of similar date, and again Athenian (Plate 5). Its main scene is this time not on the body but on the neck: a warship of the type we have seen before is shown capsized; eleven members of the crew are around it, every one clinging on either to the ship, or to a companion who in turn grasps the ship, with fishes in among them. Their torsos are cross-hatched, an early sign of the growing urge to variegate the blank silhouette of Geometric art with internal lines. The latest interpretation of this scene[4] suggests that one crewman is destined to perish, the man who lies along the keel to the right, in a pose which we have seen before, sinking downwards with strongly-flexed right arm: this, it is proposed, was a 'formula' for a dying figure. All the others, especially of course the man who is astride the keel and is even now giving aid to two companions, have on this view a chance of surviving. It is a grim scene, but less so than the previous one.

Our next example takes us away from painted pottery and away from Athens. On the neck of a transport jar, made perhaps around 700 B.C. in Homer's native region of Ionia, but actually found far to the west in the early Greek settlement of Pithekoussai on the island of Ischia, appears the impression from a stone stamp, showing an armed warrior rescuing the body of an unarmed but gigantic companion: the living warrior simultaneously brandishes two spears (Plate 6). Remarkably, a series of impressions from the very same stone was found on a terracotta plaque, this time not only made but also found in Ionia, in the sanctuary of Hera on the island of Samos. The technique of the carving is, given the difference of material, essentially the same as that in the paintings: solid figures outlined and set off against a blank background. Here, for the first time, we can go a step further in interpretation than in the earlier cases: the iconography of the scene is one that we believe we can recognise from later pictures, in which the addition of inscribed names makes identification possible. Given that the later convention for the walking or running attitude of the living figure had not yet been devised, this iconography is more or less exactly that used for the scene of Ajax heroically carrying the dead Achilles from the battlefield at Troy (Plate 7): note how the gigantic size of Achilles is emphasized throughout. This interpretation of the scenes on the early stone stamps is not quite an inescapable one: it is still possible, following a

[4] See Ahlberg-Cornell (1992) 27–28.

line of argument of which we have already heard an example, to suggest that a theme of no very distinctive import was picked up by later artists to convey a story by then well-known—an episode in fact from the *Aethiopis*, one of the 'Epic Cycle' of poems, whose action was set before, between or after the two Homeric poems and which were not held to be by Homer. We have only fragments and digests of them, but from these it is usually judged that they were composed some time after Homer. Again, I offer no comment of my own as yet.

Our final scene is equally late, around or even just after 700 B.C. A conical stand for a bowl, painted and probably found in Athens, is decorated with eleven human figures and a bird, all large in scale (Plate 8a). What was probably meant to be the central group portrays two men with what looks like a scepter between them, in the act of exchanging swords: behind each of them stands a woman, both carrying branches and the one on the right also holding a baldric which is evidently to form part of the exchange; a fifth figure, a man, comes up from the left carrying game on a stick over his shoulder. As we move round the stand to the right, we come first to the bird, next to two warriors who are engaged in combat over the fallen body of a third warrior: over him, a sword and baldric apparently hover in the air (Plate 8b). On the analogy of later convention, we should take this to represent the spoils for which the two men are fighting. Then if we move in the opposite direction from the central group, we again come upon a duel: and it is perhaps no longer a surprise that one side consists of a pair of twin figures, this time fairly clearly with their bodies joined together. A vertical spiral divides them from the other duelling group. By now, the Geometric conventions have become considerably diluted: most of the figures have visible eyes, and are no longer entirely or even mainly in silhouette technique. Yet the spirit of the representation is unchanged: the figures still obey the rule of frontal torsos and profile heads and legs; muscles may be more naturalistically indicated, but the shape of the torso, for example, still follows that of the Geometric isosceles triangle. This, and the fact that the stand may have been painted just within Homer's lifetime, will I hope excuse its inclusion here.

We have seen only a sample of the Geometric figure-painter's range: but I think it is enough to show how he adapted his composition to the different demands of burial, death in battle, after battle and at sea, rescue and truce. Every one of these themes occurs prominently in the Homeric epics; but what we have not been able to achieve is a specific reading of the narratives that is in any way comparable with our reading of Homer's. That is not to say that such a reading would have been impossible for his contemporaries too, though the conventions of Geometric art may make it hard to avoid that conclusion.

The traditional solution of the impasse, that the pictures were actually meant to illustrate the epic stories, has been referred to earlier on. It is a fact that every one of the scenes we have looked at has, by different scholars at different times and on the basis of different arguments, been claimed to do just that. To evaluate such claims, we shall need to look briefly at the sequence once again: but first let us consider what effect the claims, if validated, would have. In many opinions, including apparently those of most Classicists, they would greatly enhance the interest of the paintings: they would offer vital evidence on a question where we badly need it, namely that of the date at which familiarity with the stories told in the epics became widespread enough to feature in the art of Athens, Argos and other regions besides the poet's native Ionia. Thus a terminus would at least be fixed for the final stage of the composition of the poems. One is again reminded of the claim for the 'importance' of Claude's subjects for himself and his patrons.

But there is a price for acceptance of these claims as well. They would depreciate the achievement of the painters, not only in the obvious sense of making mere illustrators out of them, but more specifically in making them such ineffective illustrators. As we shall see again in a moment, if the prime purpose was really to recall to the viewer's mind the episodes that he or she had heard recited in the Homeric epics, then the artists cannot be said to have made a success of it: on the contrary, they alternately threw away opportunities and set up obstacles to understanding. I should say now that in my own view, none of the works that we have seen is susceptible to such a reading: only by flatly disregarding a whole series of more or less subtle signals from the artists can we maintain it. One or two of the identifications have I think been conclusively discredited. But let us test out such claims on the specific instances that we have been looking at.

With the first two paintings on funerary kraters (Plates 1–2), the issue is the same. The potential significance of the twin-figures who make such apparently casual appearances in them hinges upon a remarkable feature of Greek legend, that it does contain a pair of Siamese Twins. Their deformity is explicitly described by Hesiod (fr. 17B M–W) in a fragment of a poem of much the same date as the latest of the Geometric pictures that we saw. Homer does not dwell on their physical abnormalities, but he does twice involve them briefly in narratives (*Iliad* 11.709–710, 750–52; 23.638–40): in both cases, they feature in the accounts given by Nestor, at Troy, of the doings of his distant youth. They encounter Nestor in combat where, according to him, they are lucky to escape with their lives; and they also get the better of him in a chariot-race at some funerary games. It is the first occasion which is of potentially more direct relevance here, even though we note that the pictures offer a loose context both of chariotry and more generally of burial ritual and perhaps funeral games. But did these two artists really mean to recall the episode in Book 11 of the *Iliad* where Nestor relates his encounter with the Twins? Officially (though not in reality) the sons of Aktor, they were 'just lads, unversed in serious fighting', he says at their first mention; and presently we hear that 'I would have killed the sons of Aktor too . . . had not their father Poseidon whisked them out of the battle, shrouding them in mist.' Can these scenes have been intended to illustrate that passage? If so, the artists behaved almost as if they were covering their tracks, surrounding the incident of the Twins with much inappropriate and un-Homeric detail. It is important to note that Nestor's two reminiscences are not the only stories that we hear about the Siamese Twins: we know that they were eventually waylaid and killed by Herakles in an episode that goes unmentioned in Homer. That the twins are the same pair that is known from legend is overwhelmingly likely; but to insist that the episode chosen must be the same one that Homer chose seems to me to be an example (to use no harsher term) of wishful thinking.

With our next picture (Plate 4), it was once argued that two of the figures, nos. 5 and 8, were Ajax and Hector exchanging gifts, when their inconclusive combat was interrupted by a truce (*Iliad* 7.274–312); and that 6 and 13 were the two heralds Idaios and Talthybios who separated them. But we saw enough of this picture to realise that such an interpretation simply disregards a number of clear signals from the artist, above all the wealth of gesture: nor has the surrounding action anything in common with the staged single combat of the *Iliad*.

The shipwreck scene (Plate 5) was a predictable candidate for assimilation with the shipwreck of Odysseus as described in *Odyssey* 12.403–425; and this time the identification found much more widespread support. But it falls foul of the same criticism as in the previous case: that the artist has used subtlety of composition to indicate a very different potential outcome from that of the disaster where Odysseus alone, straddling the keel, survived. If his intention had been to portray the episode from Homer, then he could have done so very much more simply, by omitting the tell-tale feature of the hands gripping the ship and the limbs of comrades.

With the stone stamp-impressions (Plate 6), we are dealing with a different category of inference: here, for the first time, we can enlist a known later iconography in support of an identification of Ajax with the dead Achilles. As we saw, this need not be entirely conclusive: but, when all the evidence is taken into account, it does seem to me more likely than not that this is indeed the intended subject. But here we encounter a new factor of a quite different kind: of all the epic identifications we have considered, this is the only one where the episode in question is not from Homeric epic. The rescue of Achilles' body is not an event related by Homer; it belongs instead to the *Aethiopis*, an epic which Greek tradition and the surviving fragments alike suggest was composed, in its final form, well after either Homer or the date of the stamps. This is a salutary finding for two reasons: first, it reminds us that Homer was not the exclusive source for legends of the Heroic Age; and especially not for the artists since, over the whole of the first century or so of Greek figure-scenes, incorporating this period and the ensuing one, only a small fraction of the probable mythological scenes take their subject from the Iliad or the Odyssey—between 10% and 16%, according to the degree of optimism of the person counting.[5] Secondly, it hints that neither need epic poetry as a whole have been such an exclusive source. This

[5] Thus, Fittschen (1969) counts 16 from the *Iliad* and *Odyssey*, and 43 from the Trojan Cycle omitting the *Oresteia*, out of a total of 151 portrayals of legends earlier than c. 600 B.C.; while Ahlberg-Cornell (1992) arrives at the somewhat higher figures of 25:77:165. R. M. Cook (1983) extends his coverage down to c. 530 B.C., and excludes the *Oresteia* from the Trojan Cycle (though he includes the wooden Chest of Cypselus which we know only from the description in Pausanias 5.17.5–19.10). His count for the first two categories comes out in the ratio 94:324, or 29%: this is a lower proportion than Fittschen's 37% or Ahlberg's 32%. His figures suggest that, over much of the sixth century B.C., the frequency of Trojan scenes greatly increased, but that the relative popularity among the artists of the Homeric epics within the Trojan Cycle was if anything falling, not rising.

particular case is not conclusive for the latter argument: it is merely that the only epic treatment of the theme of which we know was almost certainly not yet composed at the time that this image was made.

The Homeric interpretation of our final picture, on the vessel-stand (Plate 8), brings us back to an earlier topic: for once again it has been argued that the central scene represents the truce after Ajax and Hector's single combat in the *Iliad.* Once again, I suggest, we can only accept it if we utterly disregard the inappropriate context which the artist has provided—the presence of two women, and of a hunter with game, on the battlefield at Troy—and only if we admit the logical underpinning of the identification, namely that the two warriors still duelling further round to the right are the same pair, Ajax and Hector, shown at the immediately preceding stage of the story. Again there is an iconographic obstacle, but a new one: the fallen warrior and the sword, which have no place in the staged trial by combat of *Iliad* 12. Further, to postulate that two figures should be repeated in the same zone is to confront yet other difficulties: first, that such a practice would be at variance with what we know of early Greek artistic conventions; and second, that by committing ourselves to linking two of the three scenes in this way, we are surely also committed to bringing in the third, the duel with the Siamese Twins. Yet even if this last were intended to be the fight recounted by Nestor, it occurs in a different book of the *Iliad*, a different generation of heroic genealogy, and in reported, not depicted action.

I hope that the objections I have rehearsed will suffice for my case, which is really to rehabilitate the intellectual status of the graphic artists of Homer's day. Their work was an independent art-form. It had its own tradition, much shorter than Homer's, its own objectives, and to a large extent its own subject-matter, even though this, as in the case of the Siamese Twins, may fleetingly and partially overlap with Homer's. For both kinds of artists, composition was the main concern: both used it to characterize their figures and to make more vivid their narrative. They may even have had compositional techniques in common, which there has been no time to illustrate here—most notably, in their treatment of temporal sequence, by the device of presenting as apparently simultaneous episodes which they and their public understood to be sequential. The much rarer opportunities which the visual artist enjoyed for making such figures individually recognisable, as with the Siamese Twins and, if we are right, the gigantic size of the dead Achilles, were gratefully taken: hence no doubt the otherwise remarkable popularity of the former subject. But for the most part, the goal to be aimed at was a perhaps lesser one, the creation of recognizable themes and situations, which might even have a generalized narrative content, but which even without this would strike a chord in the contemporary spectator. Subtleties of pose and gesture could contribute to this: so too could certain material 'props' whose significance is now lost on us. An example of this last, in the earlier pictures, is the distinctive form of shield to which I drew attention more than once. We want to ask why its bearers are apparently so ill-fated in battle, and why, although not all members of one side need carry such a shield, it is never shown carried by members of opposing sides: such questions may never be answerable by us, but it is surely not disingenuous or sentimental to suggest that there may be connotations here which contemporaries could readily grasp.

The artists did, however, inhabit broadly the same world that Homer lived in, and share at least some of his experience and background. Both alike partook of a present that was exciting enough, with all the intellectual and institutional developments that accompanied the expansion of the Greek world in the eighth century B.C.: but they also partook of a past which they and their patrons evidently found even more exciting. It is my conviction that this is true of the artist as well as of the poet: that their subject-matter is seldom the same, but that the world of the visual arts of this time is just as strongly suffused by the aura of story-telling about bygone days as is that of the epic—yet independently so. Less specific and circumstantial, and vastly less dominated by individuals, this art could yet charm a circle of patronage of its own: otherwise the Geometric figure-style of Athens, for instance, would not have been widely imitated across the Greek world. But it was also an art for which yet another analogy with Claude is appropriate: in the words of a critic opposed to the aims of the London exhibition of his work, 'They are not objects that tell stories, but objects to make up stories about.'

Hitherto the discussion has been almost entirely confined to the products of the Geometric style and of the transition at its end, belonging probably to the second half of the eighth century B.C. and the opening years of the seventh. As we have seen, this period has a special claim on our attention, because in part at least it coincided with the phase in which the Homeric epics reached their final form. It is thus the only period in which we can watch a parallel development occurring in the literary and the artistic consciousness of the Greek people. But at the same time, it is only the beginning of the long relationship between the visual arts and the epic in the Greek world. Over the centuries, that relationship was to undergo many changes in form and shifts of interest; yet none of these is so marked as the one that occurs now, in the first half of the seventh century—a transformation that permanently re-shaped the attitudes of the producer, the viewer and the consumer of the works of art.

It is overwhelmingly likely that the driving force behind this change lay with the two latter groups, who formed the artists' clientèle; yet we can follow its progress only through the products of the artists themselves, as the new currents carried them along. By about 650 B.C., all the important elements of the change are visible. Perhaps the earliest of these was in artistic technique: the abandonment by the vase-painters of the strict silhouette principle, with its consequent effects in the other media. This meant, above all, that artists had more scope to give individuality and recognizability to their figures: with the widespread adoption both of outline drawing and of the engraver's technique of incision, figures could be given distinctive faces and bodies, appropriate to their gender and age, and unique attributes that proclaimed their identity. But alongside this assumption of greater freedom, there grew up a practice that acted in the opposite sense: the growth of a recognized iconography, at least for the most popular and frequent subjects. We have seen one example of this already, in the depiction of Ajax carrying Achilles' body according to a repeated compositional form (Plate 7). Such conventions had already been present in Geometric art, as with the formula for the 'dying man' (above, Plate 5), but now they were applied to whole compositions rather than single figures—and, what is more, to compositions which are normally adopted for one story or episode only. These specific iconographies had a wide circulation, often crossing the boundaries of regional styles. On occasion, they could be transferred or 'misapplied' to a different story; but the fact that we can detect this practise shows the transformation that has occurred in our capacity to recognise episodes and individuals.

At times, especially in the early Archaic period, there are severe tests of this of this ability—for example, with a rather short-lived convention for showing monstrous or supernatural beings as quadrupeds. We have to forget our pre-conception of a giant as an overgrown human figure, of Medusa as a woman with a hideous grinning face, or of the Minotaur as a man with a bull's head, if we are to recognise early Archaic representations of them in the form of, respectively, a centaur-like figure, a horse with a female human head, and a bull with a man's head: yet in each case the identifications are made probable or certain by the circumstances in which they are shown—most decisively, when Medusa is in the act of being beheaded with a sword by a beardless man, who turns his face away (Plate 9).

This capacity is greatly enhanced by a third innovation that presently arrives: the gradual introduction of painted inscriptions of various kinds, among which the most significant artistically are those naming individual figures in a picture. Many a scene is thereby given an identification which might be otherwise lacking. We can seldom use these identifications as a basis for any inference about the more mysterious scenes of the preceding period: fashions in the choice of subject changed too quickly for that. But an important argument of an *a fortiori* form can nevertheless be established; it has already been mentioned in passing. This is that, even at a time when the Homeric epics were beyond all doubt enjoying wide circulation and growing prestige, and in a form at least closely resembling their final one, only a minority of the legendary subjects in art appear to be taken directly from them. In the art of the Late Geometric period, therefore, when there cannot yet be any such confidence that the Greek world at large was familiar with the poems, we have every reason to think that artistic reference to the *Iliad* and *Odyssey* would be rarer still. It is clear where the burden of proof should lie. But our concern is now with the first two generations of the Archaic period.

Opinions may differ as to what is proof of Homeric inspiration for a work in the visual arts; but the minimum requirements are surely that the episode shown should be directly treated in one of the two epics (and not merely referred to allusively, as for example with the deeds of Bellerophon or the Argonauts), and that there should be a tolerable correspondence of detail between the poetic and the visual versions. The few cases where the Homeric nomenclature for a character in a legend differs from the later one (as with Electra for instance) could also provide a useful test, with the advent of name-inscriptions. Once criteria of even this modest strictness are applied, it emerges that Homer is not the dominant influence on Greek artists that we might have expected him to be.

We may briefly survey the pattern of legendary iconography in this early phase of Archaic art. Among the prominent and recurrent legendary themes treated, first place must undoubtedly be given to the numerous deeds of Heracles. As the greatest and the most 'panhellenic' of the Greek heroes, he had a special claim on the interest of the artists—particularly of the vase-painters, who must have been increasingly uncertain as to where, within the Greek world or even beyond it, their products would find their final destination. A number of his exploits could be made visually distinctive, thanks mainly to his unorthodox weapons (club and bow) and the unique form of some of his more monstrous opponents—the Hydra, Cerberus. The pervasive convention of showing him bearded helped to differentiate him from other heroes (Theseus, Achilles) who might also be shown fighting Amazons, Centaurs, or a bull, but who were frequently portrayed as beardless. Thus it is that we can recognise, in the surviving examples of Greek art from the period before ca. 650 B.C., as many scenes involving Heracles as from the entire saga of the Trojan War and its aftermath, and three times as many as those taken from the actual subject-matter of the *Iliad* and *Odyssey*.

Three other exploits of heroes are also relatively popular, and recognizable because of the distinctive nature of the secondary participants: Perseus with Medusa (Plate 9), Theseus with the Minotaur, and Bellerophon with Pegasos and the Chimaira. Each of them is at least as common as any single scene from the Homeric epics; and, being themselves at best only fleetingly referred to in the *Iliad* and *Odyssey*, their portrayal can hardly be attributed to familiarity with the poems.

Alongside these, however, we may count a handful of portrayals which can stand as the first convincing artistic allusions to the Homeric narrative: that is, not only do they represent episodes narrated at length by Homer, but they do so in a way that is acceptably close to the Homeric accounts. The first noteworthy feature is that apparent scenes from the *Odyssey* are shown as early as, and at first more frequently than, ones taken from the *Iliad*. As examples, we may choose the three mid-seventh-century portrayals of the blinding of Polyphemus (one of them is shown in Plate 10). The first, on a complete but very worn bowl made in a Western Greek workshop and found in Etruria, shows the greatest number of points of correspondence with the version narrated in *Odyssey* 9.382–88: it alone shows the same number of attackers as in Homer—Odysseus and four companions—and picks out the hero himself and his personal rôle, holding the stake at its far end and twisting it while the others aim it into the Cyclops' eye; it alone gives the picture a Homeric setting, showing behind Polyphemus a kind of storage stand, readily identified with the cheese-crates mentioned earlier in the Homeric account (line 219). Yet it does not portray the Cyclops as gigantic in size; nor is he reclining as in Homer's version, but propped up one one hand. These two departures from the *Odyssey* passage are made good in the second piece, on a luckily-preserved fragment broken off another mixing-bowl, from Argos (Plate 10): here a huge Polyphemus lies back on a multi-colored, sloping quilt or pile of rocks. Yet this 'correction' is achieved at the cost of some of the correspondences with Homer noticed with the first piece: the picture is incomplete, but it showed three or, at most, four attackers (there was hardly room for a fifth on the vessel), and we cannot know whether the lost figure at the end of the line was recognisable as Odysseus. The third example, which is in all probability the earliest, is a picture on the neck of a huge Attic storage-jar from Eleusis, and it is the one which departs most widely from the Homeric account: there are but three attackers, and Polyphemus, though shown as gigantic, sits upright.

Besides these differentiating features, there are ways in which all three pictures alike declare their essential independence of any literary version. These can in part be explained by the dictates of the medium: the panel on the Eleusis amphora, for example, is squarish and has no room either for a reclining giant or for more than four figures in total, while the other two vessels are decorated in a zonal scheme with long horizontal panels, with a continuous base-line for the figures. This must be why all three pictures show the attack taking place horizontally, rather than vertically downwards as in Homer. Next, the Argos fragment and the Eleusis amphora combine the blinding with a clear reference to an earlier episode in the story, the intoxication of Polyphemos with Odysseus' wine (lines 345–61), by showing a cup held in the Cyclops' hand. All three pictures show the instrument of blinding as a thin spit, not an olive-wood stake as in Homer. Finally, none of the three paintings (nor even most later versions) in any way indicate the deformity and misplacement of the Cyclops' single eye, which is clearly implied in Homer by the use of the singular form and the fact that one thrust of the stake leaves him blind. Here we see at work similar factors to those detected in the account of Geometric art: an independent tradition of composition, and firm conventions as to how to draw the human figure.

As we move further into the Archaic period, the iconographic rules become clearer and more consistent, and the portrayal of episodes with some claim to a Homeric inspiration becomes ever more frequent. But another change is even more important for our purpose: this book is concerned with the elucidation of Homer and, as we move downwards in time through the seventh and sixth centuries B.C. to the Classical and later periods, the amount of light thrown directly on the Homeric poems themselves rapidly decreases. Once the impact and prestige of Homer becomes an acknowledged historical fact, rare indeed are the works of later art which can inform us directly on the diffusion of the poems or the date at which they reached the form in which we have them. Even if our aim is the less ambitious one of identifying cases where an artist gives clear proof of direct inspiration by the epic, most works of art have nothing to offer us. We shall end by looking at one or two possible exceptions.

The black-figure vase-painter Sophilos, known to us by name from his fondness for signing his pictures, worked in Athens in the decades after 600 B.C. His known output includes a few pieces with interesting provenances: one, possibly two found in the entrance-passage of a prehistoric tomb at Menidi north of Athens; another from the mound erected for the heroized Athenian dead at Marathon in 490 B.C. (which must therefore have been carefully kept as an heirloom); and a fragment of another from a mainly prehistoric site near Pharsalos in Thessaly, a place which some in antiquity identified as the royal seat of Peleus, the father of Achilles and guardian of Patroclus. It is the last of these (Plate 11) which concerns us here. The subject is a special one, and the piece may have been chosen for its appropriateness to the geographical location. The picture showed a chariot-race, with spectators watching from a tiered stand. As well as signing it, Sophilos took the much more unusual step of giving it an overall title, 'The games for Patroklos.' Though the greater part of the scene is lost, the name of Achilles survives among the spectators. The works of this painter apparently had some special appeal for use in a 'heroic' context, as their find-spots show; and in this case it is clear that we are in the general setting of book 23 of the *Iliad.* If more of the race itself survived, we could see whether the field and the sequence of runners also conformed to those in Homer; but the labelling of the picture, and the chance that Patroclus is a character whose interest was greatly enhanced by Homer himself rather than a stock figure of traditional legend, are persuasive reasons for thinking that this may have been a direct literary illustration. At least there is nothing in what survives to contradict this view.

A smaller but even clearer instance is given on a water-jar from the end of the sixth century, one of a group from Caere in Etruria whose subjects and inscriptions nevertheless suggest that they were made by a Greek. The scene is the embassy to Achilles in book 9 of the *Iliad*: there, the heroes Phoenix, Ajax, and Odysseus are accompanied by two heralds named Odios and Eurybates; and here in the picture Odios, known from no source but this single fleeting mention in Homer, is named as a herald. The geographical isolation of the artist, and the extreme obscurity of this figure who was presumably another invention of Homer's, makes this a rather powerful illustration of the range of circulation of the *Iliad.*

More often, however, there are awkwardnesses or downright obstacles to assimilating the visual and literary accounts. This was the case with the scenes of the blinding of Polyphemus that we examined; but there the way was open for explaining the differences largely by the exigences of the vase-painter's medium. In later art, the growing frequency of painted inscriptions sometimes excludes such an explanation.

No one was more generous with such inscriptions than Kleitias, who painted one of the most familiar works of art in the canon of legendary pictures, the 'François Vase,' an Athenian mixing-bowl of about 570 B.C. found at Chiusi in Etruria. Its encyclopaedic coverage runs to some twelve separate subjects from legend or divine myth, large or small in scale, on a single vessel, and they are heavily captioned. A first point to note is that, while four of the twelve scenes are taken from the Trojan Cycle, just one of these is strictly 'Homeric' in the sense that its subject figures directly in the narrative of the *Iliad* or *Odyssey*. Once again, it is the chariot-race at Patroclus' funeral games which is in question (Plate 12); the iconography used is a long-established one, first detectable in scenes of chariot-races of almost a century earlier, with a figure standing at the winning-post at the far right to await the arrival of the runners. This figure is here labelled 'Achilles,' and there can be no doubt that the occasion is meant to be the same one as in Sophilos' slightly earlier rendering: the number of competitors, five, also corresponds with Homer. But from this point on, the account in the *Iliad* is ignored: Diomedes, who wins the race in Homer after leading throughout the final stretch, is shown running third as the race approaches its end; none of the remaining four runners in the *Iliad* is even shown, their places being taken by four other named heroes: two who do not enter the race in Homer, and two who are nowhere even mentioned by him. This has occasioned much surprise: J. D. Beazley wrote 'Oddly enough, Kleitias departs widely from the Homeric account . . . Kleitias, left to himself, could not remember the field.'[6] Whether or not this last is the true explanation, one suspects that it is the profusion of inscriptions alone, here and in many other sixth-century works, which clearly exposes the discrepancy; and that many another artist, if asked to name the figures he had shown, would have proved equally oblivious or indifferent to the details of the epic texts.

The successive phases of Greek art, including the productions of Greek painters and sculptors under Roman patronage, have been treated in encyclopaedic detail by a number of works, from the standpoint of their relation to the legends in the ancient texts; and several of the books address the specific issue of the relationship with the Homeric epics.[7] But I hope that it has been made clear why, in a *New Companion to Homer*, few of these innumerable works of art demand a place. They are often helpful for us, in bringing to life a Homeric description and in showing the immense influence that Homer's works exercised at all later periods of antiquity; many of them are also works of great beauty in their own right; on occasion, they throw direct light on the reception of the Homeric poems. But seldom can they add to our knowledge of Homer himself.

---

[6] Beazley (1951) 34–35.

[7] E.g., Brillante (1983); Brommer (1973); Buitron et al. (1992); Fittschen (1973); Friis Johansen (1967); Kannicht (1982); Schefold (1966); (1981); (1992).

PLATES

Plate 1

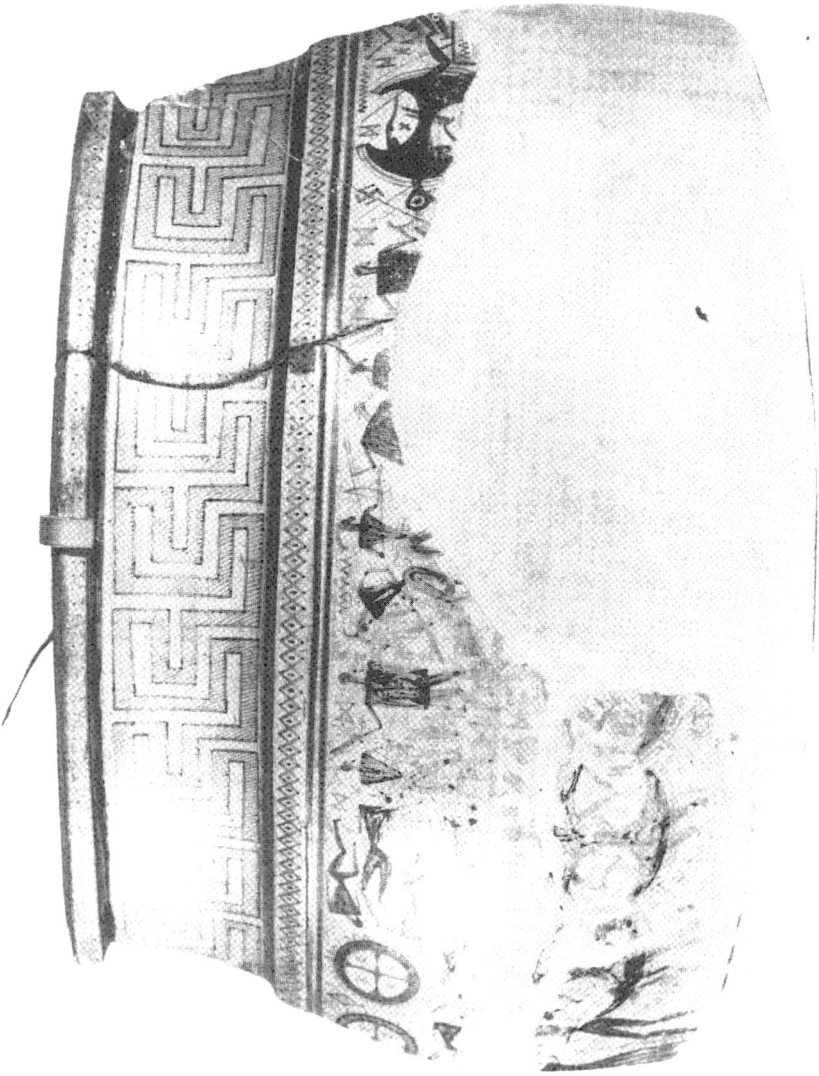

Plate 2

Plate 3

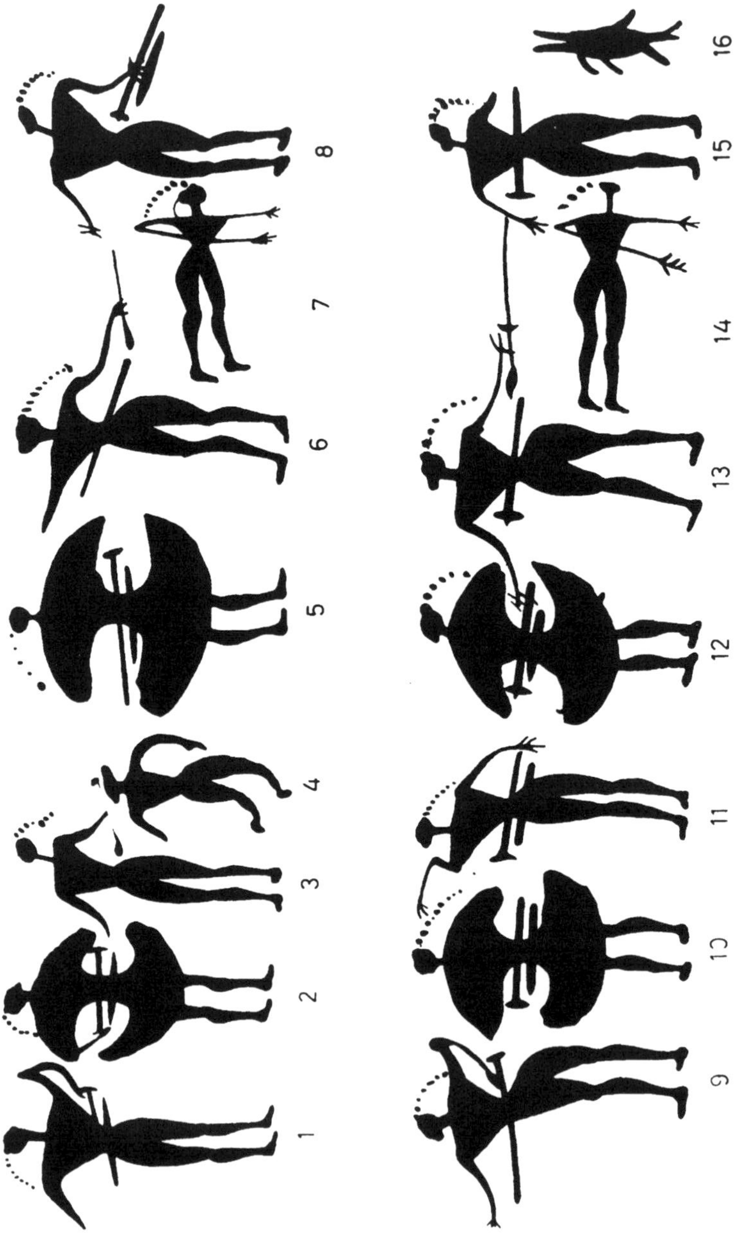

Plate 4

Plate 5

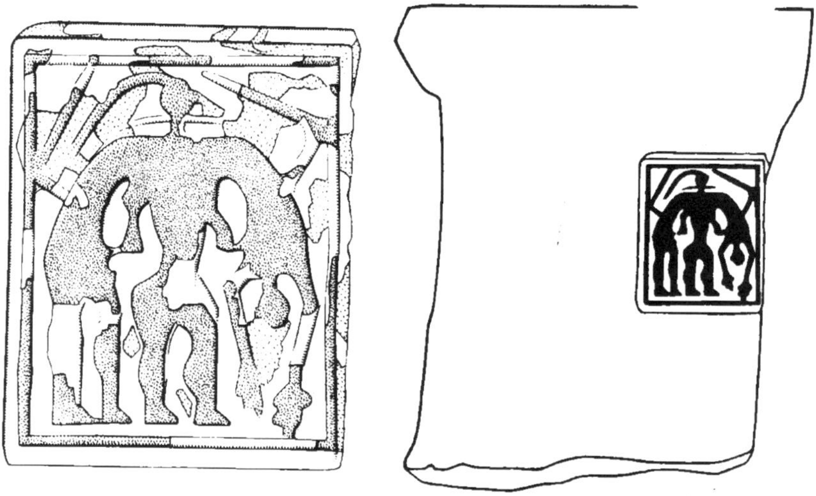

Plate 6

Plate 7

Plate 8a

Plate 8b

Plate 9

Plate 10

Plate 11

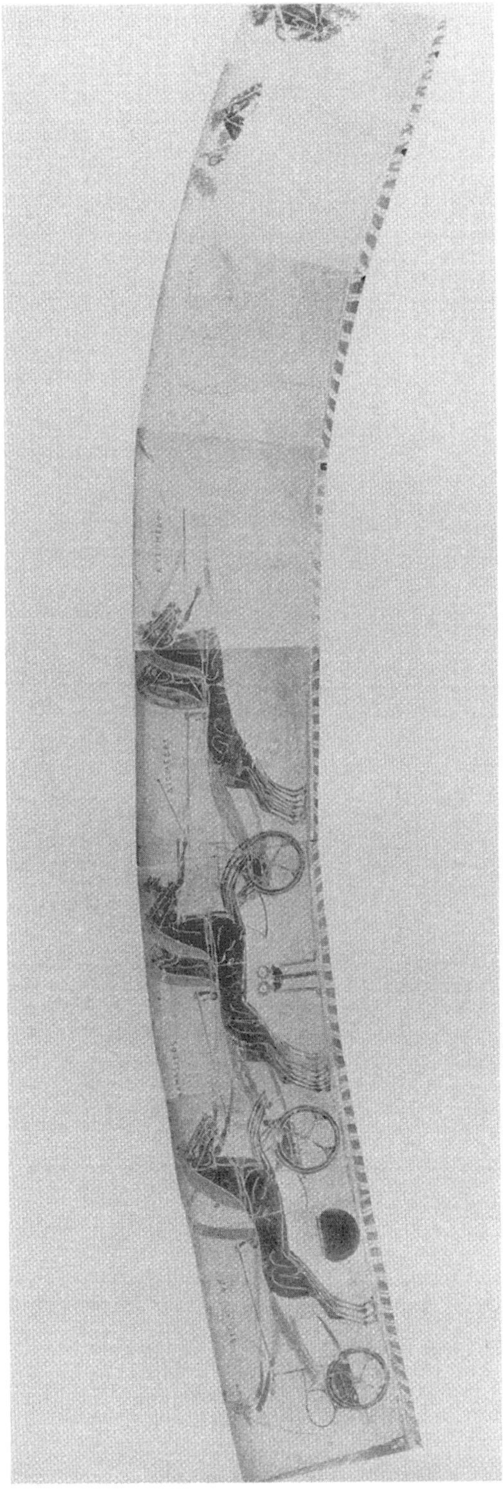

Plate 12

Sarah Morris

HOMER AND THE NEAR EAST

In their historical and literary setting, the poems of Homer and the epic cycle belong to the eastern Mediterranean: they share narrative elements with neighboring cultures since the Bronze Age, and show specific connections to Near Eastern history and mythology. Evidence for these connections has increased since the nineteenth century, with the discovery of Near Eastern texts and of archaeological evidence for the transmission of ideas.[1] This chapter will examine those discoveries, compare Near Eastern sources with Homeric themes and references, and suggest modes of contact and influence. When the Homeric corpus took final shape in the Archaic period, it incorporated centuries of oral performance and of exposure to other narratives. In their final form, the *Iliad* and the *Odyssey* are harvested from a rich heritage of stories long alive in the Bronze Age and in the Near East, reconstituted into an epic tradition of uniquely Greek heroic dimensions.

General Background and Sources

History of research

Since antiquity, readers of Homer have compared Greek epic, as a corpus of historical, theological, and narrative traditions shared by small communities united in religion and language, to the Hebrew Bible.[2] Internal similarities in poignant themes (the sacrifice of a daughter), poetic techniques (similes), and religious formulas (oaths and imprecations) also connected Homer with the Old Testament. The founder of modern Homer studies, Friedrich August Wolf, applied Eichhorn's 'documentary' hypothesis of the Pentateuch to his

---

[1] Burkert (1991) for history and bibliography.

[2] Burkert (1991); early work includes Joseph Scaliger (1540–1609) and Zachary Bogan's *Homerus Hebraizon* (1658).

'analysis' of Homer in 1795. Beyond shared features, references in the *Iliad* and *Odyssey* to Cyprus, Phoenicia, and Egypt fed modern European interests in the Orient.

This era also launched the comparative study of European languages, culminating in the identification of an Indo-European linguistic 'family' by Sir William Jones in 1786. The new kinship of Greek and European languages with India and Persia challenged philologists to explore literary connections beyond those in linguistics. The nineteenth century uncovered Near Eastern sites and deciphered their texts, such that Egyptian hieroglyphs and Mesopotamian cuneiform could be read before Homeric archaeology began at Troy. But with notable exceptions, few classicists pursued Oriental connections in the last century. The emancipation of philology from theology dissolved ties between Greek culture and the Bible, separated by the conflict between science and religion. Political and ideological attitudes toward the Orient, even anti-Semitism, also insulated Greece from the Near East until recently.

The present century added Hittite (Hurrian) and Ugaritic (Canaanite) literature to the Near Eastern library, in texts which offered a better bridge from Mesopotamia to the Aegean. Near Eastern influence on Homeric poetry only emerged fully after the Second World War, with the appearance of texts widely available to classicists[3] and the challenge to classical attitudes by controversial publications like *Homer and Bible* by C. Gordon and M. Bernal's *Black Athena*. An explosion of archaeological discoveries has made Phoenicians in the Aegean, and Greeks in the Levant, historical realities. New interest in the Bible as a work of literature introduced Homer and oral poetry to biblical criticism; comparison of narrative themes and poetic techniques has re-united the two traditions.[4] In classical scholarship, exploration of Near Eastern influence has expanded to lyric and choral poetry,[5] and Orientalia in Homeric poetry share Eastern influence with Hesiod, lyric poetry, and Archaic art; preclassical Greece has become an extension of the Near East. The challenge for both clas-

---

[3] Burkert (1992) 4–6, 88: e.g., Güterbock (1946), the first edition of Pritchard (1950; 3rd. ed. is 1974), and the first complete Atraḫasis in 1969.

[4] R. Alter, *The Art of Biblical Narrative* (New York, 1981); R. C. Culley, *Studies in the Structure of Hebrew Narrative* (Philadelphia, 1976) on the oral tradition.

[5] J. Carter, 'Masks and Poetry in Early Sparta,' in Hägg and Marinatos (1988) 89–98.

sicists and Assyriologists is to trace not only Near Eastern origins of Greek poetry, but their migration and transformation.

Primary sources

The principal narrative poems of the Near East which show close connections to Homer belong to Mesopotamia (Sumerian and Akkadian verse epics) and the Levant, especially ancient Ugarit. More distant influences and ritual traditions are detected in Egyptian documents and Hittite texts. Many evolved to survive in the Hebrew Bible, still a primary source of parallels for early Greek literature.

In 1872, cuneiform tablets from Nineveh yielded the sensational story of a flood with vivid parallels to the story of Noah in Genesis.[6] The discovery also shed light on Greek flood traditions (*Iliad* 12.1–33), especially the story of Deukalion (Apollodorus I.46 ff.). The Assyrian flood story came from twelve tablets telling a tale originally Sumerian, repeated in Akkadian, Hurrian, and Hittite versions as the epic of Gilgamesh.[7] A legendary Sumerian king of the third millennium B.C., Gilgamesh builds the walls of Uruk, fights and befriends Enkidu, defeats a monster and resists divine seduction, then loses Enkidu and travels in quest of the secret of eternal life from Utnapishtim. The latter survived the primeval flood with divine assistance, narrated in details too close to the version in Genesis (8:7–13) for coincidence. The hero's final adventure is to obtain a plant with the secret of life, before returning to Uruk. These epic themes—the nature of kingship, heroic combat and perilous journey, sexual intimacy, interaction with the gods, and quest for immortality—share much with both *Iliad* and *Odyssey*. Acquiring wisdom and self-knowledge through trials and travels is the experience of Odysseus, while the king's progression from heroic to tragic resembles the fate of Achilles.[8] The long-lived popularity of this story in the Near East, including its afterlife in the Bible, made it an heroic tradition as fundamental as Homer was to Greek culture.

The other famous surviving Akkadian poem is the Atraḫasis, both

---

[6] Foster (1993) vol. 1, 6–13 on discoveries and publication.

[7] J. Tigay, *The Evolution of the Gilgamesh Epic* (Philadelphia, 1982).

[8] J. Wilson, 'The Gilgamesh Epic and the Iliad,' *Echos du Monde Classique/Classical Views* 30 (1986) 25–41; C. Beye, 'The Epic of Gilgamesh, the Bible, and Homer: some narrative parallels,' in *Mnemai: Classical Studies in Memory of Karl H. Hulley*, ed. H. Evjen (Chico, 1984) 1–19.

a creation myth (the divine invention of the human race) and a story of divine displeasure, as man multiplied and became a nuisance.[9] Divine punishment ensued in famine, plague, and a flood, with obvious parallels to the Bible. When the gods destroy the human race, it is Atraḫasis, 'exceeding in wisdom,' who survives the flood by building an ark, as in the flood experienced by Gilgamesh, Noah, and Deukalion. Overpopulation and divine retribution also motivate the Greek epic cycle. In its lost opening poem, the *Kypria*, the Trojan war and its predecessor, the siege of Thebes, fulfill a divine purpose: relieving the earth of its excessive and impious population (fr. 1: schol. *Iliad* 1.5). A minor flood story opens *Iliad* 12 by predicting the divine destruction of the Achaean wall, punishment for sacrifices omitted (see below). As in Hesiod's *Theogony* (535 ff.), gods and men once shared the world before their disagreements; the Atraḫasis poem begins: 'When gods were (as) men. . . .' then Enki decides to create the human race from flesh, blood and clay, as divine servants. Most vividly, the division of the cosmos by lot into three domains (Tablet I.11–15)—the sky for Anu, the earth for [Enlil?], and the sea to Enki—corresponds nearly verbatim to the Homeric partition of divine rule between Zeus, Hades and Poseidon (*Iliad* 15.187–93).

Greek and Mesopotamian cosmogony converge again in the third great Near Eastern text, the Babylonian epic of creation known as Enūma Eliš for its opening words ('When on high . . .').[10] Here, the first generation of gods emerges from the mingling of the waters of Apsû (groundwater: progenitor or father) with Tiamat (saltwater: primeval mother). These watery forebears compare to Okeanos and Tethys, parental figures invoked by Hera in her famous deception of Zeus (*Il.* 14.200–11, an Oriental episode: below). Even the name of Tethys has been proposed as a Greek transcription of Tiamat (Akkadian for sea).[11] As in Hesiod's cosmic battle between Kronos and his children (*Theogony* 116–506), these divine rulers are eventually overthrown by a younger god (Ea); his son, Marduk, becomes god of Babylon and is the central figure of the poem. Like Atraḫasis, this poem anticipates more in Hesiod than Homer, enlarging Greece's debt to Near Eastern religion.

Egyptian literature, largely confined to tombs, may have circulated

[9] Foster (1993) 158–201 (four Babylonian and Assyrian versions survive).
[10] Foster (1993) 351–402.
[11] Burkert (1983) 53–55; idem (1992) 83–95.

poorly and infrequently among Greeks. But several traditions, beyond Egyptian religion, offer interesting parallels to Greek poetry, in didactic or 'wisdom' literature, tomb biographies, and lapidary accounts of pharaonic exploits. Prose tales on papyrus begin in the Middle Kingdom and include several travel stories akin to Greek ones. Most notably, the story of the Shipwrecked Sailor resembles the *nostoi* of Menelaos and Odysseus: a traveler who has returned safely comforts another with a tale of his adventures.[12] As in the *Odyssey*, the Egyptian narrator is sole survivor of a shipwreck, washes up on a strange island, subsists on fish and birds, and confronts a snaky creature with divine powers who foretells his safe return. The sailor is rescued by a ship which takes him home, after the serpent predicts: 'If you are brave and control your heart, you shall embrace your children, you shall kiss your wife, you shall see your home,' words and events evoking the *Odyssey*. In a longer prose tale of the Twelfth Dynasty, Sinuhe tells the story of his adventures abroad as a self-exiled royal 'attendant,' who prospers among Asiatics and even raises a family, but longs for home in old age. The king invites him back, he is royally received, and his tomb prepared. His fate resembles that of Odysseus and the Biblical Joseph, who long to return home despite opportunities abroad. The New Kingdom story of Wenamun follows an Egyptian merchant's difficulties in the timber trade in the Levant (Dor, Tyre, Byblos, and Alashiya), a 'fictional' account whose details of travel and trade authenticate adventures in the *Odyssey*. While some scholars discount these Egyptian parallels, their content is as striking as their context, in locales and occasions familiar to Aegean travellers.[13]

These stories resemble the *Odyssey* more than the *Iliad*, which recalls accounts of warfare, both historical and imaginary, in Egyptian art and literature of the Ramesside period. Fragments of papyrus narrate the Siege of Joppa (Jaffa), a Syrian city, by Thutmoses III.[14] Capture follows a ruse: inebriating the enemy, then infiltrating his walled city with soldiers smuggled inside baskets as 'tribute,' with obvious implications for the Trojan horse. In art, Ramesside monu-

[12] Lichtheim (1973) 211–35 ('Shipwrecked Sailor,' 'Sinuhe'); (1976) 224–30 ('Tale of Wenamun'); Gordon (1955) 98–127.

[13] Consider Greek access to Egyptian papyri: K. Sheedy, 'A Prothesis Scene from the Analatos Painter,' *Athenische Mittheilungen* 105 (1990) 142–43, or Egyptian singers like Tanetne at Byblos in 'Wenamun,' as sources of visual narratives or stories in song.

[14] Simpson (1973) 81–84.

ments long displayed images and formulas of battle to foreign visitors; the battle of Kadesh against the Hittites and their allies appeared in reliefs and narratives at numerous temples of Ramses II, and even in a papyrus 'poem.'[15] The Egyptian account is more epic than historic (the battle ended in a draw, not the glorious victory claimed); details like the capture of enemy scouts, battle at a river, divine appeal and assistance are universal to the genre but also particular to the *Iliad.*

Greek contact with the Near East was closest in north Syria, where the excavation of Ras Shamra (ancient Ugarit) since 1929 has delivered the most intriguing connections to Greek culture. Unique among inscribed documents from the city are fifteen tablets from the temple of Baal with epic poems in the Northwest Semitic dialect of Ugarit.[16] The longest is the Epic of Baal, describing his rise to power by defeating the Sea and Death to become king of the gods, the manufacture of his house, and his death and resurrection. The story shares more with Mesopotamian and Hesiodic theogonies than with Homer, but frequently recalls Greek epic poetry in poetic details and phrases (see below). Another poem narrates the birth of Danel's son, Aqhat, the divine manufacture of his weapons and his dispute over them with the goddess, Anat, who kills him through her henchman. His sister, Pagat, takes revenge on his behalf; an appended epic restores him to life, and fertility to the fields, as in other traditions (e.g., Egypt) where a sister (Isis) avenges and restores her brother (Osiris). The third Ugaritic epic chronicles the kingship of Keret (Kirta): his siege of a city for a bride leads to marriage, illness and healing by the gods, and the challenge to his throne by a son whom he curses, before the story breaks off. The role of the gods shows the closest correspondences with Greek tradition. The afterlife of these themes in the Hebrew Bible makes it difficult to distinguish Ugaritic from later influences on Homer.[17]

Partners in history with Bronze Age Achaeans are their Indo-European relatives, the Hittites, resident at Boghazköy (Hattušas) and keepers of cuneiform records, deciphered since 1915. Mythological texts claim close classical attention for their parallels to Kronos (Kumarbi) and Typhon (Illuyankaš), in stories derived from the

[15] Lichtheim (1976) 57–71; Sandars (1985) 29–38.
[16] Coogan (1992) 78–115.
[17] Gordon (1955) compiles both sets of influences.

Hurrians (resident in northern Mesopotamia) and sharing sources with Hesiod.[18] Historical and ritual texts reveal further patterns shared with Homer, especially in oaths, oracles, and mortuary rites.[19] Many traditions resemble Greek poetry in their common Near Eastern (or Anatolian) sources, not inherited Indo-European patterns.

Around twenty-five texts from Boghazköy refer to 'men of Ahhiyawa,' now widely if not universally accepted as an Anatolian name for 'Achaeans.' New studies date some of these texts to the fifteenth century; debate continues on their historical significance for Mycenaean relations with the Hittites.[20] Provocative for poetic purposes are Homeric echoes in names—Attarissiya (Atreus?), 'man of Ahhiya;' Tawagalawa (Eteokles?), Pariya-muwas (Paris, or Priam?), Alaksandus (Alexander?)—and places like Millawanda (Miletus?), Taruisa (Troy?) and Wilus(iy)a (Ilion?). These figure in border disputes between Hittite kings and their western neighbors, prehistoric conflicts which could have inspired legends of the Trojan War. For example, the earliest text, a fifteenth-century letter to Madduwattas, describes a chariot battle with a leader fallen on both sides, Hittite and Achaean, as in a Homeric duel; military patterns in the fourteenth-century annals of Mursilis II can be compared to the epic encounter of Achilles and Aeneas (*Il.* 20. 191–4).[21]

The Indic world of South Asia is too distant for historical interaction before Alexander, but its epic poems and early hymns show strong Indo-European kinship with early Greek literature. The collection of a thousand hymns known as the Rig-Veda offers divine titles and attributes, like the horse-riding Nāsatyā or 'Divine Twins' who resemble the Dioskouroi, which compare fruitfully to Homeric tradition.[22] As in Greece, the advent of writing in India led to the codification of earlier epic traditions in Sanskrit, most memorably the national battle epic Mahābhārata and the Rāmāyana.[23] Both

---

[18] M. L. West (1966) 1–31, 106–7; H. A. Hoffner, Jr., tr., *Hittite Myths*, ed. G. Beckman, Society of Biblical Literature (Atlanta, 1990). Cf. Penglase (1994); Walcot (1966).

[19] Gurney (1990) 137–40; Puhvel (1991) 9–11.

[20] Güterbock (1983) 133–8; Röllig (1992) 183–200.

[21] Smit (1988–89) 53–64. Cf. Puhvel (1987) 591–93.

[22] W. O'Flaherty, *The Rig Veda, an Anthology: One Hundred and Eight Hymns* (New York, 1982); Puhvel (1987) 45–67; Greek parallels: Frame (1972).

[23] J. D. Smith, 'Old Indian: The Two Sanskrit Epics,' in *Traditions of Heroic and Epic Poetry*, ed. A. T. Hatto (London, 1980) 48–78; Puhvel (1987) 68–93; M. C. Smith, *The Warrior Code of India's Sacred Song* (New York, 1992).

poems compile older Vedic and Indo-Iranian material often echoed in Homer. Thus the study of Sanskrit has joined classical training, and Indic meters, Vedic myths and epics have greatly enriched the reading of Homer.[24] Shared IE traditions, if not homelands, offer older original sources common to Greek and Indic literature than in countries neighboring Greece.

Historical connections and conditions

Extant Near Eastern literature is an incomplete resource for understanding Greek epic poetry: many texts were lost, and comparison depends heavily on accidents of survival. Nor was Homer the only beneficiary: Greek art and myth drew diverse and repeated inspiration from the Near East, and non-textual migration of stories and images into epic moves the pursuit of Near Eastern sources beyond literature to oral tradition and material culture.[25] Beyond coincidence or polygenesis, two methods explain the convergence of significant themes and phrases in Homer with those of neighboring cultures. Linguistic relatives like Hittite can show similarities from a comparative perspective, extrapolating to mythology in a 'monogenetic' approach for which Indo-European languages offer a unique laboratory.[26] The alternative assumes historical influence by one set of cultural forms upon another. Both methods need rigorous control of context: 'We need to compare actual records of adjacent, interacting, perhaps overlapping people, places, and times, in order to determine whether under the surface 'noise' of the text there may lurk a coherent thematic structure still discernible in formulaic petrifaction,' cautions one critic of diffusionism.[27] All these factors need attention in answering persistent modern questions: when and how Greek poets learned these stories, and under what historical and archaeological conditions.

Archaeology continues to bring Eastern Mediterranean worlds ever closer, in prehistory: frescoes of Minoan themes (bull-wrestling) in

[24] E.g., G. Nagy (1974); Puhvel (1987) 126–43; M. L. West (1988) 152–56; S. Jamison, 'Draupadī on the Walls of Troy: *Iliad* 3 from an Indic Perspective,' *Classical Antiquity* 13 (1994) 5–16; G. Nagy (1995) 163–79.

[25] Mondi (1989) 149–57.

[26] Puhvel (1987) 4.

[27] Puhvel (1991) 23, also dismisses 'vague echoes, cultural universals, and diffusional debris.'

Aegean style have recently turned up in the Egyptian delta (Avaris) and in the Levant at Tell Kabri.[28] These discoveries support close contact in the second millennium B.C., and with it opportunities for mutual influence in art and culture. By the Late Bronze Age, international connections beyond trade brought Aegean tribute to Thebes, complemented by an Egyptian itinerary of Aegean cities.[29] Mycenaean finds at Amarna and Ugarit suggest where Near Eastern cult could have inspired the pantheon of divine names and epithets in Mycenaean Greek.[30] The prehistory of epic poetry, implicit in Mycenaean lyre players and heroic images, allows early influence by the Near East upon developing Greek narrative.[31] Archaeology has illuminated the centuries between 1200 and 700 B.C., formerly a 'Dark Age,' with Orientalizing imports (including Phoenician letters) and adaptions at Aegean sites like Knossos in Crete and Lefkandi on Euboea.[32] Near Eastern influence no longer presumes the sophistication and literacy of the Bronze Age or Archaic periods,[33] but could have flourished without writing and monumental art, during the survival of Bronze Age forms into Homeric poetry. For example, the Hittites had little archaeologically visible contact with Mycenaean Greece, yet their literary and ritual texts show close parallels to Homer. Their afterlife in the northern Levant enabled translation to the formative Greek tradition, centuries after the demise of the Hittite empire. The same scenario allows the literature of Ugarit to survive its destruction after 1200 B.C., in North Syrian locales frequented by Greeks. The enormous loss of texts from the Levant, in perished writing surfaces and

---

[28] O. Negbi, 'The "Libyan Landscape" from Thera: a review of Aegean enterprises in the Late Minoan IA period,' *Journal of Mediterranean Archaeology* 7 (1994) 73–112. Tell ed-Dab'a (Avaris) reports in *Ägypten und Levante* 1 (1990); W. Niemeyer, 'Minoan Artists Travelling Overseas: the Alalakh frescoes and the painted plaster floor at Tel Kabri (western Galilee),' *Thalassa. Aegaeum* 7 (Liège, 1991) 189–201.

[29] S. Wachsmann, *Aegeans in the Theban Tombs* (Leuven, 1989); E. Cline, 'Amenophis III and the Aegean: A Reassessment of Egypto-Aegean Relations in the 14th Century B.C.,' *Orientalia* 56:1 (1987) 1–36.

[30] Kirk (1990) 1–8; cf. E. T. Mullen, Jr., *The Assembly of the Gods: The Divine Council in Canaanite and Early Hebrew Literature* (Chico, 1980); S. Morris (1992) 107–15.

[31] Webster (1958) 91–135; M. L. West (1988) 156–59; S. Morris (1989).

[32] O. Negbi, 'Evidence for Early Phoenician Communities in the East Mediterranean Islands,' *Levant* 14 (1982) 179–82; M. L. West (1988), 169–72 for impact on Homeric studies.

[33] As in A. Heubeck, 'Mythologische Vorstellungen des Alten Orients im archaischen Griechentum,' *Gymnasium* 62 (1955) 515–21; M. L. West (1988) 169; Burkert (1992) 5–6.

a history of destruction, has marginalized the importance of this area in the history of ancient literature.

The timing of Oriental influence emphasizes the early first millennium, the age of Neo-Assyrian expansion and the migration of the Phoenicians and their alphabet; this period also saw the assembly of Akkadian literature, major portions of the Hebrew Bible, and the formation of the Homeric corpus.[34] The convergence of the early Greek alphabet with the redaction of epic[35] brings contents and symbols of Near Eastern writing closer to Greek poetry. Oral literature may have accompanied religion and the art of writing from the Levant to the Aegean: popular interaction in bilingual communities and intermarriage assisted the diffusion of the alphabet and its message.[36] Mythology offers Easterners like 'Kadmos the Phoenician' who imported the alphabet to Greece, then married a Theban princess and founded a Greek dynasty.

The date of transmission from non-Greek sources is entangled with the debate over the antiquity of Homeric poetry, but recent consensus on its archaic formation should not exclude Bronze Age influences. Like the Greek alphabet, first visible in the eighth century but related to older Phoenician letter forms,[37] the corpus of epic poetry has early roots. Homeric preservation of linguistic formulae and archaeological realia long obsolete before the eighth century includes Near Eastern content.[38] For example, the iterative verb forms of East Ionic and epic dialect suggest Hittite forms obsolete in Anatolia after the Bronze Age.[39] Patterns of heroic performance replicate foreign traditions of the Bronze Age, such as the contest with the bow won by Odysseus (see below). The afterlife of Ugaritic myth in Hebrew literature makes it difficult to distinguish the legacy of Late Bronze Age Syria from early Iron Age innovation. For example, a common poetic epithet for Baal, 'Rider of the Clouds,' surfaces in Greek epic poetry as Zeus 'the cloud-gatherer.' The phrase could have migrated

---

[34] Burkert (1992) 9–40.

[35] Powell (1991), esp. 181–86, 221–33; cf. Wade-Gery (1952).

[36] M. L. West (1988) 171 (bilingual poets); J. N. Coldstream, 'Mixed Marriages at the Frontiers of the Early Greek World,' *Oxford Journal of Archaeology* 12:1 (1993) 89–107.

[37] Arguing for an early datre: J. Naveh, 'Semitic Epigraphy and the Antiquity of the Greek Alphabet,' *Kadmos* 30 (1991) 143–52 with earlier scholarship. Cf. Powell (1991) 18–20 (no earlier than 800 B.C.).

[38] See J. Bennet in this volume.

[39] Puhvel (1991) 13–20; cf. his 'Homeric Questions and Hittite Answers,' *American Journal of Philology* 104 (1983) 217–27.

to the Aegean in the Bronze Age or centuries later, a poetic corollary to the dispersal of Near Eastern bronze 'smiter gods' which also influenced Greek images of Zeus. In short, Aegean travelers, hosts and artists had frequent and intermittent contact with Near Eastern narratives, to varying effect. After extended foreign fertilization, specific historical conditions of the early Iron Age gave shape to poems like the *Iliad* and the *Odyssey*. Those very conditions were shared with the Hebrew Bible; in both areas, small city-states, often in conflict with each other while seeking new forms of community, celebrated common historical memories of a more distant past.

Near Eastern Settings in Homeric Poetry

Throughout Homer, lands and peoples east of the Aegean figure in familiar and fantastic ways in the lives of Greek heroes. Foreigners abound in Anatolia, home of Troy and its many non-Greek allies (*Il.* 4.438); their names and cities are known to Homer, but rarely fit those in history or literature.[40] The catalogue of Trojan allies in *Iliad* 2 is scantier than the roster of Achaeans which it follows, and of little historical substance beyond the Troad. For example, Miletus is home to Carians 'of barbarian speech' (2.867–9), although this area attracted Aegean migrants (Minoan, Mycenaean, then Ionian Greek) since the second millennium. The Hittites, once dominant inland, are absent from the *Iliad* but imperfectly remembered in the *Odyssey* (11.518–21) as the Keteioi—more likely Cheteioi—of Mysia, Trojan allies.[41] In recalling the siege of Troy, Odysseus tells the shade of Achilles how his son, Neoptolemos, slew Eurypylos, just as Achilles himself once wounded Eurypylos' father Telephos, a likely survival of Telipinus, son of the great Hittite (Hattic) storm god. Telipinus and his father are further linked to Greek poetry: in Hittite literature, they disappear in anger and withhold benefits—fertility—from nature, in a drama replayed in the Greek myth of Demeter and Persephone.[42] Other shadowy Trojan allies who may reflect older

[40] A. Scherer, 'Nichtgriechische Personennamen der Ilias,' in *Studien zum antiken Epos*, eds. H. Görgemanns and E. A. Schmidt (Meisenheim, 1976) 32–45; Kirk (1985) 248–63; Röllig (1992).
[41] G. Huxley, 'Hittites in Homer,' *Parola del Passato* 14 (1959) 281–82; Alcaeus, fr. 413 LP.
[42] N. J. Richardson (1974) 258–59; Hoffner (1990) 14 ff.

Hittites are the Halizones of silver-rich Alybe, possibly the Halys river (*Il.* 2.856). Legendary Easterners like the Amazons, active in the *Aithiopis* on the Trojan side, are remembered in the *Iliad* as common enemies of Phrygians near the Black Sea (3.189) and foes of Bellerophon in Lycia (6.186–87). The Lycians, prominent in the *Iliad* for the *aristeia* and death of their leader Sarpedon, can be traced to Bronze Age Lukka, fickle in loyalty to Hittites and Ahhiyawa.[43] In the Glaukos episode (*Il.* 6.150–211), marriage and *xenia* bind Greek and Lycian families in close ties: thus Glaukos and Diomedes recognize each other, refrain from combat and exchange armour. In the epic *Nostoi* or poems of return, survivors of the Trojan War like the seer, Mopsos, migrate to western and south-eastern Anatolia to found historical cities and their dynasties.[44]

Farther east, the island of Cyprus appears once in the *Iliad* as the kingdom of Kinyras, ally of Agamemnon who sends him a *xeinios*-gift, a magnificent cuirasse (11.19–28).[45] This corslet is inlaid with different metals and imported materials like tin (κασσίτερος) and κύανος (Mycenaean ku-wa-no; cf. Hittite kuwanna), blue glass or precious stone (lapis lazuli). Kinyras has a Semitic name (cf. Hebrew *kinnôr*, 'lyre,' the Akkadian god Ki-na-rum, Ugaritic knr), and his relationship with a Greek king implies traditional Near Eastern diplomacy. If Cyprus is Bronze Age Alashiya, this passage mirrors prehistoric relationships between kings of Alashiya, Ahhiyawa and the Hittites.[46] Agamemnon's Cypriote gear matches his scepter (*Il.* 2.100–8, 9.38), made by Hephaistos; its best parallel was found at Kourion. Wealthy royal tombs at Salamis on Cyprus illustrate the Iron Age afterlife of Homeric kingship, if not Achaean refugees from the Trojan war.[47]

In the *Odyssey*, the island of Cyprus figures seven times in exotic

---

[43] M. Mellink, 'Homer, Lycia and Lukka,' in Carter and Morris (1995) 33–43.

[44] Burkert (1992) 52; cf. J. Vanschoonwinkel, *L'Egée et la Méditerranée Orientale à la fin du IIe millénaire: Témoignages archéologiques et sources écrites*. Archaeologia Transatlantica IX (Louvain and Providence, 1991) 314–30.

[45] C. Baurain, 'Kinyras. La fin de l'Age de Bronze à Chypre et la tradition antique,' *Bulletin de Correspondence Hellénique* 104 (1980) 277–308; N. Richardson (1987) 125–32.

[46] M. Liverani, *Prestige and Interest: International Relations in the Near East ca. 1600–1100 B.C.* (Padua, 1990).

[47] D. Rupp, 'The "Royal Tombs" at Salamis (Cyprus): Ideological Messages of Power and Authority,' *Journal of Mediterranean Archaeology* 1:1 (1988) 111–39; *Cyprus B.C. 7000 Years of History*, ed. V. Tatton-Brown (London, 1979) 155, for gold scepter-head with falcons.

travel by Homeric heroes, on itineraries that include Phoenicia, Egypt, Africa, and Arabia. Menelaos stopped here on his circuitous return from Troy via Egypt (4.83), and the island figures similarly in the tales of Odysseus. In one adventure (17.426–44), he returns from Egypt via Cyprus as a gift (a captive in war) to a fictional ruler, Dmetor ('tamer, dominator'), son of Iasos (also a Theban patronymic: *Od.* 11.263), guest-friend of the Egyptian pharaoh. This fits a Bronze Age setting, with exchanges between rulers as in *Il.* 11.15–46. Finally, although Cyprus (Paphos) is home to Aphrodite (*Il.* 5.330; *Od.* 8.363), the *Kypria* poem of the epic cycle may owe its name not to its love themes, but to its Cypriote origins.[48]

In Homer, Phoenicia falls naturally on a maritime route with Cyprus and Egypt, and also provides superior craftsmanship in metal and textiles, especially the city of Sidon. Both Trojans (*Il.* 6.290–2) and Greeks (*Od.* 4.84) visit Sidon with Helen, and return with valuable objects, prestige goods in epic poetry. In the *Iliad*, Phoenician handiworks are offered to kings and gods, exchanged as ransom, and reward victorious athletes. Embroidered garments made by Sidonian women, a trophy of Helen's honeymoon trip from Sparta to Troy, are presented to Athena in a special appeal by the Trojan women at Hektor's request—in vain (*Il.* 6.86–98, 288–310). A silver krater proffered as first prize in the foot race at the funeral games of Patroklos (*Il.* 23.740–9) has a colorful pedigree. In their only active role in the *Iliad*, Phoenician traders brought it to Lemnos as a 'present' for king Thoas, a conflation of ancient trade and gift exchange. His grandson Euneos (son of Jason) exchanged it with Patroklos for Lykaon, captured by Achilles; in another version of the story, Achilles received a hecatomb in exchange for him from the Lemnians, who later sold him back to Eetion of Imbros for three hundred cattle (*Il.* 21.42, 79). Eventually escaping to the Trojans, via Arisbe, after this triple ransom in cattle (21.80), the unhappy son of Priam meets Achilles again, and his death, in the Greek hero's rampage after the death of Patroklos (*Il.* 21.34–135); the krater, now in Greek hands, commemorates the death of Patroklos as a prize won by Odysseus. His family also profits from Phoenician craftsmanship in the *Odyssey*, when Menelaos gives Telemachos another silver mixing bowl as a guest-gift, enhanced by the prestige of its original donor, Phaidimos,

[48] Burkert (1992) 101–4; N. J. Richardson (1987) 125–32. Note also the high incidence of 'Homeric' vocabulary in Cypriote Greek.

illustrious king of Sidon (*Od.* 4.612–9; 15.103–4). This time, the krater from Phoenicia is attributed to a Greek divine craftsman, Hephaistos, with interesting connections to the Ugaritic craftsman-god, Kothar-wa-Ḫasis.[49] The embroidered robes which join the krater as gifts to Telemachos are woven by Helen herself, but described in verses identical to the exotic ones in Hecuba's possession (*Od.* 15.105–8; cf. *Il.* 6.289–92). Greek praise of craftsmanship converges with Oriental handiwork in a poetic scenario of deceit, danger and death in these descriptions.[50] Homeric exotica resemble those described in Biblical accounts of Phoenician art (I Kings 5–7; II Chron. 2–4) and those found in Mesopotamia, Cyprus, Italy and Greece.[51] Yet Bronze Age Canaanite textiles and precious metals complicate 'dating' these passages or their Homeric setting.

In contrast to their handiwork, the Phoenicians themselves attract terms more negative than any other non-Greeks in Homer, primarily in the *Odyssey*. This portrayal once justified dating the poem 'later' than the *Iliad*, for its increased signs of Phoenician activity in the Mediterraean, and of Greek hostility.[52] As πολυπαίπαλοι seaborne traders in the *Odyssey*, unlike the πολυδαίδαλοι craftswomen in the *Iliad*, Homeric Phoenicians are greedy and deceitful: they kidnap Greeks into slavery (14.288–96; 15.403–84) and harbor stowaways (13.256–86). A recent view makes them foils for Homeric Greeks, a sign of emerging Hellenic consciousness of other Mediterranean peoples and of the divided social fabric of the early Greek *polis*.[53]

Both archaeologically and linguistically, the Aegean Bronze Age is acquainted with Egypt. Its Greek name derives from Ḫikuptaḫ, via a Near Eastern version rendering of the Egyptian name (Ḥwt k3 Ptḥ, 'House of Ptah') for Memphis, Egypt's administrative capital; compare how Mycenaean te-qa in Linear B (at Mycenae: X 508) may represent the name for Thebes, possibly a Greek corruption of Egyptian 'Ipet-sut.' At least one lord of Ithaka was called Aiguptios (*Od.* 2.15), presumably the same name as a herdman of Bronze Age

[49] S. Morris (1992) 73–100.

[50] S. Morris (1992) 10–22.

[51] Winter (1995); G. Markoe, *Phoenician Bronze and Silver Bowls from Cyprus and the Mediterranean* (Berkeley, 1985).

[52] Bernal (1987) 336–99 (history of scholarship); Carpenter (1958) 35–54, and Muhly (1970) 19–64, denied Bronze Age connections.

[53] Winter (1995) on the double meaning of these references.

Knossos (A^3-ku-pi-ti-jo: Db 1105 + 1446). More surprisingly, Bronze Age Greece also knew Egypt by its Semitic name, misr, according to another personal name, mi-sa-ra-jo (KnF841). Nothing makes these men foreigners rather than Aegean natives who acquired an Egyptian connection through travel or commerce. An expedition to Egypt for profit detains returning Trojan war heroes (*Od.* 3.300–3; 14.240–86): special adventures there color the detour of Menelaos (*Od.* 4.347–592) and the 'false tales' of Odysseus (*Od.* 14.257–97, 17.424–44). The land of the Nile was renowned for gold, silver and other wealth (*Od.* 3.301, 4.125–32) and for its organic products, like the φάρμακα which Helen adds to wine for her troubled guests (*Od.* 4.220–34). This episode demonstrates her supernatural powers as well as Egypt's reputation as a land where 'every man is a doctor, outstanding in wisdom (ἐπιστάμενος) among all men' (*Od.* 4.231–2). Bronze Age containers for opium derivatives suggest potions like Helen's, with more likely additives to wine in later sources (Plutarch *Isis and Osiris* 80).[54] Helen acquired these skills from Polydamna, wife of an Egyptian (Thon) whose people, suspiciously called the race of Paieon—Apollo's name as healing god, attested as pa-ja-wo in Linear B—specialize in healing knowledge. In these passages, Near Eastern wisdom spreads to Greeks through female friendships rather than male practitioners,[55] and Helen enjoys exotic guest-gifts from foreign women (*Od.* 4.125–32).

Two detailed Homeric adventures in Egypt offer striking correspondences with traditions native to the Nile. Beyond the profit motive which drives Homeric heroes to Egypt, Menelaos travels there for the equivalent of Odysseus' *Nekyia* (*Odyssey* 11), in his encounter with Proteus, the 'old man of the sea.' The Spartan king is marooned on a deserted island called Pharos, later the name of Ptolemy's lighthouse but here perhaps derived from an Egyptian place named Pr-Ḥr ('House of Horus') or Pr-Rʿ ('House of Re') in Egyptian. Without winds to travel on, he soon depletes his provisions and reduces his men to fishing, last resort of Homeric heroes (cf. *Od.* 12.328–32). A

[54] B. Knapp, 'Spice, drugs, grain and grog: organic goods in Bronze Age East Mediterranean trade,' in Gale, ed. (1991) 21–68; R. Germer, 'Ancient Egyptian Medicinal Plants and the Eastern Mediterranean,' in *The Healing Past: Pharmaceuticals in the Biblical and Rabbinical World*, eds. I. and W. Jacob (Leiden, 1993) 69–80.

[55] Burkert (1992) 6, on itinerant (male) professions in *Odyssey* 17.383–85: seer, healer, carpenter and singer.

goddess takes pity on him: Eidothea (invented here) advises him to capture and consult her father, Proteus 'the Egyptian,' at home elsewhere in Greek legends. His zoomorphic guise recalls the snaky family guarding the island visited by the Egyptian Shipwrecked Sailor. In his prophecy for the hero, Proteus prescribes ritual obligations much as Teiresias does for Odysseus (4.472–80), then promises Menelaos an unwordly paradise foreign, if not Egyptian, in origin (561–70).[56]

More historical than literary are the Egyptian misadventures of Odysseus in his 'false tales' to his swineherd (*Od.* 14.199–359) and the suitors (17.415–44; cf. 19.172–202). In two stories (in *Odyssey* 14 and 19), Odysseus claims to be a Cretan—most well-travelled of all Aegean peoples, the Keftiu of Egyptian fame—and a relative or comrade-in-arms of Idomeneus, hero at Troy. As a Cretan, he cannot resist an expedition to Egypt after Troy (14.243–300), but meets disaster in the Delta when his men fall to plunder and violence and are pursued by the Pharaoh. Odysseus is spared, but captured into forced labor, then lured away by a Phoenician for slavery. Only a storm saves him from this fate, and returns him to Ithaka.

These episodes could reflect historical events at the end of the Bronze Age, when foreigners of many lands attacked the Egyptian delta and engaged Pharaonic forces throughout the Ramesside period.[57] Even specific phrases echo Egyptian accounts: when Odysseus claims that 'no man dared stand against him' (the pharaoh: 14. 269–70), it recalls the same phrase used by Ramses III of foreign mercenaries in the Delta, at Medinet Habu. The Homeric supplication of the pharaoh (14.278–80) suggests Egyptian reliefs of the king in his chariot, visible for many centuries. These impressions of the Bronze Age culminate in the description of Thebes (*Od.* 4.126–7), expanded in the only reference to Egypt in the *Iliad.* When Achilles refuses Agamemnon's recompense for offense done, he rejects the treasures of Orchomenos and Thebes, 'the Egyptian one, where many goods lie stored in chambers, a city of one hundred gates, from each of which two hundred men would go forth with horses and chariots' (*Il.* 9.381–4). This image of Egypt, epitomized in its ceremonial and

[56] G. Alford, ''Ἠλύσιον: a foreign eschatological concept in Homer's Odyssey,' *Journal of Indo-European Studies* 19 (1991) 151–61; cf. Cook (1992) 253–58.

[57] Sandars (1985); V. Hankey, 'Mycenaean Pottery at Saqqara,' in Carter and Morris (1995) 70–72.

funerary capital of the Eighteenth Dynasty, must echo its Bronze Age splendors, not their revival many centuries later.[58] The many δόμοι full of κτήματα suggest Theban mortuary temples and palaces with chambers like Medinet Habu, the 'gates' could describe those pylons with images and inscriptions which inspired Homeric views of Egypt. When these monuments were observed cannot be determined, nor used to fix the date of Homeric composition.

Finally, Homeric poetry knows of more distant peoples and places, ἔσχατοι ἀνδρῶν. Libya—presumably the coast of North Africa, later colonized by Greeks—figures on the standard Homeric itinerary of the Near East with Cyprus, Phoenicia, and Egypt (e.g. for Menelaos, *Od.* 4.83–5, or the disguised Odysseus: *Od.* 14.295).[59] Like Aiguptios, Aithiops may appear in Mycenaean Greek as A^3-ti-jo-qo (Py Eb 156, Eb 846, En 74, Eo 247, Ep 301). In epic poetry, the Ethiopians ('burned faces' or 'dark skin') are Trojan allies led by Memnon, son of the Dawn Goddess, Eos (an Eastern progenitor), and their country lies in the Near East (*Od.* 4.84). At Troy, Memnon kills Antilochos, son of Nestor (*Od.* 4.187–8), but loses his life to Achilles in the eponymous lost epic poem, the *Aithiopis*. The Aithiopians are also cult hosts of Poseidon (*Od.* 1.22–6), and affiliated with Africa as the progenitor of Libyans, Pygmies, and 'Melanes' in Hesiod (*Eoiai* fr. 150, 17–19). But neither Memnon nor his Ethiopians are connected with Africa in Homer (a Persian origin persists until late: Pausanias 10.31.7) nor described with ethnic features, albeit praised for their beauty (*Od.* 11.522; cf. Herodotus 3.20). The only Homeric figure who sounds African is the herald of Ithaka, Eurybates, who travelled to Troy and back with his master; his looks are distinctive enough for Penelope to recognize his description by the disguised Odysseus (*Od.* 19. 244–8). His 'dark skin' and 'wooly hair' are consistent Negroid features in later Greek sources: Bronze Age images portray Africans as familiar to Aegean artists.[60] Yet his name is Greek—just as another Ithakan is 'Egyptian' (*Od.* 2.15)—and his ethnicity irrelevant to his important rank.

---

[58] W. Burkert, 'Das hunderttorige Theben und die Datierung der Ilias,' *Wiener Studien* 10 (1976) 6–21 uses this passage to downdate the *Iliad*.

[59] P. Haider, *Griechenland-Nordafrika: ihre Beziehungen zwischen 1500 und 600 v. Chr.* (Darmstadt, 1988).

[60] F. Snowden, *Blacks in Antiquity: Ethiopians in the Greco-Roman Experience* (Harvard, 1970); W. V. Soden, 'Die Eremboi der Odyssee und die Irrfahrt des Menelaos,' *Wiener Studien* 72 (1959) 26–28 on Homeric circumnavigation of Africa.

The sum of these passages suggests familiarity with the coastal lands of the eastern Mediterranean, with foreign names and goods as common as imported luxuries. Foreigners bear Greek names—Phaidimos of Sidon, Dmetor of Cyprus, Polydamna of Egypt—just as Trojans behave and speak like Greeks in the *Iliad.* More intriguing is how specific traditions in religion and literature penetrated the cultural life of early poets, and determined narrative elements in epic poetry.

Narrative Form and Content

A common heritage of mythological themes in Greek and Near Eastern poetry surfaces in epic episodes and as these themes are imagined in art; many have been identified and catalogued by modern scholars.[61] Greek poets adapted them into an heroic tradition and stitched them together into a smooth narrative sequence. In most instances, recombination suggests multiple sources and evolution over time, fundamental processes of epic composition.

In the *Iliad* and *Odyssey*, it is the gods and their interaction with mortals which are highly Oriental. As noted earlier (n. 30), the pantheon and its divided powers over the cosmos (*Il.* 15.187–93) are clearly Near Eastern in origin. The race of men was created by gods in Greek, Mesopotamian and Hebraic tradition and related to them through figures like Japheth, whose Homeric counterpart is Iapetos, the Titan (*Il.* 8.479; cf. Hesiod *Theogony* 507–616), and whose sons include Iavan (Ionians, or Greeks: Genesis 10:2–5).[62] Once men shared divine privileges until they abused them: this theme drives the story of Prometheus in Hesiod, Atraḫasis, and the book of Genesis. Divine modes of travel, disguise of gods and mortals, and emotional expression among Greek gods are familiar in Ugaritic epic, in particular. Communication through a dream is formulaic in Homeric and Near Eastern narrative, especially in Canaanite and Biblical tales. Homer's craftsman-god manufactures armor and buildings with Oriental details (*Il.* 18.468–82; *Od.* 7.86–94), as in Ugaritic epic Kothar makes weapons and a palace for Baal. Divine parents interact with mortal offspring in similar ways. Thus Ninsun regrets the restless heroism of

[61] Gordon (1955) and (1962) 218–77; Stella (1955); Burkert (1992) and (1991) 170–74; Dirlmeier (1955) 18–37.

[62] D. Neiman, 'The Two Genealogies of Japhet,' in *Orient and Occident. Studies presented to Cyrus H. Gordon*, ed. H. Hoffner, Jr. (Neukirchen-Vluyn, 1973) 119–26.

her son, Gilgamesh, to the god Shamash (III.2.10 ff.), just as Thetis laments her sorrows as mother of Achilles (*Il.* 1.414), both expressed as a rhetorical question. And both sons have their mothers intercede with a male god (*Il.* 1.393 ff.; Gilgamesh III.1.22 ff.). Divine protection and restraint of heroes prevails east (Epic of Baal) and west (*Il.* 1.193–8), as with divine seduction. Most famously, Odysseus resists, then exploits, the charms of Circe (*Od.* 10.281–347; cf. *Homeric Hymn to Aphrodite* 145–54, 185–90) much as Nergal behaves with Ereshkigal in Akkadian tradition; Gilgamesh refuses the advances of Ishtar, who also fails (as Šauška) to seduce Hurrian heroes in myths from Hattušas.[63] Likewise, goddesses complain in heaven when their charms fail against mortals. Ishtar appeals to her father, Anu, when she is refused by Gilgamesh (VI.1–120), or Anat protests to El when she fails to win Aqhat or his magic weapons; Aphrodite and Artemis run to Zeus when wounded (*Il.* 5.330–430; 21.505–13) and Calypso complains to Hermes of the double standard in divine seduction, when forced to relinquish Odysseus (*Od.* 5.117–44). Even when Homeric gods deceive each other they act Near Eastern: Hera 'arms' herself to seduce Zeus (*Il.* 14. 160–223) with a wardrobe and magic charms borrowed from Hittite and Near Eastern arsenals.[64]

Phrases and formulas of Homeric theology echo the Near East. In divine titles, Zeus is called 'gatherer of the clouds' (νεφεληγερέτα: *Il.* 1.511, *Od.* 1.63), like the Ugaritic 'Rider of the Clouds,' epithet of Baal. The mysterious phrase 'of tree and stone' appears twice in Homer and once in Hesiod (*Theogony* 35; *Il.* 22.126; *Od.* 19.163). A suggestive parallel is the divine secret guarded by the gods in Ugaritic epic, 'the word of the tree and the whisper of the stone.'[65] This secret is lost in Homer; in Hesiod its context still suggests some divine truth shared by the Muses and Zeus. The intimacy between God and Moses in the Hebrew Bible (Exodus 33.11) is bestowed on Homeric lawgivers (*Od.* 19.178–9): Minos of Crete is a 'familiar' (ὀαριστής) of Zeus, a term of sexual intimacy.[66] The gods build walls

[63] Crane (1988) 63–85; H. Güterbock, 'A Hurro-Hittite Hymn to Ishtar,' *Journal of the American Oriental Society* 103 (1983) 155–64.

[64] C. Faraone, 'Aphrodite's ΚΕΣΤΟΣ and apples for Atalanta: Aphrodisiacs in Early Greek Magic and Ritual,' *Phoenix* 44 (1990) 219–43. Cf. Puhvel (1991) 11–12, or Pagat's cosmetic arming scene in the epic of Aqhat: Coogan (1978) 46–7.

[65] M. L. West (1966) 167–69; M. Smith, 'Baal's Cosmic Secret,' *Ugarit-Forschungen* 16 (1984) 295–8. J. Carter, 'The Masks of Ortheia,' *American Journal of Archaeology* 91 (1987) 375–77 compares 'tree and stone' to Hebre *massēbôt* and *asherah*, Greek στῆλαι and ῥάβδοι.

[66] S. Morris (1992) 174–82 for references and discussion.

for cities of men, whether Uruk (in Gilgamesh) or Troy (*Il.* 21.446–7), but can also destroy them in anger, in Biblical or Homeric (*Il.* 12.1–32) retribution. In general, Homeric religion cannot be separated from the Near East. Greek sacrifice follows purposes and procedures for offerings (animal, cereal, and liquid) long practised in the Bronze Age, including many described in the Bible (Leviticus 1–8; Numbers 28–29). The very drink of the gods, νέκταρ, may be a Near Eastern import (Semitic nqtr describes perfumed or fragrant smoke; cf. κνίση).[67] Hittite beliefs underlie Homeric patterns in oaths (e.g. *Il.* 1.234–7, 240–2; 3.276–80)[68] and other rituals, including the consultation of the dead in *Odyssey* 11 and the celebration of funeral games in *Iliad* 23.[69] Egypt and Anatolia anticipate the famous *psychostasia* (weighing of souls), whereby Zeus decides the fate of heroes (*Il.* 8.69–72, 16.658; 22.208–13).[70]

Unlike the Bible, Homeric poetry stresses the heroic view of history without its theological overtones. As an epic of war and city siege, the *Iliad* has many literary relatives; its lost sequel, the *Ilioupersis*, suggests even greater kinship with Near Eastern accounts of the fall of cities. Military and narrative devices such as siege engines, infiltration strategies, and appeal to the gods by the defenders elaborate Near Eastern traditions.[71] The *Iliad*, devoted to one warrior and his conflicts, offers parallels to the fortunes and character of Gilgamesh. The heroes' kinship culminates in their intimate relationship to Patroklos/Enkidu, the close companion who predeceases them.[72] The bereaved hero's grief is compared, in Greek and Akkadian, to a lion's rage at the loss of its cubs (*Il.* 18.318 ff.; Gilgamesh VIII.2.18 ff.). The ghost of Enkidu appears in the final tablet of the Gilgamesh epic, as Patroklos haunts Achilles (*Il.* 23.65–107) and Achilles addresses Odysseus from Hades (*Od.* 11.465–540).

---

[67] S. Levin, 'The Etymology of νέκταρ: exotic scents in early Greece,' *Studi Miceni ed Egeo-Anatolici* 13 (1971) 31–50.

[68] Puhvel (1991) 9–10, 27–28.

[69] O. Loretz, 'Nekromantie und Totenevokation in Mesopotamien, Ugarit und Israel,' in *Religionsgeschichtliche Beziehungen zwischen Kleinasien, Nordsyrien, und dem alten Testament.* Ed. B. Janowski, K. Koch and G. Wilhelm (Göttingen, 1993) 285–318; Puhvel (1988) 26–31.

[70] Vermeule (1979) 76; cf. H. Otten, *Hethitische Totenrituale* (Berlin, 1958) 13; Puhvel (1991) 10–11.

[71] S. Morris (1995); Puhvel (1976) 60–6.

[72] As ritual substitutes for the hero, Patroklos and Enkidu also resemble a Hittite *tarpan- (Greek θεραπῶν): Nagy (1979) 33, 292–97.

Beyond the story of Achilles, the *Iliad* often points to the East. When Glaukos meets Diomedes on the battlefield, the poet's detour through Lycian mythology incorporates into the geneaology of Glaukos stories of the unfaithful wife and the fatal letter, both long popular in the Near East (*Il.* 6.119–236). Companion to the fate of Bellerophon is the story of Joseph and Potiphar's wife in the Bible (*Genesis* 39); the wife who seduces, then denounces a younger man is widespread (cf. Phaedra and Hippolytus).[73] In the *Iliad*, the young man is banished to Lycia as courier for his own death sentence, the only reference to writing in Homer. The folding tablet with 'baleful signs' now matches a find from a shipload of Near Eastern cargo wrecked off the Lycian coast, as its Greek name (δέλτος) reproduces Semitic daltu.[74] The narrative also replays the story of Uriah the Hittite, who delivers his own death warrant from David to Joab (II Samuel 11:14–21). In Lycia, Bellerophon defeats three native foes—the Chimaira, a multiform monster from Anatolian art; the Amazons, female warriors of Asian ancestry; and the fierce Solymoi of Lycia—to win a Lycian princess and her kingdom, repeating marriage alliances made in history (by the Hittites) and mythology (by Proitos himself). The passage ends with the exchange of gold armour for bronze (6.234–6), a Bronze Age pact of respect which baffles the poet but boasts a Biblical pedigree: Jonathan strikes a covenant with David and bestows on him his own clothing, armour, and weapons (I Samuel 18.1–4).[75] Further legal correspondences unite the trial scene on the Shield of Achilles (*Il.* 18.497–508) and the exchange of oaths and treaties with Near Eastern practises.[76]

The opening of *Iliad* 12 offers a brief but vivid window on the future which recapitulates the Near Eastern origins of the epic cycle. The wall of the Achaeans is destined for destruction by gods deprived of hecatombs, Zeus, Apollo and Poseidon, often enemies in the *Iliad*

[73] Burkert (1983) 51–53; Frei in Janowski et al., eds. (n. 69 above) 39–65. Hittite derivations for [B]ελλερ(ο)-οφι-φόντης as Greek slayer of Illuyankaš and Pegasus from piḫassassis argued by J. Katz; cf. C. Watkins, 'How to Kill a Dragon in Indo-European,' in *Studies in Memory of Warren Cowgill (1929–1985)*, ed. C. Watkins (Berlin, 1987) 279–87.

[74] R. Bellamy, 'Bellerophon's Tablet,' *Classical Journal* 84 (1989) 289–307; wooden tablet in Payton (1991); D. Symington, 'Late Bronze Age writing boards and their uses: textual evidence from Anatolia and Syria,' *Anatolian Studies* 41 (1991) 111–23; Burkert (1992) 30.

[75] Calder (1984) 31–35.

[76] Westbrook (1992) 53–76; Karavites and Wren (1992).

but united in anger here. The passage summons an older tradition, where divine anger at mankind motivates the Trojan war in its opening poem (*Kypria*, fr. 1).[77] War story competes with divine flood as a narrative separating the past from the present. The ἡμίθεοι or 'half-god men' link Homer with Hesiod (*Works and Days* 160) and recall the sons of God who coupled with mortal women and were eliminated by the flood (Genesis 6:1–4). In another seam of traditions, the conflux of Trojan rivers (*Il.* 12.18–23) turns a primeval flood into an epic event local to Anatolia. Such passages reveal Greek, heroic displacement of a Near Eastern, theological past, much as Hesiod emends the cycle of destruction to include an age of heroes (*Works and Days* 106–201).[78]

As a geographical and spiritual journey, the *Odyssey* parallels the story of Gilgamesh with a hero who matures, both young (Telemachos) and adult (Odysseus), encounters imaginary females, and seeks wisdom from the older generation (Utnapishtim, Teiresias). Both heroes confront loss and mortality, and re-enter their community as king. In his adventures, Odysseus meets monsters long familiar in the Near East, such as the one-eyed Cyclops, Polyphemus (*Od.* 9.105–566).[79] His encounters with supernatural women like Calypso and Circe echo Near Eastern traditions, in particular the Akkadian story of Nergal and Ereshkigal, queen of the underworld: in both poems the hero is warned of a *femme fatale*, threatens her, yields to seduction, and abandons her.[80] Odysseus embarks on another Near Eastern trip to consult the dead on Circe's advice, as Gilgamesh follows the alewife's instructions in search of Utnapishtim. The *Nekyia* invokes rituals and landscapes rich in Near Eastern overtones; unlike Nergal, the Greek hero comes back from the dead to pursue an agenda of return.[81] The island of the Phaeacians introduces an imaginary country that

---

[77] Scodel (1982) 33–50; R. Hendel, 'Of Demigods and the Deluge: Towards an Interpretation of Genesis 6:1–4,' *Journal of Biblical Literature* 106:1 (1987) 13–26, for Greek, Near Eastern and Indic versions; J. W. de Jong, 'The Over-Burdened Earth in India and Greece,' *Journal of the American Oriental Society* 105.3 (1985) 397–400.

[78] Koenen (1994) 1–34.

[79] T. Poljakov, 'A Phoenician Ancestor of the Cyclops,' *Zeitschrift für Papyrologie und Epigraphik* 53 (1983) 95–98.

[80] Crane (1988) 70–75.

[81] J. Puhvel, '"Meadow of the Otherworld" in Indo-European Mythology,' in *Zeitschrift für Vergleichende Sprachenkunde* 83 (1969) 64–69; G. Steiner, 'Die Unterweltsbeschwörung der Odyssee im Lichte hethitischer Texte,' *Ugarit-Forschungen* 3 (1971) 265–83.

evokes Aegean, Near Eastern and Indo-European traditions.[82] Their lavish palace (7.84–102) recalls not only Aegean ones but Biblical settings like the temple of Solomon (I Kings 5–7) and the Canaanite palace of Baal.[83] Their fertile land (7.112–31) resembles the imaginary paradise of Egyptian travelers (Sinuhe in Palestine, or the Shipwrecked Sailor's island). Their athletic challenge to Odysseus recasts the duel Sinuhe won abroad (cf. David's victory over Goliath: I Samuel 17) as a Greek agon (8.100–235). Even his 'false tales' apply Near Eastern military narrative to exploits fictional in the *Odyssey* but plausible in Late Bronze Age history (see above).

In his triumphant return to Ithaka, the hero regains his kingship in Near Eastern style. In an episode resembling Balthasar's feast (Daniel 5), the suitors' banquet is disrupted by an omen, from which an exiled prophet predicts doom (20.345–57); as in the Bible, the prophecy is fulfilled when the banqueters are punished and replaced by a new king. The contest with the bow and 'axes,' and battle in a banquet hall (*Od.* 21.393–421), turns several traditions into a unique heroic performance. Parallels exist in the career of the Hittite king Gurparanzaḫus who captures Akkad, defeats sixty princes and seventy heroes in archery after a banquet, and is united in bed with his wife.[84] More ingenious is the archery contest, a creative Greek misunderstanding of the image of the Egyptian pharaoh who drives arrows through bronze (ingots, which resemble double-axes: Figure 1).[85] Homeric kingship borrows freely from grander traditions of the past and the Near East, as in Agamemnon's Cypriote cuirasse and scepter (above). A foreign king with fifty sons and daughters and chambers for each, Priam of Troy (*Il.* 6.242–50; 24.495–500) emulates Ramses II, with his many sons buried in multi-chambered tombs at Thebes. Yet final recognition of the hero by his wife in devices like the bed (*Od.* 23.173–230) seems unique to Greek poetry, and perhaps to one poet.

Finally, most widely shared in Greek and Near Eastern literature

---

[82] Cook (1992) 239–67.

[83] S. Morris (1992) 83–84; Faraone (1987).

[84] E. Forrer, 'Eine Geschichte des Götterkönigtums aus dem Hatti-reiche,' in *Mélanges Cumont* (Brussels, 1936) 687–713; H. Güterbock, 'Die Historische Tradition und ihre literarische Gestaltung bei Babyloniern und Hethitern bis 1200,' *Zeitschrift für Assyriologie* 44 (1938) 83–90.

[85] Burkert (1973); underappreciated by M. Fernandez-Galiano in Russo et al. (1992) 133–47; Walcot (1984) 357–69.

FIGURE 1. SEALING FROM BETH SHEAN: RAMSES II SHOOTING THROUGH 'AXES'

is poetic nature and performance. The resemblances in poetic techniques like repetition of type-scenes and formulaic epithets, or similes from the natural world describing human action, have long been noted.[86] Another shared feature is the strong dramatic quality of direct speech; the Homeric combination of poet's voice with direct speech by heroic characters has been traced to the second millennium and Near Eastern influence.[87] The very occasion of Homeric performance offers interesting parallels to the long-lived Near Eastern tradition of the *marzeaḥ* or ritual banquet in honor of the dead.[88] Such commemorative events may have celebrated heroic deeds of the dead, prehistoric epic poems performed in groups anticipating the θίασος, Greek celebrants at functions equivalent to the *marzeaḥ*. Indeed, it has been claimed that the entire bardic tradition is more Oriental than Greek, and the shape of Homeric poems—in 24 books, corresponding to the letters of the new Oriental alphabet—more than coincidence (see M. Haslam, this vol.).

In the final analysis, it may be a greater challenge to isolate and appreciate what is Greek in Homeric poetry than to enumerate its foreign sources. Exploring the many treasures common to Homeric and Near Eastern epic, including the Hebrew Bible, enables modern readers to join archaeologists and recover the lost unity of ancient Mediterranean literature and life.

---

[86] P. Walcot, 'The Comparative Study of Ugaritic and Greek Literature,' *Ugarit-Forschung* 1 (1969) 111–118; 2 (1970) 273–75; 4 (1972) 129–33; Burkert (1991) 170; G. Hens-Piazza, 'Repetition and Rhetoric in Canaanite Epic: a close reading of KTU 1.14, III, 20–49,' *Ugarit-Forschungen* 24 (1992) 103–12.

[87] Kirk (1990) 29–30; Burkert (1991) 170.

[88] Carter (1995).

Acknowledgements: I am grateful for the assistance and counsel of Julie Laskaris, John Bennet, Barry Powell, William Schniedewind, Jaan Puhvel, and Martin West in preparing this chapter.

Kurt A. Raaflaub

HOMERIC SOCIETY

'Homeric society' is the social background against which the epic heroes live, act, excel, and suffer.[1] Hesiod believed that this society existed in a somewhat distant past, between the Bronze and the contemporary Iron Ages (*WD* 157–68); ancient tombs were venerated as those of heroes, and ancient sites and ruins attributed to them.[2] With the modern distinction between myth and history the historicity of Homeric society has become an important problem. If this society corresponds mostly not to poetic fiction but to historical reality and can be dated plausibly, historians gain a valuable literary source to illuminate a period for which they would otherwise have to rely on archaeology. Several scholars have used a commonsense approach and assumed that the poet would naturally model epic society on that of his own time.[3] Others accept this only for part of the picture; they focus on real or perceived inconsistencies, treating the supposed 'amalgamation' of heterogeneous elements as an insurmountable obstacle to the historicity of this society, which they consequently see as an artificial product of poetic tradition and imagination.[4] In the first section of this chapter, I discuss this question, turning in the second to the main features of Homeric society: polis and oikos, social groups and classes, and the political sphere. I consider economic aspects in connection with the oikos and with the appropriate groups of persons (craftsmen, traders, and gift exchange among the elite). In the third section, I draw some conclusions on the place of Homeric society in early Greek history.

---

[1] I use Richmond Lattimore's translations throughout this chapter, albeit often with substantial modifications. I do not discuss aspects of Homeric society that are treated in detail in separate chapters of this volume (e.g., religion, ethics, warfare, economy, Near Eastern connections, the archaeology of the Iron Age). For more detailed analysis of some aspects see Raaflaub (1993); (1996); (1997); forthcoming.

[2] van Wees (1992) ch. 1; Patzek (1992) pt. 3; Antonaccio (1995).

[3] E.g., Hasebroek (1931); Calhoun (1962).

[4] See n. 16 below.

Historicity and Date of Homeric Society[5]

The question of the historicity of Homeric society is related to two other much-debated problems: the 'Homeric Question,' dealing with the formation of the extant epics, and the 'Trojan War Question,' concerned with the origin of the Trojan War myth and the possibility that memories of a genuine Bronze Age war formed the core of Homer's story.[6] In this chapter I follow the conventional view that the extant epics were produced, whether or not by the same poet, roughly in the second half of the eighth century, the *Iliad* about a generation before the *Odyssey*: close enough to each other to be examined as a unit.[7]

Excavations in Troy, Mycenae, Pylos, and other sites, and the decipherment of the Linear B tablets, allow us to reconstruct the economic, social, and political structures of Aegean Bronze Age societies.[8] Many have believed, and some still do, that such essentially was the society described by Homer.[9] Yet the Mycenaean palaces are a world apart from the houses of the Homeric leaders, and the centralized, hierarchical system revealed by the tablets resembles contemporary Near Eastern civilizations but is incompatible with anything found in Homer or known from later Greek history. Comparing the evidence from the tablets and epics in the sphere of property and tenure, M. I. Finley concluded that 'The Homeric world was altogether post-Mycenaean, and the so-called reminiscences and survivals are rare, isolated and garbled. Hence Homer is not only not a reliable guide to the Mycenaean tablets; he is no guide at all.'[10]

Finley insisted that the break after the Mycenaean period was deep, complete, and permanent. By contrast, E. Vermeule suggests that 'There was no break between the Mycenaean and Homeric worlds,

---

[5] See Kirk (1975); I. Morris (1986); van Wees (1992) ch. 1; Patzek (1992); Ulf (1990) ch. 6; O. Murray (1993) 35–38; Raaflaub (1997), summarized in this section.

[6] Turner (this vol.); Finley et al. (1964); Foxhall and Davies (1984); Mellink (1986); Patzek (1992); C. G. Thomas (1993).

[7] Kirk (1985), ch. 1; Latacz (1985) 77–90. M. L. West (1995), Crielaard (1995), and others opt for the early seventh century. I use 'Homer' as a shorthand for the poet(s) who composed the extant epics.

[8] Dickinson (1994); Bennet (this vol.).

[9] This view dominates in Wace and Stubbings (1962), especially part 2B. See McDonald and Thomas (1990); I. Morris (1997).

[10] Finley (1982) 232. Cf. Finley (1970); (1982) 199–212; Austin and Vidal-Naquet (1977) 37.

only change. The degree of change is arguable.'[11] When, we ask, is 'change' profound enough to represent a 'break'? True, recent discoveries have shed welcome light on the Dark Ages; in some outlying areas (Cyprus, Crete) continuity was broad and substantial, and we now know that not all components of Mycenaean civilization were wiped out immediately when the palaces fell.[12] But it is still clear that in the Aegean most traces of this civilization had disappeared by the Submycenaean period (c. 1075–1025). In dialects (probably pointing to the influx of new populations), settlement patterns, material culture, meaning and function of terminology (despite identity of many words) and much else, despite continuity on elementary levels, the changes are deep and pervasive. The general impression remains one of a massively reduced population living in small and scattered villages, in simple conditions and in relative isolation.[13] The Protogeometric period (c. 1025–900 in Athens, but lasting a generation or two longer in some places) represents a new beginning with features that soon resemble those of Homeric society. Not surprisingly, therefore, Bronze Age survivals in the Homeric picture are rare and nonessential exceptions.[14]

Another question is whether this picture is sufficiently coherent to be historical. On sociological and anthropological grounds, Finley answered this question positively:

> A model can be constructed, imperfect, incomplete, untidy, yet tying together the fundamentals of political and social structure with an appropriate value system in a way that stands up to comparative analysis, the only control available to us in the absence of external documentation . . . The critical point is . . . that the model is so coherent, and this also rules out the common statement that what we find in the poems is either a fiction . . . or a composite drawn from different eras . . . [S]uch a composite would be blatantly artificial, unable to withstand careful social analysis.[15]

[11] Vermeule (1964) 309; C. G. Thomas (1993) 69.

[12] See Musti (1985); Musti et al., eds. (1991); Deger-Jalkotzy (1991); Ward and Joukowsky, eds. (1992); Patzek (1992) part 2; Karageorghis, ed. (1994). Van Effenterre (1985), however, goes too far.

[13] Snodgrass (1987) ch. 6; Donlan (1989a); (1989b); Blome (1991).

[14] Coldstream (1977); Patzek (1992) 104–20; I. Morris (this vol.). Survivals: n. 17 below.

[15] Finley (1978) 153.

Several other scholars have since confirmed a high degree of consistency which, overall, by far outweighs the inconsistencies and contradictions, serious as they are.[16]

The understanding of Homeric society that emerges from these discussions can be summarized as follows. First, the picture includes some anachronisms, some archaisms, and some genuine memories of the Mycenaean period and the 'Dark Ages.' The list of such items is short and under constant revision; in several cases there are alternative explanations.[17] Moreover, archaisms had their proper place in such poetry. Second, exaggeration and fantasy form important elements in heroic poetry; in most cases, they can easily be identified and do not impede serious reconstruction.[18] Third, persons, events and a few other components may have formed an old, perhaps even historical core of old traditions. Even if so, in the course of long-term transmission and constant reinterpretation, such core stories were probably transformed so profoundly that we cannot trace their beginnings. Fourth, the poet was an artist, not a historian or sociologist. He did not intend to give a complete picture, and so arguments from silence are rarely valid. As G. Calhoun said,

> Little can be said for the type of criticism . . . that fails to take account of the conventional use of numerals, of ornamental epithets, and of other formulary elements . . .; or makes no allowance for exigencies of the plot; or proceeds upon the assumption that the poet tells everything he knows upon a given subject every time it comes up, and cannot know anything that is not to be found somewhere in the poems.[19]

Fifth, most of the material used to depict the social background to heroic action is sufficiently consistent that we can recognize a society that makes sense from an anthropological perspective and can be fitted into a scheme of social evolution among early societies. This society must have existed in time and space outside of the epics. The place most likely was Ionia, but, given the panhellenic outlook and aspiration of the epics,[20] this question seems secondary.

---

[16] Confirmation: Adkins (1971) 1; (this vol.); Donlan (1981/82) 172; Carlier (1984) 211; Herman (1987) xi; Ulf (1990); van Wees (1992). Inconsistencies: Long (1970); Snodgrass (1974), contradicted by, e.g., Adkins (1971); Qviller (1981); Donlan (1981/82) 146 n. 18; (1989a) 4; I. Morris (1986) 102–120. See also n. 63 below.

[17] E.g., Kirk (1960); Patzek (1992) 186–202.

[18] van Wees (1992) ch. 1.

[19] Calhoun (1962) 431.

[20] G. Nagy (1979); Patzek (1992) 98–101.

How should this society be dated? Research on oral tradition and oral poetry is helpful here.[21] In preliterate societies, collective memories of the past are preserved beyond a period of roughly three generations only if they are important to the present; even so, they are constantly reinterpreted to fit the changing needs of the present. Despite its formulaic nature, oral epic diction is highly flexible and adaptable. Oral poetry depends on the interaction between singer and audience; in each performance the singer, using traditional diction, elaborates traditional material into a new and unique full story. Its success depends on how meaningful it is to the audience. Entertainment value is essential, but so is the potential for identification. Hence oral song focuses on typical conflict situations and ethical dilemmas. Heroic epic, nourished by historical consciousness, embeds such stories in a 'historical context,' but this context is incidental and secondary—no matter whether it is based on vague but authentic memories or results from historicizing fiction that is artificially connected with monuments of a distant past.[22] Hence heroic epic is historical in appearance but contemporary in meaning. The heroically elevated actions of individuals are set in a social context that is familiar to the audience. Many scholars believe, therefore, that Homeric society should be dated not, as Finley thought, to the tenth or ninth centuries, but to the poet's own time.[23]

Yet in many respects, as Finley recognized, this is not the late eighth-century society we know from other sources. Even taking into account some lag-time for adjustments which must have been normal in traditional poetry, the poet clearly did not want heroic society to appear blatantly contemporary. Hence his effort to preserve 'epic distance' or to use an 'alienation effect,'[24] to preserve traditional elements and to endow his social picture with a 'patina.' The social background of heroic poetry needed to be modern enough to be understandable, but archaic enough to be believable. We should therefore consider Homeric society near-contemporary rather than contemporary with the poet and date it within the time-span that could be covered by the audience's collective memory: in the late ninth and eighth centuries.

---

[21] J. M. Foley (this vol.); Vansina (1985); von Ungern-Sternberg and Reinau, eds. (1988); R. Thomas (1992).

[22] Patzek (1992) part 3.

[23] Finley (1978) 47–48. Contra: I. Morris (1986); Ulf (1990); van Wees (1992).

[24] Redfield (1975) 35–39; Vidal-Naquet (1986) 15–38; Giovannini (1989) 25–39.

Main Features of Homeric Society

Polis *and* oikos

According to Finley, 'neither poem has any trace of a *polis* in its political sense. *Polis* in Homer means nothing more than a fortified site, a town.' By contrast, F. Gschnitzer claims that the eighth-century polis was fully developed. Recent scholarship tends to disagree with both positions and argues that the Homeric polis is an early forerunner of the classical polis, that most if not all the constituent elements of the latter exist in the former, albeit in an undeveloped form, and that this polis occupies a central place in Homeric society.[25]

In fact, the epic world is full of poleis. Odysseus has seen the cities (*astea*) of many peoples (*Od.* 1.3), and the foreign visitor identifies himself by land (*gaia*), people (*dêmos*) and polis (8.555) or polis and parents (1.170). Poleis feature in similes (*Il.* 18.207–214) and on the shield of Achilles (18.490–540). The natural assumption is that people live in poleis, all important human figures are connected with a polis, and its crucial social function and symbolic significance are emphasized frequently.[26] The terminology used for these communities is consistent: *dêmos* (land, district, and people) designates the largest conceivable social unit; beyond its boundaries, there is no community. *Gaia* (land) and *patrê* (fatherland) are often synonymous with *dêmos* and polis. Polis and *asty*, interchangeably, describe the main settlement, but *polis* also refers to the larger political community (the state), comprising both town and territory. Hence Odysseus asks Nausikaa (*Od.* 6.177–78) about the people (*anthrôpoi*) who live in this land (*gaia*) and community (polis), and about the way to town (*asty*).[27]

The action of the epics takes place largely in and around four poleis, Troy and the temporary polis (fortified camp) of the Achaians[28] in the *Iliad*, Scheria (the polis of the fairy-tale Phaiakians) and Ithaka in the *Odyssey*. These poleis have considerable differences, but also share important elements. Yet is what Homer calls a 'polis' really a polis? Definitions of 'the polis' pose notorious problems. Neither

---

25 Finley (1978) 34, 155–56. Contra: I. Morris (1986) 100–104; Raaflaub (1991) 239–47; (1993) 46–59 (of which this section is a summary); van Wees (1992) ch. 2; Gschnitzer (1981) 42. See further Hoffmann (1956); C. G. Thomas (1966); Starr (1986); Scully (1990); O. Murray (1993) 42–46, 62–68.

26 Scully (1990).

27 Donlan (1970); Lévy (1983).

28 C. G. Thomas (1966) 7; Raaflaub (1993) 47–48.

independence nor an urban center, though normal, seem crucial. Minimally, the polis is a community of persons, of place or territory, of cults, customs and laws, and capable of (full or partial) self-administration (which presupposes institutions and meeting places). The Homeric polis, comprising a main settlement and its hinterland, is indeed a community of space and territory. The main settlement contains not only the homes of the inhabitants, including the large house of the overall leader (*basileus*), where the other *basileis* meet and are entertained, but also communal buildings and spaces. Walls offer shared protection. Shrines and temples (*Il.* 6.297; *Od.* 6.9–10), sacrifices and rituals (*Il.* 6.286–311; *Od.* 3.4–8) mark it as a community of cult. It certainly is a community of customs. There are no written laws but much attention is devoted to observing customary norms and procedures and to protecting justice. Most poleis are independent, self-administered entities with deliberative and decision making institutions and a meeting place (agora), often with permanent seats at least for the leaders.

The decisive question is whether the Homeric polis is, in any meaningful way, a community of citizens rather than a loose agglomeration of largely autonomous households (oikoi) banding together only in times of emergency. Many scholars consider the oikos the primary and virtually the only important social, economic, and organizational unit, which absorbs the hero's primary allegiance.

> The authoritarian household, the *oikos*, was the centre around which life was organized, from which flowed not only the satisfaction of material needs, including security, but ethical norms and values, duties, obligations and responsibilities, and relations with the gods. The *oikos* was not merely the family, it was all the people of the household together with its land and its goods.[29]

Although the *Odyssey* shows us various types of oikoi, such as Laërtes' farm in an outlying area (24.205–31) and Eumaios' pig-farm (14.5–28), that of Odysseus, paralleled on Scheria by the fairy-tale oikos of Alkinoös (6.291–94; 7.84–132), is described in most detail.[30] It is exceptional because it is the oikos of the paramount leader, the wealthiest and most powerful man in the polis. Its center is the house (*dôma*) in the town of Ithaka. It contains the great hall with fireplace (where normally, as in Scheria, the *basileus* entertains the other nobles

[29] Finley (1978) 57–58.
[30] Richter (1968) 24–32; Finley (1978) chs. 3–4; Hanson (1995) ch. 2.

and occasional guests but now the suitors hold their unruly feasts), the living quarters of family, retainers, servants, and slaves, and buildings and rooms for animals and storage. The leader's *dôma* thus is an especially large version of a farmhouse (not even the dung heap is missing, 17.297–99), the center of an extended estate which comprises gardens, orchards and fields near the town, and herds of cattle, goats, sheep and pigs (14.100–108) in the country, often independently managed by trusted servants and slaves (such as Eumaios).[31]

The system of land tenure seems clear. The most fertile land near the town and suitable for agriculture and gardens is divided up and held as private property. Outlying land suitable for pasturage is undivided and open to common use, although it is *de facto* used mostly by the elite owners of large herds. Cultivation of marginal land (*eschatia*) bestows property rights; again, elite families are most likely to profit from this opportunity (24.205–31; 18.356–61). They are also the primary recipients of a *temenos* (land cut out from undistributed territory), assigned by the *dêmos* in recognition of outstanding service to the community (*Il.* 6.194–95, 12.313–14). Wealth is still counted in herds but land obviously is important as well (section 3 below).[32]

Within his oikos, the master is in absolute control: he punishes unfaithful servants (*Od.* 22.419–77) and rewards the faithful: Eumaios and Philoitios, one certainly, the other probably a slave, are promised a wife and possessions, and a house built next to the master's own; they will be treated as companions (*hetairoi*) and brothers (*kasignêtoi*) of Telemachos (21.214–16; cf. 14.62–66). Rewards and promotion thus take place within the oikos. With good reason: the oikos offers protection; those outside the oikos (*thêtes* and foreigners) are vulnerable. Hence the oikos is populated by various categories of dependent persons, among whom free retainers or followers (*therapontes*) are especially important; they include refugees from other communities, who enjoy safety and comfort in exchange for loyal service to the master, both in war and peace.[33] All the heads of large oikoi thus have their groups of followers; their status and power is largely determined by the number of followers they can muster.[34]

---

[31] Richter (1968) 32–69; Strasburger (1953); Drerup (1969) 128–33.

[32] Gschnitzer (1981) 35–38; Donlan (1989c) Hennig (1980).

[33] Refugees: Phoenix, Patroclus (*Il.* 9.447–83; 23.84–90). *Therapontes*: Greenhalgh (1982); van Wees (1992) 42–44, 104–105, 118–20.

[34] Hence Agamemnon, leading the largest contingent, is overall leader of the Achaian army (*Il.* 2.576–80).

Undoubtedly, then, the oikos is centrally important and a primary focus of loyalty and identification. This remained true for centuries to come. But did it exclude loyalty to, identification with, and a sense of responsibility for the polis? Those who see a sharp division between oikos and polis can refer to the fact that throughout Greek history among the elite private obligations and interests clashed with the loyalty demanded by the polis, and all too often the former prevailed. Even in Homer, though, the polis plays a bigger role in people's lives than is often assumed.[35] Of course it is not a community of citizens (*koinônia politôn*) in the classical and legally defined sense, but it is developing in that direction.

Two aspects should be distinguished. One, I will show, concerns the existence of a public sphere, clearly distinguished from the private, in which the commoners are significantly involved. The other, identification with the community, is visible in the emphasis put on the individual's affiliation with a polis, and in the fact that responsibility for communal well-being is an essential part of the 'heroic code' which perhaps reflects contemporary elite ethics.[36] Distinction in the service to the community is rewarded with honors and privileges, and public status is tied to such service. Hektor is a positive model precisely because he understands his leadership primarily in terms of saving his polis (*Il.* 6.403, 441–46). Conversely, leaders who violate this code are criticized harshly (e.g., Paris, 3.39–57, 453–54) and find their position threatened by rivals and loss of followers (e.g., Agamemnon, *Il.* bks. 1–2). As Agamemnon's quarrel with Achilles shows, such conflicts among leaders and the damage they do to the community are taken seriously: efforts to prevent further splits (2.203–206) and to effect reconciliation are recounted in great detail, including a careful description of how a leader can admit his mistake, make up for it, and thereby enhance his reputation (bks. 9, 19).[37]

In sum, the individual's primary focus on family and oikos does not exclude a high valuation of service to and responsibility for the polis. Hence the praise of the just king and of the blessings he bestows on the community.[38] The hero is aware that the well-being of his

[35] Herman (1987); Strasburger (1954); Greenhalgh (1972); Walter (1993) ch. 2.
[36] *Il.* 2.233–34; 12.310–21. Redfield (1975); Adkins, this volume.
[37] Havelock (1978) ch. 7; but see Donlan (1989a) 5–6. Generally, Raaflaub (1988); Nicolai (1993).
[38] *Il.* 16.384–92; *Od.* 19.106–114; 2.230–41; 4.687–95.

family depends on that of the community. Hektor and Meleagros demonstrate in different ways how the heroic code relates to polis *and* family: 'He has no dishonor who dies defending his country, for then his wife shall be saved, and his children afterwards, and his house and property shall not be damaged, if the Achaians must go away with their ships' (Hektor, *Il.* 15.496–99).[39] Therefore, 'One omen is best, to defend the *patrê*' (12.243). Odysseus yearns for house, wife, and son, but also for *gê* and *patrê*; he is thus thinking of 'home' as oikos/family *and* country/polis. Cumulatively, the evidence suggests that the Homeric polis is indeed a community of persons or citizens and, as such, is more than the sum total of autonomous oikoi.

Social groups and classes[40]

The poet focuses on the spheres of life that are most important to the plot and to the heroic actors (war, seafaring, and the oikos); his description of society is therefore selective and informed by an elite perspective. Other spheres (such as the polis or economic activities) and other social groups enter the limelight only when it suits the poet's needs. Apparent rareness or unimportance of such groups or situations does not necessarily reflect real-life situations.

The heroes form an elite, distinguished from all others by birth, wealth, power, and skills, and who maintain close relations among each other. They are called *basileis*, but are they really 'kings' in any meaningful sense? There is much evidence to the contrary.[41] True, some passages imply a ruler who, though listening to others, makes his own decisions, who cannot be challenged effectively, and who has the power to give away entire cities if it suits him (*Il.* 9.149–56; *Od.* 4.174–77). There is also Odysseus' stern warning in the crisis of *Iliad* 2: 'Having many masters (*polykoiraniê*) is no good thing. Let there be one master (*koiranos*), one leader (*basileus*), to whom [Zeus] gives the scepter and the right of judgment, to watch over his people' (2.204–206).[42] However, during war or expeditions abroad challenges to the overall leader may threaten common success, and cannot be

[39] Lacey (1968) ch. 2; C. Patterson, *The Family in Greek History* (in preparation).

[40] Finley (1978); Gschnitzer (1981) 27–47; Donlan (1985); (1989b).

[41] Finley (1978) 83–84; Arnheim (1977); Donlan (1980) ch. 1; Gschnitzer (1981) 38–47; Cobet (1981); Carlier (1984) ch. 2; Stein-Hölkeskamp (1989) ch. 2; van Wees (1992).

[42] Easterling (1989).

tolerated.[43] Scholars disagree on how to explain the giving away of cities.[44] And whenever a paramount leader ignores the opinion of his people or fellow *basileis* (as Agamemnon in *Il.* bk. 1, and Hektor in 18.243–313), his decision leads to disaster; hence these examples are meant to describe, not the norm, but the negative exception.

Moreover, as Alkinoös says, 'twelve are marked out as *basileis* in our *dêmos* and hold power (*krainousi*) as leaders (*archoi*), and I myself am the thirteenth' (*Od.* 8.390–91). In every community there are many *basileis*; they are described functionally as leaders, councilors or elders (*prôtoi, archoi, hêgêtores, medontes, gerontes*: e.g., *Il.* 3.146–53; *Od.* 8.10–11). Despite differences in wealth, power of the oikos, personal qualities, and influence, they form a fiercely competitive group of equals, among whom the paramount *basileus* holds an inherited, though precarious, position of preeminence as *primus inter pares*—or 'a bit more.' 'How much more (or less) was a personal matter in each case.'[45] Their status is based on family, personal accomplishment, and reputation, all of which are stressed when the need arises to speak in the assembly. Their goal is 'always to be the best and to excel among the others' (*Il.* 6.208). Indeed, these are not 'rulers' or 'monarchs;' rather, they are best explained as an aristocracy-in-formation (see section 3 below).[46]

Elite ideology is exclusive; non-elite persons are not to be taken seriously. 'Sit still and listen to what others tell you, to those who are better men than you, you skulker and coward and thing of no account whatever in battle or council,' says Odysseus to the commoner, striking him with his staff (*Il.* 2.200–202). The elite seem to hold a monopoly in politics and war. This impression, though quite wrong, combined with other instances of the poet's selective focus on the elite and its ideology, has led many scholars to consider the role of the commoners negligible. Finley concludes that the decisive gap in society runs between the elite and all the rest. By contrast, C. G. Starr emphasizes that the economic gap between elite and free farmers is relatively small; he calls the latter, not very aptly, 'semi-aristocrats:' the term perhaps rather fits the former.[47] In fact, the economic gap,

[43] Patzek (1992) 131–35.

[44] Hainsworth (1993) 77–78; Raaflaub (1993) n. 35.

[45] Finley (1970) 86.

[46] Weiler (1975). How exactly to define the *basileis*' function is much debated; see nn. 40–41 and Donlan (1981/2); Qviller (1981); Ulf (1990) 223–31; Raaflaub (1991) 230–38.

[47] Finley (1978) 53; Starr (1977) ch. 6; O. Murray (1993) 68.

though varying greatly, may well be large without being decisive. Certainly, the elite families are landowners and farmers; their 'roots in the soil' are unmistakable.[48] But scale and attitude are different: although the master of the elite oikos is experienced in much of the work on his estate (*Od.* 18.365–75; 23.189–201), he usually does not work himself. Rather, he supervises the workers and makes sure they are well taken care of (*Il.* 18.550–60). In addition, plentiful resources make it possible for the elite to enjoy a refined life-style.[49] The non-elite farmer, virtually absent in the epics, probably corresponds rather to the model of Laertes in *Od.* bk. 24 or Hesiod:[50] a hard-working man, with few servants, slaves and animals, and even fewer resources to spare even if he is not constantly threatened by poverty; he relies more on his neighbors than on the elite or leaders of the polis; if he is not living in town, he goes there only when forced by specific needs (*Il.* 23.826–35).

However, these men play an important role in the assembly and warfare. On the battlefield, the *laoi* (warriors) have an equal chance to gain *aretê* and *kleos*. Apart from honorary gifts for the leaders, they receive an equal share of the booty (*Il.* 9.318–19; *Od.* 9.39–42).[51] Those who are especially successful on raiding expeditions might achieve higher status and social distinction at home as well (*Od.* 14.199–234). Hence class boundaries are not completely fixed: while noble birth is often emphasized, Calhoun rightly points to 'the conspicuous absence from both poems of specific terms for nobility of birth, of the antonyms of these terms, of words for ancestors and descendants, of the words later used in connection with the aristocratic *genê*, and the appellations later given to the lower classes.'[52] The epics reflect a transitional phase in social development 'from individual achievement, dependent solely on skill and prowess, toward the idea of a social class in which membership alone allowed one to claim excellence.'[53] Correspondingly, the relationship between commoners and elite is more complex than many scholars assume. Submissiveness and blind obedience are not typical of the *laoi*. Positive

48 Strasburger (1953); but see Hoffmann (1956) 124 n. 6, 127 n. 13.

49 Latacz (1984); Hölscher (1990) 21.

50 One of the most obvious omissions due to poetic selection. Hanson (1995) ch. 2; Millett (1984).

51 van Wees (this vol.); Detienne (1965); Nowag (1983).

52 Calhoun (1962) 438. Contra, Finley (1978) 53, 59–60.

53 Donlan (1980) 18.

terms like *agathoi* or *hêrôes* are used for them as well. Odysseus treats his followers as comrades and friends with care and respect: they are tied together by bonds of mutual dependence. The *basileus* is a 'shepherd of his people' (*poimên laôn*), not a commander or distant ruler. For high status with concomitant honors and privileges he depends on the *dêmos*.

In sum, a *dêmos* with such power cannot be negligible. On the contrary, the commoners play a significant role in the community, and it appears that the three determinants of citizen status, known from later centuries (land ownership, military capacity, political participation), although not formalized, are already in place.[54]

Outside the class of free, land owning farmers we find several categories of free persons. The retainers (*therapontes*), already mentioned, are members of the powerful elite *oikoi* and visible in a communal function only in war. *Demiourgoi* (who do *dêmia erga*, 'works for the people') form an elite of professional craftsmen and specialists, often wandering from town to town: seers, doctors, woodworkers and other builders or artists, and bards (*Od.* 17.382–86).[55] Their skills, always in high demand, compensate for their being outsiders; the ambivalence of their status is reflected in the portrait of the divine smith and artist, Hephaistos, who is envied, admired, and ridiculed at the same time.[56]

Most other craftsmen seem to belong to a specific community or oikos; they are mentioned in passing (goldsmith, carpenter, builder or shipwright, leather worker and arms manufacturer, smith, potter, etc.), and little is known about whether they are full- or part-time professionals or about other details of their situation. The impression is that the *oikos* is largely self-sufficient and most of the work is done 'in-house.'[57]

Hardly anything is said about local trade and markets, which must have existed (*Il.* 7.467; 9.71–72 for wine, 23.834–35 for iron)—another indication of the poet's selective description. Long-distance trade (*Od.* 9.125–30) is firmly in the hands of foreigners, especially Phoenicians. Trade, handled professionally and with the explicit purpose of gain, is a low-prestige occupation, often associated with

[54] Gschnitzer (1981) 35–36.
[55] Murakawa (1957); Eckstein (1974) 34–38; Finley (1978) 36–37, 56.
[56] Finley (1978) 72–73.
[57] Eckstein (1974) part 1; Rössler (1981); Schneider (1991); S. P. Morris (1992) ch. 1. On economic aspects, see also Donlan (this vol.).

piracy (*Od.* 3.71–74).[58] There is no greater offense to a traveling nobleman than to be called a trader, 'one who plies his ways in his many-locked vessel, master over mariners who also are men of business, a man who, careful of his cargo and grasping for profits, goes carefully on his way' (8.159–64).[59] Like others who are not members of the community, foreign traders are unprotected. Odysseus' Cyclops adventure in *Od.* bk. 9 and the suspicious attitude of the Phaiakians toward strangers (7.32–33) illustrate this reality; another side is visible in the common view that foreigners like other outsiders enjoy the protection of Zeus himself and should be treated hospitably (14.56–58).[60] 'Resident aliens' (*metanastai*), unless integrated in an oikos (as the refugees Phoinix and Patroklos are), are no better off: Achilles complains that Agamemnon has disgraced him in front of all the Argives, 'as if I were a *metanastês* without *timê*.' This clearly refers to the difference between citizens (*politai, astoi*) and non-citizens who, though resident in the community, do not partake in the privileges of its members.[61]

Two other forms of the acquisition or exchange of goods are highly visible in the epics. One is raiding by warrior bands led by elite leaders, as it is practiced by Achilleus in the environs of Troy (*Il.* 6.414–28; 20.188–94), by Odysseus on his way home from Troy (*Od.* 9.39–61), and by 'Odysseus the Cretan' (14.222–34).[62] Another is gift exchange among elite persons. 'There was scarcely a limit to the situations in which gift-giving was operative. More precisely, the word "gift" was a cover-all for a great variety of actions and transactions which later became differentiated and acquired their own appellations.'[63] Gift-situations and relationships include

> traders' dues, ransom, peace compacts, rewards for services, tribute to chiefs, donations from chiefs, recompense for insult, marriage transactions, and guest friendship . . . Within this diversity, all gift transactions share basic features. Gifts are given either as compensation for specific acts, positive or negative, or in expectation of some future service or favor. The gifts themselves are always things of high value . . .

---

[58] Nowag (1983); Garlan (1978); (1989) ch. 8.

[59] Finley (1978) 66–71; Coldstream (1982); Reed (1984); Kopcke (1990); von Reden (1995) ch. 3. See also Cartledge (1983).

[60] Finley (1978) 100–102; Havelock (1978) ch. 9.

[61] *Metanastai*: Gschnitzer (1981) 29; *politai*: Lévy (1985); Walter (1993).

[62] Nowag (1983); van Wees (1992) 207–258.

[63] Finley (1978) 66, and index *s.v.*; Austin and Vidal-Naquet (1977) 42–44; Donlan (1981); (1981/2); von Reden (1995) chs. 1–2.

> There is always a social element present in the transaction... [Gifts are] an exchange system whose purpose was not the maximization of material profit but the establishment and maintenance of personal relations. In such 'gift economies,' the highest premium is placed on generosity and display; superiority in gift-giving equates to superiority in social prestige.[64]

Knowing the rules of gift-giving, in part with the help of comparative anthropology, we are able to understand the great variety of possibilities in the system[65] and to 'decode' the intricacies of specific episodes, such as the ongoing competition for honor and status between Agamemnon and Achilleus (especially in *Il.* bk. 19) or the seemingly bizarre exchange between Glaukos and Diomedes of golden against bronze armor (6.119–236).[66]

Lowest on the status scale of free men is the worker for hire (*thês*). He is vulnerable and liable to be cheated and insulted by arrogant masters—as happened even to Poseidon and Apollo after they built the walls of Troy (*Il.* 21.441–52). What makes the *thês* contemptible is not the need to work but his dependence on others to earn his living, and thus his helplessness (*Od.* 18.356–75). Hence Achilleus, preferring to be last among the living rather than first among the dead, mentions not a slave but a *thês* (11.489–91).[67]

Slaves, then, are supposed to be better off.[68] In the epics they mostly are: the master's wife cares for slave children as if they were her own (*Od.* 15.363–65; 18.321–23); and, as the examples of Eumaios, Eurykleia, and Laertes' Dolios show, some slaves hold trusted positions in the oikos, and are virtually members of the family. Conversely, they have no control over their lives; they can be worked to the limits of their endurance (20.105–19); if they betray the master's trust, they are liable to cruel punishment (22.420–77). Homer is aware of the psychological effects of slavery: 'servants (*dmôes*),' says Eumaios, 'when their masters are no longer about to make them work, are no longer willing to do their rightful duties. For Zeus.... takes away one half of his quality (*aretê*) from a man, once the day of slavery closes upon him' (17.320–23). From the perspective of the free and

64 Donlan (1989a) 1, 3.

65 Overlooking this fact is the main weakness of Snodgrass' (1974) challenge to Finley.

66 Donlan (1989a).

67 Finley (1978) 57–58, 71.

68 Finley (1978) 58–59; Gschnitzer (1981) 29–33; Garlan (1988) 29–37. See also n. 70.

noble who find themselves threatened by loss of liberty, the slave's condition, of course, is utterly pitiable: no thought of future defeat is worse, says Hektor to Andromache, than 'the thought of you, when some bronze-armoured Achaian leads you off, taking away your day of liberty, in tears; and in Argos you must work at the loom of another, and carry water from the spring Messeis or Hypereia, all unwilling, but strong will be the necessity upon you' (*Il.* 6.454–58).

Still, the 'paternalistic' view of slavery prevailing in the epics is understandable: slaves, in the strict sense of the word, are relatively rare—despite the 'heroic' numbers, few are actually mentioned.[69] Men usually do not survive defeat in war; hence male slaves are victims of piracy, and female slaves are more frequent. Skilled slaves are valuable: the equivalent of four or even twenty oxen (*Il.* 23.705; *Od.* 1.430–31). Moreover, the technical terms for slaves or slavery (*doulos/ê, douleia, doulosynê*) are used rarely. The prevailing terminology for servants is functional and status neutral: *dmôs* or *oikeus* (persons working in the *dôma* or *oikos*), *drêstêr* (the 'doer'), *amphipolos* (the person 'being around' the lady). Some of these persons clearly are slaves but others are not, and unless the context makes this explicit, we cannot know. At any rate, function in the oikos and closeness to the master count for more than personal status: Eumaios and Philoitios are promoted within the oikos rather than emancipated from it (*Od.* 21.214–16).[70]

Finally, the portrait of women and wives is also ambivalent.[71] Their sphere and function are clearly marked: they produce and raise heirs, they preside over the household and supervise the slave women and storerooms, and they practice the principal women's craft, weaving (*Il.* 3.125–28; *Od.* 2.93–110). They are not confined to the women's quarters: they speak with foreigners, sometimes hear bards perform, are involved in religious rituals, especially propitiating the gods (*Il.* 6.269–80, 286–311), and move around town freely. But these same women are pointedly reminded of the separation of men's and women's spheres: 'Go back in the house, and take up your own

---

[69] The figures given (*Od.* 20.107; 22.420–24: fifty slave women, among them twelve working the mills, and twelve unfaithful) are round, presumably exaggerated to fit the splendor of a heroic oikos.

[70] Ramming (1973); Gschnitzer (1976); Wickert-Micknat (1983); Raaflaub (1985) 29–46. See also Finley (1982) chs. 7–9; Strasburger (1976).

[71] Arthur (1973); Wickert-Micknat (1982); Felson-Rubin (1994); Fantham et al. (1994) ch. 1; Blundell (1995) ch. 4; Cohen, ed. (1995).

work, the loom and the distaff, and see to it that your handmaidens ply their work also; but the men must see to discussion' or to the fighting (*Od.* 1.356–59; *Il.* 6.490–93).

While her husband is absent and her son still young, Penelope is in charge of the oikos (*Od.* 18.257–70; 19.525–27), defends it with intelligence, skill and courage (16.409–33), trying to make up for the losses caused by her suitors with the courtship gifts she extracts from them (18.274–303). Reverse similes comparing her actions and feelings with typically male situations (19.107–114; 23.233–40) indicate that hers is not an experience typical and expected of women. Arete, Alkinoös' wife, seems to play an even more powerful role (6.303–315; 7.66–77). As S. Blundell observes, 'In the utterly magical countries inhabited by Calypso and Circe, it is possible for women to be in complete control: while in a place like Scheria, midway between the everyday and the fantastic, a female can be accorded a measure of power.'[72] Helen's unusual role in Troy and Sparta (*Od.* 4.120 ff.) may also be explained by her divine descent.

To Finley 'there is no mistaking the fact that Homer fully reveals what remains true for the whole of antiquity, that women were held to be naturally inferior and therefore limited in their function to the production of offspring and the performance of household duties, and that the meaningful social relationships and the strong personal attachments were sought and found among men.'[73] True, the epics contain a few generalizing negative statements about women, most obviously provoked by Klytaimnestra's evil deed (24.191–202); even Athena, urging Telemachos to protect his mother from the suitors' aggressive wooing, says 'You know what the mind is like in the breast of a woman. She wants to build up the household of the man who marries her, and of former children, and of her beloved and wedded husband, she has no remembrance, when he is dead, nor does she think of him' (15.20–23). Otherwise, however, as M. Arthur writes, the epic 'focuses almost exclusively on the positive side of the position of women; it emphasizes women's *inclusion* in society as a whole, rather than her *exclusion* from certain roles, it celebrates the importance of the function that women do perform, instead of drawing attention to their handicaps or inabilities.' Apart from the 'marital squabbles' of Zeus and Hera—the only example of a 'war of the

[72] Blundell (1995) 55.
[73] Finley (1978) 128; Fantham et al. (1994) 39–44.

sexes' in the epics—Arthur sees the social position of women as ideologically upgraded and romanticized.[74]

Indeed, the social portrait of women is complex and rich—fuller than that of any other category of persons except the heroes. It shows them in all functions and statuses of life and in their wide range of emotions. Marital harmony is praised (*Od.* 6.180–85) and illustrated by the examples of Hektor-Andromache and Odysseus-Penelope, marital fidelity is considered the norm,[75] and in the case of Nausikaa the young woman's transition to marriage is sketched in delicate tones.[76]

Politics and the public sphere

The nature and significance of politics and the political sphere in Homeric society have been much debated among 'primitivist' and 'modernist' scholars.[77] As often in such debates, the truth lies somewhere in the middle. Finley omits a systematic analysis of the political sphere and discusses assemblies and councils in two different chapters. The community with its institutions, he argues, is a low priority after class, kin, and oikos. The epics 'are filled with assemblies and discussions, and they were not mere play-acting.' Although 'a large measure of informality . . . marked all the political institutions of the age,' the assembly's function was 'to mobilize the arguments pro and con, and to show the king or field commander how sentiment lay,' while 'the council of elders revealed the sentiment among the nobles.' The function of this council too was limited because actions and reactions were dictated by the heroic code. There were disagreements over issues or tactics, there was need for information, but there was little need for 'genuine discussion.'

> The significant fact is that never in either the *Iliad* or the *Odyssey* is there a rational discussion, a sustained, disciplined consideration of circumstances and their implications, of possible courses of action, their advantages and disadvantages. There are lengthy arguments . . . but they are quarrels, not discussions, in which each side seeks to overpower

---

[74] Arthur (1973) 13–14; Latacz (1987).

[75] *Il.* 9.446–52; *Od.* 1.429–33; Zeitlin (1995). There is much evidence that concubines and their children often were part of the household. Priam, with several wives, is a unique exception: Finley (1978) 127 n.

[76] Fantham et al. (1994) 22–27.

[77] Gschnitzer (1991) surveys both positions. Further, Gschnitzer (1983); Carlier (1984) ch. 2; (1991); Bannert (1987); Raaflaub (1993) 54–57.

> the other by threats, and to win over the assembled multitude by emotional appeal, by harangue, and by warning.[78]

Finley has persuaded many scholars, and the prevailing tendency is to emphasize the pre-political nature of the polis, the informal nature of political institutions, and the insignificance of the assembly. This picture is one-sided.

Again we should keep in mind that the epics' perspective and purpose are not those of political or historical treatises. Hence we should appreciate the fact that the epics mention so many meetings of assembly and council.[79] This reflects a basic reality: an assembly is called, often combined with a council meeting, and public debate is arranged in a polis, army, or band of warriors whenever an important issue requires discussion and decision. Informal assemblies of smaller or larger groups meet occasionally, and it seems perfectly normal for Telemachos, as for the *basileus* of the Laistrygonians and other leaders, to spend time in the *agora* (*Od.* 20.146; cf. 10.114–15; 15.466–68). The assembly thus is a traditional institution, deeply embedded in the structures and customs of society. Some of these assemblies are formalized to a considerable degree: they are convened by the herald's announcement, the 'right' to speak is determined by status, rank, and experience, and the speaker assumes a position of high communal authority by holding the leader's staff. Themis, the goddess of customary and divinely sanctioned law, and Zeus, the protector of justice, are the divine sponsors of assemblies (*Od.* 2.68–69).[80] Normally, the leader makes conscious efforts to convince the assembly (hence the great importance attributed, among the leader's qualities, to persuasive speaking)[81] and, although there is no formal vote, respects the people's opinion. If he refuses to do so and fails in executing his plan, he is liable to censure and makes himself vulnerable: in the cases of both Agamemnon (*Il.* bks. 1, 2, 9, 19) and Hektor (18.243–313; 22.99–110) the consequences are serious. The assembly has an important function in witnessing and legitimizing communal actions and decisions, from the distribution of

---

[78] Finley (1978) 78–82, 113–16.

[79] 12/12 (*Iliad*), 10/8 (*Odyssey*); Carlier (1984) 183 nn. 219–20. *Il.* 2.84–394; 9.9–79; *Od.* 2.6–257; 8.4–45 are especially important. The twenty-year hiatus on Ithaca is not to be taken literally.

[80] Gschnitzer (1991) 196.

[81] Vernant (1982) 45–50; Kennedy (1963) 35–39.

booty to 'foreign policy' to the resolution of conflicts.[82] Before the booty is distributed, it is 'common good' (*Il.* 1.124) and 'put in the middle' (*es meson*; cf. *en messêi agorêi*, 19.249). The same concept is visible in Homeric political and judicial decision making: the middle is the communal sphere (*koinon*), shared by all citizens, elite and non-elite alike.[83] Overall, although it lacks the right of initiative, free speech, and vote—restrictions which are typical of most ancient societies anyway—the assembly plays a crucial role that should not be underestimated.

Most of this is true for the council of *basileis* or *gerontes* as well. It is convened and consulted frequently by the paramount *basileus*, whether before an assembly or separately. In peace and at war, the *basileis* spend much time in consultations and at common meals. The *Iliad* describes several council debates: there is, among an elite of roughly equals, a recognizable hierarchy of speaking, and exceptions are explained carefully (*Il.* 14.109–27); the *basileis* consider it their duty to challenge the paramount leader (9.8–76), and he is expected to follow the best advice or the shared opinion of the others (9.74–76, 96–103). Two technical terms (*gerousios oinos*, the wine the *gerontes* drink in council, and *gerousios horkos*, the councilor's oath, *Il.* 4.259; 22.119) confirm that the council of *gerontes* is an established institution, and there are hints that it is, at least in some situations, held responsible for communal decisions: Hektor complains about 'our councilors' (*gerontes*) cowardice who would not let me fight by the grounded ships, though I wanted to, but held me back in restraint, and curbed in our fighters' (*Il.* 15.721–23).

Assembly and council are seen as such normal methods of communal interaction that they are attributed to divine society as well; although this society is equivalent, not to a polis, but to a family or an oikos, the gods are imagined to meet in assembly whenever discussion, decision, or announcements are necessary. E. Flaig points out that at least in one case (*Il.* 4.1–72) the principle of decision making is based on establishing consensus rather than securing victory for one side over the other. This principle is still visible in the Spartan assembly of historical times.[84] The rules applying in Homeric assemblies may thus have been very different from those familiar in later periods.

---

[82] Havelock (1978) ch. 7.
[83] Detienne (1965).
[84] Flaig (1993); (1994); cf. Patzek (1992) 131–35.

In assessing the significance of these institutions, we should keep in mind that the men (*laoi, dêmos*) meeting in the assembly are the same who fight in the army and are militarily indispensable to the community. It is the *dêmos* who assigns the prize of honor in booty (*geras*) and land (*temenos*) to the meritorious leader (*Il.* 12.310–28) and compensates the *basileis* for exceptional expenditures incurred in representing the community (*Od.* 13.13–15).[85] The *dêmos* plays a role in jurisdiction as well (*Il.* 18.497–508) and provides the forum for foreign policy decisions: the Achaian embassy demanding the return of Helen and the treasures Paris stole from Menelaos' house speaks and is rebuffed in the Trojan assembly (*Il.* 3.205–224; cf. 7.345–78); hence the Trojan *dêmos* shares the responsibility for the deed that provokes the Achaian attack, and collectively suffers for it. This is a recurrent pattern: though elevated to a heroic and panhellenic level, the Trojan War, like the war between Pylians and Epeians remembered by Nestor (*Il.* 11.668–762), reflects a conflict that begins with a private raid and escalates into a full-blown war between communities if diplomatic requests for restoration of the stolen goods (*Od.* 21.16–21) are turned down. In order to prevent such escalation, elsewhere the perpetrator's community threatens to punish him and redress the wrong he did (16.424–30). The term *thôê* designates a penalty imposed by the community on an individual for actions violating communal interests (*Il.* 13.669).[86] The essential point is that the *dêmos* is held responsible for an individual's deeds, decides whether or not to accept this responsibility, acts accordingly or bears the consequences. Procedures, sanctioned by sacrifice and oath, exist to conclude and guarantee agreements between communities (*Il.* 2.339–41; 3.67–120).[87] Not surprisingly, the epics often emphasize collective, demotic will, experience and action.[88]

Dêmos and *basileis*, then, share the political sphere: the agora is the center of the community; communal affairs (*koinon, dêmion*) are put in the middle (*es meson*), to be handled by the assembly. Private and public are clearly distinguished. The traveler is asked whether he is underway in private or public business (*Od.* 3.82), and the assembly does not deal with private matters. As an old man says when the

---

[85] Donlan (1980) 19–20; Nowag (1983) 36–40; Carlier (1984) 151–62.

[86] Vatin (1982); foreign policy: Wéry (1967); Raaflaub (forthcoming).

[87] Wickert-Micknat (1983) 18–21, 90–92; Karavites (1992); Baltrusch (1994) 104–108.

[88] Donlan (1989b) 14.

first assembly in a long time convenes on Ithaka, 'Who has perceived such an urgent need . . .? Has he perceived news of an army that is approaching . . .? Or has he some other public matter (*dêmion*) to set forth and argue?' (*Od.* 2.28–32). Political decision-making takes place in public. So does jurisdiction, which is a crucial obligation and prerogative of the *basileis*, individually and collectively.[89] The *basileis*, though holding the scepter that comes from Zeus (*Il.* 2.101–108) and thus 'sponsored' by the king of the gods, are subjected to praise and censure by the *dêmos* (*Il.* 6.401–403, 441–46; 22.104–110) and owe much of their position to the *dêmos*.

Conclusion: Homeric Society and History

Contrary to Finley and others who interpret Homeric society as a pre-polis society that gives priority almost exclusively to the individual's claims and the private sphere, I locate this society in the early polis, and emphasize the importance of the community in the individual's life, actions, and thinking. Except for the poor and landless, all citizens have a communal function in army and assembly. There are loose but well established communal structures: assembly and council, though not formalized, play an important and fairly regular role. There is a sense of a public realm, separated from the private, and an awareness of communal will and action, attributed collectively to the *dêmos*, both domestically and in dealing with other *poleis*. There is the capacity for communal accomplishment, both in war and peace (as walls and temples attest), and there is a sense of communal responsibility and solidarity. It does not seem, as Finley thought, that 'the social organization of the world of Odysseus was inadequate for the tasks we know some *poleis* contemporary with Homer to have performed.'[90]

Confirmation for all this is found in the description of the society of the Cyclopes. These, although overbearing and lawless, live in a setting of golden-age abundance. But 'they have neither assemblies for holding council (*agorai boulêphoroi*) nor laws (*themistes*), but they inhabit the crests of the lofty mountains, in hollow caves, and each one

---

[89] Hence the *basileis* are *dikaspoloi* ('realizers of law, judges:' *Il.* 1.258; *Od.* 11.186). Bonner and Smith (1930), ch. 1; Gagarin (1986), ch. 2; Havelock (1978) chs. 7–10.

[90] Finley (1978) 156.

dispenses the laws (*themisteuei*) for his children and wives, and is not concerned for the others' (*Od.* 9.105–15). This society lacks all that constitutes a polis: it has no shared settlement and communal center, no shared law and no institutionalized communication, not even a shared religion (9.273–78) or communication by ship with other communities and the outside world (9.125–30). In other words, there is no community at all, only autonomous families. This description of the ultimate 'anti-polis' represents a deliberate effort to conceptualize the polis by defining its constituent components and attitudes. Its positive counterpart appears in the ideal polis of the Phaiakians. They too are blessed by the gods and live in fairy-tale abundance, but they do everything right and fully share their communal experience; they are hospitable to foreigners and they are the ultimate sailors. As S. Scully concludes, the concept of the polis in Homer represents civilization, progress, community, justice and openness; not to live in a polis means primitiveness, isolation, fragmentation, lack of community, and lawlessness.[91]

The fact that the epics presuppose an early form of the *polis* fits well with the period suggested above for Homeric society (late ninth and eighth centuries). Archaeology dates the 'crystallization' of the polis to the eighth century; in Ionia cities may have emerged slightly earlier.[92] Colonization, beginning in the same period, both presupposed and advanced the concept of the polis. In the epics, Troy and Scheria are founded cities (*Il.* 20.215–18; *Od.* 6.3–10);[93] the latter reflects colonization, as does the description of Goat Island opposite Cyclops country (9.125–41). The earliest communal wars are attested by historical tradition for the last third of the eighth century. The earliest known polis constitution, regulating the powers of and relations between leaders, council of *gerontes* and assembly, is the Spartan Rhetra, probably dating to the mid-seventh century: an immediate descendant of the informal Homeric institutions. The list could be extended.[94]

The late ninth and eighth centuries were a period of rapid change. Within a few generations, the Hellenic world was profoundly trans-

---

[91] Scully (1981).
[92] Snodgrass (1977); (1993a); I. Morris (this vol.). Old-Smyrna: Drerup (1969) 44–47.
[93] Scully (1990) 24–25, 48.
[94] Colonization: Graham (1982); (1995); Malkin (1994); Raaflaub (1991) 218–22. Wars: Raaflaub (1991) 223–25. Rhetra: Raaflaub (1993) 64–68.

formed.[95] Old and new thus overlapped in people's experience and memory. Such *Gleichzeitigkeit des Ungleichzeitigen* made it easy for the poet to ignore very recent developments and apply to the society he was describing an archaizing patina, or to combine traditional, old-fashioned but dramatically attractive elements with more recent ones that were part of the audience's life. His listeners would have had no difficulty in understanding such mixture and juxtaposition: they knew well that things had been very different only a short time ago.[96]

Here perhaps lies at least part of the explanation for many inconsistencies that keep bothering modern scholars. The following examples all reflect a society in transition. The heroes count their wealth in herds; they are meat eaters, and conspicuous consumption of meat is crucial for sacrifices, funerals and other feasts (*Il.* 1.447–68; 23.26–34; *Od.* 3.5–8). At the same time, land is clearly important—as we know it was in the eighth century. As Donlan says, 'The Greeks of the epics were apparently stockbreeders who had adapted to farming.' Gardens, orchards and vinyards, all forming part of the great estates, are work-intensive and prestigious; they too point to the future.[97] The assignment of a *temenos* to a deserving leader is prominent in the epics, although by Homer's time increasing scarceness of land may already have eliminated this custom. In the same period, communal wars were fought between poleis for the control of fertile land. The poet describes communal wars—which, as in history, coexist with private raids by aristocratic warrior bands—but emphasizes the older, more heroic purpose of fighting about women, booty, honor and status. In war, the heroes monopolize the battlefield and the *laoi* seem little more than fodder for their killing sprees. Yet upon close inspection, the latter are constantly and equally involved in the fighting; mass fighting is the norm, the phalanx looms on the horizon.[98] In the community, institutions are informal and dominated by the elite. Yet a closer look reveals that the *dêmos*' role is significant. The individual seems almost autonomous, and foreign relations are conducted through elite guest-friendships. Yet public embassies and treaties between poleis are known and the *dêmos* is capable of taking decisive action. The elite, reflecting the contradictions of a transitional stage,

---

[95] Snodgrass (1980) 13–14; Schadewaldt (1959) 87–129.

[96] Raaflaub (1991) 251.

[97] Donlan, (1981/2) 173; (1989c) 139–43; Snodgrass (1980) 35–37; (1987) 193–209.

[98] Raaflaub (1996); van Wees (this vol.).

is an aristocracy-in-formation—as we should expect it in the time when poleis were formed, under the pressure of rapidly growing population, from clusters of little villages and follower groups, and the elite of local and regional chiefs slowly evolved into the stratified aristocracy known in the Archaic polis.[99] Gift-giving is pervasive and at the core of social relationships. Yet there are indications that the customs and values connected with it are losing importance and other considerations are taking over.[100] Again, the list could be continued.

All these seemingly contradictory elements are woven into a social picture that indeed represents an amalgam, but with very few exceptions not, as is often assumed, an artificial or unhistorical one that arbitrarily combines components from wildly divergent periods and cultures. Rather, this is a natural and organic amalgam, reflecting real historical development and perfectly understandable to the poet's listeners.

One final point. Like much else, the complex customs regulating the process of decision-making in the assembly and the equally complex rules and implications of gift-giving, though puzzling to the modern scholar, have their analogies in other cultures and can be decoded with the help of anthropology and sociology. What matters here is that the poet never explains these rules. He takes them for granted. His audience therefore must have been intimately familiar with all that was going on in these interactions.[101] Hence such customs cannot have been artificial poetic constructs or fossilized memories of things long gone. They are historical and belong to a culture that had existed in the recent past or still existed so that the poet's audience was able to recognize and understand them. The same, with few exceptions, is true for Homeric society as a whole.[102]

---

[99] Donlan (1989b) 18–26; Stein-Hölkeskamp (1989) ch. 2; Raaflaub (1991) 230–38.

[100] Donlan (1981); Starr (1977) 58–60.

[101] Donlan (1989a).

[102] I thank Walter Donlan and Gregory Bucher for valuable suggestions and assistance.

Walter Donlan

THE HOMERIC ECONOMY

An 'Embedded' Economy

Ever since the original publication of M. I. Finley's *The World of Odysseus* in 1954, scholars have become accustomed to think of the Homeric economy as submerged or 'embedded' in non-economic social relations. This concept is fundamental to understanding the Homeric economy.[1] Finley argued that the core feature of Homeric economy and society was *reciprocity*, the symbol of which was the gift. The transfer of valuables from one person or group to another both within and outside a community almost always took the form (or the guise) of gift-giving. Thus, even compulsory donations were expressed as freely given gifts. The moral foundation of a gift economy is that every act of giving, whether of things or services, incurs a debt which carries a strong obligation to repay. Inherent in this construction of give and receive is a powerful ethical bias towards fair-play.[2]

In what follows, I assume that Homeric society—the social background for the dramatic action—reflects Greek society around 800 B.C. Although it is not an 'historical society' in any sense of the word, we can, in a scientific manner, extract a real society from it. The basic economic situation is especially clear and consistent in the texts, and to some extent matches up with the archaeology of the period.[3]

The Basic Economy

Most of the free population in Homer make their livings as farmers, herders, or craftsmen. Women are completely dependent on men for their existence. Although the collapse of the Mycenaean states brought major changes in the way production was organized and distributed,

---

[1] K. Polanyi is the important figure: see Polanyi (1944); Tandy and Neale (1994).
[2] Finley (1978 [1954]) 66–67, 120–26. See also Raaflaub (this vol.).
[3] See Raaflaub (this vol.); I. Morris (this vol.); Bennet (this vol.).

many elements of the basic modes of subsistence survived unchanged. Many of the plants and animals exploited in the Late Bronze Age were available in the Dark Age; and there was probably much carry over of the tools and techniques of agriculture and stock-raising. The main crops in Homer, which grow almost everywhere in Greece, are grains (chiefly barley and wheat), olives, grapes, figs, varieties of peas and beans, and greens, along with flax (for linen), herbs, honey, and a good variety of other orchard fruits. Cattle, sheep, goats, pigs, horses, donkeys, and mules supply meat, wool, hides, cheese, manure, and traction. Fishing, hunting, and gathering supplement the diet. Wood for fuel and construction, stone, and clay, were locally available in most areas of Greece, and perhaps free for the taking.[4]

Of natural resources, metals were key. Bronze, or its constituents, copper and tin, had to be imported; iron was fairly abundant; gold was very scarce. Some regions were rich in silver, though it was not heavily mined until later. In the eighth century, metalwork meant 'large quantities of bronze and iron, a modicum of silver and gold, and a little lead.'[5] Although weapons were in most parts of Greece made of iron since the tenth century, epic convention shows weapons made exclusively of bronze.

The household (oikos) was the primary economic and social unit. Homer, Hesiod, and the scanty material remains from domestic sites suggest that individual oikoi produced what they ate, including wine and olive oil, and did their own grinding, baking, spinning, and weaving. Households were responsible even for complicated jobs like house building and tool making. Hesiod, for example, takes it for granted that a farmer might make his own wooden mortar and pestle, or a mallet for breaking up clods, build his own four-wheeled wagon, fashion a plow from scratch, and weave and sew his own clothes (*WD* 423–36; 538–46). Homer exaggerates the wealth and splendor of heroic life-styles, but his elite live merely a more luxurious version of the common farming and herding regimen.[6] Although there was undoubtedly some economic interdependence among the villages of a region, for the most part separate settlements and their countrysides may have been self-sufficient.

Homeric people have the services of three specialized craftsmen,

---

[4] van Andel and Runnels (1987); Osborne (1987); Rackham (1990); Sallares (1991); Isager and Skydsgaard (1992); Burford (1993).

[5] Snodgrass (1980) 49–50. The bronze supply increased at the end of the tenth century (see I. Morris [this vol.]).

[6] Strasburger (1953); Starr (1977) 120.

the potter (*kerameus*), the metal worker (*chalkeus*), and the carpenter-builder (*tektôn*). We should probably think of these as full-time occupations, although, of course, they might well have farmed part-time on their own or (at the least) kept a large garden. It has been suggested that they may have been itinerant workers, going from village to village. A decent-sized village, however, could have a smithy (*WD* 493–95; cf. *Od.* 18.328). A skilled carpenter, on the other hand, likely traveled from place to place, since his expertise as architect-builder would have been used mostly for building ships, the big houses of the chiefly class, and also temples, circuit walls, and other public monuments. The *tektôn*, in fact, is classified among the *dêmioergoi* ('one who works for the *dêmos*'), like the seer, healer, herald and bard, who even though they are strangers, are welcome everywhere (*Od.* 17.383–86; 19.135).

We find a number of other specific work titles in Homer and Hesiod, such as wood-cutter or fisherman, but these express either *ad hoc* activities—a man is a wood-cutter when he cuts wood—or else extended functions of an occupation, as Laerces the goldsmith (*chrusochoos*), is generically a *chalkeus* (*Od.* 3.425–38; cf. 6.232–35; *Il.* 4.110, 485–86; 7.220–23). It is possible, on the other hand, that the developed vocabulary for different types of herders represents specialized occupations. Homer's short list of full-time manufacturing occupations shows how simple the craft sphere was compared to the Bronze Age.

Trade and Commerce

The isolation of the Aegean societies from the wider Mediterranean world began to lift in the tenth century. Foreign imports became more numerous after 950; and in the eighth century there was a major expansion in imports of prestige items and artistic ideas (and quite possibly craftsmen) from the East and Egypt. Progress was not uniform across the Greek world. Euboea and Cyprus, for example, had participated in international trade since at least the tenth century, while whole regions of Greece proper long remained backward in respect to trade and commerce.[7] Domestic craftsmanship and

---

[7] Greek traders were probably active at Al Mina in Syria, about 825 (Boardman [1990]), and at Pithekoussai (Ischia) off the coast of Italy shortly after 800 (Buchner

production follow the same track. Potters and metalsmiths of the Geometric period were turning out an increasingly refined product, especially fine jewelry and other ornamental metalwork, reaching new heights of artistry and productivity in Late Geometric (c. 750–700).

The remarkable surge in commercial activity occurred in Homer's professional lifetime, yet his depiction of Greek participation in long-distance trade appears to fit the world of 800 (or earlier) better than the world of 700. Consider, for example, Mentes, the *basileus* of the Taphians, who stops at Ithaca, as guest-friend (*xeinos*) of Odysseus' family, carrying a cargo of iron to trade for bronze at the foreign port of Temese (*Od.* 1.180–84). Organized trade in bulk metals, which this seems to be, certainly fits the eighth century, yet would fit the ninth century as well, since bronze imports rose after c. 950. What gives this an archaic feel is that Mentes is a pirate-chief (the Taphians are marauders, *lēïstēres*) and a trader, a combination eminently suited to a chiefdom society, but an anachronism in the city-state.

By the end of the eighth century, Greek traders and Greek goods were competing with the Phoenicians, who were the leading merchants in the Mediterranean during the ninth and eighth centuries.[8] In the *Odyssey*, however, Phoenician trade with the Greeks is of the casual 'calling on' variety. Eumaios recounts such a visit to his home island of Syrie (*Od.* 15.415–84). 'There came Phoenician men, famed for their ships, sharpsters, bringing countless trinkets in their black ship.' They stayed a whole year, camping on the beach, selling and buying until their ship was loaded with 'much substance' (*biotos*). We would dearly love to know what was in the return cargo: probably not 'trinkets,' although local metal and ceramic goods cannot be ruled out; most likely cloth and clothing produced by the women (free and slave) of wealthy oikoi, and hides, fleeces, and possibly finished leather goods.

The Lemnians conduct opportunistic trade with the Achaean encampment at Troy, once delivering a cargo of wine, and bartering individually with the Achaeans in exchange for war-booty (bronze, iron, hides, cattle, and slaves) (*Il.* 7.467–475). The Achaean chiefs themselves dabble in trade. Achilles sells war-captives in nearby

---

and Ridgway [1993]; Coldstream [1994]). See also Coldstream (1977) 92–95, 223–33; Starr (1977) 55–73; Snodgrass (1980) 40–41, 136–37; O. Murray (1993) 69–75; Hurwit (1985) 40–41.

[8] Winter (1995).

Lemnos, Imbros, and Samos (Samothrace) in return for treasure (*Il.* 21.40–41; 23.740–47; 24.751–53). Paris brought some Sidonian women textile workers home on the same voyage on which he carried off Helen, apparently having stopped off at Sidon before coasting north to Troy. We do not know whether he traded for them or kidnapped them (*Il.* 6.288–92; see 9.70–72; *Od.* 20.381–83). There is also some indication of trading 'partnerships' between chiefs and traders.[9]

The Phoenician stereotype in Homer is a thoroughly negative one of thieving sailor-merchants who, in Eumaios' story, kidnap and sell him, with the help of his nurse, a slave woman from Sidon. As a signal that they were ready to embark, one of the sailors came to Eumaios' father's house to display a gold necklace strung with amber beads. 'This then the *dmôai* in the hall and my lady mother were handling and looking over, promising the price; and he nodded to the woman in silence.' Whereupon the nurse stole out of the house, with the child and three gold cups (*Od.* 15.461–70; cf. 14.287–98). The usual assumption is that the Dark Age Greek nobility felt contempt for the occupation of trader (*prêktêr*).[10] It should be noted, however, that Mentes is the social equal of other *basileis*, as is Euneus, *basileus* of the Lemnians, son of Jason the Argonaut. As we have seen, the Achaean warrior-chiefs take advantage of the opportunities to turn a profit from trading.

In Homer's day, the non-elite families were outside the luxury-import trade; and probably very few handled much metal, making do, as they had for millennia, with wood, stone, and bone for farm and household tools.[11] It would be incorrect, however, to say that ordinary people were not involved in truck and barter. Although Homer never mentions local markets (the *agorê* is still exclusively the place of assembly), we can assume some local exchange of farm and animal surpluses. Hesiod, writing at the end of the Geometric period, regards it as not uncommon for a farmer to load his cargo (*phortia*) in his own boat for a short to medium sail along the coast or to a nearby island (*WD* 618–94).

In short, Homer's Greeks are awake to the wider Mediterranean

[9] *Il.* 7.470–71; 23.744–45; *Od.* 4.615–19 probably refers to 'trading dues,' payments to a chief for the privilege.

[10] *Od.* 8.158–64; see Raaflaub (this vol.).

[11] The one exception would be a small amount of iron for ploughshares and spear-points, available through local trade. See *Il.* 23.832–35.

economy, but as minor players, importers of luxury products and luxury materials in exchange for agricultural and animal products and small amounts of finished goods, most of which were conveyed on foreign ships. Warrior-chiefs engage in opportunistic trade of the spoils of war, but disdain professional traders. This picture is plausible for the world of 800; it was old-fashioned when Homer made it.

Land use in Homer

There is no doubt that land was mainly agricultural by 700. A. Snodgrass makes the best case for the old idea that the Dark Age Greeks were primarily pastoralists, arguing that between 1100 and 900 Greeks practiced large-scale herding, principally of cattle, and that permanent occupation of sites 'was partially suspended.' The switch to arable farming and sedentism began in the ninth century and was completed in the eighth.[12]

Homer, though, is quite emphatic that people had always lived in permanent settlements, and defines humans as 'eaters of bread' (*sitos*, a word that is also used as a generic term for food),[13] while, at the same time, he makes herding the dominant mode of livelihood, and meat, especially beef, the principal food of chiefs and ordinary warriors alike. Snodgrass explains the Homeric emphasis on cereals as a 'thinner, and probably later, stratum of arable farming' superimposed on the earlier stock-rearing stratum.[14] Most likely arable farming was the economic basis throughout the Dark Age, and all households pastured as many animals as they could; but chiefly families kept much larger herds (especially of cattle and horses) and dominated the open grazing lands.

The wealthy cultivated more and better land than the ordinary oikoi, and gloried in their grainfields, orchards, and vineyards, as well as their livestock. Tydeus, for example, 'lived in a house rich in livelihood, and had an abundance of wheat-bearing fields and many

[12] Snodgrass (1987) 193–209; cf. Finley (1978) 60; O. Murray (1993) 46–47.

[13] E.g., *Il.* 5.341; *Od.* 8.222; 9.89; 20.108. Note Odysseus' 'agricultural' descriptions of the deserted island next to the Land of the Cyclopes and of the primitive Cyclopes, who are ignorant of agriculture (*Od.* 9.131–35, 107–11). On the mixed economy, see Richter (1968); Stubbings (1962b).

[14] Snodgrass (1980) 35–36.

orchards of trees round about and many herds' (*Il.* 14.121–24; cf. 5.612–13; 11.67–69; 18.550–57; *Od.* 14.211–12). The *temenê*, large parcels of agricultural land allotted to outstanding men by the *dêmos*, are specifically said to consist of both orchard/vineyard (*phutaliê*) and ploughland (*aroura*; see *Il.* 6.194–95; 9.533–42, 577–80; 12.313–14; 20.184–85). Alcinous' large *orchatos*, adjacent to his house, is a true wonder of fruit trees (pear, apple, pomegranate, olive, fig), grapevines, and vegetables, all ripening at different times of the year and irrigated by two springs (*Od.* 7.112–132). The capacious orchard/vineyard and garden of Laertes, in the Ithacan countryside, is a large operation, with a permanent house and sheds, producing many vines and fruit trees (fig, olive, pear, and apple) and requiring the full-time labor of Laertes and an old slave couple, and the help of their six sons (*Od.* 24.221–47, 336–44).

Undoubtedly, ordinary farmers cultivated some vines and olive trees, but only households with a large work force would manage substantial orchards and vineyards, which are labor intensive. There is no possibility of these being commercial ventures, even if we consider them to be reflections of late eighth century circumstances. Of the trees and plants mentioned, only the olive and grapevine had this potential, and significant trade in olive oil and wine came well after 700. Splendid and enviable, the orchard/vineyards were as much for display as for utility, a highly visible marker of wealth, high rank, and distinctive life-style.[15]

Ploughlands, vineyards, and orchards do not fill the Homeric landscape. Unlike in later times, but consistent with the Dark Age evidence, large areas of land are given over to flocks and herds. Homer distorts the economy for us by foregrounding the huge ranching operations of the *basileis* and other *plousioi* and pushing into the background the agricultural economy and the small and middling farmer. But the poetic selectivity also suggests that the Dark Age audiences viewed animals as the higher wealth in social terms. Common epithets of persons and places are compounds of *polu-* ('much,' 'rich in') and animals; thus, *poluarn, polurrên* (sheep), *poluboutês* (cattle), *poluïppos* (horses), and *polumêlos* (flocks). These terms are also found as proper names, like Polumelos and Polubos. Numbers are always very high.

[15] Hanson (1995) ch. 2 argues that the arboriculture and viticulture in Homer are evidence for a new agricultural regimen, instituted by ordinary farmers for the market.

Erichthonius was 'the richest of mortal men,' with 3000 mares (*Il.* 20.220–22). A young man gives as bride gifts (*hedna*) a hundred cattle, with a promise of 1000 goats and sheep (*Il.* 11.244–245). In a reprisal raid against the Eleans, the Pylians drove off fifty herds and flocks each of cattle, sheep, swine, and goats and 150 mares, with foals (*Il.* 11.677–81; cf. 4. 433–34; *Od.* 12.127–30)

Large-scale stock-raising, especially of cattle and horses, is a class divider in Homeric society, setting off the warrior-chiefs and their families from the mass of small households who had little chance of becoming 'rich in flocks.' A main constraint was manpower, as can be seen from Eumaios' description of Odysseus' wealth:

> For in truth, his livelihood was unspeakably great; no one of hero-men either on the dark mainland or in Ithaca itself had so much; no twenty men together have so much wealth; and I will count it off for you. Twelve herds of cattle on the mainland, as many flocks of sheep, as many droves of swine, as many roving herds of goats do they pasture, both strangers and his own herdsmen. And here a total of eleven roving herds of goats pasture in the backlands, and good men watch over them. (*Od.* 14.96–104).

Many animals means many shepherds. Odysseus' 960 pigs were tended by five swineherds and four dogs (*Od.* 14.21–26). Melanthius, Odysseus' goatherd, is accompanied by two other herdsmen as they bring goats to town for the suitors' dinner (*Od.* 17.212–14). Four herdsmen and nine dogs tend the herd of cattle pictured on Achilles' shield (*Il.* 18.573–78). Extra hands were always needed. Neleus takes as his chieftain's cut of the booty 'a herd of cattle and a great flock of sheep, choosing 300 and their shepherds with them' (*Il.* 11.696–97; cf. *Od.* 21.18–19).

In the underpopulated Dark Age there was more than enough land to support subsistence or small-surplus agriculture and extensive pastoralism. Even in populated areas there would have been little competition between the two modes, even considering that cattle and horse herds utilized the close-in, lusher lowland pastures, prime land for growing cereals.[16] Homer uniformly describes cattle and horses as grazing on moist meadowlands or marshlands (*leimôn, helos*).[17] This

[16] Even during the more crowded Classical period, when grazing grounds were diminished, pastoralism and arable farming coexisted fairly well. Osborne (1987) 47–52; Hodkinson (1988).

[17] Donlan (1989c) 139–40.

flood-prone ground could be, and later was, converted to arable, but not without extensive drainage work. The fact that the elite used a disproportionate share of the infield and the more marginal outfield for pasture was an ominous portent, but until about the middle of the eighth century, elite ranching and small-plot farming would have coexisted without social strain.

Although animals had commercial use, they function mainly as social wealth in Homer, given away as marriage gifts, guest-gifts (horses), or as rewards and prizes. Agricultural produce is never used in this way.[18] The commonest social use of animals is to slaughter them and give the meat away in feasts. Epic naturally emphasizes feast-giving and animal sacrifices, but since feasting is universally a major means of display and of social control in big-man and chiefly societies, we need not suspect that the narrative exaggerates its importance. The ability to furnish many victims is proof of the family's importance in the community and a burden that goes with high rank. Competition between rivals drives expenditure. Because social, not economic, considerations motivate actors, no price is too high for fame and influence, although the steady consumption of animals for feasts forces the Homeric chiefs into acquisitive behavior.

Land Tenure

The word *klêros* in Homer seems (*Il.* 15.496–99; *Od.* 11.490; 14.63–65, 211) to have much the same meaning as in Hesiod and later writings, a permanent share or allotment of the community's arable land, sufficient to maintain a family. The history of this institution is unknown; it is very unlikely, though, that it evolved out of collective ownership by a clan or a village, similar to the open fields system of early and medieval Europe.[19] But the custom of the *klêros*-family share did rest on the conceptual oneness of land and people. The *patris gaia* is the father-motherland of every sharer in the tribal name. The ideology of an essential common proprietorship of the *dêmos* (land) is a fundamental fact of Greek social and economic history. Private 'ownership' in the form of permanent possession by a lineage of

---

[18] The cost of things and slaves is stated in terms of so many 'cattle worth;' e.g., *Il.* 21.78–79; 23.702–705; *Od.* 22.56–58; Finley (1978) 67–68.

[19] Ridgeway (1885).

the land that it traditionally worked was in existence generations before Homer.[20]

We have no information about the form of a Dark Age *klêros*, whether it was a single unit (which would be consistent with small villages and hamlets or isolated farmsteads), or made up of several smaller, separated pieces—though surely not nearly so cut up as in later Greece, when the landscape had become a patchwork of small strips. We need not think that the plots were of equal value, or even that they were of equal size. The *klêroi* of the elite families were likely to have been from the best part of the fertile plain closest to the village. Land that was not cultivated was no-man's-land, or rather every man's land, available without restriction to any community member for grazing, gathering, hunting, and wood-cutting.[21]

As to inheritance, both Homer and Hesiod confirm that the traditional Greek system of equal division among all the sons was already the standard practice. The Cretan Odysseus, the son of a rich man's bought concubine, recounts that on his father's death, the legitimate sons 'divided up his living and cast lots for it, but to me they gave just a few things and allotted me a house' (*Od.* 14.208–210). The quarrel between Hesiod and his brother Perses arose after 'we had divided up the *klêros*' (*WD* 37). Partible inheritance of the *klêros*, as opposed to other forms, such as the whole going to the eldest son, functions to keep the patrilineage intact, insuring that successive generations of brothers farm the same land and perhaps live in the same house or compound. The system worked very well in a time of low population and unused arable land, when the concern was more often than not the dying out of the oikos. When population increased, and land became scarce, the custom of dividing up the *klêros* produced an economic crisis for small farmers in many parts of Greece, which became acute during the seventh century.

Scholars have long debated whether *klêroi* could be given or sold to any other oikos, or only transferred within a larger group like the kindred (*anchisteia*). The general opinion today is that plots could be alienated, but that no oikos with sons would willingly surrender the land and jeopardize the material and symbolic existence of the family. It is reasonable to assume, however, that a vacated *klêros* was legally claimed by a wider kin group.[22] This raises the question of

[20] Finley (1982) 213–32; Burford-Cooper (1977/8).
[21] Richter (1968) 12–13, 42.
[22] Finley (1968); Lacey (1968) 333–35; Starr (1977) 150–51; Gallant (1982) 113.

what force could separate a viable family from its *klêros*. One obvious force is poverty. Hesiod advises his audience to sacrifice regularly to the gods, 'that they may have a benign heart and spirit for you, so that you may buy (*ôneomai*) the *klêros* of others, and not another yours' (*WD* 340–41). The *Odyssey* has the terms *poluklêroi* and *aklêros*. The Cretan Odysseus married a 'woman from a family with many *klêroi*, because of my valor' (*Od.* 14.211–12; cf. *Il.* 5.612–13; 14.121–24). Achilles compares 'rule over all the perished dead' unfavorably with life as a hired hand (*thês*) 'for another man, a man with no lot (*aklêros anêr*), who had not much of a living' (*biotos*) (*Od.* 11.489–91). I suspect that while land was alienable before 800, the incidence of alienation, as a result of poverty, increased considerably in the eighth century.

Control and Distribution of Land

Menelaus boasts to Telemachus that as a mark of love for Odysseus,

> I would have settled him in a *polis* in Argos and built him a house, bringing him from Ithaca with his possessions and his son and all his people (*laoi*), having destroyed one *polis* [out of those] that dwell around and are ruled (*anassontai*) by me myself. (*Od.* 4.174–177)

This passage has affinities with Agamemnon's promise to Achilles of rule over and gifts from seven settlements (*ptoliethra*) in the outreaches of his chiefdom and to Peleus' gift to Phoenix of rulership and wealth among the Dolopes, a hill tribe on 'the border (*eschatiê*) of Phthia' (*Il.* 9.149–156, 479–84). Possibly, this extraordinary power over land and people merely reflects the poet's and audience's fantasy of what a Mycenaean *wanax* could do. But it may be that this simply reflects the conditions of Dark Age chiefdoms, in which paramount *basileis* might want to have able lieutenants or allies ruling over the people on the margins ('those who dwell around'), who might regard themselves as independent of the *basileus*' rule. Such maneuvers by the chief would have the approval of the *dêmos*.

But Homeric chiefs could also distribute land in and around the *astu*. Alcinous, paramount *basileus* of the Phaiakians, promises to give Odysseus an 'oikos and *ktêmata*' if he stays in Skheria and marries his daughter; Odysseus likewise promises his herdsmen, Eumaios and Philoitios, 'possessions (*ktêmata*) and houses (*oikia*) built near my own; and thereafter you two will be to my mind companions (*hetairoi*) and brothers (*kasignêtoi*) of Telemachus' (*Od.* 7.311–15; 21.214–16). Outright seizure and reallocation of another's cultivated land seems inconsistent with the *klêros*-system and the general Homeric picture of the leader-people relationship, which is one of amity and interdependence. These gifts of close-in land must refer either to the chiefs' own landholdings, or to unoccupied land. In these two cases, which emphasize the adoption of the receivers into the giver's family, the former is more likely. That is consistent with the generalizing statement of Eumaios that a 'kind-hearted master (*anax*) gives to his *oikeus* a house and a *klêros* and a much-wooed wife, when he has worked hard for him' (*Od.* 14.63–65; cf. *Il.* 6.191–95; 14.119–25)

The sole, yet decisive, example of the major role of the *basileus* in the distribution of unoccupied land is the description of the founding of Skheria by Alcinous' father Nausithous, who 'drove a wall around the polis, and built oikoi, and divided up the ploughlands (*arourai*)' (*Od.* 6.9–10). The verb 'divide' (*dateomai*) is the same used for the division of spoils from raids, distributed by lot in equal shares to each man (*Il.* 1.122–26, 366–69; 9.138; *Od.* 9.41–42, 159–60; 14.232–34). Homer does not use the word *klêros* here, but the division of *arourai*, which are located in the close-in plain (*pedion*) and outer fields (*agros*), can only refer to the allotment of *klêroi*. This matches the historical evidence that the 'founders' of the early colonies were authorized to distribute the *klêroi* and house-plots among the settlers, a mechanism that must have been based on precedent.[23]

Very likely, a similar procedure governed the allotment of land to newcomers into settled communities. Hesiod's father, 'fleeing evil poverty,' emigrated from Kyme in Asia Minor to the village of Askra in Boeotia, where he was allowed to settle and was allotted the *klêros* his sons inherited (*WD* 37, 635–40). Since the allotting of land from the arable reserve—and therefore the admission of a new family into the community—was a major event in a village's life, the decision must have been a communal one. In Homeric society, public (*dêmion*) questions of this sort are decided in the assembly, where the leading men debate (the chief having the highest authority), and the rest express approval or disapproval, but do not vote, and rarely give speeches.[24] The *temenos* is unambiguously described as the gift of the whole people, the Lykians to Bellerophon, and to Sarpedon and

[23] Graham (1964) ch. 3. On the mutual influences between the early colonies and the early city-states see Malkin (1989).

[24] See Raaflaub (this vol.).

Glaukos, the elders of the Aetolians to Meleager, the Trojans to Aeneas (*Il.* 6.194–95; 9.574–80; 12.310–18; 20.184–86). Yet the decision to 'cut out' a piece of the plainland (*pedion*) could hardly have been arrived at differently from the allocation of new *klêroi*, which in effect the *temenos* was. In these situations we can discern both the dominant authority of the chiefs and the balancing will of the *dêmos*.

Reciprocity

The gift of a *temenos* is a good example of the finely tuned reciprocity that exists between the community and its leaders in Homeric society. Like the other gifts from the people, it is a free gift, given in exchange for past and future service to the *dêmos*, yet not quite free, since it is also the chief's 'due,' his right, as leader, to something extra. As such, a *temenos* bears somewhat the same relation to the *klêros* as the *geras* does to the equal distribution (*dasmos*) of the spoils of raid and war. Neither the *geras*, which comes out of the profit, nor the *temenos*, which comes out of unallocated land, imposes a burden on the people. That is an indication of the quality of the reciprocity.[25]

The ethics and practice of leader-people reciprocity in Homer are a sort of fair inequality, in which both 'fair' and 'unequal' have understood limits. The texts make it clear that the people regularly, and by custom, gave gifts to the chiefs, although the what, when, and how are not spelled out. There are two examples of elementary taxation from the center for the public good. The leaders of the Greeks at Troy are said to 'drink at public expense' (*dêmia*), the reference being to the wine consumed in the *boulê*—known as the 'wine of the elders' (*gerousios oinos*)—which is furnished or paid for by the *dêmos* and distributed by the *basileus* to the councilors as their *geras* (*Il.* 4.259–60; 17.248–50; *Od.* 13.8). Hector complains to the allies that he is 'wearing down' (*katatruchô*) the Trojan *laoi* with exactions of 'gifts and food provisions' to pay for their services (*Il.* 17.225–26; cf. 18.290–92).

Personal gain, not public need, is the main motive for collecting gifts, however. In Homeric society, gifts from the people are materially substantial, not honorific tokens, and a chief's ability to draw on that resource is an important element of his household's economy.

[25] Donlan (1989c) 132–34, 143–45.

As young Telemachus artlessly puts it, 'For it is no bad thing to be *basileus*. Quickly one's house becomes rich and oneself more honored' (*Od.* 1.392–93; cf. *Il.* 9.149–56, 479–84; 5.78; *Od.* 14.205).

Should we see compulsory gift-giving as exploitation, that is, as what Sahlins dubbed 'negative reciprocity'?[26] To be sure, there is always the temptation for the 'shepherds of the people' to shear their flocks too closely, especially when, as in Homeric society, their expenses are great. Priam castigates his remaining sons as 'plunderers of lambs and kids among the people' (*epidêmioi harpaktêres*), which implies bullying of the populace, even if not outright robbery (*Il.* 24.262; cf. 1.231; 22.489). The overall impression from Homer, however, is that the economic demands of the *basileus* on the *dêmos* were orderly, rational, and fair. Almost all the specific situations of *dêmos* giving to *basileis* refer to the recouping of losses or heavy expenditures by the chief (*Il.* 1.133–36; *Od.* 2.74–78; 13.13–15; 19.194–98; 22.55–58; 23.356–58).

These occasions are part of an endless series of exchanges between a leader and his people. Followers and dependents give when they have to, when their chief needs it, with the expectation that it will come back in some fashion. In Homer this comes as largesse, in the form of feasts and shared sacrifices, as rewards for good deeds and favors, and as contest-prizes. We may include here what heroic poetry omits, the numberless small, banal benefits that reinforce the ties of loyalty and mutual obligation between a chief and his people.

There are people at the margin of the reciprocal relationship, who are exploited economically, principally those known as *thêtes*, laborers hired for a set wage. *Thêtes* would be men with no land or land so poor that the little wage (*misthos*) they earned, which was not much more than their keep, was better than what they could get by themselves. Some were from the group of *aklêroi*, some perhaps were 'rightless migrants' who were not given a *klêros* (*Il.* 9.648; 16.59); others were wandering beggars (*Od.* 18.357–58). Such men apply first at the wealthiest houses, which welcome the addition of cheap contract labor to their manpower (*Il.* 21.442–59; *Od.* 4.643–44). The vast majority of the unfree or semi-free workers, who probably outnumbered the free *thêtes*, also served the few wealthiest. In the fields and pastures, male *dmôes* and *thêtes* did similar work; *dmôai* worked in the

[26] Sahlins (1972).

oikos, contributing significantly to the production of cloth.[27] As has been noted often, the existence of a *dmôs/oikeus* was more secure than that of a *thês*, who performed the same hard tasks for about the same pay, but lacked the protection of membership, however lowly, in the oikos.[28]

The Treasure Economy

Reciprocity among the chiefs and other leading men in Homer is sociologically more complex than the straightforward 'generalized' system of gifts on demand from the people to the leaders, followed by unspecified returns in the form of chiefly largesse. As noted above, the economic motive in this asymmetrical relationship was great. The calls on the people's surplus sustained the *basileis* materially as well as symbolically. Gift-giving among the Homeric elite, by contrast, has maximum social and political purpose, but little economic purpose. Gifts symbolize the relationship. Each gift-act is a product both of what is appropriate and customary for the occasion and of other variables such as age and position. All offers, acceptances, or exchanges of *dôra* are instrumental, either in establishing, maintaining, or repairing a relationship, or in minimizing hostility, or validating or calibrating (and even creating) differences in rank.

Honor and prestige are the bottom line of gift transactions. In every case, the 'text' of the gift—who gives what to whom, and why, and how much and in what way—may be read as a public declaration of the relative social ranking of the participants at that moment (*Il.* 11.123–25; *Od.* 2.184–86). The emphasis on competition and display in Homeric gift-giving might seem exaggerated, had we not numerous parallels from big-man and chieftain societies world-wide. The guest-friend relationship between foreigners (*xeinoi*), which is totally free of that kind of rivalry, presents an ideal reciprocity. The host's hospitality, kind intentions, and parting gift are guaranteed a perfectly symmetrical return, with no time limit on the obligation.[29]

To talk further about gift-behavior would lead into a discussion of

[27] *Dmôes*: *Il.* 21.448–49; *Od.* 10.84–85; *dmôai*: *Il.* 1.112–15; 6.456–58; 12.433–35; *Od.* 1.356–58; 6.52–53; 20.105–10.

[28] See Raaflaub (this vol.).

[29] Donlan (1989a) 6–10; Herman (1987).

elite power relations. I will concentrate on the material and economic aspects. The material of elite gift transactions belongs to a separate form of wealth, 'treasure,' which was available in a socially useful quantity only to the elite, and circulated exclusively among them.[30] Anthropologists know many such 'multi-centric economies,' in which social-symbolic wealth circulates in a separate sphere of exchange marked by a 'different institutionalization and different moral values.'[31]

Treasure in Homer consists mainly of artifacts of metal or cloth and unworked metal (chiefly gold and iron), the generic word for which is *keimêlia*, 'things stored up,' indicating their essential nature—small items, easily transported and stored. The value of treasure goods lies in their scarcity and costliness: embroidered and dyed textiles, bronze arms and armor, gold and silver cups and ornaments, gold and (occasionally) iron in their natural states. Only cloth goods, which in fact make up a considerable portion of *keimêlia*, are produced in the oikos; the rest are specialist manufactures. Among the most valuable *keimêlia* are large, unused bronze cauldrons and tripod cauldrons, utilitarian objects elevated to purely symbolic wealth. Women and horses circulate along with treasure-gifts, since both are highest-status possessions and both produce *keimêlia*, women with their weaving, and horses as prize-winners in races.

The scarcity of treasure is inadvertently emphasized in the epics. Whereas in transactions involving animals the numbers given are very high, treasure-gifts are on a much smaller scale. Even when the poet wishes to give the impression of an enormous quantity of prestige goods, clearly exaggerating reality, the actual count is rather modest. Most treasure transactions in Homer, in fact, consist of only one to three items.[32] The same high numerical and value ratios between animals and *keimêlia* are observed in the few instances where actual equivalencies are given. A large tripod is 'worth' twelve cattle, an embossed cauldron is 'worth an ox,' a splendid silver bowl is equivalent to three horses and a chariot (*Il.* 23.702–703, 884; *Od.* 4.600–619).

It is likely that the quickening economic tempo in the ninth century reflects mainly the growing appetite of the elite for metal and

---

[30] Finley (1978) 61–62, 120–23.
[31] E.g., Bohannon (1959).
[32] Donlan (1981) 102–103.

prestige items for purposes of display and gift-giving. That requirement for success, amply documented by archaeology and the epics, spurred ambitious oikoi to increase their agricultural and animal surpluses, providing the stimulus for the spiraling growth in the crafts and trading sectors in the eighth and seventh centuries.[33] Although ordinary families were not involved directly in the prestige economy, they bore a share of the expense, as Homer shows. It is quite possible, then, that during the ninth century chieftains were already placing greater demands on the surplus of their constituents, prompting them to increase their productivity.

Wealth in animals, treasure, and female slaves is intimately tied to the institutions of war and raiding, the surest paths to personal glory and to riches in the epics. Since force of arms is the most honorable way to come into possession of these, we may suspect Homer of a selective focus. Even so, we cannot doubt that throughout the Geometric period the raid (which in the Homeric world is a cousin to trade; *Od.* 3.71–74 = 9.252–55; cf. Thuc. 1.5) was an important economic activity, and that the attacks on poleis (where the *keimêlia* lay), were partly motivated by lust for treasure and women, whatever the other reasons for enmity. The system fostered the continuing dominance of the current chiefly families, who were the organizers, leaders, and principal beneficiaries of raiding, and were already rich in flocks, and already possessed the nucleus of a raiding party in their 'retainers' (*therapontes*) and 'close companions' (*philoi hetairoi*). So, while those below them might wish to emulate them, acquisition and maintenance of a large surplus of animals, especially the luxury animals, cattle and horses, was usually possible only for the established elite.[34]

Summary and Conclusions

Homer describes an economy that is extremely simple as a functioning system, yet is fairly complex in its relationships, which are socially and ideologically constructed. In Homer, social concerns drive economic behavior. The leaders do not direct the economy; *basileis* in Homer have limited redistributive functions, and do not levy regular

---

33 Austin and Vidal-Naquet (1977) 54–56; Starr (1992) 46–49, 61.

34 The 'Cretan' Odysseus is one who did rise to chieftain status: *Od.* 14.199–234.

taxes and dues on the people. There is every indication in Homer that the 'compliance costs' to the *dêmos* for obeying the chiefs' demands for gifts are low. The practice of equal shares in the booty and the feast, with something extra for the leaders, is the paradigm of economic relations in general.

The need to consume animals and treasure to win a good reputation and create obligations operates at every level of leadership and is heaviest on the top ranks. This competition appears inefficient from the perspective of modern economic rationality, but makes perfect sense to the Homeric *basileis*, who like low-level chiefs everywhere, amass only to spend.[35] The system apparently slowed the increase of wealth differentiation, which is relatively unmarked for most of the Dark Age and becomes really severe only in the eighth century.

As I suggested earlier, little of the systemic economic changes that occurred between the end of the ninth and the early seventh centuries is found in the *Iliad* and *Odyssey*. These include, most notably, the switch from large-scale stock-raising by the elite and their transformation into an agricultural gentry with restrictive access to the land, and the erosion of the ancient principles of leader-people reciprocity, but also the waning of the animal raid as a major economic activity and the much heavier engagement of the aristocrats in organized international trade. What precipitated these and a host of other fundamental new developments, such as the 'decline' of the paramount *basileus* and the rise of city-state institutions, war for territory, and a remarkable artistic flowering, including the 'invention' of the Greek alphabet and the spread of writing[36]—all of which were coming to be during 'Homer's' own lifetime—remains a mystery.

Snodgrass has suggested the operation of a 'multiplier effect.' When major changes or innovations occur in two or more critical elements of a society, 'and the results interact, the rate of progress—both material and social—may accelerate violently.'[37] For Snodgrass and many other scholars, a primary factor of change was rapidly accelerating population growth during the early eighth century, after centuries of very low populations.[38]

These explanations make sense of the vectors of growth since 900

[35] Mauss (1966 [1925]).
[36] See Raaflaub (this vol.); van Wees (this vol.); Snodgrass (this vol.); Powell (this vol.).
[37] Snodgrass (1980) 54–55; Cf. Starr (1986) 42: 'a number of interlocked changes.'
[38] Raaflaub (1991) 215–17. See I. Morris (this vol.).

and the observable economic changes in the eighth century. The economic and social system that epic preserves supposes a 'background' world of much open land, given over mainly to large roving flocks and herds, and isolated settlements, both easy prey for marauding bands. It is people who are scarce in Homer. As soon as the land-to-people ratio began to be reversed (i.e., well before there was any serious strain on the carrying capacity of the land), the old system, which was completely maladapted to the new conditions, challenges, and opportunities, had to change. It is not surprising, therefore, that the 'structural revolution' in Greece was accomplished in the relatively short span of three or four generations; nor that the poet's audiences, living in a society in transition, could still comprehend that vanishing background world.

Hans van Wees

HOMERIC WARFARE[1]

When Homer launches into a battle narrative, many a modern reader switches off. Even those who might enjoy an elaborate fight sequence in an action movie tend to find its written equivalent overlong, repetitive, and confusing. Yet 'we must assume that the ancient audience here followed the bard as spell-bound as a modern audience follows the commentary of an exciting football match on the radio.'[2] One step toward recreating the ancient experience is to clear up the apparent confusion and reconstruct what is going on. For all their length, the battle scenes will seem far from boring once we can visualize the action.

Homeric warfare is also worth studying for its historical interest. Despite obviously fantastic elements such as divine interventions, feats of superhuman strength, and spectacular but impossible killings, it is generally and rightly assumed that, to some degree at least, Homeric scenes of combat reflect battles as they were fought by early Greek armies. It used to be commonly held that the heroes' style of fighting is quite unlike that of the Archaic and Classical Greek citizen-soldier, and that military organization, tactics, and ethics must therefore have undergone a transformation after Homer's time. The consensus was that this dramatic change in warfare was a motive force behind the rise of the city-state, tyranny, and ultimately democracy. Since the late 1970s, however, another view has gained ground. This posits that appearances deceive: on closer examination there are few significant differences between Homeric and Classical warfare, and hence military developments cannot account for the major political changes in Archaic Greece.

It is, above all, this historical debate which has lent new vitality to the study of Homeric warfare. It is not by chance that the subject has a chapter to itself in this volume, when in the old *Companion* neither 'war' nor 'battle' rated so much as an entry in the index.

---

[1] All Homeric references are to the *Iliad*, unless otherwise indicated.

[2] K. Matthiesen, in a review of S. Daitz's readings of the *Iliad* (*Gymnasium* 101 [1994] 359–60).

The Heroic Army: Warrior Bands and 'Tribal' Contingents

The story begins with a red herring: the order of battle as described in the famous *Catalogue of Ships*. Here the Greek army is drawn up in 29 contingents, varying in size but most commonly comprising about 2,000 men—that is, 40 ships, each with a crew of 50—recruited from a region embracing on average half a dozen cities. The Boiotians are stationed on the right wing (2.526), the Magnesians on the left, and Odysseus' Kephallenians hold the centre. The Trojans and their allies are similarly divided into 16 contingents according to their places of origin (2.484–877). This would seem a natural enough arrangement. Homer, however, treats the separation of 'national' contingents as an unusual notion, and he fails to sustain it.

On the Greek side, the division of the troops is first proposed by Nestor:

> Separate the men by tribes, by phratries, Agamemnon, so that a phratry may bring aid to phratries, and a tribe to tribes. If you were to act thus and the Greeks would obey you, then you might find out who among the leaders is a coward, and who is a brave man, for they would be fighting amidst their own people (2.362–66).

This is presented as a novel and excellent idea (2.370–74); Agamemnon and his closest allies personally take charge of putting it into action (2.439–46, 474–77). The surprising implication is that members of such (pseudo-) kinship groups do not fight as units as a matter of course: they would normally be found scattered across the battlefield. Meanwhile in Troy, it is pointed out to Hektor that his many allies all speak different languages. 'Let each man give orders to those whom indeed he leads, and, having drawn up his countrymen, let him lead them out' (2.803–806). The implication is that until then, forces of different ethnic origins had merged into a single, undivided army. It might be objected that this is an over-literal interpretation, that Homer is merely for dramatic effect introducing as a fresh invention a form of organization which must have been commonplace. Yet when we turn to the battle narrative, we find in fact no trace of distinct contingents and every indication that the troops mingle at will.

When on occasion the poet indicates the location of certain bodies of men on the battlefield, their positions do not remotely match those in the *Catalogue* (e.g., 4.251–421; 13.685–708). This is hardly surprising, since their leaders are extremely mobile. Hektor, having retired hurt from the centre of the battlefield (11.354–60), is next seen fighting 'on the left' (11.498) until advised to return to his previous position (11.523–42). Later, Idomeneus, who has been fighting on the left (11.498–501), meets up behind the lines with his follower Meriones who has been fighting in the center; after deliberation both decide to rejoin battle on the left (13.307–327). Hektor meanwhile stays where he is (13.674–76) until forced to move to the left again in search of support (13.735–60). There he finds Paris, whom he brings back with him to fight in the centre (13.784–94). As we shall see, leading heroes frequently respond to a call for help or to the sight of some crisis by flocking together from all over the battlefield. Such freedom of movement is obviously incompatible with fixed battle stations and distinct contingents.

A different principle of military organization is assumed throughout the narrative, although never explicitly described, and this is much more easily reconciled with the mobility of the heroes: networks of personal ties unite the army, giving it a loose and flexible structure.

The two key terms defining personal relations in the army are the egalitarian 'companion' (*hetairos*) and the hierarchical 'follower' (*therapôn*; literally 'attendant'). Everyone in the army is thought of as everyone else's 'companion,'[3] though some are inevitably closer companions than others. Being a follower, on the other hand, is neither a mutual nor a general relation, but involves one man's subordination to another. Meriones, say, follows Idomeneus and no one else. The men who form a contingent are simultaneously their commander's followers and his companions: thus the Myrmidons are variously described as Akhilleus' 'close-fighting *therapontes*' (16.272; 17.165) and as his *hetairoi* (e.g., 1.179–80). Within the contingent, though, distinctions are drawn between close personal followers and more distant ones, some of whom may have followers of their own. Some special ties of companionship may even cut across contingents. Small, fluid groups constituted by the closest of these relationships operate as units on and off the battlefield.

The best example of such a group is Akhilleus and his three most

[3] For example, Menelaos looks for Antilokhos 'everywhere among the crowd of many companions' (17.673–81), which here means the entire army, and the poet refers to the Pylians, led by Nestor and his sons, as *Menelaos*' 'worn-out companions' (17.702–703). Although in practice the term is most often applied to followers, in itself it indicates a mutual rather than a hierarchical relationship: Odysseus and Mentor are explicitly each other's *hetairoi* (*Od.* 2.225; 22.208), and in that sense Akhilleus can call his senior colleagues 'dear *hetairoi*' (19.303–313).

intimate companions and followers. Akhilleus, it is said, 'honors' Patroklos, his boyhood friend, 'above all his *hetairoi*' (18.81–82); he honors Automedon and Alkimos most 'after Patroklos' (24.574–75). Patroklos, in turn, honors Automedon most 'after Akhilleus' (16.145–46). This ranking order of respect is reflected in a hierarchy of service. Patroklos acts as Akhilleus' charioteer in battle (e.g. 17.427), while in Akhilleus' absence Automedon serves as Patroklos' charioteer (16.145). Again, Patroklos acts as personal attendant to Akhilleus at meals (9.190–220), while after his death Automedon and Alkimos take on that role (24.472–75, 573–75). We see a tiny but tightly-knit and hierarchical group of men who live and fight together.

This group is part of a larger band of companions, who share the same quarters, but sit some way apart from Akhilleus and friends (24.472–73; 9.658). We are told elsewhere that the Trojans, out in the plain, sleep and eat around campfires in 'units' (*telê*) of fifty men (8.562–63; 18.298); perhaps we may infer that the same number of men, i.e., a single ship's crew, shares a 'hut' in the Greek camp. That not all these companions are equally close to their leader is confirmed by the case of the son of Polyktor, who travelled on the same ship and is evidently supposed to be staying in the same hut, but whose only connection with Akhilleus is that he has been chosen by lot from among seven brothers to become his follower at Troy (24.396–400).

The contingent beyond this group contains a large number of men who, though they are Akhilleus' followers, are also leaders in their own right. At the call to arms, the 'leaders and lords' of the Myrmidons emerge from their quarters and 'dart' round Akhilleus (16.164–66). Their number is unspecified, but evidently considerably more than five, and includes Akhilleus' nephew Menesthios and his elderly tutor Phoinix (16.171–78, 196). Since despite their close ties to Akhilleus these two men do not share his quarters, and since Phoinix at any rate is in his own right ruler of the Dolopes (9.483–84), we may reasonably infer that they, and the other leaders of the Myrmidons, each share a hut with their own band of followers. Elsewhere in the *Iliad*, too, considerable numbers of little-known or indeed anonymous men are described as 'leaders,'[4] which presumably means that all of these have personal followers as well. In fact, contingents are

[4] As at 3.230–3: 'Idomeneus stands among the Cretans like a god, and around him the leaders of the Cretans are gathered;' cf. 16.495–96. In many passages lead-

probably envisaged as composed entirely of numerous small bands of men, with a core of the aristocratic leader's close friends and a fringe of his humbler and more distant companions.[5]

In battle, a leader is generally accompanied by at least some followers, including his charioteer of course, but also a number of other men, whose presence is mentioned only once in a while. Every so often, Homer will refer in passing to *therapontes* or *hetairoi* who are immediately at hand to pick up their leader's spoils or to lead away his prisoners. Idomeneus kills a man in pursuit: 'Idomeneus' followers plundered the body' (5.48). Akhilleus seems to be routing the enemy all by himself: then he captures twelve Trojans and we suddenly find that he has companions with him who take the prisoners off his hands (21.26–32). And so forth.

Such followers are not invented *ad hoc*, but are an implied presence throughout. Thus Aias in one episode appears to be resisting a Trojan onslaught alone, yet when Hektor comes over from the left wing specifically to deal with this pocket of resistance, we are told that 'he harassed the lines of *other* men . . . but avoided Aias in combat' (11.540–42).[6] Evidently Aias has a group of followers with him, whom the poet has previously ignored, and subsequently ignores again until, much later, he has occasion to note that 'many fine men followed him as companions, who carried his shield for him whenever his knees were overcome with exhaustion and sweat' (13.709–711). The story focuses on leading heroes so hard that one who has only his own men for company is thought of as 'alone,' but Homer takes it for granted that wherever a leader goes, his companions go with him. In the rare event of a leader actually leaving his followers, he does so only after putting someone else in charge of them (12.349–72; 17.702–706); at all other times, followers may be barely mentioned but their presence is tacitly assumed.

---

ers emerge who had not been listed as commanders in the *Catalogue*: see especially. 11.301–305, with van Wees (1986) 287–88.

[5] So Greenhalgh (1982) 82–83; Andreev (1988); van Wees (1992) 48, 337–88; (1995b) 169–74; Donlan (1994). Other scholars, however, hold that only the social elite within the army is organized into bands of leaders and personal followers, and that the common men who constitute the bulk of the forces are recruited and organized in some other, unknown, manner: Versnel (1980) 117; O. Murray (1983a) 196–98; (1983b) 259–62; (1991) 83–84, 94, 99; (1993) 47, 53–54; Welwei (1992).

[6] Aias has been 'alone' since replacing Odysseus (11.485–86), who had been alone (11.401–402); he is still 'in person' holding back the Trojans at 11.566–71. See van Wees (1986) 288–90.

It is impossible to tell, however, how many companions are supposed to be at their leader's side at any particular moment. Sometimes it seems that most of his contingent is with him; at other times, perhaps only his own band, or only a few of his closest friends. What happens in the course of battle is apparently a constant splitting, recombining, and temporary merging of groups. Take the Cretan contingent, which is clearly split into at least two parts when, as we have seen, Idomeneus and his follower Meriones are fighting in different parts of the frontline. Idomeneus subsequently leaves the battlefield with a number of companions—presumably no more than half a dozen—to carry a wounded comrade to safety (13.210–15); Meriones also leaves the battlefield, probably with a few companions of his own, although these are not mentioned (13.162–68). Both thus contribute to dividing further whatever parts of the Cretan army had been fighting with them. Then they team up and decide to rejoin the men left behind by Idomeneus, thereby reconstituting at least part of the contingent. We shall later come across examples of sizable groups merging when their leaders decide to join forces for a while.

In combat, then, the heroic army knows no cohesive and exclusive military units; accordingly, there is no technical term either for 'warrior band' or 'contingent,' and the latter can only be described in a roundabout way as an aggregate of 'tribes and phratries.'[7] Instead, battle is conducted by mobile and changing clusters of warriors, based on ties of companionship and personal subordination. Leaders and their closest followers form small but relatively stable cores which expand and contract as other followers and friends join or leave.

The Course of Battle

Homer constructs his battle scenes much as a film director might do. He opens with a panoramic image of the forces drawing up and advancing, then zooms in on the action, and thereafter cuts back and forth between close-ups of the heroes of the tale and wide-angle

[7] The word *purgos*, 'tower,' is taken by many (e.g., Latacz [1977] 52–53) in two passages to refer to a contingent (4.333–35, 347–48). It is in fact likely to refer to its leader, and in any case to be used metaphorically ('a tower of strength'), as it is in the *Odyssey* (11.556).

views of the armies at large. During close-ups, the general action recedes into the background or falls outside the frame, and a superficial impression is created of warriors fighting duels in isolation. The background, however, is never forgotten: we are regularly reminded that our heroes are not alone, but fighting 'in the crowd,' or 'among the frontline warriors,' and that they are the target of many missiles. Thus, scenes of apparent single combat in fact represent selected highlights of the action, as was established long ago by F. Albracht, and demonstrated again by G. Strasburger and J. Latacz in well-known studies.[8] Although this 'cinematic' feature of Homeric poetry has long been recognized, it cannot be emphasized enough that we must be constantly aware of it if we are to make sense of what happens in the scenes of combat.

The formation

For the long-popular idea that the bulk of the Homeric army consists of poorly armed men equipped only with light missiles, there is very little evidence. The Lokrian contingent, armed with bows and slings (13.712–18), fits the picture, but is clearly an exception. Everywhere else, images abound of troops heavily armored and equipped with spears and swords: 'it blinded eyes, the glare of bronze from shining helmets, newly polished corslets and bright shields, as they advanced in their masses' (14.340–43). These heavily armed men regularly resort to the use of arrows and stones as well. Nevertheless, the many references to such missiles flying probably indicate the presence of a significant number of light-armed troops.

A couple of passages highlight the density of the crowd as the forces stand ready for battle. Aias' men are described as 'a cloud of footsoldiers,' 'dense ranks [*phalanges*], dark and bristling with shields and spears' (4.274, 281–82). Even more strikingly, Akhilleus' troops react to his pre-battle harangue as follows: 'the lines [*stikhes*] drew closer together when they heard the prince . . . They locked together their helmets and embossed shields. Shield pressed against shield, helmet against helmet, man against man. The shining crestholders of their horsehair-plumed helmets touched when they nodded, so close together did they stand' (16.211–17). It has been argued that the

---

[8] Albracht (1886) 28; G. Strasburger (1954) 43–48, 67–68; Latacz (1977) 68–74, 83–85. Fully accepted, e.g., by Kirk (1990) 22; Finley (1978) 74.

terms *phalanges* and *stikhes*, 'ranks' and 'lines,' indicate that troops were drawn up in squares or rectangles of regular ranks and files. However, Homeric Greek appears to be as unspecific as modern English is in its use of these words, and both the image of a 'cloud' of soldiers and the spontaneous pressing together of the crowd when it is fired up suggest, not a neat formation, but an amorphous mass.[9] That it is the men of Akhilleus and Aias who are depicted in this manner is no coincidence, for they are elsewhere singled out as the two bravest contingents (8.224–26, 11.7–9): densely massed troops are clearly the Homeric ideal.

Several times, a body of soldiers is divided by its commander into five sections. Akhilleus 'appointed five leaders to whom he entrusted the giving of orders . . . and he placed all men around the leaders, dividing them well' (16.171–72, 198–99); Nestor, too, draws up his followers 'around' five named men (4.293–96). In preparation for an assault on the Greek camp the whole Trojan army spontaneously regroups: 'taking separate stations, packing themselves together, ordered in five groups, they followed their leaders' (12.86–87). A few other passages also hint at fivefold divisions.[10] Like the contingents, these sections play no part in the battle itself, except that the Trojans retain them for the duration of their assault on the Greek wall, and only resume their usual mobility after they have broken through. Unlike the contingents, however, no special advice is needed to create sections, and there is no suggestion that they are meant to be permanent units. Perhaps it is understood that such subdivisions are a common but temporary feature of military formations. They might be specifically designed to give added cohesion to the troops during the advance, but not intended to stay intact in battle.

Certainly the cohesion of their forces during the advance is a major concern for Homeric commanders. Akhilleus' men represent the ideal: 'immediately they swarmed out like wasps . . . and in their masses fell upon the Trojans' (16.259, 276). At their best, the ranks of Greeks and Trojans move forward 'one after another . . . relentlessly into battle,' 'some ahead, close together, and others behind them,' like

---

[9] Rank-and-file formation: Latacz (1977) 45–67; Pritchett (1985) 21–25; (1991) 185–86; Singor (1991); (1995) 193–99. Shapeless mass: van Wees (1986) 292–95; (1994) 3–4.

[10] Troops following commander and five others: 11.56–60; 12.139–40 (it may be significant that Agamemnon makes only five stops on his tour of the Greek army, 4.250–421).

waves whipped up by a storm (4.422–28; 13.795–800). On the other hand, entire contingents are happy to wait for someone else down the line to make the first move (4.331–35, 347–48), and Nestor finds it necessary to draw up his best troops in the rear 'to be a bulwark in battle' and force every one of the 'cowards' stationed ahead of them 'to fight even if he does not want to' (4.298–300). In order to overcome such reluctance, some other leaders make a point of personally spurring on 'the hindmost ranks' into battle (4.254; 11.65).

Leaders are generally expected to take their place 'among the foremost' and since all or most of them have chariots and charioteers to drive them to and from, and sometimes around, the battlefield, it is no surprise that Nestor stations all chariots in front of the footsoldiers (4.297). Indeed, several passages show that leaders and their chariots might advance rather faster than their followers: Patroklos and his charioteer are to be found 'in front of everyone, . . . with only one thought—to fight ahead of the Myrmidons' (16.218–20). In an earlier battle, when the armies had been separated by a truce just before coming to blows, the Greeks 'drew back their horses towards the lines' (3.113), implying that most chariots had been advancing some way in front of the infantry. It seems, in fact, that Nestor's advice to charioteers is on the one hand to stay in front of their troops rather than fall back (4.305), and on the other hand not to advance too far 'alone ahead of the others' (i.e., their followers; 4.303–304).[11]

Every effort is evidently made to keep the troops together as they move closer to the enemy, but with chariots pulling ahead, and the less eager soldiers dragging their feet, there is every chance that the army will get strung out during the advance. Even if the men do start out in regular order rather than as a mere crowd, their formation will have become fairly ragged, and certainly much less dense, by the time they reach the enemy.

The initial clash

The very first encounter sets a pattern for the action. 'When [the armies] were close, as they moved towards one another, Paris fought as frontline warrior [*promakhos*] before the Trojans, . . . walking ahead

[11] van Wees (1994) 12–13; but note that this passage is usually interpreted quite differently, as a unique reference to a battalion of chariots fighting in line (e.g., Greenhalgh [1973] 1–9).

of the mass with great strides' (3.15–16, 22). Menelaos saw him and jumped down from his chariot, 'making an appearance among the frontline warriors' (3.29–31). Paris instantly 'retreated again to the crowd of comrades' and 'plunged back into the mass of Trojans' (3.32, 36). When Hektor next stepped forward to propose a truce, 'the Greeks, aiming their arrows, shot at him and threw stones' (3.79–80). The situation is clear: although the armies are 'close,' the 'mass' are barely within reach of missiles, while *promakhoi*, of whom there are a number besides the two heroes, fight at closer range, moving in and out of the mass.

The truce is soon broken, and they advance again. This time, 'when, coming together, they reached the same ground, shields met, as did the spears and spirits of bronze-cuirassed men, and embossed shields struck one another . . .' (4.446–56). Given that commanders make an effort to lead their troops into battle in as compact an order as possible, one is inclined to infer from the 'clash of shields' that on this occasion the armies did not keep their distance but at once engaged in massed hand-to-hand combat. The narrative which follows, however, suggests otherwise.

'First Antilokhos killed a fine Trojan warrior among the *promakhoi*' (4.457–58), catching him in the forehead with a spear-cast.[12] Another Greek attempted to drag the corpse away 'from under the missiles' (4.465), but a Trojan fatally stabbed him with his spear. The poet then broadens his focus: 'over him a hard fight developed between Trojans and Greeks; they rushed towards one another like wolves, and man grappled with man' (4.470–72). We quickly zoom in again on the action: 'there Aias hit the son of Anthemion . . . as he was coming forward' (473, 480); Antiphos threw a spear 'through the crowd' (490); Odysseus 'went forward through the *promakhoi*, moving in very close, stood still and cast his spear' (495–96). The poet once more briefly surveys the action in general (505–516), before returning to individuals: 'there Diores met his doom,' when he was knocked down by a stone and then stabbed to death by Peiroos, who 'ran up to him' (524). Peiroos was hit in turn 'as he was darting away' (527). His opponent 'came close to him' (529), retrieved his spear, finished off his victim with his sword, and retreated (535). Another panoramic view ('Many others, too, were killed around them,' etc., 538–44) is

[12] ἔβαλε 4.459: the verb βάλλω is used for 'hitting' with a throw, whereas νύσσω, τύπτω and πλήσσω are used for 'striking' with a blow: Trümpy (1950) 90–111.

followed by a final close-up. 'There Pallas Athena gave spirit and daring to Diomedes,' which led to his killing a Trojan who had come towards him in a chariot and thrown a spear at him (5.1–26). This was a decisive victory which 'disturbed the spirit of all [Trojans],' so that 'the Greeks made the Trojans give way' (5.29, 37). Flight and pursuit ensued.

This narrative implies a situation in which most members of each army remain at a distance, as in the earlier sequence: the action explicitly takes place among the *promakhoi*, of whom there are many, as the poet says when he surveys the action. These 'frontline warriors' are highly mobile, moving back and forth in and out of the fight, which is mostly conducted by throwing spears (hence the reference to 'the missiles' in 4.465), though occassionally a man moves in close enough to deliver a blow with spear or sword. There even is enough space for the odd chariot to maneuver among the men. Massed hand-to-hand combat it is not.

A similar situation occurs at the start of the second battle, which again opens 'when, coming together, they reached the same ground, shields met, as did the spears and spirits of bronze-cuirassed men, and embossed shields struck one another...' (8.60–65). The next couple of lines, however, appear to suggest that there was no massed clash, indeed no close-range fighting at all: 'for as long as it was morning... missiles from both sides hit their mark, and men fell' (8.66–67). Nevertheless, the first breakthrough follows immediately. It occurs at noon when a bolt of lightning strikes panic into the Greeks, who take to flight (8.68–79).

The third and longest battle narrative describes the initial clash almost as briskly, and just as abruptly juxtaposes images of close-range and missile combat. 'Trojans and Greeks leapt at one another, and killed... The fight was evenly balanced, and they raged like wolves... For as long as it was morning... missiles from both sides hit their mark, and men fell,' until at lunchtime, 'the Greeks by their own prowess broke the enemy forces' (11.70–73, 84–85, 90–91). The fourth and final battle involves no initial clash at all, but turns into a rout from the very start, so frightened are the Trojans of Akhilleus (20.41–46).

The problem with these opening scenes is one that occurs in many later episodes as well. They appear to combine in an awkward manner three distinct elements—open order combat by *promakhoi*, close order hand-to-hand fighting, and mass exchanges of missiles.

Scholars have offered a range of solutions. The epic tradition may have incorporated two historically distinct styles of warfare: an older, Dark Age form in which *promakhoi* fight while the mass stands well back hurling missiles, and a more recent form in which the mass does all the fighting, at close range and in dense formation.[13] Another theory is that only the massed fighting is historical, while *promakhoi*-style combat is a poetic fantasy, superimposed upon it to enhance the narrative, and perhaps reflecting the imagery associated with heroes in cult.[14] Both views are tenable, if we are willing to believe that contemporary audiences were capable of suspending disbelief to the extent of not being offended by bold juxtapostions of types of warfare which they must have known from experience were incompatible.

The alternative is to assume that Homer's audience would have expected something, not wholly realistic, but more plausible and more like the battles fought by themselves. The answer may then lie in distinguishing phases within battle: perhaps a phase of missile warfare first, then a period of *promakhoi* combat, followed by massed hand-to-hand in the closing stages.[15] Or a massed clash first, during which the formations eventually disintegrate and space opens up for missile fighting and skirmishing by *promakhoi*.[16] The drawback of this approach is that neither sequence quite matches the course of events in all four episodes, and that there is no indication of any transition between phases. It is perhaps conceivable that the poet presents an abrupt short-hand version of successive stages of battle, but this would be unusual in a narrative which is normally quite expansive. Moreover, when Homer tells us who was 'first' to kill his man (4.457), he is much more likely to be speaking of the beginning of battle than of the beginning of skirmishing after a sustained massed assault has fizzled out.

---

[13] A traditionally widespread view: see, e.g., G. Murray (1907) 151; Webster (1958) 214–20. More recently, H. Singor ([1995] 193–99; cf. [1991]) adds the suggestion that the earliest forms of close order hand-to-hand fighting appearing alongside the older form of combat consist of a small number of aristocratic warriors forming up in a *single* line.

[14] A recently more popular view: e.g., Raaflaub (1993) 45-46, 53–54; Bowden (1993) 52–60, suggesting that hero cult influenced Homeric descriptions of battle; and already Kirk (1968) 111 (who, however, regarded mass fighting as a Mycenaean element).

[15] Thus Latacz (1977) 68–95, 116–212; similarly Albracht (1886).

[16] Thus Pritchett (1991) 181–90; (1985) 21–30; similarly Lang (1910) 51–59.

Finally, it is possible that the confusion is all in our minds. We may be jumping to conclusions when we take 'shields clashing' as a reference to massed close combat, or 'missiles flying' as a reference to mass long range combat. An audience familiar with the kind of warfare in which the bulk of the army keeps its distance from the enemy, as in the very first encounter, would not expect any battle to open with massed hand-to-hand fighting, and would therefore understand the clashing shields and flying spears as those of numerous *promakhoi*, 'leaping forward' and 'raging like wolves' in mobile, open-order combat. If so, all battles begin in the same style of combat by *promakhoi*, described sometimes in close-up, sometimes in panoramic sweep, with varying emphasis on handweapons or missiles. This style continues until a breakthrough is achieved.[17] If we are prepared to accept its premises regarding audience expectations of the consistency of the narrative and the nature of battle, this is an economical explanation.

Flight, pursuit and rally

A breakthrough in battle is often attributed to divine intervention, but on the human plane it is achieved either by collective effort, or by a single conspicuous killing. We are told that men have been known to win battles which they had been fated to lose, 'relying on their strength, effort, bravery, and numbers' (17.328–30); that 'the Greeks through their own prowess broke the enemy ranks, calling out to their companions across the lines' (11.90–91). Yet we are also told that 'all the Greeks were miraculously put to flight by Hektor and Father Zeus. Hektor killed only one man, Periphetes the Mycenaean' (17.636–38), and that 'Aias, son of Telamon, bulwark of the Greeks, was the first to break a Trojan rank. He brought relief to his companions by hitting the man who had proved to be the best of the Thracians' (6.5–7). The selectivity of Homer's narrative must be borne in mind, of course, and a look at its context will show that a decisive individual feat tends to occur when the winning side is enjoying collective success as well, but still the impact of such single killings is remarkable, and surely unrealistic.

[17] Thus van Wees (1994) 2–9; (1988) 2–14; similarly Kromayer and Veith (1928) 22–26. For discussions of these last three views: Cartledge (forthcoming); Snodgrass (1993b); Wheeler (1991) 126–28.

The beginning of a rout is usually clearly marked by Homer, both by phrases such as 'the Greeks made the Trojans give way' (5.37) and by indications that the character of the fighting has changed. Killings no longer alternate between the sides, but become a massacre of one side by the other, often indicated by a catalogue of how 'each of the leaders killed a man' (5.37–38). The victims normally put up no resistance. They tend to be mounting their chariots, or already mounted and turning around, as they try to escape, and they are often hit in the back. 'First Agamemnon, lord of men, hurled out of his chariot the great Odios, leader of the Halizones, who was the first to turn. He planted a spear in his back between the shoulders and drove it out through his chest' (5.38–41). Sometimes, there is a spate of killings of men in pairs, who are presumably thought of as warriors and their charioteers, caught trying to flee.[18] The slaughter during pursuit is not always a wholly one-sided affair, but the general pattern is unmistakable.

Of course the fleeing troops lose all cohesion and are scattered far and wide. In one instance, when the Trojans breach the wall around the camp, a large body of Greeks runs all the way back to their ships, and just sit there, tired and tearful, 'reviving their spirits,' while some of their comrades are still trying to resist (13.83–89). Nor do the pursuers attempt to maintain formation. The close Trojan ranks drawn up before the assault on the wall evaporate as soon as they are successful: 'now that they have surmounted the wall, some of the Trojans remain standing at a distance with their weapons, and others fight scattered among the ships, a few against many' (13.737–39). Two factors aggravate the disintegration of the troops. First, leaders taking to their chariots, including the conscientious Hektor, appear to flee and pursue as fast as they can, inevitably leaving behind their followers on foot: 'the fast horses carried Hektor and his weapons away, and he left the men of Troy,' who found their way blocked by a trench (16.367–69). Second, during pursuit, men take their time to plunder the corpses of the dead, which not only leads to further scattering of the troops, but also severely slows down the pursuit and gives the enemy a chance to get away. Accordingly, commanders try telling their men to concentrate on the chase and leave the spoils for later (6.67–71; 15.347).

---

[18] See Willcock (1993).

In these conditions it is possible for small groups to rally and create pockets of resistance. In staging a rally, individual heroes seem again remarkably effective. For instance, simply by standing their ground and killing a few men while all the other Greeks are still fleeing, Odysseus and Diomedes seem able to balance the battle (11.310–336). In the next line, however, it is suddenly revealed that there are other Greeks present (337), and we must conclude that these and other 'lone' defenders are accompanied by their followers, just as Aias turned out to be when, as we have seen, he appeared to hold back the entire Trojan army by himself. It must not be forgotten, moreover, that such individual rallies restore the balance only in one part of the front, though sometimes they can have a snowballing effect when others join in: '"Friends, leaders and lords of the Greeks, turn round, stand your ground, and save Aias, who is being overcome by missiles . . ."' Thus spoke the wounded Eurypylos, and the others came and stood close by him, leaning their shields against their shoulders and raising their spears' (11.587–94).

Army-wide rallies, by contrast, do not result from individual heroics but occur when the troops reach a defensible place, such as trench, wall, or ships, and spontaneously make a stand, or when a leader, ranging across the army and haranguing all the troops, inspires a renewed collective effort.[19] When this happens, the scattered forces regroup. The original gap between the armies is restored, the chariots which had gone ahead in pursuit fall back to rejoin the footsoldiers, and some of the cohesion of the original formation is regained.

> Immediately, Hektor in his armor jumped down from his chariot and, shaking his sharp spears, he went everywhere among the army with exhortations to fight . . . They turned round and stood facing the Greeks. (5.494–97; 6.103–106) The Greeks retreated and stopped the slaughter. (6.107) The Greeks held their ground in droves and were not afraid . . . They turned white in the shower of dust kicked up among them . . . by the hooves of the horses which rejoined them, for the charioteers turned them round. (5.498–505)

[19] Latacz (1977) 96–115, which is much more persuasive than the interpretation of mass movements as an arbitrary pattern dependent on the presumed literary conventions of the so-called *aristeia* of individual heroes suggested by Krischer (1971) 13–89.

Intensification of battle

After a successful rally, regular 'standing' combat (*stadiê husminê*) is resumed, until the next breakthrough occurs. Although the forces have regrouped, they can no longer be arranged in a regular rank-and-file structure—if they ever were. Rallies being by nature improvised and hurried, one would expect the troops to remain in a rather chaotic and scattered state, and the evidence suggests that indeed they did.

Throughout the ensuing battle scenes, the men clearly enjoy great freedom of movement, not only, as we have seen, across the front line, but also from front line to camp or city and back again. Having staged a rally, Hektor walks back to Troy (6.103–118), and when he later returns with Paris, the two of them instantly move through the army right up to the front, where each kills a man (7.1–12). Deiphobos retreats from the front to the back of the crowd, to find Aeneas and lead him to the front again (13.455–69). When Hektor is wounded, he either manages to run back to his chariot and then drive further away from the front 'into the mass' (11.354–60), or he is carried to his chariot which then removes him from the battlefield altogether (14.428–39). The wounded and dead are often helped to safety in this way. Since there is apparently always space for men and chariots to move through, the formation of the mass must be imagined as remaining fairly open during these stages of battle.

At the front, the intensity of battle tends to fluctuate over time, and to differ markedly from one part of the line to the next. Thus, during the fight over the corpse of Patroklos:

> The other Trojans and Greeks did battle in comfort, under a clear sky . . . They fought intermittently, avoiding one another's pain-inflicting missiles, standing far apart. But those in the center suffered grievously . . . For them a great fight of painful rivalry developed all day. The sweat of exhaustion constantly, relentlessly streamed into the eyes and down the arms of those who fought, and down their knees and shins and feet below . . . All the time with their sharp spears relentlessly they dashed forward and killed one another. (17.370–75, 384–87, 412–13)

What causes the intensification of battle is almost always either the need to recover a fallen comrade's dead body, or the need to help a comrade in danger. This may be achieved in two ways: either by bringing together forces from different parts of the front and concentrating them in one spot, or by calling upon men who have been hanging back to come to the front.

An example of the first method is the appeal by Menelaos to the 'leaders and lords' for help in saving the corpse of Patroklos: 'Aias son of Oileus heard him clearly and was the first to come towards him, running through the fighting, and after him Idomeneus and Meriones . . . Who could name in his mind the names of the rest, all those Greeks behind them who roused battle?' (17.246–61) In an instance of bringing help to a comrade in danger, the poet spells out what is no doubt implied elsewhere, that the anonymous multitude includes followers as well as leaders. Aineias asks Deiphobos, Paris, and Agenor to stand by him, and we are told: 'They were leaders of the Trojans together with him, but their men followed after them . . . Aineias rejoiced in his heart when he saw the crowd of men following behind him' (13.489–95).

The second method can be equally effective. At one stage, Poseidon, in the guise of the seer Kalkhas, intervenes to reinforce a rally being staged by the Aiantes. He stirs up the troops who have given up on the fight and are sitting dispiritedly by the ships.

> Going amongst them, he easily encouraged the strong ranks [*phalanges*]. He went first to Teukros and Leitos, exhorting them, and to the hero Peneleos, and to Thoas, Deipyros, Meriones and Antilokhos . . . Thus exhorting them, Poseidon spurred on the Greeks. Strong ranks went and stood around the two Aiantes . . ., for the chosen best men stood their ground against the Trojans and Hektor, forming a fence with spear against spear and shield against shield. (13.89–93, 125–30)

This is followed by the lines also used to describe Akhilleus' troops pressing together before battle, with the additional observation that 'brandished in brave hands, spears overlapped' (13.131–35). Although a more select group than Aineias' supporters, this is still clearly a large and dense crowd consisting of more than merely the nine leaders actually named.

It is by no means unusual to find warriors needing encouragement to join combat. On the contrary, at any moment during battle there are always those who choose to keep out of the fighting, because they are tired or scared, or because they hold a grudge against their leader (13.107–110, 459–61; 14.49–51). Hektor himself spends some of his time in the rear, when he is advised not to fight as *promakhos* but to 'wait among the multitude and out of the turmoil' (20.376–77). Men in general may 'shirk the fighting of their own free will'

(13.234) or 'stand off and fight not, doing as they please' (14.132). It is accordingly a major part of a leader's task to motivate as many men as possible to join battle rather than hang back, and appeals to stop 'shirking' are constantly addressed to both individuals and soldiers at large. 'Shall we shirk like this, Melanippos? . . . Follow me! We can no longer fight the Greeks from a distance' (15.553–57). 'Do not stand far away from the Trojans now, you Greeks. Come! A man must go forward against another, and be eager to fight' (20.354–55).[20]

Whether by concentrating active troops or by mobilizing those who have remained passive, assembling a dense formation is presented as a highly effective defensive tactic. The men gathered round the Aiantes, 'tightly pressing together, like a wall' (13.152), check the seemingly unstoppable advance of Hektor: 'when he ran into these dense ranks, he came to a halt very close by. The Greeks facing him struck at him with swords and spears, and pushed him away from them; he was shaken, and drew back' (13.145–48). The troops assembled in defence of the body of Patroklos have an even greater impact:

> Asteropaios went forward, he too being eager to fight the Greeks, but that was no longer at all possible. For standing around Patroklos, they enclosed him on all sides with their shields, and held out their spears before them. For Aias went round everywhere with constant exhortations; he urged that no one should retreat behind the corpse, and that no one should fight as *promakhos*, standing out from the other Greeks. . . . The earth was drenched with purple blood and crowded together lay the dead bodies of both Trojans and proud allies—and of Greeks, for they did not fight a bloodless battle. Yet far fewer of the Greeks were killed, for in the crowd they always remembered to protect one another's lives. (17.352–65)

It is significant that it is the Greeks who are most successful in applying these tactics. Their superior solidarity and co-operative obedience are highlighted elsewhere, too (3.2–9; 4.428–38).

Aias' creation of a totally cohesive body of troops is emphatically represented as the best way to stage a defence, but it is equally emphatically exceptional. In no other fight is anyone actually *forbidden* to leave the formation; nowhere else is it said that it is *impossible* for one of the enemy to attack the formation by himself; and in no other episode is a massing of troops in fact followed by an extended scene of intense mass combat without any reference to individual

[20] See van Wees (1988) 12–14.

heroics (17.366–425). Troops may mass together in other crises, but even when the Trojans renew their assault on the 'wall' of men around the Aiantes, or later when they charge at the ships, which the Greeks have 'surrounded with a fence of bronze' (15.566–67), the fighting which immediately ensues always implies a certain distance between the opposing formations, and involves men running forward, throwing missiles, and retreating, in the usual *promakhos*-style. It would appear that Aias' tactics are unique in leading to a phase of massed hand-to-hand combat, confined to the center of the line (17.370–83), and ending when a new crisis develops elsewhere (17.426–542). At all other times, despite the gathering of dense masses, men continue to be mobile and to fight in open order.[21]

Again, then, we are faced with an apparent contrast between massed and individual action, and with a range of possible solutions similar to the ones suggested for the initial clashes. Perhaps Homer juxtaposes the individualism of Dark Age warriors, or of poetic fancy, with the solidarity and discipline of contemporary armies. If so, we might wonder not only at the audience's capacity for suspending disbelief, but also at the way in which Homer on the one hand always integrates massed formations into the narrative through explicit descriptions of how they are created, and on the other hand always abruptly reverts to individual combat without any explanation. This peculiarity of the narrative casts some doubt also on the alternative view that Homeric battles proceed in distinct phases.[22] What is more, it is hard to account for the extreme rarity of actual descriptions of massed close combat, which on this view is the decisive stage of battle. One would have to assume that after the account of the build-up of troops the phase of massed combat itself is either simply skipped (as being unsuitable for poetic treatment, perhaps) or else is in fact recounted but frequently spoiled by inappropriate references to *promakhos*-style individual mobility and the use of missiles.

[21] When the fight over the body of Patroklos is resumed after the diversion of 17.426–542, the narrative does feature individual heroes, *promakhoi*, individual mobility, and the use of missiles (17.574–92); apparently the cohesion imposed by Aias has vanished. For a detailed discussion of passages featuring *promakhoi*-style combat immediately after a tightening of formations, see van Wees (1988) 7–10, but ignore the strained attempt to explain away Aias' exceptional tactics.

[22] The narrative offers no support for the suggestion that the transition to massed fighting is achieved by *promakhoi* returning to their place in the ranks of a massed formation (which had been standing at the ready while they were skirmishing) and giving the order to advance (Latacz [1977] 171–78; Albracht [1886] 39).

The remaining possibility is that we are once more jumping to conclusions when we assume that a massing together of troops is necessarily designed to lead to collective hand-to-hand combat. If, as suggested, Homer's audiences did not imagine the initial clash of armies to be anything but an encounter of numerous individual *promakhoi*, with the bulk of the army keeping its distance, then it is probable that they would not have expected a renewed build-up of troops to result in a massed clash either. Instead, they may have assumed that a densely-packed formation would merely serve as a solid defensive line and not only provide a concentration of potential *promakhoi*, but also give these men greater confidence to attack in the knowledge that the 'crowd of companions' to fall back on or call upon for help is now larger and closer at hand. This would again account for the evidence quite economically, provided one is willing to accept that, although the *Iliad* recognizes and indeed recommends the possibility of pushing the cohesion of the ranks beyond this, into actual massed combat, it is nevertheless accomplished only once, locally and temporarily, due to one leader's special initiative in an extreme crisis.

The nature of promakhoi-*combat*

However we interpret the massed formations, combat by individual *promakhoi* unquestionably dominates the narrative. Their style of fighting is conventionally described as 'duelling,' and in a few of the lenghtier confrontations there may be some justification for this. In the fullest possible sequence, the opponents challenge one another before they each let fly one or two missiles. Then they close in to fight hand-to-hand, and the fight is settled with the first or second blow. The victor may shout boasts or taunts at the enemy, and take spoils. Occasionally he mutilates his victim's corpse before retreating to the safety of the crowd of companions. This complete sequence, however, is a hypothetical composite and never actually occurs in the *Iliad.* Some encounters contain most of its elements, but most contain only a few. A single, instantly fatal spear-cast, for instance, without any run-up or follow-up, is quite common.

It is sometimes supposed that the hypothetical full sequence is the norm, and that the shorter encounters are meant to highlight only the decisive moment in it. While this is conceivable, it is more likely that even the briefest of sequences represent the full extent of a hero's intervention in the action. In a fair number of instances, at any rate, it is clear that they do:

> There Harpalion, son of king Pylaimenes, leapt at him . . . From nearby he then struck with his spear the centre of [Menelaos'] shield, but was unable to drive his weapon through it, and withdrew again into the crowd of companions to escape death, looking all round him in case someone would touch his skin with a weapon (13.642–49).

In the vast majority of cases, 'hit-and-run attack' is a much more appropriate label than 'duel,' especially since in pitched battle, as opposed to formal single combat outside it, warriors often opportunistically exploit their chances without any sign of chivalric etiquette.[23]

Both traditional and more recent interpretations hold that *promakhoi* are an elite. Traditionally, they have been seen as a small group of aristocratic 'champions,' as opposed to the commoners who form the ineffective 'multitude.' Lately, with the recognition that the poet constantly implies the presence of many more *promakhoi* than the handful of heroes mentioned by name, they have come to be seen as a rather broader group, consisting of the most heavily-armed among the warriors, who form the first line or lines of a formation otherwise composed of less well-equipped men taking part only in the massed fighting.[24] These views are just about compatible with the evidence, if we assume that appeals for help and exhortations to stop shirking, despite being addressed to 'you Greeks' or 'you Trojans' in general, are intended only for members of the elite, and if, moreover, we assume that only the higher-ranking or better-equipped of the heroes' followers and companions actually join them in combat.

It is quite conceivable, however, that exhortations to come and join battle at the front are indeed addressed to the entire mass. One passage in particular can hardly be explained any other way: 'They rebuked whomever they saw shirking the fight completely: "Friends, you who are outstanding among the Greeks, *you who are average, and*

---

[23] See Mueller (1984) 81–82, for the view that Homer selects for description the final, decisive blow only. M. Edwards (1987) 78–81, suggests that Homer describes only brief encounters 'to avoid tedium;' Griffin (1980) 90–95, 143 claims that Homer prefers immediately fatal blows to lengthy combat because he is 'interested in death far more than . . . in fighting.' I have argued that the prevalence of quick, one-sided attacks is not a literary convention but reflects a contemporary style of doing battle (van Wees [1988] 5; [1996] 36–39; implied also by Marg [1976] 10–11), and fits in with a generally non-chivalrous warrior mentality. For analyses of typical patterns within combat scenes, see Fenik (1968).

[24] See nn. 13, 15, 16 above.

you who are worse, . . . now there is work to do for everyone!" ' (12.268–71). In the light of this appeal, we should also take seriously the claim made by Thersites, the 'worst' man in the army (2.248) and a 'man of the common people' (2.198), that he and his like in fact bear the brunt of the fighting (2.231, 235–38). It would certainly be physically possible for anyone present on the battlefield to join combat actively. The openness of the formation, which allows the heroes to move anywhere along the front and through the mass, would equally allow any member of the crowd to come forward and join the *promakhoi* for a while, if he so chose. Nor need the poorer men's lack of armor be a hindrance, for besides suggesting that the possession of helmets, shields, and greaves is widespread, Homer shows unarmored archers operating in the front line, either independently (3.16–20) or in co-operation with a heavy-armed warrior (8.266–72).

If it is true that anyone in the mass is eligible to fight at the front, it would mean that the distinction between *promakhoi* and 'multitude' is merely a topographical one. Among the *promakhoi* would be reckoned anyone, from famous hero to anonymous commoner, who is currently fighting at the front; among the 'multitude' at any particular time are all those who are currently out of action, including leading heroes temporarily retired from the fray. *Promakhoi*-combat, on this view, would be a form of mass (not massed) fighting, both in the sense that numerous men fight simultaneously, and every man in the army is called upon to take his turn in the frontline, and in the sense that the common 'masses' play a major role in it.

Historical Implications

It has often been said that Homer, as a poet, cannot necessarily be expected to be consistent in his account, all the more so since he inherited a long oral tradition liable to contain material from more than one historical period. This is true, and it is therefore possible that the battle narrative is, as often claimed, a mixture of incompatible elements. On the other hand, a poet who has a clear mental image of what he is describing may very well produce a consistent narrative, even without consciously trying to, while oral traditions are often quite adaptable and may contain very little that is not new or updated. So it is equally possible that the *Iliad* might contain an internally coherent picture of heroic warfare, and indeed of the heroic world.

It has been suggested here that we can in fact reconstruct an almost wholly consistent picture of Homeric armies and battles. The heroic army is composed of many small and loosely organized bands of warriors, held together by personal ties of subordination and companionship. Battles are fought in open order; at any particular moment the majority of men remain at a distance from the enemy, while a substantial minority of individual 'front-line warriors' venture closer to fight with missiles or hand-to-hand. There is much mobility back and forth as every man in the army is expected to join combat at least occasionally, and even the bravest heroes retire from battle every so often. This picture of warfare accounts for the greater part of the narrative, and is plausible in itself: parallels may be found in 'primitive' warfare.[25]

Homer, however, goes beyond this simple image in three respects. His story adds heavy armor, chariots, and massed formations. None of these features is necessarily incompatible with the rest of the picture, as has been shown, but some would argue that their Homeric usage as reconstructed here is inefficient and therefore implausible. Heavy armor is far from ideal for the heroes' mobile style of fighting. Chariots are most effectively used in groups, and as mobile platforms to fight from, rather than singly, as transport to and from battle. Massed formations are better employed in collective close combat than as a base for individual hit-and-run sallies.

The answer to these objections must be that optimum efficiency is not by any means the only criterion governing the conduct of warfare. Heavy equipment may slow a man down, and confine him to relatively short bursts of activity, but the protection, and even the prestige, gained by wearing costly bronze armor may well have counted for more.[26] Its twin roles of status symbol and means of escape would have encouraged the use of the chariot, but at the same time the value of the horses may have inclined their owners to keep them out of the actual fighting, while the fact that each of these owners leads a band of footsoldiers would have prevented them from teaming up as a separate chariot battalion.[27] The need for solidarity in combat may have been felt keenly enough to make a

[25] Parallels: van Wees (1986) 296–97 (organization) (1994) 1, 8 (style of fighting).

[26] For recent discussions of further problems associated with Homeric arms and armor, see, e.g., the volumes *Kriegswesen* in *Archaeologia Homerica E1* (1977), *E2* (1980); van Wees (1994) 131–40.

[27] Further discussion of chariots in Homer: Van Wees (1994) 9–13, 140–41. Note

local and temporary massing of troops for defensive purposes feasible, but the loose and informal structure of the Homeric army would in all probability have failed to provide the organizational discipline required to maintain this cohesion in combat, let alone to extend it to the entire army and for the full duration of battle.

If all these elements of the heroic picture are mutually compatible and their combination not implausible, it would follow that two key features of the Classical hoplite phalanx—the bronze panoply and the massed formation—are already an integral part of Homeric warfare, but that the use made of the formation is as yet much more limited. In the *Iliad*, we may be witnessing an embryonic hoplite phalanx in the process of development. Indeed, we may be catching a glimpse of how further development was brought about, in Aias' imposition of an exceptionally cohesive order, a 'logical' but not easily accomplished extension of the heroes' regular tactics, which takes Homeric warfare another step closer to its Classical counterpart.

Ongoing military change could also account for the single certain anomaly in the Homeric picture: the contingents introduced at the outset, only to disappear immediately. The notion that allied communities fight best in separate contingents ('tribes,' or perhaps groups of tribes), and that formal kinship groups within communities ('phratries') ought to fight as distinct units, too, is a radical departure from the indiscriminate mingling, fusing, and fissioning of informally constituted warrior bands encountered everywhere else. It is conceivable but rather unlikely that this conception of 'tribal' military organization is merely a literary conceit created to describe the legendary multinational armies gathered at Troy; at the same time, the care with which it is introduced and its rationale is explained suggests that it is not a conception that the audience took for granted. Perhaps, therefore, we are dealing with a recent development in organization, one not yet fully institutionalized and certainly one not fully integrated into the epic tradition.[28] The emergence of a more formal and centralized army structure may have helped forge the greater

also the suggestion of Greenhalgh (1973) that Homer is modelling the heroic (unrealistic) use of chariot and charioteer on the contemporay use of a pair of horses and a 'squire' by mounted hoplites.

[28] This amounts to a position midway between those of A. Andrewes, 'Phratries in Homer', *Hermes* 89 (1961), 131–2, and van Wees (1986) 295–301 (which missed the point that the contingents are supposed to perform as units *in battle*, and therefore failed to recognize the incompatibility of the 'tribal' arrangement with the rest

cohesion and discipline required for the fully developed phalanx.

On the assumption that armies and battles in the *Iliad* thus reflect historical warfare and incorporate some rather advanced recent developments, they ought to belong to a period shortly before the rise of the hoplite phalanx, generally dated to the mid-seventh century B.C. This fits in well enough with the widely accepted date of 750–700 B.C. for the composition of the *Iliad*, but even better with the current trend to date this down to the early seventh century B.C. Specifically, it would tie in well with a recent suggestion that the details of Homeric arms and armor, and above all the relative frequencies of use of spear and sword in Homer, are best matched by finds of armour and by battle scenes in vase paintings of the period 700–650 B.C.[29]

None of this can be regarded as proven, of course; much depends on what one is prepared to accept as plausible military practice, and how far one is prepared to go to find internal consistency in the narrative. Yet there is one thing which all the more recent interpretations of Homeric warfare have in common, and which has come to be generally accepted: the conclusion that the anonymous masses populating the heroic battlefield are not idle spectators, but play a significant, indeed decisive, role. The poet focuses so hard on his heroes that the contribution of the masses is not immediately apparent, but a closer look establishes without a doubt that, one way or another, they are imagined as playing an active part.

Spot-lighting a few heroes is a convention of epic as a genre, of course, but Homer goes beyond this. He not merely suggests that the deeds of a single hero can have a devastating impact on the enemy and save the day for an entire army, but he even has Odysseus declare categorically that all common men are 'unwarlike, cowardly, and of no account at all in battle' (2.198–202). Homer positively fosters the impression that it is a dozen or so aristocratic leaders who are the decisive force on the battlefield. In doing so, it would seem, he reflects the self-image of contemporary aristocrats, who liked to

---

of the narrative, and which adduced only slender arguments for regarding the arrangement as a literary expedient).

[29] Van Wees (1994) 138–46; for other recent suggestions of an early seventh-century date, see Taplin (1992) 33–35; Kullmann (1992) 264; and note the more tentative conclusions of Sale (1994) and Crielaard (1995a).

claim that their power and privilege were a just reward for their outstanding services in war—a self-image which the battle narratives of the *Iliad*, on closer consideration, suggest was largely an ideological projection.[30]

The one historical conclusion which it seems safe to draw, then, is that whatever the similarities and differences between Homeric and Classical warfare, the mass played a major role in both. Insofar as established views on the rise of the *polis*, tyranny, and democracy lean quite heavily on the assumption that mass-participation was a post-Homeric phenomenon, a new development of the early Archaic age, these views now stand in need of re-examination.

[30] See van Wees (1995a) 165–70; for Homer's ideological outlook generally, see I. Morris (1986) 116–26.

A. W. H. Adkins

HOMERIC ETHICS

Introduction

The distinguished predecessor to this volume, the *Companion to Homer* edited by A. J. B. Wace and F. H. Stubbings, contains no chapter or section of a chapter devoted exclusively to Homeric ethics. G. M. Calhoun did, however, give the title 'Religion and ethics' to one sub-section of his chapter 'Polity and society' (pp. 448–50); and the title of his next sub-section, less than a page in length, is 'Ethics, manners and customs' (p. 451).

The words used in the titles of the sub-sections raise some of the basic problems which face anyone seeking a vocabulary in which to discuss such matters as ethics cross- (or multi-) culturally, particularly if we acknowledge that some virtues in one of the cultures may appear as vices in the other. Calhoun spoke of the 'mistaken belief that there is in Homer no morality: The virtues that center on Christian humility are absent or little esteemed, and their places are taken by qualities . . . that Christian ethics tends to regard as vices.'

Calhoun seems not to have seen any serious problem in these diametrically opposed evaluations of the same kind of behavior (451):

> Yet with all allowance for differences, for the conventions of Heroic epic and the actual state of society, virtues and vices in Homer are *not entirely* unlike those of today (emphasis mine . . .)
>
> The man who is generously endowed with virtues is *kalos*[1] or *esthlos* or *agathos*, the *kakos* is he in whom the virtues are deficient and vices predominate. Besides the more personal qualities, there is clear recognition of what may be called the social virtues, particularly in the case of kings or chieftains who are responsible for the welfare of their folk.

These definitions contain rules for the use of certain Homeric value-terms: 'if a person possesses *arete* or *aretai*, he may be denoted and

[1] Usually the masculine and feminine forms of *kalos* denote and commend visible beauty, the neuter being reserved for commending actions.

commended by using *agathos* or *esthlos*. They furnish no information about the content of the *aretai*, the qualities and behavior demanded of the *agathos* by the *arete*-standard if he is to be regarded as *agathos*.' For that, as Calhoun recognized, we must turn to the text of Homer, and search there for the qualities and behavior in question, being particular to note which are explicitly regarded as manifestations of *arete*.

An acquaintance with the intensive study of value terms carried on in the middle decades of this century by moral philosophers such as C. Stevenson and R. M. Hare may increase our sensitivity to questions of this kind.[2] Earlier, A. J. Ayer had introduced the doctrines of the Vienna Circle to the English-speaking world.[3] These doctrines entailed that moral judgments were irrational, in the sense that no valid reason could be adduced for espousing any moral judgment oneself or for commending it to anyone else. No one who expressed a moral judgment was saying anything more significant or objective than someone who said 'Ice cream is nice,' which could be equated with 'I like ice cream.' Anyone who dissented was in effect saying nothing more significant in reply than 'Ice cream is nasty,' or 'I don't like ice cream.' In response to those who argued that moral disagreement appeared to them to be quite different, members of the Vienna Circle would reply that a better translation of 'this is a good/honorable/just course of action' would be 'I approve of this course of action; do so too.'[4] The additional element in the moral disagreement was the command that the interlocutor should agree. It did not include any reasons that could be adduced in moral contexts but did not apply in questions agreed to be matters of taste. Presumably for anyone who felt sufficiently strongly about ice cream to attempt to impose his or her taste on others, judgments about ice cream would be in effect moral judgments.

If moral judgment were really so devoid of rationality as Ayer held in his earlier works,[5] there would be little point in studying

---

[2] Stevenson (1944); Hare (1952).

[3] Ayer (1935).

[4] I shall not discuss competing reductions of moral terms. I am concerned only with the outcome of the debate insofar as it led to the analysis of value-words in terms of informative and emotive aspects.

[5] Ayer (1982) later acknowledged that it was possible to discuss 'anthropologically' the values of a culture (and presumably of a subculture within a pluralistic modern society).

Homeric ethics or comparing it with any other, since we would be merely comparing the random and irrational with the random and irrational.[6] Hare and others refined this position. Hare observed that even in modern pluralistic societies, it would be unusual for anyone not to belong to any group, however small, whose values and beliefs he or she shared; and that within that group, the use of a value-term might convey not only approval or disapproval but also factual information, or more precisely expectations about matters of fact. Asked by one's old friend Brigadier (retd.) Tiffin to meet at the railway station someone characterized simply as 'a jolly good chap,' one would probably not approach first a bearded young man wearing sandals. The reason why is clear: one knows the kind of person whom the Brigadier is likely to call a 'jolly good chap' (and, in a reasonably familiar sense of 'why,' why he does so). One might of course be mistaken; behind the beard might be lurking a daring and skillful Secret Service operative, just as *agathos* Odysseus lurked behind the disguise of a wandering beggar, a *kakos* in his own palace. This does not exhaust the possibilities, of course. The worthy Brigadier may have had an experience on the Great North Road similar to that of Saint Paul on the road to Damascus, requiring a quite fundamental revision of goals and values. But once all is explained, 'jolly good chap' can continue to raise expectations, albeit not the same ones.[7]

Though moral philosophers have long ago turned their attention to other problems, their conclusions on this topic can still be useful in cross-cultural studies of ethics. Value-terms do possess an informative aspect, knowledge of which may be acquired by growing up in the appropriate community, by consulting native informants, or in the case of the Homeric poems, works written in a dead language, by reading and analyzing the texts. Equally there is an emotive aspect,

---

[6] Ayer rarely considered any use of moral language more complex than a simple evaluative judgment. He did not consider moral arguments conducted between persons who shared the same values.

[7] To avoid misunderstanding, let me say explicitly that I do not hold that every user of value-terms can trace his position back to his first principles, has reflected upon those principles, and can defend them, but that users of value-terms aspire to consistency. If one points out a self-contradiction to X, X is unlikely to treat the matter as trivial and what one would expect in ethical discourse. On the other side, it is not impossible for a community to be able to trace its values to a clearly envisioned goal, or for that goal to lead to conflict between a number of communities holding such values.

with the result that any value-term suggested as a translation for a Homeric value-term may be evaluated in respect of two variables.[8] Consider *arete* and 'virtue.' Insofar as 'virtue' is the most powerful English word to commend human qualities, and *arete* has a similar status in Homeric and later Greek, the translation 'virtue' is accurate; but insofar as the range of human qualities commended is not the same, it is inaccurate, and the translation may be seriously misleading. Armed with this distinction and these tools, we may discuss the topic of Homeric ethics with greater precision.

As Hare observed, even today it would be remarkable if a person were unable to find even one other person who shared his or her values, attitudes, and beliefs; and Homeric Greece was by comparison hardly pluralist at all.[9] That being so, we may reasonably hope to find in Homer (this being simply another way of saying the same thing) broad general agreement on the appropriate range of application of many of the value-terms used in the poems. We should not expect to find complete unanimity. Value-terms remain value-terms, and do not lose their emotive power. Attempted persuasion is not the only function of value-terms; but it is one function. The goal of this chapter is to present the range and emotive power of relevant Greek terms, and to link these, where possible, to other characteristics of Homeric society, enabling the reader to make informed judgments about the data.

Since the search will be conducted by studying a narrative, we will acquire also knowledge about the Homeric oikos and that much more shadowy entity, the Homeric polis. We shall discover that the Homeric *agathos*, as head of his oikos, is in a situation in which self-help must be the order of the day, so that the 'competitive' excellences, and courage above all, must appear most important in a crisis. Strictly speaking, the demand must be for 'courage leading to a successful result,' since unless a community exists and is able to defend itself, the 'cooperative' excellences cannot be practised safely. We shall discover also that the characters of the poems are aware of the social situation which furnishes these values with the attraction which they certainly possess in the Homeric poems.

---

[8] The variables vary independently, as Hare (1952) 122 observes.

[9] By this I do not mean that in post-Homeric times there was no dispute about different conceptions of the goal (*eudaimonia*), but that there was agreement that *eudaimonia* should denote and commend the goal.

We can now propose an approach to the cross-cultural study of values. We shall not be concerned with a philosophical critique, but with an 'anthropological' approach which will show features of the situation which favor the values that we discover and also any incoherences in such values which work against the goals that the members of this culture propose to themselves. The study must be of 'values,' not of 'morality:' if we single out a favored set of values—usually, of course, the set favored by our own community—by terming it the 'morality' of the society being studied, there is a danger that much will be overlooked. To treat as the society's values the whole set of values held to be important by the society—but not necessarily equally important—will be the most illuminating method. One should begin by identifying them, duly noting judgments and evaluations made by the characters and any reason assigned for making them. One should also carefully study the 'set pieces' that the poet includes in his work (e.g., Sarpedon's speech to Glaukos, *Il.* 12.310–28).

The reader should note that my use of 'values' and 'goals' from this point onwards differs from that of most scholars. 'Values' is usually employed of the ends which an agent proposes to himself or herself as those he or she intends to pursue, and it is often implied that the only link that binds these values together is that the agent pursues them. I use 'goals' in this sense, of such clearly envisioned ends as sacking Troy, creating social harmony, or reducing the national debt. 'Values,' on the other hand, signifies the value-judgments which are, or are believed to be, conducive to attaining those goals. If the goal is peace and prosperity, it makes sense to enquire whether the values are indeed appropriate, in that they—usually—conduce to the envisioned goal. They might be contained in such phrases as 'It is *aischron* to be defeated,' 'strive to make a friend of your enemy,' and 'the *agathos* must fight bravely.' The subsequent discussion will make it increasingly apparent that the values may not conduce to the attainment of the goals.

Agathos, Arete, and Similar Terms

We may now begin to study Homeric value-terms in more detail. We shall survey first some scattered passages which employ the words *agathos, esthlos, arete*, and their contraries *kakos, deilos, and kakotes*. These words, like most Greek value-terms, are untranslatable. As the most powerful terms available to commend or decry persons and their actions, they have a claim to be rendered by our 'good,' 'virtue,' 'bad,' and 'vice,' which hold a similar place in 'our' system.[10] But the qualities commended and decried are quite different, as we shall see.

The suitors selected twenty *aristoi* to commit the heinous offence of ambushing and trying to murder their host, Telemachus (*Od.* 4.778); one may possess 'all manner of *aretai* both in fleetness of foot and in fighting' (*Il.* 15.642); and Nestor advises Agamemnon to organize his troops into contingents which reflect their place of origin: he will be able to see clearly which of them is *agathos*, and which *kakos* (*Il.* 2.365). So far we have been concerned with the military excellences. But there is, not surprisingly, a 'social' use of *kakos* to match the 'social' use of *agathos*. This use is seen most clearly when Odysseus, disguised as a beggar, claims to be adept at all kinds of menial tasks 'such as the more *kakoi* do for the *agathoi*' (*Od.* 15.324).

These are not, of course, separate meanings, but different fields of action for the 'best specimens' of human being and the 'inferior specimens' of human being to show their paces.

Evidently the military competitive excellences are in the foreground, and we may expect them to take precedence over the quiet cooperative qualities.[11] Indeed, only the competitive are spoken of as *aretai*: the cooperative are not. (There is at this period in Greek no term that can be used to denote and commend the complete range of qualities that scholars are wont to regard as virtues when using English words in their customary senses.)

The connotation of *agathos*, derived from its range of usage, evidently includes military prowess, wealth, and high social status. These qualities are commended together because in the society of the Homeric poems they must occur together. The warrior must purchase his own—elaborate and expensive—panoply. In this moneyless society, wealth consists essentially in land. The result is a warrior aristocracy, reflected in the use of such words as were listed above.

There is also a group of words which denigrate actions. Words

---

[10] *Agathos* and *esthlos* are synonyms, as are *kakos* and *deilos* in Homer. *Aristos* is the superlative of *agathos*.

[11] The characters of Homer are not indifferent to suffering injustice. They would have preferred all their *agathoi* to be *pepnumenoi* as well; but the case of Telemachus at the beginning of the poem shows clearly the ineffectiveness of the *pepnumenos* who was not *agathos*, and who hence could not defend the persons, goods, and chattels of his oikos.

which commend the contrary of the kind of actions denigrated are less in evidence since the denigration occurs at times of crisis, and the consequences of defeat arouse more powerful emotions than the—comparatively—tranquil days of peace, or what passes for peace in Homeric society. So defeat is *aischron*, but *kalon* does not celebrate victory: it is used to give advice on behavior in contexts where no battle is imminent.[12]

The words concerned are the neuter adjective *aischron*, the superlative adjective *elenchistos*, and the noun *elencheie*. They do not occur very often in the poems, but they do occur where one would expect such powerful words to occur, at moments of extreme crisis. Not surprisingly, these words have a similar range of application to that of *agathos*. In *Iliad* 2, Odysseus says to Agamemnon that the Greeks are willing to make him most contemptible, *elenchistos*, in the eyes of all mortal men; and they will not fulfil the promise to return home only when they have sacked Troy. Long campaigns impose hardships, so the Greeks are to be excused for wanting to go home. Nevertheless it is *aischron* to remain for a long time and return empty-handed.

Not only failure in war is thus reprehended. Penelope rebukes Telemachus for not defending Odysseus against the suitors while the 'beggar' was in Telemachus' oikos, and threatens him with *aischos* and dishonor among men; while Eumaios would have suffered *elencheie* had his watchdogs savaged Odysseus when he unexpectedly arrived in Eumaios' farmyard.

The resemblance between the use of these words and that of the *agathos* group is evident. Failure is *aischron*, and entails *elencheie*, a feeling of shame.

Let us now return to the abundant privileges of the Homeric *agathos* and *basileus*. Sarpedon asks Glaukos why they are honored (*timasthai*) with a seat of honor, choice meats and full cups (*Il.* 12.310–28). Evidently because they make an outstanding contribution to the community, one which requires that they fight bravely in the foremost ranks against the enemy; whereupon their followers will say that their kings rule 'not ingloriously,' and enjoy the aforementioned privileges.[13]

---

[12] For example, Agamemnon in *Il.* 19.79 claims that it is *kalon* to listen to a speaker when he stands up to speak rather than to interrupt him.

[13] Sarpedon and Glaukos are Lycians, allies of the Trojans; but the values of all the contingents, whether Greeks, Trojans, or allies, are the same.

The Homeric kings are the *aristoi*, the most *agathoi*; and the grounds for applying this most powerful term of approbation to them are clear: they are (among) the most effective in the defense of their communities or in their attacks on other communities. They are expected to display outstanding prowess, and achieve outstanding success, in war and in what passes for peace, in the Homeric communities. Their effectiveness demands full armor, a necessary but not sufficient condition; they must also be courageous and skilled in its use (and must also actually succeed in battle, for the consequences of failure are appalling).

These kings were not elected because they were outstandingly brave, successful and effective in war. As heads of royal houses, they inherited wealth, essentially in the form of land, herds, and control of labor. Since most *agathoi* inherited, the Homeric society was essentially a 'landed aristocracy.'[14] It is not difficult to understand why its values seemed appropriate, to *agathos* and *kakos* alike, for the *agathos* made a contribution to the stability and survival of the community that the ill-armed *kakos* could not have made, no matter how much he exercised the cooperative excellences. Indeed his ability to contribute behavior in accordance with the cooperative excellences is less than might appear at first sight. Some contexts concerned with just behavior emphasize the justice of the judge—a person of some consequence—rather than with the justice of the quietly cooperating neighbor. The continued existence of one's oikos or polis is, not surprisingly, an unqualified good, and an unchallenged value-premise, implicit or explicit, of Greek ethics and politics.[15]

The contribution of the well-armed head of oikos was equally relevant in peace. Consider the plight of the household of Odysseus in the absence of its master at the beginning of the *Odyssey*. On the advice of the goddess Athena, Odysseus' son Telemachus calls an assembly in the second book. It quickly becomes apparent that (*a*) no assembly has been convened since Odysseus' departure for the war twenty years earlier and (*b*) not only Odysseus, or Telemachus now grown up, has a right to convene an assembly. The crucial distinction is between business that concerns the polis, the agglomeration of households on Ithaca, and business that concerns the individual oikos. Only the former (such matters as a report of an

[14] Raaflaub, this volume, offers a different picture.

[15] This is not to say that all the actions and evaluations favored by Homer's characters are *in fact* conducive to the well-being of their cities, as we shall see later.

enemy force bearing down on them) concerns the assembly; and in twenty years there has been no business of this kind. The absence of Odysseus at the war has caused many problems for the oikos of Odysseus, very few for the other oikoi of Ithaca. The first function of the *agathos* is to defend his own oikos; and this too virtually guarantees the pre-eminence of the competitive excellences.

The prime situation which brings the Ithacans together as a cohesive group is the attack of marauders from elsewhere; and here too a successful defense is vital, for reasons mentioned above. Anyone who diminishes their ability to defend themselves is likely to be treated as an enemy, as Odysseus realizes. When Odysseus kills the suitors, it is not treated as an act of retributive justice exercised by a sorely tried monarch over his unruly subjects. The judgment that the suitors have died as a result of their wrongdoings (ἀτασθαλίαι) is expressed several times (e.g., *Od.* 22.416). In killing them, Odysseus and his faithful supporters have declared war on their fellow-Ithacans, for they have slain the *herma poleos* (*Od.* 23.121–22). That is to say, the suitors, regularly referred to as *agathoi* or *esthloi*, belonged to the class of which it is demanded that they successfully defend the polis when it is attacked, and are richly rewarded with privileges when they do so. Nothing warrants killing them—*en masse*, at all events: the wrongdoings of the suitors do not harm Ithaca to the same extent that the loss of so many warriors does. In brief, they are *adikoi men, agathoi de*, with the *agathoi de* presenting a stronger consideration to the mind.[16] The reason why the possession of the competitive excellences must in the last resort take precedence over the possession of the cooperative excellences is very clear.

Time

It is important to analyze the vocabulary of reward and privilege in Homer. The central term is *time*, usually rendered 'honor.' This may be misleading, since it suggests 'honorary' and a contrast with material reward, and also something superadded to one's basic human rights, pleasant to receive but not essential to one's continued existence. Homer's *time*, however, is rooted in the material situation, and is essential to a hero's existence. Homeric values know nothing of

[16] The form of the expression belongs to classical prose rather than to Homer.

basic human rights, and *time* is usually grounded in the material, animate or inanimate.

Time goes beyond the 'material' in that to gain *time* enhances status; to lose *time* strikes at its roots. We have already discussed the material goods that Sarpedon and Glaukos receive—and deserve, if they fight bravely in their superior armor. The possession of status-enhancing material goods, derived from favored treatment in the past, the acquisition of more of the same, or at all events the avoidance of being deprived of any of it, furnishes the *agathos* or *basileus* with much of his important motivation. In *Iliad* 1 Agamemnon, deprived of Chryseis by Apollo as a result of the prayers of her father, his priest, has lost *time*, and after a heated altercation with Achilles carries out his threat to deprive him of his war-prize Briseis, thereby depriving Achilles of *time*. To recover this, Achilles prays to his mother, the sea-nymph Thetis. She prevails upon Zeus, in the light of past services that she has rendered to him, to deny victory to the Greeks until Achilles receives due *time* proportionate to his deserts.

The passage in the *Iliad* in which the material nature of *time* is most evident occurs in *Il.* 9.434–605. Phoinix is counseling Achilles to return to the fighting under certain conditions.

> It would be more *kakon*[17] for you to ward off the enemy from the burning ships. No, go back on terms of receiving gifts; for the Achaeans will *tiein* you like a god.[18] But if you go back without gifts you will no longer be equally *timeeis*.

If we translate τί *tiein* here by 'honor' and *timeeis* by 'honored,' Phoenix is telling Achilles that if he insists on gifts the Achaeans will think more highly of him, whereas if he goes back without gifts they will not rate him so highly. This seems psychologically bizarre; but if we understand *time* in a material sense, denoting the gifts, and connoting the prestige of victories won, all becomes clear. If Achilles delays his return until the ships are burning, he will receive no gifts, because he will have to take part in the fighting or perish himself.

In the *Odyssey*, the misdeed of the suitors is not simply that they have wooed Penelope while her husband was still alive (they believed that Odysseus was dead), but that they have devoured the substance

---

[17] κακόν must mean harmful, unpleasant, *for Achilles*.

[18] To 'honor like a god' has very precise implications in Homer. Those so honored are the only mortals who are given a *temenos* (*tem, compare the Latin *templum*) of land for their exclusive use. This must have been a primary source of their wealth.

(*time*) of the oikos of Odysseus (or Telemachus); and this they have done deliberately. In an oikos suffering none of the woes of the oikos of Odysseus, the idealized palace of Arete and Alcinous, Alcinous proposes that he and his elders shall each give another gift to Odysseus, and subsequently *tinusthai*, get back *time*, from the other Phaiakians: 'for it is hard for one man to give a present without reimbursement' (*Od.* 13.15).

The central importance of *time* in Homeric values should now be clear. When the system is working correctly, as described by Sarpedon, with an appropriate share of *time* distributed to each, a harmonious community is the result. But Homeric heroes are fiercely anxious about their shares (*moirai*) of *time*; and the plots of both the *Iliad* and the *Odyssey* testify to the consequences of diminishing a Homeric hero's *time*.[19] Agamemnon is accused by Achilles of leading an army in which the *agathos* and the *kakos* have the same *time* (*Il.* 9.318–19). This is evidently reprehensible. The fact that in the last resort *time* is not so much an acknowledgment of a hero's *arete* as something that a hero must use his *arete* to defend, contributes to the tension of the situation.

Time and Arete

The usage of a group of related words indicates the pre-eminent position of *time* in Homeric values. All, men and gods alike, can be placed on a scale with Zeus at the top, followed by the other gods, all of whom are higher than mortals, then by mankind from the mightiest mortal ruler to the meanest *atimetos metanastes*, the man who—clearly not voluntarily—goes elsewhere to live; and he has no *time*. He may evidently be harmed with impunity. The Homeric hero, deprived of any significant quantity of *time*, reacts violently, aware as he is of the bottom of the scale: Achilles twice complains that Agamemnon has

[19] The best example of this is not a mortal hero but the god Poseidon. When the Greeks build the wall in front of their ships, and the Phaiakians bring Odysseus home in a much better condition than Poseidon had intended, he complains that if mortals can get away with this kind of thing, he will no longer receive the *time* of sacrifice. Zeus suggests that he later wash the wall away, and immediately sink the Phaiakian ship. If it is remembered that Poseidon is both the sea god and the earthquake god, the intensity both of the anger and of the anxiety may be inferred (*Il.* 7.446–63; *Od.* 13.128–45).

treated him 'as if he were some *atimetos metanastes*.' Hyperbole, no doubt; but Achilles lived in a dangerous world, and it contained very few persons of whose aid he was, or should have been, assured.

Agathoi and *basilees* have large shares of what is distributed, for they discharge an important function. Minstrels too, as Odysseus reminds us at the court of Alkinoos and Arete in Phaiakia, have a function, and so have a share of *time* and *aidos* among mankind, since the Muse taught them songs.

Have those men who, generally or in their present circumstances, have nothing to offer in exchange for *time*, any hope of gaining from another what they cannot supply from their own resources? They have the protection of Zeus Xeinios, 'the strangers' Zeus' or Zeus Hiketesios, 'the suppliants' Zeus,' who will be discussed below.

Odysseus reminds the Cyclops that Zeus is the *epitimetor* of *hiketai*, suppliants, and *xeinoi* like Odysseus and his crew. Liddell-Scott-Jones give 'avenger' as the meaning of *epitimetor*; but the Cyclops has done nothing to require vengeance as yet. If we pay attention to the form of the word, which occurs only here, we are likely to suppose that it means 'someone who puts *time* upon' another, who would not otherwise possess it (Zeus 'puts *time* upon' the defenseless by harming those who fail to give them *time*). I return below to the more complex question of what motivates Zeus, a god more usually concerned—like the other Olympians—with his own *time*, to behave in this manner in such contexts.

Given that *time* denotes the status-conferring goods already held within the oikos of a powerful man, with the addition of those which accrue from later occasions for the distribution of booty, and that the oikos is the locus for the storing and defense of such *time*, and that the primary function of the *agathos* is to defend his *time* with all the resources at his command, it is inevitable that *arete* and *time* are two of the most important value-terms to be found in the Homeric poems, and that they are linked to one another.

Examination of the usage of other words closely linked with *time* throws light on this. The importance of *time* to the Homeric world is made clearer by two verbs derived from the same root: *tiein* and *tinein*, with its middle form *tinesthai*. *Tiein*, a synonym of *timan* 'honor,' denotes the activity of bestowing *time* on a person, the person being the object of the verb, while *tinein* denotes the transaction when the *time* is the object of the verb, something like 'paying out *time*,' and *tinesthai* denotes 'getting back *time* for oneself.' In some usages of these words and phrases, there is no particular emphasis on specified material *time*.

This fact suggests that any occasion for moving *time* in or out of oikoi is conceptualized in the same way: whatever is emphasized in translation, in Homeric Greek its most important feature is to be a transfer of *time*. Alkinoos can use *tinesthai* of his intended collection from his subjects to balance the additional valuable gifts which he and his counselors are to give to Odysseus. He seems to have sufficient authority simply to decree that this shall be done. There is a transfer of *time*, but no-one is punished, although *apotinein* in other contexts is rendered by 'be punished.' Similarly, when Achilles tries to persuade Agamemnon to return Chryseis to her father without asking anything of the Greeks in return, he adds 'But the Greeks will *apotinein* threefold or fourfold' if they capture Troy. Again, no-one is being punished. In *Od.* 3.195–98, it is said that Aegisthus '*apetise* miserably . . . since Orestes *etisato*' (Orestes killed him). Both aspects of the transfer of *time* are mentioned in the one passage. To *apotinein timen* to a *philos*, or one whom one hopes to make into a *philos*, is to enter upon a relationship of reciprocal benefits; to do the same to an enemy is something that one would do only under compulsion, as 'punishment' to oneself. In all these examples, a transfer of *time* is certainly occurring, and it is this which links the usages.

This account of the *time*-group matches the account of the *arete*-group. *Arete* in Homer is courage-and-physical-prowess-and-social-position-and-fame. It denotes and commends all these qualities together because the general needs of Homeric society demand that all should be united in certain individuals. The man of *arete* is the *agathos*, who necessarily possesses a great many goods and qualities; and he has *time*, which in some way denotes and commends his position in life. In fact, a man's *time* is his position—concretely viewed—on that scale at whose top are the immortal gods, at whose bottom is the wandering beggar. To be deprived of *time* is to be moved so much nearer to penury and nothingness, sometimes literal death. Small wonder that the response should be so violent.

Philotes and Xenie

Let us now turn to two important terms which are usually translated by 'friendship:' *philotes* and *xenie*. With *philotes* are associated the adjective/noun *philos* and the verb *philein*, and with *xenie* the nouns *xeinos* and *xeinodokos*, the adjective *philoxeinos* and the verb *xeinizein/-izesthai*. All actions and relationships which may be denoted with words from the **xein* root may also be denoted with words from the **phil* root, but not vice versa. The translation 'friendship' is not entirely satisfactory, as will appear.

The lexica offer two 'meanings' for *philos* in Homer: 'own' and 'dear.' They suggest no reason why Homeric language, which has a full set of reflexive pronominal adjectives, should feel the need of *philos* as well; but there are certainly a number of instances in which the translation 'dear' appears very strange (to say this is not to say that the remaining instances are correctly and fully translated, simply that the translation causes no problems).

If we discuss the usage of these terms in the light of the usage of *agathos* and *arete, time* and *tinesthai*, much will become clear. In our discussion of the Homeric *agathos*, his need to defend his oikos and the possessions that it contained became apparent; but no one can defend himself against a hostile or indifferent world by the strength of his right arm alone, however well-armed he may be; and the Homeric hero might well find useful a word whose function was to mark off from the rest of the contents of the world those things and persons on which he can, or should be able to, rely. This is the function of this group of terms.

We begin close to the *agathos* and work outwards. We can begin no closer than parts and aspects of the *agathos* himself. *Philos* can certainly be used of these: 'But why did my *philos* spirit (*thumos*) say these things to me?' (*Il.* 11.407). 'Their *phila* limbs were 'loosed' with grievous toil' (*Il.* 13.85). A translation of either of these phrases that uses either 'own' or 'dear' will be in a sense comprehensible; but if we compare them with the rest of Homer's usage of *philos*, what do we imagine that Homer meant? If we move a little further from the *agathos*, we find '*phila* clothing,' '*phila* bed,' '*philos* . . . *patridos aies*. . . .' 'Dear native land'? 'Own native land'? 'Own dear native land'? We might give a different answer in different examples. We might disagree. But if we focus on the Greek, it is difficult to suppose that for Homer and his contemporaries there is any difference.

Even if we consider only cases where *philos* is applied to persons, there are some puzzles. Oddest of all is the case of Eriphyle, whose shade Odysseus met in the underworld: 'hateful Eriphyle, who took . . . gold for contriving the death of her *philos aner*' (*Od.* 11.326).

Here we have to choose. Does Homer mean 'own *aner*' or 'dear *aner*'? 'Dear' hardly suits the context. 'Own *aner*,' with no connotation of affection, fits admirably, particularly since the translation of *aner* as 'husband' requires some such idea to be supplied from the context. But then how do we relate this usage of *philos* to the other, on the assumption that *philos* is generally correctly rendered by 'dear'?

There is a relevant set-piece, when the Greek Diomedes meets the Lycian Glaukos and, in the conversational manner of the Homeric warrior, asks his identity (*Il.* 6.119–65). Glaukos names his father (Hippolochus) and his grandfather (Bellerophon). To which Diomedes responds:

> Then indeed you are a *xeinos* on my father's side from olden time; for goodly Oineus entertained blameless Bellerophon in his halls, having kept him there for twenty days. And they supplied one another with fine *xeineia*, gifts to seal friendship.

Diomedes suggests that they avoid one another on the battlefield.

Diomedes and Glaukos are unknown to each other; but they are unwilling to fight against one another because of a compact made by their grandfathers. This should not surprise us. The *xeinos* is the most remote member of the group of persons linked with the *agathos* in bonds of reciprocal assistance: his *philoi*. As he is the most remote, the claim of the *xeinos* for help is likely to be invoked least often, but to be most urgent when it is invoked, for the *xeinos* is then least able to defend himself effectively. The *xeinos* is unlikely to be willing to hazard such advantages for the sake of a transient event such as the Trojan War. It also follows that *philotes* and *xeinie* are objective relationships, not dependent on the emotions of the participants. Amphiaraos was Eriphyle's *philos aner*, whatever her subsequent feelings for him. To say this is not to say that no Greek experienced any emotion in any relationship of *philotes* or *xeinie*; it is to say that emotion was not the common element that bound *philoi* together.

Homeric Ethics and the Gods

Homer's mortal characters need to avoid actions which will bring the wrath of the gods on them. Whether a god is angry or not is an empirical question: there is no punishment after death in Homeric belief, and all important[20] good and bad things, signifying the approval

[20] All good and bad things, strictly; but in practice in an epic one is only likely

or anger of deity at what one has done, must happen in life.

There is no possibility that the gods are holding an unpleasant surprise in store for a prosperous person with whom they are angry, or a pleasant one for an unsuccessful person with whom they are pleased. Success in this life may be more or less equated with divine approval, failure with divine anger.

Homer's mortal characters have an urgent practical need to discover what pleases, and what displeases, their gods. They believed that those gods had more *arete*, *time*, and strength than mankind, or in other words that they excelled in just those qualities in which mortal aristocrats outshone human *kakoi*. It seems reasonable to infer that their gods were motivated by similar considerations; and reasonable or not, it is the inference that they in fact drew. Most divine behavior in Homer can be illuminated by a comparison with the behavior of human aristocrats, rather than the behavior of disinterested judges.

The gods are respecters of persons. The Cyclops Polyphemos had behaved in a manner shocking to Greek standards of hospitality and civilized behavior. But he was Poseidon's son: he had only to pray to his father and Poseidon persecuted Odysseus, regardless of justice. Similarly, it was not for the justice of Achilles' case, or indeed for any claim that he possessed, that Zeus saw to it that the Greeks fared badly as long as Agamemon had not placated Achilles: it was a favor that Zeus owed to Achilles' mother. It was the blood-relationship between Thetis and Achilles that made the favor available for Achilles.

Moreover, it was a favor that Zeus did not wish to grant; and here again we encounter the Greek gods as immortal aristocrats. Zeus is afraid of the dissension that will ensue between Hera and himself if he helps the Trojans, whom he favors anyway, since they have always sacrificed to him abundantly. The dissension begins; and Hephaistos says 'this is a bad thing and passes what can be endured, if you two quarrel in this manner for the sake of mortals . . . There will be no delight in the goodly feast, for the worse things prevail.' The 'goodly feast' should be the constant way of life for the gods, and no mortal concerns should be permitted to threaten it.

The poet becomes more explicit at the beginning of *Iliad* 4. Hera

---

to reflect on the role of gods in important successes and disasters. See *moirai* in Adkins (1960) 17–25.

is angry because all her efforts against the Trojans seem fruitless. Zeus is willing to yield the point on this occasion; but he gives notice that when on some occasion in the future he wishes to destroy some city whose inhabitants are particularly *philoi* to Hera, she shall not attempt to resist. Hera agrees, and is satisfied. She holds that her lineage, equal as it is to that of Zeus, should guarantee that her wishes should prevail for a part of the time. Thus might two members of a mortal aristocratic family settle a dispute involving a member of their own family and an 'outsider.' No one outside the family, however abundant his deserts, can rely on a return for favors should this seriously inconvenience the members of the family.

One more example. At the beginning of *Iliad* 24, as a result of Achilles' dragging the the corpse of Hector round Troy, an altercation breaks out between the divine partisans of the Greeks and those of the Trojans. Apollo rebukes the gods for their hardness of heart: was not Hector wont to sacrifice to them? 'Perhaps, *agathos* though Achilles be, we gods may be angry with him.'

Hera replies in fury that this would be reasonable if the gods were going to assign similar *time* to Hector and Achilles.[21]

> But Hector is a mortal and suckled at a woman's breast whereas Achilles is the son of a goddess whom I myself nurtured . . . and gave as wife to Peleus. . . . And all you gods went to the wedding . . . and you feasted among the rest, you *kakos*-lover (Apollo).

Zeus mediates. There is no question of Hector and Achilles having the same *time*. But Hector was the most *philos* of mortals to the gods, since he always sacrificed copiously to them. So Priam shall be bidden to take abundant *time* to Achilles and ransom Hector's body.

This is the best that can be done for Hector. The worshipers of these gods cannot hope for an even-handed justice impartially administered.[22]

Zeus and Justice

However, there are a number of passages in the *Iliad* and *Odyssey* where the gods, and in particular Zeus, are closely linked with the

---

[21] τιμὴν τιθέναι, cf. επιτιμήτωρ.

[22] Scholars who argue that it is just that Achilles should get better treatment than Hector in terms of Homeric values seem to me to be confusing the issue, since

divine justice. For example, Eumaios says to the disguised Odysseus that it is not right (*themis*) for him to *atiman* a *xeinos*, even if one more *kakos* than the present 'beggar' should come to his door; for all *xeinoi* and beggars are from Zeus, and therefore under his protection.

This seems an unlikely role for the *time*-seeking Olympians whom we have discussed so far. It is explicable once Zeus has taken wayfarers, strangers, beggars, and guests under his protection, for then, as for the mortal *agathos*, it would be *aischron* for Zeus not to succeed in protecting them against all comers. It should be remembered that not even Zeus is omnipotent, and that if he does not keep suppliants safe, it may be insinuated that he cannot do so. But it is difficult to furnish the Zeus we have studied so far with a motive for accepting these groups in the first place.

If beggars alone stood in need of the assistance of Zeus Xeinios or Zeus Hiketesios, the belief might not have arisen. But not only beggars have such needs. Zeus 'puts *time* upon' *hiketai* and *xeinoi* in general. A *hiketes* is a 'comer,' and all 'comers' must supplicate a powerful person for protection in the new environment to which they have come.

Conclusion

From our discussions it has become apparent that Homeric values frequently do not achieve the goals of Homeric society. They do not ensure that the interests of a larger good and a larger group than the oikos may be taken into account, on the—apparently rare—occasions when these are relevant. The kings are endowed with a great deal of *time* to ensure that they will fight in the forefront of the battle on behalf of all; but it is as individuals in command of their oikoi or contingents that they possess their *time* and prestige. In *Iliad* 1, Nestor attempts to mediate by pointing out to Achilles and Agamemnon that only the Trojans will benefit from their quarrel. Neither is incapable of understanding Nestor's point, but each is afraid of being put in a bad light, competitively speaking, by the other, of being spoken of as 'a mere nobody.'

In *Iliad* 1, Agamemnon has two goals. He wishes to take Briseis

there is a word for 'just' in Homeric Greek, and Homer does not use it in such contexts as these.

from Achilles to counterbalance the loss of Chryseis, returned to her father without ransom, at Apollo's command. He also wishes to inflict a thorough defeat on the Trojans, and to sack Troy. He believes that these goals are compatible. That being the case, Agamemnon's desire to avoid loss of *time* draws him on to repair his *time* by taking Briseis from Achilles. Already in *Iliad* 2 he has discovered his mistake; and in *Iliad* 9 he tries to rectify it, by trying to placate Achilles through the medium of sending ambassadors.

In this he is completely unsuccessful. The ambassadors attempt a little private diplomacy on their own account, and try to convince Achilles that a relationship of *philotes* subsists between him and them, and with the army as a whole; but Achilles is unmoved. After all, what have they done for him in the past?[23] Phoinix, emphasizing the gifts Achilles is being promised, says that πρὶν δ' οὔ τι νεμεσσητὸν κεχολῶσθαι, 'until then, no-one would find fault with you for being angry.'

This phrase appears once in both the *Iliad* (9.523) and the *Odyssey* (22.59) at a pivotal point in the plot. The *Odyssey* passage occurs immediately after Odysseus kills Antinous with an arrow and reveals his identity. Eurymachus offers the worth of twenty oxen from each suitor to appease Odysseus; but Odysseus is unmoved.

One might perhaps have expected scholars to discuss the resemblances between the use made of the phrase in the two poems. Actual practice is different.

Achilles says that no amount of *time* would suffice to placate him; and this, we are told, puts Achilles beyond the pale. As a result of his withdrawal from the battle, an indefinitely large number of soldiers are killed who would not have been killed otherwise.

Odysseus says that no amount of *time* would suffice to placate him; and he kills considerably more than one hundred suitors who were living in what in Homeric society passes for peace. Telemachus, who is accompanied by the standard epithet *pepnumenos* as regularly as is Achilles by 'swift footed,' gives the audience plenty of opportunity to observe how ineffectual the merely *pepnumenos* is in Homeric society. In the fight in the hall Telemachus is still a junior partner, but in *Odyssey* 24 he replies confidently to Odysseus' exhortation not to

[23] As *philotes* would require. Achilles seems not to expect it; he is not angry with the Greeks in general, nor with the ambassadors in particular, merely with Agamemnon.

disgrace the family name in battle, and Laertes comments that his son and his grandson are vying with one another over *arete*. Yet this diminishes the ability of Ithaka to defend itself.

The suitors have committed *atasthaliai* against Odysseus and his oikos; yet to kill them must harm Ithaca much more than their misdeeds have done. Furthermore, since both parties would be in a very *aischron* condition were they not to fight, there seems to be no alternative to another battle, in which, says Homer, the party of Odysseus would have killed all the families of the suitors, had not Athena appeared and administered oaths to both sides. It is somewhat surprising that so many scholars find Achilles' situation more ethically complex than that of Odysseus, whose situation they hardly discuss at all. Both Achilles and Odysseus are saying that nothing could possibly be enough; and Odysseus knows (*a*) that *agathoi* are so termed because they make both their own oikos and their polis more able to defend itself and (*b*) that he and his allies have made Ithaka less capable of defending itself. Nothing can be done about the situation: the men are dead. But the comment of the aged Laertes, rejoicing that his son and his grandson are vying with one another in a contest of *arete*, may remind the audience that in killing over a hundred suitors Odysseus and his allies have been displaying *arete*.

Nor are the values of the Trojans more successfully related to their goals. Troy is to be destroyed, but not while Hector lives. At the beginning of *Iliad* 22, the majority of the Trojan army has escaped in full rout back into Troy, leaving Hector outside the gates. It is vital, if the Trojans are to live to fight another day, that Hector retreat within the walls. On the battlements, Priam tears his hair, Hecuba bares her breasts, to no avail. Hector is unmoved. What moves him is the thought of Polydamas criticising his (Hector's) ill-fated strategy. Rather than face such criticism he stays outside the Trojan wall, meets Achilles in combat, and is killed. Once again, the individualistic aspect of the *arete*-standard produces effects quite other than the goals aimed at by those who subscribed to the values.

These problems are not moral, of a kind to be solved by living up to the values of one's community. They are caused by the values themselves, and their solution calls for a kind of thought not to be expected from an epic poet. Plato was still trying to solve similar problems centuries later.

SELECT BIBLIOGRAPHY*

Aarne, A., and S. Thompson. 1961. *The Types of the Folktale: a Classification and Bibliography*. 2nd ed. Helsinki.
Adkins, A. W. H. 1960. *Merit and Responsibility: A Study in Greek Values*. Oxford.
—1971. 'Homeric Values and Homeric Society,' *Journal of Hellenic Studies* 91, 1–14.
Ahlberg-Cornell, G. 1992. *Myth and Epos in Early Greek Art: Representation and Interpretation*. Jonsered.
Albracht, F. 1886. *Kampf und Kampfschilderung bei Homer*. Naumburg.
Alexiou, M. 1974. *The Ritual Lament in Greek Tradition*. Cambridge.
Allen, T. W. 1912. *Homeri Opera*. 5 vols. Oxford.
—1923. *Homer: The Origins and the Transmission*. Oxford.
—1931. *Homeri Ilias* I: *Prolegomena*. Oxford.
Allen, T. W., W. R. Halliday, and E. E. Sikes, eds. 1936. *The Homeric Hymns*. Oxford.
Aloni, A. 1986. *Tradizioni arcaiche della Troade e composizione dell'Iliade*. Milan.
—1989. *Aedo e i tiranni: Ricerche sull'inno omerico a Apollo*. Rome.
—1992. 'Proemio e funzione proemiale nella poesia greca arcaica,' in G. Cerri, ed., *Lirica greca e latina. Atti del convegno di studi polacco italiano Poznan 2–3 maggio 1990*, 99–130. Rome.
Andersen, Ø. 1977. 'Odysseus and the Wooden Horse,' *Symbolae Osloenses* 52, 5–18.
—1987. 'Myth, Paradigm, and Spatial Form in the *Iliad*,' in Bremer et al., eds., 1–13.
—1990. 'The Making of the Past in the *Iliad*,' *Harvard Studies in Classical Philology* 93, 25–45.
Andrewes, A. 1961. 'Phratries in Homer,' *Hermes* 89, 129–40.
Antonaccio, C. 1995. *An Archaeology of Ancestors: Tomb Cult and Hero Cult in Early Greece*. Lanham, Maryland.
Apthorp, M. J. 1980. *The Manuscript Evidence for Interpolation in Homer*. Heidelberg.
Arnheim, M. T. W. 1977. *Aristocracy in Greek Society*. London.
Arthur, M. 1973. 'Early Greece. The Origins of the Western Attitude toward Women,' *Arethusa* 6, 7–58.
Auerbach, E. 1953 [1946]. *Mimesis. The Representation of Reality in Western Literature*. Trs. W. R. Trask. Princeton.
Austin, N. 1966. 'The Function of Digressions in the *Iliad*,' *Greek, Roman and Byzantine Studies* 7, 295–312.
—1975. *Archery at the Dark of the Moon*. Berkeley.
Austin, M. M. and P. Vidal-Naquet. 1977. *Economic and Social History of Ancient Greece*. Berkeley.
Ayer, A. J. 1935. *Language, Truth and Logic*. London.
—1982. *Philosophy in the Twentieth Century*. New York.

Bakker, E. J. 1990. 'Homeric Discourse and Enjambement. A Cognitive Approach,' *Transactions of the American Philological Association* 120, 1–21.
—1993a. 'Discourse and Performance: Involvement, Visualization, and "Presence" in Homeric Poetry,' *Classical Antiquity* 12, 1–29.

* This bibliography gives full references only for the most frequently cited entries.

—1993b. 'Activation and Preservation: The Interdependence of Text and Performance in an Oral Tradition,' *Oral Tradition* 8, 5–20.
—1993c. 'Topics, Boundaries and the Structure of Discourse: An Investigation of the Particle *dé*,' *Studies in Language* 17, 275–311.
—1995. 'Noun-Epithet Formulas, Milman Parry, and the Grammar of Poetry.' In Crielaard, ed., 97–125.
—1996. *Poetry in Speech. Orality and Homeric Discourse.* Ithaca, New York.
Bakker, E. and F. Fabbricotti. 1991. 'Peripheral and Nuclear Semantics in Homeric Diction: The Case of Dative Expressions for Spear,' *Mnemosyne* 44, 63–84.
Bakker, E. and A. Kahane, eds., 1997. *Written Voices, Spoken Signs. Tradition, Performance, and the Epic Text.* Cambridge, Mass.
Bakker, E. J., and N. van den Houten. 1992. 'Aspects of Synonymy in Homeric Formulaic Diction: An Investigation of Dative Expressions for "Spear."' *Classical Philology* 87, 1–13.
Bal, M. 1985. *Narratology. Introduction to the Theory of Narrative.* Trs. C. van Boheemen. Toronto.
Bannert, H. 1987. 'Versammlungsszenen bei Homer,' in Bremer et al., eds., 15–30.
Barber, R. 1992. 'The Origins of the Mycenaean Palace,' in J. M. Sanders, ed., *ΦΙΛΟΛΑΚΩΝ. Lakonian Studies in Honour of Hector Catling*, 11–23. London.
Barker, A. 1984. *Greek Musical Writings* I. Cambridge.
Barnes, H. R. 1986. 'The Colometric Structure of the Greek Hexameter,' *Greek, Roman and Byzantine Studies* 27, 125–50.
—1991. Review of Higbie (1990). *Bryn Mawr Classical Review* 2, 163–79.
Bassett, S. E. 1919. 'The Structural Similarity of *Iliad* and *Odyssey* as Revealed in the Treatment of the Hero's Fate,' *Classical Journal* 14, 557–563.
Baumeister, A., ed. 1860. *Hymni Homerici.* Leipzig.
Bäuml, F. H. 1987. 'The Theory of Oral-Formulaic Composition and the Written Medieval Text,' in J. M. Foley, ed., *Comparative Research on Oral Traditions: A Memorial for Milman Parry*, 29–45. Columbus, Ohio.
Baurain, C., C. Bonnet, and V. Krings, eds. 1991. *Phoinikeia Grammata. Lire et écrire en Méditerranée.* Namur (Collection d'études classiques VI).
Beaman, K. 1984. 'Coordination and Subordination Revisited: Syntactic Complexity in Spoken and Written Narrative Discourse,' in D. Tannen, ed., *Coherence in Spoken and Written Discourse*, 45–54. Norwood, New Jersey.
Beazley, J. 1951. *The Development of Attic Black-Figure.* Oxford.
Beck, R. 1972. 'A Principle of Composition in Homeric Verse,' *Phoenix* 26, 213–31.
Beekes, R. S. P. 1972. 'On the Structure of the Greek Hexameter,' *Glotta* 50, 1–10.
Bennet, J. 1995. 'Space Through Time: Diachronic Perspectives on the Spatial Organization of the Pylian State,' in Laffineur and Niemeier, eds., 596–601.
Bennett, E. L., Jr. 1963. 'Names for Linear B Writing and for Its Signs,' *Kadmos* 2, 98–123.
Bérard, V. 1902–03. *Les Phéniciens et l'Odyssée.* 2 vols. Paris.
Bergren, A. L. T. 1980. 'Allegorizing Winged Words: Similes and Symbolization in *Odyssey* V,' *Classical World* 74, 109–123.
—1981. 'Helen's "Good Drug:" *Odyssey* IV 1–305,' in S. Krésic, ed., *Contemporary Literary Hermeneutics and Interpretation of Classical Texts*, 201–214. Ottawa.
—1983a. 'Language and the Female in Early Greek Thought,' *Arethusa* 16, 69–95.
—1983b. 'Odyssean Temporality: Many (Re)Turns,' in Rubino and Shelmerdine, eds., 38–73.
Bernabé, A. 1988. *Poetae Epici Graeci. Testimonia et Fragmenta.* Leipzig.
Bernal, M. 1987–91. *Black Athena: The Afro-Asiatic Roots of Classical Civilization.* 2 vols. New Brunswick, New Jersey.

Bertman, S. 1966. 'The Telemachy and Structural Symmetry,' *Transactions of the American Philological Association* 97, 15–27.

—1968. 'Structural Symmetry at the End of the *Odyssey*,' *Greek, Roman and Byzantine Studies* 9:115–123.

Bertolini, F. 1989. 'Dal folclore all' epica: esempli di trasformazione e adattamento,' in D. Lanza and O. Longo, eds., *Il meraviglioso e il verosimile tra antichità e medioevo*, 131–52. Florence (Biblioteca dell''Archivum Romanicum,' Ser. 1, vol. 221).

Bethe, E. 1914–27. *Homer. Dichtung und Sage.* 3 vols. Leipzig.

Beye, C. R. 1982. *Epic and Romance in the Argonautica of Apollonius.* Carbondale, Illinois.

Blackie, J. S. 1866. *Homer and the 'Iliad.'* 4 vols. Edinburgh.

Blome, P. 1991. 'Die dunkeln Jahrhunderte—aufgehellt,' in Latacz, ed., 1991a, 45–60.

Blundell, S. 1995. *Women in Ancient Greece.* Cambridge, Mass.

Boardman, J. 1990. 'Al Mina and History,' *Oxford Journal of Archaeology* 9, 169–89.

Boedeker, D. D. 1974. *Aphrodite's Entry into Greek Epic.* Leiden (*Mnemosyne* Suppl. 32).

—1988. 'Amerikanische Oral-Tradition-Forschung. Eine Einführung.' In von Ungern-Sternberg and Reinau, eds., 34–56.

Bohannon, P. 1959. 'The Impact of Money on an African Subsistence Economy,' *Journal of Economic History* 19, 591–603.

Böhme, R. 1937. *Das Prooimion: Eine Form sakraler Dichtung der Griechen.* Bühl.

Bolling, G. M. 1925. *The External Evidence for Interpolation in Homer.* Oxford.

—1950. *Iliad Atheniensum: The Athenian Iliad of the Sixth Century B.C.* Lancaster, Pennsylvania.

Bonner, R., and G. Smith. 1930. *The Administration of Justice from Homer to Aristotle.* Chicago.

Booth, W. 1961. *The Rhetoric of Fiction.* Chicago.

Bottéro, J. 1992. *Mesopotamia.* Chicago.

Bowden, H. 1993. 'Heroes and Hoplites,' in J. Rich and G. Shipley, eds., *War and Society in the Greek World.* London.

Bowie, E. L. 1993. 'Lies, Fiction and Slander in Early Greek Poetry,' in C. Gill and T. P. Wiseman, eds., *Lies and Fiction in the Ancient World*, 1–37. Exeter.

Bowra, C. M. 1952. *Heroic Poetry.* London.

—1962. 'Style.' In Wace and Stubbings, eds., 26–37.

—1964. 'The Meaning of a Heroic Age,' in Kirk, ed., 22–47.

Boyle, A. J. 1991. 'Intellectual Pluralism and the Common Pursuit: *Ramus* Twenty Years,' *Ramus* 20:113–22.

Bremer, J. M. 1987. 'The So-Called "Götterapparat" in *Iliad* xx–xxii,' in Bremer et al., eds., 31–46.

—1994. *Greek Religion.* Oxford.

Bremer, J. M., I. J. F. de Jong, and J. Kalff, eds. 1987. *Homer: Beyond Oral Poetry. Recent Trends in Homeric Interpretation.* Amsterdam.

Brillante, C. 1983. 'Episodi iliadici nell'arte figurata e conoscenza dell'*Iliade* nella Grecia antica,' *Rheinisches Museum* 126:97–125.

Brillante, C., M. Cantilena, and C. O. Pavese, eds. 1981. *I poemi epici rapsodici non omerici e la tradizione orale. Atti del Convegno di Venezia, 28–30 settembre 1977.* Padua.

Brommer, F. 1971–76. *Denkmälerlisten zur griechischen Heldensage.* 3 vols. Marburg.

—1973. *Vasenlisten zur griechischen Heldensage.* 3rd ed. Marburg.

Brown, G., and G. Yule. 1983. *Discourse Analysis.* Cambridge.

Brown, N. O. 1947. *Hermes the Thief: The Evolution of a Myth.* Madison, Wisconsin.

Browne, H. 1908. *Handbook of Homeric Study.* 2nd ed. London.

Buchner, G., and D. Ridgway. 1993. *Pithekoussai* I. Rome.

Buffière, F. 1956. *Les Mythes d'Homère et la pensée grecque.* Paris.—Ed. and tr. 1962. *Héraclite, Allégories d'Homère.* Paris.

Buitron, D., B. Cohen, N. Austin, G. Dimock, T. Gould, W. Mullen, B. B. Powell, and M. Simpson. 1992. *The Odyssey in Ancient Art: An Epic in Word and Image.* Annandale-on-Hudson, New York.
Burford Cooper, A. 1977–78. 'The Family Farm in Greece,' *Classical Journal* 73:162–75.
Burford, A. 1993. *Land and Labor in the Greek World.* Baltimore.
Burkert, W. 1979a. 'Kynaithos, Polycrates and the Homeric Hymn to Apollo,' in *Arktouros: Hellenic Studies Presented to Bernard M. W. Knox*, 53–62. Berlin.
—1979b. 'Mythisches Denken,' in H. Poser, ed., *Philosophie und Mythos*, 29. Berlin.
—1983. 'Oriental Myth and Literature in the *Iliad*,' in Hägg, ed., 51–56.
—1985. *Greek Religion.* Trs. J. Raffan. Cambridge, Mass.
—1987. 'The Making of Homer in the Sixth Century B.C.: Rhapsodes versus Stesichoros,' in D. von Bothmer, ed., *Papers on the Amasis Painter and his World*, 43–62. Malibu, California.
—1991. 'Homerstudien und Orient,' in Latacz, ed., 1991a, 155–81.
—1992. *The Orientalizing Revolution: Near Eastern Influence on Greek Culture in the Early Archaic Age.* Trs. M. E. Pinder and W. Burkert. Cambridge, Mass.
—1993. 'Mythos—Begriff, Struktur, Funktionen,' in F. Graf, ed., *Mythos in mythenloser Gesellschaft: Das Paradigma Roms*, 9–24. Stuttgart and Leipzig.
Bury, J. B. 1913. *A History of Greece.* 2nd ed. London.
Butterworth, J. 1986. 'Homer and Hesiod,' in J. H. Betts, J. T. Hooker, and J. R. Green, eds., *Studies in Honour of T. B. L. Webster*, 33–45. Bristol.
Buxton, R. 1994. *Imaginary Greece: The Contexts of Mythology.* Cambridge.
Bynum, D. E. 1976. 'The Generic Nature of Oral Epic Poetry,' in D. Ben Amos, ed., *Folklore Genres*, 32–58. Austin, Texas.

Calame, C. 1974. 'Réflexions sur les genres littéraires en Grèce archaïque,' *Quaderni Urbinati di Cultura Classica* 17, 113–28.
—1977. *Les Choeurs des jeunes filles en Grèce archaïque.* 2 vols. Rome.
—1991. '"Mythe" et "rite" en Grèce: Des catégories indigènes?' *Kernos* 4, 179–204.
Calder, W. M., III. 1984. 'Gold for Bronze: *Iliad* 6.232–36,' in A. Boegehold, ed., *Studies Presented to Sterling Dow*, 31–35. Durham, North Carolina (*Greek, Roman and Byzantine Studies* Monograph 40).
Calder, W. M. III, and D. A. Traill, eds. 1986. *Myth, Scandal, and History.* Detroit.
Calhoun, G. 1935. 'The Art of Formula in Homer—ΕΠΕΑ ΠΤΕΡΟΕΝΤΑ,' *Classical Philology* 30, 215–27.
—1939. 'Homer's Gods—Myth and Märchen,' *American Journal of Philology* 60, 1–28.
—1962. 'Polity and Society. The Homeric Picture,' in Wace and Stubbings, eds., 431–52.
Cambitoglou, A. 1981. *Archaeological Museum of Andros.* Athens.
Cambitoglou, A., J. J. Coulton, J. Birmingham, and R. Green. 1971. *Zagora* I. Athens.
—1988. *Zagora* II. Athens.
Canciani, F. 1984. *Bildkunst.* Göttingen (Archaeologia Homerica N, Teil 2).
Cantilena, M. 1980. *Enjambement e poesia esametrica orale: una verifica.* Ferrara.
—1982. *Ricerche sulla dizione epica* I: *Per uno studio della formularità degli Inni Omerici.* Rome.
Carlier, P. 1984. *La royauté en Grèce avant d'Alexandre.* Strasbourg.
—1991. 'La procédure de décision politique du monde mycénien à l'époque archaïque,' in Musti et al., eds., 85–95.
Carpenter, R. 1933. 'The Antiquity of the Greek Alphabet,' *American Journal of Archaeology* 37, 8–29.
—1938. 'The Greek Alphabet Again,' *American Journal of Archaeology* 42, 58–69.
—1946. *Folktale, Fiction, and Saga in the Homeric Epics.* Berkeley.
Carter, J. 1995. 'Ancestor Cult and the Occasion of Homeric Performance,' in Carter and Morris, eds., 285–312.

Carter, J. B., and S. P. Morris, eds. 1995. *The Ages of Homer. A Tribute to Emily Townsend Vermeule.* Austin, Texas.
Cartledge, P. 1983. '"Trade and Politics" Revisited: Archaic Greece,' in Garnsey et al., eds., 1–15.
—Forthcoming. 'La nascità degli opliti e l'organizzazione militare,' in *I Greci.* Rome.
Cassolà, F., ed. 1975. *Inni Omerici.* Milan.
Catling, R., and I. Lemos. 1990. *Lefkandi* II.1. London (British School at Athens Supp. Vol. 22).
Cauer, P. 1923. *Grundfragen der Homerkritik.* 3rd ed. Leipzig.
Chadwick, H. M., and N. K. Chadwick. 1932. *The Growth of Literature* I: *The Ancient Literatures of Europe.* Cambridge.
Chadwick, J. 1956. 'The Greek Dialects and Greek Prehistory,' *Greece and Rome* n.s. 3, 38–50.
—1958. 'Mycenaean Elements in the Homeric Dialect,' in *Minoica: Festschrift for J. Sundwall,* 116–122. Berlin.
—1963. 'The Prehistory of the Greek Language,' in *Cambridge Ancient History* II.2, 805–819. Cambridge.
—1967. *The Decipherment of Linear B.* 2nd ed. Cambridge (1st ed., 1958).
—1976a. *The Mycenaean World.* Cambridge.
—1976b. 'Who were the Dorians?' *Parola del Passato* 31, 103–117.
—1990. 'The Descent of the Greek Epic,' *Journal of Hellenic Studies* 110, 174–77.
Chafe, W. 1988. 'Linking Intonation Units in Spoken English,' in J. Haiman and S. A. Thompson, eds., *Clause Combining in Grammar and Discourse,* 1–15. Amsterdam.
—1994. *Discourse, Consciousness, and Time. The Flow and Displacement of Conscious Experience in Speech and Writing.* Chicago.
Chantraine, P. 1933. *La formation des noms en grec ancien.* Paris.
—1953. *Grammaire Homérique: Tome II—Syntaxe.* Paris.
—1973. *Grammaire Homérique: Tome I—Phonétique et Morphologie.* 2nd ed. Paris.
Chomsky, N. 1965. *Aspects of the Theory of Syntax.* Cambridge, Mass.
Citti, V. 1966. 'Le edizioni omeriche "delle città,"' *Vichiana* 3, 227–267.
Clark, M. E. 1986. 'Neoanalysis: A Bibliographical Review,' *Classical World* 7:379–94.
—1994. 'Enjambment and Binding in Homeric Hexameter,' *Phoenix* 48, 95–114.
Clay, J. S. 1989. *The Politics of Olympus: Form and Meaning in the Major Homeric Hymns.* Princeton.
Clayman, D. L. 1981. 'Sentence Length in Greek Hexameter Poetry,' in Grotjahn, ed., 107–136.
Cline, E. H. 1994. *Sailing the Wine-Dark Sea. International Trade and the Late Bronze Age Aegean.* Oxford.
Cobet, J. 1993. 'König, Anführer, Herr; Monarch, Tyrann,' in Welskopf, ed., 11–66.
Cohen, B., ed. 1995. *The Distaff Side: Representing the Female in Homer's Odyssey.* Oxford.
Coldstream, J. N. 1968. *Greek Geometric Pottery.* London.
—1977. *Geometric Greece.* London.
—1982. 'Greeks and Phoenicians in the Aegean,' in Niemeyer, ed., 261–275.
—1994. 'Propsectors and Pioneers: Pithekoussai, Kyme and Central Italy,' in Tsetskhladze and De Angelis, eds., 47–59.
Collart, P. 1931. 'Les papyrus de *l'Iliade,*' *Revue de Philologie* ser. 3.6, 315–49.
—1933. 'Les papyrus de *l'Iliade,*' *Revue de Philologie* ser. 3.7, 33–61.
Combellack, F. M. 1959. 'Milman Parry and Homeric Artistry,' *Comparative Literature* 11, 193–208.
—1976. 'Homer the Innovator,' *Classical Philology* 71, 44–55.
—1987. 'The λύσις ἐκ τῆς λέξεως,' *American Journal of Philology* 108, 202–219.
Connelly, B. 1986. *Arab Folk Epic and Identity.* Berkeley.

Costantini, M., and J. Lallot. 1987. 'Le prooimion est-il un proème?' in *Le Texte et ses représentations*. Paris (Études de littérature ancienne 3).

Coogan, M. D., ed. and tr. 1978. *Stories from Ancient Canaan*. Philadelphia.

Cook, E. 1995. *The Odyssey in Athens. Myths of Cultural Origins*. Ithaca, New York.

Cook, R. M. 1983. 'Art and Epic in Archaic Greece,' *Bulletin van de Vereeniging tot Bevordering der Kennis van de Antike Beschaving* 58, 1–10.

Cowgill, W. C. 1966. 'Ancient Greek Dialectology in the Light of Mycenaean,' in H. Birnbaum and J. Puhvel, eds., *Ancient Indo-European Dialects*, 77–95. Berkeley.

Crane, G. 1988. *Calypso: Backgrounds and Conventions of the Odyssey*. Frankfurt (Beiträge zur klassischen Philologie 191).

Crielaard, J. P. 1995. 'Homer, History and Archaeology,' in Crielaard, ed., 201–288.

Crielaard, J. P., ed. 1995. *Homeric Questions*. Amsterdam.

Crooke, W. 1908. 'Some Notes on Homeric Folk-Lore,' *Folk-Lore* 19, 52–77, 153–89.

Crowley, J. 1989. *The Aegean and the East. An Investigation into the Transference of Artistic Motifs Between the Aegean, Egypt and the Near East in the Bronze Age*. Jonsered.

Dakoronia, F. 1987. *Marmara*. Athens.

Danek, G. 1988. *Studien zur Dolonie*. Vienna (*Wiener Studien*, Beiheft no. 12).

Danker, F. W. 1988. *A Century of Greco-Roman Philology: Featuring the American Philological Association and the Society of Biblical Literature*. Atlanta, Georgia (Biblical Scholarship in North America, no. 12).

Davies, M. 1988. *Epicorum Graecorum Fragmenta*. Göttingen.

—1989. *The Epic Cycle*. Bristol.

Davison, J. A. 1962a. 'The Transmission of the Text,' in Wace and Stubbings, eds., 215–33.

—1962b. 'The Homeric Question,' in Wace and Stubbings, eds., 234–268.

De Jong, I. J. F. 1985. '*Iliad* 1.366–392: A Mirror-Story,' *Arethusa* 18, 5–22.

—1987a. *Narrators and Focalizers. The Presentation of the Story in the Iliad*. Amsterdam.

—1987b. 'Silent Characters in the *Iliad*,' in Bremer et al., eds., 105–121.

—1987c. 'Homeric Words and Speakers: An Addendum,' *Journal of Hellenic Studies* 107, 188–89.

—1991. 'Narratology and Oral Poetry: The Case of Homer,' *Poetics Today* 12, 405–423.

—1992. 'The Subjective Style in Odysseus' Wanderings,' *Classical Quarterly* 42, 1–11.

—1993. 'Studies in Homeric Denomination,' *Mnemosyne* 46, 289–306.

—1994. 'Between Word and Deed: Hidden Thoughts in the *Odyssey*,' in I. J. F. De Jong and J. P. Sullivan, eds., 27–50.

—Forthcoming. 'Narrator Language Versus Character Language: Some Further Explorations.'

De Jong, I. J. F., and J. P. Sullivan, eds. 1994. *Modern Critical Theory and Classical Literature*. Leiden (*Mnemosyne* Supp. Vol. 130).

De Man, P. 1982. 'The Resistance to Theory,' *Yale French Studies* 63, 3–20.

De Martino, F. 1980. 'ΑΛΛΗ ΑΟΙΔΗ (in coda all' inno omerico, 545–546),' *L'Antiquité Classique* 49, 232–40.

De Polignac, F. 1995. *Cults, Territory, and the Origins of the Greek City-State*. Trs. J. Lloyd. Chicago.

Dee, J. H. 1994. *The Epithetic Phrases for the Homeric Gods (Epitheta Deorum apud Homerum); a Repertory of the Descriptive Expressions for the Divinities of the Iliad and the Odyssey*. New York.

Deger-Jalkotzy, S. 1991. 'Die Erforschung des Zusammenbruchs der sogenannten mykenischen Kultur und der sogenannten dunklen Jahrhunderte,' in Latacz, ed., 1991a, 127–54.

Deger-Jalkotzy, S. 1978. *E-QE-TA. Zur Rolle des Gefolgschaftswesens in der Sozialstruktur mykenischer Reiche.* Vienna.
—1983. *Griechenland, die Ägäis und die Levante wahrend die 'Dark Ages,'* Vienna, 1983.
Delasanta, R. 1967. *The Epic Voice.* The Hague.
Delebecque, E. 1958. *Télémaque et la structure de l'Odyssee.* Aix-en-Provence.
Denniston, J. D. 1954. *The Greek Particles.* Oxford.
Desborough, V. R. 1952. *Protogeometric Pottery.* Oxford.
—1972. *The Greek Dark Ages.* London.
Detienne, M. 1963. *Crise agraire et attitude religieuse chez Hésiode.* Brussels.
—1965. 'En Grèce archaïque: géométrie, politique et société,' *Annales, ESC* 20: 425–41.
—1986. *The Creation of Mythology.* Trs. M. Cook. Chicago.
Devine, A. M., and L. D. Stephens. 1984. *Language and Metre: Resolution, Porson's Bridge, and Their Prosodic Basis.* Chico, California (American Classical Studies 12).
—1993. 'Evidence from Experimental Psychology for the Rhythm and Metre of Greek Verse,' *Transactions of the American Philological Association* 123, 379–403.
—1994. *The Prosody of Greek Speech.* Oxford.
Di Benedetto, V. 1994. *Nel laboratorio di Omero.* Rome.
Di Luzio, A. 1969. 'I papiri omerici d'epoca tolemaica e la constituzione del testi dell'epica arcaica,' *Rivista di cultura classica e medievale* 11, 3–152.
Di Vita, A., et al., eds. 1983–84. *Grecia, Italia e Sicilia nell' VIII e VII secolo a.C.* Rome (*Annuario della Scuola Archeologica di Atene* vols. 59–61 [1981–83]).
Dickinson, O. 1986. 'Homer, the Poet of the Dark Age,' *Greece and Rome* 33, 20–37.
—1994. *The Aegean Bronze Age.* Cambridge.
Diehl, E. 1940. 'Fuerunt ante Homerum Poetae,' *Rheinisches Museum* 89, 81–114.
Diller, A. 1974. *Serta Turyniana.* Urbana, Illinois.
Dindorf, W. 1855. *Scholia Graeca in Homeri Odysseam.* 2 vols. Oxford.
—1875–88. *Scholia Graeca in Homeri Iliadem: ex codicibus aucta et emendata.* 6 vols. Oxford.
Dirlmeier, F. 1955. 'Homerisches Epos und Orient,' *Rheinisches Museum* 98, 18–37.
Doherty, L. E. 1995. *Siren Songs: Gender, Audiences, and Narrators in the Odyssey.* Ann Arbor, Michigan.
Donlan, W. 1970. 'Changes and Shifts in the Meaning of Demos in the Literature of the Archaic Period,' *Parola del passato* 25, 381–395.
—1980. *The Aristocratic Ideal in Ancient Greece. Attitudes of Superiority from Homer to the End of the Fifth Century B.C.* Lawrence, Kansas.
—1981. 'Scale, Value, and Function in the Homeric Economy,' *American Journal of Ancient History* 6, 101–117.
—1981–82. 'Reciprocities in Homer,' *Classical World* 75, 137–175.
—1985. 'The Social Groups of Dark Age Greece,' *Classical Philology* 80, 293–308.
—1989a. 'The Unequal Exchange between Glaucus and Diomedes in Light of the Homeric Gift-Economy,' *Phoenix* 43, 1–15.
—1989b. 'The Pre-State Community in Greece,' *Symbolae Osloenses* 64, 5–29.
—1989c. 'Homeric temenos and the Land Economy of the Dark Age,' *Museum Helveticum* 46, 129–145.
—1994. 'Chiefs and Followers in Pre-State Greece,' in Duncan and Tandy, eds., 39–48.
Doumas, C. 1992. *The Wall-Paintings of Thera.* Athens.
Drerup, H. 1969. *Griechische Baukunst in geometrischer Zeit.* Göttingen (Archaeologia Homerica O).
Duckworth, G. E. 1933. *Foreshadowing and Suspense in the Epics of Homer, Apollonius and Vergil.* Princeton (reprinted New York, 1966).
Duncan, C. A. M., and D. W. Tandy, eds. 1994. *From Political Economy to Anthropology.* Montreal.

Easterling, P. 1989. 'Agamemnon's *Skeptron* in the Iliad,' in Mackenzie and Roueché, eds., 104–121.
—1990. 'Constructing Character in Greek Tragedy,' in C. Pelling, ed., *Characterization and Individuality in Greek Literature*, 83–99. Oxford.
Eckstein, F. 1974. *Handwerk: Die Aussagen des frühgriechischen Epos*. Göttingen (Archaeologia Homerica L).
Eco, U. 1976. *A Theory of Semiotics*. Bloomington, Indiana.
Edmunds, L. 1993. *Myth in Homer: A Handbook*. 2nd ed. Highland Park, New Jersey.
—Forthcoming. 'Oral Story-Telling and Hexameter Poetry in Archaic Greece,' *Actas of the V Coloquio Internacional de Filología Griega*.
Edmunds, L., ed. 1987. *Approaches to Greek Myth*. Baltimore.
Edmunds, S. 1990. *Homeric Nepios*. New York.
Edwards, G. P. 1971. *The Language of Hesiod in its Traditional Context*. Oxford.
Edwards M. W. 1966. 'Some Features of Homeric Craftmanship,' *Transactions of the American Philological Association* 97, 115–79.
—1968. 'Some Stylistic Notes on *Iliad* XVIII,' *American Journal of Philology* 89, 257–83.
—1980. 'Conventionality and Individuality in *Iliad* 1,' *Harvard Studies in Classical Philology* 84, 1–28.
—1986a. 'The Conventions of a Homeric Funeral,' in J. H. Betts, J. T. Hooker, and J. R. Green, eds., *Studies in Honour of T. B. L. Webster*, 84–92. Bristol.
—1986b. 'Homer and Oral Tradition: The Formula, Part I,' *Oral Tradition* 1, 171–230.
—1987. *Homer: Poet of the Iliad*. Baltimore.
—1988. 'Homer and Oral Tradition: The Formula, Part II,' *Oral Tradition* 3, 11–60.
—1991. *The Iliad: A Commentary* II. *Books 17–20*. Cambridge.
—1992. 'Homer and Oral Tradition: The Type-Scene,' *Oral Tradition* 7, 284–330.
Effe, B. 1975. 'Entstehung und Funktion "Personaler" Erzählweisen in der Erzählliteratur der Antike,' *Poetica* 7, 135–57.
Emlyn-Jones, C. 1986. 'True and Lying Tales in the *Odyssey*,' *Greece and Rome* 33, 1–10.
Erbse, H. 1959. 'Über Aristarchs Iliasausgaben,' *Hermes* 87, 275–303.
—1960. *Beiträge zur Überlieferung der Iliasscholen*. Munich (Zetemata 24).
—1969–88. *Scholia Graeca in Homeri Iliadem* (*scholia vetera*). 7 vols. Berlin.
Evelyn-White, H. G. 1914. *Hesiod, The Homeric Hymns, and Homerica*. Cambridge, Mass.

Fantham, E., H. Foley, N. Kampen, S. Pomeroy, and H. A. Shapiro, eds. 1994. *Women in the Classical World: Image and Text*. Oxford.
Fantuzzi, M. 1980. 'Oralità, scrittura, auralita: Gli studi sulle tecniche della communicazione nella Grecia antica (1960–1980),' *Lingua e Stile* 15.4, 593–612.
—1988. *Ricerche su Apollonio Rodio*. Rome.
Faraone, C. 1987. 'Hephaestus the Magician and Near Eastern Parallels for Alcinous' Watchdogs.' *Greek, Roman and Byzantine Studies* 28, 257–80.
Fell, M., C. Schafer, L. Wierschowski, eds. 1994. *Databanken in der Alten Geschichte*. St. Katharinen (Computer und Antike b. II).
Felson-Rubin, N. 1994. *Regarding Penelope: From Character to Poetics*. Princeton.
Fenik, B. 1964. *Iliad X and the Rhesus*. Brussels.
—1968. *Typical Battle Scenes in the Iliad*. Wiesbaden.
—1974. *Studies in the Odyssey*. Stuttgart (*Hermes* Einzelschrift 30).
Fentress, J., and C. Wickham. 1992. *Social Memory*. Oxford.
Fick, A. 1885. 'Die Ursprüngliche Sprache der Homerischen Hymnen,' *Beiträge zur Kunde der Indogermanischen Sprachen* 9, 195–246.
Finkelberg, M. 1986. 'Is κλέος ἄφθιτον a Homeric Formula?' *Classical Quarterly* 36, 1–5.

—1989. 'Formulaic and Nonformulaic Elements in Homer,' *Classical Philology* 84, 179–87.
—1990. 'A Creative Oral Poet and the Muse,' *American Journal of Philology* 111, 293–303.
—1991. 'Royal Succession in Heroic Greece,' *Classical Quarterly* 41, 303–316.
Finley, M. I. 1957. 'Homer and Mycenae: Property and Tenure,' *Historia* 6, 133–59 (reprinted in Finley 1982, 213–32).
—1968. 'The Alienability of Land in Ancient Greece,' *Eirene* 7, 25–32.
—1970. *Early Greece: The Bronze and Archaic Ages*. London.
—1978. *The World of Odysseus*. Revised ed. New York.
—1982. *Economy and Society in Ancient Greece*, ed. B. D. Shaw and R. P. Saller. New York.
Finley, M., J. L. Caskey, G. S. Kirk, and D. L. Page. 1964. 'The Trojan War,' *Journal of Hellenic Studies* 84, 1–20.
Finnegan, R. 1977. *Oral Poetry: Its Nature, Significance, and Social Context*. Cambridge.
Fittschen, K. 1969. *Untersuchungen zum Beginn der Sagendarstellungen bei den Griechen*. Berlin.
—1973. *Bildkunst: der Schild des Achilleus*. Göttingen (Archaeologia Homerica N, Teil 1).
Flaig, E. 1993. 'Die spartanische Abstimmung nach der Lautstärke. Überlegungen zu Thukydides 1, 87,' *Historia* 42, 139–160.
—1994. 'Das Konsensprinzip im homerischen Olymp. Überlegungen zum göttlichen Entscheidungsprozess Ilias 4.1–72,' *Hermes* 122, 13–31.
Foley, H. P., ed. 1994. *The Homeric Hymn to Demeter: Translation, Commentary and Interpretive Essays*. Princeton.
Foley, J. M. 1985. *Oral-Formulaic Theory and Research: An Introduction and Annotated Bibliography*. New York.
—1988. *The Theory of Oral Composition: History and Methodology*. Bloomington, Indiana.
—1990. *Traditional Oral Epic: The Odyssey, Beowulf, and the Serbo-Croatian Return Song*. Berkeley.
—1991. *Immanent Art: From Structure to Meaning in Traditional Oral Epic*. Bloomington, Indiana.
—1995. *The Singer of Tales in Performance*. Bloomington, Indiana.
Ford, A. 1988. 'The Classical Definition of ΡΑΨΩΔΙΑ,' *Classical Philology* 83, 300–307.
—1992. *Homer. Poetry of the Past*. Ithaca, New York.
Forderer, M. 1971. *Anfang und Ende der abendlandische Lyrik: Untersuchungen zum homerischen Apollonhymnus und zu Anise Koltz*. Amsterdam.
Förstel, K. 1979. *Untersuchungen zum homerischen Apollonhymnos*. Bochum.
Foster, B. 1993. *Before the Muses: An Anthology of Akkadian Literature*. Bethesda, Maryland.
Fowler, A. 1982. *Kinds of Literature*. Cambridge, Mass.
Fowler, D. 1990. 'Deviant Focalisation in Virgil's *Aeneid*,' *Proceedings of the Cambridge Philological Society* n.s. 36, 42–63.
Foxhall, L. 1995. 'Bronze to iron.' *Annual of the British School at Athens* 90, 239–50.
Foxhall, L., and J. K. Davies, eds. 1984. *The Trojan War: Its Historicity and Context*. Bristol.
Fränkel, H. 1926. 'Die kallimachische und der homerische Hexameter,' *Göttinger Gelehrte Nachträge*, 127–229 (reprinted in Fränkel 1968, 100–156).
—1968. *Wege und Formen frügriechischen Denkens*. 3rd ed. Munich.
—1975. *Early Greek Poetry and Philosophy*. Trs. M. Hadas and J. Willis. New York.
Friedländer, L. 1853. *Die Homerische Kritik von Wolf bis Grote*. Berlin.
Friedländer, P. 1966. 'Das Proömium von Hesiods Theogonie,' in E. Heitsch, ed., *Hesiod*, 277–94. Darmstadt.
Friedrich, P., and J. Redfield. 1978. 'Speech as a Personality Symbol: the Case of Achilles,' *Language* 54, 263–88.
Friis Johansen, K. 1967. *The Iliad in Early Greek Art*. Copenhagen.
Fröhder, D. 1994. *Die dichterische Form der Homerischen Hymnen untersucht am Typus der mittelgroßen Preislieder*. Hildesheim (Spudasmata 53).

Gagarin, M. 1986. *Early Greek Law*. Berkeley.

Gaisser, J. H. 1969. 'A Structural Analysis of the Digressions in the *Iliad* and the *Odyssey*,' *Harvard Studies in Classical Philology* 73, 1–43.

—1974. 'Noun-Epithet Combinations in the Homeric Hymn to Demeter,' *Transactions of the American Philological Association* 104, 113–27.

Gale, N. H., ed. 1991. *Bronze Age Trade in the Mediterranean. Papers Presented at the Conference Held at Rowley House, Oxford, in December 1989*. Jonsered.

Galinsky, K. 1992. 'The Current State of the Interpretation of Roman Poetry and the Contemporary Critical Scene,' in K. Galinsky, ed., *The Interpretation of Roman Poetry: Empiricism or Hermeneutics?* Frankfurt am Main.

Gallant, T. W. 1982. 'Agricultural Systems, Land Tenure, and the Reforms of Solon,' *Annual of the British School at Athens* 77, 111–24.

Gantz, T. 1993. *Early Greek Myth*. Baltimore.

García-Ramón, J. L. 1975. *Les origines postmycéniennes du groupe dialectal Eolien*. Salamanca (*Minos* Suppl. 6).

Gardiner, J., and J. Maier, trs. 1984. *Gilgamesh. Translated from the Sîn-leqi-unninni Version*. New York.

Garlan, Y. 1978. 'Signification historique de la piraterie grecque,' *Dialogues d'histoire ancienne* 4, 1–16.

—1988. *Slavery in Ancient Greece*. Trs. Janet Lloyd. Ithaca, New York.

—1989. *Guerre et économie en Grèce ancienne*. Paris.

Garnsey, P., K. Hopkins, and C. R. Whittaker, eds. 1983. *Trade in the Ancient Economy*. Cambridge.

Garrison, D. H. 1989. 'The Great Wanderings of Odysseus: Theme and Structure,' in R. F. Sutton, Jr., ed., *Daidalikon: Studies in Memory of Raymond V. Schoder, S. J.*, 117–23. Waucanda, Illinois.

Gelb, I. J. 1963. *A Study of Writing*. Chicago.

Gelzer, T. 1987. 'Bemerkungen zum Homerischen Ares-Hymnus (Hom. Hy. 8),' *Museum Helveticum* 44, 150–167.

Gemoll, A., ed. 1886. *Die Homerischen Hymnen*. Leipzig.

Genette, G. 1980. *Narrative Discourse. An Essay in Method*. Trs. J. E. Lewin. Ithaca, New York.

Gentili, B. and P. Giannini. 1977. 'Preistoria e formazione dell'esametro,' *Quaderni Urbinati di Cultura Classica* 26:7–52.

Germain, G. 1954. *Genèse de l'Odyssée: le fantastique et le sacré*. Paris.

Giovannini, A. 1969. *Étude historique sur les origines du Catalogue des Vaissaux*. Berne.

—1989. *Vom frühen Griechentums bis zur römischen Kaiserzeit*. Stuttgart.

Givón, T. 1984. *Syntax: Functional-Typological Introduction* I. Amsterdam.

Glenn, J. 1971. 'The Polyphemus Folktale and Homer's *Kyklôpeia*,' *Transactions of the American Philological Association* 102, 133–81.

—1978. 'The Polyphemus Myth: Its Origin and Interpretation,' *Greece and Rome* 25, 141–55.

Godart, L. 1995. 'Una iscrizione in lineare B del xvii secolo a.c. ad Olimpia,' *Rendiconti dei Academei dei Lincei* series 9, vol. 6, 445–47.

Goldhill, S. 1991. *The Poet's Voice: Essays on Poetics and Greek Literature*. Cambridge.

—1994. 'The Failure of Exemplarity,' in de Jong and Sullivan, eds., 51–70.

Gonda, J. 1956. *The Character of IE Moods*. Wiesbaden.

Goold, G. P. 1960. 'Homer and the Alphabet,' *Transactions of the American Philological Association* 91, 272–291.

Gordon, C. 1955. *Homer and Bible. The Origin and Character of East Mediterranean Literature*. Cincinnati.

—1962. *Before the Bible. The Common Background of Greek and Hebrew Civilizations*. New York.

Graf, F. 1991. 'Mythenforschung und Religionswissenschaft im Zusammenhang mit Homer,' in Latacz, ed., 1991a, 331–62.
Grafton, A. 1991. *Defenders of the Text. The Traditions of Scholarship in an Age of Science, 1450–1800.* Cambridge, Mass.
Graham, A. J. 1964. *Colony and Mother City in Ancient Greece.* New York.
—1982. 'The Colonial Expansion of Greece,' *Cambridge Ancient History* III.3, 83–162. 2nd ed. Cambridge.
—1995. 'The *Odyssey*, History, and Women,' in B. Cohen, ed., 3–16.
Greenberg, N. A. 1985. 'Appendix: Language, Meter, and Sense in Theognis (The Role of *Agathos* "Noble, Good").' In T. J. Figueira and G. Nagy, eds., *Theognis of Megara: Poetry and the Polis*, 245–260. Baltimore.
Greenhalgh, P. A. L. 1972. 'Patriotism in the Homeric World,' *Historia* 21, 528–37.
—1973. *Early Greek Warfare.* Cambridge.
—1982. 'The Homeric *Therapon* and *Opaon* and Their Historical Implications,' *Bulletin of the Institute of Classical Studies* 29, 81–90.
Greimas, A. J., and J. Courtés. 1982. *Semiotics and Language: An Analytical Dictionary.* Trs. L. Crist and D. Patte. Bloomington, Indiana.
Gresseth, G. K. 1975. 'The Gilgamesh Epic and Homer,' *Classical Journal* 70, 1–18.
Griffin, J. 1980. *Homer on Life and Death.* Oxford.
—1986. 'Homeric Words and Speakers,' *Journal of Hellenic Studies* 106, 36–57.
—1995. *Homer: Iliad IX.* Oxford.
Grimm, W. 1857. 'Die Sage von Polyphem,' *Abhandlungen der Königlichen Akademie der Wissenschaften zu Berlin, philologische-historische Klasse,* 1–30 = *Kleinere Schriften* 4 (Gütersloh, 1887) 428–62.
Groningen, B. A. van. 1958. *La composition littéraire archaïque grecque.* Amsterdam.
Grote, G. 1869. *A History of Greece.* 12 vols. New edition. London.
Grotjahn, R., ed. 1981. *Hexameter Studies.* Bochum (*Quantitative Linguistics* 9).
Gschnitzer, F. 1976. *Studien zur griechischen Terminologie der Sklaverei* II. Wiesbaden.
—1981. *Griechische Sozialgeschichte von der mykenischen bis zum Ausgang der klassischen Zeit.* Wiesbaden.
—1983. 'Der Rat in der Volksversammlung. Ein Beitrag des homerischen Epos zur griechischen Verfassungsgeschichte,' in Händel and Meid, eds., 151–63.
—1991. 'Zur homerischen Staats- und Gesellschaftsordnung,' in Latacz , ed., 1991a, 182–204.
Gurney, O. R. 1990. *The Hittites.* 2nd ed. London.
Güterbock, H. 1946. *Kumarbi. Mythen vom hurritischen Kronos aus den hethitischen Fragmenten zusammengesetzt, übersetzt und erklärt.* Zürich (Istanbuler Schriften 16).
—1983. 'Hittites and the Aegean World: Part I. The Ahhiyawa Problem Reconsidered,' *American Journal of Archaeology* 87, 133–38.
—1986. 'Troy in Hittite Texts? Wilusa, Ahhiyawa, and Hittite History,' in Mellink, ed., 33–44.

Hackman, O. 1904. *Die Polyphemsage in der Volksüberlieferung.* Helsingfors.
Haft, A. J. 1984. 'Odysseus, Idomeneus and Meriones: The Cretan Lies of *Odyssey* 13–19,' *Classical Journal* 79, 289–306.
Hagel, S. 1994–95. 'Zu den Konstituenten des griechischen Hexameters,' *Wiener Studien* 107/108, 77–108.
Hägg, R., ed. 1983. *The Greek Renaissance of the Eighth Century B.C.* Stockholm.
Hägg, R., and N. Marinatos, eds. 1981. *Sanctuaries and Cult in the Aegean Bronze Age.* Stockholm.
Hägg, R., N. Marinatos, and G. Nordquist, eds. 1988. *Early Greek Cult Practice.* Stockholm.

Hainsworth, J. B. 1962. 'The Homeric Formula and the Problem of its Transmission,' *Bulletin of the Institute of Classical Studies* 9, 57–68.

—1964. 'Structure and Content in Epic Formulae: the Question of the Unique Expression,' *Classical Quarterly* 14, 155–64.

—1968. *The Flexibility of the Homeric Formula.* Oxford.

—1970. 'The Criticism of an Oral Homer,' *Journal of Hellenic Studies* 90, 90–98.

—1978. 'Good and Bad Formulae,' in B. Fenik, ed., *Homer: Tradition and Invention*, 41–50. Leiden.

—1981. 'Criteri di oralità nella poesia arcaica non omerica,' in C. Brillante et al., *I poemi epici rapsodici non omerici e la tradizione orale*, 3–27. Padua.

—1988. 'The Epic Dialect,' in Heubeck et al., eds., 24–32.

—1991. *The Idea of Epic.* Berkeley, 1991.

—1993. *The Iliad: A Commentary* III. *Books 9–12.* Cambridge.

Halliday, M. A. K., and R. Hassan. 1976. *Cohesion in English.* London.

Händel, P., and W. Meid, eds. 1983. *Festschrift für Robert Muth.* Innsbruck.

Hansen, M. H., ed. 1993. *The Ancient Greek City-State.* Copenhagen.

Hansen, W. 1976. 'The Story of the Sailor Who Went Inland,' in L. Dégh, H. Glassie, and F. Oinas, eds., *Folklore Today: A Festschrift for Richard M. Dorson*, 221–30. Bloomington, Indiana.

—1977. 'Odysseus' Last Journey,' *Quaderni Urbinati di Cultura Classica* 24, 27–48.

—1983. 'Greek Mythology and the Study of the Ancient Greek Oral Story,' *Journal of Folklore Research* 20, 101–112.

—1988. 'Folklore,' in M. Grant and R. Kitzinger eds., *Civilization of the Ancient Mediterranean: Greece and Rome* II, 1121–30. New York.

—1990. 'Odysseus and the Oar: A Folkloric Approach,' in L. Edmunds, ed., 241–72.

—1995. 'The Stuck Couple in Ancient Greece,' *FOAFtale News* 36 (January) 2–3.

Hanson, V. D. 1995. *The Other Greeks. The Family Farm and the Agrarian Roots of Western Civilization.* New York.

Hare, R. M. 1952. *The Language of Morals.* Oxford.

Harris, W. V. 1989. *Ancient Literacy.* Cambridge, Mass.

Hartel, W. 1873. *Homerische Studien* [i]. *Beiträge zur homerischen Prosodie und Metrik.* 2nd ed. Berlin.

Harvey, A. E. 1955. 'The Classification of Greek Lyric Poetry,' *Classical Quarterly* n.s. 5, 157–75.

Hasebroek, J. 1931. *Griechische Wirtschafts- und Gesellschaftsgeschichte bis zur Perserzeit.* Tübingen.

Haslam, M. 1991. 'Kleitias, Stesichoros, and the Jar of Dionysos,' *Transactions of the American Philological Association* 121, 35–45.

—1994. 'The Homer Lexicon of Apollonius Sophista I: Composition and Constituents.' *Classical Philology* 89, 1–45.

Havelock, E. 1963. *Preface to Plato.* Oxford.

—1978. *The Greek Concept of Justice.* Cambridge, Mass.

—1986. *The Muse Learns to Write.* New Haven, Conn.

Held, G. F. 1987. 'Phoinix, Agamemnon and Achilleus: Parables and Paradeigmata,' *Classical Quarterly* 37, 249–61.

Heldmann, K. 1982. *Die Niederlage Homers im Dichterwettstreit mit Hesiod.* Göttingen.

Hellwig, B. 1964. *Raum und Zeit.* Hildesheim.

Helms, M. 1988. *Ulysses' Sail. An Ethnographic Odyssey of Power, Knowledge, and Geographical Distance.* Princeton.

Hennig, D. 1980. 'Grundbesitz bei Homer und Hesiod,' *Chiron* 10, 35–52.

Henrichs, A. 1971. 'Scholia Minora zu Homer I, II, III,' *Zeitschrift für Papyrologie und Epigraphik* 7, 97–149, 229–60.

—1974. 'Scholia Minora zu Homer IV,' *Zeitschrift für Papyrologie und Epigraphik* 12, 17–43.

Herman, G. 1987. *Ritualised Friendship and the Greek City*. Cambridge.
Hermann, G. 1806. *Homeri Hymni et Epigrammata*. Leipzig.
Herter, H. 1981. 'L'Inno a Hermes alla luce della poesia orale,' in Brillante et al., eds., 183–201.
Heubeck, A. 1950. 'Studien zur Struktur der *Ilias*,' cited from reprint in J. Latacz, ed., 1991b, 450–74.
—1974. *Die homerische Frage*. Darmstadt.
—1978. 'Homeric studies today,' in B. C. Fenik, ed., *Homer: Tradition and Invention*, 1–17. Leiden.
—1979. *Schrift*. Göttingen (Archaeologica Homerica 3.X).
Heubeck, A., and A. Hoekstra. 1989. *A Commentary on Homer's Odyssey* II. *Books IX–XVI*. Oxford.
Heubeck, A., S. West, and J. B. Hainsworth. 1988. *A Commentary on Homer's Odyssey* I. *Books I–VIII*. Oxford.
Higbie, C. 1990. *Measure and Music. Enjambement and Sentence Structure in the Iliad*. Oxford.
Hiller, S. 1990. 'The Miniature Frieze in the West House—Evidence for Minoan Poetry?,' in D. A. Hardy, ed., *Thera and the Aegean World* III.1: *Archaeology*, 229–36. London.
Himmelmann-Wildschütz, N. 1961. 'Nach der Schlacht,' *Marburger Winckelmanns-programm*: 1–5.
Hodkinson, S. 1988. 'Animal Husbandry in the Greek Polis,' in C. R. Whittaker, ed., *Pastoral Economies in Classical Antiquity*, 35–74. Cambridge (*Proceedings of the Camridge Philological Society* Supp. Vol.).
Hoekstra, A. 1965. *Homeric Modifications of Formulaic Prototypes*. Amsterdam.
—1969. *The Sub-Epic Stage of the Formulaic Tradition*. Amsterdam.
—1981. *Epic Verse Before Homer*. Amsterdam.
Hoffmann, W. 1956. 'Die Polis bei Homer,' in *Festschrift Bruno Snell*, 153–65. Munich.
Hoffner, H. A., Jr. 1990. *Hittite Myths*. Atlanta.
Hogan, J. C. 1973. 'Aristotle's Criticism of Homer in the *Poetics*,' *Classical Philology* 68, 95–108.
Holoka, J. P. 1991. 'Homer, Oral Poetry Theory, and Comparative Literature: Major Trends and Controversies in Twentieth-Century Criticism,' in Latacz, ed., 1991a, 456–81.
Hölscher, U. 1990. *Die Odyssee. Epos zwischen Märchen und Roman*. 3rd ed. Munich.
—1991. 'Zur Erforschung der Strukturen in der Odyssee,' in Latacz, ed., 1991a, 415–22.
Hood, S. 1995. 'The Bronze Age Context of Homer,' in Carter and Morris, eds., 25–32.
Hooker, J. T. 1977. *The Language and Text of the Lesbian Poets*. Innsbruck.
Hope Simpson, R., and J. F. Lazenby. 1970. *The Catalogue of Ships in Homer's Iliad*. Oxford.
Horrocks, G. C. 1980. 'The Antiquity of the Greek Epic Tradition: Some New Evidence,' *Proceedings of the Cambridge Philological Society* n.s. 26, 1–11.
—1984. *Space and Time in Homer. Prepositional and Adverbial Particles in the Greek Epic*. Salem, New Hampshire.
—1987. 'The Ionian Epic Tradition: Was there an Aeolic Phase in its Development?,' in Killen et al., eds., 269–94.
Humbert, J. 1936. *Homère: Hymnes*. Paris.
Hunt, R. 1981. 'Satiric Elements in Hesiod's *Works and Days*,' *Helios* 8, 29–40.
Hunter, R. 1993. *The Argonautica of Apollonius. Literary Studies*. Cambridge.
Hurwit, J. M. 1985. *The Art and Culture of Early Greece, 1100–480 B.C.* Ithaca, New York.
Hymes, D. 1974. *Foundations in Sociolinguistics: An Ethnographic Approach*. Philadelphia.

Iakovidis, S. 1970. *Perati.* 3 vols. Athens.
Immerwahr, S. A. 1990. *Aegean Painting in the Bronze Age.* University Park, Pennsylvania.
Ingalls, W. B. 1972. 'Another Dimension of the Homeric Formula,' *Phoenix* 26: 111–22.
Isager, S., and J. E. Skydsgaard. 1992. *Ancient Greek Agriculture.* London.

Jachmann, G. 1949. *Vom frühalexandrinischen Homertext.* Göttingen (Nachrichten der Akademie der Wissenschaften in Göttingen, philologisch-historische Klasse 7).
Jaeger, W. 1939–45. *Paideia.* Trs. G. Highet. 3 vols.
Jahn, T. 1987. *Zum Wortfeld 'Seele-Geist' in der Sprache Homers.* Munich.
James, P., I. Thorpe, N. Kokkinos, N. Morkot, and J. Frankish. 1991. *Centuries of Darkness; A Challenge to the Conventional Chronology of Old World Archaeology.* London.
Janko, R. 1981. 'The Structure of the Homeric Hymns: A Study in Genre,' *Hermes* 109, 9–24.
—1982. *Homer, Hesiod and the Hymns: Diachronic Development in Epic Diction.* Cambridge.
—1990. 'The *Iliad* and its Editors: Dictation and Redaction,' *Classical Antiquity* 9, 326–34.
—1992. *The Iliad: A Commentary* IV. *Books 13–16.* Cambridge.
Jebb, R. J. 1887. *Homer: An Introduction to the Iliad and the Odyssey.* London (reprinted Port Washington, New York, 1969).
Jeffery, L. H. 1990. *The Local Scripts of Archaic Greece.* Revised ed., with supplement by A. W. Johnston. Oxford.
Jensen, M. S. 1980. *The Homeric Question and the Oral-Formulaic Theory.* Copenhagen.
Job, U. 1981. 'Annotated Bibliography on the Statistical Study of Hexameter Verse,' in Grotjahn, ed., 226–62.
Johnson, W. R. 1994. 'Information and Form: Homer, Achilles, and Statius,' in S. M. Oberhelman, V. Kelly, and R. J. Golsan, eds., *Epic and Epoch: Essays on the Interpretation and History of a Genre,* 25–39. Lubbock, Texas (Studies in Comparative Literature 4).
Jung, C. G., and K. Kerényi. 1967. 'The Psychological Aspects of the Kore,' in *Essays on a Science of Mythology: The Myth of the Divine Child,* 156–77. Princeton.

Kahane, A. 1992. 'The First Word of the *Odyssey*,' *Transactions of the American Philological Association* 122, 115–31.
—1994. *The Interpretation of Order. A Study in the Poetics of Homeric Repetition.* Oxford.
Kahn, L. 1978. *Hermès passé ou les ambiguïtés de la communication.* Paris.
Kakridis, J. T. 1949. *Homeric Researches.* Lund.
—1971. *Homer Revisited.* Lund.
Kannicht, R. 1982. 'Poetry and Art. Homer and the Monuments Afresh,' *Classical Antiquity* 1, 70–86.
Kanta, A. 1991. 'Cult, continuity and the evidence of pottery at the sanctuary of Syme Viannou, Crete,' in Musti et al., eds., 479–505.
Karageorghis, V., ed. 1994. *Cyprus in the 11th century B.C. Proceedings of the International Symposium, 30–31 Oct. 1993.* Athens and Nicosia.
Karageorghis, V., and E. Vermeule. 1982. *Mycenaean Pictorial Vase Painting.* Cambridge, Mass.
Karavites, P., and T. Wren. 1992. *Promise-Giving and Treaty-Making: Homer and the Near East.* Leiden (*Mnemosyne* Supplement 119).
Katz, M. 1991. *Penelope's Renown: Meaning and Indeterminacy in the Odyssey.* Princeton.
Kearsley, R. A. 1995. 'The Greek Geometric wares from Al Mina levels 10–8,' *Mediterranean Archaeology* 8, 7–81.

Kennedy, G. 1963. *The Art of Persuasion in Greece*. Princeton.
Kenny, A. J. P. 1982. *The Computation of Style: An Introduction to Statistics for Students of Literature and Humanities*. Oxford.
Kerényi, K. 1967. 'Kore,' in C. G. Jung and K. Kerényi, *Essays on a Science of Mythology: The Myth of the Divine Child*, 101–155. Princeton.
Keyssner, K. 1932. *Gottesvorstellung und Lebensauffassung im griechischen Hymnus*. Stuttgart (Würzburger Studien zur Altertumswissenschaft 2).
Kilian, K. 1987. 'L'architecture des résidences mycéniennes: origine et extension d'une structure du pouvoir politique pendant l'âge du Bronze récent,' in E. Lévy, ed., *Le système palatial en Orient, en Grèce et à Rome*, 203–217. Strasbourg.
—1988. 'The Emergence of *Wanax* Ideology in the Mycenaean Palaces,' *Oxford Journal of Archaeology* 7, 291–302
Killen, J. T. 1985. 'The Linear B Tablets and the Mycenaean Economy,' in A. Morpurgo Davies and Y. Duhoux, eds., *Linear B: A 1984 Survey*, 241–305. Louvain.
—1994. 'Thebes Sealings, Knossos Tablets and Mycenaean State Banquets,' *Bulletin of the Institute of Classical Studies* 41, 67–84.
—1995. 'Some Further Thoughts on "Collectors,"' in Laffineur and Niemeier, eds., 213–26.
Killen, J. T., J. L. Melena, and J.-P. Olivier, eds. 1987. *Studies in Mycenaean and Classical Greek Presented to John Chadwick*. Salamanca (*Minos* 20–22).
Kindstrand, J. F. 1973. *Homer in der zweiten Sophistik*. Uppsala (Graeca Upsaliensia 7).
Kiparsky, P. 1976. 'Oral poetry: some linguistic and typological considerations,' in Stolz and Shannon, eds., 73–106.
Kirk, G. S. 1960. 'Objective Dating Criteria in Homer,' *Museum Helveticum* 17, 189–205.
—1962. *The Songs of Homer*. Cambridge.
—1966a. 'Studies in Some Technical Aspects of Homeric Style II. Verse-Structure and Sentence-Structure in Homer,' *Yale Classical Studies* 20, 105–52.
—1966b. 'The Structure of the Homeric Hexameter,' *Yale Classical Studies* 20, 76–104.
—1968. 'War and the Warrior in the Homeric Poems,' in J.-P. Vernant, ed., *Problèmes de la guerre en Grèce ancienne*, 93–117. Paris.
—1975. 'The Homeric Poems as History,' in *Cambridge Ancient History* II.2, 820–50. 2nd ed. Cambridge.
—1976. *Homer and the Oral Tradition*. Cambridge.
—1981. 'Orality and Structure in the Homeric Hymn to Apollo,' in Brillante et al., eds., 163–81.
—1985. *The Iliad: A Commentary* I. *Books 1–4*. Cambridge.
—1990. *The Iliad: A Commentary* II. *Books 5–8*. Cambridge.
Kirk, G. S., ed. 1964. *The Language and Background of Homer*. Cambridge.
Kirk, G. S., J. E. Raven, and M. Schofield. 1983. *The Presocratic Philosophers*. 2nd ed. Cambridge.
Kitto, H. D. F. 1966. *Poiesis: Structure and Thought*. Berkeley.
Koch, P., and W. Oesterreicher. 1985. 'Sprache der Nähe—Sprache der Distanz. Mündlichkeit und Schriftlichkeit im Spannungsfeld von Sprachtheorie und Sprachgeschichte,' *Romanistisches Jahrbuch* 36, 15–43.
Koljevic, S. 1980. *The Epic in the Making*. Oxford.
Koller, H. 1956. 'Das kitharodische Prooimion: Eine formgeschichtliche Untersuchung,' *Philologus* 100, 159–206.
Kopcke, G. 1990. *Handel*. Göttingen (Archaeologia Homerica 2.M).
Korfmann, M. 1995. 'Troia: A Residential and Trading City at the Dardanelles,'

in W.-D. Niemeier and R. Laffineur, eds., *POLITEIA. Society and State in the Aegaean Bronze Age*, 173–83. Liège (Aegaeum 12).
Koster, S. 1970. *Antike Epostheorien.* Wiesbaden.
Krafft, F. 1963. *Vergleichende Untersuchungen zu Homer und Hesiod.* Göttingen.
Kraiker, W., and K. Kübler. 1939. *Kerameikos* I. Berlin.
Kretschmer, P. 1896. *Einleitung in die Geschichte der Griechischen Sprache.* Göttingen.
Krischer, T. 1971. *Formale Konventionen der homerischen Epik.* Munich.
Kromayer, J., and G. Veith. 1928. *Heerwesen und Kriegsführung der Griechen und Römer.* Munich.
Kübler, K. 1943. *Kerameikos* IV. Berlin.
—1954. *Kerameikos* V.1. Berlin.
Kühner, R, and B. Gerth. 1904. *Ausführliche Grammatik der griechischen Sprache. Zweiter Teil: Satzlehre* II. Hanover.
Kullmann, W. 1960. *Die Quellen der Ilias.* Wiesbaden.
—1968. 'Vergangenheit und Zukunft in der Ilias,' *Poetica* 2, 15–37.
—1981. 'Zur Methode der Neoanalyse in der Homerforschung,' *Wiener Studien* 15, 5–42.
—1984. 'Oral Poetry Theory and Neoanalysis in Homeric Research,' *Greek, Roman and Byzantine Studies* 25, 307–323.
—1991. 'Eregebnisse der motivgeschichtlichen Forschung zu Homer (Neoanalyse),' in Latacz, ed., 1991a, 425–55.
—1992. *Homerische Motive.* Stuttgart.
Kumpf, M. M. 1984. *Four Indices of Homeric Hapax Legomena.* Hildesheim.

Lacey, W. K. 1968. *The Family in Classical Greece.* London.
Lachmann, K. 1847. *Betrachtungen über Homers Ilias.* Berlin.
Lamberton, R. 1983. *Porphyry on the Cave of the Nymphs.* Barrytown, New York.
—1986. *Homer the Theologian.* Berkeley.
—1988. *Hesiod.* New Haven, Conn.
Lamberton, R., and J. J. Keaney, eds. 1992. *Homer's Ancient Readers.* Princeton.
Lambrinoudakis, V. G. 1988. 'Veneration of ancestors in Geometric Naxos,' in Hägg and Marinatos, eds., 235–45.
Lang, A. 1893. *Homer and the Epic.* London (reprinted New York, 1971).
—1919. *The World of Homer.* London.
Lang, M. 1989. 'Unreal Conditions in Homeric Narrative,' *Greek, Roman and Byzantine Studies* 30, 5–26.
La Roche, J. 1869–93. *Homerische Untersuchungen.* 2 vols. Leipzig (reprinted Hildesheim, 1975).
—1898. 'Zahlenverhältnisse im homerischen Vers,' *Wiener Studien* 20, 1–69.
Latacz, J. 1977. *Kampfparänese, Kampfdarstellung und Kampfwirklichkeit in der Ilias.*—1979. *Homer: Tradition und Neuerung.* Darmstadt.
—1984. 'Das Menschenbild Homers,' *Gymnasium* 91, 15–39.
—1985. *Homer. Eine Einführung.* Munich. Translated as *Homer: His Art and His World.* J. Holoka. Ann Arbor, MI, 1996.
—1987. 'Frauengestalten bei Homer: Die Frau in der Gesellschaft,' in Olshausen, ed., 43–71.
Latacz, J., ed. 1979. *Homer. Tradition und Neuerung.* Darmstadt.
—1991a. *Zweihundert Jahre Homer-Forschung: Rückblick und Ausblick.* Stuttgart (Colloquium Rauricum 2).
—ed., 1991b. *Homer: die Dichtung und ihre Deutung.* Darmstadt (Wege der Forsching 634).
Leaf, W. 1892. *A Companion to the Iliad for English Readers.* London.
—1900–1902. *The Iliad.* 2nd ed. London.
Lefkowitz, M. R. 1981. *The Lives of the Greek Poets.* Baltimore.

Lenz, J. R. 1993. 'Kings and the Ideology of Kingship in Early Greece (c. 1200–700 B.C.): Epic, Archaeology, and History.' Unpublished Ph.D. dissertation, Columbia University.

Lenz, L. 1975. *Der homerische Aphroditehymnus und die Aristie des Aineias in der Ilias*. Bonn.

Lesky, A. 1967. *Homeros* (separate publication from Supplement-Band XI of Pauly's Realencyclopaedia). Stuttgart.

Létoublon, F. 1983. 'Le miroir et la boucle,' *Poétique* 53:19–35.

Lévy, E. 1983. '*Astu* et polis dans l'*Iliade*,' *Ktèma* 8, 55–73.

—1985. '*Astos* et *politès* d'Homère à Hérodote,' *Ktèma* 10, 53–66.

Lichtheim, M. 1973–80. *Ancient Egyptian Literature*. 3 vols. Berkeley.

Lindgren, M. 1973. *The People of Pylos*. 2 vols. Uppsala.

Lohmann, D. 1970. *Die Komposition der Reden in der Ilias*. Berlin (Untersuchungen zur antiken Literatur und Geschichte, no. 6).

—1992. 'Homer als Erzaehler. Die Athla im 23. Buch der Ilias,' *Gymnasium* 99, 289–319.

Long, A. A. 1970. 'Morals and Values in Homer,' *Journal of Hellenic Studies* 90, 121–39.

Lord, A. B. 1953. 'Homer's Originality: Oral Dictated Texts,' *Transactions of the American Philological Association* 84:124–134 (reprinted in A. B. Lord 1991, 38–48).

—1960. *The Singer of Tales*. Cambridge, Mass.

—1962. 'Homer and Other Epic Poetry,' in Wace and Stubbings, eds., 179–214.

—1986. 'Perspectives on Recent Work on the Oral Traditional Formula,' *Oral Tradition* 1:467–503.

—1991. *Epic Singers and Oral Tradition*. Ithaca, New York.

—1995. *The Singer Resumes the Tale*. Ithaca, New York.

Lord, M. L. 1967. 'Withdrawal and Return: An Epic Story Pattern in the Homeric Hymn to Demeter and in the Homeric Patterns,' *Classical Journal* 62, 241–48 (reprinted in H. P. Foley, ed., 1994, 181–89).

—1968. 'Homer as an Oral Poet,' *Harvard Studies in Classical Philology* 72, 1–46.

Lorimer, H. L. 1950. *Homer and the Monuments*. London.

Lowenstam S. 1992. 'The Use of Vase-Depictions in Homeric Studies,' *Transactions of the American Philological Association* 122, 165–98.

Ludwich, A. 1898. *Die Homervulgata als voralexandrinisch erwiesen*. Leipzig.

Lührs, D. 1992. *Untersuchungen zu den Athetesen Aristarchs in der Ilias und zu ihrer Behandlung im Corpus der exegetischen Scholien*. Hildesheim.

Lynn-George, M. 1988. *Epos: Word, Narrative and the Iliad*. Atlantic Highlands, New Jersey.

—1994. '"The Stem of the Full-Blown Flower:" Homeric Studies and Literary Theory,' *Phoenix* 48, 226–53.

Lyons, J. 1968. *Introduction to Theoretical Linguistics*. Cambridge.

Maas, M., and J. M. Snyder. 1989. *Stringed Instruments of Ancient Greece*. New Haven, Conn.

MacCary, W. T. 1982. *Childlike Achilles: Ontogeny and Phylogeny in the Iliad*. New York.

MacGillivray, A., and R. Barber, eds. 1984. *The Prehistoric Cyclades*. Edinburgh.

Machacek, G. 1994. 'The Occasional Contextual Appropriateness of Formulaic Diction in the Homeric Poems,' *American Journal of Philology* 115, 321–335.

Mackenzie, M., and C. Roueché, eds. 1989. *Images of Authority. Papers Presented to Joyce Reynolds on the Occasion of her Seventieth Birthday*. Cambridge (*Proceedings of the Cambridge Philological Society*, Supp. Vol. 16).

Macleod, C. W. 1983. *Collected Essays*. Oxford.

Maehler, H. 1963. *Die Auffassung des Dichterberufs im frühen Griechentum bis zur zeit Pindars*. Göttingen.

Magoun, F. P., Jr. 1953. 'The Oral-Formulaic Character of Anglo-Saxon Narrative Poetry,' *Speculum* 28, 446–67.

Malkin, I. 1989. 'Delphoi and the Founding of Social Order in Archaic Greece,' *Metis* 3, 129–53.

—1994. 'Inside and Outside: Colonization and the Formation of the Mother City,' *Annali di Archeologia e Storia Antica* n.s. 1, 1–9.

Manning, S. W. 1995. *The Absolute Chronology of the Aegean Early Bronze Age. Archaeology, Radiocarbon and History.* Sheffield.

Marg, W. 1976. 'Kampf und Tod in der *Ilias*,' *Würzburger Jahrbücher für die Altertumswissenschaft* 2.

Martin, R. P. 1984. 'Hesiod, Odysseus, and the Instruction of Princes,' *Transactions of the American Philological Association* 114, 29–48.

—1989. *The Language of Heroes. Speech and Performance in the Iliad.* Ithaca, New York.

—1993. 'Telemachus and the Last Hero Song,' *Colby Quarterly* 29, 222–40.

Martin, W. 1986. *Recent Theories of Narrative.* Ithaca, New York.

Martindale, C. 1992. *Redeeming the Text: Latin Poetry and the Hermeneutics of Reception.* Cambridge.

Matthews, V. J. 1974. *Panyassis of Halikarnassos.* Leiden.

Mauss, M. 1966. *The Gift.* Trs. I. Cunnison. London.

Mazarakis-Ainian, A. Forthcoming. *From Ruler's Dwelling to Temple.* Göteborg.

McCarter Jr., P. K. 1975. *The Antiquity of the Greek Alphabet and the Early Phoenician Scripts.* Missoula, Montana (Harvard Semitic Monographs 9).

McDonald, W. A., and C. G. Thomas. 1990. *Progress into the Past. The Rediscovery of Mycenaean Civilization.* 2nd ed. Bloomington, Indiana.

McDonald, W. A., W. D. E. Coulson, and J. J. Rosser. 1983. *Excavations at Nichoria in Southwest Greece* III: *Dark Age and Byzantine Periods.* Minneapolis.

McGowan, J. 1994. 'Postmodernism,' in M. Groden and M. Kreiswirth, eds., *The Johns Hopkins Guide to Literary Theory and Criticism.* Baltimore.

McLeod, W. 1966. 'Studies on Panyassis,' *Phoenix* 20, 95–110.

Mee, C. B. 1984. 'Mycenaeans and Troy,' in Foxhall and Davies, eds., 45–56.

Meillet, A. 1923. *Les origines indo-européennes des mètres grecs.* Paris.

—1937. *Introduction à l'étude comparative des langues indo-européennes.* 8th ed. Paris.

Meillet, A., and J. Vendryes. 1979. *Grammaire comparée des langues classiques.* 5th ed. Paris.

Meister, K. 1921. *Die Homerische Kunstspache.* Leipzig.

Mellink, M., ed. 1986. *Troy and the Trojan War.* Bryn Mawr, Pennsylvania.

Meyer, H. 1933. *Hymnische Stilelemente in der frühgriechischen Dichtung.* Würzburg.

Miller, A. M. 1979. 'The "Address to the Delian Maidens" in the Homeric Hymn to Apollo: Epilogue or Transition?' *Transactions of the American Philological Association* 109, 173–86.

—1985. *From Delos to Delphi: A Literary Study of the Homeric Hymn to Apollo.* Leiden.

Miller, D. G. 1982. *Homer and the Ionian Epic Tradition.* Innsbruck.

Millett, P. C. 1984. 'Hesiod and his World,' *Proceedings of the Cambridge Philological Society* n.s. 30, 84–115.

Minton, W. W. 1965. 'The Fallacy of the Structural Formula,' *Transactions of the American Philological Association* 96, 241–53.

—1970. 'The Proem-Hymn of Hesiod's *Theogony*,' *Transactions of the American Philological Association* 101, 357–77.

—1975. 'The Frequency of Structuring of Traditional Formulas in Hesiod's *Theogony*,' *Harvard Studies in Classical Philology* 79, 25–54.

Mithun, M. 1992. 'Is Basic Word Order Universal?' in D. Payne, ed., *Pragmatics of Word Order Flexibility.* Amsterdam.

Mondi, R. 1983. 'The Homeric Cyclopes: Folktale, Tradition, and Theme,' *Transactions of the American Philological Association* 113, 17–38.

—1989. 'Greek Mythic Thought in the Light of the Near East,' in L. Edmunds, ed., 141–98.
Monro, D. B. 1891. *A Grammar of the Homeric Dialect.* 2nd ed. Oxford.
Monro, D. B., and T. W. Allen, eds. 1920. *Homeri Opera.* 3rd ed. Oxford.
Montanari, F. 1979. *Studi di filologia omerica antica* I. Pisa.
Moran, W. S. 1975. '*Mimneskomai* and "Remembering." Epic Stories in Homer and the Hymns,' *Quaderni Urbinati di Cultura Classica* 20, 195–211.
Morgan, C. A. 1990. *Athletes and Oracles: The Transformation of Olympia and Delphi in the Eighth Century B.C.* Cambridge.
Morgan, L. 1988. *The Miniature Wall Paintings of Thera. A Study in Aegean Culture and Iconography.* Cambridge.
Morpurgo-Davies, A. 1964. '"Doric" Features in the Language of Hesiod,' *Glotta* 42, 138–165.
—1979. 'Terminology of Power and Terminology of Work in Greek and Linear B,' in E. Risch and H. Mühlestein, eds., *Colloquium Mycenaeum,* 87–108. Geneva.
Morris, I. 1986. 'The Use and Abuse of Homer,' *Classical Antiquity* 5, 81–138.
—1987. *Burial and Ancient Society: The Rise of the Greek City-State.* Cambridge.
—1988. 'Tomb Cult and the "Greek Renaissance": The Past in the Present in the Eighth Century B.C.,' *Antiquity* 62, 750–61.
—1997. 'Periodization and the Heroes: Inventing a Dark Age,' in M. Golden and P. Toohey, eds., *Inventing Classical Culture?,* 96–131. London.
—Forthcoming. *Darkness and Heroes: Manhood, Equality, and Democracy in Iron Age Greece.* Oxford.
Morris, S. P. 1989. 'A Tale of Two Cities: The Miniature Frescoes from Thera and the Origins of Greek Poetry,' *American Journal of Archaeology* 9, 511–35.
—1992. *Daidalos and the Origins of Greek Art.* Princeton.
—1995. 'The Sacrifice of Astyanax: Near Eastern Contributions to the Siege of Troy,' in Carter and Morris, eds., 221–45.
Morrison, J. V. 1992. *Homeric Misdirection. False Predictions in the Iliad.* Ann Arbor, Michigan.
Moser, D. 1976. 'Die Homerische Frage und das Problem der mündlichen Überlieferung aus volkskundlicher Sicht,' *Fabula* 20, 116–36.
Most, G. W. 1989a. 'The Structure and Function of Odysseus' *Apologoi*,' *Transactions of the American Philological Society* 119, 15–30.
—1989b. 'Cornutus and Stoic Allegoresis: A Preliminary Report,' *Aufstieg und Niedergang der römischen Welt* 2.36.3, 2014–65. Berlin.
Mülder, D. 1910. *Die Ilias und ihre Quellen.* Berlin.
Mueller, M. 1984. *The Iliad.* London.
Muellner, L. 1976. *The Meaning of Homeric EYXOMAI Through its Formulas.* Innsbruck.
Muhly, J. 1970. 'Homer and the Phoenicians,' *Berytus* 19, 19–64.
Murakawa, K. 1957. 'Demiurgos,' *Historia* 6, 385–415.
Murnaghan, S. 1987. *Disguise and Recognition in the Odyssey.* Princeton.
Murray, G. 1907. *The Rise of the Greek Epic.* Oxford.
Murray, O. 1983a. 'The Symposion as Social Organization,' in Hägg, ed., 195–99.
—1983b. 'The Greek Symposion in History,' in E. Gabba, ed., *Tria Corda: Scritti in Onore di Arnaldo Momigliano,* 257–72. Como.
—1991. 'War and the Symposium,' in W. J. Slater, ed., *Dining in a Classical Context,* 83–103. Ann Arbor, Michigan.
—1993. *Early Greece.* 2nd ed. Cambridge, Mass.
Musti, D. 1991. *Le origini dei Greci: Dori e mondo egeo.* Rome.
Musti, D., A. Sacconi, L. Rocchetti, M. Rocchi. E. Scafa, L. Sportiello, and M. E. Giannotta, eds. 1991. *La transizione dal Miceneo al alto arcaismo: dal palazzo alla città.* Rome.

Mylonas, G. 1942. *The Hymn to Demeter and Her Sanctuary at Eleusis*. St. Louis, Missouri.
Myres, J. N. L. 1932. 'The Last Book of the *Iliad*,' *Journal of Hellenic Studies* 52, 264–96.
—1952. 'The Pattern of the *Odyssey*,' *Journal of Hellenic Studies* 72, 1–19.

Naas, M. 1995. *Turning from Persuasion to Philosophy: A Reading of Homer's Iliad*. Atlantic Highlands, New Jersey.
Nagler, M. N. 1967. 'Towards a Generative View of the Homeric Formula,' *Transactions of the American Philological Association* 98, 269–311.
—1974. *Spontaneity and Tradition: A Study in the Oral Art of Homer*. Berkeley.
Nagy, G. 1974. *Comparative Studies in Greek and Indic Meter*. Cambridge, Mass.
—1976. 'Formula and Meter,' in B. Stolz and R. Shannon, eds., *Oral Literature and the Formula*, 239–60. Ann Arbor, Michigan.
—1979. *The Best of the Achaeans: Concepts of the Hero in Archaic Greek Poetry*. Baltimore.
—1982. 'Hesiod,' in T. J. Luce, ed., *Ancient Writers*, 43–74. New York.
—1983. 'On the Death of Sarpedon,' in Rubino and Shelmerdine, eds., 189–217.
—1989. 'Early Greek Views of Poets and Poetry,' in G. Kennedy, ed., *The Cambridge History of Literary Criticism* I: *Classical Criticism*, 1–77. Cambridge.
—1990a. *Greek Mythology and Poetics*. Ithaca, New York.
—1990b. *Pindar's Homer: The Lyric Possession of an Epic Past*. Baltimore.
—1992. 'Homeric Questions,' *Transactions of the American Philological Association* 122, 17–60.
—1995. 'An Evolutionary Model for the Making of Homeric Poetry: Comparative Perspectives,' in Carter and Morris, eds., 163–79.
—1996a. *Poetry as Performance: Homer and Beyond*. Cambridge.
—1996b. *Homeric Questions*. Austin, Texas.
Nagy, J. F. 1989. 'Hierarchy, Heroes, and Heads: Indo-European Structures in Greek Myth,' in L. Edmunds, ed., 199–238.
Neitzel, H. 1975. *Homer-Rezeption bei Hesiod. Interpretation ausgewählter Passagen*. Bonn.
—1977. 'Zum zeitlichen Verhältnis von *Theogonie* (80–93) und *Odyssee* (8.166–177),' *Philologus* 121:24–44.
Nesselrath, H. G. 1992. *Ungeschehenes Geschehen. 'Beinahe-Episoden' im Griechischen und Römischen Epos*. Stuttgart.
Newman, J. K. 1986. *The Classical Epic Tradition*. Madison, Wisconsin.
Nickau, K. 1977. *Untersuchungen zur textkritischen Methode des Zenodotos von Ephesos*. Berlin.
Nicolai, W. 1993. 'Gefolgschaftsverweigerung als politisches Druckmittel in der *Ilias*,' in Raaflaub and Müller-Luckner, eds., 317–341.
Niemeyer, H. G., ed. 1982. *Phönizier im Westen*. Mainz.
Nietzsche, F. 1870–73. 'Der Florentinische Tractat über Homer und Hesiod, ihr Geschlecht und ihren Wettkampf,' *Rheinisches Museum* 25, 528–40 (part 1) and 28 (1873) 211–49 (part 2).
Niles, J. D. 1978. 'Patterning in the Wanderings of Odysseus,' *Ramus* 7, 46–60.
Nilsson, M. P. 1933. *Homer and Mycenae*. London.
Nitzsch, G. W. 1830–37. *De Historia Homeri, maximeque de scriptorum carminum aetate meletemata*. 2 vols. Hanover.
—1841. *Die Heldensage der Griechen nach ihrer nationalen Geltung*. Kiel.
—1852. *Die Sagen poesie der Griechen kritisch dargetstellt*. Braunschweig.
Norden, E. 1909. *Die antike Kunstprosa vom VI. Jahrhundert v. Chr. bis in die Zeit der Renaissance*. Darmstadt.
—1923. *Agnostos Theos*. Berlin.
Notopoulos, J. A. 1949. 'Parataxis in Homer: A New Approach to Homeric Literary Criticism,' *Transactions of the American Philological Association* 80, 1–23.
—1960. 'Homer, Hesiod, and the Achaean Heritage of Oral Poetry,' *Hesperia* 29, 177–97.

—1962. 'The Homeric Hymns as Oral Poetry: A Study of the Post-Homeric Oral Tradition,' *American Journal of Philology* 83, 337–368.
—1964. 'Studies in Early Greek Oral Poetry,' *Harvard Studies in Classical Philology* 63, 1–77.
Nowag, W. 1983. *Raub und Beute in der archaischen Zeit der Griechen.* Frankfurt.
Nyrop, Kr. 1880–82. 'Sagnet om Odysseus og Polyphem,' *Nordisk Tidskrift for Filologi* 5, 216–55.

Oesterreicher, W. 1997. 'Types of Orality in Texts,' in Bakker and Kahane, eds.
Olivier, J.-P., ed. 1992. *Mykenaika.* Paris.
Olshausen, E., ed. 1987. *Die Frau in der Gesellschaft.* Stuttgart (Humanistische Bildung 11).
Olson, S. D. 1989. 'The Stories of Helen and Menelaus (*Od.* 4.240–94) and the Return of Odysseus,' *American Journal of Philology* 110, 387–94.
—1995. *Blood and Iron. Stories and Storytelling in Homer's Odyssey.* Leiden.
Olson, D., N. Torrance, and A. Hildyard, eds. 1985. *Literacy, Language, and Learning. The Nature and Consequences of Reading and Writing.* Cambridge.
Ong, W. J. 1982. *Orality and Literacy: The Technologizing of the Word.* London.
Osborne, R. 1987. *Classical Landscape With Figures: The Ancient Greek City and its Countryside.* London.
O'Neill, E., Jr. 1942. 'The Localization of Metrical Wordtypes in the Greek Hexameter,' *Yale Classical Studies* 8, 105–178.
O'Sullivan, N. 1992. *Alcidamas, Aristophanes, and the Beginnings of Greek Stylistic Theory.* Stuttgart.

Pack, R. A. 1965. *The Greek and Latin Literary Texts from Greco-Roman Egypt.* 2nd ed. Ann Arbor, Michigan.
Packard, D. W. 1976. 'Metrical and Grammatical Patterns in the Greek Hexameter,' in A. Jones and R. F. Churchhouse, eds., *The Computer in Literary and Linguistic Studies*, 85–91. Cardiff.
Page, D. L. 1955. *The Homeric Odyssey.* Oxford.
—1959. *History and the Homeric Iliad.* Berkeley.
—1973. *Folktales in Homer's Odyssey.* Cambridge, Mass.
Palaima, T. G. 1987. 'Comments on Mycenaean Literacy,' in J. T. Killen, J. L. Melena, and J.-P. Olivier, eds., *Studies in Mycenaean and Classical Greek Presented to John Chadwick*, 499–510. Salamanca.
—1995. 'The Nature of the Mycenaean *Wanax*: Non-Indo-European Origins and Priestly Functions,' in Rehak, ed., 119–39.
—Forthcoming. 'The Origin and Ideology of Mycenaean Kingship: Homeric, Indo-European and Minoan Priest-King Models,' in T. G. Palaima, ed., *Kingship and the Organization of Power in Greek Society.* Austin, Texas.
Palmer, L. R. 1962. 'The Language of Homer,' in Wace and Stubbings, eds., 75–178.
Papadopoulos, J. 1996. 'Euboians in Macedonia? A second look,' *Oxford Journal of Archaeology* 15, 151–81.
Paraskevaïdes, H. 1984. *The Use of Synonyms in Homeric Formulaic Diction.* Amsterdam.
Parker, R. 1991. 'The Hymn to Demeter and the Homeric Hymns,' *Greece and Rome* 38, 1–17.
Parks, W. 1990. *Verbal Dueling in Heroic Narrative: The Homeric and Old English Traditions.* Princeton.
Parry, A. 1966. 'Have We Homer's *Iliad*?'. *Yale Classical Studies* 20, 175–216.
Parry, H. 1994. 'The *Apologos* of Odysseus: Lies, All Lies,' *Phoenix* 48, 1–20.
Parry, M. 1971. *The Making of Homeric Verse: The Collected Papers of Milman Parry.* Edited by A. Parry. Oxford.
Parry, M., A. B. Lord, and D. E. Bynum, eds. 1953–. *Serbo-Croatian Heroic Songs.* Cambridge, Mass., and Belgrade.

Pasquali, G. 1954. *Storia della tradizione e critica del testo*. 2nd ed. Florence.
Patzek, B. 1992. *Homer und Mykene. Mündliche Dichtung und Geschichtsschreibung*. Munich.
Patzer, H. 1990. 'Gleichzeitige Ereignisse im homerischen Epos,' in *Festschrift für H. Hörner*, 153–72. Heidelberg.
Pavese, C. O. 1974. *Tradizioni e generi poetic della Grecia arcaica. Studi sulla tradizione epica rapsodica*. Rome.
—1993. 'L'Inno rapsodico: Analisi tematica degli Inni omerici,' in A. C. Cassio and G. Cerri, eds., *Atti di un colloquio Napoli 21–24 ottobre 1993*, 155–78. Rome.
Payton, R. 1991. 'The Ulu Burun writing-board set,' *Anatolian Studies* 41, 99–110.
Pedrick, V. 1983. 'The Paradeigmatic Nature of Nestor's Speech in *Iliad* 11,' *Transactions of the American Philological Association* 113:55–68.
—1994. 'Reading in the Middle Voice: The Homeric Intertextuality of Pietro Pucci and John Peradotto,' *Helios* 21, 75–96.
Pellicia, H. N. 1985. 'The Structure of Archaic Greek Hymns.' Unpublished Ph.D. Dissertation, Yale University.
Pellizer, E. 1978. 'Tecnica compositiva e struttura genealogica nell'Inno omerico ad Afrodite,' *Quaderni Urbinati di Cultura Classica* 27, 115–44.
Penglase, C. 1994. *Greek Myths and Mesopotamia. Parallels and Influence in the Homeric Hymns and Hesiod*. London.
Peradotto, J. 1990. *Man in the Middle Voice: Name and Narration in the Odyssey*. Princeton.
Pestalozzi, H. 1945. *Die Achilleis als Quelle der Ilias*. Zürich.
Petersmann, H. 1981. 'Homer und das Märchen,' *Wiener Studien* 94:43–68.
Pfeiffer, R. 1968. *History of Classical Scholarship*. Oxford.
Phelan, J. 1990. *Reading People, Reading Plots. Character, Progression, and the Interpretation of Narrative*. Chicago.
Pierron, A., ed. 1869. *L'Iliade d'Homère*. 2 vols. Paris.
Podbielski, H. 1971. *La Structure de l'Hymne Homérique à Aphrodite à la lumière de la tradition littéraire*. Wroclaw (Archiwum Filologiczne 27).
Polanyi, K. 1944. *The Great Transformation*. Boston.
Pope, M. 1985. 'A nonce-word in the *Iliad*,' *Classical Quarterly* 35, 1–8.
Popham, M. R., L. H. Sackett, and P. G. Themelis, eds. 1980. *Lefkandi* I: *The Iron Age*. London (British School at Athens Supp. Vol. 11).
Popham, M. R., E. Touloupa, and L. H. Sackett. 1993. *Lefkandi* II.2. London (British School at Athens Supp. Vol. 23).
Porter, H. N. 1949. 'Repetition in the Homeric Hymn to Aphrodite,' *American Journal of Philology* 70, 249–272.
—1951. 'The Early Greek Hexameter,' *Yale Classical Studies* 12, 3–63.
Porter, J. I. 1992. 'Hermeneutic Lines and Circles: Aristarchus and Crates on the Exegesis of Homer,' in Lamberton and Keaney, eds., 67–114.
Porzig, W. 1954. 'Sprachgeographische Untersuchungen zu den altgriechischen Dialekten,' *Indogermanische Forschungen* 61, 147–69.
Postlethwaite, N. 1979. 'Formula and Formulaic: Some Evidence From the Homeric Hymns,' *Phoenix* 33, 1–18.
—1981. 'The Continuation of the *Odyssey*: Some Formulaic Evidence.' *Classical Philology* 76, 177–87.
Powell, B. B. 1977. *Composition by Theme in the Odyssey*. Meisenheim am Glann (Beiträge zur klassischen Philologie, 81).
—1987. 'The Origin of the Puzzling Supplementals,' *Transactions of the American Philological Association* 117, 1–20.
—1988. 'The Dipylon Oinochoe Inscription and the Spread of Literacy in 8th Century Athens,' *Kadmos* 27, 65–86.
—1991. *Homer and the Origin of the Greek Alphabet*. Cambridge.
Pratt, L. H. 1993. *Lying and Poetry from Homer to Pindar*. Ann Arbor, Michigan.

Preminger, A., and T. V. F. Brogan, eds. 1993. *The New Princeton Encyclopedia of Poetry and Poetics*. Princeton.
Preziosi, P. G. 1966. 'The Homeric Hymn to Aphrodite: An Oral Analysis,' *Harvard Studies in Classical Philology* 71, 171–204.
Pritchard, J. B. 1974. *Ancient Near Eastern Texts Relating to the Old Testament*. 3rd. ed. Princeton.
Pritchett, W. K. 1985. *The Greek State at War* IV. Berkeley.
—1991. *Studies in Ancient Greek Topography* VII. Amsterdam.
Pucci, P. 1987. *Odysseus Polutropos: Intertextual Readings in the Odyssey and the Iliad*. Ithaca, New York.
Puhvel, J. 1983. 'Homeric Questions and Hittite Answers,' *American Journal of Philology* 104, 17–22.
—1987. *Comparative Mythology*. Baltimore.
—1991. *Homer and Hittite*. Innsbruck (Innsbrucker Beiträge zur Sprachwissenschaft. Vorträge und kleinere Schriften 47).

Qviller, B. 1981. 'Dynamics of the Homeric Society,' *Symbolae Osloenses* 56, 109–155.

Raaflaub, K. 1985. *Die Entdeckung der Freiheit. Zur historischen Semantik und Gesellschaftsgeschichte eines politischen Grundbegriffes der Griechen*. Munich (*Vestigia* 37).
—1988. 'Homer and the Beginning of Political Thought in Greece,' *Boston Area Colloquium in Ancient Philosophy* 4, 1–25.
—1991. 'Homer und die Geschichte des 8. Jahrhunderts v. Chr.,' in Latacz, ed., 1991a, 205–256.
—1993. 'Homer to Solon. The Rise of the Polis, The Written Sources,' M. Hansen, ed., 41–105.
—1996. 'Citizens, Soldiers, and the Evolution of the Early Greek Polis,' in L. Mitchell and P. J. Rhodes, eds., *The Development of the Polis in Archaic Greece*. London.
Raaflaub K., and E. Müller-Luckner, eds. 1993. *Anfänge politischen Denkens in der Antike. Die nahöstlichen Kulturen und die Griechen*. Munich.
Rackham, O. 1990. 'Ancient Landscapes,' in O. Murray and S. Price, eds., *The Greek City*, 85–111. Oxford.
Radermacher, L. 1915. *Die Erzählungen der Odyssee*. Vienna (Sitzungsberichte der kais. Akademie der Wissenschaften in Wien, philologische-historische Klasse 178, No. 1).
—1931. *Der Homerische Hermeshymnus*. Vienna (Sitzungsberichte Akademie der Wissenschaften in Wien 213, no. 1).
Ramming, G. 1973. 'Die Dienerschaft in der Odyssee.' Unpublished Ph.D. dissertation, Erlangen University.
Redfield, J. M. 1975. *Nature and Culture in the Iliad. The Tragedy of Hector*. Chicago.
Reece, S. 1993. *The Stranger's Welcome: Oral Theory and the Aesthetics of the Homeric Hospitality Scene*. Ann Arbor, Michigan.
Reed, C. 1984. 'Maritime Traders in the Archaic Greek World,' *The Ancient World* 10, 31–44.
Rehak, P., ed. 1995. *The Role of the Ruler in the Prehistoric Aegean*. Liège (Aegaeum 11).
Reichel, M. 1990. 'Retardationstechniken in der Ilias,' in W. Kullmann and M. Reichel, ed., *Der Übergang von der Mündlichkeit zur Literatur bei den Griechen*. Tübingen.
Reiner, E. 1938. *Die Rituelle Totenklage der Griechen*. Tübingen.
Reinhardt, K. 1960. *Tradition und Geist: Gesammelte Essays zur Dichtung*. Göttingen.
Rengakos, A. 1993. *Der Homertext und die hellenistischen Dichter*. Stuttgart (*Hermes* Einzelschrift 64).
Richardson, N. J. 1974. *The Homeric Hymn to Demeter*. Oxford.

—1975. 'Homeric Professors in the Age of the Sophists,' *Proceedings of the Cambridge Philological Society* n.s. 21:65–81.
—1987a. 'Homer and Cyprus,' in *The Civilizations of the Aegean and their Diffusion in Cyprus and the eastern Mediterranean, 2000–600 B.C.*, 125–32. Larnaca.
—1987b. 'The Individuality of Homer's Language,' in Bremer et al., eds., 165–84.
—1993. *The Iliad: A Commentary* VI: *Books 21–24.* Cambridge.
Richardson, S. 1990. *The Homeric Narrator.* Nashville, Tennessee.
Richter, W. 1968. *Die Landwirtschaft im homerischen Zeitalter.* Göttingen (*Archaeologia Homerica* 2.H).
Ridgeway, W. 1885. 'The Homeric Land System,' *Journal of Hellenic Studies* 6, 335–3.
Riggsby, A. M. 1992. 'Homeric Speech Introductions and the Theory of Homeric Composition,' *Transactions of the American Philological Association* 122, 99–114.
Risch E. 1955. 'Die Gliederung der Griechischen Dialekte in Neuer Sicht,' *Museum Helveticum* 12, 61–76.
—1979. 'Die Griechischen Dialekte im 2. Vorchristlichen Jahrtausend,' *Studi Micenei ed Egeo-Anatolici* 20, 91–111.
—1985. 'Homerisch "ennepo," Lakonisch "epheneponti," und die alte Erzählprosa,' *Zeitschrift für Papyrologie und Epigraphik* 60, 1–9.
Robertson, M. 1951. 'The Place of Vase-Painting in Greek Art,' *Annual of the British School at Athens* 46:151–59.
Röhrich, L. 1962. 'Die mittelalterliche Redaktionen des Polyphem-Märchens (AT 1137) und ihr Verhältnis zur ausserhomerischen Tradition,' *Fabula* 5, 48–71.
Roisman, H., and M. Joseph, eds. 1993. *Essays on Homeric Epic = Colby Quarterly* 29.
Röllig, W. 1992. 'Achäer und Trojaner in hethitischen Quellen?' in I. Gamer-Wallert, ed., *Troia. Brücke zwischen Orient und Okzident*, 183–200. Tübingen.
Rose, P. W. 1992. *Sons of the Gods, Children of Earth: Ideology and Literary Form in Ancient Greece.* Ithaca, New York.
Rosen, R. M. 1990. 'Poetry and Sailing in Hesiod's *Works and Days*,' *Classical Antiquity* 9, 99–113.
Rosenberg, B. A. 1978. 'The Genres of Oral Narrative,' in J. P. Strelka, ed., *Theories of Literary Genre*, 150–65. University Park, Pennsylvania.
Rosenmeyer, T. G. 1985. 'Ancient Literary Genres: A Mirage?' *Yearbook of Comparative and General Literature* 34, 74–84.
—1988. *Deina ta Polla: A Classicist's Checklist of Twenty Literary-Critical Positions.* Buffalo, New York (*Arethusa* Monographs, no. 12).
Rösler, W. 1980. 'Die Entdeckung der Fiktionalität,' *Poetica* 12, 283–319.
Rosner, J. A. 1976. 'The Speech of Phoenix: *Iliad* 9.434–605,' *Phoenix* 30, 314–27.
Rossi, L. E. 1965. 'Estensione e valore del "colon" nell'esametro omerico,' *Studi Urbinati* 39, 239–73.
Rössler, D. 1981. 'Handwerker,' in Welskopf, ed., III.193–268.
Rowntree, D. 1981. *Statistics Without Tears: A Primer for Non-Mathematicians.* London.
Rubino, C. A., and C. Shelmerdine, eds. 1983. *Approaches to Homer.* Austin, Texas.
Rudhardt, J. 1978. 'À propos de l'hymne homérique à Déméter,' *Museum Helveticum* 35, 1–17.
—1991. 'L'hymne homérique à Aphrodite,' *Museum Helveticum* 48, 8–20.
Ruijgh, C. J. 1957. *L'elément Achéen dans la langue epique.* Amsterdam.
—1985. 'Le mycénien et Homère,' in A. Morpurgo Davies and Y. Duhoux, eds., *Linear B: A 1984 Survey*, 143–90. Louvain-la-Neuve.
—1990. 'La place des enclitiques dans l'ordre des mots chez Homère d'après la loi de Wackernagel,' H. Eichner and H. Rix, eds., *Sprachwissenschaft und Philologie. Jacob Wackernagel und die Indogermanistik heute*, 213–33. Wiesbaden.

—1995. 'D'Homère aux origines proto-mycéniennes de la tradition épique. Analyse dialectologique du langage homérique, avec un excursus sur la création de l'alphabet grec,' in Crielaard, ed., 1–96.
Russo, J. 1963. 'A Closer Look at Homeric Formulas,' *Transactions of the American Philological Association* 94, 235–47.
—1966. 'The Structural Formula in Homeric Verse,' *Yale Classical Studies* 20, 219–40.
—1976. 'Is "Oral" or "Aural" Composition the Cause of Homer's Formulaic Style?,' in Stolz and Shannon, eds., 31–54.
—1994. 'Homer's Style: Non-Formulaic Features of an Oral Aesthetic,' *Oral Tradition* 9, 371–389.
Russo, J., M. Fernandez-Galiano, and A. Heubeck. 1992. *A Commentary on Homer's Odyssey* III. *Books XVII–XXIV.* Oxford.
Rutherford, R. B. 1985. 'At Home and Abroad: Aspects of the Structure of the *Odyssey*,' *Proceedings of the Cambridge Philological Society* n.s. 31, 133–50.
Rutter, J. 1990. 'Some Comments on Interpreting the Dark-Surfaced Handmade Burnished Pottery of the 13th Century B.C. Aegean,' *Journal of Mediterranean Archaeology* 3, 29–49.
—1992. 'Cultural Novelties in the Post-Palatial Aegean World,' in Ward and Joukowsky, eds., 61–78.

Sahlins, M. 1972. *Stone Age Economics.* Chicago.
Sale, W. M. 1984. 'Homeric Olympus and its Formulae,' *American Journal of Philology* 105, 1–28.
—1987. 'The Formularity of the Place Phrases of the *Iliad*,' *Transactions of the American Philological Association* 117, 21–50.
—1989. 'The Trojans, Statistics, and Milman Parry,' *Greek, Roman, and Byzantine Studies* 30, 341–410.
—1993a. 'Homer and *Roland*: The Shared Formular Technique, Part I,' *Oral Tradition* 8, 87–142.
—1993b. 'Homer and *Roland*: The Shared Formular Technique, Part II,' *Oral Tradition* 8, 381–412.
—1994. 'The Government of Troy,' *Greek, Roman and Byzantine Studies* 35, 5–102.
Sallares, R. 1991. *The Ecology of the Ancient Greek World.* Ithaca, New York.
Sandars, N. K. 1983. *The Sea Peoples.* 2nd ed. London.
Saunders, T. J. 1991. *Plato's Penal Code.* Oxford.
Schadewaldt, W. 1959. *Von Homers Welt und Werk. Aufsätze und Auslegungen zur Homerischen Frage.* 3rd ed. Stuttgart.
—1965. *Von Homers Welt und Werk. Aufsätze und Auslegungen zur Homerischen Frage.* 4th ed. Stuttgart.
—1966. *Iliasstudien.* 3rd ed. Darmstadt.
Schaefer, U. 1988. 'The Instance of the Formula: A Poetic Device Revisited,' in R. Matthews and J. Schole-Rostosky, eds., *Papers on Language and Mediaeval Studies Presented to Alfred Schopf.* Frankfurt.
—1992. *Vokalität. Altenglische Dichtung zwischen Mündlichkeit und Schriftlichkeit.* Tübingen (*ScriptOralia* 39).
Schefold, K. 1966. *Myth and Legend in Early Greek Art.* Trs. A. Hicks. London.
—1981. *Die Göttersage in der klassischen und hellenistischen Kunst.* Munich.
—1992. *Gods and Heroes in Late Archaic Greek Art.* Trs. A. Griffiths. Cambridge.
Schein, S. 1984. *The Mortal Hero: An Introduction to Homer's Iliad.* Berkeley.
Schiffrin, D. 1987. *Discourse Markers.* Cambridge.
—1994. *Approaches to Discourse.* Oxford.
Schilardi, D. U. 1984. 'The LH IIIC epoch at the Koukounaries acropolis, Paros,' in MacGillivray and Barber, eds., 184–206.

—1988. 'The Temple of Athena at Koukounaries,' in Hägg and Marinatos, eds., 235–45.
Schliemann, H. 1875. *Troy and its Remains*. London (reprinted New York, 1976).
—1880. *Mycenae* (reprinted New York, 1976).
—1881. *Ilios*. London (reprinted New York, 1976).
—1884. *Troja*. London (reprinted New York, 1976).
—1885. *Tiryns* (reprinted New York, 1976).
Schmandt-Besserat, D. 1992. *Before Writing* I. Austin, Texas.
Schmiel, R. 1981. 'Rhythm and Accent: Texture in Greek Epic Poetry,' in Grotjahn, ed., 1–32.
Schmitt, R. 1967. *Dichtung und Dichtersprache in indogermanischer Zeit*. Wiesbaden.
Schneider, H. 1991. 'Die Gaben des Prometheus. Technik im antiken Mittelmeerraum,' in Schneider and Hägermann, eds., 17–313.
Schneider, H., and D. Hägermann, eds. 1991. *Landbau und Handwerk 750 v. Chr. bis 1000 n. Chr.*, in W. König, ed., *Propyläen Technikgeschichte*. Berlin.
Schoeck, G. 1961. *Ilias und Aithiopis*. Zürich.
Scholes, R. 1989. *Protocols of Reading*. New Haven, Conn.
Schrader, H. 1880–82. *Porphyrii Quaestionum Homericarum ad Iliadem Pertinentium Reliquias*. 2 vols. Leipzig.
—1890. *Porphyrii Quaestionum Homericarum ad Odysseam Pertinentium Reliquias*. Leipzig.
Schwenn, F. 1934. *Die Theogonie des Hesiodos*. Heidelberg.
Schwinge, E.-R. 1991. 'Homerische Epen und Erzählforschung,' in Latacz, ed., 1991b, 482–512.
Scobie, A. 1983. *Apuleius and Folklore*. London.
Scodel, R. 1982. 'The Achaean Wall and the Myth of Destruction,' *Harvard Studies in Classical Philology* 86, 33–50.
Scott, J. A. 1921. *The Unity of Homer*. Berkeley.
Scully, S. 1981. 'The Polis in Homer: A Definition and Interpretation,' *Ramus* 10, 1–34.
—1990. *Homer and the Sacred City*. Ithaca, New York.
Segal, C. 1974. 'The Homeric Hymn to Aphrodite: A Structuralist Approach,' *Classical World* 67, 205–212.
—1981. 'Orality, Repetition and Formulaic Artistry in the Homeric "Hymn to Demeter,"' in Brillante et al., eds., 107–160.
—1994. *Singers, Heroes, and Gods in the Odyssey*. Ithaca, New York.
Sellschopp, I. 1934. *Stilistische Untersuchungen zu Hesiod*. Hamburg.
Severyns, A. 1928. *Le cycle épique dans l'école d'Aristarche*. Liège and Paris.
—1946. *Homère* II: *le poète et son œuvre*. Brussels.
Shelmerdine, C. W. 1995. 'Shining and Fragrant Cloth in Homeric Epic,' in Carter and Morris, eds., 99–107.
Shelmerdine, S. C. 1981. 'The "Homeric Hymn to Hermes:" A Commentary (1–114) with Introduction.' Unpublished Ph.D. dissertation, University of Michigan.
Sherratt, E. S. 1990. '"Reading the Texts:" Archaeology and the Homeric Question,' *Antiquity* 64:807–824.
Shipp, G. P. 1961. *Essays in Mycenaean and Homeric Greek*. Melbourne.
Shive, D. M. 1987. *Naming Achilles*. Oxford.
Sicking, C. M. J. 1993. *Griechische Verslehre*. Munich (Handbuch der Altertumswissenschaft II.4).
Simonsuuri, D. 1979. *Homer's Original Genius. Eighteenth-Century Notions of the Early Greek Epic (1688–1798)*. Cambridge.
Simpson, W. K., ed., 1973. *The Literature of Ancient Egypt*. New Haven, Conn.
Singor, H. 1991. 'Nine Against Troy,' *Mnemosyne* 44:26–31.
—1995. '*Eni prôtoisi machesthai*. Some Remarks on the Iliadic Image of the Battlefield,' in Crielaard, ed., 183–200.

Sittl, K. 1884. 'Die Aeolismen der Homerischen Sprache,' *Philologus* 43, 1–31.
Slatkin, L. M. 1991. *The Power of Thetis: Allusion and Interpretation in the Iliad.* Berkeley.
—1992. 'Composition by Theme and the *Mêtis* of the *Odyssey*,' in S. L. Schein, ed., *Reading the Odyssey: Selected Interpretive Essays*, 223–37. Princeton.
Slings, S. R. 1992. 'Written and Spoken Language. An Exercise in the Pragmatics of the Greek Sentence,' *Classical Philology* 87, 95–109.
Smith, P. M. 1981a. *Nursling of Mortality: A Study of the Homeric Hymn to Aphrodite.* Frankfurt (Studien zur klassischen Philologie 3).
—1981b. 'Aineiadai as Patrons of *Iliad* XX and the Homeric Hymn to Aphrodite,' *Harvard Studies in Classical Philology* 85, 17–58.
Snodgrass, A. M. 1971. *The Dark Age of Greece.* Edinburgh.
—1974. 'An Historical Homeric Society?,' *Journal of Hellenic Studies* 94, 114–25.
—1977. *Archaeology and the Rise of the Greek State.* Cambridge.
—1980. *Archaic Greece: The Age of Experiment.* London.
—1987. *An Archaeology of Greece.* Berkeley.
—1993a. 'The Rise of the Polis. The Archaeological Evidence,' in M. H. Hansen, ed., 30–40.
—1993b. 'The "Hoplite Reform" Revisited,' *Dialogues d'histoire ancienne* 19, 49–56.
—1994. 'The Euboeans in Macedonia: A New Precedent for Westward Expansion,' *Annali di Archeologia e Storia Antica* n.s. 1, 87–93.
Solmsen, F. 1954. 'The "Gift" of Speech in Homer and Hesiod,' *Transactions of the American Philological Association* 85, 1–15.
Sommer, F. 1909. 'Zur griechischen Prosodie,' *Glotta* 1, 145–240.
Sowa, C. A. 1984. *Traditional Themes and the Homeric Hymns.* Chicago.
Stanford, W. B. 1963. *The Ulysses Theme: A Study in the Adaptability of a Traditional Hero.* Oxford.
—1965. 'The Ending of the *Odyssey*: An Ethical Approach,' *Hermathena* 100, 5–20.
Stanley, K. 1993. *The Shield of Homer: Narrative Structure in the Iliad.* Princeton.
Starr, C. G. 1961. *The Origins of Greek Civilization.* New York.
—1977. *The Economic and Social Growth of Early Greece, 800–500 B.C.* New York.
—1986. *Individual and Community. The Rise of the Polis.* Oxford.
—1992. *The Aristocratic Temper of Greek Civilization.* New York.
Stein-Hölkeskamp, E. 1989. *Adelskultur und Polisgesellschaft. Studien zum griechischen Adel in archaischer und klassischer Zeit.* Stuttgart.
Stella, L. A. 1955. *Il poema d'Ulisse.* Florence.
Sternberg, M. 1978. *Expositional Modes and Temporal Ordering in Fiction.* Baltimore.
Stevenson, C. L. 1944. *Ethics and Language.* New Haven, Conn.
Stock, B. 1983. *The Implications of Literacy.* Princeton.
Stolz, B. A., and R. S. Shannon, III., eds. 1976. *Oral Literature and the Formula.* Ann Arbor, Michigan.
Strasburger, G. 1954. *Die kleinen Kämpfer der Ilias.* Frankfurt.
Strasburger, H. 1953. 'Der soziologische Aspeckt der homerischen Epen,' *Gymnasium* 60, 97–114 (reprinted in Strasburger 1982, 491–518).
—1954. 'Der Einzelne und die Gemeinschaft im Denken der Griechen,' *Historische Zeitschrift* 177, 227–248.
—1976. *Zum antiken Gesellschaftsideal.* Heidelberg (Abhandlungen der Heidelberger Akademie, philosophisch-historische Klasse).
—1982. *Studien zur Alten Geschichte* I. Hildesheim.
Strasser, F. X. 1984. *Zu den Iterata der frügriechischen Epik.* Königstein (Beiträge zur klassischen Philologie, Heft 156).
Strömberg, R. 1950. 'The Aeolus Episode and Greek Wind Magic,' *Acta Universitatis Gotoburgensis/Göteborgs Högskolas Aarsskrift* 56, 71–81.
Strunk, K. 1957. *Die sogenannten Aeolismen der Homerischen Sprache.* Heidelberg.
Stubbings, F. H. 1962a. 'Editorial Preface,' in Wace and Stubbings, eds., v–viii.

—1962b. 'Food and Agriculture,' in Wace and Stubbings, eds., 523–30.
Styrenius, C.-G. 1967. *Submycenaean Studies*. Lund.
Suerbaum, W. 1968. 'Die Ich-Erzählungen des Odysseus: Überlegungen zur epischen Technik der Odyssee,' *Poetica* 2, 150–77.
Sutton, D. F. 1991. *Homer in the Papyri*. Atlanta (American Philological Association, computer software).
Svenbro, J. 1976. *La parole et le marbre. Aux origines de la poétique Grecque*. Lund.

Tandy, D. W., and W. C. Neale. 1994. 'Karl Polanyi's Distinctive Approach to Social Analysis and the Case of Ancient Greece,' in Duncan and Tandy, eds., 9–33.
Tannen, D., ed. 1982. *Spoken and Written Language. Exploring Orality and Literacy*. Norwood, New Jersey (Advances in Discourse Processes, 9).
—1989. *Talking Voices. Repetition, Dialogue and Imagery in Conversational Discourse*. Cambridge.
Taplin, O. 1992. *Homeric Soundings: The Shaping of the Iliad*. Oxford.
Thalmann, W. G. 1984. *Conventions of Form and Thought in Early Greek Poetry*. Baltimore.
Thiel, H. van, ed. 1991. *Homeri Odyssea*. Hildesheim.
—1996. *Homeri Ilias*. Hildesheim.
Thomas, C. G. 1966. 'Homer and the Polis,' *Parola del Passato* 21, 5–14.
—1993. *Myth Becomes History: Pre-Classical Greece*. Claremont, California.
Thomas, R. 1989. *Oral Tradition and Written Record in Classical Athens*. Cambridge.
—1992. *Literacy and Orality in Ancient Greece*. Cambridge.
Thompson, S. 1955. *A Motif-Index of Folk-Literature: A Classification of Narrative Elements in Folktales, Ballads, Myths, Fables, Mediaeval Romances, Exempla, Fabliaux, Jest-Books and Local Legends*. Revised ed., 6 vols. Bloomington, Indiana.
Todorov, T. 1969. *Grammaire du Décameron*. The Hague and Paris.
Tolstoi, J. 1934. 'Einige Märchenparallelen zur Heimkehr des Odysseus,' *Philologus* 89, 261–74.
Tracy, S. V. 1990. *The Story of the Odyssey*. Princeton.
Trahman, C. R. 1952. 'Odysseus' lies (*Odyssey*, Books 13–19),' *Phoenix* 6, 31–43.
Traill, D. 1995. *Schliemann of Troy*. London.
Trümpy, H. 1950. *Kriegerische Fachausdrücke im griechischen Epos*. Basle.
Tsetskhladze, G. R., and F. De Angelis, eds. 1994. *The Archaeology of Greek Colonisation*. Oxford.
Turner, F. M. 1981. *The Greek Heritage in Victorian Britain*. New Haven, Conn.
Tyler, S. 1987. *The Unspeakable: Discourse, Dialogue, and Rhetoric in the Postmodern World*. Madison, Wisconsin.

Ulf, C. 1990. *Die homerische Gesellschaft. Materialen zur analytischen Beschreibung und historischen Lokalisierung*. Munich (Vestigia 43).

Vallet, G., and F. Villard. 1976. *Mégara Hyblaea* I. Paris.
Van Andel, T., and C. Runnels. 1987. *Beyond the Acropolis*. Stanford.
van Effenterre, H. 1985. *La cité grecque. Des origines à la défaite de Marathon*. Paris.
Van Nortwick, T. 1975. 'The Homeric Hymn to Hermes: A Study in Early Greek Hexameter Style.' Unpublished Ph.D. dissertation, Stanford University.
van der Ben, N. 1980. 'De Homerische Aphrodite-hymne I,' *Lampas* 13, 40–77.
—1981. 'De Homerische Aphrodite-hymne 2: Ein interpretatie van het gedicht,' *Lampas* 14, 69–107.
van der Valk, M. 1949. *Textual Criticism of the Odyssey*. Leiden.
—1963–64. *Researches on the Text and Scholia of the Iliad*. 2 vols. Leiden.
van Leeuwen, J. 1918. *Enchiridium Dictionis Epicae*. 2nd ed. Leiden.
van Thiel, H., ed. 1993. *Homeri Odyssea*. Hildesheim-Zürich-New York.

van Wees, H. 1986. 'Leaders of Men?' *Classical Quarterly* 36, 285–303.
—1988. 'Kings in Combat,' *Classical Quarterly* 38, 1–24.
—1992. *Status Warriors. War, Violence, and Society in Homer and History*. Amsterdam.
—1994. 'The Homeric Way of War,' *Greece and Rome* 41, 1–18, 131–55.
—1995a. 'Princes at Dinner,' in Crielaard, ed., 147–82.
—1995b. 'Politics and the Battlefield,' in A. Powell, ed., *The Greek World*, 153–78. London.
—1996. 'Heroes, Knights and Nutters,' in A. Lloyd, ed., *Battle in Antiquity*, 1–86. London.
Vansina, Jan. 1985. *Oral Tradition and History*. Madison, Wisconsin.
Vatin, C. 1982. 'Poinè, timè, thoiè dans le droit homérique,' *Ktèma* 7, 275–80.
Ventris, M., and J. Chadwick. 1973. *Documents in Mycenaean Greek*. 2nd ed. Cambridge.
Verdenius, W. J. 1985. *A Commentary on Hesiod, Works and Days, vv. 1–382*. Leiden.
Vermeule, E. 1964. *Greece in the Bronze Age*. Chicago.
—1987. 'Baby Aigisthos and the Bronze Age,' *Proceedings of the Cambridge Philological Society* n.s. 33, 122–52.
Vernant, J.-P. 1982. *The Origins of Greek Thought*. Ithaca, New York.
Versnel, H. 1980. 'Historical Implications,' C. Stibbe, ed., *Lapis Satricanus*. The Hague.
Vidal-Naquet, P. 1986. *The Black Hunter: Forms of Thought and Forms of Society in the Greek World*. Trs. A. Szegedy-Maszak. Baltimore.
Villoison, J. B. G. d', ed. 1788. *Homeri Ilias ad veteris codicis Veneti fidem recensita*. Venice.
Visser, E. 1987. 'Homerische Versifikationstechnik. Versuch einer Rekonstruktion.' Unpublished Ph.D. dissertation, Frankfurt.
—1988. 'Formulae or Single Words? Towards a New Theory on Homeric Verse-Making,' *Würzburger Jahrbuch fur Altertumswissenschaft* n.s. 14, 21–37.
Vivante, P. 1970. *The Homeric Imagination*. Bloomington, Indiana.
—1982. *The Epithets in Homer: A Study in Poetic Values*. New Haven, Conn.
Vokotopoulou, I. 1986. *Vitsa*. 3 vols. Athens.
von Reden, S. 1995. *Exchange in Ancient Greece*. London.
von Ungern-Sternberg, J., and H. Reinau, eds. 1988. *Vergangenheit in mündlicher Überlieferung*. Stuttgart.
von Wilamowitz-Moellendorff, U. 1881. *Homerische Untersuchungen*. Berlin.
—1915. *Die Ilias und Homer*. Berlin.
—1928. *Hesiodos. Erga*. Berlin.
Voutsaki, S. 1995. 'Social and Political Processes in the Mycenaean Argolid: The Evidence from the Mortuary Practices,' in Laffineur and Niemeier, eds., 55–66.

Wace, A. J. B., and F. H. Stubbings, eds. 1962. *A Companion to Homer*. London.
Wachter, R. 1989. 'Zur Vorgeschichte des griechischen Alphabets,' *Kadmos* 29, 19–78.
Wade-Gery, H. T. 1936. 'Kynaithos,' in *Greek Poetry and Life: Essays Presented to Gilbert Murray on His Seventieth Birthday*, 56–78. Oxford.
—1952. *The Poet of the Iliad*. Cambridge.
Walcot, P. 1966. *Hesiod and the Near East*. Cardiff.
Walsh, G. B. 1984. *The Varieties of Enchantment. Early Greek Views of the Nature and Function of Poetry*. Chapel Hill, North Carolina.
Walter, U. 1993. *An der Polis teilhaben. Bürgerstaat und Zugehörigkeit im archaischen Griechenland*. Stuttgart.
Ward, G. L. 1988. *The Semantics and Pragmatics of Preposing*. New York.
Ward, W., and M. Joukowsky, eds. 1992. *The Crisis Years. The Twelfth Century B.C. from Beyond the Danube to the Tigris*. Dubuque, Iowa.
Warren, P. M. 1979. 'The Miniature Fresco from the West House at Akrotiri, Thera and its Aegean Setting,' *Journal of Hellenic Studies* 99, 115–29.
Warren, P. M., and V. Hankey. 1989. *Aegean Bronze Age Chronology*. Bristol.

Wathelet, P. 1971. *Les traits eoliens dans l'epopée grecque.* Rome.

Watkins, C. 1964. 'Preliminaries to the Reconstruction of Indo-European Sentence Structure,' *Proceedings of the 9th International Congress of Linguists*, 1035–42. Cambridge, Mass.

—1986. 'The language of the Trojans,' in M. Mellink, ed., *Troy and the Trojan War*, 45–62. Bryn Mawr, PA.

Webster, T. B. L. 1958. *From Mycenae to Homer.* London.

Weiler, I. 1975. '*Aien aristeuein.* Ideologiekritische Bemerkungen zu einem vielzitierten Homerwort,' *Stadion* 1, 199–227.

Welskopf, E., ed. 1981. *Soziale Typenbegriffe* III: *Untersuchungen ausgewählter sozialer Typenbegriffe.* Berlin.

Welwei, K. W. 1992. 'Polis-Bildung, Hetairos-Gruppen und Hetairien,' *Gymnasium* 99, 487–95.

Wendel, T. 1929. *Gesprchsanrede in Griechischen Epos und Drama der Blütezeit.* Tübingen (Tübinger Beiträge zur Altertumswissenschaft 6).

Wender, D. 1978. *The Last Scenes of the Odyssey.* Leiden (*Mnemosyne* Supplement 52).

West, M. L. 1966. *Hesiod: Theogony.* Oxford.

—1967. 'The Contest of Homer and Hesiod,' *Classical Quarterly* 17, 433–50.

—1970. 'The Eighth Homeric Hymn and Proclus,' *Classical Quarterly* 20, 300–304.

—1973a. 'Greek Poetry 2000–700 B.C.,' *Classical Quarterly* 23, 118–39.

—1973b. 'Indo-European Metre,' *Glotta* 51, 161–87.

—1974. *Studies in Greek Elegy and Iambus.* New York.

—1975. 'Cynaethus' Hymn to Apollo,' *Classical Quarterly* 25, 161–70.

—1978. *Hesiod. Works and Days.* Oxford.

—1981. 'The Singing of Homer,' *Journal of Hellenic Studies* 101, 113–29.

—1982a. *Greek Metre.* Oxford.

—1982b. 'Three Topics in Greek Metre,' *Classical Quarterly* 32, 281–97.

—1985. *The Hesiodic Catalogue of Women.* Oxford.

—1986. 'The Singing of Hexameters: Evidence from Epidaurus,' *Zeitschrift für Papyrologie und Epigraphik* 63, 39–46.

—1987. *Introduction to Greek Metre.* Oxford.

—1988. 'The Rise of the Greek Epic,' *Journal of Hellenic Studies* 108, 151–72.

—1989. 'An Unrecognized Injunctive Usage in Greek,' *Glotta* 67, 135–38.

—1995. 'The Date of the *Iliad*,' *Museum Helveticum* 52, 203–219.

West, S. 1967. *The Ptolemaic Papyri of Homer.* Köln-Opladen (Papyrologica Coloniensia 3.

Whallon, W. 1961. 'The Homeric Epithets,' *Yale Classical Studies* 17, 97–142.

—1966. 'The Shield of Ajax,' *Yale Classical Studies* 22, 7–36.

—1969. *Formula, Character, and Context: Studies in Homeric, Old English, and Old Testament Poetry.* Cambridge, Mass.

—1979. 'Is Hector *Androphonos*?' In *Arktouros: Hellenic Studies presented to B. M. W. Knox*, 19–24. Berlin.

Wheeler, E. 1991. 'The general as hoplite,' in V. Hanson, ed., *Hoplites*, 121–70. London.

White, H. 1973. *Metahistory. The Historical Imagination in Nineteenth-Century Europe.* Baltimore.

Whitfield, G. K. 1967. 'The Restored Relation: The Supplication Theme in the *Iliad*.' Unpublished Ph.D. dissertation, Columbia University.

Whitley, J. 1991a. 'Social Diversity in Dark Age Greece,' *Annual of the British School at Athens* 86, 341–65.

—1991b. *Style and Society in Dark Age Greece.* Cambridge.

Whitman, C. H. 1958. *Homer and the Heroic Tradition.* Cambridge, Mass.

Wickert-Micknat, G. 1982. *Die Frau.* Göttingen (*Archaeologia Homerica* 2.R).

—1983. *Unfreiheit im Zeitalter der homerischen Epen.* Wiesbaden.
Willcock, M. M. 1983. 'Antilochos in the *Iliad*,' in M. M. Willcock, ed., *Mélanges Edouard Delebecque*, 479–85. Aix-en-Provence.
—1987. 'The Final Scenes of *Iliad* XVII,' in Bremer et al., eds., 185–94.
—1990. 'The Search for the Poet Homer,' *Greece and Rome* 37, 1–13.
—1993. 'The Fighting in the *Iliad*,' in *Spondes ston Omirou*, 141–47. Ithaki, Greece.
Williams, B 1993. *Shame and Necessity.* Berkeley.
Winter, I. J. 1995. 'Homer's Phoenicians,' in Carter and Morris, eds., 247–71.
Wolf, F. A. 1985. *Prolegomena to Homer 1795.* Trs. and edited by A. Grafton, G. W. Most, and J. Zetzel. Princeton.
Wood, M. 1985. *In Search of the Trojan War.* London.
Woodman, A. J. 1988. *The Rhetoric of Ancient Historiography.* London.
Wright, J. C. 1995. 'From Chief to King in Mycenaean Greece,' in Rehak, ed., 63–80.
Wyatt, Jr., W. F. 1969. *Metrical Lengthening in Homer.* Rome (Incunabula Graeca 35).
—1970. 'The Prehistory of the Greek Dialects,' *Transactions of the American Philological Association* 101, 557–632.
—1975. 'Homer's Linguistic Ancestors,' *Epistimoniki Epetiri tou Aristoteliou Panepistimiou Thessaloniki* 11, 133–47.

Xenaki-Sakellariou, A., and Ch. Chatziliou. 1989. *'Peinture en metal' à l'époque mycénienne.* Athens.

Yamagata, N. 1989. 'The Apostrophe in Homer as Part of the Oral Technique,' *Bulletin of the Institute of Classical Studies* 36, 91–103.

Zeitlin, F. I. 1995. 'Figuring Fidelity in Homer's *Odyssey*,' in Cohen, ed., 117–52.
Zielinski, T. 1899–1901. 'Die Behandlung gleichzeitiger Ereignisse im antiken Epos,' *Philologus Suppl.* 8, 405–49.
Zumbach, O. 1955. *Neuerungen in der Sprache der homerischen Hymnen.* Winterthur.
Zumthor, P. 1987. *La lettre et la voix. De la 'littérature' médiévale.* Paris.
—1990. *Oral Poetry: An Introduction.* Trs. K. Murphy-Judy. Minneapolis, Minnesota.

INDEX*

abecedarium, 18, 24
Achaeans, 21, 25, 27, 31, 167, 198, 270, 291, 299, 308, 361, 402, 403, 405, 412, 421, 424, 429, 440, 461, 478, 480, 485, 602, 604, 605, 609, 610, 619, 627, 652, 653, 703
Achilles, 31, 39, 40, 75, 76, 78, 147, 164, 167–9, 175–82, 184, 185, 188, 271, 273, 275, 277, 280, 291–3, 294, 296–8, 309–11, 314–21 324, 345–52, 355–8, 375, 376, 402, 404, 407, 410, 412, 414, 416, 418, 421, 424–32, 436, 439, 453, 484, 497, 527, 560, 569, 573, 575, 576, 578, 580, 581, 601, 605, 609, 611, 614, 615, 617–9, 629, 632, 637, 638, 652, 656, 659, 703, 704, 706, 709–13
Aegisthus, 309, 706
Aeneas, 314, 405, 425, 605, 661, 683, 684
Aeneid, 58, 180, 360, 398
Aeolus, 376, 377, 378, 454
Aeschines, 33, 70, 74–8
Aethiopis, 175, 176, 178–81, 183, 185, 186, 355–7, 610, 615
Aetolia, 425
Aetolians, 311, 661
Agamemnon, 31, 177, 178, 188, 277, 295, 308–11, 319, 345, 349, 351, 352, 354, 375, 376, 388, 416, 421, 424, 425, 427, 430, 453, 484, 511, 516, 610, 614, 621, 631–4, 637, 638, 642, 659, 669, 675, 681, 699, 700, 703, 704, 706, 711
Ahhiyawa, 519, 605, 610
Aiantes, 684, 685, 686
Aithiopes, 346
Aithiopis, 175, 176, 178–81, 183, 185, 186, 355–7, 610, 615
Ajax, 27, 39, 83, 176, 177, 178, 181–3, 188, 230, 232, 355, 356, 358, 376, 453, 569, 572–4, 576, 581, 672, 674, 677, 680, 682, 684–6, 691
Akkadian language, 6, 12, 235, 601, 602, 608, 610, 617, 618, 620
Al Mina, 21, 544, 545
Alashiya, 603, 610
Alcibiades, 42, 45, 59, 74
Alcinous, 310, 414, 417, 497, 630, 634, 640, 655, 659, 660, 704–6
Alcman, 73, 81, 193
Alcyone, 430–2
Alexandria, 48, 60, 66, 68, 83, 85, 87, 88, 102, 103, 105–9, 489
alphabet, 3, 4, 7–12, 16–22, 25, 27–32, 58, 81, 194, 208–10, 227, 465, 547, 608, 623, 666
Althea, 453
Amarna, 607
Amazons, 181, 185, 578, 610, 619
Ambrosian *Iliad*, 60, 62, 88
Amphiaraus, 708
Amphidamas, 31, 474, 475, 477, 478
Analysts, 146, 147, 158
Anat, 604, 617
Andromache, 49, 169, 178, 200, 279, 320, 354, 412, 639, 641
Antenor, 354
Antia, 27, 451, 452, 459, 461
Antilochus, 176, 177, 179, 180–3, 280, 355, 357, 670, 677, 684
Antimachus, 49, 65, 69
Antinous, 363, 365, 373, 374, 379, 417, 418–20, 425, 430, 433, 712
Anu, 602, 617
aoidos, 147, 151, 403, 404, 406, 497
Apollo, 32, 33, 35, 176, 299, 308, 309, 322, 325, 345, 349, 350, 351, 356, 359, 401, 426, 427, 429, 430–3, 474, 490, 492, 493, 495, 497, 500–2, 506, 507, 613, 638, 703, 710, 712
Apollodorus, 427, 429, 601

* All names are given in their Roman form, regardless of how they appear in the text.

Apollonius of Rhodes, 318, 328, 332
Apollonius Sophista, 62, 88, 103, 117
apologue of Odysseus, 310, 312
apostrophe, 306, 307, 309
Apsû, 602
Arabic script, 8
Arcadian, 198
Archaic art, 578
Archaic Period, 26, 435
archaisms, 195, 201, 203, 216, 269
Arctinus of Miletus, 176, 182, 185
Ares, 349, 350, 370, 452, 460, 497
Arete, 321, 373, 640, 704, 705
Argives, 21, 31, 82, 350, 556, 637
Argonautica, 49, 246
Aristonicus, 73, 104, 112
Aristophanes, 429
Aristophanes of Byzantium, 33, 72, 85, 98, 102, 105, 106, 110–12, 116, 118, 121, 367, 410, 429, 474
Aristotle, 33, 35, 37, 38, 39, 43, 52, 74, 77, 82, 87, 185, 231, 396–9, 402, 423, 645
Asia Minor, 31, 200, 212, 214, 519, 660
Assyrians, 20, 28, 29, 601, 602, 608
Astyanax, 49
Athena, 40, 66, 67, 68, 147, 155, 277, 296, 301, 309, 315, 322, 323, 349, 350, 351, 353, 355, 358, 365, 366, 370–4, 379, 389, 413, 432, 456, 532, 544, 600, 611, 640, 677, 701, 713
Athenaeus, 40, 72
athetesis, 68, 72, 73, 93, 116
Atlantis, 51
Atrahasis, 439, 600, 602, 616
Augeas, 416, 423
Aulis, 25, 31, 352, 478
Automedon, 671
Avaris, 607

Baal, 28, 604, 608, 616, 617, 621
Babylon, 543, 602
Babylonian epic, 602
Bacchylides, 193, 236
basileus, 630, 633, 634, 636, 642–5, 652, 653, 655, 659, 660–3, 665, 666
Bathsheba, 28
Bellerophon, 27, 451, 452, 459, 461, 532, 577, 578, 610, 619, 708
Belshazzar, 11
Bentley, R., 96, 98 124, 227
Bible, 11, 63, 119, 142, 599–604, 608, 609, 617–19, 621, 623
Boiotia, 22, 30, 31, 533, 548, 660
Boiotians, 669
Boghazköy, 604, 605
boustrophedon, 18
Briseis, 412, 424, 484, 703, 712
Byblus, 30, 603

Cadmeans, 21
Cadmos, 20, 21, 25, 30, 555, 608
Caere, 581
caesura, 222–6, 232, 233, 236, 240, 241, 251, 255, 266, 274, 301
Calchas, 353, 684
Callimachus, 48, 49, 88, 112
Calydonian Boar Hunt, 430
Calydonians, 426, 453
Calypso, 67, 68, 277, 309, 310, 323, 333, 334, 366, 370, 373, 374, 377, 378, 617, 620, 640
Cambridge ritualists, 436
Canaanites, 8, 600, 607, 612, 616, 621, 623
Carians, 609
Carpenter, R., 18, 19, 612
Cassandra, 355
Castor, 428
Catalogue of Heroines, 418
Catalogue of Ships, 59, 83, 92, 278, 352, 434, 480, 511, 669
Cebriones, 177
Centaurs, 416, 419, 578
Cerberus, 578
Certamen, 38, 473, 474, 475, 476
Chalcis, 31, 467
Charis, 421
Charybdis, 376, 377, 378
Chimaera, 27, 28, 578, 619
Chinese writing, 5, 6, 7, 11, 151, 160
Chios, 35, 70, 81, 119, 501, 514, 533, 539
Chiusi, 581
choral lyric, 193
Chryseis, 296, 703, 706, 712
Cicero, 38, 82
Cinyras, 610
Circe, 155, 169, 373, 376, 377, 378, 424, 617, 620, 640
city editions, 69, 119, 120, 121
Cleopatra, 426, 430, 431, 432
Clitias, 118, 581, 582
Clytemnestra, 640
Cnossus, 20, 518, 522, 524, 555, 556, 607, 613
codex Sinaiticus, 89
codices, 57–63, 88, 93, 97, 101, 104, 117

Cometas, 89
Constantinople, 60, 61, 89
contraction, 195, 207, 208, 227
Corcyra, 455
Corinth, 20, 451
correption, 206
  Attic correption, 220
cosmogony, 602
Crates of Mallos, 34, 51, 58, 69, 103, 109
cremation, 23, 346, 520, 541, 543, 556, 557
Crete, 8, 16, 234, 310, 555–7, 614, 637, 658, 659, 673
Cronus, 295, 437, 602, 604
Cumae, 660
cuneiform writing, 6, 8, 12, 28, 600, 601, 604
Cup of Nestor, 23, 24, 29
Curetes, 426
Cyclops, see Polyphemus
Cynaethus, 82, 109, 501
Cypria, 25, 39, 175, 358, 407, 602, 611, 620
Cypriot, 198
Cypriote syllabary, 7
Cyprus, 7, 20, 31, 70, 119, 370, 514, 518, 540, 542, 556, 600, 610–2, 615, 616, 626, 651
Cyrus, 26, 600, 616

dactylic hexameter, 24, 35, 38, 39, 42, 50, 149, 153, 158, 164, 172, 197, 199–202, 217, 221–6, 232–46, 249, 254, 255, 260, 261, 265, 267, 268, 282, 301, 328, 329, 332, 397, 463, 464, 472, 481, 483, 489, 492, 498, 524–7, 563
Danaus, 25
Daniel, 11, 621
Dark Age, 30, 147, 197–200, 214, 397, 435, 512, 523–5, 536–8, 541, 543, 544, 547–55, 558, 607, 626, 627, 633, 650, 653–9, 666, 679, 686
David, 246, 619, 621
deconstructionism, 394
Delos, 32, 412, 499, 501
demiourgoi, 636
democracy, 668, 693
Democritus, 33
Demodocus, 41, 307, 310, 311, 370, 374, 375, 391, 393, 403, 413, 417, 480, 496, 497, 529
dêmos, 629, 631, 634, 636, 644, 645, 647, 651, 655, 657, 659, 661, 662, 666
Demosthenes, 93
Deucalion, 601, 602
dialect, 31, 46, 148, 149, 170–2, 193–205, 212–4, 217, 228, 229, 280, 326, 397, 406, 410, 463, 472, 488, 514, 525, 604, 608; Aeolic, 196–205, 209, 210–17; Arcadian, 198; Cypriot, 198; East Greek, 198–203, 214–217; Ionic, 194–200, 202, 204, 205, 208–17; Lesbian, 199, 200, 202, 205, 209–13; Mycenaean, 198; West Greek, 198–201, 203
dialectology, 195
diction, 83, 112, 121, 147, 149, 153, 156, 164, 193, 196, 203, 209, 213, 223, 227, 238–52, 256, 257, 259–61, 269, 270, 272, 274, 277, 279, 280–3, 285, 331, 340, 345, 355, 357, 399, 406, 410, 438, 463, 466, 467, 469, 471, 474, 478, 479, 484, 486, 488, 490–2, 499, 504, 505, 628
Didymus, 103, 104, 107, 110, 112, 119
digamma, 14, 29, 98, 207, 227, 228, 264, 269, 490
dikê, 484, 485, 487
Dindorf, W., 103, 117
Diomedes, 27, 58, 179, 188, 273, 308, 313, 314, 349, 350, 425, 581, 610, 619, 627, 638, 678, 682, 708
Dione, 439
Dionysius Thrax, 27, 34, 101, 108
Dionysus, 40, 489, 493, 494, 500
Dipylon Master, 564, 566
Dipylon Oinochoe, 24, 29, 30
discourse analysis, 284, 288
Doloneia, 82, 186, 349
Dolopes, 659, 671
Dorian invasion, 198

Ea, 602
Egypt, 25, 29, 30, 57, 60, 66, 70, 81, 89, 422, 518, 530, 547, 600, 604, 611–8, 651
Eidothea, 614
Eleans, 416, 656
Electra, 577
Eleusis, 499, 503, 504, 579
Empedocles, 37, 454
enjambement, 158, 267, 274, 294, 302
Enki, 602
Enkidu, 601, 618

Enlil, 602
Enuma Elish, 439, 602
Eos, 68, 281, 334, 337, 355, 615
Epic Cycle, 175, 176, 184, 185, 352, 423, 438, 570
Epigoni, 21
epos, 152, 155, 156, 168, 464, 481, 488, 492, 498
Ereshkigal, 617, 620
Eretria, 21, 22, 23, 467
Eriphyle, 707, 708
ethics, 696
Etruria, 578, 581
Euboea, 20–3, 26, 30, 31, 474, 478, 533, 607, 651
Eumaeus, 307, 311, 318, 322, 324, 363, 366, 373, 374, 378, 417, 457, 630, 631, 638, 639, 652, 653, 656, 659, 700, 710
Euphorbus, 350, 356
Euripides, 25, 64, 65, 78, 186
Euripus, 31
Eurycleia, 363, 364, 370, 371, 373, 374, 378, 638
Eurylochus, 459
Eurymachus, 712
Eurynome, 421
Eurytion, 417, 418, 419

feminism, 388, 389, 499, 503
Finley, M., 512, 625–30, 633–42, 645, 649, 674
focalization, 312–20
folktale, 391, 423, 444–50, 452, 457, 458, 460, 461
formalism, 305, 319
formulas, 23, 121, 147–57, 164, 175, 177, 188, 196, 201–4, 207, 221, 223, 226–31, 233–85, 293, 300, 302, 304, 317, 324, 326–8, 330–40, 365, 381, 399, 403, 434, 463, 472, 484, 490, 491, 493–5, 499, 524, 525, 527, 562, 565, 569, 576, 606, 608, 616, 623, 628
François Vase, 581
Fränkel, H., 240–2, 245, 255, 262, 265
Furies, 453

Galen, 38, 65, 77
Gelb, I. J., 4, 9, 10
Gelon of Syracuse, 83
genre, 52, 118, 160, 193, 214, 275, 308, 389, 393, 396–9, 403, 407, 408, 411–4, 442, 444, 445, 446, 457, 464, 471, 472, 492, 496–9, 692
Geometric style, 23, 348, 352, 537, 544, 545, 550, 553, 555, 558, 560–79, 626, 652, 653, 665
George Choeroboscus, 89
Gephyreans, 21, 31
geras, 644, 661
gerontes, 634, 643, 646
Gilgamesh, 439, 601, 602, 617, 618, 620
Glaucus, 27, 308, 610, 619, 627, 638, 700, 703, 708
Graces, 370
grammaticus, 43, 45, 46, 47, 52
grammatodidaskalos, 42, 43, 45
Grote, George, 134–6
guslar, 150, 151, 158, 161, 167, 171

Halys river, 610
Harmodius and Aristogiton, 21, 30
Harpagus, 26
Hebrew, 11, 119, 235, 451, 599, 600, 601, 603, 604, 607, 608, 610, 617, 623
Hector, 27, 37, 40, 49, 169, 177–83, 200, 232, 233, 273, 277, 279, 280, 283, 303, 315–21, 345–58, 403, 412, 413, 425, 427, 431, 432, 572, 574, 611, 632–4, 639–43, 661, 669, 672, 677, 680, 681–5, 710, 713
Hecuba, 279, 412, 612, 713
Helen, 640, 644
Heliodorus, 312
Helius, 377, 378, 464, 504
hellenism, 61
Hephaestus, 351, 421, 422, 432, 433, 440, 610, 612, 636, 709
Hera, 164, 229, 351, 353, 356, 358, 421, 432, 433, 502, 569, 602, 617, 640, 709, 710
Heracles, 560, 572, 578
Heraclitus, 36, 41, 42, 45, 51, 52
Herodian, 104
Herodotus, 21, 22, 25, 30, 33, 39, 48, 109, 307, 437, 615
Hesiod, 3, 29, 31, 32, 35, 38, 48, 49, 51, 80, 81, 83, 109, 112, 175, 245, 268, 269, 328, 359, 394, 404, 406, 408, 409, 410, 414, 437, 463–91 497, 499, 502, 523, 529, 531, 533, 542, 561, 572, 600, 602, 605, 615–7, 620, 624, 631, 635, 650, 651, 653, 657–60; his date, 465
hetairoi, 631, 665, 670–2

hiatus, 97, 98, 204, 206, 220, 231, 232, 233, 267, 642
hieroglyphic writing, 6, 8, 10
Hipparchus, 21, 41, 59, 82, 109
Hippodamia, 419
Hippolytus, 26
Hissarlik, 434
Hittites, 235, 518, 519, 551, 600, 601, 605–10, 617–21
Homeric Question, 37, 79, 103, 108, 110, 123–45, 146, 467, 557, 608, 625, 672, 675, 692, 693
Homeric society, 537, 558, 624–9, 641, 645, 646, 648, 649, 656, 660–2, 697, 700, 701, 706, 711, 712
Homeridae, 39, 81, 495, 496
hoplite phalanx, 680, 691–3
household, 372, 379, 630, 639, 640, 641, 650, 653, 701
Hurrians, 234, 235, 600, 601, 605, 617
Hydra, 578
Hymn to Apollo, 33, 35, 492, 493
Hymn to Dionysus, 489, 493, 494, 500
Hypnos, 433

Idas, 430–2
Idomeneus, 254, 255, 614, 670, 671–3, 684
Ilioupersis, 618
Illuyankas, 619
India, 235, 444, 600, 605, 606, 620
Indo-European, 606
inhumation, 520, 541, 543, 551, 556
intertextuality, 275, 392, 394, 439, 464, 465, 483, 485
Ionia, 35, 42, 200, 514, 533, 544, 548, 552, 554, 569, 571, 627, 646
Ionic dialects, 199
Irus, 365
Isis, 604, 613
Ithaca, 448, 456, 462, 612, 614, 615, 621, 629, 630, 642, 645

Jason, 611, 653
Jerome, 119, 120
Jones, Sir William, 161, 246, 310, 600, 705
Joseph, 238, 339, 451, 599, 603, 619
Josephus, 101, 107, 108, 110
Julian the Apostate, 47, 50, 54
Julius Africanus, 83

Kadesh, 604
Kakridis, J. T., 174, 175, 182, 183, 185, 186, 187, 347
Kirchhoff, A., 137
kleos, 276, 366, 426, 427, 480–7, 635
klêros, 657, 658, 660–2
koinê, 119–21
Kourion, 610
Kumarbi, 604
Kunstsprache, 149, 489, 514, 523, 537

Lachmann, K., 131–34
Laconia, 193, 550
Laertes, 364, 367, 369, 370, 371, 373, 378, 379, 449, 630, 635, 638, 655, 713
land use, 654
Laomedon, 432, 433
Lapiths, 419
Late Geometric, 545, 550, 553, 560, 562, 577, 652
lawagetas, 521
Lefkandi, 21–4, 30, 31, 541, 543, 544, 607, 626
legend; definition of, 444
Lelantine War, 31, 467
Lemnos, 353, 421, 519, 611, 653
Lesbos, 81, 200, 202, 214
Leucothea, 378
lexigraphy, 5, 9
Libation Bearers, 427
Libya, 615
Linear B, 7, 8, 25, 27, 196, 198, 199, 201, 228–30, 233, 268, 512–26, 529, 530, 536, 537, 540, 612, 625
literacy, 17, 24, 29, 31, 42, 80, 162, 165, 170, 385, 440, 491, 513, 529, 530, 532, 607, 628
logosyllabic writing, 6, 7, 8, 9, 29
Longinus, 37, 52, 112, 309
Lord, A. B., 32, 146, 149–64, 171, 183, 186, 188, 241–9, 262, 264, 269, 275, 284, 285, 304, 360, 399, 402, 438, 447, 504, 536
Lucian, 50, 119
Lycia, 27, 28, 308, 356, 451, 610, 619, 660
Lycophron, 50
Lycurgus, 77

Macedonia, 193, 552, 553, 554
Magna Graecia, 42
Mahabharata, 605
Marathon, 580, 626
Marduk, 602
Margites, 39

Marmor Parium, 434
Marpessa, 430, 431
Marseilles, 70, 119
matres lectionis, 12
Medes, 12, 217
Medinet Habu, 614
Medjedovich, Avdo, 32, 151, 162
Medusa, 577, 578
Melantho, 365, 373, 374
Meleager, 183, 310, 311, 405, 410, 416, 425–32, 452, 453, 459, 461, 633, 661
Memnon, 179–87, 281, 355–7, 615
Memphis, 612
Menelaus, 155, 177, 178, 280, 307, 321, 346, 354, 365, 375, 423, 428, 453, 454, 460, 603, 611, 613, 615, 644, 659, 670, 676, 684, 688
Menestheus, 83
Mentes, 155, 372, 374, 652, 653
Meriones, 177, 178, 234, 670, 673, 684
Messenia, 516, 517, 520, 529, 548–51
Metrodorus of Lampsacus, 43
Mezentius, 180
Milesian numbers, 26
Miletus, 176, 182, 185, 545, 547, 605, 609
Minos, 5, 617
Minotaur, 577, 578
Mopsus, 610
Musaeus, 35, 50, 466
Muses, 48, 172, 294, 306, 307, 331, 356, 369, 389, 392, 401–14, 467, 470, 475, 478, 479–81, 493, 497, 498, 502, 617, 705
Mycenae, 511, 513, 516, 517, 519, 524, 528, 531, 536, 612, 625, 679
Myrmidons, 308, 412, 670, 671, 676
myth and history, 434; and religion, 435; as oral storytelling, 418; definition, 415, 420

Naples, 21, 23, 61, 103
narratee, 306, 309, 311, 315, 316, 320, 321, 323
narratology, 305, 312, 319, 325, 380, 389, 483
Nauplius, 26, 32
Nausicaa, 309, 310, 315, 366, 370, 371, 373, 379, 411, 629, 641
Nausithous, 660
Near East, 5, 22, 30, 234, 434, 438, 439, 466, 467, 505, 530, 540, 542–7, 550, 556, 557, 599, 600–23
Nekuia, 84
Neleus, 656
Neoanalysis, 174, 175, 180–9, 438
Neoptolemus, 609
Nereids, 175, 177, 178, 188, 356, 408, 413
Nergal, 617, 620
Nestor, 23, 24, 26, 27, 29, 168, 177, 179, 180, 182, 184, 188, 309, 346, 347, 353, 365, 371, 373, 410, 416, 529, 572, 574, 615, 644, 669, 670, 675, 676, 699, 711
New Criticism, 380
Nicander of Colophon, 332
Nicanor, 57, 86, 104
Nile, 121, 613
Nimrud, 28
Ninsun, 616
Niobe, 347, 416, 418, 430
Noah, 601, 602
Nonnus, 50, 88, 237
nostos, 157, 315, 369

Ocean, 36, 327, 350, 421, 439, 602
Odios, 581, 681
Odysseus, 25, 26, 29, 39, 66, 67, 147, 153, 155, 157, 169, 175–83, 188, 270, 271, 273, 277, 296, 297, 301, 306, 307–24, 333, 334, 336, 338, 339, 346, 349, 353–6, 361–78, 389, 391, 393, 394, 402–4, 408, 411, 413, 414, 417–9, 423, 424, 428, 435, 437, 446, 448–62, 468, 469, 471, 480, 484, 512, 529, 573, 578, 579, 581, 601, 603, 608–20, 624, 627, 629, 630, 633, 634, 636, 637, 641, 645, 649, 652, 656, 658, 659, 669, 670, 672, 674, 677, 682, 692, 696, 699–713
Oedipus, 486
oikos, 624, 629–43, 650, 658, 659, 663, 664
Oineus, 425, 427
Olympus, 49, 269, 312, 320, 345, 406, 421, 428, 433, 452, 458, 494, 502, 504, 505–7, 552
oral theory, 32, 146, 148–51, 156, 157, 159, 162, 164–7, 174–6, 181, 182, 186–8, 247, 248, 261–3, 275, 276, 280, 281, 284, 285, 287, 291, 300, 304, 328, 380, 381, 467, 473, 490, 491, 513, 536, 600, 628, 713
oral-derived traditional texts, 163
Orchomenus, 528, 614
Oresteia, 25, 40

Orestes, 309, 370, 706
Origen, 119
Orion, 334
Orontes, 21, 31
Orpheus, 35, 51, 466, 495
Osiris, 604, 613
Oxyhynchus, 88

paideia, 33, 34
Palaeologan revival, 94
Palamedes, 25, 26, 28, 30, 32
Panathenaea, 59, 82
Panathenaic regulation, 59
panhellenism, 193, 194, 436, 439, 463, 499, 502, 503, 506, 550, 562, 578, 627, 644
Panyassis of Halicarnassus, 48
Paphos, 370, 611
papyri, papyrus, 28, 30, 32, 33, 34, 38, 44, 55, 57, 58, 60–9, 75–9, 85–6, 92, 94–9, 103–4, 114, 116–21, 147, 213, 229, 282, 489, 522, 603
paratactic style, 286, 399
parchment, 55, 60, 62, 63, 81, 88, 530
Paris, 69, 102, 112, 175, 176, 179, 180, 188, 321, 346, 354, 355–7, 386, 425, 428, 432, 484, 505, 545, 549, 605, 626, 632, 637, 644, 653, 670, 676, 679, 683, 684, 692
Parry, M., 32, 81, 145–53, 157, 159, 160, 162–6, 171, 175, 176, 183, 186, 238–57, 260–77, 280, 284–7, 294, 300, 302, 304, 310, 324, 328, 330–2, 341, 381, 399, 434, 490, 536, 537, 713
Patroclus, 37, 75, 78, 174, 176–82, 179–82, 188, 277, 283, 307–11, 320, 321, 350, 351, 355–7, 410, 412, 424, 426, 427, 431, 432, 532
Pausanias, 431, 456, 475, 615
Peleus, 182, 291, 293, 294, 297, 350, 356, 402, 404, 407, 425, 430, 580, 659, 710
Penelope, 67, 157, 169, 273, 307, 311, 315–9, 324, 362–75, 379, 389, 390, 391, 411, 413, 417, 418, 423, 424, 440, 448, 449, 456, 460, 462, 615, 639, 640, 641, 700, 703
Penthesilea, 181, 185
Pergamon, 51, 61, 69
Pericles, 41, 48
Perses, 409, 481, 483–6, 658
Persians, 12
Phaeacians, 311, 366, 368, 378, 379, 394, 414, 448, 455, 456, 461, 480, 620, 629, 637, 646, 659, 704
phalanges, 674, 684, 693
Pharaoh, 614
Pharos, 453, 613
Phemius, 41, 307, 310, 311, 374, 403, 404, 411, 413, 498, 529
philia, 484
Philistines, 8
Philoctetes, 352
Philoetius, 363, 364, 374, 631, 639
Phoenicians, 20–2, 28, 30, 544, 600, 608, 612, 636, 637, 652
Phoenix, 78, 240, 244, 310, 405, 410, 416, 425, 426, 427, 429, 430, 431, 432, 617, 627, 659, 703, 712
phonemes, 11, 57, 152
phonography, 5, 8, 9
Phrynichus, 427
Phthia, 431, 659
Pindar, 39, 72, 109, 179, 180, 193, 419, 463, 480, 495, 496, 501
Pirithous, 419, 430
Pisistratean recension, 79, 82, 84
Pisistratus, 34, 82, 83, 108, 109
Pithekoussai, 21, 23, 24, 29, 545, 547
Planudes, 94
Plataea, 497
Plato, 33, 36–8, 41–3, 47, 49, 51–3, 57, 64, 70, 73, 74, 78, 109, 397, 434, 713
Plotinus, 53
Plutarch, 38, 39, 42, 44, 45, 46, 51, 59, 65, 77, 78, 120, 473, 613
Podarces, 353
Poetics, 423
polis, 512, 517, 533, 546, 559, 612, 624, 629, 630, 632, 633, 635, 642, 643, 645–7, 659, 660, 665, 679, 693
Polycrates, 501
Polydamas, 189, 358, 713
Polydamna, 613, 616
Polydeuces, 428
Polyphemus, 376, 378, 391, 442, 446, 449, 450, 460, 461, 578, 579, 581, 620, 709; the Noman ruse, 450
Porphyrian, 43
Porphyry, 43, 53, 54, 59, 103, 112
Poseidon, 322, 350, 351, 359, 372, 423, 432, 433, 450, 455, 456, 572, 602, 615, 638, 684, 709
postmodernism, 380, 383–5, 390, 394, 395
Potiphar's Wife, 446, 451
Priam, 40, 168, 169, 181, 276, 280,

283, 299, 303, 314, 316, 345, 347, 354, 403, 413, 511, 605, 611, 621, 662, 710, 713
Proclus, 48, 54, 175, 176, 179, 184, 185, 355, 473
Procopius, 88
Proetus, 27, 451, 619
prolepsis, 305, 319, 320
Prooimion, 482, 494
Protesilaus, 352, 353
Proteus, 453, 460, 613
Protogeometric period, 626
psychostasia, 618
Ptolemaic manuscripts, 63, 64, 68, 75, 76
Pygmies, 353, 615
Pylians, 644, 656, 670
Pylos, 323, 365, 372, 373, 513, 516, 517, 519, 520, 522, 524, 526, 528–30, 548, 625
Pythagoreans, 42

Quintilian, 17
Quintus of Smyrna, 50, 180

Ramses II, 604, 614, 621
Ras Shamra, 604
Reinhard, K., 183, 357, 359
rhapsodes, 34, 41, 59, 69, 77, 82, 101, 102, 106, 107, 109, 110
ring composition, 347, 349, 352, 361, 363, 364, 370–6, 399

Salamis, 83, 610
Sanskrit, 251, 524, 605, 606
Sarpedon, 184, 351, 356, 357, 610, 700, 703, 704
Schadewaldt, W., 183–6, 319, 348, 354, 357, 647
Scheria, 24, 29, 312, 455, 629, 630, 640, 646, 659, 660
Schliemann, H., 139, 434, 435, 511, 512, 516, 519, 536–8
scholia, 37, 44, 49, 55, 61, 66, 69, 71, 76, 79, 88, 92, 94–6, 101–22, 282, 307, 319, 321, 489
scrolls, 57, 58, 59, 60
Scylla, 377, 378; see Polyphemus, 53, 377, 579, 620, 637, 646, 705, 709
semasiography, 5
Septuagint, 119
Shaft Graves, 516
Shamash, 617
Shield of Achilles, 527, 560, 619
Shield of Heracles, 463, 560
Sicyon, 82
Sidon, 611, 616, 653
Sinope, 70, 119
Sinties, 421
Sinuhe, 603, 621
Sirens, 377, 378, 389
Socrates, 36, 42, 45, 54, 434
Solomon, 28, 621
Solon, 82, 83, 629, 679
Sophilos, 580, 581
South Slavic oral epic, 150–2, 155–61, 167, 171, 172
Sparta, 323, 354, 365, 372, 373, 550, 551, 600, 611, 640
St. Augustine, 47
St. Basil, 47
St. Elias, 445, 456
St. Nicholaus, 457
Stesichorus, 25, 422
Stoics, 38, 51, 54, 104
structuralism, 305, 380
Submycenaean period, 541, 626, 627
Suda, 38, 58
suitors, 155–7, 177, 270, 307, 316, 320, 323, 331, 338, 363–7, 370, 372–4, 379, 390, 403, 411, 414, 418, 423, 484, 614, 621, 631, 640, 656, 699, 700, 702, 703, 712, 713
Sumerian language and literature, 6, 601
supplemental letters, 16
syllabography, 6–9, 18, 29
synizesis, 195, 206, 215, 220, 264, 269
Syrie, 652

Tanagra, 21, 22
Taphians, 652
Tartarus, 437
Telegonus, 424
Telegony, 175, 423, 424
Telemachus, 25, 155, 270, 307, 309, 316, 317, 319, 322–4, 362–75, 378, 413, 424, 484, 611, 620, 631, 640, 642, 659, 660, 662, 699–701, 704, 712
Telephus, 609
temenos, 197, 626, 631, 644, 647, 660, 661
Tethys, 36, 327, 439, 602
The Wedding of Smailagich Meho, 151, 162
Theagenes of Rhegium, 43

Thebaid, 49
Thebes, 21, 33, 39, 198, 273, 486, 513, 524, 602, 607, 612, 614, 621
Themis, 642
Theoclymenus, 428
Theogony, 29, 245, 404, 407–9, 463, 464, 466–72, 475, 479–84, 497, 499, 502, 602, 616, 617
Thera, 435, 527, 528, 607
therapontes, 631, 636, 665, 670, 672
Thersites, 689
Theseus, 83, 578
Thesprotians, 424
Thetis, 76, 169, 175–7, 179, 184, 188, 270, 296, 309, 346, 351, 355, 356, 358, 407, 413, 421, 425, 428, 431, 432, 617, 703, 709
Thoas, 311, 611, 684
Thracians, 680
Thucydides, 33, 35, 98, 307, 434, 495, 501, 547
Thutmoses III, 603
Tiamat, 602
timê, 484, 637, 644
Tiresias, 53, 375, 424, 456, 614, 620
Tithonus, 334
tmesis, 201, 202, 203, 524, 526
trade, 5, 22, 25, 613, 651
Trojan Horse, 446, 496, 603
Trojans, 176–8, 257, 270, 308, 314, 331, 346, 349, 350, 351, 353, 355, 356, 358, 421, 424, 611, 616, 661, 669, 671, 672, 675–8, 681, 683–5, 688, 709–13
Troy, 31, 33, 35, 175, 178, 181, 184, 269, 280, 310, 315, 320, 321, 338, 345–59, 366, 368, 369, 371–8, 433, 434, 448, 457, 478, 484, 486, 492, 511, 514, 518, 519, 536, 569, 572, 574, 600, 605, 606, 609, 611, 614, 615, 618, 621, 625, 629, 637, 638, 640, 646, 652, 661, 669, 671, 675, 681, 683, 691–3, 698–700, 706, 710, 712, 713
Tydeus, 308, 425, 654
Typhoeus, 437
tyranny, 668, 693
Tyre, 46, 603

Ugarit, 235, 600, 601, 604, 607, 608, 610, 612, 616–8, 620, 623
Ulu Burun shipwreck, 28, 619
Unitarians, 80, 147, 174, 182, 184
Uruk, 601, 618
Utnapishtim, 601, 620

Venetus A, 55, 61, 88, 92, 101, 104, 106
Vergil, 180, 360, 365, 396, 398
Villoison, 55, 101, 102, 105–15
von Wilamowitz-Moellendorf, U., 74, 87, 143, 183, 184, 326, 469, 486
vulgate, 33, 34, 38, 43–5, 48, 63, 64–78, 83–6, 99, 114–6, 118, 122

wanax, 516, 520, 521, 523, 529, 659
warfare, 516, 545, 603, 624, 635, 666, 668, 679, 680, 689, 690–3
Wenamun, 603
West Greek, 201
West Semitic writing, 8–12, 16, 18–21, 23, 25, 28, 29
Wolf, F. A., 3, 102, 105, 106–13, 115, 121, 125–31, 137–8, 495, 599
Works and Days, 359, 404, 407, 409, 410, 463, 464, 472–9, 481, 482–7, 620
writing boards, 28, 619

Xanthus, 432
xeinos, 652
Xenophanes, 35, 39

Yugoslavia, 148, 149, 158

Zeno, 37
Zenodotus, 65, 66, 70, 72, 73, 79, 85, 87, 93, 98, 102, 106, 110–2, 116, 118, 121
Zeus, 66, 67, 169, 172, 179, 184, 230, 269, 273, 291, 299, 308, 315, 319–22, 345, 346, 350–6, 372, 377, 409, 416, 421, 428, 432, 433, 437, 439, 454, 478, 487, 495, 496, 499, 500, 502, 504–7, 602, 608, 617, 633, 637, 638, 640, 642, 645, 680, 703, 704, 705, 709–11